MAGNALIA DEI
The Mighty Acts of God

G. ERNEST WRIGHT

MAGNALIA DEI

The Mighty Acts of God

ESSAYS ON THE BIBLE AND ARCHAEOLOGY IN MEMORY OF G. ERNEST WRIGHT

Edited by Frank Moore Cross
Werner E. Lemke, and Patrick D. Miller, Jr.

DOUBLEDAY & COMPANY, INC.
GARDEN CITY, NEW YORK

Library of Congress Cataloging in Publication Data

Main entry under title:
Magnalia Dei, the mighty acts of God.
XII, 611 p.; 24 cm
"The bibliography of G. Ernest Wright": p. 577.
Includes indexes.
1. Bible. O.T.—Addresses, essays, lectures.
2. Bible. O.T.—Antiquities—Addresses, essays, lectures.
3. Wright, George Ernest, 1909–74   4. Wright, George
Ernest, 1909–74—Bibliography.   I. Wright, George
Ernest, 1909–74   II. Cross, Frank Moore.   III. Lemke,
Werner E.   IV. Miller, Patrick D., Jr.
BS1192.M34   221.9'3
ISBN 0-385-05257-X
Library of Congress Catalog Card Number 75–29211

Preface

The volume of essays which follows is presented to G. Ernest Wright on his sixty-fifth birthday as an expression of the esteem and affection of his colleagues and his students. I take special delight in editing this volume (with the stalwart aid of my younger associates) after thirty years of friendship, the first three as his student, the last twenty-two as his colleague.

The scholarly world knows G. Ernest Wright best, perhaps, as an archaeologist. Beginning with his publication in 1937 of *The Pottery of Palestine from Earliest Times to the End of the Early Bronze Age,* he has taken a leading scholarly role in biblical archaeology, climaxed by his excavations at Shechem and at Idalion in recent years. At the same time, he has organized and directed the main thrust of American archaeology in the Near East in the last two decades, either directly, through his own expeditions, or indirectly, through his students' expeditions, and since 1966 as a uniquely active President of the American Schools of Oriental Research.

G. Ernest Wright's work as a biblical exegete and theologian also has established him as a major figure in American Old Testament studies. Some nine of the seventeen or eighteen books of which he has been author or co-author (not to mention the volumes he has edited) fall in these fields, a prodigious production had he no other scholarly interests.

Ernest Wright's closest colleagues and students know him not only as a formidable archaeological scholar, and a creative biblical theologian, but also, and not least, as a charismatic teacher whose success in recruiting and developing young archaeological and biblical scholars has made him truly the Pied Piper of American biblical scholarship.

This volume of essays is shaped to fit the interests of the scholar whose work we celebrate. The first three sections survey the history, archaeology, and religion of Israel by broad periods. Old positions are reviewed and new positions sketched out in the areas covered by general papers whose topics were assigned. Some papers on specific or limited topics have been accepted in lieu of assignments. The fourth section is devoted to biblical theology, and the fifth to the traditional, but newly active fields of canon and text. The chief difficulty in preparing this jubilee volume, given Ernest Wright's worldwide circle of scholarly friends, has been to limit the number of contributors. The selection of names has been arbitrary rather than discriminating, taken from three categories: (1) the older of our former students, (2) sometime colleagues including visiting professors at Harvard, and (3) members of the Biblical Colloquium which Ernest Wright founded a quarter century ago.

The name of the volume, *magnalia Dei* recalls a *leitmotiv* of G. Ernest Wright's authorship and teaching; it is also an expression often on his lips, echoing his Calvinist forebears of early New England.

FRANK MOORE CROSS

Cambridge, Massachusetts
March 15, 1973

Contents

PREFACE iii

LIST OF ILLUSTRATIONS ix

PRINCIPAL ABBREVIATIONS xi

I. PATRIARCHS AND JUDGES

1. *The Beginning of the Middle Bronze Age in Syria-Palestine* 3
   WILLIAM G. DEVER, WILLIAM FOXWELL ALBRIGHT INSTITUTE OF
   ARCHAEOLOGICAL RESEARCH, JERUSALEM

2. *Two Amarna Notes: The Shechem City-State and Amarna*
   Administrative Terminology 39
   EDWARD F. CAMPBELL, JR., MCCORMICK THEOLOGICAL
   SEMINARY, CHICAGO

3. *Divine Names and Titles in Early Hebrew Poetry* 55
   DAVID NOEL FREEDMAN, UNIVERSITY OF MICHIGAN

4. *Mythopoeic Antecedents of the Biblical World-View and Their*
   Transformation in Early Israelite Thought 108
   LYNN CLAPHAM, EARLHAM COLLEGE, RICHMOND, INDIANA

5. *Moses in Historical and Theological Perspective* 120
   WILLIAM FOXWELL ALBRIGHT, JOHNS HOPKINS UNIVERSITY

6. *Social Organization in Early Israel* 132
   GEORGE E. MENDENHALL, UNIVERSITY OF MICHIGAN

7. *Charismatic Leadership in the Book of Judges* 152
   ABRAHAM MALAMAT, THE HEBREW UNIVERSITY OF JERUSALEM

II. Prophets and Kings

8. *The Origins of Prophecy*   171
   HERBERT B. HUFFMON, DREW UNIVERSITY, MADISON, NEW JERSEY

9. *The "Orpheus" Jug from Megiddo*   187
   BENJAMIN MAZAR, THE HEBREW UNIVERSITY OF JERUSALEM

10. *The Organization and Administration of the Israelite Empire*   193
    JOHN BRIGHT, UNION THEOLOGICAL SEMINARY, RICHMOND

11. *Solomon, Siamun, and the Double Ax*   209
    H. DARRELL LANCE, COLGATE ROCHESTER / BEXLEY HALL /
    CROZER

12. *Israel and Phoenicia*   224
    BRIAN PECKHAM, REGIS COLLEGE, TORONTO

13. *The Megiddo Stables*   249
    YIGAEL YADIN, THE HEBREW UNIVERSITY OF JERUSALEM

14. *Of Sherds and Strata: Contributions toward an Understanding of*
    the Archaeology of the Divided Monarchy   253
    JOHN S. HOLLADAY, JR., UNIVERSITY OF TORONTO

15. *New Light on the* Na'ar *Seals*   294
    NACHMAN AVIGAD, THE HEBREW UNIVERSITY OF JERUSALEM

16. *The Way of Obedience: I Kings 13 and the Structure of the*
    Deuteronomistic History   301
    WERNER E. LEMKE, COLGATE ROCHESTER / BEXLEY HALL /
    CROZER

III. Exile and Restoration

17. *The "Olden Gods" in Ancient Near Eastern Creation Myths*   329
    FRANK MOORE CROSS, HARVARD UNIVERSITY

18. *Exodus and Covenant in Second Isaiah and Prophetic Tradition*   339
    BERNHARD W. ANDERSON, PRINCETON THEOLOGICAL SEMINARY

19. *Ezra and Nehemiah in Recent Studies*   361
    RALPH W. KLEIN, CONCORDIA THEOLOGICAL SEMINARY IN EXILE,
    ST. LOUIS

20. *Reflections on the Modern Study of the Psalms*   377
    BREVARD S. CHILDS, YALE UNIVERSITY

21. *Prolegomena to the Study of Jewish Apocalyptic*   389
    PAUL D. HANSON, THE DIVINITY SCHOOL, HARVARD UNIVERSITY

22. *Lists of Revealed Things in the Apocalyptic Literature* 414
    MICHAEL E. STONE, THE HEBREW UNIVERSITY OF JERUSALEM

IV. THE BIBLE AND THEOLOGY

23. *On Sharing the Scriptures*   455
    MOSHE GREENBERG, THE HEBREW UNIVERSITY OF JERUSALEM

24. *Faith and Ideology in the Old Testament*   464
    PATRICK D. MILLER, JR., UNION THEOLOGICAL SEMINARY,
    RICHMOND

25. *The Old Testament in "Process" Perspective: Proposal for a Way
    Forward in Biblical Theology*   480
    J. GERALD JANZEN, CHRISTIAN THEOLOGICAL SEMINARY,
    INDIANAPOLIS

26. *Historical and Canonical: Recent Discussion about the Old
    Testament and Christian Faith*   510
    JAMES MAYS, UNION THEOLOGICAL SEMINARY, RICHMOND

V. CANON AND TEXT

27. *Adaptable for Life: The Nature and Function of Canon*   531
    J. A. SANDERS, UNION THEOLOGICAL SEMINARY, NEW YORK CITY

28. *Jewish Palaeography and Its Bearing on Text Critical Studies* 561
    RICHARD S. HANSON, LUTHER COLLEGE, DECORAH, IOWA

APPENDIX: The Bibliography of G. Ernest Wright   577
INDEX OF AUTHORS   595
INDEX OF SUBJECTS   604

List of Illustrations

following p. 300

Figure 1. Some ceramic types of Palestinian MB IIA; long strokes indicate burnishing. *Vide* William G. Dever, "The Beginning of the Middle Bronze Age in Syria-Palestine."

Figure 2. The main bronze types of Palestine in MB IIA. *Vide* Dever, "The Beginning. . . ."

Figure 3. Megiddo. A restored plan of the gate and the building 2072 of Stratum VIA (second half of the eleventh century B.C.) *Vide* Benjamin Mazar, "The 'Orpheus' Jug from Megiddo."

Figure 4. The "Orpheus" Jug from Megiddo. *Vide* Mazar, "The 'Orpheus' Jug. . . ."

Figures 5a; 5b. The Siamun relief from Tanis; Montet's drawing of same. *Vide* H. Darrell Lance, "Solomon, Siamun, and the Double Ax."

Figure 6. Example of the double ax as a tool. *Vide* Lance, "Solomon, . . ."

Figure 7. Example of the double ax as a religious symbol. *Vide* Lance, "Solomon, . . ."

Figure 8. Athenian vase showing the Dipylon shield. *Vide* Lance, "Solomon, . . ."

Figure 9. Pithos stamp from Knossos. *Vide* Lance, "Solomon, . . ."

Figure 10. An Ashurnasirpal II relief in Nimrud: four horses of the royal chariot within an especially installed field-stable, a pavilion supported by pillars. *Vide* Yigael Yadin, "The Megiddo Stables."

Figure 11. An Assyrian relief from the palace of Tiglath-Pileser III: a portable and collapsible manger, its trough very shallow and placed on wooden legs. *Vide* Yadin, "The Megiddo Stables."

Figure 12. Three seals: (1) Stamped jar-handle from Tell Beit Mirsim *l'lyqm n'r ywkn;* (2) Seal of *mlkyhw n'r špṭ* (impression); (3) Seal of *bnyhw n'r ḥgy* (impression). *Vide* Nachman Avigad, "New Light on the *Na'ar* Seals."

Principal Abbreviations

(The letter N followed by a number—e.g. [N 7]— indicates in which NOTE to the same essay a more complete citation may be found. For abbreviations special to certain articles, see the NOTES appended thereto.)

AASOR — *Annual of the American Schools of Oriental Research*

AB — *The Anchor Bible, 1964–*

AJA — *American Journal of Archaeology*

ALQ² — *The Ancient Library of Qumran and Modern Biblical Studies,* by F. M. Cross, rev. ed. (Doubleday Anchor, 1961).

ANET — *Ancient Near Eastern Texts Relating to the Old Testament,* ed. James B. Pritchard, 3 eds. (Princeton University Press, 1950, 1955, 1969).

ARI — *Archaeology and the Religion of Israel,* by W. F. Albright, 5 eds. (The Johns Hopkins Press, 1942–68), 5th (1968) ed. (Doubleday Anchor, 1969).

BA — *The Biblical Archaeologist*

BANE — *The Bible and the Ancient Near East: Essays in Honor of William Foxwell Albright,* ed. G. Ernest Wright (Doubleday, 1961; Anchor, 1965).

BASOR — *Bulletin of the American Schools of Oriental Research*

BJRL — *Bulletin of the John Rylands Library*

BZAW — *Beihefte zur Zeitschrift für die alttestamentliche Wissenschaft*

CAH³ — *The Cambridge Ancient History,* I, II, 3d ed., 1970–

CBQ — *The Catholic Biblical Quarterly*

CHB — *The Cambridge History of the Bible,* I, 1970; II, 1969; III, 1963

DJD — *Discoveries in the Judaean Desert,* Oxford, 1955–

EA — *Die El-Amarna-Tafeln* by J. A. Knudtzon (Leipzig: Hinrichs, 1915)

EI — *Eretz-Israel* (The Israel Exploration Society, Jerusalem)

ET — *Expository Times*

EvTh — *Evangelische Theologie*

HTR — *Harvard Theological Review*

HUCA — *Hebrew Union College Annual*

IB — *The Interpreter's Bible, 1952–57*

ICC — *International Critical Commentary, 1899–*

IDB	– *The Interpreter's Dictionary of the Bible,* 1962
IEJ	– *Israel Exploration Journal*
JAOS	– *Journal of the American Oriental Society*
JBL	– *Journal of Biblical Literature*
JBR	– *Journal of Bible and Religion*
JEA	– *Journal of Egyptian Archaeology*
JNES	– *Journal of Near Eastern Studies*
JPOS	– *Journal of the Palestine Oriental Society*
JQR	– *Jewish Quarterly Review*
JSS	– *Journal of Semitic Studies*
JTC	– *Journal for Theology and the Church*
JTS	– *Journal of Theological Studies*
KS (Alt)	– *Kleine Schriften zur Geschichte des Volkes Israel,* by A. Alt (München, 1953–64)
KS (Eissfeldt)	– *Kleine Schriften,* by Otto Eissfeldt (Tübingen, 1962–68)
LB	– *The Land of the Bible,* by Y. Aharoni, tr. A. F. Rainey (Philadelphia: The Westminster Press, 1967)
McCQ	– *McCormick Quarterly*
McCS	– *McCormick Speaking*
NDBA	– *New Directions in Biblical Archaeology,* eds. David Noel Freedman and Jonas C. Greenfield (Doubleday, 1969; Anchor, 1971)
NEATC	– *Near Eastern Archaeology in the Twentieth Century: Essays in Honor of Nelson Glueck,* ed. J. A. Sanders (Doubleday, 1970)
OTT	– *Old Testament Theology,* by G. von Rad, tr. D. M. G. Stalker (New York: Harper, 1962–65)
PEFA	– *Palestine Exploration Fund Annual*
PEQ	– *Palestine Exploration Quarterly*
QDAP	– *Quarterly of the Department of Antiquities* (Palestine)
RB	– *Revue Biblique*
TLZ	– *Theologische Literaturzeitung*
UgS	– *Überlieferungsgeschichtliche Studien,* by M. Noth (Tübingen, 1943)
USQR	– *Union Seminary Quarterly Review*
VT	– *Vetus Testamentum*
VTS	– *Vetus Testamentum Supplement*
WB	– *The Westminster Bookman*
WHJP	– *The World History of the Jewish People,* III, ed. B. Mazar (Tel Aviv, 1971)
YGC	– *Yahweh and the Gods of Canaan* by W. F. Albright (Doubleday, 1968; Anchor, 1969)
ZAW	– *Zeitschrift für die alttestamentliche Wissenschaft*
ZDPV	– *Zeitschrift des deutschen Palästina-Vereins*
ZTK	– *Zeitschrift für Theologie und Kirche*

I

Patriarchs and Judges

1. *The Beginning of the Middle Bronze Age in Syria-Palestine*

WILLIAM G. DEVER, WILLIAM FOXWELL ALBRIGHT

INSTITUTE OF ARCHAEOLOGICAL RESEARCH, JERUSALEM

THE "MIDDLE BRONZE AGE" in Syria-Palestine, ca. 2100–1500 B.C., has been the subject of several comprehensive discussions in recent years. In two fascicles of the revised edition of the *Cambridge Ancient History* in 1965 and 1966 Kathleen Kenyon presented a thorough survey of the archaeological sites, including the generally neglected sites in Syria.[1] In 1968 Professor Benjamin Mazar offered a broad historical and cultural synthesis, based primarily on an exhaustive treatment of literary evidence from all parts of the ancient Near East.[2] These admirable discussions are so up-to-date and so definitive in their respective areas that there is little justification for another attempt at a *general history* of the entire period. Recently, however, Professor G. Ernest Wright has entered into the discussion in a review of the works of Kenyon just cited, pointing out how many scholarly issues in the literature are still unresolved. Since the writer was first introduced to the fascinating problems of the Middle Bronze Age by Professor Wright, it seems fitting to carry on that discussion in a *Festschrift* honoring him.[3]

This essay is intended to be complementary to those mentioned above, so we shall focus more narrowly on the archaeological evidence which has come to light in the last few years. However, because the material has expanded so enormously, and because much of the new evidence bears upon the forepart of the period which is less well known, we have chosen to concentrate only on the MB I and MB IIA phases. We shall organize our discussion around what we consider to be crucial problems in the current literature and promising directions for future research.

Traditionally the Middle Bronze Age in Palestine has been divided into "Middle Bronze I," ca. 2100–1900 B.C., and "Middle Bronze II," ca. 1900–1500 B.C., the latter subdivided into "IIA," ca. 1900–1750 B.C., "IIB," ca. 1750–1650 B.C., and "IIC," ca. 1650–1550/1500 B.C. To avoid confusion in our outline, we follow the conventional division and terminology for MB I and IIA (although not the dates); nevertheless it will be apparent how radically this once-useful scheme has broken down.

THE MIDDLE BRONZE I PERIOD, ca. 2200–1950 B.C.

This period was once regarded as something of a "Dark Age" in the history of Palestine, but more recently it has been sufficiently illuminated by a series of discoveries so that for the first time it appears possible to piece together a picture of the material culture. For convenience we refer to the latest and most comprehensive syntheses in 1970 and 1971, where the present writer discussed the archaeological sites and the relevant literature. Virtually all of the published sites in Palestine and the principal sites in Syria are arranged in relative sequence in a chart from these articles, updated and presented at the conclusion of this essay as Chart 1.[4] Whatever areas of disagreement remain, there is a general consensus that the MB I period represents a transitional culture, largely non-urban, between the Early Bronze period and the fully developed Middle Bronze period, spanning approximately the twenty-second through the early twentieth century B.C.

The primary question is whether this period should be discussed at all under the rubric of the "Middle Bronze" Age. The "Intermediate Early Bronze–Middle Bronze" ("EB–MB") terminology introduced in 1956 by Kenyon, and now adapted in various forms by Robert H. Smith, Paul Lapp, Moshe Kochavi, Eliezer Oren, and others,[5] reflects more than a mere departure in terminology. It is an understanding of the material culture which stresses its disjunctive features and, indeed in its more extreme forms, denies any connection whatsoever of MB I with what precedes or follows. It is only the question of the continuity of MB I and MB II that need concern us here.

A word about the origin of the terminology may help to clarify things. It is now recognized that Albright's division of periods at the type-site of Tell Beit Mirsim was worked out ceramically rather than stratigraphically.[6] But it is seldom noted that the "MB I" usage which he coined there was originally based on his observation that many basic ceramic forms—especially the pierced-rim cooking pots—seemed to continue from Stratum I through Stratum F, that is, from MB I through MB IIA.[7] Furthermore, the town fortifications and the series of domestic strata which characterized MB II proper (Strata G–D) were thought by Albright also to have begun in MB I (Strata I–H) and thus his terminology linking these periods.[8] Since this terminology was in keeping with the Classical world and since subsequent excavations tended to confirm Albright's largely intuitive sequence at Tell Beit Mirsim, the "Middle Bronze" usage for the MB I period was perpetuated, although it was increasingly recognized that by and large it was unsuitable. With the rapid accumulation of new evidence—particularly that from town sites, supplementing previous material largely from shaft-tomb cemeteries—the individual character of the MB I period has recently become more appreciated.

The point is now almost beyond dispute: the MB I period has few if any links with MB IIA and Middle Bronze proper. Only in the case of a remote common ancestry—if the two peoples responsible for these cultures were both of "Amorite" extraction—do we see a possible point of contact (below). But the break between the two in terms of their material culture is one of the most abrupt and complete in the entire cultural sequence of Palestine.[9] The contrast between the two periods could hardly be more striking, whether we look at the largely handmade and undecorated pottery of the former, and the exquisite wheelmade burnished pottery of the latter; the numerous and distinctive copper implements of the former, and the few highly sophisticated bronzes of the latter; the shaft-tombs of the former, and the cist-graves of the latter; the proliferation of seminomadic encampments and seasonal settlements on the extreme fringes of the country in the former, and the concentration of urban settlements in the central regions of the country in the latter. Indeed, the tendency to separate the two periods has become so strong that several authorities have retreated from the "Intermediate" terminology and prefer rather to connect our period with the Early Bronze Age *exclusively,* often taking up the largely abandoned "EB IV" designation to describe it.[10] The present writer proposed the composite term "EB IV/MB I" in 1966 (both to call attention to the largely overlooked EB connections and to preserve the numerical sequence of MB II), but he continues to use "MB I" for convenience, as do Wright, Amiran, and others.[11] The only thing now clear in the otherwise muddled picture is that "MB I" belongs with the Early Bronze Age *in terms of cultural phases,* whatever terminology is used; and its place in a discussion of the Middle Bronze period is largely a concession to tradition and by way of introducing "MB II."

The vexed problem of the origins of the MB I peoples has been treated frequently and in detail. The classic version of the "Amorite" hypothesis, connecting the MB I culture of Palestine with the incursions of Western Semitic peoples known in Akkadian texts of the late third millennium B.C. as the *amurrū* (Sumerian MAR.TU), was that of Albright, formulated as early as 1935.[12] Subsequent evidence has tended to make this hypothesis even more attractive, so that it has been followed by nearly all commentators on the period: Wright, de Vaux, Kenyon, and more recently by Aharoni, Yadin, and the writer.[13]

Yet it must be remembered that the correlation of the extra-Palestinian literature, however extensive, with the scanty remains from excavated sites within the country remains tenuous at best. Thus a dissenting view has gained some following recently, first advanced in 1966–1967 by Paul Lapp and Moshe Kochavi independently, then later supported by the eminent European prehistorian Marija Gimbutas.[14] This theory sees the MB I culture as intrusive in Palestine, probably derived from beyond the Caucasus and brought to Palestine by non-Semitic invaders, possibly Proto-Indo-European peoples related to the "Kurgan" migrations over east central Europe and the Balkans in the late third–early second millennia B.C. Since the writer has shown elsewhere[15] how theoretical such a reconstruction is, we may leave the discussion by pointing out that nearly all scholars adhere to the MB I "Amorite" equation and are apt to continue to do so until new evidence of a more conclusive character appears.

The chronology of MB I needs to concern us here only as the end of the period provides a convenient *terminus post quem* for the beginning of MB IIA. Albright's original date of ca. 2100–1900 B.C. prevailed astonishingly long, and there can be no doubt even today that it is substantially correct—more so, in fact, than his latest proposal to lower the end of the period to ca. 1800 B.C., which we think impossible for a number of reasons. If anything, the current tendency to *raise* the dates to ca. 2200–2000 B.C. should be supported. Our argument from the archaeological evidence has been presented elsewhere,[16] and we return to the subject below in considering the dates for the beginning of MB IIA. The point here is that MB I must have come to an end in Syria by about 2000 B.C. and scarcely later than ca. 1950 B.C. in Palestine.[17]

II. THE MIDDLE BRONZE IIA PERIOD, ca. 1950–1800 B.C.

There has never been any doubt, since Albright defined it and placed it in historical sequence after the 1932 season at Tell Beit Mirsim,[18] that the MB IIA period (Kenyon's "MB I"; cf. below) ushers in the true Middle Bronze Age in Syria-Palestine and sees the beginnings of the "Canaanite" culture and city-state system that prevailed for more than half a millennium, throughout the MB and LB periods. Albright distinguished this period, like the preceding one, first on ceramic grounds, isolating the highly burnished wheelmade wares of Strata G–F and comparing them with the few deposits known at the time, such as the "Courtyard Cemetery" at Tell el-'Ajjûl[19] in Palestine, as well as with material from Qaṭna, Ugarit, and especially from Byblos in Syria.[20] All these groups he correlated with the late Twelfth and Thirteenth Dynasties in Egypt and dated in absolute terms to ca. 1900/ 1850–1750 B.C.

As additional evidence accumulated, the picture was filled out in some detail but not substantially altered. The sites known up to the present in Palestine are few, but the following list brings them together for the first time in one publication, including several sites not previously recognized. (For tomb and stratum numbers, and for the Syrian sites, see Charts 1 and 2 at the close of this essay.) From our vantage point we can now properly assess several deposits excavated even before Tell Beit Mirsim, i.e., material from Petrie's "Amorite City" and Bliss's "City Sub I" at Tell el-Ḥesi (1891 and 1894);[21] Tombs I (lower) and III 30 at Gezer (1912);[22] a few tombs in the Jaffa Necropolis (1926);[23] and Tombs I–II at Beth-Shan (1931).[24]

Following shortly upon Albright's characterization of the period at Tell Beit Mirsim came important supplementary material from soundings at Râs el-'Ain (1936);[25] Tell Kisan (1936);[26] Beth-Shemesh (1938);[27] and especially from the excavations at Megiddo, still one of the best known sites of the period (1938).[28] In the immediate post-World War II years, evidence began to mount from a number of tombs, in the Wadi et-Tin (1947), at Tell el-Far'ah (N), and near Jaffa (1948);[29] and from a small sanctuary at Nahariyeh, on the coast (1950).[30] The publication of *Lachish* IV[31] and Hazor I[32] in the same year (1958) added small but significant stratified material from major sites. Material multiplied rapidly during the 1960s, with the publication of tombs from Khirbet Kūfīn (1962),[33] Gibeon (1963),[34] and Moza (1966)[35] in the Central Hills; a few tombs at Jericho (1965);[36] and a tomb at Barqai (1969),[37] at the southern entrance to the Megiddo pass. We may also note the stratified deposits from Shechem (1961);[38] Tell Poleg (1964)[39] and Tell Zeror (1965)[40] in the Sharon Plain; Bethel (1968);[41] and Yabneh-Yam (1969).[42] The latest notices indicate a small site on the outskirts of modern Tel-Aviv (1971);[43] a stratum not previously encountered in the excavations at Gezer (1971);[44] and a campsite near Beth-shemesh (1972).[45] Finally, unpublished tomb groups are known from Safad, Nazareth, Tell el-'Amr (Geba-Shemen), Ginosar, Dan, and 'Ain es-Sâmiyeh;[46] and surface surveys along the Sharon Plain have produced evidence of several Middle Bronze sites which began as small settlements in the MB IIA period.[47]

The basic problem in dealing with the MB IIA period in Palestine is that the excavated material is still so scant that we are unable to form a comprehensive view of the material culture. Most of the evidence we have consists of pottery, a disconcerting proportion of it at many sites, such as Tell el-'Ajjûl, Megiddo, and Tell el-Far'ah (N), from tombs and therefore not representative of the culture as a whole. Concerning the tombs themselves, those which appear to be typical are intramural burials in shallow cists which are usually stone-lined. The interments are normally of a single individual, the skeleton articulated and partly flexed. Extramural MB IIA burials are also found, mostly in reused MB I shaft-tombs in the vicinity of many sites.[48]

The pottery of MB IIA[49] is exceptionally well made on a fast wheel, evidence of which is seen in the numerous fine wheelmarks which are often left visible. The delicate and graceful forms, many of them carinated, are those which only a past mastery of wheel technique makes possible, and most of them now appear for the first time in the history of the country. The clays are well levigated and fired, and many of the wares on the smaller vessels are metallic and almost eggshell thin; even body sherds on the large storejars are so well finished that they are a delight to handle. Attention to detail is evident in the finishing of rims, handle attachments, and even the underside of the bases. Ware color ranges from brick-red to creamy white, but pinks and buffs predominate. Bowls, juglets, and all classes of jugs and pitchers are usually covered with a heavy dark red or purplish-red slip, even on the base; and the burnishing is so skillfully done that the best examples almost appear to be glazed. Painted bands or geometric designs in black, red, or in both colors decorate some vessels, and occasionally even trichrome wares appear (*Figure 1. Figures 1–12* are listed on p. ix and appear following p. 300).

The main ceramic forms are those familiar to us from MB IIB–C, since the vessels of MB IIA are actually their prototypes; but the prototypes are usually superior in form and particularly in finish. The basic repertoire is illustrated in *Figure 1*. In addition many "exoctic" and unique forms occur, still recognizable, however, by certain hallmarks of the period, such as the preference for ovoid forms and flat bases, or the frequency of painted or burnished decoration. Those who have handled this pottery will agree that it is no exaggeration to say that the MB IIA pottery of Palestine is the finest locally made pottery in the history of the country, both in its aesthetically pleasing forms and in its exquisite workmanship and finish. This pottery is all the more noteworthy because it stands in such complete contrast to the rather crude pottery of the preceding MB I period.[50]

The bronze implements are not as numerous or well known, but the basic inventory seems to consist of weapons.[51] The chief types are illustrated in *Figure 2*. Daggers with a slotted blade and a curled tang occur sporadically;[52] and the shaft-hole ax seems to begin in this period (at least to judge from Syria).[53] The metallic types are ordinarily made of true bronze with an admixture of at least 6–9 per cent of tin or lead, in contrast to those of unalloyed copper in the preceding period. They are easily distinguished from MB I in specific form—although some *general* types, such as daggers with rivets, fenestrated axes, and toggle-pins, are common to both periods.[54]

Much of the present evidence for MB IIA comes from tombs, as it does for the previous period; but that does not mean that there were few town sites or that the pattern of settlement was largely one of isolated villages, as in MB I. On the contrary, the period has always been understood, and properly so, as an urban one; and this is confirmed by the increasing stratified material from a number of major town sites which span the EB–MB periods, where MB IIA occurs in proper sequence on the mounds.[55] The relative lack of stratified material until recently is undoubtedly due to the fact that the period is not of long duration and the occupational deposits were thus fairly shallow; moreover, the remains have probably been disturbed by the massive building operations of the MB IIB–C period which followed immediately. We must also allow for the fact that excavations have simply not concentrated on appropriate sites or levels, so arguments from silence or detailed characterizations on the basis of our scanty material are dangerous.

Tell Beit Mirsim and Megiddo still remain the only town sites known in any detail.[56] Here the houses are closely grouped and give some indication of town planning, though they are by no means impressive dwellings. In general they are like those of the MB IIB–C period, which are much better attested. Neither here nor elsewhere is there monumental architecture, although at least two simple temples of the period are known: an open-air "high place" at Nahariyeh, on the coast north of Hadera; and a primitive "courtyard sanctuary" at Shechem.[57] The impressive city walls of Tell Beit Mirsim G–F and Megiddo XIII were attributed by the excavators to MB IIA, as were those of Tell Poleg more recently.[58] Recent observations, however, suggest that these fortifications may belong only to the very end of MB IIA or even to the following period.[59] Certainly at sites where the evidence is unambiguous, such as Jericho, Shechem, and Gezer, it is clear that many MB IIA settlements, although flourishing and extensive, were unfortified. (This is somewhat puzzling, especially if we contrast them to the heavily fortified sites of the following period, but we will return to this problem presently.)

The MB IIA culture was truly *urban,* however, and is best understood simply as the initial phase of the Middle Bronze period proper. We can infer this from its continuity with the fully developed urban culture of MB IIB–C, for the astonishing momentum of the latter presupposes that urban influences were already at work in the preceding period.[60] To appreciate the continuity, one has only to note that the most typical MB IIB–C ceramic forms—such as piriform juglets, carinated bowls, ovoid storejars—evolved out of their MB IIA prototypes in a continuous and almost predictable development throughout the MB II period. The same general phenomenon, though less marked, is seen in the metallic types: rilled daggers, shaft-hole axes, and toggle-pins all persist from MB IIA through MB IIB–C. However, in speaking of a continuous "evolution," it must be cautioned that we do not imply a unilinear development nor are we prejudicing the discussion with notions of "progress." One of the ironies is that while MB IIB–C does witness impressive growth in population and general prosperity throughout the period, ceramic and metallic forms undergo a steady degeneration, both technically and aesthetically, especially toward the end (although mass production does introduce a greater variety of forms). In passing, we may note that it is the continuity of the several phases in MB II which prompts us to retain the traditional "MB IIA" terminology, for it denotes the links with MB IIB–C more accurately than Kenyon's "MB I."[61]

The sudden appearance of a material culture as mature and sophisticated as that of Palestine in the MB IIA period demands explanation. This culture cannot have simply developed out of the local MB I culture which preceded it, for as we have seen the break between the two periods is one of the most abrupt and complete in the entire cultural sequence of the country. The *Vorlage* of MB IIA has been sought to the north since Albright's pioneering studies in the early 1930s demonstrated beyond doubt the links of the pottery of Tell Beit Mirsim G–F with that of sites in Syria and northern Mesopotamia. Supplementing the archaeological evidence, more recent studies by Kenyon, Mazar, and the writer[62] have emphasized the literary evidence documenting the "Amorite" expansion in the early second millennium B.C., which brought large-scale incursions of West Semitic peoples from the aforementioned areas into Palestine and probably as far south as the Egyptian Delta. These movements reached their peak in the twentieth–eighteenth centuries B.C.—precisely in the MB IIA phase in Palestine—and their effect was so powerful that southern Syria down to about the border of Palestine came to be known in Akkadian texts of the eighteenth century onward as "the land of Amurrū."[63]

It is true that we lack texts from Palestine itself, but the ethnic and linguistic situation there can safely be inferred from the well-known Egyptian "Execration Texts," of which at least the earlier (Berlin) group dates to the mid-late nineteenth century B.C. and belongs indisputably to MB IIA. The "Tale of Sinuhe" from about the twentieth century B.C. reflects essentially the same cultural environment. The "Instruction of Merykare" (ca. 2100 B.C.) and the "Wall of the Prince" built by Amenemhet I (ca. 1991–1862 B.C.) are ample witness of the threat of Asiatics entering Egypt even before MB IIA. While the peoples of Syria-Palestine are not designated specifically as "Amorites" in these texts, they are called "Amu," which certainly denotes Asiatics; furthermore they bear good West Semitic names of distinctly Amorite type, identical to those in the contemporary Akkadian texts. Finally we have the famous Beni Hasan painting (no. 3) from the early nineteenth century B.C., which depicts a trading party of Asiatics from Palestine, some members of which are shown carrying socketed spears and "duckbill" axes of precisely the type known only in MB IIA.[64]

The point is that the traditional attempt to connect the pottery of the period with Syria and northern Mesopotamia coincides remarkably with more recent interpretations of the literary evidence. The two lines of argument are thought by nearly all scholars today to converge in such a way as to identify the "Amorites" conclusively as the newcomers who introduced the material culture of MB IIA into Palestine.

However, the strictly *archaeological* data in this chain of evidence now needs to be re-examined. It should be recalled that Albright's chief argument at the time of the publication of Tell Beit Mirsim was the similarity of his MB IIA material to certain material from Byblos, particularly the "Montet Jar," which he dated to "the first half of the eighteenth century" B.C.[65] It was largely this piece of evidence which he used as a peg upon which to hang his chronology of ca. 1900 for the beginning of the period. Later he also connected "Royal Tombs" I–IV at Byblos with MB IIA in Palestine. Finally, beginning in 1962, on the basis of his identification of the princes buried in these tombs, he lowered the date for the contents to the eighteenth century B.C., thus reducing MB IIA to ca. 1800–1700 B.C. and adjusting the dates for the remainder of MB II downward accordingly.[66]

Concerning the Byblos evidence, which has been cited by Albright again and again but rarely checked by others (except Kenyon, see below), it is time to clear up some of the confusion. First of all, even if we accept Albright's date in the eighteenth century B.C. for the "Royal Tombs," the tomb contents are of no help in fixing absolute dates for MB IIA in Palestine for two simple reasons. (1) Albright's comparisons of metallic and ceramic forms were based partly on visual observations of the Byblos material, which had not been fully published.[67] A recent publication of the evidence in full by Tufnell[68] makes it clear that when the whole repertoire is considered comparisons with MB IIA are hardly conclusive. All that can be said of most of the non-Egyptian material is that it belongs generally with our MB IIA *and* B.[69] Broad comparisons may be made, but they obviously do not offer precise dates. (2) Even if the comparisons were exclusively with Palestinian MB IIA and not with IIB, this would argue at most for lowering the end of MB IIA well into the late eighteenth century B.C.; this says nothing whatsoever about the *beginning* of the period, which could still fall before the eighteenth or even before the nineteenth century B.C.

The numerous "foundation deposits" in the "Champs des Offrandes," the "Temple of Ba'alat," and the "Obelisk Temple" are no more helpful.[70] Comparisons of the deposits are apt to be facile, ignoring the fact that many of the deposits contain heirlooms and cover a time-span of two centuries or more. Furthermore, even in fairly homogeneous deposits the assemblages reflect the conglomerate and highly sophisticated culture of coastal Syria, particularly Byblos, under Egyptian influence, and the comparisons that do exist with Palestine are too distant to elucidate the material culture there in any except the most general ways. All that can be said of the majority of the deposits is that the material appears to range from the twenty-first into the early nineteenth centuries B.C. in absolute dates, and in terms of relative chronology it compares with Palestinian MB I and IIA.[71] A recent study by Tufnell, Porada, and Ward of the famous "Montet Jar"—so often cited by Albright for MB IIA parallels—indicates that the date of most of its contents may now be raised from "the first half of the eighteenth century" B.C. to the twenty-first century, with perhaps an extension of some of the scarabs into the twentieth century B.C.[72] In summary, the Byblos material as a whole, if it means anything at all, forces us to *raise,* not lower, the dates for MB IIA.

Yet we cannot stress too strongly that isolated comparisons prove nothing. The point is that since there are no absolute dates from Palestine we are dependent upon a *network* of international synchronisms for both MB I and

IIA. Today there can be little doubt about the correlation of the eclipse of town life in MB I in Palestine with the "First Intermediate" period in Egypt (Sixth through Eleventh Dynasties, ca. 2175–2040 B.C.) and in part with the "Gutian interlude" in Mesopotamia (ca. 2180–2082 B.C.).[73] The succeeding periods, the late Eleventh Dynasty (ca. 2050–1992 B.C.) and the Twelfth Dynasty in Egypt (ca. 1991–1786 B.C.), and the ascendancy of the Amorite kingdoms in Mesopotamia and Syria beginning in Ur III (ca. 2060–1950 B.C.) and accelerating in the First Dynasty of Babylon (ca. 1830 B.C.), must be correlated with MB IIA. The rapid renascence of urban life in Syria-Palestine was due to both the cultural impetus of new elements of population from Mesopotamia (the "Amorites") and to the prosperity brought about by the renewed political and economic interests of the Egyptian Twelfth Dynasty in Asia.[74] The result was a sophisticated composite culture on the Syro-Palestinian littoral which flourished in an international milieu. The "Royal Tombs" of Byblos are illustrative of this culture.[75] The developments which made this culture possible must have been under way in Syria by about 2000 B.C. or slightly later, and even allowing for the maximum cultural lag, the period cannot have begun much later in Palestine, that is, by ca. 1950–1900 B.C. Indeed, as we have shown elsewhere on the basis of actual correlations of Twelfth Dynasty Egyptian texts with the archaeological material from Megiddo and Shechem, these are the *lowest* possible dates for the beginning of MB IIA.[76]

For the end of the period, we have only to observe that MB IIB must begin by about 1800 B.C. or shortly thereafter (below), which provides a convenient *terminus ante quem*. An independent consideration is that 1950–1750 B.C. seems uncomfortably long for a period with such scant remains, and we should favor a raising of the lower limits along with the upper in order to keep the period as short as possible. In summary, Albright's drastic lowering of dates to 1800–1700 B.C. is demonstrably impossible on archaeological grounds. If anything, the dates for MB IIA should be *raised* from his original 1900–1750 B.C. to ca. 1950–1800 B.C.[77]

Having stressed the importance of international synchronisms, we must nevertheless recall that Palestine in the MB IIA period was a relatively obscure backwater, open to wider cultural influences largely via Syria.[78] It is for this reason that *direct* comparisons are difficult and even misleading, becoming more so the farther we move beyond Syria. Kenyon has recently interpreted the Syrian connections in her own way, considering chiefly the coastal area and concluding that Byblos was "the originator of the new urban civilization" of MB IIA Palestine.[79] But there are at least two difficulties with this view: the Byblian culture is itself derivative from a larger cultural sphere; and with its strong Egyptian contacts it is probably atypical (above). Let us look briefly at the broader cultural context (largely ignored by Kenyon), beginning in inner Syria, going northward along the coast, and finally into northern Mesopotamia.

To begin with the neighborhood of Byblos itself, we may note even closer parallels to the Palestinian material at coastal sites south of Byblos: from tombs at Sin el-Fil, near Beirut; and tombs at Lébé'a, Kafer-Djarra, and Kāmid el-Lōz, near Sidon.[80] Some of this material has long been known, but the almost *exact* parallels to our MB IIA pottery seem to have escaped attention. Recently E. Oren has noted many of these parallels and has made an exhaustive collection of the equally close comparisons in the bronze implements.[81] But there is much more comparative material.

The sites inland along the Orontes appear slightly farther afield in cultural relationships, but the links are still close. Much of this material has been known since the 1930s, but has rarely been utilized.[82] Moving northward precisely into the "land of the Amurrū," we find extremely close connections with our MB IIA in tombs at Tell et-Tin and Yabrud;[83] in some of the latest material in Tomb IV and especially in Tomb I at Qaṭna;[84] in Hama H;[85] at several small sites just to the north, such as Khan Sheikhoun, Tell 'As, Sourān, Maṣin, etc.;[86] especially important are the Italian excavations since 1964 at Tell Mardikh;[87] and finally in the 'Amûq.[88] Even in the northern coastal region at Ugarit[89] and Alalakh,[90] the linkages are quite close.

The connections are still recognizable as we move into Upper Mesopotamia, although naturally more distant, and because of a probable cultural lag in the diffusion of influences, some of the pertinent levels are slightly earlier. On the Euphrates and the Balikh, Carchemish and vicinity are relevant,[91] as is the famous *hypogéum* at Til-Barsib.[92] On the Khabur we have Tell Chuera[93] and Chagar Bazar.[94] Farther east near Mosul, we have reflections of this culture at Tell Billa[95] and Tepe Gawra.[96] Moving down the Euphrates, Baghouz, near Mari, has striking parallels;[97] and we may even cite material from the Diyala region.[98] Finally, to place it in its broadest setting, there are links of this whole Syro-Mesopotamian cultural complex with Iran farther east; and turning in the other direction, some basic traits extend westward as far as southeastern Anatolia, Cyprus, and the Aegean.[99]

For the latter areas the suggestion made long ago by Albright and more recently by Amiran and Wright, connecting our MB IIA painted wares with the "Khabur ware," is worthy of further investigation.[100] Kenyon alludes to some parallels in the use of painted bands at both Megiddo and Ugarit[101] but does not mention any of the "Khabur" sites or the close connections of this painted style throughout Palestine, Syria, and Upper Mesopotamia. The "Khabur" ceramic style is marked by globular bodies and a preference for handleless forms; the decoration consists of red or reddish-brown paint, applied on the upper body usually in concentric bands, or in cross-hatched chevrons between bands, in a severe geometric style. We have noted some occurrences of this ware at Megiddo, Râs el-'Ain, Gezer, Qaṭna, Hama, Ugarit, Alalakh, the 'Amûq, Til-Barsib—and, of course, at Chagar Bazar on the Khabur, where its origin is often sought.[102] Another painted style of this region, but one which is probably related, is the "North Syrian painted ware," best known from Alalakh, but occurring also in the 'Amûq ("painted simple ware"), in Cilicia ("Cappadocian ware"), and even at Kültepe beyond the Taurus range. The paint is similar to the "Khabur ware" but many include animal motifs, and the forms run more to pitchers, jugs, and wide shallow bowls (some with pedestal foot).[103] These two painted styles are contemporary in part and are undoubtedly related, although the precise connections are not yet clear. A third type of Syrian painted pottery may have been an imitation of Cypriote "White Painted" wares, for Sjöqvist, Schaeffer, and Ästrom have all maintained that this popular fabric was manufactured not only in Cyprus but was also produced very early in branch factories on the Syrian coast.[104]

While it seems certain that at least the first two painted styles influenced Palestine already in MB IIA (and the third no later than MB IIB), chronological precision could come only from a clearer understanding of the relationship between these styles. In particular, which was prior, and which way did the direction of influence go? This question cannot yet be solved, since absolute dates for the respective styles cannot be established. Two factors may point to a diffusion from west to east rather than the expected movement in the other direction. First is the fact that Syria (especially Alalakh and the coastal area) and Cilicia seem to be the center of an extraordinarily prolific painted-ware culture, as will be seen by contrasting the popularity of paint there with its relative scarcity along the Orontes (Hama J–H) or in the Upper Euphrates region (Til-Barsib), where the simple-ware tradition continued. Second is the probability that the North Syrian painted wares are the earliest and began their *floruit* in the twentieth century B.C.[105] Thus the painted wares could have originated in the west and influenced the Khabur area only secondarily.[106]

Such an explanation would correct the anomaly in current theory which has the Palestinian MB IIA painted wares of the twentieth–nineteenth centuries B.C. derived from the "Khabur" tradition, despite the fact that the excavator puts the beginning of these wares at the type-site of Chagar Bazar ca. 1800 B.C.,[107] which would correlate rather with our MB IIB. Amiran has sensed this problem,[108] but the solution is not simply to opt for Sidney Smith's "Middle Chronology" to raise the absolute dates of the "Khabur ware." Nor is this necessary, for even if the above attempt to untangle a rather complex relationship is rejected, it would still be possible to relate the "Khabur ware" to Palestinian MB IIA by simply raising the beginning of its *floruit* to ca. 1900 B.C. or earlier. It is worth recalling that Mallowan's low date seems to have rested on the assumption: (1) that there was a gap between Levels 3–2 and 1 at Chagar Bazar, following 2000 B.C.; and (2) that the tombs of Level 1, found below floors dated to the time of Shamshi-Adad I, belonged only to that period and not earlier. It would appear that both assumptions are open to question.[109]

While the assemblages in the areas we have been discussing are not of course identical, there are several *overlapping* regional cultures stretching northward from Palestine into Mesopotamia, in which ceramic and metallic types can be traced more or less continuously. Thus there is little doubt as to the origins of the MB IIA people in Palestine or of the distinctive material culture which they introduced and which was to have such a long *flourit* once established.

Today the "Amorite" background of the MB IIA period is so widely accepted[110] that the detailed ceramic comparisons we have offered only strengthen the consensus. One of the few objections offered to this view is the difficulty of explaining the nearly complete cultural break between MB I and MB IIA if *both* are to be attributed, as seems likely, to the "Amorites."[111] But elsewhere we have shown that while the earlier waves of "Amorites" came from a seminomadic culture on the fringes of Syria, by the late twentieth and nineteenth centuries B.C. succeeding waves of "Amorites" coming from the same areas had meanwhile been partly or wholly urbanized.[112] They brought with them to Palestine a material culture which appears radically new because it had no forerunners *there,* but it had been flourishing elsewhere for some time. The basic elements of this culture were undoubtedly borrowed from Mesopotamia and particularly from Syria, but once they were introduced into Palestine they were affected more strongly by local than by foreign influences. In many cases this meant a degeneration, as for instance when certain types of vessels were no longer imported but continued to be imitated, or when metallic prototypes gave way to inferior imitations in clay. Many items common in Syria were either never imported in the beginning, or soon disappeared. And, of course, there were indigenous developments, especially in utilitarian vessels.[113] In its later manifestations (MB IIB–C) the original background of this material culture becomes less and less recognizable, simply because the relative isolation and poverty of Palestine, compared to Syria, were dominant factors.

The introduction of this new culture seems by and large to have been a peaceful one, as evidenced by the fact that there is no trace of a destruction layer at any MB I site.[114] It is true that many MB I settlements were deserted at the end of the period, particularly in Transjordan and in the Negev. Small groups of people may have migrated southward, even as far as the Sinai peninsula, but most of them must have simply been assimilated, their impoverished culture swallowed up by the new and more vigorous culture of MB IIA.[115] If both populations were of West Semitic or specifically of "Amorite" stock, this should not be surprising. Further evidence that the MB I/MB IIA transition was peaceful is the fact that once settled themselves, the MB IIA newcomers apparently felt no need for massive fortifications, at least in the earliest stages (above).

We have already emphasized the continuity of MB IIA with MB IIB–C, pointing out for instance that the basic repertoire of ceramic and metallic forms of the latter is derived from MB IIA. In other areas there are, of course, distinctive features of MB IIB–C, such as multiple burials in large caves or reused shaft-tombs, rather than the single burials of MB IIA; or the development of fortress-temples which replaced the simple open-air sanctuaries of the earlier part of the period.[116] But these are natural consequences of the increasing population and prosperity which accompanied town life as it flourished. Leaving open the question of the earliest simple town walls (above), it might be argued that the only *radically* new element in the material culture of MB IIB as villages and towns grew into powerful city-states was the emergence of massive systems of fortification, particularly those of the rampart and *glacis* variety. This development, then, may be the best criterion for distinguishing MB IIB as a new cultural phase.

It is customary to attribute these rampart fortifications, along with certain other aspects of the material culture such as the "Tell el-Yehudiyeh" juglets, to the "Hyksos," partly Semitic peoples from the north who temporarily over-ran Lower Egypt in the Fifteenth through Sixteenth Dynasties. Thus one arrives at a date of ca. 1720 B.C. for the first of these fortifications, and perhaps a generation or so earlier, ca. 1750 B.C., for the beginning of the MB IIB phase.[117] Recent studies, however, have demonstrated how doubtful some of the "Hyksos" associations are,[118] and it would seem better to try to establish the date of the rampart fortifications independently. Unfortunately, the development from simple earthen embankments and mudbrick walls to elaborate glacis, revetments, and massive cyclopean walls is more complex than first thought, and the first stages cannot be isolated and dated very satisfactorily. Recently Peter Parr has judiciously surveyed all the archaeological evidence currently available and has concluded that at most Palestinian sites the first *fully developed* rampart fortifications of MB II fall between about 1725 and 1700 B.C.[119]

Another line of reasoning is to correlate the literary evidence from Mesopotamia with the emergence of flourishing city-states in Palestine. Here the evidence from Hazor and Dan (not discussed by Parr) is critical, for these two sites in northern Palestine are mentioned in the Mari letters as important centers on the established trade routes with Upper Mesopotamia. The Hazor reference has been known for some time, but recently A. Malamat has combined this with new texts mentioning Dan and has pointed out the chronological implications.[120] Excavation indicates that Hazor and Dan did not become flourishing cities until MB IIB, when the first fortifications were built,[121] so it is this period which must be correlated with the Mari texts. The earliest of these texts dates from the time of Shamshi-Adad I, so by ca. 1720 B.C. at latest (following the "Low Chronology") MB IIB is in full flower in northern Palestine. If we follow the "Middle Chronology" (Shamshi-Adad I, ca. 1815–1780 B.C.) as most Assyriologists do, then the period must begin even earlier, that is, ca. 1800 B.C. The later (Posener) group of Execration Texts, which clearly presumes a more complex social develop-

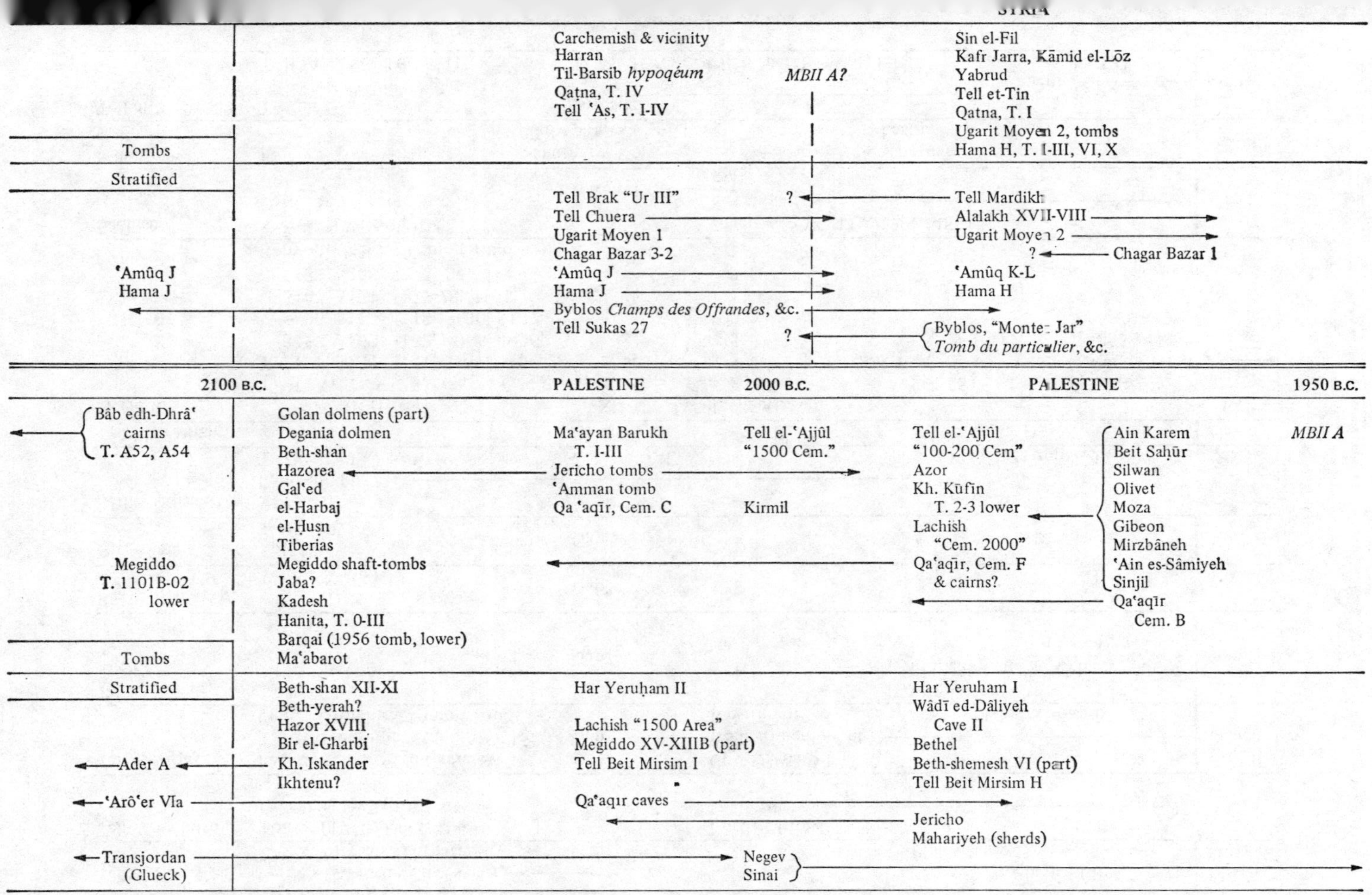

SYRIA

Tombs

Carchemish & vicinity
Harran
Til-Barsib *hypogeum*
Qatna, T. IV
Tell 'As, T. I-IV

Sin el-Fil
Kafr Jarra, Kāmid el-Lōz
Yabrud
Tell et-Tin
Qatna, T. I
Ugarit Moyen 2, tombs
Hama H, T. I-III, VI, X

Stratified

Tell Brak "Ur III"
Tell Chuera
Ugarit Moyen 1
Chagar Bazar 3-2
'Amūq J
Hama J
Byblos *Champs des Offrandes*, &c.
Tell Sukas 27

Tell Mardikh
Alalakh XVII-VIII
Ugarit Moyen 1
Chagar Bazar 1

'Amūq K-L
Hama H
Byblos, "Monte=Jar"
Tomb du particulier, &c.

'Amūq J
Hama J

MBII A?   MBII A

2100 B.C.   2000 B.C.   1950 B.C.

PALESTINE

Ma'ayan Barukh T. I-III
Jericho tombs
'Amman tomb
Qa'aqir, Cem. C

Tell el-'Ajjūl "1500 Cem."
Kirmil

Tell el-'Ajjūl "100-200 Cem."
Azor
Kh. Kūfin
T. 2-3 lower
Lachish "Cem. 2000"
Qa'aqir, Cem. F & cairns?

Ain Karem
Beit Saḥūr
Silwan
Olivet
Moza
Gibeon
Mirzbāneh
'Ain es-Sāmiyeh
Sinjil
Qa'aqir Cem. B

MBII A

Golan dolmens (part)
Degania dolmen
Beth-shan
Hazorea
Gal'ed
el-Harbaj
el-Husn
Tiberias
Megiddo shaft-tombs
Jaba?
Kadesh
Hanita, T. 0-III
Barqai (1956 tomb, lower)
Ma'abarot

Har Yeruham II
Lachish "1500 Area"
Megiddo XV-XIIIB (part)
Tell Beit Mirsim I

Qa'aqir caves

Har Yeruham I
Wādī ed-Dāliyeh Cave II
Bethel
Beth-shemesh VI (part)
Tell Beit Mirsim H

Jericho
Maḥariyeh (sherds)

2100 B.C.   2000 B.C.   PALESTINE   1950 B.C.

Tombs

Bāb edh-Dhrā' cairns T. A52, A54

Megiddo T. 1101B-02 lower

Stratified

Beth-shan XII-XI
Beth-yeraḥ?
Hazor XVIII
Bir el-Gharbi
Kh. Iskander
Ikhtenu?

Ader A

'Arō'er VIa

Transjordan (Glueck)

Negev
Sinai

Chart 1.   Relative sequence of MBI groups in Syria-Palestine ca. 2150-1950 B.C. (Syrian MBII A sites minimal and overlap with Palestinian MB I exaggerated.)

SITE	1950 B.C. MBII A	1800–1750 B.C.	MBII B	1650 B.C. MBII C	ca. 1550 B.C.
Tell el-Hesi	Petrie's "Amorite City" (part) → Bliss's "City Sub I" (part) →	Gap?		Petrie's "Phoenician City" Bliss's "City I"	Bliss's "City II"
Tell-Aviv/Jaffa	Tombs (1926, 1948, 1949) Domestic levels		Fortifications Domestic levels Tombs		?
Tell el-ʿAjjūl	Petrie's "Courtyard Cemetery" T. 1015; reuse of "100–200," "1500 Cem. Tufnell's "Tomb Groups 1–5"	Gap?	City I, Palace I Wall, embankment Revetment		City II Palace II
Tell el-Farʿah (S.)		Gap?	Wall Embankment Fosse Gate	"Tomb Group 6" "Cemetery 500" (T. 550, 551) I	Gap
Rās el-ʿAin	II Tombs 2, 4–6	Gap?			
Beth-shan	T. I, II T. 92 (1971)	Gap?		XB?	XA?
Beth-shemesh	VI (part) Campsite (1972) T. 2(=12) lower, 9	T. 3 (=13), 17		V { Wall / Gate T. 2 (=12) upper, 11	
Tell Beit Mirsim	G–F	E1	E2	D	Gap
Megiddo	XV–XIII (part) T. 911A1, D; 912B, D T.24 → T. 2151, 3138, 3141, 3147, 3150 3157, 3162, 3168, 4016, 4046, 5106, 5114, 5118, 5130, 5147 5167, 5171, 5177–78, 5181, 5183, 5268, 5275, &c. Kenyon's MB I, "Tomb Group" A	XII–XI → B C T. 3019	{Wall, Glacis, Gate 44, 644 3075 3085 4100} D E T. 3175 T. {251, 253, 257}	X F G T. {3070, 3095, 4055} T. 2031	IX → H
Lachish	Sherds, NW Section Cave 1504 (part)	T. 157, 173 Cave 6002	Glacis Revetment Fosse	T. 119, 129, 145, 153	Gap?
Nahariyeh	Sanctuary Early phases	Niveau 5	Sanctuary Last phases		
Tell el-Farʿah (N.)	Trench 692 T. B, AN, AD, 16 (part)	Niveau 5 T. A,F,H,AM,3,15,18 (part)	T. I–L, 5,11,12	Glacis Revetment Gate { T.C, E	Gap

Jericho	T. K3 "Tomb Group" ——→	I ——→	II–III	IV ——→ V ——→ ?	
			Wall, Glacis, Revetment — 3 phases ——→		Gap
Hazor	Sherds in XVII	XVII (=LC IV) Wall, gate, revetment, fosse		XVI (=LC III) T. 1-33 Area C	Gap?
		1970 Tomb → Embankment			
Shechem	Temenos 1 (XXII–XXI)	Temenos 2, 3 (XX) Wall D	Temenos 4, 5 (XIX–XVII) Wall C, Embankment	Temenos 6, 7 (XVI) Walls A, B E, NW Gates	Gap
Ta'anach		Slight remains		Wall, glacis Domestic levels } (2 phases) Intramural burials ——→	
Kh. Kūfin	T. 3-4, 6, 7	T. 3 (upper), Ch. 6, 7 (part)	T. 3 (upper), Ch.		
Gibeon	T. 31-31A (upper), 58 (upper)	15 K/LH 8, Level 4 T. 14, 15, 22, 30 36, 64A	T. 11-13, 18 35-37, 42, 57 ——→ ?	T. 19-21, 44	
Bethel	sherds?	Gap?	? } ?	Wall NW Gate Domestic levels	Gap
Beth-zur				Wall A Fields I, III, Level III }	
Gezer	XXI → Gap? T. 1 (middle), 3?	T. 1 (lower), III 30	XX ——→	XIX T. I 15, II 28	XVIII ——→ ?
Dan	Tomb		Embankment Domestic levels }	Tombs }	Gap?
Barqai	1956 Tomb (middle)	1956 Tomb (upper)			
Tell Zeror	21-20	Wall Glacis Moat } → ? 19-18		Gap?	
Tell Poleg	sherds	Brick wall Glacis } → ?			
Yabneh-yam	Domestic levels	Wall Embankment Gate, Ph III }		Gate, Ph II 1967 Tomb	

Chart 2. Major sites in Palestine in the MB II period, ca. 1950–1550 B.C. (Bold line indicates a major destruction.)

ment than the earlier group and may be correlated with MB IIB in Palestine, also mentions Hazor and Dan (Laish). Since these texts belong to about the middle of the eighteenth century B.C. at latest,[122] we have additional evidence for a *terminus ante quem* of ca. 1750 B.C. for the MB IIA/B transition. In short, Albright's latest date of ca. 1700 for the beginning of MB IIB is out of the question. Since the evidence is not yet decisive, the traditional date of ca. 1750 B.C. is still possible; but ca. 1800 B.C. is now preferred by Kenyon, Mazar, Yadin, and others.[123] If we add the evidence (above) that MB IIA must begin ca. 1950/1900 B.C. and with its paucity of material surely cannot represent a long time-span, then we may be compelled to adjust our MB IIB–C chronology upward, in fuller agreement with the Mesopotamian "Middle Chronology."

CONCLUSION

A final problem needs to be mentioned in connection with the development of the MB II fortified city-states. There is growing evidence that some sites, especially along the coast, after flourishing briefly were destroyed at the end of MB IIA or about the beginning of MB IIB.[124] Other sites inland may have had a different history, but it seems probable that even there many sites were still small and virtually undefended in the transitional MB IIA–early B period, ca. 1800–1700 B.C., and that the first effective defenses were built only after disastrous experience and recovery.[125] Whatever the explanation may be, it is clear that there was a "cultural explosion" in the MB IIC phase and that the bulk of the fortifications as well as the other impressive building operations of MB II were compressed into a relatively brief period after ca. 1650 B.C. However, the later phases of the Middle Bronze Age are beyond our scope here, and we leave the subject by simply noting the major sites and the pertinent levels in Chart 2.

NOTES

1. K. Kenyon, with G. Posener and J. Bottéro, *Syria and Palestine, c. 2160–1780 B.C.,* *CAH*[3], Fasc. 29 (1965)=part 2 of *CAH*[3], I, pp. 567–594; Kenyon, *Palestine in the Middle Bronze Age, CAH*[3], Fasc. 48 (1966)=ch. III of *CAH*[3], II.

2. B. Mazar, "The Middle Bronze Age in Palestine," *IEJ* 18 (1969), 65–97.

3. G. E. Wright, "The Archaeology of Palestine from the Neolithic Through the Middle Bronze Age," *JAOS* 91 (1971), 276–293 (a review article covering in part the second work cited in N 1). It was Professor Wright who suggested the topic of MB I for a dissertation while the writer was a doctoral student with him and guided this work to completion. Later he assigned him the responsibility of the final publication of the MB

IIA materials from Shechem (forthcoming). It was his sponsorship and encouragement that made possible the writer's work at Gezer from 1966–1971 and both the Hebrew Union College and the Albright Institute in Jerusalem. This essay is offered to Professor Wright in affection and esteem, as a small token of the writer's sense of indebtedness to him.

4. W. G. Dever, "The 'Middle Bronze I' Period in Syria and Palestine," (henceforth "Middle Bronze I"), in *NEATC,* pp. 132–163; *idem,* "The Peoples of Palestine in the Middle Bronze I Period" (henceforth "Peoples of Palestine"), *HTR* 64 (1971), 197–226. Bibliography for the sites listed in *Figure 1* will be found in these two articles; add now R. Dajani, "An EB-MB Burial from Amman," *Annual of the Department of Antiquities of Jordan* 12–13 (1967–68), 68, 69, pl. XL: 1, 2; B. Shantur and Y. Labadi, "Tomb 204 at 'Ain-Samiya," *IEJ* 21 (1971), 73–77; Z. Yeivin, "A Silver Cup from Tomb 204a at 'Ain-Samiya," *IEJ* 21 (1971), 78–81; W. G. Dever, "An MB I Tomb Group from Sinjil," *BASOR* 204 (1971), 31–37; *idem,* "MB I Cemeteries at Mirzbâneh and 'Ain-Samiya," *IEJ* 22 (1972), 75–112; *idem,* "A Middle Bronze I Necropolis and Settlement on the West Bank of the Jordan," *Archaeology* 25 (1972), 231–233 (on Jebel Qa'aqīr); O. Negbi, "Canaanite Burial Caves at Ḥanita," *Bulletin of the Ḥanita Museum,* no. 1 (Hebrew, n.d.). On the Wādi ed-Dâliyeh, see the chapter by W. G. Dever, "The MB I Pottery from Cave II," in a forthcoming *AASOR,* eds. F. M. Cross and Nancy Lapp. On the Degania and Golan dolmens, see the brief notices in *Hadashot Arkhiologiyot,* nos. 38 (1971), 7–8, and 39 (Hebrew) (1971), 10–13.

5. Cf. Dever, "Middle Bronze I," nn. 49, 84–85; M. Kochavi, "The Middle Bronze Age I (The Intermediate Bronze) in Eretz-Israel," *Qadmoniot* 2 (1969), 34–44; E. Oren, "A Middle Bronze Age I Warrior Tomb at Beth-Shan" (henceforth "Warrior Tomb"), *ZDPV* 87 (1971), 109–139.

6. G. E. Wright, "Archaeological Method in Palestine—An American Interpretation," *EI* 9 (1969), 128–129.

7. W. F. Albright, *The Excavation of Tell Beit Mirsim. I: The Pottery of the First Three Campaigns* (henceforth *TBM,* I), *AASOR* 12 (1932), 8, 11, 15. This error was obviously the result of faulty stratigraphy, but it is to Albright's credit that it was spotted and corrected in the next season; see *The Excavation of Tell Beit Mirsim. IA: The Bronze Age Pottery of the Fourth Campaign (TBM,* IA), *AASOR* 13 (1933), 64, 68.

8. Cf. W. F. Albright, *The Excavation of Tell Beit Mirsim. II: The Bronze Age (TBM,* II), *AASOR* 17 (1938), 15. Incidentally, the attribution of the first town wall to Stratum H was maintained to the end by Albright; cf. "Debir," in *Archaeology and Old Testament Study,* ed. D. Winton Thomas, (Oxford, 1967), p. 211; see also "Remarks on the Chronology of Early Bronze IV–Middle Bronze IIA in Phoenicia and Syria-Palestine," *BASOR* 184 (1966), 34, n. 34. However, the argument was one from the negative evidence and is not taken seriously by anyone today.

9. The break is stressed most strongly by Kenyon and the writer. Wright takes a more moderate position but agrees generally. Amiran first attempted to see continuity in the ceramic types, but on the basis of comparisons that were open to serious question. For the evidence and references to the opposing views, cf. Dever, "Middle Bronze I," n. 65; add now Kenyon [N 1], *CAH³,* II, 3–6; Wright, *JAOS* 91, 287; R. Amiran [see N 99]. The strongest ceramic argument is still the supposition that the distinctive pierced-rim cooking pots continued throughout both periods, but the writer will show at length the fallacy of this argument in the publication of the Dâliyeh material [N 4], where it will be demonstrated that this cooking pot type is almost exclusively MB IIA. However, the overlap of MB I and MB IIA in Syria in the twentieth century B.C. should be noted (see 13, 15 and NN 85, 86, 88, 113), a phenomenon which is not seen in Palestine probably because both cultures were derivative there and because the relative cultural isolation and poverty of Palestine did not stimulate assimilation there. On the discontinuity of bronze types, see N 54.

10. Lapp, one of the earliest proponents of the "Intermediate" terminology, in his last works abandoned this for "EB IVA–B," i.e. "EB IVB" for our period. W. F. Albright finally retained "MB I" for the main part of the period but adopted "EB IV" for the earliest phases (Amiran's Families B–C; see N 99). Wright had earlier suggested that if any new terminology were to be advanced, "EB IV" would be preferable to "MB I." For references see Dever, "Middle Bronze I" [N 4], nn. 65, 72, 84–85; add now Oren, "Warrior Tomb" [N 5], p. 109, n. 1 ("EB IVa–b"). The strongest defense to date of the continuity from EB through MB I is the writer's "Peoples of Palestine" [N 4], pp. 209–211 (also citing Lapp's independent views). It is the Bâb edh-Dhrâ' evidence that is decisive, as predicted; see now Thomas Schaub, "Bâb edh-Dhrâ' Tombs A92 and A94," and W. G. Dever, "The EB IV–MB I Horizon in Palestine," *BASOR* 210 (1973), 37–63.

11. Cf. references in N 10. Amiran's "MB I" usage seems to be a matter of conviction, but the conservatism of Wright and the writer in terminology is largely to avoid the extremely confusing usage of Kenyon, which transfers "MB I" to what is generally known as "MB IIA" (see N 61). However, Kenyon is in our opinion right *in principle*, and if agreement could be reached it would indeed be better to follow her shift. For former "EB IV" and "MB I" as a composite period we would then prefer "EB IVa–b," as does Oren [N 5]; the Bâb edh-Dhrâ' evidence [N 10] demonstrates conclusively that this is the only terminology which fits the actual ceramic sequence.

12. Cf. W. F. Albright, "Palestine in the Earliest Historical Period," *JPOS* 15 (1935), 218; for references to later works, see N 13.

13. For references to the views of Albright, Wright, de Vaux, and Kenyon, see Dever, "Middle Bronze I" [N 4], n. 53. The most extensive defense of this view to date is the writer's "Peoples of Palestine" [N 4] pp. 210–226; cf. also Y. Aharoni, *The Land of the Bible* (Philadelphia, 1966), pp. 125–126; Y. Yadin, "A Note on the Scenes Depicted on the 'Ain es-Samiya Cup," *IEJ* 21 (1971), 85.

14. Cf. Dever, "Peoples of Palestine" [N 4] pp. 220–221. An article by A. Rainey entitled "The World of Sinuhe," to appear in the forthcoming *Annual* of the Institute of Archaeology, Tel-Aviv University, vol. I, will also oppose the "Amorite" hypothesis, although primarily on literary rather than on archaeological grounds; but see our reaction in N 98.

15. "Peoples of Palestine," pp. 221–226.

16. See Dever, "Middle Bronze I" [N 4], pp. 142–144, esp. nn. 37, 38; *idem*, "Peoples of Palestine," p. 224, n. 63. Note the writer's raising of dates for MB I by about fifty years, from ca. 2150–1900 B.C. to ca. 2200–1950 B.C., as more evidence has accumulated. The latest scholar to support the higher dates (ca. 2200–2000 B.C.) is Rainey [N 14].

17. The only way to bring the end of MB I somewhat later would be to posit an overlap with MB IIA, as the writer once tentatively suggested, following Glueck and Albright; but the chronological overlap of two mutually exclusive cultures in such a small and generally homogeneous country as Palestine seems most unlikely. On a probable overlap in *Syria*, however, see N 9.

18. See *TBM*, IA [N 7], p. 68 (correcting *TBM*, I [N 7], pp. 8–18). The modest statements here conceal the fact that this was the *first* recognition and integration of an important cultural phase in the history of Palestine—at a time when there was still virtually no parallel material.

19. W. M. F. Petrie, *Ancient Gaza*, II (London, 1932), 5; for the bronzes, pl. XIV: 71–75; for the pottery, pls. XXVIII, XXX, XXXI, XXXII, XXXIV, *passim* (mostly labelled "X–XI Dynasty"); for the Plan, pl. XLVI; for the Register, pls. XLVII, LVIII. Albright's reworking of the site, described by him in "The Chronology of a South Palestinian City, Tell el-'Ajjûl," *American Journal of Semitic Languages and Literatures* 55 (1938), 337–359, is still valuable. On the "Courtyard Cemetery," see now the extremely useful re-

publication of all the material by O. Tufnell, "The Courtyard Cemetery at Tell el-'Ajjûl, Palestine," *Bulletin of the Institute of Archaeology* 3 (University of London, 1962), 1–37.

20. Albright, *TBM*, IA [N 7], pp. 69–75.

21. W. M. F. Petrie, *Tell el-Hesy* (*Lachish*) (London, 1891), pp. 41, 42, pls. V, VI, *passim* (drawings are poor, but note the high incidence of burnish); F. J. Bliss, *A Mound of Many Cities, or Tell el-Hesy Excavated* (London, 1894), pp. 40–43, pl. 3:91 (mixed with EB).

22. R. A. S. Macalister, *The Excavation of Gezer* (henceforth *Gezer*), I (London, 1912), 301, 302: III, pls. LX–LXII (T. 1); I, p. 298, fig. 158 (T. III 30).

23. L. A. Mayer, "A Bronze Age Deposit from a Cave Near Neby Rubin (Jaffa District)," Palestine Museum, Jerusalem, Bulletin 2 (1926), 2–7; cf. also NN 29, 99, 104.

24. G. M. Fitzgerald, *Beth-shan Excavations, 1921–1923* (Philadelphia, 1931), pls. XIII, XXXV:12–22. See also Oren, "Warrior Tomb" [N 5], pp. 109 ff. (T. 92 of the "Northern Cemetery").

25. J. H. Iliffe, "Pottery from Râs el-'Ain," *QDAP* 5 (1936), 116–125, pls. LXIV–LXVII (Stratum II); J. Ory, "Excavations at Râs el-'Ain. II," *QDAP* 6 (1938), 99–120 (T. 2, 3–6).

26. *QDAP* 5 (1936), 208; see also the observations of Albright in *JPOS* 15 (1935), 223, and in *TBM*, II [N 8], 24.

27. See Stratum VI, the pottery of which is mixed MB I and IIA; E. Grant and G. E. Wright, *'Ain Shems Excavations: Part IV* (Haverford, Pa., 1938), pl. XXIV: 1–11 (painted), 17–29; *idem, Part V* (1939), pp. 27, 95–99. For material from tombs, published earlier but not recognized as MB IIA, see D. MacKenzie "The Excavations at 'Ain Shems," *PEFA* 2 (1912–13), 42–46, pl. XVII (T. 9, the "High Place Grotto Sepulchre"); note also the lower levels of T. 2 (=12), E. Grant, *Beth Shemesh* (Haverford, 1929), pp. 79, 89, 137–145, 147–157, *passim* (poor description makes precise attribution difficult, but a number of forms are clearly MB IIA). See also N 45.

28. For the reused shaft-tombs, see P. L. O. Guy, *Megiddo Tombs* (Chicago, 1938), pls. 23 (T. 24, probably late MB IIA); 28–29 (T. 911A1); 31:8–21, 32:1, 2 (T. 911D); 35:1–18 (T. 912B, D). For notched chisel-axes, socketed spears, and a rilled-dagger from T. 911D, see pl. 122:1, 2, 5–7, 9. For the intramural MB IIA burials, see G. Loud, *Megiddo*, II (Chicago, 1948), pls. 7–22, where the MB IIA burials must be sorted out of Strata XV–XIII. On this task, see the valuable restudy of K. Kenyon, "The Middle and Late Bronze Age Strata at Megiddo," *Levant* 1 (1969), 25–27, figs. 1–3 ("Group I," where those tombs in our *Figure 2* and several other MB IIA tombs are listed). For the MB IIA occupation on the mound (mixed throughout Strata XV–XIII), see Loud, *Megiddo*, II, 6–8, 78–87; Kenyon, "Some Notes on the Early and Middle Bronze Age Strata of Megiddo," *EI* 5 (1955), 55–60; *idem, Levant* 1 (1969), 38ff. Wright, "The Archaeology of Palestine," in *BANE*, p. 108, n. 71; T. L. Thompson, "The Dating of the Megiddo Temples in Strata XV–XIV," *ZDPV* 86 (1970), 38–49.

29. L. H. Vincent, "Une Grotte Funéraire Antique dans l'Ouady et-Tîn," *RB* 54 (1947), 269–282 (poor descriptions, but see fig. 3, pls. V–VII, *passim,* for probable MB IIA ceramic and bronze types); A. M. Steve and R. de Vaux, "La Seconde Campagne de Fouilles à Tell el-Far'ah, Près Naplouse," *RB* 55 (1948), 571–572, fig. 11; de Vaux, "La Cinquième Campagne . . . ," *RB* 62 (1955), 549, fig. 2, nos. 4–7, 10–12; *idem,* "Les 7e, 8e, 9e Campagnes . . . ," *RB* 69 (1962), 236, 240, 248, figs. 3, 4; on Dhahrat el-Humraiya, near Jaffa, see NN 99, 104, and J. Ory, "A Bronze Age Cemetery at Dhahrat el-Humraiya," *QDAP* 13 (1948), 75–89.

30. I. Ben-Dor, "A Middle Bronze-Age Temple at Nahariya," *QDAP* 14 (1950), 1–41; see also M. Dothan, "The Excavations at Nahariya, Preliminary Report (Seasons 1954/55)," *IEJ* 6 (1956), 14–25. Cf. N 57.

31. O. Tufnell, *Lachish*, IV (London, 1958), figs. 3, 4, *passim* (esp. the cooking pots); p. 255, pls. 69:550, 86:995 (Cave 1504).

32. That there was a settlement at Hazor in MB IIA has been denied by Y. Yadin; cf. "Hazor," in *Archaeology and Old Testament Study* [N 8], p. 257 (but cf. n. 29 there, where the possibility is admitted). However, a few clear MB IIA sherds illustrated in the publication indicate at least some occupation during MB IIA; cf. Yadin et al., *Hazor*, I (Jerusalem, 1958), pls. C:1–10 (Area D³, Stratum 4), 16, 17, 19, 22 (Area D³, Stratum 3); CXII:17, 20; CXIII:1 (Area D, unstratified); *idem, Hazor*, III–IV (Jerusalem, 1961), pls. CLVI:18 ff., *passim* (Area A, Stratum XVII); CCXXXV:12–20 (Area BA, L. 4026a, Stratum 15); CCXLVI:2–15 (Area G, L. 10012, "MB II"). The local strata of these areas all equal general Stratum XVII, the earliest MB II phase recognized by the excavators. This is generally MB IIB, but the admixture of some IIA material indicates that there was at least an ephemeral MB IIA stratum, between Strata XVII and XVIII (MB I). This is now confirmed by the chance discovery in 1971 of a large tomb with "MB IIA/B" material—found *below* the MB IIB city wall; cf. Y. Yadin and Y. Shiloh, "Hazor," *IEJ* 21 (1971), 230. The writer has examined the material through the courtesy of the excavators and is convinced of the MB IIA date of the earliest material. See now Yadin, *Hazor:* (London 1972), pp. 201–206.

33. R. H. Smith, *Excavations in the Cemetery at Khirbet Kūfīn, Palestine* (1962), pp. 17–30, pls. XIII–XVII (the alabasters and a few other objects and vessels are probably MB IIB).

34. J. B. Pritchard, *The Bronze Age Cemetery at Gibeon* (Philadelphia, 1963), pp. 42, 43, 61, 62, figs. 34, 64. The excavator thought the evidence for Tomb 31–31A (Upper) pointed only to MB II generally, but the dagger and the notched ax in particular confirm the MB IIA date.

35. V. Sussman, "Middle Bronze Age Burial Caves at Moza," *'Atiqot* 3 (1966; Heb. series), 41–44, figs. 2, 3. Tombs 1 and 2 are clearly reused MB I shaft-tombs; the material is mixed and some is probably as late as MB IIC, but MB IIA is clearly represented by the notched ax (fig. 3:2) and probably also by some of the bowls and carinated cups (fig. 2, *passim;* there are no descriptions of wares, so exact attribution of vessels is difficult).

36. K. Kenyon, *Jericho*, II (London, 1965), 203–206, fig. 93; T. K3 is the only one assigned by Kenyon to MB IIA (her "MB I"). However, in addition it seems likely that most of Kenyon's "Group I" tombs (three out of four), which she attributed to MB IIB (*Jericho*, II, 172), belong rather to the end of MB IIA and the transition to MB IIB. Cf. T. A1 in *Jericho*, I (London, 1960), 302–306, figs. 112, 113; also phases 1–2 of T. A34 in all probability; ibid., pp. 352–368, figs. 140, 141, 142, 143, *passim*. T. J3 (pp. 306–315, figs. 115–118) is assigned by Kenyon to "Group I," but it is clearly MB IIB or even C and should go with "Group III" or "IV." See also *Jericho*, II, T. B48 (phases 1–3 only), pp. 206–211, figs. 95–99 (the only vessels in these early phases of T. B48 which need be later than MB IIA are those in figs. 98:1, found in the repository, and 98:9, a cylindrical juglet). On the redating of Kenyon's "Groups I–V" see the reviews of *Jericho*, I, by P. W. Lapp, *AJA* 65 (1961), 70, and of *Jericho*, II, by Wright in *Antiquity* 40 (1966), 149–150.

37. R. Gophna and V. Sussman, "A Middle Bronze Age Tomb at Barqai," *'Atiqot* 5 (1969; Heb. series), 1–13, fig. 4.

38. See the various preliminary reports by G. E. Wright et al., in *BASOR* 161 (1961), 22, 23; 169 (1963), 6, 11, 17, 18, 24–26, 31; 180 (1965), 15, 16, 26–28. See also Wright, *Shechem: The Biography of a Biblical City* (New York, 1965), pp. 111, 112, 120–122. No MB IIA pottery has yet been published, but the writer has studied the material extensively in preparation for its final publication in the Shechem series

[N 3]. The final stratum designation "XXII–XXI" in fig. 2 is from a personal communication of G. E. Wright.

39. R. Gophna, "Tel Poleg," *IEJ* 14 (1964), 109–111; *idem, RB* 62 (1965), 552, 553. On the date of the fortifications see N 59.

40. See the preliminary reports by M. Kochavi in *IEJ* 15 (1965), 254, 255; *IEJ* 16 (1966), 274, 275; cf. the final reports by K. Ohata and M. Kochavi, *Tel Zeror,* I (Tokyo, 1966), 27–28; *idem, Tel Zeror,* II (Tokyo, 1967), 23–25, also pl. IX:1 (a piriform juglet of MB IIB "Stratum 19," but probably MB IIA). On the question of the date of the fortifications, see N 59.

41. W. F. Albright and J. L. Kelso, *The Excavation of Bethel (1934–1960)* (Cambridge, 1968). On p. 56 Kelso claims some MB IIA material; but the discussion does not elucidate what is meant by this, nor is any indisputable MB IIA pottery published. (Note the complete absence of the typical MB IIA pierced-rim cooking pot, p. 56.) See the review article by the writer, "Archaeological Methods and Results: A Review of Two Recent Publications," *Orientalia* 40 (1971), 466, 467.

42. See J. Kaplan, *IEJ* 19 (1969), 121, where a date of MB IIA is claimed for the earliest MB II gate and city walls, on the basis of comparisons with the pottery of Tell Beit Mirsim G-F. But note that the pottery was all from the "lower foundations" and from "foundation trenches," so nothing more can be said than that it is in fill and provides only a *terminus post quem* for the structures above; cf. N 59.

43. J. Kaplan, *IEJ* 21 (1971), 174, reporting a primitive campsite at Sede Dov, with pottery of Tell Beit Mirsim G-F type.

44. W. G. Dever, H. D. Lance et al., "Further Excavations at Gezer," *BA* 34 (1971), 125–127.

45. A campsite with crude hovels was discovered in 1971 about one mile south of Beth-shemesh and subsequently excavated by C. Epstein; see *Hadashot Arkhiologiyot,* 41–42 (1972), 27–29 (Heb.). The excavator dates the site to early MB IIB, but personal examination of the pottery through the courtesy of Dr. Epstein has convinced this writer of a range from late MB IIA through MB IIB or later.

46. See preliminary notices in *Hadashot Arkhiologiyot,* 36 (1970), 11, 12 (Heb.); E. Oren, "Warrior Tomb" [N 5], p. 127, n. 94; R. Amiran, *Ancient Pottery of the Holy Land* (New Brunswick, N.J., 1970), p. 106. The Nazareth material is mentioned through the courtesy of D. Bahat. The writer is indebted to A. Biran for a preview of a late MB IIA or A/B tomb from Dan. C. Epstein has discussed tombs of similar date from Ginosar with the writer. Finally, on 'Ain es-Sâmiyeh, see the writer as cited in N 51.

47. These sites will be published in a dissertation being completed by R. Gophna, who has made an extensive survey of the region; the writer has seen the pottery, and there can be no question about the MB IIA or A/B date of some of it, which resembles Gezer Stratum XXI very closely.

48. For typical cist-tombs in Palestine, cf. e.g. *Gezer,* I [N 22], 298, fig. 158 (T. III 30); J. Ory, *QDAP* 6 (1938), 101–104, figs. 3–6 (Râs el-'Ain, T. 2. 4–6). For cist-tombs in Syria, see A. Assaf, "Der Friedhof von Yabrud," *Acta Apostolicae Sedis* 17 (1967), 55–68 (T. 4); R. Du Mesnil du Buisson, *Baghouz, L'ancienne Corsote* (1948), pls. XL, XLI. For reused MB I shaft-tombs, see Oren, "Warrior Tomb" [N 5], pp. 109, 110, fig. 1; Pritchard [N 34], pp. 61, 62 (T. 58); Smith [N 33], pl. V (T. 3 and references in N 33); Engberg and Shipton, *Megiddo Tombs* [N 28], T. 911–912.

49. The detailed description is offered because the pottery of MB IIA is not known firsthand to many excavators and is based on the writer's handling of the MB IIA wares from Shechem (see NN 3, 38) and Gezer (see N 45). For illustration, see Amiran [N 46], fig. 3, and further, pp. 90 ff., pls. 25–35.

50. Cf. N 9.

51. On the MB IIA weapons, see now the exhaustive treatment of Oren, with full

comparative discussion, in "Warrior Tomb" [N 5], esp. fig. 2, for an illustration of the main types (for more *typical* blood-rilled daggers, however, see for instance Pritchard [N 34], fig. 34:2). Oren [N 5] does not include the chisel-ax, which he thinks belongs only to the MB IIA/B or even the IIB horizon (cf. "Warrior Tomb," 135–136). However, one must distinguish between *two* types of chisel-axes: (1) the true "shaft-hole" chisel-ax (see N 53), which is indeed characteristic only of MB IIB–C (at least in Palestine); and (2) the simple socketless chisel-ax with a notch for thong-attachment, which is typologically earlier and occurs in clear MB IIA contexts. For examples of the latter in Palestine, see Pritchard [N 34], fig. 34:4 (T. 31–31A; contrast with the "shaft-hole" ax, fig. 51:41); Guy and Engberg, *Megiddo Tombs* [N 28], fig. 173:1, 2, pl. 122:1, 2 (T. 911); Loud [N 28], pl. 182:1 (T. 3168, with good MB IIA ceramic types); Petrie [N 19], pl. xiv:73 (T. 1015). See now W. G. Dever, "A Group of MB IIA Weapons from 'Ain es-Sâmiyeh," *BASOR* 217 (1975), 23–31.

52. The occurrences of this type in Palestine have not been heretofore recognized as belonging to MB IIA, but see Loud [N 28], pl. 178:5, belonging to L. 5061 of Stratum XIII A, which may be MB IIA. Note the extraordinarily wide diffusion of these daggers in Syria, Mesopotamia, and Anatolia, in contexts of ca. 2000 B.C. and earlier. Cf. D. B. Stronach, "The Development and Diffusion of Metal Types in Early Bronze Age Anatolia," *Anatolian Studies* 7 (1957), 107–111, figs. 5, 6 ("Type 2b–c").

53. The occurrences in Palestine all seem to be MB IIB–C, but for earlier examples in Syria, almost certainly MBI/IIA, see F. Thureau-Dangin and M. Dunand, *Til-Barsib* (1936), pls. xxviii:5, xxix:3, 5–8.

54. Here it must be borne in mind that the differences in both number and degree far outweigh the similarities. As an example, the daggers of the two periods are both identifiable as daggers, but there could scarcely be more difference, formally or technologically; contrast, for instance, Pritchard [N 34], figs. 58:6, 34:1. Fenestrated axes may appear to be nearly identical, but on the clear distinctions between the earlier ("eye") and later ("duckbill") types, see Oren, "Warrior Tomb" [N 5], 111–114, 135, 136. The point is that the distinctions are absolutely consistent: general categories may continue, but there is no overlap of *specific* types between the two periods. What is also significant is that certain diagnostic types, like the MB I pikes and javelins with curled tang, never appear in MB IIA or later contexts. The best explanation for the vague similarities in MB I and IIA weapons is that both derive from a common distant background, as does the pottery of the two periods, i.e. from Syria and northern Mesopotamia (cf. N 9).

55. Cf. Wright, *Shechem* [N 38], Dever and Lance [N 44], etc.

56. For Megiddo see references in N 28; for Tell Beit Mirsim see Albright, *TBM*, I [N 7], 14–18; *TBM*, IA [N 7], 67–75; *TBM*, II [N 8], 17–25.

57. On the Shechem courtyard temple, see N 38. For Nahariyeh, see N 30. The Nahariyeh sanctuary was dated by both excavators only to MB II generally, but the earliest phase seems certainly to belong to MB IIA. Cf. Ben-Dor [N 30], figs. 16:325 (JP); 19–22 (SJ); 23 (HK); 24:c (JB); 34 (CBB); 47 (OJP). See also Dothan [N 30], fig. 8 (JP). See N 80 for acronyms.

58. See references in NN 18, 28, 39.

59. Kenyon has already expressed doubts about the attribution of the earliest city wall at Tell Beit Mirsim to Stratum G and suggests F instead; see *CAH*³, II [N 1], 6. The same view will be defended in detail by A. Eitan in "Tell Beit Mirsim G-F—The Middle Bronze IIA Settlement," in *BASOR* 208 (1972), 19–24. Y. Yadin has recently developed the thesis that none of the known MB IIA settlements was fortified, and in a forthcoming article he will attempt to show that the city walls of Tell Beit Mirsim G-F and Megiddo XIII have both been misattributed (meanwhile see the 1972 work cited in N 32). As for the putative MB IIA date of the Tell Poleg, Tell Zeror, and Yabneh-Yam fortifications (see NN 39, 40, 42), no stratigraphic evidence linking

the MB IIA pottery to the fortifications has yet been published, and in discussions in Israel considerable doubt attaches to the opinion of the excavators on these early dates.

60. The continuity and urban character are also stressed, e.g. by Kenyon, *CAH*[3], II [N 1], 6–12. See also Mazar [N 2], 72–78.

61. Kenyon nowhere offers a defense for this terminology, and of course she herself emphasizes the continuity throughout (see N 60). The choice of terms is apparently more a matter of convenience than conviction: the former place of "MB I" having been taken by "EB–MB," it is necessary to shift "MB I" downward one phase to describe what everyone else calls "MB IIA." While this may be defensible in principle (see N 11), the unilateral introduction of new terminology simply exacerbates the difficulties already current in matters of terminology. One can hardly imagine greater confusion, even for the professional archaeologist, in reading the present literature, where the new terminology is often adopted with no explanation!

62. Kenyon, *CAH*[3], I [N 1], 60, 61 (drawing upon the superb survey of J. Bottéro and G. Posener in the first part of the same fascicle); *idem*, *CAH*[3], II [N 1], 7–12; Mazar [N 2], 69–75, 81, 82; Dever, "Peoples of Palestine" [N 4], 217–223. For recent bibliography on the Amorites, cf. n. 45 of the latter work, and esp. G. Buccellati, *Amorites of the Ur III Period* (Naples, 1966), which is now the fundamental work.

63. For references see A. Malamat, "Northern Canaan and the Mari Texts," in *NEATC* [N 4], pp. 165–166, fig. 1.

64. On the literary evidence, see principally J. Bottéro and G. Posener in *CAH*[3], I [N 1], 3–37. On the "duckbill" axes and their dating, see Oren, "Warrior Tomb" [N 5], 111–114, 133–135.

65. Albright, *TBM*, IA [N 7], 70, 74.

66. Albright, "The Chronology of Middle Bronze I (Early Bronze–Middle Bronze)," *BASOR* 168 (1962), 36–42; "The Eighteenth Century Princes of Byblos and the Chronology of Middle Bronze," *BASOR* 176 (1964), 38–46; "Further Light on the History of Middle-Bronze Byblos," *BASOR* 179 (1965), 38–43; "Remarks on the Chronology of Early Bronze IV–Middle Bronze IIA in Phoenicia and Syria-Palestine," *BASOR* 184 (1966), 26–35.

67. Cf. Albright, *BASOR* 176 (1964), 43, n. 20; "Some Remarks on the Archaeological Chronology of Palestine before about 1500 B.C.," in *Chronologies in Old World Archaeology*, ed. R. W. Ehrich (Chicago, 1965), p. 54 (henceforth *Chronologies*).

68. O. Tufnell, "The Pottery from Royal Tombs I–III at Byblos," *Berytus* 18 (1969), 5–33.

69. Cf. Tufnell [N 68], 10–17, where the comparisons are with Palestinian MB IIA–C *generally*. Note that the squat dipper juglets (nos. 32–43) are MB IIC/LB I in appearance, as are the storejars (nos. 53–57), while the single cooking pot (no. 58) is almost a classic MB IIC type. This does not prove a late date, but it does illustrate the danger of facile comparisons.

70. For the latest on these, see Albright, *BASOR* 184 (1966), 26, 27; O. Negbi and S. Moskowitz, "The 'Foundation Deposits' or 'Offering Deposits' of Byblos," *BASOR* 184 (1966), 21–26; Kenyon, *CAH*[3], I [N 1], 55–57; *CAH*[3], II [N 1], 8, 9, 12, 13.

71. This date is generally agreed to by the scholars quoted in N 70, although we should allow for a possible extension down into the mid or late nineteenth century B.C.

72. O. Tufnell and W. A. Ward, "Relations Between Byblos, Egypt, and Mesopotamia at the End of the Third Millennium B.C.: A Study of the 'Montet Jar,'" *Syria* 43 (1966), 165–241; see also E. Porada, "Les Cylindres de la Jarre Montet," ibid., 243–258. This exceedingly valuable study makes available for the first time a full and reliable publication of the rich contents of the "Montet Jar"; the original publication used by Albright (P. Montet, *Byblos et l'Egypte* [Paris, 1928, 1929], pp. 112–125;

idem, Atlas, pls. LX–LXXI) presented but a fraction of the material, most of it only in photographs. Albright's "first half of the eighteenth century" date was based mainly on the identification of the scarabs (more than one hundred) as Thirteenth Dynasty or "Second Intermediate" period; but see now Tufnell and Ward, 173–189, for a "First Intermediate" date (Sixth through Eleventh Dynasties).

73. See especially Bottéro, Posener, and Kenyon in *CAH*[3], I [N 1]. Note, however, that by "correlation" we do not necessarily imply any more than contemporaneity; artifactual evidence and direct cultural contacts are difficult enough to establish for Mesopotamia and even more so for Egypt. Cf. Dever, "Peoples of Palestine" [N 4], 212–216, 223–225.

74. This is not the place to take up again the vexed question of a Twelfth Dynasty "empire" in Asia, for even a minimalist view supports our contention that urban life in Syria-Palestine was under Egyptian *cultural* aegis. For useful and current discussions of the Egyptian material from Palestine (the earliest from the time of Sesostris I, ca. 1971–1928 B.C.), see W. A. Ward, "Egypt and the Eastern Mediterranean in the Early Second Millennium B.C.," *Orientalia* 30 (1961), 22–45, 129–155; see also W. Helck, *Die Beziehungen Ägyptens zu Vorderasien im 3 und 2 Jahrtausend v. Chr.* (Wiesbaden, 1962), pp. 43–91. An eminently balanced view will be found in G. Posener, *CAH*[3], I [N 1], 8–29; after a full review of the evidence Posener concludes (20, 21) that "in view of the progressive increase in our knowledge, we shall err less if we exaggerate than if we minimize the hold the Twelfth Dynasty had over Syria and Palestine."

75. Cf. the well-known imported artifacts bearing the names or prenomens of Amenemhet III (ca. 1842–1797 B.C.) and Amenemhet IV (ca. 1798–1790 B.C.). Some of the silver vessels from Tombs I–II (e.g. Montet, *Atlas* [N 72], pls. CXI–CXII) appear to be Minoan in inspiration. On the network of Twelfth Dynasty international contacts, cf. esp. the well-known Ṭod deposit, with silver vessels and a seal of Minoan type as well as Old Babylonian, Ur III, and earlier materials from Mesopotamia; it was dedicated by Amenemhet II (ca. 1929–1895 B.C.) and found in the temple of Montu at Ṭod, south of Luxor. Such a diverse hoard was likely put together somewhere along the Syrian coast, and it reflects very well indeed the cosmopolitan character of the MB IIA culture there; for this deposit and Twelfth Dynasty–MB IIA–MM IIA tie-ups generally, see the authoritative treatment of H. J. Kantor, "The Relative Chronology of Egypt and Its Foreign Correlations before the Late Bronze Age," in Ehrich, *Chronologies* [N 67], pp. 19–22. See further NN 89, 99, 104.

76. See N 16; our interpretation of the evidence is now followed by Wright [N 3], 289; and by A. Rainey (on chronological implications, though he differs on other points); see NN 14, 16. It follows from our rejection of Albright's lower dates that we also reject Kenyon's date of ca. 1850–1800 B.C. (cf. *CAH*[3], II [N 1], 13; lowered from ca. 1900–1800 B.C. in *Archaeology in the Holy Land* [New York, 1960], pp. 169–170), since it, too, is based largely on the Byblos "Royal Tombs."

77. Apart from absolute dates, the figures given by Albright and Kenyon are objectionable in terms of relative chronology, on the ground that they compress the period too drastically, simply because there is at present so little material. (Note that Albright in his last statement shortened his ca. 1800–1700 B.C. to ca. 1800–1725 B.C.; cf. in Ehrich, *Chronologies* [N 67], pp. 55, 56.) But see above, on the dangers of arguments from silence. In our opinion, 50–75 years is simply too brief a time-span for MB IIA; see also Wright [N 3], 289.

78. It is clear from the Egyptian texts, the onomastic evidence, the Beni Hasan paintings, the Tale of Sinuhe, etc., that there was overland traffic between Palestine and Egypt, even as early as the twenty-first century B.C. But no artifactual evidence whatsoever survives to indicate trade or cultural exchange in MB I; and what evidence there is from MB IIA appears to have come via the Syrian coast, with which Egypt

had revived a bustling sea trade by the time of the Twelfth Dynasty. Any contacts MB IIA Palestine had with Mesopotamia and Anatolia certainly came through Syria, and it seems likely that those with Egypt and Cyprus also came overland through Syria rather than by sea. Note that of all the MB IIA sites in Palestine, only Jaffa could possibly have been a seaport, and there the meagre evidence from a few tombs hardly indicates more than a small village.

79. Kenyon, *CAH*[3], II [N 1], 8.

80. M. Chehab, "Tombe Phénicienne de Sin el-Fil," *Mélanges offerts à Monsieur René Dussaud*, II (Paris, 1939), 803ff. In the following notes a code is used to simplify comparison: SJ=large ovoid storejar; OJ=small ovoid handleless jar; PB= wide shallow "platter bowl"; CB=carinated bowl; BB=biconical bowl; GB=globular bowl or vase, P=pitcher, usually with pinched mouth; LJ=large one-handled jug; J=small flat-based jug or juglet; PJ=piriform juglet; DJ=dipper juglet; C=cup; HK=holemouth krater; FL=handleless flask; L=lamp; B added to the basic abbreviation signifies "burnished," P means "painted." For the bronzes, DA="duckbill" ax; NA=notched chisel-ax; RD=rilled-dagger; SS=socketed spear or lance; A=arrowhead; TP=toggle-pin; TQ=torque. For Sin el-Fil, see ibid., T. 1; cf. figs. 3a (GBB); 4b (PJB); 7a, b (JP); 8a (PP); 8c (DJP); 9 (PB, three handles). These vessels are virtually identical to Palestinian vessels. On the bronzes (DA, RD, SS, TP) see Oren (who also notes the ceramic parallels), "Warrior Tomb" [N 5], 111–117, 121, 122.

See also P. E. Guiges, "Lébé'a, Kafer-Ğarra, Qrayé, Nécropoles de la Région Sidonienne," *Bulletin du Musée de Beyrouth* 1 (1937), 5–76; 2 (1938), 27–72. Cf. T. 1 at Lébé'a, e.g. Guiges, *Bulletin du Musée de Beyrouth* 1, fig. 3a (PJP); 3b (PJ); 3c (LJ); 3d (DJ). See also T. 3, fig. 6 (PJP). Note T. 57 at Kafer-Ğarra (Ruweise), *Bulletin du Musée de Beyrouth* 2, 30–34 (OJ, PJ, DJ, CB, SJ); also T. 66, pp. 40–50 (PJ, B and P, GBB, CBB, CB, PB); T. 73, pp. 52–59 (OJ, J, GB, CB, DJ, PJ, HK, C). The pottery from these tombs is nearly identical to that of Râs el-'Ain, for example. For the similarly close bronzes, see Oren, "Warrior Tomb" [N 5], 111–117, 119–121.

For Kāmid el-Lōz see R. Hachmann, "Rapport Préliminaire sur les fouilles au Tell Kāmid el-Lōz de 1966–1968," *Bulletin du Musée de Beyrouth* 22 (1969), 49–84; cf. T. ID15:14, pl. XVI:1–6 (PB with four handles, P, J, GB, PJ—all B). It is significant that this and other tombs are cist-tombs with flexed single burials, below the level of the city wall and *glacis*.

81. Oren seems to be the first to utilize fully some of the Syrian sites in elucidating Palestinian MB IIA (especially the overlooked Tell et-Tin tombs; "Warrior Tombs" [N 5], 112), although the indefatigable C. F. A. Schaeffer had assembled much of the older material in convenient form in *Stratigraphie Comparée et Chronologie de l'Asie Occidentale* (London, 1948). Oren's work on the bronzes of MB IIA we regard as definitive (see, however, the caveat in N 51).

82. This entire complex is ignored by Kenyon (*CAH*[3], II [N 1], 8–13), which is interesting, since it is especially damaging to her theory that Byblos and the coastal region are the ultimate sources of the material culture under consideration. Of the inland sites Kenyon mentions only Qaṭna in passing, and neither alludes to nor mentions in the bibliography the only well-stratified material we have from Syria, Hama J–H and the 'Amûq K–L (see NN 85, 88). Cf. N 81 above, referring to Schaeffer's pioneering comparative study twenty-five years ago—an astonishing piece of work and useful even today, especially on the MB I–IIA horizon.

83. Space prohibits critical discussion of the following comparisons, so we must be content merely to list the major sources for parallels. On the neglected site of Tell et-Tin, known since 1895, see Oren, "Warrior Tomb" [N 5], 122 and references there (LJ, PB, DA, SS, RD, TP). For Yabrud, cf. T. 4, a stone-lined cist-grave; Assaf [N 48], GB, CB, DJB, DA, RD, SS, TP. See N 80 for acronyms.

84. See R. du Mesnil du Buisson, *Le Site Archéologique de Mishrifé-Qaṭna* (Paris,

1935); from T. IV (ca. 2000 B.C. at latest) cf. pls. XLV:208 (OJ); XLV:274 (BB); XLVII, *passim* (C). Better comparisons come from T. I (ca. 2000–1800 B.C.); cf. du Mesnil du Buisson, "Compte Rendu de la Quatrième Campagne de Fouilles à Mishrifé-Qatna," *Syria* 11 (1930), pls. XXXI:col. 7 (PP; exact parallel for *Gezer*, I [N 22], fig. 158:7); XXXII:col. 7 (OJP, BB, FLP); XXXIII:col. 7 (FL, BB); XXXIV:col 7 (PB). See N 80 for acronyms. Our date, ca. 2200–2000 B.C., for T. IV (i.e. the latest material being transitional MB I/IIA) is generally accepted. T. I at Qatna, extremely important, was originally dated ca. 1600 B.C. by du Mesnil du Buisson, ca. 1800–1700 B.C. by Schaeffer, ca. 1800 B.C. by Albright and Ingholt, but in our opinion it follows T. IV shortly and belongs to the typical inland Syrian MB IIA horizon, i.e. twentieth or at latest nine-teenth century B.C. (as suggested long ago by Wright, *BASOR* 71 [1938], 33). See also other MB IIA tombs in the area, for example, T. I at Osmaniye (*Syria* 11 [1930], pls. XXXI–XXXIV:col. 11).

85. E. Fugmann, *Hama. Fouilles et Recherches 1931–1938. L'Architecture des Péri-odes pre-Hellénistiques* (1958); parallels in Hama H1–5 are too numerous to list, but cf. figs. 109, 110, 117, 120, 124, 126, 132, 139, *passim* (virtually all our MB IIA forms except PJ and DJ, but the GB, PB, and CB are especially close to Palestinian examples). Burnish is rare, as is paint of the "Khabur" type, but note the high incidence of combed decoration, also fairly common in Palestine in MB IIA. See also the tombs of Stratum H (T. GI, II, III, VI, X), pl. x, *passim;* here the ceramic parallels are even clearer, and in addition we have exact bronze parallels (DA, SS, RD, TP, TQ). Hama H was dated by the excavators ca. 1900–1600 (Fugmann) or ca. 2000–1750 (Ingholt). We think the latter date preferable; note the continuity and possible overlap of phases H and J (as also between the 'Amûq J–K–L, N 88 below), with J ending by general consensus around 2000 B.C. On this as the beginning date for H, see also Schaeffer [N 81], pp. 110–111; P. J. Parr, "The Origin of the Rampart Fortifications of Middle Bronze Age Palestine and Syria," *ZDPV* 84 (1968), 34–35 (although both Schaeffer and Parr *end* H at ca. 1700 B.C.).

86. On Tell 'As, see R. du Mesnil du Buisson, "Une Campagne de Fouilles à Khan Sheikhoun," *Syria* 13 (1932). TT. I–IV at Tell 'As are generally coeval with Hama J, but very close to the MB IIA horizon ca. 2000 B.C.; cf. pls. XXXIX–XL, *passim* (PB, C, OJ) for vessels which seem to antedate our MB IIA slightly (note the TP and TQ of MB I type). The Khan Sheikhoun material is mixed, but some of it is of the MB I/IIA horizon (pl. XXVI, *passim*). For nearby sites, also of this horizon, see pp. XLIX, L, *passim*.

87. See P. Matthiae, M. Liverani et al., *Missione Archeologica Italiana in Syria. Rapporto Preliminare della Campagna 1964* (Rome, 1965); *idem, . . . Rapporto Pre-liminare della Campagna 1965* (Rome, 1966); *idem, . . . Rapporto Preliminare della Campagna 1966* (Rome, 1967). While an astonishing proportion of the pottery at this important site, both from the surface and from soundings, is of the Hama J/MB I horizon (corrugated simple ware, smeared-wash ware, reserve-slip ware), it is unfortunately published only in photographs in vols. I–II, and worse still with little stratigraphic context. In vol. III, line-drawings enable us to attribute some of the pottery approxi-mately to MB IIA, especially the combed wares (figs. 11, 12, 14–17, 19, *passim*). How-ever, the opinion of the excavators that this pottery dates the fortifications and other structures to MB IIA (ca. 1800 B.C. or earlier) is certainly not substantiated by the evidence; at most this material provides a *terminus post quem*. On the problem of the Mardikh dates, see (independently) Dever, "Middle Bronze I" [N 4]; Gophna and Sussman [N 37]; Parr [N 85], 33–36. Parr disagrees with the excavators' absolute dates, and prefers to date some of this material as late as 1700 B.C., but the problem is simply that the pottery as dug and published does not date the fortifications, no matter what its own date. It is frustrating that the Mardikh evidence, so potentially decisive, cannot be used with confidence at present.

88. Unfortunately the publication of the 'Amûq pottery leaves off at present with Phase J, ending ca. 2000 B.C.; see R.S. and L. Braidwood, *Excavations in the Plain of Antioch, I. The Earlier Assemblages, Phases A–J* (Chicago, 1960). Nevertheless, it is clear that Phase J, generally belonging to MB I, already anticipates our MB IIA in some forms; cf. figs, 337:14, 15; 342:2, 3. On the dating of J and its continuity with later phases, see Braidwood, p. 523. We have also had access to the unpublished dissertation of G. F. Swift, Jr., *The Pottery of the 'Amûq Phases K to O, and Its Historical Relationships* (Chicago, 1958), where Phases K–L are described as very sparse in remains and pottery (only one vessel illustrated from K), but generally correlated with Hama H, Alalakh XVII–VIII, and the Khabur sites, and linked to Palestinian MB IIA (pp. 3, 42–47, 52, 53, the last page stressing the J–K continuity). For Phases K–L "Khabur" wares see N 90.

89. The Ugarit Moyen 2/MB IIA comparisons are only vaguely alluded to by Kenyon in reference to Megiddo (*CAH³*, II [N 1], 10–11), but in fact they are much closer generally than those from Byblos which she labors so heavily. See C. F. A. Schaeffer, *Ugaritica*, II (Paris, 1949), figs. 99–109, *passim;* pls. XV, XVI, XXXIX–XLIV, much of this material coming significantly from cist-tombs. Especially important are the *painted pitchers and juglets*, first (1) in the "Khabur" style (figs. 99:18, 19, 22; 100:12–16; 102:10; cf. Loud [N 28], pls. 11, 16, 20, *passim; Gezer*, I [N 22], fig. 158:6, 7; Ory [N 48], 117, figs. 80, 82, pls. XXV:77, 89, 90 [Râs el-'Ain]; Gophna and Sussman [N 37], figs. 4:1–3 [Barqai]); (2) the painted "eye" pitchers with flaring pinched lip of Alalakh type (figs. 100:30, 107:2; cf. Swift [N 88], fig. 2 ['Amûq L]; L. Woolley, *Alalakh* [Oxford, 1955], pls. LXXXIV:a, LXXXV:a, b; Loud [N 28], pls. 34:16, 41:29, 30); (3) the juglets with painted concentric rings (figs. 100:20, 2; cf. Loud [N 28], pl. 19:13; *Ancient Gaza*, IV, pl. LIV:60N7; Amiran [N 46], p. 112 [Ginosar]); and finally (4) the jugs of Cypriote "White Painted" III–VI type, possibly imported (figs. 100:19, 21, 25, 27; 102:3; 104:27; 105:37; 107:28; 108:19, 20, 23; cf. the Palestinian examples from Gezer, Beth-shemesh, Tell Beit Mirsim, Megiddo, and Humraiya cited in N 104). The date of ca. 1900–1750 for Ugarit Moyen 2 is well enough fixed by its levels superseding the ruins of Ugarit Ancien, by numerous XII Dynasty objects beginning with Sesostris I (ca. 1971–1928), as at Byblos; and finally by the presence of a vessel of MM IIa "Kamares" ware (ca. 1900 B.C.–) in T. LXXXVI, below the level of T. LXXXV of typical Moyen 2; see Schaeffer [N 81], pp. 25, 26, 256, figs. 108, 109.

90. Alalakh provides a wealth of material, but because of Woolley's [N 89] confused stratigraphy and his impossibly high dates for the lower levels this material has scarcely been utilized for comparisons. Nothing of Alalakh precedes the 'Amûq K–L horizon, despite Woolley's date of 3400 B.C. (!) for the basal level, and consequently Strata XVII–VIII must be drastically telescoped and fitted into the MB IIA cultural sequence in Syria; see Braidwood [N 88], p. 523, and further (especially on the links of Alalakh XVII–VIII with 'Amûq K–L) Swift [N 88], pp. 15–19, 42–62. Swift stresses the Alalakh/'Amûq L synchronisms by pointing out many close similarities in the painted wares (see also references in N 88), but we may add Phase K to the link up as well by comparing the shallow carinated bowls with painted metopes on the outside, which Swift says "seem to typify phase K most clearly" (cf. Swift, p. 14, fig. 2: Woolley, pls. XCI:below; CX:23a–c (Strata XVII–VIII). These bowls in turn are found both in Upper Mesopotamia (and even in Iran), and in Cilicia; cf. M. V. Seton-Williams, "A Painted Pottery of the Second Millennium from Southern Turkey and Northern Syria," *Iraq* 15 (1953), 57–68.

It is surprising how much of the Alalakh material can be salvaged for comparative purposes, even though it is published only by types, by going through the *Corpus* (pls. CIX–CXXV) and selecting all the forms which range through XVII–VIII (see above): note especially close parallels in types 3b (PB), 5–6a (PBB), 9 (PB), 21a (GB), 23a–c (GBP, CBP), 24 (CB), 26a (HK), 57–58 (J), 70 (PP, "eye" type), 100 (GBP, related to "Khabur" ware?), 106a (GB), 152b (HK, incised decoration), 167 (L). See N 80 for acronyms.

91. On sites near Carchemish see L. Woolley, "Hittite Burial Customs," *Annals of Archaeology and Anthropology* 6 (1913), 87–98. Note that the graves at Kara Hassan, Hamman, and Amarna are stone-lined cists, with globular wheelmade pots and bronze implements very similar to those at Til-Barsib (below N 92) and presumably dating to ca. 2000 B.C., just before our period begins; cf. pls. XIX, XXI, XXIV, XXV, *passim*. Note however, one vessel apparently of "Khabur" ware (pl. XXIII). The affinities of Hamman with Chagar Bazar 1 are seen by Mallowan, who speaks of the "closest relations." M. E. L. Mallowan, "The Excavations at Tall Chagar Bazar, and an Archaeological Survey of the Habur Region, 1934–35," *Iraq* 3 (1936), 9, 35.

On Harran, see K. Prag, "The 1959 Deep Sounding at Harran in Turkey," *Levant* 2 (1970), 63–94. The phase IV–III sherds of corrugated and combed and/or smeared-wash ware suggest a range similar to Hama and 'Amûq J, shortly before 2000 B.C.; but for slightly later material see the few sherds of early ("eggshell") "Khabur" ware, fig. 8:43–44, pl. XXXIV:a.

92. The *hypogéum* at Til-Barsib (Tell Aḫmar)—a stone-lined cist-tomb which produced 1,045 pieces of pottery—is exceedingly valuable for comparisons. See F. Thureau-Dangin, M. Dunand et al., *Til-Barsib* (Paris, 1936), pp. 96–108, pls. XX–XXXI. So many vessels might suggest a long period of use, but there were only two articulated skeletons, and the pottery is generally thought to be quite homogeneous; however that may be, the maximum range is agreed by most authorities as ca. 2300/2200–2000 B.C. (cf. Schaeffer [N 81], pp. 81–84; Braidwood [N 88], pp. 520–522). The date is a bit early for our purposes (cf. the relative scarcity of "Khabur"-style paint), and much of the pottery belongs to the regionally restricted ceramic of the Upper Euphrates; but cf. the parallels (or forerunners) of our MB IIA in figs. 29 (GB, GBP, C); 30 (GB, PB, C); 32 (P, PB). See N 80 for acronyms. Wheel striations usually show, and burnish is common on many of these vessels (p. 105). A few comparisons are striking, especially in the burnished pitchers and jugs with profiled rim and pinched mouth; cf. pl. XXV:11–13, one with the twisted or rope-handle often found in Palestine (e.g. Loud [N 28], pl. 34:11). For other cist-tombs with similar pottery, see pp. 108–119, pls. XXXII–XXXIII.

93. For Tell Chuera, see A. Moortgat, *Tell Chuēra in Nordost-Syrien. Vorläufiger Bericht über die Grabung 1958* (Köln und Opladen, 1959); ". . . über die zweite Grabungskampagne 1959" (Wiesbaden, 1960); ". . . über die dritte Grabungskampagne 1960" (Köln und Opladen, 1961); ". . . über die vierte Grabungskampagne 1963" (Köln und Opladen, 1964); ". . . über die fünfte Grabungskampagne 1964" (Wiesbaden, 1967). Very little pottery has been published as yet, and the basis of the stratigraphy has not been presented, but it is clear that much of the material is First Dynasty of Akkad–Ur III in range. For globular vases, goblets and cups similar to those of the Orontes/'Amûq/Upper Euphrates complex, which may lie in the background of our MB IIA, cf. vol. I, Abb. 19, 38; esp. vol. IV, pp. 43–50; vol. V, Abb. 27. On metals of the same horizon, see vol. I, Abb. 20; vol. II, Abb. 7, 8; vol. IV, Abb. 30. It is surprising that no "Khabur" ware has yet been published in these preliminary reports, since Tell Chuera is only some seventy miles distant from Chagar Bazar, but it may be that Tell Chuera has a gap after ca. 2000 B.C., as does Tell Brak for instance, following Ur III; cf. M. E. L. Mallowan, "Excavations at Brak and Chagar Bazar," *Iraq* 9 (1947), 25, 26.

94. The best parallels at Chagar Bazar, including the well-known painted "Khabur" ware (below), come from tombs below the floors of Level I dwellings, especially TT.

104, 111, 117, 128, 139, 141–143, 151, 154, 157, 163, 186. In addition to the painted pottery, most of these tombs yielded toggle-pins and socketed spears of distinctly late MB I/early IIA type, very similar to those at Hama, Qaṭna, Hamman, and Til-Barsib (above N 92). Cf. Mallowan [N 91]; *idem,* ". . . Second Campaign, 1936," *Iraq* 4 (1937), 102–104, 118–124 (Register), figs. 12–13, 16, 21–24, *passim.* Note that one of the tombs with painted pottery (a bowl of Alalakh type) and also with three socketed spears of Palestinian MB IIA type is T. CLIV, an intramural tomb built up of mudbrick with vaulted or corbelled roof; cf. figs. 13:10, 11, 13; 16:8. Mallowan [N 91], 36, first dated the beginning of Level I to sometime after 2000 B.C. Schaeffer [N 81], pp. 87–91, proposed ca. 1900–1750 B.C. on the basis of connections with Ugarit Moyen 2. And later, on the basis of a radical break between Levels III–II and Level I, as well as tablets of Shamshi-Adad I found on the floor associated with T. 111, Mallowan [N 93], 21–25, 83–84, lowered the date for Level I to ca. 1900–1700 B.C. and suggested that the "Khabur" ware may not have come into use *in this area* (italics mine) until ca. 1800 B.C. Cf. NN 105, 106, 109 for a higher date.

95. For Tell Billa, cf. Stratum IV and TT. 42, 48, 61; E. A. Speiser, "The Pottery of Tell Billa," *Museum Journal* 23 (1932), 255–257, 270–273, pls. LVI–LIX. Note the proliferation of painted geometric and animal motifs in the "Khabur" style in Stratum 4 (pp. 256–257), especially on the ovoid jars (pl. LIX:1, 4; cf. also pl. LXXII); and the many open bowls, carinated bowls, and globular vases (pls. LVI–LVII, *passim*). The bronzes are not illustrated, but the descriptions of a crescentric ax, daggers, spirals, and toggle-pins with decorated heads and an eye-ring (p. 271) all point to a transitional MB I/IIA date for the beginning of Stratum IV, ca. 2000 B.C. or shortly thereafter.

96. For Tepe Gawra, where the scant material of Stratum V is relevant, see E. A. Speiser, *Excavations at Tepe Gawra,* I (Philadelphia, 1935), 56–58, 101–115, 149–150, 160–161, pl. LXXI. The ceramic forms are much more Mesopotamian than previously cited parallels, although ovoid jars with chevrons on the shoulder, globular vases, and simple cups are in evidence (pl. LXXI:150, 152, 154, 161). Very little metal is present in Stratum V, but its proliferation in Stratum VI fits the evidence from Syria of a substantial metal industry ca. 2000 B.C. and generally confirms the dating of Stratum V to a period of decline following that. Speiser originally dated V to "Late Sargonid" (pp. 182–183), but a much lower date, ca. 2100–1800 B.C., is now accepted (Porada, in *Chronologies* [N 67], pp. 165–167, 179).

97. See du Mesnil du Buisson [N 48]. This important site (Baghouz) just across the Euphrates from Mari has been almost entirely overlooked, but recently E. Oren pointed out the extraordinarily close comparisons of the numerous stone-lined cist-tombs and dolmens with their bronze implements to Palestinian MB IIA; cf. "Warrior Tomb" [N 5], 125–126. Note especially the rich repertoire of bronze weapons—"duckbill" axes, riveted daggers, socketed spears, and toggle-pins, some with decorated heads (du Mesnil du Buisson [N 48], pls. LX–LXIII). The pottery is also directly comparable to our MB IIA, especially in the numerous handleless ovoid storejars with profiled rims, the globular bowls and vases, and the carinated bowls (pls. LXVIII–LXXX, *passim*). Paint is rare, but the frequent incised bands on the upper shoulder of the storejars finds good parallel in the combing of Palestinian MB IIA storejars. Cf. also Chagar Bazar 1 [N 94], Hama J–H [N 88], Qaṭna T. 1 [N 84], etc. for the same motif, and add the especially close comparisons in the rilled-rim bowls (typical of Upper Mesopotamia and Syria, but seen in Palestine only as a distant reflex, perhaps on an occasional platter bowl). Du Mesnil du Buisson [N 48], p. 62, dated these tombs at Baghouz to the fifteenth century B.C., but the date must clearly be raised to ca. 2000–1800 B.C.; cf. also Oren, "Warrior Tomb" [N 5], 126.

98. See P. Delougaz, *Pottery from the Diyala Region* (Chicago, 1952). On the pottery of the "Isin-Larsa" period see pp. 114–124; this is mostly of a thin-walled, wheel-

made fabric, rarely decorated. The assemblage as a whole is too distant for over-all comparisons, but on a few forms which do have close analogues in Palestine, see recently J. Kaplan, "Mesopotamian Elements in the Middle Bronze II Culture of Palestine," *JNES* 30 (1971), 293–307, where, significantly, most of the direct comparisons are between Diyala and our MB IIA. Such comparisons must be used with great caution, however, since the forms Kaplan cites are somewhat isolated in both cultures and are so simple that coincidence might explain the similarities. That there is a connection, on the other hand, is shown by the fact that *metallic* forms are astonishingly close from Ur all the way around the Fertile Crescent, beginning in Early Dynastic II or III; cf. Watson and Porada, in *Chronologies* [N 67], pp. 81, 166, respectively.

99. For the extension of this cultural complex into Iran see R. H. Dyson, in *Chronologies* [N 67], pp. 231–235. On the interrelationships of Syria-Palestine and Egypt with Crete in MB IIA/MM IIa, see N 75; on Cyprus see NN 89, 104.

On the links with Anatolia, see for instance Seton-Williams and Mellink [N 90], where the spread of the painted North Syrian and "Khabur" ware is documented in Cilicia and beyond. The well-known Assyrian trading colony (*Karum*) at Kültepe in Level II, ca. 2000–1900, is marked by these painted wares as well as by red-burnished wares. In Central Anatolia and the Pontic region a rich repertoire of bronze implements is linked unmistakably with the North Syrian metal industry of the MB I/IIA horizon. On the above see J. Mellaart, "Anatolia, c. 2300–1750 B.C.," in *CAH³*, I [N 1], Part 2, ch. XXIV (a), pp. 682–697. R. Amiran has demonstrated further similarities of our MB IIA to the Kültepe pottery, in such features as the distinctive flaring cut-away spouts; cf. "Similarities Between the Pottery of the MB IIA Period and the Pottery of the Assyrian Colonies and Their Implications" [N 9], figs. 1–4. Amiran also suggests a common origin for these two ceramic cultures in Upper Mesopotamia, and she adduces several parallels from Baghouz [N 48] as well as from Mari.

Two of the most striking links of Anatolia with Palestinian MB IIA do not seem to have been noted. First is the "red cross" bowls, often with loop or volute handles. See Mellaart, 692–693, for some twenty-five in Anatolia where these bowls occur ca. 2000 B.C.; and cf. *Gezer*, III [N 22], pl. LXI:16 (T. 1); MacKenzie [N 27], pl. XVII:10. 11 (Beth-Shemesh T. 9; cf. better illustration in Palestine Museum, Jerusalem, Bulletin 3 [1926], pls. V:7, VI:15; on the date, see N 27 above); *TBM*, IA [N 7], pl. V:5 (Stratum F); Ory [N 29], p. 83, fig. 22 (T. 21 at Humraiya). Note also the large MB II cemetery excavated by J. Kaplan in Tel-Aviv, where TT. 2, 3A–B, 10A, and 16 are probably late MB IIA or early IIB; for the "red cross" bowls see Kaplan, "A Cemetery of the Bronze Age Discovered Near Tel Aviv Harbour," *'Atiqot* 1 (1955), fig. 4:10 (T. II), 4:11 (T. IIIB). On the second overlooked link, see the slotted spears with bent tang, an Anatolian EB III–early MB II type, one example of which occurs in Stratum XIII at Megiddo [N 52].

100. Cf. Albright, *TBM* IA [N 7], 67–75; Amiran [N 46], pp. 113–118 and esp. pl. 35; Wright [N 3], 290.

101. Kenyon, *CAH³*, II [N 1], 10, 11.

102. Cf. NN 88–94, 104 and references there.

103. See Seton-Williams [N 90]; M. J. Mellink, in *Chronologies* [N 67], pp. 119, 120. Cf. also B. Hrouda, *Die Bemalte Keramik des zweiten Jahrtausends in Nordmesopotamien und Nordsyrien* (Berlin, 1957), pp. 22–25; Mellaart [N 99].

104. Cf. E. Sjöqvist, *Problems of the Late Cypriote Bronze Age* (Stockholm, 1940), p. 182 (on the LB period specifically); Schaeffer [N 81], pp. 349–354; P. Ästrom, *The Middle Cypriote Bronze Age* (Lund, 1957), pp. 213, 219, 222. The last two citations refer specifically to the question of the date and provenance of the Cypriote-style jugs from Ugarit, cited in N 89 and compared in the following to early MB II vessels at a number of Palestinian sites. Ästrom classifies these vessels as "White Painted III–IV

Pendent Style" and "White Painted IV–VI Cross Line Style," which he dates respectively to his "Middle Cypriote II," ca. 1750–1700 B.C., and "Middle Cypriote III," ca. 1700–1600 B.C., both of which he thinks were manufactured at Ugarit and vicinity as well as in Cyprus; cf. pp. 212–219, 268–273, fig. IX:3–7, 10–14. Ästrom's dates would put the earliest of these "Cypriote" vessels in MB IIB in Syria-Palestine, a date which is also proposed by Amiran and others (cf. Amiran [N 46], p. 121; Oren, "Warrior Tomb" [N 5], 3). But Ästrom's low dates for his "Middle Cypriote II–III" *generally* cannot be harmonized with those required for Palestine; note that he is forced to lower Tell Beit Mirsim G–F to ca. 1800–1675 B.C. and Megiddo XIV–XIII to 1750 B.C. onward (pp. 266–270). These dates and Ästrom's date of ca. 1700 B.C. for the introduction of the "White Painted IV–VI" jugs in Syria-Palestine (pp. 268–269) are probably a century and a half too low. One of the Gezer examples is from T. 1, which does indeed have MB IIB–C, but also contains clear MB IIA, not usually recognized (i.e. *Gezer*, III [N 22], pls. LX:6, 7; LXI:16, 21, 32, 33; LXII:34, 35, 41, 43, 46, 51, the last being the "Cypriote" jug). The Megiddo examples come from TT. 3086, 3111, 3128, 4107, 4109, 5068, and 5243, of which TT. 3086, 4107, and 4109 are late MB IIA or early IIB; see Loud [N 28], pls. XXVI:10, 13, 15–17; XXXIV:4, 8, 9, 12, 13 and references to the complete tomb-groups in the Register. The jug from T. 3 (=13) at Beth-Shemesh is in an early MB IIB context, but note the stratified sherd from Stratum VI, the pottery of which is otherwise MB I and IIA; cf. Grant, *Beth Shemesh* [N 27], p. 126, no. 649 (T. 13); Grant and Wright, *'Ain Shems*, IV [N 27], pl. XXIV:11 (Str. VI). In Syria, the burials of T. 57 at Kafer-Djarra (Guiges [N 80], fig. 48, for two "Cypriote" jugs) belong primarily if not exclusively to the MB IIA horizon; Oren, "Warrior Tomb" [N 5], 120, assumes later burials only because of the one cylinder-seal of the "Hammurabi or earlier" period. Cf. also T. LXXXVI at Ugarit, which contains a MM IIa bowl of "Kamares" ware, the beginnings of which are dated rather closely to ca. 1900 B.C.; this tomb was found close by and above T. LXXXV, which contained several "Cypriote" jugs, "Eye Pitchers," and typical MB IIA pottery; cf. Schaeffer, *Ugaritica*, II [N 89], figs. 108, 109; *idem* [N 81], p. 16; Mellink, in *Chronologies* [N 67], pp. 19–21. See also the ossuary-burial in Coupe I, with "Kamares" ware, "Khabur" ware, and a painted "Eye Jug"; Schaeffer [N 81], pl. V:J. Good evidence from Palestine for an MB IIA date, i.e. 1800 B.C. at latest, may be the stratified sherd from TBM G–F (accepted by Ästrom as "White Painted IV–VI Cross Line Style," Middle Cypriote III, but dated after 1700 B.C.; cf. *TBM*, IA [N 7], pl. 22:7; Ästrom, pp. 217–219). Better still is the evidence from the overlooked cemetery at Dhahrat el-Humraiya, near Jaffa [N 29]; the "Cypriote style" jugs occur in TT. 1, 2, 12, 13, 18, 34, 37, 38, 50, and 55, of which all but TT. 1 and 37 are certainly MB IIA or transitional IIA/B at latest (and see also TT. 5, 21, 29, 42, 49, 54, and 62, of the same horizon, but without these jugs). The writer is not aware that these tombs have heretofore been cited as MB IIA, but most of the rich repertoire is *classic* MB IIA. Note also that, as far as the surviving skeletal evidence indicates, all the above were single articulated burials, in shallow "cists" scooped out of the soft earth; thus there can scarcely be any question of reuse or admixture of later material in most of these tombs. Ästrom's judgment that the Cypriote jugs "do not belong to the earliest examples of this style" (p. 214) would put these tombs into the seventeenth century B.C. on his chronology, which is absurd; this only illustrates how precarious it is to date Palestinian wares by those from Cyprus in this period, when the former is better stratified and more closely dated than the latter. Note that while Ästrom, Stewart, and Catling put the Early Cypriote/Middle Cypriote I transition ca. 1850–1750 B.C., Dikaios and Karageorghis place it at ca. 2000; cf. references in O. Negbi, "Contacts Between Byblos and Cyprus at the End of the Third Millennium B.C.," *Levant* 4 (1972), 110, n. 147.

105. Cf. Alalakh, Ugarit Moyen 2, 'Amûq K–L Qaṭna T. 1, etc., with good Egyptian Twelfth Dynasty/MM IIa synchronisms. Correlations also exist with the "Cappadocian"

painted ware of Cilician MB I, in sherds at Kültepe in *Karum* IV–II, destroyed ca. 1900 B.C.; cf. references in Mellink, in Ehrich, *Chronologies* [N 67], pp. 119–121. These tie-ups provide a twentieth century B.C. date, and in turn they demonstrate connections with Upper Mesopotamia, particularly through the Assyrian trading colony at Kültepe. See also Parr [N 85], p. 36; Wright [N 3], 290. Cf. NN 88–91, 95, 99, 104, 106.

106. Cf. Porada, in *Chronologies* [N 67], p. 172. Braidwood [N 88], p. 520, implies the chronological priority and influence of the Syrian painted wares; see also Mellaart [N 99], p. 697; Mazar [N 2], p. 77; Tufnell and Ward [N 72], pp. 171–173, generally supporting an early date and a provenance in North Syria.

107. See N 94 above.

108. Amiran [N 46], pp. 113, 118.

109. Mallowan's statement [N 93], p. 22, that "there is no evidence at all to show what happened on the Khabur in the two centuries between 2000 and 1800 B.C." is clearly an assumption deriving from his hypothesis concerning the Amorite incursions and the break in the literary records, as for instance at Tell Brak. But a careful perusal of all the Chagar Bazar reports fails to turn up any real evidence for a gap between Levels 3–2 and Level 1; and note that the section in Mallowan [N 91], fig. 3, bears this out. Likewise, we can find no stratigraphic evidence that the tombs were actually *dug from* the Shamshi-Adad I floors.

110. References are too numerous to cite, but it is sufficient to note that all scholars today—even those like Lapp, Kochavi, and Rainey who deny the Amorite/MB I equation [N 14]—attribute the MB IIA culture to the "Amorites."

111. This is one of the principal objections of Lapp, Kochavi, and Rainey; cf. P. W. Lapp, "Palestine in the Early Bronze Age," in *NEATC*, pp. 116, 117; Kochavi [N 5], 44; Rainey [N 14].

112. Dever, "Peoples of Palestine" [N 4], 224, 225.

113. While many of our MB IIA ceramic and metallic forms can be paralleled in Mesopotamia, northern Syria, and the Orontes area, certain forms such as the dipper and piriform juglets, the large ovoid storejars, the saucer-lamps, and the rilled-daggers, are found to the north of Palestine only along the Syrian coast; and the pierced-rim cooking pot appears to be indigenous to Palestine proper. In addition to these elements of a more restricted regional culture, there is further evidence of a peculiarly local development in the fact that the repertoire of MB IIA in Palestine evolved (actually degenerated) rather rapidly in MB IIB–C, while the prototypes in Syria seem to have persisted unchanged for a much longer period. On the greater continuity in Syria (not in Palestine), cf. NN 85, 86, 88; cf. Parr [N 85], 35, and Amiran [N 108], with whose intuition we are in full agreement.

114. *Pace* Glueck, who simply mistook the abrupt end of many Transjordan MB I sites and their abandonment thereafter as evidence of a "destruction." Neither these nor any of the stratified sites where MB I is in proper sequence indicates anything of the sort.

115. See Dever, "Peoples of Palestine" [N 4], pp. 214–216, 224, 225.

116. Note the impressive MB IIC *migdal* temples in Megiddo XI, Shechem "Temenoi 6–7," and Hazor XVI (Area H).

117. See, for instance, Wright, in *BANE*, p. 90, summarizing Albright's long-held views, as for instance in *The Archaeology of Palestine* (Harmondsworth, Middlesex, 1949), pp. 85–87; "Palestine in the Earliest Historical Period," *JPOS* 15 (1935), 223–231; ibid. (*sic*), *JPOS* 2 (1922), 122–124, 130–138.

118. See, for instance, the brilliant *tour de force* by G. R. H. Wright, "Tell el-Yehudiyeh and the Glacis," *ZDPV* 84 (1968), 1–17. Much of the traditional association stems from Albright's pioneer works [N 117], uncritically quoted by later scholars. A semipopular statement of this view was that of R. M. Engberg in *The Hyksos Reconsidered* (Chicago, 1939), where almost all aspects of the material culture of MB II Palestine—pottery, new bronze weapons, chariotry, fortifications—are construed as

foreign or "Hyksos" elements. A strong protest was entered in 1951 by T. Säve-Söderbergh in "The Hyksos Rule in Egypt," *JEA* 37 (1951), 53–71; he has been followed by many scholars, including A. Alt, *Die Herkunft der Hyksos in neuer Sicht* (Munich, 1954=*KS*, III, 72–98); and more recently J. von Beckerath, *Untersuchungen zur politischen Geschichte der zweiten Zwischenzeit in Ägypten* (Glückstadt, 1965), pp. 119–122. See also J. Van Seters, *The Hyksos: A New Investigation* (New Haven, 1966), pp. 1–4, 181–195; Parr [N 85], 45. G. E. Wright, however, supports the traditional interpretation: [N 3], 292–293.

119. Parr [N 85], 22–27. Note, however, Parr's acceptance of the excavators' dates of ca. 1800 for the Megiddo XIII and Tell Poleg ramparts and *glacis* (pp. 26, 27), which is questionable at best; cf. N 59.

120. A. Malamat, "Northern Canaan and the Mari Texts," in *NEATC*, pp. 164–177; and more recently, "Syro-Palestinian Destinations in a Mari Tin Inventory," *IEJ* 21 (1971), 31–38.

121. See Yadin [N 32], pp. 248, 257, 258; A. Biran, *IEJ* 19 (1969), 22, 240; *idem, Qadmoniot*, IV:1 (1971), 4 ff. (on MB IIC for the fortifications).

122. Cf. Mazar [N 2], 74–75, 81, 82. Albright's date in the late nineteenth century B.C. or Van Seters' date in the early eighteenth century B.C. [N 118], pp. 78–80, would only increase the difficulty, since the references in the texts to Hazor and Dan would then have to be correlated with MB IIA, when there was no appreciable settlement at either site.

123. For Kenyon see references in N 76. Mazar [N 2], 84, 97; Yadin [N 32], p. 262, n. 29. Wright adheres to the traditional 1750–1650 B.C.; cf. [N 3], p. 290.

124. This is the thesis of the writer's colleague D. P. Cole, whose unpublished dissertation on the Shechem MB IIB pottery has been of great help in the preparation of this study. Van Seters [N 118], p. 81, thinks that the brief revival of Egypt during the Thirteenth Dynasty under Neferhotep and Sebekhotep, ca. 1740–1725 B.C., may have resulted in raids up the Syro-Palestinian coast as far as Byblos.

125. Several Palestinian sites inland show a series of destructions in MB IIB; see Albright, TBM, II [N 8], 26, 27 (mostly ceramic distinctions between Tell Beit Mirsim E_1 and E_2); Wright, *Shechem* [N 38], pp. 112–122, 237; Mazar [N 2], 86–92 (connecting a general upheaval in MB IIB with the incursions of Hurrians and Indo-Iranian peoples).

Sources for *Figure 1*

1. Small Storejar. *Megiddo*, II, pl. 12:21 (T. 5130)
2. Jug. *QDAP* 6, pl. xxv: 89 (Photograph; Râs el-'Ain. T. 4)
3. Dipper Juglet. *Megiddo*, II, pl. 17:24 (T. 5103)
4. Dipper Juglet. *Megiddo*, II, pl. 11:21 (T. 3150)
5. Juglet. *Megiddo*, II, pl. 20:18 (T. 3141)
6. Juglet. *Megiddo*, II, pl. 11:5 (T. 5183)
7. Piriform Juglet. *Ancient Pottery*, pl. 36:4 (Afula tomb)
8. Cylindrical Juglet. *Megiddo*, II, pl. 11:4 (T. 4016)
9. Jug. *Megiddo*, II, pl. 25:12 (T. 5106)
10. Jug. *Megiddo*, II, pl. 10:10 (T. 3138)
11. Piriform Juglet. *Ancient Gaza*, IV, pl. LIV:60N7 (T. 1551)
12. Piriform Juglet. *'Atiqot* 5, fig. 4:5 (Barqai, 1956 Tomb)
13. Platter Bowl. *Megiddo*, II, pl. 14:8 (same as T. 5147)

14. Cup. *Megiddo Tombs.*, pl. 28:31 (T. 911A1)
15. Platter Bowl. *Megiddo*, II, pl. 15:15 (T. 3162)
16. Carinated Bowl. *'Atiqot* 5, fig. 4:10 (Barqai, 1956 Tomb)
17. Tankard. *Megiddo*, II, pl. 11:6 (T. 5275)
18. Holemouth Krater. *TBM*, IA, pl. 5:1 (Str. G–F)
19. Globular Bowl. *Megiddo Tombs,* pl. 28:34 (T. 911A1)
20. Cooking Pot. *Megiddo*, II, pl. 9:19 (Str. XV)

Sources for *Figure 2*

1. Fenestrated ("Duckbill") Ax. *ZDPV* 87 (1971), fig. 2:4 (Beth-shan, T. 92)
2. Chisel Ax. *'Atiqot* 3, fig. 3:2 (Moza, T. 2)
3. Spear. *Ancient Gaza,* II, pl. xiv:71 (T. 1015)
4. Spear. *Megiddo*, II, pl. 178:5 (photograph; Str. XIIIA)
5. Arrowhead? *'Atiqot* 5, fig. 4:14 (Barqai, 1956 Tomb)
6. Arrowhead. *ZDPV* 87 (1971), fig. 2:3 (Beth-shan, T. 92)
7. Spear. *'Atiqot* 5, fig. 4:13 (Barqai, 1956 Tomb)
8. Spear. *Megiddo Tombs,* fig. 170:3 (T. 911D)
9. Toggle-pin. Ancient Gaza, II, pl. xviii:206 (T. 1410)
10. Toggle-pin, *'Atiqot* 1 (19) fig. 5:7 (Tel-Aviv, T. 10A)
11. Toggle-pin. *'Atiqot* 3, fig. 3:3 (Moza, T. 1/2)
12. Toggle-pin. *Megiddo Tombs,* fig. 174:6 (T. 24)

2. *Two Amarna Notes: The Shechem City-State and Amarna Administrative Terminology*

EDWARD F. CAMPBELL, JR.

MCCORMICK THEOLOGICAL SEMINARY, CHICAGO

G. ERNEST WRIGHT has succeeded in his remarkable career in combining the stringent work of a Palestinian (and now even a Cypriote!) archaeologist with the exciting task of biblical theologian. The two related studies which follow represent the efforts of an admiring disciple to do something of the same. No one will be better able to see its weaknesses than he; whatever strengths it may have are due in great measure to his inspiration, and are but a small token of esteem to a great mentor and a great human being.

I

In his celebrated *Landnahme* article of 1925, Albrecht Alt[1] underscored an important difference between the city-states of the Late Bronze Age along the coast of Palestine and in the Jezreel plain, and those in the hill country. The basic criterion was the sheer extent of the political unit—the "larger territorial formation"—in the mountains north of Jerusalem and south of Jezreel, centering undoubtedly on the city of Shechem. Recently, G. Buccellati has chosen to describe this political unit as an "expanded territorial state," and his discussion of it suggests he might better have chosen the term "expansionist."[2] For what actually defines it for him is the disruptive activity of one of the more irrepressible members of the cast of players on the stage of Amarna period Syria-Palestine, Lab'ayu. His operations can be assumed to take place at the edges of his own domain, especially since he is repeatedly accused of snatching cities to add to his own holdings. At various times, Lab'ayu threatened Biridiya of Megiddo (EA 244–245),[3] twenty-six airline miles to the NNW of Shechem, and Milkilu of Gezer (EA 253–254), thirty-three miles to the SW; formed alliances threatening Jerusalem and Keilah, thirty-one and forty-three miles to the S and SSW (EA 287, 289, and 280:30–32); and influenced, through his sons at least, Pella across the Jordan, twenty-six miles to the NE. What is indicated is a territory roughly forty miles from east to west, forty-five miles from north to south. If we assume that the Amarna archive gives a very nearly complete picture of the roster of city-states with indigenous "kings,"[4] this territory includes at least two locations which according to later (tenth century?) biblical tradition in Joshua 12 count as city-states conquered by Joshua, namely Tirṣah and Tappuaḥ,[5] neither of which are mentioned in the Amarna archive.

If the city-state of Shechem was unusually large, as Alt observed, it is not its expansionist tendencies which mark it as different in character or self-conception from the city-states on the coastal and Jezreel plains, as Buccellati proposes.[6] Lab'ayu's attempts to expand his influence and his territory are not essentially of different motivation from those of his counterparts. The Amarna archive abounds in evidence of attempted encroachments on one another's territory by many of the local rulers. Even Lab'ayu complains that someone has snipped away two of his cities (EA 252:20–22); while we may well want to question the veracity of this notorious rogue on this subject, we will do well to turn the same jaundiced eye upon the outcries of a dozen other local rulers; most of these city-state rulers were involved in the general jockeying for position characteristic of the time. The size and behavior of the Shechem city-state are probably due instead to factors of topology and population spread.

The Shechem city-state covered a zone of Palestine which was relatively forbidding in its topological character. A number of upland plains, Arabic *sahl*'s, along the hill country spine, contain eroded *terra rossa* soil from the surrounding hills, in a few places mixed with soil from eroded igneous rock; here cultivation must have been easy and fruitful. The banks of rare perennial streams, such as the Wadi Far'ah leading to the Ghor and the Wadi Janayin from the watershed at Nablus westward to the sea, were doubtless very fruitful. Other wadi beds would require more work to be rendered cultivable. Terracing of the hillsides, again a cumbersome task, would yield other cultivable patches. On the other hand, the likelihood that at least some of the region was covered by forest, probably of the dense kind called *maquis* described eloquently by M. B. Rowton in a recent study,[7] would have removed some of this cultivable land from use, at least until the forest was cleared. Both the geological character of the region and the existence of the forest contributed to the *relative* inaccessibility of the territory and thus perhaps to the ability of Lab'ayu and his people to maintain the size of their holdings.[8] What, then, can be said about the actual pattern of settlement in the region around Shechem? Archaeological excavation and topographic survey now provide enough evidence at least to suggest some things. We can look first at Shechem itself, then at its immediate environs, and finally at some of the nearby plains and valleys.

Excavations at Shechem had had little to report concerning Late Bronze Age occupation of the site until the campaigns of 1966, 1968, and 1969. Previous to those campaigns, study of the fortress-temple building in the northwestern part of the city had determined that a temple structure belonging to the Late Bronze Age rode on top of the strong foundations of the MB IIC *migdal;* it was oriented slightly differently from the earlier structure, and it had before it the famous *maṣṣebah* in a stone socket together with an altar.[9] Soil layers undisturbed by earlier excavation were minimally preserved, but enough remained to fix the fact that a late thirteenth-century temple phase had persisted into the twelfth century (Temple 2b). In addition, a few scraps of information pointed to an earlier phase, Temple 2a, which could be assigned with some diffidence to the fourteenth or even the late fifteenth century. In the East Gate of the city, and along the fortification system slightly to the north, in Field III, evidence was found for a reuse of the last MB IIC fortification system, notably with a new gate tower at the East Gate tying into what may be a new fortification wall.[10] Where limited excavation in the heart of the city, in Fields VII and IX, had reached stratification attributable to the Late Bronze Age, the situation was decidedly confused, as one can discern from the preliminary report of the 1964 campaign.[11] For this reason, a place (Field XIII) was selected for excavation just north of the temple precinct and not far inside the northwest gate in the fortifications, and was excavated during 1966, 1968 and 1969. There is no need to recapitulate the results here; suffice it to say that a well-preserved series of Late Bronze Age strata yielded excellent collections of pottery and artifacts together with enough of an idea of the architectural layout to show that Shechem was indeed a thriving city from 1450 through to roughly 1150.[12] The best preserved and in every regard the richest stratum was the one now given the over-all site designation Stratum XIII; its date is without question the heart of the fourteenth century, precisely the Amarna period. While the evidence in the temple precinct and along the fortifications has been denuded rather badly, both during a period of abandonment at the site covering roughly 1150 to 975 B.C. and at the hands of man (including archaeologists!) ever since, the evidence from Field XIII has permitted a correlation of evidence from all across the site showing Late Bronze occupation of its entire area, about sixteen acres. One further feature of Stratum XIII is important: sometime in the latter half of the fourteenth century Shechem was violently destroyed, under what circumstances and by whom we cannot be sure.

As to the richness of the finds, it should be noted that Stratum XIII yielded clear evidence of relative wealth and artistic sophistication. Walls of structures in all areas were well built and sturdy, the finest found at the site apart from those of the Middle Bronze II period and apart from a few of the Hellenistic walls. There was a wide range of pottery forms, much of it decorated, and a fair representation of imported wares. An electrum pendant, a silver toggle-pin, and one of the finest bronze figurines ever found in Palestine go with other objects to suggest relative wealth.

As an adjunct to the excavation results, we should note several tombs found in the village of 'Arâq et-Ṭayiḥ on the slope of Mount Ebal about a half kilometer north of the site. In a belt of soft limestone running beneath some of the village houses, at least two tombs have been cleared, one in late May 1966, by the Department of Antiquities of Jordan and the other by considerably less official excavators in June of that year. Pottery and metal objects from these tombs shown to the Joint Expedition staff again attested relative wealth in the LB II period, and exploration hints that there are more such tombs to be found.

Shechem sat at the east end of the throat of the pass between Mounts Gerizim and Ebal. East and south of it stretches one of the largest of the upland *sahl's* mentioned earlier. Westward a short distance, at the east edge of modern Nablus, lies the watershed and the beginning of the wadi system running west to the sea. Of interest in visualizing the Shechem city-state are sites around the plain and along the wadi which would have been closest in association with the city-state center. A topographic survey team has scoured this region for signs of ancient settlement.[13] The thoroughness of this search, conducted in the spring of 1965 and the summers of 1966 and 1968 (together with a brief exploration over the Mount Gerizim massif in November 1967 by George M. Landes), should mean that a description can be given of all LB sites in the region, within the limits to which surface survey technique is subject. That is, Late Bronze Age sherds specifically like those of the LB IIA (Amarna period) corpus established at Shechem were found at each of the sites about to be described in sufficient quantity to make the postulation of settlement during that time well-nigh inescapable. Absence of such sherds from other sites explored suggests, but hardly proves, a lack of such settlement at those sites.

West of the pass, four and three-quarter miles WNW of Shechem, lies Kûmeh (map coordinates 1707×1832). It comprises the flat top of a hillock rising some one hundred feet above the elevation of the road and the stream in the Wadi Janayin just to the south of it. A modern estate wall probably riding on the lines of ancient walling encloses an area 125 by 100 meters in extent (roughly one-quarter of Shechem's size), and there is a small spring at the NW edge. If the evidence of a large number of sherd collections is to be trusted, settlement began here in LB IIA and continued for two thousand years. From the summit the view commands both mountain flanks, a side valley leading to modern Zawâta, and the pass up to the top of the watershed in modern Nablus. Shechem itself is not visible. Two miles ESE of Kûmeh, on the south side of the valley a bit over two and a half miles from Shechem, lies Tell Sôfar (1732×1817), a small, circular tell again dominating the valley floor but not as far above it as is Kûmeh. It is much smaller—its flat top covers barely two acres—and the LB pottery thus far found is confined to its northwestern flanks. The view eastward is similar to Kûmeh's, but Sôfar is more nearly *in* the pass, in an analogous position to Shechem's. Clearly there was at least one strategically located town (at Kûmeh) in the west of the pass, dominating the main east-west travel route; Sôfar, on the other hand, may represent only a village or even an estate. Here then is one feature of the Shechem city-state, close to the central city.

Almost due east of Shechem at a distance of five and a half miles is the easternmost point of the fertile plain along its north side. Modern tracks lead from this point over a shallow pass across Jebel el-Kabîr northeastward, and to the ESE into the wadi systems leading to the Ghor. On a spur of the hills jutting into the plain here is Khirbet Bîr Shuweiḥa (1855×1785), barely eight hundred meters or half a mile north of modern Beit Dajan. The tell is small, surely not over two acres, and it is strewn with sherds of LB II and the first part of Iron I (roughly 1400–1100 B.C.); pottery of other periods is of much lower frequency. On Râs ed-Diyâr, the rise east of the modern village of Beit Dajan, more LB II pottery occurs but in no great frequency. Here, again at a strategic point, occurs the second Amarna period settlement in the immediate Shechem environs. Of tantalizing interest is the name of the modern village, which may suggest that a sanctuary of the Canaanite deity Dagon was at Kh. Bîr Shuweiḥa.

Along the fertile plain south from Shechem, extending for more than five miles to a height of land between it and the next system south, we have thus far found no site displaying clear signs of LB occupation; the best prospect is Kh. Makhneh el-Fôqa (1755×1760), two and a half miles from Shechem, and doubtless the major Early Bronze site in the area,[14] but nearly a dozen extensive sherd collections from the site have yielded precisely three uncertain LB sherds! The story is quite different, however, for Kh. el-'Urmeh (1805×1727), located on a peak two hundred meters above the floor of Wadi Yanûn, which leaves the Shechem plain just opposite Makhneh el-Fôqa and runs ESE toward modern Yanûn. Located just over five miles SE of Shechem, this is doubtless the site of Arumah of Judg. 9:41 (and 31?). Its view commands the east end of the Shechem pass and the site of the city itself, together with much of the southern branch of the Shechem plain; it also controls a minor travel route leading eastward. The enclosure on the summit is roughly two hundred by seventy-five meters in size, and pottery of LB IB through LB II is of high frequency, along with evidence of settlement from 1000 to 700 B.C. and from Roman and Byzantine times. It is an ideal spot for a military outpost.

The sites described constitute the only known settlements of the Amarna period in the entire Shechem plain. Admittedly there may have been villages here and there on the fringes of the plain at sites where explorations have discovered no LB pottery (arguments from silence in surface survey are perilous), but the likelihood is that we have here charted pretty much the character of the immediate environs of Shechem. By way of contrast, well over thirty of the fifty-six sites explored in the vicinity have late Roman and Byzantine settlements; above twenty were occupied in the Hellenistic period. In the Iron I and Iron II period, at least double the number of LB sites were occupied. And once more let it be emphasized: the known LB sites are located at strategic points in the Shechem plain.

Can anything comparable be said about regions at greater distance from Shechem? At least a few points are interesting. To the south, the nearest confidently defined site showing LB occupation is Tell Sheikh Abû Zarâd, ancient Tappuaḥ (1715×1679).[15] Three recently conducted surface surveys have each included about 10 per cent LB sherds, representing LB I and LB II. The tell again is at a strategic location, since it controls at least a part of the system of the Wadi Sarîdeh leading toward the coast, and also a pass leading NW into the Shechem plain, near modern Huwwâra.

Continuing southward, the next sure site is Shiloh, where excavation produced LB I and LB II sherds but very little clear LB stratigraphy.[16] Farther south is Bethel, perhaps close to the southern border of the Shechem city-state; here strata of LB IIA and LB IIB are clearly differentiated, and the earlier one, dated to the Amarna period, shows evidence of excellent quality of construction.[17]

North of Shechem, two excavated sites and a new find-spot are instructive. Tell el-Far‘ah (Tirṣah), six and a half miles away (considerably more by road), yields evidence of settlement in LB, although the remains on the tell are much denuded. Four tombs in the cemetery show that people were settled here both in LB I and in LB II.[18] Similarly, Dothan, fourteen miles north at the edge of the extensive and fertile Sahl ‘Arrâbeh, had LB settlement, again badly denuded, and one spectacular tomb used in four phases from LB IIA through Iron I.[19] In addition, the Shechem topographic survey team explored Kh. edh-Dhûq (1850×1940) just north of Ṭubâs, and collected enough LB II pottery to indicate that at least a village of the Amarna period was located here, roughly ten and a half miles NNE of Shechem. This ruin is the best available candidate for the site of biblical Tēbēṣ.

Now obviously this catalogue is not meant to imply that these are the only Amarna period sites in the Shechem city-state. It is a reminder, however, of how relatively few the known sites of this period are in the northern hill country. The results of one other type of investigation draw the circle just a bit tighter. Participants of the Lehrkursus of the Deutsche Evangelische Institut have subjected the small hollow west of Samaria and the flanks of the Wadi Far‘ah to more-or-less thorough investigation in connection with projects of specific students. In the Samaria hollow, none of ten sites investigated yielded any LB pottery. Only Kh. Beit Sêlûn (1666×1826), a ruin just south of modern Qûsîn, just over six miles WNW of Shechem, yielded a few LB sherds to the practiced eye of Paul W. Lapp, who read its pottery.[20] In the Wadi Far‘ah, one tell out of the ten explored clearly evidenced LB II occupation, certainly of the thirteenth century and perhaps of the fourteenth: Tell Miskeh (or Tell Misk) at 1853×1825.[21] Finally, across the Jordan just opposite the mouth of the Wadi Far'ah, surface exploration of Tell ed-Damiyeh (2017×1679) produced LB II sherds.

What conclusions are warranted from all this? At least an indication is given that sites of LB settlement were few and far between, and in most if not all instances were strategically located. A great deal more surface exploration is called for before this conclusion can be called a precise one. Nevertheless, the indications are that the Shechem city-state in the Amarna period was far from populous, no matter how extensive in area. What excavation has been done in the region suggests a second conclusion, namely that life in this period was relatively richer than some commentators have been inclined to suggest. Lab'ayu and his people may have lived comparatively well in their hill country stronghold, readily provisioned for their rather long-range forays against their neighbors. In numbers of population, it is quite possible that the Shechem city-state was no larger than such coastal city-states as Megiddo or Gezer. And so far as living under the style of administration conducted by the Egyptian overlord, Shechem may have had very nearly ideal defensive conditions of inaccessibility and isolation. It is to consideration of that administration that we now turn.

II

In recent years, a number of instructive studies have appeared which seek to describe the style of Egyptian administration in Syria-Palestine during the time of the New Kingdom, and more especially during the Amarna period. The impulse for this burst of interest is the almost unprecedented confluence of data from the diplomatic corpus being published from Ugarit, from the historical prologues of suzerainty treaties and the annals of Shuppiluliumas from the Hittite realm, and from the Amarna archive. Among many points clarified by these studies, I select several for particular attention here.

First of all, it appears that the Amarna letters chronicle less of a specific breakdown in Egyptian administration of its Syro-Palestinian holdings than has previously been maintained. History books have tended to suggest that Akhenaten's absorption with internal concerns meant that the foreign office virtually collapsed. In fact, it is becoming clearer that what the Amarna letters portray is pretty much business as usual in foreign administration, and that the Syro-Palestinian local rulers are using language in their communication with the Egyptian court which represents their normal expectancies and experience under Egyptian overlordship.[22]

Secondly, it is clear that there was a mutually established northern limit to Egyptian control in Palestine throughout the Amarna period; the Hittites remained north of it and Egyptian control pertained south of it.[28] True, city-states at or near this "border" were tempted to exchange loyalties from time to time. Nevertheless, Syria from just above Ugarit southward, and all of Palestine, oriented themselves toward Egypt and toward whatever constituted Egyptian administrative practice.

A third consideration is more complex. Broadly stated, it is that vassal kings in Syria-Palestine operated on the basis of premises about their relation to their overlord which are in many ways similar to those operative in the Hittite realm to the north. The latter, be it remembered, are made clear for us explicitly in the suzerainty-vassal treaties recovered from Boghazkoy and Ugarit. In these treaties, loyalty to overlord and to fellow vassal are stipulated as consequences of a relationship which already has a history, a history given a recital in the treaty-form as motivation for future loyalty. Now no such written treaties are known to us from Egypt, and we cannot be sure that such instruments existed. There is evidence for a powerful oath of fealty,[24] but we can only surmise that a real sense of *mutual* responsibility existed.

While the Hittite instrument provided for the vassal to retain almost complete control of the internal affairs of his own city-state, the Egyptian picture may be different. (1) The Amarna letters portray a bureaucratic superstructure in Palestine, involving territorial overseers, military commanders, and at least some garrisons of troops; at the same time, the very fact that the local rulers can appeal directly to the Pharaoh, using a courier system apparently at least partially established for the purpose, means that local autonomy existed in some form. (2) On the question of behavior in interrelations of the various local rulers under their Egyptian overlord, we cannot determine whether the oath of fealty had anything to say; Helck at one point ventured the judgment that it said nothing on the subject, apparently leaving petty rivalries to the local rulers to work out.[25] Indeed, the frequent evidence of interstate squabbling portrayed in a number of the Amarna letters would seem to argue that no Egyptian control pertained. Nevertheless, it is clear that the local rulers refer their squabbles to the Egyptian court, as though there were at least some rules of the game implied in Egyptian overlordship; resident Egyptian officials are expected by the local rulers to intervene in such interstate squabbles, and there is considerable effort expended by each local ruler involved to line Egyptian officials up on his side. (3) It appears that Pharaoh relates himself primarily to the land as his land, rather than to the rulers and their people. Even this point, however, is not entirely clear; perhaps it is applicable only to the Egyptian administrative cities, Gaza, Simyra and Kumidi, for it remains possible for a city-state ruler to indicate the completeness of his loyalty by the extravagant gift of placing his city under the direct patronage of the court, as Abimilki of Tyre does by assigning his city to the king's daughter Mayati (EA 155).[26]

The study which has sought to wrestle most thoughtfully with this ambiguous state of affairs is that of M. Liverani.[27] He contrasts the "Asian" and

"Egyptian" political conceptions (perhaps too neatly), and accounts for the fact that city-state rulers continue to press the Egyptian court for protection and support by assuming that they shared the presupposition of the Asian (including Hittite) conception, clinging to it until the realization finally got through that appeals for rights spelled out in this conception would get them nowhere. His theory is very attractive, although one wants to remember that Egyptian hegemony had been functioning in Syria-Palestine for a long time prior to the Amarna period. We are left to speculate whether Egypt had in fact a system of treaties so far lost to us,[28] which defined what vassals should expect from loyal service, or rather that the vassals operated on an understanding characteristic of the Asian policy. In any event, we have every reason to look to the Amarna letters for a range of specific terms which characterized the relationship of vassals to an overlord. And since it is clear that a suzerainty model, such as that depicted in the Hittite treaties, powerfully affected the religious formulations of the Israelites, it is worthwhile to see how the Amarna letter language related to the theological language of the Old Testament. What follows recapitulates some studies already done and suggests some new terms which show how much Old Testament usage parallels the international parlance of the Amarna letters.

As almost a regular feature of his letter, an Amarna local ruler assures his sovereign of having *heard* the words (commands) of his sovereign. Sometimes the preposition *ana* connects the word *šamû* to its object, just as Hebrew *le*- does in the Old Testament, and sometimes it does not (as also happens in Hebrew), but the semantic nuance is present that to hear him is to obey him. The local rulers also implore their overlord to hear them, with an intensity similar to that often expressed by the psalmists.

The local ruler is the servant (*ardu*) of the great king (*šarru rabû*), two terms which Jonas Greenfield has linked up with treaty terminology in the Old Testament and in Assyria.[29] The local ruler sometimes must answer to the charge of committing a transgression (*hiṭû* or *arnu*); particularly culpable in this regard are Rîb-Adda of Byblos and Lab'ayu of Shechem. As W. L. Moran has pointed out, building on an observation of V. Korošec,[30] the Akkadian verb *ra'âmu,* "to love," also belongs in overlord-vassal terminology, as, for that matter, does its opposite, "to hate." Thus, Rîb-Adda writes to the Pharaoh, "If the king my lord loves his true servant, then send the three men back; then I will live and I will guard the city for the king" (EA 123:23–28). And Abdi-Ḥeba, ruler of Jerusalem, pointedly asks the king, "Why do you show favor to (lit.: love) the Ḥabiru and oppose (hate) the (legitimate) governors" (EA 286:18–20). This love-loyalty is reciprocal; Rîb-Adda writes, in trying to move the Pharaoh, "Who will love when I have [died]?" (EA 114:68). Moran has demonstrated beyond doubt that this is precisely the conception that lies behind the Deuteronomic use of Hebrew *'āhēb,* as it does behind Judg. 5:31.

Now it is to be noted that none of the language so far cited is confined to political terminology of the Late Bronze Age. Quite the contrary; these terms and conceptions are characteristic of a long period of time and appear in other genres of literature. They appear in a treaty context with the same meanings in the Aramaic Sefire texts of the eighth century and in the Assyrian treaties of the neo-Assyrian period, especially those of Esarhaddon with his vassals. It is appropriate treaty language, or perhaps we should say language appropriate to the administration of a sovereign-vassal relationship, throughout the history of that parlance as so far attested.

There are two terms which appear in the Amarna letters, however, which tend in their precise significance to be characteristic of the Amarna period. They are administrative words which describe the combination of attitude and action hoped for by the vassal from the sovereign; in both cases, only the sovereign is the subject. They are interesting because they appear together with God as subject, sometimes in synonymous parallelism, in the Old Testament. The verbs are *nqm,* unattested as such in Akkadian, and *pqd,* widely attested in Akkadian, Aramaic, and Hebrew, with one attestation in Ugaritic.

The first of these verbs, *nqm,* was subjected to study by Mendenhall in 1948.[31] It appears in six Amarna letters a total of eight times (EA 244:26; 250:20, 48; 271:13; 274:10; 282:13; 283:16, 26); all the letters containing it come from the region from Megiddo south to the Hebron area. In each of the eight cases, the local ruler writes in the face of what he deems to be a dire threat from hostile forces, sometimes from other local rulers and sometimes from Habiru. The writers are at pains to show in what they write that they have been perfectly loyal, while their opponents are definitely disloyal. *Nqm* in six of the eight cases is an appeal directed to the sovereign to deliver his servant, dependent upon the demonstration that the loyal servant really deserves help. A letter from Shuwardata gives an eloquent example (282:11–14): "Let the king, my lord, learn that I am alone! May the king, my lord, send archer-troops in great number and deliver (*nqm*) me." In this instance, the verb is glossed with the word *yazinu,* apparently representing the causative of Canaanite *yṣ',* meaning something like "get me out of this."

What has been said applies to six of the eight Amarna usages, but the other two, both in letter 250 from a certain Ba'lu-UR.SAG, are less clear. This ruler is being pushed by other rulers to join in a reprisal attack upon the city of Qena, and he writes: "May the god of the king, my lord, *nqm* me from making war against the people of the land of Qena, servants of the king, my lord" (lines 20–22). Mendenhall implied that the term here invited not deliverance but punishment, along the lines of "May the god of the king, my lord, punish me (were I) to make war with the men of the land of Qena." This is possible, although the more likely translation is W. F. Albright's: "May the god of the king, my lord, *preserve* me from making war against the men of the land of Qena."[32] Nevertheless, I think Mendenhall's main thesis stands: the function of *nqm* is tied to the sovereign-vassal relationship and represents the help a true vassal expects from his sovereign. He expects, in short, vindication.

Several recent studies[33] have cited passages in the Old Testament where this understanding of *nqm* pertains to the use of that verb and its noun derivatives in Hebrew, especially in covenant contexts. Thus, Deut. 32:35 and 41 employ the verb with Yahweh as subject to speak of the punishment brought upon Israel's enemies because they have vaunted themselves at her expense. In Leviticus 26, where the blessings and curses consequent upon behavior in the covenant relationship are set forth, God's vindication is brought to bear upon Israel when, after due chastisement, Israel continues to walk contrary to God. "Then I too will walk contrary to you; sevenfold for your sins I will smite you. And I will bring upon you the vindicating sword, the vindication of the covenant" (vss. 24–25). Among the prophets, Jeremiah is the one who employs the term the most, and the flavor is the same. Vindication can be directed against Israel, against Jeremiah's own foes in his laments, and against Babylon (once, by the way, in parallel with *rîb*, in 51:36). On one occasion, Jeremiah's erstwhile "friends" taunt him: "Perhaps he will be deceived and we will prevail over him, and we will gain our vindication over him" (20:10). Jeremiah responds by pleading to God, who tests the righteous, to let *him* see God's vindication upon *them* (vs. 12). Equally interesting is Jeremiah 15:15, from another of the prophet's laments: "Thou knowest, O Yahweh! Remember me (*zkr*) and *pqd* me, and exercise vindication (niphal *nqm*) for me on my persecutors." The Book of Jeremiah employs the niphal, hithpael and once a piel of *nqm*, in a variety of syntactic constructions, but the nuances of the term remain the same. The literary forms here cited which contain this meaning of *nqm* are instructive: a covenant lawsuit (Deuteronomy 32), a recital of blessings and curses (Leviticus 26), and the personal complaint of a righteous man (Jeremiah 12 and 15); together with prophetic judgment speeches and prophetic salvation speeches for the future, in which the term also occurs, they should all be expected to speak of the sovereign's execution of his prerogative.

One further important point. In certain passages in the Old Testament, for example in Gen. 4:15, 24, *nqm* does mean what it usually has been claimed to mean, namely "to avenge." In the Sefire treaty III, from the eighth century, it has this meaning also: "If [any of whole group of possible enemies] seek my head to kill me, thou thyself wilt come and avenge my blood on my enemies. . . ."[34] In treaties of the first millennium, then, a different meaning from that in the Amarna letters has developed; the Amarna letters and the majority of the Old Testament passages employ what appears to be the more ancient and technical meaning for the verb.

The appearance of *pqd* in Jer. 15:15, in parallelism with *nqm*, leads us to the Amarna uses of that verb. The basic form occurs ten times in Amarna letters (the D conjugation occurs once, in a letter between equals where it means approximately "coordinate"). It also appears in a vassal letter in

Akkadian from Ugarit (*Palais royal d'Ugarit,* IV, 17.132, line 6) and in one of the fifteenth-century Ta'anach letters. Of the ten occurrences in Amarna vassal letters, five refer to the sovereign's having appointed the local ruler to the position he holds as guardian of his city. Two employ the preposition *ana* after the verb and mean "to command, direct" with the object of the action being the Egyptian bureaucrat who is the local ruler's immediate supervisor. In letter 60, however, we have Abdi-Ashirta of Amurru pleading eloquently that he has faithfully guarded all the lands of the king, and has dutifully warned his overseer about other local rulers who are not faithful. He concludes his letter: "Now may the king, my lord, know me and *pqd* me into the hand of Pahamnate, my overseer." Herbert Huffmon has shown, on the basis of Hittite treaty terminology, that the verb "to know" in this passage is an example of a technical use of that verb in a treaty sense.[35] His rendering can be paraphrased: "May the king, my lord, acknowledge me as vassal and put me under the charge of Pahamnate. . . ." The verb *pqd* here carries the nuance of "give me the protection of," since Abdi-Ashirta has no need of being appointed into the hands of his overseer; he is already under his charge. He wants, rather, the implications of the sovereign-vassal relationship to be applied. In another Amarna letter, 197, Biryawaza, who governs the Damascene region, chronicles the troubles he has been having with local rulers who are flirting with shifting their loyalty to Hatti, and after affirming by contrast "A servant of the king of Egypt am I," he writes: "So let the king *pqd* his land, so that enemies not take it."

Here are four slight variations on the meaning of one verb, all relating to the king's exercise of his prerogative and authority, and suggesting how dependent the vassal is upon the king's actually exercising that authority. One senses that the king's exercise of his prerogative is related to the vassal's behavior and his loyalty, and in this respect the term comes close to the semantic range of *nqm*. One cannot claim for the Amarna occurrences that they actually state that punishment might be a result of *pqd,* but the idea seems distinctly implied, and this prepares us for the Old Testament range of meaning for this verb.

Jack B. van Hooser, in his unpublished doctoral dissertation on the root *pqd,*[36] has developed several groupings of the Old Testament *qal* uses of this verb which correspond quite well to this variety. One group contains uses of the verb in which God looks upon his people with favor, remembers them and keeps his promise to them. An interesting illustration involves certain E-stratum passages which speak of Yahweh's visiting his people in Egyptian captivity, namely Gen. 50:24, 25 and Exod. 13:19. In each case, Joseph instructs his brothers "God will *pqd* you." In Gen. 50:24, the passage goes on "and will bring you out of this land. . . ." In the other two passages, the quotation moves directly from "God will *pqd* you" to "then you must carry my bones with you from here." Here the verb clearly implies God's sovereign activity to deliver. By way of instructive contrast, Exod. 4:16, a J passage, reads "I have *pqd*'ed you and what has been done to you in Egypt . . . ," suggesting quite a different and rather a remarkable nuance for the verb *pqd,* along the lines "I have paid attention [as one who can do something about it]."

Van Hooser describes another of his groupings as having a legal or administrative setting. Included are passages in which God appoints (or men appoint) certain officials. Also included is a grouping employing the idiom "to *pqd* iniquity (or a synonym) '*l* someone." Here one locates the familiar liturgical unit in Exod. 34:7 with its parallels in Exod. 20:5, Num. 14:18, and Deut. 5:9. In these passages God's *pqd* means "to punish": ". . . punishing the iniquity of the fathers upon the children and the children's children." A great many of the other examples in this group come from the prophets, in judgment speeches to individuals, to the nation, or to foreign nations. Again with Jeremiah, however, the term can also be used of God's vindication of his promise, as in Jer. 27:22, 29:10, and 32:5, and one can note here also Zeph. 2:7.

To these more extensive analyses, let me add briefly four other terms. The one certain appearance of the verb *zkr,* "to remember," in the Amarna letters with the overlord as subject occurs as a Canaanite gloss to Akkadian *ḫašâšu/ḫasâsu* in EA 228:19: "May the king, my lord, *remember* what has been done to Hazor, thy city, and against thy servant." As B. Childs has pointed out, the meaning here, while not directly parallel to the forms or the precise syntax constructions attested in the Old Testament, is that the great king is to remember so that recalling will issue in action, a dynamic frequent in the Old Testament.[37] Then there are two occurrences of the verb *ḥnn,* both imploring the great king to "show favor" to his vassal (EA 137:81 and 253:24). In another context, I have shown that the closest semantic parallels to the curious Hebrew form *hištaḥaweh,* "to bow down," occur in the introductions to thirty-one of the Amarna letters from central and southern Palestine.[38] Finally, in a most suggestive study, J. Wijngaards has gathered a number of passages from Hittite treaty historical prologues in which the terms "death" and "life" pertain to the condition of vassal kings in respect to the favor of their overlords.[39] Death is disfavor and life is favor; by extension "resurrection" or "giving life" is restoration to favor. Although Wijngaards did not cite them, there are several passages in the Amarna letters which have the same terminology: EA 136:43; 147:9; 198: 20, 26, 30; 215:16 and probably 152:53. What Wijngaards did do was to use this discovery to unravel the meaning of several Old Testament passages, notably Hosea 6:2 (notice here also the use of the verb "to know" in 6:3).

We have not concerned ourselves here with the complicated question of the channels for the communication of such terminology down across the centuries of Israelite tradition. Let it suffice to have claimed that the Amarna letters, and the political structures which functioned in the administration of the Egyptian New Kingdom empire as well as of the Hittite realm, are a fertile field for study of the backgrounds of Old Testament theology.[40] Lab'ayu of Shechem and his fellow city-state rulers have left us a vital legacy in their sometimes bizarre but always illuminating chronicles of local life under New Kingdom hegemony.

NOTES

1. A. Alt, "Die Landnahme der Israeliten in Palästina" (1925), reprinted with notes updated in *KS*, I (1953), 89–125; in *Essays on Old Testament History and Religion* (Garden City, New York, 1966), pp. 133–169. See esp. 100–113 in *KS*, pp. 145–157 in the English.

2. G. Buccellati, *Cities and Nations of Ancient Syria* (Rome, 1967), pp. 69–72.

3. Citations of the Amarna archive will be indicated by EA=el-'Amarna, and the numbers will follow the pattern which is now established in virtually all parts of the scholarly community, assigning 359 to 379 to texts appearing since the *editio princeps*, J. A. Knudtzon, *Die El-Amarna-Tafeln* (1915, repr. 1964), consecutively in order of their discovery and/or identification. For 359–379, see now the excellent publication of A. F. Rainey, *El Amarna Tablets 359–379: Supplement to J. A. Knudtzon, Die El-Amarna-Tafeln, Alter Orient und Altes Testament* 8 (1970). One or more easily accessible, competent English translations of each of the following letters appear in *ANET* (Albright), G. E. Wright, *Shechem* (New York, 1965) (Campbell), and Rainey: EA 137, 147, 234, 244, 245, 250, 252, 253, 254, 255, 256, 270, 271, 280, 286, 287, 289, 290, 292, 297, 298, 320, 359–371, 378. Numerous technical studies can be tracked down by starting from the notes or bibliographies of Albright in *CAH*[3], II, ch. xx; E. F. Campbell, Jr., *The Chronology of the Amarna Letters* (Baltimore, 1964), and the Rainey book just cited. New publications of the full archive in English are soon to appear.

4. Compare Campbell, *Chronology* [N 3], pp. 32–36, and F. J. Giles, *Ikhnaton: Legend and History* (1970), p. 149.

5. For a recent treatment of Josh. 12:9–24, advocating a Solomonic date for the basic list, see V. Fritz, *ZDPV* 85 (1969), 136–161.

6. See the criticisms of Buccellati's presuppositions in M. C. Astour's review of *Cities and Nations,* in *JNES* 29 (1970), 294 f.

7. M. B. Rowton, "The Topological Factor in the Ḫapiru Problem," *Studies in Honor of Benno Landsberger* (Chicago, 1965), pp. 375 ff.

8. Compare to this paragraph the description in D. Baly, *The Geography of the Bible* (New York, 1957), ch. xv, esp. pp. 175–180. While the emphasis is different, the two descriptions are based on similar data.

9. Wright, *Shechem* [N 3], pp. 95–100, 122. Details may be garnered from the preliminary reports in *BASOR* 148 (Dec. 1957), 161 (Feb. 1961), 169 (Feb. 1963), 180 (Dec. 1965).

10. Wright, *Shechem* [N 3], pp. 76–79. The proposal of K. M. Kenyon, *CAH*[3], II, ch. xi, pp. 17 ff., published in 1971, to redate the East Gate to LB is impossible, as J. D. Seger has shown in *Levant* 6 (1974), 117–130. It is troubling that Kenyon seems so seriously to mistrust the Shechem expedition's application of archaeological technique which was learned primarily from her expert and excellent example!

11. *BASOR* 180 (Dec. 1965), 10–15, 21–26.

12. *BASOR* 204 (Dec. 1971), 7–17 with fig. 8 on p. 40; 205 (Feb. 1972), 22–26.

13. See the publication of results through 1966, in *BASOR* 190 (April 1968), 19–41.

14. Albright's candidate for Michmethath (Josh. 16:6, 17:7); see *AASOR* 4 (1924), 152–153, n. 2.

15. The equation with Tappuaḥ is now virtually unanimous. See esp. E. Jenni, *ZDPV* 74 (1958), 35–40, and K. Elliger in *Archäologie und Altes Testament: Festschrift K. Galling,* eds. A. Kuschke and E. Kutsch (Tübingen, 1970), p. 98.

16. M.-L. Buhl and S. Holm-Nielsen, *Shiloh* (Copenhagen, 1969), *passim.* Lamentably, definition of Late Bronze installations is very nearly impossible; only a perusal of the plates yields a goodly smattering of LB forms.

17. J. L. Kelso et al., *AASOR* 39 (1968), esp. ch. v.

18. See R. de Vaux's preliminary reports in *RB* between 1947 and 1962, esp. 54 (1947), 576–579 and pls. xxiv–xxv; 55 (1948), 570; 58 (1951), 405–408; 59 (1952), 552–558; 62 (1955), 542–549; 64 (1957), 574–578; and, for a brief summation, de Vaux in *Archaeology and Old Testament Study,* ed. D. W. Thomas (Oxford, 1967), p. 375.

19. Preliminary reports by J. P. Free appear in *BASOR* 131, 135, 139, 143, 152, 156 and 160 between 1953 and 1960. No. 160 gives the fullest description of the tomb.

20. R. Bach, *ZDPV* 74 (1958), 41–54.

21. S. Kappus, *ZDPV* 82 (1966), 74–82; cf. A. Kuschke, *ZDPV* 74 (1958), 15 f. An ASOR team visited the site in 1964 and recovered a nearly complete LB II chalice (decorated in a style more suggestive of LB IIA than of LB IIB), along with other LB sherds, from a burn layer exposed in the side of a modern irrigation channel cutting into the north side of the mound; if the suspicion of LB IIA, i.e. the fourteenth century, is correct, this destruction would parallel the one which brought Shechem Stratum XIII to a close around 1350/1310.

22. See among others, M. W. Several, *PEQ* 104 (1972), 123–133; H. Klengel, *Das Altertum* 11 (1965), 131–137; A. R. Schulman, *Journal of the American Research Center in Egypt* 3 (1964), 51–69; Giles, [N 4], esp. pp. 141–203; and the review of Giles by E. F. Wente, *JNES* 31 (1972), 139 f. (Giles book was written on the basis of research done prior to 1960).

23. H. W. Helck, *Mitteilungen der deutschen Orient-Gesellschaft* 92 (1960), 3; Klengel, *Das Altertum* 11 (1965), 131–133.

24. H. W. Helck, *Die Beziehung Ägyptens zu Vorderasien im 3. und 2. Jahrtausend v. Chr.* pp. 256 f.

25. Helck [N 23], p. 5.

26. W. F. Albright, *JEA* 23 (1937), 191 f.; *JNES* 5 (1946), 16.

27. M. Liverani, *Revue d'Assyriologie* 61 (1967), 1–18.

28. A. Alt, *Forschungen und Fortschritte* 25 (1949), 250–251, repr. in *KS,* III (1959), 104.

29. J. C. Greenfield, *Fourth World Congress of Jewish Studies: Papers* 1 (1967), 117–119.

30. W. L. Moran, *CBQ* 25 (1963), 77–78.

31. G. E. Mendenhall, *The Wittenberg Bulletin* 15 (1948), 37–42. A new treatment of the material is in Mendenhall's volume, *The Tenth Generation* (Baltimore and London, 1973), 69–104.

32. *ANET,* p. 485.

33. G. E. Wright, in *Israel's Prophetic Heritage,* eds. B. W. Anderson and W. Harrelson, (1962), p. 31, n. 19; J. Bright, *Jeremiah,* AB, vol. 21 (1965), pp. 87, 110; E. F. Campbell, Jr., *McCQ* 20 (1967), 9.

34. Employing D. J. McCarthy's rendering, *Treaty and Covenant* (Rome, 1963), p. 193.

35. H. B. Huffmon, *BASOR* 181 (Feb. 1966), 31–37; see further Huffmon and S. B. Parker, *BASOR* 184 (Dec. 1966), 36–38.

36. J. B. van Hooser, "The Meaning of the Hebrew Root PQD in the Old Testament," doctoral dissertation, Harvard University, 1962.

37. B. S. Childs, *Memory and Tradition in Israel* (Naperville, Ill., 1962), pp. 23–24.

38. Campbell, *McCQ* 20 (1967), 8–9.

39. J. Wijngaards, *VT* 17 (1967), 226–239, esp. pp. 232–234, cf. E. F. Campbell, Jr., *Pittsburgh Perspective* 12 (1971), 110–111.

40. This should serve as a check on the excesses of some interpreters who have built upon the seminal studies of George Mendenhall in such a fashion as to evoke the charge of pan-Hittitism; Mendenhall himself has never been guilty of such a charge!

3. Divine Names and Titles in Early Hebrew Poetry

DAVID NOEL FREEDMAN

UNIVERSITY OF MICHIGAN

IN A RECENT SURVEY of early Hebrew poetry, the late Professor W. F. Albright proposed a basic sequence dating, using certain stylistic phenomena as determinative criteria.[1] Chief among these were repetitive parallelism and paronomasia or wordplay. Relative chronology is fixed by reference to Ugaritic poetry which is substantially older than practically all surviving biblical verse. Since repetitive parallelism is frequent in Ugaritic poems, its occurrence in Hebrew poetry would be an indicator of early date. On the other hand, paronomasia is rare in Ugaritic, so its occurrence in Hebrew poetry would point to a somewhat later date of composition. Albright was able to discern a pattern in early Hebrew poems exhibiting a gradual decline in the use of repetitive parallelism with a corresponding increase in the use of paronomasia.[2] This discovery permitted an arrangement of the poems in sequence, between the thirteenth and tenth centuries B.C., with more specific dates being assigned on the basis of historical allusions and other information in the poems. Albright fixed the order and dates of the poems as follows:

1. Song of Miriam (Exodus 15)—early thirteenth century
2. Song of Deborah (Judges 5)—ca. 1150
3. Oracles of Balaam (Numbers 23–24)—ca. 1200
4. Testament of Moses (Deuteronomy 33)—middle of eleventh century
5. Song of Moses (Deuteronomy 32)—ca. 1025
6. Testament of Jacob (Genesis 49)—late eleventh century
7. Song of Hannah (I Sam. 2)—late eleventh
8. David's Lament (II Sam. 1)—early tenth
9. Oracle of David (II Sam. 23)—first half of tenth
10. Royal Psalm (II Sam. 22=Ps. 18)—tenth
11. Psalm 78—tenth
12. Psalm 68—tenth

    13. Psalm 72—tenth
    14. Psalm 29[3]

The following comments about the list may be in order:

1) While the Song of Deborah precedes the Oracles of Balaam in Albright's list, he dated the Oracles earlier than the Song. On the basis of stylistic criteria, he recognized that the Song was more archaic: e.g. it exhibits extensive repetitive parallelism, while the Oracles have very little. The overriding consideration for Albright, however, was the presence of specific historical information in the Oracles, especially among the isolated utterances in Num. 24:20–24, which pointed to a date around 1200, necessarily earlier than the Song of Deborah.[4] But these utterances are not integral parts of the Oracles, and even if Albright's analysis were correct, the data would be insufficient to fix the date of the Oracles as a whole. Our investigation tends to confirm Albright's stylistic order, and points to a later date (in the tenth century) for the Oracles.

2) In further notes on the early poems, Albright expresses some reservations about his placement of the Testament of Jacob (Genesis 49), and concludes that the content is "surprisingly heterogeneous."[5] He then assigns a number of oracles to "Late Patriarchal" times, including the Joseph sayings (vss. 22–26), with which we are primarily concerned.[6]

The general purpose of the present paper is essentially the same as Albright's, to fix the chronological sequence of the early poems of Israel, as these have been preserved in the Bible. However, I expect to use an entirely different set of criteria in determining the sequence, thus providing an independent basis for comparing and evaluating results. In what follows, I wish to focus attention on the use of divine names and epithets in the poetry under consideration. The underlying assumption is that such usage, while at the option of the poet, reflects prevailing religious patterns, and the changes which took place during the creative and adaptive years of Israel's history. From an examination of the incidence and distribution of divine names and epithets, I can distinguish three phases in the development of Hebrew poetry during this early period:

1. *Militant Mosaic Yahwism* (*twelfth century*): the name Yahweh is used exclusively or predominantly.

> Exodus 15
> Psalm 29
> Judges 5

2. *Patriarchal Revival* (*eleventh century*): in addition to Yahweh, the name El is used in parallel with it. The equation Yahweh=El (i.e. the God of the Fathers) opens the way to the introduction or reintroduction of divine epithets associated with the patriarchal deity in the Genesis traditions: in particular *šadday, 'elyōn,* and *'ōlām.*

Genesis 49
Numbers 23–24
Deuteronomy 33

3. *Monarchic Syncretism (tenth century or later)*: in this period a new set of titles and epithets appears, reflecting the syncretistic tendencies of the religion of the monarchy. The date of most of these poems is secured by explicit reference to the monarchy and David in particular.

I Samuel 2
II Samuel 1
II Samuel 23
II Samuel 22=Psalm 18
Deuteronomy 32
Psalm 78
Psalm 68
Psalm 72

The variations between my list and Albright's are relatively few, especially considering the differences in method. My approach and conclusions will be defended in the analysis of the individual poems, and comments on selected divine names and epithets. The data on the incidence and distribution of the latter will be summarized in accompanying charts.

PHASE I

1. THE SONG OF THE SEA: EXOD. 15:1–18, 21[7]

Many scholars regard the poem as composite, with only the opening couplet (vs. 1, repeated with slight change in vs. 21) original, going back to Mosaic times. The rest is considered a later composition, and is dated anywhere from early monarchic to late post-exilic times. In my opinion, vss. 1 and 21 constitute a refrain, sung antiphonally by different groups at the beginning and end of the poem, and forming an envelope around the main section of the poem. A comparable arrangement is to be found in David's lament over Saul and Jonathan (II Sam. 1:19–27) in which a refrain is repeated in the opening and closing lines: *'ēk nāpᵉlū gibbōrīm.*[8] For the rest, I consider the poem a unified composition, with the possible exception of vs. 2 which seems to be a separate liturgical exordium delivered by the temple precentor, dating from the tenth century.

Returning to vss. 1 and 21, the only divine name which occurs is Yahweh, which is in accord with the hypothesis presented above. To be compared with this is the other brief war song associated with the wanderings in the wilderness, the attack on Amalek (Exod. 17:16). In the latter, the name

Yahweh appears; the abbreviated form Yah also seems to occur, but the text is difficult and may be corrupt.[9]

In addition, there are the songs of the ark, Num. 10:34–35, which probably belong to the period after the settlement in the land. The only divine appellative is Yahweh (cf. the adaptation in Ps. 68:2 which is substantially the same as Num. 10:34). The same pattern holds for the Aaronic benediction (Num. 6:24–26; Yahweh occurs three times), but this factor alone does not demonstrate an early date of composition.

In vs. 2 there is a series of divine names and epithets. The combination *'ozzī w^ezimrāt*, "my mighty fortress," occurs only here and in the parallel passages, Isa. 12:2 and Ps. 118:14.[10] Taking the terms separately, and limiting the references to poems on Albright's list, *'z* as a divine epithet is found in Ps. 29:1="Mighty One."[11] With respect to *zmrt*, the plural form *z^emīrōt* is found in II Sam. 23:1="Defense (of Israel)."[12]

The shortened form Yah also appears in vs. 2. Among the listed poems it occurs here and in Psalm 68 (twice, vss. 5, 19). Apart from these instances (and the possible occurrence in Exod. 17:16) its usage is specialized and in general late: as part of a liturgical formula in the Psalter, *hall^elūyāh;* sporadically in the Psalms and late poetry. None of these can be attested before the tenth century at the earliest (e.g. Ps. 89:9). If we suppose that the name Yahweh was introduced by Moses in the thirteenth century, we would hardly expect such an abbreviated form to be in general use before the tenth century, and the evidence generally supports this view. If the reading here is correct, then it seems to me that the verse is a later addition; or put another way, the poem in its present completed form is not earlier than the tenth century.[13]

The form *'ēlī*, "my God" (divine name with suffix), occurs in Pss. 18:3, 68:25, both of which date to the tenth century (or later) but not in any of the earlier poems on the list. Parallel to it is the expression *'^elōhē 'ābī*, "my father's God." The construct form *'^elōhē* turns up regularly on the list, but the absolute form, *'^elōhīm*=God, does not appear until the monarchic period. The combination *'^elōhē 'ābī* does not occur elsewhere in our poetry, but it does appear in prose dealing with the period of the patriarchs and Moses: e.g. Gen. 31:5, 32:10; Exod. 18:4 (cf. Gen. 26:24, 28:13, 46:3, etc.).

In the main part of the poem, vss. 3–18, the name Yahweh predominates, occurring eight times (vss. 3, 3, 6, 6, 11, 16, 17, 18). In two cases, there are parallel expressions: *n'dr, nwr', 'šh pl'* (vs. 11) and *'dny* (vs. 17). With respect to the former, *n'dr* is unique as an epithet of God, while *nwr'* occurs again in Ps. 68:36; the third expression has a parallel in Ps. 72:18, while the participle with a different object is also found in Num. 24:18 and II Sam. 22:51 (=Ps. 18:51).

The occurrence of *'dny* in vs. 17 poses a problem. While normal canons of poetic parallelism support MT (Yahweh in 17a is balanced by *'dny* in 17b), there is substantial textual evidence in favor of an original reading

Yahweh which was subsequently changed to *'dny,* i.e. a number of manuscripts of MT and the Samaritan have Yahweh.[14] There is no doubt that
'dny is a legitimate surrogate for Yahweh and is often used in combination
with it, sometimes in a parallel construction with Yahweh or *'elōhīm.* Just
when it was introduced, however, remains a question. The only attested instances in our list of poems are in Psalms 78 (vs. 65) and 68 (vss. 12,
18, 20, 23, 27, 33), neither of which can be earlier than the tenth century.
Furthermore, in view of the fact that *'dny* became a permanent substitute for
Yahweh in the reading of the text (confirmed as early as the third century
B.C. by the standard rendering of the Tetragrammaton in the LXX as
kyrios), it is very difficult to distinguish between cases in which *'dny* is
original, and in which it has been substituted accidentally for an original
Yahweh. In the present instance it seems more likely that Yahweh was the
original reading, and that *'dny* was introduced into the text secondarily. It is
more difficult to imagine the reverse.

In addition there are terms for divine beings other than Yahweh. Thus the
words *'ēlīm* and *qōdeš* occur in vs. 11, which reads:

> Who is like you, Yahweh,
> among the gods?
> Who is like you, Awesome One,
> among the holy ones?

The term *qōdeš* is an abstract or collective term, equivalent to the expected
qedōšīm, which may be reflected in the LXX of this passage.[15] The connection is well attested in Ps. 89:6–8 where both *qedōšīm* and *'ēlīm* occur in
parallel phrases. Behind the parallel pattern in poetry lies a stereotyped expression attested in a Phoenician inscription of the tenth century B.C. from
Byblos: *'l gbl qdšm,* "the holy gods of Byblos."[16] The meaning of the passage in Exodus 15 could be expressed as follows: "Who is like you, among
the holy gods, Yahweh the Awesome One?"

In the light of the data, my conclusion is that the original poem consisted
of vss. 1, 3–18, and 21 and was composed in the twelfth century.[17] The
dominant divine name is Yahweh; in addition there are a few qualifying
adjectives or epithets but these tell us very little. Subsequently, vs. 2 was
added, and with it were introduced several names and epithets, which derive
from the period of the early monarchy. In its present expanded and revised
form, the poem may be dated as late as the tenth century.[18]

Distribution

1. Yahweh: vss. 1, 3, 3, 6, 6, 11, 16, 17, 18, 21
   a. Without parallel: vss. 1, 16, 18, 21
   b. In parallel with other divine names
      1) *Adonay:* vs. 17
   c. In parallel with various terms and phrases

          1) *'īš milḥāmāh:* vs. 3
          2) *ne'dār:* vs. 11
          3) *nōrā':* vs. 11
          4) *'ōśēh pele':* vs. 11
  2. *Yah:* vs. 2
    a. In parallel with other terms:
        1) *'ozzī:* vs. 2
        2) *zimrāt:* vs. 2
  3. *Eli:* vs. 2
    a. In parallel with other terms:
        1) *'ᵉlōhē 'ābī:* vs. 2
  4. *Adonay:* vs. 17 (cf. Yahweh, 1.b.1)

2. PSALM 29[19]

Albright did not attempt to place Psalm 29 in his sequential scheme, but he speaks of it as being "very archaic" (*YGC,* p. 21) and "clearly archaic" (p. 27).[20] Nevertheless an effort can and should be made to fix a date partly on the basis of his stylistic criteria, and partly on the basis of the use of divine names. With respect to the former, Psalm 29 employs repetitive parallelism to an extraordinary extent, comparable to both the Song of the Sea and the Song of Deborah, perhaps with greater affinity for the more elaborate patterns of the latter.[21] With respect to divine epithets, the picture is very similar, though here there is a closer correlation with the Song of the Sea.[22] The name Yahweh is emphasized overwhelmingly, occurring no fewer than eighteen times in the short span of eleven verses. The only other divine designation is *'ēl,* which occurs twice (vss. 1 and 3).

In vs. 1, we have the phrase *bᵉnē 'ēlīm,* which may be rendered "sons of the gods," i.e. divine beings, like *ben-rᵉ'ēmīm,* "a calf of wild bulls," i.e. a young wild bull, or the familiar expression *bᵉnē hannᵉbī'īm,* "the sons of the prophets," i.e. members of the prophetic guild. The phrase, however, is a designation of the divine assembly, derived directly from Canaanite mythopoetic language, and should be translated "sons of El." The word *'ēlīm* should be interpreted, therefore, as the divine name, El, with the genitive case ending and the enclitic *mem.*[23] The phrase is equivalent to *'ēlīm,* "gods," in Exod. 15:11.

In vs. 3, it is combined with the term *hakkābōd.* The phrase may be rendered "the God of glory" or "the glorious God," or "El, the Glorious."[24] That a divine title is intended is shown by the usage in vs. 2: *hbw lyhwh kbwd šmw,* which may be translated, "Give praise to Yahweh, whose name is Glorious." The same term (*kbwd*) occurs in conjunction with *'z* in vs. 1: "Give praise to Yahweh, the Glorious and Victorious"; it also stands alone in vs. 9: "O Glorious One!"[25]

This generic use of *'ēl,* "God," in a construct chain, which is attested again in certain poems of Phase III, e.g. I Samuel 2 and Deuteronomy 32, is to be distinguished from its specific employment as the personal name of the deity, El, the patriarchal appellation which appears in Phase II poems, Genesis 49, Numbers 23–24, Deuteronomy 33.

In Psalm 29 reference is made to the people of Yahweh (vs. 11), but without further explicit identification. This usage corresponds to the pattern in Exodus 15 rather than that of Judges 5 where the equation with Israel is made directly. In view of its affinities with the poems in Phase I, and possible thematic dependence on the Song of the Sea, Psalm 29 should be assigned to the latter part of the twelfth century, and in any case not later than around 1100.[26]

Distribution

1. Yahweh: vss. 1, 1, 2, 2, 3, 3, 4, 4, 5, 5, 7, 8, 8, 9, 10, 10, 11, 11
   a. Without parallel (or parallel with Yahweh): vss. 1a, 2b, 3ab, 4ab, 5ab, 7, 8ab, 9, 10ab, 11ab
   b. In parallel with other divine names and epithets
      1) *El:* vs. 3
      2) *Kabod:* vss. 1, 2, 3, 9
      3) *Oz:* vs. 1
2. El: vs. 3 (cf. Yahweh, 1.b.1)

3. THE SONG OF DEBORAH: JUDG. 5:2–31[27]

In this poem there is an overwhelming preference for Yahweh, which occurs fourteen times. There are only two other epithets used: *'elōhē yiśrā'ēl*, "the God of Israel" (vss. 3, 5) and *zeh sīnay*, "the One of Sinai" (vs. 5). In all three occurrences, the terms are directly parallel with Yahweh, emphasizing the identification of Yahweh with the revelation of Mount Sinai, and as the God of Israel.

The designation, "the One of Sinai," is archaic in form, possibly pre-Mosaic in origin, and reflects the wilderness experience. If any epithet is basic and indigenous to Yahwistic religion, it is this one. The only other occurrence of that expression is in Ps. 68:9, a passage which is dependent upon Judg. 5:5.

The case is not so clear with respect to the other title, "God of Israel." It is the classical historical characterization of Yahweh, just as Israel is designated "the people of Yahweh" (vss. 11, 13; cf. Exod. 15:13, 16). While the term may also go back to Moses or the Mosaic experience, it seems to be more applicable to the community after its entry into the promised land. While the term *'am*, "people," is used repeatedly in both poems, Exodus 15 and Judges 5, and they are identified as Yahweh's people, the term Israel does not occur in Exodus 15.

It is only when they have arrived in the land that the *'am* is called Israel. According to the biblical tradition, however, both the name Israel and the designation "God of Israel" are pre-Mosaic and find their origin in the patriarchal stories. Thus Israel is the name acquired at a certain point in his career by Jacob, and continues as the name of his clan (Gen. 32:29, 35:10). Furthermore, Jacob's God, "El," is given the explicit title *'elōhē yiśrā'ēl*, "God of Israel," in connection with the erection of an altar at Shechem (33: 18–20). In view of the biblical traditions, supported by archaeological evidence, there is no reason to doubt that Israelites (i.e. *bny yśr'l*) were settled in the Shechem area during pre-Mosaic times. Their God was El, the patriarchal deity whose sway extended throughout the region, and who was worshipped at Bethel (cf. Gen. 35:7) in addition to Shechem and other places.

What is reflected in the Song of Deborah is not the equation of Yahweh with El and the blending or merging of domains, characteristics, and the like, but the attribution of El's title as God of Israel to Yahweh. This is an indication of the continuing militance of the Mosaic movement, laying claim to the loyalty of Israelites in the central highlands. They had joined the people of Yahweh in the struggle against the Canaanites on the basis of the exclusive demands of Yahweh. Only one step in the direction of accommodation to the descendants of the patriarchs was made: the appropriation of the title, God of Israel. Whatever the etymology and original meaning of the name may be, *yiśrā'ēl* is a verb compounded with the divine element *'ēl*, and must therefore derive from an El-worshiping community. That suits very well the region around Shechem in the period down to the twelfth century B.C.

The word *'elōhīm* occurs in vs. 8. The passage is difficult and so far has eluded successful analysis and interpretation. If the apparent connection between the phrase *'lhym ḥdšym* here and the same words in Deut. 32:17 is valid, then *'lhym* in both places refers to "gods," not "God."[28] There is a consistent pattern in the early poetry that the term *'elōhīm* is not used for God, although the construct form *'elōhē* and the equivalent form with pronominal suffixes are so used. It is not until we come to the Psalms in the so-called Elohistic Psalter that *'lhym* is used regularly for God, generally as a substitute for Yahweh (though Yahweh also appears in these poems).[29] The only other example of *elōhīm*, "God," from our list is found in II Sam. 23:3, *yir'at 'elōhīm*, "the fear of God," which is a stereotyped expression for "piety." The natural pair *yhwh // 'lhym* does not appear in our poetry.

In general the Song of Deborah shares with the Song of the Sea an intense concentration on the name Yahweh, to which it adds the unique but indigenous epithet *zh syny*, "the One of Sinai." In Judges 5 the people of Yahweh is explicitly identified as Israel, and Yahweh is explicitly called the God of Israel, whereas in Exodus 15, the people is called simply *'am*, though the special relationship to Yahweh is spelled out just as emphatically. In Judges 5 as well, Israel is defined as a congeries if not a confederation of tribes (i.e. territorial and political units) and a list of them is given. Except for the appropriation of the title *'elōhē yiśrā'ēl*, no link with the patriarchs or their religion is asserted, or even implied. This is the period of militant Mosaism:

Yahweh is emphasized to the exclusion of the normal parallel El; and Israel is stressed to the exclusion of the logical complement, Jacob. Those combinations were yet to be made; they belong to Phase II.

Distribution

1. Yahweh: vss. 2, 3, 3, 4, 5, 5, 9, 11, 11, 13, 23, 23, 23, 31
   a. Without parallel: vss. 2, 3a, 4, 9, 11a, 11b, 13, 23a, b, e, 31
   b. In parallel with (other) divine names and epithets:
      1) *ᵉlōhē yiśrā'ēl:* vss. 3, 5
      2) *zeh sīnay:* vs. 5

PHASE II

4. THE TESTAMENT OF JACOB: GEN. 49:1–27

Apart from the blessing of Joseph (vss. 22–26), the poem is almost entirely devoid of divine names or epithets. The only exception is the name Yahweh in vs. 18, but this verse is universally regarded as a secondary addition.

The blessing of Joseph requires special attention, not only because it is replete with archaic titles and epithets, but because this is the only clear example of non-Yahwistic El poetry in our corpus. Albright regarded this passage as stemming from late patriarchal times, and that judgment may be correct.[30] It reflects the religion of the El worshipers in the central highlands (Joseph territory) who traced their descent from the patriarchs and formed the core of the pre-Mosaic tribal league Israel. In its present form, however, the blessing has been accommodated to the historical-political realities of the eleventh century.

The key names are El and Shadday (vs. 25). According to the priestly writer the compound name El Shadday was the designation of the God of the Fathers par excellence (cf. Exod. 6:3, which is the pivotal statement about the relationship between the patriarchal name El Shadday and the new Mosaic name Yahweh) and is used by him in the patriarchal narratives: Gen. 17:1, 28:3, 35:11, 43:14, 48:3. It occurs in some of the poems of Phase II, including the present instance, Num. 24:16, and Ps. 68:15.

While Psalm 68, following Albright, is best understood as a catalogue of song titles or a compendium of opening lines, covering the whole period of our poetry from the twelfth century or earlier down to the tenth century, most of the contents must be pre-monarchic.[31] After Phase II, however, the term drops out of use, and is characteristically omitted in poetry from the monarchic period. Psalm 91, the date of which is uncertain, may be an exceptional instance from the monarchic period. In vs. 1, Shadday occurs in parallel with Elyon as is the case in Num. 24:16.

Otherwise usage is limited and follows a curious but significant pattern. It occurs in prophetic prose and poetry of the sixth century, a period of nostalgic revival in Judah and throughout the Near East, i.e. Ezek. 1:24, 10:5; Isa. 13: 6=Joel 1:15 (*yhwh∥šdy*).[32] It also occurs frequently in Job (thirty-one times), more than all the rest of the occurrences put together (seventeen times). Since Job probably dates from the same general period (seventh–sixth century),[33] the usage may reflect similar interests. It is likely that some other, stronger influence stemming from patriarchal or pre-monarchic traditions is at work here, however.

Finally we may point to the occurrence of the term twice in the Book of Ruth (1:20, 21). Naomi is quoted as referring to the deity by this title (parallel with Yahweh, vs. 21). While the date of Ruth is uncertain, the book may well be a product of the seventh–sixth centuries in its present form.[34] The pattern is therefore essentially the same as Isa. 13:6=Joel 1:15 of approximately the same date. The story, however, is about events in the period of the judges (twelfth–eleventh centuries), and may reflect actual usage of *šadday* quite accurately, since the term occurs in two poems which are dated to that period on other grounds.

To summarize: (1) The epithet *šadday* is attributed to the patriarchal period by the priestly writer. (2) It was used along with other patriarchal names during the period of the judges (eleventh century) as attested by contemporary poems, and indirectly by evidence in the Book of Ruth. (3) Then it disappeared almost entirely from use during the monarchic period (with the possible exception of Psalms 68 and 91, as noted), only to be revived in the period of national nostalgia beginning in the late seventh century B.C.

The reading El Shadday (*'ēl šadday*) in Gen. 49:25, supported by the Samaritan and the Septuagint as well as a few manuscripts of MT, is to be preferred to the standard reading of MT *wᵉ'ēt šadday* which is anomalous at best. The parallel expression is *mē'ēl 'ābīkā* which may be rendered either "From the God of your father" (so RSV), or "From El, your Father." While the former is entirely possible, the latter may be preferable, since the term "father" is a characteristic designation of El in the Ugaritic texts, and was transferred to Yahweh in Israelite tradition; cf. Deut. 32:6; Ps. 68:6.

Just as the evidence from the poems of Phase I tends to support the view that the name Yahweh was introduced by Moses and used exclusively in the early period by his followers, so the evidence from Genesis 49 points to the conclusion that the patriarchal names of God, and the compound El Shadday in particular, were used by Israelites, who claimed descent from the fathers and continued to worship the fathers' God under the name and titles of that earlier experience.

In the preceding verse (Gen. 49:24) there are two other epithets which require our attention: *'ᵃbīr yaʿᵃqōb and rō'eh 'eben yiśrā'ēl*. The former, which is commonly rendered "Mighty One of Jacob" (RSV, etc.), or "Champion," is more literally "Bull," an appropriate designation of the god El in Canaanite tradition and presumably true of the patriarchal El as well. The terms in Ugaritic and Hebrew are not identical, however; apparently certain distinctions were recognized and maintained. The phrase occurs in the royal, possibly Davidic Psalm 132 (vss. 2 and 5). It is interesting to note that the term *'ᵃbīr* otherwise turns up only in Isaiah, but in all parts of it: 1:24 (*'ᵃbīr yiśrā'ēl*), 49:26 and 60:16 (*'ᵃbīr ya'ᵃqōb*). Presumably the epithet was adopted by the early monarchy, and it remained associated with the worship of Jerusalem and its traditions thereafter.

The other phrase, *rʿh 'bn yśr'l,* poses textual and exegetical problems which so far have defied adequate analysis and solution. The essential elements are *rō'eh* and *yiśrā'ēl*="Shepherd of Israel," as comparison with Ps. 80:2 makes clear (cf. also Gen. 48:15, *hārō'eh 'ōtī,* which connects the epithet directly with Jacob/Israel). The word *'bn* may be understood as a byform of *bn,* "son."[35] Further it should be read as plural: **'ibnē* or the like. The omission of the final *yod* may be understood as an instance of early consonantal spelling, or the initial *yod* of the next word *yśr'l* may be regarded as serving double duty.[36] The rendering would then be "Shepherd of the sons of Israel"; cf. *bny y'qb* in vs. 2 of the same poem.

Other possible divine epithets may be looked for in vs. 26. As in vs. 25, *'ābīkā* may refer to El or God rather than to a human father, though such an interpretation hinges to some extent upon the proper understanding of the pair *šādayim wārāḥam* in vs. 25. If that is ultimately a reference to the Mother goddess, though somewhat generalized and demythologized, then we would be justified in seeing in *'byk* a reference to the divine Father, a more appropriate source of exceptional blessing. The following words, *gābᵉrū 'al,* are more difficult and do not make sense in the MT. Accepting the consonantal text but redividing the words (cf. the wrongly divided *'qb m'śr* in vss. 19–20), I vocalize and render as follows: *gibbōr wᵉ'al,* "Warrior and Exalted One," i.e. "the Exalted Warrior." For *gibbōr* as a divine title, see Ps. 24:8, especially the pair *'izzūz wᵉgibbōr,* "Mighty One and Warrior," i.e. "the Mighty Warrior"; and Isa. 10:21 *'ēl gibbōr,* "El the Warrior," in which *gibbōr* is an epithet of El. The second term *'al* has been identified as a divine epithet in Ugaritic, and is preserved, though not recognized as such by earlier grammarians and scholars, in several ancient poems, e.g. Deut. 33:12; I Sam. 2:10; II Sam. 23:1 (cf. the name *'ēlī* in I Sam. 1 ff. and the Northwest Semitic name *yᵉhaw-ēlī*).[37]

Finally in Gen. 49:25 we note the pair *'ad // 'ōlām.*[38] It is possible that these are divine epithets here and that the mountains mentioned are not merely aged or ancient, but specifically associated with the Ancient // Eternal God.[39] The same pair *hrry 'd // gb'wt 'wlm* occurs in the archaizing poem in Habakkuk 3 (vs. 6). The equivalent usage is found in the parallel blessing of Joseph in Deut. 33:15, *hrry qdm // gb'wt 'wlm;* cf. *'lhy qdm // zr't 'wlm* (vs. 27), already noted, which is to be rendered "the ancient

God . . . the arms of the Eternal One." The conclusion is that the term *'ōlām,* with its parallels *'ad* and *qedem,* was an ancient designation of the patriarchal God, El, and that its usage was revived or continued in the community which worshiped El, and brought its divine terminology with it when it merged with the Yahweh-worshiping group from the wilderness. Cross has established the pre-Mosaic date of the epithet *'lm* as a designation of El in the proto-Canaanite inscriptions from Sinai dating to the fifteenth century B.C.[40] Dahood has identified the divine name Olam in a number of psalms and other poetic passages:[41] cf. Isa. 40:20 and Pss. 66:7, 89:2 (*yhwh 'wlm,* "Yahweh the Eternal").

In the blessing of Joseph, there are three of the characteristic divine epithets associated with the patriarchal age in biblical tradition: El, Shadday, and possibly Olam. In addition we have *'al* (or *'ēlī*) which is derived from the same root as a fourth patriarchal title, Elyon, and semantically equivalent. The absence of the principal name Yahweh may be inadvertent, but it is more likely that this passage comes from the El-worshiping community in the Shechem area in pre-Mosaic times. In its present form, however, the Testament of Jacob reflects the formal organization of the twelve-tribe amphictyony; the repeated occurrence of the pair Jacob//Israel (vss. 2, 7, 24) confirms this view. The poem as a whole is to be assigned to Phase II, and may be dated in the first half of the eleventh century.[42]

Distribution

1. Yahweh: vs. 18 (no parallel)
2. El: vs. 25, (25)
   a. In parallel with other divine names and epithets
      1) Shadday: vs. 25
      2) *'ābīkā:* vs. 25
      3) *'ᵃbīr ya'ᵃqōb:* vs. 24
      4) *rō 'eh ('eben) yiśrā'ēl:* vs. 24
3. Shadday: vs. 25 (cf. 2.a.1)
4. Ad: vs. 26
   a. In parallel with other divine names
      1) *'ōlām:* vs. 26
5. Olam: vs. 26 (cf. Ad, 3.a.1)

5. THE ORACLES OF BALAAM: NUMBERS 23–24[43]

In these poems, the principal divine name is El, which occurs eight times, 23:8, 19, 22, 23, 24:4, 8, 16, 23. The first seven are in the major oracles, while the last occurs in one of the brief sayings appended to the oracles, and is apparently the only divine name in them (24:20–24).

The name Yahweh also occurs, but less frequently: 23:8, 21, 24:6. It is used once in each of the first three oracles, but not at all in the fourth utterance or the appended sayings.

The equation Yahweh=El appears twice: (1) Num. 23:8 where the order of MT (El//Yahweh) is reversed in the LXX which is probably original; (2) 23:21-22, where the order is Yahweh//El. This all-important identification was not present in the earlier poems of Phase I (see discussion above). It is matched by the combination Jacob-Israel, which occurs seven or eight times in these oracles (23:7, 10, 21, 23, 23, 24:5, 17, 18-19 with order reversed if the text is correct), and represents the classic designation of the tribal league.

It should be pointed out that the occurrence of Yahweh and El in parallel cola or lines does not represent the break-up of the divine name Yahweh-el (perhaps "El will create, bring to pass"), which may well have been the original full name of Yahweh, but rather the equation of separate divine names here drawn together from different traditions.[44] In our opinion, Yahweh was deliberately and explicitly separated from the El tradition with which he may have been associated earlier in pre-Mosaic times. While the story of the golden calf (Exodus 32) has been colored by reminiscences of and attitudes arising out of the division of the kingdom and the use of similar figures in the temples at Bethel and Dan, the original nucleus reflects the emphatic rejection of El worship by the militant followers of Moses during a crisis in the wilderness. Only later, after the settlement in the land, and the time of Deborah, was the breach repaired, and an agreement between the respective worshipers of Yahweh and El achieved.

The term *'elōhāw,* "his God," is joined to Yahweh in 23:21. The pronominal suffix refers to Jacob-Israel mentioned in the preceding verse, confirming the consolidation of the two segments of the confederation, and identifying Yahweh as the God of the entire community.

In the second group of oracles, other divine epithets appear: El and Shadday are associated in 24:4. In the parallel passage, 24:16, there is an additional colon which includes the title Elyon. It is clear that vs. 16 has the original form of the couplet while vs. 4 is a defective, and erroneously revised, version of the former. In any case, it is important to note the occurrence of three names or titles of the patriarchal deity in the poems, and in proximity to each other.

The names El and Shadday have already been discussed, though it may be emphasized that together they are the basic designation of the God of the fathers. Along with it we have Elyon which is associated specifically with Abraham and the dialogue with Melchizedek at Salem (Gen. 14:18, 19, 20, 22; note the combination El Elyon). Besides its occurrence in the Oracles of Balaam, Elyon also is found in Deut. 32:8 (probably an extract from an older cosmogony), II Sam. 22:14=Ps. 18:14 (to which should be compared I Sam. 2:10 where we have the epithet *'lw* for original Al or Eli in place of Elyon in the same clause), and Ps. 78:17, 35, 56.

The Oracles of Balaam are representative of Phase II. We may isolate the following features:

1) identification of Yahweh with El, the God of the fathers;
2) the divine epithets used are those associated with the patriarchs: specifically Shadday and Elyon, while others are avoided or employed sparingly. The occurrence of Shadday is especially noteworthy, since this term was in use mainly during the period of the judges and apparently fell into disfavor during the monarchy. It does not reappear until the seventh–sixth centuries in biblical usage.

In view of the evidence a date in the eleventh century for the Oracles is entirely reasonable.

Distribution

1. El: 23:8, 19, 22, 23; 24:4, 8, 16, 23
   a. Without parallel: 23:19, 22, 23; 24:8, 23
   b. In parallel with other divine names and epithets
      1) Yahweh: 23:8
      2) Elyon: 24:(4), 16
      3) Shadday: 24:4, 16
   c. In parallel with other terms
      1) *mōṣī'*: 23:22; 24:8
2. Yahweh: 23:8, 21; 24:6
   a. Without parallel: 24:6
   b. In parallel with other divine names
      1) El: 23:8 (cf. El, 1.b.1)
      2) *'ᵉlōhāw:* 23:21
3. Elyon: 24:(4), 16 (cf. El, 1.b.2)
4. Shadday: 24:4, 16 (cf. El, 1.b.3)

6. THE TESTAMENT OF MOSES: DEUTERONOMY 33[45]

The distribution of divine names and epithets in Deuteronomy 33 is very similar to that in Genesis 49 and Numbers 23–24. The patriarchal terms El and Olam occur as well as Eli (which is equivalent to Elyon). Only Shadday is missing, and this may indicate that Deuteronomy 33 is slightly later in date than the other two, a view which may be sustained on other grounds as well.

The principal divine name in this poem, unlike both the preceding ones, is Yahweh which occurs eight times: vss. 2, 7, 11, 12, 13, 21, 23, 29. Unlike the Testament of Jacob, the name Yahweh occurs repeatedly in the individual sayings concerning the tribes: Judah, Levi, Benjamin, Joseph, Naphtali. It also appears in the opening and closing units showing that the entire composition is thoroughly Yahwistic.

The opening verses are admittedly difficult and obscure if not corrupt. It is possible that there is a divine epithet in the phrase *ḥōbēb 'ammīm,* "lover of peoples" (vs. 3), but if so, it is unique in our collection.

In vs. 12 it is possible to read *'lyw* in either position as the divine title Al or Eli, "the Exalted One." The sequence is similar to I Sam. 2:10 where *'lw,* "the Exalted," is parallel to Yahweh.[46]

The sequence *hrry qdm // gb'wt 'wlm* occurs in vs. 15. This pair has been discussed earlier in connection with the Joseph saying in Genesis 49 where a similar combination appears (vs. 26). It remains a question whether the phrases are best rendered "ancient mountains // eternal hills" or "mountains of the Ancient One // hills of the Eternal," but the latter is at least plausible if not probable.

In vs. 16 we have the unique designation *šōk^enī s^eneh,* "the dweller in the bush," apparently a reference to the episode of the burning bush (cf. Exod. 3:1–5). The archaic and poetic character of the epithet is indicated by the survival of the genitive case ending on the participle (*šōk^enī*) which is grammatically correct.[47]

The expression *marḥīb gād,* "the enlarger of Gad," occurs in vs. 20. Although the sentiment is echoed repeatedly in connection with the occupation of the land, the word *marḥīb* does not occur again in the Bible.

In vs. 26, we meet the traditional patriarchal name El, and along with it the phrase *rōkēb šāmayim,* "Rider of the skies." With this is to be compared the expression *lārōkēb bišmē š^emē qedem,* "O Rider of the ancient and most remote skies," lit. "in the skies of the skies of antiquity" (Ps. 68:34). Cf. also Ps. 68:5, *lārōkēb bā'^arābōt,* "O Rider of the clouds."

In the following verse we find *'lhy qdm,* "the ancient God," and *zr't 'wlm,* "the arms of the Eternal One." The parallelism confirms the interpretation of *'wlm* as the divine epithet, while *'lhy qdm* is simply the extended form of *qdm,* "the Ancient One."

In both the framework and the blessings, Deuteronomy 33 exhibits a range of divine names and epithets comparable to the Testament of Jacob and the Oracles of Balaam. Yahweh is emphasized as in the Song of the Sea and the Song of Deborah. The combination Jacob-Israel occurs several times, vss. 4–5 (not parallel, but associated), 10, 28, as in Genesis 49 and Numbers 23–24. The name Israel occurs independently (vss. 21, 29), however, which reminds us of the Song of Deborah.

There is an interesting reference to Moses (vs. 4) which is unique in the early poetry. Although several poems are attributed to Moses including this one, the connection is late and editorial. The next verse (5) speaks of a king, which suggests, if the verse itself is not secondary, that the framework was added in the monarchic period, or that the poem as a whole reflects the transition period from tribal confederacy to monarchy, i.e. the time of Saul. This historical situation presupposed in the individual sayings, and the description of Benjamin especially, point to the latter part of the eleventh century as the time of composition.[48]

It may be added that the unusual designation $y^e\check{s}\bar{u}r\bar{u}n$ for Israel which occurs twice in the poem (specifically in the framework—vss. 5 and 26) occurs again only in Deuteronomy 32 among our poems, which on other grounds should be dated to the monarchic period. The term must have had special and rather exclusive connotations because it is dropped entirely until Second Isaiah picks it up at the height of the nostalgic period (Isa. 44:2).

Characteristic of the Phase II poems is the continued use of the name Yahweh, but not the overwhelming preponderance evident in Phase I. It is frequent in Deuteronomy 33, but in Numbers 23–24 it is less common, preference being shown for the designation El. In Genesis 49 it does not appear at all in the sayings, though it occurs once in a secondary insertion (vs. 18). In this respect Genesis 49 is unique among all the poems in the list; the general omission of Yahweh must be the result of some special circumstance about which we can only speculate at this point.

All of the poems have the name El, and one or more of the epithets explicitly associated with the patriarchs: Shadday (Genesis 49 and Numbers 23–24), Elyon (Numbers 23–24), and Olam (Genesis 49 and Deuteronomy 33). It would be appropriate to speak of a revival of patriarchal religion or religious terminology during this period. Several indicators point to the eleventh century as the date of composition for these poems, with their strong emphasis on the tribal confederation (Genesis 49 and Deuteronomy 33), but there are some hints as well of the earliest phases of the monarchy (Numbers 23–24 and Deuteronomy 33).

Distribution

1. Yahweh: vss. 2, 7, 11, 12, 13, 21, 23, 29
   a. Without parallel: vss. 2, 7, 11, 13, 21, 23, 29
   b. In parallel with other divine names
      1) 'al or '$\bar{e}l\bar{i}$: vs. 12
2. Al or Eli: vs. 12 (cf. 1.b.1)
   a. In parallel construction or combination
      1) $\hbar\bar{o}p\bar{e}p$: vs. 12
3. El: vs. 26
   a. In parallel with other terms
      1) $r\bar{o}k\bar{e}b$ $\check{s}\bar{a}mayim$: vs. 26
4. '$^e l\bar{o}h\bar{e}$ $qedem$: vs. 27
   a. In parallel with other divine names
      1) '$\bar{o}l\bar{a}m$: vs. 27
5. Olam: vss. 15, 27
   a. In parallel with other divine names and epithets
      1) $qedem$: vss. 15, 27 (cf. '$^e l\bar{o}h\bar{e}$ $qedem$, 4.a.1)

PHASE III: TENTH CENTURY OR LATER

7. THE SONG OF HANNAH: I SAM. 2:1–10

The predominant divine name in this poem is Yahweh, which occurs nine times in MT (eight, if we substitute *bē'lōhay* for the second *byhwh* in vs. 1 with LXX, which is reasonable). No other epithet or qualifying term occurs more than once, except for *'lhy* which appears twice with suffixes; *'lhy* in vs. 1 and *'lhynw* in vs. 2.

The term *qādōš*, "holy," appears in vs. 2. While the expression is an old one, deriving from Canaanite mythology, and is used as a collective singular or plural of the divine beings who participate in the heavenly council (cf. Exod. 15:11 *qdš//'lym;* Deut. 33:2[?], 3; Ps. 89:6, 8), it is not used of God in any of the poems so far considered. It appears in our corpus only in Ps. 78:41, where we have *qᵉdōš yiśrā'ēl//'ēl*, i.e. El, the Holy One of Israel. The expression becomes dominant in Jerusalem usage of the eighth century and is very frequent in First Isaiah. It is also common in the later prophets, especially Second Isaiah.

The term *ṣūr*, "mountain," also makes its appearance as an epithet of God for the first time (vs. 2). This is one of the more common titles in Phase III poems, and is distinctive of songs associated with the monarchy: cf. II Sam. 23:3; II Sam. 22:2, 32, 47, (47)=Ps. 18:2, 32, 47; Ps. 78:35; it also occurs frequently in Deuteronomy 32. Apart from these occurrences, the term as a divine epithet (either *ṣūr, ṣūrī,* or the like) occurs only in a number of psalms and prophetic materials: Isa. 17:10, 30:29; Hab. 1:12. There are no occurrences in the Pentateuch or Historical Books (apart from the poems in our group), showing there was no tradition associating the epithet with patriarchal religion. This is supported by the fact that although the equivalent term occurs in the Ugaritic texts it is not used as a divine title. There remains the curious, apparently archaic name *ṣūrīšadday,* "Zurishaddai" ("Shadday is my Mountain"; Num. 1:6, etc.) which was borne by the father of the tribal leader of Simeon at the time of the census. In our poetry, however, the two terms *šadday* and *ṣūr* do not occur in the same composition. Just as *šadday* is typical of Phase II poems, so *ṣūr* is characteristic of Phase III.[40] Since the terms are nearly equivalent in meaning, it would appear that Canaanite (=Hebrew) *ṣūr* displaced older Amorite *šadday* during the period of the monarchy.

In vs. 3 Yahweh is identified as *'ēl dē'ōt*, "the God of knowledge." The formation reminds us of similar constructions, e.g. *'ēl hakkābōd*, "the God of glory" (Ps. 29:3);[50] *'ēl 'ᵉmūnāh*, "the God of faithfulness" (Deut. 32:4); the patriarchal formula *'ēl ro'ī*, "the God of my vision"(?) or "El who sees me" (Gen. 16:13); *'ēl qannā'*, "the God of zeal (or passion)"

(Exod. 34:14); *'ēl raḥūm wᵉḥannūn,* "the God of love and grace" (Exod. 34:6).

In vss. 6–8 a long series of participles is associated with the name Yahweh: *mmyt, mḥyh, mwryd, mwryš, m'šyr, mšpyl, mqym.* A similar arrangement occurs in the Royal Psalm, II Sam. 22:2–3=Ps. 18:3 though the specific terms are different. The multiplication of qualifying adjectives has a liturgical character and may well reflect temple practice.

The term *'lw* (vs. 10), Al or Eli, "the Exalted One," has been noted.

A monarchic date for the poem is established by vs. 10 (i.e. *malkō // mᵉšīḥō*=his anointed king), assuming that it is an original part of the poem. That a distinct series of divine epithets and adjectives is associated with poems of the monarchy seems evident.

Distribution

1. Yahweh: vss. 1, [1], 2, 3, 6, 7, 8, 10, 10
   a. Without parallel (or with Yahweh as parallel): vss. 1ab, 8, 10a
   b. With other divine names
      1) *'ᵉlōhay:* vs. 1
      2) *'ᵉlōhēnū:* vs. 2
      3) *'ēl (dē'ōt):* vs. 3
      4) *'al:* cf. *'lw*
      5) *qādōš:* vs. 2
      6) *ṣūr:* vs. 2
   c. With other terms
      1) *mēmīt:* vs. 6
      2) *mᵉḥayyeh:* vs. 6
      3) *mōrīd:* vs. 6
      4) *mōrīš:* vs. 7
      5) *ma'ᵃšīr:* vs. 7
      6) *mašpīl:* vs. 7
      7) *mᵉrōmēm:* vs. 7
      8) *mēqīm:* vs. 8
2. El: vs. 2 (cf. Yahweh, 1.b.3)
3. Al: vs. 10
   a. With parallel divine names
      1) Yahweh: vs. 10
4. Qadosh: vs. 2 (cf. 1.b.5)
5. Ṣur: vs. 2 (cf. 1.b.6)

8. DAVID'S LAMENT OVER SAUL AND JONATHAN: II SAM. 1:19–27[51]

Unfortunately for our purposes, no divine names or epithets appear in this poem. This is especially regrettable, since the date of the poem can be fixed with reasonable certainty at about 1000 B.C.

9. THE LAST WORDS OF DAVID: II SAM. 23:1–7[52]

Unlike the preceding item, this short poem is practically a compendium of current divine names and epithets: the direct association with David ensures a tenth-century date.

In the opening line of vs. 1 we find the divine title *'l*, "the Exalted One": i.e. "oracle of the man, raised up by the Exalted One."[53] This term has been discussed in connection with Gen. 49:26; Deut. 33:12; and I Sam. 2:10.

In the second line of the same verse, we find the terms *'lhy y'qb // zmrwt yśr'l*, "the God of Jacob // the Defense of Israel." The formal pattern is very much like that of Deut. 33:27 *'lhy qdm // zr't 'wlm*, "the ancient God // the arms of the Eternal." For the expression *zmrwt*, "defense," see the comments on *zmrt* in Exod. 15:2.

In vs. 2 Yahweh appears for the only time in the poem.

In vs. 3 MT has *'lhy yśr'l*, "the God of Israel," but it is likely that the original reading was *'lhy y'qb*, "the God of Jacob," since we have "Israel" in the parallel expression, *swr yśr'l*, "the Mountain of Israel," and one would expect the same pairing of Jacob and Israel here as in vs. 1. It has already been observed that the use of *swr* as a divine epithet is characteristic of Phase III poems.

The word *'elōhīm*, "God," in the absolute form appears for the first time in our poetry in vs. 3. It occurs in the expression *yir'at 'elōhīm*, "the fear of God," which is quite rare; cf. Gen. 20:11 and Neh. 5:15. The phrase, which conveys the basic idea of "piety" or "reverence," describes the attitude and behavior of a *saddīq*, "righteous one" (which is the parallel or complementary term in our passage). The common expression is *yir'at Yahweh* which occurs frequently in the wisdom literature and later poetry (note Isa. 11:2–3, where it is used of the ideal king of the house of David). The word *'elōhīm* occurs in Judg. 5:8, but there it must be a numerical plural and refer to "new gods."[54] A similar usage occurs in Deut. 32:17 (where *'lhym* is parallel to *hdšym*); in Deut. 32:39 *'lhym* is also probably a numerical plural, and in any case refers to a god or gods other than Yahweh.[55] It is interesting to note that the construct form *'lhy* and the form with suffixes invariably refers to Yahweh in the early poems, cf. Exod. 15:2; Judg. 5:3, 5; Num. 23:21; Deut. 33:27; I Sam. 2:(1), 2; etc. while the absolute form *'lhym* is not used at all of God, but only as a numerical plural referring to other gods.

The divine name *'ēl*, "El, God," occurs in vs. 5, and parallel to it is the term *'ōlām*. I take this to be the divine epithet, "the Eternal One" forming part of the traditional combination *'ēl 'ōlām* (cf. Gen. 21:33), "El the Eternal."[56] The word *'ōlām* is usually construed with *berīt* and rendered "an eternal covenant." Since the expression occurs frequently in the Bible, it cannot be ruled out. Nevertheless it should be noted that the other occurrences of the expression in the Bible are all late. It appears only in the prose of the Pentateuch and is used only by P: Gen. 9:16; 17:7, 13, 19; Exod. 31:16; Lev. 24:8; Num. 18:19. For the rest it is found only in exilic and post-exilic prophecy: Isa. 24:5, 55:3, 61:8; Jer. 32:40, 50:5; Ezek. 16:60, 37:26; and a late Psalm (105:10=I Chron. 16:17). Under the circumstances it would be unusual, though not impossible to find it in an early Davidic poem, especially since the covenant with David is not elsewhere called a *bᵉrīt ʿōlām,* "everlasting covenant": cf. Pss. 89:4, 29, 35, 40; 132:12; Jer. 33:21. What is to be everlasting is the promised kingship. The idea but not the wording occurs in Ps. 89:29—"For ever will I maintain my kindness toward him / and my covenant will stand firm for him." Isa. 55:3 echoes a similar sentiment though it speaks of a future rather than a historic covenant: "I will make with you an everlasting covenant (*bᵉrīt ʿōlām*), my steadfast sure love for David." Hence, I would render II Sam. 23:5 as follows:

> Utterly secure is my dynasty with El
> For the Eternal has executed a covenant in my behalf.

In estimating the date of this poem consideration should be given to the opening formula: *nᵉʾum dāwīd ben-yišay / ūnᵉʾum haggeber . . . ,* "The oracle of David ben-Jesse / yea the oracle of that man . . ." The formula is the same as that of the Oracles of Balaam (Num. 24:3–4, 15–16):

nᵉʾum bilʿam bᵉnō-bᵉʿōr	The oracle of Balaam the son of Beor
ūnᵉʾum haggeber . . .	yea the oracle of that man . . .

Except for Prov. 30:1 which has an abbreviated form of this introduction (*nᵉʾum haggeber*) in an obscure context and Ps. 36:2, these are the only instances in which *nᵉʾum* is used of a human speaker. Otherwise it is always used of God.

The opening formula in the Oracles of Balaam and David's Testament belongs to a formal style which seems to have flourished in the eleventh–tenth centuries. Then it dropped out of use in relation to human beings, surviving only in combination with God in liturgical formulae. It is restricted almost entirely to prophetic utterances (cf. the exceptional *nᵉʾum Yahweh,* Ps. 110:1; the psalm may be of early date).

Distribution

1. Al: vs. 1
2. *ᵉlōhē* ——: vss. 1, 3
   a. In parallel with other divine names and epithets
      1) *zᵉmīrōt:* vs. 1.
      2) *ṣūr:* vs. 3
3. Yahweh: vs. 2
4. Elohim: vs. 3

5. El: vs. 5
   a. In parallel with other divine names
      1) '*ōlām:* vs. 5
6. Ṣur: vs. 3 (cf. 2.a.2)
7. Olam: vs. 5 (cf. 5.a.1)

10. A ROYAL SONG OF THANKSGIVING: II SAMUEL 22=PSALM 18[57]

This poem, which is preserved both in the books of Samuel and of Psalms was considered by more than one editor to be characteristically Davidic. Among other features, it shares with II Samuel 23 and I Samuel 2 a similar selection of divine names and epithets.

The name Yahweh dominates the poem, occurring sixteen times in the Samuel version (S) and in the Psalms edition (P).

In the opening verses (2–3), after the initial occurrence of Yahweh, there is a series of qualifying nouns, including participles, all referring to the deity and having the first person pronominal suffix:

S		P
1. *sal'ī*	My Rock	*sal'ī*
2. *mᵉṣūdātī*	My Stronghold	*mᵉṣūdātī*
3. *mᵉpalṭī*	My Deliverer	*mᵉpalṭī*
4. '*ᵉlōhay* [MT '*ᵉlōhē*]	My God	'*ēlī*
5. *ṣūrī*	My Mountain	*ṣūrī*
6. *maginnī*	My Suzerain	*maginnī*
7. *qeren yiš'ī*	The Horn of My Salvation	*qeren yiš'ī*
8. *miśgabbī*	My Redoubt	*miśgabbī*
9. *mᵉnūsī*	My Refuge	————
10. *mōšī'ī*	My Savior	————

The series may be compared with the list of participles detailing Yahweh's powers and activities already noted in I Samuel 2. This group, however, has a devotional and personal quality lacking in the other.

From this list, the terms that are of particular interest to us are '*ᵉlōhay* (S)='*ēlī* (P), and *ṣūrī,* which occur elsewhere in this poem, and others of our collection:

The construct form '*ᵉlōhē* occurs in combination with *yiš'ī* in vs. 47 (P), "the God of my salvation."[58] The parallel terms are Yahweh and *ṣūrī.* The form with first person singular suffix, '*ᵉlōhay,* occurs in vss. 7, 22, and 30. In vss. 7 and 22 it is balanced by Yahweh, while there is no correlative in vs. 30. In vs. 32, we have the form with the first person plural suffix '*ᵉlōhēnū.* Parallel terms are '*ēl* (S)='*ᵉlōah* (P), Yahweh, and *ṣūr.* We note the first appearance of '*ᵉlōah* in our group of poems. It occurs twice in Deut. 32 (vss. 15, 17) but otherwise is not present. It is very common in Job (forty-two times) and occurs in other archaizing poetry of the later period: e.g. Hab. 3:3; cf. Pss. 50:22, 114:7, 139:19; Prov. 30:5; Isa. 44:8. The distribution is similar to that of *šadday,* already noted, though 'ᵉlōah is not genuinely archaic in the same sense as šadday which has roots in patriarchal times. The term 'ᵉlōah does not seem to have been used earlier than the monarchy and then only for a brief period, presumably in the tenth–ninth centuries. After a gap, it was revived in the nostalgic era, previously mentioned.

The name El (in addition to the suffixed form in Ps. 18:3) occurs in vss. 31, 32 (S), 33, and 48. In vs. 31 hā'ēl, "the God, El himself," is parallel to Yahweh and māgēn, "Shield," or "Suzerain, Benefactor."[59]

The pronoun hū', "He," is used as a designation for God in conjunction with māgēn. A random distribution of this term among the poems in our list might have been expected, but in fact it is restricted entirely to Phase III, and particularly to the last four poems in this group. Besides the occurrence here, it appears in Deut. 32:4, 6, 6, 39; Ps. 78:38; Ps. 68:36. In view of the unusual and consistent pattern displayed, we may regard its use as a feature of Phase III poetry. In vs. 33, hā'ēl has mā'uzzī, "my Refuge," as a complement in S, but in P there is a participial expression ham'azzᵉrēnī, "the One who girds me."

The epithet ṣwr, "Mountain," occurs in vss. 2, 32, 47 (S has it twice). These instances have all been noted previously.

The epithet 'elyōn occurs in vs. 14 in parallel with Yahweh. The verse itself echoes I Sam. 2:10 in part, where we have the divine name Al which is related to Elyon. Its occurrence in the Oracles of Balaam has been noted.

The term nērī, "my Lamp," occurs in vs. 29, in parallel with Yahweh and 'ᵉlohay (P).

More participles turn up in vss. 34–35: mᵉšawweh, "the One who sets," and mᵉlammēd, "the One who teaches." In vs. 49, we have mōṣī'ī, "the One who brings me out" (S), and mᵉpalṭī, "the One who delivers me" (P).

The closing verse, if part of the original poem, fixes the date of composition in the monarchy and attaches it to David and his posterity. The parallel terms malkō // mᵉšīḥō are the same as in I Sam. 2:10.

Distribution

1. Yahweh: vss. 2, (3P), 4, 7, 14, 16, 19, 21, 22, 25, 29, (29S), 31, 32, 42, 47, 50
   a. Without parallels: vss. 4, 16, 19, 21, 25, 29ab(S), 42, 50
   b. With divine names and epithets:
      1) sal'ī: vs. 2
      2) mᵉṣūdātī: vs. 2
      3) mᵉpalṭī: vs. 2
      4) 'ᵉlōhay: vss. 3(S), 7, 22, 29(P), 30
      5) 'ēlī: vs. 3 (P)
      6) ṣūrī: vss. 3, 47

      7) *maginnī:* vs. 3
      8) *qeren yiš'ī:* vs. 3
      9) *miśgabbī:* vs. 3
     10) *mᵉnūsī:* vs. 3
     11) *mōšī'ī:* vs. 3
     12) *'elyōn:* vs. 14
     13) *nērī:* vs. 29
     14) *hā'ēl:* vs. 31 (cf. El 2.a.1)
     15) *'ᵉlōhēnū:* vs. 32 (cf. El 2.a.2)
     16) *'ᵉlōhē yiš'ī:* vs. 47
   c. With other terms
      1) *mᵉhullāl:* vs. 4
      2) *māgēn:* vs. 31
      3) *magdīl:* vs. 51
      4) *'ōśeh-ḥesed:* vs. 51
  2. El: vss. 31, 32(S), 33, 48
   a. With divine names and epithets
      1) Yahweh: vss. 31, 32
      2) *ṣūr:* vs. 32
      3) *'ᵉlōhēnū:* vs. 32
      4) *mā'uzzī:* vs. 33
   b. With other terms
      1) *māgēn:* vs. 31
      2) *hū':* vs. 31
      3) *hannōtēn nᵉqāmōt:* vs. 48
      4) *mōrīd:* vs. 48
      5) *mōšī'ī:* vs. 49
  3. Ṣur: vss. 3, 32, 37, 47(S)
   a. With other divine names
      1) Yahweh // *'ᵉlōhay:* vss. 2–3 (cf. 1.b.6)
      2) El // Yahweh // *'ᵉlōhēnū:* vs. 32
      3) Yahweh // *'ᵉlōhē yiš'ī:* vs. 47 (cf. 1.b.16)
  4. Elyon: vs. 14 (cf. 1.b.12)
  5. Eloah: vs. 32(P)
   a. In parallel with divine names and epithets: (cf. 2.a.2)
      1) Yahweh: vs. 32
      2) Ṣur: vs. 32
      3) *'ᵉlōhēnū:* vs. 32
  6. *Hū':* vs. 31 (cf. 2.b.2)

11. THE SONG OF MOSES: DEUTERONOMY 32

The pattern of selection and distribution of divine names and epithets in Deuteronomy 32 is very similar to that of the poems just considered and of Psalm 78. We may have in these data an additional and possibly helpful clue to the dating of this poem, which has proved a difficult problem to scholars, who have tested an assortment of dates from Moses to the exile and beyond.[60]

The principal divine name is Yahweh which occurs eight times, as was also the case with Deuteronomy 33 and I Samuel 2 (on a corrected basis).

In vs. 3, we have *'elōhēnū,* "our God," which is parallel to Yahweh. In vs. 37 the archaic form *'elōhēmō,* "their God," occurs, in parallel with *ṣūr,* "Mountain."

The term *ṣūr* occurs seven times; in six instances the reference is to the God of Israel: vss. 4, 15, 18, 30, 31, 37. In vs. 4, the word *haṣṣūr,* "the Mountain," has a parallel in *'ēl 'emūnāh,* "the God of truth." In addition the terms *ṣaddīq,* "Righteous One," and *yāšār,* "Upright One," are used of God. In vs. 15, *ṣūr* is paralleled by *'elōah,* "God," which has already been discussed in connection with its appearance in Ps. 18:32. In vs. 18, *ṣūr* is balanced by *'ēl,* "El, God," while in vs. 30, the matching term is Yahweh. In vs. 31, *ṣūr* occurs twice in the sequence *kī lō' keṣūrēnū ṣūrām,* "For their mountain is not like our Mountain." A comparison of deities is involved, though it is interesting that the same epithet is used of both the true and a false god. Verse 37 combines *ṣūr* with *'elōhēmō,* "their God," as already mentioned.

The divine name or qualifying designation *'ēl* is also common in this poem, occurring a total of five times (vss. 4, 8, 12, 18, 21), including a highly probable reading in vs. 8 on the basis of the LXX and a Qumran document of Deuteronomy 32, i.e. *bny 'l* (or *'lhym*) for *bny yśr'l.*[61]

In vs. 12, *'ēl* is modified by *nēkār,* "strange, foreign," in reference to another god as a possible companion of Yahweh: "Yahweh alone guided him / and there was no strange god with him." In vs. 21, there is a different sort of negative formulation: *lō'-'ēl,* "a no-god," i.e. a false deity. The line reads: "They aroused my resentment with a no-god / they provided me with their vanities (i.e. idols)." It will be seen that the term *'ēl* in this poem is not restricted to the divine appellation "El" (vs. 18, already noted) but is used in a more generic sense as well: e.g. *'ēl 'emūnāh* (vs. 4), "God of truth" or "the faithful God"; *'ēl nēkār,* "a strange god"; *lō'-'ēl,* "a no-god."

In vs. 8, the patriarchal epithet *'elyōn* makes its appearance; its occurrence in Numbers 23–24 and II Samuel 22=Psalm 18 has already been noted. The passage here has an archaic ring, reflecting mythologic traditions about the origins of the nations: a poetic version to be compared and contrasted with the story of the tower of Babel (Gen. 11:1–9). There is an apparent equation of Elyon with El, if we accept the reading of LXX and 4Q Deuteronomy: cf. Gen. 14:18, 20, 21, where the combination occurs. The identification of this God with Yahweh is certainly intended by the poet (cf. vss. 12 and esp. 39), though vs. 9 has been interpreted as reflecting a subordinate status for Yahweh in the pantheon headed by Elyon.

The term *'elōah,* "God," occurs twice, once in parallel with *ṣūr* (see

above), once in vs. 17 where it stands for the true God in contrast with
šēdīm, "demons, evil spirits," and *'ᵉlōhīm,* "gods."

In vs. 39, *'ᵉlōhīm,* "gods," (though possibly "god") is comparable to *'ēl
nēkār* in vs. 12:

> And there was no strange god with him (12)
> And beside me there are no gods (39).

Additional terms for "God" (*'l* or *'lhym*) and "gods" (*'lhym*) probably
occurred in an earlier form of vs. 43 which is truncated in MT (cf. LXX
and 4Q Deuteronomy).[62] If *'lhym,* "God," is the correct reading here (and
possibly vs. 8), then these instances would parallel the usage noted in
II Sam. 23:3.

On the basis of the selection and distribution of divine names and epithets in this poem, I would assign it to the latter part of Phase III, and
date it in the latter part of the tenth century at the earliest, or in the ninth
century. At the same time, it should be noted that there is no explicit reference to the monarchy or historical events later than the settlement. There
are other affinities with earlier poems, especially the Blessing of Moses and
the Oracles of Balaam. Apparently the poet had in mind a setting in the
pre-monarchic period and composed his piece accordingly. A later editor
correctly perceived this intention and quite naturally attributed the utterance to the principal figure of early Israel, Moses himself.

Distribution

1. Yahweh: vss. 3, 6, 9, 12, 19, 27, 30, 36
   a. Without parallels: vss. 9, 19, 27, 36
   b. In parallel with divine names and epithets
      1) *'ᵉlōhēnū:* vs. 3
      2) *hū'* vss. 6ab
      3) *'ābīkā:* vs. 6
      4) *'ēl nēkār:* vs. 12
      5) *ṣūrām:* vs. 31 (cf. *ṣūr,* 2.a.7)
2. Ṣur: vss. 4, 15, 18, 30, 31, 37
   a. In parallel with other divine names
      1) *'ēl 'ᵉmūnāh:* vs. 4
      2) *ṣaddīq:* vs. 4
      3) *yāšār:* vs. 4
      4) *hū':* vs. 4
      5) *'ᵉlōah:* vs. 15 (cf. 6.a.1)
      6) *'ēl:* vs. 18
      7) Yahweh: vs. 30
      8) *'ᵉlōhēmō:* vs. 37
   b. In parallel with other terms

　　　1) *ṣūrām:* vs. 31 (*kᵉṣūrēnū*): I assume that Israel is speaking
　　　　in this verse. In any case one term refers to the God of Israel
　　　　and the other *ṣūr* refers to another god.
　　3. El: vss. 4, (8), 18
　　　a. Without parallel: vs. 8 (but linked with Elyon)
　　　b. In parallel with divine names
　　　　1) *haṣṣūr:* vs. 4 (cf. 2.a.1)
　　　　2) *ṣaddīq // yāšār:* vs. 4
　　　　3) *hū':* vs. 4
　　　　4) *ṣūr:* vs. 18 (cf. 2.a.6)
　　4. *Hū':* vss. 4, 6, 6, 39
　　　a. In parallel construction
　　　　1) *haṣṣūr:* vs. 4 (cf. 2.a.1)
　　　　2) *'ēl 'ᵉmūnāh:* vs. 4 (3.b.3)
　　　　3) *ṣaddīq // yāšār:* vs. 4
　　　　4) Yahweh: vs. 6 (cf. 1.b.2)
　　　　5) *'ābīkā:* vs. 6
　　5. *Elyon:* vs. 8
　　6. *Eloah:* vss. 15, 17
　　　a. Without parallel: vs. 17
　　　b. In parallel construction
　　　　1) *ṣūr:* vs. 15

12. PSALM 78

Since this Psalm is located in the Elohistic Psalter, the dominant divine
name is Elohim (eight times) instead of Yahweh (twice). Almost as frequent as Elohim is El which occurs seven times. The name Yahweh appears in vss. 4 and 21; in both verses it stands by itself, without a parallel
term.

In the Elohistic Psalter, the name Elohim is used where in the same or similar lines in a Yahwistic compendium the name Yahweh would appear.[63]
As we have seen, the emergence of Elohim as a distinctive name for God is
rather late in our poetry (II Samuel 23 and perhaps Deuteronomy 32);
its use in the Elohistic Psalter is rather unusual and reflects the special circumstances under which that part of the Psalter was composed or com-
piled. It occurs in vss. 7, 10, 19, 22, 31, 35, 56, 59. Thus in vs. 7, Elohim
is set in parallel with El as elsewhere in our poetry it is Yahweh and El that
are conjoined. The same pairing of Elohim and El occurs in vss. 19 and 35.
In the latter verse, two additional terms occur, forming double pairs:

　　　　'elōhīm ṣūrām　　　God (was) their Mountain
　　　　'ēl-'elyōn gō'ᵃlām　　El-Elyon (was) their Redeemer

In vs. 56, Elohim is paired with Elyon: "And they tested and rebelled
against God Most High." In vs. 59, Elohim is paralleled by *m'd,* "the

Mighty One." The passage may be rendered: God heard and was angered /
and the Mighty One rejected Israel."[64] In the other instances, Elohim has no
explicit parallel (vss. 10, 22, 31).

El occurs in vss. 7, 8, 18, 19, 34, 35, 41. Several of these have already
been noted (vss. 7, 19, 35). El in vs. 18 balances Elyon in vs. 17. In vs. 41,
El is identified as $q^e d\bar{o}\check{s}$ $yi\acute{s}r\bar{a}'\bar{e}l$, "the Holy One of Israel." The occurrence
of $q\bar{a}d\bar{o}\check{s}$ in I Sam. 2:2 has already been noted, as well as its distribution
in the Bible. The combination $q^e d\bar{o}\check{s}$ $yi\acute{s}r\bar{a}'\bar{e}l$ is the distinctive title used by
I and II Isaiah; but it also occurs in Ps. 89:19 which is a royal psalm of ap-
proximately the same date as this poem.[65] In vss. 8 and 34, El stands
alone.

The epithet Elyon occurs three times (vss. 17, 35, and 56), all of which
have been noted previously: (1) parallel to El in vs. 18; (2) combined
with El and parallel to Elohim (vs. 35); $\dot{s}\bar{u}r\bar{a}m$, "their Mountain," also occurs in this verse, parallel to $g\bar{o}'^a l\bar{a}m$, "their Redeemer"; (3) linked with
Elohim (vs. 56).

The term Adonay occurs once, in vs. 65. The only other instance in the
poetry studied so far is the disputed occurrence in Exod. 15:17 (MT).
There are several more examples in Psalm 68. It is clear in any case that
Adonay was not in general use before the tenth century which is the earliest possible date for this Psalm and Psalm 68 in their present form.

The general selection and distribution of divine names and epithets in
Psalm 78 correlate well with the other poems in this group, and tend to
support a date in the early monarchy. The specific references to Judah,
Zion, and David confirm the supposition. The shift in usage away from
Yahweh to Elohim seems to reflect the special circumstances of the editorial
format of the Elohistic Psalter and is not necessarily a reflection of the original pattern of the poem. The same is true of the other poems from this section of the Psalter which are yet to be examined.

Distribution

1. Elohim: vss. 7, 10, 19, 22, 31, 35, 56, 59
   a. Without parallel: vss. 10, 22, 31
   b. In parallel construction
      1) '$\bar{e}l$: vss. 7, 19, 35
      2) $\dot{s}\bar{u}r\bar{a}m$: vs. 35
      3) '$ely\bar{o}n$: vss. 35, 56
      4) $g\bar{o}'^a l\bar{a}m$: vs. 35
      5) $m'd$: vs. 59
2. El: vss. 7, 8, 18, 19, 34, 35, 41
   a. Without parallel: vss. 8, 34
   b. In parallel construction
      1) '$^e l\bar{o}h\bar{\imath}m$: vss. 7, 19, 35 (cf. 1.b.1)
      2) '$ely\bar{o}n$: vss. 17 (cf. 3.a.1), 35

    3) *ṣūrām // gō'ᵃlām:* vs. 35
    4) *qᵉdōš yiśrā'ēl:* vs. 41
  3. Elyon: vss. 17, 35, 56
    a. In parallel construction
      1) El: vss. 17, 35 (cf. 2.b.2)
      2) Elohim: vss. 35, 56 (cf. 1.b.3)
      3) *ṣūrām // gō'ᵃlām:* vs. 35
  4. Yahweh: vss. 4, 21
  5. Adonay: vs. 65
  6. *Hū':* vs. 38
    a. In parallel construction
      1) *raḥūm:* vs. 38

13. PSALM 72

This poem begins with the word *'ᵉlōhīm,* "God," a usage which is to be expected in this section of the Psalter. There are no other divine names and epithets, however, until the concluding lines of the poem, vss. 18–19. These do not appear to have been part of the original poem, but constitute a liturgical conclusion to this second book of the Psalter. In any case the divine names and titles are as follows: (1) Yahweh; (2) *'ᵉlōhīm;* (3) *'ᵉlōhē yiśrā'ēl.* The phrase "Yahweh, the God of Israel" goes back ultimately to the Song of Deborah. Apparently *'ᵉlōhīm* was inserted in keeping with the character of the Elohistic Psalter; the combination Yahweh Elohim is reminiscent of the curious pattern in the J source at the beginning of Genesis (2:4 ff.).

The evidence is insufficient to make a judgment, but there is nothing in the poem, and certainly in the divine nomenclature to preclude a tenth-century date.

14. PSALM 68[66]

Albright described this poem as a catalogue of *Incipits* or first lines of early Israelite songs dating from the period between the thirteenth and tenth centuries. On the basis of our analysis and grouping of divine titles, Psalm 68 exhibits similar heterogeneous characteristics, with a varied collection of such terms belonging to all three phases of early Israelite poetry. In other words, the diversity of divine names conforms to the hypothetical model posited by Albright. Furthermore the distribution, with few exceptions would point to a collection of songs that was predominantly pre-monarchic in date (i.e. before Phase III).

For reasons already adduced, the principal name of God used in this Psalm is Elohim (twenty-four times); in many if not most cases, it can be shown that the more original form of the line or couplet had the name Yahweh. Nevertheless, Yahweh does appear three times; and El is present in five places. The construct form *'ᵉlōhē* occurs twice and *zh syny,* "the One of Sinai," once; *šadday* also appears once. The relatively late term *'dny,* "my Lord," appears six times (in some cases apparently as a substitute for a more original Yahweh). The short form Yah occurs twice. In such a catholic collection, certain omissions are surprising: *'elyōn,* "Most High," *ṣūr,* "Mountain," and *'elōah,* "God," do not occur. The absence of the latter two suggests that few of the opening lines derive from the period of the monarchy, though the compilation can hardly antedate the tenth century in view of vss. 30 ff. which mention Jerusalem and presuppose the existence of the temple. A more detailed study of the divine names and epithets follows:

In vs. 2 there is a clear echo of the Song of the Ark (Num. 10:35), but Elohim has been substituted for the original Yahweh. There is no parallel term, as is also true in vss. 3 and 4.

In vs. 5, there is a parallel expression for Elohim: *lārōkēb bā'ᵃrābōt,* "O Rider of the Clouds," which is derived from a Canaanite expression used of Baal.[67] The term Yah also occurs in this verse, but the exact meaning of the passage is unclear. In vs. 6 Elohim is designated *'ᵃbī yᵉtōmīm,* "Father of the fatherless," and *dayyan 'almānōt,* "the Legal Guardian of the widows." In vs. 7, Elohim serves as subject of two participles: *mōšīb,* "Who settles singles in households," and *mōṣī',* "Who brings forth prisoners."

In vss. 8–9, there is an adaptation of a well-known passage in the Song of Deborah (Judg. 5:4–5), in which Elohim has been substituted for the more original Yahweh (three times). In addition we have the familiar *zh syny,* "the One of Sinai," and *'lhy yśr'l,* "the God of Israel."

In vs. 10, Elohim stands by itself, without a parallel term. The same is true of vs. 11. In vs. 12 Adonay, "my Lord," occurs, in place of the expected Elohim. In vs. 15, we have the only occurrence of Shadday in the poem.

In vss. 16–17, Elohim occurs twice; the second is balanced by Yahweh. In vs. 18, Elohim occurs in the first colon, and Adonay in the second. Since the second colon is evidently a slightly corrupted version of the first colon of Deut. 33:2, *yhwh msyny b',* "Yahweh came from Sinai," it is probable that Adonay has been substituted for a more original Yahweh here. I render the colon as follows:

'dny b' msyny	My Lord came from Sinai among the
bqdš	holy ones

The term *bqdš* is to be interpreted as a collective: holy ones. The same usage occurs in vs. 25 of this psalm, and in Exod. 15:11; cf. also *rbbt qdš,* "myriads of holy ones" (Deut. 33:2).[68]

In vs. 19 we have the unusual combination *yh 'lhym.* The initial term (*yh*) is probably the exclamation, "O!" rather than the divine name Yah.[69]

In vss. 20–21, there is a chiastic arrangement featuring Adonay and El, as follows:

$$\text{'}^a d\bar{o}nay /\!/ h\bar{a}\text{'}\bar{e}l \text{ (20)}$$
$$h\bar{a}\text{'}\bar{e}l /\!/ \text{'}^a d\bar{o}nay \text{ (21)}$$

In vs. 21, enclosed within the outer pair is another combination: El and Yahweh.

In vs. 22, we have Elohim alone; in vs. 23, the divine name is Adonay. In vs. 25, Elohim is matched by *'ēlī,* "my God," which in turn is in apposition with *malkī,* "my King." The passage as a whole may be rendered:

> Behold the marches of God
> The marches of my God,
> My King among the holy ones.[70]

In vs. 27, Elohim is balanced by Yahweh. In vs. 29, *'ᵉlōhēkā,* "your God," is in parallel construction with Elohim. In vs. 30, the divine appellative *'l,* "Exalted One," occurs. I follow Dahood generally in analyzing and rendering: "Your temple, Exalted One, is in Jerusalem."[71] In vs. 32, Elohim has no parallel. In vs. 33, Elohim is balanced by Adonay. In vs. 34, the epithet, *rōkēb,* occurs in the expression: *lārōkēb bišmē šᵉmē-qedem,* "O Rider of the most ancient skies." Cf. vs. 5.

In vs. 35, Elohim occurs in parallel with *'l yśr'l,* "the Exalted One of Israel." In vs. 36, Elohim occurs with the participle *nwr',* "the Terrible One"; it is balanced by the expression *'ēl yiśrā'ēl,* "the God of Israel," which reminds us of the patriarchal *'ēl 'ᵉlōhē yiśrā'ēl,* "El, the God of Israel" (Gen. 33:20) as well as the common expression *'lhy yśr'l,* "the God of Israel." The Psalm ends with Elohim (*bārūk 'ᵉlōhīm,* "blessed be God").

Distribution
1. Elohim: vss. 2, 3, 4, 5, 6, 7, 8, 9, 9, 10, 11, 16, 17, 18, 19, 22, 25, 27, 29, 32, 33, 35, 36, 36
    a. Without parallel: vss. 2, 3, 4, 8, 10, 11, 22, 32, 35, 36
    b. In parallel with other divine names
        1) Yah: vs. 5, cf. vs. 19 (?)
        2) Yahweh: vss. 17, 27
        3) Adonay: vss. 18, 33
        4) El: vss. 25 (*'ēlī*), 36 (*'ēl yiśrā'ēl*)
        5) Elohim: vs. 9 (*'ᵉlōhē yiśrā' ēl*); cf. vs. 29 (*'ᵉlōhēkā*)
        6) Al: vs. 35 (*'l yśr'l*)
    c. In parallel with various epithets and phrases
        1) *rōkēb:* vs. 5 (*lārōkēb bā'ᵃrābōt,* "O Rider of the clouds"; cf. vs. 34)
        2) *'ᵃbī yᵉtōmīm wᵉdayyan 'almānōt:* vs. 6
        3) *mōšīb yᵉḥīdīm* and *mōṣī' 'ᵃsīrīm:* vs. 7
        4) *zeh sīnay:* vs. 9
        5) *malkī:* vs. 25
        6) *nōrā':* vs. 36
        7) *bārūk:* vs. 36

2. Adonay: vss. 12, 18, 20, 21, 23, 33
   a. Without parallel: vss. 12, 23
   b. In parallel with other divine names
      1) El: vs. 20 (*hā'ēl*); cf. vs. 21
      2) Elohim: cf. vss. 18, 33
3. El: vss. 20, 21, 21, 25, 36
   a. Without parallel
   b. In parallel with other divine names
      1) Adonay: vs. 21, cf. vs. 20
      2) Yahweh: vs. 21
      3) Elohim: cf. vss. 25, 36
4. Yahweh: vss. 17, 21, 27
   a. Without parallel
   b. In parallel with other divine names
      1) Elohim: cf. vss. 17, 27
      2) El: cf. vs. 21
5. Al: vss. 30, 35
   a. Without parallel: vs. 30
   b. In parallel with Elohim: vs. 35
6. Shadday: vs. 15 (no parallel)
7. Yah: vss. 5, 19 (both instances are uncertain)

SUMMARY: THE CHRONOLOGY OF THE POEMS

From the data on divine names and epithets and certain other key terms assembled and analyzed in the foregoing presentation it is possible to present certain conclusions about the relative and absolute chronology of the poems under consideration.

First of all, the selection and distribution of divine names do not appear to be haphazard but follow a traceable evolutionary pattern. We believe that we can distinguish three major phases during the period from the twelfth through the tenth–ninth centuries B.C., and arrange the poems in a general chronological sequence according to specific criteria. We restrict ourselves to divine nomenclature and a few other terms, but recognize that there are a number of other factors to be considered in making a determination of date, whether relative or absolute or both. Such factors include content and style in the broad sense as well as numerous details of different kinds. But our purpose here is to present the case for the particular criterion described and to show its relevance for arranging the poems chronologically.

Secondly, we have assumed generally the integrity and accuracy of the received Hebrew text (MT), i.e. that the poems are unified compositions and that the text has been transmitted faithfully, in particular with respect to the divine names and epithets. With certain exceptions, the data support the presupposition: there has been very little tampering or alteration. With respect to integrity, the danger zones are at the beginning and ending of the poems, where introductory or concluding matter could have been and occasionally may have been added (Exod. 15:2 is the single most striking example though there are others). With respect to accuracy, there are two principal difficulties both having to do with the substitution of one appellation for another though each occurred or developed under different circumstances and presumably at a different time:

1. The substitution of Adonay for Yahweh, which ultimately became universal in reading the Scriptures and examples of which crept into the text as a result. The title Adonay must also have had an independent history so it is difficult to determine when it is an original reading and when it is a secondary substitution for Yahweh. Again with a rare exception or two, the evidence from our poems is that Adonay was not in use in Israelite poetry until Phase III.

2. The substitution of Elohim for an original Yahweh. This practice, which is evident in the so-called Elohistic Psalter, presumably reflects the same ambience and literary usage that we find in the E-source of the Pentateuch, and may date back to the tenth–ninth centuries. While the term *'elōhīm* was certainly known and in use from earliest times, its specific employment as a name for God (as against the numerical plural "gods") is not attested until Phase III in our collection of poetry. Even then we must distinguish between its natural appearance (e.g. II Sam. 23:3) and its extensive use as a surrogate for a more original Yahweh in Psalms 68 (especially) and 78. In spite of these difficulties, what is surprising is the degree to which the nomenclature remains characteristic and distinctive; the inevitable conclusion is that there has been no wholesale substitution or alteration of names. A good illustration of the very limited extent of such changes may be seen in the comparison of II Samuel 22 with Psalm 18: in vs. 3, S has *'elōhē* while P has *'ēlī* (probably the better reading); in vs. 29, S has Yahweh, while P reads *'elōhay* (again the preferred reading); in vs. 32, S has *'ēl* while P reads *'elōah* (presumably a secondary reading and a sign of later compilation); in vs. 47, S has *ṣūr,* while P omits the word (also correct, since *ṣūr* is intrusive in the passage). Otherwise the distribution of divine names is the same.

Thirdly, the pertinent data have been assembled on a chart, to indicate at a glance the distribution and arrangement of the terms which have been isolated in this study. In setting up the chart the list of terms has been coordinated with the list of poems. The sequence of poems has been derived essentially from Albright with occasional rearrangement as indicated by the occurrence or absence of key epithets. These adjustments reflect the theory on which the investigation is based and in turn affect the conclusions. In other words, a certain degree of circular reasoning is inevitable as well as desirable in formulating the hypothesis. By this process of double approximation, a greater precision is achieved in organizing the material and ordering the poems. The test of the theory is likewise twofold: (1) inner consistency, which may be a matter of scholarly ingenuity, but not less important for that reason; and (2) conformity to external data, that is, data external to the hypothesis or the materials used in arranging the poems: e.g. historical references and allusions, independent scholarly reconstructions and conclusions, etc.

Taking the group of poems as a whole, it is immediately obvious that there are a plethora of names, epithets, and other terms descriptive of the deity, so many, in fact, that it would be very difficult if not impossible to handle them effectively in trying to determine chronological relationships among the poems. A striking illustration would be the long lists of participles and similar expressions used of God in the Song of Hannah (I Samuel 2) and the Royal Song of Thanksgiving (II Samuel 22=Psalm 18). The available information is outlined in Chart A (pp. 103–104).

Once the over-all pattern has been established, then important but incidental details of this kind shed significant light on the nature of Israelite hymnody in the period to which these poems belong. In general, however, terms which occur in only one of the poems in the group are not immediately pertinent to our investigation and these have been excluded from a more concentrated summary of the evidence provided in Chart B (pp. 105–106).

Even this compilation is too cluttered and confusing, though the basic data are present. Further reduction in the number to a select group of diagnostic and determinative expressions is necessary, along with appropriate adjustments in the sequence of the poems, in order to produce a consistent evolutionary and intelligible sequence dating. We have restricted the study to the dozen key terms in categories A and B under divine epithets, and half-a-dozen other terms which bear on the questions of order and chronology. Similarly, we have reduced Albright's list of poems from fourteen to twelve because two of the compositions have insufficient data to allow for adequate analysis and comparison (David's Lament, II Sam. 1:19–27, and Psalm 72). The resultant correlations and adjustments are presented in Chart C (p. 107). The following comments are in order:

The Terms:
    A. Terms for God
        1. Names
           a. Yahweh and Yah

In these poems the name Yahweh is practically ubiquitous, and generally dominant. Since there is every reason to believe that the name was introduced into general use in the course of the thirteenth century B.C., and not before, a clear *terminus a quo* is provided for the poems in which Yahweh appears. No serious scholar has ever suggested otherwise, and the tradition uniformly assigns the poems to Moses, his contemporaries, or successors. The single exception is all the more striking because not only is the poem in Genesis

49 attributed to a pre-Mosaic figure (the patriarch Jacob) but the name Yahweh is conspicuously absent.[72] Since this is not the case even with the Elohistic Psalms 78 and 68 in which Elohim predominates, or the Oracles of Balaam in which El has the leading role (Yahweh occurs two or three times in each of the three poems mentioned), the omission as well as the tradition behind it may be significant, and may point to a non-Yahwistic origin for the Testament of Jacob.

The short form Yah, in contrast with Yahweh, is rare, occurring three times in all (as against ninety plus for Yahweh): once in Exodus 15, twice in Psalm 68. All three examples are suspicious, and its absence from the rest of the poems indicates that the form was not known or not in use for most of the period. One would normally expect an abbreviated form to be introduced after the full form had been in use for some time. Its appearance in Psalm 68, which is placed at the end of the sequence, would be in conformity with this expectation.[73] The problem of its appearance in Exodus 15 has already been mentioned. Essentially the conclusion is that the poem in its present final form including vs. 2 (with Yah and '$\bar{e}l\bar{i}$) and the title Adonay in vs. 17 reflects a monarchic setting and should be dated in the tenth century. However, there is excellent reason to believe that the poem in a more original form consisted of an opening and closing (vss. 1 and 21) and a corpus beginning with vs. 3 and extending through vs. 18. In addition there is convincing textual evidence to support the reading Yahweh instead of Adonay in vs. 17. Under the circumstances, an earlier date, and a position at the head of the line would be appropriate for this song.

b. Elohim

1) The independent form, '^{e}lōhīm, occurs only once in these poems, with the exception of the Elohistic Psalms, 78, 68, where it is the dominant name (eight times in Psalm 78, and twenty-four times in Psalm 68). It appears in II Sam. 23:3, which cannot be earlier than the second quarter of the tenth century. It should be added that the word '^{e}lōhīm with the meaning "gods, divine beings" occurs in some of our poems: Judg. 5:8 and Deut. 32:17, 39, but there is no overlap. In poems where '^{e}lōhīm means "God," the word is not used for "gods," and vice versa.[74] The conclusion is that until the tenth century the term '^{e}lōhīm was used only as a numerical plural, and applied to other gods. From the middle of the tenth century on, its predominant use was as a designation of God, and a surrogate for Yahweh. It would be fair to link this usage in the Elohistic Psalms, especially 78 and 68, with the practice of the Elohist in the Pentateuch: the dates would be reasonably close as well.

2) If the independent or absolute form '^{e}lōhīm is used as a numerical plural in early poetry and only later as a name of God, the same cannot be said of the construct form '^{e}lōhē, which is used of God in several early poems, i.e. from the beginning of our sequence: the form '^{e}lōhē yiśrā'ēl occurs twice in the Song of Deborah, as well as in Psalms 68 and 72, while

its counterpart *'elōhē ya'aqōb* appeared twice (in all probability) in II Samuel 23.[75] Other forms are attested in Deuteronomy 33 (*'elōhē qedem,* vs. 27) and Exodus 15 (*'elōhē 'ābī,* but this is in vs. 2). In any event the construct form is present in poetry from all three phases, stretching from the twelfth through the tenth centuries. It should be added that the suffixed form *'elōhāw* in Num. 23:21 is equivalent, since the antecedent for the pronominal suffix is Jacob/Israel of the same verse. The same argument can be used in connection with other plural pronominal suffixes: *'elōhēnū* and *'elōhēmō* which occur in third phase poems I Samuel 2, II Samuel 22 =Psalm 18, and Deuteronomy 32.

3) Two other suffixed forms remain: *'elōhay* which has a personal, devotional tone, and is more appropriate for the king than the nation. Typically this form occurs in Royal Psalms: I Samuel 2, and II Samuel 22=Psalm 18. The remaining form *'elōhēkā* occurs in Ps. 68:20 in an obscure passage. It is difficult to say just who is meant by the pronoun, or if, finally, it is the pronominal suffix.[76]

c. El (and *hā'ēl*)

1) The independent form *'ēl* (or *hā'ēl*) occurs in most of the poems in the group, showing that the divine name or designation El is second in importance only to Yahweh in these poems. Thus it is present in all three of the poems in Phase II, and five of the six in Phase III.[77] A point of major interest is that the independent form does not appear in any of the poems of Phase I: Exodus 15, Psalm 29, and Judges 5. It is to be noted that the suffixed form *'ēlī* occurs in Exod. 15:2, a verse which has already been discussed. The suffixed form also appears in Pss. 18:3 (but not in II Samuel 22) and 68:25, pointing to a somewhat later date for the introduction of this form than the independent form. Furthermore, the independent form *'ēl* also appears in both Psalms 18 and 68, along with the suffixed form, which is not the case with Exodus 15. We reserve judgment about *'ēlī* in Exodus 15 on two grounds: (1) that it is not the same as *'ēl*=El, and (2) that it may be a secondary intrusion (i.e. as part of vs. 2). The conclusion is that the divine name El was not in use during the earliest phase of Israelite poetry: neither Exodus 15 nor Judges 5, which are overwhelmingly Yahwistic in character and tone, have it. With respect to Psalm 29, the title occurs only in the phrase *'ēl hakkābōd* (vs. 3), which should be analyzed as a construct chain and rendered "the God of glory" or "the glorious God." In defense of this analysis we may point to the parallel expression *melek hakkābōd* in Ps. 24:7–10 which is also to be interpreted as a construct chain. In addition, there is no traditional association of El with the term *kābōd,* as there is with *'elyōn, 'ōlām,* and *šadday;* (3) the imagery and allusions of the poem are associated with the figure of Baal, rather than El; the former is more likely to have been the model for "the God of glory."

2) There are a handful of other instances of the term *'ēl* in a construct

relationship. Considered alphabetically, the first of these, *'ēl 'ābīkā* (Gen. 49:25) is a doubtful case. The normal rendering: "the God of your father" (RSV) is possible but not likely. The translation should reflect the apposition of the two nouns: "El, your Father." The term *'ābīkā* in vs. 26 also has a divine reference in our opinion: "the blessings of your father . . ." The identification is unmistakable in Deut. 32:6, "Is not He your Father . . . ?" The forms *'ēl 'ᵉmūnāh* (Deut. 32:4) and *'ēl dē'ōt* (I Sam. 2:3) are more clearly construct chains, and here the meaning is "God of truth or faithfulness," and "God of knowledge." The same is true of *'ēl hakkābōd*, "the God of glory," in Ps. 29:3, as already observed. The use is generic, and *'ēl* in these passages is equivalent to Elohim, or rather the construct *'ᵉlōhē*. That seems to be the only reasonable way to interpret the peculiar form *'ēl yiśrā'ēl*, "the God of Israel." The original form of this patriarchal designation was *'ēl 'ᵉlōhē yiśrā'ēl*, "El the God of Israel" (Gen. 33:20). Apparently it has been telescoped in Ps. 68:36. Three of the four occurrences of *'ēl* in a construct chain are in Phase III poems, indicating that the widespread use of this formation was relatively late, and raising a question, perhaps, about the date of the final version of Psalm 29.

3) The suffixed form *'ēlī* has already been discussed. Two of the three occurrences of this form are found in Phase III poems: Psalms 18 and 68. The form in Ps. 18:3 is matched by *'ᵉlōhē* (to be corrected to *'ᵉlōhay*) in II Sam. 22:3, showing that the terms were equivalent in meaning. Our conclusion about the suffixed form is that in general its use is a later development than the use of the independent form. It is a feature of Phase III poems, while the appearance of El as an independent form belongs to Phase II.

d. Eloah

1) The term, which is the formal singular of *'ᵉlōhīm*, is not at all common in Biblical Hebrew, and very rare in the group of poems under consideration. It occurs twice in Deuteronomy 32 (vss. 15, 17), and once in Psalm 18 (vs. 32; II Sam. 22:32 has *'ēl*, presumably the more original reading). The inference to be drawn on the basis of admittedly limited data is that the name Eloah was not in use during Phases I and II of the early poetry, and makes its first appearance around the middle of Phase III (late tenth century). Beyond this it appears sporadically in a few Psalms, Habakkuk, and Second Isaiah; but very frequently in Job (forty-two times out of a total of fifty-seven in the Hebrew Bible). The pattern resembles the distribution of Shadday at least superficially: some early use (though Shadday has much better attestation) and a revival in the nostalgic period (seventh–sixth centuries), with a heavy concentration in Job, a strongly archaizing poetic work.

2. Principal titles and epithets

a. Elyon

The title Elyon, which biblical tradition traces back to patriarchal times (cf. Gen. 14:18, 19, 20, 22) is well attested in our list, occurring in four poems: Numbers 23–24, II Samuel 22=Psalm 18, Deuteronomy 32, and Psalm 78. The combination El Elyon, which is found in Genesis, recurs in Ps. 78:35, while the pair is split in Num. 24:16 (cf. 24:4), a common device in Hebrew poetry. To summarize: Elyon as an epithet for God does not appear in poetry of Phase I, but does occur in Phase II along with other archaic (i.e. patriarchal, according to the tradition) names and titles: El, Shadday, and Olam. It continues in use in Phase III, and occasionally thereafter in a number of Psalms (including Psalms 47 and 91, which employ other archaic and archaizing terms).

b. Al (or Eli)

The related term Al (or Eli), "the Most High," has a similar distribution through Phases II and III, appearing in Genesis 49, Deuteronomy 33, I Samuel 2, II Samuel 23, and Psalm 68. Curiously enough the form Al does not occur in the poems in which Elyon appears, and Elyon does not appear in the poems which have Al. They appear to be alternate forms of the same basic attribute of God. That the expressions are equivalent and interchangeable is shown by the parallel passages:

I Sam. 2:10	II Sam. 22:14=Ps. 18:14
'al baššāmayim yar'ēm	*yar'ēm baššāmayin Yahweh*
Yahweh yādīn 'apsē 'āreṣ	*wᵉ'elyōn yittēn qōlō*

The different forms *'al, 'lyw, 'lw* may reflect an original **'aliyu>'alu>'al,* though the variety may be due in part at least to the fact that the later editors and scribes did not recognize the existence of the epithet and invariably read the term as a form of the preposition *'al,* by itself or with suffixes. Our vocalization is hypothetical, though the form is derived from the root *'ly,* which also underlies *'elyōn.*[78]

c. Shadday

The designation Shadday, like Elyon, is traced to patriarchal times in the biblical tradition, specifically by the priestly writer or editor, who states that the name of God par excellence for the patriarchs was El Shadday (Exod. 6:3). At the same time he asserts that the name Yahweh was first revealed to Moses and by him to the people. The compound form El Shadday is standard usage in the P material of the Pentateuch (Gen. 17:1, 28:3, 35:11, 43:14, 48:3; Exod. 6:3); it also occurs in Ezek. 10:5 (but cf. Ezek. 1:24 where Shadday alone appears). In Num. 24:4, 16, Shadday occurs by itself, but in parallel sequence with El and Elyon, suggesting a break-up of the traditional combination. In this case, El forms a natural pair with both Elyon and Shadday (as in the patriarchal narratives). In Gen. 49:25, El and Shadday are in parallel cola according to MT, but the reading *wᵉ'ēl šadday* for *wᵉ'ēt šadday* is attested by some manuscripts of MT, the Samaritan and Septuagint, and is to be preferred: *'ēl 'ābīkā // 'ēl šadday.* In Ps. 68:15 Shadday stands by itself.

For the rest, the term occurs in Psalm 91 in parallel with Elyon (vs. 1), a poem of uncertain but possibly early date, since the same pair of terms occurs in the Oracles of Balaam. It also occurs in Isa. 13:6=Joel 1:15, both of which can be dated in the sixth century, during the nostalgic period. As in the case of Eloah, the majority of occurrences of Shadday is in Job (thirty-one out of a total of forty-eight). Finally, we note the occurrence, twice, of the title in Ruth (1:20, 21). While in its present form Ruth is relatively late, perhaps seventh–sixth centuries B.C.,[79] it purports to deal with the period of the judges. Apparently the use of Shadday was intended to reflect actual practice in that period, and was probably accurate in that respect. It is precisely in the poetry of Phase II (eleventh century) that we find Shadday, so the evidence of the poems corroborates the data in Ruth, which in turn support the proposed dating of the poems.

d. Olam

This is another term with roots in the patriarchal tradition: cf. Gen. 21:33, where the combination El Olam, "El the Eternal," appears. Since 'ōlām is a common noun to begin with, and the divine title is indistinguishable from it in form, the identification of the latter cannot be regarded as certain in all cases, though in some it is highly probable. The best example is Deut. 33:27 in which 'ōlām is in parallel construction with 'elōhē qedem, "the ancient God."[80] It may well be that the construct 'elōhē is intended to serve double duty, controlling 'ōlām as well as qedem, i.e. "the God of eternity." But the difference between that and "the Eternal One" would be slight, and in time the term Olam would gain independent status as in fact it did in later Phoenician tradition. Whether the phrases combining 'ōlām with gb'wt//hrry are also to be interpreted in this fashion, "the hills of the Eternal One" rather than in the customary way, "the eternal hills," depends partly on the interpretation of the rather vague translation "eternal hills" and partly on the degree to which mythological notions of the sacred mountain (-range), i.e. the mountains//hills of the gods are reflected in this poetry (cf. Gen. 49:26=Deut. 33:15—gb'wt 'wlm). The remaining instance, in II Sam. 23:5, is also debatable, but there is a strong case for rendering the clause "for the Eternal has ordained a covenant for me" rather than "He has ordained an eternal covenant for me."[81]

The divine term 'ōlām, like the other patriarchal epithets of El, is found in the poetry of Phase II (Deuteronomy 33 and Genesis 49), and may also appear in Phase III (cf. II Sam. 23:5). It was never very popular and did not catch on as a title of God, though it was used extensively in liturgical phrases preserved in the Psalms. Its use as a divine epithet seems to be concentrated in the latter part of Phase II, and the first half of Phase III, roughly 1050–950 B.C.

e. Ṣur

The next term to be considered is ṣūr, the basic meaning of which is "mountain." As a title or name for God, its use is concentrated in the poetry of Phase III. It is found in practically all the poems of that phase, but not at all in the poems of Phases I and II. Comparison between *ṣūr* and its apparent cognate *šadday* is instructive and may be important.[82] Its presence in poetry which cannot be earlier than the tenth century gives it a reasonable connection with the monarchy, while its absence from all twelfth- and eleventh-century poetry is equally significant. The frequent occurrence of *ṣūr* in Deuteronomy 32 also helps to fix the date of that elusive poem.

1) The independent forms *ṣūr* and *haṣṣūr* occur in I Sam. 2:2; II Sam. 22:32=Ps. 18:32; II Sam. 22:47 (omitted in Ps. 18:47, which is the superior reading); and Deut. 32:4, 15, 18, 37. These poems are concentrated in Phase III, and if we add the construct form in the phrase *ṣūr yiśrā'ēl*, "the Mountain of Israel," which appears in II Sam. 23:3, we would have a solid group of four consecutive poems from the beginning of Phase III to a point well past the middle.

2) The distribution of suffixed forms of *ṣūr* (e.g. *ṣūrī, ṣūrēnū, ṣūrām*) is also restricted to Phase III, but there seems to be a slight shift toward a later date for these forms. While the independent and construct forms occur in the first four poems of Phase III, the suffixed forms occur in the third, fourth, and fifth poems in the group. Thus the two earliest poems in Phase III (I Samuel 2 and II Samuel 23) have the independent form only, while the fifth poem (Psalm 78) has the suffixed form only. The third and fourth poems, II Samuel 22=Psalm 18, and Deuteronomy 32, have both independent and suffixed forms:

Ps. 18=

	I Sam. 2	II Sam. 23	II Sam. 22	Deut. 32	Ps. 78
(h) ṣūr	X	X	X	X	—
ṣūr+suff.	—	—	X	X	X

The divine title *ṣūr* is characteristic of Phase III poetry. The independent form seems to have flourished earlier in this period and the suffixed form somewhat later though there is a considerable overlap, which is hardly surprising. The general picture conforms to what we have seen to be the case with *'ēl* and its suffixed form.

f. *hū'*

Since *hū'*, "he, that one," is a pronoun which could have been substituted for, or used in parallel with, any divine name or title, a random distribution among the poems in our group might have been expected. On the contrary, it is entirely absent from Phases I and II; and its use is concentrated in Phase III. It appears in the last four poems on the list: II Samuel 22=Psalm 18, Deuteronomy 32, Psalm 78, and Psalm 68, and nowhere else in the group, indicating that its use is characteristic of Phase III, especially the middle and latter part of that period.

g. Adonay

The last title to be considered is Adonay, which occurs three times in the poems on our list. Aside from the example in Exod. 15:17 already considered, it appears only in the last two poems of Phase III: Psalms 78 and 68. It occurs once in Psalm 78 (vs. 65), and six times in Psalm 68 (vss. 12, 18, 20, 21, 23, 33). On the whole, it appears to be a substitute for another divine name, usually Yahweh, rather than a new title, though it may well have served the latter function as well. As a surrogate, its distribution is much like that of Elohim and the pronoun *hū'*. During the latter part of Phase III, there was a significant development in the use of equivalent or substitute terms for the principal name, Yahweh, along with the general proliferation of divine names and epithets already described. It would be entirely reasonable to associate this development with the worship at the temple and the adaptation of the rich Canaanite musical and poetic traditions for liturgical use there.

As previously indicated we will not deal with the long list of qualifying nouns and participles applied to the deity in the poems. They deserve more detailed classification and analysis than is possible in the present paper, though such analysis should yield supporting or corrective data for the conclusions drawn from the primary evidence provided by the principal divine names and titles.

There is a group of other terms in the poems which may provide clues to the proposed sequence dating. An examination of words used for other divine beings is not particularly fruitful, chiefly because there are very few of them, and they do not exhibit any clear pattern of distribution. Thus *'ēlīm*, "gods," turns up in Exod. 15:11. Ps. 29:1 has *bᵉnē 'ēlīm*, probably "sons of El" (with enclitic *mem* attached to *'ēli*, singular with genitive case rather than the plural ending). The singular *'ēl nēkār*, "foreign god," occurs in Deut. 32:12, however. The collective term *qdš*, "holy ones," also appears in Exod. 15:11, and apparently in Deut. 33:2; the plural form occurs in the latter, vs. 3. Finally *'ᵉlōhīm* as a numerical plural, "gods," appears in Judg. 5:8 and Deut. 32:17. All these terms appear early in the list, and reappear later, but the incidence is too sporadic and the distribution too scattered to offer a basis for making useful inferences.

The case is somewhat different with certain other nouns, proper and common. If we concentrate attention on the words referring to the people of Yahweh, we find the following data of interest. The term *'am*, "people," is used throughout Phases I and II, appearing in all six poems of those groups. In Phase III the use is less consistent, though the term turns up in Deuteronomy 32 and Psalm 78. It does not appear in the three poems which mark the initial period of Phase III, but these focus explicitly on the anointed one, the king, who displaces the people as the immediate object of divine attention: I Sam. 2:10 and II Sam. 22:51=Ps. 18:51 have the parallel terms *malkō∥mᵉšīḥō*. In II Sam. 23:1, *mᵉšīaḥ* (construct) occurs but not *melek;* however, David the king is referred to by name. The shift from people to king is made evident by the following comparison:

Ps. 29:11	I Sam. 2:10
Yahweh *ʿōz leʿammō yittēn*	*weyitten-ʿoz lemalkō*

It may be added that the term *mšyḥ* occurs only in the three poems in which the term *ʿam* does not. None of these terms occurs in Psalm 68, which is distinguished by other special features.

The name Israel appears for the first time in our poetry in the Song of Deborah (eight occurrences: vss. 2, 3, 5, 7, 7, 8, 9, 11). It does not occur in Exodus 15 or Psalm 29, though in both of these poems the term *ʿam* is used with direct reference to Yahweh as possessor and/or creator of his people. In Judges 5, the expression *ʿam Yahweh* is used along with Israel, but the name Jacob is conspicuously absent. In practically all the other poems in our list, the two names are linked: e.g. Numbers 23–24, Genesis 49, Deuteronomy 33, II Samuel 23, Deuteronomy 32, Psalm 78. The exceptions are Pss. 68:9 and 72:18. In those passages, the formula used is *ʾelōhē yiśrāʾēl,* "the God of Israel," which is the same as in Judg. 5:3, 5. Thus the pair Jacob//Israel is typical of Phases II and III, but does not appear in Phase I. It is tempting to see the reflection of historical developments in the shifts in usage from *ʿam* alone, as in Exodus 15 and Psalm 29, to the pair *yaʿaqōb//yiśrāʾēl* (along with *ʿam*) in Phases II and III. In addition, there is the exotic term *yešūrūn* which occurs only three times in our poetry, and once thereafter in the Hebrew Bible.[83] These occurrences are in Deuteronomy 33 (vss. 5 and 26), and Deuteronomy 32 (vs. 15), which represent Phases II and III respectively. The selection and distribution of the terms for the people of Yahweh, *ʿam, yiśrāʾēl, yaʿaqōb,* and *yešūrūn* are almost exactly the same in Deuteronomy 33 and Deuteronomy 32, and following Albright, it would seem logical to date their composition in the same period. On the other hand, there is a significant divergence in their use of divine names and epithets, which justifies the somewhat greater gap in time between them that I have estimated, and their assignment to different phases. The explanation of these apparently conflicting or divergent tendencies may lie in the presumed effort of the poet to imitate an older style and set his poem in an earlier historical setting.

The remaining terms *melek//*mašīaḥ* appear in poems of the monarchy (both in I Samuel 2 and II Samuel 22=Psalm 18, *mšyḥ* alone in II Samuel 23). The term "king" appears as well in Num. 24:7 (*malkō*) and Deut. 33:5 (*melek*). In neither case is it entirely clear whether the divine or a human king is meant, but we must allow for the latter possibility. If so, and if the reference is to the Israelite monarchy, then we must reckon with a date of composition during the monarchy in both instances. In my opinion Deuteronomy 33 as a whole reflects the election and consecration of Saul as king by the tribal confederation, and vs. 5 in particular contains an allusion to the inauguration of his reign. The passage in the Oracles of Balaam is more obscure and it is better to suspend judgment about that particular question. A date in the eleventh century for the Oracles of Balaam seems probable to me, as also for Deuteronomy 33.

CONCLUSION

To summarize: comparison with the conclusions of Albright and Robertson show relatively modest divergences in the ordering of the poems, and their chronology, both relative and absolute, although the approach and criteria employed were very different. In the following table I have listed the poems once more, giving the dates proposed by Albright, Robertson, and me.

Poem	Albright	Robertson[84]	Freedman
Exodus 15	1. 13th century	1. 12th century	1. 12th century
Judges 5	2. 1150	2. end of 12th	3. 12th
Numbers 23–24	3. 1200		4. 11th
Deuteronomy 33	4. mid 11th		6. late 11th
Deuteronomy 32	5. ca. 1025	3. 11th–10th	11. 10th–9th
Genesis 49	6. late 11th		5. 11th
I Samuel 2	7. late 11th		7. 11th–10th
II Samuel 1	8. early 10th		8. early 10th
II Samuel 23	9. first half 10th		9. first half 10th
II Samuel 22-Psalm 18	10. 10th	4. 11th–10th	10. 10th
Psalm 78	11. 10th	5. 10th–9th	12. 10th–9th
Psalm 68	12. 10th		13. 10th–9th
Psalm 72	13. 10th		14. 10th–9th
Psalm 29	14. [5th]		2. 12th

The essential differences in order are as follows:

1) Albright discusses Psalm 29, describes it as very archaic, but finally suggests that it dates in final form from the fifth century B.C.[85] In my opinion it is very archaic and belongs to Phase I, in the twelfth century.

2) After placing Genesis 49 sixth in his list, and dating it late in the eleventh century, Albright modified his views and suggested that parts of it may be considerably older, going back to late patriarchal times. I have placed it fifth, and dated it to the eleventh century.

3) Albright has Deuteronomy 33 before Genesis 49, while I reverse the order since I believe, as Albright suspected, that Genesis 49 is more archaic.

4) There is a major divergence in dealing with Deuteronomy 32. Albright puts it fifth, and dates it about 1025, but I find many marks of later composition, and put it eleventh in order, placing it in Phase III, not earlier than the tenth century, and very likely the ninth century.

5) I have insufficient data to place or date II Samuel 1 and Psalm 72 but have no reason to disagree with Albright's dates.

6) Albright places Judges 5 before Numbers 23–24 on stylistic grounds, but dates Numbers 23–24 before Judges 5. My data support Albright's stylistic analysis, but not his dating, so I date Judges 5 earlier than Numbers 23–24.

With respect to specific dates, there are some variations. Albright dates Exodus 15 to the thirteenth century and Numbers 23–24 to 1200, while I find nothing earlier than the twelfth century, to which period I assign both Exodus 15 and Judges 5. Numbers 23–24, on the other hand, belongs to the eleventh century in my opinion. I date Deuteronomy 33 slightly later than Albright and Genesis 49 slightly earlier. I also put Deuteronomy 32 at least a century later than Albright does. The rest are the same, or practically so.

There is a striking agreement with Robertson on the poems to which he is willing to assign dates. Thus we agree on a twelfth-century date for Exodus 15 and Judges 5, as well as on the order of composition of these poems. We also agree on a tenth-ninth-century date for Psalm 78. We diverge slightly on II Samuel 22=Psalm 18, which he dates a little earlier than I do, and more seriously on Deuteronomy 32. He is closer to Eissfeldt and Albright, dating the poem in the eleventh–tenth centuries, whereas I am closer to Wright and Cross, placing it in the tenth–ninth centuries.

While the order of the poems cannot be fixed with certainty, and all proposed dates are approximate, a consensus on the corpus of early Hebrew poetry and the broad outlines of its chronology seems to have emerged.

A NOTE ON THE NAME YAHWEH

In all the poems, the term *yhwh* functions clearly as a proper noun both grammatically and syntactically. Its original verbal form and force have left no trace in the poetry under consideration, any more than such factors survive in names like *ya'ᵃqōb* and *yiśrā'ēl*. This fact is both interesting and a little disturbing, especially if the name were of recent origin (thirteenth century), and if it still retained its verbal force for some time after its adoption.[86]

There are several expressions in which the verbal force has been preserved, and which can only be understood in the light of the original meaning of the form *yhwh*:[87] e.g. such phrases as *yhwh ṣᵉbā'ōt*, "he creates the hosts," *yhwh šālōm*, "he inaugurates peace" (Judg. 6:24). Neither of these appears in any of our poems, nor anything like them, so we must suppose that these expressions while correctly reflecting the etymology of the term *yhwh* do not underlie its use as a name, but were introduced secondarily, i.e. after the adoption of Yahweh as a name, the name of God. The expression *yhwh ṣᵉbā'ōt*, "he creates the hosts," does not occur in the Pentateuch at all, but first appears in the stories in the books of Samuel (cf. I Sam. 1:3, 11,

4:4, 15:2, etc.). According to repeated testimony, it was part of the legend on the ark (cf. I Sam. 4:4; II Sam. 6:2), and there is little reason to doubt that this was the original locus of the expression in pre-monarchic times. The expression *yhwh šālōm* (Judg. 6:24) seems to come from the same period. Of these expressions, only *yhwh ṣᵉbā'ōt* became a factor in Israelite poetry and its appearance is largely late and secondary since in the majority of instances it has the form *yhwh 'ᵉlōhē ṣᵉbā'ōt*, "Yahweh, the God of hosts," in which the verbal force of *yhwh* has been lost entirely. Nevertheless, the verbal force is preserved in the original form, reflected in the prose tradition, and some account must be taken of this.

Our proposal is briefly as follows:

1) The original form *yahweh* was a verb, and was used in a variety of liturgical utterances relating to the patriarchal God El.[88] Thus El was the God who created the hosts, peace, and the rest. During the period of the judges some of these expressions were introduced at the time that the name El was itself officially accepted by Israel and identified with Yahweh the God of Moses.

2) Yahweh as the personal name of God had been introduced earlier by Moses and it was used and understood as a name. Afterwards, when Yahweh and El were identified, the archaic expressions which originally described activities of El were adopted along with the divine titles and epithets associated with patriarchal El. The expressions containing the verb *yahweh* were introduced but there must have been some confusion about their meaning and significance. Very soon the verbal element was interpreted as the name, and the result was the misinterpretation of the expression. This comes out clearly in the modification of the original *yhwh ṣᵉbā'ōt* to *yhwh 'ᵉlōhē ṣᵉbā'ōt*, a necessary change on the part of those who saw in *yhwh* only the sacred name of God, and not a verb previously associated with a different theological tradition.

3) As already indicated, our poetry is entirely unaffected by this development, indicating that the traditions on which the earliest Israelite poems rested began with Yahweh as the personal name of God and only later incorporated the expressions which retained the verbal force of the underlying root (the hiphil form of *hwy).

NOTES

1. W. F. Albright, *YGC*, pp. 1–28, 42–52. The individual poems were analyzed in a series of articles spanning his career as a scholar: e.g. "The Earliest Forms of Hebrew Verse," *JPOS* 2 (1922), 69–86; "The Oracles of Balaam," *JBL* 63 (1944), 207–233; "The Psalm of Habakkuk," *Studies in Old Testament Prophecy* (Edinburgh, 1950), pp. 1–18;

"A Catalogue of Early Hebrew Lyric Poems (Psalm 68)," *HUCA* 33, Part 1 (1950–51), 1–39; "Some Remarks on the Song of Moses in Deuteronomy XXXII," *VT* 9 (1959), 339–346. For discussion of the dates of various poems in the group, see F. M. Cross and D. N. Freedman, *Studies in Ancient Yahwistic Poetry* (henceforth *SAYP;* Baltimore, 1950), and D. A. Robertson, *Linguistic Evidence in Dating Early Hebrew Poetry* (henceforth *LEDEHP;* New Haven, 1966).

2. *YGC,* pp. 10 ff.

3. Albright makes several comments about the age of the poem, but does not fix a date; see discussion, p. 60.

4. *YGC,* pp. 15–16. 5. *YGC,* p. 265.

6. *YGC,* p. 266. See the discussion of Genesis 49, p. 63.

7. There is a number of recent and forthcoming studies of this poem: *YGC,* pp. 11–13, 45–47; *SAYP* [N 1], pp. 83–127; F. M. Cross and D. N. Freedman, "The Song of Miriam," *JNES* 14 (1955), 237–250; Cross, "The Song of the Sea and Canaanite Myth," in *God and Christ: Existence and Province, JTC* 5 (1968), 1–25; note the references in fn. 27, pp. 9–10; P. C. Craigie, "An Egyptian Expression in the Song of the Sea (Ex. XV 4)," *VT* 20 (1970), 83–86, with a bibliographical summary on p. 83; the same author has an extensive study of the poem which will be published in the near future. See also "Strophe and Meter in Exodus 15," my lengthy study of the structure of the poem in *A Light Unto My Path,* the J. M. Myers *Festschrift* (Temple University Press, 1974), pp. 163–204. Cf. G. W. Coats, "The Traditio-Historical Character of the Reed Sea Motif," *VT* 17 (1967), 253–265; B. S. Childs, "A Traditio-Historical Study of the Reed Sea Tradition," *VT* 20 (1970), 406–418.

8. Cf. D. N. Freedman, "The Refrain in David's Lament over Saul and Jonathan," in *Ex Orbe Religionum (Studia Geo Widengren),* Studies in the History of Religions, No. 21 (1972), 115–126.

9. The older printed editions of the Hebrew Bible have *ks yh* as two words, but Kittel, *Biblia Hebraica*[3], reads *ksyh* as a single expression. Neither the form nor the meaning is clear, though the verbal root *ksy* may be discerned (as suggested by Cross).

10. Cf. Cross and Freedman, "The Song of Miriam" [N 7], 243.

11. For discussion on the structure and meaning of Psalm 29, see D. N. Freedman and C. F. Hyland, "Psalm 29: A Structural Analysis," *HTR* 66 (1973), 237–256.

12. Cf. H. N. Richardson, "The Last Words of David: Some Notes on II Samuel 23:1–7," *JBL* 90 (1971), 257–266, esp. pp. 261–262.

13. See Cross, "The Song of the Sea and Canaanite Myth" [N 7], p. 13, fn. 42.

14. Ibid., p. 16, fn. 57. 15. Ibid., p. 14, fn. 49.

16. Cf. Albright, "The Phoenician Inscriptions of the Tenth Century B.C. from Byblus," *JAOS* 67 (1947), 153–160; the phrase occurs in the Yeḥimilk inscription, lines 4–5, dated by Albright to the middle of the tenth century, pp. 156–157.

17. This date is supported by Cross, "The Song of the Sea and Canaanite Myth" [N 7], p. 11 (late twelfth or early eleventh century; Robertson, *LEDEHP* [N 1], p. 231 (twelfth); P. C. Craigie, unpublished monograph.

18. It is likely that many if not most of the poems in our list appeared in one or the other of two early anthologies which are mentioned in the Bible: the Book of the Wars of Yahweh (Num. 21:14), and the Book of Jashar (Josh. 10:13; II Sam. 1:18). The earliest editions of these collections may well go back to the time of the judges, but the final published form must be dated in the monarchic period. In fact there is a reference to the Book of Jashar in the LXX of I Kings 8:13, as the source for a poetic utterance attributed to Solomon at the dedication of the temple.

19. For recent discussion of Psalm 29, see P. C. Craigie, "Psalm XXIX in Hebrew Poetic Tradition," *VT* 22 (1972), 143–151, and literature cited. Cf. Hyland and Freedman [N 11].

20. Albright also states that it is impossible to date accurately but suggests a "fifth(?) century B.C." date for its final redaction (*YGC*, p. 255).

21. On the similarities and differences between Exodus 15 and Judges 5, see Albright, *YGC*, pp. 12–14.

22. On the similarities between Psalms 29 and Exodus 15, see Craigie [N 19].

23. Cf. M. Dahood, *Psalms I*, AB, vol. 16 (1966), pp. 175–176; and on Ps. 89:7, *Psalms II*, AB, vol. 17 (1968), p. 313.

24. In Ps. 24:7–10, the equivalent expression *melek hakkābōd*, "the king of glory" or "the glorious king," occurs five times as a title of Yahweh. This evidence strengthens the view that *'ēl hakkābōd* should be analyzed as a construct chain. The passage in Psalm 24 belongs to the same genre as Psalm 29, and may also date to the pre-monarchic period.

25. See discussion in Hyland and Freedman [N 11].

26. H. L. Ginsberg, "A Strand in the Cord of Hebraic Hymnody," *EI* 9 (1969), 45–50, dates it to the pre-monarchic period (p. 45), while Cross, "The Song of the Sea and Canaanite Myth," [N 7], 10, and Craigie [N 19], 144, place it somewhat later.

27. For recent discussion see P. C. Craigie, "The Song of Deborah and the Epic of Tukulti-Ninurta," *JBL* 88 (1969), 253–265; and "Some Further Notes on the Song of Deborah," *VT* 22 (1972), 349–353. Cf. also R. G. Boling in *Judges*, AB, vol. 6A (1975).

28. Following A. Weiser, "Das Deboralied," *ZAW* 71 (1959), 75, and D. R. Hillers, "A Note on Judges 5:8," *CBQ* 27 (1965), 124; against Craigie, "Some Further Notes on the Song of Deborah" [N 27], 350–351.

29. Cf. Albright, *YGC*, pp. 31–34, citing work by Boling, "'Synonymous' Parallelism in the Psalms," *Journal of Semitic Studies* 5 (1960), 221–255.

30. *YGC*, pp. 255–256.

31. *YGC*, pp. 26–27, and references in fn. 60 on p. 26.

32. The passage in Isaiah is generally dated to the sixth century B.C. or later; cf. R. B. Y. Scott, "Isaiah: Chapters 1–39," IB, V (1956), 254–255. On the date of Joel, see J. M. Myers, "Some Considerations Bearing on the Date of Joel," *ZAW* 74 (1962), 177–195; his conclusion (p. 195) is that a date around 520 B.C. is the most likely.

33. On the date of Job, see D. N. Freedman, "Orthographic Peculiarities in the Book of Job," *EI* 9 (1969), 35–44. Albright's conclusions as to the date of Job are given on pp. 43–44.

34. E. F. Campbell, Jr., recommends an earlier date (in the ninth century) for the composition of Ruth; cf. *Ruth*, AB, vol. 7 (1975), pp. 23–28.

35. See M. Dahood, *Psalms III*, AB, vol. 17A (1970), p. 324; cf. Isa. 14:19 and Job 5:23. The same word, with prosthetic *aleph* occurs in Phoenician.

36. For discussion and evaluation see D. N. Freedman, "The Structure of Psalm 137," in *Near Eastern Studies in Honor of William Foxwell Albright*, ed. Hans Goedicke (Baltimore, 1971), p. 195 and fn. 9; and Freedman, "Prolegomenon," *The Forms of Hebrew Poetry*, by G. B. Gray (New York, 1972), p. liv, fn. 6.

37. For discussion of the term, see F. M. Cross and D. N. Freedman, "The Blessing of Moses," *JBL* 67 (1948), 194 and 204–205, fn. 38; also Richardson [N 12], 260–261, and fns. 16–18.

38. The word *hwry* may be an error for *hrry*, "mountains" (to be vocalized *harᵉrē* as a construct before *'ad*, which has mistakenly been interpreted as the preposition and linked with the following word *ta'ᵃwat*), in parallel with *gib'ōt*, "hills." See *SAYP* [N 1], pp. 141 and 182, fns. 82, 83.

39. The use of *'ōlām* as a divine epithet is even more probable in Deut. 33:27; cf. Cross and Freedman [N 37], pp. 196 and 209, fn. 85. Another possible instance occurs

in II Sam. 23:5; cf. Richardson [N 12], 259, 263–264. See the discussion of this verse, p. 73.

40. F. M. Cross, "Yahweh and the God of the Patriarchs," *HTR* 55 (1962), 238–239.

41. Cf. *Psalms I*, Index, p. 322; *Psalms II*, Index, p. 386 [N 23].

42. Cf. *SAYP* [N 1], pp. 129–233.

43. The best study of this poem is still that of Albright, "The Oracles of Balaam," *JBL* 63 (1944). More recent comments are to be found in ch. 1 of *YGC*.

44. On the original form of the name Yahweh, see Dahood, *Psalms I*, Index, p. 320; *Psalms II*, Index, p. 384 [N 23]; *Psalms III* [N 35], Index, p. 472. Cf. also D. N. Freedman, "The Name of the God of Moses," *JBL* 79 (1969), 151–156, esp. p. 156; and Cross [N 40], pp. 250 ff.

45. For detailed discussion, see Cross and Freedman [N 37].

46. See discussion p. 65, and N 37.

47. Cf. Cross and Freedman [N 37], pp. 194 and 206, fn. 53.

48. On the date of composition, "The Blessing of Moses" [N 37], p. 192.

49. As already noted *šadday* appears in Psalm 68 (vs. 15), which we have assigned to Phase III. However, Psalm 68 contains much older material and the passage in question may derive from an earlier period. The absence of *ṣūr* from Psalm 68 is another indication of its archaic character.

50. See discussion of this expression and the general formulation, p. 60.

51. For recent discussion of this poem and bibliography, see Freedman [N 8].

52. For recent discussion, see Richardson [N 12], and D. N. Freedman, "II Samuel 23:4," *JBL* 90 (1971), 329–330.

53. For *'l* in MT, the reading in 4QSam[a] is *'l*, "El, God," which may be more original (so Cross). See Richardson [N 12], pp. 260–261.

54. See discussion p. 62 and N 28.

55. At Deut. 32:8, the reading in MT, *bny yśr'l*, "sons of Israel," is secondary. The original Hebrew was *bny 'l* (or possibly *'lym* or *'lhym* since the manuscript breaks off after the letters *'l*), "the sons of El." See P. W. Skehan, "A fragment of the 'Song of Moses' (Deut. 32) from Qumran," *BASOR* 136 (1954), 12. At Deut. 32:43, the Qumran scroll has the phrase *kl 'lhym*, "all the gods," clearly the numerical plural. Skehan, ibid., pp. 13–15, restores a line with the phrase *benē 'ēlīm*, while F. M. Cross, *ALQ²*, pp. 182–183, supplies *bny 'lhym*, "sons of God." The reading is based on an unpublished 4Q reading.

56. See Richardson [N 12], pp. 263–264.

57. For detailed discussion, see F. M. Cross and D. N. Freedman, "A Royal Song of Thanksgiving: II Samuel=Psalm 18," *JBL* 72 (1953), 15–34.

58. The parallel passage (S) has *'elōhē ṣūr yiš'ī*, a contaminated text in which the word *ṣūr* is intrusive.

59. On this meaning of *mgn*, perhaps *māgēn* or *māgōn*, see Freedman [N 8], pp. 122–123. Cf. Dahood, *Psalms I*, Index, p. 321, and *Psalms II*, Index, p. 384 [N 23].

60. For discussion of the problem and various solutions, see the following: Albright, *YGC*, pp. 17 ff., and "Some Remarks on the Song of Moses in Deuteronomy XXXII," pp. 339–346 [N 1]; O. Eissfeldt, *Das Lied Moses Deuteronomium 32, 1–43 und das Lehrgedicht Asaphs Psalm 78 samt einer Analyse der Umgebung des Mose-Liedes*, Berichte über die Verhandlungen der Sächsischen Akademie der Wissenschaften zu Leipzig. Phil.-hist. Klasse, 104–5 (Berlin, 1958); P. W. Skehan, "The Structure of the Song of Moses in Deuteronomy," *CBQ* 13 (1951), 153–163; G. E. Wright, "The Lawsuit of God: A Form-Critical Study of Deuteronomy 32," in *Israel's Prophetic Heritage*, eds. B. W. Anderson and W. Harrelson (New York, 1962), pp. 26–67; Robertson, *LEDEHP* [N 1], p. 231.

61. See Skehan [N 55], p. 12.

62. See ibid., pp. 13–15; Cross, *ALQ²*, pp. 182–183; Albright, *YGC*, p. 18 and fns. 46 and 46a.

63. Cf. Boling, [N 29], pp. 221–255; Albright, *YGC*, pp. 31 ff.

64. See my note "God Almighty in Psalm 78:59," *Biblica* 54 (1973), 268. A parallel instance occurs in Ps. 46:2; cf. Dahood, *Psalms III*, pp. 136 and 318–319, correcting his analysis in *Psalms I*, p. 278.

65. Cf. Ps. 71:22.

66. For discussion see Albright, *YGC*, pp. 26–27; "A Catalogue of Early Hebrew Lyric Poems (Psalm 68)" [N 1].

67. Ibid.

68. Cf. Cross and Freedman [N 37], pp. 193, 198–199, fns. 8–9. The emendation of *qdš* to *qdšm* is not necessary.

69. I owe this observation to F. M. Cross.

70. For the rendering of *bqdš*, "among the holy ones," see N 68. Contrast Dahood, *Psalms III* [N 35], p. 147, who translates "from his sanctuary."

71. *Psalms III*, pp. 132, 149. The same epithet occurs in vs. 35 in association with Israel, "the Exalted One of Israel."

72. The single line, vs. 18, which contained the name Yahweh is not a part of the original poem, but a later insertion.

73. See comments p. 83 on the examples in vss. 5 and 19.

74. On a possible exception in Deuteronomy 32, see discussion p. 73, esp. N 55. It is important to emphasize that the reading *'lhym*, "God," is not directly and explicitly attested in any manuscript or version available to us.

75. See comments p. 73 on the reading in II Sam. 23:3; cf. Richardson [N 12], p. 262.

76. See the discussion of this point by Dahood, *Psalms II* [N 23], p. 149.

77. While it does not occur by itself in I Samuel 2, it appears as a construct with *dēʿōt*, "the God of knowledge," or "the (all-) knowing God."

78. That the third stem consonant was *yod* is confirmed by Ugaritic *'ly;* cf. Gordon, *Ugaritic Textbook* (Rome, 1965), p. 456; Dahood, "The Divine Name *'ēlî* in the Psalms," *Theological Studies* 14 (1953), 452–457; *Psalms I*, Index, p. 322; *Psalms II*, p. 386 [N 23]; *Psalms III* [N 35], p. 475.

79. See discussion p. 64, and N 34.

80. See discussion p. 65, and N 39.

81. See discussion pp. 65, 73 and NN 39, 56.

82. See discussion p. 71, and N 49.

83. It occurs in Isa. 44:2, from the nostalgic period (sixth century).

84. *LEDEHP* [N 1], p. 231. Robertson regards only five of the poems listed as demonstrably or probably early.

85. See discussion p. 60, and N 20.

86. Albright's effort to read the verb *yahweh* in Exod. 15:3 *yahweh 'īš milḥāmāh*, "he creates the army," i.e. the men of war (*YGC*, p. 13, fn. 34), deserves consideration, but is hardly compelling when the normal reading makes reasonable sense in the context. The poem is about Yahweh as the Divine Warrior, who unaided, destroys the Egyptians and strikes terror in the hearts of all other enemies of his people, so it is difficult to see the rationale or purpose in a reference to the creation of fighting hosts whether divine or human.

87. See Albright, *YGC*, p. 33, and review of B. N. Wambacq, "L'épithète divine *Jahvé Seba'ôt*: Étude philologique, historique et exégetique," *JBL* 67 (1948), 377–381; F. M. Cross, "Yahweh and the God of the Patriarchs," *HTR* 55 (1962), 250–259; D. N. Freedman, "The Name of the God of Moses," *JBL* 79 (1960), 151–156.

88. See Cross [N 87].

CHART A: THE TERMS

I. Terms for God
  A. Names
    1. Yahweh and Yah
    2. Elohim
      a. Independent form
      b. Construct chain:
        1) *'elōhē* yiśrā'*el*/ya'*ᵃqob*
        2) *'elōhē 'ābī*
        3) *'elōhē qedem*
      c. Suffixed forms:
        1) *'elōhay*
        2) *'elōhēkā*
        3) *'elōhāw*
        4) *'elōhēnū*
        5) *'elōhēmō*
    3. El (and hā'ēl)
      a. Independent form
      b. Construct chain
        1) *'ēl 'ābīkā* (?)
        2) *'ēl 'ᵉmūnāh*
        3) *'ēl dē'ōt*
        4) *'ēl yiśrā'ēl*
        5) *'ēl (hak)kābōd*
      c. Suffixed form: *'ēlī*
    4. Eloah
  B. Principal titles and epithets:
    1. Elyon
    2. Al
      a. Independent forms: *'l, 'lw, 'lyw*
      b. Construct chain: *'l yiśrā'ēl*
    3. Shadday
    4. Olam
    5. Ṣūr (and haṣṣūr)
      a. Independent form
      b. Construct chain: *ṣūr yiśrā'ēl*
      c. Suffixed forms
        1) *ṣūrī*
        2) *ṣūrēnū*
        3) *ṣūrām*
    6. Hū'
    7. Adonay
  C. Qualifying Nouns and Phrases
    1. Nouns
      a. Independent forms
        1) *zmrt*
        2) *yāšār*
        3) *kābōd*
        4) *m'd*
        5) *māgēn*
        6) *melek*
        7) *'ad*
        8) *'ōz*
        9) *ṣaddīq*
        10) *qedem*
        11) *qādōš*
        12) *raḥūm*
      b. Suffixed forms
        1) *'ābīkā*
        2) *ḥizqī*
        3) *māginnī*
        4) *malkī*
        5) *mᵉnūsī*
        6) *mā'uzzī*
        7) *mᵉṣūdātī*
        8) *miśgabbī*
        9) *nērī*
        10) *sal'ī*
        11) *'ozzī*
    2. Phrases
      a. *'ᵃbīr ya'ᵃqōb*
      b. *'īš milḥāmāh*
      c. *zeh sīnay*
      d. *qeren yiš'ī*
  D. Participles
    1. Qal (G-stem)
      a. *bārūk*
      b. *gō'ᵃlām*
      c. *ḥōbēb*
      d. *ḥōpēp*
      e. *(han)nōtēn*
      f. *'ōśeh ḥesed*
      g. *'ōśeh niplā'ōt*
      h. *'ōśeh pele'*
      i. *rōkēb*
      j. *rō'ēh*
      k. *šōkᵉnī sᵉnēh*
    2. Niphal (N-stem)
      a. *ne'dār*
      b. *nōrā'*
    3. Piel - Pual (D-stem)
      a. *mᵉhullāl*
      b. *mᵉḥayyeh*
      c. *mᵉlammēd*
      d. *mᵉpalṭī*
      e. *mᵉrōmēm*
      f. *mᵉšawweh*

4. Hiphil (H-stem)
   a. *magdīl*
   b. **mōṣī'*
      1) *mōṣī'ī*
      2) *mōṣī'ō*
      3) *mōṣī'ām*
   c. *mōrīd*
   d. *mōrīš*
   e. *mōšī'ī*
   f. *mēmīt*
   g. *ma'ăšīr*
   h. *mēqīm*
   i. *marḥīb*
   j. *mašpīl*

II. Other terms
   A. For divine beings
      1. *'ēl (īm)*
      2. *qdš (īm)*
      3. *'elōhīm*
      4. *šēdīm*
   B. Proper nouns
      1. *'edōm*
      2. *ya'ăqōb*
      3. *yiśrā'ēl*
      4. *yešūrūn*
      5. *kena'an*
      6. *mō'āb*
      7. *miṣrayim*
      8. *sīnay*
      9. *pelešet*
      10. *šē'īr*
   C. Common nouns
      1. *melek*
      2. **māšīaḥ*
      3. *ne'um*
      4. *'am*

	Exod. 15	Judg. 5	Num. 23-24	Deut. 33	Deut. 32	Gen. 49	I Sam. 2	II Sam. 1	II Sam. 23	II Sam. 22 / Ps. 18		Ps. 78	Ps. 68	Ps. 72	Ps. 29
										S	P				
יהוה	10[b]	14	3	8	8	1	8[c]		1	16	16	2	3	1	18
עז	1														1
זמר[ו]ת	1						1								
יה	1												2		
אל	1		8	1	4[d]	2[e]	1		1	4	4	7	5		1
אלהים	1	2	1	1	2		2[f]		3	6	6	8	26	3	
נורא	1												1		
אדני	1[g]											1	6		
זה סיני		1											1		
מלך			1										1		1
מוציא			2							1	0	1			
עליון			2[h]		1					1	1	3			
שדי			2		1								1		
על[י]ו				1		1	1		1				2		
רכב				1									2		
עולם				1					1						
צור					6	1			1	4	3	1			
אב					1	2									
הוא					4					1	1	1	1		
אלוה					2					0	1				

[a] This chart includes divine names and epithets which occur in more than one poem in the group. The order of the poems follows Albright's arrangement. The numbers are derived from MT except where otherwise indicated.

[b] For statistical purposes I consider vs. 21 to be part of the poem. If we accept the reading *yhwh* for *'dny* in vs. 17, the total would be 11.

[c] Reading *b'lhy* for *byhwh* in vs. 1; in MT the total is 9.

[d] Including the reading *'l* in vs. 8, on the basis of 4QDeut. and LXX, but excluding *'l* in vs. 12, which is listed in B.2 under other gods.

[e] Reading *'l šdy* in vs. 25 with Samaritan, LXX, etc. against MT, *'t šdy*.

[f] See fn. c.

[g] If *yhwh* is the original reading in vs. 17, then *'dny* would be dropped.

[h] Restoring *'lywn* in Num. 24:4 on the basis of Num. 24:16.

CHART B.2

	Exod. 15	Judg. 5	Num. 23-24	Deut. 33	Deut. 32	Gen. 49	I Sam. 2	II Sam. 1	II Sam. 23	Ps. 18 / II Sam. 22 S	P	Ps. 78	Ps. 68	Ps. 72	Ps. 29
אל]ים[	1				1										1
קדש]ים[	1			2											
עם	3	4	2	3	4	1						5		3	2
אלהים		1			2										
נאם			6						2						
מלך			1	1			1			1	1				
משיח							1	1	1	1	1				
דוד									1	1	1	1			
אדם	1	1	1												
כנען	1	1													
מואב	1		2												
ישראל		8	8	5	1	4		1	2 ᵃ			7	3	1	
שעיר		1	1	1											
סיני		1		1									2		
יעקב			8	3	1	3			2 ᵇ			3			
מצרים			2									3	1		
ישרן				2	1										

ᵃ Reading *'lhy y'qb* for *'lhy yśr'l* in vs. 3, on the basis of the parallel construction in vs. 1.

ᵇ Cf. fn. a.

CHART C

	PHASE I — 12th Century			PHASE II — 11th Century			PHASE III — 10th Century		Ps. 18 (II Sm. 22)		9th Century		
	Exod. 15	Ps. 29	Judg. 5	Gen. 49	Num. 23-24	Deut. 33	1 Sam. 2	II Sam. 23	S	P	Deut. 32	Ps. 78	Ps. 68
יהוה	X	X	X	(X)[a]	X	X	X	X	X	X	X	X	X
אל [b]	(X)[c]	X					X			X	X		X
אלהי	(X)[c]		X		X	X	X	X	X	X	X		X
אל [d]				X	X	X	X	X	X	X	X	X	X
שדי				X	X								
על[י]				X		X	X	X					X
עליון					X				X	X	X	X	
צור							X	X	X	X	X	X	
אלהים								Ẋ				X	X
הוא									X	X	X	X	X
אלוה									X	X			
אדני	(X)[e]											X	X

	Exod. 15	Ps. 29	Judg. 5	Gen. 49	Num. 23-24	Deut. 33	1 Sam. 2	II Sam. 23	S	P	Deut. 32	Ps. 78	Ps. 68
עם	X	X	X	X	X	X					X	X	
ישראל		X	X	X	X		X				X	X	X
יעקב				X	X	X					X	X	
מלך					X	X	X		X	X			
משיח							X	X	X	X			
דוד							X	X	X		X		

The poems are listed in order of composition and the terms in order of appearance.

a The name Yahweh appears only once, in vs. 18, which is a secondary insertion.

b The term *'lhym* here is generic, i.e. "God." It occurs either as a construct, *'elōhē*, or with the suffix -*y*, "my God."

c These forms occur in vs. 2, which is not part of the original poem in my opinion.

d The term *'l* here is the personal name of the deity, "El."

e The word *'dny* occurs once in Exodus 15 (vs. 17) and is textually suspect. The original reading probably was *yhwh*.

4. Mythopoeic Antecedents of the Biblical World-View and Their Transformation in Early Israelite Thought

LYNN CLAPHAM

EARLHAM COLLEGE, RICHMOND, INDIANA

ONE OF THE problems of concern to G. Ernest Wright is that of the emergence of Israel's faith from her mythopoeic environment. Until a few decades ago many would have subscribed to the "evolutionary" or "developmental" view which held that the lower spiritual values of mythopoeic culture gave way to the higher insights of biblical religion which, in turn, passed through its own successive stages of refinement. This school of thought has few supporters now,[1] although occasionally one may still detect reminiscences of the same typological pattern in some reconstructions of biblical traditions. Wright publicly announced the demise of this view in *The Old Testament Against Its Environment* (1950). No metaphor of growth or evolution can account for the strong preoccupation with God's history of redemption which lies at the center of Israel's faith, Wright argues. Israel defines herself in relation to a God of history who is transcendent from the powers of nature embodied in the gods of adjacent culture. The contrast with Israel's mythopoeic environment is sufficiently strong that, if the metaphor can be used at all, we should speak of a "mutation" which yields, in effect, a new species.

It is disappointing that few have risen to the challenge set forth by Wright. Some have argued that the concept "history" in the "God who acts" approach to biblical theology raises more problems than it solves. However, this does not seem to be the chief obstacle in the path of a new reconstruction of the relation between Israel and her environment. The greater problem seems to be the bifurcation within biblical studies between those who stress strong continuities between Israel and mythopoeic culture and those who stress Israel's particular and unique concern with "salvation history."

Those in the first group point to strong similarities between Israelite and contemporary ancient Near Eastern cultures. Those usually associated with the "myth and ritual" school stress the period of the monarchy in Israel where kingship and temple and their associated cult find strong parallels in Canaan and Mesopotamia. Others can point to mythopoeic backgrounds for the "clan-deity" relation of the patriarchs to Yahweh, the holy war and divine warrior ideology of the period of the League, the institution of prophetism, and the vigorous imagery of apocalyptic.[2] How, then, does one account for Israel's concern with salvation history? Although rarely articulated, the implication of this approach is that there is a development from myth to history in Israel, a remnant of the old evolutionary view of Israel's origins. The fundamental question remains unanswered: What precipitated the movement from myth to history? Why did Israel not simply continue in the mythopoeic pattern common about her?

Those of the second group in contemporary biblical studies stress the primacy of the historical element in Israel's world-view. Finding their strongest evidence in the period of the tribal League, the German "school" of Noth, von Rad, Kraus, and their British and American associates argue that Israel comes into being about a common historical tradition of the Exodus and Conquest. The covenant renewal festival is the primary cultic activity preserving these traditions, and it comes into being in response to the historical memories which it carries. The "salvation historical" approach thus differs from the "myth and ritual" in that it insists upon the primacy of "historical" over the "mythological" elements in Israel's world-view. However, it is in no better position to account for Israel's departure from its mythopoeic environment. It sees the break occurring at an earlier point but can offer no explanation for it. We are left with the same basic question: How do we account for the movement from myth to history in Israel?

This division in biblical studies has pushed far into the background the old question of the origins of Israel's world-view. Until a wider consensus is achieved on the question of the relation of myth and history *within* Israel's thought, we are in no position to investigate the question of Israel's departure from ancient Near Eastern cultural patterns. This study proposes that the time is right to reopen this question. Recent work in the history of Israel's religion has overcome the division between the two dominant schools of biblical study cited above, offering a reconstruction doing justice to both historical and mythopoeic elements in biblical thought. Further, recent work in the nature of ancient Near Eastern mythopoeic thought has brought us to the point where a new hypothesis relating Israel to her environment is possible.

I

In a recent study, F. M. Cross provides an analysis of early Israelite traditions which permits us to move behind the divisions of the myth-and-ritual and history-of-redemption schools of thought. In "The Divine Warrior in Israel's Early Cult,"[3] Cross argues that these two approaches have compatible strengths and weaknesses. The myth-and-ritual school draws heavily upon the period of the monarchy, stressing the royal psalms in its reconstruction of the cult. As suggested above, this approach is not able to account for the strong historical elements found in the royal ideology nor the even stronger ones found in older epic and poetic traditions from the period of the tribal League. It also stumbles upon the methodological difficulty of distinguishing between the Israelite royal cult in which the psalms were used and the old Canaanite cult from which they were borrowed and modified. On the other hand, Cross points out, the myth-and-ritual school is quite right in stressing strong continuities between monarchical Israel and her immediate mythopoeic environment. "There must have been an *Anknüpfungspunkt,* a suitable matrix into which Canaanite lore could be grafted and in which it would remain alive" (p. 14).

The history-of-redemption school draws upon Israelite traditions of the League and the strong historical motifs to which the myth-and-ritual approach cannot do justice. Although it is incorrect in seeing separate origins for the themes Exodus-Conquest and revelation of the Law and Sinai, it is basically correct in arguing that Israel's early cult comes into being in response to traditions of God's saving events which created the community. With this stress upon historical motifs, however, the history-of-redemption school is not able to account for the strong resurgence of mythological motifs during the monarchy. "The question of how this historical cult arose out of the mythopoeic culture which preceded it is left unanswered, as is the problem of the receptivity of Israel's religion and cult to the increment of mythological symbols and motives in the imperial and monarchic era" (p. 15).

Cross shows that Israel's early traditions are shaped strongly by the imagery of Yahweh the Divine Warrior and King and the language of the holy warfare. The Divine Warrior has strong continuities with the Canaanite notion of the Divine Warrior-King who defeats his enemies in cosmic battle and establishes himself as supreme executive power among the assembly of the gods in his newly created temple on the mount of assembly. Not only in the royal psalms but also in the earliest traditions of the Exodus and Conquest (e.g. Exodus 15; Judges 5), Yahweh is described in language of the glorious Warrior and King. This means that the primary language of salvation history dominant in the early period is couched in terms drawn from a mythopoeic background. In the early period some of this background shows through, but it is dominated by *heilsgeschichtlich* motifs. In the period of the monarchy the cosmic and universal dimensions of the material undergo a resurgence which moves the royal cult closer to its Canaanite counterpart. Thus myth and history stand in various relations of tension in Israel's history. The history-of-redemption school is correct in its insistence that the primary language of Israel's self-understanding is historical, although they fail to perceive the mythopoeic background out of which this language emerged. The myth-and-ritual school is correct in its analysis of the royal cult and theology, although its failure to understand the transformation of mythopoeic themes in early Israel prevents an adequate understanding of the historical framework which always controlled the use of myth in Israel.

This reinterpretation of the history of Israel's early religion permits us to reopen the question of its origins in mythopoeic culture in a new way. If the imagery of the Divine Warrior is central in Israel's early traditions, how did this theme come to be available in mythopoeic thought for such vigorous reuse? Was there any *praeparatio* in myth from which such a move might have been made? Further, while Israel's use of the Divine Warrior and King imagery has strong continuities with myth, there are some noteworthy discontinuities as well. What are these changes and what, in myth, may have permitted or given rise to them?

II

That the Divine Warrior and King should prove to be a theme common to the Bible and contemporary Canaanite culture suggests a fact seldom noted in discussions of Israel and her environment: there are strong political and historical elements in both mythopoeic and biblical thought. The usual contrast between "myth" and "history" seems to be a too simple manner of juxtaposing the two world-views in question. For example, if one scans the section "Historical Texts" of James Pritchard's *Ancient Near Eastern Texts*, it is clear that ancient rulers and nations often interpreted their historical and political fortunes with direct reference to the role played in them by deities of the Divine Warrior type. In Mesopotamia, there is frequent mention of Enlil, Marduk (Bel), Dagan, Adad, Ninurta, Ashur, etc. The Moabite stone interprets the fortunes of Mesha as the doings of Chemosh. In Ugaritic literature, the Keret and Aqhat epics show that the events of men and nations were understood to be shaped by El, Baal, and Anat. In the Homeric epics, perhaps the most strongly "politicized" of ancient mythopoeic material, the progress of the Trojan War is understood to be the reflex of machinations among the Olympian deities, with Zeus the principal determiner of historical events.[4]

To be sure, the primary emphasis in mythopoeic thought is upon the powers, structures, and processes of nature. These aspects of nature present themselves to man in a plurality of personal forms, the gods, those beings in whom man attempts to deal with nature. Something of the range of these powers of nature embodied in the gods is revealed in synopses of selected ancient Near Eastern and early Greek creation myths. In the first tablet of the Babylonian *Enuma Elish,* we find the following generations of the gods:

> Before there was anything else, there was only Apsu [fresh water] and Tiamat [salt water], mixing their waters together.
> They begot Lahmu and Lahamu [fresh and salt water silt].
> They in turn had Anshar and Kishar [heaven and earth "horizons"].
> They produced Anu [heaven].
> Anu fathered Ea [the quick-wit of fresh water].
> Ea produced Marduk [the storm wind].

A Canaanite creation account preserved in the *Praeparatio evangelica* of Eusebius of Caesarea (I.10.7–14) lists several generations of gods, beginning with elemental substances and moving to the more complex personalities of the pantheon:

> Everything begins with the East Wind and "Baau" [wet, chaotic stuff].
> These beget Aion ["Eternity"].
> Aion produces Light, Fire, and Flame.
> From these come four cosmic mountains: Cassius, Lebanon, Anti-Lebanon, and Amanus.
> These, in turn, beget two temple sites of cosmic attributes: "Highest Heaven" and Ushu (two old temple districts in Tyre).
> They produce Heaven and Earth.
> Heaven and Earth bear El and Dagan ["God" par excellence and "Grain"].
> El and Dagan then father all the other gods of the pantheon: Baal, Yamm, Mot, Anat, etc.

A formally similar account of origins is found in the *Theogony* of Hesiod:

> First, "Chaos came into being,"
> Followed by Earth, Tartaros [the Deep Underworld], and Eros.
> From Chaos came Erebos [the entrance of the underworld] and Night.
> Earth then produced her mate Heaven and the [cosmic] Mountains.
> She also produced Pontos [Sea] and Okeanos.
> Heaven and Earth begot Kronos and Rhea.
> They, in turn, produced Zeus, Hades, Poseidon, and the other Olympians.

In each of these accounts the same general pattern may be seen: the old generations of the gods are the large substances, structures, and components of the universe as it now stands (Water, Air, Light, Mountains, etc.); the younger generations are the more refined powers of nature which tend to operate within the larger structures provided by their ancestors (Storm-Wind, Grain, the power of Death in the Underworld, etc.).

A further distinction of importance may be made between these two classes of gods in mythopoeic thought. The old gods tend to be much less active in the immediate affairs of men and nature. They may be called the "theogonic gods": they do little more than produce other gods, rarely participate in the cult, are cited infrequently in the epics, and almost never appear in human personal names. The younger deities, usually the offspring of Heaven and Earth where they appear, are much more active in the seasonal and daily affairs of men and nature. These we shall call the "political gods": they form a political assembly the decisions, loves, intrigues, and conflicts of which affect directly the life of men and nations and determine the seasonal and daily fluctuations in nature. They embody powers of nature, to be sure, but have an added political or "historical" dimension to their activities. Without exception, it is the gods of this class through whom the ancients interpreted historical events, as suggested above. Important among these deities, understandably, are those possessing special abilities in divine warfare and executive power.

Although it has not often been noted, there is some evidence that in the second millennium the old theogonic deities increasingly were viewed as ineffective, even otiose, while the political gods were increasingly vigorous. This is somewhat less true of Mesopotamia than Canaan but we can see the tendency at work. In *Enuma Elish* the older gods are rendered confused and powerless by Tiamat's threat upon the divine community. They must turn to a vigorous young political deity (Marduk) and a new form of political organization (kingship) to re-establish order. The demise of the last vigorous theogonic deity is achieved when Marduk defeats Tiamat and reshapes her inert corpse into the completed universe now occupied by gods and men. This in turn permits the placement of the gods in dependable circuits for seasonal reckoning and the creation of the human race. From the Ugaritic texts of the fifteenth and fourteenth centuries we hear only of the younger ("political") deities in the Canaanite pantheon. We must go to old divine witness lists in treaties and the traditions preserved in Eusebius and Damascius to reconstruct the old generations of the gods. In fact, these sources and biblical evidence suggest that by the ninth century even El, the son of Heaven and Earth and first executive of the divine assembly, is no longer an effective political force among gods and men, a fate very much like that of Kronos, his equivalent in Greek mythology. From Homer we learn of many exploits of the political deities, but we must go to Hesiod and second-millennium Hittite and Hurrian sources to learn of the old theogonic generations.

Further evidence of the change in status of the two classes of gods is provided in those traditions which show that the younger deities function within and exercise control over those very portions of the universe embodied in the older gods. In *Enuma Elish* Enki and Marduk refashion Apsu and Tiamat into disciplined strata of the cosmos in preemptory fashion. Enki reduces Apsu to the controlled fresh water now found underground, building upon him the palace in which he and his wife produce Marduk (Tablet I.60–78). Marduk splits the inflated body of Tiamat "like a clam shell," making from it the sky, earth, and underworld in which he now exercises supreme control over the affairs of men and gods (Tablet IV.128 ff.). In Greek tradition, Zeus, Hades, and Poseidon divide and rule over those realms of heaven, underworld, and sea which in Hesiod's *Theogony* consist of several primordial deities (*Iliad* 15.190). The Homeric epics presume that these are fixed and inert arenas within which the political gods interact. In the Ugaritic epics, El, Baal, Mot, and Yamm similarly divide and govern affairs in heaven, earth, sea, underworld, and the cosmic mountains, all structures of nature embodied in old theogonic gods in the traditions reported in Eusebius. In the "first cycle" in Eusebius (I.10.1–7) we find the very striking situation in which the old theogonic gods have been reduced to impersonal substances, treated in proto-philosophical fashion, while the political deities continue to function in their mythopoeic manner.[5]

This suggests that during the second millennium, the period including part of the patriarchal period, the time of Moses, and the early Tribal League, mythopoeic thought in the ancient world exhibited some characteristics similar to those of the biblical world-view:

1) The most important figure is the Divine Warrior and King, the vigorous leader of the divine world who assembles the cosmic host about him, routs the forces of disorder and evil, establishes his kingship on the cosmic mountain, and, chairing the divine assembly, guarantees justice among gods and men. About the figure of the Divine Warrior are concentrated the political and historical motifs of the younger deities in mythopoeic thought; in the figure of Yahweh Israel finds the origin and understanding of its salvation history.

2) The most important disruption to this schema is the challenge to the chief executive of the divine assembly which comes from other political deities. In both mythopoeic thought and the Bible, historical enemies present little real challenge to this hegemony and are dispensed with in cursory fashion. The more important challenges come from Tiamat or Kingu for Marduk, Yamm or Mot for Baal, Hades or Poseidon for Zeus, and the chief political gods of Canaan or Babylon for Yahweh. In every case, the basic challenge is to the divine kingship and its control of the divine assembly, the local powers of nature, and the destiny of mankind.

3) The larger structures of the universe (those embodied in the old theogonic gods in myth) tend to be viewed as inert and fixed structures in which the political activities of the younger gods and the daily and seasonal changes in nature occur. The biblical narrative before the exile proceeds on the confident assumption that heaven and earth and the major appurtenances thereto remain essentially fixed and dependable and upon this stage Israel's salvation history is worked out. As in much of mythopoeic culture of the time, there are only slight hints of the old personalities and independence of the old gods, and in both cultures these tend to occur in treaty contexts. In Deut. 4:26, 30:19, and 31:28 Moses calls Heaven and

Earth to witness against Israel should she violate the stipulations of the Mosaic covenant, very much as, for example, the Sefire treaty is concluded in the presence of both political deities and ". . . Heaven and Earth, the (Abysmal) Springs and Sources, and Day and Night" (Text A, 11–12). When the prophets indict Israel for covenant violation, we also find references to cosmic powers with theogonic antecedents as though they too had been invoked as treaty witnesses. Isaiah summons "heaven and earth" (1:2), Jeremiah "the heavens" (2:12), and Micah the "mountains, hills, and foundations of the earth" (6:1–2) in prosecuting Israel in covenant lawsuit.

Within the context of a stable cosmos, the biblical world-view permits unpredictable daily and seasonal changes in the lesser aspects of nature, much as is the case in mythopoeic thought. As in myth, this is understood to arise from political developments within the divine council, usually developments initiated or conducted by the Divine Warrior and King figure. Decisions in the council generate correlated activities in nature and history. In the "Lamentation over the Destruction of Ur" the behavior of weather, flock, and field are inextricably interwoven with that of the rampaging enemy armies.[6] When Baal is defeated by the challenger Mot, his descent into the underworld means both the end of weather favorable for crops and increased vulnerability for his people.[7] Ancient Near Eastern treaties often contain curses which bring upon the offending party, subject to determination by the divine council, a variety of political and natural disasters.[8]

In the biblical tradition actions of the Divine Warrior occasion coordinated abrupt changes in nature and history. The two occasions on which this is most likely are Holy Warfare and covenant violation. Traditions of the Exodus (Exodus 7–15) and the Conquest and defense of the land (Joshua and Judges) stress the military role played by the sun, wind, hail, rivers, the Reed Sea, and other aspects of nature. Covenant violation may mean not only loss of land and people to enemies serving as Yahweh's agent of punishment, but also cessation of the productive powers of the land (cf. I Kings 17:1 and 18:1–2; Isa. 3:1; Jer. 14:1–6).

III

To this point it has been argued that there are elements in the biblical world-view which find strong antecedents in the mythopoeic world-view contemporary with Israel's formative years. The shift in emphasis toward the younger political deities, with the figure of the Divine Warrior and King as the most potent expression of this emphasis, and the corresponding downgrading of the older gods may be seen as a *praeparatio* for the central biblical concern with Yahweh the Divine Warrior and King who deals with

Israel politically and historically in the context of an essentially stable natural order.

At this point, however, we must recognize and deal with an element in biblical thought which sets it apart from its mythopoeic environment. Although depicted as the Divine Warrior and King, Yahweh is never a manifestation of or encompassed within any part of nature. The notion that the divine transcends every aspect of the universe is always assumed in Israel's treatment of Yahweh's relations with both history and nature. This feature alone radically distinguishes the Divine Warrior in biblical tradition from the same motif in adjacent cultures and produces important consequences. Athough Yahweh is free to use the storm wind and associated meteorological phenomena in holy warfare, he stands over and separate from them (cf. Exodus 15), unlike the divine warriors Baal, Marduk, or Zeus. If necessary, Yahweh may be explicitly disassociated from these aspects of nature (cf. I Kings 19:9 ff.). This means that Yahweh's political hegemony cannot seriously be challenged by one or another power of nature, whatever form it may take. Unlike Baal, for example, whose supremacy must be defended against the power of chaos in the sea or the power of death emanating from the underworld, Yahweh's kingship stands above the fluctuations of seasons or cycles in nature. This also means that relations between Yahweh and Israel may take political and historical forms of long duration, permitting the structure of covenantal relationships (both promissory and conditional) which govern that relationship. It also means that even in those periods in Israel's history in which the imagery associated with the Divine Warrior permitted the strong resurgence of mythopoeic themes (principally the ideology of the monarchy and apocalyptic), the actions of God in the historical continuum provide the important clues for Israel's self-understanding.

Are there mythopoeic antecedents to this notion of the transcendence of the divine? There is some evidence that there are subtle but incomplete tendencies in this direction in ancient thought. In his essay "Formative Tendencies in Sumerian Religion," Thorkild Jacobsen outlines the development of early Mesopotamian myth.[9] He traces the responses to the divine from the early "intransitive" stage, in which the numinous is largely circumscribed by and limited to the natural form of which it is the embodiment, to the later anthropomorphic stage, in which the gods assume more vigorous political and social functions and begin to transcend their earlier localized forms. At no time, however, is the earlier totally supplanted by the later, even if the first survives only as an emblem of the deity used in its iconography. Jacobsen points out that in some cases the human form of the divine developed an open hostility toward its earlier form, as in the case of Aspu and Enki or Ninurta and the Zu-bird.

We can see that the movement from "intransitivity" toward "transitivity" is accelerated in the second millennium by the increased importance of the political deities, as noted earlier. Among these political deities we may detect different degrees of attachment to the natural form or power of which they are the embodiment. Figures such as Marduk, Ishtar, Baal, Mot, or Anat, although politically active members of the divine assembly, function in ways closely related to the natural power they represent, for example, the storm wind, the capricious spring fertility, the power of death, etc. Deities such as Enki, Kothar, or Zeus are further removed from their antecedents in nature. Most of their activity in traditions from this period is better understood, however, when their natural roots are kept in mind. A few figures seem to be purely political in activity, leaving few if any hints of the aspect of nature which once may have more vigorously informed their character. Most important for our purposes here is the Canaanite senior executive deity El. His name and common epithets, such as "Father of Years," "Creator of Heaven and Earth," etc., allude to his strong political interests and his involvement with important aspects of nature, but resist efforts to determine what part of nature he represents in himself.[10] In the third cycle of traditions preserved in Eusebius and Hittite sources we catch a glimpse of El in his earlier, more vigorous years, plotting, warring, and making love. The Ugaritic texts allude to his earlier exploits (see especially the text "Birth of the Gods"), but it is clear that his old powers are slipping. Allusions in the Bible to Baal and Baal's consort Asherah, the former mate of El, suggest that El has been supplanted in the Canaanite pantheon of the Iron Age.[11] It is entirely possible that we are victims of our lack of information here, but the available evidence suggests that in El we encounter the most strongly "transitive" deity in the ancient Near East proximate to Israel. His entire character seems to be defined by political and social activities. In the end, however, he too is succeeded by other, more vigorous political deities with clearer antecedents in nature. The transcendent dimensions of El's character thus have their own particular limitation.

The above suggests that there is in mythopoeic thought a tendency toward the quality of divine transcendence from nature fundamental to the biblical world-view. No figure seems to reach the dimensions of "transitivity" expressed in Yahweh, but again one may detect a *praeparatio* for this strong biblical theme in myth. It is understandable that this and the emphasis upon political and historical activity by the divine should accompany one another in biblical thought and that both should be susceptible to emphasis and transformation in the formative years of Israel.

IV

This leads us to a final matter, the question of the specific vehicle by which Israel's appropriation, emphasis, and subtle transformation of these mythopoeic elements might have occurred. Our proposal is that it was the special "clan-deity" or "God of the Fathers" relationship between the patriarchs and Yahweh which provided the "mutation" from mythopoeic to salvation-historical world-view.

We know something of the kind of relationship which seems to have existed between Abraham and his ancestry and Yahweh from studies of Mesopotamian and Amorite "clan-deity" relationships in the second millennium.[12] The Ugaritic texts provide some examples of this same relationship in a milieu more proximate to Israel. In the Keret and Aqhat epics we have two instances in which prominent clan chieftains find themselves without heirs and appeal to El to provide them offspring. Although other deities are involved, the implication of both texts is that the individuals in question enjoy a special clan relationship with the senior executive deity such that the future of the family is a legitimate object of El's special concern. Although fragmentary, both epics reveal the intimate involvement of the deity in the political fortunes of the family through more than one generation. The parallels with the patriarchal traditions in Genesis are obvious.

In another study, F. M. Cross provides a careful study of the divine epithets in the patriarchal traditions of Genesis.[13] Updating and proceeding beyond the helpful work of Alt, Cross determines that the "El epithets" of Genesis, El, Olam, El Shadday, El Elyon, and the like, can be shown to be epithets of the Canaanite god El. It even seems likely that *Yahweh* is a shortened form of a sentence epithet of El. This makes excellent sense of the biblical tradition in Exodus 3 and 6 that Yahweh is identified with the deity with whom the patriarchs enjoyed a promissory covenantal relationship. Cross concludes by outlining several important features of biblical tradition "which are best explained if Yahweh is recognized as originally a cultic name of El, and if we suppose that the god Yahweh split off from El in the radical differentiation of his cultus, ultimately ousting El from his place in the divine council, and condemning the ancient powers to death (Psalm 82)" (pp. 256–257).

Here we seem to have evidence of precisely the kind of bridging mechanism which would permit and explain the emergence of the biblical worldview from its mythopoeic environment. In a period when the political deities are on the ascendancy in myth, Israel's founding clan enjoyed a special relationship with the chief executive and warrior deity of West Semitic culture. This is also the deity who seems to portray the most heightened form of transcendence over the natural manifestation of the gods in myth. The unusually good fortune of the patriarchs over several generations and especially the events of the Mosaic period, demonstrating Yahweh's clear dominance over the powers of nature and history, pushed the political and transitivizing tendencies of mythopoeic thought into a qualitatively new order of relationship between man and the divine. Thus there are both continuities and discontinuities between biblical and ancient Near Eastern thought. Israel's fundamental claims about the nature of reality had antecedents in mythopoeic thought, but these underwent sufficient emphasis and transformation to produce a new world-view.

The author expresses his thanks to the Humanities Development Fund of Earlham College for the support which permitted the research and writing of this article.

NOTES

1. A striking recent example of this view may be found in the Introduction to E. A. Speiser's *Genesis,* AB, vol. 1 (1964); see esp. pp. XLIII–LII.

2. A recent work of some note stressing Israel's similarity with her environment is that of Bertil Albrektson, *History and the Gods* (Lund, 1967).

3. *Biblical Motifs: Origins and Transformations,* ed. A. Altmann, *Studies and Texts,* III (Cambridge, Mass., 1966), 11–30.

4. A more detailed discussion of the relation between myth and history and a helpful typology by which to describe shifts in this relation may be found in Paul D. Hanson, "Jewish Apocalyptic Against Its Near Eastern Environment," *RB* 78 (1971), 31–58.

5. This has important implications for our understanding of the emergence of philosophical thought from its mythopoeic background, on which see my forthcoming article, "The Transformation of Myth in the Early Presocratics."

6. See the translation of S. N. Kramer, in *ANET,* pp. 455 ff.

7. Text 67. v–vi; see H. L. Ginsberg's translation in *ANET,* p. 139.

8. A handy summary of this phenomenon and its appearance in the Bible is found in D. H. Hillers, *Treaty Curses and the Old Testament Prophets* (Rome, 1964).

9. *BANE,* pp. 353–368.

10. See the article "'El" by F. M. Cross in *Theologisches Wörterbuch zum alten Testament,* Band I (1970), 259–279.

11. The most important study here remains M. H. Pope, *El in the Ugaritic Texts* (Leiden, 1955), with supplements by P. D. Miller, "El the Warrior," *HTR* 60 (1967), 411–431.

12. Much remains to be done here by those who control the primary material. The comments by T. Jacobsen in the last note of the article by Cross cited immediately below are most suggestive.

13. "Yahweh and the God of the Patriarchs," *HTR* 55 (1962), 225–259.

5. Moses in Historical and
Theological Perspective

WILLIAM FOXWELL ALBRIGHT

JOHNS HOPKINS UNIVERSITY

MOSES, probably born in the late fourteenth century B.C. and died about the middle of the thirteenth, was the founder of ancient Israel, according to all biblical testimony. He is said to have led his enslaved people out of Egypt through the deserts of Sinai and Midian to the border of Canaan, which had been promised to their forefather Abraham. As founder, he established Israel's religious and civil organization. This tradition is doubted even today, but it is strongly supported by historical analogy, and is now being confirmed by a rapidly increasing mass of evidence uncovered by archaeologists and philologians. Post-biblical religious tradition has often treated him as the author of the entire Pentateuch.

In the late eighteenth and early nineteenth centuries there grew up in Germany an increasingly critical approach to the problems of Pentateuchal tradition. Following earlier suggestions about the use of the divine names *Elohim,* "God," and *Yahweh,* which became the personal name of the one God of Israel, they were used as clues to the authorship of different prose portions of the Pentateuch.

This approach was then combined with a rigid theory of the evolution of Israelite religion and literature along Hegelian lines. W. Vatke, followed by J. Wellhausen (1878), were the founders of the school of radical critics who still dominate the field of research in some countries. Wellhausen was a brilliant Arabist and Hebraist who did not dispute the ultimate historicity of Moses, but lowered the date of the composition of the various "documents" of the Pentateuch (J, E, D, P) to the ninth–fifth centuries B.C. This extreme view gradually won the day in most scholarly circles until about forty years ago, when the archaeological reaction set in, proving that such low dating

This paper, originally designed as an article for an encyclopedia, replaces a paper on "Moses in Historical and Theological Perspective" being prepared by Albright at the time of his death. [F.M.C.]

and extreme skepticism about the historical traditions of Israel will not stand serious analysis.

Soon afterwards such outstanding scholars as M. Noth recognized that the "documents" were really different editions or recensions of the same original traditions and not independent sources. At the same time the tendency toward earlier dating of much Pentateuchal prose and Hebrew verse in general found increasing support among Old Testament scholars. This tendency has been powerfully reinforced by a flood of new archaeological data which have affected every possible approach to Pentateuchal problems.

Here we accept the view that the prose documents are different editions or recensions of common source material. That is, they generally reflect the same original oral and written tradition, which was edited by men entrusted with the task of passing on normative tradition by word of mouth or in manuscript form. In view of the well-known fact that all over the Old World history was first transmitted in poetic form and either sung or chanted to the accompaniment of music, it would be very strange indeed if the late dates that used to be assigned to early Hebrew poetry could be maintained against clear archaeological evidence. Independent traditions are of special value, since they enable historians to see events and personalities in proper perspective, and thus expand our understanding of their historical meaning.

ARCHAEOLOGICAL LIGHT ON THE MOSAIC PERIOD

Our knowledge of the ancient East has been increasing steadily in all areas. We can now draw on established fact to tell whether an episode or allusion to life and customs is characteristic of a given period or environment. We can generally fix the language and period to which an ancient Oriental name belongs.

The importance of cuneiform sources has recently been increasing rapidly. The Amarna tablets (fourteenth century B.C.) became known about 1890. In 1907 came the first cuneiform tablets from the Hittite capital at Boğazköy, east of Ankara, followed by many thousands more (sixteenth–thirteenth centuries B.C.). The sensational tablet finds at Ugarit on the North Syrian coast (fourteenth–thirteenth centuries B.C.) began in 1929. These finds and a host of others span the lifetime of Moses. In 1901 came the Code of Hammurabi. Since this code dated at least four centuries before Moses, the extraordinary similarity of some of its content to the Book of the Covenant (Exodus 21–23) aroused tremendous interest. This find has since been followed by discovery of many other cuneiform codes of law, including another Semitic Babylonian code (from Eshnunna) dating less than a century before the Hammurabi Code and also showing many similarities to Mosaic legislation. The Middle Assyrian laws (late twelfth century B.C.) and the somewhat earlier Hittite laws are useful for perspective. Remains of three still earlier Sumerian law codes (between 2100 and 1800 B.C.) have been recovered; they give us the background of all the other codes, including the Hebrew (see below). These laws are supplemented by great masses of legal and business tablets now numbered in hundreds of thousands. Thanks to all this rich material we can place the legal institutions of Moses in proper perspective and can distinguish between successive stages in its early development.

The Old Assyrian tablets (nineteenth and eighteenth centuries B.C.), the Mari tablets (eighteenth century B.C.), the Nuzi tablets (fifteenth century B.C.), and the Alalakh tablets (mostly from the seventeenth and fifteenth centuries B.C.) illuminate social organization and commercial relations of the early Hebrews. Tablets from these sites as far as excavated already number tens of thousands.

The Hebrew Egyptian Experience

There can no longer be any reasonable doubt as to the antiquity of the Patriarchal tradition. We now know the general course of Northwest-Semitic history in Mesopotamia, Syria, and Palestine from the twentieth century B.C. on down, and Hebrew traditions fit very well into successive phases of this history. The seminomadic tribes and clans were already settling down in different parts of the Fertile Crescent, and were actively engaged in trade and commerce, like the biblical Patriarchs in Israelite tradition. The personal names are often the same, and nearly all belong to the same or closely related dialects. Many of the tribal and clan names recur contemporaneously in Mesopotamia, Syria, and Palestine, as well as in the Pentateuch. The religion of the Patriarchs is now fairly well known, as far as it can be gleaned from personal names and contemporary cuneiform tablets from Mari. We find most of the old Semitic appellations of the supreme deity not only in Patriarchal and late pre-Mosaic names, as well as in the early poetry of Israel, but also in contemporary cuneiform and Egyptian sources. Great emphasis was laid on the importance of the ancestral divinity of the clan or tribe by these seminomads, and this is reflected in the Mosaic tradition by references in Exodus 3 and elsewhere to the "God of the Fathers."

The most archaic covenant forms in the Bible go back to this period, in which the covenant structure of society was governed by intertribal relations and especially by agreements between merchants, caravaneers, and rulers of countries of origin and destination as well as of intermediate districts on caravan routes. It is no accident that the three cities most intimately connected with Patriarchal tradition, Ur, Haran (Harran), and Nahor, are specifically mentioned as caravan centers in early cuneiform tablets.

There is now ample evidence that the Hebrews of Moses' time were far from being barbarians. For one thing, we now have the oldest known inscriptions in alphabetic script, based partly on Egyptian, which was the forerunner of all historical alphabets of the East and West. This "Proto-Sinaitic" script is now well documented in inscriptions from Sinai itself as well as from Palestine and Egypt.

We now have independent evidence for the close connection of the Hebrews with Tanis (biblical Zoan and Rameses), as well as for the intensive settling of the previously almost unoccupied northeastern Delta by Semites and other foreigners after 1700 B.C. Among the occupations and kinds of labor which we can now connect specifically with the Hebrews were mining in Sinai and Nubia, transportation for the state, production of wine. Biblical tradition confirms these three kinds of labor and adds building operations for the king.

It was once thought by most critical scholars that the names of persons mentioned in Exodus and Numbers were mostly fictitious. Now this cannot be said any longer, since the names of Israelites contemporary with Moses are nearly all typical of the people and period. For instance, the names of the two midwives, Shiphrah and Puah (Exod. 1:15), were quite recently labeled "later inventions" by a leading authority on Hebrew proper names, but they are now known to be quite authentic.

It is particularly significant that the sculpture and carved representations associated with Northwest-Semitic inscriptions in Sinai (fifteenth century B.C.) are invariably Egyptianizing in character, with no trace of direct influence from Palestine or Syria. Similarly, the personal names in these same Proto-Sinaitic inscriptions are in part Egyptian. We cannot, therefore, be surprised to find Egyptian names in the immediate circle of Moses.

MOSES IN EGYPT

The name of Moses (Hebrew *Moshe*) is derived from Egyptian *mōse* (earlier *māse*), "is born," which occurs as the second element in many personal names of the age, such as Remose, "the sun-god is born." The abbreviated form was especially popular in this very period, and the slight phonetic shifts took place within Hebrew. The names of several other members of the family of Moses and Aaron were also Egyptian, as has long been known. Particularly instructive is *Phinehas,* which stands for the common Egyptian name *Penahse,* "The Negro."

Just what Moses' relationship with the Egyptian court was, we do not know, but there seems no reason to doubt that he was indeed brought up in close connection with it, and that he was a bright lad who received an exceptionally good education. Even if much later traditions about Moses' learning are exaggerated, it is difficult to imagine that anyone without an exceptional background could produce the enduring structure of religion, law, and organization which Moses left to posterity.

MOSES AND MIDIAN

The Midianite adventure of Moses is one of the most controversial episodes in biblical history. It is now also one of the best supported traditions in the earlier books of the Old Testament. Toward the end of the fourteenth century B.C., as we know from the latest archaeological discoveries of Beno Rothenberg (1969), Egypt developed copper mining in the region then occupied by Midianites and their subject tribes. His excavations at the ancient copper-mining site of Mene'iye (Israeli Timna) have brought to light remains of a small Egyptian temple founded by Sethos I (1315–1304 B.C.) and occupied by succeeding Pharaohs until the mid-twelfth century B.C. Here we find, as in other parts of Edom during this period, that even the pottery shows strong Egyptian influence. Now evidence also shows that the Midianites were the leading caravaneers of western Arabia, and further explains why they were so much interested in controlling the trade routes through Edom, Moab, and Sinai. Careful re-examination of the passages where the relationship between Moses and the priest of Midian and his family are mentioned shows clearly that the latter have been misunderstood. Jethro was himself a member of the Midianite and Edomite clan of Reuel, and Hobab, who is often identified with him, was Moses' son-in-law. In view of this situation, Moses' intimate relationship with the Midianite metalworkers (Kenites) and his marriage to Jethro's daughter, as well as his close attachment to Jethro and Hobab, are highly significant.

THE EXODUS

Fortunately we have several slightly divergent accounts of the Exodus, which are preserved in the Song of Miriam in Exod. 15:1–18 as well as in other prose and verse forms. In vs. 21 the first line (by which well-known poems were usually identified in the ancient Near East) is specifically attributed to Miriam. The Exodus proper is described in prose in Exodus 13, 14, and 15: 19 ff., as well as more briefly in some other passages. The prose texts all belong to the so-called J E P complex, which consists of prose narrative written down on the basis of written and oral material, both prose and verse, about the tenth century B.C. and later re-edited.

The discovery at Ugarit of long Canaanite epics and hymns, copied in the fourteenth and thirteenth centuries B.C., clearly shows that the Song of Miriam must have been composed under the influence of Canaanite poetic style and phraseology in the then-spoken Hebrew dialect. Owing to its extraordinary popularity, it is probable that this poem has survived in virtually its original form, except that ancestral Hebrew was still in an early stage of development and its pronunciation in the time of Moses would be about as different from that of Classical Hebrew as Chaucer's English is from the English of today. Other shorter and longer poems and snatches of verse are strewn through the prose account of the Exodus and wilderness wanderings, making it very clear that we have to deal with extremely ancient tradition preserved orally and sung when the past of Israel was rehearsed.

A comparison of the verse and prose traditions of the Exodus proves clearly that the prose tradition rests on original poetic sources, and that if we compare the surviving Israelite traditions, we read of a strong southeast wind which blew the shallow swamp water of the Sea of Reeds northwards, making it possible for the Israelites to cross. It was then followed by a strong north wind which drove the sea water in billows over the pursuing Egyptians.

An interesting fact which could not have been recognized before the publication of the Qumran (Cave 4) Scrolls, with their testimony as to the existence of sometimes sharply divergent recensions of the later Hebrew Bible, is that the list of stations along the wilderness route of escape was originally couched in fixed verse form, with some verses from the beginning and end of the original recapitulation still preserved. This means that the list itself was extremely old and probably goes back to the Mosaic period or soon afterwards. Important recensional variants are, however, preserved only in the portion of the list which begins with Rameses, later Tanis (biblical Zoan) but not, as sometimes thought, identical with the second Hyksos capital, Avaris.

SINAI AND KADESH

In the time of Moses, the peninsula of Sinai was not a complete desert, as most of it is now. In those days charcoal burners, goats, and camels had not yet destroyed the forests of scrub tamarisk and other vegetation which then dotted the peninsula wherever there was some subsurface water. There was much more such water, which was preserved by vegetation cover and which in turn provided food for a great many game animals, such as wild cattle, wild sheep and goats, and antelopes, as well as large and small fowl. There were also a great many more small animals, and much more fish in the surrounding arms of the Red Sea.

Owing to the vastly greater stand of tamarisks, there was, in favorable years, a great deal of manna, shown by F. B. Bodenheimer to have been excreted, like honey, by two related species of scale insects on the branches of the trees and generally collected under the trees. In a favorable season this sweet, nutritive substance would support a considerable number of people. In any case, the manna and the "windfall" when migrating quail were blown inland were enough to sustain the Israelites until they were able to find game animals and feed their own flocks. Among the followers of Moses must have been some who, like him, were already familiar with the desert. His son-in-law, the Midianite Hobab, became their guide, as vividly described in a verse quotation (Num. 10:31).

Two places in the desert wanderings are especially stressed: Mount Sinai and Kadesh-barnea. The latter complex consisted of two adjacent oases, each of which had an abundant flow of water. In antiquity they were surrounded by fortresses and semipermanent settlements (especially in the early Patriarchal Age and the period beginning with the thirteenth century B.C.). Because of the quantity of available water they were exceedingly important caravan stations on the early route from Palestine to Egypt, which did not yet follow the coast (since northeastern Egypt was mostly swampland before the Hyksos period), but went straight across from Arad and Beersheba in southern Palestine by way of these oases to the southern end of the Isthmus of Suez. This caravan route is now well attested for the First Egyptian Dynasty as well as for the twentieth–nineteenth centuries B.C.

The question of the number of Hebrews involved in the Exodus is impossible to settle, especially since the total population of Palestine can scarcely have exceeded a quarter million at that time. Nor can we say just what was implied by the terms *asafsuf* and *'erebrab,* which meant roughly "unorganized mob" and "mixed crowd." This presumably means that most of the escaped serfs had no definite tribal status. They may well have included people of quite different ethnic origins. We now know, however, from better understanding of the Testament of Jacob (Genesis 49) and from data unearthed by archaeologists, that biblical tradition is quite correct in putting back the settlement in Palestine of some Hebrew tribes in the Patriarchal Age—possibly several centuries before the Exodus.

Egypt and Palestine were both parts of the same empire, whether Hyksos or native Egyptian, during virtually this entire period. Consequently there must have been normal communication back and forth, and tribal kinship might be just as well defined as among Arab tribes of the Middle Ages. There was great emphasis on tribal and clan relationships, which were often remembered for centuries, just as among other seminomadic groups which have reached a certain stage of culture but are still without definite territorial connection. Tribal and clan affiliation therefore takes the place of the territorial bond which is so important for both animals and men at relatively advanced stages of evolution. There was, therefore, no great difficulty in selecting twelve groupings to receive tribal names. In other words, it is highly probable that the traditional tribal names (though not entirely consistent in any two independent lists) date back in general to the Mosaic period or earlier. The twelve-tribe confederation was analogous in some important respects to the early Greek and Italic amphictyony, where tribes or towns were grouped together as a national unit around a central sanctuary. That this confederation was suggested to Moses by his Midianite father-in-law is quite possible, since the Ishmaelites were also divided into twelve tribes (Gen. 25:12 ff.).

There is no good reason why Mount Sinai should have been a volcano— much less that it should have been situated in Hejaz (West Arabia), as held by some. The name has nothing to do with the Sumerian moon-god *Zuen,* later *Sin,* but may well be a dialectal variant of Hebrew *seneh,* "thorn bush," especially since Moses is said to have received his first revelation at such a bush. In any case, it was located on one of the most convenient caravan routes leading from the Straits of Tiran northwest to the turquoise mines at Serabit el-Khadim and from there to Suez.

MOSES IN TRANSJORDAN

In order to escape easy Egyptian pursuit, Moses had to avoid the northern coast of Sinai, where there was then a well-built and much used chariot road to Gaza from Sile (near Qantara). At some time in the period of desert wandering an attempt was made by part of the Mosaic confederation to attack Palestine from Kadesh. But this attempt failed. Moses may also have had to avoid the Arabah Valley south of the Dead Sea between later Edom and Judah, because of Egyptian copper-mining colonies there (see above).

We are told in separate accounts of the Conquest of Transjordan in Numbers and Deuteronomy that the Israelites were refused permission to go through Edom and Moab. At that time there seems to have been some kind of condominium in which power was shared by Egyptians and Midianites, and the Edomites were vassals of both. The Israelites turned eastward toward the desert and went around Edom and Moab until they reached the territory of Sihon king of Heshbon. At that time Moab was evidently a very small country, and its northern part was in the hands of a ruler of unknown background. Unfortunately archaeology has not yet shed any light on either Sihon "the Amorite" or Og king of Bashan, though Heshbon has been partly excavated by Siegfried Horn, and Og's capital at Ashtaroth (Tell Ashtarah) by a Syrian expedition, the results of which are not yet known.

There is no way of determining just how long Moses lived after his conquest of central and northern Transjordan. The three divisions of forty years each in Moses' life are in accordance with much other Israelite chronological practice, closely paralleled by Phoenician and early Greek historical theory. According to a very ancient tradition, Moses survived the Balaam episode as well as the subsequent war between Israel and Midian, which decided to protect its sphere of power (Numbers 31).

The Balaam episode is of very great significance, since here again we have very archaic oracles in verse, which must go back, in part, at least, to the time of Balaam himself. He was apparently one of the first important converts to the religion of Moses after the adhesion of the Kenites. Later he defected to the Midianites.

The narrative of Moses' death provides a very interesting illustration of early Israelite popular beliefs about great heroes. There is no tradition anywhere in the Old Testament about the exact burial place of Moses. This omission probably reflects his own effort to prevent his burial place from becoming a paganizing sanctuary where the hero would receive semidivine honors, according to widespread Northwest-Semitic practice at that time.

The Work of Moses

The contribution of Moses has been a subject of controversy since the early nineteenth century. Opinions vary all the way from traditional acceptance of Moses as the towering figure he is represented in Orthodox Jewish and Christian tradition to the almost totally negative approach of many radical critics, both Christian and Jewish. The vast mass of material bearing on the ancient Near Eastern religions which has been uncovered by archaeologists and interpreted by philologians, shows clearly that Israelite monotheism, as represented by the writing prophets of Israel from the eighth to the sixth century B.C., has no real parallel anywhere else in the ancient world. It is just as unique as the discovery of generalized conceptual thought by the Greeks in the sixth century B.C. It has almost nothing in common with the polytheism and pantheism of either Hinduism or Buddhism. There was nothing passive or contemplative about the recorded faith of ancient Israel.

The view that Moses may best be compared to a pre-Islamic Arab diviner was strongly defended by the late Yehezkel Kaufmann, who considered Moses as the founder of Israel and its religion, but was skeptical about details of the historical tradition. To Kaufmann, Moses was a religious genius belonging to a people with native religious genius, just as Greek philosophy arose, he thought, among a people with native philosophical genius. Kaufmann, however, neglected the results of archaeology and modern research on the ancient Near East almost entirely.

In the light of our present knowledge about the background of Mosaic faith, a quite different approach is necessary. Moses was not, so far as we can tell from the verse and prose tradition, a conscious innovator, but a man on fire with reforming zeal. He endeavored to restore the faith of Israel in the God of the Fathers, who was identified with Yahweh, the appellation of God which was selected by Moses as best suited to his resolute monotheism. The fact that the oldest laws of Israel, as far as preserved, are inheritances from the Hebrew past in Mesopotamia, and that the sacrificial ritual appears to have been drawn in large part from earlier Hebrew and possibly Midianite sources, does not suggest deliberate innovation, but adaptation.

It can scarcely be accidental that the only consciously monotheistic system which can be proved to have existed in the entire ancient Near East outside of Israel was the solar monotheism of Amarna. Egypt was dominated by it during the reign of Akhnaten (or Ikhnaton), who reigned about 1375–1357 B.C., and it continued for a few years after the death of the king. In the following century it influenced the orthodox solar cult of Amun. Since the early life of Moses in Egypt may safely be placed in the latter part of the same fourteenth century B.C., it is very likely that Moses was familiar with vestigial remains of the Aten cult. The possible relation between this solar monotheism and the religion of Moses has been grossly exaggerated or caricatured by some writers. It is quite true that the monotheism of Amarna was not a philosophical system, but neither was the faith of Israel. It is also true that there were many survivals of polytheism in the relief paintings and inscriptions of Amarna. Amarna theology was centered around a threefold manifestation: the solar disk (Aten), divested of mythological trappings; the representation of the Aten in his temple at Amarna; and the king as earthly embodiment of the solar disk. The Aten is addressed as "the only god, beside whom there is no other" and as "creator of everything." There was, however, a world of difference between the morality of Amarna and that of the Mosaic tradition. In the Egyptian Aten cult we find no apparent interest in the common man; it was concentrated on the royal family and courtiers.

The personal name of Moses' God was probably selected from already recognized Hebrew liturgical appellations of deity. The consonants *YHWH* (pronounced *Yahweh*) may be shortened from the liturgical formula "He creates what comes into existence." Some scholars have objected to the translation of Yahweh as "Creator" on the ground that it is too abstract and philosophical a concept for early Israel. But in all early Afro-Asian languages, including Egyptian, Babylonian, and Northwest Semitic, such causatives of abstract verbs, meaning "to cause to be" and "to bring into existence," were common. No abstract "philosophical" thinking is involved.

It is probable that both the cultic and the secular legislation of Moses' time was simple in comparison to the development we find in the completed Pentateuch, and much simpler than the theory of early Judaism in the time of the Mishna (second century A.D.). We must not, however, jump to the opposite extreme. For instance, F. M. Cross has shown that the account of the tabernacle in Exodus refers to different stages of its development from the original Tent of Meeting in Sinai through the tabernacle in Shiloh. A similar development is probably true of both cultic and secular legislation of Moses. H. M. Wiener, a British jurist who was also a strong opponent of German historico-literary criticism, once pointed out that the original Mosaic legislation may not have included more than a third or so of the Pentateuchal legislation which has reached us, and that the remaining two-thirds includes later commentary and court decisions, as well as executive orders. Of course the same is true of the British constitution—as well as the Constitution of the United States, which is both the same as—and quite different from—what it was originally.

Mosaic legislation plainly distinguishes between case law and "apodictic" law (to use Alt's term) in the Pentateuch. The case law is identical in structure with early cuneiform case law, and many individual laws sometimes identical in content with similar laws in the two best known Semitic codes, those of Eshnunna (no later than 1725 B.C.) and Hammurabi (about 1690 B.C.). That the Hebrew case laws in the Pentateuch actually antedate the settlement of Israel in Palestine and are probably pre-Mosaic in large part is shown clearly by references to a distinction between Hebrew and non-Hebrew slaves. Since the term "Hebrew" included much more than Israel, and since it is never used by post-Mosaic Israelites of themselves, it is almost certainly a survival from earlier times, as already pointed out by Alt. A number of other references are also very archaic, especially those to oaths by the gods. The references in the Book of the Covenant (Exod. 21:6 and 12) are almost certainly a survival from older polytheistic times, though they later received a monotheistic interpretation.

Apodictic laws are variously formulated in the Pentateuch, and never have the conditional structure of the ancient Near Eastern case laws. They consist largely of moral and ethical commands and precepts. The Ten Commandments are the best illustration of this form of law. While there are antecedents in the Hittite treaties (which also contain the earliest examples of the covenant form—suzerainty treaty—which appears already in Joshua 24), in general they are morally and socially more advanced than anything yet known in ancient Near Eastern legislation, whether cultic or secular. In this respect Mosaic law is not only very ancient but more advanced than any comparable material in the ancient world.

Another important distinction made by various scholars is that between the *mishpatim* or the ancient customs and practices (applying to what we should call "common law") and the rules and regulations governing cultic, civil and military life. These laws are called by the generic name *hoq*, which means literally "what is carved or inscribed." We are now familiar with discoveries of inscribed walls (or remains of them) at the citadel of Amman (ninth century B.C.), Nora in Sardinia (ninth century B.C.), Gortyn in Crete (seventh century B.C.), the Agora in Athens (Draco's laws of homicide), and Shechem (Mount Ebal) in Israel at the time of the Conquest. These are enough to show that inscribing of specific laws, rules, and decrees on prominent stone structures was common among Ammonites, Phoenicians, and Greeks, as well as Israelites.

To some it may seem unlikely that the laws, rules, and regulations of the Pentateuch should belong to different periods and that the process of adding to them should have continued for many centuries after the Pentateuch was put into its present form. It has, however, been shown that some basic laws which one might expect to have in the Pentateuch appear first in later biblical literature. Several eminent rabbinic scholars have recently shown that some rabbinic legislation goes back to pre-exilic times, and fits perfectly into otherwise incomplete biblical texts. Most significant of all, perhaps, is the discovery of the so-called Temple Scroll from the Qumran area, already described by Y. Yadin; it contains a large number of miscellaneous laws and rules about festivals and military organization, etc., which must go back in part to quite early times, though the manuscript itself dates from about the Christian era.

Moses is the first great individual in history whose life and personality we can sketch with any degree of clarity. It is now reasonably certain that Akhnaten of Egypt was a tool in the hands of others and was not himself a great personality in any sense of the term. In the history of human progress it may safely be said that the two earliest outstanding personalities to emerge in their respective civilizations were Moses and Thales. To Moses we owe the emergence of higher religious life and moral culture in Western civilization. To Thales, seven centuries later, we owe the great leap forward in systematic conceptual thinking, just as Moses had pioneered in founding a religious structure with which scientific method could coexist.

6. Social Organization in Early Israel

GEORGE E. MENDENHALL
UNIVERSITY OF MICHIGAN

SINCE 1930 the system of "Twelve Tribes" of ancient Israel has been described either within the framework of Martin Noth's hypothesis that called upon Greek amphictyonies as an analogy,[1] or it has been rejected. So far as I have become aware, no one has come up with a viable alternative; though it is not, so far as I know, argued with any responsible scholarship, it seems to be assumed by the opponents of Noth's thesis that some sort of mystical racial identity came into existence with Abraham and has continued to the present day, complete with deity and territorial identity.

There are so many viable alternatives to the impasse presently characteristic of biblical studies that one hardly knows where to begin. Perhaps it would be best to point out that even the title of this paper is highly misleading from the point of view of the person (or scholar) who is innocent of contamination from recent anthropological literature. For what is meant by "social organization" by modern politicians, or the complex of academic organizations intent upon promoting their particularistic interests, is radically different *in kind* from social structures and relationships that have characterized most of mankind since the dawn of historical recording—and still do.[2] Therefore, the term "social organization" here does not refer to power structures with "rights and duties" stipulated in advance, but with a complex of mutually interacting social solidarities that were and are constantly changing. The primary problem is simple to ask, but extremely difficult to answer: Why was there any tradition of the "Twelve Tribes" of Jacob/Israel at all? To be sure, it was a part of the "orthodox" ideology, probably at the time of the united monarchy. It is the question because the later tradition was not interested at all in the historical and social problem of the *genesis* and function of the system, but only in its political utilization.[3] Therefore, we have an enormous problem of trying to penetrate the propaganda screen of the later political organization to ascertain some historical and religious foundations that could explain the existence of a surprisingly large—and persistent, as we know from the prophets—social and religious tradition that survived even the political cynicism of several centuries of the "united" and divided monarchies.

Noth's work on the "amphictyony" of the early Greek political alliances has been both extremely stimulating, and, it seems, increasingly under attack. H. M. Orlinsky "proved" in 1962[4] that ancient Israel was not a Greek amphictyony, which should not be surprising to anyone who has any concept at all of contrasts between ancient and modern history and social systems, or between a religious community and political expediency. The point of the historical and therefore religious problem is to understand, not merely to label, the functioning of a surprisingly large social solidarity that had seemingly a minimum of permanent political power structures or military organization and resources.

It should be clear by now that social structure, or social organization, is a product of many factors in which kinship is a relatively minor element.[5] Any culture of the ancient world is a complex of economic-technological, social, and ideological factors that have succeeded in maintaining an economic base for continuity through time. Some have succeeded in a degree high enough to have come to the attention of our contemporary world together with some sort of label. Since the preservation of records in writing in the ancient world is almost always the function of a highly specialized group in the broader culture, the documentation gives usually a minimum of information about non- or minimally literate sub-cultures. Therefore the attention of the scholarly world has been enormously dominated by the usual urban, specialized, groups of bureaucrats, priests, and merchants whose activities produce most of the surviving inscriptions. The result is that scholars are most poorly prepared to understand so historically important a society and culture as the ancient Twelve Tribes that contrasted in every way to the ancient pagan urban polytheisms and the attendant social polytomy that was held together by not much more than economic interests and military force. It is not surprising that for a century Old Testament scholars and now archaeologists have tried to explain everything non-urban by labeling it "nomadic," now demoted to the status of "seminomadic."

The proper starting point has been almost totally ignored, even though it is admitted by all ancient historians that it furnished the economic foundations of all the ancient empires: namely, the village peasantry. Theories about hordes of "land-hungry" nomads infiltrating the "sown" to become sedentary, or driving out whole populations in order to take over their fields are completely groundless, anachronistic, and even absurd. It is even comic in light of the fact that governments have been trying to force sedentarization upon nomadic groups ever since the Ottoman empire with minimal success. As one young teenager in the Syrian Desert told us explaining why he had run away from school in the city to return to his father's tent, "It is much better out here." The process in the Bronze Age was a gradual progression in the reverse direction: an increasing *withdrawal* from control of the central government, and an eventual adaptation to the desert environment made possible by the introduction of the domesticated camel.

A far more productive and stimulating approach is furnished by modern ethnography and anthropology that has developed to a point at which valid generalizations about peasant village culture can be utilized. The now typical analysis of peasant culture recognizes three interrelated factors to which it is necessary to add a fourth particularly when we deal with the ancient Twelve Tribe system of Israel.

Eric R. Wolf[6] has rightly emphasized the enormous importance of peasantry that has constituted the majority of all mankind from the dawn of history, and yet has been both exploited and despised by urban populations and establishments. We now know of village society highly developed already in the pre-pottery Neolithic, of enormous concentrations of villages in north-eastern Syria in the Chalcolithic period, and we have hundreds upon hundreds of names of villages and towns from the administrative archives of nearly every ancient empire. Whether or not the prehistoric villages should be labeled as "peasantry" is a matter of definition. According to Wolf, the difference between a "primitive" economy and a "peasant" economy lies in the fact that the latter has lost control of the means of production. It has passed "from the hands of the primary producers into the hands of groups that do not carry on the productive process themselves, but assume instead special executive and administrative functions, backed by the use of force."[7]

In other words, if the existence of the power superstructure is essential to the *definition* of a peasantry, the latter is essential to the very existence of a power structure. Someone has to produce the goods and services that the power structure redistributes, first to themselves, then to the various urban specialists who form the bureaucracy, the priesthoods, the artisans that make the luxury goods, and above all the military elite and their supporting crafts-men of the weapons industry. All these things are illustrated most abundantly in the various archives, as well as the correspondence of Syro-Palestinian city-states, and need not be further discussed here. What has been most inadequately realized is the fact that the "normative" present form of the ancient narratives about early Israel has been concocted precisely by such a power structure and its "intellectuals."

This description seems to apply with very little modification to the states of the Middle and Late Bronze Ages, the period immediately preceding Moses. But it applies equally well to the period of Solomon (if not David), and the results of the structure are seen in the events that followed the attempt of Rehoboam to become completely "modern."[8]

The problem that faces us is to understand the structure and functioning of a socioreligious organization that occupied the brief two centuries between those two political structures. For it seems clear that those two centuries saw the introduction and successful functioning of a socioideological complex that has had immeasurable impact upon the whole of Western civilization to the present day. The biblical traditions, meager as they are even supplemented by archaeological evidence, nevertheless strongly support the thesis that what modern scholarly endeavor has classified as interconnected economic-technological, social, and ideological factors are inseparably bound up also with a historical (i.e. nonstructured socially and therefore unpredictable) factor, all of which must be taken into consideration in any attempt to understand ancient Israel in the period of the "judges." It should perhaps be pointed out with an emphasis that verges upon offense, in view of widely accepted racist ideologies of the present, that "ethnic" factors are completely dismissed as historical factors. For an "ethnos" is the *product* of many factors, and the *cause* of nothing, to paraphrase an anthropologist speaking of social organization.[9] However, there can be no doubt that a pseudo-ethnic *ideology* has often been a most important political/military factor in history for some centuries, and in spite of the racist ideologies of the nineteenth and twentieth centuries and their horrible results seems in the present time actually to be increasing in popularity and political power. (One can only expect that some day the various Witch/Bitch organizations will concoct a genealogy that "proves" they are the authentic descendants of the mythical Amazons.)

The misuse of the traditional past has been explored by J. H. Plumb,[10] but the similar exploitation of the archaeologically recovered "past" has hardly had a voice in recent times except for an academic protest against a few incompetent enthusiasts.

If we can bring ourselves to let ancient man be irrelevant to the present —to have *his own* life and reality, his own context and concerns, without saddling him with the obligation to lend support to modern inanities and insanities—then we may very well have much to learn from him, as he did from his own experience that we call "history."

In what follows it is not possible to do much more than offer further discussion and some new insights that elaborate upon the thesis I have presented in chapter VII of *The Tenth Generation,* "Tribe and State in the Ancient World." This is particularly appropriate in a tribute to G. Ernest Wright, since the discussion must center largely in the examination of the relationships between historical events and the economic and social factors of ancient Israelite culture. But in order to do so in a manner appropriate to a separate article in a *Festschrift,* it is necessary to summarize some of the main points made in my chapter. First, even in so-called "primitive" societies, it is generally true that as soon as a social organization receives a *name,* it has already transcended kinship ties as the basis of a larger solidarity.[11] Second, again in primitive society, a "tribe" is a *residential* unit characterized at least by geographical proximity. In other words, *contra* de Vaux who takes it to be evidence of Bedouin origin,[12] it has nothing to do with nomadism even among truly "primitive" tribes. Third, there is no evidence that the Twelve Tribes of ancient Israel have much if anything to do with the modern anthropological definition of a primitive "tribe."[13] On the other hand, they have considerable similarity to early forms of noncentralized social organization of Mediterranean cities from Nippur to Rome, from Bronze Age Byblos to Hellenistic Anatolia.[14] The tribes are administrative units each under a *nasi'* who is sacrosanct[15]—and could be such only under the covenant relationship with Yahweh. The cursing of Yahweh and the *nasi'* prohibited by the Covenant Code could only mean breach of covenant and therefore loss of status within the larger community.

The triumphant discovery by Orlinsky that the Twelve Tribes were not a Greek amphictyony is therefore completely devoid of historical perspective and irrelevant to any historical method. The implicit comparative method that he uses, assuming that post-biblical Jewish tradition and exegesis are the only sources for understanding Late Bronze or Early Iron Age cultures and structures, needs to be relegated to the Middle Ages together with similar methods of interpreting the Old Testament by Christian theologians who found in it all the various doctrines of the Medieval Church.

To point out a few facts: the Greek amphictyonies were alliances of Greek cities, while the Israelite Federation (which term I much prefer, to *avoid* too close an identification with the specifically Greek cultural adaptation of a much earlier Oriental form of social organization, and to emphasize the connection with Latin *foedus* which means both "league" and "covenant"), was an oath-bound unity of the village populations of ancient Palestine that was oriented first toward the realization of the ethical rule of Yahweh as the only Suzerain, and secondly toward the avoidance of the reimposition of the imperialism of the foreign-dominated regimes of the Palestinian power structures—the city-states. The distinction between formal analysis and functional purpose is one that seemingly is either entirely foreign to traditional biblical scholarship or avoided like the plague as a threat. Similarly, the critical analysis of what, in our range of ancient phenomena, are causes and what are effects needs much more attention. Most foreign and domestic biblical scholarship seems to regard ancient Israel as the "cause" of archaeological and social history, while it seems now perfectly clear that it is the "effect" of a complex of historical events. Even the "biblical theology" cannot be comprehended rationally apart from an understanding of the historical process, even though it was obscured to become a mere prostitute for the political establishment in biblical times—as the prophets point out with considerable gusto.[16]

Nevertheless, both the Greek and ancient Israelite federations had a (necessarily?) military orientation or function, but ancient Israel was not, at first, dominated by the military function—that came only with the state and short-lived empire. But the contrast between the two is functionally unbridgeable: one was for political power, led by an urban elite, while the other was for the warding off of political and military force, by a peasant community.[17]

The theology, ethic, and social organization of ancient Israel thus finds an almost complete harmony with modern ethnological description in the thesis that I presented some years ago. The ancient Palestinian *ḫupšu* of the Late Bronze Age were unified into a population of the *ḥopšī,* "freemen," by the religious movement that stemmed from Moses and the dramatic event of the Exodus. The movement had incredible impact upon the future course of Western and Middle Eastern civilization, but its basic principles were and are usually rejected for political and economic interests.

As Wolf describes it, the typical peasant "runs a household, not a business concern."[18] This brief statement describes probably the overwhelming majority of all mankind since before the dawn of history, and probably the majority of humanity today. There are a number of types of peasant society that we need not discuss here. But the Mediterranean type of peasantry based upon what is termed "short-term fallowing" that utilizes animal traction to produce cereals in combination with livestock raising is well attested since the Early Bronze Age and describes with admirable precision what all of our biblical traditions and sources convey. When one adds to this the traditional description of "each one under his vine and under his fig tree"[19] we have the complete range of the typical "scratch-plow" type of peasant society that is presupposed already for Syria in the Sinuhe story from Middle Kingdom Egypt.[20] If it had not been for the romantic biblical English of Doughty, and the equally romantic fantasies of Musil and others that found in the bedouin the original prototype of "semitic" civilization, it is impossible to imagine how biblical scholarship could have been so absolutely dominated by the "bedouin mirage" for nearly a century. For the bedouin type of cultural adaptation to environment is so minimally productive economically that it can survive only in some sort of symbiosis with the more productive villages and towns. Only in times of minimal political effectiveness could it even approach becoming an important historical factor, and even then it formed a sort of military aristocracy that dominated a subjected peasantry—and was like all such, extremely short-lived.[21] The accompanying cultural traits of glorification of genealogical lineage and prowess in battle that also seem to be characteristic of bedouin culture since pre-Islamic times are very questionably of Syro-Palestinian origin, but have their closest analogues in the barbarian, semiprimitive chiefdoms of Anatolian cultures that are reflected most clearly in the poems of Homer—the *Fürstenspiegel* for most of Western aristocracy since the Renaissance.[22] Aristocratic lineage, military prowess, and the domesticated camel probably came already associated into the Eastern Mediterranean area from the semi-savage regions far to the north about the time the "sea-peoples" established their domination of the lucrative urban social organizations.[23]

In contrast, the typical peasant-village society of the Mediterranean world was pragmatic, egalitarian, and concerned with productivity sufficient to make survival possible faced with the constant series of (usually foreign) military aristocracies that demanded most of their produce as "taxes" and a considerable part of their labor for "public works" and warfare.

There is no evidence and no argument of any plausibility that could neutralize the leading hypothesis that the Twelve Tribes of early Israel constituted much of the indigenous village-peasant population of Late Bronze Age Palestine, which was *unified* by a religious movement stemming from Moses and the dramatic events of the Exodus, and subsequently succeeded in throwing off the tyranny of foreign exploiters. A peasantry typically has very little resources for innovations (which are, incidentally, usually very expensive both in time and economic resources—a point that needs to be kept in mind in view of the tired old cliché that demands "social change")— and therefore the enormous changes of all sorts that characterized the *entire* Eastern Mediterranean region at the transition from the Late Bronze to the Early Iron Age furnishes us with an intensely interesting historical challenge[24] that has been evaded by the traditional theories of "invasion of barbarian nomads" and the like, based upon completely naïve concepts of the identity of "race," language, and culture[25] and the seemingly absolute inability on the part of Western scholars to conceive of processes of cultural change in "traditional" Eastern societies. When Wolf speaks of the peasants' "inability or unwillingness to give up their traditional social and political autonomy for the role of a dependent peasantry in asymmetrical relationships with dominant overlords"[26] we have a paradigmatic illustration of the historical process that took place at each threshold of the ancient Near Eastern Dark Ages. The statement is the more impressive since it has the context of Southeast Asian peasants' abandoning their assigned intensive hydraulic plots in favor of swidden cultivation,[27] i.e. cultivation of frontier lands after clearing it of natural vegetation including forest (cf. Josh. 17:15–18). Again the modern and ancient situations are radically different. The "Joseph" tribes demanded more agricultural land since it was, under the Yahwist covenant, tax free except for minimal ritual and humanitarian obligations. Clearing of forest land, on the other hand, demanded enormous amounts of labor. The modern parallel from Southeast Asia is comprehensible since the amount of labor involved in clearing swiddens was compensated by the escape from centralized political and economic control and taxation. It does not demand much imagination to see why the ancient Yahwist community was so enormously attractive to most of the existing Palestinian peasantry: it offered tax-exempt tenure of the fields they worked without the "demands and sanctions of power-holders outside his social stratum. . . ."[28]

The economic/technological foundations of the ancient *foedus* of Twelve Tribes are therefore absolutely inseparable from the ideology/theology, and also from the history. Yahweh as the one who succeeded to the various petty kings as owner of the territory allotted fields to the various families, not as possession but as fief to be enjoyed in perpetuity so long as the vassal obeyed his obligations under the covenant (Lev. 18:28). Since Yahweh until the united monarchy had no need or use for the ruinous tax upon the peasants, the major dilemma of the peasants was temporarily solved. Yet Wolf's statement about peasantry still holds true: "A peasantry is always in a dynamic state, moving continuously between two poles in search for a solution of its basic dilemma."[29]

For not only was its autonomy constantly challenged by the remnants of the old empire and city-state system, it was threatened also by those successful peasants[30] who wanted often enough to make themselves a new military aristocracy and succeed to the old royal tradition—notably Abimelech, Jephthah, and eventually David. Against these threats, both external and internal, the only counterforce was the larger unity centered upon Yahweh and the covenant. Any reversion to pre-Yahwist cults of local nature could only have the effect of weakening the whole in its perpetual struggle against ambitious politicians, the main theme of the Book of Judges which is essentially historically correct, even though the traditions have been used in an exactly opposite context: for the purpose of enhancing "national" solidarity under the kingship.

Because of the constantly changing nature of the total context of life in an unstable period, and in view of the fact that "tribal" organizations are themselves very weakly bonded,[31] it is not at all surprising that tribal names in the period of the judges have a rather vivid diversity, and most of them disappear entirely from real-life context after the establishment of the monarchy. It is exactly what we should expect. For peasant coalitions are not only ubiquitous and ephemeral, they are also strongly goal oriented, and when the goal of freedom from external military and economic control is achieved the "organization" has only an ideological existence. Unlike a modern political party or even a religious denomination that has a professional bureaucracy that continues the legal fiction of the community of the faithful with certain powers (especially over the community treasury), a peasant organization disappears into the body whole, like a virus. Consequently, the often remarked "crisis theology" that seems to characterize the narratives of the period between pagan political structures—from about 1200 to 1000 B.C.—is again exactly what we should expect. After all, it is the ancient pagan sociopolitical structure that had rigid bureaucratic and class definitions, that is both irrelevant and virtually impossible to a village-peasant society, that characteristically has a minimum of occupational specializations. At most, the distinction between the man who has a field to cultivate and the man who has flocks of sheep or goats to pasture is still recognized in modern Near Eastern villages.[32] Any further specialization is likely to be a part-time sideline, such as building, metalworking, or pottery-making.[33]

It is at this point that it must be emphasized that there is one specialization well attested in the archaic narratives. This is the priest/Levite. It is assumed here, since there is hardly adequate evidence to the contrary, that the *functions* of prophet (or prophetess—Deborah) or "judge" are not occupational specializations, though I will cheerfully admit that Abimelech and Jephthah had ambitions in that direction. The Gideon story illustrates the opposite, as does also the "parable of Jotham." From the story of Micah and the Danites in Judges 18 we can infer beyond doubt that religious specialists were in some demand in Palestinian culture of the twelfth century, but from the narrative as we have it there is very little reason to believe that the "Levite" in question was much different from the magi of the Hellenistic period—merely a specialist in religious ritual. But one must wonder whether the narrative is really typical of the Yahwist *foedus*. It is a record of the deplorable origins of the cult at Dan under the divided monarchy that was certainly unashamedly pagan both in origin and nature.[34] On the other hand, it is clear from passages like Hosea 3:6 that priests were *supposed* to be repositories of the normative religious tradition[35]—in which they evidently had little interest. In other words the *function* of the *hieromnēmones* (an *office* in the Greek amphictyonies) was disvalued during the divided monarchy in favor of purely ritual functions for which there was much more demand and therefore income, to judge from the prophetic denunciations of such ceremonial labors. There is good reason then to believe that the destruction in 587 B.C. may well have led the priestly groups to attempt a recovery of their role as the preservers of sacred tradition. However, it is abundantly evident that their concept of the past was dominated by their ritual functions and almost completely devoid of historical insights or understanding of the real past.[36] Therefore in P, Moses becomes the inspired legislator who delivered to the complete Twelve Tribes the entire corpus of tradition, including that which was brought in with the return to Bronze Age paganism under David and especially Solomon.

It is little wonder, then, that we have so few authentic materials and usable traditions that actually reflect realities of life under the Twelve Tribe system. The shift of dominance of the religious culture from the family and village centered peasantry to the pagan and power-mad urban centers meant an almost complete disvaluation of the old Yahwist tradition and the covenant that alone furnished a vehicle for a larger unity. What was preserved was so radically transformed by the political ideology derived from baal worship that it takes very subtle and skillful discrimination to see the original Yahwist functioning tradition under the Yahwistic[37] veneer of the pagan temple system. That Yahwisticism reduced the Mosaic Yahweh to a mere baal symbol of still another ambitious city-state intent on becoming an empire.

It succeeded for a brief time, but the peasantry that demanded a king found within two generations that the warning of Samuel was all too well grounded. They again had become a peasantry; having lost control of their own productivity and even the grass-roots large organization, most of the "tribes" disappeared forever, as they usually do when centralization of power takes place. The loss of most of the empire under Solomon meant that the expense of maintaining the ostentatious palace, temple, bureaucracy and army could no longer be met by the systematic looting of bordering lands, and therefore Rehoboam had no choice but to run for king on the platform of an enormous increase in taxation and forced labor. As at the end of the Late Bronze Age, there was ultimately a limit to the ability of the peasantry to endure the confiscation of most of their produce. What Rehoboam probably did not contemplate was the sudden resurgence of prophetic spokesmen for the old *pax Yahweh* that made it impossible for him to assert his authority by military force. The episode can hardly have been calculated to increase his love for the old Mosaic Yahwism.

The biblical history as it can now be reconstructed thus forms an almost perfect paradigm of a peasantry that succeeds in throwing off the "traditional liens on (their) funds of rent."[38] As Wolf has pointed out, "when the power structure through which funds have been siphoned off to traditional overlords has become ineffective," then there is characteristically a large increase in productivity.[39] This I believe to be illustrated in the increase in the number of Early Iron Age archaeological sites in Palestine and Transjordan in comparison with those of the Late Bronze Age. It correlates as well with the impoverishment or temporary disappearance of the cities, and the consequent radical deterioration in the quality of luxury goods, especially pottery.

Again as Wolf puts it, "the peasant retains both autonomy and capacity to survive when urban populations seek sustenance in the garbage cans of crumbling towns."[40] In view of the virtually universal destruction of civilization at the transition from the Late Bronze to the Early Iron Age, the statement has an impressive pregnancy. But our sources and other data indicate very strongly that the urban populations are not likely long to be content with the garbage cans when it is so easy to use force to obtain valuables from the defenseless. So land and sea piracy become the "in" thing, and a peasant population *must* form larger social relationships to ward off both the "legitimate" political as well as the illegitimate foreign pirates. One thinks of the Midianite raids to which Gideon was able to mount an effective counterforce, but only after converting his village to the Yahwist federation.[41] The traditional village self-sufficiency simply cannot cope with organized force of foreign origin, and therefore must form larger social units, willy-nilly.[42] The best example comes from Mari where the Benjaminites form an effective coalition against the Mari pirates *after* their respective indigenous sociopolitical organizations had been destroyed by superior military force, as we know from the Yaḫdun-Lim foundation deposit inscription that everyone has ignored since it demolishes the modern scholarly obsession with the "nomadic" origins of all Near Eastern culture groups.[43] The transient violence of ancient pagan states merely reinforces the equally Near Eastern observation that "the meek shall inherit the earth."[44] The urban garbage cans furnish little hope for continuity: political fanaticism may work for a brief period, but it is self-destructive since it cannot produce anything *essential* to human life —merely a peasantry that always would prefer to remain autonomous and productive of the necessities of life.

With these comments on the historical aspects of the ancient Palestinian peasantry and their "dynamic state" illustrated by the very brief existence of the Twelve Tribe Federation that constituted the Imperium of Yahweh, we may return to the main topic—the social organization in the time of the Judges.

Peasant society is typically at the subsistence level largely because of the enormous exactions of the superior monopoly of force to which it is subjected. Therefore, all aspects of peasant organization that exist are oriented toward quite specific goals or values. Elaboration of symbols and symbolic ideologies may be present, but they contrast totally to those of urban society. Symbols in urban society are essential to *status,* while peasant symbols are and must be constantly oriented toward *functions.* Perhaps the worst fraud ever perpetrated upon humanity is the fateful transference of the old "divine charter" of Mesopotamian paganism to Palestine. In the irrigation culture of Mesopotamia it was completely incontrovertible that apart from the centralized control of the king and his bureaucrats, the peasantry could produce little in that particular environment. There was, thus, a certain plausibility in that sort of theology, since the monopoly of force was essential to the maintenance of the irrigation canal system upon which most of the society depended. But when that ideology was transferred to Syria and Palestine (lands of rainfall culture), best illustrated by the so-called "Davidic covenant," it was entirely irrational and absurd. For the state was a producer of nothing but war and taxes—plus a superstratum of a parasitic elite that had a superior ability to extract goods from those unable to defend themselves. This is the context in which the alleged "social gospel" of the prophets should be re-examined. It is quite opposite to the tired "liberalism" of modern politics that calls for *increased* oppression of the producers in order to support a non-productive clientele of the incompetent and lazy both at the top and the bottom of social strata upon which the political power of the "liberals" depends. It is no accident that it is the non-productive incompetents that are most vociferous about the necessity of a "revolution" in the United States both at the "grass roots" and in the radical circles of university Social Science departments. It is probably also a most intriguing solution to an otherwise insoluble puzzle of history—namely, the anti-iconic nature of early Yahwism. For non-productive political ideologies *must* use symbols in order to obtain the support necessary to their existence and success—literary, graphic, and linguistic. It contrasts in every way to that which characterized early Yahwism that may be described as the symbolization of historical *events,* inseparably bound up with *qualitative* concerns, that is, with concerns about the contrast between good and evil. In a peasant society such a contrast is much clearer than in a typical urban environment, for it is the contrast between life and death.

If we grant that the Twelve Tribes of that ancient religious solidarity that called its social organization *"Yiśrā'ēl"* actually constituted a large majority of the village population of Palestine of the Late Bronze Age, then there is almost nothing of the archaeological and linguistic facts we have that does not fall properly into place. The problem that we have not been able to cope with is the social organization, and this is the major objective of the present paper.

That historical events and the religious ideology inseparable from them brought into being a large community at the end of the Late Bronze Age is incontrovertible. That attempts were made in late post-exilic times to identify that large community with a genealogical relationship is equally incontrovertible, but the absurdity of that epigonic attempt to misuse the past has hardly been questioned since John the Baptist.[45] In the light of much recent ethnological, linguistic, historical, and archaeological evidence a new look at ancient "Israel" is long overdue, particularly when very old traditions are being misused for political purposes at the present time, just as "Aryan" myths were misused by racist apologists for the Nazi regime.

Social organization defined as the ordered world of the Palestinian villages that had a large solidarity from the desert fringe in the south to the spring-fed valleys of the Biqa' of Lebanon in the north—from Dan to Beer-sheba—was certainly a very complex and multi-faceted phenomenon, as is any large social order. But it must be emphasized with the utmost force that any concern with that ancient social organization is inseparable from the normative (and despised) ideology that alone constituted its foundations, as well as those of all of Western and Near Eastern civilizations to the present day in readapted forms: Christianity, Islam, and Judaism in statistical order. Most of the issues that faced the ancient religious solidarity are just as alive—and just as vicious—today as they were in biblical times. But since the intent here is the description of social organization in ancient Israel, other modern issues may be left to find their own solution, hopefully having learned something from history—a forlorn hope indeed.

As in any large social organization, the large structure consists of a complex of concentric circles centering upon the nuclear family: the parents and offspring. It is at this level that the ancient Israelite religious system had its most powerful support, for the family could exist in prosperity only when it could survive in undisturbed enjoyment of its field and its "fig tree and grapevine" that it held as a fief from Yahweh under the covenant to obey the unconditional obligations of response to the call to war and the ethical obligations to refrain from actions incompatible with the social solidarity.

We are in no position at present to determine whether or not the *rô'š bêt 'āb* attested in biblical sources justifies the conclusion that an extended family system existed in the time of the Judges. At any rate, in view of the five-generation system that seems characteristic of biblical kinship, there could have been no *obligatory* family relationship between two persons who did not have a common traced ancestor within the five-generation pattern other than those of the covenant. Such a kinship system that formed some kind of unit under the oldest surviving ancestor could well have been a quite large factor in society during the period of the Judges, particularly in the circumstances described above when the peasantry was immune from the exactions of the urban tax collector. There seems to be little reason to question that the basic unit of society was such kin-bound groups, but the larger society can by no means be explained on such a basis—this structure is virtually universal in peasant cultures.

The next larger unit than the kin group was the village. As is true of many other Eastern Mediterranean cultures, most gentilics in biblical Hebrew derive from such local designations.[46] The village formed a social solidarity based upon geographical and cultural proximity, not upon kinship reinforced by the Yahwist covenant. As in the modern Near East, villages regarded themselves as segments of still larger units of society in which kinship was completely nonfunctional.[47] Though such larger relationships were and are often described in terms derived from kin terminology, as a matter of fact the actual ties derived either from common interests and therefore necessity as described above—the problem of achieving a larger unity for common defense against a common foe, usually the centralized state—or, in the case of ancient Israel, from a common ideology that had demonstrated an ability to create a solution to the perpetual "peasants' dilemma."

It is the form and function of these larger units that constitute the problem of the so-called Israelite amphictyony that Orlinsky and Yeivin[48] have so strongly attacked—but without putting anything at all in its place other than the utterly modern, anachronistic, and vicious concept of some mythical "racial" identity.

As it has been argued above, peasant societies beyond the immediate kin or village group tend to be nonexistent until a specific problem or goal appears. This is precisely what is most characteristic of the narratives we have of the period of the judges. To be sure, most of the specific goals have to do with the warding off of foreign attacks, and of this we have abundant illustration from the old poem fragment of Joshua 10 to Judges 5 and the Gideon story. In every case it is the glory of the central ideological, functional symbol that is celebrated—Yahweh. Here we have the *functioning* symbol of unity that underlay the supra-village unity that made the warding off of foreign domination possible, and simultaneously prevented the development of the war-hero type of pagan military dictatorship from arising from within—cf. the Gideon story.

It is the ideological, covenant substratum that constituted whatever basis there was for supra-kin and supra-local larger unities. Those larger unities existed only insofar as they had specific goals or functions to meet, but in order to preserve even these potential functions there had to be periodic reinforcement of the ideological foundations. Therefore, the central shrine centered on the Ark of the Covenant (which most certainly *could* not have been invented by the monarchy or its pagan priesthood) wherever it may have been located. For there can be no question that the old pagan tendency toward local aggrandizement at the expense of groups beyond the tribal border continued even under the *pax Yahweh*.[49] This tendency was enormously elaborated at the beginning of the monarchy, particularly, it seems, as a result of the competition between David and the Saulides, notably David's piracy. The competition only enhanced the paganization of the population, for the Mosaic covenant *could* not be geographically located. Sinai of course would be much too remote to be ritually functional to Palestinian villagers, and *no other* location could be of particular or peculiar religious value without becoming a mere appendage of some pagan cult or enhancing the status of some locality—exactly what happened with the ritual establishment of Jerusalem, Bethel, and Dan. Sacred places are irrelevant to a sacred covenant, though seemingly irredeemably necessary to pagan religiosity, as M. Eliade has well described.[50] The concept of a "holy people" and a "holy land" is absolutely incompatible in authentic biblical Mosaic Yahwism with the concept of a "holy place." The latter is nothing but pure partisan politics parading as authentic religion, and usually at the expense of some group that is consequently assigned the role of "productive peasant" for the purpose of producing the goods necessary for maintaining the glory of the "holy place" and its minions. It is for this reason that all the scholarly argument about the "holy place" of the Ark during the time of the judges simply demonstrates the incompetence of recent scholarship in understanding the Yahwist religious structure. For the millennium-old conflict between local power centers of Palestine was precisely what the Yahwist federation brought (temporarily!) to an end, or at least muted the competition for a few centuries. For the identification of power centers with religious centers is one of the oldest pagan political propaganda ploys known to mankind.[51] Its economic as well as political functions are well illustrated by the enormous prosperity of the Greek temple cities of the early Christian era[52] as well as by the current fad of (largely) American tourism that seems obsessed with looking at old churches all over Europe. It would seem, to me at least, obvious that the idolization of sacred places is as universal to paganism as it is foreign to the premonarchic biblical faith, whether of the Old Testament or of the New.[53]

Again, we can see why the authentic Yahwism of the interim period from the demise of the Late Bronze Age city-states until the resurgence of the old paganism with the political triumph of the Jebusite bureaucrats has been radically obscured in the Old Testament narratives. The older, highly unfashionable, Mosaic faith survived with only the prophets as its spokesmen, often at the risk of their lives, and no doubt a considerable part of village populations as its living practitioners and embodiments.

It is for this reason—the constant battle between the new and revolutionary religious understanding of God and man that stemmed from Moses and the old pagan political ideologies—that modern scholarship, increasingly conditioned by political power concerns, has been impotent to deal with the biblical system of thought, society, and adaptation to environment. But the conflict was certainly not merely one of "ethnic groups." There could have been no important ethnic or linguistic contrast between the "Canaanites" and "Israelites" in 1200 B.C. There was, however, an enormous contrast of value systems. The Canaanite one was based upon political power derived from some political divine symbol called "baal," while the Israelite was based upon a covenant the stipulations of which furnished the foundations for a large and interchangeable peasant community on a voluntary basis.[54]

That larger community was subdivided into local segments that have traditionally been termed "tribes" in the English language and with equivalent terms in the various languages of biblical scholarship. Yet no one seems to have asked the most important question: What *was* an ancient Israelite *šēbeṭ* and what were its foundations and functions? One observation we can make with certainty: the "history" writers of the time of the monarchy cannot have been concerned to preserve the traditions of the tribes since the latter are perpetually inimical to the centralized power structure, just as the religious structure of the old covenant Yahwism was absolutely incompatible with the absolutism of the Solomonic pagan dynasty. We cannot answer with certainty at present the leading question, but the old traditions and laws at least strongly support the conclusion that a *šēbeṭ* was actually a unit of society under the authority of a *nasī'*, in other words, an administrative unit. Biblical sources like almost all of our other sources for the ancient world are, and should be expected to be, extremely meager when it has to do with local, grass-roots social structures. The latter emerge into historical view only after they have become radically changed and have developed specialists in writing, archives, and bureaucratic administration. But by the time these latter aspects of social organization that modern scholars usually identify with "civilization" have developed, the personnel involved have almost always become alienated from their social origins, or have actually had an alien origin. It is for this reason that virtually all our ancient documents that have survived are in a language that is alien to the population of the political structure under whose auspices they were produced.

The territorial-administrative nature of a "tribe" is further reinforced by a look at the map. In the Amarna period, Palestine was misruled by a series of petty city-states nominally under the crumbling Egyptian empire. The major power centers from Megiddo to Keilah were constantly harassing each other and each others' peasantry across the boundary line.[55] Presumably,

though we have no direct evidence, each city-state was the *center* of a territory it dominated including the villages within the boundary line. To illustrate: the conflict between Shechem and Megiddo so well narrated by the
Amarna letters means there was a political boundary line somewhere, perhaps halfway between the two power centers. The early Israelite administrative (and militia) units took place in such a way that the territory formerly
claimed by the city-states was entirely broken up. Instead of being at the
center of a territory, the old pagan cities were at the boundary line between
"tribes," and the population between Shechem and Megiddo, for example,
was unified as the "tribe" of Manasseh. The same is true south of Shechem
where the territory to Bethel became Ephraim and from Bethel to Jerusalem
became Benjamin. Again, south of Jerusalem became Judah. The same
phenomenon by which the old power centers became peripheral pagan en-
claves is illustrated at Beth-Shan, Gezer, Heshbon, Rabbath-Ammon, possibly
Dibon, and Pella. All this illustrates most beautifully the fact that the village
peasantry *between* two (or more) power centers were unified so that they
could ward off by common effort *either* of their two traditional overlords,
with a maximum of quick response, and if need be, call upon the neighboring
"tribes" for military support, so that any armed force of the old power centers
would be automatically faced with an impossible two-front war in which
guerrilla tactics were used evidently with enormous effectiveness. It is no
wonder that the city-states that were completely surrounded by the "tribes"
of the unified peasantry worked out some sort of *modus vivendi* with the
village populations or became at least nominally Yahwist for a time. The
best examples are Hebron, Bethel, and Shechem, and somewhat later, Dan
—all of which were centers for the reintroduction of the old pagan political
religion during the monarchies.

The successful withdrawal of the very large peasant population from control of the city-states can be understood only upon two presuppositions. The
first is a most powerful ideological system that succeeded both in forming
such a widespread unity and maintaining it intact. A corollary is of course
some simple instrument by which that unity was concretely given form and
continuity—and that can be only the *foedus,* the covenant. Second, the
success of an unarmed peasantry with no training in warfare can be explained only upon the assumption that the old power centers had already
been greatly weakened by the destructions of the thirteenth century that
are now so well attested from archaeological evidence. Those destructions
can hardly be interpreted as anything else but a civilization-wide response
to the entire bankruptcy of political organizations and functions as they
existed in the Late Bronze Age—for the process is attested from Mycenae to
Egypt. The "great wars" of the Israelite "conquest" cannot have been much
more than guerrilla skirmishes involving little more than a few hundred
peasant militia in most instances.[56] As Orlinsky, among others, has pointed
out, there is hardly a case before Saul in which there was a complete mobili-

zation of the entire Twelve Tribe Federation. In fact, it seems to me now very probable that the "census lists" of Numbers 1 and 26 reflect the very early military organization inherited by King Saul and continued by David, prior to the complete bureaucratization of the kingdom under the impact of the old Jebusite political structure that he took over: the Davidic "census."

Since the resistance of peasant populations to innovation is both well-known and well-grounded (any change is likely to be for the worse, except one that delivers them from the royal landlord), it goes without saying that military organization under the king would necessarily continue, at first, traditional modes of social organization. Therefore, the traditional tribal recruiting district, the *'eleph,* is the fundamental structure of the military organization—and well illustrated in the early stories of David.[57] It is this that David's census destroyed forever—and the plague that broke out was evidently regarded as the divine punishment that ensued. The result was the introduction of the cult of Yahweh into Jerusalem—and simultaneously the introduction of the old Jebusite/Canaanite idea that rituals *are* an adequate and effective substitute for obedience to the covenant obligations to Yahweh.

NOTES

1. An analogy should not be expected to be an identity. It is absurd a priori to proceed under the assumption that all traits must be formally and functionally identical before it is justified to conclude that there is a useful parallel. The best proof for this principle is the often ridiculous and uncontrolled "parallelomania" that draws upon formal traits to reach all sorts of conclusions concerning relationships between ancient and modern societies. The function and context of the formal trait may well be exactly opposite.

2. Note K. Boulding's observation about the lack of organizations in American culture a mere century ago. *The Organizational Revolution* (New York, 1953), p. 3.

3. In other words, the then fashionable view of the society that promoted a fictitious genealogical unity for political purposes was the opposite of the covenant value system that unified the village population against political power structures.

4. H. M. Orlinsky, "The Tribal System of Israel and Related Groups in the Period of the Judges," *Oriens Antiquus* 1 (1962), 11–20.

5. E. R. Service, *Primitive Social Organization* (New York, 1962), p. 116. On p. 131 Service comments on the frequency of transfer of kinship criteria to sociocentric status terms in tribal society. To this must be compared the virtually universal application of kinship terms to political relationships in our ancient Near Eastern sources from the Mari alliances to the genealogy of the Hammurapi dynasty.

6. E. R. Wolf, *Peasants,* Foundations of Modern Anthropology Series (Englewood Cliffs, N.J., 1966).

7. Ibid., p. 3.

8. I Kings 12.

9. Service [N 5], p. 180.

10. J. H. Plumb, *The Death of the Past,* p. 17: "Nothing has been so corruptly

used as concepts of the past." It is not only biblical studies and theology in general that seem to have worked under the assumption that, as Plumb put it, "History is the exegesis of a dogmatic past." Virtually all the special minority "culture studies" and ethnic history programs that are sprouting up in American universities like mushrooms after a rain illustrate this same concept of history.

11. Service [N 5], p. 116.

12. Ibid., p. 114. Among all the difference between truly "primitive" tribes and those of the ancient Israelite *foedus* one of the most important is mentioned also on this same page. "Wrongs to individuals are punished by the corporate group, the 'legal person.'" There can be no question that in the period of the Federation, it was Yahweh who was the "legal person." The various tribes or judges acted merely as agents.

13. See G. E. Mendenhall, *The Tenth Generation* (Baltimore, 1973), ch. VII.

14. Ibid.

15. Exod. 22:28.

16. Note the deliberate use of prostitution figures of speech throughout the Bible, esp. in Ezekiel 16.

17. One wonders what the prehistory of the Greek amphictyonies may have been, particularly since we have attestation for them only at a relatively late period by Near Eastern standards. The so-called "Dorian invasion" could easily have been just such a historical red herring as the "Israelite conquest."

18. Wolf [N 6], p. 2.

19. I Kings 4:25.

20. Wolf [N 6], p. 32. Cf. *ANET*, p. 19, for an inventory of the Syrian land of Yaa, that includes the classical categories of cereals, fruits, wine, and livestock. Note also Hans Goedicke's demonstration that the Egyptian term "sand-dwellers" that has always been unquestioningly assumed to mean "desert nomads" in truth designates a culture possessed of fortresses, orchards, and oxen. Biblical and ancient Near Eastern scholarship has always been characterized by incredible naïveté where socioeconomic ecotypes are concerned.

21. A. Jaussen vividly describes such a situation in *Coutumes des nomades de Moab* (Paris, 1908), pp. 162–64, 240–42.

22. This is very probably an oversimplification. The Sinuhe story certainly does glorify military prowess in ritual single combat that is *very* reminiscent of the David and Goliath story. It again illustrates the typical attitude of ancient populations that which "Big-Man" (i.e. Sumerian LU.GAL) ruled over them was a matter of indifference, as it must have been since the result was always the same. The "war-gods" who produced the victory of the "big-man" who won is a function of this sort of social structure. A modern, "scientific" warfare, on the other hand, is able to predict with great accuracy the outcome of any potential battle, and therefore needs no "war-gods," except perhaps at the level of the individual who doesn't know what is going on, does merely what he is told to do, and has no inkling of the statistical chances of his becoming one of the predicted casualties.

23. Compare the nomadic Scythians described by Herodotus IV 46 and elsewhere.

24. On the difficulty of radical change in peasant ideology see Wolf [N 6], p. 103. Peasants have no monopoly on this trait: Jer. 13:23; Isa. 6:10.

25. See E. Pulgram, "Mycenean Linear B, Greek, and the Greeks," *Glotta* 38 (1960), 171–81, esp. 172.

26. Wolf [N 6], p. 24.

27. Ibid. Aharoni's Early Iron villages of Upper Galilee are most probably to be interpreted in this context.

28. Ibid., p. 11.

29. Ibid., p. 17.

30. Ibid., p. 30. Compare also the aristocratic pretensions of the English *nouveaux riches* in early English history in Plumb [N 10], pp. 31–35.

31. Service [N 5], p. 114.

32. E.g. Cain and Abel. When we were looking for a young man to act as guard of an antiquities site in the Euphrates Valley, a certain young man was recommended to us on the ground "that he had neither a field or sheep" and therefore nothing to take him away from his new duties.

33. Wolf [N 6], p. 40 ". . . the economic specialty is carried on part-time by people who farm. . . ."

34. W. F. Albright, *From the Stone Age to Christianity*, 2d ed. (Baltimore, 1946), pp. 229 f.

35. Perhaps Jer. 2:8 belongs here as well.

36. If the Zadoqite priesthood of Jerusalem was actually the old Jebusite priesthood maintained in office (beside the Yahwist priest Abiathar), then their ritual tradition would *have* to be legitimized in later times by a fictitious "Mosaic" origin, and their Yahwist origin by genealogy (I Chron. 5:34—with which compare the genealogy of the Hammurapi dynasty).

37. The distinction made here between the Mosaic Yahwism and the monarchic syncretistic Yahwisticism follows by analogy the demonstrated similar process that took place in the Persian empire under Darius and Xerxes, resulting in a distinction between Zarathustrianism and Zarathustricism made by I. Gershevitch, *JNES* 23 (1964), 12–38.

38. Wolf [N 6], p. 16.

39. Ibid.

40. Ibid., p. 17.

41. Judges 6.

42. Wolf [N 6], p. 77.

43. Yaḥdun-Lim, *RA* 33 (1936), 49 ff.

44. Matt. 5:5; Ps. 37:11.

45. Matt. 3:9.

46. A large percentage of all gentilics in biblical Hebrew, or better, South Canaanite, are toponyms. A hasty sample count would indicate some 50 per cent. The same is true of "Les ethniques hittites et louvites," ch. III of E. Laroche, *Les Noms des Hittites* (Paris, 1966), pp. 255 ff. The best commentary on the situation is given in "Coins of al-Yaman 132–569 A.H.," *Al-Abḥath* 23 (1970), 11: "Memories of pre-Islamic kings and the terminology used by Yamanī sources have given rise to the belief that al-Yaman possessed a monarchical tradition. Nothing could be further from the truth. Yamanī society—like all others in the Middle Ages—was molecular in structure. The loyalty of the individual was torn between the family, the tribe, and the village, but it was never granted to the province. In such a society, authority tends to be justified by power."

47. The kin-bound structure was associated with the five-generation system of tracing kinship. Anything beyond this was of public, over against the private kin system, function having to do particularly with the normal political functions of law (in the local community) and war (involving tribal and supratribal public units for which the common Yahwist ideology was the only foundation).

48. Orlinsky [N 4]. Sh. Yeivin, *The Israelite Conquest of Canaan* (Istanbul, 1971), p. 122. Neither work has any but minimal contact with historical or social reality other than present ideologies.

49. The best illustration is the conquest of Laish by the Danites in Judges 18. Similar tendencies are illustrated by the futile Ephraimite attempt at control of Gilead (Judg. 12:4), and the similar Ephraimite resentment of Gideon's success against the Midianites (Judg. 8:1). Compare also the very elaborate and late version of the East Bank/West Bank conflict of Joshua 22. The almost pathetic disavowal of the idea that

the altar was built for making sacrifices is amusing (vs. 23) in view of the universal prophetic condemnation of the sacrificial ritual. But the function of the altar as an '*ēd* is *most* interesting in view of the fact that the "second giving of the law" is located in the Jordan Valley in the time of Moses, and this narrative is extremely careful to make the location (Shittim) extremely vague. The "Reform" of Josiah underlies the present form of this narrative that preserves authentic local traditions about the end of the Mosaic period. It was the site where the Transjordanian groups were incorporated into the Yahwist community prior to the first intervention in Palestine proper, and therefore was a most formidable danger to the ideology of Josiah, who had a most tenuous claim (in Jerusalem!) to the authentic continuity of the Mosaic tradition. So, both the altar and the no doubt local tradition of Moses' burial site *had* to be negated—by negating the sacral nature of the first and the authenticity of the second, even denying its existence, which may very well have been true.

50. M. Eliade, *The Sacred and the Profane* (New York, 1961).

51. Anthropological literature does an infinitely better job of describing the real functions of such ideologies; e.g. Wolf [N 6], "The role of the city," pp. 10 ff.: ". . . the sites of famous shrines, functioned primarily as religious centers, attracting devotees in periodic pilgrimages to its temples." This statement refers specifically to India. It goes without saying that there is enormous profit in combining with this the "castle and power apparatus of military rulers, and . . . administrative centers." Nowadays we call it "tourism."

52. Note the very modern reaction of Demetrius the silversmith of Ephesus to an attempt at downgrading the local religious establishment in Acts 19:23 ff. Demetrius evidently succeeded, for the real prosperity of those pagan sacral cities took place in the second century A.D. Their reduction to ghost towns took place gradually after the identification of Christianity with Byzantine politics beginning with Constantine.

53. In view of the universal prophetic condemnation of the cult of the dead, the undeniable Transjordanian location of the tomb of Moses would have had most complex reactions among the proponents of the "reform" of Josiah. It could be described as a threefold problem: (a) the genuine concern for the Mosaic covenant-ethical tradition that badly needed support; (b) the cultic-touristic celebration of national shrines (in alien-held territory); (c) the cultic-ritual obsession with clannish/tribal symbols; cf. N 48. The only solution possible was the one chosen—that no one knew the burial site of Moses.

54. A phenomenon that needs further investigation is the fact that a high percentage of really significant religious movements stemmed from what can only be termed low prestige countryside, often villages. Most of the OT prophets, the early Maccabees, Zarathustra, Jesus of Nazareth, Luther of Eisleben, and many others stem from small communities of no prestige whatsoever. Those that do come from high prestige urban centers exhibit "withdrawal" either physically (Moses, Buddha, Francis of Assisi) or ideologically (Paul of Tarsus).

55. Mendenhall [N 13], *TTG*, chs. III, IV.

56. Notably Gideon.

57. G. E. Mendenhall, "The Census Lists of Numbers 1 and 26," *JBL* 77 (1958), 52–66.

7. Charismatic Leadership in the Book of Judges

ABRAHAM MALAMAT

THE HEBREW UNIVERSITY OF JERUSALEM

THE HISTORY of Israel from the conquest of Canaan in the thirteenth century B.C. to the establishment of the monarchy at the close of the eleventh century was characterized by a unique political system. This regime of judges, which has no extant parallel among the peoples of the ancient Near East, was a response to a chronic state of war imposed upon the Israelites by their neighbors. It is not surprising, therefore, that its main manifestations are in the military sphere. In times of distress, charismatic leaders in the form of deliverer-judges arose sporadically among the Israelites and brought them out from under the hands of their oppressors. The Book of Judges, which is the principal source for observing this historical phenomenon (it is also intimated in the stories concerning Saul, in I Samuel), contains a collection of folk tales on the deliverer-judges, each of which portrays an encounter with an adversary of a particular type, as well as the specific challenge confronting the judge. The Book of Judges also attests to another kind of leader, known in biblical scholarship as the "minor judge" in contradistinction to the deliverers, the "major judges."

Since our discussion is devoted primarily to the historical category of charismatic leadership, we shall not delve into such specific problems of biblical criticism relating to the Book of Judges as the editorial strata, the technical terms *šopeṭ*—which we following convention shall render "judge" —and *mošia'*, "deliverer," or the relation between the "major" and the "minor judges."[1] Nor are we concerned with the "minor judge" per se, for he does not embody the characteristics of a deliverer, at any rate not according to the stereotyped chronicle sources drawn upon in the Book of Judges (10:1–5; 12:8–15). It should be noted, however, that at least some of the five "minor judges" may have engaged in military activities and relieved their people from oppression.[2] Further, the root *yš'*, "to deliver, save," is employed in each of the narratives of the "major judges" with the exception of Deborah and Barak, either in an epithet, "deliverer" (applied to Othniel and Ehud—3:9, 15), or in the verbal form *hošia'* (besides in the account of Othniel, it is found relating to Gideon—6:14, etc.; 8:22; to Jephthah—12:2–3; to Samson—13:5; and to Tola, the first of the "minor judges"—10:1; but also to Shamgar the son of Anath—3:31, for which see below). On the other hand, the root *špṭ,* in the senses "to rule," "to champion," "to judge," occurs in these stories in relation to Othniel, Deborah, Jephthah, and Samson (3:10; 4:4; 12:7; 15:20; 16:31) and regularly to all five "minor judges."[3]

I

The first of the deliverer-judges is Othniel, who defeated an invader who had penetrated deep into southern Palestine, the mysterious Cushan-Rishathaim, king of Aram-Naharaim. Because of the vague, schematic formulation of this account, material details of the actual war are lacking. The episode of Deborah and Barak epitomizes the confrontation with the autochthonous Canaanite population in the northern part of the country. The chief military challenge in this case was the chariot-force of the Canaanites, confronting the Israelite foot soldiers who, moreover, were poorly equipped (5:8). By reading between the lines of the biblical account, we can reconstruct the Israelite plan of operation in overcoming the situation: exploiting climatic and topographical factors, they rendered the Canaanite chariotry inoperable. The story of Gideon illustrates the conflict with desert marauders headed by the Midianites, who were making incursions into the cultivated region from the eastern fringes of Transjordan. In this instance, the military problem was twofold: the numerical superiority of the enemy and his skilled use of the camel in warfare, which necessitated the adoption of special tactics to which the Israelites were unaccustomed. Gideon found a solution by planning a night attack, enabling him to nullify both these factors. The narratives linked with the names of Ehud and Jephthah describe wars against Moab and Ammon, national states which arose in Transjordan in the thirteenth century B.C. and whose inhabitants, in contrast to the Israelites, were already organized under monarchical regimes at an early stage of their settlement. Finally, the Samson cycle represents the clash with the Philistines in the western part of the country, an enemy which by virtue of its superior technology and its military aristocracy (*sᵉrānim*) was destined to jeopardize the very existence of Israel.[4]

We are confronted by the conspicuous fact that in none of the episodes in the Book of Judges is there a recurrence of either the type of enemy fought or the arena of battle, or the ethnic-tribal origin of the "deliverer," who arises in each instance from a different tribe. Concerning the latter aspect, we long ago noted in an unpublished study a point generally overlooked—that the sequence of narratives in the Book of Judges may have been based essentially on a geographical scheme which presents the judges in the order of their tribal-territorial affiliations, from the south of the country to the north: Othniel from Judah, Ehud from Benjamin, Deborah from the hill country of Ephraim (drawing along with her Barak of Naphtali), Gideon from Manasseh (so, too, Abimelech, on whom see the last part of this paper), and Jephthah the Gileadite, which brings us to the area of Gad in Transjordan. Likewise, the two "minor judges" wedged in between the stories of Abimelech and Jephthah—Tola of the tribe of Issachar, and Jair of Gilead, who represents the eastern half of the tribe of Manasseh—are in keeping generally with the tribal-territorial scheme of the book. It is true that Samson, the last of the "major judges," belonged to the tribe of Dan and was active in the southern part of the country, but his cycle of tales constitutes a separate literary pericope within the book. Moreover, from the viewpoint of the later redactor, it was only proper to place the Danite hero at the end of the sequence of judges, for his tribe had long since migrated to the northern extremity of the land. Thus, too, it can hardly be accidental that in Judges 1, where the Israelite tribes are listed also in a principally geographical order from south to north, Dan (in a southern context) appears at the very end of the list.[5] If we posit, however, the tribal-territorial principle as a guideline in the present structure of the Book of Judges, the chronological credibility of the actual sequence of historical events, as presented in the book, is naturally impaired (and see below).

The absence of duplication in the type of enemy and the tribal affinity of the judges raise the possibility that the compiler of the book endeavored to portray only models of oppressors, on the one hand, and of deliverers, on the other hand, emphasizing the features specific to each particular confrontation. In other words, in selecting the stories in the Book of Judges, we deem that the compiler wittingly restricted his choice so as to obtain a paradigmatic scheme of Israel's wars in the premonarchical period. These paradigms would serve a didactic purpose, seemingly alluded to at the beginning of the body proper of the book (3:1–2): "Now these are the nations which the Lord left, to test Israel by them . . . that he might teach war to such at least as had not known it before."[6]

An exception to this scheme, insofar as the identity of the enemy and the military action are concerned, is the heroic exploit of Shamgar the son of Anath: he "smote of the Philistines six hundred men with an ox-goad; and he also delivered Israel" (3:31), an event which recalls Samson's smiting a thousand Philistines with the jawbone of an ass (15:15–16). But it is generally conjectured that this event occurred in the north, and not in the area of Samson's exploit. It may well be that, precisely because of the paradigmatic intent of the Book of Judges, the redactor did not feel the need to give a full account of this event, contenting himself with a mere reference to Shamgar, apparently because his name occurs later, in the Song of Deborah (5:6). At all events, it is reasonable to suppose that not all the deliverers active in the twelfth to eleventh centuries B.C. have found mention in the Book of Judges. This assumption is supported by Samuel's farewell address, in which he counts among Israel's deliverers, alongside Jerubbaal (i.e. Gideon) and Jephthah, the enigmatic Bedan (I Sam. 12:11), a deliverer who is otherwise unknown[7] and whose deed of deliverance is lost to us.

The Book of Judges "compensates" us for its material defects and limitations as a comprehensive, multi-faceted historical source by providing a conceptual schema regarding the unfoldment of the events of the period generally, and the appearance of the deliverer-judge in particular. This schema, unparalleled in the other biblical books for systematic consistency, is founded upon a pragmatic theological interpretation which forms both the general introduction to the events of the period (2:11–19) and the setting into which the narratives of the individual judges were integrated. In this manner, the episodes are concatenated into a single historical chain. It is true that the pragmatic, historiosophic framework is to be ascribed only to an editorial stage of the book—and, according to the prevalent view, to its last redactor, the so-called Deuteronomist. Nevertheless, the content of this framework is not necessarily the expression of a later ideological concept, as most scholars hold. It possibly, and even probably, contains authentic reflections and preserves elements of ancient historical reality.[8]

The following two doctrines are basic to the pragmatic exposition.

a) The concept of historical periodicity. According to this doctrine the events of the period of the judges formed a chain of recurring cycles, each comprising four successive stages: the people sinned by reverting to idolatry, which brought in its train subjugation by an adversary; thereupon the people invoked the Lord to deliver them and ultimately their redemption came about by the hand of a deliverer. The deliverer-judge secured for his people a protracted period of "rest"; to use biblical terminology—"The land was at rest for [twenty, forty, eighty] years." But "whenever the judge died, they turned back and behaved worse than their fathers, going after other gods, serving them and prostrating themselves to them" (2:19). This cyclic view imposes a picture of linear development in which the judges appear in succession, from Othniel to Samson, with gaps between, when there was no leader. In this manner a historical-chronological sequence was created, which cannot be accepted *prima facie* as reflecting actual reality, unless the order of events is corroborated by additional factors. Furthermore, this approach negates the possibility—which cannot be excluded *a priori*—of the contemporaneous existence of two or more judges, active in separate parts of the country.

On the other hand, it seems that the historiosophic framework expressed an immanent truth in regard to the conditions prevailing in the premonarchical period, when it emphasizes the frequent vicissitudes befalling the people politically and militarily, which to a great extent were the outcome of the national-religious consciousness; its decline aggravated the nation's position, while its reinforcement led to consolidation and prosperity. Moreover, it is a universal phenomenon that in time of danger and crises there is an upsurge of charismatic sensitivity among the people, which seizes upon a personality which is able to satisfy, as one sociologist phrases it, "the charismatic hunger"[9] of his contemporaries. This explains the recurring dependence of the Israelites upon deliverer-leaders in times of trouble.

b) The concept of the pan-Israelite dimension. On the basis of this doctrine the tribal events of the period—including the scope of the judge's activity—were elevated to a broad, national level encompassing the entire people and country. Hyperbolic as this may be, the prevalent approach of biblical criticism is likewise unsatisfactory inasmuch as it holds that the judge's action was of only a restricted local and tribal background and confined his authority to a single tribe or even less. It would seem that this radical narrowing of horizon is equally a distortion of the reality of the period.[10] In the actual situation, the individual tribal framework was of little significance to the Israelite judge (see below), and of even less to the external enemy who was not consciously attacking a specific tribe or its territory, but rather Israelites per se. Generally, several tribes were affected simultaneously, and the act of liberation from the foreign pressure, which exceeded the strength of any solitary Israelite tribe, necessitated the cooperation of a confederacy. Thus, any relatively local incident could readily reach a more national plane.

Indeed, the internal evidence within the narratives of the judges clearly reflects these conditions. Thus, for instance, Gideon assembles for his battle against the Midianites not only members of his own clan, Abiezer, and his fellow Manassite tribesmen, but also troops from Asher, Zebulon, and Naphtali (6:35) and, at a later stage, he even seeks the assistance of the Ephraimites (7:24f.). This is also true of other judges, although the scope of their activities was at times more limited. The high point in national solidarity in the period of the judges was achieved at the battle of Deborah and Barak. Here, according to the Song of Deborah, six tribes united in a concerted action—from Benjamin in the south to Naphtali in the north, who came "to the help of the Lord among the fighting men." Thus, the significant epithet "mother in Israel," bestowed upon Deborah (5:7), was quite appropriate.

To sum up, the authority of the deliverer-judge transcended the ambit of the individual tribe and was not confined to a restricted locale. It was only natural that his influence should embrace a tribal confederacy, whether broad or limited; and thus his mission and his charismatic attribute also assumed a national dimension, instead of retaining a mere tribal flavor. The judge's action within the intertribal and supratribal framework, therefore, justifies historically the use in the Book of Judges of the designation "Israel" for the object of the judge's act of deliverance and rule; hence, this appellation should not be regarded as a later artificial amplification, under tendentious, pan-Israelite influence.[11] Although this is still a far cry from pan-

Israelite rule, the judges were blazing the path to a new era of leadership—
the Israelite monarchy.

II

The best starting point in examining the nature of the judges' regime and
the specific characteristics of the deliverer-leader is the theory developed at
the beginning of this century by Max Weber concerning the several types
of leadership and domination, including charismatic rule. Weber was not
the first to resort to the term *charisma* as indicating unique qualities—
deviating from the common and routine. He expressly states that he borrowed the term from the church historian Rudolph Sohm (1841–1917).
But he was the first to place the phenomenon of charismatic rule on a broad
sociological and political plane, and to present it as a defined model of one
of the types of authority or leadership wielded by extraordinary, singular
persons within a society. Thereby he paved the way for the term to become
common currency not only in the social and political sciences, but also in
daily speech (frequently employed in doubtful usages). Weber himself used
the word charisma primarily in the connotation of the New Testament,[12]
namely, as a gift of divine grace. It is particularly his appraisement of the
charismatic order as essentially a religious transcendental category—in contradistinction to the majority of his followers, who infused the concept with
secular content—that makes Weber's analyses supremely relevant for the
biblical phenomenon. Although biblical terminology does not contain the
exact semantic equivalent for charisma, it approximates to the expression
"spirit [*rūaḥ*] of the Lord," which is bestowed upon the leader and stirs him
to action.

In his treatment of charismatic leadership, Weber unfortunately gave only
marginal attention to the Israelite judge, for this personality could have
served as an exemplar of his *Idealtypus*. In his empirical analyses he was
less concerned with the military leaders than with another distinctly charismatic figure which appears in the Bible and in numerous societies, namely,
the prophet and the various kinds of diviners. On the other hand, those Bible
scholars who in dealing with the period of the judges have adopted Weber's
concept of charisma—such as Alt, Buber, Eichrodt, and Albright, to mention
only the most outstanding pioneers—have relied mainly on his book *Das
antike Judentum*.[13] In the latter, though indeed he did treat the Israelite
judge per se, he did little to elucidate his views on charisma. And Bible
scholars, on their part, have not generally consulted Weber's brilliant over-all
analyses of the phenomenon, to be found in his monumental *Wirtschaft
und Gesellschaft*, which presents his most comprehensive and systematic
formulation of the types of domination.[14]

The concept of charisma has taken on further dimensions, especially in the last decade or so, through the renewed interest in and reappraisal of Weber's *oeuvre*,[15] as well as under the impetus of the emergence of the new states of Asia and Africa. The recent applications in the latter direction are of particular relevance to charismatic leadership in the Bible, despite the considerable differences in time and historical circumstances. The contemporary phenomenon—especially in Africa—has evolved out of tribal society still largely subject to religious-magical motivation and is in that respect closer to the biblical environment than Western civilization, from which most of the analogies hitherto adduced have been drawn.[16]

In order to comprehend the particular quality of the charismatic rule of the judges, we must juxtapose it to the two other basic forms of leadership or authority, included in Weber's classical tripartite typology of legitimate domination.[17] (1) The traditional authority; this was represented in Israel from earliest times by a patriarchal-tribal system, in which authority descended through family heads and resided in a gerontocracy. (2) The legal-rational authority; this approached realization among the Israelites upon the establishment of the monarchy and a budding bureaucratic apparatus (albeit patrimonial) which evolved around it.[18] By their very nature, these two types of rule are mutually antagonistic and are motivated by opposite aims. Traditional authority is inclined toward conservatism and endeavors to maintain the status quo in the life pattern, whereas legal authority is activated by dynamic and rational-utilitarian forces and seeks to adapt the pattern of life to ever-changing circumstances, despite sanctified tradition. But they have a common denominator in their desire for stability and permanence, inasmuch as the leadership is uninterrupted and conventional, and conforms with prevailing interests.

Diametrically opposed is charismatic authority, distinguished primarily by its exclusive, personal character, entirely independent of the hierarchic structure. It is sporadic, unstable, and transient by its very nature and is not subject to the accepted laws of government and the routine social system. In Weber's words, "[this authority] is expressly non-rational in the sense that it conforms to none of the rules." However, the emphatic statement "none of the rules" is undoubtedly exaggerated, as is the apparent rigidity of a threefold typology of authority and leadership.[19] In reality, these types do not appear in their pure and pristine form, but in some measure mix and overlap. In other words, the other two legitimate forms do also contain charismatic traits, a phenomenon which Weber himself clearly acknowledged.[20] But both his followers and his critics have emphasized that the real problem lies in the degree of the charismatic quality—intense or attenuated—present in the several forms of domination.[21] These qualifications of the Weberian tripartite scheme fully apply to Israelite society in the biblical period.

According to Weber's definition, the charismatic leader was endowed from birth with physical and mental traits that differed from the ordinary and commonplace qualities (his *Ausseralltäglichkeit*). Both the charismatic individual and his following regard these attributes as emanating from a higher force; in this sense, he possesses supernatural gifts and is a leader *Dei gratia*. The charismatic leader arises, in Weber's words, "in times of psychic, physical, economic, ethical, religious, or political distress." This maxim, now regarded as classic, together with the characteristics just mentioned, aptly suits the Israelite judge and the circumstances of his emergence, as revealed in the Book of Judges. The deliverer-judge, distinguished by extraordinary qualities and gifts, appeared in his own estimation and in that of his devotees as a divine agent delivering his people from national crisis, an act which imbued him with supreme authority within his society.

This brings us to the other aspect of the charismatic phenomenon—the prerequisite of a society willing to recognize this type of authority. Without such recognition, charisma lacks all substantiality and remains meaningless. Hence, this phenomenon is to be regarded as a process of interaction between the personality of the leader, on the one hand, and his followers seeking to achieve desired objectives, on the other hand.[22] Viewed in this light the concept of charisma gains a socio-political dimension, which biblical scholarship, with its express theological interest, neglected.[23] Only in a given socio-historical context, the "situation" of the sociologists, could the charistmatic person prevail and his mission come to fulfillment. The specific conditions or situational aspects conducive to the charismatic emergence were not particularly treated by Weber in his comparative analyses, though this facet has drawn great attention in post-Weberian investigation, especially in connection with the nature of leadership in the developing countries.[24]

III

A climate favorable to the emergence of charismatic leadership in Israel's history matured in the era of the judges. The "situation" entailed a dual crisis: externally, enemies made for constant insecurity, with succeeding disasters befalling the Israelites (as seen above); internally, traditional authority was progressively undermined. Increasing sedentation in this period, with its consequent adjustments to the conditions of permanent settlement alongside partial adaptation to the Canaanite urban environment, led the Israelite tribes to a preference for territorial principles over gentilic bonds and consanguinity. Thus, the tribal institutions—indeed the entire inherited societal framework—were on the wane.

Although the routine social system and day-to-day affairs continued under the jurisdiction of the clan heads and the institution of the elders, the traditional elite could no longer maintain its own prestige let alone cope with the task of maintaining Israelite autonomy. Ineluctably, a crisis of trust was created, and with it a crisis of authority. The existing leadership which was held responsible for the people's straits was forced aside, to make way for leaders of a new kind who were able to inspire confidence, to steer a course for the people, and to shoulder the task of deliverance. The very weakening of traditional authority within clan and tribe resulted in individuals breaking away from the tight bonds of kinship, freeing them to exercise personal initiative which could eventually lead to attaining a national commission.[25] This polar relationship within Israelite society—the decline of traditional authority and the rise of individuals outside the old order—finds ample expression in the Book of Judges:[26]

Deborah, as a woman, had no standing in the agnatic-patriarchal order; it was she, however, who roused the people to fight for their freedom, who stirred Barak to action and, in short, who was the driving force behind the battle. Gideon, "whose clan is the weakest in Manasseh" and who himself was "the least in his family" (6:15), initiated and stood at the head of the forces of liberation—he, not his father or senior brothers, or the representatives of more renowned families. But the most indicative example of the incompetency of the traditional leadership and the rise of a fringe personality is the episode of Jephthah, who stood outside the normal social framework. The elders of Gilead sought in their hour of peril a leader from their own midst, but in vain. Hard-pressed, they turned to Jephthah the outcast, "the son of a harlot"—who had been ousted by his brothers from his patrimony—for he possessed the requisite military qualifications, having gathered around him a band of fighters. The traditional rulers were forced to accede to Jephthah (11:6 ff.) and appoint him not only as "commander" (qāṣîn), that is, as leader for the duration of the war, but also as "head" (rôš), that is, as supreme ruler in peace as well—all of which involved surrendering their authority and the powers vested in them.

In the social and political vacuum created by the crumbling of traditional authority, before the requisite instruments of the legal-rational establishment had been fashioned—such as a standing army and a bureaucratic apparatus—the "floruit" of the Israelite judge was born. The Israelites despaired of deliverance through the existing leadership and languished for a deliverer-leader. This protracted yearning under the harsh conditions of distress, which increased the emotional strain, generated a deep religious-national awakening among the people—intensifying the charismatic susceptibility. Yet the "situation" of collective crisis alone is insufficient to trigger a charismatic emergence, as is shown by the lengthy periods of oppression and subjugation preceding the deliverance. In any event, in no instance did a deliverer-judge arise immediately upon the inception of a crisis (see below). Clearly, therefore, a further prerequisite is the appearance of the potential leader, a personage able to alleviate the people's frustration and apathy, to define for them their national goals, and to serve as a catalyst for their collective desires.[27] Only the integration of these conditions, in each and every case, could lead to charismatic leadership, personified in Israelite history by the deliverer-judge.

IV

We shall now outline the qualities and principal components inherent in the personality of the Israelite deliverer-judge and his charismatic rule, as can be deduced from Weberian and post-Weberian theories. Apart from and above these, emphasis must be placed, from the outset, on the focal element peculiar to the Israelite phenomenon, namely the politico-military facet of deliverer-leadership integrated with the religious aspect[28] and usually involving personal bravery. The schematic outline below[29] does not intend to minimize the variety and diversity indeed found in the personalities and deeds of the individual judges, just as the absence of one quality or another in a given judge cannot invalidate the basic model of his charismatic leadership. The lack of a particular constituent can be ascribed merely to the manner of presentation by the literary source.

a) A prerequisite for the maturing of the charismatic attribute is a situation of major crisis, above all one induced by an infringement upon national and territorial integrity, in other words, subjugation by an enemy.[30] The appearance of each of the deliverer-judges occurred only after oppression by an alien people, which lasted many years—for eight years prior to Othniel (3:8); eighteen before Ehud (3:14); twenty before Deborah (4:3); seven before Gideon (6:1); eighteen before Jephthah (10:8); and forty before and during Samson's time (13:1, and cf. 15:20).

b) The charismatic trait involves direct contact with transcendental powers and identification with the symbols held most sacred by a people.[31] In Israel such experiences were realized in the intimate relationship of the charismatic personage with God, expressed in religious revelations and in the spirit (*rûaḥ*) of *YHWH* with which the hero has come to be associated, by himself and by the people. Running through the Book of Judges like a thread are the phrases: "And the spirit of the Lord came upon [Othniel]" (3:10); "But the spirit of the Lord took possession of Gideon" (6:34); "Then the spirit of the Lord came upon Jephthah" (11:29); "And the spirit of the Lord began to stir [Samson]" (13:25); and "And the spirit of the Lord came mightily upon [Samson]" (14:6, 19; 15:14).

c) Sometimes the divine contact required public signs and acknowledgment prior to the act of deliverance, to affirm the authority of the charismatic person both in his own eyes and in the consciousness of the people. The outstanding example is the case of Gideon, who appeals to God, upon being consecrated for his mission, for "a sign that it is Thou who spokest with me" (6:17); and on the eve of his action he twice requests additional signs (the episode of the fleece of wool). There are numerous signs mentioned in the stories of Samson, who was designated for his task even prior to his birth (13:3 ff.). The signs in the "call narratives" of these two deliverers were associated with the apparition of an angel of the Lord announcing the mission of the deliverer, a motif intended to enhance the credibility of his mandate.[32]

d) The authority bestowed upon the charismatic leader is characteristically spontaneous. The judges were appointed for their task *ad hoc,* and their nomination was specifically personal and consequently non-hereditary or non-transferable. (The sole exception, Abimelech's inheritance of Gideon's authority, is a case of usurpation; see below).

e) The authority of charismatic leadership, by nature, is not dependent on social class or status, nor on age-group or sex. This is attested to by such figures as Jephthah, who was of dubious descent, the "lad" Gideon, who was the youngest of his family, and Deborah, the judgess and prophetess. An indication that the deliverer-judges were not of noble lineage is the conspicuous fact that they or their forebears (except Othniel's and Ehud's fathers; see immediately below) do not find mention in the tribal genealogies of the Bible. On the other hand, an inferior social status is not, of course, an essential feature of the rise of a deliverer-judge. Besides Othniel the putative "son of Kenaz, Caleb's younger brother" (3:9), Ehud the son of Gera was a scion of a noble Benjaminite family (Gen. 46:21; I Chron. 8:3, 7), which was still renowned in David's time (II Sam. 16:5). Furthermore, it appears that even prior to his charismatic emergence Ehud held a prominent role within his tribe, for he stood at the head of the delegation bringing tribute to the king of Moab—precisely like a vassal chief would appear before his suzerain. This seems to be a rare instance of a leader who acquired the charismatic quality in the course of his official career, a phenomenon found at times also in other charismatic regimes.[33]

f) The rise and activity of charismatic leaders are not necessarily linked to important religious or civil centers. In this respect it is noteworthy that not even one of the Israelite judges arose in a place of special status in Israel's history, and certainly not at any site of cultic significance such as Shechem, Bethel, or Shiloh. Deborah judges "between Ramah and Bethel in the hill country of Ephraim" (4:5); Gideon's residence, Ophrah, became an Israelite cultic seat only after the act of deliverance; Jephthah found refuge in the land of Tob, a fringe area, and only after his appointment did he move to Mizpah and make it his permanent abode (11:16, 34); while Samson's birthplace was at Zorah, and the beginning of his activity was "in the encampment of Dan, between Zorah and Eshtaol" (13:25).

g) Finally, the specific relationship between the charismatic leader and the people, which is not based upon formal rules or administrative organization, and certainly not on coercion; rather, it rests upon emotion, the personal reverence toward the charismatic individual on the part of his devotees. A following gathered around the Israelite judge of its own free will, placing its entire dependence upon him with unshaken faith in his mission (an exception here is Samson the Nazirite). The mustering of warriors took on the form of a voluntary militia—in contrast to a mercenary force—dedicated to the leader with no rational remuneration or predetermined material reward.

In the Book of Judges there is one exceptional figure of a leader who represents the complete antithesis of the above scheme—namely, Abimelech the son of Gideon. His detailed story (Judges 9) was probably included in the book because of its paradigmatic value—in this case, to furnish the model of what I would call an "anti-judge" or "anti-deliverer." Indeed, comparing Abimelech to the typical charismatic leader, following the above outline, we find diametrically opposed traits or no corresponding traits whatsoever:

a) Abimelech's rise was not preceded by a period of foreign subjugation necessitating an act of deliverance, and consequently it did not result in an era of tranquillity.

b–c) Abimelech did not act under divine inspiration, and received no religious revelations. His military engagements, daring as they may have been, hardly constitute acts of deliverance from a foe, but aimed at conquest, oppression, and destruction.

d) Abimelech did not come upon the scene spontaneously, but paved his way to power by political maneuvering, including the slaughter of his brothers. He based his demands for authority on the inheritance of his father's position as ruler (9:2).

e) In his climb to power, Abimelech was aided not only by his paternal pedigree, but also by familial ties on his maternal side since his mother was of the Canaanite nobility of Shechem.

f) In contrast to the other judges, Abimelech became ruler in a key urban center, the city of Shechem, a site long-sanctified even in Israelite tradition.

g) Abimelech's authority was cast in a conventional pattern, that of kingship; the local oligarchy, the "lords of Shechem" (*ba'⁼lê š⁼kem*), "made him king" (9:6). He instituted an administration in the city, as is indicated by his appointment of Zebul as "official" (*pāqîd*) or "governor of the city" (*śar ha'îr;* 9:28, 30). Initially, Abimelech utilized a mercenary troop of "idle and reckless men," paid from the temple treasury of Baal-berit, the city's deity (9:4).

Abimelech's rule did not, therefore, emanate from any charismatic quality. His system of government, drawing in great measure upon the Canaanite concept of the city-state, was of a dimorphic structure, a combination of rule over a foreign urban center, on the one hand, and over the Israelite

rural, tribal elements, on the other hand.[34] In seizing the reigns of government he acted solely out of personal greed for power—a motive far removed from any legitimate form of domination, most especially charismatic.
Indeed, in Israelite tradition, Abimelech's abortive regency was excoriated
as a despotic usurpation of power. In summing up his rule, the biblical
author avoids calling him king or judge, but employs the unique phrase:
"he held sway [wa-yāśar] over Israel for three years" (9:22).

The natural desire to stabilize the sporadic leadership of the judges strength-
ened the tendency among the Israelites to give fixed and permanent form to
the charismatic attribute that it might become a stable, organized, and
hereditary function—a universal phenomenon known as the "routinization
of charisma." Indeed, it is against this background that the kingship offered to Gideon by "the men of Israel" must be viewed: "Rule over us,
you and your son and your grandson also; for you have delivered us out of
the hand of Midian" (8:22). However, the time was not yet ripe for
transmuting the Israelite order. Individual freedom and the egalitarian
structure of Israelite society were still major obstructions to change, alongside the deeply rooted belief in the supremacy of the Heavenly Kingdom.[35]

It was only toward the end of the eleventh century B.C. that the requisite
internal conditions in Israel matured for the establishment of a new regime,
a process accelerated by weighty external factors—principally the Philistine
threat. At this stage, charisma ceased to function in its pure, concentrated
form and became institutionalized within the framework of the Israelite
monarchy.[36]

This paper is based on a lecture given at a symposium on "Types of Leadership in the
Biblical Period" held at the Israel Academy of Sciences and Humanities on 15 Decem-
ber 1971. Throughout this paper, references by chapter and verse alone are to the
Book of Judges.

NOTES

1. For a general survey, see A. Malamat, "The Period of the Judges," in *Judges,
WHJP*, III, 129–163, 314–323. For the composition of the Book of Judges and its
Redaktionsgeschichte, see the cited literature, ibid., p. 314, n. 1, and p. 350 (General Bibliography). Like its West Semitic cognates from the early second millennium B.C. on, the root *špṭ* in the Book of Judges signifies more than merely "judging";
it covers the broad concept of rulership, including the aspects of judge and champion.
Contrary to the generally accepted critical view, its presence in the deliverer narratives
is no less primary than that of *yš', mošia';* see ibid., pp. 130 f.

2. The different representations of the "major" and the "minor" judges in the Bible

may be merely a carry-over from the literary sources drawn upon by the compiler—colorful folk narratives on the one hand, and schematic family chronicles on the other hand. See ibid., p. 131. Y. Kaufmann, *The Book of Judges* [Hebrew] (Jerusalem, 1962), pp. 47 f., entirely assimilated the "minor" to the "major" judges, assuming that the stories of deliverance once associated with the former had been lost. But this is an extreme view.

3. For the literature on *špṭ, šopeṭ,* see *WHJP,* III, 314 f., nn. 6–7; and see now also H. Reviv, "Types of Leadership in the Period of the Judges," in *Beer-Sheva. Annual, Studies in Bible* . . . [Hebrew] 1 (1973), 204–221 and T. Ishida, "The Leaders of the Tribal League 'Israel' in the Pre-Monarchic Period," *RB* 80 (1973), 514–530. On *yšʿ,* see now J. F. A. Sawyer, *Semantics in Biblical Research—New Methods of Defining Hebrew Words for Salvation* (London, 1972), esp. pp. 57 f., 94 f.

4. For an extensive historical survey of the above military encounters, see *WHJP,* III, 135–159. For the possible identification of King Cushan-Rishathaim, see our remarks in ibid., pp. 25–27; on the Philistine threat see B. Mazar, "The Philistines and Their Wars with Israel," ibid., pp. 164–179.

5. The biblical lists of tribes arranged on a geographical principle have been treated most recently by Helga Weippert, "Das geographische System der Stämme Israels," *VT* 23 (1973), 76–89, where, *inter alia,* Dan's ultimate position in the list of Judges 1 is attributed to a late redactor, ascribing the order there to the period of the united monarchy; for this same dating, see Z. Kallai, *Proceedings of the Fifth World Congress of Jewish Studies* [Hebrew] (Jerusalem, 1969), p. 133, n. 12. By analogy, we can perhaps ascribe the north-to-south sequence of the structure of the Book of Judges as a whole, as outlined above, to the same period.

6. "To test" (*lᵉnassot*) in 3:1 is the subject of an exegetical controversy. One view (exemplified by Kaufmann [N 2], p. 100) holds that a religious trial of Israel is intended, in the face of heathen temptation. It is preferable, however, and in keeping with the context of vss. 1–2 here, to regard the expression as referring to military experience; cf., for example, C. F. Burney, *The Book of Judges*[2] (London, 1920), p. 54; and esp. M. Greenberg, *JBL* 79 (1960), 276 and n. 5 (where the term is translated as "to give [Israel] experience"). See now also J. Licht, *Testing in the Hebrew Scriptures and in Post-Biblical Judaism* [Hebrew], (Jerusalem, 1973), pp. 15 ff.

7. For the attempts to identify this personage, see *WHJP,* III, 315, n. 15.

8. This has been stressed in particular by Kaufmann [N 2], p. 33, who, however, is too fundamentalistic in his regarding the framework as an early, primary "historical document," like the deliverer narratives themselves. On the literary complexity of the framework proper, including pre-Deuteronomic strands, cf. W. Beyerlin, "Gattung und Herkunft des Rahmens im Richterbuch," in *Festschrift A. Weiser* (Göttingen, 1963), pp. 1–29; for the relationship between the framework and the Book of Judges as a whole, see esp. W. Richter, *Die Bearbeitungen des "Retterbuches" in der deuteronomischen Epoche* (Bonn, 1964).

9. E. H. Erikson, quoted by D. A. Rustow, in *Philosophers and Kings: Studies in Leadership* (New York, 1970), p. 15.

10. Cf. Kaufmann [N 2], pp. 36 ff.; *WHJP,* III, 129.

11. As widely held by Bible critics; contrasting this, see the references in the previous note, and now Ishida [N 3], p. 165. Attention should be drawn to a similar phenomenon regarding leadership in today's developing nations: the expansion of dimensions in tribal leaders and their becoming "nationalized," tribe being "transcended, while the sacred earth [i.e. the optative domain] retains its sacredness, its charisma, although it is no longer circumscribed by the area within which one's particular tribe—one's kinship and ethnic group—dwells" (E. Shils, "The Concentration and Dispersion of Charisma, Their Bearing on Economic Policy in Underdeveloped Countries, *World Politics* II [1958–59], 1–19, quotation on p. 4).

12. Almost exclusively in the Pauline epistles (Romans and esp. Corinthians); see most recently H. Conzelmann, *Theologisches Wörterbuch zum Neuen Testament*, IX, Lief. 7 (Stuttgart, 1971), 393–397, s.v. *charisma*.

13. *Gesammelte Aufsätze zur Religionssoziologie* III: *Das antike Judentum* (Tübingen, 1923). English translation by H. H. Gerth and D. Martindale, *Ancient Judaism* (Glencoe, 1952), index, s.v. *charisma, šopeṭim*. For the literature of the Bible scholars, see N 28.

14. *Grundriss der Sozialökonomik: Wirtschaft und Gesellschaft* (Tübingen, 1925); we use here the 4th edition (henceforth *WuG*), critically revised and with excerpts from Weber's other writings, by J. Winckelmann (Tübingen, 1956), I, 122–176; II, 541–615. English edition by G. Roth and C. Wittich, *Economy and Society, an Outline of Interpretive Sociology* (New York, 1968), I, 212 ff.; III, 1111 ff. Earlier publications in English of sections on charisma appear in *Max Weber: The Theory of Social and Economic Organization*, ed. T. Parsons, trs. A. M. Henderson and T. Parsons (New York, 1947), pp. 358–392; and *Max Weber: On Charisma and Institution Building*, ed. S. N. Eisenstadt (Chicago-London, 1968).

15. Of the abundant recent literature on Weber's conception of charisma, we may note the following: the numerous publications of T. Parsons (a most recent treatment is his *Politics and Social Structure* [New York-London, 1969], ch. 5, pp. 98–110); the introductions by Parsons and Eisenstadt in the works edited by them [N 14]; R. Bendix, *Max Weber—An Intellectual Portrait* (New York, 1962; repr. University Paperbacks, London, 1966), ch. x; P. M. Blau, "Critical Remarks on Weber's Theory of Authority," *American Political Science Review* 57 (1963), 305–316; W. H. Friedland, "For a Sociological Concept of Charisma," *Social Forces* 43 (1964), 18–26; K. J. Ratman, "Charisma and Political Leadership," *Political Studies* 12 (1964), 341–354; K. Loewenstein, *Max Webers staatspolitische Auffassungen in der Sicht unserer Zeit* (Bonn, 1965), pp. 74–88; W. J. Mommsen, "Universalgeschichtliches und politisches Denken bei Max Weber," *Historische Zeitschrift* 201 (1965), 557–612, esp. 586 ff.; the articles by D. A. Rustow, "The Study of Leadership," pp. 1–18, and R. C. Tucker, "The Theory of Charismatic Leadership," pp. 69–94 in *Philosophers and Kings: Studies in Leadership*, ed. D. A. Rustow (New York, 1970); *The Iron Cage—An Historical Interpretation of Max Weber* (New York, 1970); J. Séguy, "Max Weber et la sociologie historique des religions," *Archives de Sociologie des Religions* 33 (1972), 71–103, esp. 94 ff.; and see the works by E. Shils, cited below [N 21] and by Ann R. Willner [N 24].

16. Loewenstein [N 15], pp. 78 ff., considers genuine charisma as particularly inherent in those political milieus characterized by "magical-ritualistic or mystical-religious elements," as in the pre-Cartesian West and in large parts of Asia and Africa still today.

17. Cf. *WuG* [N 14], pp. 122 ff. Weber's concise formulation of his scheme, included only in the 4th edition of *WuG*, pp. 551–558, did not belong originally to this work and was therefore removed from the subsequent editions (cf. *Studienausgabe*, I [Köln-Berlin, 1964], p. xv, and the English edition of 1968). The development of Weber's concept of charismatic rule is traced in Mitzman [N 15], index, s.v. *charisma*.

18. Strictly according to Weber, however, *true* legal rationality was achieved only in modern Western civilization (cf. Bendix, [N 15], pp. 385 ff.). My colleague S. N. Eisenstadt has pointed out to me that the Israelite monarchical regime was essentially patrimonial (a traditional rather than legal-rational feature); and besides, all "old bureaucracies were essentially patrimonial in character" (J. Freund, *The Sociology of Max Weber* [New York, 1968], p. 236).

19. See several of the authors mentioned above in N 15, e.g. Eisenstadt (introduction, esp. pp. xxi ff.); Blau; Ratman (esp. p. 344); Rustow (pp. 14 ff.); and further, Shils' "Charisma, Order and Status" and his entry on "Charisma" in *International Encyclopedia of the Social Sciences*, II, esp. p. 390; both cited in N 21, below.

20. Hence Weber's introduction of the concepts *Gentilcharisma* (lineage charisma) and *Amtscharisma* (charisma of office) for the "depersonalization" of the charismatic quality in traditional domination, on the one hand, and the rational-legal domination, on the other hand. See *WuG* [N 14], pp. 681 ff., 700 ff.; and cf. also Bendix [N 15], pp. 308 ff.

21. See principally Shils' "The Concentration and Dispersion of Charisma" [N 11]; "Charisma, Order and Status," *American Social Review* 30 (1965), 199–213; and "Charisma," in *International Encyclopedia of the Social Sciences*, II (1968), 386–390.

22. Cf. W. E. Mühlmann, *Max Weber und die rationale Soziologie* (Tübingen, 1966), pp. 18–21; Friedland [N 15], pp. 20 f.; Rustow [N. 15], pp. 15 ff.

23. This interpretation may serve to mollify recent questioning of the application of "charisma" to the Israelite judge, as notably in G. Fohrer, *Geschichte der israelitischen Religion* (Berlin, 1969), pp. 87 f., 138. For the stress on the theological aspect, see the literature cited below toward the end of N 28.

24. See notably A. R. Willner and D. Willner, "The Rise and Role of Charismatic Leadership," *Annals of the American Academy of Political and Social Science* 358 (1965), 77–88; A. R. Willner, *Charismatic Political Leadership: A Theory* (Princeton, 1968), ch. III: "The Charismatic Phenomenon—Convergence and Catalyst"; and e.g. D. A. Rustow, *A World of Nations* (Washington, 1967), pp. 148–169 (Charisma and the Founding of States).

25. For a similar process in the developing states, see Shils, [N 11], pp. 1, 16.

26. The relationship between the "establishment" and the charismatic leaders in the period of the judges was insufficiently elaborated upon in Weber's *Antike Judentum* [N 13], pp. 21 ff., 92 ff.; cf. now Reviv [N 3], who, however, puts too much weight on the role of the elders *vis-à-vis* the judges.

27. Cf. A. R. Willner, *Charismatic Political Leadership* [N 24], pp. 44 ff.

28. There may well have been a gradual strengthening and emphasis on the religious aspect, due to later tendentious reflections upon the early historical events in the Bible; cf. the conclusions, though extreme, in L. Schmidt, *Menschlicher Erfolg und Jahwes Initiative* (Neukirchen-Vluyn, 1970); F. Stolz, *Jahwes und Israels Kriege* (Zürich, 1972) esp. pp. 100 ff., 172 ff.; and the more cautious treatment in I. L. Seeligmann, "Menschliches Heldentum und göttliche Hilfe," *Theologische Zeitschrift* 19 (1963), 385–411, esp. 397 ff. The primeval nature of "charisma" within Yahwistic faith, already existent in the period of the judges, has long been noted in literature: A. Alt, *Die Staatenbildung der Israeliten in Palästina* (Leipzig, 1930), p. 9; M. Buber, *Königtum Gottes* (Berlin, 1932); W. Eichrodt, *Theologie des Alten Testaments*, I (Leipzig, 1933), 150 ff., 237 f. (in the seventh edition, 1962, 190 ff., 298); and G. von Rad, *Theologie des Alten Testaments*, I (Munich, 1957), 100 ff.; and most recently, W. Zimmerli, *Grundriss der alttestamentlichen Theologie* (Stüttgart, 1972), pp. 68–72.

29. I am indebted to Professor U. Tal for certain features in the outline, which he pointed out during a lecture before a seminar on the regime of the judges, conducted by the author at the Hebrew University in 1959. Of course, Professor Tal could not then utilize the recent abundance of literature on the application of charisma.

30. Cf. A. R. Willner, *Charismatic Political Leadership* [N 24], p. 41, noting the ensuing effects of subjugation.

31. Cf. Shils' "Charisma, Order and Status" and "Charisma" [both in N 21].

32. Contrasting critical analyses of the literary relationship between the themes of "sign," "call," and "theophanic angel," especially in the Gideon episode, are given by W. Richter, *Die sogenannten vorprophetischen Berufungsberichte* (Göttingen, 1970) and Schmidt [N 28]; earlier literature is noted in both works.

33. Cf. A. R. Willner, *Charismatic Political Leadership* [N 24], p. 12.

34. For Abimelech's rule and its peculiar nature, see *WHJP*, III, 149 ff. Its course of development can also be analyzed in the light of Weber's theorems on modes of

domination (though *Antike Judentum* [N 13], p. 16, n. 2, and p. 23, mistakenly we believe, refers to Abimelech as a charismatic leader): Abimelech initially sought support of the "lords of Shechem" and later clashed with them, exemplifying Weber's notion that early kings, originally rural war leaders, had to rely upon the support of cities but, once established, came into conflict with the urban oligarchy. Further, Abimelech attempted to neutralize the influence of the city aristocracy by appointing his own retainers as officials and by mobilizing troops from among the (loyal) Israelites; this conforms with the Weberian king counteracting his dependence upon the local oligarchy by installing personally devoted officials from the ranks of the populace and by recruiting mercenaries from outside. Cf. Bendix [N 15], p. 211, basing on *WuG* [N 14].

35. See esp. Buber's *Königtum Göttes* [N 28], where he uses Gideon's rejection of the offer of kingship as a point of departure.

36. Such "routinization" into charismatic kingship is treated in general in Weber's *WuG* [N 14], pp. 678 f., 684 f.; for the phenomenon in Israel—beyond the scope of the present study—see in particular, recently, J. A. Soggin, *Das Königtum in Israel* (Berlin, 1967), which gives the earlier literature, and now also F. M. Cross, *Canaanite Myth and Hebrew Epic* (Cambridge, Mass., 1973), pp. 219 ff.

II

Prophets and Kings

8. *The Origins of Prophecy*

HERBERT B. HUFFMON

DREW UNIVERSITY, MADISON, NEW JERSEY

IT IS A COMMONPLACE in biblical criticism to find the origins of prophecy among Samuel and his successors, however that prophecy be evaluated. In this opinion, of course, biblical criticism merely represents the basic picture given by the Bible itself. Deprived of one of the secret pleasures of critical scholarship, namely, arguing that the traditional picture is altogether wrong, the task remaining is to present the common view in the framework of our constantly increasing knowledge of the historical background and setting of the rise of Israelite prophecy and of the processes and techniques of change and development that are involved. Such a presentation may serve both to support and to supplement the common view.

There is a sense, however, in which a topic such as this is somewhat misleading. To single out the "origins" of prophecy as a topic or problem may suggest to some that there is a special difficulty involved in understanding why prophecy should "originate" in some individual culture. First of all, change—and social change in particular—is in no way unusual. It is one of the basic givens of human existence, in spite of the myth of the "unchanging East" or the notion of "age-old" beliefs.[1] Second, prophecy is really a rather widespread human phenomenon and might even be called universal. Although at least in the Western world prophecy is peculiarly associated with ancient Israel, that view represents more a value judgment on the content and significance of Israelite prophetic activity than an appraisal of the actual distribution of prophetic activity throughout all human history.[2] But then this anticipates our definition of prophecy.

It is difficult to determine who is a prophet and who is not. Recent books have proclaimed such diverse figures as Mark Twain, Leon Trotsky, and Charles F. Kettering as "prophets." And Elijah, who fearlessly challenged the four hundred and fifty prophets of Baal at Mount Carmel, not to mention the four hundred prophets of Asherah, might well have hesitated before the ten thousand prophets recently reported to have gathered in Boston. But then the newspaper headline turned out to refer to a convention of economists. Apparently anyone connected with social reform, innovation, or prediction can be called a "prophet." It may be that the continuing use of this imprecise term creates problems in understanding the Israelite prophets.

The Greek term *prophētēs,* "one who proclaims," "speaker," is not necessarily of much help in this regard. First, the range of activities of the *prophētēs* does not tally very well with that of Near Eastern "prophets" in terms of the means of reception, the form, and the content of the oracles. Second, as a translation word the Greek term is used for phenomena as diverse as the Egyptian priestly office, *ḥm-nṯr,* "servant of the god," whose primary liturgical and administrative roles were coupled with the preparing of oracle questions and interpreting of oracle signs, and the Hebrew *nābī'.* The Classical terms and the phenomena to which they refer cannot be taken as parallel to the ancient Near Eastern phenomena without prior consideration, just as the categories into which the activities are classified by commentators such as Cicero (*De Divinatione*) cannot merely be presumed to be universally useful. The center of attention must be what actually transpired in the ancient Near East itself.

In terms of ancient Near Eastern religious circles a useful definition of "prophet" seems to be that the prophet is a person who through non-technical means receives a clear and immediate message from a deity for transmission to a third party. The contrast is with learned, technical divination and the use of interpretative skills, or what Plato calls "the rational investigation of futurity" (*Phaedrus*), even though the divination may well relate to past events.

Although at one time prophecy, typically seen as ecstatic prophecy, was related exclusively to a Canaanite background, the rise of Israelite prophecy must now be seen in light of a considerably wider framework. First, prophecy in the ancient Near East, though still a marginal phenomenon, is now known to be far more widely attested than was previously thought. Second, recent studies by historians of religion and anthropologists of millenarian or "revitalization" movements and of spirit-possession and even shamanism help to provide new insights into the development and role of prophecy in the ancient Near East.[3] For in spite of the involvement of our own convictions, the origins of prophecy in Israel cannot be separated from either the rest of the surrounding world or similar developments at other times elsewhere.

In terms of the brief definition of prophecy already offered, the earliest attestation of prophetic revelations come from the archives of Mari. From the Mari letters of the latter part of the eighteenth century B.C. we learn of an astonishing variety of prophetic activity. And, we are told, there are yet more letters about prophetic activity presently unpublished in any form.[4] From the nearly thirty letters already published in one form or another, reports tell of prophets in a wide area from Aleppo to at least Mari, and there are even connections with Sippar, not far north of Babylon itself.

The prophets divide into two groups, those with official titles and those without. Those persons designated by titles as *āpilu, assinnu,* or *muḫḫū* bear titles of cultic functionaries or at least of persons who are connected with various deities and who may receive royal support. These titles are known also from lexical texts which collect titles of various occupations. The titles in question, however, do not refer to cult priests or priestesses in the strict sense of those directly involved in the care and feeding of the gods.[5] Those persons who do not bear titles such as *āpilu* are apparently lay or private persons, some of whom indeed are well known from other texts.

As for the titles, two, *āpilu/āpiltu,* "Answerer," and *muḫḫū/muḫḫūtu,* probably meaning "Ecstatic," occur with both men and women, though the men predominate. Moreover, one text suggests that "Answerers" might exist and operate in groups. The third title, *assinnu,* of uncertain meaning and found only with men, is later at least especially associated with the cult of Ishtar. There is also some information about the circumstances of the oracles. The "Answerer" at times delivered the oracle in the temple, once following upon the royal sacrifice of Dagan of Tuttul. The "Ecstatic" also spoke in the temple on occasion and once there is reference to a preceding sacrifice. On another occasion the "Ecstatic" came to the king's representative, presumably outside the temple. In a text describing a ritual for the cult of Ishtar at Mari there is mention of a *muḫḫū* becoming ecstatic (*a-na ma-ḫi-e-im*), but it is the *assinnu* who in one letter is said to have "become ecstatic (*im-ma-ḫu*)" and given an oracle, not the *muḫḫū.* Then again it is an "Ecstatic" who concludes a temple oracle with the assurance that "I will continue to answer (*a-ta-na-ap-pa-al*)." These three titles do occur outside the Mari archives, although *āpilu* seems restricted to lexical lists (assuming that it cannot be separated from the *a-pi-lu-u, a-pil-lu-ú* who has a similar identity). But nowhere do the titles occur in connection with the giving of oracles.

Several of the Mari letters report oracles given by private or lay persons, of whom the majority are women. These persons come from various ranks of the Mari society. Typically they report revelations by way of dreams which either take place in a temple or involve a dream visit to a temple. There is no hint of incubation, however. Once a lady "became ecstatic (*im-ma-ḫi*)" in a temple and delivered an oracle, and twice—or once if the apparent name, Qamatum, is actually a title, *qabbātum,* "Speaker"—a lady merely came and gave an oracle.

Due perhaps to the nature of the Mari archives, the oracles reported relate primarily to the king. One or two oracles, though, are addressed to the people of Terqa. In regard to the content of these oracles, it is important to note that within the framework of Mesopotamian religious practice—and the Mari area represents a western province of that tradition—the oracles are often critical of the king for failing in his duties to various gods and temples. Once the king is even reminded of his obligation to promote justice. Mostly, however, the oracles are favorable to the king. But even with favorable oracles there are at times clear indications of the marginal standing of prophetic oracles. The royal official or agent often advises the king to have a proper extispicy made, i.e. to resort to learned divination, and the role of the symbolic hair and hem surrendered by various speakers is presumably to aid in another means of verification.

Some of the oracles give indication of having been solicited, whereas others seem to be quite unsolicited. In this connection it is reasonable to conjecture that on occasion the oracles from "official" sources were a scheduled response, a means by which the deity could signal a reaction to the preceding cultic activity, such as a sacrifice. But even if some of the oracles were solicited at some appropriate moment in the cult it seems clear that the response was sometimes at least not quite what had been expected. In terms of style the oracles feature such introductory phrases as "thus says god so-and-so," or "god so-and-so sent me." There is at least one "woe oracle" against the king's enemy.

Apart from the Mari archives the extensive textual remains of the Old Babylonian period have yielded only one more or less comparable oracle text, the oracle from Uruk. This text, although somewhat obscure, involves direct address by Nanaya-Ishtar, whose message is understood as intended for the king.[6] This lack of evidence does suggest that oracle giving was a marginal phenomenon. It is quite possible that the muḫḫū (twice), or LÚ.GUB.BA (five times), who is mentioned in Old Babylonian texts other than from Mari was not associated with prophetic oracles in Babylonia proper. (For that matter the closely related or variant title maḫḫū/maḫ-ḫūtu, presumably also meaning "Ecstatic" and which is known from later texts, is never explicitly associated with prophetic oracle speaking.) Prophetic oracles may have been virtually limited to the Mari sphere during the Old Babylonian period. The prominence of prophets in the Mari archives as opposed to the rest of the Old Babylonian texts does suggest that it may have been congenial to Amorite religious tradition.

In between the Old Babylonian and the first millennium texts reporting prophetic activity we have two isolated sources. The first is the prayers of Mursilis II (latter part of the fourteenth century B.C.) concerning the plague and how it might be averted. Mursilis lists the various means by which he might learn the reason for the god's anger: (1) through a dream of the king himself or some other person; (2) through technical divination; (3) through incubation, apparently, by priests or female mediums; and (4) through inspired speaking.[7] Specifically, the last-mentioned option is "let a man of god (come and) declare it." But there is no further information about this "man of god." The second source is the well-known Wen-Amun Report from about the middle of the eleventh century B.C.[8] While in Byblos, Wen-Amun, the Egyptian representative of the god Amun, was rescued from a forced departure by an oracle. A Byblian court page apparently became ecstatic and cried out (to the king of Byblos), "bring up (the) god! Bring up the messenger who is carrying him. Amun is the one who sent him out." Although this instance in an Egyptian report has been regarded by some scholars, most notably G. Hölscher,[9] as partial justification for the derivation of Israelite prophecy from Canaanite sources, it is striking that in form and content the Byblian oracle is rather different from those of the Israelite prophets, or, for that matter, the Mari or Neo-Assyrian prophets. It is also interesting that so far there is no explicit evidence for prophetic oracles in the texts from Ugarit.

In the first millennium there are scattered reports about prophetic activity in Syria and Palestine, apart from the Yahwistic prophets, and an impressive amount of information about prophetic oracles during the reigns of the Assyrian kings Esarhaddon and Ashurbanipal. The earliest reports concern the prophets of Baal (and of Asherah) who were active in northern Israel in the ninth century. They engage in frenzied behavior but are not associated with oracles, so far as their activities are described. It is possible that they did not give oracles.[10] The next report is in the Zakir stele which dates from the early eighth century. Zakir, king of Hamath and Lu'ash, prayed to Baal-shamayn while under siege. Baal-shamayn answered him by means of *ḥāziyīn*, "Seers," and *'-d-dīn*, presumably diviners of some kind. The oracle itself, "Fear not, for I have made [you ki]ng [and I will sta]nd by you and rescue you from all [these kings who] have thrown up (?) a siege wall against you . . . ," is similar in style to the Neo-Assyrian oracles and to some of the biblical oracles.[11] The circumstances of the solicited oracle suggest a parallel to Zedekiah and the four hundred (I Kings 22).

Although virtually all the texts relating to Neo-Assyrian prophecy have been published for well over fifty years, they have had the benefit of but little attention. This inattention partly reflects the marginal character of the texts from the point of view of the dominant Mesopotamian religious tradition and partly testifies to a difficult combination of poor editions and obscure content. Presently, however, with the aid of fresh collations in the British Museum, several studies are under way.[12]

The known oracles all date from the reigns of Esarhaddon (681–668) and Ashurbanipal (668–ca. 630). This may be somewhat accidental, since at least one of the titles involved, *rāgintu*, "Announcer," occurs in a Middle Assyrian text from Tell Rimah.[13] None of the titles used with oracle speakers is a title also found in the Mari texts; all are different. The titles used are *raggimu/raggintu*, "Announcer," and *šabrū/šabratu*, apparently "Seer," found with both men and women. These two titles are identified with each other in a list of professions, where they occur together with cultic functionaries. But their own cultic role is unknown. In addition, one oracle giver is identified as a *šelūtu*, "(Lady) Votary," a title known from some contracts referring to temple votaries,[14] but there is no further information about her function. In some oracle collections, however, we find the ascription "from the mouth of so-and-so, citizen of such-and-such a town." Once in such a collection a speaker is identified as "so-and-so, a *šelūtu* of the king," without reference to her city, but otherwise in these texts no titles are given. It is probable that these persons without any title, among whom women are in a slight majority, were ordinary persons who had no special status in regard to the temple cult. If so, the Mari prophets would parallel the Neo-Assyrian prophets in the mixture of professional and lay persons.

Only in the case of the *šabrū,* who received a revelation in a dream and whose revelation is not fully parallel to those of the other oracle givers, do we have any information as to how the revelation was received.[15] The *raggimu,* although fairly well attested in the texts, received the messages in some unspecified fashion. It is rather speculative to describe these oracle givers as ecstatics or as priests in the strict sense, in view of the lack of explicit information.

Formally the Assyrian oracles are predominately first person speeches by the deity. They feature the phrase "fear not," particularly at the beginning of the oracle. The oracles are addressed to the king or the queen mother for the main part, though it should be noted that they come largely from what seem to be official collections. In content the oracles are primarily reassuring. Some, however, are critical of the king. For example, the king may be accused of ignoring a previous oracle. There are indications that some of the oracles were solicited, but for the majority of them it is an open question as to whether they were solicited or not.

There is, then, ample evidence for the existence of official and unofficial prophetic messengers in the ancient Near East. Apart from the texts surveyed above there is an impressive group of phenomena that have been labeled "prophetic" in terms of a definition other than that used in the present study. But because they reflect a different understanding of the nature of prophecy they are left aside in this discussion. The evidence presented should suffice to show that as defined here the prophetic activity recorded in the Hebrew Bible is not a unique or isolated happening in the world of the ancient Near East.

Actually, whereas the biblical scholar is commonly embarrassed in the presence of the abundant and growing sources available to colleagues in ancient Near Eastern studies, with regard to the origins of prophecy the biblical scholar has the advantage. Modern anthropological studies permit us to see the unfolding of various prophetic movements or prophetic roles, but only in the biblical material can we see with some clarity the background and setting of the rise of prophecy in a community of the ancient Near East. Mari and Assyria permit us to glimpse prophetic activity; in Israel we can study its development.

The rise of prophecy is widely acknowledged to have taken place with

Samuel and his successors. This is the picture presented in the biblical texts, at least in regard to prophetic continuity, and it seems to be essentially correct. The time of Samuel is certainly an appropriate period for the development of new roles, for Samuel lived during one of the great crises in Israelite history. Indeed, the widely observed connection of new or renewed religious movements in general and prophecy in particular with times of stress or crisis is well illustrated by Samuel's age.[16] It is during such a crisis that the traditional wisdom and authority may more easily be challenged by non-institutional means and that people are more receptive to new departures. Also, a crisis often brings with it a reallocation of social roles and the development of new roles.[17] During a period of stress there may even be a "psychic epidemic," with large groups of people engaging in such phenomena as mass ecstasy.[18] The prophetic "bands" in Israel seem to illustrate the point. The Ghost Dance of the American Indians is another case. It is a common phenomenon.

It is of course obvious that in the period of Samuel, Saul, and David there were dramatic changes in the allocation of roles. The new roles naturally are not without precedent in the past, for unless there is at least some use of pre-existing models and techniques new departures generally have little chance of gaining wide acceptance.

Among the factors that led to Israel's crisis toward the end of the eleventh century were the changing character of Israel itself in terms of territory and populace, the development of an adjacent power with long-range economic and territorial ambitions in the person of the Philistines, the ultimate fall of Shiloh and the central shrine, and the unstable character of Israelite political authority. This last factor is especially pertinent.

Israel had survived for two hundred years, more or less, without rulers, i.e. without any particularly discernible centralized authority.[19] The temporary and geographically limited role of the charismatic *šōpēṭ*, which means "Hero" or "Leader" rather than "Judge," was unpredictable, had no clear succession, and related to flurries of activity rather than standing authority. But the question as to whether Israel could long endure without a more pervasive and predictable political structure had arisen from many quarters by the time of Philistine power. The attempt to institutionalize authority and provide for regular succession in the line of Gideon was rejected by him (Judges 8). Subsequently one of Gideon's numerous sons, Abimelech, tried to establish a dynasty, but he met with only local and temporary success (Judges 9). Yet the problems and difficulties remained. Indeed, there was another abortive attempt to institutionalize authority. In his old age, Samuel himself "appointed his sons as *šōpᵉṭîm* (I Sam. 8:1–3)." But Samuel's two sons, whose center of activities was in Beer-sheba, proved no more worthy than had Abimelech or, for that matter, Eli's two priestly sons. The notice that Samuel's sons took bribes and perverted justice points to a judicial role in their case. Presumably they were but a modest reflection of Samuel's activities, but their appointment does seem to represent an attempt to transfer authority by means of hereditary succession. Samuel's hope for his sons or at least his loaning of prestige to them is another indication of the extent of the breakdown of the more informal patterns of leadership in vogue during the period of the League. The cumulative stresses and strains that Israel was experiencing by the latter part of the eleventh century were preparing the way for a somewhat drastic redefinition of some basic roles. It is not a mere matter of chance that at the same time that a king (*melek*) emerges for Israel, the prophet (*nābī'*) does also.

During the period of the Yahwistic League the religio-political role structure was rather simple. Apart from the priests associated with various shrines there were apparently no accepted religious specialists. The *nāśī'*, a tribal leader of some kind, presumably had an administrative role, but no details are preserved. Indeed, in his study "Office and Vocation," Martin Noth refers to only one real office in pre-monarchic Israel, that of "judge."[20] The holders of this office are also known as the "minor judges," partly at least because nothing more is known about them than their names and their title, *šōpēṭ* (Judg. 10:1–5, 12:7–15), which is widely taken to refer to a judicial role. They may have been something like intertribal arbiters, a role that Deborah, the "prophetess," seems to have accumulated (Judg. 4:4–5) as perhaps Jephthah did later. But any precise description of their role is speculative, since the clearest connection with a judicial function is the bribes received by Samuel's sons. The role that is most important for later developments is that of the better known *šōpᵉṭīm* such as Gideon and Jephthah. These leaders have two basic qualities. First, their authority is charismatic in the classical sense. That is, they were "set apart from ordinary men and treated as endowed with supernatural, superhuman, or at least specifically exceptional powers or qualities."[21] Their authority derives from their revelation, mission, or charismatic designation as in the case of Deborah and Barak. Such a charismatic leader must offer a relevant task or message, as one cannot lead without followers. At the same time, a charismatic leader is permitted an unusual degree of innovative initiative. He may transmit a traditional message, but he—or she—may also to some extent modify or redefine the message.[22] Second, these leaders are military heroes who meet a threat to public security by armed force. The victory, of course, is due to God's intervention.

In terms of the later role structure, the one role of the *šōpēṭ* is redistributed into the roles of the *nābī'*, the charismatic messenger, and the *melek*, the permanent war leader. The new roles are not merely a subdivision of the old role, but each comes in a new combination. The *melek*, for example, quickly becomes a permanent military, administrative, economic, and religious leader. What the *nābī'* continues is the utilization of charismatic authority, particularly the inauguration or legitimation of a new ruler—for a period at least from Samuel to Elisha—much as the *šōpēṭ* inaugurated a major military campaign. Of course, the acceptability of the new role of *nābī'* was partly due to some of the features of the activity of Moses, at least as traditionally seen. Moses concentrated in himself virtually all the major roles. He was a charismatic messenger, a priest, a military and judicial leader. He cannot be adequately described in terms of the later structure of roles, as acknowledged in a way by the Deuteronomist's description of him as the *nābī'* without parallel. Moses was clearly more than a prophet, but he provided a model for the later acceptance of the charisma and innovative initiative shown by the prophets.

While the new roles of *nābī'* and *melek* were taking their initial shape the process was apparently reflected in some terminological variation. The title *nāgīd* is used for Saul, David, Solomon, Jeroboam, Baasha, and Hezekiah, especially in legitimation statements. Presumably it points to a leadership role that was conceived somewhat differently than that of the *melek,* which designated the Canaanite and Aramaean royal office. The use of *nāgīd* in statements by Samuel, Nathan, Ahijah, and Jehu ben Hanani—though others used it as well—suggests that they found it congenial because of its less grandiose connotations.[23] At the least it indicated something other than the borrowing of the neighboring royal office.

Also, in the case of Samuel, who accumulated or concentrated in himself a variety of roles rather as Moses had earlier and who likewise cannot be described by any one title, we find more than one title in use. He is called *šōpēṭ* (by implication) and *nāzīr,* "Votary" (LXX, Dead Sea Scrolls), as well as *rō'eh,* "Seer," *'īš 'ᵉlōhīm,* "Man of God," and *nābī'.* The threefold range of titles in connection with his prophetic role suggests some uncertainty as to how to identify this role. Samuel and Hanani a century later (II Chron. 16:1–10) are the only persons given the title *rō'eh.* And Hanani conducts himself as a typical *nābī'* in his only known activity. (He may be the same Hanani who is mentioned as the father of Jehu, variously called *nābī'* or *ḥōzeh,* "Visionary," in which case we would have the only case of known heredity among persons called prophets.) Moreover, derivatives of *r'h,* "to see," are frequently found in connection with the later prophets. There is no reason to take *rō'eh* as a technical term, such as shaman, nor is there any real basis for differentiation between *rō'eh* and *nābī'.*

It is in the time after Samuel that we find persons whose special roles are restricted basically to prophecy itself. Yet already under David there seems to be something of a bifurcation among those called *nābī'.* The *nābī'* Nathan both advises the court and delivers prophetic oracles. He is responsible for the oracle confirming God's choice of David and his house (II Samuel 7) and also delivered the oracle condemning the treatment of Uriah and Bathsheba (II Samuel 12). And there is also Gad, who gives advice and delivers oracles to the king and who is variously described as *nābī',* (I Sam. 22:5), as *hannābī' ḥōzēh dāvīd,* "the prophet, David's 'visionary'" (II Sam. 22:11), as *ḥōzēh dāvīd/hammelek,* "David's/the king's 'visionary'"

(I Chron. 21:9//II Sam. 24:11; II Chron. 29:25), or as merely *ḥōzeh* (I Chron. 29:29). It is noteworthy that a phrase such as *nābī' dāvīd/hammelek* does not occur, so that although the title *ḥōzeh* may well point to prophetic activity, as it does in the case of Jehu ben Hanani (II Chron. 19:2), in some general references, and in the *ḥāziyīn* of Zakir, the combination *ḥōzēh dāvīd/hammelek* suggests some different understanding. The same combination occurs with Heman (I Chron. 25:5), presumably the same as the celebrated wise man (I Kings 5:11[4:31E]), and Yeduthun (II Chron. 35:15), and Asaph also is called a *ḥōzeh* (II Chron. 29:30). The temple musicians deriving from these three are described as "those who prophesy (*hannibbᵉʾīm*, Q) with lyres, harps, and cymbals," and some are specifically said to act under royal direction (I Chron. 25:1–3). Gad, together with Nathan and David, is given credit for the later Levitic musicians (II Chron. 29:25). There presumably was some connection between Gad and cultic musical groups which may become frenzied, much as the "band" of prophets in the Samuel-Saul narratives who are frenzied musicians connected with a shrine. This connection of Gad, which has been discussed so well by A. R. Johnson,[24] could be a parallel to the Mari and Neo-Assyrian prophets who also have a cultic role. It is worth mentioning that the Mari *assinnu* later appears as a singer in the cult of Ishtar. Also striking is the parallel in form and content between the oracle of Jahaziel, the Levite of the line of Asaph upon whom God's spirit came (II Chron. 20:14–18), and some of the Neo-Assyrian oracles. It is important to bear in mind also the apparent antiquity and Canaanite background of the temple musicians and "visionaries."[25] This direction of development may well have had Canaanite influence in terms of music (and frenzy?).

Nathan illustrates a different development of the *nābī'*, or of the *nābī'* as opposed to the *ḥōzeh*. He has a special role in regard to the king, a role continued particularly in the north. For unlike the *šōpēṭ* the *melek* is not directly commissioned as a charismatic leader. Rather, the prophet as the charismatic messenger installs and legitimates the *melek* or, perhaps preferably, the *nāgīd*. We find such activity either before or during the reign, in the case of Samuel for Saul and David, Nathan for David, Ahijah for Jeroboam, Jehu for Baasha, and one of the members of the prophetic band, acting for Elisha, for Jehu. Likewise the prophet can announce the rejection of a king, as for example Samuel did for Saul, Ahijah for Jeroboam, Jehu—in the same oracle in which legitimation is expressed—for Baasha, and Elijah for Ahab and, in a fashion, for Ahaziah. Obviously such a relationship was fraught with danger for the king, as an oracle expressing God's rejection is but a slightly veiled invitation to intrigue and assassination, and with frustration for the prophet, who may announce both choice and termination. It is not surprising that gradually northern and southern prophets turn away from the apparent policy of dealing primarily with the king (if our sources do not mislead us; cf. Mari and Assyria), the head of the people, and deal more directly with the people. We can see this already with Elijah.

The relationship between (a) the large groups of prophets who are mentioned in connection with Samuel and Elisha in particular and who are associated with music and frenzy and attached to various shrines or cult centers and (b) the official (temple) musicians and "prophets" is largely a matter for speculation. The official group is best known in connection with Jerusalem and the prophetic "bands" are associated mainly with northern shrines, so there may well be some geographical variation. But then to what extent the "sons of the prophets" should be differentiated from Zedekiah and the four hundred and similar groups cannot be said. It is quite possible that these types represent to some extent an institutionalization of the "psychic epidemic" that can be produced in periods of crisis. And we cannot say whether inspired oracle giving was a primary or a secondary role within these groups. It may well have been secondary. In any case, the activities of these groups provided a setting within which individual participants might become clothed with God's spirit and deliver a prophetic oracle. On occasion it is reported that a member of a prophetic band individually gave an oracle (I Kings 20:35-42; cf. II Kings 9:1-10), and Zedekiah of course speaks for the four hundred (I Kings 22). But we are also told that the "spirit of the Lord came upon Jahaziel," a Levite in the line of Asaph, who thereupon delivered a prophetic oracle. Thus there perhaps was a reservoir in the more or less official groups out of which there might arise individuals who broke through the normal boundaries of their role. Likewise those prophets who stood apart from such circles—or who transcended them —would provide some impetus for such activity. In spite of the polemic against "official" prophets or prophets who did not behave or give messages consistent with the leading "canonical" prophets, there may often have been a fruitful interrelationship between the various types.

A basic continuity between the early prophets such as Ahijah and Elijah and the later prophets should be quite clear. The prophets continue in their call and in their experience; they continue to be charismatic messengers who announce "thus says the Lord"; they continue to represent the old Yahwistic traditions; they continue to be "seized upon" from a wide variety of everyday stations and roles; and they continue to demonstrate the innovative capacity of the charismatic. That the innovations in understanding, appropriating, and modifying the tradition lead ultimately to new departures in the message does not separate in type the early and the later prophets.[26]

Perhaps two further issues may be discussed by way of illustration. First, there is the question of prophecy and divination recently raised again by H. M. Orlinsky in a study that reflects, in more forceful fashion, the tendency since J. G. Herder to separate the earlier and later prophets.[27] Orlinsky takes divination to mean primarily prediction. He characterizes the diviner-seer, who is closely related to the priest (the same person may be both), as "a craftsman"—"he offered sacrifices, he interpreted dreams, he predicted events, he performed miracles, and sometimes he was in charge of a shrine and of apprentices" (pp. 158–159). In short, the diviner as seen by Orlinsky is a skilled religious specialist. Orlinsky then proceeds to classify the Near Eastern prophets, specifically the Mari prophets known before the publication of *Archives royales de Mari* (1967) and the biblical prophets up to and including Elijah and Elisha, as diviners, affirms that there is an immovable barrier between divination and prophecy (otherwise described as the division between men of deeds—seers-diviners—and men of words— the later prophets), and leaves aside the question of the rise of prophecy. The later prophets he pictures as debaters, using "argument, reasoning, exhortation" (p. 159). There is no transition between the two groups.

Divination might be understood as the process of apprehending the pleasure or will of the gods or as "cognizing and recognizing the holy in its appearances,"[28] and in such a sense one could discuss the early prophets in terms of divination. But if the stress is on a craft such as interpreting dreams and predicting events, then it is hard to see how that applies to the *nābī'* of early Israel or to the Mari (or Assyrian) prophets. Divination in the ancient Near East, and especially wherever Mesopotamian culture had much influence, was a learned, technical, and, in ideal at least, hereditary profession. Technical divination was widely practiced in ancient Syria, as is attested by the number of liver models found in excavations as well as by literary references. Where we are well informed about divination—discerning the future—in early Israel, it is priestly divination by the sacred lots, a procedure having a well-defined form. The few occasions in which the older prophets are consulted about such matters as lost animals (Samuel, as initiated by Saul's servant) or a child's health (Ahijah) may reflect a popular understanding of them as some kind of clairvoyant, yet one must note that the occasions are put to a very different use by the prophets. The "cures"— bringing back to life—brought about through Elijah or by Elisha may reflect an accumulation of roles by a "man of God," but in the case of Elijah in particular it serves as a means of accreditation or legitimation for the prophet. (Elisha may well represent a different type of prophet.) Micaiah appealed to historical vindication; others healed. There is no close parallel, for example, between the prophetic cures and those effected by such figures as trained and officially initiated shamans.

In the process of conveying God's reaction to the deeds of the king or other persons or his will and pleasure, the early prophets make statements about the future. These might be understood as predictions, but they are not comparable to the typical oracle question and answer found in ancient Egypt, Mesopotamia, or Greece. The prophet states God's implicit or explicit judgment on the previous conduct of the person(s) involved, as in the case of Micaiah's message against Ahab. If we compare the practitioners

of the "natural divination" described by Cicero, they commonly made predictions in an obscure form so as to leave an escape by way of ambiguity.
Micaiah did not do that. Learned Mesopotamian diviners would say whether
the omens were favorable or unfavorable, but they also had a simple means
of overturning an oracle. Merely try again was their answer. They did not
risk their person; their hair and hem were not taken. But when Zechariah,
son of Jehoiada, the priest, was clothed with God's spirit and delivered a
prophetic oracle against the people of Judah, King Jehoash had him stoned
to death (II Chron. 24:20–22). That was not the fate of diviners, whose
main risk was in deceiving people. It may be that the older prophets were
at times clairvoyants as well as charismatic messengers, since those roles could
be combined in the same person, but there is no indication that they made
use of organized divination. And of course the later prophets cannot be disassociated from any insight into God's plans for the future.

Orlinsky's view denies any movement from divination to prophecy and
offers no concept of the origins of prophecy in Israel other than, one supposes, as a miraculous mutation in the people of Israel. Apart from the
consideration that even though divination, as understood by Orlinsky, may
not easily develop into prophecy, yet the roles of diviner and prophet—or
priest and prophet—could be combined in the same gifted religious person, the option of a miraculous growth without precedent or forerunner is
not an attractive hypothesis concerning the origins of prophecy.

Second, there is the problem of true and false prophecy. Ecstasy—in a
non-technical sense—or possession is an easily induced experience. Given
the proper circumstances, diet, and/or exercises such as dancing and sing-
ing, an ecstatic experience can be produced for virtually any person or
group, just as almost anyone can be "brainwashed" given sufficient time
and technique. Attendance at any carefully directed revival meeting or pop
festival should illustrate the point. The wide availability of ecstasy is both
an advantage and a disadvantage. It is distinct from the technical preparation
of the divination expert or the necessary heredity or purity of the priest,
but it can be used by all kinds of persons. To the extent that prophecy
involves ecstasy or frenzy—as we are explicitly told in some cases for
Mari and Israelite prophets—it utilizes an unstable factor. An interesting
illustration is the story of the "man of God" from Judah who was deceived
by the prophet of Bethel and was killed by a lion (I Kings 13). This story
seems to reflect a test to persevere in the revelation one has received in
spite of contrary claims by other prophets. Claims are too easily made.
Likewise Micaiah, when confronted with the proper experience and behavior of the four hundred led by Zedekiah, said that though Zedekiah was
speaking for God, yet God had sent a lying spirit to him so as to deceive
Ahab. In reply to Zedekiah's question as to how God's spirit went from
him to speak to Micaiah, Micaiah can only appeal to subsequent events
to indicate whether God was supporting or opposing Ahab. The onlookers

could not distinguish true prophecy from false prophecy on the basis of appearance, as Micaiah acknowledges. And this problem became increasingly important in the history of prophecy. For example, Jeremiah presents considerable polemic against prophets who can be accused of prophesying their own dreams or in the name of Baal rather than the word which Yahweh might put in their mouth. But this presumably is not the way that these prophets presented themselves. Jeremiah also appeals to vindication in time of true prophecy that accurately reflects God's intentions (Jer. 28:9; cf. 37:19), which again acknowledges that there is no formal distinction. Prophecy thus has a precarious quality, as ultimately only internal and subjective confessional criteria can distinguish true and false prophecy. Deut. 18:21–22 tells us that false prophets can be separated from others because they prophesy in the name of other gods (conviction) and their words do not come to pass. Deut. 13:1–3 stresses the point that even if a prophet arises and gives signs or wonders that do come to pass and then invites the people to follow other gods, he is a false prophet and God is testing the people. So the people are left on their own, apart from the advice not to heed any prophet who does not speak in the name of Yahweh. Subsequent events may be consistent or inconsistent with some prophetic oracles, but as the people who ascribed the fall of Jerusalem to the anger of the Queen of Heaven correctly saw, history is ambiguous (Jer. 44:15–19). God cannot "act" without interpreters.[29]

NOTES

1. See L. Mair, *Anthropology and Social Change* (London, 1969), pp. 120–134; W. Howells, *The Heathens: Primitive Man and His Religions* (New York, 1948), p. 259.

2. Cf. K. O. L. Burridge, *New Heaven, New Earth: A Study of Millenarian Activities* (Oxford, 1969), pp. 11–12, 153–164, for both restrictions and general discussion. For broad coverage see also G. Guariglia, *Prophetismus und Heilserwartungs-Bewegungen als völkerkundliches und religionsgeschichtliches Problem* (Vienna, 1959), and *Chiliasmus und Nativismus*, ed. W. E. Mühlmann (Berlin, 1961).

3. In addition to the works cited in N 2, see M. Eliade, *Shamanism. Archaic Techniques of Ecstasy*, tr. W. R. Trask (Princeton, 1964); V. Lanternari, *The Religions of the Oppressed*, tr. L. Sergio (New York, 1963), together with the comments in *Current Anthropology* 6 (1965), 447–465; I. L. Lewis, *Ecstatic Religion. An Anthropological Study of Spirit Possession and Shamanism* (Harmondsworth, 1971); A. F. C. Wallace, "Revitalization Movements," *American Anthropologist* 58 (1956), 264–281; P. Worsley, *The Trumpet Shall Sound*, 2d ed. (New York, 1968).

4. See J.-G. Heintz, *VT* 21 (1971), 529, n. 1. For the texts and discussion with references see the translations by W. L. Moran in *ANET*, 3d ed. (1968), 623–625, 629–632; F. Ellermeier, *Prophetie in Mari und Israel* (Herzberg, 1968); H. B.

Huffmon, in *The Biblical Archaeologist Reader*, III, 199–224; and W. H. Ph. Römer, *Frauenbriefe über Religion, Politik und Privatleben in Māri* (Neukirchen-Vluyn, 1971).

5. For a study of the Old Babylonian priesthood see J. Renger, *Zeitschrift für Assyriologic* 58, N.F. 24 (1967), 110–188; 59, N.F. 25 (1969), 104–230.

6. Tr. R. D. Biggs, in *ANET*, p. 604.

7. Tr. A. Goetze, in *ANET*, pp. 394–396.

8. Tr. J. A. Wilson, in *ANET*, pp. 25–29, esp. 26.

9. G. Hölscher, *Die Profeten* (Leipzig, 1914), pp. 129–143; *Geschichte der israelitischen und jüdischen Religion* (Giessen, 1922), pp. 83–84.

10. Lucian in *De Dea Syria* makes no reference to spoken oracles, whereas Apuleius in *The Golden Ass* refers only to oracles in the Greek style (ix 8). Jeremiah's polemical references (2:8; 23:13) are presumably not to be taken seriously as literal truth.

11. Tr. F. Rosenthal, in *ANET*, pp. 655–656. The recent study of this text by J. F. Ross, "Prophecy in Hamath, Israel, and Mari," *HTR* 63 (1970), 1–28, fails to make a case for any particular continuity between Hamath and Mari and passes by the Assyrian parallels. '*š 'nh* is still best taken as "humble man," since Hana is not attested as a geographical name in contemporary texts and would presumably be transcribed *ḥnh* anyway. Moreover, Mer (Wer) is already known in a personal name from Ugarit (*Palais royal d'Ugarit*, III, 16.249, 14). Mesopotamian gods need no special apology to appear in the west.

12. For the present see S. A. Strong, *Beiträge zur Assyriologie* 2 (1894), 627–643; S. Langdon, *Tammuz and Ishtar* (London, 1914), pp. 128–147 (and pls. II–IV); Th. Bauer, *Das Inschriftenwerk Assurbanipals* (Leipzig, 1933), pp. 79–82; and the translation of one of the main texts by Biggs, in *ANET*, p. 605. There are also some oracles reported in the Harper letters; see the letter translated by Moran, in *ANET*, pp. 625–626.

13. H. W. F. Saggs, *Iraq* 30 (1968), 161–162, pl. xlvii (2031.6).

14. B. Parker, *Iraq* 16 (1954), 39–40, pl. vii (2309.9; 2316.2, 4).

15. See the translation by Biggs, in *ANET*, p. 606, and the parallel text in M. Streck, *Assurbanipal*, II (Leipzig, 1916), 188–195 (K.2652.25 ff.).

16. See the general comments by S. N. Eisenstadt in his introduction to *Max Weber on Charisma and Institution Building* (Chicago, 1968), pp. xxvii–xxix. Eisenstadt emphasizes that the connection with stress situations does not exclude transition or conflict periods within an orderly social life. See also the works cited in NN 2–3.

17. T. Parsons, *The Social System* (London, 1951), pp. 503–520.

18. For this term see George Rosen, *Madness in Society. Chapters in the Historical Sociology of Mental Illness* (Chicago, 1968; New York, Harper Torchbook, 1969), pp. 179–182, 195–225, and his discussion of the prophetic bands (pp. 59–60).

19. See the discussions in *Tribes Without Rulers* eds., J. Middleton and D. Tait (London, 1958), especially the introductory chapter.

20. M. Noth, *The Laws in the Pentateuch and Other Studies*, tr. D. R. Ap-Thomas (Philadelphia, 1967), pp. 229–249.

21. M. Weber, quoted from the volume edited by Eisenstadt [N 16], p. 48.

22. See the excellent discussion by Worsley [N 3], pp. ix–xxi.

23. See the comments by W. F. Albright, *Samuel and the Beginnings of the Prophetic Movement* (Cincinnati, ca. 1961), pp. 15–16.

24. Johnson, *The Cultic Prophet in Ancient Israel*, 2d ed. (Cardiff, 1962), esp. pp. 69 ff.

25. Albright, *YGC*, pp. 244–253; *ARI*, pp. 122–124, with notes.

26. See the excellent study by R. Rendtorff, "Erwägungen zur Frühgeschichte des

Prophetentums in Israel," *ZTK* 59 (1962), 145–167, tr. P. J. Achtemeier in *History and Hermeneutic, JTC* 4 (1967), 14–34, and the helpful review by I. Engnell, *A Rigid Scrutiny,* tr. J. T. Willis with H. Ringgren (Nashville, 1969), pp. 123–179.

27. H. Orlinsky, "The Seer in Ancient Israel," *Oriens Antiquus* 4 (1965), 153–174.

28. R. Otto, *The Idea of the Holy,* tr. J. W. Harvey, 2d ed. (London, 1950), p. 144.

29. The present writer is currently preparing a larger and more detailed study on the general topic considered here. In this forthcoming study the pertinent texts will be cited and translated and perhaps some of the cryptic or obscure statements here will become clearer.

9. The "Orpheus" Jug from Megiddo

BENJAMIN MAZAR

THE HEBREW UNIVERSITY OF JERUSALEM

THE SETTLEMENT represented by Stratum VIA at Megiddo can be considered a good example of a city under Philistine rule in the second half of the eleventh century B.C. The excavations there have shown that in this period—corresponding to the latest Philistine level at Tell Qasile (Stratum X), as well—Megiddo was a fortified city which flourished as a Philistine stronghold in the Jezreel Valley and as a trade center on important caravan crossroads.[1] This stronghold seems to have been founded by the Philistines after the battle of Ebenezer, and to have been destroyed by David after he crushed the Philistines and gained control of the Via Maris. An unfortified Israelite settlement (Str. VB) was built in the time of David over the remains of the Philistine city. Under Solomon, a "city of store" (cf. I Kings 9: 19) arose here, with fortifications on a plan similar to those of Hazor and Gezer (I Kings 9:15).[2]

The most important structure discovered in Stratum VIA at Megiddo is the large building 2072, near the northern gate in area AA.[3] This brick-built structure is of notable plan; as far as it can be determined from the remains (see the restored plan in *Figure 3*), it may perhaps be compared to the private houses of Stratum X at Tell Qasile, with the difference that it is much larger. A winding stairway near the northwest corner may indicate that it had a second story. A vast number of finds were made in the various rooms. In one room, 2102, a jug was found with a peculiar strainer spout (*Figure 4*). The finds are indicative not only of the high status of the dwellers in this house, but also that they were of the Philistine aristocracy.[4] Therefore, we may perhaps assume that this was the residence of the Philistine governor at Megiddo in the days of Saul and early in the reign of David.

It should be noted that the spouted jug, peculiar as it may be, is still clearly Philistine, of the eleventh century B.C. This can be seen from its shape, the white slip, the black and red ornamentation, and the character of the ornamentation, reflecting Late Mycenaean traditions (Mycenaean IIIC:1). Indeed, all this is most typical of the hybrid style of the Philistine pottery.[5] The jug may have been used as a decorative vessel for some time; it could have been made prior to the decline of the Philistine ceramic tradition, as seen in Stratum VIA at Megiddo, and especially in Stratum X at Tell Qasile.[6]

The scene on the side of the jug (see *Figure 4*) shows the figure of a bearded man, stepping to the right and holding a harp; flanking him are various animals, all of whom face right toward a stylized palm tree (only the upper part of which remains).[7] Comparison with similar figures in Late Mycenaean art[8] aids in identifying most of these animals, though some are doubtful, being overstylized. Before the man are a lion(?), a dog, and a crab, seemingly in a row. Before them, between the palm and the lion, is a fish. Following the lion, between him and the man, is a gazelle, with a fish above her horns. To the left of the man's head is a scorpion. At the end of the column, to the left of the man, there seems to be a horse, with a large bird on its back and a fish above. Between the man and the horse is a large fish. The artist seems to have intended depicting a group of various animals, including beasts of the earth, birds, creeping things, fowl, and creatures of the waters (cf. Gen. 1:20–24).

A scene similar to that on the Megiddo jug appears on a seal from Tarsus in Cilicia, found in what seems to have been a Late Bronze Age stratum.[9] This seal depicts a man kneeling on one knee and holding a harp, surrounded by various animals. Hetty Goldman has already suggested that both scenes depict the familiar motif of Orpheus playing before the animals. This explanation, acceptable *prima facie,* is doubtful for various reasons. On the Megiddo jug, the animals are not facing the man, and nothing in the composition would indicate that the artist intended to show the animals as listening to the music. Besides, the Orpheus motif is not known in Greek poetry or art earlier than the sixth century B.C.[10]

In seeking to explain this scene, we must first note that complex compositions depicting various motifs of daily life, or mythology and epic literature, are by no means uncommon in the art of Canaan and the neighboring lands in the Late Bronze Age and in the Early Iron Age. Especially interesting in this context is the large group of ornamental ivory plaques found in the Stratum VIIA palace at Megiddo, dating to the thirteenth–twelfth centuries B.C.[11] Some of these ivories depict scenes of everyday life, such as drinking scenes, battles, hunting, etc., and even a victory ceremony in which a man is playing a harp before his master, who is sitting on a throne.[12]

The artist may have intended, in the scene on the present jug, to depict a common subject, a known motif among the Philistine potters: a bard accompanying himself on a harp, the subject of his poem being the tree and the animals shown around him. This is reminiscent of what is related of Solomon: "For Solomon's wisdom excelled the wisdom of all the children of the east, and all the wisdom of Egypt. For he was wiser than all men, than Ethan the Ezrahite, and Heman, and Chalcol and Darda, the sons of

Mahol. . . . And he spoke three thousand proverbs; and his songs were a thousand and five. And he spake of trees, from the cedar tree that is in Lebanon even unto the hyssop that springeth out of the wall; he spake also of beasts, and of fowl, and of creeping things, and of fishes" (I Kings 4: 30–33).

The similarity between the motifs of Solomon's proverbs, especially the various animals, and the scene on the Megiddo jug is certainly not incidental. Moreover, the various types of wisdom proverbs (proverbs, riddles, and especially proverbs on animals and plants) had always been common in the ancient world.[13] It is principally to these that the Israelite historiographer refers in speaking of the "wisdom of all the children of the east (*benê Qedem*), and all the wisdom of Egypt."[14] Many such proverbs were popular in the Aegean regions as well, and were crystallized within the collection of Greek proverbs ascribed to Aesop. Such literary forms were, of course, well known in Israel and among the peoples of this region. Thus, in the Bible, it is not surprising to find a very considerable amount of wisdom literature, taken from various sources and having principally a didactic and ethical character.[15] There is also no doubt that proverbs (*měšalîm*) and riddles (*ḥîdôt*) were presented on festive occasions and at banquets, and that they were often delivered with musical accompaniment.[16] We must especially note the riddle which Samson posed to his Philistine companions at his wedding feast (Judg. 14:10 ff.). This example, taken from daily life, is certainly indicative of a general trend. At the beginning of the first millennium B.C., when Israel and Tyre both rose to prominence, sharing in the general growth of international trade at this time, wisdom literature came to be cultivated even more than before, especially in the royal courts and among the aristocracy. Among those uttering proverbs were now also the rulers and their courtiers.[17]

The biblical reference to Solomon's wisdom—"For Solomon's wisdom excelled the wisdom of all the children of the east and all the wisdom of Egypt" (I Kings 4:30)—is surprisingly followed by a reference to several unknown persons. Scholarly interest in these otherwise unknown sages, who must have been well known in the days of David and Solomon, is understandable. Albright has suggested that Mahol had a meaning similar to that of the Greek *orkēstra*, and that "the sons of Mahol" represented a sort of musicians' guild;[18] he differentiated, however, between Ethan the Ezrahite and the other three, specified as the sons of Mahol. The text would seem to indicate, though, that all four were sons of Mahol; the designation "Ezrahite," here and in Ps. 89:1 applied to Ethan, is also used in relation to Heman in Ps. 88:1.[19] The latter designation, meaning "citizen of the land" (cf. LXX *avtóchtōn tēs gēs*), refers to a free man, whether Israelite landholder or free artisan, or a member of a noble Gentile family which had become attached to the Israelites and included within the recognized genealogical lists. The First Book of Chronicles mentions Ethan (also called Jeduthun) and Heman as heads of families of bards serving in the temple in Jerusalem—ascribed to Levite clans, in keeping with the tendency to connect genealogically all the free families involved in cultic duties in the temple with the tribe of Levi.[20] Moreover, later tradition held that David gave Asaph, Heman, and Ethan (or Jeduthun) and their descendants the status of bards "for the service of the house of God, according to the king's order"; "who should prophesy with harps, with psalteries, and with cymbals"; "in the words of God, to lift up the horn" (I Chron. 25:1–7, etc.). We may also mention that, among the sages, "the sons of Mahol" in I Kings 5, only Ethan (Jeduthun) and Heman are also mentioned in I Chronicles 25 and Psalms. Further, the relationship between Ethan and Jeduthun remains questionable, especially since the latter appears as a musical term in Psalms (39:1; 77:1; etc.).

The onomasticon of these four names—Ethan, Heman, Chalcol, and Darda—is also obscure. They certainly are not common Israelite private names, nor are they known from sources outside the Bible.[21] This in itself casts a shadow on their origin, especially since their relationship to the Judahite family of Zerah (I Chron. 2:4) is putative, and the appending of Ethan and Heman to the Levites served merely to indicate the status of their descendants in the temple service. Their appearance as bards serving the kings of the united monarchy can be understood, since David and Solomon recruited not only officials and mercenaries into the royal service but also bards and singers from among the Gentiles. These took upon themselves to serve the God of Israel and the king of Israel, and became part of the royal and temple administration. The "sons of Mahol" may at first have been a "guild" of bards and singers who became famous for their "wisdom," similar to other specialized fraternities or "guilds" known from the Ugaritic texts and biblical literature (including fraternities of prophets; I Sam. 9:5, etc.). And it is probable that among their poetic creations were proverbs on animals and plants.

NOTES

1. For Stratum VIA at Megiddo, see G. Loud, *Megiddo* II (henceforth: *Megiddo* II), (Chicago, 1948), pp. 33 ff.; and for its dating and character, see B. Mazar, *BASOR* 124 (1951), 21 ff.; *Proceedings of the Israel Academy of Sciences and Humanities*, I, 7, (1964), p. 10, n. 17; and G. E. Wright, *BASOR* 155 (1959), 13 ff. Yadin's recent excavations at Megiddo have proven Stratum VIA to belong to the second half of the eleventh century B.C. and that it was a Philistine stronghold at that time. See now Y. Yadin, *BA* 33 (1970), 77 ff. For a different opinion, see Y. Aharoni, in *NEATC*, pp. 363 ff., where Stratum VIA at Megiddo is interpreted as an Israelite city.
2. Cf. Y. Yadin, *BA* 23 (1960), 62 ff.; 33 (1970), 66 ff.

3. See *Megiddo* II [N 1], p. 37, figs. 83 and 386.

4. The finds were published in *Megiddo* II; besides the jug, found in the large room 2101 (pls. 76 and 142:20), there were a seal with a schematic figure of a man in Philistine style (pl. 163:16), two adzes and a copper lugged axe (pl. 183:19–20, 22), typical of the Early Iron Age, a limestone statuette (pl. 367:9), the head of an Astarte figurine (pl. 243:23), and much fine pottery (including Cypriot imports), almost all of which is typical of the second half of the eleventh century B.C. (e.g. pls. 75:8, 10; 79: 5; 80:7).

5. For the Philistine pottery, see T. Dothan, *The Philistines and Their Material Culture* (Hebrew) (Jerusalem, 1967).

6. See B. Mazar, *IEJ* 1 (1950–51), 61 ff.

7. See *Megiddo* II [N 1], pl. 76:1.

8. Cf. A. Furumark, *The Mycenaean Pottery* (Stockholm, 1941); and T. Dothan, [N 5], pp. 132 f.

9. See H. Goldman; *Excavations at Gozlu Kule, Tarsus* II, 1 (Princeton, 1956), p. 239, figs. 394:35; 400:35; and Edith Porada, in *The Aegean and the Near East, Studies Presented to Hetty Goldman*, ed. S. Weinberg (New York, 1956), p. 204.

10. For details, see K. Ziegler, in Pauly-Wissowa: *Realencyclopaedie* XVIII, 1 (1942), pp. 1200 ff., and esp. p. 1215; *idem*, in *Der Kleine Pauly* (Stuttgart, 1970), pp. 351 ff.

11. See G. Loud, *The Megiddo Ivories* (Chicago, 1939), esp. pls. 10, 22 and 32–33.

12. See ibid., pl. 4:2. In this context, we may also note two Philistine seals from Tell el-Far'a (South) and from Tell Qasile: Fl. Petrie, *Beth-pelet* I (London, 1930), p. 10 and pl. XXIX: 257; and B. Mazar, *Bulletin of the Israel Exploration Society* 31 (1967), 64 ff., pls. 4–5 (Hebrew). These bear a series of depictions which are organically related.

13. Proverbs on animals and plants are prominent already in Sumerian literature; see E. I. Gordon: *Sumerian Proverbs* (Philadelphia, 1959), pp. 286 ff.; for Babylonian proverbs, see E. Ebeling, *Die Babylonische Fabel* (Leipzig, 1927); and especially W. G. Lambert, *Babylonian Wisdom Literature* (Oxford, 1960); and on the wisdom literature of the ancient Orient in general, J. Nougayrol: *Les Sagesses du Proche-Orient* (Paris, 1963).

14. See A. Alt, "Weisheit Salomons," in *KS* II (1956), 90 ff.—an attempt to show a connection between the wisdom of Solomon and the *Listenwissenschaft* of the Babylonians and Egyptians, e.g. the Onomasticon of Amenope, of the eleventh century B.C., which according to the introduction is supposed to be the "law" of all existence, as created by Ptah and recorded by Thoth; see A. Gardiner, *Ancient Egyptian Onomastica* (Oxford, 1947); cf. R. B. Y. Scott, *Wisdom in Israel and the Ancient Near East* (Presented to H. H. Rowley) *VTS* 3 (1955), 262 ff.

15. See N. H. Tur-Sinai, in *Encyclopaedia Biblica*, III (Jerusalem, 1962), pp. 127 ff. (Hebrew); *VTS* 3 (1955); W. McKane, *Proverbs* (London, 1970) and bibliography there, pp. xi–xxii.

16. Cf. Ps. 49:4.

17. In this context, the biblical episode of the Queen of Sheba is enlightening: she came to Solomon to prove him with riddles (I Kings 10:1). Josephus cites Dius and Menander on the wisdom contest between Solomon and Hiram of Tyre, and Abdemon, a Tyrian who excelled in solving riddles (*Contra Apionem* 18, 1). On the *ummânu* in Mesopotamia who was not only a craftsmaster or a sage, but also a high official, see E. Reiner: *Orientalia* (1961), 1 ff.

18. W. F. Albright, *ARI* (1942), pp. 127 and 210. A similar suggestion was already made by the medieval commentator Rashi.

19. This approach is in evidence also in I Chron. 2:6, though the compiler of the genealogical lists included Ethan, Heman, Chalcol, and Dar'a (i.e. Darda) among the

sons of Zerah the Judahite, supposing "Ezrahite" to mean the Zerahite. This genealogical listing is certainly contrived.

20. For the genealogical lists, see K. Möhlenbrink, *ZAW* (1934), 202 f. and 229 f.; A. Lefèvre: *Récherches de science religieuse* (1950), 287 ff.; Sh. Yeivin, in *Encyclopaedia Biblica*, IV (Jerusalem, 1962), pp. 45 ff. (Hebrew).

21. In one opinion, Ethan and Heman were of the abbreviated type of names ending in *-ân;* another opinion holds that the meaning of Ethan is simply "strong," and that Heman stems from *Nehêmân*, "faithful," or that it stems from the root *YMN*. Whatever the case, these names are unknown as private names in any source prior to the Persian period. This is true of Chalcol and Darda, as well. See also Albright [N 18], pp. 210 and n. 100, where he compares biblical Chalcol with Krkr (Klkl), the name of a female musician in the temple of Ptaḥ at Ashkelon, mentioned in Egyptian inscriptions on ivory plaques discovered in the palace at Megiddo; this comparison is not certain, since it is not impossible that the name stems from the root *krkr,* in the sense of "dance" (cf. II Sam. 6:16). The Ugaritic names (*bn*)'*atn* and '*atnprln* should not be connected with biblical Ethan (cf. Gordon, *Ugaritic Textbook,* Glossary, p. 368). Albright has recently suggested connecting Ethan with the Ugaritic name Attuyânu (alphabetic '*atyn*), apparently of Hurrian origin; see W. F. Albright, *YGC,* p. 250.

10. *The Organization and Administration of the Israelite Empire*

JOHN BRIGHT

UNION THEOLOGICAL SEMINARY, RICHMOND

IT IS FITTING that a volume prepared in honor of G. Ernest Wright should include an article on this subject, for it is one to which he has himself made important contributions, as will appear below. The subject is a broad one. It has been discussed both in general works and in specific treatments too numerous to mention here.[1] We can in this brief article make no attempt at an independent investigation, but rather shall seek to present a summary of what has been said on salient aspects of the subject in the hope that the reader may gain an idea of the present state of the discussion.

The Israelite empire was, of course, the creation of David. Before him there was no empire, and no organized government in any proper sense of the word. In the days of the judges Israel had existed as a sacral league of tribes[2] which, though a powerfully cohesive force, was without central government, permanent leadership, standing army, or bureaucracy of any sort. To be sure, the election of Saul as king had given Israel leadership on a permanent basis. But Saul's entire reign was spent at war. Although we may see in his policy of attaching likely young soldiers to his person for permanent service (I Sam. 14:52) the beginnings of a standing army, Saul made no change in the tribal organization, and set up no bureaucracy or administrative machinery of which we have knowledge.[3] It was the achievement of David, which transformed Israel within and without, that made the development of structures of government inevitable, indeed imperatively necessary.

It is not our task to trace David's brilliant career. But the state that he built was a very complex structure, to a high degree centered in David's own person. The union of Israel and Judah after the death of Ish-baal was a personal one: David, already king over Judah, was accepted as king by the northern tribes also (II Sam. 5:1-3).[4] The capital city, Jerusalem, had been taken (II Sam. 5:6-9) by David's personal troops (vs. 6) and became his personal holding—as Ziklag already was (I Sam. 27:6).[5] After the defeat of the Philistines, city-states along the coastal plain, in the Plain of Esdraelon, and elsewhere, which had previously been under Philistine control, transferred their allegiance to David and were incorporated into Israel; but, except perhaps in isolated instances, these were not absorbed into the tribes, but were subject directly to the crown. Moreover, David's foreign empire had been won, and was held, thanks largely to his professional troops (though the tribal levies were used at least to some extent; cf. II Sam. 11:11), and it owed its allegiance to, and had to be governed by, David himself. The whole structure was so centered in David's person that dynastic succession became a political necessity. The empire was passed on to David's son, Solomon, who, fighting no major wars that we know of, devoted himself to consolidating his power over it and developing its economic potentialities. That numerous innovations and changes in the structures of government should accompany these events is only what one would expect.

I

Our knowledge of how David ruled his foreign empire must be pieced together from isolated notices here and there and is, at best, inadequate. But it seems clear, and is generally agreed, that he did not govern all parts of it in the same way. Rather, he chose in each case the means of control which, for reasons we cannot know, seemed to him the most suitable.[6]

1) There can be little doubt that the Transjordanian states of Moab, Edom, and Ammon were controlled under various arrangements. The statement (II Sam. 12:30) that the Ammonite crown was placed on David's head is most naturally understood as meaning that David himself assumed the throne as king of Ammon—though no doubt exercising his authority through a native vassal-deputy (cf. II Sam. 17:27 and 10:1 f.). As for the Moabites, we read (II Sam. 8:2) that they "became servants to David and brought tribute," which would seem to indicate that the Moabite king was left on his throne to rule as David's vassal. With Edom he pursued a different course, for (II Sam. 8:14) "he put $n^e\d{s}\bar{\imath}b\bar{\imath}m$ in Edom." The word is most naturally translated as "garrisons,"[7] which points to a military occupation of that land. Since garrisons would hardly have reported individually to Jerusalem, but must have been controlled locally by some higher central command, it appears that Edom was ruled by a (military?) governor as a conquered province.[8]

2) Regarding conquered territory in northern Transjordan and Syria, our information is again meagre and spotty. The dominant state in Syria at the time was the kingdom of Zobah, which lay north of Damascus both east and west of the Anti-Lebanon range, and which exercised hegemony over the various Aramaean states and tribes from southern Syria to the Eu-

phrates valley. Its king, Hadadezer, was apparently of a house that stemmed from Beth-rehob (he is called ben Rehob in II Sam. 8:3, 12). We are told (II Sam. 10:6–19) that when David attacked Ammon, the Ammonites hired the Aramaeans of Zobah and Beth-rehob, as well as troops from Maacah (south of Mount Hermon) and Tob (somewhere in southern Syria) to come to their aid. But David beat them; subsequently he moved into Syria and broke the power of Hadadezer completely (II Sam. 8:3–8). He then took over all this area and administered it under various arrangements.

A. Malamat[9] has advanced the attractive hypothesis that Zobah was not the mere head of a coalition, but was actually a state as complex in its structure as David's own. It consisted of Beth-rehob and Zobah (which were united in Hadadezer's person), conquered territory ruled by governors (such as Damascus), and vassal states and satellites (Maacah, etc.). Malamat believes that David took over Zobah not only territorially, but structurally: i.e. he took over its component parts each for itself and governed each under the arrangement that seemed most suitable. This hypothesis, though it cannot be proved correct in every detail, accords well with the meagre biblical evidence. We are told (II Sam. 10:19) that, after the Aramaean defeat in Transjordan, "the kings who were Hadadezer's servants . . . made peace with Israel and became their servants." This would suggest that Hadadezer's southernmost vassal-allies (Maacah, Tob) surrendered at this time and became, in turn, vassals of David.[10] Geshur (east of the Sea of Galilee), with which David was already allied by marriage (II Sam. 3:3), apparently remained neutral in this affair and continued to preserve its identity (cf. II Sam. 13:37), though no doubt obliged to acknowledge David's overlordship. As for Damascus, II Sam. 8:6 tells us that David placed garrisons there, which suggests that he governed it, as he did Edom, as a province of the empire: i.e. it had (so Malamat) the same status under David as it had had under Hadadezer. How David administered the territory of Zobah and Beth-rehob we are not told. Some surmise that Hadadezer became David's vassal;[11] but Malamat argues that these areas were incorporated into Israel and ruled as occupied territory, presumably through governors appointed by David. We lack the evidence to decide.

The precise nature of David's relationship to the kingdom of Hamath in northern Syria is likewise uncertain. We are told (II Sam. 8:9 f.) that after David had crushed Hadadezer, the king of Hamath sent him lavish gifts— i.e. a treaty of some sort was concluded. But it is difficult to be sure whether this was a parity treaty—as the treaty with Tyre, made by David (II Sam. 5:11 f.) and renewed by Solomon (I Kings 5:15–26[10:1–12E.]) apparently was[12]—or one between suzerain and vassal. Opinion has usually inclined to the former alternative:[13] that the king of Hamath, happy to be rid of the menace of Hadadezer and wishing to head off further Israelite expansion to the north, established friendly relations with David, at the same time recognizing his rights in southern Syria and northeastward to the Euphrates. Others, however, disagree. Malamat, in particular, argues that both the value of the gifts sent and the fact that they were delivered by the king's son points to a suzerainty treaty, and believes that the name of the younger prince (Hadoram in I Chron. 18:10, but Joram in II Sam. 8:10) suggests that he took a Yahwistic throne name in token of his subordinate position.[14]

3) The position of David *vis-à-vis* the Philistines is far from clear. That he drove them from Israelite soil is certain (II Sam. 5:17–25). That he administered them yet further defeats which effectively broke their striking power is likewise certain, for otherwise his wars of conquest would not have been possible. The language of II Sam. 8:1, 11 f., which state that David "subdued" the Philistines, would suggest that they were reduced to a position of helplessness and forced to recognize Israelite supremacy, and this may be supported by the fact that Philistine troops (Cherethites and Pelethites) subsequently formed the backbone of David's mercenary corps (II Sam. 8:18; 15:18 etc.). Complete ascendancy over the Philistines must be assumed.

Nevertheless the precise extent of David's conquest remains uncertain. The Bible gives us only the cryptic text of II Sam. 8:1, the meaning of which has never been satisfactorily elucidated. The parallel text in I Chron. 18:1 says that David took Gath and its villages and, although this reading is scarcely to be preferred, it seems to be factually correct, and is supported by the fact that Gittite troops later formed a special contingent among David's mercenaries (II Sam. 15:18). To be sure, not only is the location of Gath disputed,[15] but there were several Gaths; some scholars doubt that it was the Philistine city-state of that name that David took.[16] But it seems entirely likely that it was, and that its king, Achish, whose vassal David had once been (I Samuel 27), became in turn David's vassal.[17] To the north, David occupied the coastal plain from Mount Carmel to a point south of Joppa; at least, this area was later parcelled out among three of Solomon's provinces, of which we shall speak below. Since it was probably David's aim to annex all territories claimed by the tribes, and since the tribal claim of Dan (Josh. 19:40–46) reached from Beth-shemesh to the sea in the neighborhood of Joppa (including Ekron), it is likely that David drastically restricted the territory of Ekron, if he did not occupy it altogether.[18]

On the other hand, we are nowhere told that David reduced the Philistine coastal cities of Ashdod, Ashkelon, and Gaza. Moreover, I Kings 9:16 suggests that the Canaanite city of Gezer, which had been under Philistine control, did not pass into Israelite hands until the reign of Solomon. This seems strange. It is hard to believe that David, in view of his undoubted military superiority, was simply unable to take these cities. True, one could argue that the Philistines capitulated, making attacks upon their chief cities unnecessary. But, in that event, it is equally strange that the Bible should say nothing about it. Malamat has advanced the hypothesis that David refrained from attacking the Philistine heartland because he knew that Egypt still claimed suzerainty over it and was reluctant to involve himself in possible difficulties with the Pharaoh.[19] Malamat further believes that when the Pharaoh (probably Siamun of the Twenty-first Dynasty) later marched into Palestine and took Gezer, it was not just to do a favor for Solomon; rather, hoping to re-establish Egyptian ascendancy in Palestine, he had launched a campaign against Philistia (over which he claimed suzerainty) in the course of which the frontier city of Gezer was taken, but then, finding himself confronted by a stronger force than he had bargained for in the form of Solomon's army, he thought it wiser to yield the city (and, in Malamat's view, other areas as well) to Solomon, make peace and withdraw. Y. Aharoni, however, argues that Gezer, like other city-states that had been subject to the Philistines, had already submitted peacefully to David, and that the Pharaoh's attack upon it was regarded by Solomon as a direct infringement on his territory.[20] He therefore reacted with sufficient force to cause the Pharaoh to conclude a treaty of peace, saving face by yielding the city as a dowry to his daughter, whom he gave in marriage to Solomon. Short of further evidence the details will perhaps never be clear; but Malamat's hypothesis, in its broad outlines, seems most illuminating.

The empire built by David was passed on to Solomon, who presumably administered it just as his father had. To be sure, at some time during his reign the province of Damascus was lost, and never recovered (I Kings 11: 23–25). But how extensive this loss was, and what effect it may have had on Solomon's administration of such lands as he still held, we do not know. In Edom, too, one Hadad stirred up trouble for Solomon and may have removed parts of that land, at least temporarily, from Israelite control. But how serious this trouble was, and how the administration of this province may have been affected, we again do not know.

II

1) Concerning the internal administration of Israel and Judah under David we have almost no direct information. But that David was forced to take steps toward the setting up of structures of government is certain. It was inevitable that he should have. The nation could not be administered solely on the basis of the old tribal system, for it now consisted not merely of the twelve traditional tribes, but also embraced, as we have said, the territories of the various city-states which, on the collapse of Philistine power, had transferred their allegiance to David and been incorporated into Israel. Moreover, though David depended increasingly on his professional army, his wars of conquest must have imposed a heavy and continuing demand for troops which it would have been difficult, if not impossible, to meet by

means of the traditional rally of the clans. And, although we may suppose that David was able to defray the cost of his wars and the expenses of state in good part from booty and tribute taken from conquered peoples, and from the income from crown property, it is all but certain that he was obliged to give thought to the finding of new sources of revenue. That David ever resorted to conscription, or imposed systematic taxation on his people, is nowhere specifically stated. But the fact that he ordered a census to be taken (II Samuel 24) indicates that he had some such steps in mind, for the major purpose of the census in the ancient world was always to lay the basis for levying taxes and registering men for military service (or corvée).[21] In spite of textual corruptions, it is clear from vss. 5–7 that the census included all of "greater Israel"—i.e. both the Israelite tribes and the newly annexed city-states. Some administrative reorganization of the whole land was clearly intended.

Whether or not David ever carried this out is unknown. Some scholars think that he did, and that the administrative system described in I Kings 4:7–19 was actually set up by David.[22] Others believe that David tried to organize the heartland of his realm within the framework of the traditional pattern of twelve tribes.[23] Still others argue that he was able to carry out a reorganization in Judah but, because of opposition, was unable to do so in Israel.[24] We cannot be sure. But in view of the fact that the census had strong opposition from the beginning, plus the fact that a plague that struck the land at the time was undoubtedly blamed upon David's action in taking it, it seems doubtful that David was ever able to carry out his intentions completely.

2) It is certain, however, that by the latter part of Solomon's reign a sweeping administrative reorganization had been made. This we know from the list of Solomon's twelve provinces and their governors—two of whom were the king's sons-in-law—found in I Kings 4:7–19. The authenticity of this list is not in dispute. Its significance was first made clear by A. Alt in an article published in 1913.[25] Several years later W. F. Albright published a study which he described as a supplement to Alt's, in which, by combining two of the provinces listed, he allowed place (as Alt had not) for Judah within the twelve-province system.[26] Since then, various scholars have studied the list, most of whom have been in general agreement with Alt.[27] Alt's understanding of the geographical order of the provinces has been generally accepted. The list begins with Mount Ephraim (Province 1) in the north-central part of the land. Then follow the provinces adjacent to it on the west (nos. 2, 3, 4), on the north (no. 5), and on the east (nos. 6, 7); then three provinces in Galilee (nos. 8, 9, 10); and, finally, two to the south of Mount Ephraim, east and west of the Jordan (nos. 11, 12). Alt also noted that the first seven of these provinces are designated by the names of areas or towns, while the last five (reading "Gad" for "Gilead" in vs. 19 with LXX and most scholars) bear the names of Israelite tribes. He concluded that

Solomon's reorganization aimed at being as conservative as possible; it respected tribal lines where this was at all feasible, and formed new provinces mainly to include areas recently absorbed into Israel. And in this conclusion he has been rather generally followed.

Recently, however, in an important article, G. Ernest Wright has challenged this conclusion.[28] He argues that the new system represented a far more radical shift than Alt had believed, and aimed at a division of the land into twelve districts of approximately equal economic capacity. True, where tribal lines were preserved the province was so named. But, says he, this occurs in only three cases: Naphtali (and even here, one might add, northern Dan must have been included in this province), Issachar, and Benjamin; the province of Asher included Zebulun (he reads "Zebulun" for "Bealoth" in vs. 16, as others have), while Gad (so reading in vs. 19, as most scholars do) is not the tribe of Gad but "the land of Gad," which is a territorial, not a tribal, designation. Actually, the three Transjordanian provinces (nos. 6, 7, 12) all cut across tribal lines. The debate, however, centers on the dimensions of Province 3 and, therewith, of Province 1. Alt, and most others, have regarded the latter (Mount Ephraim) as comprising roughly the tribal territory of Ephraim and western Manasseh, and have located the former in the central Sharon plain, where Socoh (vs. 10) was in all probability located. Wright, while accepting Alt's identification of Socoh (Shuweikeh, north of Tulkarm), doubts that in ancient times Sharon alone could have constituted a viable province because of its generally poor soil, and believes that Province 3 reached much farther inland to include most of western Manasseh. With F. M. Cross,[29] he locates the land of Hepher (cf. vs. 10) in northeastern Manasseh, north of Shechem (Hepher is bracketed with Tappuah in Josh. 12:17, and is listed as a sub-clan of Manasseh in Josh. 17:2), and suggests that Arubboth, apparently the capital of the province, is to be found not far from Dothan. Conversely, he believes that Province 1 embraced the territory of Ephraim, plus appreciable portions of Manasseh, including the agricultural areas around Shechem and Tirzah. A further cutting across tribal lines is thus indicated.

If Wright's conclusions are correct—and the writer believes that they are —Solomon's reorganization represented a far more radical break with the tribal system than has been supposed. It appears that he disregarded tribal lines far more often than he followed them. His aim, then, must have been not merely to assure the regular forwarding of provisions to the court (I Kings 5:7 f.[4:27 f.E.])—and to provide a basis for conscription (in his case, probably more for corvée labor than for military service)—but also to weaken tribal ties and to centralize power in the crown in a manner unprecedented.

3) But was Judah a part of this system? As we said, Albright long ago argued that it constituted one of the twelve provinces; but he has not been generally followed in this. The name "Judah" does not occur in MT of

I Kings 4:19, which ends "and there was one $n^e \bar{s} ib$ in the land"; it must be assumed to have slipped accidentally to the beginning of vs. 20 or to have dropped out by haplography. Yet, however one understands the text of vs. 19, it is difficult to believe that Judah was so blatantly favored as to be exempted from taxation altogether. The general opinion seems to be that it was not, but, the monarchy being a dual one, was administered under a separate system. As we shall see, some believe that it was, like the north, divided into provinces, the list describing which has not been preserved. It is impossible to be certain; but there is strong evidence that it was so divided in the days of the divided monarchy, and the system was in all likelihood much older. It is today generally agreed that the list of the towns of Judah in Josh. 15:21-62 (to which LXX adds a further group of towns after vs. 59) and of Benjamin in 18:21-28 (or at least vss. 25-28)—and, in the opinion of some, that of Dan in 19:41-46—reflect an administrative division of the kingdom of Judah into twelve provinces. Differences have chiefly to do with the geographical limits of some of these provinces, and with the historical situation which the lists presuppose. We need not debate these questions at length, since the lists as we have them could not possibly come from the days of the empire (to mention but one thing, some of the towns listed did not come into existence till the ninth century).[30] We shall, therefore, summarize briefly.

Once again the discussion was set off by Alt, who (in 1925) was the first to discern in these lists twelve administrative districts into which the kingdom of Judah had been divided.[31] Alt included in his analysis the northern district of Benjamin (Josh. 18:21-24), which trenches rather deeply upon Ephraimite territory, and the area of Dan (19:41-46), which reaches all the way to the sea in the vicinity of Joppa, and he concluded that the lists could only have come from the reign of Josiah, when Judah, once again free, was embarking upon its expansionist policy; the northern bulge into Ephraim he connected with Josiah's activity in Bethel (II Kings 23:15-20), and saw it as reflecting the first step toward his subsequent annexation of the whole of Samaria. Alt's study was closely reasoned and won widespread acceptance. His approach was subsequently taken up and developed by M. Noth,[32] and his understanding of the province list of Judah became, perhaps especially in Germany, well-nigh the consensus.

In 1956, however, Alt's position was questioned at certain important points in a penetrating article by Cross and Wright.[33] Specifically, these scholars criticized Alt for his delineation of certain of the provinces (his no. 11, their nos. 11, 12) and, especially for his inclusion of the Danite list as a province in the system. In this they seem to be correct, as subsequent studies have agreed. Although one can no longer hold it against Alt that there is no evidence that Josiah ever controlled this area, for such evidence now exists (Yabneh-yam!), it is certainly true that the Danite list is formally different from the rest and is, moreover, difficult to fit in with the Judahite list in ch. 15, as Cross and Wright make clear. In seeking a date for the list, these scholars note the northern bulge of Benjamin (Josh. 18:21–24), and relate this to the conquests of Abijah (II Chron. 13:19 f.) which, though lost by Asa, were, they believe, subsequently recovered by him and passed on to his son Jehoshaphat (cf. II Chron. 17:2), in whose reign the administrative reorganization reflected in the list was made.

Subsequent to this article the discussion has gone to and fro. In 1958, Z. Kallai-Kleinmann[34] argued that the lists (plural!) are separate documents, not necessarily all of the same date. The Benjamite list reflects the conquests of Abijah, the Danite list is based on Solomon's second province, while the Judahite list in its present form dates to Hezekiah, though it may have originated with Jehoshaphat, or even earlier. In 1959, Y. Aharoni argued that the list comes from the reign of Uzziah (he excluded Josh. 18:21–24 from the system), though agreeing that an administrative reorganization must have been carried out by Jehoshaphat.[35] Subsequently, however, Aharoni altered his position and, while disagreeing with Cross and Wright on various details, accepted a date in the reign of Jehoshaphat.[36] Still other scholars, though refusing to commit themselves to a firm decision, have allowed the reign of Jehoshaphat as a possibility.[37]

But none of this answers our main question: When was an administrative division of Judah first carried out? Virtually every scholar who has discussed the subject has expressed the belief that the system is much older than the lists themselves, and not a few have ventured the opinion that it may have originated with Solomon, or even David.[38] Cross and Wright point to tenth-century palaces and storehouses discovered at Beth-shemesh (IIa) and Lachish (V), which suggest that those cities were even then centers of provincial administration; since they would date the erection of these buildings to David, they believe that some sort of administrative system had been set up in Judah during his reign. But it must be said that the date of these buildings is disputed, and that other scholars would attribute them to Solomon.[39] The writer is not competent to offer an opinion. In either case, however, it seems probable that under the united monarchy Judah was governed through a provincial system similar to that which is known to have existed in Israel. But of its details we can say nothing.

III

A structure as complex as the one we have described naturally could not be supervised by the king personally; the development of a central administration was necessary. And, though we have very little direct information as to the ways in which it functioned, there is evidence that an administrative structure was set up by David which burgeoned considerably under Solomon. Moreover, there seems to be a fairly general agreement today that, in many of its features, this was patterned on Egyptian models.[40] This is in no way surprising. The newly created state had no native precedents for such things, and would have had to have borrowed from outside.

We have two lists of David's cabinet officers (as we would say)—one (II Sam. 8:16–18) apparently from earlier in his reign, one (II Sam. 20: 23–26) apparently from later—and one of Solomon's (I Kings 4:1–6).[41] In II Sam. 8:16–18 we find the following listed (the order of listing seems to be haphazard): the commander of the army, the *mazkīr* (in most EVV unfortunately translated as "recorder"), the two chief priests, the *sōphēr* (the secretary), and the chief of the foreign mercenaries. The list of II Sam. 20:23–26 records the same officials, but adds an officer over the *mas* (chief of corvée).[42] Solomon continued these offices, but added an officer *'al hannissābīm* ("over the governors") and one *'al habbayit* ("over the house," i.e. the palace); a "king's friend" is also listed. Notably, however, no special commander of mercenary troops is mentioned, which may well indicate that by Solomon's day the army consisted largely of professionals, so that this office could be combined with that of the commander-in-chief.

Though our information is at many points limited, there seems to be a rather general agreement with regard to the functions of these officers. Indeed, in some instances (the chief priest, the army commander) these may be said to be in the broad sense fairly obvious. The fact that the chief priest was a member of the king's "cabinet," and responsible directly to the king, illustrates the intimate way in which religion and state were integrated with one another in ancient Israel (and elsewhere in the ancient world). Though we may assume that the routine management of religious affairs was normally left to the high priest, the temple cult was a national cult, and the king its titular head. As for military affairs, though the king doubtless left matters of army administration, training, and the planning of tactics to his commander-in-chief, the latter was directly responsible to him; the king could, and sometimes did, assume command in the field if the situation seemed to warrant it.[43]

The duties of the chief of corvée are likewise in general obvious, and they must have become rather onerous as Solomon enlarged the use of forced labor on his various building projects (I Kings 5:27 f.[13 f.E.]; 9:15 ff.). This labor force was presumably raised by conscription out of the various provinces, in each of which there probably was a chief corvée officer who worked with the governor.[44] Under him, in turn, there would have been a staff of labor bosses who actively superintended the work; the grand total of these is given as 550 in I Kings 9:23, as 3,300 in 5:30 [16E.]).[45] The function of the officer *'al hannissābīm* ("over the governors") is likewise more or less clear from his title. He was the one to whom the governors of the various provinces reported, and whose responsibility it doubtless was to see to it that they remitted their taxes as stipulated, and on time, and otherwise conducted affairs in their provinces in accordance with the king's wishes. Whether governors of conquered territories, such as Edom and Damascus, likewise reported to him is unknown. Since these were possibly military governors supported by occupation troops, they may have reported through the commanding general.

Since the appearance of the articles of de Vaux and Begrich,[46] it has been generally agreed that the offices of *'al habbayit, sōphēr,* and *mazkīr* were patterned on Egyptian models. Texts such as II Kings 18:18, 37 suggest that, at least at a later date, they were (and in that order) the king's three chief ministers. The *mazkīr* (lit. "the one who brings to remembrance, makes known, announces") was not a "recorder" (so many EVV), but the royal herald. His counterpart in Egypt had charge of palace ceremonies and was the one who admitted persons to the king's presence for audiences; but he was more than a chief of protocol, for he also reported to the king regarding affairs in the land and officially transmitted the royal commands to the people. He also accompanied the king on journeys, watched over his person, and had charge of his quarters and provisions. The *sōphēr,* as his title implies, was at once the king's private secretary and secretary of state. He handled all official correspondence, both external and internal, and he may also (cf. II Kings 12:11[10E.]) have had the task of recording revenues received at the court from taxes, tolls, tribute, and the like. We may assume that he had a sizable staff of scribes working under him. De Vaux suggested[47] that David's secretary may actually have been an Egyptian, his name—which appears variously as Seriah (II Sam. 8:17), Sheva (II Sam. 20:25) Shavsha (I Chron. 18:16), and Shisha (I Kings 4:3)—being the Egyptian šš or the like, while that of his son, Eliḥoreph (I Kings 4:3), who served under Solomon, may originally have been (cf. LXX[B]) Eliḥaph ("Apis is my god").[48] The suggestion is attractive but, owing particularly to uncertainties in the textual tradition, it has not gained universal acceptance.[49] The office of *'al habbayit* was one of those instituted by Solomon. The title ("over the house") would suggest that this functionary was originally the major-domo of the palace and the king's steward who managed the crown property—which by Solomon's day must have been considerable. But there is evidence that, at least at a later date (cf. II Kings 18:18, 37; 19:2, etc.), he was much more than that and served, in fact, as the king's chief minister—like the Egyptian vizier, who was likewise governor of the palace.

In the opinion of most scholars, further evidence of Egyptian influence is to be found in the title of "the king's friend" (I Kings 4:5).[50] This personage is mentioned only in texts relating to David and Solomon (cf. II Sam. 15:37; 16:16 f.; I Chron. 27:33), and it is difficult to say what his precise function was. But, in view of the fact that he is listed among Solomon's high officials, it seems unlikely that the title was a purely honorary one. H. Donner has plausibly suggested[51] that he was a sort of privy counselor, and that the title later fell from use because the functions of its holder could no longer be distinguished from those of a *yōʻēṣ* (counselor). It is likewise possible that evidence of Egyptian influence is to be found in that body of picked soldiers about David's person, known as the "Thirty" (II Sam. 23:24–39). In 1935, K. Elliger[52] made an exhaustive study of this list, and argued that the Thirty was a royal bodyguard modeled on a similar organization which existed in Egypt. Elliger's views won wide acceptance and, so far as the writer is aware, for many years went uncontested. In 1963, however, B. Mazar[53] pointed out that the number "thirty" is frequent in pre-monarchical Israelite tradition, and argued that the assumption of Egyptian influence is unwarranted. Caution would seem to be indicated. But, whatever the truth of the matter in this regard may be, Egyptian influence upon the development of the bureaucracy of the Israelite empire seems undeniable.

IV

Further administrative measures on the part of David or Solomon may lie concealed behind the list of cities of refuge in Joshua 20, and the list of Levitic cities in Joshua 21. The former list has received little discussion outside of the commentaries. Though the chapter was given its present form possibly in the late seventh century, the institution itself is surely older. It represents the attempt to curb those private feuds and clan vendettas to which all tribal societies are liable by providing cities to which any who had taken life unintentionally might flee. Since vendettas are things that no stable government can tolerate, it is entirely reasonable to suppose, as a number of scholars do, that such a system was set up by David or, at the latest, by Solomon.[54] But we lack the information to say more.

The list of Levitic cities has received more discussion. Scholars of an earlier generation usually regarded this list as a post-exilic priestly Utopia, of minimal historical value. And, more recently, Y. Kaufmann has regarded it as a Utopia, but one that comes from the very beginning of the Israelite occupation of Palestine.[55] But in recent years one detects a growing tendency to accept it as reflecting actual historical circumstances. The basic study here was that of Albright in 1945.[56] Albright convincingly demonstrated that the lists in Joshua 21 and I Chronicles 6 go back to a common original; pointing out that not all the towns listed were Israelite before David, and that a number were lost soon after Solomon's death, he saw the list as reflecting a resettlement of Levites which was carried out late in David's reign or early in that of Solomon (before his administrative reorganization, which disregarded tribal lines)[57] Albright's conclusions were brilliantly developed, and they gained widespread acceptance. It is true that in 1951, and again in 1952, Alt sought to relate the list to the reign of Josiah.[58] But more recent discussions of the problem have tended to a tenth-century date.[59] We are left to guess what the purpose of this resettlement of Levites was. It is noteworthy that, aside from a concentration in Benjamin, their cities were located in good part in peripheral areas, in many instances areas newly incorporated into Israel. It may be, therefore, that the aim was primarily to promulgate the official cultus and to promote national solidarity and loyalty to the crown in "less secure" parts of the realm.[60] If this was the purpose of the project, it probably did not survive the division of the monarchy on Solomon's death.[61]

But we must close. The organization and administration of the Israelite empire is a subject upon which our knowledge is far from complete. In fact, it rather resembles an iceberg, most of which is not visible to the eye. One wonders if many significant breakthroughs will take place short of the discovery of new information. Our review has been of necessity a summary one —and, I fear, at many points superficial—but I trust that what has been said will allow the reader some idea of the major problem areas and of the present state of the discussion. It is both a pleasure and an honor to be able to present this paper to George Ernest Wright, whose scholarship I have always admired, and whose friendship and encouragement over the years has meant more to me than I can readily say.

NOTES

1. Cf., *inter alia*, K. Galling, *Die israelitische Staatsverfassung in ihrer vorderorientalischen Umwelt,* Der Alte Orient, XXVIII, 3–4 (Leipzig, 1929); A. Alt, "The Formation of the Israelite State in Palestine" (1930) in *Essays on Old Testament History and Religion,* tr. R. A. Wilson (Oxford, 1961), pp. 171–237; more recently, G. Buccellati, *Cities and Nations of Ancient Syria* (Rome, 1967); also, R. de Vaux, *Ancient Israel: Its Life and Institutions* (tr., New York, 1961; paperback ed., 1965), where rather full bibliography on most aspects of the subject will be found.

2. Cf. esp. M. Noth, *Das System der zwölf Stämme Israels* (1930; repr. Darmstadt, 1966). The existence of such a league has been disputed, e.g. by H. M. Orlinsky, *Oriens Antiquus* 1 (1962), 11–20, and G. Fohrer, *TLZ* 91 (1966), cols. 801–816, 893–904, but, in my opinion, not successfully.

3. Y. Aharoni, *LB,* pp. 255–257 (cf. also Hebrew article cited in n. 4, but not available to me), sees in the names in II Sam. 2:8 f. five administrative districts (in addition to Judah) which Saul had set up. But this seems less than certain.

4. Since the fundamental treatment of Alt [N 1], this has been the generally accepted opinion. It has been contested, however, by Buccellati [N 1], pp. 148–155, who believes that the dualism emerged later.

5. Again the commonly accepted opinion; cf. Alt [N 1]; "Jerusalems Aufstieg" (1925), in *KS* III, 243–257; questioned, however, by Buccellati, pp. 160–168.

6. Again compare the work of Alt cited in N 1; also his "Das Grossreich Davids" (1950), in *KS* II, 66–75.

7. In some contexts it could be understood as "prefects," "governors." The reader who troubles to check will find that there is occasional textual confusion between this word and *niṣṣāb,* "governor."

8. I Kings 22:48[47E.] states that Edom was ruled by a *niṣṣāb* ("governor," RSV

"deputy") in the days of Jehoshaphat. But the text may be corrupt; cf. LXX and the commentaries.

9. A. Malamat, "Aspects of the Foreign Policies of David and Solomon," *JNES* 22 (1963), 1–17 (esp. 1–6).

10. Perhaps with some reduction of territory; Abel-beth-maacah was Israelite later in David's reign (see II Sam. 20:14, 18 f.). On Maacah and Geshur, see B. Mazar, *JBL* 80 (1961), 16–28.

11. E.g. Alt, *KS*, II, 72; Mazar [N 10], 28. One might argue from II Sam. 8:6, where it is stated that "the Arameans became servants to David and brought tribute," that all the various Aramean lands except Damascus (cf. vs. 8a) became vassal states of David. But this may be pressing language too far.

12. On this treaty, cf. F. C. Fensham, *VTS*, 17 (Leiden, 1969), 71–87.

13. E.g. Alt, *KS*, II, 72 f.; Mazar, *BA* 25 (1962), 103; O. Eissfeldt, "The Hebrew Kingdom," (in *CAH³*, II:34 (1965), 47.

14. [N 9], 6–8. Malamat also refers to an eighth-century king of Hamath, whose name appears alternatively as Ilubidi or Yaubidi, as evidence of continuing Israelite influence in that land. But on these names cf. most recently E. Lipiński, *VT* 21 (1971), 371–373.

15. The problem cannot concern us here; see G. E. Wright, *BA* 29 (1966), 78–82, for a discussion of various possibilities (he opts for Tell esh-Shariʻah) and further references.

16. E.g. Mazar, *IEJ* 4 (1954), 227–235; Malamat [N 9], 15; Aharoni, *LB*, pp. 261, 292.

17. This is not contradicted by I Kings 2:39 f., as some, e.g. Malamat, Aharoni, believe. We need not assume that the king of Gath mentioned there was an independent ruler and not a vassal of Solomon; cf. Wright [N 15], 81 f.

18. Cf. Wright [N 15], pp. 83 f.; also Aharoni, *LB*, p. 261. Malamat [N 9], 15–17, however, reckons with a large-scale transfer of Philistine territory (Ekron, Gath) to Israel in Solomon's reign. Whether the summary notices in I Kings 5:1, 4[4:21, 24E.]) are sufficient evidence that Solomon also ruled Gaza, as Malamat suggests, is to me an open question.

19. Malamat, N 9, 10–17. O. Eissfeldt had earlier (*ZDPV* 66 [1943] 118) advanced a similar suggestion; cf. *KS*, II, 455 f.

20. Eissfeldt, p. 272.

21. Cf. G. E. Mendenhall, *JBL* 77 (1958), 52–66 (esp. 53 f.), on the subject.

22. Cf. Mazar, *IEJ* 10 (1960), 71.

23. Cf. Aharoni, *LB*, pp. 264–267.

24. Cf. F. M. Cross and G. E. Wright, *JBL* 75 (1956), 224–226. We shall return to this subject on p. 200.

25. Alt, "Israels Gaue unter Salomo"; cf. *KS* II, 76–89.

26. Albright, "The Administrative Divisions of Israel and Judah," *JPOS* 5 (1925), 17–54.

27. Detailed treatments have been few; cf., *inter alia*, F.-M. Abel, *Géographie de la Palestine*, II (Paris, 1938), 79–83; de Vaux [N 1], pp. 133–135; M. Noth, *Könige* (Neukirchen, 1964), pp. 55–75; Aharoni, *LB*, pp. 276–280.

28. Wright, "The Provinces of Solomon," *EI* 8 (1967), 58–68.

29. See Cross's map in Wright and Cross [N 24], p. 63.

30. I.e. in the wilderness province (Josh. 15:61 f.); cf. F. M. Cross and J. T. Milik, "Explorations in the Judean Buqêʻah," *BASOR* 142 (1956), 5–17.

31. Alt, "Judas Gaue unter Josia"; cf. *KS*, II, 276–288.

32. Cf. Noth, "Studien zu den historisch-geographischen Dokumenten des Josuabuches," *ZDPV* 58 (1935), 185–255; also *Das Buch Josua* (Tübingen, 1938; 2d ed., 1953), pp. 73–123.

33. Cross and Wright, "The Boundary and Province Lists of the Kingdom of Judah," *JBL* 75 (1956), 202–226.

34. Kallai-Kleinmann, "The Town Lists of Judah, Simeon, Benjamin and Dan," *VT* 8 (1958), 134–160.

35. Aharoni, "The Province-list of Judah," *VT* 9 (1959), 225–246. A similar position was later taken by K.-D. Schunk, in *Benjamin, BZAW* 86 (1963), 153–159.

36. Cf. Aharoni, *LB*, pp. 296–304.

37. E.g. de Vaux [N 1], pp. 135 f.

38. E.g. Cross and Wright [N 33], 224 f.; de Vaux, ibid.; Schunk, *Benjamin* [N 35], p. 160. II Chron. 11:23 might suggest that such a system existed at least in the reign of Rehoboam.

39. See e.g. the articles of Kallai-Kleinmann and Aharoni in NN 34 and 35, respectively; also Mazar [N 22], 69 f.

40. The basic studies are: de Vaux, "Titres et fonctionnaires égyptiens à la cour de David et de Salomon" (1939; repr., *Bible et Orient* [Paris, 1967], pp. 189–201); J. Begrich, "Sōfēr und Mazkīr" (1940/41; repr., *Gesammelte Studien zum A.T.* [Munich, 1964], pp. 67–98). These scholars' conclusions have been widely accepted.

41. We cannot delay on textual problems relative to these lists; cf. the commentaries.

42. De Vaux, *Ancient Israel* [N 1], p. 128, doubts that Adoram was in office under David, or that this post was established before Solomon. But David at least put conquered peoples to forced labor (II Sam. 12:31), and must have needed an officer to supervise them. If Adoram had entered David's service late in his reign as a young man, he could have been perhaps in his sixties, and still active, after Solomon's death (I Kings 12:18).

43. On all matters pertaining to the army, its organization, administration, weapons and tactics, cf. esp. Y. Yadin, *The Art of Warfare in Biblical Lands*, 2 vols. (tr., New York, 1963).

44. Jeroboam is said to have been in charge of "the *sēbel* of the house of Joseph" (I Kings 11:28). Does this mean Solomon's first province or a larger area? On the word *sēbel* (not the usual one for corvée), cf. M. Held, *JAOS* 88 (1968), 90–96.

45. They are called *śārē hannissābīm*, an expression that occurs only in these verses (and II Chron. 8:10), and would most naturally be translated as "officers of the governors."

46. See N 40.

47. De Vaux [N 40], pp. 192–196.

48. In this last, de Vaux followed J. Marquart, *Fundamente israelitischer und jüdischer Geschichte* (1897), p. 22—a work to which I do not have access.

49. A. Cody, "Le titre égyptien et le nom propre du scribe de David," *RB* 72 (1965), 381–393, has argued that David's secretary had the good Hebrew name of Seriah, and that the other names are corruptions of his Egyptian title (*sḥ-š't*, or the like, the first word meaning "scribe," the second "dispatch," "letter"); he was addressed by this title, which was then mistaken for a proper name. Not being in command of Egyptian, the writer is not competent to express an opinion.

50. Cf. de Vaux [N 40], pp. 198–201; most recently, H. Donner, "Der 'Freund des Königs'," *ZAW* 73 (1961), 269–277. This view is widely accepted; cf. the commentaries. A. van Selms, however, argues for a Mesopotamian origin; *JNES* 16 (1957), 118–123.

51. *ZAW* 73 (1961), 270 f.

52. K. Elliger, "Die dreissig Helden Davids" (repr. *Kleine Schriften zum A.T.* [Munich, 1966], pp. 72–118).

53. Mazar, "The Military Elite of King David," *VT* 13 (1963), 310–320. Y. Yadin [N 43], p. 277, believes that the Thirty was not a bodyguard, but a supreme army council, members of which served as permanent commanders of the militia when it was called up.

54. Cf., *inter alia*, M. Löhr, *Das Asylwesen im A.T.* (Halle, 1930), pp. 209 f.; Albright, *ARI*, pp. 120 f.; de Vaux [N 1], pp. 160–163.

55. Y. Kaufmann, *The Biblical Account of the Conquest of Palestine* (Jerusalem, 1953), pp. 40–46.

56. W. F. Albright, "The List of Levitic Cities," *Louis Ginzberg Jubilee Volume* (New York, 1945), pp. 49–73. Albright (p. 50) refers to an earlier article by S. Klein (1934, in Hebrew) to which I do not have access.

57. In *ARI*, pp. 117–121, Albright argues strongly for a Davidic date.

58. Alt, "Bemerkungen zu einigen judäischen Ortslisten des Alten Testaments" (1951; cf. *KS* II, 289–305); "Festungen und Levitenorte im Lande Juda" (1952; cf. *KS* II, 306–315).

59. Cf. Mazar, "The Cities of the Priests and the Levites," *VTS* VII (1960), 193–205, who dates the list to Solomon; Aharoni, *LB*, pp. 268–273, who dates it to David; also for a tenth-century date: de Vaux, *Ancient Israel* [N 1], pp. 366 f.; J. A. Soggin, *Josué, Commentaire de l'Ancien Testament* (Neuchâtel, 1970), pp. 151–154.

60. Cf. Aharoni, Mazar [N 59], who see also an administrative function.

61. Aharoni (*LB*, p. 273), possibly correctly, sees evidence of the ejection of these Levites in II Chron. 11:13 f.

11. *Solomon, Siamun, and the Double Ax*

H. DARRELL LANCE

COLGATE ROCHESTER/BEXLEY HALL/CROZER

OVER THE PAST two decades the influence of G. Ernest Wright as archaeological teacher and organizer has been extraordinary. The number of younger scholars now at work in Palestinian and Cypriote archaeology who were trained directly or indirectly by him, and the number of archaeological projects which were conceived, inspired, and organized by him rival those of his own teacher, Albright. It was Wright, for example, who first suggested the re-excavation of Gezer and who persuaded the late Nelson Glueck over dinner one evening at the Desert Inn in Beer-sheba to adopt the site as the long-range project of the Hebrew Union College Biblical and Archaeological School (recently renamed the Nelson Glueck School of Bible and Archaeology). The present study, a small footnote to the historiography of Gezer, grew directly out of that project and represents but one product of the kind of archaeological and historical investigation that has rippled across many sites, problems, and periods from an energetic center.

In I Kings 9:16 we read that "Pharaoh, king of Egypt, went up, took Gezer, burned it with fire, and slaughtered the Canaanites who lived in the city. Then he gave it as dowry to his daughter, the wife of Solomon." Suggestions for the identification of the anonymous Pharaoh mentioned in this intriguing passage have ranged from Shishak, the first king of the Twenty-second Dynasty, back through several of his predecessors; but recently the name of Siamun, the penultimate king of the Twenty-first Dynasty has found increasing favor, particularly as a result of the discovery by Montet of a relief of this king which has been interpreted as indicating military activity by Siamun in Asia.[1] It will be the basic contention of this article that the Siamun relief has been badly misunderstood and must be eliminated from the discussion with the consequence that the question of the Pharaoh's identity is still open. But first let us see why the problem cannot yet be solved on the basis of chronology.

I

We can establish with some probability the period within the reign of Solomon in which the events of I Kings 9:16 took place. The clear implication of the story, reinforced by other mentions of Pharaoh's daughter in I Kings 3:1, 7:8, and 9:24, is that Solomon was already reigning when the marriage took place. Even more decisive is Horn's point that Solomon was not the obvious heir-apparent until shortly before David's death; and, given the extreme rarity of marriages between daughters of Pharaoh and foreign kings, it is inconceivable that the match would have been made before Solomon's hold on the throne was assured.[2] Hence, we are not being bold if we take Solomon's accession for our *terminus a quo*. Fortunately we also have a clear *terminus ad quem*, for I Kings 3:1b states that Solomon brought his royal bride into the City of David until he should finish building the temple of Yahweh, his palace, and the wall of Jerusalem. If this verse is correct and the temple was not completed at the time of the marriage, this places the marriage and the concomitant conquest of Gezer sometime before Solomon's eleventh year since the temple was finished in that year (I Kings 6:38).[3] Moreover, I Kings 3:1b permits the interpretation that Solomon's building projects were already under way when Pharaoh's daughter arrived in Jerusalem. If that is the case, then our *a quo* date is reduced to Solomon's fourth year (I Kings 6:1), bringing us to a tentative range of Solomon's fourth to eleventh years, i.e. the period of the building of the temple.

The problem now becomes the identification of the Pharaoh of Egypt who was reigning during Solomon's fourth to eleventh years. Unfortunately, we have only one fixed point to guide us. In I Kings 14:25–27 we read that Shishak, king of Egypt, came up against Jerusalem and looted the king's palace and the temple. This event took place in the fifth year of Rehoboam and at the minimum tells us that Rehoboam and Shishak (Shoshenq I) were contemporaries. It follows that if we know (1) the length of Solomon's reign, (2) when in the reign of Shishak his raid took place, and (3) the length of the reigns of Shishak's predecessors, i.e. the last kings of the Twenty-first Dynasty, we should be able to determine which Pharaoh was on the throne in the early years of Solomon's reign when the conquest of Gezer occurred. It is at this point, however, that the difficulties arise.

1. Although the biblical record attributes forty years to the reign of Solomon (I Kings 11:42), the highest year date recorded for him is the twenty-fourth, i.e. the year of completion of his building projects in Jerusalem (I Kings 9:10).[4] The clear implication of the stories of Solomon's latter days, however, is that he had grown old (I Kings 11:4) and that there had been sufficient time for the religious fervor that must have ac-

companied the building of the temple to cool considerably (I Kings 11). Thus the figure of forty years is probably within the correct range.

2. The biblical synchronism of I Kings 14:25–27 tells us in what year of Rehoboam's reign Shishak looted Jerusalem, but we do not know what was the corresponding year of Shishak.[5] Some light is shed, however, by an inscription from year twenty-one of Shoshenq found in a quarry at Gebel es-Silsilah commemorating the quarrying of the stone used in his additions to the Karnak temple.[6] Although the projected building projects mentioned in the inscription are quite extensive, comparatively little was actually accomplished. In particular, the relief which commemorates Shishak's victories during his campaign into Palestine was left incomplete. This plus the fact that Manetho reckons only twenty-one years for the reign of Shishak strongly suggests that the Pharaoh died in his twenty-first or twenty-second year.[7] Since it is unlikely that a great deal of time would elapse between Pharaoh's campaign and its commemoration in stone, one may estimate that the foray took place no later than his twenty-first year and probably no earlier than about his eighteenth.[8] Subtracting the intervening years of Rehoboam, we see that Shishak and Solomon ruled contemporaneously for no more than the last seventeen years of Solomon's life.[9] Even if the figure of forty years for Solomon's reign is rejected as a round number, he cannot have ruled fewer than thirty years at the very least. This would put Shishak's accession at the very earliest in Solomon's fourteenth year, well after the *terminus ante quem* of his eleventh year which we have already established for the marriage. The earlier in Shishak's reign that the raid on Palestine occurred or the longer that Solomon's reign exceeded the absolute minimum of thirty years, the further apart would grow the gap between Solomon's eleventh year and the accession of Shishak. Thus regardless of the system of absolute chronology adopted and despite the advocacy of a number of distinguished scholars, Shishak cannot possibly have been Solomon's father-in-law.[10]

3. As we move back into the final reigns of the Twenty-first Dynasty, our uncertainties increase. The chronology of this dynasty remains unclear despite a number of recent studies.[11] The crucial question is the length of the reign of the final king of that dynasty, Psusennes II. If he reigned twenty-five or more years, then he would have already become Pharaoh at the time of the death of David and would be the prime candidate for the conqueror of Gezer. A shorter reign would mean that his predecessor, Siamun, was still on the throne. Unfortunately, almost nothing is known of the reign of this Psusennes. It is possible that a year twelve may be attributed to him in one list[12] and a year thirteen in another,[13] but both of these are uncertain. Africanus and Eusebius do not agree on a Manethonian number, the former giving Psusennes fourteen years and the latter thirty-five. Although the Eusebian number appears artificially inflated by the standard twenty years, it is

interesting to note that only if thirty-five years are attributed to Psusennes is the total of 130 years attained, the total which both traditions preserve for the dynasty as a whole.[14] Most Egyptologists agree that the total of 130 years for the Twenty-first Dynasty is a minimum; estimates range from 130 upward to 150 years.[15] Therefore, to choose the lower of the two numbers for the reign of Psusennes II only increases the difficulty by decreasing the total for the dynasty to less than 130 years. Even the extra years of Siamun's reign (perhaps the Psinaches of Manetho) which is known to have lasted at least seventeen years as against the nine attributed to Psinaches would not fill the gap.[16]

The evidence, therefore, for the reign of Psusennes II is inconclusive. Either Africanus' fourteen years or Eusebius' thirty-five could be correct or the true figure could be something else. Consequently it becomes impossible on the basis of our present information to solve the problem from a chronological approach. The chronological data allow either Siamun or Psusennes to be the Pharaoh of I Kings 9:16; any choice between them on the basis of present information is premature.

II

The current preference for Siamun is usually not based on chronological considerations but on the aforementioned relief found by Pierre Montet in his excavations at Tanis in 1939 (*Figure 5a*).[17] Although only one block survives, it bears the broken but recognizable cartouche of Siamun.[18] The scene portrayed is one sufficiently familiar to allow us to reconstruct the general picture. The king is holding a prisoner (or prisoners) by the hair with his left hand while he prepares to execute the unfortunate with a mace or sickle-sword which he raises behind him in his right hand. The position of the prisoner is puzzling; the hand which is raised in the usual appeal for mercy seems to appear from behind the back of the prisoner under the other arm, and there may thus have been more than one prisoner in the original relief.[19] In the hand of the arm extending downward there is an object which appears to have two crescentic blades, the left one slightly larger than the right. In his drawing (*Figure 5b*) Montet shows a handle extending from the bottom of the object although this detail is questionable, judging from the photograph.[20]

When Montet first published the Siamun piece in *Le Drame d'Avaris*, he pointed out that sculptors of such scenes often placed in the hand of the prisoner being executed a weapon typical of the defeated people; and he proposed that the object held by the figure in the Siamun relief is such a weapon.[21] He identified the weapon as a double ax which he stated was of Aegean origin and a weapon which the Sea Peoples continued to use. He went on to propose that Siamun must have conducted a war against the

Philistines in the course of which he conquered Gezer. According to his chronology, Siamun was more a contemporary of David than of Solomon, and so Montet conjectured that Gezer was held by the Egyptians for some time before being given to Solomon.

In his definitive publication of the block, Montet repeated substantially the views put forth in *Le Drame d'Avaris*.[22] But in *Egypt and the Bible,* Montet made his position more precise, stating that although it was Siamun who conquered Gezer, it was not handed over as dowry to Solomon until the time of Psusennes II.[23] As documentation for his position that it is the double ax which is portrayed on the Siamun relief, Montet refers the reader to an illustration in a work by Dussaud which turns out to be the double ax used as a decorative motif on a Minoan vase from Gournia in Crete.[24]

The basic analysis of the Siamun relief by Montet as depicting a victory over the Philistines which is to be connected with the conquest of Gezer has found favor among a number of scholars, among them Goldwasser,[25] Elgood,[26] Yeivin,[27] Malamat,[28] Černý,[29] and Horn.[30] Indeed, no dissenting voices have been raised; and Montet's interpretation of the relief appears to be approaching adoption by consensus.[30a] However, it is the argument of this study that Montet's argument is based on three assumptions, all of which are demonstrably false.

The first assumption is that the double ax of the shape shown on the Siamun relief was used as a weapon in the Aegean world. On examining the available evidence, however, one finds the case to be quite the contrary. In the first place one must point out that there were two quite different types of double axes in the Aegean world. The first was a tool similar to the modern double-bladed woodsman's ax. A typical example is shown in *Figure 6*.[31] Sometimes the edges or the long sides are more curved,[32] but its basic form is a solid one intended for heavy work. This form of the double ax is found throughout the Aegean world in the Late Helladic and Early Iron Ages, and examples are known from Palestine, including one from Gezer.[33] The second form taken by the double ax is quite different; both the sides and the edges are much more curved, and the ends of the cutting blades are sharply pointed (*Figure 7*).[34]

One can see at a glance that if the object portrayed on the Siamun relief is a double ax at all, it can only be compared to the second or flaring form. Numerous examples of the double ax in this flaring shape also are found in the Aegean, the vast majority in Crete; but whenever they occur in metal, the examples "are unfit for practical use, either through being made of thin sheet bronze which cannot stand any wear or because they are so small that they cannot have been a tool (they often have, for example, nothing but a small bronze pin for a handle)."[35] Sometimes they are even found in gold or silver like some of those from the great hoard of Arkalochori.[36] It has long been recognized that these flaring double axes were not intended for actual use but were votive objects connected with Minoan religion. To quote the famous dictum of Nilsson: "Of all the religious symbols and emblems that appear in the Minoan civilization, the double ax is the most conspicuous, the real sign of Minoan religion and as omnipresent as the cross in Christianity or the crescent in Islam."[37]

The flaring double ax thus is primarily a symbol of Minoan religion; and as in the case of the Minoan vase to which Montet referred, it frequently serves as a decorative motif. However, when we look for evidence of the double ax of the flaring shape used as a weapon, we search in vain. There is not one single example from the period around the turn of the second millennium B.C. in the Aegean, Anatolia, or the Levant of a double ax of the flaring shape which is used as a weapon.[38] This is true not only of arti-factual remains but of pictorial or monumental representations as well.[39] Before one begins to find axes of this shape from even roughly contemporary periods which were actually intended for use in battle, one has to go across the Caucasus or to Iron Age Italy.[40] The flaring double ax, as already mentioned, does occur frequently as a motif in Minoan art and to some extent in Mycenaean art as long as it was under Minoan influence, but in no case is it shown being used as a weapon.[41] The similarity which Montet noticed between the object on the Siamun relief and the pictorial representa-tions from the Aegean is one of form alone; a similarity of function is ab-sent.[42]

But we may go even further. No only does the flaring double ax never occur as a weapon in the Aegean world, but battle axes of any sort at all are nearly unknown in Mycenaean Greece and are almost as rare in the Dark Age.[43] Thus to speak confidently as does Černý of the borrowing of the battle ax by the Sea Peoples from the Aegean world becomes most difficult, and to speak of the borrowing of a battle ax of the flaring type well-nigh impossible.[44]

The second assumption of Montet's analysis of the Siamun relief is that the battle ax was the characteristic weapon of the Sea Peoples in general and of the Philistines in particular. To test this assumption we have three sources of information: (1) representations of Sea Peoples in the monuments, (2) materials recovered from excavated Philistine sites, and (3) the rather com-plete description of Goliath's armor in I Samuel 17.

1. Various groups of the Sea Peoples are pictured both in reliefs of Rameses II and Rameses III. In the reliefs of Rameses II depicting the battle with the Hittites at Kadesh the Sherden appear as mercenary soldiers bearing as their weapons swords, spears, and round shields.[45] In the Medinet Habu reliefs of Rameses III groups of Sea Peoples appear in a number of roles— as mercenaries in battles against the Libyans,[46] against cities in Asia,[47] and against other Sea Peoples, notably in the famous land and sea battle reliefs.[48] In all these representations, the Sea Peoples, regardless of the group to which they belong as indicated by their headdress, carry the same sort of weapons—a round shield and a sword, sometimes long, sometimes

short, sometimes with scarcely any pommel, sometimes with a pronounced crescentic one.[49] In none of these scenes do any members of the Sea People groups carry anything resembling a battle ax. The one possible exception to this rule is the figure portrayed on the ivory gaming board found at Enkomi on Cyprus.[50] Although the figure is bearded in contrast to the clean-shaven Sea Peoples pictured on Egyptian reliefs, his headdress and kilt are very similar to those of the Sea Peoples. In his hand he bears what appears to be a single-bladed ax, but it is quite different in shape from the object portrayed on the Siamun relief.

2. As for actual weapons found at Philistine sites or in Philistine tombs, the situation can be quickly stated: no weapon resembling the object on the Siamun relief has been discovered. Of course the quantity of weapons found in these contexts is not great, and this argument alone would not be conclusive. It is interesting to note, however, that Petrie found in a Philistine tomb, No. 542, at Tell Farah(S) a short sword with the crescent-shaped pommel similar to those shown on the Medinet Habu reliefs.[51] Also from near Jaffa comes an example of a long sword compared by Hall, Yadin, and Mrs. Dothan to the longer sword carried by the Sea Peoples.[52] Given the Medinet Habu reliefs and these actual remains, the sword would appear to be a far better candidate for the weapon characteristic of the Philistines than a totally hypothetical battle ax.

3. In I Samuel 17:5–7 there occurs a detailed description of the armor and weapons of Goliath. He wears a helmet of bronze (*kôba‘ nᵉḥōšet*) and a suit of mail (*širyôn qaśqaśśîm*). Upon his legs are bronze greaves (*miṣḥat nᵉḥōšet*),[53] and on his shoulders is a *kîdôn nᵉḥōšet*, traditionally translated as "javelin" or the like but according to O'Callaghan and Yadin, a sword.[54] Finally, he carried a spear (*ḥănît*) with a heavy point and for the actual fight would take his shield (*ṣinnāh*) in hand which was carried out to the field for him by a shield bearer. Although some of the pieces of armor are not completely understood, it is plain that none of them is a battle ax.

In short, the statement that an ax was a typical weapon of the Philistines has not a single piece of evidence in its support.

The final assumption of Montet's analysis and which is of course the primary one is that the object shown on the relief is indeed a double ax. The published drawings show two lines running from the fist of the prisoner down to the edge of the block (*Figure 5b*). One's suspicion is immediately aroused by the asymmetry of the lines as shown: the "handle" of the ax does not meet the head at right angles. This would mean that the hole for the haft would have to run through the head at an angle, an unprecedented arrangement for a double ax. Unfortunately the photograph of the relief published by Montet (see *Figure 5a*) is not sufficiently clear in its details to be certain, but it appears quite likely that the "handle" (which, if present, would admittedly have to be much less deeply carved than the rest of the relief) is simply not there. But this cannot finally be settled without new photographs or an inspection of the actual relief.

The strongest reason for doubting that the object is a battle ax, however, lies in the way the prisoner is gripping it, *viz.* around the middle of the "head." As stated below in N 42, when the double ax of the Minoan cult is represented as carried, it is grasped by the handle. The same must be said for the far more numerous representations of persons holding a battle ax which in contrast to the situation in the Aegean was a common weapon of the Egyptians and many other Near Eastern groups.[55] Sometimes the haft is grasped close to the head for balance and ease of carrying when not in use,[56] but the handle is never totally ignored as would be the case in our relief. In Egyptian reliefs this literalism is maintained even when execution scenes such as the one under discussion are portrayed; the prisoner always holds the weapon in the proper way. Even if the weapon is shown as broken as is sometimes the case with the bow, still the prisoner grasps it at the proper point for use.[57] Given this consistent correctness in the representation of weapons and their handling, the conclusion seems inescapable that the object in the hand of the prisoner on the Siamun relief is not intended to represent a battle ax of any sort. What is in fact represented is a question which can be left to Egyptologists since there is now no reason to believe that the relief has anything to do with a campaign of Siamun against Philistia or Gezer. However, a few observations may be made.

Since there is no trace of a blade protruding from the object, it cannot be an elaborate hilt of a sword or dagger. Although there are problems with the proposal, in some ways the most attractive suggestion is that it is some kind of shield, either a small parrying shield or a miniaturized one representing a shield of full size.[58] Nothing is known of the shape of Philistine shields; but judging from the Medinet Habu reliefs, they were probably round. From the Near Eastern world the closest parallels for a shield approximating this shape would be those borne by Hittites in the Egyptian reliefs of the battle of Kadesh.[59] However, the Hittite shield is much less sharply curved at the ends and is more substantial through the middle. If the Hittite shield should indeed lie behind the Siamun relief, it would of course mean that the tenth-century sculptor is merely copying and that the Siamun relief portrays a fictitious episode.[60]

An even more striking parallel is afforded by the Dipylon shield represented on later Greek art of the eighth century. Best known from funeral and war scenes on Athenian vases, it is basically oval in shape with large pieces cut out symmetrically, leaving an exaggeratedly crescentic top and bottom joined by a narrow wasp waist (*Figure 8*).[61] This shield bears a strong resemblance to the object in the Siamun relief although the crescentic ends of the Dipylon shield are much larger in relation to the center than they are in the object on the relief. Since as already mentioned, miniaturization of weapons in the hands of captives is a common feature of Egyptian relief art, the reduction in size here would not create a problem. There is strong difference of opinion, however, among those competent to judge whether the Dipylon shield ever existed as an actual piece of armor in the form portrayed in Geometric art. Lorimer who assumes that the form existed and was used admits that by the Geometric period it had become a symbol of days of yore with religious and heroic connotations. Webster and Snodgrass have argued that the ceremonial use of the Dipylon shield is the primary one and that it never was used in actual combat.[62] In support of his argument, Snodgrass adduces a number of representations in which the shield is shown too small to have been of any practical use. One of his examples, a stamp found on a Cretan pithos of about 700 B.C., is reproduced here (*Figure 9*) as the most striking visual parallel the writer was able to find for the object on the Siamun relief.[63] But whether the object on the relief represents a Dipylon shield in particular or indeed a shield of any kind is a problem which may now be left for solution to Egyptologists.

The conclusions of this study, therefore, must be essentially negative. Given the chronological uncertainties of the period, the Tanis relief was the only "firm" evidence to connect Siamun with the events of I Kings 9:16; but we have seen that the object on the Siamun relief bears no resemblance to any weapon which can be connected with the Philistines. The presence of a scarab of Siamun at Tell el-Far'ah, cited by Malamat and Horn as evidence for activity of this Pharaoh in the area, means only that someone brought a scarab of Siamun from Egypt, nothing more.[64] This could have been done by a peaceful traveler in the reign of Siamun, Psusennes II, or even later, and in no way indicates military activity. In short, although the Pharaoh of I Kings 9:16 was almost certainly one of the last kings of the Twenty-first Dynasty, that is all that our present evidence permits us to say.

Acknowledgments: The research for this article took the author well beyond the bounds of his primary area of competence, and he would like to express his gratitude for the generous assistance of those who guided him to materials Aegean and Egyptological: George M. A. Hanfmann, Miranda M. Marvin, N. B. Millet, Emily T. Vermeule, and Jane C. Waldbaum. These are by no means responsible for oversights, nor do they necessarily endorse the conclusions of the study. Special thanks are due Prof. Millet for his kind permission to be quoted (NN 42 and 60). Finally, the author would like to thank Prof. J. Maxwell Miller for an important bibliographical reference.

Appreciation is expressed to the following for permission to reproduce the illustrations which accompany this article (see NOTES, below, for original publication): *Figure 5a* (N 17) Mme. C. Beaucour-Montet; *Figures 5b* (N 20) and *6* (N 31) Librairie Orientaliste Paul Geuthner, S.A.; *Figure 7* (N 34) Cambridge University Press; *Figure 8* (N 61) Macmillan, London and Basingstoke; *Figure 9* (N 63) Managing Committee, British School at Athens.

NOTES

1. For a review of proposals for the identity of the Pharaoh, see Siegfried H. Horn, "Who Was Solomon's Egyptian Father-in-Law?" *Biblical Research* 12 (1967), 3–5. In addition see NN 25–30 below for references to the recent studies which favor Siamun.

2. Horn [N 1], 8. For a discussion of the apparent uniqueness of this marriage, see A. Malamat, "The Kingdom of David and Solomon in Its Contact with Egypt and Aram Naharaim," *BA* 21 (1958), 97–99.

3. Malamat, "Aspects of the Foreign Policies of David and Solomon," *JNES* 22 (1963), 11. Malamat calls the completion of the temple in the eleventh year the *terminus post quem* for the marriage, an obvious *lapsus calami*. Horn [N 1], 8–9, who does not mention the reference in 3:1, places the *terminus ante quem* unnecessarily late, about Solomon's twentieth year.

4. D. N. Freedman, citing I Kings 9:10, states that Solomon's highest recorded year is twenty; "The Chronology of Israel and the Ancient Near East," in *BANE*, p. 209 and n. 28. But the building projects which took twenty years to complete were begun in Solomon's fourth year, not his first (I Kings 6:37).

5. Since Egyptian chronology is dependent on the synchronism with Rehoboam for one of its fixed points in this uncertain era, it is of no independent help here. Nor is the problem affected by different choices among the various alternatives for the absolute dates of Solomon's reign.

6. R. A. Caminos, "Gebel es-Silsilah No. 100," *JEA* 38 (1952), 46–61. Also see the comments by W. F. Albright in *BASOR* 130 (1953), 6; also 141 (1956), 26–27.

7. Caminos [N 6], 59–60; Manetho, *Ægyptiaca, etc.* tr. W. G. Waddell, Loeb Classical Library (Cambridge, Mass., 1940), fragments 60 and 61, p. 159.

8. So Albright [N 6], 7, and E. Hornung, *Untersuchungen zur Chronologie und Geschichte des Neuen Reiches* (Wiesbaden, 1964), p. 24. Gardiner thinks that the Bubastite portal was constructed earlier than the projects mentioned in the Silsileh inscription and so would place the campaign of Shishak about his fifteenth year; *Egypt of the Pharaohs* (Oxford, 1961), pp. 328–329, 448.

9. These calculations assume the use in Judah of the antedating system at this time. See Freedman, *BANE*, pp. 208–209; and W. F. Albright, "The Chronology of the Divided Monarchy of Israel," *BASOR* 100 (1945), 20, n. 14. The period of contemporaneity would be sixteen years if with E. R. Thiele one assumes a post-dating system in use in Judah from the beginning of the monarchy; *The Mysterious Numbers of the Hebrew Kings*, rev. ed. (Grand Rapids, 1965), ch. 2.

10. First demonstrated by J. Goldwasser, "The Campaign of Siamun to Palestine" (Hebrew), *Bulletin of the Jewish Palestine Exploration Society* 14 (1949), 82–83.

11. For a helpful summary of recent bibliography, see S. Wenig, "Einige Bemerkungen zur Chronologie der Frühen 21 Dynastie," *Zeitschrift für Aegyptische Sprache und Altertumskunde* 94 (1967), 134–139. A new work by K. A. Kitchen on the chronology of the period, *The Third Intermediate Period in Egypt*, was not yet available for this study.

12. Hornung [N 8], p. 105 and n. 35.

13. K. A. Kitchen, "On the Chronology and History of the New Kingdom," *Chronique d'Égypte* 40 (1965), 321–322.

14. For a discussion of the tendency of Manethonian numbers to be increased by

twenty or forty, see W. Helck, *Untersuchungen zu Manetho und den Aegyptischen Königslisten* (Berlin, 1956), pp. 73, 81–82.

15. See the comments by Gardiner [N 8], p. 324. For a convenient summary of scholarly opinion on the matter, see the table following p. 120 in Hornung [N 8]. In addition, see J. Černý, *Egypt from the Death of Ramesses III to the End of the Twenty-first Dynasty*, (*CAH*², II, ch. xxxv [Fasc. 27], 1965), inside back cover.

16. Horn's conclusion ([N 1], 12) that the chronological data make it "almost certain" that Siamun is the Pharaoh in question follows from his acceptance of Africanus' figure of fourteen years for the reign of Psusennes II. But he does not deal with the problem that this creates for the length of the dynasty.

17. P. Montet, *La Nécropole Royale de Tanis: I, Les Constructions et le tombeau d'Osorkon II* (Paris, 1947), pl. IXA. Montet describes the piece briefly as "un fragment de bas-relief en calcaire, de petit module" (p. 36). His description of the find-spot is not clear, but apparently the relief was found under some mudbrick houses of the Ptolemaic period which had been built against the south wall of the main temple. He describes the find-spot as "entre l'immeuble XIV [one of the mudbrick houses] et un mur de briques visible sur notre planche XI,B" (p. 36). But neither the description nor the plate helps to clarify the matter, especially as no reduced elevations are given on any of the plans. Most likely the block was found somewhere in the triangle formed by numbers 1, 2, and 11 on his Planche I. He identifies the nearby Building 11 on Planche I as the foundations of a temple of Dynasty XXI and proposes that the relief came from that building.

18. See H. Gauthier, *Le Livre des rois d'Egypte, Tome III*, Mémoires Publiées par les Membres de l'Institut Français d'Archéologie Orientale du Caire, Vol. XIX (Cairo, 1913), 296–98.

19. Cf. pls. 105 and 114 in H. H. Nelson et al., *Medinet Habu, II: Later Historical Records of Rameses III*, Oriental Institute Publications [henceforth OIP], Vol. IX, Chicago, 1932. Here two figures are being held by the king; and the artist, seemingly unclear how to position the four arms of the prisoners, has solved the problem awkwardly by putting the arm of one prisoner around the neck and down across the chest of the other. The confused position of the arms on the Siamun relief may reflect something of this sort. The relief portrayed in *Medinet Habu, II*, pl. 114, can also be found in Y. Yadin, *The Art of Warfare in Biblical Lands* (New York, 1963), p. 350.

20. The line drawing (*Figure 5b*) is from P. Montet, *Le Drame d'Avaris* (Paris, 1941), p. 196. Another drawing of the relief appears in Montet, *Egypt and the Bible* (Philadelphia, 1968), p. 37. This second drawing differs in some details from that in *Le Drame d'Avaris*. The first has been chosen for reproduction here since the shape of the object in the hand of the captive appears to be a more accurate rendition of the lines visible in the photograph. In any case, the differences do not appear to be crucial. For other examples of such execution scenes from the New Kingdom, see e.g. W. Wreszinski, *Atlas zur altägyptischen Kulturgeschichte* (Leipzig, 1914–), Teil II, Taf. 184a, Beibilt 7 (Thuthmosis III); Taf. 3 (Thuthmosis IV); Tafs. 50a and 53a, Abb. II (Seti I); Tafs. 182 and 184a (Ramęses II). Also see Yadin [N 19], pp. 232–233, 350, *et passim*.

21. Montet, *Le Drame d'Avaris*, 196. Cf. the scenes from Wreszinski and Yadin cited in N 20.

22. Montet [N 17], I, 36.

23. Montet, *Egypt and the Bible* [N 20], pp. 36–40. In a confusing passage in this book (p. 40) Montet appears to raise the question of whether Psusennes II might have been the conqueror of Gezer as well as Solomon's father-in-law.

24. Ibid., p. 38, n. 12. The reference, cited slightly incorrectly by Montet, should be

René Dussaud, *Les Civilisations Préhelléniques dans le Bassin de la Mer Égée*, 2d ed. (Paris, 1914), p. 340, fig. 247.

25. Goldwasser [N 10], 82–84.

26. P. G. Elgood, *Later Dynasties of Egypt* (Oxford, 1951), p. 34 and n. 1.

27. S. Yeivin, "Did the Kingdoms of Israel Have a Maritime Policy?" *JQR* 50 (1959–60), 202, n. 48.

28. Malamat [N 3], 12.

29. Černý [N 15], 54.

30. Horn [N 1], 14–17.

30a. An earlier version of this paper was read before the Society of Biblical Literature in New York in December 1970 under the title "The Conquest of Gezer and the Double Ax." The Traditional interpretation of the Siamun relief has now been challenged also by R. Giveon in a footnote to a study which appeared after the completion of the present draft: see "An Egyptian Official at Gezer?" *IEJ* 72 (1972), 145, n. 4.

31. J. Deshayes, *Les Outils de bronze de l'Indus au Danube,* Institut Français d'Archéologie de Beyrouth: Bibliothèque Archéologique et Historique, Vol. LXXI (Paris, 1960), Vol. II, pl. xxxiv, 8.

32. See e.g. ibid., 14, 15. The latter of these two examples is also reproduced in E. Vermeule, *Greece in the Bronze Age* (Chicago, 1964), p. 229, fig. 39.

33. See the discussion in Deshayes [N 31], I, 253–261. See also the example from a hoard found at Mycenae in G. Mylonas, "Three Late Mycenaean Knives," *AJA* 66 (1962), pl. 121, fig. 5, and *Mycenae and the Mycenaean Age* (Princeton, 1966), pp. 147–148. For the evidence from Cyprus, see H. W. Catling, *Cypriot Bronzework in the Mycenaean World* (Oxford, 1964), pp. 88–89. For examples from the Iron Age, see J. K. Brock, *Fortetsa* (Cambridge, 1957), p. 138, no. 1641, pl. 172; also P. Courbin, "Une Tombe Géométrique d'Argos," *Bulletin de Correspondance Hellénique* 81 (1957), 367–368, figs. 50, 51. For Palestinian examples see e.g. G. Loud, *Megiddo II: Seasons of 1935–39*, OIP, Vol. LXII (Chicago, 1948), pl. 182, no. 7 (from Str. XIII), and pl. 183, nos. 14, 15 (from Strata VIB and VI, respectively). The Gezer example is found in R. A. S. Macalister, *The Excavations of Gezer*, II (London, 1912), 242, fig. 394. The unusual shape of the Gezer example plus the fact that part of the wooden shaft was found still attached to the ax causes one to wonder if the ax was actually ancient. The double ax referred to by Horn [N 1], 15, which was found in the tenth-century tomb of a Phoenician warrior at Achzib, is not described by Prausnitz in his report (*IEJ* 13 [1963], 338) but probably falls into this category.

34. A. B. Cook, *Zeus: A Study in Ancient Religion*, reprint (New York, 1965), Vol. II, Part 1, p. 640, fig. 566c. Reproduced by permission of Cambridge University Press.

35. M. P. Nilsson, *The Minoan-Mycenaean Religion and Its Survival in Greek Religion* [henceforth *MMR*], rev. ed. (Lund, 1950), p. 194.

36. *MMR*, pp. 60–61. See also E. Vermeule, "A Gold Minoan Double Axe," *Bulletin, Museum of Fine Arts, Boston* 57 (1959), 5–6.

37. *MMR* [N 35], p. 194. See Nilsson's thorough discussion of the archaeological evidence and his interpretation of the ax as a cult symbol in ch. vi. His conclusion is that the ax was the instrument used to stun the beast of sacrifice before it was hoisted onto a sacrificial table for the actual cutting of the throat (pp. 227–235). This interpretation is accepted by Hutchinson although with some misgivings (R. W. Hutchinson, *Prehistoric Crete* [Baltimore, 1962], pp. 224–225). For an alternate interpretation, *viz.* that the ax is the emblem of the male sky god, see Cook [N 34], pp. 513–704. The religious significance of the double ax appears to be Minoan as distinguished from Mycenaean. See Mylonas, *Mycenae and the Mycenaean Age* [N 33], pp. 169–172.

38. See the discussions of the material in H.-G. Buchholz, *Zur Herkunft der kretischen Doppelaxt* (Munich, 1959); Catling [N 33], p. 88; V. R. A. Desborough, *The Last*

Mycenaeans and Their Successors (Oxford, 1964), pp. 66–69; Deshayes [N 31], I, 253–255 and II, pls. xxxiv and xxxv; S. Przeworski, "Die Metallindustrie Anatoliens in der Zeit von 1500 bis 700 vor Chr.," *Opera Selecta* (Wroclaw-Warsaw-Krakow, 1967), 128–131; C. F. A. Schaeffer, *Stratigraphie comparée* (London, 1948), *passim;* A. Snodgrass, *Early Greek Armour and Weapons* (Edinburgh, 1964), 166–167; Yadin [N 19], pp. 41–44.

39. The only possible exception known to the writer is in the frieze of the procession of the Hittite gods at Yazilikaya. In the drawings which have been made of the scene one deity appears to be carrying a double ax with flaring blades. See e.g. O. R. Gurney, *The Hittites,* rev. ed. (London, 1962), p. 143, or H. Gressmann, *Altorientalische Bilder zum Alten Testament,* 2d ed. (Berlin and Leipzig, 1927), fig. 338. But Bittel, who has repeatedly studied the relief itself, is of the opinion that the weapon is of the "spincback" type similar to the one borne by the warrior from Boghazköy, conveniently illustrated in *The Ancient Near East in Pictures,* no. 38. Przeworski, who reports Bittel's opinion, has also visited the monument but was unable to decide what sort of ax was represented; see Przeworski [N 38], 181, n. 86. Thus it is not clear whether this frieze offers an exception to the general situation or not. Excellent photographs of the frieze can be found in E. Akurgal, *The Art of the Hittites* (New York, 1962), pls. 76 above and 77 below.

40. See Deshayes [N 31], I, 218, and II, pl. xxviii, 8; also F. Petrie, *Tools and Weapons* (London, 1917), p. 13 and pl. xii, no. 24.

41. *MMR* [N 35], pp. 199–216; also Mylonas, *Mycenae and the Mycenaean Age* [N 33], pp. 169–172, esp. 172.

42. Given the possibility, long proposed by Albright, that there was a colony of Cretans on the coast south of Gaza, and also given David's use of "Cherethites" or Cretans as mercenaries (e.g. II Sam. 8:18, 20:7, etc.) could the double ax on the Siamun relief be the Minoan religious symbol, indicating Siamun's triumph over these transplanted Cretans on his northeast border? See Albright, "Syria, the Philistines, and Phoenicia," *CAH*[2], II, ch. xxxiii (Fasc. 51), 29; "A Colony of Cretan Mercenaries on the Coast of the Negeb," *JPOS* 1 (1921), 187–194; "Egypt and the Early History of the Negeb," *JPOS* 4 (1924), 131–142. The writer finds such a possibility unlikely for a number of reasons, of which perhaps two are the most important. In the first place, in the few Minoan cult scenes in which the double ax is being carried by someone, it is grasped by the handle, not around the blade as the figure in the Siamun relief would be doing. See e.g. *MMR* [N 35], pp. 225–226, fig. 112; also A. Evans, *The Palace of Minos* (London, 1931–35), I, 435, fig. 312a. For later representations on coins, see Cook [N 34], 561 *et passim.* In the second place, a search through Egyptian reliefs of prisoners holding characteristic objects reveals no case in which the object held could be construed as representing the prisoner's religion. N. B. Millet has expressed orally to the writer his opinion that such a representation would be unprecedented.

The tradition represented by Amos 9:7 and the feather-headed man on the Phaistos disk are often cited as evidence that the Philistines themselves came from Crete (e.g. Horn [N 1], 15; Yadin [N 19], p. 344). But there are strong arguments for an Anatolian as against a Cretan background for the disk. See Hutchinson [N 37], pp. 66–70, and M. J. Mellink, "Lycian Wooden Huts and Sign 24 on the Phaistos Disk," *Kadmos* 3 (1964), 1–7. An Anatolian origin also for the Philistines is argued by Albright, *CAH*[2], II, ch. xxxiii (Fasc. 51), 29–30; also see R. D. Barnett, "The Sea Peoples," *CAH*[2], II, ch. xxviii (Fasc. 68), 15–16. For other viewpoints see Desborough [N 38], pp. 213, 237–241, and Vermeule [N 32], pp. 271–274.

43. The writer does not claim to have perused all the available material himself, but there are a number of excellent recent surveys of the period. None of them claims that the battle ax was a typical or characteristic weapon. In their discussions of Mycenaean

weapons, Desborough [N 38], pp. 66–69; Mylonas, *Mycenae and the Mycenaean Age* [N 33], pp. 197–198; and A. J. B. Wace, *Mycenae* (Princeton, 1949), p. 112, make no mention of the ax at all. Vermeule in her discussion of the LH IIIB period, on the basis of some of the Linear B texts, lists the ax as a possible weapon of the nobility though nothing more than that [N 32], p. 260. A mold for making winged axes of Italic type was found at Mycenae, again in a LH IIIB context, but Stubbings describes it as "a type of implement (or weapon) otherwise unknown in Late Helladic or other contemporary Aegean contexts": F. H. Stubbings, "A Winged Axe Mould," *Annual of the British School at Athens* 49 (1954), 297. In Catling's discussion of the Cypriote material, there is no mention of battle axes in his section on weapons [N 33], ch. v. He does mention one double ax of the straight-sided variety which may have been used as a weapon (pp. 88–89, fig. 9:1 and pl. 6m). In short, although there are isolated examples of battle axes in the Aegean and surrounding territories at the end of the Late Bronze Age, they are extremely rare. Marinatos appears to be alone in his undocumented statement that an ax was part of the normal arms of the noble Mycenaean warrior: S. Marinatos and M. Hirmer, *Kreta und das Mykenische Hellas* (Munich, 1959), p. 59.

As for the Greek Dark Age, Snodgrass, who has collected all the available evidence, in a recent study concludes cautiously that "an axe of some form may have been wielded by the Geometric warrior and his predecessors," and that the present evidence makes it "a reasonable contention that in the somewhat irregular style of warfare of the Dark Age, the battle axe was among the weapons known to the Greek warrior" (Snodgrass [N 38], pp. 166–167). However, the paucity of possible examples of battle axes which he cites in contrast to the evidence for the sword, the spear, and the bow and arrow makes it clear that it was not a common weapon. This is indicated also by the scant reference to the battle ax in Homer. Lorimer finds only two mentions, *Iliad*, N 611–612 and O 711): H. L. Lorimer, *Homer and the Monuments* (London, 1950), pp. 305–306.

44. Černý, *CAH²* [N 15], p. 54.

45. Wreszinski [N 20], Teil II, Taf. 19.

46. The Epigraphic Survey, *Medinet Habu, I: Earlier Historical Records of Rameses III*, OIP, Vol. VIII, 1930), pls. 19, 70; also Yadin [N 19], pp. 334–335.

47. *Medinet Habu, II* [N 19], pls. 88, 94.

48. *Medinet Habu, I* [N 46], pls. 32–34, 37–41; also Yadin, *The Art of Warfare* [N 19], pp. 336–340.

49. For an example of such a crescent-pommeled sword found at Mycenae, see Mylonas, *Mycenae and the Mycenaean Age* [N 33], pl. 144.

50. Originally published in A. S. Murray, A. H. Smith, and H. B. Walters, *Excavations in Cyprus* (London, 1900), pp. 12–13, fig. 19, pl. I. See also Yadin [N 19], p. 338.

51. F. Petrie, *Beth-pelet*, I (London, 1930), pl. XXI, no. 90. Tomb 542 belongs to the later or true Philistine group of the two groups of Sea People tombs recognized at Tell Farah(S) by Waldbaum; see J. C. Waldbaum, "Philistine Tombs at Tell Fara," *AJA* 70 (1966), 331–340. For a challenge to Waldbaum's theory of origins, see W. H. Stiebing, Jr., "Another Look at the Origins of the Philistine Tombs at Tell el Far'ah(S)," *AJA* 74 (1970), 139–143.

52. This is the one published in H. R. Hall, *The Civilization of Greece in the Bronze Age* (London, 1928), p. 254, fig. 329, as coming from Gaza. But Barnett, who has evidently looked up the records in the British Museum, says that this is mistaken (*CAH²* [N 42], 12). See also Barnett, *Illustrations of Old Testament History* (London, 1966), p. 29 and fig. 16; T. Dothan, *The Philistines and Their Material Culture* (Hebrew; Jerusalem, 1967), p. 14, and Yadin [N 19], p. 344.

53. The word *miṣḥat*, read by the versions as plural is a *hapax legomenon*. The LXX translates as *knēmides*, the normal Greek word for "greaves"; and given the context, this meaning seems clear. See the comments of Yadin in *The Scroll of the War of the*

Sons of Light against the Sons of Darkness (Oxford, 1962), pp. 122–123; also in *The Art of Warfare* [N 19], p. 354.

54. See R. T. O'Callaghan, "The Word *ktp* in Ugaritic and Egypto-Canaanite Mythology," *Orientalia* 21 (1952), 43, and Yadin, *The Scroll of the War*, pp. 130–131. This proposal is attractive since otherwise Goliath would be carrying two throwing weapons but no sword. Given the detailed nature of the description in the narrative and the clear evidence that the sword was a common Philistine weapon, this omission would be strange. The Greek practice of carrying two throwing spears does not seem to have originated until well after the close of the Bronze Age. See Lorimer [N 43], pp. 254–258.

55. See Yadin [N 19], *passim*. Representations from Late Bronze or Early Iron Age Greece of axes being handled are very rare; but see the seal from Vaphio which portrays a priest holding a fenestrated ax of the Syrian type by the handle and resting the head on his shoulder, in Mylonas, *Mycenae and the Mycenaean Age* [N 33], fig. 127, no. 36, and p. 164.

56. E.g. Yadin [N 19], pp. 137, 185, 222.

57. E.g. ibid., pp. 232–233.

58. For an example of such a small shield see the Neo-Hittite relief from Zinjirli (*The Ancient Near East in Pictures*, no. 36). See also what is probably a small irregularly shaped shield borne by the central warrior on the Megiddo sherd (ibid., no. 60; Yadin [N 19], p. 242). For examples of miniaturization of weapons held by prisoners in this type of relief, see the scenes in Wreszinski listed in N 20.

59. Wreszinski [N 20], Tafs. 21, 21a, 83–89. See also Yadin, pp. 238–239.

60. N. B. Millet has expressed to the writer the opinion that although one would normally expect such a scene to be based in fact, the contrary would not be surprising by the time of the Twenty-first Dynasty.

61. Lorimer [N 43], p. 157, fig. 12. For other examples, see ibid., pp. 156–161, figs. 11–14 and pls. XX:1a, XXV:3, XXVI:2–3. Also see Snodgrass [N 38], pls. 1, 2, 3, 27.

62. Lorimer [N 43], pp. 155–167; T. B. L. Webster, *From Mycenae to Homer* (New York, 1964), pp. 169–170; Snodgrass [N 38], pp. 58–60.

63. The stamp was originally published by J. Boardman, "Archaic Finds at Knossos," *The Annual of the British School at Athens* 57 (1962), 31–32. The resemblance may of course be purely coincidental.

64. Malamat [N 3], 12; Horn [N 1], 16.

12. Israel and Phoenicia

BRIAN PECKHAM

REGIS COLLEGE, TORONTO

THE RELATIONSHIP between Israel and Phoenicia is known principally from incidental convergence of evidence,[1] but the history of their relationship is elusive. Mainland Phoenicia is buried in its own obscurity, and is revealed uncertainly in its extraterritorial and overseas enterprises.[2] The only systematic and continuous source for the history of Israel and Phoenicia is Israelite historical tradition. This complex tradition cannot eliminate all the notable interstices in the data, but can situate in proper historical perspective otherwise random evidence and vagrant conjecture.

In the beginning Israel and Phoenicia were contemporary. Both had remote origins, Israel its patriarchal period, Phoenicia its Canaanite ancestry. Each acquired a new or revolutionary territorial circumscription ca. 1200 B.C., partly of their own doing, partly through the collapse of empires, the intrusion of the Philistines, the Aramaean migrations. Both, and the Aramaeans with them, survived and developed in a pre-monarchical era[3] which persisted until the abrupt and simultaneous emergence of empire ca. 1000 B.C. The history of Israel and Phoenicia begins at this time.

This proposed congruity of origins, development, and final establishment is the basis for the interpretation of the pre-national involvements of Israel and Phoenicia. Despite the evident continuity between Canaan and Phoenicia,[4] they are not to be identified. In chronological terms, the transition from "Canaan" to "Phoenicia" did not occur ca. 1200 B.C. as is commonly supposed.[5] This opinion could be sustained only if Phoenicia were considered the immediate and sole heir of Canaan. However, this emphasizes the continuity between Canaan and Phoenicia and obscures the particularity of the latter.[6] Further, it excludes Israel as collateral beneficiary of Canaan, an exclusion hardly reconcilable with what is known of early Israelite culture. The alternative, therefore, is to consider the troubles of the times and the late thirteenth-century upheaval in Canaan as the earliest historical antecedents of what eventually became Phoenicia. These Canaanite antecedents of Phoenicia can be described with varying degrees of probability.

Among the notable developments which preceded and surely contributed to the rise of Phoenicia—and then of Israel—was the gradual alphabetization of Canaan. The pictographic evolved into the linear script in the twelfth century B.C.; by the end of that century horizontal writing had replaced writing in vertical columns; about the same time the use of Canaanite cuneiform was abandoned; somewhat later, right-to-left writing became normative.[7] It is possible that extraneous influences were operative in this development,[8] but the gradual normalization and simplification of the alphabet and writing was undoubtedly a significant factor in the cultural transition from Canaan to Phoenicia.[9]

The most important development, obviously, was the collapse of Canaan. In the Amarna period this Egyptian province comprised three administrative districts: in the northwest, Amurru with its capital at Sumur; in the northeast, Upe with its capital at Kumidi; in the south, exclusive of the Transjordanian regions and of Byblos which belonged to Amurru, Canaan with its capital at Gaza.[10] When the Hittites finally acquired unchallenged control of Amurru in 1300 B.C.,[11] the province included only the districts of Canaan and Upe (Damascus). It was deprived of a northern buffer when the Hittite empire submerged in the latter part of the thirteenth century.[12] With the death of Ramesses III (1166 B.C.) and the total collapse of Egyptian imperial capabilities and design, Canaan lost its already meagre political homogeneity and was left to its own inadequate resources and progressive disintegration. The whole district of Damascus, at least, was gradually overrun by the Aramaeans, and although neither the precise chronology nor the exact sequence of events are known, this infiltration most probably began early in the twelfth century and was consolidated by the mid-eleventh century B.C.[13] Thus, only the district of Canaan was left, and it was open and vulnerable on two fronts.

There was, first, the invasion of the Sea Peoples.[14] The initial wave, including the Sherden, allied itself with the Libyans and was defeated by Merneptah ca. 1232 B.C. This group bypassed, and apparently had no designs on, Canaan,[15] although in the same year there was a revolt in Canaan—now including Israel—which was also suppressed by Merneptah.[16] The second wave attacked in the eighth year of Ramesses III (ca. 1190), by sea and by land down the coast of Canaan, and was defeated on the borders of Egypt. There is no evidence that in its southward sweep this group was opposed by the Canaanites, and none that they pillaged as they went. Their destination was Egypt, and it was there they intended to settle. However, it is known that after their defeat some of this group settled in southern Canaan, probably as mercenaries or vassals of Ramesses III.[17] The main contingent, the Philistines, acquired the coastal area from Gaza to Joppa, and were perhaps garrisoned at Sharuhen. Dor and its vicinity was taken over by the Tjekker. The intervening area was most probably occupied by the Danuna, the later Israelite tribe of Dan, the *dnnym* of the Karatepe inscriptions.[18] There is no trace of the other two peoples (Sheklesh and Weshesh), but a member of the earlier wave, the Sherden,[19] had also settled in Canaan, perhaps at Megiddo and Beth-shan, in their traditional role as Egyptian mercenaries.[20] As a result of this second invasion, therefore, all of Canaan south of Tyre and the plain of Ācco was controlled by the Sea Peoples, two of whom—the Danuna and the Sherden—became integral to the relationship between Israel and Phoenicia, and to the latter's expansion into the north (western Anatolia) and into the west (Sardinia).[21] Northern coastal Canaan, on the other hand, was relatively unaffected by the settlement of the Sea Peoples.[22] Initially these held, possibly against the invading Israelites, the perimeter marked on the north by the Jezreel valley (Megiddo, Beth-shan), and on the east by the Jordan valley (Tell es-Sa'idiyeh, Deir 'Alla). By the end of the twelfth or the early eleventh century, the Philistines had occupied the major part of the territory of Judah,[23] so that it was they, and not the Canaanites, who later became Judah's principal antagonist. That is, the Sea Peoples were concentrated in southern Canaan, and under the gradual ascendancy of the Philistines were mainly intent on territorial acquisition.[24] What is evident, moreover, is that northern Canaan only profited from these foreign intrusions. By the beginning of the eleventh century, Byblos had declared its independence from, but was free to continue its traditional economic relation with, Egypt.[25] Tyre and Sidon had established a commercial syndicate with the Philistines,[26] and had furthered their maritime interests by some sort of agreement with Asher, Zebulun, Issachar,[27] and probably with Dan which presumably had migrated northward by this time.[28] In this conglomerate Canaan was continuing a naval tradition which can be traced at least to the fourteenth century B.C.,[29] when its fleets cruised the Mediterranean from Egypt to Cyprus, Cilicia, Crete, and Greece.[30] Canaanite supremacy on the seas continued at least to the end of the thirteenth century.[31] In the twelfth century the Sea Peoples were competitors or associates of the Canaanites but, after their defeat by the Egyptians, and given their instinct for the land, there is no reason to suppose that they menaced Canaanite commercial ventures. Finally, the only serious evidence from the eleventh century clearly testifies to the peaceful cooperation of Canaanites and Sea Peoples and suggests a considerable development of Sidonian interests.

The invasion of the Sea Peoples, therefore, was an important phase in the transition from Canaan to Phoenicia. Apart from it, the provincial conglomerate known as Canaan would never have achieved national status. The northern region retained its autonomy, but was divided by its political and commercial ties: Byblos, as tradition prescribed, aligned itself with Egypt; the Sidonians lived in closer symbiosis with the Philistines and with elements of the Israelite tribal complex. The whole southern region was lost, but a new international policy—fully verified when Judah had overcome and replaced the Philistines—adequately compensated for the geographical restriction.

The contribution of the Sea Peoples to the rise of Phoenicia did not consist in turning Canaan to the sea, but in introducing it to the newly emerging cultures of the settled land.

The second challenge to Canaan was Israel. The victory stele of Merneptah's fifth year (ca. 1232 B.C.) celebrates his triumph over an Israel which was apparently situated in the northern region of Canaan, since it is mentioned after Gaza (?), Ascalon, Gezer, and Yeno'am.[32] This Israel may have comprised mainly the tribe of Asher which is known in approximately this area of Canaan from the time of Sethos I (1318–1304 B.C.) and of Ramesses II (1304–1237 B.C.),[33] although elements of Issachar[34] and perhaps Zebulun may also have been included in the single designation. At this time, and into the twelfth century, there was no conflict between Canaanites and Israel. The peace was broken for the first time, it seems, in the days of Shamgar ben 'Anat. Although relatively little notice is given to this Canaanite defeat of a Philistine force,[35] the hero's exploit defined an era of hostility between Israel and Canaan. No later than the mid-twelfth century, Israel had expanded to include—in Canaan—at least Asher, Ephraim, Benjamin, Machir, Issachar, Naphtali, and Zebulon.[36] The earliest wars were in the north above the perimeter established by the Philistines.[37] Despite the complexity of the texts and traditions which are the evidence for these wars,[38] their general thrust can be sketched with some probability. The first assault was led by Sisera, commander under Jabin of Hazor, and was beaten back in the vicinity of Tabor; in the second battle the Canaanites, now led by Jabin himself, were met and defeated farther north, near Merom; finally Hazor itself was destroyed, and the united Canaanite front collapsed. More important than this conjectural reconstruction of the wars was their total result. Some Israelite tribes were more securely established in the land but at the same time they had weakened or destroyed any possible indigenous competition with coastal Canaan. The whole coastal region with its adjacent territories remained uncontested, as is evident in Asher's fidelity to its maritime commitments and its refusal to join in the wars, as well as in the later list of unconquered Canaanite cities. This list[39] makes it clear that the Israel of this time, apart from its occupation of Galilee, did not, and probably did not try to, alter the geopolitical situation established by the Philistines and the northern Canaanites: thus Dor, the cities of the plain of Ācco (Acre) and northward, cities of Upper Galilee which probably belonged to the Sidonians, and the Jezreel valley remained "Canaanite." Further, although Israel's general boundary descriptions correspond to those of the province of Canaan, the northern Canaanite region—apart from the territory attributed to Asher, traditional confederate of the Sidonians— was not allotted to any tribe.[40] In short, the initial occupation of the land was hardly disadvantageous to coastal Canaan: much of Canaan was still intact; the coastal cities and their possessions were never an objective of this inchoate Israel; their supremacy was assured by the defeat of the Hazor

coalition; their political and commercial interests in the interior were maintained with the new settlers at least through their contacts with Asher, Zebulon, and Issachar. In return, Israel had the advantage of the land and its
culture.

There is some evidence, therefore, that early Israel was a positive influence on Canaan. The expansion of this nuclear Israel and its further contribution to the rise of Phoenicia can only be surmised. Canaan remained
the projected territorial claim of Israel, and it seems certain that the land
was settled and occupied on a tribal basis, but there is very little information on intertribal relations, on multitribal organization, or on the governmental system of the individual tribes. There were presumably incidental
confederacies as well as permanent alignments of tribes, and it would be
exceptional if these were not constituted by pact or treaty.[41] But the political,
religious, economic, and cultural affiliations of the tribes remain obscure.
It has become increasingly evident, however, that pre-monarchical Israel
was never organized as a twelve-tribe amphictyony.[42] The amphictyonic
theory is a second-order hypothesis, depending on questionable historical
analogy,[43] and based on prior theories of the conquest,[44] of holy war,[45] of
covenant,[46] of Yahweh's self-revelation and accompanying theologies. These
traditions stand without the hypothesis. The historical evidence, however,
and specifically the relation between Israel and Canaan, is easily distorted
by the amphictyonic hypothesis. Apart from suggesting an inaccurate description of the growth of Israel, it tends to exclude the possibility of creative
self-determination in Canaan, to produce an ideological Canaan symbolic of
Israel's profane interests, and to reduce Phoenicia to a degenerate heritage
molded into respectability by the confluence of foreign interests. But in
fact there is no evidence that Canaan was confronted by a united coalition
of twelve tribes, either in the earliest period of Israel's settlement, or in the
era of the judges, or, indeed, as late as the reign of Saul.[47] Judah, especially,
had its peculiarly autonomous history. Along with elements of Levi and
Simeon, it shared the religious traditions of Israel,[48] and on this basis was
for a time part of the kingdom of Saul. But its origins, settlement, affiliations, and development were quite distinct from those of the other tribes,
and it was only in the early reign of David at Hebron that it achieved
tribal cohesion.[49] It was in relation to, and by agreement with, the kingdom
of Judah that the northern tribes, already affiliated in diverse ways, acquired
their national identity.[50] Thus the final unification of the twelve tribes
was accomplished only in the reign of David and was coincident with the
national status of Judah and of Israel.[51] It was at the same time, and by
deliberate association with this Israelite amalgam commensurate with its
own possibilities, that Phoenicia assumed its proper dominion.

The role of Byblos in the development of Canaan and in the later history
of Phoenicia seems to have been marginal. In the Amarna period Byblos
was included in Amurru. Later, although there is no evidence one way or the

other, it may have been one of the ports from which the first wave of Sea Peoples attacked Egypt. It was an autonomous city-state in the latter part of the twelfth century: although it is listed along with Arvad and Sidon among those who paid tribute to Tiglathpileser I (1116–1078 B.C.), Assyria could make no real political claim on the west at this time; in the Report of Wenamun (ca. 1060 B.C.) Zakarba'al reminds the Egyptian envoy that Byblos had effectively declared its independence from Egypt in the reign of his father. However, despite this political independence, it is clear from the same Report that Byblos, alone among the Canaanite cities, had gone its own way and maintained its traditional economic ties with Egypt. The same pro-Egyptian policy is also verified by the tenth-century Byblian inscriptions.[52] Toward the end of this century, and perhaps earlier, Byblos began to rely more seriously on Egypt as a counterbalance to the increasing pressure of the Sidonian empire.[53] The abortive Philistine campaign of Pharaoh Siamun (ca. 976–958)[54] intended to reestablish Egypt's political and commercial interests and could have eased the economic strain on Byblos. Shishak's campaign (ca. 918 B.C.) certainly meant to destroy or undermine the Tyrian and Israelite trade monopoly and would have been advantageous to Byblos if Tyre had not already achieved imperial status. The fact of Tyrian predominance is indicated by the inclusion of Byblians in the work crews of the Solomonic temple,[55] and is attested in Ezekiel's lament over Tyre.[56] Byblos' pro-Egyptian policy, and the failure of Egypt to establish any viable alternative to the Phoenician-Israelite trade monopoly, undoubtedly contributed to the increasing insignificance of Byblos in the later history of Phoenicia. In 876 B.C., along with Tyre, Sidon, and Arvad, it paid tribute to Assurnasirpal II, but continuing relations with Egypt are confirmed by the discovery of a statue of Osorkon II (870–847 B.C.) at Byblos.[57] Sometime between 887 and 856 B.C. Tyre founded Botrys, but was unopposed by Byblos which by now certainly accepted Tyrian supremacy in Phoenicia.[58] Whether or not Byblos was aligned with Egypt at the battle of Qarqar,[59] it is certain that Byblos retained its association with Egypt into the mid-ninth century, thereby effectively dissociating itself from the Phoenician empire. In the eighth and seventh centuries Byblos is known only from Assyrian texts, Šipţiba'al II (ca. 740) paid tribute to Tiglathpileser III, 'Ormilk I (ca. 701) to Sennacherib, and Milk'asap (ca. 670) to both Esarhaddon and Asshurbanipal.[60] It was only in the sixth century, when the Tyrian empire had crumbled, that Byblos began to extend its interests. Early in the century it founded a colony at Amrit[61] and, perhaps about the same time, at Larnax tes Lapethou in Cyprus.[62] The Pyrgi inscription, which has affinities to the inscriptions from Cyprus, seems to have more specific parallels in the inscriptions of Larnax tes Lapethou,[63] and may be evidence for Byblian, or Byblian-inspired expansion to the western Mediterranean at the end of the sixth century. From the fifth and fourth centuries there are a number of inscriptions and other epigraphic materials which supply a complete king list but very little other information.[64] What is noteworthy about Byblos, therefore, is its alignment with Egypt and its consequent isolation from the main line of Phoenician development, indeed, its quasi-exclusion from the Phoenician empire. The evidence is surely incomplete, but what there is agrees that Byblos did not assert itself in the period between the end of the eleventh and the beginning of the sixth century B.C., that is, during the ascendancy of Tyre and Sidon.

There is still less information on the other Phoenician cities. Nothing is known of Beirut.[65] Arvad is listed in various Assyrian texts but the most significant information is that, unlike Tyre and Sidon, it was an ally of Irhuleni of Hamath at the battle of Qarqar,[66] and that in the seventh century it was incorporated in the Assyrian province of Simyra. It is possible that, like Byblos, it remained somewhat aloof from the Phoenician empire. At any rate, the history of Israel and Phoenicia concerns mainly the relations of Israel and Judah to Tyre and Sidon.

In the second half of the eleventh century Phoenicia maintained its commercial ties with the Philistines and was on relatively good terms with Israel. But at the same time Philistine expansion—Dor and the other Sea Peoples were not involved—threatened the integrity and growth of Israel. The response to this threat was the adoption of the monarchical system under Saul (ca. 1020 B.C.).[67] Saul seems to have been able to protect the eastern frontier against the Ammonites and others, but despite sporadic victories failed against the Philistines. Nevertheless, the shift toward empire can be dated to his reign: he established a limited tribal unity, however rudimentary its administrative organization; for the first time in the history of the tribes there was an incipient state which included the territory of Judah. This political cohesion which Saul achieved against a common enemy endured beyond the reduction of the Philistines and was the preface to empire.

The empire was finally established under David (ca. 1000–961 B.C.). The first step was the defeat of the Amalekites, the traditional enemy who had opposed the tribes entering the land from the south.[68] Although Saul fought against them, the transferal of the kingdom is attributed to his unwillingness or inability to destroy them.[69] His military policy and neglect of political priorities cost him the total allegiance of the southern tribes. David, protégé of the Philistines, capitalized on this political blunder and campaigned against the Amalekites until they were finally routed.[70] Consequently, "the elders of Judah" acknowledged David's leadership, and anointed him king at Hebron over the fully constituted "house of Judah."[71] David's first move, then, was the consolidation of the tribe and kingdom of Judah. Next, he ventured to absorb the house of Saul, with which he was already associated by his marriage with Michal and by his agreement with Jonathan, and whose authority had been weakened after Saul's death and by the formation of the southern kingdom. He accomplished much more. Not only the house of Benjamin, Saul's kingdom, but all the tribes of Israel made a treaty with David, and accepted his kingship on the understanding that he would free them of the Philistine tyranny.[72] There followed David's defeat of the Philistines. Very little information on this phase has been preserved. It would seem that it was preceded by the absorption of the remaining Canaanite cities into the united kingdom: since there is no evidence that any of these cities was conquered, it is likely that they forfeited whatever autonomy they still retained for neutrality under David. The Philistines were then defeated and restricted to the territory of their five cities.[73] The fourth step was the creation of a commercial empire. This included Moab and Edom who became David's servants and paid tribute;[74] the third district of Canaan, which now consisted of Aramaean principalities under the hegemony of Zobah, and which David conquered and incorporated into his kingdom;[75] Ammon, which had broken its earlier treaty with David and had entered the war as ally of the Aramaeans, and which also was incorporated into the Davidic kingdom;[76] Geshur, which was already in treaty relationship with David and remained neutral in the Aramaean wars;[77] and Hamath, no longer menaced by Zobah, which recognized Israel's annexation of the Aramaean states and, maintaining its independence, concluded a treaty with David.[78] This process of consolidation and unification, of conquest, subjugation and federation, probably occupied most of David's reign, but he eventually controlled or had free access to every major trade route and resource between Egypt and Anatolia. The project of empire was completed late in David's reign by the alliance with Hiram of Tyre.[79] Details of the treaty are wanting, but there were probably concessions made on both sides, although territorial claims do not seem to have been an issue for either party.[80] The Davidic empire was the unopposed heir of the land of Canaan, which it had forged into a political unity with unlimited commercial possibilities. Phoenicia was no longer compelled to thrive on its maritime prowess, but could take full advantage of the system of alliances in which it was now associated.

From the early tenth century Phoenicia was attracted, and perhaps influenced, by the military and political progress of Israel. The confinement of the Philistines increased its share of the trade receipts and assured Phoenician monopoly of the seas. The political stability imposed by the empire liberated and transformed the market potential. The first to recognize the possibilities of the new era was Hiram of Tyre (ca. 969–936). At the accession of Solomon (ca. 961 B.C.), the treaty between Israel and Tyre was renegotiated.[81] There was, first, the commercial accord whereby Phoenician materiel and expertise was exchanged for Israelite food supplies. According to this agreement, Tyre was probably given free entry to all the major ports as far south as Joppa.[82] The commercial relationship, however, was only a part of the formal treaty drawn up between the two empires: it is at least unlikely that the explicit reference to peace and treaty-making included only the stipulations covering Solomon's building operations. This treaty seems to have included a clause according to which Israel would cede agricultural and coastal land to Phoenicia: at any rate, the land of Cabul, most of the coastal and adjacent territory which had been reckoned to the tribe of Asher, was given to Hiram.[83] Clearly, Hiram was aware of Tyre's enormous potential and was determined not only to adjust its position *vis-à-vis* Israel, but to establish its imperial status in the Near East and eventually throughout the Mediterranean.

There is some evidence for this intention in the extrabiblical records of Hiram's early reign. He rebuilt and enlarged the mainland city of Tyre and joined it to the island fortress by some sort of causeway. He then demolished the ancient shrines, set up a golden pillar in the sanctuary of Baal Shamem, and built new temples to Melqart and Astarte.[84] In short, Hiram built a capital that could rival Solomon's Jerusalem,[85] and for his imperial design found it necessary to break with the religious traditions of Canaan. Similarly, the Solomonic temple—built on the Phoenician model since there was none other to follow[86]—was the religious symbol of the empire, and entailed an analogous departure from the Canaanite heritage of tribal religious traditions.[87] The subsequent history of Israel and Phoenicia in the tenth century is that of two empires bound by common culture, mutual interest, and formal treaty.

The evidence for the continuing relations between Solomon and Hiram concerns mainly their commercial ventures. In Israel this required the administrative changes effected by Solomon, whereby Judah retained its relative independence while the rest of the empire was organized into twelve provinces, distributed according to economic and not tribal convenience.[88] At the same time, it is conceivable that Tyre had imposed upon or come to some agreement with the other cities and ports of Phoenicia. At any rate, development of trade and the prosperity of the empires depended on Phoenician naval superiority and on Israelite control of the overland routes. Thus, for instance, the expeditions to Ophir[89] included ships built by Solomon and operated from Israel's port at Ezion-Geber, but they were commanded by Tyrians and belonged to Hiram's fleet.[90] Similarly, the triennial voyages to Tarshish depended on Tyrian initiative, although they obviously expected Israelite cooperation.[91] Solomon's control of the overland routes resulted from the system of alliances made by David, but extended as far as South Arabia[92] and northward to Anatolia.[93] Nor was it liable to Philistine or Egyptian interference since at the beginning of his reign Solomon had defeated Pharaoh Siamun and had contracted a marriage alliance with Egypt.[94] The magnitude of this international commerce and the enormous prestige which accrued especially to Tyre may be gathered from the "trader's catalogue" in Ezek. 27:12–25 which has been inserted into the later lament over Tyre.[95] This catalogue includes five geographical regions[96] which seem to have been grouped with regard to the trade routes on which they lay. The first area lists places in Anatolia that were reached directly by sea. The second and third areas, which included the territory from Edom through

Judah, the land of Israel, Ammon and Damascus into northern Syria, could have been handled by the King's Highway. The fourth and fifth areas, which stretched from South Arabia into northern Mesopotamia, were probably covered by the inland routes that traversed Judaean territory and continued along the Via Maris. This vast trade monopoly hardly outlasted the dissolution of the Israelite empire at the death of Solomon, but it established a precedent which survived and was adapted in the Phoenician empire and later Tyrian expansion.

The commercial alliance between Israel and Tyre further disintegrated as a result of the invasion of Shishak (935–914).[97] This campaign was surely prompted by the collapse of the empire and the inauguration of the separate kingdoms of Judah and Israel. It was also preceded by significant diplomatic preparations. During the reign of Solomon, Hadad of Edom escaped to Egypt where he was accepted at the court of Shishak,[98] and was rewarded for his intrigue by the destruction of Ezion-Geber.[99] Neither Egypt nor Edom exploited the port facilities, but it was a respite for Edom and a serious loss to Judah. The Egyptian court had also entertained Jeroboam when his royal pretensions brought him into conflict with Solomon.[100] The negotiations carried on at this time must certainly have influenced Shishak's policy to some extent, and may have determined him to launch his campaign. At any rate, he destroyed the Negeb installations and disrupted the Tyrian-Judaean transit trade with South Arabia. Whether or not he could have completely overrun Judah, he was satisfied to bypass it on receipt of a substantial payment from Rehoboam.[101] In fact, his objective was the Northern Kingdom, most of which was covered by his line of march. It is hardly credible that all the towns on his itinerary were destroyed. Rather, he was obviously intent on terminating the commercial empire established by Solomon, and on replacing it with an Egyptian-Philistine-Israelite conglomerate which might rely on Tyrian resources, but which would definitely exclude Judah. Thus, his "campaign" in the north, in which he neither demanded nor received tribute from Jeroboam, amounted to little more than a show of power. Shishak's maneuver, ultimately, was a rather stupid little episode with some important consequences: the relations between Judah and Tyre were terminated; Tyre may have continued dealing with the Northern Kingdom for a short time, but with Judah excluded it preferred to expand its empire in other directions; the conflicts between Judah and Israel were aggravated to the profit of no one, least of all Egypt or Philistia.

The continuous wars between Israel and Judah, and the line of fortifications built by Rehoboam, mainly against the Philistines,[102] support the conjecture that Israel had come to some sort of agreement with the Philistines and intended to control as much of the remaining trade potential as it could. Judah was on the defensive. In the reign of Baasha (ca. 900–877), Israel tried to encroach on Judaean territory or at least to hamper its trade, and was probably acting in concert with the Egyptians who attacked from the south.[103] Judah survived by defeating the Egyptians and by allying itself with Damascus:[104] Israel lost all its territory adjacent to Phoenicia, and Damascus, which had already revolted in the reign of Solomon, was on its way to becoming a major power. If Israel relied on the Philistine-Egyptian axis,[105] it succeeded mainly in isolating Judah, severing any lingering connection with Phoenicia, and launching the Tyrian empire on its program of overseas expansion and colonization. The empire established by David and Solomon was finished, and although it lingered on as an ideal or ideology in Judah, its substance was acquired and transformed by Tyre.

The question of Phoenician colonization has become entangled with the obvious contradiction between the chronology of the Classical sources and the evidence of archaeology.[106] However, a date in the latter part of the tenth century for the beginning of Tyrian colonization can be maintained with some probability on the basis of the history of Israel and Phoenicia. The collapse of the Israelite empire and the subsequent disruption of commerce forced Tyre to consider new sources of trade. It was at this time, and in order to assure the stability of its trade, that the Phoenician empire turned to colonization. The process itself is another matter. Colonization involves at least a certain deliberateness of policy, some continuity of settlement, and a minimum of cultural tradition in the settled area.[107] Where these conditions are only partially fulfilled, there can be sufficient evidence for an outline of the general thrust, but not for a history, of early Phoenician colonization.

From Canaanite times Cyprus was on the route to Anatolia and the west. About the mid-tenth century, Hiram campaigned against Kition, which had refused to pay tribute, and forced the town to submit to Tyrian rule.[108] Until this time Kition had not been a Phoenician settlement[109] or a colony, since these did not pay tribute to the mainland. It was a foreign port of call expected to pay a tax on the profit it made from Phoenician trade. The colonization of the town, and then of the whole island, began after its subjection to Tyre when it came under Phoenician administration. The earliest Phoenician epigraphic material from the island is the Honeyman funerary inscription from the first half of the ninth century.[110] The Ba'al Lebanon inscription from the mid-eighth century was dedicated by a lieutenant responsible to Hiram II of Tyre, and confirms the colonial status of the island administered by this governor of Carthage. Although Phoenician colonization of Cyprus ended at the close of the eighth century when Kition declared its independence and perhaps assumed the jurisdictional role of Carthage, there is an almost uninterrupted series of Phoenician inscriptions from the island which reflects the continuous settlement and cultural tradition established by Tyre.[111]

Another area of Phoenician settlement in the late tenth and early ninth centuries was Asia Minor and Anatolia. The evidence for colonization as such is less conclusive, but it is not unlikely that initial Phoenician expansion took place in those regions already familiarized by trade, and that one specific reason for this expansion northward was to take over the earlier Philistine monopoly on iron. The trader's catalogue in Ezekiel begins with places and areas reached by the Phoenician fleet. Tarshish, which heads the list and is noted for its export of metals including iron, can be identified in this context with Tarsus in Cilicia.[112] The list also includes Ionia and Rhodes, and between them Tabal, Meshek, and Bet Togarmah. The earliest evidence for settlement is in the latter region. The Kilamuwa inscription from Zinjirli (ca. 825 B.C.) mentions four earlier reigns of kings with Phoenician names, and hence it is quite certain that Phoenician rule in this area began in the early ninth century at least.[113] As the inscription affirms, the Phoenicians encountered prolonged resistance from the local rulers, but maintained their position with Assyrian help. In the latter part of the eighth century Aramaean influence predominated—as the language of the inscriptions attests[114] —and the Phoenicians became a minority at Zinjirli. Nevertheless, the adjacent kingdom of Karatepe, whose relation to Phoenicia can perhaps be traced to the earlier Sidonian associations with the Danuna and the tribe of Dan, remained Phoenician until its subjugation by Assyria in the early seventh century: the continuity of Phoenician interests in this area is confirmed by the help Sidon supplied to Que in its revolt against Assyria, and by the abortive alliance between Sidon and Que in the reign of Esarhaddon.[115] In short, there were certainly early settlements in Anatolia—such as would be required by the ivory industry;[116] there is some evidence for colonization; analogy suggests that both originated at the time of the dissolution of the Israelite-Tyrian commercial association.

Although Phoenicia inherited the navigation of the Mediterranean from the Canaanites, and from them or the Sea Peoples became familiar with the western routes,[117] Phoenician colonization of the western Mediterranean can be traced only to the same era.[118] The earliest evidence is the Nora stone, dated to the first half of the ninth century. It has been considered a fragment of a monumental inscription, and therefore essentially unintelligible. Those who have accepted its completeness have regularly been misled by the assumption that it commemorates the building of a temple in Sardinia; occasional misreading of several letters has contributed to the confusion and disagreements. Read correctly, the inscription is a dedication to the god Pumay in remembrance of a specific historical incident:[119] a large Phoenician force had been driven from Tarshish after some period of settlement, and out of gratitude for finding asylum in Sardinia dedicated a stele to their god. Thus, the inscription is evidence that early in the ninth century Phoenicians had tried and failed to establish a colony at Tarshish. The fact that Tarshish was not in Sardinia,[120] and that Sardinia lay on a known route but was not the main objective of the colonists, requires a date considerably earlier than that of the inscription for the attempted colonization of Tarshish. The importance of the inscription, therefore, is that Tyre adopted a policy of westward expansion at the same time and for the same reasons as its colonization of Cyprus and Anatolia. However, the Nora stone may be an index of a more generalized failure to colonize the west in the ninth century, and it is possible that the Phoenicians became content with settlements along their trade routes. At any rate, the substantial evidence for earlier colonization is not invalidated by the fact that the history of these settlements and of Phoenicians in the west begins in the eighth century B.C.[121]

The earliest Tyrian colonization occupied the half century of its dissociation with Israel and Judah. However, the conflict between Israel and Judah, which was at least partially motivated by economics but which had achieved mainly the alienation of the Tyrian empire, came to an end with the accession of Omri (ca. 876–869 B.C.).[122] There was already an uneasiness over the domestic and foreign policy of Baasha and of Elah his heir, which was expressed but could not be resolved in Zimri's destruction of the whole line of Baasha. Apparently Tibni had assumed the throne but soon abdicated in favor of Omri.[123] Although no reason is given for the shift in public opinion which led to Israel's acceptance of Omri, it is conceivable—as later events would confirm—that the decision was made because of Omri's pro-Phoenician policy, or perhaps even because of the positive intervention of Ittoba'al of Tyre (ca. 887–857 B.C.) At any rate, Omri's construction of Samaria should be interpreted both as a decisive break with the Tirzah policies of Baasha, and as a deliberate effort to reconstruct the Northern Kingdom around a new capital which was strategically located and did not prejudice relations with either Tyre or Judah. Nothing more is known of his reign, but the ultimate success of his initiative is indicated by the Assyrian designation of Israel as the House of Omri or Samaria,[124] and by the prosperity of the dynasty he founded.

International policy was probably inaugurated by Omri, but certainly had become a firmly established program under Ahab when, for the first time, a semblance of the Solomonic empire was restored. Israel's alliance with Tyre, by the marriage of Ahab and Jezebel and the acceptance of the cult of Melqart in Samaria, perhaps was concluded by Omri when he moved his capital from Tirzah.[125] It might have been at the same time that a treaty, represented by the marriage of Athaliah and Jehoram, was concluded between Israel and Judah.[126] The unifying force in this system of alliances was undoubtedly Tyre whose commercial hegemony was still intact and indispensable to the prosperity of both kingdoms. Nevertheless, it was Judah which contributed most to the renewal of commercial relations with Tyre. Jehoshaphat (ca. 873–849) reorganized the administrative districts of Judah in which he built fortresses and store-cities and instituted judicial reform.[127] In his reign Edom was administered by a Judaean viceroy, Ezion-Geber was rebuilt with the intention of renewing the Ophir trade,[128] and some Philistines along with neighboring Arab tribes paid tribute. It seems fairly certain, therefore, that Judah had assured control of the southern and Arabian trade routes, including most probably those which debouched at Gaza. Ahab's main contribution to the alliance was military, as Moab's recognition of Israel's sovereignty over most of its territory[129] and later events would indicate. Although the Old Testament incorrectly dates the Aramaean wars to the reign of Ahab, instead of to the era of the Jehu dynasty and more specifically the reign of Jehoahaz,[130] it is clear that Israel maintained good relations with Damascus throughout his reign. The dedication to Melqart in the Ben Hadad inscription probably supposes a similar understanding between Damascus and Tyre. Further, since Hamath was allied with Damascus and Israel in the anti-Assyrian coalition, it can be concluded that the northern routes through Syria and Anatolia were also kept open. The second quarter of the ninth century, therefore, was a time of substantial commercial revival and of renewed cooperation between Tyre, Judah, and Israel.

However, this alliance did not survive much beyond mid-century when it was overwhelmed first by the Assyrians and then by the Aramaeans. It began to be threatened soon after the accession of Shalmaneser III (ca. 859–825 B.C.). His early campaigns ended with the defeat and annexation of Bit Adini and the dispersion of the northern coalition.[131] In his advance against Hamath he again received tribute from these northern states. At the battle of Qarqar and in subsequent campaigns (849, 848, 845 B.C.) Hamath was the main objective, but the Assyrian army was unable to defeat the united front led by Damascus and Israel. There were no campaigns between 845 and 841 B.C., and sometime in this period Hamath had come to terms with Assyria and was conceded its neutrality. Damascus, now ruled by the usurper Hazael, relied chiefly on Israel whose policy was significantly determined by Jezebel the Queen Mother.[132] When Joram and Ahaziah tried to stop the Assyrian advance at Ramoth-Gilead, Jehu, in an attempt to rescue Israel, rebelled, destroyed the pro-Aramaean ruling houses, and paid tribute to Assyria.[133] This coup gave Assyria free passage through Israel into Phoenicia at least as far as Ba'ali Ra'ši[134] where Ba'almanzer II of Tyre (ca. 849–830) had to pay tribute to Shalmaneser. It is conceivable that relations between Israel and Tyre could have survived Jehu's desperate political compromise, but they did not. After destroying the southern coalition, Shalmaneser III's pressure on the west ceased, but the Jehu dynasty was totally absorbed in its wars with the Aramaean empire established by Hazael. Israel lost much of its territory,[135] and was on the defensive until the Aramaeans were crushed by Adadnirari III in his campaign against Mansuate (796 B.C.).[136] Throughout this period, Phoenicia had nothing to gain from further association with Israel. Tyrian interest in Judah might have continued through the reign of Athaliah (842–837), but Edom had revolted and the kingdom had to pay tribute to Hazael.[137] The commercial prospects which had initially contributed to the triple alliance were wiped out, and the economic consequences for Phoenicia must have been considerable. Henceforward Tyre avoided all but the most incidental involvements with either kingdom and turned definitively to its western Mediterranean holdings: first, as tradition attests, to Carthage;[138] later, under increasingly oppressive Assyrian domination in the eighth century, to other western sites.[139]

The disaffection of Tyre is indicated by its exclusion from the Davidic-Solomonic empire which was restored, for the second and last time, by Uzziah (ca. 783–735) and Jeroboam II (786–746).[140] The fact of empire resulted in an explicit Judaean imperial policy, exemplified by Uzziah's leadership of the northern coalition[141] which he undertook with the intention of maintaining the whole empire, including Israel, against Assyria. Both the fact and the theory of empire are presupposed by the oracles of Amos against the nations, and the condemnation of Tyre for treaty violation confirms Phoenicia's abstention, and may suggest deliberate opposition to the restoration.[142] If this was the case, it was a serious miscalculation since Phoenicia had grown up with the empire and could not survive without it. In fact, before the end of the century the Tyrian empire was destroyed, and it was only by tradition of leadership and sheer tenacity that Tyre and Sidon remained the predominant powers in Phoenicia.

Phoenician mainland enterprise was severely restricted by the development of the Assyrian provincial system instituted by Tiglathpileser III and expanded by Sargon II.[143] Further, under Hiram II (774–738) and Mittin II (738–734), Tyre had to pay tribute to Assyria and was excluded from Philistia and the southern markets which Assyria had decided to monopolize.[144] Finally, Tyre's situation became intolerable and Luli, taking advantage of the upheaval in Judah and Philistia, rebelled. In 701 B.C. Sennacherib attacked, and partly because of the defection of Sidon and other Phoenician cities, Tyre was defeated. Luli escaped to Cyprus but was assassinated by the Kitians; Ittoba'al II was named king by Sennacherib and Tyre was forced to pay annual tribute to Assyria.[145] Not only had Phoenicia lost its independence, it was divided by the divergent interests of Tyre and Sidon. Early in the reign of Esarhaddon (680–669) Abdimilkut of Sidon concluded an alliance with Que and rebelled. The city was captured in 667 B.C., Abdimilkut was killed, and Sidon became an Assyrian province administered by an Assyrian governor.[146] Although Ba'al of Tyre had concluded a treaty with Esarhaddon and had recovered some of Sidon's territory, he allied himself with Tirhaqa (685–663) and revolted in 671 B.C. When Esarhaddon defeated Ba'al, and conquered Egypt and Ethiopia, Tyre was incorporated into the Assyrian provincial system, but Ba'al retained his throne, as well as the security and arrogance to rebel again in the time of Ashurbanipal (668–633).[147] Throughout this period of decline Phoenician contact with Judah was incidental if anything, and the meagre evidence does not really suggest that either Tyre or Sidon was involved: a sanctuary excavated at Jerusalem may be representative of the Phoenician cults introduced by Manasseh;[148] the *lmlk* stamps were introduced into Judah via Phoenicia in the reign of Josiah;[149] the *ktym* of the Arad inscriptions may have been Phoenician mercenaries from Kition.[150]

As Israel and Phoenicia emerged at the same time, and each prospered only with the other, so both succumbed together to the Babylonians. Tyre under Ittoba'al III surrendered after a siege of thirteen years (586–573), and Ba'al II (573–563) acquired the throne as vassal of Nebuchadrezzar.[151] These and the later kings up to Hiram III (552–532) probably ruled over both Tyre and Sidon, but by the beginning of the fifth century each had its own king.[152] In the mid-fifth century Sidon, as vassal of Persia, had acquired the plain of Sharon from Dor to Joppa and renewed some form of relation with Judah.[153] The Revolt of Tennes (351–345) involved not only Sidon,[154] but Palestinian towns as well,[155] and perhaps the whole coastal area which belonged to Sidon, including Shiqmona[156] and Tell Abu Hawam.[157] In effect it was a revolt of the satrapy, and its suppression put an end to whatever symbiosis Judah and Sidon had enjoyed during the Persian period.

NOTES

1. Cf. W. F. Albright, *YGC.*

2. Cf. S. Moscati, *The World of the Phoenicians,* tr. A. Hamilton (London, 1968).

3. Saul's reign began ca. 1020 B.C. The Aramaean (mainly Damascene) king list can be reconstructed from OT sources, and does not antedate the tenth century. The Tyrian and Byblian king lists begin about the turn of the tenth century: cf. Albright, "The New Assyro-Tyrian Synchronism and the Chronology of Tyre," *Annuaire de l'Institut de Philologie et d'Histoire Orientales et Slaves* (*Mélanges Isidore Lévy*) 13 (1953), 1–9; "The Phoenician Inscriptions of the Tenth Century B.C. from Byblus," *JAOS* 67 (1947), 153–160. The designation "pre-monarchical" is used on the basis of this evidence, but also intends that even if the monarchy existed it was not a significant influence on the transition from Canaan to Phoenicia. Although Zakarba'al was king of Byblos ca. 1060, Byblos is not typical of Canaanite-Phoenician development.

4. Cf. Albright, "The Role of the Canaanites in the History of Civilization," in *BANE,* pp. 328–362; "Syria, the Philistines and Phoenicia," in *CAH²,* vol. II, ch. xxxiii (Cambridge, 1966).

5. Cf. Moscati, "La questione fenicia," *Atti della Accademia Nazionale dei Lincei. Rendiconti, Classe di Scienze morali, storiche e filologiche* 18 (1963), 483–506. It is proposed (p. 490) that the history of Phoenicia as such begins about 1200 B.C. and ends with the conquest of Alexander in 332 B.C.

6. Cf. Moscati, "I Fenici come problema," *Kôkalos* 10–11 (1964–65), 525–538, where it is noted that the precise nature of Phoenician civilization is usually presupposed as known rather than critically studied.

7. Cf. F. M. Cross, "The Evolution of the Proto-Canaanite Alphabet," *BASOR* 134 (1954), 15–24; "The Origin and Early Evolution of the Alphabet," *EI* 8 (1967), 8*–24*.

8. Cf. B. Mazar, "The Philistines and the Rise of Israel and Tyre," *The Israel Academy of Sciences and Humanities. Proceedings,* I, 7 (Jerusalem, 1964), 7.

9. Cf. J. Naveh, "The Scripts in Palestine and Transjordan in the Iron Age," in *NEATC,* pp. 277–283.

10. Cf. W. Helck, *Die Beziehungen Ägyptens zu Vorderasien im 3. und 2. Jahrtausend v. Chr.*, Ägyptologische Abhandlungen, 5 (Wiesbaden,[2] 1971), 248–255.

11. Cf. A. Goetze, "The Hittites and Syria (1300–1200 B.C.)," *CAH*[2], vol. II, ch. xxiv (1965).

12. Cf. G. A. Lehmann, "Der Untergang des hethitischen Grossreiches und die neuen Texte aus Ugarit," *Ugarit-Forschungen* 2 (1970), 39–73.

13. Cf. Albright, "Syria, the Philistines and Phoenicia" [N 4], sec. 4; J. A. Brinkman, *A Political History of Post-Kassite Babylonia, 1158–722 B.C.*, Analecta Orientalia 43 (Rome, 1968), pp. 267–285.

14. Cf. R. D. Barnett, "The Sea Peoples," *CAH*[2], vol. II, ch. xxviii (1969); M. C. Astour, "New Evidence on the Last Days of Ugarit," *AJA* 69 (1965), 253–258.

15. Cf. R. de Vaux, "La Phénicie et les Peuples de la Mer," *Mélanges de l'Université Saint-Joseph* 45 (1969), 479–498, esp. 483.

16. Cf. *ANET*, pp. 376–378; R. O. Faulkner, "Egypt: From the Inception of the Nineteenth Dynasty to the Death of Ramesses III," *CAH*[2], vol. II, ch. xxiii (1966), 18–21.

17. Cf. G. E. Wright, "Fresh Evidence for the Philistine Story," *BA* 29 (1966), 70–86.

18. Cf. Y. Yadin, "'And Dan, Why did he Remain in Ships?'" *The Australian Journal of Biblical Archaeology* 1 (1968), 9–23; G. Huxley, *Crete and the Luwians* (Oxford, 1961), p. 55.

19. Cf. F. Schachermeyr, "Hörnerhelme und Federkronen als Kopfbedeckungen bei den 'Seevölkern' der ägyptischen Reliefs," *Ugaritica* 6 (Paris, 1969), 451–459.

20. They are known from the Amarna letters (EA 122:35; 123:15), perhaps as mercenaries in the service of Rib-Addi of Byblos. They served as mercenaries of Ramesses II in the battle of Qadesh (*ANET*, p. 225). They were settled by Ramesses III somewhere in southern Canaan, and are listed in the Onomasticon of Amenope after the tribe of Asher and before the Tjekker: cf. Y. Aharoni, *LB*, pp. 245–253, esp. 248.

21. The Sherden had settled in Sardinia and southwestern Corsica sometime in the fourteenth century; cf. R. Grosjean, "Recent Work in Corsica," *Antiquity* 40 (1966), 190–198, pls. 29–31, and G. Daniel and J. D. Evans, "The Western Mediterranean," *CAH*[2], vol. II, ch. xxxvii, 31–34. Their familiarity with the western routes was undoubtedly important for the Canaanites and the Phoenicians who followed them.

22. Cf. de Vaux [N 15], pp. 489–498.

23. Cf. Wright [N 17], 70–78.

24. It was perhaps late in this period of expansion that a king of Ascalon "destroyed" Sidon and that Tyre became the most important of the Sidonian cities (Justin, *Epitome of Trogus Pompeius* xviii 3, 5). This episode may be related to Tiglathpileser I's (1116–1078) expeditions to the west, in which he claims to have received tribute from Byblos, Sidon, and Arvad. However, Assyria was incapable of any sustained effort in Canaan at this time, and if there was conflict between Ascalon and Sidon it was short lived.

25. Cf. J. Leclant, "Les relations entre l'Egypte et la Phénicie du voyage d'Ounamon à l'expédition d'Alexandre," in *The Role of the Phoenicians in the Interaction of Mediterranean Civilizations*, ed. W. A. Ward (Beirut, 1968), pp. 9–31.

26. Cf. Mazar [N 8], pp. 3–6.

27. Asher: Judg. 1:31–32, 5:17; Zebulun: Gen. 49:13; Deut. 33:18–19; Issachar: Deut. 33:18–19. Cf. H. J. Zobel, "Stammesspruch und Geschichte," *BZAW* 95 (1965), 80–104.

28. Cf. Yadin [N 18], 21–22. The migration would have been due partly to Philistine pressure, partly to the settlement of Israelite tribes, and partly to the possibility of a closer association with Sidon. On the enigmatic texts concerning Dan and the Sidonians (Judg. 18:7, 28), cf. A. Malamat, "The Danite Migration and the

Pan-Israelite Exodus-Conquest: A Biblical Narrative Pattern," *Biblica* 51 (1970), 1–16, esp. 5, n. 3.

29. J. M. Sasson, "Canaanite Maritime Involvement in the Second Millennium B.C.," *JAOS* 86 (1966), 126–138; Helck, "Ein Indiz früher Handelsfahrten syrischer Kaufleute," *Ugarit-Forschungen* 2 (1970), 35–37.

30. Cf. de Vaux [N 15], 490–496; C. G. Thomas, "A Mycenaean Hegemony? A Reconsideration," *Journal of Hellenic Studies* 90 (1970), 184–192.

31. G. F. Bass, *Cape Gelidonya: A Bronze Age Shipwreck*. Transactions of the American Philosophical Society, 57, 8 (Philadelphia, 1967).

32. *ANET*, p. 378.

33. Cf. Aharoni, *LB*, pp. 168, 170, 171, 175. Asher certainly maintained its particular relations with the Sidonians at least into the eleventh century, and probably later.

34. Cf. *LB*, pp. 175, 200.

35. Judg. 3:31. Cf. W. Richter, *Die Bearbeitungen des "Retterbuches" in der deuteronomischen Epoche*, Bonner Biblische Beiträge, 21 (Bonn, 1964), 92–97. Richter considers this entirely the work of the Deuteronomist, whose only basis in the tradition is Judg. 5:6 where the secondary insertion of Jael transformed Shamgar into an ally of Israel rather than the enemy he was. Historical considerations are deliberately avoided (96, n. 44).

36. Cf. *LB*, pp. 192–200.

37. From the start there is no evidence of conflict between the northern tribes and the Philistines. If Gen. 9:25–27, whose original form is not easily reconstructed, is early, it indicates that Israel's objective was Canaan and that Philistine settlement in its territory was unopposed. Cf. D. Neiman, "The Date and Circumstances of the Cursing of Canaan," *Biblical Motifs: Origins and Transformations*, ed. A. Altmann (Cambridge, 1966), pp. 113–134.

38. Cf. *LB*, pp. 200–211. The earliest texts are Judges 4, 5, independent witnesses both in their origins and developments. Cf. Richter, *Traditionsgeschichtliche Untersuchungen zum Richterbuch*, Bonner Biblische Beiträge, 18 (Bonn, 1963), 29–112. Josh. 11:1–9, with its appendix in vss. 10–13, is apparently later and was used in the editorial contamination of Judges 4.

39. Judg. 1:21–36 and the corresponding passages of Joshua 15–19. Cf. *LB*, pp. 212–215, 227–239. According to Aharoni ("New Aspects of the Israelite Occupation of the North," in *NEATC*, pp. 254–267) it concerns only the tribes of Ephraim, Manasseh, Benjamin, Zebulun, and Naphtali, and is to be dated sometime before 1125 B.C.

40. Cf. *LB*, pp. 61–70, 215–217. According to Josh. 19:24–29 (*LB*, pp. 237–238) the territory north of the Carmel up to and including Tyre was allotted to Asher, although it was not "conquered" until the time of David. However, under Solomon's administrative system its territory was considerably diminished, and was further reduced when Cabul was ceded to Tyre. That is, the inheritance of Asher was properly Sidonian and was manipulated according to political interest.

41. Cf. E. F. Campbell, Jr., and Ernest Wright, "Tribal League Shrines in Amman and Shechem," *BA* 32 (1969), 104–116; R. E. Clements, "Baal-Berith of Shechem," *JSS* 13 (1968), 21–32.

42. Cf. G. Fohrer, "Altes Testament—'Amphiktyonie' und 'Bund'," *TLZ* 91 (1966), 801–816, 893–904.

43. Cf. de Vaux, "La thèse de l' 'Amphictyonie Israélite'," *HTR* 64 (1971), 415–436. The evidence for the Delphic amphictyony is collected by H. Bengston, *Die Staatsverträge des Altertums, II: Die Verträge der griechisch-römischen Welt von 700 bis 338 v. Chr.* (Munich, 1962), 3–4.

44. Cf. M. Noth, *Das System der zwölf Stämme Israels* (Stuttgart, 1930).

45. Cf. R. Smend, *Yahweh War and Tribal Confederation*, tr. M. G. Rogers (Nashville, 1970).

46. Cf. G. W. Anderson, "Israel: Amphictyony: *'am; kāhāl; 'ēdāh*," in *Translating and Understanding the Old Testament*, eds. H. T. Frank and W. L. Reed (Nashville, 1970), pp. 135–151.

47. Cf. *LB*, pp. 254–258.

48. Cf. Smend, "Gehörte Juda zum vorstaatlichen Israel?" in *Fourth World Congress of Jewish Studies. Papers*, I (Jerusalem, 1967), 57–62.

49. Cf. R. de Vaux, "The Settlement of the Israelites in Southern Palestine and the Origins of the Tribe of Judah," in *Translating and Understanding the Old Testament* [N 46], pp. 108–134. There are no early and authentic traditions on a conquest by Judah; Judah's "conquest" followed on settlement in the land. It is probable that the Yahwist transformed a number of traditions on the settlement of the southern tribes into narratives on the wilderness wanderings. Cf. V. Fritz, *Israel in der Wüste*, Marburger Theologische Studien, 7 (Marburg, 1970).

50. Cf. G. Buccellati, *Cities and Nations of Ancient Syria*, Studi Semitici, 26 (Rome, 1967), 111–125.

51. Cf. S. Herrmann, "Autonome Entwicklungen in den Königreichen Israel und Juda," *VTS* 17 (1969), 139–158.

52. Cf. W. Herrmann, "Der historische Ertrag der altbyblischen Königsinschriften," *Mitteilungen des Instituts für Orientforschung* 6 (1958), 14–32.

53. Cf. Albright, *CAH*² [N 4], 38. Albright suggested that the inscriptions of Abiba'al (ca. 930) and Eliba'al (ca. 920) on statues of Shishak I and of Osorkon I indicated that these two kings regarded themselves as vassals of the pharaohs.

54. Cf. Malamat, "Aspects of the Foreign Policies of David and Solomon," *JNES* 22 (1963), 1–17, esp. 10–17. If Yeḥimilk of Byblos (ca. 950) founded a new dynasty, it may have been in view of this more aggressive policy.

55. I Kings 5:32.

56. Ezek. 27:9. Cf. W. Zimmerli, *Ezechiel*, Biblischer Kommentar, 13 (Neukirchen, 1962), 624–661, esp. 634–642; H. J. Van Dijk, *Ezekiel's Prophecy on Tyre (Ez. 26, 1–28, 19)*: *A New Approach*, Biblica et Orientalia, 20 (Rome, 1968), 48–91.

57. Cf. Leclant [N 25], pp. 9–31, esp. p. 13. The statue of the enthroned king should be considered more reliable evidence of Egyptian presence than the alabaster jars with the cartouche of Osorkon II found at Samaria and Almuñécar.

58. Josephus *Antiquities* VIII 324. Botrys was approximately ten miles north of Byblos. It is doubtful that Byblos had been defeated by Tyre, as was suggested by Albright, in *CAH*² [N 4], p. 39.

59. Cf. H. Tadmor, "Que and Muṣri," *IEJ* 11 (1961), 143–150. Tadmor makes a plausible case for the correction of *Gua to Gu[bal]a*, and then identifying the following Muṣri with Egypt. However, if the scribe was as incompetent as Tadmor shows, it is just as likely that *Gu-a-a* is a scribal error for the normal *Qu-a-a*, "Que." Further, I Kings 10:28, II Kings 7:6, and Sefire I A 5 all require the existence of an Anatolian Muṣri associated with Que.

60. *ANET*, pp. 282, 287, 291, 294.

61. The evidence is mainly the script tradition; cf. B. Peckham, *The Development of the Late Phoenician Scripts* (Cambridge, 1968), pp. 130–131 and indeed s.v. "Amrit stele."

62. Cf. W. R. Lane, "The Phoenician Dialect of Larnax tes Lapethou," *BASOR* 194 (1969), 39–45. On the script, cf. Peckham [N 61], p. 40, n. 73.

63. Cf. J. A. Fitzmyer, "The Phoenician Inscription from Pyrgi," *JAOS* 86 (1966), 285–297, *passim* but esp. 296. The verbal suffix *-w* is typically Byblian. The usual order in date formulae in Cyprus is (day)-month-year, *lmlky/lmlk*. Not only does Pyrgi reverse this order, but it lists events in a sequence which is peculiar to Larnax tes Lapethou (cf. A. M. Honeyman, *JEA* 26 (1940) 56–67, esp. 60, n. 3): first, the

latest dedication in time, which provides the occasion for the inscription, and which is dated to the day (Pyrgi, line 5; *bmtn 'bbt*); then the other dedications in chronological order and with the date given only to the month (Pyrgi, lines 8–9, gives the date to the day: *bym qbr 'lm*). The Pyrgi inscription records first the date of the completion and dedication of the shrine, which is the occasion for the inscription, and then the date of the construction of the shrine.

64. Cf. J. Starcky, "Une inscription phénicienne de Byblos," *Mélanges de l'Université Saint-Joseph* 45 (1969), 257–273, pl. 1. It is an inscription of an unnamed king who belongs between Yeḥawmilk (ca. 450) and 'Elpa'al (early fourth century). It is notable for its designation of the Persian king as *'dn mlkm*, as well as for its unfortunately enigmatic reference to a naval detachment. (In line 3 the word following *wdrkm* is *wdrkm*: the scribe erased it when he noticed his mistake).

65. There is an unpublished ninth-century inscription from Khan el-Khalde just south of the city, inscribed *ptty*, probably an Anatolian personal name; cf. Ph. H. J. Houwink Ten Cate, *The Luwian Population Groups of Lycia and Cilicia Aspera During the Hellenistic Period*, Documenta et Monumenta Orientis Antiqui, 10 (Leiden, 1965), 158.

66. *ANET*, pp. 279, 282, 287, 291, 294, 296. From the time of Shalmaneser III until the reign of Ashurbanipal, all that is known of the city is the names of the kings who paid tribute to Assyria. There is also some later epigraphic evidence for Arvadites at Abydos and at Carthage.

67. Cf. K.-D. Schunck, *Benjamin. Untersuchungen zur Entstehung und Geschichte eines israelitischen Stammes*, BZAW 86 (Berlin, 1963), 108–138.

68. Exod. 17:8–16 (cf. Num. 13:29; 14:25, 43, 45); Num. 24:20; Deut. 25:17–19; I Sam. 15.

69. I Sam. 14:48, 15:28, 28:18.

70. I Sam. 27:8–12, 30; II Sam. 8:12.

71. I Sam. 30:26–31; II Sam. 2:4, 10.

72. II Sam. 5:1–3. The conquest of the Philistines as condition of the treaty is explicit in Abner's negotiations with Israel (II Sam. 3:18), and implicit in the introduction to the treaty (II Sam. 5:2) which refers to I Samuel 18:16 and to David's victories over the Philistines (e.g. I Sam. 18:30).

73. II Sam. 5:17–25, 8:1, 12.

74. II Sam. 8:2, 13–14. Cf. J. C. Greenfield, "Some Aspects of Treaty Terminology in the Bible," in *Fourth World Congress of Jewish Studies. Papers*, I [N 48], 117–119.

75. Cf. Malamat, "Aspects of the Foreign Policies of David and Solomon" [N 54], 1–17, esp. 1–6.

76. II Sam. 10, 12:26–31. Albright ("Notes on Ammonite History," in *Miscellanea Biblica B. Ubach*, ed. R. M. Díaz [Montserrat, 1953], pp. 131–136, esp. 133) suggested that Nahash had joined David in the struggle against the house of Saul.

77. Cf. Mazar, "Geshur and Maacah," *JBL* 80 (1961), 16–28.

78. II Sam. 8:9–10; I Chron. 18:9–10. This can only be construed as a parity treaty. The reference to the treaty is the sending of the embassy, in this case the king's son, since "to send a messenger" or the equivalent often connotes the making of a treaty; cf. II Sam. 5:11, 10:2=I Chron. 19:2; II Kings 16:7, 17:4. When Toi's son ascended the throne, probably in the time of Solomon, he adopted the alternate regnal names Joram and Hadoram. Both are incongruous for the ruler of a neo-Hittite state, and if the Yahwistic name confirms the close relationship between Israel and Hamath, it is not an argument for the vassal status of the latter.

79. II Sam. 5:11; I Kings 5:15. Cf. F. C. Fensham, "The Treaty Between the Israelites and Tyrians," *VTS* 17 (1969), 71–87. Since Hiram's rule is calculated ca.

969–936 B.C. the treaty must have been made in the last decade of David's reign (ca. 1000–961).

80. If Tyre recognized David's authority over the theoretical territory of Asher, it was a diplomatic gesture with no practical consequences, since the area remained as much Phoenician as Israelite.

81. I Kings 5:15–26.

82. II Chron. 2:17; cf. Ezra 3:7.

83. I Kings 9:10–13; cf. II Chron. 8:1–2. The precise extent of the territory and its twenty towns cannot be determined. In its present position in the biblical text, the transfer of Cabul compensates for the supply of foodstuffs which had continued throughout Solomon's building period.

84. Josephus *Contra Apionem* I 112–120; *Antiquities* VIII 144–149; cf. R. D. Barnett, "Ezekiel and Tyre," *EI* 9 (1969), 6*–13*. On the cult of Baal Shamen, cf. Albright, *YGC*, pp. 197–202.

85. Cf. M. B. Rowton, "The Date of the Founding of Solomon's Temple," *BASOR* 119 (1950), 20–22; cf. H. J. Katzenstein, "Is There any Synchronism between the Reigns of Hiram and Solomon?" *JNES* 24 (1965), 116–117.

86. Cf. G. R. H. Wright, "Pre-Israelite Temples in the Land of Canaan," *PEQ* 103 (1971), 17–32.

87. Cf. J. A. Soggin, "Der offiziell geförderte Synkretismus in Israel während des 10. Jahrhunderts," *ZAW* 78 (1966), 179–204; S. Terrien, "The Omphalos Myth and Hebrew Religion," *VT* 20 (1970), 315–338. A sensible corrective to exaggerated notions of syncretism can be found in M. Pye, "Syncretism and Ambiguity," *Numen* 18 (1971), 83–93.

88. Ernest Wright, "The Provinces of Solomon (I Kings 4:7–19)," *EI* 8 (1967), 58*–68*. Cf. also T. N. D. Mettinger, *Solomonic State Officials. A Study of the Civil Government Officials of the Israelite Monarchy* (Lund, 1971).

89. Cf. V. Christidès, "L'énigme d'Ophir," *RB* 77 (1970), 240–247.

90. I Kings 9:26–28, 10:11–12; cf. S. Yeivin, "Did the Kingdom of Israel have a Maritime Policy?" *JQR* 50 (1959–60), 193–228.

91. I Kings 10:22; II Chron. 9:21.

92. I Kings 10:1–10, 13, 15. Cf. Albright, "Was the Age of Solomon without Monumental Art?" in *EI* 5 (1958), 7*–9*; G. W. Van Beek, "Frankincense and Myrrh," *BA* 23 (1960), 76–77.

93. I Kings 10:28–29. Cf. Noth, *Könige,* Biblischer Kommentar, 9 (Neukirchen-Vluyn, 1967), pp. 234–237.

94. Cf. H. D. Lance, "Gezer in the Land and in History," *BA* 30 (1967), 39–42.

95. Cf. Zimmerli, *Ezechiel* [N 56], 649–661. This has been dated to the tenth–ninth century by Mazar [N 8], 21.

96. Cf. J. Simons, *The Geographical and Topographical Texts of the Old Testament* (Leiden, 1959), pp. 456–457; Van Dijk [N 56], 48–82. Phoenicia itself is not included in the catalogue, since the editor omitted names already mentioned in the lament; cf. Zimmerli [N 56], p. 659.

97. Cf. Aharoni, *LB*, pp. 283–290; S. Herrmann, "Operationen Pharao Schoschenks I. im östlichen Ephraim," *ZDPV* 80 (1964), 55–79; Helck, *Die Beziehungen Ägyptens zu Vorderasien im 3. und 2. Jahrtausend v. Chr.* [N 10], 238–245.

98. I Kings 11:14–22. Cf. W. J. Martin, " 'Dischronologized' Narrative in the Old Testament," *VTS* 17 (1969), 185.

99. Cf. N. Glueck, "Ezion-Geber," *BA* 28 (1965), 82.

100. I Kings 11:40.

101. I Kings 14:25–28; II Chron. 12:1–12. For another interpretation of the discrepancy between biblical and Egyptian sources cf. Y. Elizur, "The Biblical Account of

Shishak's Invasion: Prophetic Historiosophy versus Reality," in *Fourth World Congress of Jewish Studies. Papers*, I [N 48], 29–31 (English summary, p. 252).

102. I Kings 14:30; II Chron. 11:5–12. Cf. *LB*, pp. 290–294.

103. I Kings 15:16–22; II Chron. 14:8–14.

104. I Kings 15:18–20.

105. Cf. I Kings 15:27, 16:15. Both Nadab and Baasha were supplanted because of some conflict with the Philistines over Gibbethon. The reasons for the conflict are not given, but it is not impossible that it was due to some disagreement over trade rights.

106. Albright, *CAH²* [N 4], 39–40, attempted to reconcile the two sources by reducing the forty-year generation span on which the ancient chronologies were based to a more realistic mean of twenty-five years. De Vaux appealed to the fact that the archaeological evidence is incomplete, but his catalogue of more recent finds hardly reduces the chronological gap between the two sources ("On Right and Wrong Uses of Archaeology," *NEATC*, pp. 64–80, esp. 70–72).

107. On the definition of colonization cf. L. L. Orlin, *Assyrian Colonies in Cappadocia*, Studies in Ancient History, 1 (The Hague, 1970), 161–183.

108. Josephus *Contra Apionem* I 119; *Antiquities* VIII 146. The reading "Kition" was suggested by Albright, "The Role of the Canaanites in the History of Civilization" [N 4], p. 361, n. 101. The date of the campaign is based on the supposition that the joint commercial operations of Israel and Tyre were already established and were jeopardized by the revolt of Kition.

109. Cf. V. Karageorghis, "Chronique des fouilles à Chypre," *Bulletin de Correspondance Hellénique* 84 (1960), 242–299, esp. pp. 285–286; "Chronique des fouilles et découvertes archéologiques à Chypre en 1964," *Bulletin de Correspondance Hellénique* 89 (1965), 231–300, esp. 266–268.

110. H. Donner and W. Röllig, *Kanaanäische und aramäische Inschriften*, 2d ed. (Wiesbaden, 1968), no. 30. A short note by O. Masson and a new photograph can be found in *Bulletin de Correspondance Hellénique* 92 (1968), 379–380, pl. 21.

111. Cf. Peckham [N 61], pp. 13–24. The defection of Kition (p. 15, n. 13) is also recorded in Isaiah 23:12.

112. Cf. G. Garbini, "Tarsis e Gen. 10, 4," *Bibbia e Oriente* 7 (1965), 13–19.

113. Cf. Donner and Röllig [N 110], no. 24:1–4; cf. no. 25. Cf. also Y. Yadin, "Symbols of Deities at Zinjirli, Carthage and Hazor," *NEATC*, pp. 199–231.

114. Cf. Donner and Röllig [N 110], nos. 214–221: all of these are written in Aramaic.

115. Cf. J. D. Bing, "Tarsus. A Forgotten Colony of Lindos," *JNES* 30 (1971), 99–109; also *ANET*, p. 290.

116. Cf. Barnett, "Phoenician and Syrian Ivory Carving," *PEQ* 71 (1939), 4–9; "Phoenicia and the Ivory Trade, *Archaeology* 9 (1956), 87–97; *A Catalogue of the Nimrud Ivories* (London, 1957); "Hamat and Nimrud," *Iraq* 25 (1963), 81–84.

117. Cf. L. Breglia, "Le antiche rotte del Mediterraneo documentate da monete e pesi," *Rendiconti Accademia di Archeologia, Lettere e Belle Arti di Napoli* 30 (1955 [1956]), 210–326; Garbini, "L'espansione fenicia nel Mediterraneo," *Cultura e Scuola* II/7 (1963), 92–97.

118. P. Cintas (*Manuel d'archéologie punique*, I [Paris, 1970]) is inclined to restore the traditional dates of colonization in the west.

119. Cf. B. Peckham, "The Nora Inscription," *Orientalia* 41 (1972), 457–468.

120. In the light of this inscription, the tradition according to which Nora was founded from Tarshish in Spain (cf. Moscati [N 1], pp. 206–207) may deserve some consideration.

121. On Phoenicians in Spain, cf. H. G. Niemeyer and H. Schubart, *Toscanos. Die altpunische Faktorei an der Mündung des Río de Vélez*, Madrider Forschungen 6

(Berlin, 1969); J. M. Blázquez, "Relaciones entre Hispania y los Semitas (Sirios, Fenicios, Chipriotas, Cartagineses y Judios) en la Antiguedad," *Beiträge zur Alten Geschichte und deren Nachleben,* eds. I. R. Stiehl and H. E. Stier (Berlin, 1969), pp. 42–75. On the other western sites, cf. *Ricerche Puniche nel Mediterraneo Centrale,* Studi Semitici 36 (Rome 1970); Moscati, *Fenici e Cartaginesi in Sardegna* (Milan, 1968).

122. Cf. J. M. Miller, *The Omride Dynasty in the Light of Recent Literary and Archaeological Research* [1964], (Ann Arbor, 1971).

123. Cf. Miller, "So Tibni Died" (I Kings 16:22), *VT* 18 (1968), 392–394.

124. The earliest Assyrian mention of Samaria is from the time of Adadnirari III; cf. S. Page, "Joash and Samaria in a New Stela Excavated at Tel al Rimah, Iraq," *VT* 19 (1969), 483–484. It became the designation of an Assyrian province in the reign of Sargon II, and is referred to as such in II Kings 23:19.

125. The sources (I Kings 16:31–33; Josephus *Antiquities* VIII 316–318) refer only to Ahab's marriage and apostasy.

126. The treaty between Jehoshaphat and "the king of Israel" is recorded in I Kings 22:45, but II Chron. 18:1 identifies the king as Ahab. The same problem underlies the designation of Athaliah as daughter of Omri (II Kings, 8:26; II Chron. 22:2) or as daughter of Ahab (II Kings 8:18; II Chron. 18:1, 21:6). According to J. Bright (*A History of Israel* [Philadelphia, 1959], p. 222, n. 41) she was not the daughter of Ahab; M. Noth (*The History of Israel,* 2d ed. [New York, 1960], p. 236, n. 4) explains that she was the daughter of Ahab and is called daughter of Omri because she was of the house of Omri; a compromise position is adopted by H. J. Katzenstein, "Who Were the Parents of Athaliah?" *IEJ* 5 (1955), 194–197. It is preferable to consider her Omri's daughter, and to construe her association with Ahab as a secondary and tendentious repudiation.

127. Cf. F. M. Cross and G. Ernest Wright, "The Boundary and Province Lists of the Kingdom of Judah," *JBL* 75 (1956), 202–226. Cf. also II Chron. 17:12–13, 19:5.

128. I Kings 22:48–49. According to Josephus (*Antiquities* IX 17) the ships were too large to be seaworthy. If this is the real reason for the wreck of the fleet, it is safe to assume that the yards were not operated by Phoenicians. Apparently, this was strictly a Judaean enterprise and when it failed, Jehoshaphat refused Israelite help; cf. I Kings 22:50 and II Chron. 20:35–37.

129. II Kings 3:4; the Mesha stele, lines 4–11; cf. Donner and Röllig [N 110], no. 181; J. C. L. Gibson, *Textbook of Syrian Semitic Inscriptions:* I, *Hebrew and Moabite Inscriptions* (Oxford, 1971), 71–83.

130. Cf. J. M. Miller, "The Elisha Cycle and the Accounts of the Omride Wars," *JBL* 85 (1966), 441–454; "The Fall of the House of Ahab," *VT* 17 (1967), 307–324; "The Rest of the Acts of Jehoahaz (I Kings 20; 22:1–38)," *ZAW* 80 (1968), 337–342; "Geshur and Aram," *JNES* 28 (1969), 60–61.

131. Cf. W. W. Hallo, "From Qarqar to Carchemish: Assyria and Israel in the Light of New Discoveries," *BA* 23 (1960), 37–39.

132. Cf. O. H. Steck, *Überlieferung und Zeitgeschichte in den Elia-Erzählungen,* Wissenschaftliche Monographien zum Alten und Neuen Testament, 26 (Neukirchen-Vluyn, 1968), 53–71; N. Avigad, "The Seal of Jezebel," *IEJ* 14 (1964), 274–276, pl. 56C; O. Eissfeldt, " 'Bist du Elia, so bin ich Isebel' (I Kön. 19:2)," *VTS* 16 (1967), 65–70.

133. Cf. Astour, "841 B.C.: The First Assyrian Invasion of Israel," *JAOS* 91 (1971), 383–389.

134. Cf. E. Lipiński, "Ba'ali Ra'ši et Ra'šu Qudšu," *RB* 78 (1971), 84–92. Ba'ali Ra'ši is located at Ras Naqura, the promontory just north of Achzib and south of Tyre.

135. II Kings 10:32–33. Cf. H. Tadmor, "The Southern Border of Aram," *IEJ* 12 (1962), 114–122.

136. Adadnirari III is commonly identified as the savior mentioned in II Kings 13:5 and alluded to in 13:23. The chronology has been complicated by the Tell al Rimah stele: cf. Page, "A Stela of Adad-nirari III and Nergal-ereš from Tell al Rimah," *Iraq* 30 (1968), 139–153; A. Cody, "A New Inscription from Tell al-Rimāḥ and King Jehoash of Israel," *CBQ* 32 (1970), 325–340. However, this inscription probably refers to the events of a "single year" rather than to his "first year"; cf. Tadmor, "A Note on the Saba'a Stele of Adad-nirari III," *IEJ* 19 (1969), 46–48. Between 805 and 803 B.C. Adadnirari was occupied in the north against Arpad, Hazazu and Ba'li. His campaign of 802 probably refers to the submission of the Chaldaeans, and the entry for this year should be read "to the Sealand" rather than "to the Sea"; Brinkman [N 13], pp. 216–217 and n. 1359. There is no evidence, therefore, for a campaign against the Aramaeans before that of 796 B.C.

137. II Kings 8:20–22; 12:17–18.

138. Cf. Cintas [N 118], 1–24, 99–242.

139. Cf. Garbini, "I Fenici in Occidente," *Studi Etruschi* 34 (1966), 111–147. Albright's contention ("The Role of the Canaanites in the History of Civilization" [N 4], p. 348) that Phoenician colonization came to a close at the end of the eighth century, and that Carthaginian influence became predominant in the west is contradicted at least by the art-historical evidence; cf. S. Moscati, "Art phénicien d'Occident," *Mélanges de l'Université Saint-Joseph* 45 (1969), 381–390, pls. 1–4; J. M. Blázquez, *Tartessos y los origenes de la colonización fenicia en Occidente* (Salamanca, 1968).

140. Cf. Aharoni, *LB*, pp. 313–315.

141. Tadmor, "Azriyau of Yaudi," *Scripta Hierosolymitana* 8 (1961), 232–271; cf. also J. Mauchline, "Implicit Signs of a Persistent Belief in the Davidic Empire," *VT* 20 (1970), 287–303.

142. Amos 1:9–10. This section, as well as the oracles against Edom and Judah, is regularly considered Deuteronomistic or exilic; cf. W. H. Schmidt, "Die deuteronomistische Redaktion des Amosbuches," *ZAW* 77 (1965), 174–178. None of the arguments, including the attempt to find a suitable historical situation, is conclusive. Thus, the oracle against Judah, as any thorough study of the language would reveal, does not contain any typically Deuteronomistic terminology. The divergence of these three from the regular structure of the oracles has a literary function, since these are the only oracles which contain a specific reference to treaty and covenant; cf. M. Fishbane, "The Treaty Background of Amos 1:11 and Related Matters," *JBL* 89 (1970), 313–318; R. B. Coote, "Amos 1:11; *rḥmyw*," *JBL* 90 (1971), 206–208.

143. Cf. *LB*, pp. 331–335; Tadmor, "The Campaigns of Sargon II of Assur: A Chronological-Historical Study," *Journal of Cuneiform Studies* 12 (1958), 22–40, 77–100; Moscati [N 2], pp. 18–23.

144. Cf. Tadmor, "Philistia under Assyrian Rule," *BA* 29 (1966), 86–102.

145. *ANET*, pp. 287, 288; Josephus *Antiquities* IX 284–287. According to Menander, Sidon and mainland Tyre were among the numerous cities that revolted from Tyre. According to the Annals of Sennacherib, Greater Sidon, Lesser Sidon, Bit-Zitti, Sarepta, Mahalliba, mainland Tyre, Achzib, and Ācco all submitted to Assyria.

146. *ANET*, pp. 290–291.

147. *ANET*, pp. 295, 297. It is not unlikely that Phoenician emigration to the western colonies accelerated rapidly at this time; cf. W. Culican, "Almuñécar, Assur and Phoenician Penetration of the Western Mediterranean," *Levant* 2 (1970), 28–36, esp. 32, 35.

148. Cf. K. M. Kenyon, "Israelite Jerusalem," *NEATC*, pp. 244–246.

149. Cf. Cross, "Judean Stamps," *EI* 9 (1969), 20–22.

150. The common opinion is that the *ktym* were Greek mercenaries, such as were garrisoned at Yabneh-Yam in the latter part of the seventh century: cf. Aharoni, "Hebrew Ostraca from Tel Arad," *IEJ* 16 (1966), 4–5; "Forerunners of the Limes:

Iron Age Fortresses in the Negev," *IEJ* 17 (1967), 14; K. S. Freedy and D. B. Redford, "The Dates in Ezekiel in Relation to Biblical, Babylonian and Egyptian Sources," *JAOS* 90 (1970), 478, n. 79.

151. Josephus *Contra Apionem* I 156–159.

152. Herodotus VII 98.

153. Sidonians and Tyrians are mentioned in Ezra 3:7; only the latter in Nehemiah 13:16. On "Hebraisms" in the early fifth century Sidonian inscriptions cf. Greenfield, "Scripture and Inscription: The Literary and Rhetorical Element in Some Early Phoenician Inscriptions," *Near Eastern Studies in Honor of William Foxwell Albright*, ed. H. Goedicke (Baltimore, 1971), pp. 258–260.

154. The ostraca from Sidon are probably to be dated to this period; cf. A. Vanel, "Six 'ostraca' phéniciens trouvés au temple d'Echmoun, près de Saïda," *Bulletin du Musée de Beyrouth* 20 (1967), 45–95, pls. 1–4; "Le septième ostracon phénicien trouvé au temple d'Echmoun, près de Saïda," *Mélanges de l'Université Saint-Joseph* 45 (1969), 345–364.

155. Cf. D. Barag, "The Effects of the Tennes Rebellion on Palestine," *BASOR* 183 (1966), 6–12. Elath should also be included in this list; cf. F. M. Cross, "Jar Inscriptions from Shiqmona," *IEJ* 18 (1968), 229, n. 22.

156. Shiqmona had a very brief occupation level starting somewhere around the middle of the century; cf. *IEJ* 19 (1969), 181–182.

157. Cf. E. Stern, "The Dating of Stratum II at Tell Abu Hawam," *IEJ* 18 (1968), 213–219.

13. *The Megiddo Stables*

YIGAEL YADIN

THE HEBREW UNIVERSITY OF JERUSALEM

G. ERNEST WRIGHT has contributed much to the solving of the intricate problems of Iron Age Megiddo; let this short note, dealing with an important aspect of Israelite Megiddo, be taken as a humble tribute in appreciation of Wright's great contributions.

Recently, J. B. Pritchard published an important article dealing with the nature of the two huge building complexes at Megiddo, Stratum IV, popularly known as "Solomon's Stables."[1] Pritchard—accepting the evidence of my excavations at Megiddo as proving that the stables (in fact the whole of Stratum IV) do not belong to Solomon's times—further suggests that these complexes be regarded not as stables but as storehouses or barracks. Thus, if Pritchard's suggestion is accepted too, the buildings are neither Solomon's nor stables. Pritchard should be congratulated on raising the issue, as the "stable" interpretation was unanimously accepted by all scholars since first put forward by P. L. O. Guy. However, it seems to me that his stimulating suggestion must, as yet, be weighed with caution. While it is true that the biblical references to Solomon's activities concerning horses influenced Guy and his colleagues in attributing the buildings to Solomon, it was the *nature* of the buildings which prompted the Megiddo excavators to identify them as stables. Pritchard raises several doubts concerning the interpretation of some architectural elements as belonging to a stable. On some of these I would like to comment:

It is true that the plan of the individual structures of the Megiddo buildings resembles very much those of the pillared buildings of Hazor VIII, Tell es-Sa'idiyeh, Beer-sheba,[2] etc. However, the similarity in itself is not decisive, since the two rows of pillars could have been a common architectural solution for large buildings whatever their functions.[3] One should mention also an additional element in the southern complex, a huge square court. This feature indicates the military nature of the building, rather than a storehouse. However, the most characteristic elements of the Megiddo structures, which do not appear in any of the other pillared buildings, are the huge, manger-like ashlar blocks found in both the northern and southern complexes. They are situated between the pillars (which in many cases have holes for tethering). It was these manger-like stones which convinced the Megiddo excavators that the buildings were indeed stables. Anyone who looks at these huge, beautifully dressed blocks, still lying on the site, cannot but come to the conclusion that there must have been a very important reason for the builders to produce these blocks; much labor and effort were invested in their production. Pritchard's main objection to the "manger" interpretation is the fact that the trough is only fifteen centimeters deep: "It is obvious that such a shallow trough—only six inches—would scarcely be the most practical container for grain or other food for a horse."[4]

On this point I should like to be more cautious. Some experts in horse breeding to whom I showed these troughs were of the opinion that this was the ideal solution to control the amount of grain, and yet not force the horses to lower their heads into a deep trough. It would be interesting to have a reaction to this problem by other experts on horse breeding. The weight of the stone (several hundred kilograms) was an additional asset, as it prevented the horses from moving the mangers and turning them over. It is also conceivable that movable wooden troughs were inserted into the depressions of the stones. Of course it could be argued that no such sophisticated mangers were used in antiquity, or that mangers were not used at all. This theoretical objection leads me to the other query of Pritchard's: "Is there evidence that horses were kept in stables and not in open enclosures?"[5] Pritchard answers this question in the negative. This is indeed a strange assertion, since even on an *a priori* assumption, we should have come to the conclusion that the highly prized animals would not have been exposed to the rain, wind, cold, and occasional snow typical of the winters in Palestine and the neighboring countries to the north.

Fortunately we do not have to speculate. There is much evidence for horses' stables, mangers, and tethering stones from el-Amarna. The subject is treated in detail by A. Badawy.[6] The following excerpts should suffice for our purpose: "stables feature a built-up manger with tethering stones on one side and a feeding passage on the opposite side, accessible from outside."[7] "The police barracks, identified as such on account of the extensive accommodation for horses . . . the entrance leads into a large central court surrounded by mangers and tethering stones with a row of deep contiguous stables on the east."[8]

It is also worth quoting Pendlebury's description of the stables in the private houses at el-Amarna: "The stables often occupy part of one side of an estate. They consist of a cobbled standing space for the horses with a tethering stone let into the ground. The square mangers are built up and behind them runs a feeding passage so that they can be filled from outside."[9] It is also interesting to compare the layout of the royal barracks at el-Amarna with the Megiddo buildings: "the great parade ground with a deep well in the middle, long cobbled stables with mangers and tethering stones to the East. . . ."[10]

Even more important to our discussion is, perhaps, the evidence from Ashurnasirpal II reliefs in Nimrud—contemporary with Megiddo Stratum IV. On one of these orthostats[11] we have a unique depiction (here *Figure 10*) of the four horses of the royal chariot within an especially installed field-stable, a pavilion supported by pillars. Two of the horses are shown eating from a manger strikingly similar in shape and dimensions to the mangers of Megiddo. The artist even emphasized the shallowness of the trough by the position of the horses' heads and necks.

The interest in this depiction lies in the fact that it indicates that even under field conditions stables were erected at least for the royal team. The shallowness of the troughs of the manger is shown on yet another Assyrian relief, from the palace of Tiglath-Pileser III.[12] Here (*Figure 11*) we see a portable and collapsible manger; its trough is very shallow and is placed on wooden legs. The trough's height from the ground is approximately like that at Megiddo.

Y. Shiloh has reminded me of the royal stable at Ugarit, partially published by C. Schaeffer.[13] Not only was a horse's bit found in this stable, but the four mangers are made of stone, and their dimensions are identical with those of Meggiddo, as indicated by Schaeffer in a letter to me, dated 20 May 1973.

In conclusion I should like to stress again the importance of Pritchard's article in casting doubts on a well-accepted theory; yet it seems to me that the above submitted evidence should caution one against rejecting the stables theory without further study. Surely the time has not yet come to declare the Megiddo stables "myths created by modern archaeology."[14]

NOTES

1. J. B. Pritchard, "The Megiddo Stables: A Reassessment," in *NEATC*, pp. 268 ff.

2. *IEJ* 20 (1970), 228.

3. Cf. Y. Shiloh, "The Four-Room House in the Israelite City," *IEJ* 20 (1970), 182.

4. Pritchard [N 1], p. 267.

5. Ibid., p. 274.

6. A. Badawy, *A History of Egyptian Architecture: The Empire* (Berkeley, 1968).

7. Ibid., p. 151.   8. Ibid., p. 125.

9. J. D. S. Pendlebury, *Tell el-Amarna* (London, 1936), p. 113.

10. Ibid., p. 41.

11. A. H. Layard, *The Monuments of Nineveh* (London, 1849), pl. 30. For a good photograph, see R. D. Barnett, *Assyrian Palace Reliefs* (London, n.d.), pl. 21.

12. [N 11], pl. 63. Cf. also Barnett and M. Falkner, *The Sculptures of Tiglath-Pileser III* (London, 1962), pl. LXIII and p. 24.

13. Cf. Schaeffer, *Syria* (1938), 313 ff.; (1939), 284; *idem, Illustrated London News* 6 Jan. 1940, p. 26, and *Ugaritica,* IV 3 (Paris, 1962), fig. 13.

14. Y. Aharoni, "A Prospectus for *The Beer-Sheba Excavations*" (Tel Aviv, 1972), p. 7. It is interesting that Aharoni tried to explain away the difference between the Solomonic defenses at Hazor and Gezer and those of Megiddo IV by the fact that Megiddo was a chariot city; *BASOR* 154 (1969), 35 ff.

14. Of Sherds and Strata:
Contributions toward an Understanding of
the Archaeology of the Divided Monarchy[1]

JOHN S. HOLLADAY, JR.

UNIVERSITY OF TORONTO

IN MANY WAYS our understanding of the basic archaeology of the period of the Divided Monarchy has progressed surprisingly little past the point to which it was advanced by G. Ernest Wright's seminal analysis of the material from the Haverford Excavations at Beth-shemesh. We have, indeed, recouped the Ahabic stables at Megiddo from King Solomon's fabled reign, and important work has been done at a great many sites over the lands of ancient Judah and Israel. Yet a basic synthesis still eludes our grasp. The final dates of the Megiddo stratification remain as shadowy as ever, controversy rages over the various destruction levels and tombs of Lachish, uncertainty besets our dating of eighth- and ninth-century remains in Judah and our control of post-722 B.C. strata in the north, while tombs and archaeological sites on the fringes of the country seem to be capable of being dated more or less according to taste. Symptomatic of the situation is the fact that, in a period in which historical events are debated in terms of years, the archaeological "controls" often can be debated in terms of more than a century. That this ought not to be is obvious. Generally accepted dates for individual strata do exist, and others presumably can be hammered out. Yet the fact remains that the major authority on the ancient pottery of the Holy Land, working with only slightly fewer materials than those presently available, could find cause in 1964 to divide the pottery of the period of the Divided Monarchy only four ways: one division being chronological, at about 800 B.C.; and the other being geographical, into "northern" and "southern" traditions.[2]

As in many fields of study, only a little more information helps to turn the scales decisively. And while only a relatively little new information has indeed been published since 1964, that information has been pivotal. Additionally, a change of perspective with regard to the character of ceramic deposits has gradually come about through the introduction of new techniques of field investigation, starting with Kathleen Kenyon's work at Jericho. This combination of just a little new, but well-dated pottery plus a deepened understanding of the differing chronological implications of various types of archaeological deposits now make it possible to attempt a synthesis of Palestinian ceramic chronology which was simply unattainable a decade ago.

THE THEORETICAL BASIS OF THE INVESTIGATION

No period in the history of Palestine has better archaeological attestation than the early sixth century B.C. The relentless advance of the Babylon army in 597 B.C. and its ruthless campaign of destruction and deportation following the ill-fated nationalist movement under Zedekiah not only produced great layers of sealed destruction debris at every Judaean settlement of note but ensured that the bulk of this debris would remain untouched by rebuilding efforts of any survivors, so that neither the usual programs of wholesale clearance and restoration or casual squatter reoccupation could take their toll of the archaeological evidence. Thus, almost every occupied Judaean city or village acquired the character of an archaeologically sealed destruction deposit, and when most sites were reoccupied, the ceramic and other items in the material-culture complexes of the succeeding Persian and Hellenistic periods were sufficiently distinctive so that most later intrusive elements can be identified at a glance. Two recently excavated strata in particular, En Gedi V and Ramat Raḥel VA, stand out in this context. Each was built at the very end of the Judaean monarchy, and each suffered massive destruction at the hands of the Babylonians. Thus, at neither site are the outlines of the ceramic typology of the period ca. 609–587 B.C. blurred or distorted by significant quantities of either earlier or later materials.[3]

From the standpoint of studies in ceramic chronology, there is a special character to corpora of pottery stemming from well-sealed destruction deposits which sets them off from other chronologically significant assemblages such as groups from cisterns, tomb groups, midden deposits, or sealed earthen fills. Particularly for the period in question, and probably for most others as well, this distinctiveness lies in the great homogeneity of the materials. In striking contrast to the broad variety of bowls, jugs, and other types of pottery for which we have witness in the typical plates of any given stratum at continuously occupied sites such as Megiddo (Str. IV–II) or Hazor (Str. X–VI), Judaean deposits of the early sixth century B.C. are regular and strictly limited in terms of typical forms, colors, and decoration. They generally are so predictable as to be uninteresting.[4] Nor does this uniformity appear to be merely a lack of creative impulse on the part of the late seventh/early sixth-century potter, but a characteristic of sealed, simultaneously destroyed deposits in general. The 725 B.C. destructions at Shechem and Tell el-Far'ah (N) have exactly the same repetitive, monotonous character, as do some 90 per cent of the items figured in the Stratum V plates in *Hazor I–IV* and Samaria Pottery Period VI, all witnesses to similar destructions in the third quarter of the eighth century B.C.

Upon reflection, the reasons for this are clear. Pottery forms naturally evolved over a period of time, producing deposits of much richer variety of form in situations where the work of successive generations of potters would be preserved in a diachronic sequence, i.e. in successions of sealed fills, midden heaps, family tombs, and cisterns. But at any one period in history the range of forms available to the local householder must have been infinitely more limited. Even the most casual inspection of a modern sales exhibit of "kitchen pottery" in any Middle or Far Eastern country should serve to drive home the point. Local potters produce items designed to fill specific "ecological niches" in the material-culture complex of their immediate village or trading area. As a general rule, one potter produces only one item for each "niche" or else produces only a limited range of items. Tradition and availability of materials combine to limit the number and character of forms produced in any one atelier. Other workshops in the surrounding area, using different clays or techniques, may seek to expand their market through export to neighboring cities, while local villages may from time to time depend upon importations of job lots for the bulk of their purchases, with local merchants carrying over remnants of these lots for sale during the intervening period. Nor is this mere hypothetical reconstruction. The writer has witnessed exactly this pattern in traditional villages and towns in Turkey (shipment by trucks, ox carts, and camel trains), Jordan (truck transport), and Egypt (middlemen on large fellukas selling tightly packed cargoes of heavily built medium-red deep bowls and jars, complementary to locally produced off-white, thinner wares sold at one or two exhibitions in one or two quarters of the city).[5]

The above observations both support and contradict traditional practices of dating by ceramic parallels. On the one hand, the often repeated claim that "ninety per cent of the pottery from a given stratum comes from its last ten years" certainly holds true for destruction deposits. In fact, the present writer would prefer to say that, if only items stemming from the actual destruction levels could be isolated from the stratification, and if all post-destructional fills and intrusions were recognized and separately treated in both the field processing and the publication, probably something like 98 per cent of the restorable forms should date to the last ten or fifteen years of the city's life. The life of the average clay pot in daily use is not long. If, on the other hand, post-destruction intrusions and pre-destruction fills and midden deposits cannot be segregated, then the materials from that particular "stratum" obviously come from such a broad and uncertain chronological period or set of periods as to make them of qualitatively different worth as chronological determinants to those from sealed destruction deposits.

This does not mean that tomb groups, midden deposits, carefully isolated fills, or even casually excavated "strata" are of no chronological value. But it does mean that they are completely different from and of a less precise order of worth as chronological determinants than groups which can be identified as simultaneous in their occurrence. Much of the chronological confusion apparent in the archaeological literature has its roots precisely in this failure to distinguish between these quite different orders of ceramic evidence.

Tomb groups may be of longer or shorter chronological duration. Frequently objects from totally different archaeological periods are found in the same tomb group. Nor do most tomb deposits, not to mention clearance procedures, allow one to distinguish between successive burials of different periods. In short, tomb groups depend for their definition upon stratigraphically derived typology, and the incautious use of tomb materials in establishing absolute dates poses more problems than it solves. Unfortunately, for some periods or localities, tomb groups constitute the only available evidence.

Midden deposits, silo groups, and *rubbish pits* are of a different order entirely, and their usefulness depends upon the sharpness of the excavator's powers of observation: How do these deposits relate to observed earth layers, i.e. to balk-controlled stratigraphy? Are the contents more or less simultaneously deposited, or are they gradual accumulations over a period of years? Can one distinguish between the primary deposit in a pit or silo and the leveling fill with its associated items? Properly observed, excavated, presented, and analyzed, these groups present a number of different sorts of chronologically significant data.

Imported fills are of yet another order of usefulness. Generally unrecognized and confused with earlier occupational deposits in traditional "stratigraphically" excavated sites, their utility is nonetheless very great, as Principal Kenyon proved in her programmatic treatment of the Iron Age and Hellenistic pottery from Samaria. And, although many of the published results are still in the offing, substantial gains in ceramic chronology have been made through the utilization of these materials by pupils both of Principal Kenyon and especially Professor Wright, whose modified application of the Wheeler-Kenyon techniques at Tell Balaṭah provided a training ground from which two generations of younger field archaeologists have emerged.[6,7] For the purposes of the present study all that needs to be said about imported fills is that (if properly isolated and excavated) sub-floor fills or other "sealed" fills contain materials earlier than the constructional phase of features by which they are sealed.[8] A stratified series of fills, for example, beneath successive floors or buildings at a particular site may yield chronological information of a relatively high order, but in few cases can the entire ceramic contents of a fill be unequivocally equated with the culture complex either of the preceding or succeeding building periods. A case in point is the survival, long past their time, of quantities of early ninth-century (and earlier?) cooking pot rims together with one typically late eighth-century cooking pot rim in Samaria "Period IV."[9]

In the absence of stratigraphically isolated occupation or destruction deposits showing pottery forms extant at any one time or during any given period, one can say little about the duration or variety of forms present in any one archaeological period attested only in terms of imported fills. At any given site, so much of any particular fill may be comprised of material excavated from a sufficiently earlier stratum that the result could be totally misleading.[10] Even more misleading, however, would be a sub-floor fill comprised of materials uniformly only fifty to seventy-five years earlier than the associated structure. In this case, lacking closely dated, simultaneously destroyed groups with which to control the analysis, the typologist could only speculate about the degree of chronological relationship between sub-floor and above-floor deposits.[11]

A caveat: in the above discussion it has been assumed that, contrary to the practice of most excavations in the published literature, all intrusions, pits, graves, caches, have been recognized and related to their proper stratigraphic context by the excavator. At present, however, it seems only honest to admit that no excavator has successfully identified *all* such intrusions. To be sure, some, either by virtue of habits of observation and close control of the actual digging process and/or by the close application of techniques designed expressly to facilitate such recognition, are better than others. And the consistency of materials relating to any given stratum, fill, etc. in the plates of their publications often stands in striking contrast to the stratigraphic confusion evident in the published results of other sites. Nevertheless, even with the very best of excavations, a certain amount of negative feedback must be employed to overcome the effects of unavoidable contamination of the basic data.

Unless one postulates specialized trade relationships, tomb robbing, antique collecting by the ancients, one potter a hundred years ahead of his time, or the like, it simply does not make sense for 99 per cent of the evidence to point to one conclusion while 1 per cent points toward another. In the case of the Samaria Pottery Period IV fill referred to above, it is not reasonable to suggest that tenth/ninth-century cooking pots were still being used in the eighth century. Nor were distinctively new vessel ware-form modes developed and used in minuscule quantities in one or two individual homes a hundred or more years ahead of their general use in the rest of the country. A case in point for the latter observation would be the curious presence of two high-based lamps in a "Stratum VA" context (Locus 3146) at Hazor.[12] Both

Tufnell and Aharoni have argued, and with some reason, that this lamp form does not come into being in the south until the period exemplified by Lachish Stratum II. Since the form is not attested in Lachish Stratum III, the terminal date of which can no longer be placed before 609 at the earliest and in all probability dates to 597 B.C. (see below), nor is it encountered in any other well-attested context prior to the late seventh or early sixth century, it is highly unlikely that its presence in this one locus from Hazor represents a genuine eighth-century occurrence of the form. Similar illustrations could be multiplied from any adequately published site.[13] In short, the more we know of a period, the more we can say with certainty which forms truly belong in groups attributed to that period and which are there accidentally, either "persisting" in fills or "intrusive" in pits and foundation trenches. Certainly it is far from proper analytic technique to support a weak hypothesis (e.g. a possible eighth-century dating of some other site) by reference to uncritically assessed parallels (the two lone high-based lamp examples from Hazor). By the same line of reasoning, i.e. by citing evidence from Tell Abu Hawam "Stratum III," one could argue that the immediate forebear of this most distinctive and ubiquitous early sixth-century lamp actually had its genesis prior to Shishak's 918 B.C. raid upon Palestine,[14] but that the form somehow managed not to come into commercial production until more than 250 years later. Alternatively, one could seek to bring the entire Tell Abu Hawam Stratum III grouping down to a lower date on the basis of the presence in published material attributed to that stratum of a very few easily recognized, but intrusive vessels.[15]

The foregoing analysis eventuates in three general observations and two proposed terminological distinctions which we will seek to apply to the refinement of the ceramic chronology of seventh/sixth-century Palestine.

1. Dating by ceramic parallels must proceed on the basis of sufficiently and securely dated materials of common and sufficiently widespread occurrence so that their chronological attribution is not open to serious question. Isolated "earliest occurrences" and "late survivals" may occasionally represent a historical reality, but in the absence of overwhelming evidence to the contrary, these isolated examples cannot be taken seriously for the purposes of establishing the framework of a ceramic chronology. In a mass-produced, utilitarian item, one should not expect to find anachronisms. Nor do securely stratified materials often produce evidence suggestive of anachronisms.

2. Midden heaps and stratified fills, or successive layers of occupational accumulation (probably including localized areas of imported fill) i.e. the typical "stratum" of most excavation reports, produce random examples of ceramics of several different "product-years." Thus, the pottery forms are those of a certain diachronistic period, together with earlier materials persisting in fills, and should be so designated. For this class of data, the writer has proposed the term "period" pottery.[16] That is, pottery from the *period*

of duration of the stratum in question. Assuming a constant feeding back of information regarding the typical constituents of the stratum so as to eliminate—or at least bracket—earlier fragments persisting in fills and late intrusive elements not recognized as such during the actual excavation process, materials of this sort form the bulk of our presently available data for many periods of Palestinian history. Normally ceramic remains in this category would be *expected* to be more fragmentary than those from destruction groups, and more variable in form and decoration—in direct proportion to the length of duration of the stratum. For close dating purposes the value of "period" remains varies considerably, but is inevitably less than ideal. This factor must always be considered when evaluating proposed datings based on parallels with such materials. Tomb and cistern groups likewise are varied and uncertain in terms of their absolute dating, generally cover a span of time (i.e. are "period" groups), and should always be utilized in combination with stratigraphically attested materials if these are at all available.

3. Pottery groups consisting of in-use pottery simultaneously destroyed at the time of a sudden catastrophe offer the only certain evidence as to the standard repertory of the pottery in use at any given point in time and should, for this reason, receive special designation. For this category of pottery, which can be extended (again assuming proper vetting of the data to eliminate later intrusions, stratigraphic misattribution of certain loci, squatter reoccupation, etc.) to cover most of the restorable pottery of strata terminated by violent destruction, the writer has proposed the use of the term "horizon," e.g. pottery of the 918, 733, 722, 597, and 587 B.C. horizons.[17] Pottery of this class is characterized by a relatively limited number of common forms (cf. the repetitiousness of the plates of Ramat Raḥel Str. VA, and En Gedi Str. V). It is significant that differences between various sites exhibiting destruction layers of the same horizon tend to be much less evident than between published "period" groups of similar periods.

PALESTINIAN CERAMIC CHRONOLOGY OF THE SEVENTH
TO EARLY SIXTH CENTURIES B.C.

During the past several decades there has been a growing tendency to separate the ceramic chronology of the south from that of the north during the course of the late eighth through early sixth centuries. The basic concept of this division seems to have been that of W. F. Albright,[18] who was followed in this respect by J. C. Wampler.[19] More recently, this understanding of the data was restated in Aharoni and Amiran's widely accepted joint article, "A New Scheme for the Sub-Division of the Iron Age in Palestine[20] and presented in a full, though not strongly argued, fashion in Mrs. Amiran's invaluable *Ancient Pottery of the Holy Land.*[21]

The appeal of this "northern"/"southern" theory, as we may term it, lies in its ability to account for the observed distribution patterns of a great many distinctive ceramic forms—e.g. a northern distribution for the double-rimmed, unburnished decanter, a southern distribution for the single-rimmed, ring-burnished "southern" decanter;[22] a northern distribution for the simple, unburnished saucer form, a southern distribution for the wheel-burnished "southern" sauce;[23] etc. The elegance of the explanation, however, is flawed by its failure to deal seriously with any possible alternative explanations for the phenomena in question. Nor are all the available data taken into consideration in the formulation of this theory. In lumping together, for the most part, all ceramic materials from ca. 800 B.C. to the early sixth century, the analysis in fact begs the question of whether these observed distinctions are actually geographical or chronological.

The stratigraphical/chronological facts are remarkably clear. At the present time, there are no published southern (Judaean) sites with strata dating to the eighth or first half of the seventh century B.C.[24] On the other hand, the pottery assemblages characterized as typically "northern" stem, for the most part, from sites with major datable stratification ending either around the last quarter of the eighth century or at some slightly later indeterminate period.[25]

Thus, even at this stage of analysis it seems reasonable to suggest that "northern" eighth-century assemblages should, in point of fact, be more suggestive of what might be expected from "southern" sites of the same period than theoretical extrapolations from Judaean sites of the late seventh/early sixth centuries. Certainly it would seem odd if such closely interrelated cultures as ninth- and eighth-century Judah and Israel did not reflect this interrelatedness as well in their material cultures. Prior to the Syro-Ephraimitic War, there is no reason to suppose that Judaean pottery differed radically from that of the north, and good reason to assume that it was very similar, though local differences may have appeared from time to time in certain categories of ware. But, while Israelite pottery of the 733 and 725–722 B.C. horizons is well known, we simply do not know enough of the pottery of eighth-century Judah to test this hypothesis.[26]

On the other hand, the ceramic repertory of very closely dated Judaean sites of the late seventh/early sixth centuries is not only well known, thanks in great measure to Prof. Aharoni's excavations at Ramat Raḥel and Profs. Mazar, T. Dothan and I. Dunayevsky's excavations at En Gedi (Tell el-Jurn/Tel Goren), but a considerable quantity of post-733–722 B.C. material from "northern" and "Trans-Jordanian" sites has been published. While the absolute dates of most of these northern strata and Trans-Jordanian groups are a matter of scholarly dispute, it would seem at least possible to test the parallel hypothesis that *"Judaean" ceramic indices of the late seventh/*

early sixth centuries B.C. *may give some indication of similarly dated materials in the north.*[27]

The final results of an extensive analysis of this material are presented in Chart 1 below. Twenty-one typical late seventh- to early sixth-century "southern" forms were selected on the basis of their regular occurrence in three main sites: Ramat Raḥel Stratum VA (post-609 to 587?), with the bulk of the restorable pottery coming from the last decade of that period;[28] En Gedi (Tell Goren) Stratum V (bulk of restorable material dating to 587 B.C.),[29] Lachish Strata III and II (dated either to 609 and 587 B.C. or, more plausibly, 597 and 587 B.C. respectively).[30] It must be emphasized that none of these forms is characteristic of critically analyzed 733–722 B.C. horizon "northern" strata. To these was added, as a test element, the so-called "northern decanter," well-attested in 733–722 B.C. stratification. Occurrences of these twenty-two forms were then noted in analyzing published materials from virtually every published Palestinian and Trans-Jordanian site. The results of this preliminary analysis cannot, for reasons of space, be given here, but they furnished clear proof of the regular appearance of all of the "southern" test forms in northern and Trans-Jordanian Iron Age II contexts.

In the interpretation of this particular aspect of the study it is important to note that, although some indication of the quantity of items relating to any given vessel form at a particualr site might be inferred from the quantity of published examples, the mode of analysis is basically a "presence/absence" testing of the data. As long as the constituent types are clearly defined and well separated from similar—but chronologically distinct—forms, the study of all but the three type-sites is completely independent of stratigraphic attributions or the claimed dates of individual excavators. And since examples of all but one of the twenty-one basic forms appear in at least two of the type-sites, a strong internal control is established over the test forms as well. Occasional misinterpretations of forms from published drawings or descriptions, while probably inevitable, or at least open to debate, in no way detract from the cumulative weight of the evidence as a whole.

The reasoning behind this analysis can be outlined as follows:

a) *If* a–n occur in early sixth-century destruction levels in the south

b) *and* if these materials do not appear in stratigraphically assured 733–722 destruction levels in the north

c) *then* occurrences of a–n or a large proportion of these types in any other loci, whether southern or northern, should indicate roughly synchronous late seventh–early sixth-century deposits.[31]

d) A strongly skewed distribution of certain forms (e.g. a site with quantities of "a," "k," and "n" but no "b–j" or "l–m") probably should become the occasion for special investigation to determine whether this reflects (1) the earlier pre-597 development of that

	Ramat Raḥel	En Gedi	Tell Beit Mirsim	Beth-shemesh	Lachish	Beth Shan	Bethel	Tell el-Far'ah (N)	Hazor	Megiddo	Samaria	Shechem
"Assyrian" bowls	VA	V		T.5	? T.1002 / ? T.218 / ? T.224					III	PP VI* / PP VII	VI
"Rice Bowls"	VA,B	V & Clark	A2	II b / Ts. 2, 8 / Rep. T. 7	III / II		"Iron II"	I	?IV	IV-II	PP VII	do.
Burnished saucers	do.	do.	do.	?Ts. 5,7,8 / ?Rep. T.2	do.	do.	do.	do.	VIII-IV	III-II	do.	do.
Curved rim bowls	VA	V	A2	?II / ?T.7 / II b	?III	? Level IV	? "6th c."	do.	?IV / VI		PP IV* / E 207 / Qz, Qy	do.
"Half moon" rim bowls	VA	V	A1 / A2	?II / Rep.T.7 / Ts. 2, 5-8	III / II	Level IV	"Iron II" / "6th c."	do.	V, / IV	III-I	PP VIII	do.
Large handled bowls (A)	? VA,B	? V	? A2	II a-b / II b	do.		do.	do.			do.	do.
Large handled bowls (B)	VA,B	V	A2	II b-c / II b-c	do.	? Level IV	? "Iron II" / ? "6th c."	do.	? VI	III	do.	do.
"Judaean" c-pots	VA ? / VB	V & Clark	do.	II c, Rep. / II c; Rep. / T.2;Ts.5,7,8	do.		"Iron II"	do.	? V		? PP VII / ?PP VIII	do.
Flared-rim c-pots	VA	V	? A2	II	II		? "Iron II"	do.	VA	I	? PP VII / ?PP VIII	? V
Handleless necked jars	do.	do.	? A2		T.106		? "L.B."	do.			? PP VIII	"V" ? (VI prob.)

H-mouth jars, wide rim	do.	do.	A2	II b-c, IIc	III, II		"6th c."			IV filling, IV-I	PP V?, PP VIII	VI
Bag-shaped jars	do.	do.	do.		II						PP VIII	
Four handled jars ($\simeq$ lmlk)	VA,B	do.	do.	II b-c, IIc	III, II?		do.		III	II, III-II, II,1	E 207, Z deep pit, Qn	do.
"Neckless" jars	VA	V, IV	do.	T.14	III		do.		II	III, II	PP VII	do.
Pointed bottles	Pit 48<	V, IV	do.	T.218	T.106	Level IV	"Iron II"	III, "Fer II"	VA	III, II	E 207	VI
"Phoenician" juglets, a-c	VA	V	do.	IIc. Ts.1,2,7,8 Rep.T.8	II		do.	III, "Fer II"	VA	III, II	E 207	do.
"One-handled" jugs	?Va	Clark	do.	IIc. Ts.1,2,7,8 Rep.T.8	III				V	III, III-II, II,1	E 207, Z deep pit, Qn	
"Red Jugs"	VA	V		Rep.T.8	T.106, T.1010		"6th c."		?VI			
"Northern" decanters				II a-b, b-c Rep.Ts.2,8		do.	do.	II	VII, VI, VB,VA	IV filling, IV, III	PP VI+, Z deep pit, E 207, Qn	VII
"Southern" decanters	do.	do.	do.	IIc. Ts.2-8,14 Rep.T.2,8	III, II		"Iron II", "6th c."	I	VI, V,VA, IV	II, T.219	E 207	VI
"Low-based" lamps	VA,B	V, Clark	do.	IIc. Rep.Ts.2,7,8 Ts.2,5-8	II		"6th c."		VA	III	Dj	VI, "V"?
"High-based" lamps	do.	do.	do.	IIc, T.14, Rep.Ts.2,4 Ts.2,6-8	II		do.	do.	VA	III		

form, (2) regional influences, (3) selectivity in publication, (4) relatively greater local utilization of that form, or (5) some other factor.

One of the drawbacks of the presence/absence/rough quantification mode of analysis undertaken as the preliminary stage of the investigation was that the stratigraphic attribution of the various occurrences of the forms under analysis was deliberately ignored, and, in the space limitations of the present article, it would not be possible to document the stratigraphic affinities of the thousands of references. Yet, if the preliminary inference suggested by that analysis was that the commonly held "northern"/"southern" dichotomy of ceramic forms in fact represents primarily a *chronological* rather than *geopolitical* distinction, it necessarily follows that great interest attaches to the actual stratigraphic attribution of each "southern" or seventh/sixth-century item witnessed in "northern" stratification. A concomitant of this focusing upon actual stratigraphic attribution is that interest centers only on published sites with adequately observed stratification. Thus the initially all-encompassing investigation narrows down to the relatively small number of northern and southern sites analyzed in Chart 1, the documentation of which is presented in the appendix to the present article.

Abbreviations and Conventions

c-pots	cooking pots
do.	*ditto*
H-mouth jars	Hole-mouth jars
PP	Pottery Period (Samaria)
Rep. T.(s)	Repository of Tomb(s)
*	intrusive?
~ *lmlk*	jars similar to (and including) typical *lmlk*-stamped wine jars
? . . .	indicates some doubt on the part of the writer that the vessel cited is actually of the type under analysis
. . . ?	indicates some doubt as to the actual stratigraphic separation.

In the light of the methodological considerations outlined above (pp. 258–259) some observations must be made concerning specific sites analyzed in Chart 1.

1) *Ramat Raḥel:* No pottery forms are illustrated which, in my opinion, would indicate occupation prior to the last quarter of the seventh century. This judgment would include all published sub-floor fills and "Stratum VB" materials with the possible exception of *RR* II, fig. 35:10.

2) *En Gedi:* The Tell Goren Stratum V materials seem to reflect destruction materials of the 587 horizon, equalling Lachish II (and the latest Lachish tomb deposits) in almost every respect.[32] Together with carefully

selected Lachish II materials, and Ramat Raḥel VA, these pottery forms should furnish the type-series to test for materials of this horizon. Note particularly the presence at Ramat Raḥel and En Gedi of such late forms as "Red Jugs," pre-Hellenistic "Bag-shaped Jars" and flattened flared-rim cooking pots as well as the distinctively ridged thin-ware sub-type of the rilled-rim "Judaean" ["deep"] cooking pot, all lacking in reasonably secure Lachish III stratification.[33] The almost total absence of the ubiquitous earlier "one-handled" wide-mouthed jug in these strata is also noteworthy, especially in view of its prominence in Lachish Stratum III.

The *Clark Collection* vessels from En Gedi, on the other hand, clearly exhibit "period" characteristics stretching from the 587 B.C. horizon[34] back at least to the 597 horizon, although with the exception of the tenth/ninth-century forms of *'Atiqot* V, fig. 32:3 (and 4?) the present writer sees no forms he would regard as significantly earlier than ca. 609–600 B.C.[35]

3) *Tell Beit Mirsim:* The "stratigraphic" nature of the excavations makes control of this material equally as difficult as that from most other similarly excavated sites, but items characteristic of the 587 B.C. horizon are conspicuously absent, or else present only in very limited quantities (high-based lamps [?] of sub-standard type). In view of the great quantity of published material this is surely indicative of, at best, a very minor "squatter" reoccupation following 597 B.C. The great majority of published (drawn) items from Stratum A2 correspond fully with 597 "horizon" categories as these are defined by Lachish Stratum III, but some vessels betray eighth-century and even earlier characteristics, indicating at least some mixing of 597 destruction-loci with earlier materials, probably including a 701 B.C. horizon and stray items derived from fills. As would be expected, the sherd materials illustrated by photographic plates appear much more heterogeneous than the drawn, intact or reconstructed forms, suggesting "persistence" of earlier materials in imported fills.

4) *Beth-shemesh:* Only Wright's exceptional gifts as a ceramic typologist saved the publication of the stratified material from this site from total chaos. Even within "rooms," recent materials make it easy to distinguish intrusive elements. The writer's impressions of the horizon materials present in the published materials are indicated in Chart 3, but the picture is made much more complex by the undoubted presence of considerable amounts of "period" pottery falling between the main horizons.

Tomb 1, as Wright noted already in 1939, consists largely of pottery covering the period of the late tenth to early ninth century (Wright's "Str. IIb"),[36] but materials from the eighth (?) century[37] and (middle ?) seventh century are also present.[38] Pottery from the repository of Tomb 2 now appears so close to the Clark Collection materials from En Gedi that its attribution to the period stretching from the late seventh century into the first decade of the sixth century seems automatic, while sufficient quantities of "Red Jugs," high-based lamps and flat flared-rim cooking pots serve to indicate continued use of Tombs 2–8 down to the end of Stratum IIc and the final destruction of the Judaean state.[39] The date of Tomb 14 must be settled by further advances in the ceramic indices of the early "Persian Period" but, as Wright noted, it continues so many early sixth-century ceramic traditions that it is difficult to date its beginning phase much after ca. 575–550 B.C., with no obvious necessity for the group as a whole to extend beyond 500 B.C.[40]

5) *Lachish:* It is impossible within the confines of this study adequately to discuss the complexities of establishing even relatively sure criteria for the separation of Strata III and II loci. The Bastion area contains so many later intrusive elements as to limit its usefulness as a primary source, but relatively secure Stratum II loci founded on burned Stratum III brick debris including Loci 1019, 1059, 1060 (?), 1064, 1067 (with caution), 1068 (do.), 1069, Pit 1074, 1075 (?) and 1077 seem to offer the best opportunity of isolating typically 587 horizon materials, although the excavators' tendency to include sub-floor materials and items from stratigraphically ambiguous loci considerably clouds the investigation. At the suggestion of Prof. Aharoni, who has long supported Miss Tufnell in her dating of Lachish Stratum III to the end of the eighth century, the writer has carefully reviewed the entire ceramic repertory of even reasonably secure Strata III and II loci, and found very few differences indeed, certainly nothing that could not be attributed to a ten-year development period following the nation-wide shock of a massive destruction and the local stimulus of the resettlement of many sites, including Lachish. The difference between Lachish Stratum III pottery and that of known 733 and 725–722 B.C. horizons from the northern sites is, however, marked and general throughout the repertory. On the other hand, with very few exceptions, differences between Lachish Strata III and II appear only after long and patient study. In Stratum III, examples of the late eighth-century shallow cooking pot persist in modified form,[41] but are being replaced with a more flaring rim of the same general type.[42] A special high-necked form seems characteristic of a brief period just prior to the III destruction.[43] In Stratum II the flat, flared-rim (often notched) becomes the dominant "shallow" cooking pot rim-form mode. It is, however, but an exaggerated modification of the earlier flaring thickened rim, perhaps serving better as a lid-device. "One-handled" wide-mouth jugs are common in III loci, but seem to be replaced by the very distinct, but related, "Red Jug" series in post-597 B.C. contexts. In Stratum II the smaller high-based, poorly flanged lamp emerges, partially (?) replacing the larger, well-flanged "shallow disc base" lamp.[44] None of these differences is very marked, however, and others which might be hazarded are even less distinctive. In fact, the "Red Jug" seems to

be the only really new form, with the others simply representing the unfolding of evolutionary tendencies along lines already laid down in Stratum III. Certainly, from a purely ceramic point of view, no hundred years is required to account for such small changes. Nor, as has often been noted, is the miserable domestic architecture of Stratum II indicative of a century of growth and rebuilding, while the bastion rebuilding is more than adequately accounted for by the events of 592–587 B.C. In any event, the brilliant and incisive work of H. Darrell Lance in analyzing the find spots of the Type III stamped jar handles from Lachish and his remarks on the III–II stratigraphic relationships have, in the writer's opinion, settled the vexed matter once and for all.[45] Henceforth the burden of proof is on anyone who wants to argue an earlier date and the demonstration will have to assume as its first order of business the carrying back of the entire series of royal stamped jar handles into the eighth century.

6) *Beth Shan:* As Mrs. James has conclusively demonstrated, this site was finally destroyed in the late eighth century, probably either at 733 B.C. or with the 721 B.C. deportations.[46] An exceedingly low level of casual squatter occupation would account for all subsequent Iron Age remains.

7) *Bethel* may have been within the orbit of Judah during the reign of Josiah, but there is no good evidence for this, and, as Lance indicates, neither the biblical nor the archaeological evidence favors such a view.[47] Taken together with Hazor, Tell el-Far'ah (N), Shechem, and Samaria, the amount of "southern" material at Bethel in no way stands out. All alike either have "southern" *and* seventh/sixth-century components or they simply have seventh/sixth-century occupation.[48]

8) The striking limitation of clearly defined late seventh/early sixth-century materials in the north to these two pottery periods at Samaria, one squatter stratum at Shechem and one limited stratum of a similarly ephemeral nature at Tell el-Far'ah (N) in contrast to the situation at Megiddo and Hazor calls for comment. The first two sites were excavated following the Wheeler-Kenyon techniques of observed earth-layers and closely defined locus groupings. At Tell el-Far'ah, de Vaux found a well-defined though disturbed reoccupation stratum overlying his coherent (ca. 725 B.C.) "niv. 2" stratum, the upper stratum, "niv. 1," being clearly set off from the earlier one by a heavy layer of ashes.[49] Here, conventional "stratigraphic" techniques, coupled with de Vaux's very powerful ceramic instincts, proved adequate to the task of stripping off the "stratum."[50]

9) At *Hazor* and *Megiddo,* the situation seems rather different from that described in (8) above. At Megiddo, a relatively limited number of late seventh/early sixth-century forms appear consistently in locus groupings of forms otherwise known primarily from eighth-century deposits. Mostly these items appear as clear intrusions into Stratum IV loci, or in hardly less clearly intrusive association with the predominantly late eighth-century

Stratum III horizon materials or slightly later "Stratum II" (period ?) groupings, the bulk of whose associations still are with eighth-century forms. Either these late forms represent the final horizon materials from the destruction of a small Stratum II community, which seems unlikely, or they represent squatters' occupation of II and III remains, with some intrusions penetrating down to the earlier Stratum IV layer. Needless to say, the excavation and recording techniques employed at Megiddo would have been unable to make the separation. At Hazor, coherent general stratification begins only with Stratum III with II reuse (Area B), or Stratum IV (Area A).[51] Lacking sufficiently distinctive stratigraphic separation of many loci and utilizing the "stratigraphic" technique of excavation,[52] the excavators' inclusion of a certain amount of intrusive later material in Strata IV, V, and even "VI" locus groups would be inevitable. This seems to be what we find portrayed in the tabulation. The series "VII, VI, VB, VA" for the eighth-century "northern decanter" versus the seventh-century "southern decanter" "VI, V, VA, IV" series is instructive, and, coupled with the relatively small number and scattered location of the majority of the "southern" forms, well illustrates the point.

CONCLUSIONS

The hypothesis that securely dated "Judaean" materials of the 597–587 B.C. horizons may be used to identify similarly dated materials in northern Palestinian sites is confirmed by the appearance of substantial quantities of most forms and some quantities of all forms in northern strata generally regarded as seventh century,[53] late seventh century,[54] and strata whether attributed to the late eighth–seventh centuries or open to intrusions from the late seventh/early sixth centuries B.C.[55]

STRATIGRAPHY OF THE PERIOD OF THE DIVIDED MONARCHY

The analysis that follows (in Chart 3 below) is based upon (a) the results of an intensive stratigraphic, historical, and typological re-examination of four stratified Israelite sites: Tell el-Farʻah (N), Hazor, Samaria, and the unpublished Iron II materials from Shechem (see Chart 2 below); (b) the materials and perspective presented in the preceding sections of the present article; (c) an intensive re-examination of the Megiddo Iron II materials in the light of "a" and "b" above, since, given the usual dating of Strata IV–II, the ceramic repertory of this site alone seemed to be in conflict with the emerging picture of ceramic developments during the late eighth to early sixth centuries B.C. The key stratification and assigned destruction or closing dates for the period 918–722 B.C. are as follows:[56]

Chart 2

Samaria	Tell el-Far'ah (N)*	Hazor*	Shechem
	Niv. III (elements) 918†	X 918	
		IX ca. 880	
PP I ca. 860	*Niv.* III (elements) ca. 860		Str. IXʙ 860
PPs II & III ca. 842	*Niv.* intermédiaire ca. 840	VIII ca. 841	
			Str. IXᴀ ca. 810
		VI ca. 760	
PP V ca. 745 or 735		Vʙ ca. 745	Str. VIII ca. 745
		Vᴀ 733	
PP VI ca. 722	*Niv.* II 723		Str. VII ca. 724

* Utilizing critically selected loci only.   † All dates are B.C.

Abbreviations
PP   Pottery Period (Samaria)
Niv.   Niveau

Chart 3.   Stratigraphy of the Perio[d]

Date	Hazor	T. Abu Hawam	Ein Gev	Megiddo	Taanach	Tell 'Amal	Beth Shan	Tell el Far'ah (N.)	Samaria	Shechem	Tell Qasile	Bethel	Gezer	Tell en-Nasbeh
950	X	III		VA/IVB	"Cultic Structure"	III	Lower V	III[B]	elements	XI?	IX,1 [some earlier mtls.]		VIII	
918	XI		V							X?			VII	Ts. 32, 54
ca. 880					occupation						VIII [918 B.C. mtls. in published pottery]			
ca. 860	VIII		IV			II?	Upper V ? ?	III[A]	PP I	IXB				?
							Niv. interméd.							
842 / ca. 840	VII		III					PP II 842		VII[2] ?			
ca. 810			II						PP II	IXA	VII[1] ?	scattered elements		T.32
ca. 810										ca. 810			VI[B]	T.5
ca. 760 VB	VI							PP IV						
ca. 745 VA				IVA		I?	IV	PP V ? — ?	VIII ca. 745				scattered elements
733 / 722				III		? = ?		II PP VI	VII			[or] ?	
	IV		I				squatters	E207			2 ostraca		
ca. 680				II?					PP VII				VI[A] ?	T.5
III					occupation					VI				
ca. 645		squatter occupation?	?	squatter occupation				PP VII					
609		slight occupation					I ? ?	PP VIII		lamp	elements		
597													
587										?		?	V

Abbreviations and Conventions

Clark Coll. mtls.	Clark Collection materials	*Niv. interméd.* PP	niveau intermédiaire Pottery Period

Divided Monarchy (ca. 922-587 B.C.)

Columns (left to right): [Ful], Ramat Raḥel, Beth-shemesh, el-Buqê'ah, Beth-zur, Lachish, 'En Gedi, T. Beit Mirsim, Arad, T. Beer-sheba, Ashdod, Tell Jemmeh, 'Adoni Nur T., 'Amman Tombs, Meqabelein Tomb, Sahab Tomb

Beth-shemesh: II a; II b elements; II b elements; scattered elements (few); II c; elements; elements

el-Buqê'ah: elements in "Grain Pit"

T. Beit Mirsim: B3; = ? = ? =; scattered elements, A1; Late A1 elements; A2; elements

Arad: XI?; VIII?; VII?

T. Beer-sheba: store-house

Ashdod: Area D Str. 4; -? — ?-; Loc. 119?; D-3; ca. 630?-; D-2; -? ↕ ?-; D-1?

Tell Jemmeh: elements; elements; 604 Fort el Residency

'Adoni Nur T.: -ca. 650-; ?; ?

Beth-shemesh / Ramat Raḥel (bottom): VB; VA; II c; BASOR 142; elements; elements

el-Buqê'ah: ?; ? ↕ ?; ?

Beth-zur: III; III; II

Lachish: Clark Coll.

'En Gedi: V

'Amman Tombs: ?; ?; ?

Meqabelein Tomb: ?; ?; ?

Sahab Tomb: ?

A double line across a column indicates a destruction.   A single line across a column indicates a stratigraphic separation.

COMMENTS

Tell Jemmeh and the Dating of "Assyrian Palace Ware" in Palestinian Contexts. The absence of large numbers of foreign forms such as "Assyrian Bowls" in the Assyrian provincial capital of Megiddo and the garrisoned site of Hazor contrasts strangely with the situation obtaining at Tell el-Far'ah (N), *Niv*. I, Tell Jemmeh (esp. the DZ 194 grain pit filling), and the Assyrian provincial capital of Samaria, Pottery Period VII. Further, the ceramic corpora of Megiddo II and III and Hazor Strata III–IV show relatively closer affinities with Megiddo IVA and Hazor V than with Samaria Pottery Period VII, Tell el-Far'ah (N), *Niv*. I, etc., which are closely allied with securely dated seventh/sixth-century Judaean pottery. This regular conjunction of "Assyrian" wares with late seventh-century forms raises the question of the proper dating and historical attribution of the "Assyrian Palace Ware" found in Palestinian sites. In the past, it has generally been attributed to the Assyrian occupying forces of the late eighth century B.C.[57] Recent studies based on the Nimrud excavations, however, suggest that the floruit of ware like that at Tell Jemmeh, Tell el-Far'ah (N), Samaria, Shechem VI, Ramat Raḥel VA, En Gedi, etc.,[58] should be placed in *and following* the last days of the Assyrian empire.[59] Since it is becoming increasingly clear that Assyria was forced back into her own heartland early in the second half of the seventh century, the presence of these late forms of "Assyrian" ware in unquestionably late seventh-century Palestinian stratification (e.g. Ramat Raḥel, En Gedi and Tell el-Far'ah (N), *Niv*. 1) becomes an embarrassment unless we recognize them as actually *post*-Assyrian in date. That is, we must recognize them as witnessing to a *Babylonian* influence in at least the aforementioned sites. In the cases of Ramat Raḥel and En Gedi this is the obvious solution to the chronological problem. In the case of Tell Jemmeh, a comparison between *Gerar*, pl. LXV, and the illustrations and descriptions in *Iraq* 16 (1954), 164–167, pls. XXXVII–XXXIX, and *Iraq* 21 (1959), 130–146, pls. XXXIV–XXXIX, strongly suggests that the "Fort" and "Residency" at Tell Jemmeh were the work of Nebuchadrezzar, who logically should have established a garrison there following his defeat of the Egyptian army in 605–604 B.C. (II Kings 24:7).[60] This construction of the events also fits well with the observation that the slightly earlier "Assyrian Ware" of the Trans-Jordanian tomb groups is considerably different (less flaring, shorter rims) than the highly developed forms which characterize the end of Nimrud and the early sixth-century Palestinian sites.[61] The two Hazor examples[62] fit well earlier in the typology and presumably should be dated to the first half of the seventh century. The lone Samaria Pottery Period VI example[63] is probably intrusive from Pottery Period VII, while it is entirely possible that some of the pottery forms figured in Pottery Period VII cover a rather longer time span than originally thought.[64]

MEGIDDO

Only a methodological suggestion can be offered here. In her perceptive and cogent analysis of the Megiddo stratification in *Samaria-Sebaste* III, Principal Kenyon analyzes the occurrences of several eighth-century forms in Megiddo Stratum IV loci. Typical of this analysis is the statement, apropos of the filling beneath Stable 1576 and the associated courtyard:

> [Jugs] nos. 99 and 100, again only sherds, are examples of water-decanters. This is again a class of vessel with an overwhelming preponderance of occurrences in Stratum III, only one example of the twelve types being recorded in IV, though the occurrences of type 100 are not listed as it is so common. The Samaria evidence confirms a late date for the appearance of the class, for it first occurs in Period VI. . . ."[65]

On the face of it, this is an eminently logical analysis, and, in view of the known shortcomings of the Megiddo excavations, the obvious implication is that one can ignore this lone Stratum IV occurrence (the "IV" filling materials are almost certainly intrusive) either as an early example or—more plausibly—as intrusive. *Conclusion:* Megiddo IV ends before or just at the introduction of this form.

Upon closer examination, however, this analysis, and others like it, dissolves. In the first place, can one legitimately overlook occurrences of the most common decanter form? While these occurrences are not listed in the distribution tables[66] they *are* listed in the "Register of Finds."[67] Two registered items, P2355–56 from Locus 637, and sherds from Loci 1593 (in 1482) and –1601 (III) appear in Stratum IV loci. These, taken together with the sherds of Type 107 from Locus –1416 (III) add up to five occurrences of the "northern" decanter form in IV loci. A similar search through Strata III, II, and I locus lists reveals two registered vessels in two loci (508 and 1001) and sherds from twelve more loci in Stratum III, one registered vessel (Locus 543); and sherds from three other loci in Stratum II and five registered vessels in "Stratum I" (Loci 308, 560, 568, 603, 1346). The pattern, then, for the Type 100 distribution would seem to be: Stratum IV, 4 exx.; Stratum III, 14 exx.; Stratum II, 4 exx.; Stratum I, 5 exx. But, and this is a second weakness in the analysis, it must be noted that these are raw statistics, and not directly comparable, for there are only some 75 loci listed for Stratum IV versus about 391 loci for Stratum III and 166 and 99 loci for Strata II and I respectively. Assuming roughly the same ratio of vessels per locus in each stratum, Stratum IV examples must be multiplied by a factor of 5.21, Stratum II by a factor of 2.23, and Stratum I by a factor of 3.94 to get equivalent figures. The following tabulation shows the differences between rounded-off weighted and unweighted occurrences.

Megiddo I	*Str. IV*	*Str. III*	*Str. II*	*Str. I*
Jug Type 100: unweighted exx.	4	14	4	5
weighted exx.	21	14	9	20

The Stratum I examples point to an obvious difficulty in either phasing or stratification which cannot be examined here, but the clear implication of the other figures is that Type 100, far from "having an overwhelming preponderance of occurrences in Stratum III," actually seems to be a *typical* Stratum IVA form continuing into the Strata III and II periods.

Taking all occurrences of the well-developed "northern" decanter form into consideration (Types 99–100, 102–107) and ignoring examples in the "IV filling" or listed only by squares, the comparable figures would be:

	Str. IV	*Str. III*	*Str. II*	*Str. I*
unweighted	5	43	12	9
weighted	26	43	27	35

From this, and a separate analysis of Type 107 (Str. IV: 1 ex.; Str. III: 4 exx.; Str. II: 1 ex.) the preliminary judgment would seem to be that Types 100 and 107 appear in IV and III loci almost equally, while the other forms are typically III or III and II in their occurrence.

Whether or not the Megiddo stratification will support this degree of analysis is an open question. But, in the light of the disparity between the numbers of loci and, therefore, pottery forms recorded from the individual strata, it is self-evident that simple comparisons of examples from various "strata" cannot be held to represent their relative frequency and unweighted comparisons of the type usually made are not only meaningless but misleading.[68]

Application of the principle of "weighting" listed examples, particuarly between Strata IV and III occurrences, has demonstrated to the writer's complete satisfaction that the forms typical of Stratum IVA loci are fully in keeping with other 733 B.C. horizon materials (e.g. Hazor Str. V/VA). The closeness of typical Stratum III items to forms current at 722 B.C.[69] has been noted and discussed at some length by Kenyon[70] and perhaps should be taken even more seriously than either Principal Kenyon or the present writer have. That is, it is entirely possible that an argument could be made for an Assyrian rebuilding of the destroyed Stratum IV city along lines familiar to Assyrians, but foreign to Palestine, during the period 733–722.[71] This city (Str. III), along with much of northern Palestine, may then have been largely depopulated during the mass deportations inaugurated by Sargon, with elements of Strata "III," "II," and "I" reflecting a greatly lessened and more dispersed occupation dependent upon the Assyrian administrative and military establishment during the last decades of the eighth century and first half of the seventh century B.C. Other elements of "Strata II and I" could then reflect a declining population during the period of Assyrian weakness, with a total abandonment of the site probably following Josiah's defeat in 609 B.C.

TELL QASILE

In the absence of an adequate publication of the results of the excavations at Tell Qasile, it is difficult to be certain of any conclusions regarding the stratification of the site. Nevertheless, since materials from Tell Qasile have been used to restructure much of the Iron I and early Iron II stratigraphy of northern Palestine,[72] it is necessary at least to emphasize that none of the published material, with the exception of the two fine late eighth-century ostraca, need be dated later than the end of the ninth century B.C.[73] Nor is the writer aware of any evidence in the unpublished material which would contradict this judgment.[74]

TELL ARAD AND TELL BEER-SHEBA

Since very little has been published from either of these sites, the dating given reflects a tentative evaluation of both published and unpublished materials generously made available by Prof. Aharoni and Mrs. Amiran and may require slight modification in the light of final publication of the data. But, if the analyses attempted in the present study have any validity, it seems to the writer that neither Arad VIII nor the final Judaean phase at Tell Beer-sheba can be dated before the last half of the seventh century B.C.[75]

ASHDOD

In view of the great number of parallels cited by the excavators (pp. 134–137) with Lachish Strata III and II, Tell Beit Mirsim Stratum A, Samaria Pottery Period VII, late seventh-century Nimrud, the Sahab tomb, Ramat Raḥel, the Amman tombs, Beth-shemesh Stratum II (note 30!), etc., the suggestion of a date in the late seventh century for Stratum 3 of Area D can hardly come as much of a surprise.[76] If this dating can be supported, it then follows that the characteristic elements of Strata 2 and 1 must be even later. The following tabulation (Chart 4) presents some, though by no means all, of the correspondences between Ashdod, Area D, Strata 3, 2, and 2–1 and the late seventh-century[77] coastal site of Meṣad Ḥashavyahu[78] and late seventh/early sixth-century materials from Lachish. The very high number of correlations, particularly in forms peculiar to the late seventh–early sixth centuries, seems to the present writer to be decisive for the general range of dates proposed in Chart 3 above.

Chart 4

Vessel or Feature	Ashdod[79]	Meṣad Ḥashavyahu[80]	Lachish[81]
	— Str. 3 —		
Bowl with horizontal loop handle	36:2	7:1-8, 11-12, 14	—
Wheel burnished bowl with ribbed exterior walls	36:3, 37:12; 40:5 (Str. 2)	4:4	??[82]
Round-shouldered neckless craters with short, sharply everted rims	36:6	5:8	—
Wide-rimmed deep bowl-crater	36:9	—	102:653 655 (III) 657 (III?)
Saucer with drooping rim	37:5	4:1-2	80:62 (III?)
Handleless necked jars	37:18 19	5:9	90:388 (T 106
Pointed dipper juglet with high loop handle	37:24 39:6	—	88:303 (T 10(cf. 103:671 (I
Dipper juglet	37:25	—	88:298-290 304-305 (T 1(
"One-handled jug"	37:22	—	84:170 (T 10(176 (III?)
do?	38:1	5:7	84:198-191 (I
Cooking pot	39:5	—	93:443 (III?)
	— Str. 2 —		
Bowl	40:6	—	80:74 (III)
Pointed dipper juglet	40:14	—	103:671 (III)
Cooking pot	40:19	5:1	104:691 (II)
Holemouth jar	40:21	5:11	97:544 (III,
	— Str. 2-1 —		
Bowl	41:8	4:10	
Bowl	41:9	4:11	
Cooking pot	41:10	41:12 (similar)	similar in typ 104:689 (II)

NOTE ON THE EẒ-ẒAHIRIYYEH TOMB GROUP

In the light of new data, particularly from En Gedi,[83] it now seems reasonably clear that the span of this tomb group is far too long for it to be utilized as a primary source of parallels for dating purposes. The following all appear to be late seventh/early sixth-century elements: (all items listed from the left) *QDAP* IV (1934–35), pls. LXI: 1 lower left; LXI: 2 top row, nos. 1, 2 (?), 4 (?), 5, 6; LXII: 1, nos. 1, 2 (?); LXII: 2 upper row center (?); LXIII: row 1, nos. 3–5, 7 (?); row 2; row 3, center.

NOTES

1. Abbreviations, bibliography, and acknowledgments:

AASOR 38	Sellers, *Beth-zur 1957*
AASOR 39	Kelso, *The Excavation of Bethel*
AS IV, V	Grant and Wright, *Ain Shems Excavations* IV, V
'Atiqot V	Mazar et al., *En Gedi*
'Atiqot VII	Dothan and Freedman, *Ashdod* I
. . . *Beth Shan*	James, *The Iron Age at Beth Shan*
CBZ	Sellers, *The Citadel of Beth-zur*
Gezer I (HUC)	Dever, Lance, and Wright, *Gezer I*
H I–III/IV	Yadin et al., *Hazor* I to III–IV
Jericho II	Kenyon, *Excavations at Jericho II*
M Tombs	Engberg, *Megiddo Tombs*
M I	Lamon and Shipton, *Megiddo* I
M II	Loud, *Megiddo* II
PNP	Holladay, "The Pottery of Northern Palestine during the Ninth and Eighth Centuries, B.C."
RB 54, 58	de Vaux, ". . . Fouilles a Tell el-Far'ah . . . ,"
59, 62, 64	*RB*, vols. 54 (1947) to 64 (1957)
RR I, II	Aharoni, *Ramat Raḥel* I, II
SS III	Crowfoot et al., *Samaria-Sebaste* III
TBM I, III	Albright, *The Excavation of Tell Beit Mirsim, AASOR* 12, 21–22
TN I, II	McCown and Wampler, *Excavations at Tell en-Naṣbeh*

Many bibliographic citations are made ad loc. Bibliography basic to the study or related to Charts 1 and 3, but not cited in the notes, is as follows:

Y. Aharoni, "Arad: Its Inscriptions and Temple," *BA* 31 (1968), 2–32; *Excavations at Ramat Raḥel* (Rome, 1962, 1964). Y. Aharoni and Ruth Amiran, "A New Scheme for the Sub-Division of the Iron Age in Palestine," *IEJ* 8 (1958), 171–184; "Excavations at Tel Arad, 1962," *IEJ* 14 (1964), 131–147; *Ancient Arad:* Introductory Guide to Exhibition Held at the Israel Museum, Jan.–Apr. 1967 (Jerusalem, n.d.). W. F. Albright. *The Excavation of Tell Beit Mirsim, AASOR* 12, 21–22 (New Haven, 1932, 1943).

D. C. Baramki, "An Early Iron Age Tomb at eẓ-Ẓāhiriyye," *QDAP* 4 (1934),

109–110. Marie-Louise Buhl and Svend Holm-Nielsen, *Shiloh: The Danish Excavations at Tall Sailūn, Palestine* (Copenhagen, 1969), F. M. Cross and J. T. Milik, "Explorations in the Judaean Buqê'ah," *BASOR* 142 (1956), 5–17. J. W. Crowfoot, G. M. Crowfoot, and Kathleen M. Kenyon, *Samaria-Sebaste III: The Objects from Samaria* (London, 1957).

W. G. Dever, H. D. Lance, and G. E. Wright, *Gezer I: Preliminary Report of the 1964–66 Seasons, Annual of the Hebrew Union College Biblical and Archaeological School in Jerusalem* I (Jerusalem, 1970). W. G. Dever et al., "Further Excavations at Gezer, 1969-71," *BA* 34 (1971), pp. 94–132. M. Dothan and D. N. Freedman, *Ashdod I: The First Season of Excavations, 1962, 'Atiqot,* VII, English Series (Jerusalem, 1967). Gershon Edelstein, *The Weaver's Quarters at Tel Amal in the Period of the United Monarchy,* Hebrew with English summary (Nir David, n.d.).

R. M. Engberg, *Megiddo Tombs* (Chicago, 1938). J. P. Free, "The Second Season at Dothan," *BASOR* 135 (1954), 14–20. Elihu Grant and G. E. Wright, *Ain Shems Excavations,* IV, V (Haverford, Pa., 1938, 1939). R. W. Hamilton, "Tall Abū Hawam: Interim Report," *QDAP* 3 (1934), 74–80; "Excavations at Tell Abu Hawām," *QDAP* 4 (1935), pp. 1–69. G. L. Harding "An Iron-Age Tomb at Sahab," *QDAP* 13 (1947), 92–102; "An Iron-Age Tomb at Meqabelein," *QDAP* 16 (1937), 44–48; "Two Iron-Age Tombs in Amman," *Annual of the Department of Antiquities of Jordan,* I (1951), 37–40; "Two Iron Age Tombs from 'Amman," *QDAP* 11 (1944), 67–74.

E. Henschel-Simon, "A Note on the Pottery of the 'Amman Tombs," *QDAP* 11 (1944), 75–80. J. S. Holladay, Jr., "The Pottery of Northern Palestine in the Ninth and Eighth Centuries, B.C." unpub. Harvard Th.D dissertation (1966) scheduled to appear as vol. IX of the Shechem series. S. H. Horn and L. G. Moulds, "Pottery from Shechem Excavated in 1913 and 1914," *Andrews University Seminary Studies,* VII (1969), 17–46. The Institute of Archaeology, Tel Aviv University, *The Beer-sheba Excavations* (Tel Aviv, 1971).

Frances W. James, *The Iron Age at Beth Shan* (Philadelphia, 1966). J. L. Kelso et al., *The Excavation of Bethel (1934–1960),* AASOR 39 (Cambridge, Mass, 1968). Kathleen M. Kenyon, "Megiddo, Hazor, Samaria and Iron Age Chronology," *Bulletin of the London Institute of Archaeology,* 1964, pp. 143–156; Kenyon et al., *Excavations at Jericho II: the Tombs Excavated in 1955–58* (London, 1965). R. S. Lamon and G. M. Shipton, *Megiddo I: Seasons of 1925–34, Strata I–V* (Chicago, 1939).

P. W. Lapp, "The Pottery of Palestine in the Persian Period," *Archäologie und altes Testament: Festschrift für Kurt Galling,* eds. A. Kuschke and E. Kutsch (Tübingen, 1970). G. Loud, *Megiddo II: Seasons of 1935–1939* (Chicago, 1948). D. Mackenzie, *The Excavations at Ain Shems,* 1911, PEFA 1 (1911), 1–94; *Excavations at Ain Shems* (Beth-shemesh) PEFA 2 (1912-3).

B. Maisler (Mazar), "The Excavations at Tell Qasîle, Preliminary Report," *IEJ* 1 (1951), 61–76, 125–140, 194–218. B. Mazar, *Excavations in the Old City of Jerusalem Near the Temple Mount . . . 1969–1970* (Jerusalem, 1971); B. Mazar, Trude Dothan, and I. Dunayevsky, *En-Gedi: The First and Second Seasons of Excavations, 1961–1962, 'Atiqot,* V English Series (Jerusalem, 1966). C. C. McCown, *Tell en-Naṣbeh I: Archaeological and Historical Results* (Berkeley, 1947).

Sir W. M. Flinders Petrie, *Gerar,* Publications of the British School of Archaeology in Egypt, no. 43 (London, 1928). J. B. Pritchard, *Winery, Defenses and Soundings at Gibeon* (Philadelphia, 1964). G. A. Reisner, C. S. Fisher, and D. G. Lyon, *The Harvard Excavations at Samaria,* Text and Plates (Cambridge, Mass., 1924). Fr. Silvester J. Saller, O.F.M., "Iron Age Tombs at Nebo, Jordan," *Liber Annuus* 16 (1966), 165–298. O. R. Sellers, *The Citadel of Beth-zur* (Philadelphia, 1933); Sellers et al., *The 1957 Excavation at Beth-zur,* AASOR 38 (Cambridge, Mass., 1968).

L. A. Sinclair, *An Archaeological Study of Gibeah (Tell el-Fûl),* AASOR 34–35,

(New Haven, 1960), 1–52. Olga Tufnell, "Hazor, Samaria and Lachish: A Synthesis," *PEQ* (1959), 90–105; Tufnell et al., *Lachish III: The Iron Age* (London, 1953). A. D. Tushingham, *The Excavations at Dibon (Dhībân) in Moab: The Third Campaign, 1952–53, AASOR* 40 (Cambridge, Mass., 1972); "Tombs of the Early Iron Age," in Kenyon et al. *Jericho II.*

R. de Vaux, O.P., "La Première Campagne de Fouilles a Tell el-Far'ah, près Naplouse," *RB* 54 (1947), 394–433 and 573–589; "La Troisième Campagne . . . ," *RB* 58 (1951), 393–430; "La Quatrième Campagne . . . ," *RB* 59 (1952), 551–583; "Les Fouilles de Tell el-Far'ah, près Naplouse—Cinquième Campagne," *RB* 62 (1955), 541–589; "Les Fouilles . . .—Sixième Campagne," *RB* 64 (1957), 552–580. J. C. Wampler, *Tell en-Naṣbeh II: The Pottery* (Berkeley, 1947), F. V. Winnett and W. L. Reed, *The Excavations at Dibon (Dhībân in Moab), AASOR* 36–37 (New Haven, 1964).

G. Ernest Wright, "Archaeological Fills and Strata," *BA* 25 (1962), 34–40; "Israelite Samaria and Iron Age Chronology," *BASOR* 155 (1959), 13–29; *Shechem: the Biography of a Biblical City* (New York, 1965). Y. Yadin, Y. Aharoni, R. Amiran, T. Dothan, I. Dunayevsky, J. Perrot, *Hazor I: An Account of the First Season of Excavations, 1955; Hazor II: An Account of the Second Season of Excavations, 1956; Hazor III–IV, An Account of the Third and Fourth Seasons of Excavations, 1957–1958, Plates* (Jerusalem, 1958, 1960, 1961).

The list of those who have been generous with both their time and unpublished materials is long and perilously subject to momentary oversight, but I have benefited immeasurably from the insights and perspectives into the mysteries of Iron II pottery afforded through the kindnesses and professional courtesies of Yohanan Aharoni, Ruth Amiran, Nachman Avigad, Avram Biran, Rudolph Cohen, Moshe and Trude Dothan, William G. Dever, Avi Eitan, Paul and Nancy Lapp, Benjamin Mazar, Walter Rast, James Sauer, Yigal Shiloh, Olga Tufnell, G. Ernest Wright, Yigael Yadin and the late Père de Vaux, O.P. Special thanks are due Père Jean P. Prignaud, O.P., for permission to cite certain critical unpublished Tell el-Far'ah (N) materials.

2. Ruth Amiran, *Ancient Pottery of the Holy Land* (Jerusalem, 1969), pp. 15, 191 ff.

3. *'Atiqot* V, pp. 16–21; *RR* II, pp. 122–124. This evaluation of the chronological worth of the En Gedi Str. V materials is in conscious disagreement with the opinion implied by Lapp in his review of Pritchard's *Winery . . . (AJA* 72 [1968], 391–393), p. 393. Whether the flat flared-rim cooking pot of *Winery . . .* fig. 34:2 continues into the later part of the sixth century is not the question. Evidence for this is, in the present writer's opinion, not decisive (cf. also N 33 below). The form is, however, characteristic of precisely the period to which En Gedi V is assigned, i.e. the final decade of the Judaean kingdom. Cf. the references cited in the appendix of the present study to occurrences of the form at Lachish and, especially, Ramat Raḥel. This is not to imply that all items attributed to En Gedi Str. V are to be dated to the Babylonian destruction. A certain amount of post-destructional material is included in the En Gedi figures, e.g. the wavy-sided mortaria of *'Atiqot* V, fig. 16:1, 2, but for the most part, such misattributions are obvious and present little hindrance to the effective use of the bulk of the Str. V finds as indicators of the latest Judaean material-culture complex. Cf. already *'Atiqot* V, pp. 27, 31.

4. As Prof. Aharoni has repeatedly observed in personal communication and public addresses, within this context even minor differences in the indices of certain forms (e.g. lamps, cooking pots) at different sites in the same general geopolitical area must surely be of some chronological significance. I would only disagree in noting that the range of forms (e.g. cooking pots) made by any one potter's shop was probably even more limited than the general spectrum of simultaneously available forms, and that

geographical proximity to various manufacturers or preferential purchasing (e.g. by government contract) undoubtedly played a role in the range of products bought for use or resale in any given place.

5. The remarks of H. J. Franken, "Analysis of Methods of Potmaking in Archaeology," *HTR* 64 (1971), 227–255, especially pp. 249 ff., are suggestive in this regard, although for reasons which cannot be entered into here, the present writer would not concur with all of Franken's conclusions or his caveats with regard to more "traditional" methods of ceramic analysis. For a description of contemporary potters' activities in traditional Lebanese society, see V. Hankey, "Pottery-making at Beit Shebab, Lebanon," *PEQ* (1968), 27–32. The need for further investigation into such traditional industries in the Levant and Egypt is obvious. A note of urgency also is introduced by the growth of the modern plastics industry which may make such operations either obsolete or more specialized within a very short time. With regard to Palestine proper, there is an especial need for ethnological and technological documentation of the potteries of the Hebron region, which are perhaps more nearly akin to those of Iron Age Judah than the smaller cottage-industry operations which have been described elsewhere, e.g. Grace M. Crowfoot, "Pots, Ancient and Modern," *PEQ* (1932), 179–187. Studies of Aegean potters' practices, e.g. Stanley Casson, "The Modern Pottery Trade in the Aegean," *Antiquity* 12 (1938), 464–473, point up both the historical craft continuity in a given area and the great disparity between the practices of different geographical areas.

6. Among these studies may be cited works by Paul Lapp: *Palestinian Ceramic Chronology 200 B.C.–A.D. 70, AASOR* 38, chs. IV, VI with Nancy Lapp (New Haven, 1961); "The Pottery of Palestine in the Persian Period" [N 1]; Nancy Lapp, "Pottery from Some Hellenistic Loci at Balâṭah (Shechem)," *BASOR* 175 (1964), 14–26; J. D. Seger, "Two Pottery Groups of Middle Bronze Shechem," in Wright, *Shechem* [N 1], pp. 335–337; J. B. Hennessy, *The Foreign Relations of Palestine during the Early Bronze Age* (London, 1967); Dever and Lance, *Gezer* I [N 1]; and J. A. Sauer in Sauer and Lugenbeal, "Seventh–Sixth Century B.C. Pottery from Area B at Heshbon," *Andrews University Seminary Studies,* X (1972). Major unpublished studies scheduled for publication in the Shechem series include: D. P. Cole, "The Stratified Pottery of Middle Bronze IIB from the Courtyard Temples of Shechem (Drew Seminary Th.D. dissertation); J. S. Holladay, Jr. PNP; and J. D. Seger "The Middle Bronze IIC Pottery of Shechem. In the *Gezer* (HUC) series, the forthcoming study of the Gezer High Place by Anita Walker depends almost entirely upon data of this sort for its conclusions. In connection with the present occasion it is worthy of mention that the three last-mentioned investigations are Harvard dissertations prepared under Prof. Wright's direction, as was the original of Lapp's *Palestinian Ceramic Chronology 200 B.C.– A.D. 70*

7. A partial corrective to Kenyon's conclusions as they apply to conventions of dating prevalent among Palestinian archaeologists has been provided in an important series of articles by Wright: "Israelite Samaria and Iron Age Chronology" [N 1], esp. pp. 20 ff.; "Comment on Yadin's Dating of the Shechem Temple," *BASOR* 150 (1958), 34–35; "Archaeological Fills and Strata," *BA* 25 (1962), 34–40, esp. pp. 36 ff.; "Archaeological Method in Palestine—An American Interpretation," *EI*, vol. 9, The W. F. Albright Volume (Jerusalem, 1969), 120–133.

8. Cf. *SS* III, pp. 90–91.

9. Cf. *SS* III, fig. 6, no. 39, with nos. 25–38. Cf. also Kenyon's description of the mixed stratigraphic nature of much of the Early Bronze Age pottery from the site, p. 91.

10. A good example is the difficult stratigraphy beneath the Hellenistic House in Field II at Shechem. Cf. Wright, "Archaeological Fills and Strata" [N 7], p. 35.

11. For an analysis of a similar situation, cf. Paul Lapp's discussion of the debris layers from Rooms 1 and 2 of the Field II Hellenistic House at Shechem, *Palestinian Ceramic Chronology* [N 6], pp. 41–48.

12. *H* III/IV, pl. ccxxxii:9, 10.

13. Cf. for example, T. Dothan's evaluation of the chronological significance of the two En Gedi mortaria apparently found on a Str. V floor (*'Atiqot* V, p. 27).

14. Cf. Tell Abu Hawam Str. III, no. 94, a distinctive seventh-century "low-based" lamp (*QDAP* 3 [1934], 23). Note the exposed nature of the find-spot.

15. The certain items are Lamp 94 and "Bath" [Coffin] 100. Pilgrim Flask 89 is probably also later, cf. already Gus Van Beek ("The Date of Tell Abu Hawam, Stratum III" *BASOR* 138, pp. 34–38, esp. 35, the rest of Van Beek's attempted division is not convincing). Jugs 67 and 78 are of uncertain provenience and should at least be bracketed in critical discussion. Cf. PNP, pp. 136–137.

16. PNP, pp. 19–28.   17. Ibid.   18. *TBM* I, pp. 82–83.

19. *TN* II, pp. 17–18, 21–22 etc.   20. *IEJ* 8 (1958), 171–184.

21. Amiran [N 2], pp. 191 ff.   22. Ibid., pp. 259–262.   23. Ibid., pp. 200–206.

24. Regarding the date of Lachish Str. III the only published stratum which is a candidate (attributed to the late eighth century by Aharoni and Amiran), see p. 266 below.

25. Megiddo Strata III–II. Hazor IV–III.

26. Certainly Arad VIII coforms too closely to the known 597 and 587 B.C. horizon groupings to be dated a hundred years earlier and no earlier post-Str. XI materials have yet been published. See below, p. 275.

27. In fact, it was precisely the occurrence of very large quantities of so-called "southern" forms in the post-724 B.C. pottery of Shechem which provided the initial impetus for the present investigation.

28. See above, p. 259.

29. Cf. p. 259 above and *'Atiqot* V, p. 38.

30. *Cf.* Lance [N 45 below], pp. 321–330.

31. It hardly needs to be noted that this is the basic methodological presupposition underlying all dating by means of pottery parallels.

32. Cf. *'Atiqot* V, p. 38b.

33. This evaluation of the chronological significance of the flat, flared-rim cooking pot fits well with all known stratification, with the major exception of the material from Meṣad Ḥashavyahu which is generally dated to the last quarter of the seventh century B.C. (J. Naveh, "The Excavations at Meṣad Ḥashavyahu," *IEJ* 12 [1962], 89–113, esp. 99.) Dissatisfaction with this narrow dating has been expressed by Paul Lapp in the Galling *Festschrift* [N 1], p. 184, n. 28. The present writer shares in this uneasiness, although, in the absence of adequate publication, it is impossible to do more than express an opinion that the vessels figured in 5:1–3 (and possibly the lamps 5:18, 21 on p. 103) should be added to the list of post-600 B.C. materials cited by Lapp. The possibility that the major occupation is to be dated to the first quarter of the sixth century cannot, however, be completely disregarded.

34. Omitting the obviously later fig. 33 assemblage.

35. *Cf.* *'Atiqot* V, p. 57a, where, however, the period is extended over the entire seventh century, conflicting severely with the evidence derivative both of 722 B.C. horizon materials in the north as well as with ca. 650 (to ?) period materials from the Adoni-Nur tomb.

36. *AS* V, p. 136.

37. The three-handled jar of *PEFA* 2 (1912–13), pl. xxii:15.

38. The pillar-based figurine, *PEFA* 2, xxii:9, xxiii, and the "one-handled" jugs (?) and late black juglets on pl. xxiv.

39. Cf. *AS* V, p. 136. *Note: PEFA* 2, pls. xliv:11 (T.6), liv:14 (T.8), lvi:15 (T.8), and lvii:20 (T.8) presumably postdate the "Persian" form from the En Gedi portion of the Clark Collection (*'Atiqot* V, fig. 33, pl. xxxvi:6).

40. *AS* V, pp. 144–145.

41. E.g. *L* III, pl. 93:442, the type seems slightly later than *RR* II, fig. 35:10 (Str. Vʙ).

42. E.g. *L* III, pl. 93:443.

43. E.g. *L* III, pl. 104:698.

44. In view of the ubiquity of this form in late Judaean tomb groups, the writer confesses a distinct uneasiness at dating the form so late, preferring instead an emergence in the last quarter of the seventh century or so. The evidence from Lachish and unpublished materials from Tell Beer-sheba, however, indicate otherwise.

45. Cf. H. Darrell Lance, "The Royal Stamps and the Kingdom of Josiah" in the Lapp Memorial Volume, *HTR* 64:2, 3 (1971), 315–332. For the previous history of the discussion, see the convenient summary in Lance, p. 321, to which may be added O. Tufnell, "Hazor, Samaria and Lachish," *PEQ* (1959), 90–105.

46. James, *The Iron Age at Beth Shan*, [ɴ 1], pp. 125 ff., esp. pp. 129–132.

47. Lance [ɴ 45], p. 332.

48. Regarding the evidence for a supposed "sixth century" occupation at Bethel, cf. the writer's analysis in W. G. Dever, "Archaeological Methods and Results: A Review of Two Recent Publications," *Orientalia* 40 (1971), 469. Cf. also Paul Lapp's remarks in the Galling *Festschrift* [ɴ 1], p. 181, n. 14.

49. *RB* 58 (1951), 417–420 and pls. vɪ, vɪɪ, and vɪɪɪ.

50. But note the intrusive late Hellenistic fusiform bottle, ibid., pp. 418–419, 12:9.

51. Cf. *H* I, p. 21 (Area A), pp. 45 ff. (Area B), *H* II, pp. 31–32 (Area A) and p. 58.

52. See the comments above p. 257.

53. *SS* III, Pottery Period VII.

54. *SS* III, Pottery Period VIII, Tell el-Farʿah (N) *Niv.* I, Shechem Str. VI.

55. Hazor Strata III–IV with possible odd intrusions into Strata VI–VIII, Megiddo Strata I–III, with intrusions into Str. IV and Str. IV filling.

56. For the historical analysis generating these dates and the bases for the critical selection of loci, see "PNP," pp. 31–133.

57. So Petrie, *Gerar* [ɴ 1], pp. 23–24; Kenyon, *SS* III [ɴ 1], pp. 97–98. Amiran, *Ancient Pottery* [ɴ 2], p. 291, is more cautious, noting only that "it [always] appears in strata of the period following the Assyrian Conquest of Samaria, that is, after 721 ʙ.c."

58. Cf. the appendix below, *Assyrian bowls and beakers*.

59. Cf. especially the comments by Joan Oates in "Late Assyrian Pottery from Fort Shalmaneser," *Iraq* 21 (1959), 130, to the effect that the pottery of the final 612 ʙ.c. destruction "is identical with . . . groups found at a higher level that can confidently be attributed to reoccupation by squatters." Cf. also ibid., n. 1, which extends the dates of tablets from TW 53 room 19 at Nimrud from ca. "666 ʙ.c.–626 ʙ.c." (*Iraq* 16 [1954], 164) to "perhaps as late as 616 ʙ.c." In other words, the pottery from these two groups (*Iraq* 16 and 21) is to be dated very closely to 612 ʙ.c. and later, instead of to the late eighth and early seventh centuries ʙ.c.

60. The Smithsonian Excavations at Tell Jemmeh under Gus Van Beek have recently found "Palace Ware" pieces *in situ* in the remains of a large brick building of Assyrian (or neo-Babylonian) style which apparently formed part of the "Residency," proving their connection with these buildings.

61. Compare e.g. the bowl no. 70 and the beaker no. 88 in the Adoni-Nur tomb group (*PEFA* 6 [1953], fig. 21) with *Iraq* 16 (1954), pls. xxxvɪɪ:7–8, xxxvɪɪɪ:2–5 and *Iraq* 21 (1959), pl. xxxvɪɪ:59, 60–67.

62. Cf. appendix below, *"Assyrian" bowls and beakers*.

63. *SS* III, fig. 10:9.

64. *SS* III, fig. 11.

65. *SS* III, p. 203.

66. *Megiddo* I, pp. 173 ff.

67. *Megiddo* I, pp. 109 ff.

68. The writer is under no illusion that the picture created by "weighting" one or two examples of a type to "five" or "ten" "equivalents" is an accurate representation either of the true stratigraphic attribution of that particular type or its relative proportion with regard to other forms attributed to that stratum. Weak and imperfect as the adjusted data are, however, they are nevertheless more in keeping with the actual claimed facts of the excavation results than a clumsy comparison of raw numbers, and probably represent about as good data as the excavation reports are capable of yielding. Statistical manipulation cannot, in this instance, make up for faulty data collection. But it can at least enable us to compare the results of that data collection process in terms more or less consistent with the sampling techniques employed.

69. Compare e.g. *M* I Jugs 108–110 with *SS* III Pottery Period VI forms, figs. 9:5, 10:17, 18(?), 19.

70. *SS* III, pp. 124, 203–204.

71. Cf. the independent conclusions of K. Kenyon, *Archaeology in the Holy Land* (London, 1960), pp. 282 ff.; Y. Aharoni, review of the above in *IEJ* 11 (1961), 90; Y. Yadin, "Megiddo of the Kings of Israel," *BA* 33 (1970), 96.

72. B. Maisler (Mazar), "The Stratification of Tell Abū Hawâm on the Bay of Acre," *BASOR* 124 (1951), 21–25.

73. For an exhaustive review of the published and representative unpublished evidence, cf. "PNP," pp. 162–172.

74. If the form figured in *IEJ* 1 (1951), pl. 36:A:6 is actually a "half moon rim," as it appears to be, it would go along with an unpublished high-based lamp as one of two intrusive elements from a now-lost late seventh/early sixth-century stratum.

75. For Arad, cf. the strap-handled, burnished "Judaean" decanters of Arad VIII in *IEJ* 14 (1964), pls. 36A and B, the royal-stamped jar-handles of either VII or VIII (ibid., p. 138) and the four-handled jar of the *lmlk* type from Str. VIII (ibid., pl. 33:D). For materials from Beer-sheba, see Y. Aharoni, *Excavations at Tel Beer-sheba: Preliminary Report on the First Season, 1969* (Tel Aviv, 1970), esp. figs. 1–9; "The pottery vessels found in the storehouse." These vessels, sealed in the debris of the final destruction of the Judaean stronghold, correspond almost exactly to the Lachish Str. III corpus, and have been compared by the excavator with the pottery of Arad VIII (*IEJ* 14 [1964], 6). Note especially the three-handled jars with cup level with rim and strap-handles (as in Arad VIII), figs. 4:47, 48, 50; "southern" decanters (9:88); four-handled store jars of the *lmlk* type (6:66); tall crater/store jars (8:75–78); "Rice bowls" (figs. 1:1–2, 4 [type A] and figs. 1:3, 6–8 [type B]—for "types" see the appendix below, *"Rice bowls"*); "Judaean" cooking pots of earlier type than En Gedi V (cf. fig. 3:40–46 with the tall, flaring necks and different neck ridging of the thin-ware En Gedi forms of *'Atiqot* V, fig. 17); wide-rimmed holemouth jars, either doubly or triply-ridged (fig. 7); "Half moon" rimmed bowls (fig. 1, esp. no. 25); large four-handled bowls with half-moon rims (our "type B," fig. 2:26–28); "one-handled" jugs (8:80–81?); the late, high-necked, deep-bodied variant of the "late shallow" cooking pot form (cf. fig. 3:37 with the somewhat shorter-necked *L* III, pl. 104:689); and low-based lamps (9:92–93).

76. Taking into account only Str. 3 pottery parallels with sites having reasonably secure stratigraphy and ignoring sites like Tell en-Naṣbeh, Tell el-Farʿah (S), etc., the ratio of seventh century to earlier parallels given in the text is on the order of 20:12.

77. And/or later? Cf. N 33 above.   78. *IEJ* 12 (1962), 89–113 [N 33].

79. *'Atiqot* VII.   80. *IEJ* 12 (1962), 89–113.   81. *Lachish* III.

82. Many *L* III exx. are formally closer to *'Atiqot* VII, figs. 36:3 and 40:5, than is the Meṣad Ḥashavyahu example; compare pl. 81:103, 104 (cf. also *'Atiqot* VII, fig. 37:10, possibly a "Str. 4" form persisting in fill) and pl. 99:591–598. These are all irregularly hand-burnished, however, except for 594. Most come from the "Level V–IV" excavations near the Citadel (cf. p. 140). These forms, all hand-burnished on a dark red slip,

appear in great quantity in some of the late tenth–early ninth-century roadways of the Solomonic Gateway at Gezer, but it is still too early to set specific time limits on their range there. They do not, however, seem to persist into the eighth or seventh centuries, nor are they ever wheel-burnished. Thus it seems unlikely that they are directly ancestral to the Ashdod 3–2 forms.

83. D. C. Baramki, "An Early Iron Age Tomb at eẓ-Ẓāhiriyye," *QDAP* 4 (1934), 109–110, pls. LXI–LXIV.

APPENDIX

DOCUMENTATION FOR CHART 1 ON PP. 262–63

"Assyrian" bowls and beakers: (burnish indicated by *) Ramat Raḥel: *RR* I, fig. 11:15? (VA); *RR* II, fig. 18:21–23 (Va). En Gedi: *'Atiqot* V, pl. 25:7*, 8, cf. p. 26 (both V). Beth-shemesh: *PEFA* 2, pl. XLI:4 (T. 5). Lachish (?): LIII, pl. 81:92? (T. 1002), 97? (T. 218). Tell el-Far'ah (N): *RB* 58, pp. 418–49, fig. 12:1*, 2, 3*, 4*, 6* and several unpub. exx., all *Niv.* 1; fig. 12:12 may be the lower half of a beaker (*niv.* 1). Hazor: *H* I, pl. XXIV:3* (V); *H* II, pl. XCVIII:44* (IV). Megiddo: *M* I, pl. 9:12 (III). Samaria: *SS* III, figs. 10:9, 10 (intrusive? in Pottery Period [PP] VI "pit i"); 11:15, 17, 22, 23* (all PP VIII); 18:9, 10 (PP VII). *HE* p. 280, fig. 156:21 a*–c*; p. 292, fig. 169:18b? Shechem: *BASOR* 169, fig. 22:2* and many unpub. VI examples.

"Rice bowls": (close interior wheel burnish indicated by *, interior and exterior burnish by **). Two types are analyzed: type A (no base) is typified by En Gedi fig. 15:6; type B (low disc or ring base) is typified by En Gedi fig. 15:7 (*'Atiqot* V, p. 63). As is evident from the arrangement of the forms on the *TBM* plates, this type tends to interact with other small bowl forms in such a way that it is difficult to do justice both to the full range of variability of the vessel ware-form mode and to its integrity as a definite type at the same time. Ramat Raḥel: *RR* I, figs. 11:5–9 (Va, type B); 27:1 (Vb, type B); 28:20 (Va, type A), 21 (Va, type B). *RR* II, fig. 17:53–56 (Va, type B). En Gedi: *'Atiqot* V, fig. 15:6 (type A), 7, 8? (type B, all Str. V); Clark Collection, ibid., fig. 29:10, 13, 14 (type A), 15?, 16? (type B). Tell Beit Mirsim: *TBM* I, type A: pls. 64:14, 17*, 18*, 19*; 67:1*, 2, 3*, 11*, 12*, 14*, 16, 19. Type B: pls. 67:4*, 5*, 6*, 8*, 9, 13*, 15 (all Str. A2). *TBM* III, type A: pl. 25:1*, 2*, 3*, 6*, 7*, 8*, 9*, 10*, 12*, 13* (nos. 8 and 9 from the 33–15 cache of phase *gamma* of the West Tower, the rest Str. A2). Type B: pls. 24:3*?, 6?, 7*?, 8, 9, 16, 18, 20, 25*, 26*, 27*?; 25:4*, 5*, 11*, 16* (nos. 24:6 and 25:16 from the 33–15 cache, all others Str. A2). Beth-shemesh: *AS* IV, pl. LXIII:23–25, 26*, 27 (type B, Str. IIb); *PEFA* 2, pls. XXXVII:9? (curved sides, type A?, T. 2); XLVI:5 (type unclear, repository T. 7). *L* III, type B: pls. 79:16 (Str. III), 17, 45 (III); 98:572 (III), 573, 574?, 576 (III). Type A: pl. 81:89 (some in III? loc.), 90 (irr. hnd. burn. int., III?), 91**, 95 (II). Bethel: *AASOR* 39, pls. 63:16*; 64:7?, 10 (all probably type B). Hazor (?): *H* II, pl. XCVIII:7?, 8? (both type B?, both IV). Shechem: Several unpublished examples, including B62.VII.21.167.1476 figured in "PNP," p. 551:A (type B?) parallel *TBM* III, pl. 24:7, 8.

Burnished saucers: the form, with disc base or concave disc base, is typified by En Gedi fig. 15:3–4 (*'Atiqot* V, p. 63) and *RR* II, fig. 16:1–28 (excluding nos. 6, 15, 20 and 22 which are formally the same, but do not have any mention of burnish in the description). The burnishing is usually semicontinuous ring burnish where it is fully described or shown in plates. Some possibility exists that a very few 733–722 B.C. horizon saucers have widely spaced lines of wheel burnishing (*cf. SS* III, pp. 113 and

141, but note also that many loci considered pre-722 B.C. have later components: e.g. Z Deep Pit, E 207 and the S. Tombs). None of the saucers in the critically selected pre-722 B.C. loci included in "PNP" is burnished, nor do I find any record in my notes that any of the numerous *niv.* 2 saucers or saucer fragments from Tell el-Far'ah (N) were burnished. The drooping rim, e.g. *RR* II, fig. 16:14–28, is restricted to post-722 B.C. *loci*. Note particularly that the form is both temporally and formally distinct from the burnished platter-bowls of Samaria Pottery Period III. Ramat Raḥel: *RR* I, figs. 11:1–3; 26:1 (for burnish, see p. 40); 28:2–8, 10–12 (all Va). *RR* II, figs. 16:1–5, 7–14, 16–19, 21, 23–28 (Va); 18:13? (Va, probably ring based, but note rim-form mode and burnish typical of form under analysis); 20:5 (Va); 35:6 (Vb). En Gedi: *'Atiqot* V, fig. 15:3, 4 (Str. V). Note that fig. 5:7 is included in this category on p. 26a and pl. 25–3 suggests burnish. Clark Collection: ibid., fig. 29:9. Beth shemesh (?): *PEFA* 2, pls. XXXIII:24 (repository T. 2); XLI:12 (T. 5); XLVI:4 (T. 7); LVI:10 and LVII:1 (T. 8) all appear to be examples of the form. Lachish: *L* III, pls. 79:1 (parallel in III loc.); 80:60, 64 (exx. in both III and II loc.); 98:560 (ex. in II loc.). Bethel: *AASOR* 29, pl. 63:15, cf. *RR* II, fig. 18:13. Hazor: *H* I, pls. LXIX:18 (IV); LXXI:1 (V, note drooping rim); Hazor III–IV, pls. CLXXXI:38 (VI); CCXIV:3 (VII); CCXIX:7 (VI); CCXXV:23 (Va, all other items from locus have excellent 733 horizon parallels); CCLIV:28 (IV). *M* I, pl. 24–42 (III–II), 43 (IV–II), 44 (IV–III). Samaria: *SS* III, fig. 6:2 (P. Period IV), widely spaced ring burnish int. on red slip. See introductory note above. Despite the excavator's comments on p. 113, no other examples of burnished saucers are published from the secure loci selected for the stratified pottery series (figs. 1–10). Nor do any appear in the Pottery Period VII pottery assemblage (fig. 11), but burnished examples were noted from Loci E 207, Qz, Qy, each of which contains substantial quantities of seventh-century pottery forms. *SS* III, fig. 13:1, see comments on p. 139 of the text, exx. from Qz, Qy and E 207. The saucers shown in fig. 13:10–13 seem often to have been burnished (p. 143) and, except for the ring base, are typical of the late seventh/early sixth-century forms from Judaean sites. Cf. also the high-based highly burnished saucers from E 207 (*SS* III, fig. 14:2–4) which exhibit similar drooping rim-form modes. *HE*, p. 280, fig. 156:9a; the saucers nos. 16 and 19 on p. 286, fig. 161, fall into a group of vessels described (p. 284) as "usually pebble-burnished," but it is not noted whether these particular forms are burnished or not. Shechem: several unpublished exx. from Str. VI, some very finely wheel burnished on a dark red slip.

Curved rim bowls: (Burnish indicated by *, int. and ext. burnish **) The type is defined on the basis of parallelism with *RR* I, fig. 11:4, 14 and En Gedi fig. 15:2 (*'Atiqot* V). Vessel ware-form modes which seem similar to these forms come in a variety of gradations. These forms are indicated by a question mark following the reference, e.g., *'Atiqot* V, figs. 14:17?; 15:1?. Ramat Raḥel: see above, both Va, both **. En Gedi: see above, all are V, 15:1 is "irreg. burn. int. and ext." and 15:2 is **. Tell Beit Mirsim: *TBM* I, pls. 62:3; 65:20a**? ("probably A1"), 20b*?, 21*?, 24*?, 25*; 66:3*?, 7*. *TBM* III, pl. 21:8*?, 15*?. Beth-shemesh (?): *AS* IV, pl. LXVI:1?, 3?; *PEFA* 2, pls. XLVI:3? (repository of T. 7); XLVII:9? (T. 7). Lachish (?): *L* III, pls. 79:51*? (exx. in *loci* predominately III in character); 99:603? (III), 605*?. Beth Shan (?): . . . *Beth Shan* fig. 67:7?; 68:1?. Hazor: *H* II, pl. XCVIII:15? (IV); *H* III/IV, pl. CCXLIX:11*, 12* (both possibly **, both VI). Samaria: *SS* III, figs. 11:9?, 11, 12, 13*, 14 (P. Period VII, note the interaction with the "Assyrian" bowl form); 19:10?* *HE*, p. 278, fig. 154:17?.

"Half moon" rim bowls: this group forms the most common single bowl type of the late seventh/early sixth centuries B.C. It regularly is spirally wheel-burnished int. and for about half to two-thirds of the ext. rim, most frequently on an unslipped ("self-slipped") surface. The type is Kenyon's "triangular folded rim" bowl, cf. *SS* III, pp. 127, 193–195, 206, the present nomenclature being chosen to suggest the normally rounded character of the external rim thickening, which may range from semi-circular

to triangular in section. The Ramat Raḥel exemplars below illustrate the normal range of forms. Bowls apparently burnished int. and on rim on unslipped or "self-slipped" wares are indicated by the sign @. Ramat Raḥel: *RR* I, figs. 11:12@, 13@, 14@; 12:2; 26:2; 28:22–27 (all @), 28, 29, 30@, 31 (slipped and burnished int.). *RR* II, figs. 16:35–60 (all @ but nos. 42, 48, 50, 51, 54, 56, 57 for which no burnish is noted and no. 48, which is recorded as having a "light" slip); 17:1–49 (all @ except for lack of burnish notes for nos. 14, 20, 22–23, 32, 37, 38, 44); 20:1–2, 4@; 35:1, 7@ (ext. also burnished [?]), 8. All but the last two items are str. Va. En Gedi: '*Atiqot* V, figs. 8:1–5; 14:1–11 (all V, all @ except 8:1, which is wheel-burnished all over, including the base). Clark Collection, ibid., fig. 29:1 (red slipped and burnished int. and rim), 2–4 (all @). Fig. 29:5–6 probably also relate to type. Tell Beit Mirsim: (*N.B.*, the descriptions given are unsatisfactory. Burnish indications on the drawings are indicated * for interior only and ** for interior and exterior.) *TBM* I, pls. 61 (most exx.); 62:1, 6*, 7*, 15*, 19*; 63 (all except no. 2?); 64:1*, 3*, 12*; 66:5, 8*?, 9*, 10*. *TBM* III, pls. 20:1*, 2*, 3*, 4?, 5?, 6*; 21:2*, 9*?, 13*, 14*; 22:10*, 11*, 12*; 23:2, 3*, 4, 5*, 6*, 8*?, 9. All exx. are apparently Str. A2. *Note:* the *TBM* plates exhibit very nearly the full range of thickened-rim bowl ware-form modes from the 733–722 B.C. horizon types to the 597–587 B.C. forms. Compare *RR* II, figs. 16:35–60; 17:1–51, which exhibit much of the same variability. Crucial dating criteria, such as details of ware, burnish patterns and slipping techniques, details of the exterior rim-form mode, etc., may not always be sufficient to date certain individual published items. Nevertheless the difference between the overall impression created by the vessel ware-form modes of, e.g. *H* II, pl. LXXXI:17–28 and the Ramat Raḥel examples is marked and unmistakable. Some seventh-century examples may look earlier, but few eighth-century folded-rim (!) bowls could be mistaken for later "half moon" rims. Beth-shemesh: *AS* IV, pls. LXIV:19 ("IIb type," bright red slip int. and to carination ext.); LXVII:11 (IIc, red burnished slip int. and over rim); *PEFA* 2 (descriptions generally wanting), pls. 37:8, 16?, 18 (all T. 2, no. 18 has chocolate-brown slip, burnished int. and ext., cf. p. 68); 41:1?, 7, 11? (T. 5); 44A:4 (T. 6); 47:11 (T. 7); 54:6, 18 (Repos. T. 8); 56:8, 57:3, 58:8 (T. 8). Lachish: *L* III (*N.B.* in the earlier plates slips—usually pink or red—seem to be indicated perhaps more often than would normally be expected for the form. Items marked + are described as burnished on such a slip.), pls. 80:69+ (Str. III and II exx.), 70, 71+, 73+ (III), 75+ (III), 77+ (prob. III), 78+ (II), 79 (III, II loci), 81+ (III, nos. 82 and 83 are even farther from the type under discussion, but are of the same type and range as 81); 101:627@ (III), 628, 629@ (III and II), 630 (as pl. 80:81–83), 631+ (III), 632+ (III), 633 (III), 634@ (II), 635@ (mostly III, one II?), 636 ("hand burnished," 1 ex., II), 637 (III, II), 638 (III), 639 (II?), 643+ (III), 646. Beth Shan: . . . *Beth Shan*, fig. 68:9. Bethel: *AASOR* 39, pls. 62:4–16; 63:19–21, 24, 27; 79:5; 80:1, 6–8 (both "Iron II" and "sixth century" identifications; @ items would seem to be 62:8, 11, 12–15, 16?; 63:20–21, 24; 79:5; 80:6). Tell el-Far'ah (N): unpublished exx. from *niv.* 1 loc. 111, F 1367 (int. bottom of bowl with triangular impressions inside a circle, cf. *RB* 58, pp. 418–419, fig. 12, nos. 14, 16) and another unregistered sherd of the same type. In contrast to nearby Shechem and Samaria, bowls of this type were relatively uncommon in good *niv.* 1 loci. Hazor: *H* I, pl. LVIII:2@, 3? (IV); LXIII:7? (V), LXXV:1, 2 (V). *H* II, pls. XCII:19 (Va); XCVIII:16@?. *H* III/IV, pls. CCXXX:2@, 5@, 6@, 7?, 8 (Va); CCXLIX:10? (VI); CCLI:20? (V). Megiddo: *M* I, pl. 23:5@ (I, 1 ex., cf. *SS* III, fig. 32:8, 6), 6 (III-3 exx., II-1 ex., I-2 exx.), 7@ (III-2 exx., I-2 exx.), 8@ (III-5 exx., I-1 ex.), 9@ (III-2 exx.), 10@ (III-1 ex., II-1 ex.), 12 (II-1 ex.), 18@ (III-1 ex., II-1 ex.), 19 (III-1 ex., II-2 exx., I-1 ex.). Samaria: *SS* III (*Note:* many *SS* III exx. are not closely parallel to the 597–587 type under analysis. The ones marked ! are the most characteristic for the present type.) figs. 11:1@, 3@, 4?, 6!, 7 (Pottery Period VII); 32:6@, 7!, 8 (P. Period VII). Shechem: *BASOR* 169, fig. 22:3 (VI), plus many unpublished exx., all from Str. VI, cf. "PNP," p. 551:H.

Large handled bowls (A): bowls with two or four handles are, at best, exceedingly rare before the end of the eighth century B.C. Only one example of such a bowl, as distinguished from craters such as *H* II, pls. LXVII:13; LXVIII:2, 11; LXXXIII:13, etc., appeared in the loci selected for inclusion in "PNP." That example, *H* II, pl. LXXXII:1, appeared in a somewhat suspect locus (L. 3115a), has a typical seventh-century unslipped burnished surface (int. only?), and probably is intrusive from a later period. Bowls of type "A" (e.g., *AS* IV, pl. LXIV:1, 6, 10) seem to form a continuum with those of type "B" below, the principal distinction being the more generally incurving or horizontal rim of type "A" and the closer generic relationship of the "B" rims to the "Half moon" rim series. Spaced wheel burnish in both series is generally limited to the interior and the upper portions of the rim, and is indicated by *. Clear "A" forms seem to be earlier than clear "B" forms. Ramat Raḥel (?): *RR* II, fig. 18:1* (Va) is close to type, but continuity with nos. 2–6, all of the same vessel ware-form mode, indicates placement in the "B" series. Fig. 35:9* (Vb) is similar. En Gedi (?): *'Atiqot* V, fig. 16:6 (V, 4 handles) is closely similar to the *RR* II exx. Tell Beit Mirsim (?): *TBM* I, pl. 60:1*, 8*, 9*, 10* could be treated similarly to the above items. Beth-shemesh: *AS* IV, pl. LXIV:1*, 2*–5*? (no. 2 is "IIa–b"), 6*, 7*?, 10* (IIb), 11*?. Lachish: *L* III, pls. 81:120 (III, four handles); 102:650* (III, four handles?), 651, 652 (III), 653, 654 (II), 657* (III? four handles). Bethel: *AASOR* 39, pls. 62:1*, 2, 8*, 18* ("Iron II," nos. 1–2 prob. continuous with 62:3, which has been placed under type "B"); 64:1*, 2 ("sixth century," related to "B" forms). Tell el-Far'ah (N): an unpublished ex. in the unregistered sherd collection from Locus 111 (*niv.* 1): handle, broadly oval and slightly ridged, spaced int. wheel burnish. Hazor: *H* II, pls. LXXXII:1* (Va); XCVIII:13* (IV). Megiddo: *M* I, pl. 27–85 (III–5 exx. everted rim unlike either "A" or "B"), 86 (III-2 exx. form intermediate between bowl and typical eighth-century crater, e.g., ibid., no. 84). Samaria: *SS* III, figs. 12:3 (P. Period VIII); 20:1* (four handles, E 207 and one ex. from Z deep pit, note that center handle is incompletely drawn). Shechem: unpub. exx., Str. VI.

Large handled bowls (B): See comments above. Ramat Raḥel: *RR* I, figs. 11:17*, 18, 19*, 21* (all Va, no. 17 rim atypical); 27:3 (Vb); 28:17 (as 11:17), 32*?, 34 (all Va, no. 33 is a crater, cf. ibid., fig. 12:9). *RR* II, figs. 18:1*?, 2* 3, 4*, 5*, 6 (all rest. with four handles, all Va); 20:3* (rest. with four handles, Va). Cf. discussion of Ramat Raḥel "A" forms above. En Gedi: *'Atiqot* V, fig. 16:3*, 4*, 5* (no. 5 has four handles, all Str. V, cf. discussion of En Gedi forms under "A" above). Tell Beit Mirsim: *TBM* I, pl. 60:2*, 3*, 4–7, 10b*, 11*, 12?, 13 (all A2). Beth-shemesh: *AS* IV, pl. LXIV:8* (IIb), 9* (IIb–c), 12* (IIb), 13*–16*, 18 (IIb–c) (handles missing on preserved portions of nos. 8, 15). Lachish: *L* III, pls. 81:121 (III, four handles); 102:647* (II), 648* (II), 649* (III), 655 (III). Beth Shan (?): . . . *Beth Shan*, fig. 35:1, termed "cooking pot." Form is that of the bowls under discussion, although smaller, Level IV. Bethel: *AASOR* 39, pls. 62:3*? ("Iron II"); 64:1*?, 2? ("sixth century"). Cf. discussion of Bethel exx. under "A" above. Tell el-Far'ah (N): unpublished fragment from Loc. 124 (*niv.* 1) with flattened handle, strongly rounded carination, spaced wheel burnishing int. and over rim to upper handle attachments. Samaria: *SS* III fig. 12:2 (P. Period VIII, hand burnished. Cf. comments ibid., p. 131.) Shechem: *BASOR* 169, fig. 22:4, 5* (VI) plus many unpub. exx. (VI).

"Judaean" cooking pots: the form is Aharoni and Amiran's "Deep Type" (*IEJ* 8 [1458], N 1, pp. 174–175). Ramat Raḥel: *RR* I, figs. 11:22; 25:3. Cf. *RR* II, pp. 30–31, where this type is said to be exclusively from sub-floor deposits, despite the fact that this one published example seems to be from a Va locus (the excessively generalizing indications of find spots in *RR* I, pp. 13–15, however, make it impossible to be sure that some elements of fig. 11 are not sub-floor). Fig. 25:3 is expressly stated (p. 40, b, 1) as coming from the large courtyard, i.e. from above its surface (contrast the statement in ibid. p. 40, b, 3). En Gedi: *'Atiqot* V, figs. 8:11; 17:1–5, cf. p. 28 (V). Clark Collection: ibid., fig. 29:20–23. Tell Beit Mirsim:*TBM* I, pls. 55:1, 3, 6, 8, 10,

11, 12; 56:12–14. *TBM* III, pl. 19:5–11, cf. § 155. Beth-shemesh: *AS* IV, pls. 64:27–31 (27, 29, 31 "IIb–c," 30 "IIc"), cf. *AS* V, p. 138; 67:17, 19 may be one-handled examples or jugs modeled on cooking pot prototypes, probably the latter. Lachish: *L* III, pl. 93:446 (transitional?), 447–459, 462. Hazor (?): *H* III/IV pl. CLXXXIV:11? (VI, cf. *L* III, pl. 93:446–448, 455, 457). Samaria: *SS* III, figs. 11:33? (P. Period VII "jar," ware color seems wrong for a cooking pot, but the form is anomalous for a seventh-century jar); 12:11–12 (PP VIII, cf. comments on pp. 131–132). Shechem: unpublished exx. from Str. VI. E.g., several exx. closely similar to En Gedi (*'Atiqot* V) fig. 17:2: pottery registry numbers 5046, 5117, 6332, 7141.

Flared-rim cooking pots: this type seems to have been unrecognized as a distinct form prior to the excavations at Ramat Raḥel and En Gedi (Tel Goren). Aharoni (*RR* II, pp. 30–31) and Amiran (*Ancient Pottery* [N 2], p. 232) classify it as a variant of the "Late Shallow Type" (*IEJ* 8 [1958], N 1, p. 174). In accord with this judgment is the observation that rims of many seventh-century exemplars of the "Late Shallow Type" flare outward (e.g., *TBM* I, pl. 56:1), in contrast to the inward stance of eighth-century exemplars. Present indications limit the type to the period after 597 B.C. Ramat Raḥel: *RR* I, figs. 11:20 ("tau" potter's mark on handle), 23, 24 (all Va, only no. 24 has a grooved rim indicated on the drawing); 28:35–37, 38? (Va). *RR* II, figs. 18:7–12; 20:8–9 (no grooves indicated), 10 (all Va). En Gedi: *'Atiqot* V, fig. 18:1–8, cf. pl. 28b (V). Beth-shemesh: *AS* IV, pl. LXIII:41? (not datable within II, cf. *RR* II, pl. 18:10, 12). *PEFA* 2, pl. XLIV:1 (T. 6, cf. descr. p. 79). Lachish: *L* III, pls. 93:460; 104:691 (both II). Bethel: *AASOR* 39, pl. 65:4 ("Iron II"). Hazor (?): *H* I, pl. LV:5?, 7? (V). *H* III/IV, pl. CXC:4? (V). Shechem: many unpublished VI exx. Cf. also Lapp, in the Galling Festschrift [N 1], p. 190, fig. 3:13–17 and discussion on p. 186. Cf. p. 180, where it is clear that this "Str. V" material, though well-dated by Greek vase fragments, is a wholly artificial collection of "Pre-IV" materials considered later than "Str. VI." Whether or not this particular cooking pot form actually is attested in the late sixth century must remain, for the present, questionable.

Handleless necked jars: the form is typified by *RR* I, fig. 12:3 and *IEJ* 12 (1962), 102–103, fig. 5:9 from Meṣad Ḥashavyahu. Ramat Raḥel: *RR* I, figs. 12:3 ("burnished"); 28:40 ("wheel-burnished," both Va). En Gedi: *'Atiqot* V, fig. 15:11 (wh.-burnished. ext.), 12 (wh.-burnished. rim, but cf. p. 28, 13 (ext. and int. of rim wh.-burn.), 15? (wh.-burn. ext., all V, see p. 28). Lachish: *L* III, pl. 90:388 ("ring hd.-burn. all over," T. 106). Bethel: *AASOR* 39, pl. 77:8? ("Late Bronze," but vessel is from Loc. 408, dug 24 July 57. All other published items from L. 408, including 407/408 exx., are dug on 27 July 57 or 30 July 57 and are uniformly Iron II.) Tell el-Farʿah (N): unpub. ex. from Loc. 124 with spaced wheel burnish ext., becoming almost continuous below neck. Wheel burnish continues over rim and slightly down into the neck. Dia. 20.5 cm. at mouth. Megiddo: *M* I, pl. 13:66 (I-1 ex.). Samaria (?): *SS* III, fig. 12:32? (PP VIII). Clark Collection: *'Atiqot* V, fig. 32:5 is a different, much smaller "miniature jar" type similar to exx. from *TBM* I, pl. 67:20–21, 22?, 23–28 (24 wh.-burn. ext.); Beth-shemesh (*AS* IV, pl. LXVI:45); *L* III, pl. 90:377–378; and Beth-zur (*CBZ*, pl. XIII:22, 24–25). All these seem to be closely related to a small Assyrian handleless necked jar form witnessed at Fort Shalmaneser (*Iraq* 21 [1959], pl. XXXVII: 72–77) in the 612 and post-612 B.C. destruction levels.

Holemouth jars, wide-rimmed: the early forms seem to be those typified by *M* I, pl. 11: 54, with simple rim and an obtuse angle at the juncture of the rim with the vessel sidewall. The triply-ribbed form of *M* I, pl. 11:57 appears to be typologically intermediate between this form and the thinner, wider ribbed rims of Ramat Raḥel Va (e.g. *RR* I, fig. 12:4) and En Gedi V (*'Atiqot* V, fig. 21:6). The early sixth-century rim-form modes seem regularly to be characterized by a sharp exterior angle at the shoulder and (generally) a more nearly right angle juncture of body and rim. Note that many so-called "holemouth jars" are actually either neckless jars (*RR* I, fig. 12:5) or tall crater/store jars (cf. ibid. no. 8 with *'Atiqot* V, fig. 21:3–5, 7–8). Ramat

Raḥel: (all exx. Str. Va) *RR* I, figs. 12:4, 6; 25:10, 12; 26:5–8; 29:4–11. *RR* II, figs. 19:1–3; 21:1–8, 10–12; 35:5. En Gedi: *'Atiqot* V, figs. 21:1, 2, 6, cf. p. 32 (all V). Tell Beit Mirsim: *TBM* I, pl. 52:1–7, 9 (all apparently A2; note major differences between these and those of the 587 horizon). Beth-shemesh: *AS* IV, pls. xlvii:15–18? (IIc), 5?; lxv:18, 21, 24, 28–30, 31–33 (IIc where identified, cf. *AS* V, p. 143). *PEFA* 2, pl. xix:1, 2, 3, 5 ("re-occupation period"). Lachish: *L* III, pls. 90:391–392 (III); 97:537–541 (all II?), 543 (do.), 544 (III and II loci), 545, 546 (II), 548 (III), 549 (III), 550 (III—and II,), 551 (*N.B.*, 548–551 are not really very "wide-rimmed," but do form a continuum with examples that are "wide-rimmed"), 554. Note the similarity of Str. III exx. to *TBM* I exx. Bethel: *AASOR* 39, pl. 66:4–6, 11–12 ("Sixth century"). Tell el-Far'ah (N): *RB* 58, pp. 418–419, fig. 12:19, 21 (*niv.* I). Megiddo: *M* I, pl. 11:54 (IV filling-1 ex., IV-1 ex., III–31 exx. incl. one with seal impression of Shabaka, ca. 710–696 B.C., II-6 exx., I-4 exx.), 57 (IV-2 exx.). *M Tombs*, pl. 38:26. Samaria: *SS* III, figs. 12:21 (PP VIII); 8:4 (PP V, intrusive? or crater rim? Note other "VII–VIII" elements in *hk*, e.g. fig. 8:8); 21:10? (possibly a crater). Shechem: unpublished exx., Str. VI or later, mostly of the medium-width triply-ridged variety.

Pre-Hellenistic bag-shaped jars: the type is relatively uncommon, although a more full recovery of whole jar forms might yield a different picture. Ramat Raḥel: *RR* I, figs. 12:1?; 29:1–3 (all "?"). *RR* II, fig. 19:4, 5 (all Va). En Gedi: *'Atiqot* V, fig. 22:3 (V, cf. p. 32). Fig. 22:4 is a degenerate "Hippo jar" form tending toward a bag shape, possibly indicating the influence of the "bag-shaped" jar form. Lachish (?): *L* III, pl. 96:518, 528? (both II, cf. *'Atiqot* V, fig. 22:4 and 3, respectively). Samaria: *SS* III, figs. 12a:1?; 32:1 (both PP VIII).

Four-handled store jars, including LMLK wine jars: Ramat Raḥel: *RR* I, figs. 14:2; 15:1–8; 26:3?; 31:4–9 (all Va). *RR* II, pls. 38–39 (all Vb), cf. pp. 33 ff. and 61 ff. and *RR* I, p. 47. En Gedi: *'Atiqot* V, fig. 22:2; pl. 19 and pp. 32–35. Note also the four-handled tall crater/store jar of fig. 21:7. Tell Beit Mirsim: *TBM* I, pls. 52:10–11 (A2); 32:4; 40:3–5. *TBM* III, pls. 13:2 (A2); 29:8, 10. Note also the tall four-handled crater/store jars, *TBM* III, pl. 13:1–2, 4. Beth-shemesh: *AS* IV, pl. 46:23, 25 (cf. *AS* V, pp. 79, 82, 84). Note also the tall crater/store jar with four handles, *PEFA* 2, pls. l (T. 7); lviii (T. 8) and cf. the discussion concerning handles on p. 89. Lachish: *L* III, pl. 95:482, 483, 484 (all III), Cf. pp. 340 ff. Note also the four-handled tall crater/store jars of pls. 95:491–492; 96:499, 501–502. Bethel: *AASOR* 39, pl. 80:10, 12, ("sixth century"). Shechem (?): doubly-ribbed handles similar to the above appear in Str. VI, but the vessel ware-form mode is unclear.

Neckless jars: cf. the discussion by Paul Lapp, *AASOR* 38 (Beth-zur), pp. 58–59, and note that parallels brought forward here constitute a modification of his conclusions regarding the geographical distribution of the form. Ramat Raḥel: *RR* I, fig. 12:5 (cf. left-side drawing), 7? (Va). Tell Beit Mirsim (?): *TBM* I, pl. 52:12, 13 (A2). *TBM* III, pl. 13:7, 9. See the discussion by Lapp cited above. Beth-shemesh: *AS* IV, pl. lxv:1–12 (no. 5 is IIc, 7 and 12 are IIb–c). Lachish: *L* III, pl. 94:466 (1 ex. in III locus). Bethel: *AASOR* 39, pl. 67:9 ("sixth century"). Hazor: *H* I, pl. lxxvii:31 (III, cf. *AASOR* 38, fig. 15:10–11). Megiddo: *M* I, pl. 12:63–65 (all I) appear to be later developments of the form with high loop handles or horizontal handles. *M* I, pl. 12:60 may be an atypical rim, but the form is characteristically undecorated. Samaria: *SS* III, figs. 12:20? (PP VIII); 21:23 (E 207, others Qz, Qx). Shechem: *BASOR* 169, fig. 22:8; many other unpublished Str. VI (and later?) exx., including B62:VII.8.2.1227 and B62.VII.5.34.428 (cf. "PNP" p. 549: P, R).

Pointed bottles: cf. Sahab Tomb B, *QDAP* 13 (1948), p. 98, nos. 31–37, p. 99, nos. 42–43. Although the form appears only at En Gedi among the critical strata selected for generation of the type-series of late seventh/early sixth-century pottery, it is a wide-ranging, well-attested form in the late seventh/early sixth-century Trans-Jordanian tomb series. Similarly, it appears as an import in late seventh-century stratification at Fort Shalmaneser (*Iraq* 21 [1959], pl. xxxvIII:88, 90, cf. p. 144). Since the form appears at virtually all the "northern" sites but nowhere in eighth-century stratification, the determination was made to include it among those analyzed. The chronological range of the vessel seems somewhat longer than most of the forms under investigation, with degenerate unpainted examples probably extending well into the Persian Period. Burnished examples indicated by *: Ramat Raḥel: *RR* II, fig. 14:39, 40*, 41. Probably these are all or mostly all post-587 B.C. in date, since "Refuse Pit 484" (1961) contained materials dating from the fifth/sixth century down well into the second century B.C. En Gedi: *'Atiqot* V, fig. 19:14, 15 (possibly IV, but cf. p. 31, which discusses the typological development of the pointed bottle and mentions a finely made painted example from V). Beth-shemesh: *AS* IV, pl. LXVIII:10* (T. 14, typologically degenerate). Lachish: *L* III, pl. 90:383, 384 (both T. 106). Bethel: *AASOR* 39:4 ("Iron II"). Tell el-Far'ah (N): *RB* 58, pp. 418–419, fig. 12:10, 13 (*niv.* I). Hazor: *H* I, pl. LXXX:22 (II, cf. pp. 58–59). Megiddo: *M* I, pl. 9:6, 7* (Str. II, nos. 4–5, 8–9 appear to be late derivatives). Samaria: *SS* III, fig. 11:34 (PP VII). *HE* I, fig. 163:III:4. Shechem: S. H. Horn and L. G. Moulds, "Pottery from Shechem Excavated 1913 and 1914," *Andrews University Seminary Studies* 7 (1969), pls. VIII, IX, no. 188, cf. remarks on p. 44. Several other unpublished Str. VI fragments are directly comparable to the Tell el-Far'ah exx. cited above.

"Phoenician" juglets with two handles (a), one handle (b) and no handles (c): these are easily distinguished from the familiar tenth-century forms by the disc base-form mode. The form is especially common in Trans-Jordanian tomb groups of the late seventh century B.C., cf. Silvester J. Saller, "Iron Age Tombs at Nebo, Jordan," *Liber Annuus* 16 (1966), 225 ff. and *Dhībân* II, 88 ff. Ramat Raḥel: *RR* II, fig. 11:28 ("b", Va). En Gedi: *'Atiqot* V, fig. 19:12(b)?, pl. XVII:10 ("a", both V, cf. p. 30). Tell Beit Mirsim: *TBM* I, pl. 66:17–20 (all "a," A2). *TBM* III, pl. 15:1–3(A), 4 ("b", all A2 with the exception of 15:4, which Albright considered somewhat earlier, cf. § 157). Lachish: *L* III, pl. 88:331 ("b", T. 218). Beth Shan: . . . *Beth Shan*, pls. 34:5 ("b"); 70:19 ("b", ware color unusual for type, both Level IV); 72:8 ("a", Level IV). Tell el-Far'ah (N): *RB* 54, pp. 582–583, fig. 4:1 ("b"), *"Fer* II"). *RB* 58, pp. 410–411, fig. 10:5 ("a", *"niv.* III", probably a *niv.* I intrusion into the eastern end of Loc. 217, unrecognized because of the similarity to tenth-century juglets. Cf. Sahab Tomb B, no. 64 [*QDAP* 13 (1947), 101]). Hazor: *H* III/IV, pl. CCXXVIII:21, 22 (type unclear, both Va; no. 23 ["a"] may be an eighth-century form). Megiddo: *M* I, pls. 1:30, 39–42 (all "b", all III); 9:2–3 ("a", II). Samaria: *SS* III, fig. 23:7("b"), 5?("b"), 8("a"), 15?("a") (all E 207).

"One-handled" jugs with wide mouth and rounded bottom: cf. *L* III, pl. 84:165–187, 189–192. Some of the larger forms are formally very close to tenth/ninth-century cooking jugs such as *RB* 58, pp. 410–411, fig. 10:19, although ware distinctions generally may be noted. The earlier chronological range of the type is not known, although no "northern" parallels from the 733/722 horizons are known to the writer. Post-597 exx. are rare. Burnished vessels indicated by *: Ramat Raḥel: *RR* I, fig. 11:31? (Va, cf. *L* III, pl. 84:169, 175, 180). En Gedi: Clark Collection, *'Atiqot* V, fig. 31:11–12. Tell Beit Mirsim: *TBM* I, pl. 57:1–8, 10–12, 14–17 (A2, no. 16 appears to have been used as a cooking jug, cf. p. 135). Pl. 57:9, 13 would appear to be related forms, transitional to the "Red Jug" form. *TBM* III, pl. 17:7–13, 15 (nos. 9, 13 from W. Tower, phase *gamma* cache 33–15, rest A2, cf. § 154: nos. 7, 8, 12, 15 are described as "smoked"). Beth-shemesh: *AS* IV, pl. 67:2, 13–16 (no. 2 is "IIc"). *PEFA* 2, pls. 24:1–5, 6(?) (T. 1); 33:23, 25(?) (all T. 2, no. 21 may be transitional to the "Red Jug" type); 39A:11, 12 (T. 4 repos.); 46:9, 13 (T. 7); 47:6, 10, 19 (T. 7); 56:14, 57:9 (T. 8), cf. pp. 81–82. Lachish: *L* III, cf. above; items from good Str. III loci include 167, 177, 183, 187, 189, 190, 192. Hazor: *H* II, pl. LXXV:5* (V, cf. *L* III, pl. 84:171, 174, 176, 180, though burnish is moderately unusual). Megiddo: *M* I, pls. 1:31? (I, painted bands unusual, base prob. wrongly restored) 2:58*–60*?

(III, II, III respectively, all vertically burnished as in dipper juglets, apparently a by-form of the dipper-juglet series, but cf. *L* III, pl. 84:174, 176); 5:112 (III), 118 (III–II, looks like a tenth/ninth-century cooking jug but cf. *L* III, pl. 84:167, 173). Samaria: *SS* III, fig. 22:10 (Z deep pit, E 207–2 exx., Qn; cf. comments on p. 168).

"Red Jugs": the term is Wampler's for his types 606–614 (*TN* II, pls. 34–35). As utilized here, it comprises the class of jugs with tall, flaring necks, simple rims, handle from shoulder to rim, slightly convex base only occasionally becoming flat and almost invariably heavily red-slipped. The range is well represented by *TN* II, pl. 34:606–610, 611?. At present, the form is attested only for post-587 loci. Ramat Raḥel: *RR* I, fig. 28:44, 45, 46 (pierced base). *RR* II, fig. 19:9–12. Contrary to the descriptions, all are red-slipped and burnished ext., cf. *RR* I, p. 41 and pl. 23:3, which seems to show the jug figured in fig. 28:44. All are Str. Va. En Gedi: *'Atiqot* V, fig. 19:11 (V, cf. p. 30). Tell Beit Mirsim (?): *TBM* I, pl. 57:9, 13 and *TBM* III pls. 16:5, 17:16 appear to be "one-handled" jugs with flattened bases, perhaps partly transitional to the "Red Jug" type. No true "Red Jugs" occur. Beth-shemesh: *PEFA* 2, pls. XXXVII:13 (T. 2, burnished slip, cf. p. 67); XLVII:8 (T. 7); LIV:12 (Repos. of T. 8); LVI:3, LVII:8 (T. 8). Lachish: *L* III, pl. 84:193, 194, 198, 199 (all T. 106–9 exx. except for one ex. from T. 1010). Bethel: *AASOR* 39, pl. 78:5 ("sixth century", note attributions and excavation dates of other Loc. 403 materials). Hazor (?): *H* III/IV, pl. CLXXXII:21 (Str. VI, cf. *L* III, 84:198, although "one-handled" jugs 170–172, 177–179, 181 also offer strong points of similarity). It must be emphasized that the form, with its convex base and tall flaring neck, is not typical of the eighth century, but is both common and quite variable in details of body and neck-form modes in early sixth-century deposits.

Note: *M* I, pl. 3:81–82 (IV–III, IV resp.) are probably *not* influenced by this form. Certainly the slightly-formed ring base is foreign to the form, as are the relative neck-body proportions.

"Northern" decanters: the type, characteristic of the second half of the eighth century B.C., is well epitomized by . . . Beth Shan, fig. 71:7–9, 11. See also *M* I, pl. 4:99–100, 102–107. The form has a doubly-ridged rim, trapezoidal body-form mode, oval to round to "hogback" handle section and, generally, a ridged neck. Shoulder grooves often occur. It was apparently never burnished during the eighth century. The only burnished example known to the writer, *M* I, pl. 4:100, comes from a "Str. I" locus, and it is highly improbable that all other examples "typed" to Jug 100 are burnished (Loc. 603 also contained typically II–III Jars 54 and 81, and probably is to be dated to the first half of the seventh century, by which time the burnished "southern" decanter has already made its appearance at Hazor in Str. IV). Neither this nor the following form should be confused with the globular decanter, which first appears in northern sites in the 733/722 destruction levels (cf. *SS* III, fig. 10:17, 19 and *H* I, pl. LVI:16–18, *H* II, pl. LXXXVII:6). This form is similar in respect of handle section and neck ridge, but always has a globular body and a single-ridged or "beaked" rim. . . . Beth Shan, fig. 71:12–14 are characteristic of the form and serve to corroborate James's conclusion that Beth Shan Level IV was destroyed in 733 B.C. See the discussions by Kenyon, *SS* III, p. 124 and Wampler, *TN* II, pp. 21b–22a. The typological progression from the "northern" decanter to the "southern" decanter is difficult to demonstrate other than from appearance or non-appearance in dated stratification especially since so little eighth-century stratification has been published for the south. In addition to the seventh-century "southern" decanters at "northern" sites cited below, two other important complementary distributions should be noted. The "northern" decanter appears in tomb groups at both Tell en-Naṣbeh (T. 5) and Jericho (T. WH.I, Level 5 front) characterized by other eighth-century materials: *TN* I, pp. 83–84, 98–100, cf. also W. F. Badè, *Some Tombs of Tell en-Nasbeh*, Palestine Institute Publication, no. 2 (Berkeley, 1931), pls. XVI–XXIII and *Jericho* II, fig. 258:3 and accompanying discussion. "Southern" decanters appear in quantity at both sites, but in-

variably in association with seventh- to sixth-century materials: e.g., Badè, pls. XIII–XV (*TN* II types 735–3 exx., 740), *Jericho* II, T. WH.I, Jug type E.I,a (Levels 1 and 3), fig. 258:1–2, 4 and accompanying discussion. Cf. also Sellin and Watzinger, *Jericho* Bl. 33:A 16c and 15c.

Beth Shan: . . . *Beth Shan*, figs. 10:1–5, 22:8; 36:2; 46:1; 66:5; 71:7–9, 11 and other exx. ("Level IV"). Bethel: *AASOR* 39, fig. 64:17 ("sixth century"). Tell el-Far'ah (N): *RB* 59, fig. 9:7; *RB* 58, fig. 11:23 (*Niv.* II). Hazor: *H* II, pls. LXIV:20–21 (VII); LXX:19–20 (VI); LXXIX:18 (Vb); LXXV:10 (V); LXXXVII:4–5 (Va), other exx. *passim* *H* I, *H* III/IV. Megiddo: *M* I, pls. 4:99–100, 102–107. *M* II, pl. 91:1 (IV). Cf. discussion below. Samaria: *SS* III, figs. 10:18; 22:1, 2?, 4 (Pottery Period VI, E 207, S Tombs 108, Qz, Qn, Qd, Stadium, Z deep pit). Shechem: "PNP," fig. 104:G, H (both Str. VII).

"Southern" decanter: the type tends toward simpler body lines than the above, although it is always trapezoidal. The rim is single-ridged or "beaked", handles are flat or strap-like, with a central broad depression on the upper surface. Most are wheel-burnished below the handle attachment down to the lower carination, with vertical hand burnish in the area of the handle. Post-597 B.C. examples often have a "stepped" ridge (probably a constructional feature, caused by insertion of the neck and rim into the lower neck) in place of the earlier "folded" ridge. *TN* II, pls. 38:675–676; 39:734–740, 750 well illustrate the type. Late exx. from En Gedi (*'Atiqot* V, figs. 9:7–8 and 20:1–5) exhibit the "stepped" ridge feature. A special sub-form of interest is that of the un-burnished type illustrated in *PEFA* 6 (1935) from the Adoni Nur tomb, fig. 22:103–104, probably dating to the last half of the seventh century B.C. Mention of burnish in the descriptions is indicated by *. Ramat Raḥel: *RR* I, figs. 11:26–27; 25:4; 28:41*, 43* (all Va). *RR* II, figs. 20:12, 16–17 (latter two parallel Adoni Nur nos. 103–104, see above), 35:4*. All exx. are Str. Va. En Gedi: *'Atiqot* V, figs. 9:7–8; 20:1–5, all wheel burnished, all Str. V, cf. pp. 31–32. Tell Beit Mirsim: *TBM* I, pls. 59:1–6; 66:27?. *TBM* III, pl. 16:6, 8. All are Str. A2, except for 59:4, from the abandoned dye-plant in SE 32 A-10 found with a medium high-based lamp, pl. 70:8, which Albright dated to "about the end of the eighth century B.C." Beth-shemesh: *AS* IV, pls. XLV:13, 14*, 15*, 16; LXVII:7*, 8* (IIc); LXVIII:2*, 6*, 13, 14 (T. 14, exx. typologically degenerate, cf. *AS* V, p. 141). *PEFA* 2, pls. XXXIII:28 (note older rounded handle with central ridge, Repos. T. 2); XXXVII:14 (T. 2); XXXIXB:5** (T. 4); XLI:14*, 16**, 18** (T. 5); XLIVA:6, 7** (T. 6); XLVII:12**, 13** (T. 7); LIV:16*, 18*, 21* (Repos. T. 8); LVI:13**, 16 (T. 8); LVII:13**, 16**, 18 (T. 8). *N.B.* attempted identification of burnish from the preceding plates is marked ** and may be erroneous in some cases. For descriptions, see pp. 66–67 (ibid.). Lachish: *L* III, pls. 87:264, 273*–279*, 281*; 103:665*, 668 (III and II loci, mostly the latter, all but 264, 278 and 668 are described as burnished). Bethel: *AASOR* 39, pls. 78:3* ("sixth century"); 79:1*–2 (burnished? both "Iron II"). Tell el-Far'ah (N): an unpublished sherd* from Locus 124 (*Niv.* I). Hazor: *H* I, pl. LXIX:8* (V); *H* II, pls. LXXXVII:12, 13*?, 22 (all Va); C:18–20, 32* ("Adoni Nur" type, see introduction to form above and Amiran, *Ancient Pottery* [N 2], p. 296), all are Str. IV. *H* III/IV, pls. CLXXXIV:23*, CCXIX:21 (both VI loci but both have other seventh-century elements, e.g. burnished saucers, pls. CLXXXI:38 and CCXIX:7). Megiddo: *M* I, pls. 2:67* (closely parallel to Adoni Nur 102); 3:101*? (both II). *M Tombs* 42:30 (=141:11, T. 219). Samaria: *SS* III, p. 167 comments on decanters near in type to fig. 22:2 indicate three burnished examples from Z deep pit, E 207 "fragments . . . closely ring burnished on body with vertical hand burnish on handle and neck" and Qn "fragments . . . burnished on rim." All loci cited have other seventh-century materials. Shechem: unpublished materials studied by the writer (Str. VI), e.g. B60.VII.7.87.4655 neck fragment parallel

to En Gedi fig. 20:1 (*'Atiqot* V, p. 73), cf. also the handle section *BASOR* 169 (1963), fig. 22:13.

"Low-based" lamps: the separation of this type from the following "high-based" form is, to a certain extent, subjective and dependent upon which elements of the vessel ware-form mode are selected for analysis. *L* III, pl. 83:150–152 are closely related forms characterized by a flat (formed) base and a broad flange clearly distinguished from the sidewall of the vessel. This feature sets the seventh-century B.C. form apart from the LB to 918 B.C. (?) low-based lamps such as . . . *Beth Shan*, figs. 52:12; 122:10 (Level VI); *M* I, pl. 38:18 (V); *RB* 56, p. 128, fig. 9:10 ("Moyen-Bronze II"), p. 132, fig. 11 ("Récent Bronze"), *H* III/IV, pl. CLXIX:9–10 (XII), Bethel (*AASOR* XXXIX) pl. 55:11 ("Iron I"). In general, the "high-based" lamp forms tend to have a flange less clearly defined and more nearly continuous with the sidewall. "Low-based" lamps also tend to be somewhat larger than their "high-based" related forms. Ramat Raḥel: *RR* I, figs. 11:35, 33? (both Va); 27:5–6, 7? (all Vb). En Gedi: *'Atiqot* V, fig. 23:3 (ring base), 4 (do?) (both V), see p. 35. Clark Collection: ibid., fig. 22:6–7. Tell Beit Mirsim: *TBM* I, pl 70:1–3, 6–7 (all A2); *TBM* III, pl. 15:5–9?, 10 (nos. 6, 8, 9 from W. Tower, phase *gamma* cache 33–15, others A2). Beth-shemesh: *AS* IV, pls. XLV:21 (IIb–c), 22 (IIa–b), 23, cf. *AS* V, p. 141; LXVII:20, 23. *PEFA* 2, pls. XXXIII:2–3, 6, 11 (Repos. T. 2); XXXVII:1–2 (T. 2); XLI:2 (T. 5); XLIVA:8 (T. 6); XLVI:6 (Repos. T. 7); XLVII:1–2 (T. 7); LIV:1? (Repos. T. 8); LVI:4? and LVII:6 (T. 8). One "low-based" lamp (possibly the L.B.-Iron I type) may have been found in T. 1, cf. *PEFA* 2, p. 65. Lachish: *L* III, pl. 83:150, 151, 152 (III and II loci). Note the unusually well-articulated base on no. 152 (cf. also *TBM* I, pl. 70:9; *TBM* III, pl. 15:7, 9?) a feature which sets it apart from most "low-based" lamps and one which may show influence of the "high-based" form. Bethel: *AASOR* 38, pl. 65:21 ("sixth century"). Shechem: *N.B.* Lapp's statement in *AASOR* 38 (Beth-zur), p. 68, is incorrect. There were no footed lamps of any kind in the stratified eighth-century materials from Shechem.

"High-based" lamps: cf. discussion of "low-based" lamps above. At Lachish, the "high-based" lamps, typified by *L* III, pl. 83:153, are restricted to Str. II contexts. Notable in most examples of this form is the distinctly articulated base and the lack of clear demarcation between the flange and the sidewall of the lamp. Note also the relatively smaller width of the lamp *vis-à-vis* the width of the base. These three characteristics also fit the Str. II lamp form *L* III, pl. 83:149, which would hardly be called "high-based" on any other grounds. Ramat Raḥel: *RR* I, figs. 11:36–38 (Va); 27:8 (Vb); 28:50 (Va). En Gedi: *'Atiqot* V, figs. 11:upper; 23:5–7 (moderately low, but of "high-based" type), 8–9 (all V), cf. p. 35. Clark Collection: ibid., fig. 32:8–9. Tell Beit Mirsim: *TBM* I, pl. 70:4–5, 8–9, 11 (all A2) all have features relating to the form under discussion, although only the curious little no. 11 has a high base. Beth-shemesh: *AS* IV, pls. XLV:25–27 (no. 26 "II-c"), cf. *AS* V, p. 141; XLVIII:8, 12 (T. 14, cf. *AS* V, p. 142). *PEFA* 2, pls. XXXIII:4, 5 (Repos. T. 2); XXXVII:3, 4 (T. 2); XXXIXA:4 (Repos. T. 4); XLIVA:8 (T. 6); 46:10, 12 and XLVII:3, 4 (T. 7); LIV:4–5 (T. 8); LVI:18, 20 and LVII:10, 11, 15, 16, 19 (T. 8). Lachish: *L* III, pl. 83:149, 152?, 153 (all stratified exx. II or later, most exx. from tombs, esp. Ts. 106 and 1002). Tell el-Far'ah (N): *RB* 58, fig. 12:17 (*Niv.* I). Hazor: *H* III/IV, pl. CCXXXII:9, 10 (Area B, Str. Va Loc. 3146, which has other seventh to sixth century forms: e.g. pl. CCXXX:2, 12?, 21, 29). Megiddo: *M* I, pl. 37:6, 7 (only 1 ex. each, both from "Str. III"). Samaria: *SS* III, fig. 27:4 (Dj, only 1 ex. found). Shechem: *BASOR* 169, pp. 52–3, fig. 22:14 (VI), several other unpub. exx.

15. New Light on the Na'ar Seals

NACHMAN AVIGAD

THE HEBREW UNIVERSITY OF JERUSALEM

The purpose of this paper is to discuss two new Hebrew seals of the *na'ar*-class and to examine their bearing on the accepted interpretation of the category of seals and seal-impressions inscribed with the formula X *na'ar* Y.

This formula has been amply discussed by the late Professor Albright in his thorough treatment of the seal-impressions *l'lyqm n'r ywkn* found on jar-handles at Tell Beit Mirsim (*Figure 12,* 1) and at Beth Shemesh in 1928–1930.[1] In 1961 a fourth impression of the same seal was discovered at Ramat Raḥel.[2]

There is little to be added to the basic and generally accepted interpretation of this seal by Albright. For a better understanding, we shall repeat here some of his arguments. This seal evidently belongs to the well-known category of seals bearing the inscription X *'ebed* Y, since the words *'ebed,* "slave, servant, officer" and *na'ar,* "youth, attendant, servant, steward" are roughly synonymous, and the formulae are thus parallel. The two titles seem however to indicate different ranks and functions. *'Ebed* is known to have been the title of high-ranking officers of the royal court, whereas the title *na'ar* is never mentioned in the texts among the highest officials of the realm.[3]

The use of *na'ar* in Hebrew is manifold. The word means originally "lad, youth, young boy," a sense in which it occurs repeatedly in the Bible. It then comes to mean "young attendant, personal servant," e.g. of Elijah (I Kings 8:43), of Elisha (II Kings 5:20, 8:4); it is often used in the plural, *nĕ'ārīm,* e.g. of Abraham (Gen. 18:7); of David (I Sam. 25:9–25); of Absalom (II Sam. 13:28–29); of the King of Assyria (here soldiers are obviously meant [II Kings 19:6; Isa. 37:6]); of King Ahasuerus (Esther 2:2, 6:3), etc. Further, *na'ar* appears in the sense of "armor-bearer," e.g. of Gideon (Judg. 7:11); of Abimelech (Judg. 9:54); of Jonathan (I Sam. 14:1).

Obviously the *nĕ'ārīm* of these categories were servants in the ordinary sense of the word and they had hardly anything to do with seals. Only a *na'ar* who held a responsible office would be in need of a seal and could eventually own one. A man of this type might have been the *na'ar* of Boaz, the Bethlehemite farmer, "a mighty man of wealth." This *na'ar* was an overseer in charge of the reapers (Ruth 2:5–6).

However, *ṣībā'* (Ziba) the *na'ar* of King Saul held a distinguished position (II Sam. 9:9–10). He is the only *na'ar* who is mentioned in the Bible by name. He is also called *"na'ar bêt Šā'ūl"* (II Sam. 19:18) which can best be translated as "steward (or intendant) of the house of Saul." Ziba was evidently the custodian of the personal property of Saul and his family. The eminence of his position is indicated by the fact that he had fifteen sons and twenty servants of his own. Being himself a servant of Saul's family, Ziba later became the *na'ar* of Mephibosheth, Saul's grandson, when David bestowed half of Saul's property upon him.

Albright, of course, pointed to Ziba, the steward of Saul, as the most striking illustration which provides a complete and satisfactory explanation of the usage of the seal of *'Elyāqīm na'ar Ywkn. Ywkn,* which should be vocalized *Yawkin,*[4] is the abbreviated form of *Yĕhôyākīn* or *Yôyākīn*— the name of the next to the last King of Judah. The inscription should therefore be interpreted: "Eliakim steward of Jehoiachin (or Joiachin)," i.e. the administrator of the personal or crown property of King Jehoiachin.

So far, this was the only known seal of this class of which, however, only impressions were found. Recently, two *na'ar* seals proper were published, bearing the inscriptions *lbṭš n'r brk'l*[5] and *l'bd' n'r 'lrm*[6] respectively. Both seals originate from Transjordan and are probably Ammonite. We do not know all the kings of the neighboring border states by name. The present writer suggested that these *nĕ'ārīm* were in the service of tribal chieftains. In a semi-nomadic society, each chieftain was a sort of petty king having his attendants. This, however, could not be said about the centralistic monarchy of Judah in the eighth–seventh centuries. There, it seemed, a *na'ar* occupying a position and owning a seal must have been in the king's service, just as an *'ebed* was.

It is here that the new finds mentioned at the beginning of this paper come in. They are the first known Hebrew seals of the *na'ar* class, since, as we saw, we have only imprints from the Eliakim seal. Both seals were recently acquired by collectors and their exact provenience is unknown. They form a most important addition to the otherwise scanty epigraphic evidence on our specific subject. We shall treat these seals in full.

The seal of *Malkîyāhū na'ar Šāpāṭ* (*Figure 12,* 2)

This is a scaraboid of polished yellow limestone, perforated lengthwise, 16 mm long, 7.5 mm wide, and 9 mm thick. The flat oval bottom is divided by double lines into three horizontal registers.

In the upper register there is a figure of a fish with a prickly body, remarkably well carved in a molded, naturalistic style.[7] In front of it, there seems to be a representation of a fishing hook. The fish as a major motif is rare on Hebrew or related seals.[8] So far it has appeared only once on a Hebrew seal as part of an assemblage of Egyptian symbols.[9]

The two lower registers are occupied by the following inscriptions:

mlkyhw	Belonging to Malkiyahu
n'r špṭ	steward of Shaphat

The engraver ingeniously managed to include the last two words in the exergue by inserting the *shin* in the empty space between the *resh* and the *pe*.

Both Malkiyahu and Shaphat are common biblical names. Malkiyahu, "Yahweh is my king," in its full form occurs only once (Jer. 38:6). Incidentally, this man was also a functionary bearing the title "son of the king" who was in charge of the prison where Jeremiah was confined. The shortened form Malkiyah (both forms are written Malchiah in the A.V.) is common to several persons mentioned in the later books of the Bible. Malkiyahu also appears on another seal[10] and on a Hebrew ostracon from Arad.[11]

The title *na'ar* is discussed above.

Shaphat is a hypocoristicon of Jehoshaphat, "Yahweh has judged," and is held in common by several persons in the Bible:

a. One of the spies who were sent out to spy the Land of Canaan (Num 13:5)
b. Father of the prophet Elisha (I Kings 19:16)
c. Son of Adlai, David's overseer of the herds (I Chron. 3:22)
d. A Gadite in Bashan (I Chron. 5:12)
e. A son of Shemaiah (I Chron. 27:29)

The name Shaphat also occurs on another Hebrew seal: *lšpṭ*.[12]

It appears that neither the owner of the seal nor his master can be identified with any persons mentioned in the Bible. Clearly, Shaphat is not a known king. It would be highly speculative to identify him with King Jehoshaphat on the grounds that his name is a hypocoristicon of the latter's. Besides, an early ninth-century date would be too early for our seal because of palaeographical reasons. The script belongs to the horizon of the seventh century's formal cursive. Noteworthy features are the *lamed* with its flat and bent bottom line, and the *he* with its slanting lower horizontal strike.

The seal of *Běnāyāhū na'ar Ḥaggî*[13] (Figure 12, 3)

This is a scaraboid of polished stone with irregular brownish-red and white stripes; pierced lengthwise; 16×14×6 mm. Exceptionally, this seal is inscribed on its domed back and not on the flat bottom as usual.

The seal is divided by double lines into three horizontal registers. The two upper ones contain the inscription. The lower register displays a design consisting of two volutes springing from a triangle. This is a well-known motif in Phoenician art and architecture, widely adopted by the same arts in Israel. It frequently figures as a volute-capital supporting palmettes and "sacred trees," particularly in ivory carvings of the ninth–eighth centuries B.C.[14]

On our seal this design is apparently meant to represent a proto-Aeolic capital as found in Israelite buildings at Samaria,[15] Megiddo,[16] Jerusalem,[17] and Ramat Raḥel.[18] The corresponding capitals at Hazor have no triangles.[19] A representation of the proto-Aeolic capital is also preserved on an ivory plaque from Samaria.[20]

Here, this motif makes its first appearance on a seal. A recently published Phoenician seal shows a similar architectural motif—a capital in Egyptian style.[21]

The two-line inscription reads:

lbnyh	Belonging to Benayahu
w n'r ḥgy	steward of Ḥaggi

Several letters are slightly defective, but the reading is quite clear. The last letter of the first name is transferred to the second line.

The name Benayahu (in the A.V., Benaiah), "Yahweh has built," is common to a number of persons of rank mentioned in the Bible (one Benaiah held high military offices in the latter part of David's and in Solomon's reign), but none of these is likely to have been the owner of this seal. One wonders whether there is an intentional connection between the name of the seal-owner and the architectural motif which he chose for his seal.

Na'ar, "steward," has been discussed above.

Ḥgy, vocalized *Ḥaggî*, "festal" (probably abbreviated from Ḥaggiah, "festival of Yahweh"), occurs once in the Bible as the son of Gad and founder of a tribal family (Gen. 46:16; Num. 26:15). In the post-exilic period the name of the prophet *Ḥgy* is pronounced Ḥaggai. *Ḥgy* appears several times on Hebrew seals and seal-impressions.[22]

Here again we may conclude that neither Benayahu nor his master Haggi can be identified and that the latter was certainly not a king or any other known royal personage.

Palaeographically the seal may be dated approximately to the eighth century B.C. The double volute design is also in keeping with this date.

The two seals discussed above have much in common: a similar layout of design; rare motifs of decoration; both seals belong to functionaries of the same rank; the names of their superiors belong to neither Israelite nor Judaean monarchs. It is the last-mentioned characteristic which lends particular interest to these seals.

Obviously both Shaphat and Ḥaggi were wealthy men. They may have been just rich landowners, or they may have belonged to the class of high ranking officials who enjoyed a privileged position and perhaps received land from the king—as the practice sometimes was. In any case, they employed stewards for the administration of their estates. Judging from their attractive seals, these stewards—Malkiyahu and Benayahu—apparently occupied distinguished positions, although in a private capacity.

After establishing the private character of these seals, we might, excursively, consider their bearing on some other seals or seal-impressions.

It may be remembered that the many known Hebrew *'ebed*-seals bear two formulae: X *'ebed hammelek,* or X *'ebed* Y where Y is always the name of a known king. Other title bearers on seals were regularly also royal officials, e.g. *ben hammelek* and *'ašer 'al habbayit.* When the first *na'ar* seal impressions appeared, and the name of Eliakim's master happened to be a hypocoristicon of the name of a known king, this *na'ar* was consequently also regarded as being in the service of the king. This may, of course, still be true. But in the light of the new evidence, an *a priori* assumption that every *na'ar* seal must belong to an official of the royal household is not in place anymore. *Inter alia,* it should be noted that, so far, the designation *na'ar hammelek* has not been found on seals.[23]

It therefore seems in place to question whether *Yawkin* of the Eliakim seal-impressions was indeed the king Jehoiachin, or rather a private estate owner. The answer to this question depends on a reconsideration of the whole subject which would require a separate paper. We should like to point out one serious difficulty which Albright had to overcome in his interpretation.

The young king Jehoiachin occupied the throne only for three months, mostly during the siege of Jerusalem when the country lay at the mercy of the Babylonians (II Kings 24:8–12). After this brief rule, Jehoiachin was taken prisoner to Babylon and never returned from his exile. Albright himself regarded it as improbable that the seal-impressions of Eliakim were struck during the short reign of Jehoiachin. It could be argued that they were prepared perhaps before his reign, when he was a crown prince and owner of estates. However, Albright dated the Eliakim seal-impressions to the very last phase of Tell Beit Mirsim, between the years 598 and 589 B.C.,[24] i.e. after Nebuchadnezzar's invasion in 598. He therefore suggested that the jars were stamped during the first years of Jehoiachin's captivity, when he was still considered as king *de jure* by the people of Judah,[25] although Zedekiah occupied the throne. This interpretation, however, involves political problems which cannot be discussed here.[26]

The wide distribution of the Eliakim seal-impressions is generally considered as an argument in favor of the accepted view that they belong to a crown estate. But this is not necessarily true. By now, we possess a number of private seal-impressions which were also found in different sites—e.g. "Menahem (son of) Yôbanah/Yehobanah" (found at Tell el-Judeideh, Bethshemesh, Ramat Rahel,[27] and lately also in the Jewish Quarter of the Old

City of Jerusalem); or "Shebna (son of) Shaḥar" (Lachish, Tell en-Naṣbeh, Ramat Raḥel,[28] etc.). A recent trend has been felt among scholars to attribute this type of private seal also to royal officials.[29]

However, we must allow the existence of organized private enterprise in the country's economy, side by side with royal enterprise. Large estates, belonging to wealthy private landowners and administered by stewards, distributed their products all over the country. A clarification of this point of economic and social organization is, I think, the main contribution of our new *na'ar* seals.

It gives me great pleasure to dedicate this study to Professor G. Ernest Wright—eminent scholar and great friend.

NOTES

1. W. F. Albright, " 'The Seal of Eliakim and the Latest Pre-exilic History of Judah,' with Some Observations on Ezekiel," *JBL* 51 (1932), 77–106.

2. Y. Aharoni, *Excavations at Ramat Raḥel, 1961–1962* (Rome, 1964), p. 33.

3. Cf. R. de Vaux, *Ancient Israel, Its Life and Institutions* (London, 1961), pp. 124–126.

4. For this vocalization see Albright, *Tell Beit Mirsim. III, AASOR* 21–22 (1943), 66, n. 9.

5. M. F. Martin, "Six Palestinian Ancient Seals," *Rivista degli studi Orientali* 36 (1964), 203 ff., n. 3.

6. N. Avigad, "Seals and Sealings," *IEJ* 14 (1964), 192 f.

7. The fish appears to be inspired by a member of the family *Diodontidae,* perhaps *Diodon hystrix* found in all tropical seas. [F.M.C.].

8. It appears on another, yet unpublished seal.

9. Avigad, *IEJ* 4 (1954), pl. 21:2.

10. A. Reifenberg, *IEJ* 4 (1954), p. 140.

11. Aharoni, *EI* 9 (1962), 11.

12. I. Ben-Dor, *QDAP* 13 (1947–48), 64 ff.

13. This seal is said to come from the Hebron area. It was acquired in 1969 by Mr. Amiel Brown to whom the writer is indebted for permission to publish it.

14. J. W. Crowfoot and Grace M. Crowfoot, *Early Ivories from Samaria* (London, 1938), pls. XVII, XXI; R. D. Barnett. *A Catalogue of the Nimrud Ivories* (London, 1957), fig. 1.

15. J. W. Crowfoot, K. M. Kenyon, E. L. Sukenik, *The Buildings at Samaria* (London 1942), pl. XXIX, 2.

16. R. S. Lamon and G. M. Shipton, *Megiddo I* (Chicago, 1939), fig. 67.

17. K. M. Kenyon, *Jerusalem* (London, 1967), pl. 20.

18. Aharoni [N 2], pl. 42:1.

19. Y. Yadin et al., *Hazor III–IV* (Jerusalem, 1961), pls. CCCLXII–CCCLXIII.

20. Crowfoot [N 14], pl. XXII:1.

21. N. Avigad, "An Unpublished Phoenician Seal," in *Hommages à André Dupont-Sommer* (Paris, 1971), p. 3.

22. Two *ḥgy* seals were found in Jerusalem: D. Diringer, *Le iscrizioni antico-ebraiche palestinesi* (Roma, 1934), no. 20; J. Prignaud, *RB* 70 (1964), 374. Another seal was

published by N. Avigad, *Bulletin of the Israel Exploration Society* 25 (1961), 244. For a stamped handle, see Diringer, p. 120.

23. A slip of the pen occurred when the late Père de Vaux referred erroneously to the seal-impression of "Eliakim *na'ar* of the King."

24. Albright, *Tell Beit Mirsim. III* [N 4], pp. 66 f.

25. Ibid., p. 66, n. 9.

26. Cf. E. F. Weidner, "Jojachin König von Juda in babylonischen Keilschrifttexten," in *Mélanges Syriens offerts à M. René Dussaud*, II (Paris, 1939), 923–935; Albright, "King Joiachin in Exile," *BA* 5 (1942), 49–55; A. Malamat, "Jeremiah and the Last Two Kings of Judah," *PEQ* (1951), 81–87.

27. Aharoni [N 2], p. 60, with earlier literature.

28. Aharoni, *Excavations at Ramat Raḥel, 1959–1960* (Rome, 1962), p. 18, with literature.

29. Aharoni [N 2], p. 61.

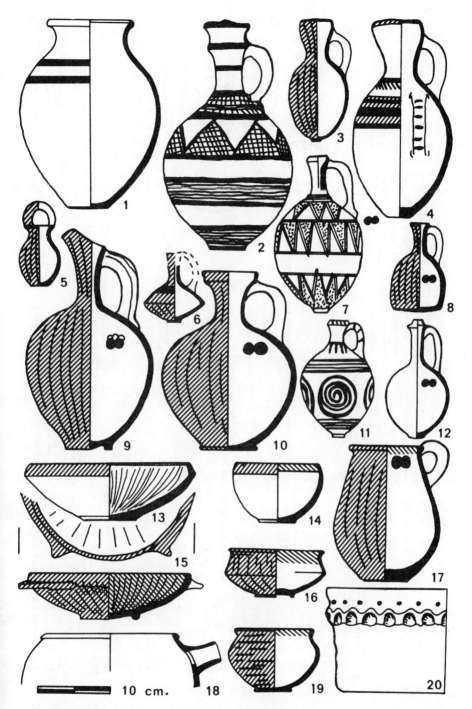

Figure 1. Some ceramic types of Palestinian MB IIA; long strokes indicate burnishing. *Vide* William G. Dever, "The Beginning of the Middle Bronze Age in Syria-Palestine."

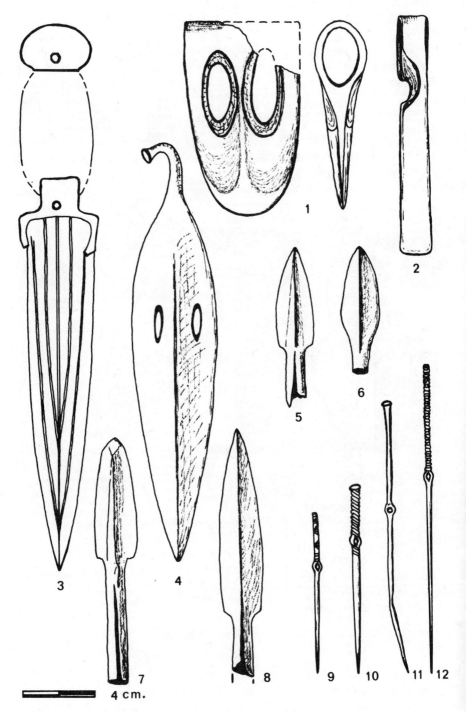

Figure 2. The main bronze types of Palestine in MB IIA. *Vide* Dever, "The Beginning. . . ."

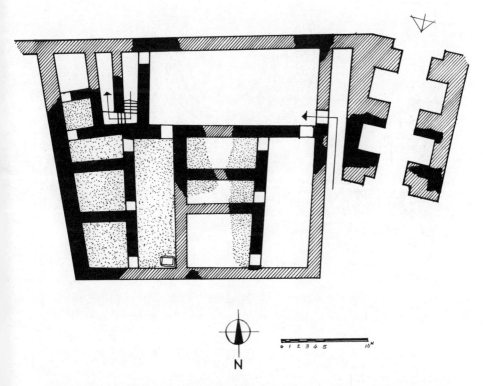

Figure 3. Megiddo. A restored plan of the gate and the building 2072 of Stratum VIA (second half of the eleventh century B.C.). *Vide* Benjamin Mazar, "The 'Orpheus' Jug from Megiddo."

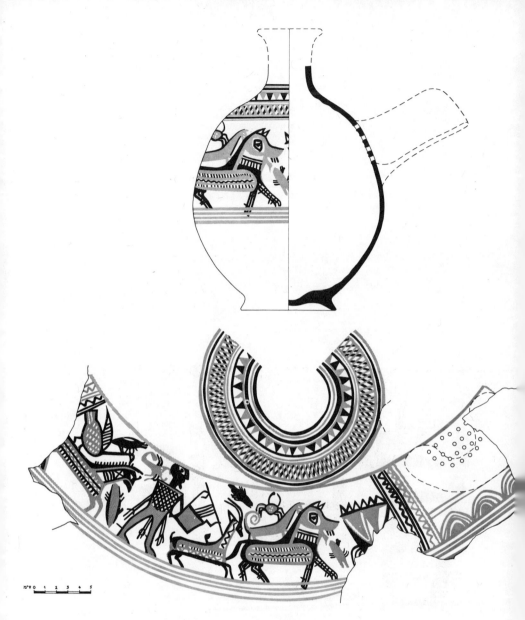

Figure 4. The "Orpheus" Jug from Megiddo. *Vide* Mazar, "The 'Orpheus' Jug. . . ."

Figures 5a. The Siamun relief from Tanis; *5b.* Montet's drawing of same. *Vide* H. Darrell Lance, "Solomon, Siamun, and the Double Ax."

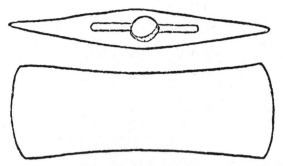

Figure 6. Example of the double ax as a tool. *Vide* Lance, "Solomon, . . ."

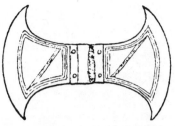

Figure 7. Example of the double ax as a religious symbol. *Vide* Lance, "Solomon, . . ."

Figure 8. Athenian vase showing the Dipylon shield. *Vide* Lance, "Solomon, . . ."

Figure 9. Pithos stamp from Knossos. *Vide* Lance, "Solomon, . . ."

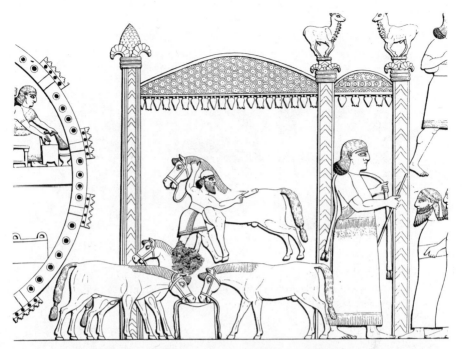

Figure 10. An Ashurnasirpal II relief in Nimrud: four horses of the royal chariot within an especially installed field-stable, a pavilion supported by pillars. *Vide* Yigael Yadin, "The Megiddo Stables."

Figure 11. An Assyrian relief from the palace of Tiglath-Pileser III: a portable and collapsible manger, its trough very shallow and placed on wooden legs. *Vide* Yadin, "The Megiddo. . . ."

Figure 12. Three seals: (1) Stamped jar-handle from Tell Beit Mirsim *l'lyqm n'r ywkn;* (2) Seal of *mlkyhw n'r špṭ* (impression); (3) Seal of *bnyhw n'r ḥgy* (impression). *Vide* Nachman Avigad, "New Light on the *Na'ar* Seals."

16. The Way of Obedience:
I Kings 13 and the Structure of
the Deuteronomistic History

WERNER E. LEMKE

COLGATE ROCHESTER/BEXLEY HALL/CROZER

I

IT HAS BEEN roughly thirty years now since the first appearance of Martin Noth's monumental *Überlieferungsgeschichtliche Studien,* in which he advanced the theory that the books of Deuteronomy through II Kings constitute a larger unified historical work, the so-called Deuteronomistic History, which is distinct in outlook and composition from the Tetrateuch or Priestly Work.[1] His views have gained a wide following among Old Testament scholars and have led to a burst of literary activity on that important segment of Old Testament literature.[2]

Such widespread acceptance of Noth's thesis in its broad outlines, however, must not be allowed to obscure the fact that subsequent investigations have raised anew a number of important questions, upon which no general agreement has as yet been reached. These unresolved questions center chiefly on two areas: (1) the unity of authorship and date of composition of the Deuteronomistic History; and (2) its over-all structure and basic theological perspective.

With regard to the former, many scholars no longer accept Noth's basic contention that the Deuteronomistic History derives essentially from one exilic author whose work subsequently received only minor additions but no thoroughgoing revisions. Pointing to numerous seams and differences in perspective throughout the Deuteronomistic History, they feel that these could be better accounted for by a successive edition theory, involving at least two, possibly more, authors.[3] When it comes to dating these historically, opinions are divided as to where they should be placed. Some would place the first edition in the late pre-exilic period, with subsequent revisions following during the exile.[4] Others would locate all editions in the exilic, or even early post-exilic, period.[5] Some would even go so far as to argue that we should no longer speak of major and distinct authors, but view the work as the product of a whole Deuteronomic school, whose editorial work was an ongoing process extending over several decades or even generations.[6] One may be permitted to observe that if this were in fact so, then one of the most fundamental and attractive aspects of Noth's thesis would have to be abandoned altogether.

With regard to the second main area of contention, relating to the over-all structure and basic theological perspective of the Deuteronomistic History, here, too, much work has been done since the appearance of Noth's influential work. Among the questions relating to this area which have been the object of subsequent investigations are such issues as the relationship of the Deuteronomistic author(s) to the code of Deuteronomy and the extent to which their hand is present in the Book of Deuteronomy itself;[7] the role of the Davidic theology or royal messianism in the perspective of the Deuteronomist(s);[8] and the pivotal or structurally significant loci in the Deuteronomistic History;[9] to mention only some of the more significant issues in regard to which Noth's work has been modified or advanced by recent studies.

In the light of these developments, it has become abundantly clear that much work remains to be done, before anything approaching a consensus on this important body of Old Testament literature may be achieved. Not only will it require a more systematic sifting and assessment of the vast literature already produced, but also a continuation of the investigation, through articles and monographs, of more narrowly focused themes and segments of the Deuteronomistic History. The author's own investigation of I Kings 13 in the following pages is offered as a modest contribution to the ongoing study of the structure and theology of this monumental work.[10]

II

Our story in I Kings 13 is one of the more fascinating, though in many respects puzzling, prophetic narratives found in the Deuteronomistic History.[11] As it now stands, the story tells of a nameless man of God from Judah, who came to Jeroboam I at Bethel and delivered an oracle which foretold the destruction of the altar, upon which Jeroboam was about to offer sacrifices, some three hundred years later by Josiah. Having authenticated his oracle by two miraculous signs, and having declined an invitation by the king to stay and refresh himself, the nameless man of God departed as abruptly as he had appeared. On his journey home, however, he was induced by a prophet who lived at Bethel to depart from his divinely ordained way, as a result of which he was slain by a lion when he resumed his journey. Upon hearing of this, the prophet from Bethel went and brought back the corpse of the man of God. He buried it in his own tomb and instructed his sons to bury him upon his own death in the same tomb with the man of God, in the belief that the latter's prophecy against the altar of Bethel would surely come to pass some day.

This story has been subject to widely divergent scholarly estimates. As yet no consensus has emerged in regard to such basic questions as its date of composition, authorship, form-critical classification, tradition history and significance within the larger structural and ideological framework of the Deuteronomistic History. It is particularly the latter issue with which we shall be concerned in this paper, but before we turn to that, it might be useful for the sake of the discussion to provide a concise résumé of some representative past scholarly discussion.

Many commentators consider our story a late legend or midrash which was inserted only secondarily, and at a relatively late stage, into its present context. Thus, Wellhausen called it, "eine Legende im Stil des Midrasch" and assigned it to a late post-exilic and post-Deuteronomic hand.[12] Benzinger, agreeing essentially with Wellhausen, considered this story a reflection of a rather mechanistic concept of Prophetism in later Judaism.[13] In his extensive analysis of I Kings, A. Jepsen assigned our pericope to a Levitical and post-Deuteronomic redaction of the late sixth century B.C., that is, during the period of the building of the Second Temple.[14] In a more recent study of this chapter, Jepsen still prefers this view, but allows for the possibility that an exilic Deuteronomistic hand could have been responsible for the inclusion of this chapter.[15] Eissfeldt believes that it is a secondary insertion into the Book of Kings, which is not to be ascribed to the Deuteronomistic compiler.[16] A similar view is maintained by Jörg Debus, though without any significant discussion of the evidence.[17] All of these commentators have this in common: they consider the story to be a secondary, post-Deuteronomistic interpolation. If their view should prove to be correct, then, of course, our story would be of no significance for an assessment of the structure and theology of the Deuteronomistic History.

Other commentators, however, assign the story's present position, though not its composition, to a Deuteronomistic redaction. Montgomery, who calls it a midrash of dubious historical value whose documentary fixation it is impossible to date, follows Šanda in assigning its redaction to the time of Josiah.[18] Snaith assigns its present position to a Deuteronomic compilation around 610 B.C., but goes on to say that "there is no adequate reason for doubting that this is an ancient tale; the Deuteronomic compiler revived it in order to show that Jeroboam had received full warning and, incidentally, that Judeans should avoid all relations with northerners."[19] Snaith, however, adduces no evidence to support his contention that the story is an ancient tale. The same, unfortunately, is true of W. F. Albright who on one occasion expressed a similar conviction with respect to the antiquity of the tale.[20] Martin Klopfenstein in his recent study of I Kings 13 likewise defends the possible antiquity of the story, the final form of which, however, he too would assign to the time of Josiah.[21]

Some have questioned the unity of our story, seeing it rather as a combination of two independent traditions of unequal historical value. Morgenstern, for instance, considers vss. 11–32 a secondary expansion of a primary narrative found in vss. 1–10, 33–34.[22] John Gray, who in the first edition of his commentary on Kings viewed the story as a composite of two separate traditions, has since reverted to accepting the unity of the story, which he now characterizes as a "prophetic legend in saga style, transmitted by the Deuteronomistic compiler."[23] The unity of the story is also defended by Martin Noth, though with a certain amount of ambivalence when it comes to defining the extent of its Deuteronomistic redaction. In his earlier monograph, he viewed our story as an individual legend, originating in prophetic circles at Bethel and incorporated by the Deuteronomist into his history because of its immediate relevance to the reform measures of King Josiah.[24] In his more recent, and regrettably unfinished, commentary on Kings, however, Noth seems more inclined to reduce the Deuteronomist's share in the redactional process of the story, by suggesting that it may already have been a part of the pre-Deuteronomistic stage of the Jeroboam tradition.[25] The Deuteronomist's share in this story is reduced by Noth to the following verses: 13:2b f., 33–34, and possibly 13:32b. For the ultimate origins of the story, Noth looks to North-Israelite prophetic circles from the time of the last days of the Northern Kingdom.[26]

As is eminently clear from this concise survey of the literature, our story is beset with a number of problems which have been widely debated, but concerning which no general agreement exists as yet. Its unity and antiquity have been both denied and defended. Its ultimate origins have been the object of much speculation, which more often than not has been based on a paucity of factual data. Above all, its place and theological significance within the over-all structure of the Deuteronomistic History have received only insufficient attention, even by those commentators who would assign its present shape and position to a Deuteronomistic editor. We wish to argue that I Kings 13 forms an integral part of the structure and theology of the Deuteronomistic History and that while its ultimate origins may most likely be traced to northern prophetic circles, its present position and formulation owes more to the hands of a Deuteronomistic editor or author than has hitherto been allowed.[27]

We shall begin our own investigation with a structural analysis of the story, along with its immediate literary framework.

III

The immediate literary framework of our story, which is found in 12:26–33 and 13:33–34, gives the impression of being overloaded with secondary expansions and repetitive glosses. Jeroboam's ascending upon the altar, for instance, is mentioned three times (12:32 and twice in 12:33), while his establishing of a festival on the fifteenth day of the eighth month is mentioned twice (12:32, 33). His appointment of non-Levitical priests at the high places is likewise mentioned twice (12:31 and 13:33). For these reasons, it is generally recognized that our story seems to have been inserted into a previously existing narrative. Opinions are divided, however, as to where the seam is to be placed.[28] It by no means follows, though, that the narrative is therefore a secondary insertion, made subsequent to the Deuteronomistic edition of the Book of Kings, as some commentators have maintained.[29] The present disorder and overloading of the framework may equally well have resulted from glossing, or even scribal errors, made subsequent to the insertion of our story by a Deuteronomistic editor.[30] Since the words 'aḥar haddābār hazzeh in 13:33 clearly presuppose knowledge of our story and, furthermore, since the rest of the verse reflects the language and thought of 12:31, it is to be assumed that the editorial hand discernible in 12:31–33 and 13:33 was responsible for the insertion of our story. This suggestion is further supported by the consideration that 13:34 seems to be a resumption and completion of the thought temporarily abandoned in 12:30.[31] That the hand responsible for the inclusion, and possibly even partial shaping of our story, was that of a Deuteronomistic editor we shall try to argue in a subsequent section below. Before we do that, however, we must turn to a brief delineation of the structure of our story and an identification of its dominant motifs.

As is generally recognized, the story seems to fall quite naturally into two main parts, each of which has its distinct, though not unrelated, focus: (1) vss. 1–10 and (2) vss. 11–32. Each part has two major protagonists around whom the main action revolves, and several minor or incidental characters.

The first part focuses upon the fate of the altar of Jeroboam as foretold by the nameless man of God from Judah. The latter is the chief protagonist, with the king being his antagonist, and between the two, all of the action and dialogue takes place. Not explicitly mentioned but assumed as incidental characters are the king's servants and people (vs. 4), among whom, according to the information contained in vs. 11, must have been the sons of the old prophet in Bethel. The action in this part proceeds rather rapidly to its climax and resolution. The man of God appears, delivers his oracle against the altar of Jeroboam, and authenticates it by means of a sign. His divine authority is further underscored by the fact that the king's hand, which was raised against him, was paralyzed and that it was restored only upon the prophet's intercession with the Lord on his behalf. The scene ebbs off with the king's invitation to the prophet to come home with him and the prophet's refusal to have table fellowship with him. Verses 9b–10, beginning with the words "nor return by the way you came . . . ," serve a transitional function in that they look forward to the sequel which follows in vss. 11–32.

The second part focuses upon the fate of the man of God. It is developed more broadly and introduces a new antagonist in the person of the old prophet from Bethel. The latter, upon hearing from his sons about the events which had transpired at the Bethel sanctuary, set out after the man of God, and having caught up with him, he induced him to return to his home, contrary to his previously given divine command. The consequences of this act of disobedience are announced immediately in vs. 20, which may be viewed as the climax of this story. From there on, the tensions quickly resolve and the story takes its inevitable course. The man of God is killed by a lion on his homeward journey, brought back and buried by his prophetic colleague from Bethel. Verse 32 looks back to the first part of our story, thus providing a bracket which holds both parts together. The structure of our story could be outlined as follows:

Part I: The Oracle against the Altar of Jeroboam at Bethel. Verses 1–10
    A. Introduction. Vs. 1
    B. The Oracle and Sign against the Altar. Vss. 2–3
    C. The Exchange between the King and the Man of God. Vss. 4–9a
    D. Transition to Part II. Vss. 9b–10

Part II: The Disobedience of the Man of God and Its Consequences. Verses 11–32
    A. Introduction of the Old Prophet from Bethel. Vs. 11
    B. The Man of God is Induced to Depart from His Divine Commission. Vss. 12–19
    C. The Man of God is Judged for His Disobedience to His Divine Commission. Vss. 20–26
    D. The Man of God is Brought Back and Buried by the Prophet of Bethel. Vs. 30
    E. Concluding Resumption of the Major Theme of Part I. Vss. 31–32

On the basis of the foregoing structural analysis, it should be apparent that this story revolves around two dominant motifs: a polemic against the cultic establishment of Jeroboam and a discursive narrative about the importance of obedience to the divine word.[32] Since these two themes correspond roughly to the two major sections of our story, it is not surprising that many commentators have seen fit to question the unity of our story. There is no law, however, that says that a story can only have one major theme. Nor are these two themes entirely unrelated, at least in the perspective of certain Old Testament traditions, as we shall see below. Furthermore, if these two themes were in fact ever part of two separate narratives, this could only have been possible in the earliest pre-literary stages of the traditions. As the story now stands, it can only be considered a literary unit, because of the integral relation between the two parts and the uniformity of language which characterizes it throughout.[33]

IV

We shall now address ourselves to the question of whether there exists a more integral relationship between our story, along with its immediate literary framework, and the larger structure and theology of the Deuteronomistic History. We believe that such a relationship does in fact exist and propose to demonstrate this by means of an analysis of certain key expressions and dominant motifs in our story which are paralleled elsewhere in the Deuteronomistic History.

1) 'ārê šōmrôn, "cities of Samaria" (13:32)

Although this expression occurs only once in our story, it is of interest because of both its chronological implications and its connection with other pivotal passages in the Deuteronomistic History. As the phrase "cities of Samaria" suggests, "Samaria" here can only be the name of a country or region, which linguistic usage, however, did not come into existence prior to the late ninth century B.C.[34] In the Old Testament, it seems to have come into prominence only subsequent to the fall of the city of Samaria in 722 B.C. and the creation of the Assyrian province by that name. Thus at least this reference, if not the entire story, cannot antedate the late ninth century and in all likelihood derives from a time subsequent to the late eighth century B.C. Moreover, similar references to the "cities of Samaria" occur in only two other passages in the entire Old Testament. In II Kings 17:24–28 we are told how following the fall of Israel, the king of Assyria settled other nations in the "cities of Samaria" (vss. 24 and 26).[35] The story goes on to tell how these were plagued by lions [!], because of their failure to worship Yahweh, until the Assyrian king sent back a Yahweh priest who, residing at Bethel [!], taught them how they should fear the Lord.[36]

The other reference to the "cities of Samaria" comes from the account of Josiah's reform in II Kings 23:19, where we are told that Josiah removed all the shrines of the high places that were in the "cities of Samaria."[37] The account goes on to state that "he did to them according to all that he had done at Bethel." It should be noted that both of the other passages in which the "cities of Samaria" are mentioned are found in chapters which occupy a key role in the structure and theology of the Deuteronomistic History, as is generally recognized, the one having to do with the demise of the Northern Kingdom and the other with the reform of Josiah.

The same interconnection between these passages is further supported by the next two expressions which we shall examine.

2) kōhănê habbāmôt, "priests of the high places" (12:32, 13:2, 33)[38]

Four times in our pericope the expression "priests of the high places" is used in a derogatory manner to refer to the priesthood which Jeroboam installed at Bethel and throughout his realm. This expression occurs only three times elsewhere:[39] once in II Kings 17:32, where it refers to the priests which the resettled pagan peoples of Samaria appointed for themselves subsequent to the fall of the Northern Kingdom; and twice in the account of Josiah's reform (II Kings 23:9, 20).[40] Like the preceding one, this expression is found only at three key points in the Deuteronomistic History: in the account of Jeroboam's cultic innovations (I Kings 12–13), in the reflections following the fall of the Northern Kingdom (II Kings 17), and in the account of Josiah's reform (II Kings 23). Surely such a relationship cannot be accidental, but must point to some larger purpose or design.

3) *bāttê habbāmôt,* "shrines of the high places" (12:31, 13:32)

This expression occurs twice in our pericope and only three times elsewhere. As in the case of the previous two expressions, all the other occurrences are confined to the same pivotal passages in the Deuteronomistic History. Twice it appears in the peroration on the occasion of the fall of the Northern Kingdom (II Kings 17:29, 32); and once in the account of Josiah's reform (II Kings 23:19). Thus this expression also, as the two preceding ones, suggests that there exists a close relationship between these three pivotal passages in the Deuteronomistic History, which is most readily explained if we assume a common authorship and design. Their general flavor and outlook is Deuteronomistic and presupposes the reforms of Josiah.[41] It should be noted that these expressions appear in both the story proper (13:2, 32), as well as in its immediate literary framework (12:31, 32; 13:32, 33), suggesting that the same editorial hand was at work in both. Thus, while the story proper may have had earlier written or oral antecedents, its present formulation and position is due to a Deuteronomistic editor writing subsequent to the Josianic reform. That this conclusion is essentially correct is confirmed by our analysis of some other expressions and motifs, to an examination of which we must now turn.

4) *limrôt 'et pî yhwh,* "To rebel against the mouth of the Lord" (13:21, 26)

Twice the nameless man of God from Judah is accused of having rebelled against the command (lit. "mouth") of Yahweh. The idiom is striking and bears further investigation. The verb *mrh,* "to rebel, be stubborn or obstinate, disobey," occurs forty-three times in the Old Testament. With but one exception, it is always used in a theological sense of man's rebellion against God.[42] In conjunction with the expression *pî yhwh,* "mouth" or "command of Yahweh," our idiom occurs ten times, seven of which fall within the Deuteronomic literature.[43] The latter appear all within paranetic sections so characteristic of Deuteronomic style. I Sam. 12:14–15 is of particular interest and may serve to illustrate this:

> If you will fear the Lord and serve him and hearken to his voice and not rebel against the commandment of the Lord (*wĕlō' tamrû 'et pî yhwh*), and if both you and the king who reigns over you will follow

the Lord your God, it will be well; but if you will not hearken to the voice of the Lord, but rebel against the commandment of the Lord (*ûmrîtem 'et pî yhwh*), then the hand of the Lord will be against you and your king.

This passage is patently Deuteronomistic, as is generally recognized by most scholars.[44] Moreover, it occurs in another key passage or structural pivot of the Deuteronomistic History, marking the transition from the era of the Judges to the period of the monarchy. Its affinities to our story are remarkable, not only in terms of the commonality of the idiom employed, but in the emphasis upon the proper worship of Yahweh and the strict obedience to his will, upon which hinges the fate of both the people as well as their king.

In the light of this, the presence of a Deuteronomistic hand in I Kings 13 is again strongly suggested, and the structural lines which connect our story to its larger framework within the Deuteronomistic History extend not only forward to II Kings 17 and 23, but backward to I Sam. 12 as well.

5) *lišmōr 'et hammiṣwāh*, "To keep the commandment" (13:21)

Like the preceding expression, this idiom points strongly to the presence of a Deuteronomistic hand. The verb *šmr*, "to guard, keep," is frequently used in the Old Testament in conjunction with abstract nouns in the sense of "to keep, observe, obey."[45] The combination of *šmr* followed by *miṣwāh*, either singly or in combination with synonymous terms, occurs seventy-three times. The vast majority of these occurrences are concentrated in two books: Deuteronomy (thirty-three times)[46] and Kings (sixteen times),[47] with four more occurrences elsewhere in the Deuteronomistic History.[48] If we subtract one occurrence of this idiom in II Chron. 34:31, which is taken from II Kings 23:3, we are left with only nineteen instances in which the idiom occurs outside the Deuteronomistic History.[49] And nearly all of these are demonstrably later or dependent upon Deuteronomic usage.[50] In the light of these statistical data, the Deuteronomistic provenance of the phrase in I Kings 13 is strongly suggested. It becomes even more certain when we compare it with many occurrences in other key passages generally assigned to the Deuteronomistic Historian.[51] Of these, it may suffice to cite II Kings 17:13 as an example:

> Yet the Lord warned Israel and Judah by every prophet and every seer, saying: "Turn from your evil ways and keep my commandments and my statutes (*wěšimrû miṣwōtay wěḥuqqôtay*), in accordance with all the law which I commanded your fathers and which I sent to you by my servants the prophets.[52]

This passage comes from the well-known peroration of the Deuteronomistic Historian on the occasion of the fall of the Northern Kingdom. According to him, Israel's demise was due, among other things, to her failure to keep the commandments of God, as revealed in the Torah and reiterated through the mouth of the prophets. In spite of repeated warnings by the prophets, Israel failed to obey God and as a consequence met with destruction.

This passage is also of interest because of its affinity to the next expression which we shall examine.

6) lāšûb min/bĕ hadderek, "To turn from/return by the way" (13:9, 10, 17, 26, 33)

One is struck by the frequent occurrence of the root šûb in this story; sixteen times to be exact, which is more than in any other chapter in the entire Old Testament, except for Jeremiah 3 where the root occurs an equal number of times.[53] The root has a wide range of meaning and is used in our chapter in at least four different ways: (1) to return an object to its former position or state, as in vss. 4 and 6; (2) to go back in the direction from which one came, as in vss. 9, 10, 16, 17, 18, 19, 20, 22, 23, and 29; (3) to repeat or continue an action, as in vs. 33; and (4) in a transferred sense to depart from a course of action or mode of behavior, as in vs. 33. Five times the verb occurs in combination with the noun derek, "way," and it is this latter combination in particular which we shall examine more closely.[54] Three times the words are conjoined by means of the preposition bēt, and in each of these instances, the expression has a literal or physical meaning, that is, the man of God from Judah was forbidden to return by the way he had come to Bethel.[55] Twice the two words are conjoined by means of the preposition min, and in at least one of these instances, if not in both, the expression has a transferred or metaphorical meaning, as in definition (4) above. In this latter sense the idiom is clearly used in vs. 33:

> After this thing Jeroboam did not turn from his evil way (lō' šāb yārob'ām middarkô hārā'āh), but continued to appoint from all sorts of people priests for the high places; whoever so desired, he appointed as priest for the high places.

Verses 33–34 are generally ascribed to a Deuteronomistic editor.[56] This suggestion is further supported by the fact that the idiom in question occurs once more in the context of another pivotal passage in Kings, the affinity of which to our story we had occasion to point out earlier.[57] Elsewhere the idiom šûb min hadderek occurs eighteen more times.[58] Most of these are concentrated in the books of Jeremiah and Ezekiel, and while we do not wish to posit any strict literary dependence, we may safely venture the suggestion that the idiom in question was characteristic of the late pre-exilic or exilic prose tradition which found its literary deposit in the books of Jeremiah and Ezekiel.[59]

In the light of this meaning of šûb min hadderek in vs. 33, we must now turn to examine its meaning in vs. 26, which appears more ambiguous. The RSV translates it as follows:

And when the prophet who had brought him back from the way heard of it, he said, "It is the man of God, who disobeyed the word of the Lord; therefore the Lord has given him to the lion, which has torn him and slain him, according to the word which the Lord spoke to him."[60]

This translation suggests that the idiom is to be understood in the literal sense of physical motion, and this in fact is how it is understood by virtually every commentator. But is this the only possible, or even most likely, translation? We should like to suggest that the idiom in this instance as well might more correctly be translated in its metaphorical sense of "to depart or turn from one course of action or mode of behavior to another," whether this be for good or ill. Thus understood vs. 26 would be translated: "And when the prophet who had made him depart from the way heard of it, he said: 'It is the man of God. . . .'" The way from which the man of God had departed, of course, was the divine command which had been given him. In support of such a translation and interpretation we would cite the following facts. First of all, wherever *šûb* is used in conjunction with the preposition *min* and the noun *derek*, the idiom has never a literal meaning, but is always used in a metaphorical sense.[61] Thus, if the idiom were to have a literal meaning here, it would be the only instance in the entire Old Testament. Secondly, the presence of another idiom in the same verse (i.e. *mārāh 'et pî yhwh*), whose Deuteronomistic flavor we have noted above in this section at (4), makes it all the more likely that the idiom under discussion is likewise used in a theological sense. And thirdly, the noun *derek* in its non-literal and theological or metaphorical sense is a favorite term of the Deuteronomic and Deuteronomistic writers and appears in such related expressions as "to walk (or not to walk) in the way(s) of N," where "N" can be either human,[62] or divine,[63] and the related expression "to turn or depart (*sûr*) from the way."[64]

Quite conceivably the author of vs. 26 intended to play on the various nuances of the meaning of *šûb* in conjunction with *derek,* leaving it purposely ambiguous in order to facilitate the transition from the literal sense (as in vss. 9, 10, 17) to the metaphorical one (as in vs. 33).[65] This intricate play on the meaning of the root *šûb* within the story inevitably brings to mind the importance which this root has in the larger theological perspective of the Deuteronomistic History. H. W. Wolff has shown how the theme of repentance, of turning away from false gods in order to turn to Yahweh in singular devotion, appears at important junctures in the Deuteronomistic History.[66] He sees this appeal to repentance as part of the basic kerygmatic thrust of the Deuteronomistic Historian, who thereby provided a limited ray of hope on the basis of which Israel's continued, or renewed, existence as the people of God might be assured. Our story thus could be seen as a negative illustration of this theme, pointing to the dire consequences which ensued when a man on the one hand turned from his divinely ordained way, and on the other failed to turn from his evil ways and persisted in them in spite of all warnings.

Our linguistic analysis of the preceding six expressions has shown that there exists in fact an integral relationship between our pericope and the larger structure and theology of the Deuteronomistic History. The same conclusion is further supported by the manner in which the two dominant motifs of our story, which we isolated in our structural analysis above, find echoes in the wider perspective of the Deuteronomistic History. For one, the polemic against the cultic establishment of Jeroboam, whose sin becomes the major reason for the eventual demise of the Northern Kingdom, is a well-known. Deuteronomistic theme. It runs like a red thread through the Deuteronomistic History of the Divided Monarchy, until it reaches its climactic fulfillment and resolution in the account of Josiah's reform in II Kings 23. In the light of the ample treatment which this theme has received elsewhere, we need not enter into it here at any greater length.[67]

The second main theme of our story likewise finds echoes elsewhere in the Deuteronomic traditions. The demand for obedience to the divine command occupies a prominent place in the Deuteronomic literature.[68] Failure to heed the divine command leads to dire consequences, as illustrated not only by our story, but by many other passages in the Deuteronomic corpus.[69] To be sure, there is a difference between our story and most of the other Deuteronomic passages which we cited, in that in the latter, the divine command is usually mediated through the Mosaic Torah, whereas in our story it is seen as coming through a prophetic *dābār*. But this difference is more apparent than real and presents no insurmountable obstacles for the point which we wish to make, for in the Deuteronomistic perspective these two entities are not entirely distinct and unrelated. Not only is Moses seen as a prophet par excellence (Deuteronomy 18), but the prophets in general were understood to be guardians and interpreters of the Mosaic Torah, as illustrated by the following passage taken from the Deuteronomist's peroration on the occasion of the fall of the Northern Kingdom.

> Yet the Lord warned Israel and Judah by every prophet and every seer, saying, "Turn from your evil ways and keep my commandments and my statutes, in accordance with all the law which I commanded your fathers, and which I sent to you by my servants the prophets." But they would not listen, but were stubborn, as their fathers had been, who did not believe in the Lord their God. They despised his statutes and his covenant that he made with their fathers, and the warnings which he gave them. They went after false idols and became false, and they followed the nations that were round about them, concerning whom the Lord had commanded them that they should not do like them (II Kings 17:13–15).

It is interesting to observe how the prophets in this perspective have become bearers of the Mosaic Torah, and how Israel's failure to heed their repeated warnings led to the nation's eventual downfall. Thus the theme of obedience and disobedience to the divine command is likewise seen to be congenial and integrally related to the theology and structure of the Deuteronomistic History.

By this we do not mean to suggest, however, that a Deuteronomistic editor invented either of these themes, or that our story is simply a theological construct of his. In all likelihood, he was utilizing a pre-existing tradition which was congenial to his purposes and which he adapted and included for reasons of his own at this particular juncture in his history. That this is actually so we hope to demonstrate in the next section, in which we shall trace briefly the pre-Deuteronomistic tradition history of our story.

V

We shall begin by analyzing two of the most prominent expressions which run throughout this story, followed by a discussion of the possible antecedents of its major motifs and certain other features.

1) *'îš hā'elōhîm,* "Man of God" (13:1, 4, 5, 6, 7, 8, 11, 12, 14, 21, 26, 29, 31)

This expression occurs fifteen times throughout our story. It is consistently applied to the nameless prophet from Judah, whereas the old prophet from Bethel is always designated by the term *nābî'*.[70] Apparently the author of the story meant to differentiate clearly between the two. But whether this differentiation was merely one of convenience, that is, to keep the two prophets from being confused, or tendentious, is less easily determined. The two designations as such do not bear any inherent contrast, for elsewhere they are used synonymously to designate true Yahweh prophets.[71] The term *'îš hā'elōhîm* occurs seventy-six times in the Old Testament and seems to designate a being or person who possesses divine powers or stands in a peculiar relationship to the deity.[72] Thus it may be used to designate the "angel" of God,[73] Moses,[74] David,[75] Samuel,[76] or other prophets. It should be noted that the expression always refers to Yahweh prophets and never to other prophets, such as those of Baal. When we look at the distribution of the term, a significant pattern emerges. The vast majority of all occurrences of the term are confined to the Deuteronomistic History.[77] Yet to be determined remain its usage and distribution within that tradition complex. In virtually every instance it is used to designate a prophet.[78] Furthermore, the term is most heavily concentrated in the Elijah-Elisha traditions, occurring thirty-seven times between I Kings 17 and II Kings 13.[79] Four times the term occurs in the early Saul tradition with reference to Samuel (I Sam. 9:6,

7, 8, 10).[80] On the basis of these statistics, it would appear that the term originated in Northern prophetic circles and that it was characteristic of those prophetic traditions which were remembered and handed down among these circles. It is only natural to conclude, therefore, that the provenance of our story must be sought among these same circles.[81]

2) bidĕbar yhwh, "By the Word of the Lord" (13:1, 2, 5, 9, 17, 18, 32)

This expression, which occurs seven times in our story, is not characteristically Deuteronomistic. Wellhausen cited it as an indication of the supposed lateness of our passage.[82] But this is far from certain as we shall see. The expression most likely suggests agency and is intended to underscore the divine origin and authority of the prophetic mission.[83] The expression is relatively rare, occurring in this form only five times elsewhere.[84] In I Sam. 3:21 we read: "And the Lord appeared again at Shiloh, for the Lord revealed himself to Samuel at Shiloh bidĕbar yhwh." In II Chron. 30:12 the phrase suggests divine authorization for King Hezekiah's reform measures: "The hand of God was also upon Judah to give them one heart to do what the king and the princes commanded bidĕbar yhwh." Slightly different from these passages is the use of the phrase in Jer. 8:9, where the use of the preposition bĕ is dictated by the verb: "The wise men shall be put to shame, they shall be dismayed and taken; lo, they have rejected the word of the Lord (mā'ăsû bidĕbar yhwh) and what wisdom is in them?" Different also is the use of the idiom in Ps. 33:6, where the phrase refers not to the prophetic word, but rather to the creative word of the Lord: "By the word of the Lord (bidĕbar yhwh) the heavens were made, and all their host by the breath of his mouth." This leaves I Kings 20:35, which, aside from I Sam. 3:21, provides the closest parallel to the use of this expression in our story. It is found in the context of another prophetic story in which the judgment of God is pronounced upon Ahab for having spared the life of Benhadad.[85] The passage which is of particular interest in connection with our story in I Kings 13 reads as follows:

> And a certain man of the sons of the prophets said to his fellow at the command of the Lord (bidĕbar yhwh), "Strike me, I pray." But the man refused to strike him. Then he said to him, "Because you have not obeyed the voice of the Lord, behold, as soon as you have gone from me, a lion shall kill you." And as soon as he had departed from him, a lion met him and killed him (I Kings 20:35–36).

The parallels to our story are most remarkable, as seen not only in the use of the same expression, but also because of certain other features which both stories have in common. Both involve an exchange between two prophets; both revolve around the theme of unquestioning obedience to the divine word; and in both the prophet who disobeyed the word of the Lord was slain by a lion as a consequence of his disobedience. Such striking similarities are surely not coincidental, unless, of course, we wish to argue that the stories do in fact reflect fairly accurately two separate historical incidents. Those who are not too impressed by the probability of such an alternative are forced to explain these striking affinities by either positing literary dependence, or assuming that what we are dealing with here are two distinct literary deposits of a common motif or tradition. We are inclined toward the latter alternative. Since the story in I Kings 20:35 ff. must undoubtedly be derived from Northern prophetic circles,[86] it is only natural to conclude that the provenance of our story in I Kings 13 must be sought among these same circles. The same conclusion is also suggested by certain other features and motifs in our story.

For one, there is the dominance of miraculous features in our story, which finds its closest parallel in the Elisha traditions. Not only was the altar rent in twain, but Jeroboam's hand was miraculously paralyzed and restored; and the normally ferocious lion did not attack the donkey, but stood calmly beside him after he had slain the man of God. Incidentally, the miraculous utilization of animals in our story calls to mind the story in II Kings 2:23 ff., where two she-bears are said to have killed a group of boys who had mocked the prophet Elisha for his baldness, as he journeyed from Jericho to Bethel.[87]

Several features of our story, thus, suggest that it has pre-Deuteronomistic antecedents and that its ultimate provenance points to Northern prophetic circles.[88] Can the same conclusion be demonstrated with reference to the dominant theme of the first half of our story, namely, the polemic against the altar of Jeroboam? The answer to this question is more complicated.

We might begin by observing that the motif of the prophetic threat against the altar or shrine of Bethel has at times been linked with the message of Amos, in the sense that I Kings 13 has been viewed as a popular or legendary reflex of the latter.[89] Indeed, the two traditions exhibit some tantalizing similarities which may be enumerated as follows:

1. Both Amos and the nameless man of God came from Judah to prophesy at the sanctuary of Bethel.
2. Both came into conflict with the authorities there.[90]
3. Both foretell the destruction of the altar and/or sanctuary at Bethel.[91]
4. Both prophets exercised their ministry under a king by the name of Jeroboam.[92]
5. Both traditions are concerned to differentiate the Judaean prophet from other *nĕbî'îm:* I Kings 13 by designating the Judean prophet consistently by the term "man of God," in distinction to the *nābî'* of Bethel, and Amos 7:14 f. by Amos' explicit assertion that he was not one of the *nĕbî'îm* or guilds of prophets who ordinarily plied their trade at the sanctuary.[93]

On the other hand, we must not overlook a number of differences that exist between our story and the Amos tradition:

1. The story in I Kings 13 is dated to the time of Jeroboam I, whereas the oracles of Amos come from the time of Jeroboam II.

2. Amos' immediate adversary at Bethel was not Jeroboam II, but his high priest Amaziah.
3. I Kings 13 speaks of an immediate destruction of the altar, whereas no such event is recorded for us in the Book of Amos.
4. There is no correspondence in the Amos tradition to the withering of the King's hand in I Kings 13.
5. The sequel to the incident at Bethel in I Kings 13:11–32 has no counterpart in the Amos tradition.[94]

Not all of these differences, of course, are equally significant. It is in the nature of the development of legends or popular traditions to telescope time, alter or confuse incidental features, such as names of personalities and places, or to expand upon the miraculous features of a story. Thus the possibility of some connection between this story and the figure of Amos cannot be ruled out simply on the strength of these differences. Conversely, however, the similarities between these traditions are sufficiently general and diffuse so as not to allow us to elevate the possibility of a connection into a certainty or even strong probability, and for this reason we would be inclined to go along with most commentators who deny or seriously question the thesis that the antecedents of our story lie in the Amos tradition.[95] After all, it is not entirely inconceivable that Jeroboam's cultic establishment at Bethel should have been subject to the denunciation of more than one Judaean prophet, whose words and deeds were remembered in subsequent tradition. In view of the widespread hostility with which Jeroboam's cultic innovations were received by certain Yahwistic circles in Israel, it is neither possible, nor necessary, to trace the antecedents of our story too specifically. Amos was not the only one who inveighed against Bethel, nor was such an invective the exclusive prerogative of Judaeans, as the example of Hosea so amply demonstrates.[96] In this connection, we might also mention the strong condemnation of Jeroboam in the older Ahijah tradition underlying I Kings 14:1–18.[97] Thus, while the evidence is not as clear or unambiguous as one might wish, there is nothing in the first part of our story that prevents us from adopting the position arrived at on other grounds, namely, that the ultimate provenance of our story is to be sought among Northern prophetic circles.

We shall conclude with a brief summary of our findings and an assessment of the larger function and role of our story within the structure and theology of the Deuteronomistic History.

VI

In the foregoing analysis, we have tried to show that our story in I Kings 13 is integrally related to its immediate literary framework in 12:31–33; 13:33, as demonstrated by both structural and linguistic considerations, and that the editorial hand responsible for the latter was also responsible for the partial shaping and inclusion of the former.[98] On the basis of the linguistic evidence, as well as certain thematic and structural affinities to other key passages in the Deuteronomistic History,[99] we have argued that the editorial hand responsible for the partial shaping and inclusion of our story must have been that of a Deuteronomistic author, to whom we should attribute essentially the following passages: 12:31–33; 13:2, 9b–10, 21, 26, 32–33.[100] For the rest, we can no longer be certain as to how much should be ascribed to him and how much to the underlying tradition which he utilized and which, as we saw, he most likely received from Northern prophetic circles. What the original shape of this tradition was is less easily determined. Most likely the narrative contained a prophetic threat against the altar of Jeroboam at Bethel,[101] followed by a sequel which told how the prophet who had become disobedient to his divine commission by having table fellowship in Bethel was punished by an untimely and miraculous death, thus underscoring the importance of unquestioning obedience to the divine command. The story undoubtedly concluded with a reference to the prophet's burial by his colleague at Bethel.[102]

The Deuteronomist took over this story and adapted it in the light of the subsequent history of Israel, adding to it those features which are more specifically related to the reforms of Josiah and providing it with those reflective comments that tie it to the larger perspectives of his history. Affinities with such other key Deuteronomistic passages as I Samuel 12 and II Kings 17 and 23 suggest that our story in its present context is to be viewed as another pivotal passage in the Deuteronomistic History, which is illustrative of the Historian's theology and over-all proclamation.[103] For one, it fits admirably into the larger scheme of prophecy and fulfillment observable throughout the Deuteronomistic History. It provides one of the more impressive examples of the realization of the divine word as mediated through the prophets, which brackets virtually the entire history of the divided monarchy.[104] Moreover, the story provided him with an opportunity to condemn those religious practices in Israel which he considered deviant and in which he saw the root causes of all of Israel's troubles, from the era of the Judges to the end of the monarchy. Above all, our story provided him with a paradigmatic example of the importance of unquestioning obedience to the divine will. Proleptically, the fate of the man of God from Judah points beyond itself to that of the nation. Like the former, Israel too had received a command from Yahweh, as revealed in the Mosaic Torah and reiterated repeatedly by his servants the prophets. Like him, she had rebelled against the mouth of the Lord by turning from her divinely ordained way, thus sealing her ultimate downfall and destruction and confirming the warning which the Deuteronomist had uttered, on the occasion of the institution of the monarchy, through the mouth of the prophet Samuel:

"But if you still do wickedly, you shall be swept away, both you and your king" (I Sam. 12:25).[105]

What Yahweh had foretold by his prophets had indeed come about in the demise of the nation Israel and in the disappearance of her monarchy. The lessons to be learned from Israel's history in the promised land were obvious, and the implications to be deduced from it were clear to anyone who had eyes to see and ears to perceive that which the Lord had done.

NOTES

1. M. Noth, *Überlieferungsgeschichtliche Studien: Die Sammelnden und Bearbeitenden Geschichtswerke im Alten Testament* (Tübingen, 1957; first published in 1943). Hereafter cited as Noth, *UgS*.

2. The literature which has appeared during the past three decades, and which continues to appear unabated, is too vast to be surveyed within the confines of this article. The author hopes to do this at greater length in the not too distant future in a forthcoming monograph.

3. G. von Rad already, in discussing the editorial processes leading to the formation of the Deuteronomistic History, voiced that opinion when he observed: "It is difficult to think that the editing of the Book of Judges and that of the Book of Kings could have taken place as a single piece of work": *OTT*, I (1962), 347. W. Richter, in his detailed analysis of the Book of Judges, discerns three stages in the Deuteronomic edition of the Book of Judges, of which only the last is assigned to the exilic Deuteronomistic Historian. Cf. his *Die Bearbeitung des "Retterbuches" in der deuteronomischen Epoche*, Bonner Biblische Beiträge, 21 (Bonn, 1964), 85 f., 140 ff. Most recently R. Smend argued for at least two successive major editions of the Deuteronomistic History. Cf. his article "Das Gesetz und die Völker: Ein Beitrag zur deuteronomistischen Redaktionsgeschichte," in *Probleme Biblischer Theologie*, ed. H. W. Wolff (Munich, 1971), pp. 494–509.

4. So e.g. Richter, cited in N 3. Further, J. Gray, who dates the first edition "between the outbreak of Jehoiakim's revolt against Nebuchadrezzar in 598 and his death in 597": *I and II Kings: A Commentary*, 2d ed. (London, 1970), p. 7. Unless otherwise noted, all references are to the second edition. Others would place the first, and major, edition in the time of Josiah, followed by an exilic supplementation. So, for instance, Georg Fohrer in his *Introduction to the Old Testament* (Nashville, 1968), p. 236; and F. M. Cross in his article "The Structure of the Deuteronomic History," in *Perspectives in Jewish Learning*, III (Chicago, 1968), 9–24.

5. So e.g. A. Jepsen, *Die Quellen des Königsbuches*, 2d ed. (Halle, 1956), pp. 76, 95 ff., 104. Jepsen distinguishes between an early exilic priestly redaction, a late exilic nebiistic redaction, which corresponds roughly to Noth's Deuteronomist, and a minor post-exilic Levitic redaction.

6. This seems to be the view of E. W. Nicholson, who argues that "the Deuteronomistic history represents the work of a circle who were the direct descendants of the authors of the book of Deuteronomy and who, working in Jerusalem, adopted various aspects of the Jerusalemite traditions and re-interpreted them on the basis of their own specific traditions": *Deuteronomy and Tradition* (Oxford, 1967), p. 113. A similar, though somewhat more tentative, suggestion is made by J. Debus in his monograph *Die Sünde*

Jeroboams: Studien zur Darstellung Jeroboams und der Geschichte des Nordreichs in der deuteronomistischen Geschichtsschreibung (Göttingen, 1967), pp. 109–115. R. A. Carlson, in his *David the Chosen King: A Traditio-Historical Approach to the Second Book of Samuel* (Stockholm, 1964), speaks of a "D-group," by which he means a group of exilic redactors responsible for the final shape of the Deuteronomistic History. In the author's judgment, however, Carlson assigns far too much to their hand, making insufficient allowance for the existence of pre-exilic source materials.

7. In addition to Nicholson's book cited in N 6, and the numerous publications by N. Lohfink, cf. esp. G. Minette de Tilesse, "Sections 'Tu' et sections 'Vous' dans le Deutéronome," *VT* 12 (1962), 29–87.

8. In addition to Cross, "Structure" [N 4], and Carlson, *David* [N 6], see esp. G. von Rad, "The Deuteronomic Theology of History in I and II Kings," in *The Problem of the Hexateuch and Other Essays* (New York, 1966), pp. 205–221.

9. Cf. e.g. H. W. Wolff, "Das Kerygma des Deuteronomistischen Geschichtswerks," *ZAW* 73 (1961), 171–186. Further, D. J. McCarthy, "II Samuel 7 and the Structure of the Deuteronomic History," *JBL* 84 (1965), 131–138.

10. It is also offered as a token of the author's deep and abiding esteem for G. Ernest Wright as a scholar, teacher, and friend. Parenthetically, the author may be permitted to observe that his interest in I Kings 13 and the larger problems of the Deuteronomistic History was first aroused many years ago in the context of a graduate seminar with Dr. Wright. It is only fitting therefore that our study of I Kings 13 is dedicated to the man to whose stimulating influence it owes so much.

11. The author throughout this paper has deliberately used the more general designations "story," or "(prophetic) narrative," rather than more narrow form-critical terms like "legend," "midrash," or even "parable," all of which have been used by different commentators at one time or another. Since the author has not been able to find commonly accepted definitions of the terms mentioned above, and in order not to prejudice the question of the historicity of the narrative, it seemed preferable to use more neutral and inclusive form-critical designations, especially since our argument is not materially affected by what we call our pericope.

12. J. Wellhausen, *Die Composition des Hexateuchs und der Historischen Bücher des Alten Testaments* (Berlin, 1889), p. 280.

13. I. Benzinger, *Die Bücher der Könige*, Handkommentar zum Alten Testament, IX (Tübingen, 1899), pp. 90–93.

14. Jepsen, *Quellen* [N 5], p. 104.

15. Cf. Jepsen's article, "Gottesmann und Prophet. Anmerkungen zum Kapitel 1. Könige 13," in *Probleme Biblischer Theologie* [N 3], pp. 171–180.

16. O. Eissfeldt, *The Old Testament—An Introduction* (New York, 1965), p. 290.

17. His evidence is summed up in one sentence in a footnote: "Dass es sich um eine nachdtr. Einfügung handelt, geht sachlich aus dem übertrieben wunderhaften Charakter der Erzählung, literarisch aus der schlechten Einfügung in den Kontext hervor." Debus, *Sünde Jeroboams* [N 6], p. 35.

18. J. A. Montgomery, *Kings*, ICC (Edinburgh, 1951), pp. 41, 261. Cf. also A. Šanda, *Die Bücher der Könige* (Münster, 1911), p. 359.

19. N. H. Snaith, *Kings*, IB, III (1954), 120. Whether Snaith's statement regarding the intentions of the Deuteronomic compiler is adequate remains to be seen.

20. "Two very early stories reported in I Kings 13–14 illustrate the hostility of the nascent prophetic movement toward the shrines of Jeroboam I." W. F. Albright, *ARI³*, p. 156.

21. M. A. Klopfenstein, "1. Könige 13," in *Parrhesia. Karl Barth zum 80. Geburtstag am 10. Mai 1966*, ed. E. Busch, J. Fangmeier, and M. Geiger (Zürich, 1966), pp. 639–672. Klopfenstein's study is of particular interest for its summary and critical assessment of Karl Barth's exegesis of our chapter, without which no review of the relevant

secondary literature would be complete. Barth's valuable study of our pericope first appeared in his *Kirchliche Dogmatik*, vol. II, 2, pp. 434–453. Subsequently it was reprinted under the title, 'Exegese von 1. Könige 13," in *Biblische Studien, Heft 10*, ed. H. J. Kraus (Neukirchen, 1955), pp. 12–56. Subsequent references to Barth's study are cited from this latter edition.

22. J. Morgenstern, *Amos Studies*, I (Cincinnati, 1941), p. 161.

23. Cf. Gray, *I & II Kings* [N 4], p. 324.

24. Noth, *UgS* [N 1], p. 81. Followed by I. Plein, "Erwägungen zur Überlieferung von I Reg 11:26–14:20," *ZAW* 78 (1966), 8–24. Plein, however, adduces no further evidence to support this view.

25. M. Noth, *Könige*, Biblischer Kommentar, IX, 4 (Neukirchen, 1968), 293.

26. Ibid., 295.

27. For the purposes of this article, we shall disregard the question of the possible multiplicity of Deuteronomistic editors or authors of the larger history, which at any rate could not be settled on the basis of an examination of so narrow a scope.

28. Noth, *Könige* [N 25], 292, places it after 12:32; as do Gray, *I & II Kings* [N 4], p. 318, and others. Montgomery, *Kings* [N 18], p. 259, and Eissfeldt, *Introduction* [N 16], p. 290, place it already after 12:31.

29. So e.g. Eissfeldt [N 16], along with several other commentators.

30. This, for instance, is surely the case with the gloss found in 12:33: *bāhodeš 'ăšer bādā' millibbô*. Its late and secondary nature is suggested by the use of the rare verb *bādā'*, which occurs only here and in Neh. 6:8, as well as by the consideration that it introduces an extraneous note in the narrative, which bears no relation to either the story or the rest of the narrative. The story is not concerned with the festival at all, but with the fate of the altar; and the reference to the date of the festival in 12:32 contains no hint that it was the date which was objectionable among Jeroboam's cultic innovations.

31. Note the twofold recurrence of the identical phrase *wayĕhî haddābār (Qerê) hazzeh lĕhattā't*. We seem to have here another example of the operation of the literary-critical principle of resumption, identified and discussed at length by C. Kuhl, "Die 'Wiederaufnahme'—ein literarkritisches Princip?" *ZAW* 64 (1952), 1–11.

32. The writer cannot agree with those who would see only one major theological theme in this story. This can only be done by subordinating drastically the one in favor of the other. Thus, Jepsen, *Gottesmann* [N 15], pp. 181 f., emphasizes Yahweh's rejection of Bethel as the only dominant theme of our story. Others shift its major emphasis to the second half, seeing the story arising out of the conflict between true and false prophecy. So, for instance, G. Quell, *Wahre und Falsche Propheten. Versuch einer Interpretation* (Berlin, 1952). J. L. Crenshaw likewise stresses the significance of I Kings 13 for a study of false prophecy. Cf. his *Prophetic Conflict: Its Affect Upon Israelite Religion* (Berlin, 1971), pp. 39 f.

33. Cf. e.g. the expressions "man of God," "by the word of the Lord," and "priests of the high places," which occur in both parts of our story.

34. The earliest known reference to Samaria as a country or region comes from a recently discovered stela of Adad-Nirari III: "He received the tribute of Ia'asu the Samaritan (mIa-'u-su matSa-me-ri-na-a-a). Cf. S. Page, "A Stela of Adad-Nirari III and Nergal-Ereš from Tell Al Rimah," *Iraq* 30 (1968), 139–153. The author is indebted to his colleague Prof. R. A. Henshaw for this reference.

35. The source analysis of these verses in II Kings 17 is debated. Jepsen, *Quellen* [N 5], assigns vss. 24–33, 41 to a post-exilic Levitical redactor. Noth, *UgS* [N 1], p. 85, sees in vss. 24, 29–31 an excerpt from the royal annals, but derives vss. 25–28 from a local Bethel story. Gray, *I & II Kings* [N 4], p. 650, simply designates vss. 24–28 as an addendum, possibly from an account by a priest of the restored cult of Bethel. The present writer is inclined, with Burney and Montgomery, to view vss. 24–34a as

embodying pre-exilic source materials, which were incorporated by a Deuteronomistic editor. Cf. Montgomery, *Kings* [N 18], p. 477, and C. F. Burney, *Notes on the Hebrew Text of the Books of Kings* (Oxford, 1903), pp. 333 f.

36. The reference to lions as agents of Yahweh's judgment, as well as the mentioning of the locale of Bethel, represent some further tantalizing affinities to our story. Unfortunately, they are vague and general, so as not to allow us to do more than raise the issue of a possible connection.

37. The source analysis of the account of Josiah's reform in II Kings 23:4–25 is complicated, and the provenance of vs. 19 is debated. Thus, Burney, *Notes* [N 35], p. 355, finds Deuteronomic phrases in vs. 19, and Gray, *I & II Kings* [N 4], p. 738, assigns all of vss. 16–20 to a Deuteronomistic redactor. Montgomery on the other hand considers vss. 15–20 a "passage of generalities dependent upon the midrash in I Kings 13": *Kings* [N 18], p. 534. Jepsen, *Quellen* [N 5], assigns vss. 16–20 to his post-exilic Levitical redactor; whereas Noth, *UgS* [N 1], p. 86, sees in vss. 4–20a excerpts from the royal annals which the Deuteronomist appended after 23:3.

38. It should be noted that this expression occurs in both the story proper as well as in its literary framework, thus confirming the results which we arrived at in our structural analysis above, namely, that the same editorial hand at work in the framework (12:31–33, 13:33) was also responsible for the inclusion and, we must now add, present formulation of our story.

39. A related, but slightly different, expression, "priests for the high places" *kōhănîm labbāmôt*, occurs in II Chron. 11:15, which is the Chronicler's parallel version to the account in I Kings 12:32.

40. It should be noted that vs. 20 could hardly derive from the same hand as vs. 9, since it clearly contradicts it. According to vs. 9, "the priests of the high places did not come up to the altar of the Lord in Jerusalem, but they ate unleavened bread among their brethren," whereas vs. 20 asserts that all the priests of the high places were slaughtered. The account of Josiah's reform must therefore be composite. We are inclined to view vs. 9 as being part of the original account of Josiah's reform, and vs. 20 as a subsequent addition from the hand of a Deuteronomistic redactor whose hand can also be discerned in I Kings 12–13 and II Kings 17.

41. The fact that there is a discrepancy between II Kings 23:9 on the one hand and II Kings 23:20, along with I Kings 13:2, on the other, would suggest that our Deuteronomistic author completed his work some time subsequent to the original account of that reform. How much later, we cannot determine with any degree of certainty at this point.

42. In Deut. 21:18, 20 it is used in reference to the rebellion of a son against his parents.

43. Cf. Num 20:24; 27:14; Deut. 1:26, 43; 9:23; I Sam. 12:14, 15; I Kings 13:21, 26; and Lam. 1:18. Lam. 1:18 comes from a sixth-century context, and the two passages in Numbers are generally assigned to P. Thus even these three passages could be dependent on Deuteronomistic usage.

44. Cf. e.g. Noth, *UgS* [N 1], pp. 59–60, and, most recently, the extensive analysis of this chapter by H. J. Boecker in his monograph, *Die Beurteilung des Königtums in den Deuteronomistischen Abschnitten des I. Samuelbuches, Wissenschaftliche Monographien zum Alten und Neuen Testament* 31 (Neukirchen, 1969), 61–88.

45. The abstract nouns occurring most commonly as objects of either singly or in various combinations, are: *miṣwāh* (73 times), *ḥōq/ḥuqqāh* (55 times), *mišpāṭ* (30 times), *mišmeret* (30 times), *běrît* (15 times), *dābār* (16 times), *tôrāh* (10 times), *derek* (11 times), and *'ēdût* (9 times).

46. Cf. Deut. 4:2, 40, 5:10, 29, 32, 6:2, 17, 25, 7:9, 11, 12, 8:1, 2, 6, 11, 10:13, 11:1, 8, 22, 13:5, 19, 19:9, 26:17, 18, 27:1, 28:1, 9, 13, 15, 45, 30:10, 16.

47. Cf. I Kings 2:3, 43, 3:14, 6:12, 8:58, 61, 9:6, 11:34, 38, 13:21, 14:8; II Kings 17:13, 19, 37, 18:6, 23:3.

48. Cf. Josh. 22:3, 5; I Sam. 13:13, 14.

49. Gen. 26:5; Exod. 12:17, 16:28, 20:6; Lev. 22:31, 26:3; Jer. 35:18; Pss. 89:32, 119:16; Prov. 4:4, 7:2, 19:16; Qoh. 8:5, 12:3; Neh. 1:7, 9, 10:30; I Chron. 28:8, 29:19.

50. Only five passages may antedate Deuteronomic usage: Gen. 26:5; Exod. 12:17, 16:28, 20:6; Ps. 89:32.

51. Cf. e.g. Deut. 30:10, 16; I Kings 3:14, 8:58, 61, 9:6, 11:34, 38, 14:8, 17:13, 19, 37; II Kings 23:3; and compare with I Sam. 13:13.

52. The same expression occurs twice more in the same chapter. Cf. vss. 19, 37.

53. For a comprehensive analysis of the meaning and distribution of the root *šub,* cf. W. L. Holladay, *The Root Šûbh in the Old Testament* (Leiden, 1958).

54. In addition, *derek* is used six more times singly. Cf. vss. 12, 24, 25, 28.

55. Cf. vss. 9, 10, 17; elsewhere in the Old Testament the combination of *šûb* with *derek* in a literal sense appears also in Gen. 33:16; I Kings 19:15 (with *lāmed*); Deut. 17:16, 28:68; II Kings 19:28, 33=Isa. 37:29, 34 (with *bēt*); and Ezek. 46.9 (without preposition).

56. So, for instance, Noth, *Könige* [N 25], p. 293; Gray, *I & II Kings* [N 4], p. 303; Burney, *Notes* [N 35], p. 184; a.o. We have tried to suggest, however, that we need to distinguish two different hands or successive redactional stages in these two verses. Cf. Section III above.

57. Cf. II Kings 17:13: "Yet the Lord warned Israel and Judah by every prophet and seer, saying, 'Turn from your evil ways (*šûbû middarkêkem hārā'îm*) and keep my commandments and my statutes, in accordance with all the law which I commanded your fathers, and which I sent to you by my servants the prophets.' "

58. Cf. Jer. 15:7, 18:11, 23:22, 25:5, 26:3, 35:15, 36:3, 7; Ezek. 3:19, 13:22, 18:23, 33:9, 11; II Chron. 7:14; Zech. 1:4; Jonah 3:8, 10. Most of the occurrences in Jeremiah are assigned by Holladay, *Root Šûbh* [N 53], pp. 128–139, to the so-called "Deuteronomistic" prose sections, or C-source, of the book, though 15:7 is attributed by him to Jeremiah's genuine oracles. Conceivably, the expression originated with the prophet and was then picked up by subsequent exilic writers.

59. Other related expressions utilizing the verb *šûb* in the sense of "to turn or repent from evil," but without *derek,* point to the same conclusion. Cf. e.g. Jer. 18:8, 23:14, 44:5; Ezek. 23:21, 27, 28, 30, 33:12, 14, 19; and compare with I Kings 8:35.

60. The second half of vs. 26, beginning with "therefore the Lord . . . ," as well as all of vs. 27, are absent from many Greek recensions.

61. See all the instances listed in N 58 and compare with this the instances listed in N 55. In the latter, the preposition *min* is never used.

62. Cf. I Sam. 8:3, 5; I Kings 15:26, 34, 16:2, 19, 26, 22:43, 53; II Kings 8:18, 27, 16:3, 22:2.

63. Cf. Deut. 8:6, 10:12, 11:22, 19:9, 26:17, 29:9, 30:16; Judg. 2:22; I Kings 2:3, 3:14, 8:58, 11:33, 38; II Kings 21:22.

64. Cf. Deut. 9:12, 16, 11:28, 17:11, 31:29; Judg. 2:17; I Kings 22:43. Cf. also F. J. Helfmeyer, *Die Nachfolge Gottes im Alten Testament,* Bonner Biblische Beiträge, 29 (1968), 162, who argues that the formula *sûr min hadderek* is of Dt.-Dtr. provenance.

65. Incidentally, this expression would become another piece of evidence which supports our contention that the author of the literary framework in 12:31–33, 13:33 is also responsible for the inclusion and at least partial formation of our story.

66. Cf. Wolff, "Das Kerygma des deuteronomistischen Geschichtswerks," in his *Gesammelte Studien zum Alten Testament* (Munich, 1964), pp. 308–324.

67. For an extensive analysis of this theme and its function within the Deuteronomistic History, cf. Debus, *Sünde Jeroboams* [N 6], esp. pp. 93–95. In the light of the importance of this theme in the Deuteronomistic perspective, which Debus quite clearly recognizes, it is astonishing how he can be so blind to its presence in our story, which he

dismisses with a few lines as a late prophetic legend, inserted in post-Deuteronomistic times. Cf. p. 35. More recently, F. M. Cross called attention to the importance of this theme in his article, "Structure" [N 4], 9–24. In contrast to Debus, Cross assigns the insertion of this story to the hand of a Deuteronomic editor of the Josianic era. Cf. pp. 12 ff. If our observations concerning the structural seams and linguistic expressions are correct, however, we may have to view our pericope as the result of two successive Deuteronomistic editions, 12:26–30, 13:34 belonging to the first, and 12:31–13:33 belonging to the second. The first editor knew already about the sin of Jeroboam, but the second illustrated and underscored that sin further by means of the inclusion of our story.

68. Cf., for instance, Deut. 5:32–33, 11:13–17, 30:1–10, 15–20, 31:27–29; Josh. 1: 7–8; Judg. 6:7–10; I Sam. 7:3–4; I Kings 3:14, 9:4–5, 12:21–24; II Kings 21:7–8. In this connection, it may be appropriate to recall von Rad's observation: "The question of obedience is the one fundamental notion underlying deuteronomistic historical writing": "Deuteronomic Theology" [N 8], p. 208. Surprisingly, however, von Rad failed to draw any connections between our story and that fundamental Deuteronomistic notion.

69. Cf. e.g. Deut. 28:15 ff., 30:15–20; Judg. 2:1–5, 20–23; I Sam. 12:14–15, 13:13–14, 15:10–23; II Sam. 12:7–15; I Kings 9:6–9, 11:9–11, 14:7–11; II Kings 2:10–15, 22:13.

70. The only apparent exception to this is vs. 23: "He saddled the ass for the *nābî'* whom he had brought back." The absence of this phrase in the versions (LXX, Syriac, Old Latin), however, suggests that it is a secondary explanatory gloss.

71. Moses, Elijah, and Elisha, for instance, are all referred to by both terms, *'îš hā'elōhîm* and *nābî'*. Cf. also Albright, *Samuel and the Beginnings of the Prophetic Movement* (Cincinnati, 1961), p. 7, who makes the following assertion: "In the early Monarchy 'man of God' was apparently a synonym for *nāvî.*"

72. In this latter sense it is analogous to the designation "man of N," where N is a proper name, which usually designates a person who stands in some kind of vassal relationship to a superior. Cf. M. Noth, *Die Israelitischen Personennamen im Rahmen der gemeinsemitischen Namengebung* (Stuttgart, 1928), p. 138.

73. Judg. 13:6, 8. There is some confusion in this passage whether he is thought of as human or divine, which may represent a shift in Israel's understanding of angelology.

74. Cf. Deut. 33:1; Josh. 14:6; Ps. 90:1; Ezra 3:2; I Chron. 23:14; II Chron. 30:10.

75. II Chron. 8:14; Neh. 12:24, 26.

76. I Sam. 9:6, 9, 10.

77. To be exact, 64 out of 76 instances. Of the remaining 12, 8 are demonstrably dependent upon Deuteronomistic usage, leaving only 4 occurrences of the term which are without parallel in the Deuteronomistic History: Jer. 35:4; II Chron. 8:14; Neh. 12: 24, 26. In the isolated reference in Jeremiah, the term refers to an otherwise unknown "Hanan ben-Igdaliah," who may have been the head of a prophetic guild associated with the Temple in Jerusalem. The remaining three references all come from the Chronicler's History and refer uniformly to David, who, in the perspective of the Chronicler, was a man of God *par excellence.* With reference to the question of the provenance of our story it should also be pointed out that the Chronicler himself, apart from his *Vorlage*, never uses the term "man of God" to designate a prophet. Cf. also R. Hallevy, "Man of God," *JNES* 17 (1958), 243.

78. The only apparent exceptions are two occurrences in Judg. 13:6, 8, where the term seems to alternate with the expression *mal'āk yhwh*, and in Deut. 33:1 and Josh. 14:6, where it refers to Moses. Since Moses, however, was considered a prophet in the Deuteronomic tradition, this exception is more apparent than real. As for the Judges passage, A. Rofé has suggested that this may actually represent an anti-angelogical polemic, whereby at some stage in the Israelite tradition angels came to be replaced by prophets as Yahweh's messengers. Cf. his "Israelite Belief in Angels in the Pre-Exilic Period as

Evidenced by Biblical Traditions," Hebrew University Dissertation, 1969. Rofé's dissertation was available to the writer in abstract form only.

79. Cf. I Kings 17:18, 24, 20:28; II Kings 1:9, 10, 11, 12, 13, 4:7, 9, 16, 21, 22, 25, 27, 40, 42, 5:8, 14, 15, 20, 6:6, 9, 10, 15, 7:2, 17, 18, 19, 8:2, 4, 7, 8, 11, 13:19.

80. Apart from two isolated references in I Sam. 2:27 and I Kings 12:22, all the remaining occurrences in which the terms are used to designate a prophet, seventeen to be exact, are confined to our story and its sequel in II Kings 23.

81. It is, of course, always possible to argue that a Deuteronomistic editor could have used this term in I Kings 13 in free imitation of earlier prophetic models. But that possibility has much less to commend itself in the light of further considerations offered below.

82. Cf. Wellhausen, *Composition* [N 12], p. 280.

83. Noth, *Könige* [N 25], p. 296, translates it as "Kraft des Wortes Jahwes." Montgomery feels that it is best rendered with "invested with the word," and compares it to the New Testament expression *en dunamei pneumatos* "in or by the power of the spirit." *Kings* [N 18], p. 263.

84. Cf. I Sam. 3:21; I Kings 20:35; Jer. 8:9; Ps. 33:6; II Chron. 30:12. Related but slightly differing expressions occur in II Sam. 16:23; I Chron. 25:5; II Chron. 29:15.

85. Cf. I Kings 20:35–43. This story is strangely reminiscent of the one in I Sam. 15: 1–23, where Saul was faulted by the prophet Samuel for having spared Agag, king of the Amalekites. Their common theme and outlook suggest that they most likely derive from similar circles of Northern prophets, among whom the traditions of holy war were kept alive.

86. Jepsen, *Quellen* [N 5], p. 78 and synopsis, assigns it to his source N, by which he means prophetic stories circulated and handed down among *nabis*. While the story in I Kings 20 in its present context is dated to the time of Ahab, it is likely that it originated during the period of the Aramaean wars of the late ninth century B.C. Cf. O. H. Steck, *Überlieferungs und Zeitgeschichte in den Elia-Erzählungen* (Neukirchen, 1968), p. 50, n. 1.

87. Other parallels frequently mentioned in this connection are Balaam's ass and Jonah's fish. For a fuller discussion of the animal motif, with citation of both biblical and extrabiblical parallels, see esp. Klopfenstein, "1. Könige 13" [N 21], pp. 661–665.

88. Such considerations clearly refute the arguments of those commentators who, on the basis of the legendary and credulous features of the story, consider it to be a late midrash of the type found in the Chronicler's history. We wish to argue that the legendary features of our story in I Kings 13 are much more akin to the Elijah-Elisha traditions, than to anything which the Chronicler brings. To see how different in outlook and stylistic features a typical midrash of the Chronicler is, one need only take a look at II Chronicles 13. This story, which is likewise assigned to the time of Jeroboam I and deals with the same theme of condemnation of the Northern cultic establishment, may be considered the Chronicler's counterpart to I Kings 13, which, incidentally the Chronicler omits from his narrative altogether.

89. Wellhausen already made a passing comment to that effect; *Composition* [N 12], p. 280. More recently, this theory was revived with considerable elaboration by Morgenstern, *Amos Studies*, I [N 22], 146–179. He sees in I Kings 13:1–10 essentially a legendary reflex of Amos' prophetic activity at Bethel and the tradition of the great earthquake in the days of Uzziah (Amos 1:1). Most recently the theory has been defended by O. Eissfeldt, who sees in I Kings 13 a popular Judaean tradition about the prophet Amos. Cf. his "Amos und Jona in volkstümlicher Überlieferung," in *KS*, IV, 137–142. The theory is also supported by Crenshaw, in *Prophetic Conflict* [N 32], pp. 41 f., where he states, "Despite the differences the probability is that Amos is the prophet behind I Kings 13."

90. Cf. Amos 7:10–13.

91. Cf. Amos 3:13–15: ". . . that on the day I punish Israel for his transgressions, I will punish the altars of Bethel, and the horns of the altar shall be cut off and fall to the ground . . ." Cf. also the vision in 9:1 ff.: "I saw the Lord standing beside the altar and he said: 'Smite the capitals until the thresholds shake, and shatter them on the heads of all the people.'" Compare also with these the further denunciations of Bethel in 4:4 f. and 5:5f. Amos 7:9 speaks of the destruction of the high-places and sanctuaries, along with the house of Jeroboam.

92. There is some question, however, of whether the king in the story was originally mentioned by name. The identification with Jeroboam may be secondary. Cf. Noth, *Könige* [N 25], pp. 293 f.

93. Other, but much less obvious and more speculative, points of contact have been suggested. So, for instance, Morgenstern's suggestion that the rending of the altar in I Kings 13 was occasioned by the earthquake during the days of King Uzziah. The same is true of some of Crenshaw's suggested parallels listed on p. 42 of *Prophetic Conflict* [N 32].

94. Morgenstern gets around this difficulty by considering I Kings 13:11–32 a secondary insertion which had nothing to do with the story: *Amos Studies* [N 22], p. 161. A diametrically opposite conclusion is drawn by Eissfeldt when he ventures the opinion that I Kings 13 may have preserved some historical information not found in the Book of Amos, and that in fact the tomb of the unknown prophet in Bethel was none other than the tomb of Amos. *KS*, IV, 139.

95. Cf. e.g. Wolff, "Das Ende des Heiligtums in Bethel," in *Archäologie und Altes Testament*, eds. A. Kuschke and E. Kutsch (Tübingen, 1970), pp. 287–298. See further Noth, *Könige* [N 25], p. 295, and Jepsen, *Gottesmann* [N 15], p. 180; a.o. It is possible, however, that while our story did not originate in the Amos tradition, it may have been partly influenced by the latter.

96. That Hosea rejected Jeroboam's cultic establishment as one of the root causes of Israel's unfaithfulness to Yahweh is clear from such passages as Hos. 4:15–19, 8:4–6, 11, 10:1–8, 13:1–3. Bethel was consistently and derisively designated by him as *bêt 'āwen*, and the bulls which Jeroboam had set up were denounced by him as idolatrous images.

97. While I Kings 14 in its present form shows many traces of a Deuteronomistic hand, it undoubtedly preserves older materials inimical to Jeroboam I. Cf. Noth, *Könige* [N 25], pp. 310 ff.

98. Cf. Sections III and IV, 1–3, 6, above.   99. Cf. Sections III and IV.

100. We further suggested that this Deuteronomistic author most likely should be distinguished from the one found in 12:26–30 and 13:34, not only because of the obvious seams in the immediate context of the story, but elsewhere as well. Cf. e.g. the obvious seams and secondary expansions in II Kings 17 and 23.

101. Since 13:2 derives in all likelihood from the Deuteronomist, the question arises as to what the content of the original prophetic oracle against the altar might have been. It probably did not contain any reference to the slaughtering of the priests of the high-places, but a simple prediction of the destruction and/or defiling of the altar. Thus the content of the original oracle against the altar is more likely to be found in 13:3, rather than in 13:2. Did the Deuteronomistic editor make a sign out of that which originally constituted the oracle itself? If so, then vs. 5, which is often felt to be intrusive by commentators, should be ascribed to him as well.

102. Conceivably, it may have been concerned thereby to underscore the religious unity of the prophetic movement in Israel, which, while politically frequently divided, recognized no religious boundaries in the service of their common God.

103. Thus it fills a vacuum which has been keenly felt by many. It would be remarkable, to say the least, if as important an event in the history of Israel as the division of the kingdom, with its ensuing religious schism, and the establishment of those cultic

practices which led to the eventual downfall of Israel should have received only passing attention from the Deuteronomistic Historian. Thus, in his study of the prayers and speeches in the Deuteronomistic History, O. Plöger once expressed himself to this effect:

> Es fällt nämlich auf, dass in der Darstellung des Zeitabschnittes von der Tempel-weihe bis zur ephraimitischen Katastrophe keine zusammenfassende Betrachtung aus der Feder des Deuteronomisten mehr anzutreffen ist, obwohl etwa ein Ereignis wie das der sog. Reichstrennung unter Salomos Nachfolger Rehabeam schwerwiegend genug gewesen wäre.

"Reden und Gebete im deuteronomistischen und chronistischen Geschichtswerk," in *Aus der Spätzeit des Alten Testaments* (Göttingen, 1971), p. 52. If we are correct, however, I Kings 13 fulfills precisely the kind of function Plöger was looking for. To be sure, it is not a speech like I Sam. 12, nor a prayer like I Kings 8, nor a free commentary like II Kings 17:7–20. Rather, it is a narrative with considerable action, suspense and movement, but heavily interlaced with dialogue and speeches by its main characters. The particular vehicle chosen by the Deuteronomist to make his point was dictated, here as elsewhere, by his available sources. By virtue of its particular character and concerns, the story was a most suitable vehicle for the expression of his basic perspectives and concerns.

104. This pattern of promise and fulfillment in the Deuteronomistic History is so well known that we need not elaborate upon it any further. Cf. von Rad, "Deuteronomic Theology" [N 8]. To von Rad's list of prophecy-fulfillment pairs, however, we should like to add two which were apparently overlooked by him: I Sam. 2:27–36—I Kings 2:26–27 and II Kings 10:30—II Kings 15:12.

105. Whether a nation whose bones lay in the grave of exile could ever live again is an interesting question raised by our story, but one which is not answered by it in any explicit fashion. Elsewhere in the Old Testament, as well as in the Deuteronomistic History, that possibility was affirmed quite explicitly. Cf. Ezek. 37:1–14; Deut. 4:25–31, 30:1–10.

III

Exile and Restoration

17. The "Olden Gods" in Ancient Near Eastern Creation Myths

FRANK MOORE CROSS

HARVARD UNIVERSITY

IN A PAPER published some years ago, I found it useful to distinguish two genres or ideal types of creation myth in Canaanite and related ancient Near Eastern cycles.[1] One type is the *theogony,* the birth and succession of the gods, especially the old gods. Only at the end of the theogony proper do we reach the active or young deities, the great gods of the cult. The second type is the *cosmogony,* characterized by a conflict between the old and the young gods out of which order, especially kingship, is established in the cosmos. The theogonic myth normally uses the language of time; its events were of old, at the beginning. Yet the time language points beyond itself to "eternal" structures which embrace even the gods and which constitute reality at all times. The cosmogony is a libretto to the rites of the cult. It may or may not use time language. Yet the myth always delineates "primordial" events, that is, events which constitute cosmos, and hence are properly timeless or cyclical or "eschatological" in character.

To both the theogony and the cosmogony belong a special class of deities, the "olden gods." This class had a precise designation in Hittite, *šiuneš karuileš,* "the olden gods," in Akkadian translation *ilānū ša dārūti* or *ilānū ša dārātim,* "primeval gods" (Urgötter).[2] In Egypt the Ogdoad of Hermopolis had a similar title, *nṯr.w pꜣw.ty.w,* "primeval gods."[3] In the theogony, the olden gods are the focus of attention; in the cosmogony, the olden gods are pitted against the young god(s) in a titanic struggle. "Titanic" here is used in the original sense; the Titans were among the olden gods of Greece.

1. In the theogony, creation is described utilizing the language of sexual procreation. Characteristically, we find a series of pairs of gods, most pairs made up of a male and female, frequently with rhyming or etymologically related names. For example, the primordial gods of Egypt, the Ogdoad of Hermopolis, consisted of four symmetrical, theogonic pairs: Nūn and Nawnet, Ḥūḥ and Ḥawḥet, Kūk and Kawket, Amūn and Amawnet.[4] An old Babylonian list begins with the names of fifteen matched pairs which constitute the

genealogy of Enlil: Enki and Ninki, Enmul and Ninmul, Enul and Ninul, Ennun and Ninnun, Enkur and Ninkur . . . Enmešarra and Ninmešarra.[5]

The theogonic divine pairs are often binary opposites: Heaven and Earth (*Šamêm* and *'Arṣ*) in the Phoenician theogony of Sakkunyaton; *Ouranos* and *Gē* in Hesiod, etc.; in the the theogony introducing the Babylonian Creation Epic *Enūma eliš* we find *Apsu* and *Tiāmat,* "the sweet waters" (male) and "the salty abyss" (female); *Anšar* and *Kišar,* the opposing horizons of heaven and earth. Included are the oppositions male/female, heaven/earth, sweet/salt, day/night (light and darkness); less transparent is the opposition in the Hittite natural pairs: mountain and rivers, spring and the Great Sea, Heaven and Earth, winds and clouds. The olden gods may bear highly abstract names. Striking are the Egyptian pairs: "Inertness" (*Nūn,* a name of the primordial waters), "Unbounded" (*Ḥūḥ,* infinite in space, presumably used of the primordial space), "Primeval Darkness" (*Kūk,* the darkness before the rising of the stars), "Invisibility" (*Amūn,* evidently the air or wind originally), "Nothingness" (*Nyз.w,* an alias of *Amūn*). Here belong also Greek Xáos, and as well Sumerian *Enmešarra* and *Ninmešarra,* "Lord world order" and "Lady world order."[6]

The olden gods may be described in some sense as "dead" gods. To be sure, a dead god does not cease to exist or to function. The old gods, at any rate, are placed in the Netherworld. The Hittite *šiuneš karuileš* dwelt in the Underworld and were also called "lords of earth."[7] The Hermopolite Ogdoad were dead and had their necropolis (*t3-ḏśr*) in Medinet Habu.[8] Zeus cast Cronos and the Titans into deep Tartaros, bound in chains. The ancient gods which make up the genealogies of Anu and Enlil also appear to be "dead" gods or, in any case, gods confined to the Underworld.[9]

A newly published theogony from Babylon gives us new insights into this aspect of the old gods.[10] Seven generations are listed before one comes to the great gods, the living gods of the cult. For six generations there is repeated an oedipal pattern of patricide and incest. The first pair, of which only one name *Erṣitu* (Earth) is certain, gives birth to Sumuqan (ᵈAMA.GAN.DÙ), and *Tāmtu* (Sea). Sumuqan killed his father and took to wife his mother Earth and his sister Sea. Sea kills her mother for good measure. Incest and patricide persist generation after generation until the seventh when the old god is merely chained by his son in taking power.

Incest marks the uncivilized, disordered behavior of the old gods. Of course incest was as inevitable at the beginnings of the family of the gods as among the children of Adam. Reflections of the pattern of patricide occur also in the theogonies of the Hittites (Hurrians), the Greeks, and the Canaanites, especially at the transitional generation or generations between the olden gods and the young cult gods. In the *Theogony* of Hesiod, Cronos emasculated his father Heaven (*Ouranos*), with the connivance of his mother Earth (*Gē*), and Zeus in turn defeated Cronos. In a Hurrian theogony[11] Alalu was defeated in battle by his son Anu and fled into the Underworld; Anu was emasculated by his son Kumarbi who in turn appears to have been over-thrown by the storm-god Tešup. Under the label "olden gods," the Hittites regularly listed two series of foreign deities: Naraš, Napšaraš, Minki, Tuḫuši, Ammunki, Ammizzadu of uncertain origin, Alalu, Anu, Antu, Apantu, Enlil, and Ninlil, all Mesopotamian gods. Appended was a third group, mountains and rivers, springs and Great Sea, Heaven and Earth, winds and clouds.

In one of the theogonies of the Phoenician hierophant Sakkunyaton (San-chuniathon),[12] the god 'Ēl, son of Šamêm, Heaven, avenged his mother Earth by castrating Heaven, leaving him to die. Here the oedipal pattern stops. In Canaanite lore 'Ēl remained head of the pantheon, judge over the council of the gods, and was not ousted by the young storm-god Ba'l (alias Haddu). Rather, Sakkunyaton relates that 'Ēl associated Astarte and Adod (that is, Ba'l-Haddu) in his rule. In a newly published text this relation is confirmed:

> *'Ilu yaṭaba ba-'aṭṭart<šadi>*
> *'Ilu ṭapaṭa ba-Haddi rā'iyu*
> *dū yašīru wa-yaḏammiru ba-kinnāri . . .*

> 'Ēl sits enthroned with Astarte <of the steppe>
> 'Ēl sits as judge with Haddu his shepherd
> Who sings and plays on the lyre . . .[13]

Ba'l stands at the right hand of 'Ēl his father. He is crown prince or coregent, the young warrior and musician whom 'Ēl associates in his rule. Astarte, 'Ēl's mistress, forms the divine triad. So 'Ēl remained at the head of the pantheon and ruled from his seat on the mount of assembly.

The oedipal pattern also is largely absent from the theogony which intro-duces the late Mesopotamian creation myth *Enūma eliš*. Old gods Apsu and Tiāmat are killed by young gods Ea and Marduk, the first pair separated by a number of generations from the young gods who dispatch them.

The lists of the olden gods exhibit great variation in the number of gen-erations and in the names of the theogonic pairs. Five generations separate Enlil from the first generation in *Enūma eliš*, at least seven in the Lambert theogony; the Genouillac list counts fifteen pairs, and the series AN:*Anum* lists even more. Sakkunyaton gives three theogonies. The first, however, called the theogony of Taauth (Thoth), is directly borrowed from the Hermopo-lite theogony of the Ogdoad as shown persuasively by Albright.[14] The latter two, however, are fragments to be pieced together to make six or seven generations to 'Ēl, the head of the pantheon of the active deities of the cosmic state.

Some confusion has resulted in the failure of scholars in the past to recog-nize the two classes of deities, the old god and the young god. Names of old gods may overlap with those of young gods. For example, Enki in the pair

Enki and Ninki bears the same name as the cult god Enki, but the two gods are not identical. The same is probably to be said of the god of the Ogdoad, Amūn, who in origin was unrelated to Amūn of Heliopolis, the king of the gods.[15] 'Ôlam (Oulōmos of Mochus) is the name of a Phoenician old god, "the ancient one" literally. The epithet 'Ôlam, and its equivalent Saeculum, Senex, and Gerōn in the Punic world,[16] also was used of 'Ēl, but the two must not be confused. Similarly, there is an old god name 'Elyôn, "Most High," to be distinguished carefully from the god of the Jerusalem cult called 'Elyôn.[17] One should not mix dead gods with living gods, even those with identical epithets or names.

We may conclude our remarks on this divine type by observing that the olden gods ordinarily had no temples or cults.[18] They rarely received sacrifices, to judge from extant texts, and were not the objects of hymns of praise. In the pantheon lists of Ugarit they go unrecorded thus far. 'Ēl heads the pantheon and his genealogy is ignored. Nor do the olden gods appear normally as theophorous elements in personal names.[19] This is as it should be. Who desires an inert or dead god as his patron?

2. The olden gods also play a role in the second type of creation myth, the type we have called the *cosmogony*. The great cosmogonic myths of Mesopotamia and Canaan were associated with the central rites of the cult and as such are of much greater importance than the theogonic myths for our understanding of ancient, mythopoeic religion. The cosmogonies recount the warfare between the olden god or gods and the young god, or gods, a conflict out of which emerges victory for the young god and the establishment of kingship among the gods, an orderly, cosmic government. Kingship and its hierarchical institutions are thus fixed in the orders of creation, and human kingship, patterned after the cosmic government, gains religious sanction.

In the Babylonian creation epic *Enūma eliš*,[20] the conflict emerges from a clash between the primordial gods and the young gods. The old, inert gods are disturbed by the activity of the youngsters. They want sleep and silence. The struggle reflects the duality of reality: stagnation, sterility, death, chaos are ranged against life, violence, fertility in the cosmos. Tiāmat, the sleepy dragon, and Apsu, her watery spouse, are goaded to fury and determine to destroy their offspring. Apsu is finished off early by wise Ea, and the ultimate struggle is between Sea and the young champion of the gods, Marduk. Tiāmat meanwhile has exalted her son Kingu in her assembly and he becomes her new spouse after the incestuous pattern of the old gods.

Marduk, invested with provisional kingship, is armed with weapons appropriate to the storm-god: the cloud chariot, lightning bolts, a bow and a magical club. With his irresistible weapons he slays the ancient dragon. He splits her carcass to form the heavenly ocean and the nether sea, and the bubble of order in between becomes the ordered universe. The climax of the cosmogony comes with the return of the divine warrior in triumph and his enthronement as king. The gods greet him on his return to the assembly.

"Assembled were the Igigi, they prostrated themselves before him altogether, as many as they were, the Anunnaki kissed his feet. Their assembly [came] to pay him reverence, and stood before him, did obeisance (saying): 'He is king indeed.' "[21] Marduk then took up his royal insignia and was invested as king. He also announced his building project: the construction of his temple and residence in Babylon in the pattern of his cosmic temple. The foundation of the temple is equated in mythic dualism with creation. The establishment of Babylonian rule becomes identical with the establishment of cosmic order. Kingship, divine and human, is fixed in the orders of creation, properly eternal. Finally, the gods feast in the royal temple, celebrating the banquet of the divine king, the archetype of the royal enthronement festival on earth. In these lines the myth and the cultic drama, libretto and rite become plain, and the political and propagandistic features of the cosmogonic myth emerge clearly. The cosmic state of the gods and the political community of Babylon are institutions fixed in eternity. The myth records primordial events; the drama also actualizes the creation ever anew. It is not astonishing that at the end of *Enūma eliš* we find the petition: "May [Marduk] shepherd all the gods like sheep, May he subdue Tiāmat . . ." The primeval event, celebrated in the cultus, now is also the new creation. Sacred time is fluid. Unhappily, there is no space here to deal with the several creation stories in the cosmogonic form. However, the form and function of these cosmogonies of Mesopotamia and Canaan[22] are well known, and we are more interested here to examine the function and history of the theogonic form in Near Eastern mythology.

3. Commonly the theogony may serve as a prologue to the cosmogony pointing to the primeval nature of the mythic events by using the language of time. The dualism of the binary oppositions, male and female, heaven and earth, and so on, supports and turns into the dualism of the cosmogony which opposes the old gods and the new, the dead or inert and the living or active, the gods of chaos and the gods of order. This is not the only context in which we find the listing of the theogonic pairs, and both the theogony and the cosmogony may stand alone. As a matter of fact, the cosmogonies introduced by theogonies are mostly late, sophisticated texts: *Enūma eliš,* the *Theogony* of Hesiod, the third theogony of Sakkunyaton, all reflecting impulses to systematize the divine powers. The Ugaritic cosmogonic cycle (in which Ba'l battles with Sea and Death to secure kingship) is not prefaced by a theogony. Indeed no theogonic myth is extant in the Canaanite cuneiform texts. This circumstance has led certain scholars to claim that there is no creation myth at Ugarit. Such a view is wholly wrong-headed in my judgment. The absence of a theogonic prologue is merely a primitive feature of the Ugaritic cosmogonic cycle. Otherwise, it bears all the traits of the cosmogony. The conflict between Ba'l and Yamm-Nahar (Sea and River), Môt (Death), and Lôtān are alloforms reflecting the usual conflict between the old gods and the young gods of the cult. The primary focus of the cycle is the emergence of kingship among the gods. Ba'l the divine warrior returns victorious to the

divine assembly, receives kingship, builds his royal temple on Mount Ṣapōn, and invites the gods to the royal banquet. The pattern of the cosmogonic myth could not be more evident. Moreover, one remembers that in biblical lore the defeat of Sea or the dragon is properly placed in time, at creation, or, to say the same thing, in the new creation. In the banquet of the end-time, the faithful feast on the flesh of Leviathan.

The theogony may also stand alone in Phoenician mythopoeic lore as is the case with the first theogony of Sakkunyaton or the Hermopolite theogony.

Interesting also is the use of the theogonic pairs in lists of witnesses in Hittite and West Semitic treaty texts. In the treaties they are named following the patron gods of the parties to the treaty and after the great gods and the gods of the cult places. They are often designated by the rubric "olden gods" in Hittite texts, distinguishing them from the principal, active gods. Heaven and Earth form the pivotal pair, often, between the executive gods and the old gods, followed by mountains, rivers, sea, and so on. It is not surprising to find that the order of the theogonic pairs is reversed in many treaty texts as is natural since the "living" deities are named first: thus the eighth-century treaty of Sefire lists ". . . 'Ēl and 'Elyōn, Heaven and Earth, Abyss and Sources, Night and Day."[23] Evidently there is revealed here the desire for completeness in listing witnesses to the treaty. Also even the young gods are bound by or contained in the prototypic structures of the universe represented by the primeval powers.

This function of the theogonic pairs survives in attenuated form in Israel in the context of the covenant lawsuit. Witnesses to Israel's covenant or treaty with Yahweh are called upon to attend the cosmic legal proceedings in which Israel is prosecuted for breach of treaty. The classical formulae of the prophetic process include the address to the olden gods: "Hear O Mountains the lawsuit of Yahweh, and <give ear> O Foundations of the Earth" (Micah 6, 2a); "Listen O Heavens, give ear O Earth" (Isaiah 1, 2a); "Be astonished, O Heavens, on this account, be greatly appalled <O Mountains>" (Jer. 2:12; cf. Jer. 2:9 f.).[24]

The speculative and classificatory function of the theogonic pairs alluded to earlier needs to be further underlined. The theogony was created by a mythopoeic mind enchanted by binary opposites that seemed fixed in the structure of reality.

It is not by chance that in the proto-philosophic speculations of the pre-Socratics of the Milesian school, lists of opposites played a fundamental role.[25] One thinks particularly of the pairs, cold (wind/air) and hot (fire), wet (water) and dry (earth), which separate out from the substratum "the Unbounded" (apeiron) in the thought of Anaximander. The abstraction vividly reflected in the theogonic genre of gods no doubt gave impetus to philosophical abstraction and classification. In any case, the linkage and continuity between theogonic speculation and the cosmological speculation of the Milesian school is difficult to deny. As for the substratum of Thales (primordial water), of Anaximander (the Unbounded), and of Anaximenes (air-wind-vapor), all are found in the theogonies of Phoenicia and Egypt.[26]

4. I wish to turn finally to a discussion of the Phoenician theogony and its transformation in the biblical account of creation. As noted above, Sakkunyaton's lore as preserved by Philo Byblius contains three theogonic cycles, the first the theology of Thoth which need not detain us, the second and third fragments of a single theogony transformed under Euhemeristic influences into a history of culture. Together the fragments permit us to piece together a substantial part of a canonical Phoenician theogony.

The first pair are the wind *Qodm*[27] and his spouse *Baau* (biblical *bōhū*). "Qodm the Wind" may mean either the east wind or the primordial wind, or still more likely, both. The second pair is *'Ôlam* (later Phoenician *'ūlōm*) and his female counterpart, perhaps **'Ôlamt*.[28] In early Phoenician, *'Ôlām* means only "the ancient one" or the "eternal one." The Greek term is *Aiōn*, Mandaic *'ālmā* in later Gnostic systems. *'Ôlām,* the child of *Baau,* is identical with the Gnostic *yaldabaōt,* that is "the child of Chaos." The third pair is listed in Greek as *Genos* and *Genea* and imitates the Phoenician by being derived from the same stem. *Yald* and *Yaldat* are possible names suggesting that this pair is a doublet of the second pair. From them stem Light, Fire and Flame, and the giants, Mount Casius, Lebanon, Hermon and Amanus (the cedar mountain, βαραθυ, Hebrew *běrōš*). Here the series breaks off to be taken up again in the third fragment[29] with the pair *Elyūn* (Hebrew *'Elyōn*) and *Bērūt* (Hebrew *bě'ērōt*). The pair is not symmetrical: "The Most High" and "Springs." There may be confusion or an omission in the transmitted lore. The final pair is Heaven and Earth (Samêm and 'Arṣ) before the appearance of the great gods, 'Ēl, Dagon, 'Aštart, and so on, the children of Heaven and Earth. To this theogony is attached only a brief reference to the establishment of kingship among the gods, enough, however, to recognize the linkage between the two types of creation myth in Phoenicia.

The biblical account of creation in the first chapter of Genesis belongs clearly to the theogonic genre, not to the cosmogonic form. It begins with the theogonic formula, "When God began to create heaven and earth . . . then he said, 'Let light come into existence. . . .'" In a parenthesis we are told that the earth was chaos and disorder: *tōhū wā-bōhū,* Sakkunyaton's *Baau,* Hesiod's *Chaos.* Darkness was on the face of the Deep *těhōm,* Babylonian *Tiāmat,* Egyptian *Nūn,* and the divine wind soared over the surface of the waters of the deep, the primordial wind of Sakkunyaton and Anaximenes. Thus allusion is made to several of the theogonic pairs: wind and watery chaos, heaven and earth, darkness and light. To be sure, the olden gods are here natural pairs, abstracted like the elements of the Ionian cosmologists. More important, there is in the Genesis creation story no element of cosmogonic conflict, no linkage to a cosmogony. God creates by fiat. On the other hand, the creation account is a prologue attached to an epic account of the call of the fathers, the victory of the Divine Warrior in the Exodus and Conquest, and the creation of the convenantal political order at Sinai. The creation story provides a universal context and a temporal setting to the Israelite epic. We have argued that the theogonic myth used the language of time to point to the primordial or eternal dimension of the cosmogonic myth. That is, the time language refers to fluid, cyclical time, not to ordinary linear time, in the creation cycles of Mesopotamia and Canaan. In Israel time is linear, a radical transformation of the older Near Eastern tradition. Creation is merely a first event—without significance—in a linear series of epic events.

The history of the theogony comes to an end, so to speak, in two transformations, in the monotheistic creation story of Genesis 1, and in the cosmology of the Ionian philosophers. It is of considerable interest that the composition of the Hebrew creation story and the activity of the Greek philosophers coincided in time, in the course of the sixth century B.C. when the ancient Semitic empires were brought to an end, and the age of Persia and Greece was dawning.

NOTES

1. See F. M. Cross, "The Song of the Sea and Canaanite Myth," *JTC* 5 (1968), 9 and n. 26. Cf. *idem, Canaanite Myth and Hebrew Epic* (Cambridge, Mass., 1973), pp. 39–43.

2. See esp. O. R. Gurney, "Hittite Prayers of Mursili II," *AAA* 27 (1940), 81f., and his references, esp. E. Forrer, "Eine Geschichte des Götterkönigtums aus dem Hatti-Reiche," *Annuaire de l'institut de phil. et d'hist. orientale* (*Mélanges* Franz Cumont) IV (1936), 687–713.

3. For this and other designations including "the old(est) gods," see K. Sethe, *Amun und die acht Urgötter von Hermopolis* [Abh. der preuss. Akad. der Wissenschaft, 1929], pp. 45–48.

4. For the last-named pair often a substitution is made of the names Ny3.w/Ny3.t. The vocalization of the series is ascertained by the series in Greek transcription: *Noun, Nouni*, etc.

5. This series comes from the Genouillac List, published in *Textes cunéiformes du Louvre* (=Textes religieux sumériens du Louvre 10), and discussed by H. de Genouillac in his paper, "Grande liste de noms divins sumeriens," *Revue d'Assyriologie* 20 (1923), 89–106; 25 (1928), 133–139. For this and other lists see provisionally W. G. Lambert, "Götterlisten" and "Göttergenealogie" in the *Reallexikon der Assyriologie* and his forthcoming *Babylonian Creation Myths*.

6. T. Jacobsen translates the name, "Lord *modus operandi* of the universe" and "Lady *modus operandi* of the universe," *Toward the Image of Tammuz* (Cambridge, Mass., 1970), p. 116.

7. See the remarks of Gurney, "Hittite Prayers" [N 2], 81, and n. 4 where he refers to the phrase *kat-te-ir-ri-eš ka-ru-ú-e-li-e-eš* DINGIR.MEŠ, "infernal and ancient gods."

8. See Sethe, *Amun und die acht Urgötter* [N 3], pp. 53 ff.

9. Cf. S. N. Kramer, "The Death of Gilgamesh," *BASOR* 94 (1944), 12 and n. 30. Jacobsen in *Image of Tammuz* [N 6], p. 115, writes of the old god En-uru-ulla, "The lord of the primeval city" as follows: "Since this deity is known . . . to be located in

the nether world, we may assume that 'the primeval city' is the city of the dead. . . . Death it would appear was and ruled before life. . . ."

10. W. G. Lambert and A. R. Millard, *Cuneiform Texts from Babylonian Tablets* (*CT*), 46, 43. See also W. G. Lambert and P. Walcot, "A New Babylonian Theogony and Hesiod," *Kadmos* 4 (1965), 64–72, A. K. Grayson in *ANET*, p. 517; I have also had access to an unpublished paper of Thorkild Jacobsen, who has been able to reconstruct much more of this text than his predecessors. I owe much to his interpretation.

11. The basic treatments are those of Forrer, "Götterkönigtums" [N 2], and H. G. Güterbock, *Kumarbi, Mythen vom hurritischen Kronos* (New York, 1946).

12. See the edition of K. Mras, *Eusebius Werke* 8. Band I. Teil *Die Praeparatio evangelica* (Berlin, 1954), 10.1–44; and C. Clemen, *Die phönikische Religion nach Philo von Byblos* (Leipzig, 1939).

13. J. Nougayrol, C. Virolleaud et al., *Ugaritica* V (Paris, 1968), 2 (RS 24.252), lines 3 f. My student, Dr. Conrad L'Heureux, has discussed the text in detail in his unpublished Harvard dissertation, "El and the Rephaim" (1971).

14. See Albright's paper (published posthumously), "Neglected Factors in the Greek Intellectual Revolution," *Proceedings of the American Philosophical Society* 116 (1972), 225–242.

15. It is clear that in this case the Egyptians confused them, and indeed the confusion produced finally four Amūns. See Sethe, *Amun und die acht Urgötter* [N 3], p. 60, and esp. W. Helck, *Wörterbuch der Mythologie* (ed. H. W. Haussig), I, 3, 331.

16. See my discussion in *Canaanite Myth and Hebrew Epic* [N 1], pp. 24–35.

17. Gen. 14:19, 20, 22.

18. The funerary cult of the Egyptian Ogdoad is in point of fact the exception that proves the rule. For other possible exceptions, see W. L. Moran, *Biblica* 43 (1962), 319 and n. 2.

19. The names *'Abd-Ṣapōn* and *'Abd-Ḥamōn* are apparently exceptions, mountains (Cassius and Amanus) being reckoned as old gods. However, the names may be hypocoristica for 'Abd-ba'l-Ṣapōn and 'Abd-ba'l-Ḥamōn.

20. See now W. G. Lambert and S. B. Parker, *Enūma Eliš* (Oxford, 1966). Citations from Tablet V are after B. Landsberger and J. V. Kinnier Wilson, "The Fifth Tablet of *Enuma Eliš*," *JNES* 20 (1961), 154–179.

21. Tablet V, 85–88.

22. On the Ugaritic cycle, see *Canaanite Myth and Hebrew Epic* [N 1], pp. 112–144.

23. *Kanaanäische und aramäische Inschriften* 222, A.11 f.; cf. J. A. Fitzmyer, *The Aramaic Inscriptions of Sefîre* (Rome, 1967), pp. 37–39. On the pairs, Heaven and Earth, and Day and Night, see Moran, *Biblica* 43 [N 18], 317 ff., and references.

24. See also Deut. 32:1 and Ps. 50:4, hymns which echo the covenant-lawsuit formula.

25. See Albright, "Neglected Factors in the Greek Intellectual Revolution" [N 14], pp. 236–238.

26. O. Eissfeldt in his paper "Phönikische und griechische Kosmogonie," *Éléments orientaux dans la religion grecque ancienne* [*Travaux du Centre d'Études supérieures spécialisé d'histoire de religions de Strasbourg*] (Paris, 1960), 1–15, has argued for direct influence of the Phoenician theogony of Taaut (Thoth) found in Sakkunyaton (*Praep. evang.* I.10.1), noting among many resemblances the key term *apeiron* used in Anaximander of the substrate, and Sakkunyaton's characteristic description of elements of primordial chaos as *apeira* and *mē echein peras*. W. F. Albright (in the paper cited in N 14) has demonstrated further that the first theogony of Sakkunyaton is taken over as a whole from the Hermopolite theology. We note the pair *Ḥūḥ* and *Ḥawḥet*, "Lord Unlimited-in-Space" and "Lady Unlimited-in-Space."

27. The emendation of Κ Ο Λ Π Ι to Κ Ο Δ Μ is that of Albright, *JBL* 43 (1923), 66 f. Cf. L. Clapham, "Sanchuniathon: The First Two Cycles (unpublished Harvard dissertation, 1969), p. 83.

28. Compare the Mesopotamian theogonic pair Dūri and Dāri, whose names have the same meaning.

29. *Praep. evang.* 10, 14.15.

18. *Exodus and Covenant in Second Isaiah and Prophetic Tradition*

BERNHARD W. ANDERSON

PRINCETON THEOLOGICAL SEMINARY

IN RECENT YEARS there has been wide agreement that two major covenant theologies were operative in the history of Israel's traditions: a conditional covenant associated pre-eminently with Moses, and an "everlasting covenant" (*berît 'ôlām*), more unilateral and unconditional in character, which was identified primarily with David and perhaps antecedently with Abraham.[1] Ever since the time when David brought the Ark into his new capital of Jerusalem, thereby seeking to combine the symbolism of the Mosaic tradition with the alien institutions of king and temple, these two covenant theologies existed in relation to, if not in tension with, one another. Indeed, one of the chief tasks of biblical theology is to understand how the two interacted in the history of traditions.[2] In an essay which sets forth a proposal for the presentation of Old Testament theology, G. Ernest Wright observes: "It is not altogether clear precisely how the Mosaic covenant and the Jerusalem theology of the Davidic monarchy were adjusted to one another." He goes on to say: "It is clear, however, that in Exilic and Post-Exilic religious expression, it was the covenant with David that now gave ground to hope and was deemed centrally important," as evidenced by the "everlasting covenant" with Abraham (which reflects the Davidic covenant), by the prophecies of Ezekiel, Haggai and—to some extent—Zechariah, and above all by the Chronicler's history.[3] I should like to pick up on his reflections at this point and to concentrate mainly on the theological contribution of Second Isaiah in the context of prophetic traditions. Since the interrelationship of Exodus and Covenant in Israel's faith has always been at the center of Professor Wright's interest, it is a pleasure to present this essay to him as a token of gratitude for the impact of his writings upon my thinking ever since the beginning of my teaching career and in appreciation of the cordial relationship which has developed across the years, during the initial stages of the re-excavation of Shechem, the annual discussions in the Biblical Colloquium, and other forms of collaboration.

I

It is appropriate to launch into a study of Exodus and Covenant in Israel's theological traditions by turning to the unknown prophet of the Exile (Isaiah 40–55), known among scholars as Second Isaiah. For no prophet of the Old Testament draws more deeply upon the wealth of Israel's traditions. He is a debtor to the Israelite sacred story (*Heilsgeschichte*) found classically in the Pentateuch, to the prophets who preceded him, to wisdom circles, to the liturgical traditions of the Psalter, and to the royal theology of Zion.[4] In his prophecy all of the traditions of Israel came together and, under the alchemy of his poetic and theological insight, were given a new synthesis.

While the ecumenical achievement of the prophet has been generally recognized, insufficient attention has been given to the fact that one major motif of the Israelite tradition is minimized or even neglected in his prophecy. Nowhere does Second Isaiah place any stress upon the Mosaic covenant.[5] There are, to be sure, a few references to *tôrâ* in the sense of divine "teaching" or even "revelation":

1) *42:4.* Of the Servant it is said:

> Never flagging, never breaking down,
>   he will plant justice (*mišpāṭ*) on the earth,
>   while distant shores wait for his torah.

2) *42:21* In a context dealing with Israel, the Servant, it is said that Yahweh's intention to manifest his revelation through Israel is frustrated by the people's blind and captive condition.

> It pleased Yahweh, for the sake of his righteousness,
>   to enhance and glorify his torah,
> but this is a people plundered and despoiled . . .[6]

3) *42:24.* In the same poem (42:18–25) it is announced that Israel's blindness has prevented her from understanding the meaning of what had happened:

> Who delivered Jacob to despoilers,
>   Israel to plunderers?
> Was it not Yahweh against whom we sinned
>   [in whose ways they would not walk,
>   and to whose torah they would not listen?][7]

4) *51:4.* In a context dealing with the call of Israel, we read:

> Hearken to me, you peoples,
>   and give ear to me, you nations![8]

> For torah will proceed from me,
> and my judgment (*mišpāṭ*) as a light to the peoples.

5) *51:7*. In the same poem (51:1–8), Israel is addressed at the opening:

> Listen to me, you who know what is right (*ṣedeq*),
> you people in whose heart is my torah.

In the latter case, the language is reminiscent of Jeremiah's prophecy of the new covenant (Jer. 31:33f.; cf. Ezek. 36:27), a passage which, of course, belongs in the tradition of Mosaic theology.

In short, with the clear exception of 42:24c, whose authenticity is questionable, Second Isaiah seems to use the term *tôrâ* in a rather broad sense, practically equivalent to divine revelation which was given to Israel and, through Israel or the Servant, was to be mediated to the nations. At any rate, in none of these cases is there a clear allusion to Moses, the Sinai theophany, the decalog, or the conditional covenant.

There is one passage (48:17–19) which, at first glance, seems to suggest the conditional Mosaic covenant.

> Thus says Yahweh your Redeemer, the Holy One of Israel:
> I am Yahweh your God who teaches you for your profit,
> who guides you in the way wherein you should walk.
> If only you had hearkened to my commandments,
> your well-being (*šālôm*) would have been like a river.
> your salvation (*ṣᵉdāqâ*) like the surge of the sea.
> Your descendants would have been like the sand,
> and your offspring like its grains.
> Their name would never be blotted out,
> nor destroyed from my presence.

This passage is strongly reminiscent of the covenant renewal liturgy in Psalm 81, especially the concluding admonition (vss. 14–15[13–14]):

> O that my people would listen to me,
> that Israel would walk in my ways!
> Soon I would subdue their enemies,
> and against their foes would turn my power.

There is a big difference, however, in the way the promise of blessing is treated in the two contexts. The psalm is addressed to the cultic situation of the *present*, appealing for a covenant renewal now which could affect God's future action. Accordingly, the psalm begins with a summary of Yahweh's gracious acts: the deliverance from oppression, the revelation "in the secret place of thunder" (Sinai), and the testing in the wilderness (vss. 5b–7[6b–8]). The divine oracle, apparently delivered by a temple priest or prophet, then leads to an admonition (vss. 9–11[8–10]), including the prohibition of worshiping any "strange god" (an allusion to the first commandment of the decalog), Yahweh's self-predication as the God who brought his people out of Egypt, and his promise that covenant obedience will bring well-being. The remainder of the psalm, which contains an indictment for past behavior and an appeal for covenant faithfulness, indicates that the future prosperity of the people is contingent upon their willingness to change their ways *now*.

Second Isaiah may have been influenced by this cultic form, If so, he modifies the promise of blessing by taking it out of the context of covenant renewal in the present and referring it to past behavior which had led to the catastrophic event of the fall of Jerusalem and the exile of the people. Conceivably things could have been different—in fact, the promise made to Abraham concerning a posterity as numerous as the sands of the sea might have been realized, if only Israel had hearkened to Yahweh's commandments. The past, however, is irrevocable, and the recollection of it can only prompt an expression of divine anguish about what might have been, had Israel acted differently. In any case, the recollection of Israel's behavior which leads consistently from the past into the present does not provide the basis for future hope. Unlike Psalm 81, Second Isaiah does not think of Israel's future salvation as being contingent upon the renewal of the Mosaic covenant in the present.[9]

It is strange that a prophet who drew so deeply upon the sacred traditions of Israel is silent about the Sinai revelation and gives no great weight to the conditional promises of the Mosaic covenant (cf. Exod. 19:3b–6). This lack is especially surprising in a prophet whose imagination is stirred by the symbolization of Israel's sacred story: the call and promises to the fathers (41:8–10, 43:27, 51:1–2), the deliverance from Egypt (43:16–17, 51:9–10, etc.), the journey through the wilderness (40:3–5, 43:19–21), and the (re)-entrance into the promised land.[10] Moreover, he knows the larger tradition (*Urgeschichte*) which reaches back through the Noachian covenant (54:9–10) to the creation, when Yahweh stretched out the heavens and laid the foundations of the earth (40:12–31, 42:5, 44:24, 45:9–13, 18, 48:13, 51:13, 16). In what seems to be a reference to the priestly creation story, he declares that it is not Yahweh's intention to allow the earth to return to pre-creation chaos, the *tôhû* of Gen. 1:2 (45:18–19). He must have known the Pentateuchal tradition in approximately the form given to it by the Priestly Writer.

It is true that Second Isaiah was also profoundly influenced by the theology of the Jerusalem circle. For him Zion is the urban symbol of the people Israel, the herald of good tidings to the broken and desolate cities of Judah (40:9). Moreover, in the second part of his prophecy (chs. 49–55) there are a number of Zion poems which elaborate some of the motifs of the Jerusalem cult, above all the theme of Yahweh's kingship (see 52:7–10) as expressed in the so-called enthronement psalms (Psalms 47, 93, 95–99). On the other hand, Second Isaiah gives virtually no weight to the two fundamental tenets of Davidic theology (cf. Psalm 132): Yahweh's election of the Davidic king and his election of the Jerusalem temple as the place of his sacramental presence. (The only reference to the temple in Isaiah 40–55 is found in 44:28b.) Nor does he refer to any of the historical events which were important in royal covenant theology, such as the rise of David to be king, the escorting of the Ark into Jerusalem, and the plan to build a temple. Instead, he relies heavily upon the Pentateuchal traditions, the core of which is the exodus from Egypt. "The place which Deutero-Isaiah gives to the Exodus is so conspicuous," observes Westermann, "that all the other events in Israel's history recede into the background."[11]

It is hardly accidental or insignificant that the prophet, writing at a time when Exodus and Sinai were firmly united in Israel's sacred story, ignored the Mosaic covenant altogether and at the climax and conclusion of his work emphasized the "everlasting covenant" typified by the covenants with Noah (54:7–10) and with David (55:3–5).[12] It would be helpful, therefore, to approach this matter by reviewing briefly the place of the Exodus-Covenant motif in Israel's theological traditions.

II

The story of the deliverance of Hebrew slaves from bondage to Pharaoh has had a powerful appeal to the religious imagination, even to the present day when oppressed groups have reappropriated its symbolism. As David Daube observes, "this habit of looking on the exodus as a prototype, as a mould in which other stories of rescue from ruin may be cast, goes back to the Bible itself" where the exodus story constitutes the basic "pattern of deliverance" to whose presuppositions all other liberation motifs are accommodated.[13] This is clearly the case with Second Isaiah in whose poetry the Exodus is both the classical instance of Yahweh's redemptive activity and, at the same time, the type of the new exodus of salvation that was about to take place. Broadly speaking, the message of the prophet was an exposition of the theological meaning of the Exodus for the time of Israel's Babylonian bondage. Other prophets, such as Hosea and Ezekiel, also engaged in this kind of theological thinking.[14]

The stress upon the theological significance of the Exodus does not necessarily minimize its historicity, that is, its place in the actual course of events which formed Israel as a people. The theologian, however, is interested primarily in what makes the Exodus eventful, that is, laden with meaning which could exert a powerful and creative influence in the history of traditions. Wright has helped us to understand how the Exodus has symbolic, revelatory power.

An event is an attribute of an active subject which reveals itself only to the degree that inferences can be properly deduced from what it does. Since in the Bible God is the central subject, there is no attempt to penetrate what he is in himself. There is only the testimony of what he has done, together with the body of "inferences" or assumptions as to what may be deduced from the events. Thus a happening or tradition about a happening may be charged with meaning. The event may have, as it were, a semantic field around it which contains an inexhaustible source of energy as worshipers recall it in their own particular historical situations.[15]

It is in the prophecy of Second Isaiah, above all, that we can appreciate the rich "semantic field" of this event, one charged with such theological meaning that it illuminated Israel's knowledge of Yahweh, her vocation and witness in the world, and her hope for a future in which all mankind may participate.

In the creative period of the origin of the Pentateuchal tradition, that is, the two centuries before David, the Exodus was the primary confession of the Israelite community.[16] In the traditions from this period the event was charged with such meaning that other episodes and motifs were drawn into its semantic field. This is evident, for instance, in the account of the crossing of the Jordan (Joshua 3–4) which, as Daube reminds us, "is full of elements designed to recall the crossing of the Red Sea under Moses."[17] Moreover, early Israelite poetry, such as the Song of the Sea (Exod. 15: 1–18), shows that Canaanite imagery was drawn into the semantic field of the Exodus, perhaps in the context of a cultic re-enactment of the crossing of the Sea celebrated at the shrine of Gilgal.[18] In this early period Exodus and Sinai, redemption and covenant belonged essentially together. Sinai was regarded as the place from which Yahweh came to deliver his people (Judg. 5:4–5), just as it was the place where he established his covenant with Israel on the basis of his commandments (Exod. 24:3–8). His action on behalf of Israel was that of a sovereign whose deeds of benevolence "imposed lasting obligations on those on whose behalf he intervened."[19] Thus Israel's experience of salvation was connected essentially with the demand for social justice as the only appropriate response to the kind of action Yahweh had performed (cf. Micah 6:1–8). And in the terms of the Mosaic covenant, the promise of Yahweh was conditional: "If you will obey my voice and keep my covenant . . ." (Exod. 19:5–6).

The question is what happened to the Israelite mythos (Exodus, Sinai, wilderness, promised land) when this pattern of symbolization encountered the new way of thinking introduced by Davidic theology, with its twin convictions of the enduring covenant with David and the election of Zion as Yahweh's dwelling place. Under the influence of Rost's essay on "Sinaitic Covenant and Davidic Covenant," referred to previously, there has been a tendency to think of the two covenant theologies (Mosaic and Davidic) as "northern" (Ephraimitic) and "southern" (Judaean) respectively. It is alleged that the new royal theology, being based on the alien institutions of kingship and temple, had the effect of suppressing the ancient Mosaic tradition.[20] In reaction to the dynastic theology of the Davidic court, it is said, Jeroboam I returned to the Exodus-Covenant tradition of the ancient tribal league. Northern prophets, especially Elijah and Hosea, belong in the Exodus-Sinai tradition, while the southern prophet, Isaiah of Jerusalem, avoids the Exodus and concentrates, rather, on the key issues of royal theology: the Davidic Messiah and Yahweh's inviolable dwelling place in Zion. It was only later, according to this reconstruction, that the two covenant theologies were harmonized, chiefly by the Deuteronomist.

The separation of covenant theologies on the basis of geography is undoubtedly an oversimplification.[21] Insofar as the Davidic covenant legitimated a single dynasty, in the face of the threat of social disruption that accompanied a change of administration, it undoubtedly provided a measure of social stability in the south which was lacking in the north, where no single dynasty was able to maintain itself in unbroken continuity. II Sam. 7, at least in its present form, justifies the continuance of the line of David (vss. 11b–16; cf. Ps. 89:4–5, 30–38[3–4, 29–37]) by saying that Yahweh made a firm commitment to David (II Sam. 23:5, a $b^e r\hat{\imath}t$ '$\hat{o}l\bar{a}m$). This view, of course, is consonant with the royal psalms of the Psalter which give expression to Yahweh's special favor to the reigning king. Moreover, Psalm 78, which originally may have had a different conclusion after vs. 66, in its present form intends to justify the transfer of leadership from the northern tribes ("the tent of Joseph") to Judah, specifically to the Davidic king and the Jerusalem temple (vss. 67–72), if not to account for the schism between Samaria and Judah.[22] It would be going too far, however, to move beyond these claims of legitimacy, which undoubtedly figured prominently in the Jerusalem circle, and to say that the Davidic theology brought about a complete suppression of the Exodus-Covenant theology of Mosaic tradition. After all, David took pains to escort the Ark, the palladium of the tribal league, into Jerusalem, thereby symbolically laying claim to the previous religious tradition (cf. Ps. 24:7–10). Furthermore, if the ancient Israelite epic, known as J, was given written formulation in the time of the Davidic-Solomonic renascence, the Mosaic pattern of symbolization, that is, the Exodus story including Sinai, must have had a significant place in the new theological interpretation. In Jerusalem the question was not either Moses or David but, rather, how the semantic field of the Exodus would exert its power in the new situation of worship.

An immediate point of contact between the early Israelite cult and the cult of Zion was the theme of the Divine Warrior's victory at the Sea, a victory which established Yahweh's sovereignty as cosmic King over the peoples and Creator of the world.[23] In the psalms of the Jerusalem cult (e.g. Psalms 29, 77, 114; Habakkuk 3) the Divine Warrior wages battle, not against pharaonic enemies of flesh and blood, but against mythical powers—floods,

Sea, Rahab—which defy his kingly rule. No longer is the sea a passive natural element which Yahweh used to accomplish his deliverance of Israel; rather, the waters were "afraid," they "fled," and were "rebuked" by Yahweh's wrath. In these contexts the meaning of the Exodus is enhanced by mythical motifs, derived primarily from Canaan, with the result that Yahweh's historical deeds are seen in the spacious perspective of his cosmic rule. To be sure, this cosmic dimension was present in early poems celebrating the wars of Yahweh; but the new situation occasioned by the rise of David prompted a new understanding of Yahweh's sovereignty in areas of thought and experience which were more or less strange to the kind of worship practiced at confederate sanctuaries: Shechem, Bethel, Gilgal, Shiloh.[24] It is against the background of the Jerusalem cult that we can understand Second Isaiah's use of the motif of Yahweh's kingship (52:7–8) or his interpretation of the victory at the Sea as the Divine Warrior's triumph over the powers of chaos represented by Rahab (51:9–11). The prophet's thought seems to break beyond the confines of Israel's *Heilsgeschichte,* which provides the source of much of his poetic imagery, and to ground hope for the future transcendentally in the sovereign decree of the God who is the cosmic King.

While the semantic field of the Exodus profoundly influenced the Jerusalem cult, it is not clear how the conditional Mosaic covenant was accommodated to the "everlasting covenant" with its promises of grace to David. The problem is solved too easily by saying, as Rost argued, that the Exodus-Covenant tradition was preserved in the north and was not incorporated into the Jerusalem theology until the "Deuteronomic" reform of Josiah. It is significant that Psalm 50, which has affinities with the (northern?) Psalm 81, portrays Yahweh "dawning" from Zion, manifestly an allusion to the old tradition of his epiphany from Sinai (Ps. 68:8–11, 18[7–10, 17]; Deut. 33: 2–5). Yahweh comes in a theophany of fire and storm to judge his people who have concluded a covenant with him (vs. 5) but who have ignored his decalogic instruction, as evidenced in their condoning of stealing, adultery, and slander (vss. 16–21). On the other hand, while there can be no doubt that "the Sinai tradition was brought to Jerusalem along with the Ark,"[25] we have no clear evidence that the Mosaic and Davidic covenants, before the Deuteronomist's work, were reconciled in the Jerusalem cult. It is true that some of the texts dealing with the Davidic covenant introduce a conditional note. In Psalm 89, for instance, Yahweh makes an absolute promise to David that his line would endure *'ad 'ōlām,* in perpetuity (vss. 4–5[3–4]), that his throne would have a permanence like the cosmic stability of the heavens (vss. 36–38[35–37]), though this commitment is qualified by the responsibility of Davidic kings to the commandments, presumably the Mosaic torah.

> If his sons reject my torah,
>   and fail to follow my ordinances,
> If they violate my statutes,

> fail to observe my commandments,
> then I will punish their transgressions with the rod,
>> and their offense with scourges;
> but I will not terminate my loyalty (*ḥesed*) to him,
>> or go back on my faithfulness.
>>> Ps. 89:31–34[30–33]

This conditional language is also found in II Sam. 7 (esp. vss. 14–15) which in its present form has a strongly Deuteronomic cast, and also in Psalm 132 which stands in even closer proximity to the early theology of the Davidic court:

> Yahweh made an oath to David,
>> a lasting promise from which he will not swerve:
> "One of your own descendants
>> I will place on your throne.
> If your descendants keep my covenant,
>> and my testimonies which I teach them,
> then their sons too in perpetuity
>> shall sit upon your throne."
>>> Ps. 132:11–12

It is impossible to determine the degree to which the qualification of the unconditional commitment to David was influenced by Deuteronomic revision of the royal theology or, alternatively, by a pre-Deuteronomic accommodation to the Mosaic covenant theology. It is noteworthy that Isaiah of Jerusalem, who virtually ignored the Exodus tradition[26] and who concentrated, rather, on the theology of Zion, introduced a strong admonition based on the conditional "if . . . then . . ." formulation (Isa. 1:19–20). Furthermore, the genre of the covenant lawsuit was employed by prophets of the pre-exilic period (cf. Micah 6:1–8). In any case, in none of the Zion texts mentioned above does the conditional element fundamentally affect Yahweh's absolute commitment to David's dynasty. Nathan's prophecy is understood to mean that Yahweh's pledge to David remains unalterable, even though Davidic kings proved faithless, and this is "the direct contrary" of the Mosaic covenant form, as McCarthy rightly observes. Indeed, this covenant in principle was "simply a promise of God and was valid despite anything that Israel might do."[27]

III

Against this background, it is significant that Second Isaiah, whose prophecy is bound up in the same scroll with Isaiah of Jerusalem and who presumably stood in the same prophetic tradition, turns not to the conditional Mosaic covenant which from the first had been associated with the Exodus but, rather, to the *bᵉrît ʿôlām* which is grounded solely in Yahweh's unalterable promises of grace. This happens twice, toward the conclusion of the corpus of his prophecy. In the first instance (54:7–10) the prophet turns to the *bᵉrît ʿôlām* (Gen. 9:16) or the *bᵉrît šālôm* (Ezek. 34:24, 37:26; cf. Num. 25: 12) of priestly tradition in order to emphasize the permanent validity of Yahweh's promises of grace. The superb poem found in 54:1–10 reaches its climax with this proclamation of salvation:

> For a brief instant I forsook you
>   but with tremendous compassion I will gather you.
> In bursting wrath for a moment
>   I hid my face from you,
> but with everlasting loyalty (*ḥesed*) I'll have compassion on you,
>   says Yahweh, your Redeemer.
>
> For like the days of Noah is this to me:
>   just as I vowed that the waters of Noah
>   should never again pass over the earth,
> so I have sworn not to be angry with you
>   or to rebuke you any more.
> For even though the mountains were to vanish,
>   and the hills were to totter,
> still, my constant loyalty would not vanish from you,
>   and my covenant of peace not waver,
>   says Yahweh, who has compassion on you.
>
> Isa. 54:7–10

It is significant that here the prophet announces hope for the future on the basis not of the Mosaic covenant with its emphasis upon human obligation but, rather, of a covenant which stresses God's "unilateral and unconditional commitment" to mankind, "in full view of man's ineradicable tendency to do wrong."[28] Yahweh's faithfulness to his people, though momentarily eclipsed by the shadow of his judgment, is more secure than the enduring mountains (cf. Ps. 46:1–3). Salvation is not grounded on the behavior of the people or upon historical contingencies but solely on a covenant of commitment made by the Creator.

In the next chapter the prophet reiterates the proclamation, this time basing it upon the irrevocable covenant with David (55:1–5). With a surprising reinterpretation of royal covenant theology, however, the promises of grace are transferred from the Davidic dynasty to the *people,* as indicated by the plural suffix in 55:3b (*lākem*).[29] The passage begins with a gracious invitation which is reminiscent of scenes in the marketplace where vendors sell their wares. However, what is "for sale," namely, fullness of life, is available *gratis,* "without price." The prophetic proclamation then continues:

Give ear and come to me,
  listen, that you may have life to the full!
I will make an enduring covenant with you,
  the reliable manifestations of my loyalty to David.[30]
Even as I made him a witness to the peoples,
  a leader and commander of peoples,
so you shall call a nation you do not know,
  nations unknown to you shall hasten to you,
on account of Yahweh your God,
  because of the Holy One of Israel who has honored you.

                                           Isa. 55:3–5

The poem continues with a plea to respond to Yahweh's invitation without delay in the recognition that his forgiveness is abundant, that his grace exceeds the grasp of human comprehension, and that his word accomplishes its purpose as surely as the rain makes the earth fertile (vss. 6–11). It concludes by sounding the theme with which the prophecy opens: the new exodus through a marvelously transformed wilderness.[31]

These are the only two places where *berît* is used in the prophecy of Second Isaiah, leaving out of account the references to the "everlasting covenant" in the related passage Isa. 61:1–11 (vs. 8), and the usages in 42:6 and 49:8 which extend the meaning of the term to describe the evangelical role of the Servant as "a covenant to the people." Westermann observes that in Old Testament theology the function of the covenant is to confirm the relationship between God and people which is based upon a prior act of deliverance and that, in this respect, Second Isaiah's use of *berît* is "exactly the same as in Ex. 34 and Josh. 24."[32] It is true, of course, that the biblical covenants, despite their differences in type, have in common an emphasis upon the anterior grace of Yahweh which establishes the relationship. Due attention must be given, however, to the theological differences between the two major covenant theologies if we are to understand why Second Isaiah ignores the Mosaic covenant and turns instead to the Noachian and Davidic covenants (and the promise to Abraham) to give ground for hope. This matter deserves more careful attention.

IV

Mosaic covenant theology, as expressed classically in the conditional formulation of Exod. 19:3–6,[33] placed a heavy burden of responsibility upon the human partner. It was essentially "a covenant of human obligation."[34] According to this way of thinking, Israel's future was contingent upon her own behavior. In any moment of decision she faced the alternatives of blessing or curse, weal or woe, life or death. The problematic character of this covenant is expressed forcefully in the covenant renewal ceremony at Shechem, as described in Joshua 24. After reciting Yahweh's prior deeds of benevolence and summoning the people to respond to his claim upon them, Joshua issues this stern warning:

> You are unable to serve Yahweh, for he is a holy
> God, he is a zealous God. He will not forgive your
> violations and your infractions. If you forsake Yahweh
> and serve alien gods, then he will turn and bring
> disaster upon you, after having brought you good (religious).
>
> Josh. 24:19–21

As Gerhard von Rad points out, the statement that Israel is unable to serve Yahweh is unparalleled in the Old Testament; and in some way it relates to the verdict, to which prophets like Jeremiah and Ezekiel were driven, that Israel lacks the capacity "to live with and belong to God."[35] This pessimistic appraisal of the human situation is understandable especially within the framework of Mosaic covenant theology. The question arises: Can a covenant which places great emphasis upon human obligation, that is, upon the contingency of human decision, provide any firm assurance that the covenant relationship will last and therefore give any ground for future hope? It is well known that this covenant theology made ample use of the literary genre of the *rîb* or covenant lawsuit in which the suzerain, after recalling his benevolent deeds, indicts his people through a prophetic messenger for their betrayal of the covenant.[36]

Israel's covenant relationship with God became acutely problematic in the message of two precursors of Second Isaiah who stood primarily in the Mosaic covenant tradition: Hosea and Jeremiah. Hosea's message is based on a profound awareness of the prior divine acts which initiated the covenant relationship. No prophet before Second Isaiah gave more eloquent witness to the conviction that Yahweh is the God of Israel from the time of the Exodus, the crucial event which called the people into being and endowed them with a future (2:16–17[14–15], 11:1, 12:9, 13, 13:4–5; cf. 9:10). Yet he is also the prophet who takes with utmost seriousness the contingent element of the Mosaic covenant with its call to covenant obedience under the sanctions of the blessing and the curse (welfare or disaster). In his interpretation, Israel's history from the time of the entrance into Canaan was a history of covenant failure, owing to the "harlotrous spirit" which gripped the people with such power that they were held helplessly in bondage to their false style of life (Hosea 5:3–4). Hence the prophet pressed Mosaic covenant theology to its inevitable conclusion: if there was human betrayal of the covenant, Yahweh himself would abrogate the relationship, even to the point of inverting the ancient covenant formula by saying: "You are not my people and I am not your God" (Hosea 1:8).

> Put the trumpet to your lips!
>   A vulture [?] is over the sanctuary of Yahweh;
> because they have broken my covenant,
>   and transgressed my torah.
> To me they cry:
>   "My God, we recognize you."
> Israel has rejected good relations (*ṭôb*):
>   the enemy shall pursue him.[37]
>
>   Hosea 8:1–3

Hosea believed, however, that in the last analysis Yahweh's love for his people is "irrational" in that it exceeds the strict limits of the Mosaic covenant. His faithfulness to his people is analogous to a father's anguished love for his prodigal son (ch. 11), or to a man who buys back an adulterous woman (ch. 3). Hence the prophet, within the context of conditional covenant theology, presses toward an understanding of Yahweh's permanent covenant, despite the infidelity of his people. The last word is not that of divine judgment which formalizes the termination of a relationship which Israel has already ended by her own behavior. Using the imagery of the sacred tradition, the prophet ventures to speak of Israel's new beginning in the wilderness (2:16–17[14–15]) and of a new covenant which, unlike the Mosaic covenant, will last in perpetuity (*le'ôlām;* 2:21[19]) for it will be based upon a new disposition of the people characterized by righteousness and justice, *ḥesed* and mercy.[38]

The prophecy of Jeremiah, akin to that of Hosea in many ways, belongs fundamentally within the Mosaic covenant tradition. To be sure, there are a few passages which indicate that he knew and made limited use of Davidic covenant theology but, as von Rad rightly observes, it was really "something quite alien" to him.[39] His message was dominated by the Exodus-Covenant tradition from first to last. This is evident from the covenant lawsuit in chapter 2 which charges that the people have defected from Yahweh who brought them out of Egypt, led them through the wilderness, and brought them to the promised land. No longer characterized by the loyalty (*ḥesed*) of their youth (2:2), they have turned from Yahweh, the fountain of living waters, to satisfy their thirst at the cracked and leaky cisterns of false religious loyalties (2:4–13). The same Mosaic theology is evident in Jeremiah's temple sermon (ch. 7) which boldly criticizes the premises of royal theology with its deceptive confidence in the temple as Yahweh's dwelling place and sets before the people the "if" of the covenant.

> For if you really amend your ways and your deeds,
> if you really practice justice one toward another,
> if you don't oppress the resident alien, the orphan,
> and the widow, or shed innocent blood in this place,
> or follow after other gods to your own detriment,

> then I will let you dwell in this place, in the land
> which I gave to your fathers for all time.
>
>   Jer. 7:5–7

Here the promises of the covenant are contingent upon the people's behavior, specifically obedience of the commandments of the decalog (vss. 9–10). If they fail in this, the curse of the covenant will be experienced. A temple which had become a robbers' hideout would suffer the fate of the central sanctuary of Shiloh which perished during the Philistine wars.

Speaking from the standpoint of the Mosaic covenant, Jeremiah appealed for a corporate change in the people's style of life, a radical reorientation in response to the "if" (4:1–2!) of the covenant. In doing so, he was just as profoundly aware as Hosea before him of the bondage of the will from which the people apparently were powerless to free themselves. While the Deuteronomic reinterpretation of the Israelite tradition was based on the confidence that Israel could enjoy fullness of life if she hearkened to the invitation to covenant renewal, the prophets of the same period, especially Jeremiah and Ezekiel, were more pessimistic about Israel's capacity to fulfill the obligations of the covenant.[40] Jeremiah said that Israel could no more change her ways than the Ethiopian could change the color of his skin (Jer. 13:23); and, with an insight which anticipated modern psychology, he insisted that the "heart" is "deceitful" and "desperately sick" (Jer. 17:9). Ezekiel went so far as to say that Israel's whole history, beginning with the Exodus, was an *Unheilsgeschichte,* a history of failure, in which the people had displayed a shocking incapacity to be faithful to the covenant (Ezekiel 20). The words of Joshua, spoken in the context of a covenant renewal ceremony, had an ominous realism: "You cannot serve Yahweh."

Nevertheless, prophets who were active during the period of the fall of Jerusalem were not driven into pessimism about the future. To be sure, insofar as the future is contingent upon man's covenant faithfulness they saw little hope. Perhaps their announcements of the inevitable coming of the day of judgment are understandable in our time when some political philosophers are not sanguine about man's capacity to fulfill the conditions for the survival of human civilization. Be that as it may, prophetic hope came to be grounded upon God's covenant commitment which is not limited in the last analysis by the Mosaic covenant with its heavy emphasis upon human freedom and obligation.

Jeremiah's prophecy of the new covenant (Jer. 31:31–34) sets forth an "optimism of grace" within the framework of the Mosaic covenant. He envisions a "metastatic change" in Israel, that is, a reform through "a change in the constitution of being,"[41] with the result that the torah will be implanted in the heart and there will be a complete identity between man's will and God's will (see 24:7!). What is more, Jeremiah announces that the new age will be inaugurated by Yahweh's forgiveness, which gives evidence of his persistent faithfulness despite the broken covenant relationship of the past. This note is sounded in another eschatological passage:

> With an everlasting love I have loved you,
>> therefore I have prolonged loyalty (*ḥesed*) to you.[42]
>>> Jer. 31:3b

Jeremiah's final understanding of the covenant relationship, then, exhibits a polarity: on the human side the covenant was broken and, given the desperately sick "heart" (i.e. mind and will, volitional being) of Israel, could not be repaired by renewal ceremonies; on the divine side, however, the relationship was grounded in Yahweh's *'aḥᵃbat 'ôlām,* his everlasting love which is not conditioned by human behavior. Considering this polarity, it is not surprising that the prophet's theology begins to move away from the Mosaic covenant toward the Davidic covenant with its unconditional promises of grace. This is evident when the prophecy of the new covenant is placed in parallel with a related passage:

Behold, days are coming—the oracle of Yahweh—when I will conclude with the house of Israel a new covenant: not like the covenant which I concluded with their fathers on the day when I took them by the hand to bring them out of the land of Egypt, which covenant of mine they broke, though I was their master—the oracle of Yahweh.

But this is the covenant I will conclude with the house of Israel after those days—the oracle of Yahweh. I will put my torah in their inward being and upon their heart I will inscribe it. Then I will be their God and they shall be my people. No longer will a man teach his neighbor or a man his brother, saying, "Know Yahweh," because all of them will know me, from the least of them to the greatest—the oracle of Yahweh; for I will forgive their iniquity, and their sin I will remember no longer.

Jer. 31:31–34

Behold, I am going to gather them from all the countries to which I banished them in my anger and my wrath and my great indignation, and I will restore them to this place and will settle them in security.

They shall be my people, and I will be their God, and I will give them a single heart and a single way of life, so that they may fear me constantly, for their own good and for the good of their children after them. I will conclude with them an everlasting covenant (*bᵉrît 'ôlām*), never to swerve from doing good to them. I will put the fear of me in their heart, so that they may not turn away from me. I will take delight in doing them good, and I will plant them on this land faithfully with all my heart and all my being.

Jer. 32:37–41

To von Rad these parallel passages suggest that Jeremiah spoke of the new covenant in different ways on two occasions and that both have been revised subsequently.[43] What unites these passages, however, is the awareness of a divine commitment which creates a new and permanent relationship, unaffected by the contingencies of human behavior. This new relationship, which provides the ground for future hope, is specifically called a b°rît 'ôlām, an enduring covenant. It is noteworthy that Jeremiah was not concerned merely with a new relationship with God but with its outward manifestation, namely, Israel's restoration to the land and the resumption of normal activities (see vss. 42–44!).

Before turning again to Second Isaiah, it should be observed that there are striking affinities between the prophecy of Jeremiah and that of Ezekiel who specifically described the new relationship as a "covenant of peace" or an "everlasting covenant" (34:25, 27:26). The essential features of Jeremiah's prophecy concerning the new covenant are recapitulated in Ezek. 36:28–32: the heart of the people will be miraculously changed so that they may obey the torah inwardly (vss. 26–27) and they will be cleansed (forgiven) of their past sins (vs. 25). As a result of Yahweh's gracious action, the word is spoken: "you shall dwell in the land which I gave to your fathers and be my people, and I will be your God" (vs. 28). While Ezekiel shows great preference for the Exodus-Sinai tradition, as indicated by the covenant formula "you . . . my people, I . . . your God" (34:23–24, 30, 37:23, 27), he is much more positive in his adoption of the Davidic theology than was Jeremiah who stayed essentially within the Mosaic covenant theology, though pressing it to its very limits.[44]

V

The proclamation of Second Isaiah begins on the very note with which Jeremiah's prophecy of the new covenant concludes: the free offer of divine forgiveness which is the ground of Israel's hope and consolation. This is the announcement which the King makes in his heavenly council and which is to be heralded on earth:

> "Comfort, comfort my people,"
>   says your God.
> "Speak tenderly to Jerusalem,
>   and proclaim to her
> that her sentence is completed,
>   her penalty is satisfied,
> that she has received from Yahweh's hand
>   double for all her sins."

Isa. 40:1–2

For Second Isaiah salvation is not something held in store for the future, contingent upon the people's behavior; rather, it is a new life which God has decreed as an accomplished intention, empowered to go into effect immediately. While both Jeremiah and Ezekiel anticipated a metastatic change, a transformation of the human heart to make the people capable of obeying God's torah, Second Isaiah speaks good news into a human situation which, by any prophetic measurement, remains unchanged. The Israel who hears the message of consolation is still blind, insensitive, and rebellious "from birth" (48:8). The ground for hope, therefore, is not a change on the side of man but, so to speak, on the side of God. The opening announcement of chapter 40 is echoed later on in a climactic passage, where the theme is the constancy of Yahweh's *ḥesed*.

> In bursting wrath for a moment
> I hid my face from you,
> but with everlasting loyalty (*ḥesed*) I'll have compassion on you,
> says Yahweh, your Redeemer.
>
> Isa. 54:7–8

It is doubtful whether this language should be pressed to mean that "a change had come over God" so that he ceased from wrath and displayed mercy.[45] It is not that Yahweh has changed within himself; rather, his *ḥesed* is not bound by what men have a right to expect or what they regard as possible. This understanding of God's faithfulness is at least implicit in the ancient liturgical formulation found in Exod. 34:6–7. In that cultic confession, which is echoed in various places in the Old Testament, Yahweh is proclaimed as the God who is "rich in *ḥesed* and fidelity," and this is preceded by the expressions "compassionate and gracious" and "slow to anger." My colleague Katharine Sakenfeld maintains that this collocation suggests that *ḥesed* means "so great in faithfulness that Yahweh is willing to forgive even a breach of relationship," though she points out that the aspect of *ḥesed* as mercy was brought out fully in exilic and post-exilic writings.[46] Clearly Second Isaiah intends to say that Yahweh's faithfulness is permanent precisely because he is free to act as he will, even to the point of maintaining a relationship which, in the strict terms of Mosaic theology, should have been abrogated. His forgiveness is the expression of *ḥesed* which creates a new historical possibility for his people.

> It is I, I, who blot out your sins for my sake,
> and your iniquities I will remember no more.
> Isa. 43:25 (cf. Jer. 31:34c)

The constancy of Yahweh's faithfulness is the theme which runs throughout the poems of Second Isaiah. In various contexts the prophet affirms that the good news deals with what is "everlasting." Yahweh's word is not characterized by the impermanence of the grass that withers or the flower that fades but it stands *lᵉ'ôlām*, in perpetuity (40:8). The salvation proclaimed to Israel is not a transient state but is *tᵉšû'at 'ôlāmîm*, everlasting salvation (45:17; cf. 51:8), even as the joy of the redeemed is *śimḥat 'ôlām*, gladness without end (51:11). Furthermore, Yahweh's affection for his people is not conditioned by reciprocal love; rather, it is the compassion of *ḥesed 'ôlām*, unwavering loyalty, which outlasts periods of estrangement (54:8). It follows, then, that Yahweh's covenant with his people is not one that could be qualified or invalidated by their behavior; rather, it is a *bᵉrît 'ôlām*, a covenant of divine commitment like that which was made with David or, in the priestly tradition, like the one that was made with Noah.

Thus Second Isaiah's rhapsody is based upon a vision which soars above the mundane plane which is characterized by the transience of all human achievements and the fallibility of human performance and perceives the dimension of divine transcendence or, in the language of mythical symbolism, the cosmic realm of the heavenly council where the solemn decrees affecting human destiny are made. He employs effectively the symbolization of Israel's *Heilsgeschichte* in his portrayal of the new exodus of salvation; but his hope for the future is not grounded, in the final analysis, upon anything historical. Even Israel's history is significant only insofar as it points beyond itself and bears witness to the Creator whose faithfulness embraces the whole sweep of history, from creation to consummation. Before the Creator's cosmic majesty the rulers of the earth are as nothing (40:24); and the gods of the world are reduced to impotent silence before his sovereign word which has the force of an irrevocable decree (55:10–11). It is significant that Second Isaiah's predications of Yahweh's majesty do not employ the old hymnic formula "who brought Israel up out of Egypt," but are cast in hymnic forms which ascribe praise to the God who created the heavens and the earth, who formed Israel as a people, and who declares the end from the beginning (42:5, 44:2, 45:18, 51:15 f.). Nothing contingent, nothing historical can express fully the mystery of his grace and faithfulness.

Viewed in this theological perspective, it is understandable that Second Isaiah turns not to the Mosaic covenant with its conditional promises but to the type of covenant which expresses Yahweh's gracious and faithful commitment to his people. Like the everlasting covenant with Noah which assured the permanence of the natural order, Yahweh's commitment is made unilaterally and unconditionally. Like the covenant with David, Yahweh's promises are made for the sake of his own name (43:25; cf. 45:9), without regard to human conditions. The Mosaic covenant is appropriately absent from Second Isaiah's prophecy, for obedience to commandments is not regarded as a prerequisite for blessing and welfare. Commenting on Isa. 55:5, Westermann pertinently observes: "The new, lasting covenant with Israel is made 'because of Yahweh, your God.' The covenant is altogether an act of God's grace towards Israel; there is no suggestion of Israel's being laid under any obligation."[47] As we noticed at the beginning of this study, the torah which Israel (or the Servant) is to mediate to the world is not the Mosaic commandments but, in a broader sense, the revelation of Yahweh's purpose for all mankind and the whole creation. Israel's "obligation" is to be a witness to grace which is freely given, "without price," and thereby to attract nations to Zion, the world center from which the word or torah of Yahweh goes forth (cf. Isa. 2:3).

In conclusion, the prophecy of Second Isaiah provides a vantage point from which to survey the interaction of the two major covenant theologies in the history of Israel's traditions. Creatively reinterpreting Israel's traditions for the situation of the people in exile, the prophet blends the Mosaic and Davidic theological perspectives. He adopts the Exodus pattern of symbolization, though separating it from the conditional Mosaic covenant with which it had been bound from the very first; and he adopts the unconditional covenant with David, though separating it from the unhappy history of the Davidic dynasty and transferring its promises of grace to the people. This was not a mere compromise between two radically different theologies, but a synthesis in which the whole was greater than the sum of its constituent parts. On the basis of his reinterpretation of Israel's traditions, the prophet proclaims a salvation based upon Yahweh's *ḥesed* which endures despite human failure, upon Yahweh's word which stands forever despite historical transience. He is rhapsodically and doxologically aware, as was Paul in Rom. 11:33–36, that God's thoughts are not men's thoughts, that he remains free to show mercy upon whom he will show mercy, and that his word accomplishes what he purposes (Isa. 55:6–11). The mystery of history, to which Israel's whole existence bears witness, is illumined by divine faithfulness expressed in forgiveness, that is, the granting of a new historical possibility which exceeds all human expectation or merit. According to the prophet, Yahweh was on the verge of doing a "new thing," indeed even in the present it was bursting forth (Isa. 43:18–19). Therefore, what was required was a new theological understanding of Israel's traditions in the present situation. The new wine of the gospel could not be contained adequately in the old wineskin of the Mosaic covenant but was best suited to the theology of the everlasting covenant. By placing the Exodus—the crucial event of Israel's history—in this new theological context, the prophet transposed the meaning of the event into the higher key of the announcement of a new creation into which Israel and all the people are summoned to enter at the gracious invitation of Yahweh, the Holy One of Israel. Indeed, the role of the Servant is to be "a covenant to the people, a light to the nations" (42:6, 49:8) and thus to include mankind within the embrace of the everlasting covenant.

NOTES

1. Discussion was stimulated by two seminal essays: L. Rost, "Sinaibund und Davidsbund," *TLZ* 72 (1947), cols. 129–134, and G. E. Mendenhall, *Law and Covenant in Israel and the Ancient Near East* (Pittsburgh, 1955), pp. 24–50. For a summary of the subsequent scholarly discussion see D. J. McCarthy, *Old Testament Covenant: A Survey*

of Current Opinions (Richmond, 1972). In a recent book, *Bundestheologie im Alten Testament*, Wissenschaftliche Monographien zum Alten und Neuen Testament, 36 (Neukirchen-Vluyn, 1969), L. Perlitt has challenged the basis of the whole discussion by maintaining that *berît* refers to "obligation" rather than a "relationship" and by arguing that *berît* theology was first introduced by the Deuteronomic school. For an effective reply, see the review essay by D. J. McCarthy, *Biblica* 53 (1972), 110–121.

2. This issue receives central attention in Gerhard von Rad's *OTT*, I and II. See also the essay by J. C. Rylaarsdam, "Jewish-Christian Relationship: The Two Covenants and the Dilemmas of Christology," *Journal of Ecumenical Studies* 9 (1972), 249–270, where the attempt is made to understand the relation between Christianity and Judaism on the basis of the two covenants.

3. G. E. Wright, "Reflections Concerning Old Testament Theology," *Studia Biblica et Semitica Theodoro Christiano Vriezen Dedicata* (Wageningen, 1966), pp. 387 f.

4. For discussions of the influence of traditions upon Second Isaiah, see J. Begrich, *Studien zu Deuterojesaja,* Theologische Bücherei 20 (Munich, 1963), 80–95; C. Westermann, *Isaiah 40–66,* Old Testament Library (Philadelphia, 1969), pp. 21–27.

5. This fact is noted and briefly discussed by J. Muilenburg, "Israel, the Covenant People," in *IB*, V, 405.

6. 42:21 is sometimes regarded as a gloss. Westermann [N 4], p. 111, for instance, regards it as "an extremely typical addition" by a writer who, like the author of Psalm 119, "cultivated a legal piety." C. R. North, *The Second Isaiah* (London, 1964), p. 118, maintains that the language here and in vs. 24 is "Deuteronomic in tone," indicating that the passage has been revised editorially. Muilenburg [N 5], 477, however, defends the authenticity of the verse.

7. The bracketed portion of this verse, which introduces a change in person from "we" to "they" and reflects Deuteronomic language, is often regarded as an editorial expansion. Westermann [N 4], p. 113, regards it as a misplaced continuation of the legalistic addition in vs. 21. J. McKenzie, *Second Isaiah,* AB, vol. 20, 46, however, defends the text by saying that "the speaker slips out of his identification with the people after the first verb."

8. Some manuscripts and the Syriac read plurals in vs. 4a: "peoples"/"nations," instead of MT "my people"/"my nation." This is probably correct, since *le'ōm* is not used elsewhere of Israel. It is noteworthy that *tôrâ* and *mišpāṭ* are paralleled in 42:1–4.

9. Westermann [N 4], pp. 203–204, who maintains that Second Isaiah announced "salvation and salvation alone," argues that 48:18–19 shows that the prophet's words were supplemented with an admonition appropriate to post-exilic services of worship. Exegesis of the passage, however, does not make this conclusion necessary. North, [N 6], p. 182, rightly points out that the passage refers to the past, not to the future. "The past is irrevocable, but there is nothing in the passage to suggest that there is no longer any hope for Israel. That would be a negation of Deutero-Isaiah's message. . . . Divine grace is ever renewed. The sense of the whole is 'Would that you had (but you did not), and yet you still may . . .' " [receive the promises to Abraham].

10. For a summary of the *Heilsgeschichte* in Second Isaiah, see my "Exodus Typology in Second Isaiah," in *Israel's Prophetic Heritage: Essays in Honor of James Muilenburg,* eds. B. W. Anderson and W. Harrelson (New York, 1962), pp. 182–184.

11. Westermann [N 4], p. 22.

12. The covenant with Abraham (Genesis 15 and 17) is not explicitly mentioned, though the promise to Abraham receives great stress, especially in 51:1–3.

13. D. Daube, *The Exodus Pattern in the Bible* (London, 1963), p. 11.

14. In addition to my essay on exodus typology in Second Isaiah, referred to above, see W. Zimmerli, "Le nouvel 'exode' dans le message des deux grands prophètes de l'exil," in *La Branche d'Amandier, Hommage à Wilhelm Vischer* (Montpellier, 1960), pp. 216–227; J. Blenkinsopp, "Scope and Depth of Exodus Tradition in Deutero-Isaiah

40:55," in *The Dynamism of Biblical Tradition,* Concilium 20 (Paramus, N.J., 1967), 41–50.

15. Wright [N 3], p. 383.

16. See M. Noth, *A History of Pentateuchal Traditions,* tr. B. W. Anderson (Englewood Cliffs, N.J., 1971), pp. 47–51. He writes: "In the case of the 'guidance out of Egypt' we are dealing with a primary confession (*Urbekenntnis*) of Israel, one that is expressed rather strictly in hymnic form, and at the same time with the kernel of the whole subsequent Pentateuchal tradition" (p. 47). See my introduction to the volume, especially pp. xx–xxiii, xxviii–xxxii.

17. Daube [N 13], p. 11.

18. See the illuminating essays by F. M. Cross, "The Divine Warrior in Israel's Early Cult," in *Biblical Motifs,* ed. A. Altmann (Cambridge, Mass., 1966), pp. 11–30, and "The Song of the Sea and Canaanite Myth," in *God and Christ: Existence and Province, JTC* 5 (1968), 1–25. See also P. D. Miller, Jr., *The Divine Warrior in Early Israel* (Cambridge, Mass., 1973).

19. Daube [N 13], p. 13. For the analogy of the Mosaic covenant to ancient suzerainty treaties, see the monograph by G. E. Mendenhall [N 1], and K. Baltzer, *Das Bundesformular* (2d ed., 1964); Eng. tr. *The Covenant Formulary* (Philadelphia, 1971).

20. See N. Poulssen, *König und Tempel im Glaubenszeugnis des Alten Testaments,* Stuttgarter Biblische Monographien 3 (Stuttgart, 1967), reviewed in *CBQ* 31 (1969), 45–52.

21. See A. H. J. Gunneweg, "Sinaibund und Davidsbund," *VT* 10 (1960), 335–341.

22. See R. P. Carroll, "Psalm LXXVIII: Vestiges of a Tribal Polemic," *VT* 21 (1971), 133–150.

23. In addition to the articles by Cross cited above [N 18], see my *Creation versus Chaos* (New York, 1967), ch. 2.

24. Gunneweg [N 21], p. 339, remarks: "The history of the Yahweh religion can be regarded as a constant broadening of the scope of authority of the ancient God of the covenant, who claims for his sole sovereignty new areas which originally must have been alien to his worshipers."

25. H.-J. Kraus, *Worship in Israel* (Oxford, 1966), esp. pp. 188–200.

26. The authenticity of references to the Exodus in Isa. 4:2–6, 10:24–26, and 11:16 is not certain.

27. D. J. McCarthy, "Covenant in the Old Testament: the Present State of Inquiry," *CBQ* 27 (1965), 236, 238.

28. See D. N. Freedman, "Divine Commitment and Human Obligation," *Interpretation* 18 (1964), 425 f., who rightly points out that the Noachian covenant, with its promise of the orderly processes of nature, is not contingent upon human behavior.

29. See O. Eissfeldt, "The Promises of Grace to David," in *Israel's Prophetic Heritage* [N 10], pp. 196–207. There was some precedent for this in the Deuteronomic History. McCarthy, *Old Testament Covenant* [N 1], p. 48, observes: "Already in Nathan's promise, that is, in the covenant with David, the grace given David was extended to the whole people."

30. The expression *ḥasdê Dāwīd* is unusual in that the second member of the construct refers to the recipient, rather than the performer, of *ḥesed* although, as K. D. Sakenfeld, "Studies in the Usage of the Hebrew Word Ḥesed," Harvard dissertation (1970), pp. 212–215, points out, it has a grammatical parallel in expressions like *bᵉrît 'am* and *'ôr gôyîm* where the construct is construed with a dative meaning.

31. W. Brueggemann, "Isaiah 55 and Deuteronomic Theology," *ZAW* 80 (1968), 191–203, attempts to understand this chapter in relation to Deuteronomic appeals for the renewal of covenant. However, Second Isaiah's "orientation to the future," in my judgment, is based upon the theology of Yahweh's *enduring* covenant, not upon Israel's renewal of the covenant as in Deut. 4:29–31 (cf. Isa. 55:6–9).

32. Westermann [N 4], pp. 275 f.

33. See the excellent essay by J. Muilenburg, "The Form and Structure of the Covenantal Formulations," *VT* 9 (1959), 347–365. This "covenantal *Gattung*," he observes, "is *in nuce* the *fons et origo* of the many covenantal pericopes which appear throughout the Old Testament" (p. 352).

34. Freedman [N 28], p. 420, properly distinguishes between a covenant of human obligation in which the Suzerain imposes terms or stipulations on the human partner, and a covenant of divine commitment in which "the roles are partly reversed" and God takes upon himself obligations, that is, binds himself to the people by an oath.

35. Von Rad, *OTT*, II, 268, 399.

36. One of the important studies of this genre is G. E. Wright's essay, "The Lawsuit of God: A Form-critical Study of Deuteronomy 32," in *Israel's Prophetic Heritage* [N 10], pp. 26–67.

37. Covenant (treaty) terminology seems to be employed in vs. 2 ("know"=acknowledge sovereignty, be loyal to) and vs. 3 ("good" [*tôb*]=amicable relation between parties or comity). The same applies to Josh. 24:19–21, quoted above. Cf. McCarthy, *Biblica* 53 [N 1], 114.

38. In Hosea's usage the term *hesed* refers only to Israel's side of the covenant relationship, according to the study of Sakenfeld [N 30], pp. 178ff. In later prophetic tradition (Micah, Isaiah, Jeremiah) the term is also used with respect to the divine side of the relationship.

39. Von Rad, *OTT*, II, 192. The Davidic messianic tradition is found in 23:5–6 and 30:8–9. 17:24–27 is undoubtedly an editorial expansion of an oracle by Jeremiah on the Sabbath; 33:14–26, which contains three passages dealing with Yahweh's promises to David, is lacking in the LXX and may represent later expansion (J. Bright, *Jeremiah*, AB, vol. 21, 120, 298). For a discussion of this whole question, see M. Sekine, "Davidsbund und Sinaibund bei Jeremiah," *VT* 9 (1959), 47 ff.

40. See *OTT*, II, 269.

41. The term "metastasis" is used in this sense by Eric Voegelin in his volume, *Israel and Revelation* (Baton Rouge, 1956). See my review article, "Politics and the Transcendent," *The Political Science Reviewer*, 1 (1971), esp. pp. 20–25. Von Rad, *OTT*, II, 214, speaks of "a miraculous change in man's nature."

42. On this passage K. Sakenfeld [N 30], p. 205, comments: "*Hesed* here is God's persistent faithfulness to Israel: despite punishment the covenant relationship has not ended."

43. Von Rad, *OTT*, II, 214 f. See his whole discussion of the new covenant, pp. 212–217.

44. At the conclusion of his treatment of Ezekiel, von Rad remarks (*OTT*, II, 236): "Thus Ezekiel fuses the Sinai tradition and the Davidic tradition which Jeremiah still kept essentially separate. But the Sinai tradition dominates his thought—under the new David, Israel will obey the commandments (Ezek. 37:24)."

45. Commenting on 54:7–8, Westermann [N 4], p. 274, writes: "Here we have the heart of the matter, the basic factor in Deutero-Isaiah's proclamation—with God himself and in God himself the change has already taken place, and therefore everything must alter. A change has come over God. He ceases from wrath, and again shows Israel mercy. This makes everything all right again."

46. Sakenfeld [N 30], pp. 129 ff., observes that forgiveness in this context does not mean "merely being freed from some inner mental anxiety rooted in feelings of guilt," but signified "deliverance from some actual physical threat." Therefore "in cases where deliverance is coextensive with forgiveness, the people's sin should have ended the relationship, thus relieving God of any responsibility for them. The greatness of his *hesed* consists in his refusal, even in the face of rejection, to give up on his people, to set aside the responsibility which he took upon himself in choosing them as his people."

47. Westermann [N 4], p. 285.

19. Ezra and Nehemiah in Recent Studies

RALPH W. KLEIN

CONCORDIA THEOLOGICAL SEMINARY IN EXILE, ST. LOUIS

STUDENTS OF EZRA and Nehemiah are indebted to the late H. H. Rowley for his comprehensive surveys of critical research,[1] although these now must be supplemented to bring them up to date.[2] This essay will examine some of the latest *exegetical* contributions that seem to be most likely to form the lines of discussion in the future. Mention must be made in passing to archaeology and especially to Miss Kenyon's excavations in Jerusalem which have demonstrated that Nehemiah probably built his wall on the eastern *crest* of Ophel, because the terraces (*millō'*) on the eastern slope had collapsed and become irreparable after 587 B.C. We now can see that it was because of the small size of the city that Nehemiah could finish his work with such speed.[3]

I. The Work of Ezra and Nehemiah

Ulrich Kellermann has made a provocative attempt to fit Ezra and Nehemiah into the history of the divided post-exilic community.[4] Building on the work of Otto Plöger and Aage Bentzen, Kellermann distinguishes between two major parties: one was eschatological, Zionistic, messianic, and dedicated to the law; the other was priestly, theocratic, without interest in national expansion or in the laws forbidding marriage to foreigners.[5]

Kellermann finds himself able to say little about the details of Ezra's career since he believes that Ezra 7:12–23, 25 f. was the only source for the Ezra story available to the Chronicler. The rest of the biblical material is the Chronicler's propaganda. He concludes that (1) Ezra returned with a group of people from the exile to set things right according to the law; (2) he met opposition from leaders in Palestine who were oriented toward Samaria; (3) he failed. The Zionist or eschatological party subsequently tried to rebuild the walls of Jerusalem (4:7 ff.) because they realized that reform could come only if they broke their ties with the Samaritans. Outside pressures thwarted this effort (4:23) resulting in the dispatch of an unofficial Jewish delegation to the Persian court in order to enlist the help of Nehemiah, the cupbearer of the king,[6] who was descended from a side branch of the Davidic family.[7] Artaxerxes I agreed with the plan to upgrade Judah not only because of the influence of Nehemiah, but also because of the danger to the empire from Egypt.

Kellermann assigns the expulsion of Tobiah (13:4–9)[8] and the reordering of the sacrificial cult and the Levites (13:10–14) to a period between Nehemiah's first preparations and the beginning of the wall rebuilding itself. When the neighboring provinces protested his innovations, Nehemiah excluded the Samaritans from the cult (2:19 f.) and annulled the possession rights of the neighbors. In order to negate the despair caused by threats of military assault, Nehemiah called the *Volksheerbann* back into existence and encouraged the people with the ideology of Holy War (4:7 ff.). After appealing to the nobility in regard to the indebtedness of the people, he assumed a right used by pre-exilic kings, cancelled the civil law, and even forced the return of property taken in pledge (5:1–13). This gained him the undying enmity of the upper class. As reformer of the cultic and religious life according to these and other passages, Nehemiah is the last known representative of the so-called "Nasi institution" (Ezek. 44:1–3, 45:21a, 22 ff., 46:1–10), which was being steadily displaced by the theocracy headed by the high priest.

In a series of letters Sanballat accused Nehemiah of wanting to be king, a charge which Nehemiah branded as a total invention (6:8). Tobiah also incited prophets against him according to the somewhat obscure account of 6:10–14.[9] In the time between the completion and the dedication of the walls, Nehemiah carried out a series of reforms dealing with the Sabbath, mixed marriages, and temple supplies. The favorable political situation, the rebuilding of the walls, and the Davidic descent of Nehemiah fanned smoldering messianic hopes, probably against the will of Nehemiah. But his social reforms and his observance of the law seemed to fit the eschatological program marked out in Trito-Isaiah (cf. Neh. 1:5–11, 13:15–22, 5:1–13) and Malachi (cf. Neh. 13:4–14, 28–31).

This allowed the Samaritans and the Jerusalem upper classes to make a case with the Persian court and get Nehemiah recalled after twelve years as governor.[10] Nehemiah was in desperate straits. Therefore he called on Yahweh for help in the Nehemiah Memoirs (our terminology) and also provided evidence for his innocence by listing how he had merely carried out the king's orders and administered the law which had been made binding by the crown. Nehemiah failed because of the excessive enthusiasm of his own party and because of the opposition of the theocrats, but his failure was tempered by a partial success: even in the theocracy, the law now became the basis for life.

Although accused by Samaritans and by some within Judah of rebellion and messianic pretensions (6:6), Nehemiah asserted before God that all charges were groundless—he had strictly followed the direction of the king in giving a capital city to the land and had restored the walls of the capital in addition to carrying through needed reforms. The Chronicler included the Nehemiah Memoirs in his history and saw in Nehemiah the final example of help from the Persian kings in founding the theocracy of which he was a partisan. The Chronicler liked the anti-Samaritan bias of the materials now contained in Nehemiah 13, but elsewhere he tried to paralyze the figure of Nehemiah by having Ezra anticipate his every reform and by bracketing the Nehemiah Memoirs with Ezra material in Ezra 7–10 and Neh 8–10. Kellermann thus dismisses almost all of the Chronicler's material on Ezra as conscious invention meant to relegate Nehemiah to a shadowlike role. Two lines of Nehemiah tradition stand in a dialectical relationship in later non-canonical documents. One view understands him as a priestly founder of cult or royal founder of the state; the other denies him any major share in either. Some writings emphasize the messianic element while others refute it. Study of this later tradition history is often used by Kellermann to support the vague evidence for Nehemiah's role in the Nehemiah Memoirs and in the Chronicler.

Kellermann's views have considerable merit. He has offered new and exciting evidence for the Davidic ancestry or, at the least, eschatological orientation of Nehemiah. But his interpretation of the purpose and value of the Chronicler is inadequate especially since he discounts everything of Ezra except for chapter 7. According to the thesis of Karl-Friedrich Pohlmann, to be discussed below, the original edition of the Chronicler did not include the Nehemiah materials and therefore cannot be an anti-Nehemiah polemic. Furthermore, Kellermann's disassociation of the Chronicler from "Zionistic" circles is puzzling. Again, why did the Chronicler include so much of the unrevised Nehemiah Memoirs and break up his Ezra story by doing so? If the Chronicler represented theocratic, non-messianic circles, how can we explain the prominence given to David? Study of III Ezra also raises questions about his ascription of many passages to a post-Chronistic redactor living in the second century since many of these passages are already present in III Ezra which antedates (!) the addition of the Nehemiah Memoirs to the Chronicler's history.

Kurt Galling's reconstruction of the historical setting of Ezra places great emphasis on the political side of the Persian policy and denies that the Persians determined the content of the law of Ezra.[11] To demonstrate that this was characteristic of Persian policy he reconstructs the first part of the Passover Papyrus as a *political* ruling to the effect that the leadership of the satrapy should not give in to the Egyptians who were protesting the Jewish sacrificial systems; the second half is an *inner-Jewish* ruling on Passover—*maṣṣot*. Nehemiah's appointment as governor was also politically motivated since Artaxerxes I wanted a man whom he could trust next to the always untrustworthy Egypt, especially after the revolt of Megabyzos, the satrap of Syria. Bagoas, whom Galling interprets as a Persian in both name and religion, was sent as a confessionally neutral figure after the heightening of tensions between Jerusalem and Samaria that attended Nehemiah's second governorship.

From Elephantine papyri 30 and 32, Galling concludes that Delaiah of Samaria and Bagoas authorized the rebuilding of the Yahu temple in Egypt whereas the Jerusalemite officials Johanan and Ostanes opposed it. Bagoas tried to meet this opposition by showing friendship to Jeshua, the brother of Johanan, and by promising him the high priesthood. But Jeshua was killed by the high priest Johanan. In retaliation, Bagoas vented his anger on the Jews for seven years until they finally sought a clarification of the situation through a royal decision. This was the hour of Ezra.[12]

Ezra was sent by the Persians to clear up the polarized situation and to relieve the financial hardships caused by Bagoas' punishment (7:15–18), but the conduct of his activities was determined solely by the law he brought. Thus according to 7:14 he was given a free hand in sacred matters.[13] Ezra had nothing to do with Bagoas' administration nor with the enforcement of Judaism by Persian penalties (*pace* E. Meyer) for Galling links 7:26 (emended) to 7:21–23. In fact, Ezra kept an exceedingly low profile! Although he was a priest, he did not carry out priestly functions lest that create tensions with the Jerusalemite priests, nor did he ever meet with Johanan. Similarly, his treatment of the mixed marriage question was limited to advice; all actions proceeded from the Jerusalemites and Judaeans. Only after Shecaniah urged Ezra to act, did he begin to play a role, but even then the nobles and elders completed the work. Finally, the ceremony in Nehemiah 8 was not the publication of a previously unknown law, but an attempt to actualize the existing law by proclaiming it. The constituting and consolidating of the theocracy was the crown and end of Ezra's mission. The theocratic principle meant that Israel could gather behind her secure walls to dedicate herself to the cult and the doing of the divine will. Since such a theocracy excluded (messianic) eschatology, people later saw prophecy as ending with Ezra.

Galling, therefore, finds himself able to say much more about Ezra than does Kellermann, partly because of his use of the Passover Papyrus and the material from Josephus. His reconstruction rests in part, however, on a questionable literary rearrangement of Ezra 7 and would be denied by anyone unable to accept an early fourth-century date for Ezra. In addition, it has recently been pointed out that Bagoas may have been a Jew (cf. Ezra 2:2) and that Josephus calls Bagoas a *strategos,* thus probably meaning the general of the same name who served under Artaxerxes III.[14] Finally, his identification of Pethahiah (Neh. 11:24) as the successor of Bagoas must be evaluated in the light of Rudolph's claim that Pethahiah fulfilled the same function as Ezra the scribe.

In a recent article Robert North has departed from the commonly held interpretation of the offices of Ezra and Nehemiah.[15] He too is critical of the alleged Persian governmental title "Secretary of the Law of the God of Heaven" (Schaeder) or "Undersecretary of State for Jewish Affairs" (Galling). Ezra's commission to appoint judges (7:25 f.) is interpreted as religious authority exercised under the king's approval while the king's copious financial support (7:15–24) is dismissed as patron donations, tax exemption, and special ration coupons. Ezra's mission was to exercise his religious calling freely in accord with his conscience and his special talents and thus foster submissiveness and cooperativeness welcome to the Persian authorities.

Far more controversial is his denial of the governor's office to Nehemiah and even to Sanballat. Nehemiah was a mere page or a youthful favorite of the king (not a eunuch!), and he became a building contractor in Judaea. His authority among the Judaean *segānîm* and *ḥōrîm* is limited to genial persuasiveness, backed by friends in the capital. North's basic criticism is leveled at 5:14: "I was appointed to be their *governor*." While there are some textual and exegetical difficulties here, he seems to be unwarranted in emending *peḥām* to *bāhem* ("I was appointed to be among them") in the face of such clear passages as 5:14 and 18 where Nehemiah is surely referring to his own office when he relates that neither he nor his brothers ate the food allowance of the governor. North understands Nehemiah's reference to not eating the "governor's bread" to be a reference to the low quality of his diet. Finally, North denies the office of governor to Sanballat, claiming that officeholders of this name in Josephus and the Samaria papyri were thirty-five to one hundred years after him. Sanballat and the other enemies of Nehemiah are even classified as Judaeans. While the omission of the word "governor" in Nehemiah's account of Sanballat is remarkable, Kellermann's suggestion that this silence is a sign of the enmity Nehemiah felt for him seems to be much more plausible.[16]

II. LITERARY PROBLEMS

One issue on which opinion has not changed a great deal is the dependence of Nehemiah primarily on Deuteronomy alone, although recent publications have spelled out the case in greater detail.[17]

THE FORM OF THE NEHEMIAH MEMOIRS

Scholars have long endeavored to classify the form of the Nehemiah Memoirs. Mowinckel compared it with ancient Near Eastern royal inscriptions; Ernst Sellin and W. Schottroff have adduced parallels from dedicatory inscriptions or from patrons of sanctuaries; others have seen in it a copy or a translation of a copy of the report sent to the Persian court.[18]

Two recent contributions are worthy of note. Gerhard von Rad compared it with certain biographical inscriptions from late periods in Egypt.[19] But it must be noted that these are often copied on statues in temples or on steles in graves, not on a scroll. What is more, they have a pedagogical tone lacking in Nehemiah. Nehemiah's attitude toward his opponents and his use of the *zokrâ* formula also distinguish him from the alleged Egyptian parallels. According to Kellermann, most of the best parallels suggested by von Rad are from 5:14 ff. and 13:4 ff., which are either secondary or at least not central to the makeup of the document. Perhaps the most striking parallel is the biographical similarity between Nehemiah and Udjahorresnet, but in style and form, and even in the idea of merit (*Verdienstgedanke*), they are much different.

Kellermann, on the other hand, compares the Nehemiah memoirs with the prayers of the falsely accused as studied by H. Schmidt,[20] in which the Psalmist prays to God for legal help and for proof of his innocence. Kellermann corrects Schmidt by asserting that this form was not only used in cases involving God (*Gottesgericht*), but also by persons who were oppressed by false witnesses at the gate and therefore could only cry to God. He suggests that the priesthood and the nobility of Judah and the leaders of Samaria were the legal opponents of Nehemiah. According to 2:19 and 6:6 f. they accused Nehemiah of high treason and revolt against the king. Because of the multitude of his opponents and their serious charges, Nehemiah had to appeal directly to God. The Nehemiah *Quelle,* as Kellermann calls it, is unique in two respects: its length, and its written character. He accounts for the former by Nehemiah's need to report on the prehistory of the king's appointment and on his carrying out of his office; the latter is required since the priests, who would usually have been the ones to speak the accused's prayers before God, were part of the opposition in this case. Kellermann also raises the question whether Job does not also offer a parallel to a written appeal to God for help in legal difficulty. Kellermann issues a special warning about the probable biased nature of this document. Perhaps we can conclude that everything he mentions "to God" is true, but, for apologetic reasons, much would be passed over in silence.

EZRA'S LAW

What is the "law of your God," which was in the hand of Ezra (Ezra 7:14 and 25)? Four basic hypotheses have been advanced (with infinite variations!): Ezra's law is (1) the Pentateuch; (2) the priestly code; (3) a collection of laws probably now included in the Pentateuch, but whose precise identification is impossible; (4) the Deuteronomic code.[21] The following paragraphs will outline only the most recent suggestions.

Sigmund Mowinckel believed that this law was the Pentateuch, but that Ezra was not its editor. The Pentateuch, whose authority grew gradually rather than through one promulgation, existed both in Palestine and Babylon before Ezra's time. According to Mowinckel, Ezra may well have been sent to bring certain practices into line with those of the Babylonian community, especially such institutions as the feast of tabernacles (Nehemiah 8), just as the Passover Papyrus attempted to regulate the nature and length of the feast of unleavened bread at Elephantine. Hence he is willing to grant that Ezra may have brought a slightly different recension of an already existing law.[22]

J. G. Vink, on the other hand, challenges the existence of P in early post-exilic times and links it instead with Ezra's mission which he dates in 398.[23] In certain respects he builds on the work of H. Cazelles and P. Grelot who had argued in a series of articles that the laws containing the so-called *gēr/'ezrāḥ* formulas were Ezra's contribution to the Pentateuch.[24] According to Cazelles the *gērîm* were the exiles who wished to resettle in Palestine while the *'ezrāḥîm* were the Samaritans who claimed continuous possession of the land. Ezra attempted to unite both of these groups by a series of revised laws. Subsequently, factions loyal to either Ezra or Nehemiah arose, and the Chronicler attempted to heal this breach. At the same time the Chronicler gave support to the Levites and vented his anti-Samaritan bias. Grelot's theory is similar, but he identified the *gērîm* as Jews from the dispersion who came to Jerusalem for the celebration of the regular feasts while the *'ezrāḥîm* were the Judaean and Samaritan Jews. Vink differs from both, not only in that he suggests a third definition for *gērîm and 'ezrāḥîm* (the former are the leading classes in Samaria who are under strong Persian influence; the latter are the Israelites) but especially in his linking of the *entire* Priestly Code to the mission of Ezra. His thesis is based, in part, on Albrecht Alt's view of the post-exilic forms of government, that is, that the north had been provided with a new, foreign upper class that naturally was always in some tension with the native Israelites in the south.[25] Nehemiah heightened the tension between the Judaeans and the Samaritan ruling class with the result that the laws of Deuteronomy were given diametrically opposite interpretations in the two parts of the country. Nehemiah's expulsion of one of Jehoiada's sons threatened the Deuteronomic alliance between the priests of North Israel and Jerusalem and stirred up a desire for a sanctuary in the north. The Persians met this crisis with a two part plan: they replaced Nehemiah with Bagoas whose Persian name indicates his "neutrality" in religious matters (*pace* Kurt Galling); and they ordered loyal Babylonian Jews to prepare new legislation aimed at a greater unity of the Palestinian community. Basic to Vink's position are two highly debatable presuppositions: (1) Ezra had an ecumenical attitude toward Samaria, a conclusion made possible by assigning most of Ezra 9 and 10 to a Maccabean redactor; and (2) an interpretation of the Priestly Code (which he finds also in the Book of Joshua) as the etiology of Ezra's reform. The analogy he finds between the Persians' attitude toward Ezra's reform and the imposition of Jewish traditions on the colony at Elephantine is rendered dubious by Galling's study referred to above. Many will be unpersuaded by the late date and suggested place of origin for P, not to mention the highly questionable etiological connection between many parts of P and the time of Ezra.

Finally, Ulrich Kellermann has contended that the law of Ezra was only a (slightly expanded) form of the Deuteronomic code.[26] Kellermann's argument begins with two admitted presuppositions: (1) Ezra preceded Nehemiah, coming to Jerusalem before 448; and (2) the Chronicler's account of Ezra is largely untrustworthy. Only Ezra 7:12–23, 25 f. is deemed dependable and from its vs. 25a Kellermann deduces that Ezra had nothing to do with the proclamation of a new law, but only with a visitation of the cultic community according to the standard of a definite Jewish law. For one reason or another the Pentateuch, P, H, and the Book of the Covenant are ruled out as candidates for Ezra's law, and he notes also that the Nehemiah Memoirs seem to use only Dt and Dtr (cf. N 17). So Ezra, who preceded Nehemiah, would not have used laws going beyond Deuteronomy, just as Malachi is limited to the latter law code. When the Passover Papyrus reforms the rules from Passover on the basis of P, this appeal to the Priestly Code was an innovation. In short, P is interpreted by Kellermann as the counter thrust of the theocratic hierarchy to the Zionist-Messianic-Eschatological tendencies of the historical Ezra and Nehemiah.

III. THE CHRONICLER'S ORIGINAL EDITION

While Martin Noth and Ulrich Kellermann have ascribed the arrangement of the Ezra-Nehemiah materials to the Chronicler himself,[27] and Wilhelm Rudolph contends that the original order of the Chronicler can be reconstructed from the present disarray,[28] G. Hölscher and Sigmund Mowinckel have ascribed the present arrangement (and amount) of materials to a post-Chronistic redaction.[29] This last hypothesis is supported by the arrangement of materials in III Ezra (I and II Chronicles, Ezra 1–10, Nehemiah 8), an arrangement for which Karl-Friedrich Pohlmann has recently offered support as the original shape of the Chronicler.[30] Pohlmann believes that III Ezra, which shows no trace of the Nehemiah tradition, is a fragment of a translation of an original recension although the interpolation of the story of the three pages in III Ezra caused some disarrangement. III Ezra breaks off in the middle of the equivalent of Neh. 8:13, but Josephus, who is clearly indebted to this work, seems to have known a work that included everything up to 8:18. Ezra dies before the appearance of Nehemiah in Josephus, but his extensive knowledge of the source behind Neh. 1:1–7:4 can be demonstrated. In any case, Josephus did not use a recension of the Chronicler in which the Ezra story had been tied with the Nehemiah account.

According to Pohlmann the purpose of Nehemiah 8 is not the promulgation of the law, but to hold up the attitude of the post-exilic community as an ideal for the Chronicler's readers. Because of the similarity between Nehemiah 8 and the later synagogue worship, he assumes that the Chronicler was dependent on the synagogue worship of his time. This chapter is the climax of his work and it is impossible to imagine that the Chronicler would have followed this by such controversial and sad subjects as the mixed marriages in Nehemiah 13. In fact, Pohlmann suggests that the structure of the Chronicler's history can only be properly understood if Nehemiah 8 is its final chapter. Observing that the Chronicler records major festivals after all major building or repair of the temple and after cult reforms, he outlines the following sequences: dedication of the temple—tabernacles (II Chron. 7:8–10); Hezekiah's restoration of the cult—Passover (II Chron. 30); Josiah's reforms—Passover (II Chron. 35); initial sacrifice after exile—Passover (Ezra 3:1); dedication of temple—Passover (Ezra 6:19–22). If Nehemiah 8 originally followed Ezra 9–10, as Pohlmann suggests, a typical sequence results: reform of mixed marriages—tabernacles.

Furthermore, it is possible to argue that Neh. 8:17 is the climax toward which the entire work is building. According to this verse, "All the assembly . . . made booths and dwelt in booths; for from the days of Jeshua the son of Nun to that day the people of Israel had not done so." When this is compared with II Chron. 30:6 and 35:18 we find that three of the greatest cultic moments are matched with outstanding figures of early Israel, and that Ezra's work is linked to the period of Exodus-Conquest (cf. Ezra 1:1):

	Hezekiah–Solomon	
Josiah	–	Samuel
Ezra	–	Joshua

Pohlmann attributes the arrangement of materials in the canonical books of Ezra and Nehemiah to a later redactor who linked an account of the rebuilding of Jerusalem's wall (=Nehemiah Memoirs) to the Chronicler's account of the establishment of the post-exilic Jerusalem cultic community.

One of the serious objections that could be raised to Pohlmann's reconstruction is the similarity of III Ezra 9:37 to Neh. 7:72. Some scholars have concluded from this that III Ezra presupposes the list in Nehemiah 7 and probably most of Nehemiah 1–7 and that no significance can therefore be placed in the sequence of Ezra 10–Nehemiah 8 in III Ezra. But Pohlmann argues that the contents[31] of III Ezra 9:37 are needed to link 9:18–36 (=Ezra 10:18–44) and the following pericope, 9:38 ff. (=Neh. 8:1 ff.), since we are told there that the priests and Levites had resettled in their former dwellings, from which they could reassemble in Neh. 8:1. When the Ezra and Nehemiah materials were finally combined, the Hebrew *Vorlage* behind III Ezra 9:37 was excised because of its general similarity to Neh. 7:72.[32]

Pohlmann has presented a convincing case that the materials of Ezra 1–10 were originally followed in the Chronicler's history by Nehemiah 8. While this does not preclude that the historical sequence of events might call for an arrangement such as Ezra 7–8, Nehemiah 8, Ezra 9–10, Nehemiah 9–10,[33] it does help to isolate more directly the Chronicler's intention. Furthermore, it raises very serious questions about the Noth-Kellermann contention that the Ezra materials were composed as an explicit refutation of Nehemiah and his followers. Consequently the alleged bias of the Chronicler disappears and his historical value is at least potentially restored.[34] Finally, if the Ezra and Nehemiah materials were composed to legitimate the cult community and to appeal to God for legal defense respectively, then perhaps little should be inferred—one way or the other—from the silence about Nehemiah in the Ezra story and *vice versa.*

IV. THE DATE OF EZRA AND NEHEMIAH

For years scholars have tried to elucidate the figures of Ezra and Nehemiah by reconstructing the historical setting in which they operated. Recently Galling, as we have noted, has attempted to fit Ezra into the crisis caused by the Persian official Bagoas. With the discovery of the Elephantine papyri, the date of Nehemiah's arrival in Jerusalem has been generally fixed as 445. One letter (Cowley 30/31) dated to the seventeenth year of Darius II or 408 B.C., was sent to Bagoas (the successor of Nehemiah?), and reference is made to Johanan, the second high priest (Neh. 12:10f., 22) after Nehemiah's contemporary Eliashib (Neh. 3:1 and 13:28), and to the sons of the governor of Samaria Sanballat, presumably Nehemiah's arch rival. From this it has been concluded that the king in whose twentieth year Nehemiah began his career is Artaxerxes I (465–425).

No such consensus prevails with regard to Ezra. In Ezra 7:7f. his arrival is dated to the seventh year of Artaxerxes, but this has been complicated by two crucial questions: (a) which Artaxerxes is meant, Artaxerxes I (465–425) or Artaxerxes II (404–358); and (b) is the figure 7 reliable and correct? We list here the three major alternatives:[35]

    1) Ezra came in the seventh year of Artaxerxes I or 458.
    2) Ezra came in the seventh year of Artaxerxes II or 398.
    3) Ezra came in the thirty-seventh year of Artaxerxes I or 428.

Thus the date of Ezra's appearance and his relationship to Nehemiah have been the point of considerable debate. Because there is really very little evidence to suggest they were contemporaries, and because of the arbitrariness of the emendation in alternative (3), an increasing number of scholars have opted for a 398 date for Ezra.

But in two of the most recent studies, Ulrich Kellermann and Richard Saley[36] have offered support for the order Ezra-Nehemiah although they differ widely both on method and conclusions.

Kellermann discounts the evidence of Ezra 7:7f. and dates Ezra on the basis of the relationship of his work to Nehemiah.[37] Trito-Isaiah, Malachi, and Neh 13:4ff. offer evidence for a rift between the rigorous and the lax Jews in the post-exilic community. Kellermann argues that Ezra's mission was in support of the rigorists. He also takes Ezra 4:12 and Neh. 1:2 f. as referring to the group returning with Ezra (Ezra 7:13) and he dates this to some time prior to 448, or at least in connection with the Megabyzos disturbance. But this reconstruction is unsatisfactory both because it ignores the date given in our sources and because it is too skeptical toward the Chronicler in general. He finds it unnecessary to explain the sequence of the reforms of Ezra and Nehemiah outside of a simple theory that the spiritual activities of Ezra preceded the government-supported reforms of Nehemiah.

Richard Saley shows no such suspicion of the biblical dates. His solution, though radical and, in a sense, narrowly based, is potentially epoch making and therefore must be surveyed in this prospectus of current studies on Ezra and Nehemiah. Saley argues that the references to Nehemiah in the Ezra materials and vice versa are secondary,[38] and that the original Chronicler followed the Ezra 1–10–Nehemiah 8 sequence discussed above with regard to Pohlmann. He is convinced that the Chronicler came after Ezra, but before Nehemiah.

Before going on to his concrete suggestions, however, we must note the impact of the Samaria papyri from the Wâdi Dâliyeh and Josephus on recent investigations of the Persian period. On the basis of data contained in the papyri, Frank M. Cross has suggested the following sequence for the house of Sanballat:[39]

> Sanballat I, mid-fifth century
> Delaiah 407 (Elephantine)
> Sanballat II
> (Yeshūaʿ)
> Hananiah—governor in 354
> Sanballat III—appointed by Darius III (335–330); cf. Josephus

Saley suggests that Nehemiah's trouble with Sanballat refers to Sanballat II who served under Artaxerxes II. He adduces evidence from Josephus[40] where it is reported that the high priest Johanan murdered his brother Jesus who was a friend of the Persian general Bagoas. Later Manasseh, the brother of Johanan's successor Jaddua, married Nikaso, the daughter of Sanballat who had been appointed by Darius III. Manasseh's father-in-law subsequently promised to establish a temple for him, a promise he made good at the time of Alexander. Professor Wright has shown the plausibility of the latter events.[41] Saley argues for the reliability of the former and attempts to establish the date for it.

First he identifies the general Bagoas to whom Josephus refers as the infamous eunuch of the Persian court in the mid-fourth century who in 343 was appointed vizier of Egypt after the reconquest of that country, and who later was responsible for the assassination of two Persian monarchs.[42] Bagoas would seem to have been acting in character when he carried through reprisals after the murder of his friend Jesus. But if this is so, when are the high priests Johanan and Jaddua to be dated?

The crux of Saley's argument is Neh. 12:22–23. While details of the argument must await the completion of his thesis, a basic point is derived from the following contrasting lists:

vs. 22 Eliashib	vs. 23 Eliashib
Joiada	Johanan
Johanan	
Jaddua	

The compiler of Nehemiah 12 identified the Johanan of vs. 22 with Johanan of vs. 23 just as scholars have usually understood Johanan ben Eliashib of Ezra 10:6 to mean Johanan the grandson of Eliashib. If these are, in fact, different men (note the use of papponomy in the Samaria papyri) then the actual sequence of post-exilic high priests might be as follows: Jeshua, Joiakim, Eliashib I, Johanan I, Eliashib II, Joiada, Johanan II, Jaddua.

Saley therefore suggests the following historical reconstruction: Ezra came in the seventh year of Artaxerxes II (398), had associations with Johanan I (Ezra 10:6), who together with the Persian governor Bagoas is mentioned in the Elephantine papyri of the late fifth century. Nehemiah came in the twentieth year of Artaxerxes II (384), when Eliashib II was high priest. During Nehemiah's time (13:28) one of the sons of Joiada married the son of Sanballat II. Some time after Nehemiah, Johanan II murdered his brother Jesus who was in league with Bagoas the officer of Artaxerxes III. When Jaddua became high priest, his brother Manasseh married Nikaso, the daughter of Sanballat III, who had been appointed by Darius III and who received permission from Alexander to erect a Samaritan temple. The compiler responsible for inserting the high priestly list of Neh. 12:1–26 into the Chronicler's History has, by his seeming confusion of the two Eliashibs and the two Johanans, helped to set the scene for the lengthy modern argument over the date of these men and their relationship to one another.

The thesis is provocative because it moves Ezra and Nehemiah to the fourth century. If correct, it cancels the historical settings suggested above by Kellermann, Galling, and everyone else and it therefore would necessitate a whole new schedule for post-exilic developments. Because Saley's work is not yet finished, criticisms must be brief and tentative. He gives extraordinary weight to an obscure passage like Neh. 12:22–23 which itself is located in a secondary chapter. Furthermore, he assumes not only papponomy in general, but the existence of two Eliashibs and two Johanans, in addition to three Sanballats (so also Cross) and two men named Bagoas. While many would be willing to accept multiple Sanballats and Bagoas's, the evidence is thin for creating a new Eliashib and a new Johanan, for positing two marriages between the Jerusalem high priestly house and the family of Sanballat, and, perhaps, for moving Geshem to the fourth century.[43]

V. TEXTUAL CRITICISM

Finally, space permits only passing reference to conclusions drawn from my re-examination of I Esdras (=III Ezra) in the wake of Qumran.[44] Analysis of all differences in textual length between this version and the later Septuagint (=G), on the one hand, and the MT, on the other, failed to sustain critics who have dismissed the omissions in the versions as abbreviations made by the translator. In almost seventy readings, for example, a Hebrew or Aramaic expression omitted by I Esdras is also omitted by G, by the Syriac, or by the independent evidence of II Kings.[45] Agreements of I Esdras with the text of Nehemiah against the text of Ezra in Ezra 2/Nehemiah 7 demonstrates the reliability of I Esdras.[46] Nearly a score of conflations in the MT and numerous other additions were detected via retroversion from I Esdras alone. If we judge by similar, although less numerous, readings in G, both Greek translations antedate the rabbinic Bible. The many pluses in I Esdras do not invalidate these conclusions. The use of double translations and hendiadys reveals an attempt to give a full representation of the *Vorlage*. Many other pluses, particularly in I Esdras, must now be considered original readings and/or bona fide Hebrew-Aramaic readings.

NOTES

1. H. H. Rowley, "The Chronological Order of Ezra and Nehemiah," *Ignace Goldziher Memorial Volume*, Part I, eds. D. S. Löwinger and J. Somogyi (Budapest, 1948), pp. 117–149. "Nehemiah's Mission and its Background," *BJRL* 37 (1954–55), 528–561. "Sanballat and the Samaritan Temple," *BJRL* 38 (1955–56), 166–198.

2. See J. M. Myers, *Ezra•Nehemiah*, AB, vol. 14 (1965), XIX–LXXXIII, and the prolegomenon by W. F. Stinespring in the reprint of C. C. Torrey's *Ezra Studies* (New York, 1970), pp. xi–xxviii.

3. K. M. Kenyon, *Jerusalem: Excavating 3,000 Years of History* (New York, 1967), and "Israelite Jerusalem," in *NEATC*, pp. 232–253.

4. U. Kellermann, *Nehemia: Quellen, Überlieferung und Geschichte*, BZAW 102 (Berlin, 1967).

5. O. Plöger identified an eschatological and a theocratic party in Israel while Bentzen saw a conflict between the priestly aristocracy and the reform-minded laity. P. D. Hanson has modified these notions and correlated them with the origin of apocalyptic in his recent Harvard dissertation; see provisionally his "Jewish Apocalyptic against its Near Eastern Environment," *RB* 78 (1971), 31–58, and "Old Testament Apocalyptic Re-examined," *Interpretation* 25 (1971), 454–479.

6. Kellermann, in *Nehemia* [N 4], has raised objections to the theory that Nehemiah was a eunuch. He believes that the Persians would have honored the provisions of Deut. 23:2 since Nehemiah was also to be involved with the cult, pp. 154–155. W. T. In der Smitten contends that the word *tiršātā'* does not mean eunuch (*pace* E. Meyer) but "the

circumcised one," and that this nickname was given first to Zerubbabel and, only in secondary passages, to Nehemiah: "Der Tirschātā' in Esra-Nehemia," *VT* 21 (1971), 618–620.

7. The following cumulative evidence for Davidic descent is adduced: (a) he comes from a rich, noble family, Neh. 5:14, 17f.; (b) his family graves are inside Jerusalem, 2:3, 5; (c) he confesses the guilt of his father's house, 1:6, just as the Deuteronomic Historian dwelled on royal sins; (d) the charge that he wanted to be king would be most credible if he came from the royal line; (e) his high position at court corresponds to the usual policy of the Persians to elevate leaders from the royal families of captured nations. Kellermann, *Nehemia*, pp. 156–159.

8. Tobiah was a subordinate official in the Samaritan provincial administration. When Nehemiah became governor and formed Judah as a separate province, he took the place of Tobiah and eventually decided to clear out his room in the temple; ibid., pp. 167–170.

9. Kellermann, ibid., pp. 180–182, believes that Shemaiah was trying to designate Nehemiah as king on the urging of the Zionists. When Nehemiah sought him out to stop this, Sanballat suspected that Nehemiah was going to be crowned in secret like Zerubbabel. Nehemiah tried to obscure the issue by conflating this incident with the sending of terrorists by Tobiah.

10. Kellermann, ibid., does not allow for a second term in office and ascribes part of Neh. 13 to a post-Chronistic redactor who was trying to explain that the conditions described in 13:4 f. could have arisen only if Nehemiah had been absent.

11. K. Galling, "Bagoas und Ezra," in *Studien zur Geschichte Israels im Persischen Zeitalter* (Tübingen, 1964), pp. 149–184.

12. Galling, ibid., p. 161, makes extensive use of Josephus *Antiquities* xi vii 1 ff. He raises the possibility that the seven-year punishment inflicted by Bagoas may be reflected in the Chronicler's dating of Ezra to the seventh year of Artaxerxes (II).

13. Galling, ibid., criticizes E. Schaeder's interpretation of *spr* as a Persian state office and sees in it only an office acknowledged by the Jewish diaspora. S. Mowinckel considers Schaeder's interpretation unnecessary and prefers a translation *Schriftgelehrter: Studien zu dem Buche Ezra-Nehemia,* III (Oslo, 1965), 124. Generally little space will be given to this three volume work since it primarily supports old positions already put forward in 1916. For R. North's critique of the Schaeder hypothesis, see N 15 below.

14. B. Porten, *Archives from Elephantine* (Berkeley, 1968), p. 290.

15. R. North, "Civil Authority in Ezra," in *Studi in onore di Edoardo Volterra,* VI (Milan, n.d.), 377–404. North admits that he has departed from some of the views set forth in his commentary on Ezra and Nehemiah in the *Jerome Biblical Commentary,* eds. R. E. Brown et al. (Englewood Cliffs, N.J., 1968), pp. 426–438.

16. Kellermann, *Nehemia* [N 4], p. 167. Compare also the references to him as the Horonite, 2:10, 19, which may be ascribing to him Moabite affiliations.

17. See H. Cazelles, "La Mission d'Esdras," *VT* 4 (1954), 120–122; and Kellermann, "Erwägungen zum Esragesetz," *ZAW* 80 (1968), 381–383. Myers, *Ezra·Nehemiah* [N 2], p. LX, believes that Nehemiah used a combination of D and P, but evidence for the latter source is slight.

18. For bibliography and history of research, see Kellermann, *Nehemia* [N 4], pp. 76–88.

19. G. von Rad, "Die Nehemia-Denkschrift," *ZAW* 76 (1964), 176–187.

20. H. Schmidt, *Das Gebet der Angeklagten im Alten Testament,* BZAW 49 (Giessen, 1928).

21. For a survey of research see Kellermann, "Esragesetz" [N 17], *passim.*

22. Mowinckel, *Studien,* III [N 13], 124–141.

23. J. G. Vink, "The Date and Origin of the Priestly Code in the Old Testament," *Oudtestamentische Studien* 15 (1969) 1–144.

24. Cazelles, "La Mission d'Esdras" [N 17]. P. Grelot, "Le Papyrus Pascal d'Eléphantine," *VT* 4 (1954), 349–384; "Le Papyrus Pascal d'Eléphantine et le problème de Pentateuque," *VT* 5 (1955), 250–265; "La dernière étape de la rédaction sacerdotale," *VT* 6 (1956), 174–189.

25. A. Alt, "Die Rolle Samarias bei der Entstehung des Judentums," in *KS*, II, 316–337.

26. Kellermann, "Esragesetz" [N 17], 379 ff. The equation of wisdom and law in Ezra 7:25 recalls Deut. 4:6. The reference to the law of the king in Ezra 7:26 reflects the Persian custom of codifying old monarchical laws of conquered regions, and D had become such a state law through the reform of Josiah.

27. Noth, *Überlieferungsgeschichtliche Studien*, I (Tübingen, 1943), 123; Kellermann, *Nehemia* [N 4], p. 32.

28. W. Rudolph, *Esra und Nehemia samt 3 Esra*, Handbuch zum Alten Testament I, 20 (Tübingen, 1949), xxii.

29. G. Hölscher, *Die Bücher Esra und Nehemia*, Die Heilige Schrift des Alten Testaments (Tübingen, 1923), pp. 493 ff., and Mowinckel, *Studien zu dem Buche Ezra-Nehemia*, I (Oslo, 1964), 29 ff.

30. K.-F. Pohlmann, *Studien zum dritten Esra* (Göttingen, 1970).

31. Pohlmann deletes *tē noumēnia toū hebdomou mēnos;* ibid., p. 70.

32. The presence of a translation for *hattiršātā'* in III Ezra 9:49 (=Neh. 8:9) is mildly embarrassing, but Pohlmann offers a pair of plausible hypotheses to account for this; ibid., pp. 64 ff. In any case, Ezra seems to have been the only leader in the original recension of Neh. 8.

33. Myers surveys a variety of attempted reconstructions; *Ezra•Nehemiah* [N 2], pp. XLII–XLVIII.

34. For a similar critique of alleged bias, using text-critical arguments, see W. E. Lemke, "The Synoptic Problem in the Chronicler's History," *HTR* 58 (1964), 349–364. S. Japhet has recently challenged the unity of the Chronicler's work on the basis of linguistic and stylistic differences between Ezra-Nehemiah and Chronicles. Since she takes inadequate account of the fact that the Nehemiah Memoirs *per se* are irrelevant to the Chronicler's style and that significant sections of Nehemiah are post-Chronistic, her contention that Ezra and Nehemiah antedate Chronicles is not convincing; see "The Supposed Common Authorship of Chronicles and Ezra-Nehemiah Investigated Anew," *VT* 18 (1968), 330–371.

35. Complete discussions can be found in Rowley, "The Chronological Order of Ezra und Nehemiah" [N 1], and Kellermann, "Erwägungen zum Problem der Esradatierung," *ZAW* 80 (1968), 55–87.

36. R. Saley's Harvard dissertation was not complete at the time of the writing of this article. Gratitude is hereby expressed for several oral and written communications from him.

37. The number "seven" is interpreted as an attempt to make Ezra's work last at least as long as Nehemiah's twelve-year term (Ezra was still functioning in the twentieth year according to Neh. 8), or as the next logical number after the sixth year of Darius (!) in Ezra 6:15.

38. So also Myers, *Ezra•Nehemiah* [N 2], p. XLIII.

39. F. M. Cross, "Aspects of Samaritan and Jewish History in Late Persian and Hellenistic Times," *HTR* 59 (1966), 201–211, and "The Discovery of the Samaria Papyri," *BA* 26 (1963), 110–121.

40. Josephus *Antiquities* XI vii 1–2.

41. G. E. Wright, "The Samaritans at Shechem," *HTR* 55 (1962), 357–366. Cf. J. D. Purvis, *The Samaritan Pentateuch and the Origin of the Samaritan Sect* (Cambridge, Mass., 1968). Purvis also dates the final Samaritan schism to Hasmonaean times.

42. See A. T. Olmstead, *History of the Persian Empire* (Chicago, 1948), pp. 437–

440. Thus there are two men involved named Bagoas: one is a governor of the fifth century; one a military official of the fourth.

43. Saley has informed me that he plans to offer a solution for the latter problem in his dissertation.

44. Ralph W. Klein, "Studies in the Greek Texts of the Chronicler," unpublished Th.D. dissertation, Harvard Divinity School, 1966.

45. R. W. Klein, "New Evidence for an Old Recension of Reigns," *HTR* 60 (1967), 93–105, and "Supplements in the Paraleipomena: A Rejoinder," *HTR* 61 (1968), 492–495.

46. R. W. Klein, "Old Readings in I Esdras: The List of Returnees from Babylon (Ezra 2 // Nehemiah 7)," *HTR* 62 (1969), 99–107.

20. *Reflections on the Modern Study*
of the Psalms

BREVARD S. CHILDS,
YALE UNIVERSITY

CRITICAL STUDY of the Old Testament psalms has been so extensive within the last several decades that it is an overwhelming task to attempt to cover the subject even in a cursory manner. However, the fact that there have been several excellent reviews of the history of research has greatly reduced the necessity of another comprehensive survey of the field.[1] The concern of this essay is a more modest one. It is to suggest that there are some important reasons why the direction of psalm research needs to shift from those questions which have tended to dominate the study of the Psalter.

I

Scholarly interest in the Old Testament psalms since the end of World War II has been preoccupied with certain major interests. One of the most obvious concentrations has been in continuation of the form critical, traditio-historical approach which Hermann Gunkel inaugurated. Whereas in the decade of the thirties British and American scholarship virtually ignored the form critical approach—one thinks of such commentaries as Barnes (1931) or Buttenwieser (1938)—during the last two decades dozens of introductions[2] have appeared which sought to popularize Gunkel's approach. Indeed the wide international and interconfessional consensus respecting the importance of Gunkel's work has become a hallmark of the modern period.

Interest in pursuing Gunkel's program has frequently focused on two areas in particular, those of literary genre and sociological function (*Sitz im Leben*). Obviously these two questions often overlap. First of all, there have been several major attempts to refine or to alter Gunkel's literary classification of the psalms.[3] Unquestionably from such work there have emerged many new insights into the literary problems and several weak points of Gunkel's classification have been convincingly demonstrated. Particularly

Begrich's early essays have been impressive.[4] In general, however, few of the proposed corrections have managed to convince a wide audience in the way Gunkel's did, nor has any new consensus emerged. The reason for the general inability of the form critical method to make steady progress remains a puzzling question. Some have suggested that the recent attempts have been too narrowly based and lacked the broad *religionsgeschichtliche* context of Gunkel's original program.[5] Others have been far more radical in criticizing the form critical method itself.[6] The criticism of scholars such as Weiss[7] or Alonso-Schökel[8] would propose shifting the focus away from Gunkel's emphasis on an *Urform* within a given sociological setting to concentration on stylistic features and the individuality of each psalm. Even such studies as those of Boling[9] and Culley[10] which continue to stress the oral dimension grow out of a dissatisfaction with the older form critical approach. In sum, the classic form critical method for the study of the psalms associated with Gunkel which permanently stamped the face of Old Testament research seems now to be offering diminishing returns. No method has been widely accepted to replace it.

A somewhat similar development has accompanied the more recent research in regard to the search for the *Sitz im Leben* of the various psalms. To be sure, Mowinckel's early criticism in *Psalmenstudien* of Gunkel's approach to the cult has received wide acceptance. Even his well-known, more controversial theory of a coronation festival was accepted, by and large, by even such conservative scholars as Eichrodt. But beginning with the fifties an increasing number of scholars sought to modify the theory or abandon it altogether.[11] Actually what is surprising is how few of the subsequent attempts to refine aspects of the cultic setting of the psalms have been sustained. One thinks, for example, of Hans Schmidt's early attempt to isolate a particular type of complaint psalm,[12] of the theories associated with the "Myth and Ritual" school,[13] or the "patternism" of Engnell.[14] Indeed the steady stream of learned monographs on the psalms which continue to emerge from Germany only goes to confirm the impression that the law of diminishing returns has set in.[15] These observations are not intended to call into question the advances which have been made, or to denigrate the genuine insight of the traditio-historical method which have become common scholarly property, but rather to raise the question as to how much further the one method should be pressed. Much of the exegetical gain of determining the original setting of a psalm is jeopardized when the proposed *Sitz im Leben* rests on an extremely fragile and hypothetical base. Moreover, the function of a secondary setting often seems to be more significant for exegesis than a fixation with an alleged original *Sitz*.

Another major focus of psalm research during the last several decades, and one which also seeks to recover the *Vorlage,* is the comparative philological method which has been mainly developed by American and British scholars. The early essays of Albright[16] and Ginsberg[17] broke new ground in seeking to recover the early forms of Hebrew poetry particularly on the basis of Northwest Semitic epigraphy. In the early fifties the several articles of Cross and Freedman[18] sought to perfect the method. Certainly Dahood's massive commentary[19] stands well within this same tradition, even though his particular execution of it has received substantial criticism from within the same school.

Although few scholars would doubt the solid achievements of this method, it remains a question whether the practice of this approach has not also reached a certain impasse in spite of the "threshold" rhetoric. While Dahood has demonstrated that projected readings on the basis of Ugaritic seem almost inexhaustible, increasingly the need to establish sound philological and semantic controls has been voiced. [20] Moreover, the issue of on what level one reads the psalms has become increasingly acute. Can the Masoretic or Septuagintal tradition be so quickly dismissed or ignored in the enthusiasm of recovering an alleged original archaic level? At least for an increasing number of scholars the problem of understanding the present shape of the Psalter including both the consonantal and vocalic traditions emerges as a more pressing problem than the reconstructed original form of the text. But surely the two approaches, the diachronic and synchronic, are not antithetical if properly executed.

There is an even more important reason which would call for a shift in the focus of psalm research in the coming decades. The new texts from Qumran have opened up a whole new set of possibilities for understanding the late period of Hebrew psalmody. Now for the first time there is solid extra-biblical evidence by which to trace the final stages in the formation of the Old Testament Psalter. Indeed, even the older collections such as Ben Sira and the Psalms of Solomon have received a new importance in the light of the Qumran discoveries. Whereas in the previous generation, scholars such as Mowinckel tended to denigrate the last stages in the development, the period of late Hebrew psalmody now appears to be one of the most exciting and, in many ways, creative eras of Israel's history. In my judgment, the real challenge of psalms study lies in this period which has been largely neglected up to now.

II

At the outset it is necessary to recognize some of the basic studies which have been made in the field of late Hebrew psalmody. As early as 1924 Mowinckel, in volume VI of his *Psalmenstudien,* had criticized at length the theory of Gunkel and Causse who had attributed the late psalms to a private, non-cultic origin. He defended his cultic theory and assigned the composition of the late psalms to a temple personnel for use in the cult.

The most thoroughgoing response to Mowinckel's interpretation came from H. Ludin Jansen.[21] The strength of Jansen's approach lay in exploiting the full range of available parallel material from the Apocrypha and Pseudepigrapha, especially Sirach and the Psalms of Solomon. He developed his theory that the late psalms were not cultic in Mowinckel's sense of the term because of the fixed form of Jewish worship in the early Hellenistic period, but performed an edifying, didactic role for the synagogue and temple.

Another contribution of significance which attacked the larger problem of late psalmody was the lengthy article of Holm-Nielsen[22] in 1960. The author first attempted to break out of the impasse which he felt had been caused by too narrow a view of cult, and cautioned of the need for recognizing the complexity of the concept. He argued that a psalm could have a role in the cult and function didactically as well. Above all, Holm-Nielsen investigated the way in which the older psalms had achieved a normative character and were reused in the later psalms. He thus raised the whole question of Scripture and canon which, surprisingly enough, had seldom been brought into the discussion.

Mention should also be made of the revised English edition[23] (1962) of Mowinckel's *Offersang og Sangoffer* (1951). In an important chapter on "The Learned Psalmography," Mowinckel took into consideration the criticisms of his earlier position and did offer some modifications by allowing a larger role for non-cultic poetry within Israel; but his general approach remained basically the same. Although Mowinckel has a brief chapter on the Qumran psalter, his position was obviously formed without taking the new material seriously into consideration.

III

If one turns now from the broad treatment of the subject to the detailed issues involved in the study of late Hebrew psalmody, one gains immediately the impression that there are a great variety of issues which will have to be explored before a new synthesis is possible.

A. THE PRESENT SHAPE OF THE PSALTER

For the school of Gunkel the question of understanding the present shape of the Psalter was considered irrelevant and unimportant. The more recent standard commentaries of Weiser and Kraus virtually ignore the topic. Nevertheless the issue of how the psalms were finally collected and given their present shape has important implications for late psalmody.

First of all, the number and order of the psalms within the Psalter has emerged with new significance from the Qumran Psalms Scroll and touches directly on the problem of canon (see below). Clearly no consensus has emerged to explain the present order beyond the recognition of the role of earlier collections.[24] The attempt to use the present order in determining the function of the Psalter within the synagogue has sparked a steady stream of literature since the beginning of the twentieth century which tried to work out the cycle of lectionary readings lying behind the sequence of the Psalter.[25] The theory has received its most thorough, recent exposition by A. Arens.[26] Unquestionably this approach to the problem has raised a whole set of issues which have been often ignored. At times the evidence is striking in its ability to explain many features. Still the hypothetical nature of the various reconstructions along with sharp disagreement among the experts continues to pose serious problems and prevents anything resembling a consensus from emerging, even on basic issues.

In a much more modest and tentative way Westermann's brief article on the collection of the psalms[27] offers many fresh insights into the redactional history of the Psalter. Westermann stresses that the Psalter as a final collection has lost its primary cultic function and reflects its new role as Sacred Scripture on which the pious of Israel study and meditate. Nevertheless he feels sure that at a certain stage in the development of the tradition a consciousness of the original function of genres was retained. The question is an interesting one and needs further exploration. In my judgment, one could go further than Westermann in tracing the new function which Psalm 1 as an introduction to the collection served, as well as recognizing other signs of reinterpretation by means of their positioning within the various collections. It is of interest that certain genres such as individual complaint psalms have been retained in a collection (cf. Book I), whereas the royal psalms have been scattered throughout the Psalter.

B. THE ISSUE OF CANON

Closely allied to the above issue is the whole problem of the development of the Psalter as canonical scripture, which involves both the collection of psalms and the establishment of the text. H. Ludin Jansen[28] represented the scholarly consensus in the thirties when he assumed that the Psalter had been closed by the beginning of the second century B.C.E. because of the evidence from the prologue of Sirach and the sequence and scope of the Septuagint. Further he argued that the use of an original individual psalm of thanksgiving (Psalm 30) at the dedication of the temple in 165 would suggest that no new composition could rival the older traditional psalms.

The discoveries at Qumran, particularly the psalms from Cave XI, have raised the issue in a new and forceful way. Not only is the order different from the canonical psalter, but there are a number of new psalms and a prose tradition about the psalms which challenges the adequacy of the older understanding of canon. Particularly J. A. Sanders[29] has continued to raise the issue whether the Qumran psalter does in fact represent a variant form which is distinct from that of the Masoretic or "canonical" tradition. He argues that "the last third of the Qumran Psalter indicates a still open-ended Psalter in the first century."[30] Sanders' view has called forth a vigorous response from Goshen-Gottstein.[31] He argues that rather than positing a different canon, the Qumran evidence suggests a "liturgical collection," which he feels satisfies both the canonical and textual issues involved.

More recently Peter Ackroyd[32] has tried to put the question of canon into a broader context while taking into consideration the arguments of both Sanders and Goshen-Gottstein. Ackroyd also acknowledges his debt to the discussion by G. Ernest Wright.[33] Ackroyd raises the question as to whether the canonical psalter itself is not really to be defined as a "liturgical collection" and to what extent a somewhat arbitrary section from a larger body of material by part of the Jewish community should be binding on the Christian faith.[34] He does not suggest a final answer, but clearly the issue of canon has moved to the center of the discipline and affects a wide range of subjects including text criticism and theology.

C. INNER BIBLICAL EXEGESIS

Hertzberg[35] once employed the term *Nachgeschichte* to describe the process by which an Old Testament text—not simply a tradition—continued to reverberate throughout the rest of the Bible. The concept was later picked up and brilliantly developed by Seeligmann[36] who quite correctly joined the process of inner biblical exegesis with a *Kanonbewusstsein*. Indeed, perhaps one of the most fruitful avenues by which to explore the problem of canon is by closely investigating how in fact Old Testament texts began to function normatively within the various parts of the Jewish community. Although some very good work has already been done in the area of inner biblical exegesis,[37] it is clear that much more needs to be done before the evidence can be related to the broader issues.

The problem of an adequate methodology remains an acute one in this area of study. It is an obvious error to project into the pre-exilic psalms a midrashic method which flowered in the Hellenistic period. Yet it is also evident that the concept of a normative scripture unleashed a new set of forces which were different in kind from those influencing the development of oral tradition in the pre-exilic period.

There is another indication within the Psalter that the traditional psalms of Israel had assumed a new function as Sacred Scripture of the community. It has long been noticed that certain psalms are actually only compilations of other psalms. Thus Psalm 108 consists of two parts made by joining Psalms 57 and 60. In other psalms, such as 86, almost every line of the psalm has been picked up from another portion of the Hebrew Bible and fashioned into a poem. Mowinckel discussed this feature as characteristic of late psalmody[38] and judged it as a sign of the breakdown of spontaneous piety. The real credit, however, for understanding the significance of this development goes to the French scholars associated with the school of Robert.[39] These scholars used the term "relecture" or "anthological style" to describe the process by which a later biblical writer made use of an earlier writing to produce a new form with its own individual integrity.

Unquestionably this French school has discovered an important side of late psalmody which the classic German form critical school underestimated in its significance. However, it is also the case that the method needs considerable refinement and further controls. The variety of ways in which early scripture was reused along with its historical development within Israel needs to be carefully examined.

The interesting thing to note is that already by the time of the Chronicler one can discover at least one form of the reuse of earlier psalms. I Chronicles 16 describes the bringing of the ark into Jerusalem and David's appointing Asaph and his choir to render thanksgiving to God. The liturgical nature of the service is made clear by the concluding Amen response of the people (vs. 26). The actual hymn which is cited as providing the service of thanksgiving is made up of a catena of psalms, namely, parts of 105, 96, and 106. Likewise, in II Chronicles 6 and 7 Solomon is described as including in his prayer a citation from Psalm 132 and the people respond with the refrain from 136. The point to be stressed is that within late Israel, the psalms have been loosened from their original cultic context and the words assigned a new significance as Sacred Scripture for a new and different function. Far from being a sign of a loss of piety or an attachment to the past, this move testified to Israel's desire to articulate fresh praise to God through the mediation of older forms.

Recent study of the reuse of the psalms has received a major impetus, of course, from the Qumran discoveries. Already there has been some excellent work in showing the new use of old psalms in the *Hodayot*.[40] But there is now the need to restudy the whole question of the use of the Old Testament in late Hebrew psalmody by employing all the comparative literature available which would include the full range of the apocryphal and pseudepigraphical corpus. Many of the standard editions of such works as the Psalms of Solomon—one thinks of Ryle or Viteau—definitely need reworking in the light of modern form criticism and the recent discoveries.

D. SUPERSCRIPTIONS TO THE PSALMS

Surely the most far reaching alteration with which the collector shaped the canonical psalter was in his use of superscriptions. Little interest has been paid to these titles in recent years.[41] The New English Bible has even chosen to omit them from the translation. The reason for this lack of interest is clear enough. A wide consensus has been reached among critical scholars for over a hundred years that the titles are secondary additions, which can afford no reliable information toward establishing the original historical setting of the psalms. However, although the titles are relatively late, they represent an important reflection on how the psalms as a collection of sacred literature were understood and how this secondary setting became normative for the canonical tradition. In addition, the titles are significant in dealing with the perennial problem of the *Sitz im Leben* for late Hebrew psalmody.

It is important to distinguish the various elements within the titles. The titles are of a wide variety and reflect different functions. Some are of a liturgical nature and designate the manner in which the psalm was to be rendered by the choirmaster. Many of these technical terms can no longer be understood and appear to have been unintelligible even to the early Greek translators.[42] Quite recently Sawyer has made out a good case for the antiquity of certain of the liturgical elements in the titles which have a striking continuity with Akkadian parallels.[43] However, the present form of the superscriptions is undoubtedly late. I have argued in an article that the historical references to David are the result of a development of inner biblical exegesis closely akin to later midrashic techniques which sought to establish the setting from the content of the psalms.[44] The development of this use of superscriptions can be also fixed in time. The form does not appear until after the Chronicler and is fully developed by the time of the Qumran Psalms Scroll.

How is one to understand this move toward historization which took psalms once functioning within a cultic context and placed them within the history of the "canonical" David? It is important to note that the incidents chosen as evoking the psalms were not royal occasions nor representative of the kingly office. Rather David is pictured simply as a man, indeed chosen by God for the sake of Israel, but one who displays the strengths and weaknesses of all men. By attaching a psalm to a historical event the interpretation of the psalm is made to focus on the inner life of the psalmist. An access is now provided the reader into David's emotional life. Later Israel is offered a guideline on how the faith relates to the subjective side of its life.

The effect of this new context has implications for the much discussed problem of the *Sitz im Leben* of the Psalter. The psalms are transmitted as the sacred psalms of David, but they testify to all the common troubles and joys of ordinary human life in which all men participate. These psalms do not need to be cultically actualized to serve later generations. They are made immediately accessible to the faithful. Through the mouth of David, the representative man, they become a personal word from God to their own situation. The titles, far from tying these poems to the ancient past, serve to contemporize and individualize them for every generation of suffering and persecuted Israel.

IV

Finally a brief summary is in order on the subject of the Psalter and the Christian faith. One of the most characteristic features of the last twenty-five years of Psalms study has been the continuous attempt to relate the Old

Testament psalms to Christian theology.[45] Naturally the concern is not new and extends back to the inception of the Christian Church. The new feature consisted in the attempt, first to read the psalms critically through the eyes of Gunkel and then go beyond the form critical stage to develop a more theologically relevant interpretation. As a result the new form of theological interpretation differs sharply from the many nineteenth-century theologies of the Psalter. It is not necessary to review in detail the various stances employed during the last few decades. They varied from existential categories, to those of *Heilsgeschichte* and typology, to traditional allegory. Usually the main lines of Gunkel's scheme emerged intact with only a few suggested minor alterations.

In my judgment, these theological attempts have been only partially successful. The difficulty of moving from an original cultic setting to the contemporary scene remains enormous. Likewise, the move from a critical reading to a modern, devotional application has generally seemed highly forced and subjective. Certainly the frequent attempt to *Vergegenwärtigung* in terms of a rather direct extension of Israel's cult into Christian litany runs into many obvious problems.

I would argue that the need of taking seriously the canonical form of the Psalter would greatly aid in making use of the psalms in the life of the Christian Church. Such a move would not disregard the historical dimensions of the Psalter, but would attempt to profit from the shaping which the final redactors gave the older material in order to transform traditional poetry into Sacred Scripture for the later generations of the faithful.

NOTES

1. Cf. J. J. Stamm, "Ein Vierteljahrhundert Psalmenforschung," *ThR* 23 (1955), 1–68; J. Coppens, "Études Récentes sur le Psautier," in *Le Psautier,* ed. R. de Langhe (Louvain, 1962), pp. 1–91; E. Lipinski, "Les psaumes de la royauté de Yahwé dans l'exégèse moderne," in *Le Psautier,* pp. 133–272; A. S. Kapelrud, "Scandinavian Research in the Psalms after Mowinckel," *Annual of the Swedish Theological Institute* 4 (1965), 148–162; J. Schildenberger, "Die Psalmen. Eine Übersicht über einige Psalmenwerke der Gegenwart," *Bibel und Leben* 8 (1967), 220–231; D. J. A. Clines, "Psalm Research since 1955: I. The Psalms and the Cult. II. The Literary Genres," *Tyndale Bulletin* 18 (1967), 103–125; 20 (1969), 105–125; L. Sabourin, *The Psalms. Their Origin and Meaning,* II (Staten Island, N.Y., 1969), pp. 337–367.
2. S. Terrien, *The Psalms and Their Meaning for Today* (New York, 1952); A. R. Johnson, "The Psalms," in *The Old Testament and Modern Study,* ed. H. H. Rowley (Oxford, 1951), pp. 162–209; J. Muilenburg's introductory essay in H. Gunkel, *The Psalms* (Philadelphia, 1967); cf. also the many translations of European popularizations such as P. Drijvers, *The Psalms, Their Structure and Meaning* (New York, 1965); C. Barth, *Introduction to the Psalms* (New York, 1966).
3. Cf. e.g. the studies of C. Westermann, *The Praise of God in the Psalms* (1953;

Eng. tr., Richmond, 1965); J. W. Wevers, "A Study in the Form Criticism of Individual Complaint Psalms," *VT* 6 (1956), 80–96; A. Descamps, "Les Genres littéraires du Psautier," in *Le Psautier* [N 1], pp. 73–88; R. Murphy, "A Consideration of the Classification 'Wisdom Psalms,'" *VTS* 9 (1962), 156–167; L. Sabourin, *Un Classement littéraire des Psaumes* (Bruges, 1964).

4. J. Begrich, "Das priesterliche Heilsorakel," *ZAW* 52 (1934), 81–93; "Die priesterliche Tora," *BZAW* 66 (1936), 63–88. Both reprinted in *Gesammelte Studien zum Alten Testament* (Munich, 1964).

5. Cf. E. Gerstenberger's review of C. Westermann, *JBL* 81 (1961), 207 f. But certainly an essay such as W. W. Hallo's "Individual Prayer in Sumerian. The Continuity of a Tradition," in *Essays in Memory of E. A. Speiser* (New Haven, 1968), pp. 71–89, is a model of the comparative approach.

6. Cf. A. Szörenyi, *Psalmen und Kult im Alten Testament* (Budapest, 1961), cited by Clines, "Psalm Research" [N 1], p. 114.

7. M. Weiss, "Wege der neuen Dichtungswissenschaft in ihrer Anwendung auf die Psalmenforschung," *Biblica* 42 (1961), 255–302.

8. L. Alonso-Schökel, *Estudios de Poética Hebrea* (Barcelona, 1963); a German translation has been announced: *Das Alte Testament als literarisches Kunstwerk*.

9. R. G. Boling, "Synonymous Parallelism in the Psalms," *JSS* 5 (1960), 221–255.

10. R. C. Culley, *Oral Formulaic Language in the Biblical Psalms* (Toronto, 1967).

11. Typical attempts are those of A. Weiser, "Zur Frage nach den Beziehungen der Psalmen zum Kult," in *Festschrift A. Bertholet* (Tübingen, 1950), pp. 513–532; H. J. Kraus, *Die Königsherrschaft Gottes im Alten Testament* (Tübingen, 1951); cf. the full discussion in Lipinski, "Les psaumes" [N 1], pp. 133 f.

12. H. Schmidt, *Das Gebet des Angeklagten im A. T.* (Giessen, 1928).

13. S. H. Hooke, ed., *Myth and Ritual* (Oxford, 1933); *The Labyrinth* (London, 1935); *Myth, Ritual, and Kingship* (Oxford, 1958). A. R. Johnson, *Sacral Kingship in Ancient Israel* (Cardiff, 1955).

14. Cf. I. Engnell, *Studies in Divine Kingship in the Ancient Near East* (Uppsala, 1943); "Planted by the Streams of Water," in *Studia Orient. Io. Pedersen* (Hauniae, 1953), pp. 85–96; "The Book of Psalms," in *A Rigid Scrutiny* (Nashville, 1969), pp. 68 ff.; E. R. Dalglish, *Psalm 51 in the Light of Ancient Near Eastern Patternism* (New York, 1951); G. W. Ahlström, *Psalm 89. Eine Liturgie aus dem Ritual des leidenden Königs* (Lund, 1959).

15. G. Wanke, *Die Zionstheologie der Korachiten in ihrem traditionsgeschichtlichen Zusammenhang* (Berlin, 1966); L. Delekat, *Asylie und Schutzorakel am Zionheiligtum* (Leiden, 1967); W. Beyerlin, *Die Rettung der Bedrängten in den Feindpsalmen der Einzelnen auf institutionelle Zusammenhänge untersucht* (Göttingen, 1970).

16. W. F. Albright, "The Earliest Forms of Hebrew Verse," *JPOS* 2 (1922), 69 ff.; "The Psalm of Habakkuk," in *Studies in Old Testament Prophecy* [T. H. Robinson Volume], ed. H. H. Rowley (Edinburgh, 1950), pp. 1 ff.; "A Catalogue of Early Hebrew Lyric Poems (Ps. LXVIII)," *HUCA* 23 (1950), 1–40; "Notes on Psalms 68 and 134," in *Interpretationes ad Vetus Testamentum pertinentes S. Mowinckel* (Oslo, 1955), pp. 1–12.

17. H. L. Ginsberg, "A Phoenician Hymn in the Psalter," *Atti del XIX Congresso Internazionale degli Orientalisti* (Rome, 1935), pp. 472–476.

18. Cf. among others, F. M. Cross and D. N. Freedman, "A Royal Song of Thanksgiving: II Sam. 22=Ps. 18a," *JBL* 72 (1953), 15–34; "The Song of Miriam," *JNES* 14 (1955), 237–250. Also, D. N. Freedman, "Archaic Forms in Early Hebrew Poetry," *ZAW* 72 (1960), 101–107; F. M. Cross, "The Divine Warrior in Israel's Early Cult," in *Biblical Motifs*, ed. A. Altmann (Cambridge, Mass., 1966), pp. 11–30.

19. M. Dahood, *Psalms, I–III*, AB vols. 16, 17, 17A (1966–70).

20. Cf. such typical reviews as D. A. Robertson, *JBL* 85 (1966), 484; H. Donner, "Ugaritismen in der Psalmenforschung," *ZAW* 79 (1967), 322–350; J. Barr, *Comparative Philology and the Text of the Old Testament* (Oxford, 1968).

21. H. Luden Jansen, *Die Spätjüdische Psalmendichtung. Ihr Entstehungskreis und ihr 'Sitz im Leben'* (Oslo, 1937); cf. also P. A. Munch, "Die jüdischen 'Weisheitspsalmen' und ihr Platz im Leben," *Acta Orientalia* (1936), 112–140.

22. S. Holm-Nielsen, "The Importance of Late Jewish Psalmody for the Understanding of Old Testament Psalmodic Tradition," *Studia Theologica* 14 (1960), 1–53.

23. S. Mowinckel, *The Psalms in Israel's Worship*, I–II (Oxford, 1962).

24. Cf. the survey in C. T. Niemeyer, *Het Problem de Rangschikking der Psalmen* (Leiden, 1950).

25. Cf. such articles as E. G. King, "The Influence of the Triennial Cycle upon the Psalter," *JTS* 5 (1904), 203–213; I. Abrahams, "E. G. King on the Influence of the Triennial Cycle upon the Psalter," *JQR* 16 (1904), 579–583; H. St. J. Thackeray, "Psalm 76 and other Psalms for the Feast of Tabernacles," *JTS* 15 (1913–14), 425–431; L. Rabinowitz, "Does Midrash Tehillim Reflect the Triennial Cycle of Psalms?" *JQR* 26 (1935–36), 349–368; A. Guilding, "Some Obscured Rubrics and Lectionary Allusions in the Psalter," *JTS*, N.S. 3 (1952), 41–55.

26. A. Arens, "Hat der Psalter seinen 'Sitz im Leben' in der synagogalen Leseordnung des Pentateuch?" in *Le Psautier* [N 1], pp. 107–131; *Die Psalmen im Gottesdienst des Alten Bundes*, 2 Aufl. (Trier, 1968).

27. C. Westermann, "Zur Sammlung des Psalters," in *Forschung am A.T.* (Munich, 1964), pp. 336–343.

28. Jansen [N 21], pp. 98 f.

29. J. A. Sanders, *The Psalms Scroll of Qumran Cave 11 (11QPsᵃ)*, DJD, IV (Oxford, 1965); "Variorum in 11QPsᵃ," *HTR* 59 (1966), 83–94; *The Dead Sea Psalms Scroll* (Ithaca, 1967), pp. 9 ff., 155 ff.; "Cave 11 Surprises and the Question of Canon," in *NDBA*, pp. 113–130.

30. Sanders, *The Dead Sea Psalms Scroll*, p. 158.

31. M. Goshen-Gottstein, "The Psalms Scroll (11QPsᵃ). A Problem of Canon and Text," *Textus* 5 (1960), 22–33. Cf. also the article of S. Talmon, ibid., 11–21.

32. P. R. Ackroyd, "The Open Canon," *Colloquium. The Australian and New Zealand Theological Review* (May 1970), 279–291.

33. G. E. Wright, *The Old Testament and Theology* (New York, 1969), pp. 166–185.

34. Ackroyd, "Open Canon" [N 32], p. 279.

35. H. W. Hertzberg, "Die Nachgeschichte alttestamentlicher Texte innerhalb des Alten Testaments," BZAW 66 (1936), 110–121.

36. I. L. Seeligmann, "Voraussetzungen des Midrashexegese," *VTS* 1 (1953), 150–181.

37. For example, Holm-Nielsen, "The Importance of Late Jewish Psalmody" [N 22], pp. 24 ff.; N. M. Sarna, "The Psalm for the Sabbath Day (Ps. 92)," *JBL* 81 (1962), 155–168; "Psalm 89: A Study of Inner Biblical Exegesis," in *Biblical and Other Studies*, ed. A. Altmann (Cambridge, Mass., 1963), pp. 29–46.

38. S. Mowinckel, *Psalmenstudien*, I–VI (Kristiania, 1921–24), vol. VI.

39. Cf. such representative articles and monographs as the following: A. Robert, "Le Psaume CXIX et les Sapientiaux," *RB* 48 (1939), 5–20 (Robert's full bibliography is listed in *Melanges bibliques rédigés en l'honneur de A. Robert*, 1959); A. Deissler, *Psalm 119 (118) und seine Theologie. Ein Beitrag zu Erforschung der anthologischen Stilgattung im A.T.* (Munich, 1955); A. Gelin, "La question des 'relectures bibliques' à l'intérieur d'une tradition vivante," in *Sacra Pagina*, Bibliotheca ephemeridum theologicarum lovaniensium, 12 (Paris, 1954), 303–315; H. Cazelles, "Une Relecture du Psaume XXIX?" in *A la Rencontre de Dieu. Mémorial A. Gelin* (Le Puy, 1961), pp. 119–128; J. Becker, *Israel deutet seine Psalmen* (Stuttgart, 1968), pp. 9 ff.

40. Holm-Nielsen, *Hodayot. Psalms from Qumran* (Aarhus, 1960).

41. Cf. the following articles: J.-M. Vosté, "Sur les titre des Psaumes dans la Pešittā," *Biblica* 25 (1944), 210 ff.; N. H. Tur-Sinai, "The Literary Character of the Book of Psalms," *OTS* 8 (1950), 263 ff.; H. D. Preuss, "Die Psalmenüberschriften," *ZAW* 71 (1959), 44 ff.; L. Delekat, "Probleme der Psalmenüberschriften," *ZAW* 76 (1964), 280 ff.; J. J. Glueck, "Some Remarks on the Introductory Notes of the Psalms," *Studies on the Psalms* (Potchefstroom, 1963), pp. 30–39.

42. Cf. Mowinckel's various attempts: *Psalmenstudien,* IV [N 38], and *The Psalms in Israel's Worship,* II [N 23], 207 ff.

43. J. F. A. Sawyer, "An Analysis of the Content and Meaning of the Psalm-Headings," *Transactions of the Glasgow University Oriental Society* 22 (1967–68), 26 ff.

44. B. S. Childs, "Psalms Titles and Midrashic Exegesis," *JSS* 16 (1971), 137–150.

45. The following examples are representative: Terrien, *The Psalms and Their Meaning for Today* [N 2]; R. B. Y. Scott, *The Psalms as Christian Praise* (London, 1954); A. Gelin, *La Prière des Psaumes* (Paris, 1961); T. Worden, *The Psalms are Christian Prayers* (London, 1962); Drijvers, *The Psalms, Their Structure and Meaning* [N 2]; Barth, *Introduction to the Psalms* [N 2].

21. *Prolegomena to the Study of Jewish Apocalyptic*[1]

PAUL D. HANSON

THE DIVINITY SCHOOL, HARVARD UNIVERSITY

THE TITLE of a recent book by Klaus Koch aptly describes the posture of most students of the Bible before the literature which concerns us in this essay: *Ratlos vor der Apokalyptik*.[2] Among students of both Testaments, Jewish apocalyptic remains an unsolved riddle. While it would be rash to claim that that riddle is about to be broken, there are new bits of data which raise hopes that the groundwork is being laid for penetration into the dark riddle of apocalyptic from a new perspective. That groundwork is located not on virgin territory, however, but on the scarred battleground of old controversies; that is to say, it is being worked out in lively dialogue with the works of previous generations of scholars. In our attempt to describe that groundwork, it seems prudent to begin with the dialogue with earlier scholarship, and only with the insights gained from that dialogue to proceed to outline a program for the restudy of apocalyptic from the new perspective opening before us.

I. The Study of Jewish Apocalyptic in Past Scholarship

As in so many areas of biblical research, in the area of apocalyptic the name of Julius Wellhausen assumes an imposing position. All of the strengths and weaknesses of the "school" approach to research are manifested by the influence which Wellhausen's evaluation of apocalyptic had on succeeding generations of scholars. The light which he and his followers shed on the literary history of the apocalyptic writings is not insignificant. Yet one finds deeper insights into the nature and history of apocalyptic literature among several scholars of the generation before Wellhausen, insights lost to the world of scholarship for decades in the wake of the current set in motion by Wellhausen.

The first comprehensive study of the subject was conducted by Friedrich Lücke.[3] Though hindered by a dogmatic position which allowed only a negative judgment on the extra-canonical apocalyptic works, his analysis of the biblical apocalypses is impressive for such an early work. Apocalyptic develops out of prophecy, and what influence from Hellenism and Zoroastrianism can be detected is limited mainly to the form, affecting substance very little.[4] The essence of apocalyptic he recognized in its view of history, from which center all of its other characteristics could be understood. This grasping for the core of apocalyptic is noteworthy, as is his explanation of the causes giving rise to apocalyptic, including the disillusioning experiences after the return from exile, the oppression under foreign powers, and tensions within the community.[5]

Many of the ideas of Lücke were developed further by Eduard Reuss,[6] such as the view that apocalyptic develops out of prophecy, and the explanation of the rise of apocalyptic as a response to the disappointments of the post-exilic period. While freeing himself from the dogmatic view of canon held by Lücke, Reuss himself operates within a new "dogma," that of rationalism, leading him to distinguish between prophecy derived from man's intelligence and apocalyptic from his phantasy.

Adolf Hilgenfeld[7] outlined an approach to the study of apocalyptic which he intended to correct flaws in Lücke's study: he set out to describe the inner unity from which all of the characteristics of Jewish apocalyptic became intelligible, and insisted that the only means by which one could accomplish the task was through the historical investigation of the rise of apocalyptic.[8] It was only to the great loss of scholarship that this attention to the origins and development of apocalyptic was neglected among subsequent generations of scholars. While seeking to replace the dogmatic perspectives of Lücke and Reuss with a historical approach, however, Hilgenfeld himself applied a philosophical construct in tracing the development of apocalyptic, that of Hegelian idealism;[9] an irresistible rational spirit was seen developing through prophecy, apocalyptic, and Christianity. Hilgenfeld's reconstruction, nonetheless, lifted apocalyptic to an honorable position in the area of biblical studies, a position which, unfortunately, it was soon to lose because of the powerful influence of Wellhausen and Duhm.

Julius Wellhausen based his evaluation of apocalyptic upon De Wette's theory of a sharp division between pre-exilic Israelite religion and post-exilic Judaism, the latter being dominated by the law and a tradition of interpretation which stifled the prophetic spirit.[10] The favorite term used by Wellhausen and his followers in describing the apocalyptists was "Epigonen," imitators who borrowed from prophetic and Persian sources alike in writing documents which represented a distinct fall from the heights attained by the great prophets ending with Second Isaiah. In Wellhausen's reconstruction of the relation of the Old and New Testaments, the spiritual predecessors of Jesus were found in the classical prophets, thus passing over the intervening five centuries and the entire corpus of Jewish apocalyptic.[11] Both the exclusive attention of this school to the question of authorship and historical setting and its theory of a fundamental break between prophecy and apocalyptic made it impossible for those writing from the Wellhausenian perspective—whether in Germany or in the English-speaking world[12]—to advance beyond Hilgenfeld in tracing the development of apocalyptic from its earlier origins.

Among the literary critics of the era at the turn of the century R. H. Charles defies easy categorization.[13] To be sure, he operated with the tools developed by Wellhausen, and joined his contemporaries in dating compositions like Zechariah 14 and the Isaiah Apocalypse in the second century B.C.[14] and in speaking of "the benumbing yoke of the Law" in the post-exilic period which killed the dynamic relationship between prophet and his world.[15] There is, however, another dimension of his study which resisted the literary critic's characteristic condemnation of apocalyptic: because of his careful attention to the message of the apocalyptic writings themselves, the organic connection between prophecy and apocalyptic was very clear to him.[16] When seeking to trace the development of Jewish and Christian apocalyptic, he begins with the teachings of pre-exilic prophecy, finding "that apocalyptic has not only its roots and early growth in the Old Testament: it has already arrived at a high degree of maturity within the Canon of the Old Testament, and that without including in our purview the Book of Daniel."[17] This sense of the prophetic roots of apocalyptic leads Charles to resist the increasingly influential Iranian theory: for example, regarding resurrection, he insists: "It is the genuine product of Jewish inspiration, and not derived from any foreign source."[18]

This view of the organic connection between prophecy and apocalyptic also leads Charles to reject the "prophetic connection" theory of Wellhausen and his students. Important here is Charles's view of Judaism in the pre-Christian era, which, contrary to the dominant view of scholars in his time and ours, was not characterized by antagonisms between apocalyptic and legalistic factions; rather, apocalyptic was an essential part of Judaism, and was at one with the spirit of Judaism in its devotion to the Law.[19] This view of pre-Christian Judaism is the basis for his interpretation of Christian origins. Christianity did not hark back to classical prophecy, skipping over five centuries of post-exilic Judaism, but rather, "inasmuch as prophecy had died long before the Christian era, and its place had been taken by apocalyptic, it was from the apocalyptic side of Judaism that Christianity was born. . . ."[20] The theological integrity and importance of apocalyptic is thus established from two sides in Charles, in its organic connection with classical prophecy and in its parental relationship to Christianity. In tracing the development of the Judaeo-Christian tradition, Charles was thus a clear spokesman claiming that apocalyptic must not be passed over; in fact, it developed beyond prophecy in several respects: in its universal scope, and in its "great idea that all history, alike human, cosmological, and spiritual is a unity. . . ."[21]

Unfortunately, Charles's reconstruction suffers from serious drawbacks as well: he was not free from an evolutionary scheme which sometimes determines his dating of the material. That the "rational Spirit" of Hegelianism lives on is seen, for example, in his tracing the development from a materialistic and mechanical view of the future life to a spiritual and dynamic view. Since the teaching of the future life finds its fulfillment in the New Testament, Jewish apocalyptic is ultimately superseded. In his treatment of the Synoptic Gospels, it becomes apparent that even this scholar is not free at times from the disparagement of apocalyptic in favor of classical prophecy which we noted in Wellhausen. Jesus ultimately stands in the tradition of Jeremiah and his followers.[22] Pure elements of apocalyptic, such as are found in Mark 13 and the Apocalypse of John, are regarded in the category of lower, older ideas lingering on in the New Testament from its roots in Judaism. Thus one ultimately finds a contradiction in Charles between his careful attention to the development of the intertestamental literature up to the New Testament and his rejection as a part of true Christianity of the genuinely apocalyptic elements in the New Testament.[23]

More characteristic among the literary critics than the appreciation of apocalyptic found in Charles is an even greater disparagement of this literature than found in Wellhausen; for, once the latter had denied any authentic prophetic spirit in the work of the apocalyptists and had denigrated them to the role of imitators of the prophets, the way was prepared for denying all connections between prophecy and apocalyptic. This step, adumbrated by Noack and Dillmann, was taken in a clear manner by G. Hölscher, who denied that apocalyptic developed out of prophecy, but looked to wisdom instead for apocalyptic's origins. The new literary mode of the post-exilic scribes was the legend, which drew upon biblical material and folk traditions as well as esoteric and foreign sources.[24]

The negative attitude toward apocalyptic which came to characterize the literary critics finds a different form of expression in George Foot Moore's great work, *Judaism*. The aim of Moore's study is to describe the nature of "normative Judaism," that is, "to exhibit the religious conceptions and moral principles of Judaism, its modes of worship and observance, and its distinctive piety, in the form in which, by the end of the second century of the Christian era, they attained general acceptance and authority."[25] In elucidating his critical principles, Moore states that he gives primacy to the sources which Judaism itself recognized as authentic; applied to the apocalyptic writings, this principle implies that "it is a fallacy of method for the historian to make them a primary source for the eschatology of Judaism, much more to contaminate its theology with them."[26] Moore thus uncritically accepts the judgment on the apocalyptic writings which was passed by the authorities of a later period, the Tannaic, a judgment largely representing a bitter reaction by the rabbis against the apocalyptic writings because of the calamity of A.D. 70, for which those writings were held in part responsible.[27] In other words,

Moore applies the dogmatic criterion of "normative Judaism" to a period which knew no such norm, but was characterized instead by various streams of tradition competing for acceptance. Therefore, the only aspect of apocalyptic which is studied by Moore is that which ultimately found its way into the "normative Judaism" of the Tannaic period, namely, the belief in the re-vivification of the dead in the Messianic age.[28] All other segments of the vast mosaic of apocalyptic are ignored as "imaginative presentation."[29] Given his method, it was impossible for Moore to treat the phenomenon of Jewish apocalyptic as a whole and on its own merit, even as it was impossible for him to add to the understanding of the origins of apocalyptic and the circumstances in the Jewish community within which the apocalyptic literature flourished.

After having traced the manner in which the literary critics came to interpret apocalyptic, we move back in time to note the inception of another approach to the subject. It was the work of Hermann Gunkel which brought into the field whole new possibilities of advancing the understanding of the nature of apocalyptic literature, many of them through implication, some taking the form of pregnant suggestions never developed by the master himself, others neglected in succeeding generations and to this day not fully exploited. Gunkel's program—set out as a harsh criticism of the onesidedness of Wellhausen's concern with the creativity of the authors, which concern he felt excluded consideration of the pre-literary history of the material—precipitated a methodological revolution.

In distinguishing between the traditional material incorporated into an apocalyptic work and the creativity of the composer, Gunkel countered the view of most literary critics that the images and symbols of the apocalyptic works were the products of phantasy to be dismissed as devoid of theological significance.[30] The apocalyptists were not lapsing into subjectivism, but were summoning a prestigious authority comparable to, and in fact more ancient than, that of the classical prophets. That authority was a lively tradition of myth which spoke of creation, cosmic conflict, and Yahweh's central part in the primordial events. In *Schöpfung und Chaos* Gunkel demonstrated the manner in which the form-critical method could utilize telltale features in the writings (narrative elements left unexplained by the context, features not derivable from earlier biblical tradition but found in ancient myth)[31] to discern and trace back traditional elements drawn from mythic lore by the composer.[32] This mythic tradition is found not only in foreign religions but lives on throughout the history of the religion of Israel, a fact established by Gunkel through a study of the hymnic passages in Psalms, Job, Jeremiah, and the apocalyptic writings, passages reflecting the primordial conflict against Sea, Leviathan, Rahab, *et cetera*.[33]

This new traditio-historical method Gunkel applied in a harsh polemic against the allegorical manner of treating the mythic fragments in the apocalyptic writings which was customary in his day, whereby those mythic fragments were subjected to a search for the key which would unlock the riddle propounded by the author. When discovered, that key was used to disclose the historical events to which the episodes of the myth were supposedly referring. Gunkel insisted instead that apocalyptic writers took over mythic episodes without attempting to interpret every point.[34] Thus many features, and even entire apocalyptic units of tradition, remained totally unrelated to historical events.[35] Since Gunkel finds such historicizing interpretation highly arbitrary and uncontrolled by the original intention of most compositions, he defines the circumstances under which episodes in apocalyptic can be related to events of the historical order: (1) if the material itself contains clear reference to historical situations; or (2) if a clear chronological application is suggested by the recognizable relationships within a vision.[36] These conditions lacking, the explanation of mythic features must be sought in the traditions drawn upon by the writer. Though rigorously applied by Gunkel to his study of the Book of Revelation, this iconoclastic aspect of his method subsequently was virtually lost among students of apocalyptic.

Besides turning attention toward earlier sources, Gunkel's concern with writing the history of the tradition provided an impetus toward tracing the history of genres from the prophets down to apocalyptic. This task, in our mind one of the most promising aspects of a new approach to the riddle of apocalyptic, was never systematically carried out by Gunkel or his disciples; indeed, there remained flaws in his reconstruction which would have made completion of this task impossible, especially his failure to identify correctly the historical carrier of the mythic traditions in Israel and his late dating of many early apocalyptic compositions.

Another aspect of Gunkel's form-critical program is of great significance for the study of apocalyptic; the inquiry into the sociological matrix of the literature. This inquiry was neglected by the school of Wellhausen because of its exclusive interest in the narrower historical question of the relation between the author and the national and international events of his time. Gunkel, however, was not content merely to identify the ancient sources of tradition and to trace the development of the genres utilized; he went on to study the *Sitz im Volksleben Israels,* that is, he sought to explain what in the sociological environment of the people invited the application of the ancient conflict myth. Basically his investigation does not get beyond the general observation that the post-exilic Jewish community and the early Christian Church, in posing rueful questions—why do the innocent suffer and yet the Lord tarries, leaving his people in the hands of oppressors?—found comfort in the message of myth: the enemies of the primordial time are identical to those now threatening the community, and even as Yahweh defeated the powers of chaos then, so too will he destroy the enemies of the people now threatening to destroy them; hence the application to apocalyptic of the concept *Urzeit wird Endzeit.*[37] Here too a very promising avenue of inquiry is left undeveloped by Gunkel; in fact, at times his attention narrows to the problem of the individual composer to the neglect of the problem of sociological setting, at other times the appropriation of mythic material is attributed to the lack of theological creativity on the part of the authors.[38] The apocalyptic literature is still not considered on its own merit, and potentially promising methodological principles are not allowed free application due to the lingering influence of the early literary critical school.

There is, however, one aspect of his investigation where Gunkel did not stop short of full and consistent application; regrettably, it is an aspect which involves a serious error, this being the identification of the ultimate source of myth in apocalyptic with the Babylonian conflict myth. This error is to be understood in the context of that time: the *Enūma eliš* had been newly discovered by George Smith; lively discussion was being carried on with regard to problems of translation, and serious lacunae still marred thorough understanding of the myth. Other important sources of our knowledge of ancient Near Eastern myth were yet unknown. It is not difficult to understand, in the wake of the discovery of the *Enūma eliš,* how such extravagant claims were made for the importance of this myth in the study of the Old Testament and intertestamental literature. Thus Gunkel studied various psalms, Genesis 1, Daniel 7, and Revelation 12, and concluded that all were based on the Babylonian myth.[39] We thus recognize an aspect of Gunkel's study which must be modified on the basis of more recent discoveries. The Ugaritic Baal cycle gives us another version of the conflict myth which is geographically closer to the Old Testament traditions, is historically prior to the *Enūma eliš,*[40] and which betrays parallels, many verbal, closer to the biblical material than the Babylonian myth utilized by Gunkel. Not only will his exclusive attention to Babylonian origins have to be modified, but many details of interpretation will have to be corrected as well, for example, (1) his failure to recognize the significance of *parallelismus membrorum* in passages like Isa. 51:13 and Isa. 27:1 where parallel names for the enemy of Yahweh are taken to refer to two different beings corresponding to Tiamat and her general Kingu, and (2) his argument that Mesopotamian origin is indicated by climatic considerations.[41]

Other errors in Gunkel's reconstruction were related to the broken nature of his Babylonian texts. For example, he replaces the historicizing interpretation of Revelation 12 with an equally speculative traditio-historical interpretation, reading into the Babylonian myth a Marduk nativity which ends up being the basis for a hypothetical Christmas festival vying with the Babylonian New Year's feast in importance![42] Gunkel unfortunately did not apply controls to his new method, which matched in stringency the controls he prescribed for the literary critics in his polemic against their method of *Zeitgeschichte.*[43]

Another conclusion based on speculation which has not withstood the test of further discoveries is Gunkel's conclusion that the ancient myths already contained an eschatological orientation.[44] The future element in the ancient myths, whether Canaanite or Mesopotamian, is different from the future element in apocalyptic, the former being tied to the cycle of the agricultural calendar, the latter being teleological in nature.

Finally, Gunkel's account of the origin of myth in apocalyptic suffers from his failure to identify the historical carrier of myth in Israel from the period of the league down to the exile. Nowhere does he identify an institutional vehicle, but rather refers vaguely to the influence of Babylonian myth on folk-circles who were busy asking Gunkel's beloved aetiological questions.[45] This failure is astonishing in light of the careful attention Gunkel paid to the element of myth in the Psalms and other hymns.

Gunkel, like Moses, was a pioneer who did not reach his destination. By 1913 he had left the study of apocalyptic in disappointment, not finding there the explanation of New Testament origins which he had expected.[46] But here the parallel ends, for while Joshua succeeded in arriving at the goal of his master, Gunkel's students did not. In the area of Pentateuchal studies his challenges were taken up effectively by form critics like Alt and Noth; in the area of Jewish and Christian apocalyptic, however, the form-critical and traditio-historical tasks remain to be completed.

It is impossible here to trace the program outlined by Gunkel through the work of his disciples. One of his concerns especially continued to exercise biblical scholars, the search for the antecedents to the traditional material incorporated by the apocalyptists into their works. Though introducing a profoundly important element into the total task of the historical method, it opened the door to many reconstructions which were more imaginary than accurate. In question were the origins of elements like mythopoeic motifs, dualism, division of history into epochs, angelology, numerology, and cosmic speculation. Gunkel himself contributed to a very dubious development in his nearly exclusive devotion to and often purely hypothetical defense of his Babylonian theory.[47] Turning away from Babylonian cosmology, however, the majority of scholars, applying the same history of religions approach, turned with enthusiasm to a new source to explain the rise of apocalyptic, Persian dualism.[48] The Persian theory found a forceful protagonist in the twenties in R. Reitzenstein, who argued that the main teachings of apocalyptic could be understood only as derived from the Iranian mystery religions.[49] Thereafter, recourse to Zoroastrianism as an answer to the problem of origins became fashionable among scholars, including R. Otto, H. S. Nyberg, A. Bertholet, E. Meyer, W. Bousset, and A. von Gall.[50] The last-mentioned, for example, wrote that ". . . the home of Jewish eschatology was the religion of Zarathustra. . . ." Apocalyptic is thus "unjewish in every respect according to form and content."[51]

Closely associated with Gunkel's approach, but proceeding more cautiously in the search for antecedents than the history of religions group, is Hugo Gressmann.[52] Gressmann argues that the eschatology of the prophets can be understood only by recognizing its antecedents, and he warns against hasty recourse to outside influences such as Persian dualism to account for Israelite eschatology.[53] Rather, priority must be given to the task of "more clearly working out the nature of Israelite religion itself, testing in the case of each passage whether it arose in Israel itself or entered from the outside."[54] Seeking the origin of Israelite eschatology, he first considers "judgment eschatology," and in the study of passages like Ezekiel 38–39, Zechariah 14, Revelation 9, and the Book of Job he finds elements which reflect origin in ancient myth. While concluding that these fragmentary elements can be explained only if they entered Israel at an early pre-prophetic period, he is hesitant to define their source of origin, because of the fragmentary nature of the evidence.[55] Similarly, when he comes to consider "salvation eschatology," he recognizes a source in early myth which entered Israel, most likely already in fragmentary form, in the pre-prophetic period. Another point which Gressmann makes is significant: the common source of both salvation and judgment eschatology in ancient myth indicates that the two cannot be divided —as the critics of his time were wont to do—into two separate bodies, the former post-exilic, the latter coming from pre-exilic times.[56]

The main problem in Gressmann's reconstruction is tied to a confusing identification of eschatology with myth. Gressmann's study is valuable in directing the attention of scholarship toward the early contact between the religion of Israel and ancient myth. What he obscures is the profound change which occurred when those mythic elements were removed from the cyclical world-view of which they were a part and absorbed into the prophetic tradition, that change involving precisely a process of eschatologization, whereby the conflict and creation of the myth came to be construed as something non-recurrent and final. Like Gunkel, Gressmann also fails to recognize the important role played by the royal cult of Jerusalem in preserving those early mythic traditions in a largely unbroken form, thus serving as a native vehicle by which they were transmitted to the point of their re-entry into the prophetic tradition after the exile. Failing to recognize this native institutional carrier of myth during the monarchic period, Gressmann must posit a second major influx of myth from a foreign source to account for the presence of myth in apocalyptic.[57]

The new direction of research made possible by the work of Gunkel and Gressmann was carried on most effectively in relation to apocalyptic not in Germany but in England and Scandinavia by S. H. Hooke (in collaboration with the scholars associated with his "Myth and Ritual" approach),[58] Ivan Engnell,[59] and Sigmund Mowinckel, to mention only the most important. It was Mowinckel who perhaps made the most enduring contribution, for he brought together many of the ideas originating with the older History of Religions School (Winckler, Gunkel, Gressmann), the Myth and Ritual School, and Ivan Engnell, refining and synthesizing them into a comprehensive picture of Israel's royal cult in its relation to the royal ideologies of the ancient Near East while at the same time exercising greater care than his predecessors not to emphasize the common pattern spanning the cultures of the ancient world to the point of obscuring the distinctiveness of the individual religions.[60] In his studies on the royal psalms[61] and the prophetic oracles growing out of the royal ideology[62] he drew attention to the rich body of mythological motifs which were very much alive in Israel during the monarchic period in the royal cult of Jerusalem. Besides reconstructing the features of that cult[63] he demonstrated the influence which its mythic elements began to exert on prophecy. Though not applying these insights to the problem of the rise of apocalyptic because of reasons to be mentioned below, Mowinckel in fact did much to clarify the nature of the carrier of the mythical traditions upon which the late prophetic tradition drew and which were so influential in transforming prophetic eschatology into apocalyptic,[64] a carrier native to Israel's religious experience and thus offering an alternative to the recourse to Persian dualism being taken at that time by most scholars. Although those mythical elements traced ultimately to ancient Near Eastern myth (especially and most immediately Canaanite myth),[65] they were borrowed by Israel's late prophets not directly from foreign cults, but through the mediation of the native traditions of the royal cult.[66] Since that borrowing became especially strong after the demise of the royal cult in 587, Mowinckel correctly draws attention to the profound changes effected in Yahwism by the Babylonian destruction and emphasizes the role played by Second Isaiah in introducing the cosmic imagery of myth into the prophetic tradition.[67]

While thus recognizing the monumental nature of Mowinckel's contribution to our subject, we must note several aspects of his study which require modification. One concerns definitions. Taking the position opposite that of Gressmann, he argues that eschatology becomes a part of Yahwistic faith only in the post-exilic period.[68] Before that period Mowinckel speaks of "future hope," admitting, to be sure, that "out of the future hope eschatology developed."[69] His argument is tied to his notion that only a disappointment of the magnitude of the catastrophe of 587 could effect the transformation of a future hope tied to concrete events into an eschatology announcing the creation of a new order. This distinction is unnatural for two interrelated reasons: (1) before 587 Israel knew profound disappointments which rudely drew attention to the contradiction between Yahweh's promises and Israel's experiences, for example, at the point of the division between the northern and southern kingdoms, during Syrian and Assyrian domination, at the fall of Samaria, during the reign of apostate kings like Manasseh; (2) in the pre-exilic prophets as well Yahweh's final, decisive (i.e. eschatological!) act is awaited as a part of the promises of the covenant.[70] Hence what Mowinckel calls future hope we would designate eschatology, and we would contrast somewhat differently prophecy in its pre-exilic and post-exilic modes on the basis of a distinction between prophetic eschatology and apocalyptic eschatology, the former envisioning Yahweh's final act of fulfillment primarily on the mundane plane, the latter increasingly in the cosmic realm of myth.[71] Because Mowinckel makes eschatology and apocalyptic such late arrivals in Yahwism, he must turn finally to Chaldaean syncretism (as a late outgrowth of Persian religion) to account for the elements of dualism, cosmological speculation, etc.[72] If Mowinckel had recognized how early the essential elements of apocalyptic were present in Israel's literature,[73] we feel that he would not have turned to Chaldean sources, but—in a manner more consistent with his overall reconstruction—would have recognized in these features of late prophecy and apocalyptic evidence of the influence of the mythic tradition of the royal cult of Jerusalem upon the closing chapter of the prophetic movement.[74]

Among the scholars that pursue a line similar to Mowinckel's is Aage Bentzen.[75] In a clearer manner than Mowinckel he draws attention to the royal cult in Jerusalem as the carrier of mythical motifs which were absorbed by apocalyptic. Also, on the basis of the Ugaritic corpus, he looks to Canaanite religion for the original source of many themes and concepts of apocalyptic (e.g. the *ab šnm* of Daniel 7).[76]

Recently the new approach to apocalyptic which we have seen developing has been given a higher degree of precision by F. M. Cross who has affirmed the ancient (especially Northwest Semitic) mythic source of the "new" elements in the apocalyptic literature and then gone on to demonstrate how the royal cult in Jerusalem was the institution which absorbed these elements into the religion of Israel, thus becoming the mediator through which they reached the late prophets and apocalyptic seers.[77]

Complementing this new approach and neglected only with great risk to a balanced understanding of apocalyptic is a theme which has persisted among some writers throughout the study of the subject, namely, the roots of apocalyptic in Old Testament prophecy. This theme was reiterated very clearly by H. H. Rowley,[78] and receives attention in D. S. Russell's study as well.[79] In our consideration of recent works in English, S. B. Frost's treatment of the subject should receive comment.[80] Frost traces apocalyptic back to Old Testament roots, leaving room, however, for Iranian influence to account for such elements as its dualism.[81] In a subsequent article Frost describes apocalyptic as the result of a blending of eschatology (an indigenous Israelite phenomenon of pre-exilic prophecy depicting Yahweh's fulfillment of the historical process) and myth (a foreign element providing the rationale for the status quo), although he does not describe the manner in which the latter entered Yahwism.[82] We agree with Frost that the influx of mythical materials into prophetic eschatology is a major factor in the rise of apocalyptic, though more must be said about the role played by the sociological and historical circumstances which abetted this transformation and about the source of that recrudescent myth. In describing pre-exilic eschatology, however, Frost narrows his definition too severely when he excludes the expectation of Yahweh's fulfilling acts within the events of history. Rather than argue as Frost does that Isa. 29:1–9 is not eschatological whereas Isa. 2:10–14 is, we would recognize the same basic eschatological vision of Yahweh's final decisive action underlying both, with the difference being in the degree to which that vision was translated into historical categories, Isa. 2:10–14 being left largely on the cosmic level, 29:1–9 being related intimately to historical events.

As we will have occasion to mention again, one of the most promising facets of Gunkel's program which has been neglected in subsequent research is his investigation of the sociological conditions within which apocalyptic was born. One important study which appeared in 1959 is a notable exception, that of Otto Plöger.[83] In inquiring what type of developments within post-exilic Judaism could account for the borrowing of the Persian elements which he recognizes in a book like Daniel, Plöger recognizes a sharp division between theocratic and eschatological elements within the community. It is from the latter that the ḥasidim emerged and from the ḥasidim came the writer of Daniel. The most valuable aspect of Plöger's work is found in his attempt to move back from the second century to the roots of apocalyptic. But his results are finally forced and unconvincing, as seen in his critical fourth chapter which deals with Isaiah 24–27, Zechariah 12–14 and Joel. The main thrust of the book is aimed at getting the parties concerned down to the second century, when the important foreign elements can be brought into the religion of Israel which will finally explain the rise of apocalyptic. The result is that all of his pre-Daniel passages are dated much too late, with the further consequence that his entire reconstruction of the rise of apocalyptic is grossly inaccurate. Plöger's method of inquiry will bear fruit only when scholarship frees itself from its infatuation with Zoroastrianism and turns greater attention to the wealth of mythic material which came down to the apocalyptists from channels running deep within the religion of Israel, channels tracing ultimately to Canaanite sources of the Late Bronze Age, and not to Iranian sources of the third and second centuries B.C.

Another weakness of Plöger's study, the tendency to divide too neatly between parties within post-exilic Judaism, is found in exacerbated form in a work appearing the following year by D. Rössler.[84] Though some of his observations regarding the contrasting views toward law and history held by apocalyptic and rabbinic writers are valid, by and large his rigid separation does not withstand the test of historical investigation. Moreover, a grave methodological flaw is found in his method of comparison: his rabbinical material derives from a period several centuries later than the apocalyptic writings with which comparison is made![85]

We shall conclude this discussion of past research by referring to two avenues of inquiry which we regard as counterproductive. Since the first has been discussed above, it can be mentioned with brevity, it being the lingering preoccupation with Persia as the primary source of the "new" element which gave rise to apocalyptic. In the conclusion to his book, J. Schmidt refers to one of the certainties established by apocalyptic research, namely, the very strong influence which Persian concepts had on apocalyptic literature. Rather than enter into a polemic against the Persian theory of apocalyptic's origin, we refer to the decisive refutation of this theory by an Iranian specialist, R. N. Frye.[86] The Persian theory grew on the basis of an inaccurate and in large part imaginary reconstruction of the Persian material, which material was characterized by sufficient ambivalences and historical problems to allow it to become a complete explanation for every problem raised by Jewish apocalyptic.

A second avenue of inquiry which we should regard as counterproductive is not so ubiquitous in the literature as the above, although it is not absent even in the early stages of the study of apocalyptic:[87] the attempt to explain apocalyptic as a late, decadent outgrowth from wisdom. The latest major protagonist of this view is G. von Rad, who denies strenuously that the apocalyptists follow in any way in the tradition of the prophets.[88] That wisdom was drawn into apocalyptic and given a prominent position within that literature cannot be denied. That wisdom, however, accounts for the origin and circumscribes the essence of apocalyptic is an untenable hypothesis. K. Koch sees von Rad's extreme position against the background of the latter's view that Israel's *Heilsgeschichte* ends with Ezra.[89] Basically, von Rad's position remains the prophetic connection theory of nineteenth-century German scholarship. The post-exilic period is a dark age to be vaulted over as one moves from the outpouring of the Spirit in the prophets to the renewal of the Spirit in Christianity.

II. SUGGESTIONS FOR THE RESTUDY OF JEWISH APOCALYPTIC

Although our dialogue with past scholarship on apocalyptic gives hints of movement toward a new perspective, current essays indicate that that new perspective is still clouded by disagreements on matters as basic as definitions and as comprehensive as the origins and significance of this literature. The safest course suggested by this situation would be to describe objectively current alternative interpretations; we choose another course, however, that of taking clues from the best insights of past scholarship in an attempt to move toward the new perspective from which the restudy of our subject can be undertaken, at the same time spelling out the methodological implications of that perspective.

Past scholarship has secured certain results which provide a reliable foundation upon which new studies can base themselves. Already earlier literary critics progressed a long way toward clarifying the literary structure of the apocalyptic writings, and textual studies like those of Charles, though now in need of updating on the basis of new evidence, set that aspect of the study on a secure footing. Likewise those same older critics cast much light on the historical backgrounds of many apocalyptic compositions. And who can belittle the contributions of Gunkel and his followers, opening as they did a whole new dimension in pointing to the pre-literary history of traditional material embedded in the apocalyptic books, in embarking on the task of tracing the history of genres from the prophets down to the apocalyptists, and in inquiring into the sociological setting of the various writings. Moreover, the errors of past scholars serve warning of the pitfalls which await the unwary pilgrim in the fascinating field of apocalyptic.

1. TEXTUAL AND LITERARY CRITICISM

As Gunkel maintained in introducing his new method for the study of apocalyptic, the literary critical and form-critical approaches are not mutually exclusive; rather, the critic must discern when the nature of the material calls for application of the one, when for the other.[90] Besides making every possible effort to base itself on a thorough investigation of the text, any new study of apocalyptic must carefully take into consideration the question of literary criticism, questions of separate sources which have been combined in the present redaction and of interpolations, the problem of authors, date of composition, and allusions to historical events. Whereas the applicability of literary critical methods may be disputed by some in earlier biblical writings on the basis of the hypothesis that the entire tradition history of the material was oral, this caveat does not apply to the apocalyptic writings, which without exception betray a literary character.

At the same time, the history of literary criticism in the area of apocalyptic literature is replete with errors, including the division of sources often to the point of absurdity, and the eager, often whimsical connection of compositions to historical events on the basis of alleged historical allusions. Especially in a literature which professes to be esoteric in nature, which is replete with mythopoeic and thus by nature supermundane material, and which embodies traditional stock from diverse periods, connections may be drawn to historical events only with utmost caution.

2. FORM-CRITICAL INVESTIGATION: THE ANALYSIS OF GENRES AND OF THE HISTORY OF TRANSMISSION

Only when every component unit of an apocalyptic work is carefully analyzed with regard to its genre can one begin to move toward an analysis of the work as a whole. Of the many tasks urgently in need of attention in the area of apocalyptic, the thorough form critical analysis of this entire class of material must be given top priority. Many continuities are visible between classical Hebrew genres and those found in apocalyptic; most characteristic, however, are genres which have developed beyond the classical forms, many by way of fusing what were separate types into hybrid forms. This level of investigation is of critical importance *vis-à-vis* many of the perplexing problems remaining in the realm of apocalyptic research; for example, the problem of the relation between prophetic and wisdom traditions in this literature cannot be addressed apart from a thorough form critical analysis.

Such analysis of form will open the door to another area which has been neglected in the literature to the detriment of our understanding of the subject, the area of the sociological matrix within which apocalyptic arose. We hesitate to use the designation *Sitz im Leben* for this inquiry, since the original scope of Gunkel's *Sitz im Volksleben Israels* has been narrowed and weakened in nearly all scholarship since his time; whereas Gunkel could speak of dealing, in the question of the *Sitz im Leben,* with the movements of the masses,[91] the term has come to apply almost exclusively to the *cultic* setting of Israel's genres. Such a narrowing of the concept is illegitimate especially in the investigation of apocalyptic where the typical setting is not related to a cultic place but is intertwined with movements among the masses. We must broaden the scope of form-critical research so as to investigate this broader setting, thereby uncovering the tensions both within the community and from the outside which transformed old genres into new and produced new modes of expressing traditional beliefs. Investigation of the settings which are discernible behind the genres will lead to a deeper understanding of the conditions which gave rise to this literature. For example, the ubiquitous elements of polemic will shed light on the nature of the struggle from which apocalyptic arose and developed. Application of insights from sociology, and even cautious application of modern analogies, promise to make more intelligible the background and thus the essential nature of apocalyptic.

Although the history of the genres in apocalyptic usually does not span so large a segment of time as much of the earlier biblical material, the problems raised by the history of transmission must not be neglected. In those cases where units have passed restlessly from one form and setting to another, each stage of transmission must be investigated and, insofar as possible, reconstructed.

3. HISTORY OF RELIGIONS

Gunkel's methodology, concerned as it was with the search for the pre-literary history of traditional material embedded in apocalyptic compositions, and combined as it was with the excitement over recent archaeological discoveries of other ancient Near Eastern religious literatures, led to an animated search for the antecedents of the "new" elements in apocalyptic. The new enthusiasm brought with it many reckless conclusions based on a parallelomania which increased the persuasiveness of its argument in proportion to the ambivalence of its comparative material. The corrective must come not by giving up the search for antecedents, but by a more controlled method of comparison. No longer is it sufficient to isolate feature y in Jewish apocalyptic, compare it to feature x in a foreign religion—be it Iranian, Canaanite, Babylonian, or Egyptian—and on the basis of similarities draw the conclusion that y derives from x. We are not concerned primarily with the objection already raised by some scholars that the direction of influence may be the reverse, since the validity of this objection is obvious. Our concern is more basic, and seeks to eliminate conclusions based on fortuitous resemblances. As in the realm of comparative linguistics, a relation between x and y can be maintained only if one can demonstrate the path along which x passed to y. In connection with the most basic mythopoeic concepts of apocalyptic, such a path has not been traced from Zoroastrianism to apocalyptic, or from Egyptian religion to apocalyptic. We believe, however, that such a path *can* be traced along its various stages from the ancient sources (especially Canaanite) whence mythic materials were absorbed into Yahwism early in Israel's history, which path is then discernible running through the early hymnic compositions of the league, on through the literature of the royal cult, finally reaching late prophecy and early apocalyptic in the sixth and fifth centuries. This more controlled use of the comparative method we feel will reveal the source of the essential components of apocalyptic much closer to the native traditions of Israel than suggested in the past by scholars hastily turning to foreign literatures.

Current discussion on the subject of apocalyptic raises the specter of a new and equally dangerous parallelomania which must be cautioned against, one arising from the popularity of the subject in contemporary literature. Modern analogy can in fact throw light on the stages of the development of apocalyptic thought, inasmuch as certain basic sociological conditions lie at the base of all apocalyptic movements. But the peculiarity of Jewish apocalyptic, in contrast to contemporary modes of apocalyptic, must not be obscured: it did not involve flight into a purely subjective consciousness, but harked back to a well-defined cosmology.

4. TYPOLOGY

In studying Jewish apocalyptic, we are not studying a timeless phenomenon which could be analyzed like a piece of granite to determine its component parts, or a phenomenon circumscribed by one historical period.[92] We are dealing rather with a development over a period of several centuries, and thus the method of approaching this literature must not be static, but must have built into it a means of tracing that development. The method must also be fashioned so as to be applicable to another peculiarity of this material: whereas a small amount of it can be secured to historical pegs (e.g. Daniel), most of it eludes dating on the basis of historical allusions (most of the alleged "historical" references of the older literary critics are imaginary);[93] indeed, some of the most important compositions, from the point of view of understanding apocalyptic, fall into the latter category. Must this material be disregarded in a new reconstruction of the development of apocalyptic, inasmuch as the older "historical" allusions in large part prove untenable, or is there another method which will open up this otherwise undatable material for utilization in this task? Progress within the realm of typological investigation of this material allows us to answer affirmatively the latter question.

Typological study of the material should take place simultaneously on several levels, including prosody, literary types, concepts, and sociological setting; in this way each level of inquiry acts as a check on the results of the others.

The development of a typology of prosody is in its infant stages. It is now possible to identify genuinely archaic Hebrew poetry on the basis of poetic canons isolated in the Ugaritic literature and found in a very pure form in early Yahwistic poetry.[94] Then follows a period of several centuries where innovations are found alongside lingering archaic features, a period, however, which remains in need of thorough, systematic study. The sixth century is a crucial one in the development of prosody as in each of the other typologies. It was a period of tremendous disruption, when new forces came to bear on all structures, from the political and social realm to the realm of literary forms. The fields of pottery chronology and palaeography indicate that during periods of stress forms tend to develop with greater rapidity than in stable periods, when development occurs at a slower pace. It is in periods of such rapid change that the resulting typology allows one to date within narrower time limits than during periods of stability. To be sure, great caution must be exercised, inasmuch as absolute chronology may relate to relative chronology differently in different localities, and even within different parties or schools of tradition. The sixth-century corpus of prophetic material in Isaiah 56–66 is thus of immense value, being of such homogeneity of form, theme, and sociological background that it gives the critic an opportunity to follow the development of prosody within one "school" relatively free from outside contamination. On the basis of this corpus, a prosodic development can be followed from a very archaizing imitation of early Hebrew canons to a new, baroque prosody which already points to the complete collapse of poetry into prose narrative.[95]

The value of such typological investigation of prosody in the study of the development of apocalyptic is obvious. Unfortunately it can be applied only within bodies of literature where the homogeneity of origin found in Isaiah 56–66 is manifested, and where the prosody is genuinely in a state of development and not in a period of mere imitation of various earlier models. The latter becomes increasingly the mark of late apocalyptic poetry (and of course much late apocalyptic has lapsed into pure prose); hence the usefulness of prosodic analysis diminishes as one moves into the later material.

The value of the typological study of genres (*Gattungsgeschichte*) has been recognized since Gunkel's time. Within the realm of apocalyptic, however, this study has fallen far behind the analysis which has been directed toward pre-exilic material. The new study of Jewish apocalyptic will demand a unit-by-unit form critical study of all apocalyptic works which will seek, in addition to the usual form critical purposes mentioned above, to develop a typology of genres in this late material. A precursory study of the material indicates that this literature is characterized by an increasing preponderance of hybrid genres, fusing the purer types of earlier periods into mixed forms. Typological study on this level promises also to cast much new light on the origin and nature of Jewish apocalyptic.

Always at the center of the discussion about apocalyptic has been the problem of the development of concepts, and, whether individual critics were aware of the fact or not, much of their interpretation was guided by this consideration. Though much abused as a tool when guided by philosophical theories like Hegelianism, new efforts at grasping the meaning of apocalyptic cannot afford to ignore the fact that concepts do develop in time. Caution must be exercised, however, not to overlook the complexity of this development, for of all the typologies involved in this study, the typology of concepts is the most intricate. The investigation on this level must be rigorously historical, and free from a philosophical or dogmatic notion of the goal toward which the "universal spirit" is guiding the development of ideas, whether that goal be German Idealism, normative rabbinic Judaism, or orthodox Christianity. Moreover, not too much can be demanded of this level of inquiry, especially when it comes to detailed dating. The typology of concepts will never be amenable to distinguishing between years or even decades; the unit of measurement will most commonly be the century, except in periods of unusually rapid development.

The usefulness of the typology of concepts will generally be restricted to major ideas which span centuries in their importance. For example, the tension between mythopoeic and historical views of divine action in the history of Israel's religion promises to supply proto-apocalyptic and apocalyptic works with relative dates. To the warning mentioned above two more may be added: those concepts which are most likely to have universal validity among all segments of a nation (not being restricted to particular sects or having vastly different meanings among different parties) will be most free from hazards, i.e. concepts which are a part of the world-view of an entire people. Where ideas are used which have meaning only within a particular segment of a population, utmost care must be exercised to utilize comparative material stemming only from that segment, and conclusions drawn must not then be applied to the rest of the nation. Where deep divisions fragment a community, ideas may develop at different rates on the various sides of those divisions.

We introduce a fourth typological tool, the sociological setting visible behind the material. Some of the most penetrating analyses of the phenomenon of apocalyptic have come from modern sociologists.[96] Rather clearly definable sociological circumstances have given rise to apocalyptic movements throughout history, ancient and modern. In conjunction with form-critical conclusions concerning the community setting of individual compositions, these sociological analyses aid one in recognizing the significance of socio-political conditions reflected by apocalyptic compositions and in reconstructing the essential features of the matrix within which apocalyptic originated and developed.

As a conceptual aid toward perceiving the significance of the socio-political dimension in the rise of apocalyptic we favor a study of the polarity, manifested throughout the history of the post-exilic community, between a realistic or pragmatic view of reality and a visionary view. Involved are two different perceptions of divine action, the realist identifying divine activity with historical institutions and events, the visionary looking for cosmic events which break into the mundane order with destructive power unseating the powerful and exalting the weak. The visionary view tends to be carried by members of the community who are of low station or are disenfranchised from the community structures, individuals awaiting fulfillment of delayed divine promises which will establish them in positions of power which the existing order had denied them; the pragmatic view is espoused by the religious and civil community leaders, those both charged with the day-to-day supervision of the institutional structures and having a vested interest in their perpetuation. Jewish literature throughout its history is characterized by the tension between these two perceptions of reality, and the apocalyptic works down to the medieval period can be studied in relation to this polarity.[97] By tracing the history of this polarity it becomes possible to define the relation of certain apocalyptic compositions to the social forces operative within the community, and to begin to reconstruct the broad lines of a typology ranging from sixth-century proto-apocalyptic to the full-blown apocalyptic of succeeding centuries.

The advantages of this approach to the problem of the sociological matrix of apocalyptic over that of Plöger and Rössler are significant. In tying the development of apocalyptic to actual parties within the Jewish community their approach proves untenable on two accounts. First, no Jewish party maintained a static position throughout its history. To take one example, in the sixth and fifth centuries early apocalyptic compositions arose within a visionary group comprising a mixture of prophetic and Levitical elements which was opposed by a Zadokite-dominated priesthood, the latter being in firm control of the Jerusalem temple cult. In the second century the Zadokite party's fortunes were reversed, for they found themselves excluded from the temple cult by the Hasmonaeans and taking refuge instead with the apocalyptically oriented community at Qumran. Apocalyptic writings thus are not the monopoly of one party throughout the history of Judaism, and the common denominator which ties together the various groups producing apocalyptic writings must be defined in terms other than rival parties. Secondly, no group at any time in Jewish history is purely apocalyptic, nor is any totally legalistic in orientation. This dichotomy promulgated especially by Rössler is artificial, the rabbinical writings being devoid of apocalyptic notions no more than the apocalyptic writings are bereft of devotion to the Torah.

For these reasons we adopt a conceptual framework lacking the clear lines of that used by Plöger and Rössler, but remaining more sensitive to the complexities of historical realities: within the post-exilic community we discern two basic perceptions of reality, one realistic and pragmatic, the other visionary. While no party is ever characterized purely by one of these perceptions, under definable sociological circumstances certain segments of the population are dominated by one or the other. Especially in periods of crisis and internecine struggle the community becomes polarized, with the visionary and realistic perceptions being adopted by rival groups (e.g. the end of the sixth century and the first half of the second century B.C.). These are periods of apocalyptic fervor and proliferation. In other periods the visionary and realistic tendencies are held together within the community, and apocalyptic activity is at a low level, the writings of such times typically bringing together elements of both perceptions into a balance (e.g. the period of the Chronicler).

The method which we have outlined above for the restudy of the Jewish apocalyptic literature can be designated "contextual-typological analysis," inasmuch as it utilizes the tools of form criticism to interpret a composition within its historical and sociological context, and adds to this the tools of typological analysis to explain the development of a literature which, while eluding a direct method of dating, is developing on several levels which can be analyzed with significant results. Yet there is no denying that typological analysis is fraught with hazards. When abused it can lead to a viciously circular kind of argument. But here one must distinguish between circular argument and cumulative argument, for it is the latter which characterizes the method here being outlined. Conclusions are drawn only when the material has been investigated from the several perspectives defined above, and of course conclusions must be regarded as tentative in proportion to the degree of certainty or uncertainty which this multi-faceted investigation yields in a given case. As the investigation is carried on, adjustments will be made repeatedly in detail as well as in the overall reconstruction on the basis of new evidence. And mistakes will be made, but hopefully mistakes which are fewer and less serious than those issuing from studies dominated by a dogmatic or philosophical view of religious history, or from investigations guided by intuition unchecked by a critical methodology.

NOTES

1. For two reasons especially this essay seems an appropriate form of paying tribute to my beloved teacher and friend, Professor Wright. It was due to his well-known pedagogical ability to introduce his students to new frontiers that I was first brought into contact with the riddle of apocalyptic. Moreover, Professor Wright's lifelong in-

terest in biblical theology will be served by the restudy of Jewish apocalyptic, for the biblical theologian is able to move authentically between the Testaments not by vaulting over the labyrinth of apocalyptic, but by attempting to pass through the intertestamental literature as a pilgrim seeking understanding, in the knowledge that not the pre-exilic prophets alone, but those prophets in concert with their post-exilic successors represent the *praeparatio* for the new acts of God which unfold in the New Testament.

2. K. Koch, *Ratlos vor der Apokalyptik* (Gütersloh, 1970), now translated under the title *The Rediscovery of Apocalyptic,* Studies in Biblical Theology 22 (London, 1972).

3. F. Lücke, *Commentar über die Schriften des Evangelisten Johs.* IV. Theil, 1. Band, *Versuch einer vollständigen Einleitung in die Offenbarung Johannis und in die gesammte apokalyptische Literatur,* 1832.

4. Ibid., p. 25.   5. Ibid., pp. 33 f.

6. E. Reuss, "Johannes Apokalypse," in J. S. Ersch und J. G. Gruber, *Allgemeine Enzyklopädie der Wissenschaften und Künste,* II/27 (1850), 79–94.

7. A. Hilgenfeld, *Die jüdische Apokalyptik in ihrer geschichtlichen Entwicklung* (Jena, 1857).

8. Ibid., p. 8.

9. See J. Schmidt, *Die jüdische Apokalyptik* (Neukirchen, 1969), p. 142, who points to Hilgenfeld's frequent use of terms like *natürliche Entwicklung, sukzessive Fortbildung,* and *stetiger Fortschritt.*

10. J. Wellhausen, *Prolegomena to the History of Ancient Israel* (New York, 1957 [originally published in German in 1878]), pp. 422–425.

11. This notion is referred to in the literature as the *Profeten-Anschluss-Theorie,* "prophetic connection theory."

12. E.g. C. H. Toy, *Judaism and Christianity* (Boston, 1890) and T. K. Cheyne, *Jewish Religious Life after the Exile* (New York, 1898).

13. The monumental contribution of R. H. Charles to the study of the Apocrypha and Pseudepigrapha through the collecting and editing of the manuscripts available at his time needs no discussion; it remains the basis for the study of the field [N 20]. Regarding his interpretation of apocalyptic, the most concise study is found in his *Eschatology: The Doctrine of a Future Life in Israel, Judaism and Christianity* (New York, 1963 [first printed in 1899]).

14. Ibid., pp. 86, 130.   15. Ibid., pp. 101, 123 f.   16. Ibid., pp. 123 f.

17. Ibid., p. 200.

18. Ibid., p. 133. On p. 139 Charles formulates a principle which has been overlooked in the study of apocalyptic to the detriment of the field: regarding the theory of a direct borrowing from Zoroastrianism he argues that "in the case of any religion such a method of explanation is mechanical, and only to be admitted when it is clearly proved that the elements for an internal and organic development were wanting." On this basis he finds elements derived from Zoroastrianism to be few and late.

19. Ibid., pp. 193–195. On p. 195 we read: "I have emphasized the original and fundamental identity of apocalyptic and legalistic Pharisaism in respect to devotion to the Law, because Jewish scholars in the past, and to a great extent in the present, have denied to apocalyptic its place in the faith of pre-Christian orthodox Judaism."

20. Ibid., p. 193. Statements like the above strike a familiar chord for the reader familiar with E. Käsemann's dictum that "apocalyptic . . . was the mother of all Christian theology": "The Beginnings of Christian Theology," *JTC* 6 (1969), 40. Or again, "Thus apocalyptic Pharisaism became, speaking historically, the parent of Christianity . . ." (Charles, *Eschatology* [N 13], p. 196). Repeatedly Charles emphasizes that the apocalyptists were more than epigones; in his introductory remarks to the Book of Enoch he writes: "Some of its authors—and there were many—belonged to the true succession of the prophets, and it was simply owing to the evil character of the period, in which their lot was cast, that these enthusiasts and mystics, exhibiting on occasions

the inspiration of the O.T. prophets, were obliged to issue their works under the aegis of some ancient name" (*The Apocrypha and Pseudepigrapha of the Old Testament*, ed. Charles, II [Oxford, 1913], 163).

21. Charles, *Eschatology* [N 13], p. 183.

22. Ibid., pp. 363–364.   23. Ibid., pp. 387–390.

24. L. Noack, *Ker Ursprung des Christenthums* (Leipzig, 1857); A. Dillmann, *Das Buch Henoch übersetzt und erklärt* (Leipzig, 1851); G. Hölscher, *Die Entstehung des Danielbuchs,* Theologische Studien und Kritiken, 92, 1919. This manner of dismissing the prophetic and theological value of apocalyptic has been taken up anew by G. von Rad, *OTT,* II, 303 f.

25. G. F. Moore, *Judaism,* I (Cambridge, 1927), 125.   26. Ibid., 127.

27. Moore, *Judaism,* II (1927), 346, 352. Moore follows the ancient dictum of Akiba in regarding the apocalyptic writings as among the "outside books," and thus he virtually disregards them; see ibid., II, 281.

28. In terms of the structure of Moore's two-volume work, this means that the apocalyptic writings enter the discussion only at the very end of the second volume (Part VII, "The Hereafter").

29. Moore, *Judaism,* II, 323.

30. ". . . die Apokalypse will Wahrheit geben; sie kann daher nicht zu einem grossen Teile Schöpfungen der Phantasie ihres Verfassers enthalten" (H. Gunkel, *Schöpfung und Chaos in Urzeit und Endzeit* [Göttingen, 1895] p. 253).

31. E.g. Gunkel seeks to demonstrate point for point how features in Revelation defy explanation until brought into relation with Babylonian myth (*Schöpfung,* pp. 257–272).

32. Gunkel contrasts his traditio-historical theory of the origin of the apocalyptic writings with the "great creative composer" theory of the literary critics: "Ganz andersartig aber sind Schriften, die im wesentlichen Codificationen einer Tradition darstellen; der eigentliche Urheber des in ihnen niedergelegten Stoffes ist nicht der Schriftsteller, sondern eine ganze Reihe von Geschlechtern; und der Stoff setzt in der Form, in der er gegenwärtig existiert, eine vielleicht jahrhundertjährige Geschichte voraus, in der auch mündliche Tradition eine Rolle spielen mag" (*Schöpfung,* p. 208).

33. Nowhere in the biblical material or in the pseudepigrapha does Gunkel argue for direct borrowing from Babylonian sources. Rather the Babylonian material had been mediated for centuries through Israelite tradition before reaching the writers of e.g. Genesis 1, Revelation 12, or IV Ezra 14 (Gunkel, *Schöpfung,* pp. 146–149).

34. Gunkel felt that his study established the fact "dass die traditions-geschichtliche Erklärung berufen ist, die zeitgeschichtliche in Zukunft zu ersetzen" (*Schöpfung,* p. 233).

35. Gunkel, *Schöpfung,* pp. 212–217. See a discussion of the misguided application of the historicizing method to one early apocalyptic composition in P. D. Hanson, "Zechariah 9 and the Recapitulation of an Ancient Ritual Pattern," *JBL* 92 (1973), 37–59.

36. Gunkel, *Schöpfung,* p. 220. To these two points may be added a third: "'Zeitgeschichtliche' Erklärung aber ist nur da berechtigt, wo es sich um ein von dem Schriftsteller frei componiertes oder wenigstens umgearbeitetes Material handelt" (*Schöpfung,* p. 209).

37. See e.g. Gunkel's explanation of the sociological setting of Ps. 74:12–19 on pp. 42 f. and of Revelation on pp. 302 ff. of *Schöpfung.*

38. E.g. Gunkel, *Schöpfung,* p. 397. On this point, see J. Schmidt [N 9], p. 197.

39. Gunkel, *Schöpfung,* pp. 41 ff., 112–114, 328, 379 ff. Cf. J. Jeremias, *Theophanie* (Neukirchen, 1965), pp. 92–94.

40. T. Jacobsen, "The Battle between Marduk and Tiamat," *JAOS* 88 (1968), 104–108.

41. A conclusion opposite that of Gunkel seems to be true; the storm god language of these allusions points to the Mediterranean coast (Jacobsen [N 40], 107 f.).

42. Gunkel, *Schöpfung*, p. 385.

43. W. Bousset already recognized this vulnerability in Gunkel's method when he noted that it is false to assume that in each case where the *zeitgeschichtliche* Method did not bring clear results, the traditio-historical method could. There were cases where *neither* method could lead to assured solutions, and questions would have to be left open: Bousset, *Der Antichrist in der Überlieferung des Judentums, des neuen Testaments und der alten Kirche* (Göttingen, 1895), p. 7. Gunkel would have avoided some enormous errors had he recognized this limitation to his method in cases like Revelation 12.

44. Gunkel, *Schöpfung*, pp. 87 and 371.   45. Ibid., pp. 131, 157–158.

46. W. Klatt, *Hermann Gunkel*, Forschungen zur Religion und Literatur des Alten und Neuen Testaments 100 (Göttingen, 1969), 36 ff.; and *idem*, "Ein Brief von Hermann Gunkel . . . ," *ZTK* 66 (1969), 4.

47. Occasionally he also referred to Persian and Old Testament influence, e.g. Gunkel, *Schöpfung*, 290 ff.

48. Cf. E. Bölken, *Die Verwandschaft der jüdisch-christlichen mit der persischen Eschatologie* (Göttingen, 1902).

49. R. Reitzenstein, *Das iranische Erlösungsmysterium* (Bonn, 1921).

50. R. Otto, *The Kingdom of God and the Son of Man* (London, 1938 [originally published in German in 1934]); H. S. Nyberg, *Die Religionen des alten Iran* (Osnabrueck, 1938 [originally published in Swedish in 1937]); A. Bertholet, *Daniel und die griechische Gefahr*, Religionsgeschichtliche Volksbücher, II/17 (Tübingen, 1907); E. Meyer, *Ursprung und Anfänge des Christentums*, II (Stuttgart, 1921); W. Bousset, *Die Religion des Judentums im späthellenistischen Zeitalter*, Handbuch zum Neuen Testament, 21 (Tübingen, 1926).

51. A. von Gall, *Basileia tou Theou, eine religionsgeschichtliche Studie zur vorkirchlichen Eschatologie* (Heidelberg, 1926), p. ix. What von Gall could not derive from Persia he sought to find in Egyptian religion (p. 265).

52. H. Gressmann, *Der Ursprung der israelitisch-jüdischen Eschatologie* (Göttingen, 1905).

53. Only with greatest caution does Gressmann refer to specific foreign sources, and then characteristically in footnotes (e.g. ibid., pp. 247, 291).

54. Ibid., p. 5.   55. Ibid., pp. 174–192.   56. Ibid., p. 245.   57. Ibid., pp. 247f.

58. Cf. S. H. Hooke's essay, "The Myth and Ritual Pattern in Jewish and Christian Apocalyptic," in *The Labyrinth* (London, 1935).

59. I. Engnell, *Studies in Divine Kingship in the Ancient Near East* (Uppsala, 1943).

60. Cf. S. Mowinckel, *He that Cometh* (New York, 1955 [originally published in Norwegian in 1951]), p 25.

61. See esp. S. Mowinckel, *Psalmenstudien*, I–VI (Amsterdam, 1966 [originally published in 1921 ff.]), and *The Psalms in Israel's Worship*, I–II (New York, 1962).

62. Mowinckel, *He that Cometh* [N 60], pp. 102–137, *inter alia*.

63. While Mowinckel, ibid., often goes beyond the evidence in his reconstruction (especially in describing the details of the Enthronement Festival) the general lines of his description of the royal Jerusalem cult and the ritual pattern upon which it was based remain, in the mind of this writer, convincing.

64. Note, however, that Mowinckel, ibid., does not use the terms "prophetic eschatology" and "apocalyptic eschatology" in the sense in which we apply them.

65. Ibid., p. 56.   66. Ibid., pp. 102–124.   67. Ibid., pp. 139–144, 263.

68. Ibid., pp. 126–133, 155, 158.   69. Ibid., p. 133.

70. See S. B. Frost, "Eschatology and Myth," *VT* 2 (1952), 76–79; H. W. Wolff,

Hosea, Bibel und Kirche, 14/1 (Neukirchen, 1965²), 78 f., and H. D. Preuss, *Jahweglaube und Zukunftserwartung* (Stuttgart, 1968), pp. 205–214; Preuss writes: "Eschatologie ist damit innerhalb des Alten Testaments weder ein Fremdkörper noch eine Entstellung des Jahweglaubens noch ein Spätling, noch ist ihre Entstehung nur durch fremde Einflüsse zu erklären, sondern der Jahweglaube selber ist der Wurzelgrund der Eschatologie, da er durch den Charakter seines Gottes und dessen Offenbarung in Wort und Geschichte, in Verheissungen und weiterführenden Einlösungen, stets zukunftsbezogen gewesen und geblieben ist" (p. 208).

71. For a more complete description of this distinction see P. D. Hanson, "Jewish Apocalyptic against its Near Eastern Environment," *RB* 78 (1971), 35 f.

72. Mowinckel, *He that Cometh* [N 60], pp. 432 f.

73. All of the essential features of apocalyptic were present within native Jewish traditions by the beginning of the fourth century B.C.; cf. P. D. Hanson, "Old Testament Apocalyptic Reexamined," *Interpretation* 25 (1971), 468–473.

74. Also in discussing the apocalyptic figure of the "Son of Man" Mowinckel pursues foreign sources in a highly speculative fashion, which leads him to the conclusion that the Son of Man derives from the "oriental, cosmological, eschatological myth of Anthropos": [N 60], p. 425. Never does he supply solid primary evidence to support his theory, but he repeatedly quotes Bousset, Reitzenstein, Volz and Nyberg (e.g. in n. 2 on p. 422), all of them writers whose conclusions in the area of apocalyptic fail to stand in the face of new evidence. Mowinckel himself goes on to qualify his derivation theory almost to the point of refuting his own position; for example, he states, "Judaism, then, was unaware that the Son of Man was really the Primordial Man. . . . It is, therefore, not without justification that Sjöberg claims that the difference between the Primordial Man and the Son of Man is greater than the similarity" (p. 436). It is very doubtful whether even the starting point of Mowinckel's theory—the attempt to draw a distinction between two Messiahs, one earthly and the other transcendental—can be justified. Mowinckel himself must admit that in the Jewish sources the two types are fused. We believe that the tension between the earthly-national and the transcendental-cosmic emphases in Jewish reflection on the future deliverer is best explained in terms of a dialectic which characterized the entire history of post-exilic Judaism between a "pragmatic" view which recognized as the sphere of divine activity the historical order and a "visionary" view which regarded divine activity as occurring primarily on a cosmic plane. Circles which accentuated the "visionary" view tended to see the future deliverer in cosmic terms (e.g. Daniel 7; IV Ezra 13), while those who stressed the "pragmatic" view depicted him in earthly-national terms (Haggai-Zechariah, the Targums, the Psalms of Solomon, the Testaments of the Twelve Patriarchs). This is not to claim that two different sources were being drawn upon, one native, one foreign (*contra* Mowinckel); rather, two different perspectives from Israel's own past were stressed in varying degrees by different circles.

75. See esp. A. Bentzen's commentary *Daniel,* Handbuch zum Alten Testament, 19 (Tübingen, 1952) and *King and Messiah* (London, 1954 [first published in German in 1948]).

76. Bentzen, *Daniel,* 61 f.

77. F. M. Cross, "The Divine Warrior in Israel's Early Cult," *Biblical Motifs,* ed. A. Altmann (Cambridge, Mass., 1966), pp. 11–30. See also F. M. Cross, "New Directions in the Study of Apocalyptic," *JTC* 6 (1969), 157–165. For an attempted reconstruction of the development of apocalyptic out of its roots in ancient Near Eastern myth, as mediated by the royal cult and prophecy, see Hanson, *RB* 78 (1971), 31–58.

78. H. H. Rowley, *The Relevance of Apocalyptic* (London, 1944).

79. D. S. Russell, *The Method and Message of Jewish Apocalyptic* (Philadelphia, 1964).

80. S. B. Frost, *Old Testament Apocalyptic* (London, 1952).

81. Ibid., pp. 19 and 234.

82. Frost, "Eschatology" [N 70], pp. 70–80.

83. O. Plöger, *Theokratie und Eschatologie* (Neukirchen, 1959).

84. D. Rössler, *Gesetz und Geschichte, Untersuchungen zur Theologie der jüdischen Apokalyptik und der pharisäischen Orthodoxie* (Neukirchen, 1960).

85. See the criticism of Rössler's study in Koch, *The Rediscovery* [N 2], pp. 40–42.

86. R. N. Frye, "Reitzenstein and Qumrân Revisited by an Iranian," *HTR* 55 (1962), 261–268.

87. See N 24.

88. G. von Rad, *OTT*, II, 303 f.

89. Koch, *The Rediscovery* [N 2], p. 45.

90. Gunkel [N 30], pp. 207 f.

91. Gunkel, *Zum religionsgeschichtlichen Verständis des NT*, Forschungen zur Religion und Literatur des Alten und Neuen Testaments, 1 (Göttingen, 1910²), 12.

92. Many of the attempts by earlier scholars to understand the nature of apocalyptic have been misdirected because apocalyptic was treated as a phenomenon strictly contained within one period. Its nature was explained by searching for foreign parallels belonging to that period, such parallels being located within Zoroastrianism. This static approach blinded the researchers to roots reaching far back into Israel's own religious past, allowing them to deny in many cases any primary connections with the classical prophets, permitting them to denigrate apocalyptic as a degenerate play of the phantasy without intrinsic religious worth and without meaningful connections either to pre-exilic Yahwism or Christianity. See Hanson, "Jewish Apocalyptic" [N 71], 31–33.

93. Cf. Hanson, "Zechariah 9" [N 35].

94. Cf. Cross, "The Song of the Sea and Canaanite Myth," *JTC* 5 (1968), 1–25.

95. Cf. Hanson, "Studies in the Origins of Jewish Apocalyptic," (unpublished Ph.D. dissertation, Harvard University, 1969), pp. 92 f. *inter alia*.

96. See K. Mannheim, *Ideology and Utopia, an Introduction to the Sociology of Knowledge* (New York, 1936 [first published in German in 1929]); M. Weber, *The Sociology of Religion* (Boston, 1963 [first published in German in 1922]); E. Troeltsch, *The Social Teaching of the Christian Churches*, 2 vols. (New York, 1960 [first published in German in 1911]).

97. The tension which we are describing is not limited to Jewish religious literature, but is present in all ethical religions. A gauge to the health and vitality of a confessional community is the degree to which it is able to maintain this tension in a constructive balance, enriching its life in the real world with its vision of realities too vast to be comprehended by its institutions, and yet insisting with prophetic zeal that its vision find application in the real world. One example of this creative tension is seen in the dialectic between "essence" and "existence" in Paul Tillich's treatment of Christian theology in *Systematic Theology*, II (Chicago, 1957), 29–44.

22. Lists of Revealed Things
in the Apocalyptic Literature

MICHAEL E. STONE

THE HEBREW UNIVERSITY OF JERUSALEM

IN A NUMBER of places in the apocalyptic literature there occur lists between which a striking similarity may be observed. This relationship cannot be explained away on the basis of coincidence alone. A comparative examination of the lists in the light not only of details of content and language, but also of their function and place within the vision structure puts this relationship beyond doubt.

These lists might be characterized as catalogues of the subject matter of apocalyptic speculation. They form an integral part of the apocalyptic vision and, as will be shown in detail below, stand at the center of the revelatory experience. Among the subjects they comprehend are astronomy and meteorology, uranography and cosmology, the secrets of nature and Wisdom as well as other aspects of esoteric lore not easily classified in accepted categories.

I

One such list is to be found in II Baruch 59, presented as the contents of the revelation made to Moses on Sinai.[1] The chapter falls into two parts. The first, vss. 1–4, contains a general statement that, together with the revelation of the Torah, Moses received additional information about the end of days, eschatological reward, and the pattern and measurements of Zion. In these verses there may be observed a progression from general statement toward a list form. From a literary point of view this section moves from the full sentence form of vs. 2 to the three shorter phrases of vs. 4:

> Many admonitions together with the principles of the Law,
> And the consummation of times, as also to thee,

And likewise the pattern of Zion and its measure and
the pattern of which the sanctuary of the present
time was to be made.

In vs. 5 the list proper commences with its typical short one or two word
phrases:

the measures of fire,
the weight of the winds, . . .

This list contains twenty-nine phrases composed of nouns in a genitival
relationship.[2] It is important to observe that the statements in vs. 4, which do
not show the list form common to vss. 5–11, seem to represent a different
block of material. Except for one element (the "consummation of the ages,"
vs. 4; cf. vs. 8), the features mentioned are not found in the list 5–11. In this
context it should perhaps be observed that the reference to the "pattern of
Zion and its measures" and "the pattern of the Sanctuary" (vs. 4) seems to
reflect a continuing tradition having to do with the heavenly "model" of Zion
or Jerusalem.[3] To judge from the Qumran "Description de la Jérusalem Nouvelle" and from the material in II Baruch, this tradition dealt with speculations about the plan and dimensions of the heavenly city and temple. It
seems to be significant that this tradition is not included in the revealed
materials in 5–11, nor anywhere else in the lists. Indeed, this interest in
the "measures of Zion" seems curiously unstressed in the apocryphal and
Rabbinic literatures. This may also be an additional indication of the need
to separate the materials in vs. 4 from those in vss. 5–11.

The list in II Bar. 59:5–11 is formed therefore, of twenty-nine phrases
identical in their structure. After the point of juncture with vss. 1–4, i.e. after
the phrase "But then he showed him" (vs. 5a), no verb is to be found. Further, as will become evident below when the contents and scope of the lists
are analyzed, the phrases fall into groups characterized by their contents.

II

It is important to observe the context in which this list in II Bar. 59:5–11
is presented. It is given in the context of a historical recital, in an overall
view of human history. In the *Heilsgeschichte* which is contained in the
vision of the black and bright waters, when the revelation at Sinai is mentioned, the scope is extended in such a way as to include this formulaic list. In
this, incidentally, it is possible to see the heart of the difference between vss.
4 and 5–11. Verse 4 seems to contain those elements which could be associated with the giving of the Torah, vss. 5–11 add a list, formulaic in nature,
which has virtually nothing in common with vs. 4. It should be observed that
of the three elements related in vs. 4, two are clearly derived directly
from the Book of Exodus, "many admonitions together with the principles

of the Law" and "the pattern of Zion." The first stems, naturally, from the revelation at Sinai and the second from the Sanctuary material in Exodus. It is precisely the third element, also to be found as part of the Mosaic revelation in IV Ezra 14:4, which is common to vs. 4 and to the list in vss. 5–11. This derivation from Exodus, incidentally, does not make the existence of a speculative tradition of the Heavenly Jerusalem any less real; it merely indicates one of its points of origin.[4]

Lists of similar formulaic nature are found elsewhere. From many points of view the list in Baruch is close to a list found in II Enoch 23:1 (Vaillant [N 1], p. 27). Here the seer has been elevated to the highest heaven and placed before God. He is transformed into an angel by having his earthly garments removed and being annointed with the fragrant divine oil.[5] Then Enoch is ensconced as scribe, and, given the reed and book, records what the angel Vreveil, himself the Heavenly Scribe, reveals to him at divine command. The contents of this revelation include cosmology, meteorology, calendar, angelology, and the knowledge of the angelic songs. This lore he writes down during thirty days and thirty nights, recording it in 360 [366 *Vetus Latina (VL)*] books. This list, like that in II Baruch 59, is in the form of a catalogue of nouns and here, generally, in the same form of two nouns in genetival relationship. Thus, in vs. 2:

> les montées des nuages,
> et les sorties des vents, . . .

Similar lists, as the high points of apocalyptic revelations, are found elsewhere, although the basic literary form indicated here is sometimes expanded or varied.

Thus a further list may be observed in I Enoch 60:11 ff. This passage is assigned by Charles [N 22] to the Noachic section of Enoch. The text of chapter 60 is disjointed and unclear, and some disarrangement has entered into the text. Nonetheless the passage in which the list is situated is quite coherent. The revelation is a communication of what is hidden, of the heavenly secrets (60:11). Unfortunately the more general context of the list is not preserved, and it is impossible to clarify the broader functional role of this catalogue. Yet it remains quite clear that that list is the contents of the revelation to the seer, by an angel, of "what was hidden."

This list falls into two sections. The first, vss. 11–13, has the basic literary form of the two lists which have already been mentioned. But here, in many phrases, where two nouns occur in other lists, the first of them appears as a verb. Thus, for example:

II Bar. 59:5	the weight of the winds	I Enoch 60:12 how the winds are weighed,
II Enoch 23:2	the exits of the winds	and (how) the portals of the winds are reckoned.

STONE: *Revealed Things in Apocalyptic Literature*   417

Similar examples could be multiplied. Furthermore, this list places great emphasis on the regular or measured function of each of the elements. Its general bias is meteorological and astronomical, but cosmological interest is to be observed in vs. 11 which, in its general nature can well be compared with the opening of II Enoch 23. In both places the emphasis is on the knowledge of the secrets of the universe.

In I Enoch 60:14–22 we have what is evidently a reworking of a similar list, or even of the second part of the list lying behind vss. 11–13, or else an expansion of the list in vss. 11–13. In these verses a further series of meteorological phenomena is dealt with. These phenomena are described in a rather unique fashion consistently throughout these verses. Each is described in terms of the spirit, the guardian angel which regulates its conduct. It is enough here to note that the list in I Enoch 60: 11–13 (?+14–22) and the lists in II Baruch 59 and II Enoch 23 share a basically common scope, content, and context, although varying somewhat in form.

There is one further similar list in I Enoch 41:1–7 with which is perhaps to be associated 43:1–2. Here, as in chapter 60 we are dealing with what are, in contrast to II Baruch 59 and II Enoch 23, expanded formulae. Here, once more, we find the same emphasis on the regularity and proportionality of the natural phenomena. The list of natural and meteorological phenomena, found in I Enoch 41:3–7 and 43:1–2 is preceded in 41:1–2 by a revelation of "all the secrets of the heavens"—including primarily information on eschatological reward and punishment and their place. The material here revealed is called "secrets" and, as above, it fulfills the function of summarizing or epitomizing the revelation made to Enoch.

These two bodies of material in I Enoch are very similar to a second list in II Enoch 40:1–13. The context of this passage is Enoch's return to earth after his heavenly journeys (cf. ch. 38). Upon his return he opens a discourse to his children following in general a pattern of moral admonition similar to that placed in his mouth in the final section of I Enoch. To this body of moral teaching he prefaces a summary of all that he saw and recorded in heaven. This summary is again in the list form. It varies somewhat in the different recensions of the book, but its basic weight, like that of the material in I Enoch mentioned above, is toward the astronomical, calendarical, and meteorological. Here too, in vs. 12, we find the same reference to the final judgment as in I Enoch 41:1–2. From the literary viewpoint this list also represents the expanded type.

One other list is to be found in Pseudo-Philo, *Liber Antiquitatem Biblicarum (LAB)* in general parallel to that in II Baruch 59. The passage reads:

> *Tunc ostendit ei Dominus terram et omnia que in ea sunt et dixit: Haec est terra quam dabo populo meo. Et ostendit ei locum unde elevant nubes aquam, ad irrigandam omnem terram, et locum unde accipit fluvius irrigationem, et terram Egypti, et locum firmamenti unde bibit sola terra sancta. Et ostendit ei mensuras sanctuarii et numerum oblationum et signa in quibus incipient inspicere celum* (*LAB* 19:10).

This passage deals with the things revealed to Moses before his death, basing itself, of course, on Deut. 32:49, 34:1 ff. It contains, with the exception of the last sentence, items which can be construed mainly as an expansion of what Deuteronomy says was revealed to him (Deut. 34:1–3). As a separate sentence introduced by its own verb, we find certain matters relating to the Sanctuary. In particular the *mensuras sanctuarii* are found as in II Bar. 59:4. There they seem in place, since the revelation of the details of the Tabernacle are the context of the material there. Just why they appear in *LAB* is hard to tell, for by any reading of the biblical story, they were revealed to Moses well before his death. The same is true of *numerum oblationum*. In II Bar. 59:9, however, the phrase "number of the offerings" is completely cryptic, for it occurs in the list proper, in the context of the revelation of cosmological and other secrets. In *LAB* this term is transparent, and refers, presumably, to the sacrificial cult and its regulations. The broader meaning of the sentence in *LAB* is, as noted, rather difficult in context, for in the passage all is made basically subservient to the revelation to Moses of Deuteronomy 34.[6] Thus even cosmological elements such as *locum unde elevant nubes aquam* or *locum firmamenti* are clearly made to serve the main aim of the passage. Moses is not shown these various sights for any intrinsic interest they might have. They are part, without doubt, of the revelation to Moses of the Holy Land before his death. Thus they are complemented by the phrases *ad irrigandam omnem terram* and *unde bibit sola terra sancta.*

Together with the two elements connected with the Sanctuary, the final phrase *signa in quibus incipient inspicere celum,* which refers perhaps to some sort of astronomical or astrological knowledge, is equally curious. It is apparent, therefore, that this is a special formulation within the general list type with the elements in it subject to the general purpose and biblical origin of the passage. The repetition of *locum* at the start of each of the phrases is notable and it is found with one exception (*terram Egypti*) through the end of the revelation of the land. This technique is to be observed in other lists, such as "the secrets" in I Enoch 41:3 and "the chambers" in I Enoch 41:4–5, et al.

It is clear, therefore, that in the sources here adduced so far a common function can be observed for the lists. They all occur at the high point of a revelation, where a brief statement of its contents is desired, or else as a summary of what is revealed to the seer. It seems likely, therefore, that by examining in detail the information which the lists claim to have been revealed to the seers, a view can be reached of what the writers of the apocalypses thought to lie at the heart of apocalyptic revelation itself. Yet the formulaic nature of the lists raises the serious question whether they might not present pre-existing materials. Thus not only might the lists represent, as it were, a summary listing of the speculative concerns of the apocalyptic schools, but it is also possible that the pre-existing catalogues of subjects, if indeed the lists are such, played a role in determining just what those concerns would be. It is also alternatively possible that formulaic, traditional lists were included in the apocalyptic books without having more than partial overlap with the actual concerns of the apocalyptic authors.

III

Before approaching the complex of problems which has been raised in the preceding paragraph, there are certain further materials which must be brought into account. Elsewhere, the writer drew attention to the interesting materials to be found in IV Ezra 4:5-8 with which are associated 5:36 f.[7] These verses appear to show a clear relationship to the lists here being discussed, and in particular to II Baruch 59. The angel says to Ezra that he will ask him three questions and if he can answer them then he will reveal that which Ezra wishes to know. To this Ezra responds:

IV Ezra 4	*II Baruch 59*
5 And I said: Speak my Lord.	
And he said to me:	
Come, weigh me the weight of fire	5a the measures of fire
Or measure me the measure of wind	5c the weight of the winds
Or recall for me the day which	
has passed	
6 And I answered and said:	
Which of mortals can do this,	
that you ask me about these things?	
7 And he said to me:	
If I had asked you, saying,	
How many dwellings are there in the	
heart of the sea	
or how many streams in the source	5b the depths of the abyss
of the deep,	
or how many ways above the	
firmament,	
or which are the exits of Sheol,	10 the mouth of Gehenna
or which are the paths of	10 the place of faith, the
Paradise?[8]	region of hope
	8 the greatness of Paradise

8   You would perhaps have said to me:
Into the deep I have not descended,
Nor into Sheol have I yet gone down,
Neither to heaven have I ever ascended,
Nor have I entered Paradise.

9 Now, however, I only asked you
about fire and wind and the
day
through which you have passed (Latin)/
which has passed (Orig. Vers.)
and without which you cannot exist.

IV Ezra 5

36 And he said to me:
Number for me those who (*VL,* the   9   the earths which have
days which) have not yet   not yet come
come,[9]
And collect for me the scattered rain   5   the number of the drops
drops,   of rain
And make withered flowers bloom for me,
37 And open for me the closed chambers,
And bring forth for me the winds/spirits
shut up in them,
or show me the face of a person whom you
have never seen,
or show me the appearance of a voice.

Now, it has been shown in detail elsewhere that these verses from IV Ezra can best be understood against the background of lists such as those outlined above.[10] The very point of this passage is indeed fully evident only in this light. In the structure of the first vision in IV Ezra, the verses in chapter 4 cited above serve to express the limitation of human knowledge. Three riddles are posed, Ezra cannot solve them, so how can he hope to solve the basic theological issues which he has raised, the "way of the Most High" (vs. 11). The issues he has raised are the problems arising from the existence of evil and the concurrent problem of the suffering of Israel—in short, problems of theodicy. Now such issues were, in the normal course of events, answered for the apocalypticists by revelations.[11] Here, however, the writer wishes to emphasize the limits of human knowledge, to deny the possibility of such revelations. To do this he does not simply have the angel ask the seer some riddles, to show him how limited his knowledge is. He chooses those riddles, and adduces other elements of knowledge, from a complex of ideas—a catalogue of those very subjects which in the normal run of events apocalypticists considered as central to their revelatory experiences. When seen in this light, the passage receives its full dramatic dimension. It is a denial, daring, perhaps even polemical, of the availability of certain types of special knowledge, a denial therefore of a specific part of apocalyptic tradition.

This interpretation, it seems, is forced upon us, not only because of the inner logic of IV Ezra itself, but by the very parallels with the material in

II Baruch 59 which have been indicated above. If the riddles of IV Ezra were merely self-evident insoluble "silly questions," how could the same subjects be attributed to the divine revelation to Moses on Sinai? If they were not invested with speculative content, or at least if they did not represent a formulaic list used in the context of revelation, then their place in II Baruch becomes incomprehensible, and the usage of IV Ezra far less convincing.

Yet, the interrogative formulation in IV Ezra is by no means unique. Elsewhere the same sort of information as is referred to in IV Ezra and in II Baruch is formulated as questions. But, in contrast to the questions in IV Ezra, the use of the questions elsewhere is very different.

It is clear that many of the elements mentioned in the lists in IV Ezra and in II Baruch are drawn from the important chapters 28 and 38 of the Book of Job. In an interesting essay von Rad has dealt with Job 38.[12] There he pointed to the similarities existing between the *Ostrakon of Amenope* and Job 38–39. These similarities are primarily in the list of the elements of creation. Von Rad [N 15] discerns similar lists in Sirach 43, Psalm 148, and the Song of the Three Children. Yet he observes that the use of the lists of natural elements varies in the different sources. Addressing himself to the literary form of Job 38, he observes that it cannot be regarded as hymnic, for hymns are not formed of rhetorical questions alone. At this point he turns his attention to *Papyrus Anastasi I*. Here he finds some interrogative formulations similar to those in Job 38 and questions, like those there, raised with ironical purpose. In the large complex of rhetorical questions of Job 38, therefore, von Rad discerns two elements, the lists of natural phenomena and the ironical questions. Both, he would maintain, go back to Egyptian Wisdom forms, but stem from varying contexts.[13] Now it may well prove to be the case that advancing scholarship on the notoriously problematic book of Job will force modification of this stance of von Rad.[14] In his recent work on Wisdom he has broadened this treatment of the interrogative formulations in the Wisdom literature, regarding them as stylistic remnants of a type of catechetical or paedagogical school teaching.[15] In this treatment, he does not discuss the Egyptian origins of the rhetorical question form.

Now, in passages analogous to our lists we find rhetorical questions. Naturally, such questions are to be found at many points in the Wisdom literature. Thus we may point to such general statements of the inaccessibility of Wisdom, and of the greatness of divine Wisdom as Ben Sira 18:4–5:

> 4 *outheni exepolēsin exaggeilai ta erga autou;*
> *kai tis exichniasei ta megaleia autou;*
> 5 *kratos megalōsunēs autou tis exarithmēsetai;*
> *kai tis prosthēsei ekdiēgēsasthai ta eleē autou;*

Such rhetorical questions as these are not surprising, although the emphasis on weight and measure is suggestive for our purposes. The point of such

passages is to state the limitlessness and unknowability of the divine wonders.[16] Similarly, but with an interesting reversal of this denial of knowledge
which is implied in Ben Sira, is Wisd. Sol. 9:13–18:

> 13 For what man shall know the counsel of God?
>   Or who shall conceive what the Lord willeth?
> 14 For the thoughts of mortals are timorous,
>   And our devices are prone to fail.
> 15 For a corruptible body weigheth down the soul,
>   And the earthly frame lieth heavy on the mind
>   that is full of cares.
> 16 And hardly do we divine the things that are on earth,
>   And the things that are close at hand we find with
>   labor;
> 17 And who *ever* gained knowledge of thy counsel,
>   except thou gavest wisdom,
>   And sentest thy holy spirit from on high?
> 18 And it was thus that the ways of them which are on
>   the earth were corrected,
>   And men were taught the things that are pleasing
>   unto thee;
>   And through wisdom were they saved.

Interestingly, beyond the influence of Greek thought patterns which may be
found in vss. 14–16, the point of this passage is similar to that in Ben
Sira 18 quoted above. Yet here another conclusion is drawn from the unknowability of God's way: the conclusion that God has the power to make
his way known. The denial of the possibility of knowledge of "the counsel of
God" is reversed. It is indeed impossible "except thou gavest wisdom, and
sentest thy holy spirit from on high."

Now such passages as these, as has already been observed, are a fairly
common feature of Wisdom literature.[17] Their function is to emphasize the
value and the worth of Wisdom. Von Rad points to the strong sense of
the limits of Wisdom to be observed in the Wisdom literature and the
correspondingly profound sense of the mysteries of God. These latter stand
in opposition to the teaching of Wisdom. The wonders and mysteries are
often spoken of, he would maintain, in hymnic form. The questions here
being considered also serve to emphasize the unknowability of God's ways.[18]
A similar passage is to be found in the Syriac Apocalypse of Baruch 14:8–9:

> 8 But who O Lord, my Lord, will comprehend Thy judgment?
>   Or who will search out the profoundness of Thy way?
>   Or who will think out the weight of Thy path?
> 9 Or who will be able to think out Thy incomprehensible
>   counsel?

> Or who of those that are born has ever found
> The beginning or end of Thy wisdom?

This passage occurs in the context of a prayer in which Baruch poses the dilemma arising from the destruction of Zion. This explains the second person formulation here as opposed to the third person in the passages in Ben Sira and Wisdom of Solomon. In content and in general tone the passage is very close to IV Ezra 4:10–11, where the same language concerning the "way of the Most High" is to be observed. Here the comparison with the Wisdom of Solomon ch. 9 also suggests itself, where vss. 13, 16 17 are composed of the same types of question, but there in vss. 17b–18 the possibility of knowledge is admitted. It is clear that, for Ezra and for Baruch, the knowledge of the "way of the Most High" means more than just general information about his conduct of the world: it implies understanding of the principles which can explain the problems which are agitating the seers, knowledge which is, to this extent at least, saving knowledge.

Now, while the passage in II Baruch examined in the preceding paragraph could be considered as a special use of a type of formulation which we found to be common in the Wisdom books, and as such is merely evidence for the well-known penetration of Wisdom language and ideas into apocalyptic circles, there is a passage in I Enoch which is of far greater implications. In I Enoch 93:11–14 we find the following:

> 11 For who is there of all the children of men that is able to hear the
>   voice of the Holy One without being troubled?
>   And who can think His thoughts?
>   And who is there that can behold all the works of heaven?
> 12 And how should there be one who could behold heaven?
>   And who is there that could understand the things of heaven,
>   And see a soul or a spirit and could tell thereof,
>   Or ascend and see all their ends,
>   And think them or do like them?
> 13 And who is there of all men that could know what is the breadth and
>   the length of the earth?
>   And to whom has been shown the measure of all of them?
> 14 Or is there any one who could discern the length of heaven,
>   And how great its height,
>   And upon what it is founded,
>   And how great is the number of the stars?
>   And where all the luminaries rest?

In this passage we find an interesting movement away from the use of the question to pose a general query about the possibility of knowledge of the way to God to a series of questions concerning "the heaven," "the things of heaven," "a soul or a spirit" and their doings, "the breadth and length of the earth," "their measure," the "length of the heaven," "its height," upon "what it is founded," "the number of the stars" and "where all the luminaries rest." Now this list of subjects bears a very close resemblance to the lists discussed above. This is not merely a matter of general resemblance, but one which can be traced to specifics. Thus we may compare "the length of heaven," "its height," and "upon what it is founded" (I Enoch 93:14) with "what is first and last in heaven in the height, and at the ends of the heaven and on the foundation of heaven" in I Enoch 60:11. Individual elements of this complex are also to be found elsewhere. Thus the idea of the measures of the heaven may be found in II Bar. 59:8, "the height of the air"; in Armenian IV Ezra 5:6, "the height of the heavens"; and in Ben Sira 1:3, "the height of heaven . . . who can investigate."[19]

The phrase "length of heaven" is best compared with II Enoch 40:2, "the ends of the heaven and their plenitude"; likewise the "breadth of the earth" and "its length" may be compared with Job 38:18, *hitbōnantā ʿad raḥăbê ʾareṣ;* Armenian IV Ezra 5:36, "the extension of the earth or the thickness of the earth"; Ben Sira 1:3, "the breath of the earth . . . who can investigate?" The "number of the stars" is also often revealed in the lists. Thus in II Enoch 40:2, Enoch says, "I have measured the number of the stars, the great, countless number of them. For not even the angels see their number while I have written their names." Likewise, the numbers or the names of the stars are included in the list in I Enoch 60:12, "the division of the stars according to their names."[20]

The same emphasis on dimensions, measuring, counting, and so forth can be observed throughout the lists we discussed above and in the passage in I Enoch 93. Further, even the seemingly odd expression "to see a soul or spirit" in vs. 12 can be compared with the similarly curious "face of a person whom you have never seen" and the "appearance of a voice" in IV Ezra 5: 37.[21]

This passage is found at the end of the seventh week in the Apocalypse of Weeks. Charles comments on vss. 11–14:

> These verses are quite out of place in their present context and suit rather the Book of the Heavenly Luminaries lxxii–lxxix, lxxxii; but are foreign to the whole tone of this book, xci–cvi.[22]

Now it will not be maintained here that they are original in their present place. The complexities of the Apocalypse of Weeks are well known, and in particular the tension existing between the seven-week apocalypse and the ten-week form of the same. It may be by no chance that weeks one through seven are separated from weeks eight to ten in the Ethiopic MSS. For, it should be borne in mind that the form of the apocalypse which has been made familiar to us is the result of modern editorial rearrangement. Again, it should be noted that here we recognize the basic justification for this re-ordering of the text; but with I Enoch 93:11–14 in mind, it should be

remembered that at least in one form of the transmission they stood independently, following the end of what looked like a seven-week apocalypse,
and the misplaced three final weeks occurred preceding this in the text as
it is found in the MSS.

The last verse of the seven-week apocalypse, 93:10, reads as follows:

> And at its [the seventh week's] close shall be elected
> The elect righteous of the eternal plant of righteousness,
> To receive sevenfold instruction concerning all His creation.

It is surely significant that this verse precedes 11–14 in the present form
of the text. For the present paper 93:10 is important in its own right. It is
an assertion of the coming revelation of knowledge to the "elect righteous."
This knowledge is described as "sevenfold instruction." And the cosmological
aspect of this knowledge is stressed in the text, so that it can be described
as "sevenfold instruction concerning all His creation."[23]

Now, evidently this verse has drawn to it the passage vss. 11–14 which,
given its present context, therefore, cannot be regarded as a total denial of the
possibility of such knowledge, but only of its availability to ordinary men
under ordinary circumstances. It is primarily an assertion of the eschatological
reversal of this ordinary situation.

But, even if the passage is separated from its present context, it is very
significant. In contrast to the Wisdom sources, here the contents of the question have changed. In the Wisdom texts examined above, the meaning of
the question was probably not greatly different from that of II Bar. 14:8–9;
who can understand God's way in governing the world and creation?
Alternatively, it might be said that II Baruch is a special formulation of the
general question found in the Wisdom books. The answer implied, in either
formulation, is: "no human being, for this is the essence of wisdom which
is unknowable," or at least, as in Wisd. Sol. 9:17 no one unless God reveals
it. In I Enoch 93, however, the question has been invested with another
meaning. It refers, not to God's way with the world, but to a catalogue of
heavenly secrets. This catalogue is identical, in nearly all its parts, with the
lists noted above, of those things revealed to the apocalyptic seers. The use
originally made of this "interrogative list," as I Enoch 93:11–14 may be
designated, is not clear. In its present context it implies that just these things
will be those which will be revealed eschatologically to the righteous, a meaning demanded by the preceding verse. This is thus the third element of a
clear pattern. The secret knowledge which was revealed in the historical past
to Moses on Sinai, the same knowledge which is unveiled before the apocalyptic seer in the present, is also that which will be made known at the escha-
ton to the elect righteous.

A further point arising from the reformulation is the new, specific content
with which the old Wisdom terminology and forms have been filled. Taking
von Rad's analysis as a point of departure, it may be said that the significance

of I Enoch 93 is that an interrogative formulation can be moved from a pure Wisdom context to one in which, in both content and form, it refers to and is relevant to the secret tradition of apocalyptic speculation. This particular transformation of a Wisdom form and of Wisdom language is part of a general movement in the apocalyptic writings toward reinterpretation and reuse of Wisdom language. "Wisdom" is invested, therefore, with a new meaning. The fuller implications of this will be discussed below.

IV

When this material is to be assessed from the point of view of its origins and contents, it is of considerable interest to investigate first certain select elements and certain complexes of ideas and their development from early biblical origins through psalmodic and Wisdom forms to our lists. Since, at least in part, the lists deal with various phenomena of nature, they run parallel to the forms and the types of literature with which von Rad dealt in the above-mentioned paper, especially to hymns of praise to God the Creator.

First, therefore, the references to the stars will be discussed. Since there are a large number of references to the stars in the early sources, it will be most convenient if first those aspects of the knowledge of the stars which came to play a role in the lists are isolated.

The place of astronomical information within the realm of revealed knowledge is, of course, very clear and no more evidence need be cited than the "Book of the Heavenly Luminaries" (I Enoch 72–82), and the astronomical sections of other apocalyptic books.[24] "The Book of the Heavenly Luminaries" is presented in the form of a celestial revelation by Uriel to Enoch and the special nature of the information revealed is strongly stressed.

Again in II Enoch, we find the following:

> J'ai comblé (le compte) des étoiles, grande multitude sans nombre. Quel homme concevra les circuits de leurs changements ou leurs mouvements ou leurs retours, ou leurs guidés ou les guidés? Les anges euxmemes ne connaisent pas (même) leur nombre; moi, j'ai ecrit leurs noms (40:2–3).[25]

In his comment on this verse, Vaillant suggests that the last phrase is corrupt and that it should read "leur nombre" or "ses noms," in this latter case meaning the names of the sun which is mentioned in the next sentence (cf. I Enoch 78:1). Yet in this latter case the syntax would be most difficult. Vaillant appears to be puzzled by the statement that Enoch wrote down the names of the stars. Yet this assertion is far from a surprising phenomenon as will be shown. Without Vaillant's suggested emendation, therefore, the passage in II Enoch claims that Enoch counted and recorded the number of the stars and their names—a feat beyond the powers of the very angels.

Moreover, he apparently claims knowledge of the orbits of the stars and—
evidently this is what "leurs guidés ou les guidés" means—of their angelic
guides (cf. I Enoch 80:1, etc.).

The items counting and naming stars deserve further attention. Thus, in
the "interrogative list" in I Enoch 93, it may be observed that one of a series
of measures inquired about is the number of the stars. Similarly in I Enoch
60:12 the "names" and "divisions" (constellations?) of the stars are among
the revealed secrets. Speculation about the names of some of the stars is to
be found in I Enoch 82:7–19. Likewise II Enoch 11 gives information
about the numbers of the stars.[26]

It is by no means an innovation of these particular types of apocalyptic
lists that the knowledge of the number or names of the stars is a sign of the
special status or role of him who knows. Indeed, in Ps. 147:4–5 we find
asserted of God himself that he it is who:

> môneh mispār lakkôkābîm
> l*e*kullām šēmôt yiqrā'
> gādôl '*a*dônênû w*e*rab-kôaḥ
> litbûnātô 'ên mispār

The same theme, the juxtaposition of the counting and the calling by name
in the context of the exaltation of God is to be observed in Isa. 40:26:

> š'w mrwm 'ynykm wr'w my-br' 'lh
> hmwṣy' bmspr ṣb'm lklm bšm yqr'
> mrb 'wnym w'myṣ kḥ 'yš l' n'dr

Here the counting and the calling by name are given a particular sense,
perhaps a sort of "numbering off" or taking count, which image might have
been drawn from the military sphere.

A later development, in a Wisdom passage, but doubtless based on the
biblical verses celebrating God's counting or naming of the stars, is to be
found in I Bar. 3:34 f. Here the calling by name is given a new orientation
when the text states, once more in the context of the praise of God's wondrous
action in nature:

> hoi de asteres elampsan en tais phulakais autōn kai euphranthēsan,
> ekalesen autous, kai eipon paresmen. elampsan met'
> euphrosumēs tō poiēsanti autous.

Here, the idea of God's naming of the stars, is to be seen rather as a
development of the concept of calling from "calling by name" to "summoning." In any case, the two concepts are close to one another.

A similar idea is to be found in a passage of praise to God in *LAB* 21:2.
This passage shows various of the elements to be observed in the lists, but
they are mentioned in the context of praise of God. The phrase relevant to
the present point of the discussion is *et tu investigasti astra et numerasti*

stellas. This takes us no further, substantially, than do Ps. 147:5 f. and Isa. 40:26. It is of interest, however, to see this typologically old type of usage in an indubitably later text. Moreover, this passage includes certain other elements, the establishment of the rain and the number (reading, as John Strugnell suggests *sensum* as *censum*) of all generations which are similar to those observed in the lists.[27]

What is of particular interest in the material described above is the shift in the subject of the action. In passages of praise of God from the works of nature, as a mode of highlighting his role as the Creator and Lord of the forces of nature, we are told that he called the host of the stars by name and that he knows their number. That this is indeed an activity beyond human achievement is clear from the fact that the innumerable multiplicity of the stars is paradigmatic in popular usage in biblical Hebrew for numbers which are infinite, beyond any human ken, or even for a very large number. Thus Gen. 22:17

> *whrbh 'rbh 't-zrʿk kkwkby hšmym.*[28]

The element of counting is even more explicit in what are apparently literary re-formulations of this expression. Thus Gen. 15:5

> *wywṣ' 'tw hḥwṣh wy'mr hbṭ n' hšmymh*
> *wspr hkwkbym 'm twkl lspr 'tm wy'mr*
> *lw kh yhyh zrʿk*

Jer. 33:22

> *'šr l' yspr ṣb' hšmym wl' ymd ḥwl hym*
> *kn 'rbh 't zrʿ dwd 'bdy w't-hlwym*
> *mšrty 'ty*[29]

It is evident that when the hymnic praises of God's activity in nature proudly proclaim that he it is that counts the stars and calls them by name, this statement receives an added point and emphasis when it is seen set against the background of the type of popular expression emphasized here.

When the statements in the apocalyptic lists are examined in light of the preceding, as well as of the well known astronomical interests of the apocalyptic books, they take on a heightened and provocative sense. That which is impossible for man, that which is proclaimed as a parade example of God's dominion over His creation, precisely that is revealed to the seer and recorded by him. Once more the far-reaching nature of the apocalyptic claim is most striking.

Yet another implication of the apocalyptic materials bearing on this subject is to be found in I Enoch 43:1-4.

1 And I saw other lightnings and the stars of heaven, and I saw how He called them all by their names and they harkened to Him.

2 And I saw how they are weighed in a righteous balance according to

their proportions of light; [I saw] the width of their spaces and the day of their appearances, and how their revolution produces lightning; and [I saw] their revolution according to the number of the angels, and [how] they keep faith with each other.

3 And I asked the angel who went with me who showed me what is hidden, "What are these?"

4 And he said to me, "The Lord of Spirits hath showed thee their parabolic meaning [lit. "their parable"]: these are the names of the holy who dwell on the earth and believe in the name of the Lord of Spirits for ever and ever."[30]

In this passage we find not only the calling of the stars by name and their harkening (cf. in particular I Bar. 3:34 f.), but also the revelation of their light, their orbits, and the angelic guides who determine these latter, as well as the regularity of the balance and proportion between them.

These verses resemble, in general, II Enoch 40:2–3. Two new elements are introduced. One is that the regularity of the movements of the celestial bodies is called "how they keep faith with one another" which implies not only a personification of them, but also the ascribing of an ethical or moral quality to their regularity. The same language of the relationship between the sun and the moon is employed in I Enoch 41:5 where, moreover, this keeping of faith is said to be "in accordance with the oath by which they are bound together."[31]

In an important, but unfortunately partly fragmentary passage in I Enoch 69:16–21, 25, the oath is discussed by which all the structures of nature are regulated. The preceding vss. 13–15 are sadly unclear. If they are connected with vss. 4–12 they have to do with the forbidden teachings imparted by the satans to men. The passage apparently relates the revelation of a hidden name and oath by Michael to the Angel Kâsbeêl, and it then goes on (vss. 16 ff.) to describe the function of this oath. Some sort of name speculation probably lies behind it. Of particular interest are vss. 19–21:

19 And through that oath are the depths made fast,
     And abide and stir not from their place from eternity
         to eternity.[32]
20 And through that oath the sun and moon complete their
         course,
     And deviate not from their ordinance from eternity to
         eternity
21 And through that oath the stars complete their course,
     And he calls them by their names,
     And they answer him from eternity to eternity.

The calling by name and answering here appear to be sureties or functions of the regular workings of the natural order.

In general the concept expressed in these passages may be compared with I Enoch 2–5:3 where the regularity of the works of nature serves as a paradigm of obedience and submission to God. This is contrasted in 5:4 ff. with man's disobedience and transgression.

Somewhat similar ideas are to be found in T. Naphthali 3:2:

> *Hēlios kai selēnē kai asteres ouk allaiousin taxin autōn, houtōs*
> *kai humeis mē allaiōsēte nomon Theou en etaxią praxeōn humōn.*

In these verses the point is substantially identical with that made in I Enoch 2–5. Similar views are already to be found in Ben Sira 16:26–28. Especially is vs. 28 striking in our context:

> *hekastos ton plēsion autou ouk exethlipsen,*
> *kai heōs aiōnos ouk apeithēsousin tou*
> *rēmatos autou*[33]

The second aspect of the passage in I Enoch 43 is the statement that the parabolic meaning of the stars is "the names of the holy who dwell on the earth and believe in the name of the Lord of Spirits for ever and ever." This important statement opens up a number of lines of investigation. The connection implied between the righteous and the stars in this passage is not a direct identification. On the face of it the comparison, the *mašal,* appears to arise from the obedience of the stars to their Maker and their faithfulness to their covenant, which are not only paradigmatic for the righteous, an example for them to follow, but are also like the very qualities of the righteous.

The relationship between the righteous and the stars, however, is not an isolated occurrence in this passage. It is quite a widespread phenomenon. The best known passage is, perhaps, Daniel 12:3

> *hmśklym yzhrw kzhr hrqy‘*
> *wmṣdyqy hrbym kkwkbym l‘wlm w‘d*

This is not alone. In a series of passages we find the righteous likened to the stars, in particular the eschatological context. In Sifre Pārāsheth Děbārîm 10 (ed. Friedmann 67a) and parallel in Lev. R. 20:2 we read that the faces of the righteous in the future will be like seven things, the sun, the moon, the firmament, the stars, the lightning, roses, and the Temple candelabrum. In IV Ezra 7:125 the faces of the righteous are said to shine above the stars, while 7:97b says that they are as the light of the stars.[34] Moreover, yet another series of passages says that the righteous will be like stars or are intimately connected with stars. In IV Macc. 17:5 the seven sons are said to be "star-like, with God" and in Ass. Mos. 10:9 Israel is said to be exalted by God and caused to approach the stars in their place of habitation. As in Jer. 51:9, Isa. 14:13, so also Ps. Sol. 1:5 describes the overwhelming pride of the wicked as the attempt to reach the stars. In light of this, the versions of Isa. 14:13 are most interesting. MT and Syriac read *wm'l lkwkby 'l 'rym*. For *kwkby 'l* LXX reads "stars of Heaven," but in the Targum we find *'myh d'lhh*. This again suggests the relationship between the righteous and the stars.

Since the stars stand in a clear relationship to the angels, and at the same time a number of passages indicate also that the blessed righteous are compared to and occasionally even transformed to the likeness of angels, a clear relationship appears to exist between these three. This may, in part at least, lie behind the statements made in I Enoch 43:1–4.[35]

V

In order to show the complexities involved in tracing traditions such as these, in this section certain other elements will be explored. This will strengthen the point illustrated in the preceding section, that many of the terms, found in formulaic lists, do in fact have speculative content, which can often, though not universally, be documented with great specificity in apocalyptic vision materials. It will become equally evident that the origins of some of these materials are to be sought in Wisdom passages, or in hymns of praise to God as Creator.

Indeed, the close connection between some forms of these latter types of materials has been observed above.

II Bar. 59:5

The measures of fire, the depths of the abyss, the weight
of the winds, the number of the drops of rain.

Job 28:23–26

23   *'lhym hbyn drkh whw' yd' 't-mqwmh*
24   *ky hw' lqṣwt h'rṣ ybyṭ tḥt kl hšmym yr'h*
25   *l'śwt lrwḥ mšql wmym tkn bmdh*
26a *b'śtw lmṭr ḥq*

Ben Sira 1:1–3

1   *Pasa sophia para kuriou*
   kai met' autou estin eis ton aiōna
2   *ammon thalassōn kai stagonas huetou*
   kai hēmeras aiōnos tis exarithmēsei
3   *hupsos ouranou kai platos gēs*
   kai abusson kai sophian tis exichniasei.

In these passages from Job 28 and Ben Sira 1 are found nearly all the elements contained in the four phrases of II Bar. 59:5. The measures of fire

(?=lightning) are missing, but they are integral to the tradition of II Baruch as will be shown below. Both Job 28 and Ben Sira 1 are designed primarily to state either things which God alone can know, or things which man cannot know. Baruch comes to assert that these very things were revealed to Moses.

Closely connected with this text is II Bar. 48:4 ff. This is not a Wisdom-question passage as are the two cited above, but a passage of praise for God's acts in and power over nature. II Baruch 48, in its first ten verses in particular, shows a close relationship with the apocalyptic lists. The verses relevant to the passage under discussion are:

> 4 Thou makest known the multitude of fire,
>   And thou weighest the lightness of the wind.
> 5 Thou explorest the limit of the heights,
>   And thou scrutinizest the depths of the darkness.

Similarly close are IV Ezra 4:5, 5:36

> 4:5 Come weigh me the weight of fire,
>   Or measure me the measure of wind,
> 5:36 Collect for me the scattered raindrops.

These are the only places where the weight of fire is mentioned. The meaning of the phrase remains sealed, unless it refers to lightning or to the fire around the divine throne. "The weight of the winds," however, is much more broadly attested. In I Enoch 60:12 one aspect of this is made explicit. Enoch, under the guidance of the angel sees,

> The chambers of the winds, and how the winds are divided, and how they are weighed, and [how] the portals of the winds are reckoned, each according to the power of the wind.

From this it is evident, therefore, that the weighing of the wind has to do with the proper distribution of the power or strength of the wind. This knowledge belongs to the realm of meteorological and uranographical revelation.[36]

From Jub. 2:2 it is clear that there are angels appointed over the winds, and the actual process of weighing, "how they are weighed" in the words of I Enoch, is described in the list in II Enoch 40:

> Moi j'ai écrit les chambres des vents, moi j'ai observé et j'ai vu comment leurs gardiens apportent des balances et des mesures: d'abord ils les mettent sur la balance, ensuite dans la mesure, et c'est à la mesure qu'ils les lâchent sur toute la terre, pour que d'un souffle rude ils n'enbranlent pas la terre (vs. 11, Vaillant [N 1], p. 43).

The circle is completed![37]

The depths of the abyss is a basic cosmological element. It is to be found in many contexts. Above, Ben Sira 1:3 was quoted, with which Ben Sira

42:18 may be compared. In Job 38:16, in a passage which is important for tracing the origin of a number of these elements, we read, in a Wisdom question passage whose subjects are cosmographic:

> *hb't 'd nbky ym*
> *w bhqr thwm hthlkt*[38]

II Baruch 48:5, a poem of praise to the Creator, emphasizing his profound Wisdom, has been quoted above. One of the features of God's Wisdom is that he "scrutinizes the depths of darkness." Since this stands in contrasting parallelism to the exploration "of the limit of the heights" the reference is clear.

In IV Ezra 4:7 f. reference is found to the sources of the deep as a potential subject of knowledge, thus:

> 7 *Quantae habitationes sunt in corde maris?*
>   *aut quantae venae sunt in principio Abyssi?*
> 8 *dicebas fortasne mihi*
>   *In Abyssum non descendi*
>   *neque in infernum adhunc (penetravi* [L])[39]

The actual speculative content of this material is to be found in various sources. In Enoch 17 and 18, in describing the first of Enoch's journeys through the cosmos, the depths are revealed to him, with details of their structure and contents. In this context too, perhaps the materials in ch. 21 should be considered. It is of interest, moreover, that in these chapters information touching on other parts of the revealed information is to be found —the winds, the firmament, and other features.[40]

A final passage again serves to remind us that there is, as was true too of the stars, no real distinction between the meteorological and other eschatological or religious spheres. In I Enoch 61:1–4, the element of measuring is clear and explicit, but the righteous are measured. In it too the secrets of the depths of the earth are referred to but this implies not some cosmological information, but rather the righteous buried in it. The passage at least in part seems to be modeled after Zech. 2:5 ff.

The number of the drops of rain is apparently the most anomalous of the four elements revealed to Moses according to the verse in II Baruch. In IV Ezra 5:36 the seer is asked whether he can gather the scattered raindrops. This appears to be a curious request indeed.

Still, this subject returns again in the various forms with which we have become familiar. In II Bar. 21:8, in a prayer in praise of God, the seer says:

> Who causest the drops of rain to rain by number upon the earth.

In a very similar context, *LAB* 21:2 as observed above, a number of the same elements are found. The passage reads:

Et dixit Ihesus: Tu pre omnibus scis Domine quid agat cor maris ante quam irascatur, et tu investigasti astra, et numerasti stellas, et constituisti pluviam, tu scis sensum<emend. J. Strugnell: *censum*>*omnium generationum antequam nascantur.*

Here although the numbering is not mentioned specifically, the combination of elements clearly indicates that the same material is involved.[41] Equally appropriate to the pattern is what was found in Ben Sira 1:2 above, where it is said that man cannot number the raindrops. The same pattern is to be observed.

Moreover, the speculative content of this term is more explicit where the raindrops form part of the subject of revelation in II Enoch 40:8 (Vaillant [N 1], p. 41): "Les sejours des nuages et leurs bouches et leurs ciels et leurs pluies et les gouttes, mai je les ai explorés." And Vaillant notes the interesting *Vetus Latina* "et leurs ciels et comment ils portent la pluie, et toutes les gouttes de pluie," which is even more to the point.

In II Enoch 47 (Vaillant, p. 49) once more the idea of the counting of the drops of rain occurs. Moreover, the combination of elements in this passage resembles that to be found in Ben Sira 1:3 and II Baruch 59. Although the verse seems to be in the line of the praises of God, it appears from the context that these secrets are those revealed by Enoch in his books. This is particularly clear in the text published by Vaillant. The relevant passage, coming in Enoch's address to his children, is:

> prenez ces livres, les livres écrits de la main de votre père et en eux connaissez les oeuvres du Seigneur: qu'il n'y a pas en dehors du Seigneur seul . . . qui a fait seul la création innombrable—qui a compté la poussière de la terre ou le sable de la mer ou les gouttes des nuages? . . .

The idea of numbering drops of rain, or a measuring of the rain, is to be found in I Enoch 60:21–23. This also suggests that, as with the measure of the winds, the measure of the rain has a meteorological function. Moreover it is connected with a guardian spirit.[42]

The idea lying behind this element in II Baruch 59 appears to be analogous, therefore, to that observed with regard to the wind. Perhaps taking its departure from the formulations like Job 28:25–26a, *wmym tkn bmdh b'štw lmṭr ḥq,* the counting or gathering of the raindrops is, first and foremost, a part of God's function as Creator and Lord of nature (cf. also Job 36:27). The very paradoxical nature of this action seems to have attracted the attention of the apocalyptic authors. For this reason, perhaps, it becomes invested with speculative content.

PRELIMINARY CONCLUSIONS

In the preceding sections the following points have been analyzed:
  1) There exists a list form which occurs in a number of apocalypses.

These lists share a common function, and a common content. There are two basic types of formulation—a short one and a long one.

2) These lists occur as summaries of information revealed to the seers. Such lists are to be found either as the high point of visionary experiences or as summaries of the subject matter revealed in the context of later recapitulations of visionary experiences.

3) With these lists must be associated certain types of interrogative lists. These interrogative lists take their origin apparently in the interrogative Wisdom formulations such as Job 38 and Ben Sira 1:3 ff.

4) Von Rad has shown the Wisdom origins of the lists of materials from which Job 38 is constructed, as well as the rhetorical question form in which that chapter is written. The same lists of elements of creation are also to be found in psalmodic literature in what we have dubbed "Hymns to God as Creator."

5) The close examination of the contents of the lists in the apocalypses, both the declarative and the interrogative ones, was undertaken. An analysis of certain selected elements which at first appeared paradoxical showed that they refer to the subjects of speculative activity whose content can usually be documented in the surviving sources.

VI

From this formulation it might be assumed that the lists here discussed, showing as they do the elements of form and contents common with the Wisdom lists of Job 38, etc., seem to imply a direct descent from Wisdom sources. This should, perhaps, be examined somewhat more closely, particularly in light of recent views which derive the whole of "apocalyptic" from Wisdom sources.[43] Von Rad in his study of Job 38 discovers that he can arrange tables for the sources discussed by him and demonstrate that not only the idea of a list of the elements of creation, but the very range of elements chosen by the authors of the various sources and the actual order in which they appear are practically identical. That is to say, he shows not merely a general similarity of select elements, but also a relationship extending into the particulars of choice of elements and their ordering. This cannot be demonstrated to exist between the apocalyptic lists and any biblical source, including Job 28 and 38.[44] Such may perhaps be discerned with respect to a few items in Ben Sira 1:3 ff. and the similar terms in the lists in II Baruch 59 and IV Ezra. These, however, form a short and isolated unit of material which is, in any case, best explained as a common element of tradition.[45] At the most, certain isolated cosmological elements are common to the apocalyptic lists and to Job 38. Further, the apocalyptic lists are primarily of the declarative type, Job 38 and associated Wisdom materials are interrogative in formulation. The lists in the apocalypses are not merely inherited units of Wisdom material; they comprise rather catalogues of actual subjects of speculative investigation, study, and perhaps even of the contents of ecstatic experiences of the apocalyptic authors. If they derive ultimately from Wisdom list materials then the elements included in them and their ordering appear to have been profoundly influenced by the actual speculative concerns and activity of the apocalyptic authors.

One might be tempted to go further and regard the interrogative form as primary—after all it has the supposed Wisdom antecedents—and, building on von Rad's suggestion that it derives from a "catechetical" or paedagogical context, one might suggest something similar for the origins of the present lists. To do this for the apocalypses, however, is to enter a realm where the historical underpinnings of the hypothesis are nonexistent. There is, in actual fact, no information at all about how the speculative materials found in the apocalypses were developed, preserved, and transmitted.[46] It would be positively misleading, therefore, to put forward such suggestions. To judge from the apocalypses themselves, perhaps the declarative lists were primary and served to recount the contents of real or supposed visionary experiences. The role of both types in their pre-literary life remains completely mysterious.

Gerhard von Rad has claimed for some years that the apocalyptic itself is a child not of prophecy but of Wisdom.[47] Beyond the questions discussed above it seems proper to enquire how the sort of speculative material represented in the lists relates to the Wisdom tradition. It appears that most of the subjects mentioned in the apocalyptic lists are not represented in the biblical or apocryphal Wisdom books. Perhaps in response to this, as well as for other reasons, in his recent work on Wisdom von Rad strongly emphasized the view that that which is preserved of biblical and apocryphal Wisdom literature represents only a small portion of the subject matter which was part of the teaching of the wise.[48] He wishes to see the great variety of Wisdom interests in the later period reflected in the interesting catalogue preserved in Wisd. Sol. 7:17–21:

17   For he hath given me an unerring knowledge of the things that are,
       To know the constitution of the world and the operation of the elements,
18   The beginning and the end and the middle of the times,
       The alternations of the solstices and the changes of seasons,
19   The circuits of years and the positions of stars,
20   The natures of living creatures and the ragings of wild beasts,
       The powers of spirits and the thoughts of men,
       The diversities of plants and the virtues of roots,
21   All things that are either secret or manifest I learned,
22   For she that is the artificer of all things taught me, even Wisdom.

He admits that in fact the evidence for the astronomical knowledge claimed in this passage is slim, in spite of the central position of the claims of vss. 18

and 19 (vs. 18 is surely calendaric and not eschatological). Observe, of course, the interesting reversal of the older Wisdom denials of the possibility of the knowledge of secrets in vs. 22.

Now, the subject matter of this list is in the realm of natural science, medicine, magic, and the control of nature and of man. That this "constitution of the world and operation of the elements" included the sort of intense interest in cosmic geography reflected in the apocalypses is not borne out by anything in the Wisdom books. Most significantly, aspects of magical, medical and demonological knowledge found in vs. 20 occur nowhere in the apocalyptic lists.[49] Still, this list of subjects in Wisd. Sol. 7:17–21 has obvious points of contact and meeting with the apocalyptic lists as well as, and this should be stressed, these very real points of difference.

Another consideration is to be derived from the fact that Wisd. Sol. 7:17–21 is clearly a description of Solomon's knowledge. When it speaks of his knowledge of the "spirits" and of his other extraordinary knowledge of plants and roots, of animals and beasts, this passage seems to be presenting the oldest known form of the later traditions, familiar already to Josephus, of Solomon's remarkable magical and demonological knowledge and control of nature. If this is so, then of course this list would tell us little about the scope of the Wisdom tradition, for no one could claim that this later Solomon figure represents an ideal Wisdom type or the like.[50]

Now von Rad may well be right that in the scope of the learning of the Wisdom teachers much more was included than is apparent in the extant Wisdom books. Yet the fact remains that for the very existence of most of the branches of learning he cites, the main Israelite Wisdom source is the Wisdom of Solomon itself, in the list here discussed.[51] Moreover even the Wisdom of Solomon, the book which alone claims for Wisdom the comprehensive revelation of the secrets, nowhere provides us with the clear evidence for the actual speculation or learning pursued under these very general rubrics. It may reasonably be assumed that the scribes and the wise were the tradents of a goodly segment of the intellectual culture of ancient Israel, but just what its contents were remains problematic.[52]

The interrogative list in Wisd. Sol. 9:13–18 is equally elusive when one wishes to find out what are the more precise referrents of the general terms it comprehends. Again the books of Wisdom literature themselves are of no great assistance. The author of Qohelet says that he went to investigate "everything which happens under the heavens" (1:13). The author of Wisdom of Solomon is more daring. The heavenly and the secret, he claims, can be revealed to Solomon through Wisdom or God's holy spirit (=Wisdom). The contents of this revelation of the secret or heavenly, except perhaps for the hints offered by the parallelism of 9:16b and 17, remain unknown:

16b   But the things that are in the heavens who ever traced out?

17   And who ever gained knowledge of thy counsel?
       Except thou gavest wisdom
       And sentest thy holy spirit from on high.

Equally instructive is the result of this revelation of Wisdom given in 9:18.

> 18   And it was thus that the ways of those who are on the earth were corrected.
>
> And men were taught the things that are pleasing unto thee,
>
> And through wisdom they were saved.

In short, what appears to be clear is that in the Wisdom literature which antedates the apocalypses we do not find anything which helps us directly to explain the more curious and less obvious objects of apocalyptic speculation. It seems most probable that part of this speculative concern of the apocalyptic lists derived from Wisdom sources, although the lines of connection may prove difficult to trace. It is impossible, however, to see the Wisdom tradition as the only source from which the interest in these subjects sprang.[53]

In two recent articles Hans Dieter Betz has entered a strong plea for the renewed consideration of the historico-religious approach to the apocalyptic religious literature.[54] He wishes to treat apocalypticism in the context of the religious syncretism of the Hellenistic-Oriental type. Thus he states clearly: "We have to free ourselves from the idea of treating apocalypticism as an isolated and purely inner-Jewish phenomenon. Rather, we must learn to understand apocalypticism as a peculiar manifestation within the entire course of Hellenistic-Oriental syncretism."[55] In this connection he mentions with approval von Rad's rejection of the common derivation of apocalypticism from prophecy. Emphasizing the Wisdom elements that von Rad stresses, he seeks to explain them as part of a contemporary type of religious creativity, not as deriving from the Israelite Wisdom tradition.[56]

It is beyond doubt true that the apocalypses will have to be studied as part of broader movements in Hellenistic religion and thought. In stressing this Betz has rendered a most valuable service to the advance of scholarship. It may be that through this will emerge the understanding of elements of the apocalypses not explicable by other means. Yet, as will become evident, Betz's formulation is perhaps too extreme, for the "inner-Jewish" features of the phenomenon must be granted their full measure.

Another major attempt to provide an explanation for the origins and complexity of the apocalyptic phenomenon is that of Martin Hengel. At considerable length he argues for the origins of apocalypticism in the circles of the Chasidim and sees as its most typical characteristic its concept of history.[57] With this is combined a belief in immortality or resurrection and final reward[58] and most typically this is presented as revealed Wisdom of heavenly secrets whose scope is determined by the encyclopaedic range of late Wisdom.[59] He regards this concept of revealed Wisdom together with pseudepigraphy as common features of Hellenistic religiosity also to be observed in the apocalypses.[60] In spite of the very suggestive Hellenistic evidence he adduces, Hengel does not wish to venture beyond the observation of the existence of the common features to the positing of direct Hellenistic-Oriental influence on the Jewish apocalyptic. He admits, of course, the possibility of this influence in specific matters.[61]

The Hellenistic literary and religious types pointed out by Hengel seem to be indicative of the potential contribution of the Hellenistic-Oriental religious world to the understanding of the apocalyptic.[62] Specifically, however, no explanation appears immediately of the role or origin of the type of speculative material represented by our lists. The point of the theory of revealed Wisdom as expounded by Hengel is that the teaching of the books is regarded as revealed, and speculative matters such as those in the lists do not play a central role in this complex.[63] Hengel's theories may be regarded, therefore, as strengthening Betz's plea for a detailed re-examination of the Hellenistic-Oriental sources. These are not the total explanation of the phenomenon, as is patent from his comments and from what we will say below.

POSTSCRIPT

Since the study presented in the previous sections appears to bear on the subject of definition and categorization of this literature which has been the subject of considerable scholarly debate in the last decade, some observations are added here which extend beyond the conclusions that can properly be drawn from the argument presented above. The writer is moved to add these speculative comments since the matter has been under such close scrutiny in recent years.

It must be stated at the outset that a great deal of the current discussion of apocalypticism and of the apocalypses is being carried on in the midst of a semantic confusion of the first order.[64] The confusion turns on the relationship of apocalypticism (also called apocalyptic) and the apocalypses. By the terms "apocalyptic" or "apocalypticism" (and this latter is employed throughout this section) a certain pattern of ideas is designated and the debate had centered primarily on the relationship obtaining between this pattern of ideas and certain aspects of early Christian and New Testament thought.[65] By the term "apocalypse" the literary works are designated, and while a good deal still remains to be done in the working out of the literary form of the apocalypse and its relationship to other associated materials, in particular the Testament genre, the general characteristics of the literary form are clear and one is generally able to decide whether a given work is an apocalypse or not.[66] Recent years have not seen any particularly great advances in the study of the apocalypses as a genre, although the criticism of various individual works has been advanced at divers points.[67] Confusion has entered at the point at which the relationship between apocalypticism and the apocalypses has been obscured.

The two phenomena have names derived from the same Greek word and this appears, *prima facie,* to imply that a relationship of dependence or identity exists between the two. It will be maintained here that this is not necessarily the case and, indeed, only by maintaining a clear distinction between the two can a series of problems be solved.

If as a point of departure any of the recent attempts to state the nature of "apocalypticism" is taken, then there are some of the books which are conventionally regarded as apocalypses which are for all practical purposes devoid of apocalypticism. Thus, for example, Koch lists as basic characteristics of "apocalypticism" the following features:

1. The acute expectation of the fulfillment of divine promises.
2. Cosmic catastrophe.
3. A relationship between the time of the end and the preceding human and cosmic history.
4. Angelology and demonology.
5. Salvation beyond the catastrophe.
6. Salvation proceeds from the Divine Throne.
7. A Savior figure with royal characteristics.
8. A number of other characteristics that he sums up in the *Stichwort* "glory."[68]

Koch does not claim, of course, that *all* these features must be found before the presence of "apocalypticism" is demonstrated, for he does not pretend to have here a definition but merely a list of prominent characteristics. Yet, even with this proviso, it is clear that a list of traits of this type is a most inadequate sort of description of the phenomenon and certainly nothing like a definition, and it adds nothing to our understanding of it. Furthermore, and this is the major issue to be discussed here, certain literary works which are apocalypses as well as large sections of others, present so few of these characteristics or present them in a way so incidental to the body of the content of the work, as to be no more repositories of "apocalypticism" than the books of Maccabees or Ben Sira. Thus, for example, the Greek apocalypse of Baruch is almost totally lacking in all the eschatologically orientated characteristics of Koch's list. Conversely many of them are to be found in works which are not apocalypses, such as the Testaments of the Twelve Patriarchs or certain Qumran *pesharim.* Moreover, and we shall return to this below, these features of apocalypticism do not provide any sort of explanation for major literary and formal characteristics of the apocalypses such as pseudepigraphy, the symbolic vision, esotericism (or pseudo-esotericism) of the revelation, *et alia.*

There are various ways of trying to resolve the issue here made evident. Koch attempts to do this by delimiting tremendously the number of works to be included as apocalypses for the discussion.[69] He will admit to the discussion as prime witnesses only Daniel, I Enoch, II Baruch, IV Ezra, the Apocalypse of Abraham, and the Apocalypse of John. To do this is to stack the deck in a fashion that is not particularly helpful. Furthermore, I Enoch in particular, and to a lesser extent II Baruch and the Apocalypse of Abraham still remain full of unexplained material. Admittedly Koch does not set out to explain it.

Hans Dieter Betz in his articles considered above proceeds in another direction. Deriving his concept of apocalypticism from the apocalypses, he is struck by the fact that conventional views of apocalyptic do not emphasize sufficiently the elements of knowledge in the texts. This stance is, in principle, as valid as that taken here.[70] It will become evident, however, in the following paragraphs that, in spite of his views, the phenomenon of "apocalyticism" in the commonly accepted sense can be derived from Israelite sources and it is, in our view, helpful to make the distinction. The apocalypses still must be explained (see below).

Frank Moore Cross published in 1969 an important article taking a position which appears to be diametrically opposed to that of Betz. He maintains the profoundly Israelite character of apocalyptic (meaning "apocalypticism" in the usual sense).[71] The central part of Cross's argument was taken up in one of the most interesting and important recent contributions to the study of apocalypticism, the volume by Paul D. Hanson, *The Dawn of Apocalyptic* [N 47]. In this work Hanson deals with the question of the development of "apocalyptic" (to be corrected, he assures us in a footnote on p. 7 to "apocalyptic eschatology") from prophecy. Focusing on the late sixth and the fifth centuries B.C., he attempts to show the development and growth of what he calls "early" and "middle" apocalyptic." He cites, early in his work, D. S. Russell's list of the characteristics of "apocalyptic" which, since it does not differentiate the apocalypses from apocalypticism, is far less helpful than that proposed by Koch. It is a mélange of literary, conceptual, theological, and formal characteristics.[72] Hanson points out the uselessness of these catalogues of traits for advancing our understanding of the phenomenon and attempts his own definition which arises from his analysis of this "early" and "middle" apocalyptic material.[73] Apocalyptic, he assures us, is "the disclosure (usually esoteric in nature) to the elect of the prophetic vision of Yahweh's sovereignty (including his future dealings with his people, the inner secrets of the cosmos, etc.), which vision the visionaries have ceased to translate into the terms of plain history, real politics and human instrumentality because of a pessimistic view of reality growing out of the bleak post-Exilic conditions in which the visionary group found itself, conditions seeming unsuitable to them as a context for the envisioned restoration of Yahweh's people" (p. 7).[74] He then proceeds to demonstrate the truth of this very significant contention, or at least all of it except the phrase "the inner secrets of the cosmos." Hanson succeeds in demonstrating, beyond a doubt, the origins of apocalyptic eschatology in prophecy, and of its "re-mythologization" in the dual loci of the mythologizing royal cult and ancient league traditions. With these basic contentions there is no argument here, only agreement. Yet, we must maintain that Hanson has not explained the origins of the apocalypses and of many of the features that characterize them. He has provided a contribution of capital importance to the study of "apocalypticism" or "apocalyptic eschatology."

On the one hand many of the formal features of the apocalypses have their direct ancestry not in the "visionary" tradition of the group responsible for the development of "apocalyptic eschatology" but in priestly and "hierocratic sources such as Ezekiel and Proto-Zechariah.[75] On the other, the part of the apocalypses called "speculative" in our paper, is clearly an embarrassment to Hanson. He introduces the phrase "inner secret of the cosmos" into his definition, although this is, in fact, the only phrase in the definition not demonstrated in the thesis. On p. 5 he speaks of "outside influences (e.g. Persian dualism and Hellenism)" which play a role after the basic character of "apocalyptic" is set. On p. 13, at apparent variance with his own definition on p. 7, he speaks of "the absorption of Wisdom materials" leading to "the unveiling of secrets of the universe." Clearly here this scholar feels that while what he has demonstrated is crucial to the development of "apocalyptic," it does not explain certain features of the apocalypses. Owing to the confusion of "apocalyptic" with "apocalypses," he feels that he should have explained these features of the apocalypses. He thus attempts to show his consciousness of the material unaccounted for as stated above. Yet we would maintain that this is unnecessary, for Hanson's thesis bears on "apocalypticism," not on the apocalypses. It should be stressed that this observation in no way invalidates the major contentions of Hanson's thesis, but constitutes a clarification of an issue which is preliminary to his discussion.

Bearing the above in mind, and in view of the fact that "apocalypticism" does not appear either to be the ideology of the apocalypses or to exhaust the contents of the apocalypses, we can pose another type of question and suggest another focus. If the point of departure is the apocalypses and then not predominantly those two which managed to get themselves considered canonical—Daniel by the Jews and the Apocalypse of John by the Christians —what is it that makes sense of these products of the human spirit? Clearly they are not transparently simple works, and one is more than justified in asking: What ideological, theological, or conceptual patterns can be discerned which provide a basis of coherence for them? What central concerns motivate their authors?

Manifestly, apocalypticism is not adequate. It makes no sense of at least two of the five independent works bound together under the name of I Enoch: parts I and III. Equally large parts of II Enoch, most of III Baruch, sections of II Baruch and of the Apocalypse of Abraham are completely irrelevant if judged by the criterion of "apocalypticism" or "apocalyptic eschatology."

At least one major factor which must, we venture to suggest, be taken into account is the sort of statement presented by the lists whose existence was pointed out in the first part of this paper. This speculative concern may derive in part from the tradition of Wisdom. It may, as I. Grünwald, following directions suggested by Scholem and initial perceptions of Scholem, pointed out in a recent dissertation, be quite correct to highlight the lines of connection, valid and significant as they are, which link parts of the Qumran materials, certain texts in the apocalypses, some hints and suggestive passages in Rabbinic literature and the Hechalot and Merkabah mystical texts.[76] In the Wisdom texts and traditions this knowledge had its function and its purpose, bound up with the status of the scribe or teacher of Wisdom, be it a court role or another. In the Hechalot texts as in the later mystical traditions the knowledge provides the map or the needed instruments for the ascent of the soul or the analogous theosophical aim of the particular movement. What is the function or role of this speculative knowledge in the apocalypses? It is hard to consider it some sort of "pure" scientific concern. The present writer must admit that he does not know the answer to the question. One thing is clear beyond doubt, however; this is a part, an integral and most significant part of the apocalypses and of the religious world-view whose expression they are. The apocalypticists, as is indicated by the functions the lists play, consider them to be central. Any theory which wishes to explain the apocalypses and to reach an understanding of the religious outlook of their authors must take account of them.

The historico-religious approach proposed by Betz has the virtue of taking its departure from the need to provide an explanation for the sort of material here considered. It is clearly potentially a contributor to our understanding and deserves the most serious attention of scholars seeking to resolve these issues. That, in the writer's view, it will not provide the only key to the mysteries of the texts is sufficiently evident from what has been said above.

Finally, it may perhaps be suggested that the terms "apocalyptic" and "apocalypticism" be abandoned altogether. They will continue to confuse the issue as they tend to imply an identity between the way of thought they designate and the apocalypses. The writer does not deny the tremendous importance of this pattern of thought in the apocalypses, yet it is not exclusive to the apocalypses. Indeed the "truly apocalyptic" apocalypses are the exception rather than the rule. Daniel, Revelation, and IV Ezra (which as has been demonstrated elsewhere is polemically opposed to speculations)[77] exhaust the list. Just what term should be substituted for "apocalyptic" and "apocalypticism" is not clear. Perhaps Hanson's "apocalyptic eschatology" will prove serviceable.[78] It is to be hoped that the distinction can be preserved, for the apocalypses remain one of the greatest conundrums in the history of Jewish thought, religion, and literature. As long as we remember that by explaining "apocalyptic eschatology" we have not explained the apocalypses, there is hope for the future of the discussion.[79]

The writer is indebted to Ithamar Grünwald of Jerusalem, in discussion with whom the initial ideas for the study of the lists were worked out. In particular some very interesting observations on the lists in the Merkabah literature were communicated to me by him and his study of this material is well advanced. Naturally the responsibility for the article is all my own. John Strugnell, Frank Moore Cross, and other friends kindly offered comments.

NOTES

1. The idea that the revelation made to Moses on Sinai encompassed additional lore extending beyond the normally accepted range of the revealed Torah is a fairly widespread one. It may be observed in an unmistakably apocalyptic context in the first chapter of the Book of Jubilees which makes the very clear claim that the Book of Jubilees itself was revealed to Moses on Sinai. This claim, which is difficult to dismiss as mere literary "window dressing," is of course no more (and no less) astounding than other statements in apocalyptic books. Compare with it, by way of example, the introduction to II Enoch. It is by no mere chance that the first verses of I Enoch (1:1–3) are based on the Blessing of Moses (Deut. 33:1) and the Song of Balaam (Num. 24:3–4), with apparent reference also to Ezek. 1:1. In this association of verses and, one suspects, in the implied claim of the writer, Enoch combines the qualities of the greatest prophet of Israel, the greatest prophet of the nations, and perhaps Ezekiel, whose very first chapter later proves to be of great mystic import. Enoch's direct receipt of revelation from God is equally explicit in 106:19, and an even more radical claim is made in II Enoch 22:4–12; A. Vaillant, *Le Livre des Secrets d'Henoch* (Paris, 1952), pp. 25 f. From the study of these and other similar passages, important conclusions may be drawn bearing on various aspects of the apocalyptic phenomenon. It is the writer's hope to do this in the future. For the present subject, the nature of the Mosaic revelation, we must revert to other texts.

The typology of the Mosaic revelation permeates IV Ezra 14 which tells of the second giving of the Torah. Ezra is summoned by a voice from a bush as Moses was (14:1–3) and indeed the parallel is made explicit by the author in vs. 4. Here too the revelation to Moses is said to contain "many wondrous things . . . secrets of the times . . . end of the seasons." Ezra requests a new revelation of Torah (vss. 20 ff.). He addresses the people, opening his discourse with the typically Mosaic "Hear, Israel" (e.g. Deut. 5:1, 6:4, etc.) and to him are made known both an esoteric revelation (the twenty-four books) and a secret one (the seventy books), all during a forty-day period (vss. 45 ff.). It is highly significant that of the secret books it is said, "for in them is the spring of understanding, the fountain of wisdom and the stream of knowledge." The claim here is basically like that in Jubilees.

These examples and others exhibit clearly the claim that the Mosaic revelation extends beyond "the written Torah." Moreover, they are analogous to the views of the origins of the Oral Torah in Rabbinic literature, but are more radical than they, in spite of views in Rabbinic sources which highlight the role of the Oral Torah. See in general: E. E. Urbach, *The Sages: Their Concepts and Beliefs* (Jerusalem, 1969), pp. 254–278, and particularly pp. 270 ff. [in Hebrew]. This difference is typified and expressed in part by the attitude of the biblical text, as was pointed out by I. Heinemann, *Darkē Ha-Agadah* [*Ways of the Aggada*] (Jerusalem, 1949), pp. 176 f. The reformulation of the biblical stories as connected narratives, using the language of the biblical text, and the introduction into this reformulated biblical text of additional extraneous materials as is done by the author of Jubilees, is utterly different in character from the treatment of that text possible in the Rabbinic world. This reflects, it is maintained, not merely a different literary convention or exegetical technique, but a different attitude toward inspiration. The Temple Scroll of Qumran is, according to published reports, even more extreme in this respect, rewriting parts of Pentateuchal legislation in terms of sectarian *halachah,* in a form and a language designed to resemble that of the Pentateuch, and rephrasing third person divine utterance in the first person. It is in view of phenomena like these that the claims of the apocalyptic authors as to the sources and nature of the revelations made in their works must be read and evaluated. This problematic complex bears too on the viewpoints lying behind apocalyptic pseudepigraphy. It is hoped to devote a full discussion to these issues in the future. They bear however, in the present discussion, on the attribution of the list to Moses, which should, therefore, be regarded as more than a stylistic device. See for a recent summary of views on the problem, without real penetration into the issues, D. S. Russell, *The Method and Message of Jewish Apocalyptic* (Philadelphia, 1964), pp. 127 ff., 158 ff. On the revelation to Moses, see also the prologue to the Greek *Apocalypsis Mosis.* On pseudepigraphy as a typically Hellenistic phenomenon see the comments of M. Hengel, *Judentum und Hellenismus* (Tübingen, 1969), pp. 206, 238, 392 f.

2. Of the list in II Baruch 59, only vs. 9b, which is problematic, is not composed of nouns in genitival relationship. Even here B. Violet, *Die Apokalypsen des Esra und des Baruch in deutscher Gestalt* (Leipzig, 1924), ad loc. suggests a Hebrew original *btym b'm* which, if correct, would not imply major deviation from the norm. See most recently the comments of P. Bogaert, *Apocalypse de Baruch,* II (Paris, 1969), 112 f. He does not consider Violet's emendation convincing.

3. While the exact interpretation of the word *tabnit* in Exod. 25:9, 10 is subject to argument, it is clear that it was later understood in this fashion; cf. I Chron. 28:19; Ezek. 40–48, esp. 40:2. Perhaps Zech. 2:5–9 also reflects this idea; cf. E. Kaufmann, *History of the Religion of Israel from Antiquity to the End of the Second Temple,* VIII (Tel Aviv, 1956), 236 f. [in Hebrew]. Compare, however, B. Uffenheimer, *Visions of Zechariah, from Prophecy to Apocalyptic* (Jerusalem, 1961), pp. 91 f. [in Hebrew]. This type of speculation is explicit in the *Description de la Jerusalem Nouvelle* discovered in a number of manuscripts at Qumran; cf. DJD, I, 134 (1Q 32), DJD, III, 84 (2Q 24), 184 (5Q 15), and in the Apocalypse of John (Book of Revelation) 21:9–27. *Re* this latter see D. Flusser, "Qumran und die Zwölf" in *Initiation,* ed. C. J. Bleeker, Studies in the History of Religions, 10 (Leiden, 1956), 134–146, and more recently, *idem,* "The Pesher of Isaiah and the Twelve Apostles," *EI* 8 (1967), 52–62 [in Hebrew]. The exact relevance of the newly discovered Temple Scroll (see Y. Yadin, *BA* 30 [1967], 135–139) to this tradition is not clear. Yadin says, p. 138, "The Scroll's Temple is not, strictly speaking, the eschatological "ready-made" God-built Temple, which is also the subject, *inter alia,* of the Qumran *Pesharim* ('That is the house which he will make in the end of days'; cf. *Israel Exploration Journal* 9 [1959], 95 ff., articles by Flusser and myself). In fact, a badly-preserved part of our Scroll . . . seems to refer to the Scroll's Temple as the one to be built until the day that I shall create Myself My Temple. . . .'" We must await publication of the text before it can be evaluated in light of the speculative tradition here indicated. Rabbinic thought, in well-known passages, also shows the idea of a pre-existent "concept" of temple in the thought of God; see e.g. Gen. R. (ed. Theodor-Albeck), p. 6. See further E. Bischoff, *Babylonische Astrales in Weltbild des Thalmud u. Midrasch* (Leipzig, 1906), pp. 22–28. Bogaert [N 2]. 111f., thinks that, with a slight emendation, this should be read, "l'image et les dimensions de Sion qui serait construite et l'image du Sanctuaire actuel." This does not affect the fact that the idea of the heavenly sanctuary or Jerusalem is operative here. See also V. Aptowitzer, "The Heavenly Temple in the Agada" *Tarbiz* 2 (1932), 137–153, 257 [in Hebrew]. Bogaert in his commentary alludes to certain of the parallels mentioned here to elements of the list, but suggests as

comparative material to this list only the lists found in the Midrashim of the things created before the world. These are not responsive to the material in II Baruch. See Bogaert, [N 2], 111–113.

4. The Heavenly Jerusalem and its relationship to the Mosaic revelation on Sinai are amply illustrated in II Bar. 4:2–6:

> 2. Dost thou think that this is that city of which I said: "On the palms of my
> 3. hands have I graven thee?" This building now built in your midst is not that which was revealed with me, that which was prepared beforehand here from the time when I took counsel to make Paradise and showed it to Adam before he sinned, but when he transgressed the commandment it was removed 4. from him as also Paradise. And after these things I showed it to my servant 5. Abraham by night among the portions of the victims. And again I showed it to Moses on Mount Sinai when I showed him the likeness of the tabernacle and 6. all its vessels. And now, behold it is preserved with me, as also Paradise.

This passage furnishes, as it were, a summary of the views about the heavenly Temple as revealed in the past. Some of the material on this matter, insofar as it is related to a possible speculative tradition of the measures of the heavenly Jerusalem, was quoted in the preceding note. For lists of further sources see Bogaert [N 2], 14–18; Violet [N 2], p. 208. See also Wisd. Sol. 9:8.

5. See J. Z. Smith, "The Prayer of Joseph," in *Religions in Antiquity, Essays in Memory of Erwin Ramsdell Goodenough*, ed. J. Neusner (Leiden, 1968), pp. 290 f.

6. "The Temple and the order of the sacrifices" are among the things revealed to Abraham in Genesis 15 according to Mekilta, Jethro 9 (ed. Horovitz-Rabin, p. 236).

7. M. E. Stone, "Paradise in IV Ezra iv. 8, and vii. 36, viii. 52" *Journal of Jewish Studies* 17 (1966), 85–88.

8. The expression "paths of Paradise" is strikingly paralleled in *LAB* 19:10 quoted above, p. 417; *usque ad semitas paradysi*. There, however, the expression serves a different function. Moses is shown the *locum unde pluit manna populi usque ad semitas paradysias* part of the revelation touching on the Holy Land and the sacrifices. The final sentence of this passage is similar to material in II Baruch 59; see the discussion of this on p. 418.

9. Cf. *LAB.* 21:2; *tu scis sensum*<emend. J. Strugnell: *censum*>*omnium generationium antequam nascantur*. This perhaps adds some support to the reading "those who have not yet come."

10. Stone [N 7].

11. See e.g. the Similitudes of Enoch, *passim*. This is strikingly the situation in that apparently most "rational" of the apocalypses, IV Ezra, where the resolution of each dialogue is a vision and the resolution of the three dialogues—three visions. See also: Michael E. Stone, "Features of the Eschatology of IV Ezra," unpublished Ph.D. dissertation, Harvard University, Cambridge, Mass., 1965, pp. 25 ff.

12. G. von Rad, "Hiob und die altägyptische Weisheit," in *Gesammelte Studien zum Alten Testament* (München: 1958), pp. 262–272, reprinted from *VTS* 3 (1955), 293–301.

13. Ibid., esp. pp. 267–270.

14. See e.g. the extremely interesting and suggestive comments on Job in connection with apocalyptic by F. M. Cross, "New Directions in the Study of Apocalyptic," *JTC* 6 (1969), 157–165.

15. G. von Rad, *Weisheit in Israel* (Neukirchen-Vluyn, 1970), pp. 32 f. He regards the questions in IV Ezra 5:43 ff. which were discussed above, as well as other interrogative materials found elsewhere in IV Ezra as "didaktische Dialog," p. 33, n. 12.

16. The same idea, in another form, is expressed in Ben Sira 31:18 ff.

17. Cf. e.g. Job 11:7 ff. et al.

18. Von Rad, *Weisheit* [N 15], pp. 134–137, 372 f. He would see this sense of the mysteries of God as one of the sources from which the apocalyptic sprang.

19. The importance of the Ben Sira passage is discussed on p. 431. For the idea of the height of the heaven, see also II Bar. 48:5, II Enoch A, 40:12. Compare also Bogaert [N 2], 112. In a folk tale quoted by St. John D. Seymour, *Tales of King Solomon* (Oxford, 1924), p. 53, appears what is perhaps a curious reflection of this tradition: "Once in the pride of his heart he swore that he would measure the height of heaven. So he caused to be made a machine in the shape of an enormous circle." The tale continues to relate his ascent in this flying machine until warned by Saint Peter not to continue farther. The story continues: "Then the king said to himself, 'If I may not measure the height of heaven, at least I can measure the depth of the ocean." He then has a glass bathyscope made but is prevented from completing his descent by a giant lobster which warns him off.

20. We shall return to the question of the place of this tradition below, but it should be noted that it can be found also in Wisd. Sol 7:19; Armenian IV Ezra 5:36; I Bar. 3:34 f., etc. For interest in the names and numbers of the stars we may compare already Ps. 147:4; Isa. 40:26.

21. See N 41.

22. *The Apocrypha and Pseudepigrapha of the Old Testament,* ed. R. H. Charles, 2 vols. (Oxford, 1913), II, 264.

23. It is very likely that the Apocalypse of Weeks is connected with the sectarian literature from Qumran. In this case, the reference in I Enoch 93:10 probably has to do with the founding of the sect; see J. P. Thorndike, "The Apocalypse of Weeks and the Qumran Sect," *Revue de Qumrân* (1961), 163–184. Certainly once the separation of the last three weeks has taken place, 93:10 receives, albeit secondarily, a fully and purely eschatological import. It is interesting that in ch. 91, where the last three weeks of the Apocalypse are to be found in the manuscripts, the verse preceding them, i.e. 91:10 (91:11 is an editorial addition), also raises the theme of the eschatological granting of wisdom: "And the righteous shall arise from their sleep, and wisdom shall be given unto them." Is it possible that this played a role in the misplacement of these three weeks? Hengel [N 1], p. 377, regards the Apocalypse of Weeks as the oldest part of I Enoch. He also speaks of the eschatological granting of wisdom (p. 378).

This argument is not substantially affected by the new materials adduced by J. T. Milik. Concerning the Apocalypse of Weeks, he notes that 4Q Heng shows the ten weeks consecutively. He also observes, "de même, la section 93:11–14 (elle-même assez differente de texte ge'ez) était précedée d'un texte analogue trois fois plus long que le passage éthopien." No indication is given, however, of where these verses or the longer additional passage do actually occur in the Aramaic manuscript from Qumran. A final assessment must await his publication of the texts. One wonders whether the occurrence of something in the Qumran manuscripts of necessity forecloses the possibility that a reading of the Greek or Ethiopic tradition reflects the original. See: J. T. Milik, "Problèmes de la Littérature Hénochique à la Lumière des Fragments Araméens de Qumrân," *HTR* 64 (1971), 333–378, esp. p. 360.

24. The chief astronomical texts in the apocalypses other than I Enoch are II Enoch 11–16, III Baruch 6. For a more exhaustive treatment of the sources see H. Bietenhard, *Die himmlische Welt im Urchristentum und Spätjudentum* (Tübingen, 1951), pp. 1–52. On the intense Jewish interest in astronomy in the period, see the sources assembled by Hengel [N 1], p. 168 and n. 256. Interestingly, the material in the apocalypses has very little astrological coloring, its basic motif being apparently calendaric. Hengel, pp. 427–442, deals in particular with astrology and its position in Qumran

and in Hellenistic thought. In spite of some evidence for zodiacal interests in I Enoch, there do not appear to be any major true astrological texts among the apocalypses. It is of further interest to observe that the lists do not contain any of the "forbidden" sciences revealed by the Watchers according to I Enoch 7–8, 69; Jub. 8:3 f. The material in I Enoch 69 from vs. 8 on is of a curious type, overlapping not with the forbidden teachings of I Enoch 7–8, etc. but with other traditions like Jub. 4:17 ff. The points of contact between this material and the medical traditions of Jub. 10:1–15 are clear, but the distinction which must be drawn between these two bodies of learning is equally evident.

25. Vaillant [N 1], p. 41.

26. Some discussion of the number of the stars is to be found in Bereshit 32b: '*mr lh hqdwš brwk hw' bty šnym 'šr mzlwt br'ty brqy' w'l kl mzl wmzl br'ty lw šlšym ḥyl w'l kl ḥyl wḥyl br'ty lw šlšym lgywn w'l kl lgywn br'ty lw šlšym rhṭwn w'l kl rhṭwn wrhṭwn br'ty lw šlšym qrṭwn w'l kl qrṭwn wqrṭwn br'ty lw šlšym gsṭr' w'l kl gsṭr' wgsṭr' tlyty bw šlš m'wt wššym wḥmšh 'lpy rbw' kwkbym.* See also Bischoff [N 3], pp. 44 f.; Bietenhard [N 24], pp. 32 f.

27. On the terms in this list see N 9 and Section V.

28. Cf. Gen. 26:4; Exod. 32:13; Neh. 9:23. An alternative form of this expression is *kwkby hšmym lrb;* see Deut. 1:10, 10:22, 28:62.

29. The sand of the sea and the dust of the earth serve a similar function in popular proverbial expressions for large numbers. See e.g. "sand of the sea" in Gen. 32:13; Josh. 11:4; Judg. 7:12; Jer. 33:22, etc., and "dust of the earth" in Gen. 13:16, 28:14; II Sam. 22:43; II Chron. 1:9; Job 27:16, etc. "Sea" and "dust," however, do not seem to undergo the special development which takes place with the stars. This may indicate that the development of this last concept is not by chance. Cf. the passage from II Enoch 47 quoted on pp. 434.

30. For the understanding of the heavenly mechanics see Bietenhard [N 24], pp. 19 ff.

31. See also on this idea: E. Pfeiffer, *Studien zum Antiken Sternglauben* (Leipzig and Berlin, 1916), pp. 17 f.

32. Cf. Prayer of Manasses, vs. 3:

> ho pedēsas tēn thalasson tǭ logǭ tou prostagmatos sou
> ho kleisas tēn abusson kai sphragisamenos tǭ phoberǭ
> kai endoxǭ onomati sou.

Alongside a passage like I Enoch 69:14–21 this verse receives a new dimension. See Apocalypse of John 20:3.

33. Another similar passage is the passage at the end of Ps. Sol. 18 which deals with the praise of God's action reflected in the regularity of the astronomical bodies as a sign of their submission to him.

34. The features of the shining of the faces of the righteous and also the elements to which this shining is compared are much more complex than is indicated here. There is also a group of passages comparing the righteous with angels. In detail see Stone, "Eschatology" [N 11], pp. 206–211. On the possible connection of these ideas with concepts of astral immortality, with citation of the extensive previous bibliography, see Hengel [N 1], pp. 358 f. and notes there.

35. See Stone, "Eschatology" [N 1], pp. 210 f. and references there. In particular observe Job 38:7; cf. also Jer. 19:13, 33:22; Judg. 5:20; Ps. 148:2 f.; Neh. 9:6; II Kings 23:5, cf. 21:15; Deut. 4:19. Cf. also Joseph's dream, Gen. 37:9. In the later books see I Enoch 104:6, 86:1, 3, 90:21. Stars are a symbol of the righteous in I Enoch 46:7; Dan. 8:10 f.

36. On the portals see e.g. I Enoch 33–36; II Enoch 40:10f. (Vaillant [N 1], p. 43) et al. See Bietenhard [N 24], pp. 25 ff., and full references there.

37. On the winds see further in a list in I Enoch 41:2–4.

38. The depths or springs of the deep appear as the basic cosmological element throughout the Bible. For the present discussion note e.g. Gen. 1:2; Prov. 8:24, cf. 28.

39. See Stone, "Paradise" [N 7], 85–88.

40. It should be observed that in these passages in I Enoch the actual measure of the depth is not given. Yet, although a chief interest in these chapters is the fate of the "stars"—the fallen angels—their scope extends beyond this limited subject, as the revelation of the winds, the firmament, and other such matters indicates.

41. The expression *tu scis sensum<*or: *censum>omnium generationum antequam nascantur* is perhaps to be compared with "the earths which have not yet come" in II Bar. 59:9, and perhaps with "seeing a soul or spirit" in I Enoch 93:12, and "the face of a person whom you have never seen" and "the appearance of a voice" in IV Ezra 5:37. Its connection with IV Ezra 5:36 was observed in N 8.

42. Thus I Enoch 60:21–22 (Charles [N 22], II, 225):

> And when the spirit of the rain goes forth from its chamber, the angels come and open the chamber and lead it out, and when it is diffused over the whole earth it unites with the water on the earth. And whensoever it unites with the water on the earth . . .
>
> For the waters are for those who dwell on the earth . . . : therefore there is a measure for the rain, and the angels take it in charge.

Revelation as to the workings of the rain is also to be observed in I Enoch 76:11, 13.

43. Thus in particular G. von Rad, *Theologie des Alten Testaments*, 4th ed. (Munich, 1965), pp. 315–337. See further N 47.

44. See von Rad, "Hiob" [N 12], esp. 264.

45. See pp. 735 ff.

46. See Stone, "Eschatology" [N 11], 17–21. Although some statements there would be modified today, nothing has emerged to change the central observations bearing on the projecting of the Qumran type of setting onto the non-Essene material.

47. Von Rad, "Hiob" [N 12], 315–337, has made his claim most emphatically. His stance is challenged on the question of the origins of apocalyptic eschatology implicitly by P. D. Hanson, *The Dawn of Apocalyptic* (Philadelphia, 1975). Hanson sets forth certain aspects of his thesis in "Old Testament Apocalyptic Re-examined," *Interpretation* 25 (1971), 454–479. Some of the programmatic material was also published in his article, "Jewish Apocalyptic against Its Near Eastern Environment," *RB* 78 (1971), 31–58. Here reference will be made primarily to the far more detailed presentation in his dissertation. Von Rad was explicitly challenged by K. Koch, *Ratlos vor der Apokalyptik* (Gütersloh, 1970), pp. 40–46, and others. In his book on Wisdom, von Rad devotes a lengthy chapter to the determination of the times in Wisdom and apocalyptic; *Weisheit* [N 15], pp. 337–353. This is worthy of detailed treatment separately. A critique of his position is also to be found in Cross [N 14], p. 159, n. 3.

48. Von Rad, *Weisheit* [N 14], pp. 29 ff., 154 ff., 364 ff.

49. See the observation made in N 24.

50. This interpretation is also supported by C. C. McCown, *The Testament of Solomon* (Leipzig, 1922), p. 91. The magical tradition associated with Solomon is early and of profound importance for the development of Jewish, pagan, and Christian magic. It was also known in the Hellenistic world; Hengel [N 1], p. 239 and n. 173. This tradition was already well developed in the time of Josephus, as in *Antiquities* VIII 2, 5 where there are remarkable parallels to our passage, including the magical cutting of roots. See also possibly *LAB* 60:3 which may well refer to Solomon's power over the demons. For a sampling of later sources, see McCown, pp. 92–104. [For attestation of

the early date of this tradition—the apparent use of Solomon's name for expelling demons in the apotropaic psalm scroll from Qumran—see the most recent publication, "Un petit rouleau de psaumes apocryphes (11 QPsApᵃ)," by J. P. M. van der Ploeg, in *Tradition und Glaube: Das frühe Christentum in seiner Umwelt*, Fs. K. G. Kuhn, eds. G. Jeremias, H.-W. Kuhn, H. Stegemann (Göttingen, 1971), pp. 128–139, esp. 130–131, col. i.

51. See von Rad, *Weisheit* [N 15], pp. 364 ff., esp. 154 ff.; cf. 30.

52. Hengel's theory on the development is alluded to below; see also Hengel [N 1], pp. 210–318.

53. The question of the genesis of the lists is not at the heart of our concern here. Thus, the issues dealt with in this section should be regarded as *sub judice* pending a new, major study of Wisdom materials in light of this problem. Hengel [N 1], p. 380, has again drawn attention to earlier observations of the "pre-scientific" character of much apocalyptic cosmology and uranography. This point will have to be taken into account in the formulation of future views on the role of the speculative tradition in the formation of apocalyptic.

54. Hans D. Betz, "On the Problem of the Religio-Historical Understanding of Apocalyptic," *JTC* 6 (1969), 134–156, originally published as "Zum Problem des religionsgeschichtliche Verstandnisses der Apokalyptik," *ZTK* 63 (1966), 391–409; Eng. tr. "The Concept of Apocalyptic in the Theology of the Pannenberg Group," *JTC* 6 (1969), 192–207.

55. Betz, *JTC* 6 (1969), 138.

56. Betz, ibid., pp. 134–137, 200 f.

57. Hengel [N 1], pp. 330–357, 456.   58. Ibid., pp. 357–369, 457.

59. Hengel, pp. 369–381.   60. Ibid., pp. 381–394.   61. Ibid., pp. 391 f.

62. Hengel's study is, of course, based on material which he regards as having been written down to the Maccabean revolt. Moreover, his work is of remarkable scope and deals with an extensive range of problems. Here, no evaluation is being offered of his general theory of the origins of apocalyptic. Rather, examined here are those aspects of his theory which apparently reflect an interest in secret knowledge, while the rest is not subjected to a critique.

63. Hengel [N 1], pp. 369–381, esp. 374 ff. That encyclopaedic wisdom which he recognizes plays, in his view, a role subordinate to that of *Heilsgeschichte*. Thus he says, on p. 377:

> Freilich ist diese apokalyptische "encyclopädische" Weisheit keinesfalls Selbstzweck. Die kosmologischen Geheimnisse von 1. Hen. haben eine deutliche eschatologische Ausrichtung . . . Der ganze Kosmos steht im Dienste einer eschatologisch bestimmten Heilsgeschichte.

If this is even partly right then the lists, their scope, and their function remain completely incomprehensible.

64. Koch [N 47], pp. 15 ff. This book provides an excellent summary of recent debate on the subject. Naturally the distinction between apocalypticism and the apocalypses has been mentioned by a number of recent writers on the subject. They generally do not draw any conclusions from it. See e.g. G. Ebeling, "The Ground of Christian Theology," *JTC* 6 (1969), 52 f. He spends all his article, however, discussing apocalypticism without any concern for apocalypses. Betz, "Problem" [N 54], 134 f., draws the distinction, but defines apocalypticism in accordance with the contents of the apocalypses. Von Rad, *Weisheit* [N 15], in fact does the same, but his presentation is distorted by his insistence on the exclusive Wisdom origin of apocalyptic. Koch [N 47] draws the distinction, but not the implications.

65. Chief documents for the debate of the N.T. scholars are to be found conveniently in English translation in *JTC* 6 (1969). Here too some contributions by American scholars are to be found. Some more recent American contributions are to be found in *Interpretation* 25 (1971). Other than Hanson's study mentioned above [N 47], particular interest is to be found in A. N. Wilder, "The Rhetoric of Ancient and Modern Apocalyptic," *Interpretation* 25 (1971), 436–453. His attempt to state something about the various levels at which "apocalyptic" is discussed is thought-provoking. There is a critical discussion of a great deal of the literature in Koch's book [N 47] and in Betz's articles [N 54].

66. Cf. the suggestion of Koch [N 47], pp. 19–24.

67. It is beyond our aim to give a bibliography of studies on the various apocalypses. The most recent introduction to all this literature is by A.-M. Denis, *Introduction aux Pseudepigraphes grecs de l'Ancien Testament,* Studia in Veteris Testamenti Pseudepigrapha, I (Leiden, 1970). See also J. Schreiner, *Alttestamentlich-Jüdisch Apokalyptik* (Munich, 1969). This work adds so little to what has been said on the subject that one wonders whether it was worth writing.

68. Koch [N 47], pp. 24–30. His discussion of each of these features is, of course, rather fuller than could be reported here.

69. Koch's statement, pp. 19 f., is as follows: "Um eine historische Anschauung vom Hintergrund der apokalyptischen Gedankenbildung und einen brauchbaren, allgemein benutzbaren Begriff von Apokalyptik zu gewinnen, hat man von denjenigen Schriften auszugehen, die hebräisch oder aramäisch abgefasst sind oder in denen zumindest hebräischer oder aramäischer Geist dominiert." To this category he attributes the books mentioned in the text, describing the Apocalypse of John as Semitizing. This is, naturally, an impossible position, for beyond the fact that quite reputable scholars have maintained the Semitic origin of other works, e.g. II Enoch, just how is the category of those "in denen zumindest hebräischer oder aramäischer Geist dominiert" to be fixed?

70. See Betz, "Problem" [N 54], 134 f.

71. See Cross [N 14], 157–165. Hanson does not discuss or develop Cross's highly suggestive observations on the Book of Job, ibid., pp. 162 f. It is to be hoped that he will spell these out in full detail soon.

72. Hanson, [N 47], p. 4; Russell [N 1], p. 105. On the origins of Russell's list, see Hanson, ibid.

73. The same observation was made by Betz in "Problem" [N 54], 135.

74. Observe a similar formulation by Hengel [N 1], p. 378.

75. These categories are those of Hanson, *Dawn of Apocalyptic* [N 47], *passim*.

76. See G. Scholem, *Jewish Gnosticism, Merkabah Mysticism and Talmudic Tradition* (New York, 1960); I. Grünwald, "Apocalyptic and Merkabah Mysticism: A Study of Jewish Esoteric Literature in the Time of Mishnah and Talmud," unpublished dissertation, Hebrew University, 1969 [in Hebrew]. Grünwald has also kindly made available to the writer an unpublished paper in English on "The Esoteric Essence of Jewish Apocalyptic" which provides further bibliography. The lists studied in the present article have their continuation in materials found in the Hechaloth books and also in *Sefer Harazim*. Grünwald's study of these latter materials is well advanced. Betz also remarks on the connection between the apocalypses and the esoteric tradition, in "Concept" [N 54], 199 f.

77. See above, pp. 419 f. See also Stone, "Paradise" [N 7]. That Daniel is not a typical apocalypse was long ago remarked (as a point in its favor) by L. Ginzberg, "Some Observations on the Attitude of the Synagogue towards Apocalyptic-Eschatological Writings," *JBL* 41 (1922), 135, n. 48; see also Betz, "Concept" [N 54], 199.

78. If the distinction is to be made between the pattern of thought and the literary form of the works, the question may be raised as to whether this pattern of thought indeed finds its best or most explicit or clearest place of expression in the apocalypses.

If an examination reveals that it is at least as prominent in works other than the apocalypses, then even the formulation "apocalyptic eschatology" should perhaps be reconsidered. Moreover, even if the nouns are kept distinct, the adjective "apocalyptic" will remain impossibly ambiguous.

79. It may well eventuate that various types are to be distinguished among the apocalypses, but it is clear that our understanding will be advanced only by the study of them in all the rich variety of the material they present of the subjects that concerned them. Betz, "Concept" [N 54], 199 f., also observes that there are different types of apocalypse. Other major aspects of the apocalypses of which there is little real understanding include, *inter alia,* pseudepigraphy, the claim of inspiration, the presence or absence of a real experiential basis behind the vision form, and numerous other issues of literary, tradition, and form criticism.

IV

The Bible and Theology

23. On Sharing the Scriptures

MOSHE GREENBERG

THE HEBREW UNIVERSITY OF JERUSALEM

A SALIENT CHARACTERISTIC of George Ernest Wright is his constant endeavor to attain to clarity in his religious and theological thought. Not content with archaeological-historical inquiry, he has exerted himself over the decades to integrate it with his spiritual concerns, thus producing thoughtful writings stimulating to others in the highest degree. I do but acknowledge a debt in dedicating to him this paper—the opening address to the Jerusalem Congress on Black Africa and the Bible, held in Jerusalem, 24–27 April 1972. I was encouraged to grapple with this theme in no small measure by the example given by G. E. Wright that scholarship does not require a choice between historical inquiry and religious concern, but that both can be manifest harmoniously in one and the same man.

What is the meaning of this gathering in Jerusalem of men from the land that, in Isaiah's language, is "beyond the rivers of Ethiopia" (Isa. 18:1) to discuss with Israelis the place of the Bible in Africa?

Let us consider first the spiritual cargo borne by each of the faiths that are party to this discussion, especially their relationship to the Hebrew Scriptures, which they venerate in common. My remarks on African Christianity are perforce tentative, and put forward with much diffidence; if I offer them at all it is only to reveal my understanding (and perhaps that of my colleagues) of our partners in this discussion at its inception, so that if wrong, wholly or in part, the error may be corrected at once. This is how I conceive the mind of our partners at the outset of this discussion, and by this conception, right or wrong, my following remarks have been shaped. In describing the spiritual cargo of the Jewish party to the discussion I have a similar purpose: to reveal to our guests, many of whom are not likely to have a knowledge of the spiritual state of the Jewish faith-community, something of our positions with respect to the Holy Scriptures, and the question of their significance outside Jewry.

Our partners are Christians of Africa; each of these attributes is momentous.

As Christians, they and we share a common library of sacred books, but the history of our attitudes toward these books is very different.[1] For Christians, our sacred books have always been the Old Testament, a repository of stories, admonitions, prophecies and psalms borne by ancient Israel until, in the fullness of time, their ultimate meaning and fulfillment were manifest in Jesus the Christ. The subsequent worth of that repository has been debated in the Church from its inception as a Gentile institution. In early times, the Old Testament was deemed valuable chiefly for its prophetic evidence for the coming Jesus and his role in salvation. Its message of salvation was wholly appropriated by the Gentile Church, who denied to Israel in the flesh any further role in God's scheme of salvation after they denied the Savior. Indeed, the Church appropriated the very title of "true Israel" along with the Old Testament. But though it held on to the Old Testament, since the heart of the Christian message was freedom from the law, the binding quality of the bulk of God's commandments as set forth in the Old Testament was annulled, its moral admonitions were superseded by the sublimer ones of Jesus, and its stories treated as little more than records of ancient Israel's sinfulness. Although the extreme (but logical) conclusion of Marcion, that the Old Testament was to be excised from Christian sanctity as the work of an inferior deity, was rejected by the Church, it was mainly through allegory and spiritualizing—that is, through a refusal to take the Old Testament in its real, concrete terms—that the Church was able to continue to treasure it among its sacred writings. To be sure, scholars through the centuries maintained an interest in the plain meaning of the text, and its edificatory value—when carefully screened—was acknowledged. But for the mass of Christians, the spiritual essence of the Old Testament emerged only when it was presented as an allegory or a prefiguration of Christian saints and doctrines.

No little ingenuity was expended on such interpretation, because the obvious, other reality of every page of the Old Testament cried out against its wholesale Christianization. Moreover, the pilgrimages to the Holy Land undertaken throughout the Middle Ages served time and again to remind Christians of the earthy reality of land and people—if only through the sacred sites at which Bible events were commemorated in Palestine.

In modern times, the acceptance—especially by the Protestant churches— of a historical view and of criticism of the Old Testament has opened new avenues of appreciation of the Old Testament which do not require allegorization of its content. Modern theology has attempted to justify the retention of the Old Testament in Christian Scripture on the basis of the insight it gives into the meaning of Jesus' work through its progressive revelation of the divine plan; through its providing a foil for Jesus' message (precisely because it is law it can show the full sense of the liberation by the gospel); in general, through providing such understanding of the New Testament that only background, antecedent development, and foil can provide (and in modern times, understanding of every phenomenon is not deemed complete without its history). To be sure, this has not seemed to all a sufficient ground for calling the Old Testament a sacred book, and its word a still living word of God. But it has awakened a lively interest in the life and literature of ancient Israel. As theology is replaced on the popular level with curiosity and noncommittal interest in the past, insight into the background of Jesus remains a partial justification of Old Testament study among modern Christians.

On a deeper level, some modern theologians have noted the greater richness of the Old Testament in comprehending more aspects of life in this world than the New, and in displaying the religious attitude to a larger variety of experiences. We shall have more to say of that later.

Throughout this entire period, Jews resolutely maintained their title to their sacred book as the manifest heirs, by virtue of unbroken succession to Abraham, Isaac, and Jacob and the community of the covenant at Sinai. Its story was their history, its commandments and admonitions their guide to life and constitution, its psalms their prayers. To be sure, no less than the Christians could the Jews remain insensible to the discrepancies between their outlook, their doctrines, their behavior, and those of the Scriptures (distant as they were from their origins by centuries). Yet they did not resort to the drastic expedient of annulling the sense by allegorization; rather they devised hermeneutics that enabled them organically, as it were, to extend the sense of Scripture, to adapt it, to adjust it to new times, without denying its patent human subject—the people of Israel in the flesh—or its patent overarching message—God's requirement that Israel obey his special commandments.[2] The manifest rationality of this interpretation was its strength and accounts for its hold over the minds of Jews until our time. Its limitation is equally patent: the denial of the significance of Hebrew Scripture to any but Jews.

Owing to this widely divergent appreciation of Hebrew Scriptures, Christians as a rule had little reason to look to the Jews for illuminating their meaning, and Jews had no reason to consult the Christians. A trickle of Christian scholars inquiring of the Jews after the plain meaning of the Hebrew persisted through to modern times, but for the most part such Christians did not conceal their contempt for Judaism. There could be no common ground of faith between the Christocentric, denationalized reading of the Old Testament pursued in the Church and the bipolar, theoethnocentric reading of the same text by the Jews.[3] While a good number of our guests here are academic scholars, interest in the plain sense of Hebrew alone cannot account for the curiosity, indeed the expectation of spiritual reward, that moved this group of Christians to come this long way to Jerusalem.

The African factor may have something to do with that.[4] Christianity in Black Africa has settled among peoples whose outlook is in several ways analogous to the Israel described in Hebrew Scriptures. Obligations and loyalties are largely local and tribal—the tribe being a fundamental societal unit. The traditional religions, the substrate of Christianity, share with the

Hebrew religion several important concepts: (a) the idea that conduct should follow principles God gave to the founding fathers of the clan; (b) the unity of the realm of values—there being no separation of sacred from profane; (c) what has been called the life-affirming character of religion —its positive evaluation of vital forces, fertility, self-expression in dance and song; (d) the dual character of the Supreme Being, majestic ruler, yet near, kind, "one on whom men may lean and do not fall"; (e) a certain informality and popularity of religion, with holders of spiritual office often being part-time (rather than full-time) professionals and dependent on gifts from those who consult them. All these traits are to be found in the Israel of Hebrew Scriptures and must make their reception among Africans easier than someone coming from the European forms of Christianity might imagine. A telling indication of the affinity African Christians feel toward the Old Testament is criticism voiced of the independent churches that they are too much weighted toward the Old Testament.

It seems as though the social and spiritual background of Africans brings them close to the Old Testament, while their Christian outlook divests it of its Jewishness, so that they are in the unique position of being able to appropriate the Old Testament as it is, with its concreteness and reality so congenial to them, without Judaizing. And since this process goes on along with the emergence into nationhood of African states, it would seem that the Jews, whose possession of the Old Testament is coeval with their existence but whose emergence into nationhood is equally new, should offer an instructive example of the interaction of Scripture and modern nationality.

From the Jewish side, two conditions must be met for fruitful discussion to take place: (1) the Jews must indeed furnish an example of scriptural life in a modern state; or, failing that, there must at least be among them spokesmen for such a conception with whom Africans may speak; (2) Jews must be able to discern the universal dimension of their Scripture, that which is not dependent upon or applicable to Jews only, in order to be able to participate in a discussion ventilating the non-specifically Jewish implications of Holy Scripture. To what extent can these two conditions be fulfilled today?

1) Although government and people, taken as a whole, are agreed that modern Israel is a Jewish state, confusion reigns over the ideological and political implications of that concept (much less over its physical basis). As regards the constitutionality of Scripture as expressed in its law (whether the original or the highly developed later Jewish elaboration of it in the so-called oral law), official policy and the bulk of public opinion resolutely oppose it, a concession being made only in the realm of personal status law (e.g. marriage and divorce), for the sake of folk unity. Outside of the law of personal status, which is scripturally derived and religious, the state does not enact or enforce any religious law—though in fact there is no consistently clear separation of church and state, owing to the peculiar nature of Jewish life and culture, in which willy-nilly the two are intertwined. Thus

by the Western touchstone of separation of realms, the fact that Holy Scriptures are taught in every grade of the public schools would make Israel appear to have an established religion. Public sabbath observance is another confused realm, with political-power considerations uppermost (the coalition with religious parties determining concessions along these lines). In the realms of social welfare and international politics, the influence of Scripture is usually not even nominal—save as socialist or welfare state policies are more congenial (perhaps) to a population raised on Scripture, or nationalism is leavened by scriptural appeals.

It is true, nonetheless, that the presence of Scripture haunts the public consciousness even at its most secular, and that debate, often very articulate, goes on in the public media, and in journals, on many aspects of the problem of relating life in the state to Scripture. As nowhere else, Scripture is on the agenda of public affairs in Israel. Only this morning (24 April 1972) the aristocratic-liberal newspaper *Ha'aretz* carried a feature on the scripturally based legal-religious problem of defining a Jew.

It is therefore possible to find here people who are ready and equipped to speak on the possibility, the problems and the limitations of realizing today a Scripture-based state.

2) During the course of their long history, Jews have not had much occasion to regard their Scriptures as a potentially universal possession of mankind. The prophets were extremely vague about the status of the special commandments in their visions of a united mankind of the future. Rabbinic Judaism expressly limited the obligation to observe the commandments of the Torah to Jews, and found only seven particular commandments laid upon the rest of mankind for whom the special revelation to Israel was unnecessary. Evidence for exposition of the Torah as a potentially universal rule comes from the Alexandrian Jewish community in the last centuries of the pre-Christian era. Jewish apologetes flourished in the Egyptian diaspora, with Philo of Alexandria at their head. Thereafter, adversity and enmity closed the Jews off from prolonged, ideological, personal intercourse with the nations. Not that Jews were inattentive to the ideological currents of their environment, they were highly attentive; but that personal involvement in that environment and in those currents was restricted to a very small circle, and then it was one-way: Jews discussed the Gentile world, not the other way around. The case of German Jewry during the nineteenth to early twentieth centuries is a shining example.[5] The ideal terms of Jewish involvement in the world without loss of identity and integrity were never part of the curriculum of Jewish schools. The Gentile world as a value was unknown; the Gentiles were not integrated into the Jewish world-view except as a negative, hostile quantity. Typical of this situation was the Talmudic-Rabbinic exclusion of Gentiles from the study of the Torah and condemnation of the Jew who taught him Torah for breaching the rule, "Do not put a stumbling-block before the blind."[6] Jerome tells how one of his teachers,

the Tiberian Jew Baraninas, used to come to his house only at night for fear of the wrath of the Jews (a reflex of the Christian pretension to being the sole custodians of the Scripture). This rule was not strictly followed at any time (as the case of Jerome proves); needless to say, modern secularization of the Jews has brought about a total neglect of it. Nonetheless, Jewish instruction of Scripture to non-Jews has as a rule been purely philological, the teaching of language, text and history. The religious significance of Scripture remained a private, internal affair which Jews were not concerned to teach and Gentiles not interested to learn.

Ecumenical activity since the Second World War has changed matters somewhat. Jews have been invited to discuss aspects of Judaism, especially Jewish understandings of Scripture, with Christians. The object of such invitations has not always been clear; it is clear only that Christians wish to learn how Jews read their Scripture, but just why is not. I think it must be said that something of this unclarity surrounds this meeting as well, chiefly owing to a lack of preliminary acquaintance and discussion of the parties. But that is no fatal flaw. Let us proceed on the assumption that Christian conviction and the hope of religious illumination are the motive of this pilgrimage-conference: what aspects of Jewish appreciation of Scripture can Jews offer as suggestive and serviceable to Christians of Africa—indeed to Christians at large? It is not a question many Jews have asked themselves; in seeking answers I have had to learn from the wrestlings of Christian theologians with the Old Testament. Here, then, is an agenda of a Jewish-Christian consideration of the timeless and universal issues of religion that are posed by Hebrew Scripture.

1) The Testament as a "bridge to the world." New Testament Christianity stands under the impression of the imminent return of Christ and the end of the historical order; this affects deeply its teaching on ethics, law, and the state. Toward the latter two it adopts an almost careless stand: these institutions are on the verge of disappearance; to be concerned with them is idle; hence only the radical rule of love between men is important, and any infringement of it by considerations flowing from justice, law, or the state is ill-advised. But our world has not yet been redeemed by the returned Christ, and so we find ourselves more in the situation of the Old Testament community than that of the New. We must have institutions that regulate relations between men, and between groups of men. The Old Testament alone of the canonical books of Christianity contains specific rules and regulations aimed at fashioning a righteous society. Christian reluctance to accept the validity of the law may be countered by the Jewish appreciation of the law as but the consequence, in human terms, of the divine assertion "I am the Lord your God." Man's acceptance of God's lordship is realized and displayed in his shaping life in accord with the righteous will of God. This acceptance on the part of man is not motivated by a system of rewards and punishments; it is man's response of gratitude both for God's announced in-

tent to take him for his own, and for the salvation of God that he has experienced. "You have seen what I did to the Egyptians, how I bore you on eagles' wings and brought you to me; now, if you will obey me . . . you will be my treasure from among all the peoples . . ." (Exod. 19:4–5).

2) A kingdom of priests; a holy nation. God's law is given to a people. It is not the property of a sanctified clergy, or a class, but it is the "heritage of the congregation of Jacob" (Deut. 33:4). For man in the world cannot be righteous when he is alone and solitary. He is a social being, and his improvement needs a community to be realized. The interrelations of the members of the family, the interrelations of tribes with one another, the relation of the state to its neighbors in war and peace; the obligation of the state, not merely of the individual, to God—these are concerns that life in this world forces upon us and it is inconceivable to the God of the Old Testament that on such matters men be left without instruction or admonition.

A particular problem is the boundary between human and divine authority in this world. The Old Testament contains a record of centuries of struggle between man and God concerning that elusive and crucial boundary. No Christian citizen can in conscience avoid the issue.[7]

It is of the essence of the laws of the Old Testament that they are made public, taught to the populace by the prophet and then by priests, and not kept to a sacred caste. The realization of a "kingdom" and "nation" of holy persons requires it. This idea is the wellspring of the great educational institutions of Judaism and Christianity, and of the repeated liturgical proclamation of God's word at set times and festivals. The publicity of the laws is also the basis of communal responsibility and the duty of the individual to protest wrongs in his community.

Fundamental to the Old Testament is the moral unity of the world of man. The domain of God is the whole of man's world and the drive of the religious impulse of the Old Testament is to dedicate every part of man's life to God. This is a scandal of western modernism, which seeks to give scope to man's autonomy; but Christian and Jew alike, as they draw their values from Scripture, must confront the consequences of the commandment "You shall love the Lord your God with all your heart and soul and might" (Deut. 6:4). In one form or another its realization entails the dedication and regulation; it is total; it is communal. The clash with anthropocentric modern thought is direct and total as well.

3) Paradigms of human behavior. Character is influenced and formed more by example than by precept. It is the Old Testament that contains a treasure of examples of behavior, good and bad, viewed from the angle of man's creaturehood. Faith in the justice of God or his mercy is tested time and again in the lives of Old Testament personages. Contemplation of their responses trains us in our own. National history is also passed in review, and is judged; the sentiments of patriotism are set against various sentences of God upon the nation. All this is indispensable guidance for a man and for a

people for whom the end of the world is not at hand, but who will be living in history as far as they can see ahead.

4) Finally, the praises of God, the laments and supplications made to him by the poets of the Old Testament are paradigms of our address to God and our unspoken wishes and prayers directed to him as well. To take an example: it is significant that the psalmists do not make of God's praise a preface to a request from him. Praise in the psalms is celebration, the enthusiastic admiration of one whose eye is open to the goodness and majesty of God in the world, or to his saving acts, private and public, in the past. Properly speaking there is not even "thanksgiving" in the psalms, but only admiring celebration of bounties received.[8]

In all these matters, the Jewish understanding of Scripture has grown with the trials of national and personal history. The bulk of Jewish literature is in the form of commentary on Scripture, and whether this form is always justified or not (often the pretense of commentary disguises a full-fledged original personal viewpoint) it is nonetheless true that Jewish literature is a monument to the continuous, living power of the word of Scripture in the life of a people.

The current scene in Jewry does not encourage an insider to exclaim upon the spirituality, the insight, and the devotion of this people to their Scripture and its literary afterlife. Much of it is unknown, much needs sifting and evaluation. All of it is in various stages of decrepitude, needing renovation and ventilation in the brisk air of engaged controversy—the controversy of men engaged in the life of the times, ready to shoulder the responsibility of shaping public policy (or at least trying to influence it) in the light of their sacred heritage. Perhaps only such astonishing events as the gathering of men from far off exotic lands to seek the word of God in Jerusalem can move this people, too familiar with their God and his word, to fresh, wondrous contemplation of it again.

Isaiah concludes his address to "the land of whirring wings, which is beyond the rivers of Ethiopia . . . a nation tall and smooth . . . whose lands rivers divide" with a vision of the latter days.

> At that time gifts will be brought to the Lord of hosts
> from a people tall and smooth
> from a people feared near and far,
> a nation mighty and conquering
> whose land the rivers divide
> to mount Zion, the place of the name of the Lord of hosts.

What better gift than to give occasion to a stirring of minds to study the question of the universal significance of Scripture in our time, to force a people dulled by toil and adversity to behold its treasure through the eyes of new admirers! That is a gift to the Lord of hosts that only men of Africa can bring.

NOTES

1. Most of what I know ot the history of the Old Testament in the Church is derived from these works: A. Harnack, *The Mission and Expansion of Christianity*, tr., ed. J. Moffatt (London, 1908; repr. New York, 1961), esp. chs. v, vii, viii; G. H. Gilbert, *Interpretation of the Bible: A Short History* (New York, 1908); M. Simon, *Verus Israel* (Paris, 1948), esp. chs. iii, v, and vi; E. G. Kraeling, *The Old Testament Since the Reformation* (London, 1955). One may now consult further the pertinent chapters in *CHB*, II, III.
2. For a recent compendious survey of medieval Jewish exegesis, see E. I. J. Rosenthal in *CHB*, II (1969), 252–279.
3. Jewish rebuttals of christological readings of Hebrew Scripture are described by E. I. J. Rosenthal in "Anti-Christian Polemic in Medieval Bible Commentaries," *Journal of Jewish Studies* 11 (1960), 115–135, and "Jüdische Antwort," in *Kirche und Synagoge*, eds. K. H. Rengstorf, S. von Kortzfleisch (Stuttgart, 1968), pp. 307–362; both reprinted in *Jewish Themes*, Studia Semitica, I (Cambridge, 1971), 165–243. The latest account of Christian Hebraists is by R. Loewe in *Encyclopaedia Judaica*, 8 (Jerusalem, 1971), cols. 9–71, with an astonishingly generous listing of persons and an excellent bibliography.
4. The following remarks have been distilled from Geoffrey Parrinder, *Religion in Africa* (Harmondsworth, 1969); current research and bibliographical information is published in the periodical *Journal of Religion in Africa*, Leiden.
5. See G. G. Scholem, "Jews and Germans," *Commentary* 32/5 (Nov. 1966), 31–38; repr. in *The Jewish Expression*, ed. J. Goldin (New York, 1970), pp. 465–483.
6. *Tosafot, Ḥagigah* 13a, rubric *'En.*
7. Prophetic utterances on this theme have often been analyzed; see e.g. N. K. Gottwald, *All the Kingdoms of the Earth* (New York, 1964). Closer to the modern situation are the examples of disobedience to illegal royal orders collected and elaborated in the light of rabbinic exegesis by M. Greenberg in "Rabbinic Reflections on Defying Illegal Orders: Amasa, Abner, and Joab," *Judaism* 19 (Winter 1970), 30–37.
8. C. Westermann, *The Praise of God in the Psalms*, tr. K. R. Crim (London, 1966), pp. 1–51.

24. Faith and Ideology in the Old Testament

PATRICK D. MILLER, JR.
UNION THEOLOGICAL SEMINARY, RICHMOND

THE INSIGHTS and analytical tools of sociology have made a significant contribution to the study of the Old Testament during the twentieth century. Herbert Hahn has summarized the major contributions of this approach in his book *The Old Testament in Modern Research*.[1] The basic works in this area, however, have largely been in the first half of the century, even though sociological studies have expanded during the last twenty-five years at a rapid pace.[2] That may be because of a current mutual disinterest on the part of sociologist and biblical interpreter alike. Whatever the reason, the following essay is a modest attempt to look at the Old Testament with some of the insights given to us by sociology, or, to put it more precisely, one area of that discipline, the sociology of knowledge. The writer should admit at the beginning that his particular field of study is the Old Testament and not sociology. Sociological analysis of biblical materials is fraught with difficulties and pitfalls, especially for one who is not a sociologist, but such analysis remains a *desideratum* in the field and is worth the risk. One can always be confident others will correct and carry the discussion further.

By "sociology of knowledge" is meant in simplest terms the examination of the relationship of thought or ways of thinking to social context, i.e. "the social roots of our knowledge,"[3] or "the social construction of reality."[4] Religion, of course, plays a major role in both the construction of reality as a group perceives it and the maintenance of that reality.[5] It participates in the process of legitimation, the explanation and justification of the social order. It "legitimates social institutions by bestowing upon them as ultimately valid ontological status, that is, by *locating* them within a sacred and cosmic frame of reference."[6] That happens in terms of individual and group, both for the everyday experiences of life as well as for "those marginal situations in which the reality of everyday life is put in question."[7]

Since Karl Mannheim's major work, *Ideology and Utopia,* the phenomenon of ideology has been a basic concern of the sociology of knowledge—"the understanding that no human thought . . . is immune to the ideologizing influences of its social context."[8] It is that phenomenon in its religious manifestation which is the particular focus of this paper. One finds in the scholarly literature concerned with the Old Testament and its ancient Near Eastern background references to "ideology," e.g. "national ideology," "royal ideology," "convenantal ideology," "ideology of kingship," or simply "ideology."[9] In many instances the term appears in a proper context. Sometimes it appears to mean no more than a complex of ideas. But the word "ideology" is a fairly precise and technical term appearing more frequently in such disciplines as political science and sociology than in Near Eastern studies. Consequently, the Old Testament scholar may use the term "ideology" carelessly without full awareness that it is technical and therefore to be used in a specific sense.

The contention of the following discussion, however, is not that the word "ideology" should be removed from Old Testament critical studies. To argue for a careful use is not to say that it has no place. On the contrary, it is precisely my point that a proper understanding of the development of Israel's history and religion involves a recognition of the presence and the effect of ideological factors. And an honest and critical evaluation or estimation of Israel's religion should take the ideological factor more into account than previous studies have tended to. An examination of the extent to which ideology is a part of or in conflict with Israel's faith is thus an important task for the historian of Israel's religion as well as the Old Testament theologian. The following remarks can only be an initial attempt to lay out some guidelines, define the problem, and suggest tentatively areas in which the ideological character of the faith of Israel may be seen.[10] Some of these areas have already been noted by others and even more can be said than one will find in the brief scope of this particular discussion which seeks to take a broad view rather than focus on one particular area or era.

Ideology is a complex word whose meaning has a long history.[11] It may be used in a pejorative sense, implying a negative judgment. Since Napoleon, who used the word as a term of contempt, this has been the connotation it has borne in its general use.[12] But ideology may also be used in a more neutral way as a description of the way things are in a society, the values, ideas, and conceptions of a society which cause it to do or act as it does. A value judgment does not necessarily have to be made by the designation "ideology."

The term, however, does imply that the picture or view entertained by the group or society that has the ideology is partial, that there are factors underlying or hidden that may not have been articulated or completely realized by the group but that are influential in its thought and action. This aspect of ideology is most crucial and in fact helps determine what is meant when the word is applied to a system of thought, a point of view, or a program, whether religious, political, or social. To use Talcott Parsons' terms: selectivity and distortion take place.[13] The distortion and selection may not be entirely intentional. The ideologist may not even be aware of his distortions. Furthermore, what he says may belie his actual intentions or motives whether they be conscious or not. For this reason one must not depend entirely on what is said to reach a true understanding of the meaning and intention of the individual or group propounding an ideology. One has to probe beneath the surface and use what Mannheim calls "the indirect method of analysing the social conditions of the individual or his group." Or, to put it in another way:

> The ideas expressed by the subject are thus regarded as functions of his existence. This means that opinions, statements, propositions, and systems of ideas are not taken at their face value but are interpreted in the light of the life-situation of the one who expresses them. It signifies further that the specific character and life-situation of the subject influence his opinions, perceptions, and interpretations.[14]

One may not necessarily be dealing with calculated lies, but with unintentional error and distortion arising out of the individual or group's social situation.

It may be appropriate at this stage to define the word "ideology" inasmuch as various nuances and meanings have been given to it. For purposes of further clarification, therefore, two basic and generally similar definitions of ideology are given here. The first is that of Winston White, which is helpful because of its succinctness and brevity: "An ideology is a selective interpretation of the state of affairs in society made by those who share some particular conception of what it ought to be."[15] The second and more elaborate definition is that of James Luther Adams who defines ideology as:

> that composite myth by which a society or group identifies itself, not only for itself but also for other societies and groups. An ideology posits the group's goals and the justification of these goals in terms of which the group deals with other groups and with conflicts within the group; it defines and interprets the situation; aims to overcome indifference to the common good; it reduces excessive emphasis on individual action. It makes possible group action.[16]

Further:

> In its full mythical corpus, an ideology articulates a myth of origin and a myth of mission—a Whence and a Whither—for the group, not merely in a general way (so as to express the group's sense of values and of vocation) but also in relation to the situation in which the group finds itself.[17]

There are other ways of speaking of ideology, such as a way of life, a political program, a tool of action. All these definitions contain some element of truth but are vague and subject to distortion. It is also possible to see the development of an ideology as a response to strain, as do Parsons and White. The strain is in the discrepancy between the way things are and the way they ought to be in the eyes of the group. But perhaps even more important is to recognize in the understanding of an ideology that it usually involves a philosophy of history or an attitude toward history. The movement between Whence and Whither, origin and goal, the way things are and the way they ought to be, forces the ideologist, whatever his point of view, to some conception or understanding of history.[18]

It may seem that the above analysis of ideology has wandered far afield from the Old Testament. In the most obvious sense that is true. Yet it is this analysis—when used as spectacles through which one views the history of Israel's religion—that can enable one to see more clearly the ideological aspects of Israel's faith.

The roots of ideology in Israelite thought are to be found in the earliest period, particularly in the election and covenant theology of Israel. A fully articulated and worked-out ideology, however, does not really manifest itself until the Yahwist's presentation of Israel's history when it becomes considerably retrospective. The notion of a chosen people and the belief in the divine promises, which are at the center of his interpretation, contain almost by definition ideological qualities. For here is a group, in this case an ethnic and later national group, pictured as bound together in common cause, assuming for ideological reasons a common origin, i.e. Abraham, and having moved toward a common goal—the "utopia" of the Promised Land. In this context faith and ideology are closely intertwined. An elaborated, compelling, strong theology is permeated with hidden causes and underlying motives that center in Israel's self-interest, but the theology of the Yahwist is more than that. The line between faith and ideology is never drawn completely, but in the early period of Israel's history the two are less clearly differentiated than at later stages.

It is rather difficult to define that which I have called the faith element in distinction from the ideological. It may be best to speak of it in terms of those impulses which force Israel's theology out beyond the limits of its own self-interest. Or, to come at definition in terms of differentiation, ideology can be thought of as the ego extension of the group whereas faith refers to that process whereby the ego is transcended. The criteria here would seem to be at least three (though not necessarily always appearing together):

1. The possibility and presence of self-criticism which means also the possibility of judgment as the end of Israel's history.
2. The positive relationship of Israel with the other nations of the world. A sense of responsibility *vis-à-vis* other people so that Israel's own particular interests do not totally define its goal or mission and Israel's place in the world is set at least in part for the well-being of the nations.

3. The moral demand for justice and righteousness as the central characteristics of human conduct.

The designation of such factors as representing something other than the ideology of the group may be in part an arbitrary decision but they can be argued. For example, the first of the criteria represents a critique of one of the basic functions of an ideology, the support of the group. The second criterion functions as a critique of ideology's primary interest in the ego of the group. The presence of universal norms provides a rule to measure the life of the group and one that does not come solely from within the ideology. That criterion also serves as a critique of the uniqueness or exclusive character of the ideology. It accepts within itself the possibility of judgment by norms that belong also to those not sharing the national ideology.[19]

Keeping what has been said to this point in mind, I would like now to look at the Old Testament material quite broadly—and inevitably incompletely—beginning with the early poetry, then the Yahwist, and the conquest traditions which are a complex mixture of earlier material and later interpretation, followed by a brief look at the prophetic criticism.

If we try to examine the Old Testament material from some sort of historical perspective—and it is not always possible because of the complexities of the history of tradition—the first place to center one's attention is on the corpus of early poetry. What sort of picture is given here of Israel in terms of goals and aims, attitudes toward other groups? In the blessing of Isaac (Gen. 27:27b–29), for example, we have Israel described as beneficiary of the blessings of God in terms of fertility and prosperity, a rich land. Israel is to be master and lord of the peoples. The ancient victory hymn of Exodus 15 depicts the Hebrews as the redeemed of Yahweh (vs. 13) who has manifest his *ḥesed* upon them, has mightily overthrown all who stand in Israel's way on the journey to the Promised Land, has led them into the land and planted them there in his holy abode. We have here in poetic form the ideology of conquest. The oppressors of Israel have been overthrown and now as the elect people of God the Israelites march forth in conquest with Yahweh leading—to take the Promised Land.

That sort of picture dominates the early poetry and partially hides the fact that underlying this is a history of motley groups of people related in various ways but seeking and manifesting a basis for unity as well as a rationale for the acquisition of land and conflict with neighbors. Along with Exodus 15 one might cite Judges 5 and more especially the conclusion to the hymnic framework of Deuteronomy 33. The conquest is viewed in these hymns both as divine action and divine command to Israel. Israel is to destroy "the enemy" and live in prosperity and happiness and safety under the protection of Yahweh. The other peoples, i.e. "your enemies," shall be totally subject to the "saved" people of Yahweh.

In the early poetry, therefore, we have in effect an identification of faith and ideology, an identification of Yahweh's goals and interests with those of

Israel: land and the growth of a people. Or we might say that the early poetry sets forth an ideology for the beginnings of the nation in the land, but not in any systematic fashion. There is no critical element present,[20] and Israel's attitude toward the nations is summed up in the word "enemies."

With the Yahwist the situation is somewhat different. As already suggested, the rather complete picture of Israel's early history which he gives provides for a carefully worked out ideological rationale. The origin and unity of the people are rooted in their "common" ancestor Abraham and his obedience to the divine call. They are also rooted in the promise of a son and posterity. The growth of the people Israel is seen as a divine gift and a reward to the faithful Abraham. It is not viewed as the coming together of disparate elements with common needs and common enemies for sociopolitical purposes. The land is Israel's by virtue of the promise. It is a divine gift also. Furthermore, the account of origins as the Yahwist tells it plays a role in the developing royal ideology.

This is the ideology, the theological rationale for the union of the tribes, the acquisition of the land at least in part by the displacement of prior inhabitants, and the development of a strong national state under a powerful monarchy. The ideology does not spring up full blown. It grows and develops in the process of the history of tradition.[21] But there are also elements here which keep Israel's theology from being simply ideology or enable it to transcend ideology. The criteria cited earlier are present in the Yahwist's history. H. W. Wolff has demonstrated quite clearly the thematic character of the blessing motif in the Yahwistic epic and particularly the blessing of the peoples of the earth through Israel.[22] This note is sounded five times in the Yahwist's account (Gen. 12:3, 18:18, 22:18, 26:4, 28:14), and Wolff dares to call it the kerygma of the Yahwist to the Israel of his time. In his concluding statement Wolff shows how the Yahwist has transcended the merely ideological statement of Israel's Whence and Whither:

> It must have been a cutting word to the *hubris* of those who lived ostentatiously in Solomon's day to learn that their greatness would be attained as a blessing of Yahweh only when through them all nations had found blessing as deliverance to a free, productive life. Thus, for the sake of this high purpose, the Yahwist takes the blasé back to Yahweh's beginnings with Israel by reinterpreting the traditions for his own time with compelling power.

The Yahwist's history, therefore, manifests the possibility of criticism of Israel's ideology and its potential for pride and, furthermore, proclaims that Israel's goal or mission is not simply in terms of self-interest but ultimately and primarily in being the means of blessing and good for *all* the peoples of the earth. Thus two of the criteria for transcending ideology—even if still essentially within an ideological framework—are fulfilled.

The third criterion—the moral demand for justice and righteousness as the central characteristics of human conduct—is also found in the Yahwistic history, specifically within an election context. In the account of Abraham's intercession for Sodom[23] Yahweh says (Gen. 18:17b–19):

> "Shall I hide from Abraham what I am about to do, seeing that Abraham shall become a great and mighty nation, and all the nations of the earth shall bless themselves by him? No, for I have chosen (*yāda'ti*) him, that he may charge his children and his household after him to keep the way of the Lord by doing righteousness (*ṣᵉdāqāh*) and justice (*mišpāṭ*); so that the Lord may bring to Abraham what he has promised."

Verse 19 may be theological reflection on the Yahwist's part, although it is frequently attributed to a redactor because of the "theological formulations which are quite foreign to the other narrators."[24] Whether it is the work of the Yahwist or a later addition reading back into the Abraham story the covenant demands, the writer of this verse sets forth the universal norms of justice and righteousness as Yahweh's way and the way of his people. These act as controls or checks on the conduct and ideology of the Israelites and have in them also the potential for criticism and judgment both of the ideology and the conduct, a potential that is realized in the prophecy of Amos.

When we turn to the conquest traditions beyond the early poetry, matters become more complex. Deuteronomic influence is strong and contributes to the formation of ideology. Primitive elements and later theological reflection are present side by side.

The question of Israel's settlement in the land continues to be one of the most debated matters in Old Testament studies.[25] The date, the length of time involved, the very nature of the process of settlement particularly with regard to its military or non-military character are all matters of considerable debate. We do not have a detailed, definitive, historical picture of this period and probably never will have. Both the literary evidence and the archaeological evidence are debatable. The canonical picture of the taking of the land is clearly retrospective and involves considerable later reflection. Which is to suggest also that the ideology of conquest here is at least in part interpretation, vindication, and rationale after the fact, a justification of Israel's actions in securing a land, an accounting for its later understanding of its elect position on the basis of a picture and interpretation of the earlier history.

At the same time it may be suggested that the practices and conceptions of Israel's holy wars actually had their primary roots in an ideology of conquest. Less rationale was needed for wars of protection and defense, and it is highly unlikely that such an involved one with its many theological and cultic elements would have developed merely as a basis for self-defense.[26] On the contrary, the type of activity and theological interpretation which was involved in Israel's sacral warfare is best understood as being based upon an ideology that gave reason, motive, and goal for Israel's action. That ideology saw Israel as a chosen people, the *'am yhwh*. The goal toward which the action and the ideology moved was the Promised Land, a place where the people could live in contentment and serve Yahweh. Underlying all this was the continuing need for land or place and the recognition that drastic or very aggressive measures would have to be taken to achieve that end. One notes also the process of selectivity and distortion taking place in that some contexts make the takeover of the land seem total whereas other accounts indicate this was not so.

In any event, the picture that one receives of the early history, which is a mixture of primitive and later interpretations, is in the technical sense of the term ideology: the people's conceptions and rituals of war; their understanding of their election; the view that God and the angels were on their side; their participation in battle seen as going to the help of Yahweh; and an interpretation of victory as Yahweh's giving the enemy into their hands—all this being a part of the Whence and Whither, a part of the group's conceptions of the way things were in order to bring about the way things ought to be, i.e. that Israel might have a land. Partially hidden was the basic fact that tribal groups were in need of land, had been both slowly and quickly moving in on territory occupied by others, coming into hostile contact with the prior occupants and seeking to move them out. There were political and sociological factors (not all of them discoverable) which caused the formation of an ideology.[27]

An important element in Israel's early sacral wars and in the ideology growing out of them was the *ḥērem,* the ban, according to which the booty and captives were consecrated to Yahweh and totally destroyed.[28] The *ḥērem,* which is obviously a problem for the person who seeks to appropriate the Old Testament theologically, was to some extent a problem for the ancient Israelites. Building on the work of Brekelmans, one may cite it as an interesting example of the growth or development of ideology. Brekelmans makes a good case for the conclusion that the historical cases of the carrying out of the *ḥērem* took place in three offensive endeavors (two of them in the conquest traditions) recorded in Numbers 21; Joshua 6–7; and I Samuel 15. The number of instances may be debated, but he makes a good case for these. He interprets the war *ḥērem* in the early period as a vow made to Yahweh in very dangerous and difficult battles in order to make certain of his help. Three things happen to the interpretation of the *ḥērem* as the Deuteronomic traditions elaborate an ideology for the *ḥērem:*

1. The practice of *ḥērem* is levelled through the conquest traditions (though there may have been in actuality more cases than the three cited by Brekelmans, there are also signs of this later expansion) in order to make it a standard element of the conquest wars.
2. The *ḥērem,* which appears originally to have been an act initiated by

      man is made into a divine command (Josh. 10:40 and 11:20; explicitly and implicitly in Deuteronomy).

3. Most important, the Deuteronomist seeks to show that the purpose of the *ḥērem* was to remove all aspects of the pagan Canaanite religion and culture so that Yahwism might not be corrupted.

Thus in the light of the later situation the role of the *ḥērem* in Israel is reinterpreted, giving it a more significant and fundamental place and transforming the early conflicts of the conquest into a forthright *Religionskampf* with the *ḥērem* at the center as a divine command to avoid Canaanite contamination. The real purposes of the *ḥērem* and the conflicts have been covered over as the ideological interpretation of Israel's beginnings has developed.[29]

Two other passages having to do with the Deuteronomic interpretation of the conquest of the land illustrate the interplay of ideological factors in the faith of Israel at this point.

Jephthah in his dispute with the Ammonites over the plain of Moab is instructive in this regard. The territory between the Arnon and Jabbok rivers was throughout the centuries a disputed area (see e.g. the Meša' Stele). In his message to the Ammonites Jephthah explains the historical circumstances of Israel's present occupancy of the land. The Amorites had sought to block Israel's passage and were defeated, i.e. "Yahweh the God of Israel gave Sihon and all his people into the hand of Israel" (Judg. 11:21). Israel's claim to the land is legitimate. She had taken it from the Amorites who had earlier taken it from Moab (Num. 21:26 f.). Jephthah establishes his claim in a theological-ideological fashion, which he knows the king of the Ammonites will understand because it is traditional language (see again the Meša' Stele): "So then Yahweh, the God of Israel, dispossessed the Amorites from before his people Israel; and are you to take possession of them? Will you not possess what Chemosh your god causes you to possess? And all that Yahweh our God has dispossessed before us, we will possess" (Judg. 11:23–24). In the Deuteronomic account (ch. 2) the basis for Israel's occupancy is even more thoroughly ideological; Sihon's decision to block Israel's passage was as a result of Yahweh's hardening his heart precisely in order that Israel might get hold of his territory.[30]

The intermingling of faith and ideology as well as the struggle between these two forces is clearly seen in Deut. 9:4 ff., where Israel is enjoined as a nation not to assume that it was because of the people's innate goodness that they were being given the land. Experience had given the lie to any notion of election because of worthiness. Israel was a stubborn people, who had provoked Yahweh to wrath countless times from the very beginning (Deut. 9:6 ff.). The "gift" of the land to Israel was for two reasons: (a) Yahweh loves Israel (Deut. 7:8), and (b) Yahweh is driving out the nations because of their wickedness (Deut. 9:5). There can be little doubt that Israel or elements within Israel took this last reason at face value and were convinced both of the accuracy of the statement and the legitimacy of Yahweh's action.

But the ideological character of the ascribed motive must also be recognized. Israel's acquisition of the needed land cannot be ascribed to her own faithfulness, and it is apparently not enough to say that Yahweh gives the land out of love. The present occupants of the land (i.e. prior to Israel's occupation) are wicked and deserve to lose the land through divine wrath although one might be hard-pressed in an objective analysis to prove the greater wickedness of the Amorites, Canaanites, Girgashites, Perizites, etc.

We have suggested ways in which an ideological analysis of the accounts of Israel's origins and early history is possible. But we have also noted that there were factors at work keeping the ideology somewhat in check. Israel's life could come under scrutiny and possible criticism. Imperatives of obedience, righteousness, and justice kept the faith of Israel from becoming purely ideological or worked to redeem it when it did so. Covenant responsibility was the context in which all of Israel's faith and history was to be set. Failure to hold on to that primary fact led to the ideological distortion of Israel's faith in the later history of the nation and brought about the harshest condemnation of the prophets, who perceived that the popular or national theology was simply an ideology without controls, without any checks and balances.

In the later history of Israel under the monarchy the interrelationship, indeed the conflict, between faith and ideology is further seen. The Davidic covenant and promises became the basis for a national ideology. In fact it is here apparently that Old Testament scholarship most often makes reference to ideology. Within various expressions of the David-Zion theology there were some checks and balances as one can see, for example, in Psalms 89 and 132. There were calls for obedience in the promises of an eternal house and the rule of Zion. But these tended to play a minor role in the theology of the monarchy as apparently was the case with the Sinai covenant with its demands for obedience (though the interrelationship of Davidic covenant and Sinai covenant in the monarchy is a difficult matter). A sign of the strongly ideological character of the national theology was the tenacious hold upon it by the nation despite the fact that actual circumstances raised serious questions about its validity. Such tenacity can be and perhaps in part was a characteristic of faith. But there was no attempt to re-evaluate this theology to discover where ideological but false security had replaced faithfulness. The people were content to repeat "The temple of the Lord." The divine imperatives of justice, mercy, and righteousness were easily forgotten.

There was present in this situation a process of selectivity and distortion taking place which made the Davidic promises and covenant increasingly ideological, a program for action suitable to the views of the people about what they wanted in their society and about what God was doing in the world and in history. Ideological elements prevailed to the neglect of those characteristics which belong to genuine faith and right religion. The eternal promise was selected. The chastening with the rod of men (II Sam. 7:14) was for all intents and purposes ignored, though it took place. The Davidic covenant was selected; the Sinaitic covenant fell to the side. The inviolability of Zion was an unquestioned presupposition; the fate of Shiloh was ignored.

It was the task of the prophets to point out this selectivity and distortion, the error on the part of people and kings whether intended or unintended. It was the function of the prophets to puncture the identification of faith with ideology. They were able to do this because to a large extent they stood outside the power structures—a stance that best allowed a vigorous attack upon the popular ideology.

The prophet Amos placed the traditions of election and covenant at the very heart of much of his preaching. He believed firmly in the ancient promises of Yahweh to his people. But he did not hesitate to pick the most appealing part of the popular ideology about Israel's destiny and use it as a basis for judgment against the very proponents of that ideology:

> You only have I known
> of all the families of the earth;
> *therefore* I will punish you
> for all your iniquities.
>
> Amos 3:2[31]

The theology of election and promise is turned against Israel and no longer permitted to be the guarantor of the *status quo* or the basis for a utopian or ideal future. It now becomes the motive for doom and destruction because of the absence of that which points to genuine faith, justice, and righteousness.[32]

Jeremiah also wrestled with this problem. Despite his priestly ancestry he attacked the easy and deceptive security of those who felt that as long as the temple existed on Zion everything would be all right. He bade them take another look at Shiloh where Yahweh's dwelling had once been. There they would see the tenuousness of their ideology apart from obedience and trust. Those who centuries before had been "given" the land were now told by the very God who had provided for their need for land: "Amend your ways and your doings, and I will let you dwell in this place" (Jer. 7:3).[33] Whatever had been the motives and reasons—apparent and hidden—for the earlier conquest and settlement of the land, Judah's occupation of her territory was seen by Jeremiah as anything but permanent. The ideology which contributed to a theology of the gift of the land could now be used against the people and made the basis for the removal of the land. Even as the earlier occupants were wiped out because of their wickedness, according to the Deuteronomist, so now the present occupants would suffer a similar fate for a similar reason.

One recognizes, therefore, with Berger and others that the prophetic message before the exile was not non-ideological.[34] The prophets contributed a rationale for the coming experience of Israel. But the old ideology was changed and criticized by a perspective that transcended it and yet stood in continuity with it. This fact is recognized by Berger implicitly if not indeed explicitly. With reference to A. Gunneweg's monograph, *Mündliche und schriftliche Tradition der vorexilischen Prophetenbücher als Problem der neueren Prophetenforschung* (Göttingen, 1959), Berger makes the following comment:

> The position that Gunneweg represents very well thus gives up the traditional attempt to set the canonical prophets off in a special sociological category, making their distinctiveness *a strictly theological one.* They stand out against their common background of Nabiism in terms of the astounding *novum* of their message. This message, *while largely based on the older traditions of Israel* as transmitted in the cult, *radicalized* the latter—and thus also transformed the office held by the prophets. And indeed *"radicalization"* is also a good term to describe the place of the canonical prophets in the general development of Israel's religion (italics mine).[35]

What Berger describes here as a "strictly theological" distinctiveness or a "radicalization" appears to conform in large part to what has been described here as the element of faith, involved with but not simply identical to the national ideology. Berger also admits that at this point the prophets were in continuity with the traditions before them, in which faith and ideology constantly interacted.

When viewing the fate of the Israelites at the hand of the Assyrians and Babylonians, one might expect to find in Deutero-Isaiah the end of ideology as far as the history of Israel's religion is concerned. But this prophet of the exile does not renounce ideology completely. Rather he reinterprets it in the light of the hard lessons of history. Israel is again in need of land and a home. And once again the promise of land as a divine gift is made. The ideology conforms to the history that is taking place. The notion of Israel as a chosen people and the conception of history from beginning to end as the working out of Yahweh's purpose are nowhere more clearly present than in Deutero-Isaiah. But now the element of the future rises more sharply to the fore. The ancient "myth"—in the ideological sense—of origin is re-enacted in a new creation and a new exodus. The people is formed again. The universal and trans-Israel dimensions of her "myth" of mission are accentuated. In primary and secondary strata of Deutero-Isaiah Israel's future is seen in terms of the nations. Part of her *raison d'être* is precisely witness and mission.

> Behold, you shall call nations that you know not,
>   and nations that knew you not shall run to you,
> because of Yahweh your God, and of the Holy One of Israel,
>   for he has glorified you.
>
> Isa. 55:5

The prophet speaks of one who "will bring justice to the nations" (Isa. 42:1) and one who is given as "a covenant to the people, a light to the nations"

(Isa. 42:6).[36] Thus in a sense with Deutero-Isaiah the history of the religion of Israel in its ideological content comes around full circle. The earlier intermingling of faith and ideology takes place once again, only now with the experience of divine chastisement and divine comfort the ideology is redirected, and the theocratic structure of Israel's existence is universalized to a high degree.[37]

NOTES

1. H. F. Hahn, *The Old Testament in Modern Research*, 2d ed. (Philadelphia, 1966), pp. 157–184, 275–276. More recently S. T. Kimbrough has presented some interpretive articles focusing specifically on the work of Antonin Causse: "Une conception sociologique de la religion d'Israel," *Revue d'histoire et de philosophie religieuse* 49 (1969), 313–330; and "A Non-Weberian Sociological Approach to Israelite Religion," *JNES* 31 (1972), 195–202.

2. There are some notable exceptions, e.g. G. E. Mendenhall in "The Hebrew Conquest of Palestine," *BA* 25 (1962), 66–87; "The Relation of the Individual to Political Society in Ancient Israel," in *Biblical Studies in Memory of H. C. Alleman*, eds. J. M. Myers, O. Reimherr, and H. N. Bream (Locust Valley, N.Y.: J. J. Augustin, 1960), pp. 89–108; and more recently in a paper, "Abraham in the Light of History," presented at the Society of Biblical Literature meeting of 1972 in Los Angeles. From the side of the sociologist one should mention P. Berger, "Charisma and Religious Innovation: The Social Location of Israelite Prophecy," *American Sociological Review* 28 (1963), 940–950. The supplement to the second edition of Hahn [N 1] reflects the more recent situation. There are few works cited under the "sociological" approach and most of those listed do not qualify as interdisciplinary studies where the constructs and analytical tools of sociology are applied to Old Testament studies.

3. K. Mannheim, *Ideology and Utopia*, trs. L. Wirth and E. Shils (New York, 1966), p. 6.

4. The title of one of the more important works in the field by P. Berger and T. Luckmann; see N 8.

5. P. Berger, *The Sacred Canopy* (Garden City, N.Y., 1969), chs. 1, 2.

6. Ibid., p. 33.   7. Ibid., p. 42.

8. P. Berger and T. Luckmann, *The Social Construction of Reality* (Garden City, N.Y., 1966), p. 9.

9. A purely random and sample perusal of several Old Testament works produced the following references: S. Mowinckel, *He That Cometh* (New York, 1956), pp. 52, 55, 57 *et passim* ("royal ideology"); J. Bright, *A History of Israel* (Philadelphia, 1959), p. 273 *et passim* ("national ideology"); G. Widengren, "Early Hebrew Myths and Their Interpretation," in *Myth, Ritual, and Kingship*, ed. S. H. Hooke (Oxford, 1958), p. 169 ("royal ideology"); "Methodological Aspects of Old Testament Study," in *Congress Volume, Oxford 1959*, VTS, VII (1960), 13–30; G. E. Wright, "Cult and History," *Interpretation* 16 (1962), 17 ("covenant ideology"); F. M. Cross, "The Divine Warrior in Israel's Early Cult," in *Biblical Motifs*, ed. A. Altmann (Cambridge, Mass., 1966), pp. 18, 27, 28; R. A. Carlson, *David the Chosen King* (Stockholm, 1964), *passim* ("Deuteronomic ideology"). Cf. G. E. Wright, *God Who Acts* (London, 1952), p. 45. Wright is correct that the ideology of holy war was more than a mere

rationalization of the nation's wars. But that does not mean we can ignore the dimension of rationalization and ideology.

10. I am aware of the apparently simplistic and as yet undefined distinction between faith and ideology that is implied in these sentences. Effort at definition and differentiation is made further on. Even so, one should admit from the start the difficulties and the somewhat arbitrary character of any distinction at this point. It may be ultimately an impossible task to distinguish between ideology and faith. That is, such an approach may be an attempt to combine an anthropological perspective with a theological perspective. Peter Berger brings both perspectives to bear on his analysis of the nature of reality, but does so in *separate* books: *The Social Construction of Reality* [N 8] and *The Sacred Canopy* [N 5] (anthropological), and *A Rumor of Angels* (theological). Cf. D. W. Shriver, Jr., "For Faith and Ideology," *The Christian Century* 79 (1962), 774–776.

11. On the history of the meaning of the term "ideology" see K. Mannheim's major work, *Ideology and Utopia* [N 3], pp. 59 ff. *et passim*. Cf. G. Lichtheim, "The Concept of Ideology," *History and Theory* 4 (1965), 164–195. A thoughtful discussion of Christianity and ideology from an apologetic viewpoint is found in A. Richardson, *Christian Apologetics* (London, 1947), pp. 65–88. The present paper is similar to Richardson in some ways but departs from it in others.

12. Mannheim [N 3], p. 72; J. L. Adams "Religion and Ideologies," *Confluence* 4 (1955), p. 75.

13. T. Parsons, "An Approach to the Sociology of Knowledge," in *Transactions of the Fourth World Congress of Sociology*, offprint of the International Sociological Association (1959), IV, 25–49.

14. Mannheim [N 3], p. 56.

15. W. White, *Beyond Conformity* (New York, 1961), p. 6. White's book is an interesting study in the field of sociology of knowledge involving an analysis and critique—largely on the basis of Parsons' theories—of the ideology of contemporary American intellectuals. Note also the similar brief definition given by Shriver [N 10], p. 774: "Sociologists nowadays tend to define an ideology as a set of interpretations and a program of action relevant to the problems of a particular historical cluster of social circumstances."

16. Adams, "Religion and Ideologies" [N 12], 72.   17. Ibid., 73.

18. Cf. Michel Philibert, "Existentialism and Marxism," *The Student World* 51 (1958), 140–156.

19. The faith component spoken of here is of course not something confined to the Old Testament or Israelite religion. It may be present in other theological frameworks along with their ideological dimension. Indeed, the criteria proposed here may play a part in other religious formulations.

20. If Deuteronomy 32 were included in the early (tenth century and before) corpus, this statement would have to be modified in part. But its inclusion is still questionable. See G. E. Wright, "The Lawsuit of God: A Form-Critical Study of Deuteronomy 32," in *Israel's Prophetic Heritage*, eds. B. W. Anderson and W. Harrelson (New York, 1962), pp. 26–67.

21. This is best demonstrated by the analysis of C. Westermann of the types of promise narratives and the history of their tradition where he seeks to show that the promise narrative originally involved only one promise, either a son or land. Later this is expanded with the promise of progeny in great numbers and the blessing of the peoples through the name and seed of Abraham. Although Westermann is not concerned with ideological analysis in his treatment, he has demonstrated the history of the growth of ideology. See "Arten der Erzählung in der Genesis," in *Forschung am Alten Testament* (München, 1964).

22. H. W. Wolff, "The Kerygma of the Yahwist," *Interpretation* 20 (1966), 132–158.

In his treatment of Gen. 12:1–3 as the basic pericope, Wolff shows how the syntactical arrangement of the passage leads to a climax in the promise of blessing for the families of the earth through Abraham:

> Here (vs. 3b) the series of five imperfect cohortative consecutive clauses is interrupted by a clause with a perfect consecutive. Thus verse 3b is clearly set off as the sequel to the consequences (vss. 2–3a) of the departure of Abraham (vs. 1); it is the real result and it is, therefore, confirmed definitively by the perfect. The abrupt change in the final clause is further clarified by the fact that in verse 3b the subject is no longer Yahweh but "all the families of the earth." In so doing it he set down conclusively whom Yahweh's action, already manifoldly described, ultimately concerns and what this action is to accomplish for them. Thus the syntactical gradient of the long period hastens quite clearly to this concluding clause. It is the terse, concise *conclusio* of the whole" (p. 138).

The history of the tradition leads to the same conclusion:

> Analysis of tradition history thus emphasizes the clarity of the concluding sentence and its accentuated one-sidedness, showing that the history writer, as a witness, really wants to culminate with this very utterance: ". . . all the families of the earth can gain a blessing in you." Even though the Yahwist, by the manner and location of his formulation says that he is only testifying to the will of God, who has always been proclaimed in Israel, we still have no proof that it was ever expressed that way before" (pp. 144–145).

23. Wolff [N 22], 148, points to this as one of the Yahwist's examples of how Abraham/Israel brings blessing to the peoples of the earth.

24. G. von Rad, *Genesis* (Philadelphia, 1961), p. 204.

25. See e.g. P. W. Lapp, "The Conquest of Palestine in the Light of Archaeology," *Concordia Theological Monthly* 38 (1967), 283–300; and M. W. Weippert, *The Settlement of the Israelite Tribes in Palestine,* Studies in Biblical Theology, II (London, 1971), 21.

26. It should be acknowledged that that ideology once established would have functioned as an essential factor in motivating the tribes to a common response in defensive engagements.

27. The same would be true, *mutatis mutandis,* if Mendenhall is correct in seeing the "conquest" as "a peasant's revolt against the network of interlocking Canaanite city-states."

28. The basic study of the *ḥērem* is that of C. H. W. Brekelmans, *Die Ḥērem in Het Oude Testament* (Nÿmegen: Centrale drukkerij, 1959).

29. See Berger, *The Sacred Canopy* [N 5], pp. 44 f. for discussion of the place of religious legitimations in time of war and other marginal situations.

30. J. Van Seters has also recognized the ideological character of this material albeit with some debatable historical judgments:

> The narratives are ideological documents which only seem to come to the fore at a very late stage in the dispute. The basis of the claim is that Israel's land was taken from the ancient Amorites who no longer exist to dispute this claim. Deuteronomy (2:5, 9, 19) states that at the time of Israel's settlement they never made claim or contested as much as a single 'footbreadth' of territory belonging to Edom, Moab, or Ammon. The Judges account emphasizes that the territory claimed by Israel was undisputed by Moabite kings through three hundred years of settlement. The Numbers version further indicates that Moab lost its claims to the land of Sihon who subsequently lost it to Israel. The accounts do not serve the purpose of preserving ancient traditions but function as ideological claims to the land.

"The Terms 'Amorite' and 'Hittite' in the Old Testament," *VT* 22 (1972), 77–78.

31. See J. L. Mays, *Amos* (Philadelphia, 1969), pp. 56–57 for a discussion of the relation of this passage to Gen. 18:17b–19.

32. See e.g. Amos 5:4–6, 14–15, 21–24, where the act of seeking Yahweh, commonly identified with the acts and attitudes of worship, is equated with the establishment of justice and the continuing presence of righteousness.

33. Jer. 7:3 is capable of another interpretation and one which is followed in some commentaries e.g. by J. Bright (AB, vol. 21, 1965) and W. Rudolph (Handbuch zum Alten Testament, 12, 1947) i.e. the Piel forms of *škn* are revocalized as Qal forms (in agreement with Aquila and the Vulgate) so that "I will let you dwell" becomes "I will dwell with you." There is substantial argument for this change in that the emphasis of the passage is on what happened to Shiloh—where formerly Yahweh caused his name to dwell—because of the people's wickedness. In this case it would be the Zion ideology that Jeremiah turns back against the people, rather than the conquest ideology.

I have read with the MT as it stands, however. The same point is made in vs. 15 where the prophet says, "I will cast you out from my face as I cast out all your brothers, all the seed of Israel."

34. Berger sums up the matter thus: ". . . the prophets provided that rationalizing (in Weber's sense) 'theodicy' that served to interpret religiously the political history of Israel through the catastrophe of the exile and furnished part of the foundation for Israel's future existence as a 'pariah community' in the world of nations," ("Charisma and Religious Innovation" [N 2], 941).

35. Ibid., 948.

36. See the comment of C. Westermann on this verse: "The sense is that God has designated Israel to be a light to the world and to mediate salvation to it; she is to bring enlightenment and liberation to others" (*Isaiah 40–66* [Philadelphia, 1969], pp. 100–101).

37. This is an arbitrary but not unnatural stopping point. The kind of ideological analysis proposed here can and should go on with the later Old Testament period.

25. The Old Testament in "Process" Perspective: Proposal for a Way Forward in Biblical Theology

J. GERALD JANZEN

CHRISTIAN THEOLOGICAL SEMINARY, INDIANAPOLIS

I. INTRODUCTION

A. BIBLICAL THEOLOGY IN CRISIS

The appearance, within a year (1970), of Brevard Childs's *Biblical Theology in Crisis,* and the Twenty-Fifth Anniversary issue of *Interpretation,* only emphasized from within the ranks of biblical scholarship what had already become evident to and among theologians generally, that "the interest seems to have shifted away from Biblical studies."[1] The earlier resurgence of interest in biblical theology, Childs reminds us, was borne on the crest of the theological wave of neo-orthodoxy; and though by no means all who shared this resurgent interest would have styled themselves as neo-orthodox in their thinking, yet the movement did create a general climate much more congenial to the pursuit of biblical theology, whether conceived as a strictly descriptive task or as a hermeneutical engagement of the text for its contemporary "cash value." For a time this pursuit seemed securely afloat upon the theological tide which, like the Sea of Faith in Matthew Arnold's "Dover Beach,"

> Was once, too, at the full, and round earth's shore
> Lay like the folds of a bright girdle furled.

Yet in the past decade the tide has turned, and what Childs calls the Biblical Theology Movement appears to be stranded, or in danger of being stranded, by neo-orthodoxy's

> . . . melancholy, long, withdrawing roar,
> Retreating, to the breath
> Of the night-wind, down the vast edges drear
> And naked shingles of the world.

Now, it seems to be a valid inference from Childs's historical analysis, that biblical theology cannot be sufficient unto itself, but must come to terms with, even as it is influenced by, the more general currents of thought in the present day. Admittedly, the present theological scene is in great flux, and it may strike some that

> . . . we are here as on a darkling plain
> Swept with confused alarms of struggle and flight,
> Where ignorant armies clash by night.

At least some contemporary theological programs may appear to offer little help to the biblical theologian, or request any help from him in the work of constructive theology. Nevertheless, if biblical theology is to be carried on elsewhere than in a backwater, new proposals must be based upon more than an appeal to the exegetical spirit of Matthew Henry, or even of Calvin and Luther. Theologically rich as their exegesis was, its power in no small part was due to the recovery of what might be called literal historical exegesis, in contrast to exegetical modes prevalent in preceding centuries. In that respect, their exegesis reflected the general interests of the period.[2] If subsequent critical exegesis at times has been boxed into a positivistic corner, its presuppositions and methods may need correcting. But they must be revised in dialogue with general perspectives of our own time. Whereas, though I for one resonated to the warm passion of Childs's concern for an exegetical approach with greater "cash value," I could not escape the recurrent feeling that his own proposal is, in effect, an attempt to raise a past epoch from the dead. The question is, how to move forward in biblical theology in full view of the contemporary situation generally. The purpose of this paper is to propose a way forward, which I will introduce by taking another look at the historical context within which Childs has placed the rebirth of biblical theology.

B. A WIDER PERSPECTIVE

In a retrospective article entitled "The New Realism in Religious Inquiry,"[3] Bernard E. Meland places the neo-orthodox era in fresh light. Cautioning against a tendency to view this theological renascence merely in terms of its reaction against liberalism, and its recurrence to Reformation insights, he argues that its true significance is to be seen in relation to "currents of thought that were to effect a revolution in fundamental notions as these bear upon every form of disciplined thought" (p. 311). He acknowledges that, for the most part, neo-Reformation theologians "seemed only mildly aware of, or concerned with, this vaster intellectual upheaval that was manifesting itself in the sciences and in new expressions of metaphysics" (p. 311). Nevertheless, he asserts,

> a line of protest and inquiry, extending from Barth to Whitehead *forms a new frontier of realism,* breaking free of the enclosure of mentalism which was imposed upon Christian thinking for more than three hundred years and which had shaped the imagery of theological liberalism since the time of Kant (p. 312; italics mine).

That there are marked differences of theological opinion along this frontier, Meland readily concedes. But these differences, he insists, emerge primarily at the point of the constructive task of doctrinal interpretation; while at the prophetic stage of protest and reaction they form a consensus over against the older liberalism. For, as Meland goes on to argue, the older liberal tradition had settled into a rationalistic orthodoxy of its own, closed within its own presuppositions and methodologies; and it was now the so-called neo-orthodox thinkers who, along with others, were carrying forward "the restive and liberating dynamic of Protestantism that once spoke through historic liberalism" (p. 314).

As he compares this "new frontier of realism," in both its wings, to "the break through Scholasticism in the sixteenth century" (pp. 312–313), Meland is strongly reminiscent of Whitehead, who wrote:

> The Reformation and the scientific movement were two aspects of the historical revolt which was the dominant intellectual movement of the later Renaissance. The appeal to the origins of Christianity, and Francis Bacon's appeal to efficient causes as against final causes, were two sides of one movement of thought. . . . It was the return to the contemplation of brute fact; and it was based on a recoil from the inflexible rationalism of medieval thought.[4]

According to this analysis, at the beginning of the modern period scientific, philosophical, theological, and biblical interests all were pursued in a common mode of inquiry, and on the basis of shared fundamental presuppositions. It is the argument of the present paper, building upon Meland's analysis, that perhaps for the first time in centuries biblical interpretation may find itself in a situation analogous to that of the Protesant reformers; and that a reconception of interpretation, within the perspective of certain new modes of thought, may indeed recover an exegetical tradition, in its spirit and its depth, though not in its specific form or results.

Now, the waning of the neo-orthodox wing of the new realism, it would seem, is due in some measure to the fact that it was not sufficiently aware of movements along the rest of the "front"; that it did not fully appreciate the extent to which fundamental notions of western thought were being subjected to radical critique and revision from within; and that it therefore tended to assume the character of a negative reaction against the world of liberalism, rather than the role of a midwife helping this world through to a rebirth of its basic notions. Viewed in narrow perspective, then, the passing of neo-orthodoxy might be compared to earlier movements of protest against the main drift of modern thought, and, in its decline, like them may be thought simply to have failed. One thinks, for example, of "the literary romantic movement at the beginning of the nineteenth century [which], just as much as Berkeley's philosophical idealistic movement a hundred years earlier, refused to be confined within the materialistic concepts of the orthodox scientific theory" (Whitehead, SMW, p. 88). The nature poetry of this movement Whitehead describes as "a protest on behalf of the organic view of nature, and also a protest against the exclusion of value from the essence of matter of fact. . . . The romantic reaction was a protest on behalf of value" (SMW, p. 94).[5] It is in terms of this comparison of movements of protest that the use of Arnold's "Dover Beach" at the beginning of this paper has its point.

But the comparison is only partially apposite. For, whereas earlier movements of protest either foundered before the relentless progress of scientific materialism, or issued in modes of thought divorced from it, "when . . . we come to the twentieth century, we . . . find a movement in science itself to reorganize its concepts, driven thereto by its own intrinsic development" (SMW, p. 88). The argument is that this reorganization of concepts is, in its radical character, comparable to that of the sixteenth and seventeenth centuries, in which were laid down the fundamental notions which, directly or indirectly, have shaped the course of investigation and thinking in the sciences, philosophy, and Protestant theology, until our own day. Now, if Meland is correct in his characterization of neo-orthodox thought as a part of this "new frontier of realism," then its passing need not signal the demise of the biblical theology movement to which it gave such impetus. Rather, I suggest, this movement has the opportunity to enter a new phase in which, carrying forward the realistic emphases of neo-orthodox thought, and establishing close working relations with the other wing of the new realism, it can break fresh ground in the task of interpreting the biblical mythos for the coming age. In saying this I am urging, from the side of biblical studies, what Meland envisaged from the side of a Process-oriented constructive theology, when he wrote:

> Because the new metaphysics, giving to scientific categories their full and imaginative meaning, rises out of the living experiences of men in which decisions are made, and where events of tragedy and triumph are forged, it finds an immediate rapport with the imagery and poetic symbolism of the Biblical writers. What this ancient lore set forth through parable and poetry, the metaphysician—attuned to the qualitative meaning of every concrete event—finds himself expounding in what he understands to be more definitive terms. The interrelating of these ancient and modern sources has not gone far as yet; but the possibilities of their interpenetration give promise of a vigorous structure of faith which will at once have cognitive force and poetic appeal (FC, p. 19).

C. METAPHYSICS AND THE BIBLE

Some remarks are in order, at this point, concerning the relation between metaphysics, and biblical theology as an interpretive, or hermeneutical, venture.

A few sentences ago, I used the term *mythos* to characterize the Bible. In so doing, I intend to suggest that the relation between the Bible and metaphysics is an instance of the relation generally between *mythos* and *logos*. As I hope will become evident in Part II of this paper (especially II, c), my understanding of this relation is consistent with, and I think required by, the metaphysics here being considered.

In at least one respect, *mythos* and *logos* are alike: the function of both is to cut away the welter of sheer detail and to "lay bare the lines" in nature and life. They differ in the way they attempt to do this; and thereby they differ in the manner of their utility. *Mythic* exposition is synthetic, *logical* is analytic. *Mythic* expression is concrete, *logical* is abstract. The power of *logical* language is its ability to articulate the relations of things in universal terms, barren of reference to particulars, and thereby to lay bare the harmony of things as devoid of inconsistency. The power of *mythic* language is its ability to depict the relations of things in terms of particulars (what Philip Wheelwright calls "concrete universals"), with their innumerable associations, intimations, and emotional qualities, and thereby to convey the harmony of things as inclusive of all the contrasts that endow life with its intensity and width of value. Both modes of thought and expression are indispensable to one another and tend to cohere. For mythic modes (as Eliade has argued) reveal an implicit but often sophisticated logic; and logical modes, however rigorously analytical in their procedure, end as they begin, with "metaphors mutely appealing for an imaginative leap" (see below, p. 493). But of the two, the *mythic* is capable of fuller depiction of reality as a whole. For its manner of "laying bare the lines" is such as to "preserve the spirit of the whole—so that all that one has suppressed and cut away is there to the reader's consciousness as much as if it were in type on the page" (Willa Cather, *On the Art of Fiction*).

Metaphysics, as *logos,* constitutes "a coherent, logical, necessary system of general ideas in terms of which every element of our experience can be interpreted" (PR, p. 5). So understood, metaphysics can serve biblical theology in its hermeneutical task, by providing it with general ideas and terms for its analysis and explication of the Bible. Moreover, it provides a critical control on inconsistencies, apparent or real, between basic metaphors, tradition complexes, and theological trajectories in the Bible.

For its part, the Bible, as *mythos,* constitutes part of the total evidence—along with that which "is to be found in law, in moral and sociological habits, in literature and art as ministering to human satisfactions, in historical judgments on the rise and decay of social systems, and in science" (MoT

p. 70; cf. p. 165)—upon which a metaphysical system should be constructed. In so serving metaphysics, the Bible may become its critic, whenever it is in danger of becoming shallowly empirical and so tends to overlook some of the evidence in favor of a thin consistency.

Metaphysics and biblical theology, then, stand in a reciprocally constructive and critical relation to one another; and, in my view, it is only when this relation is sustained in tensive balance that either can achieve maximum results.

The "new metaphysics," with which Meland has associated neo-orthodoxy in a "new frontier of realism," has received several weighty formulations. The most comprehensive and systematic is that of Whitehead, and it is his metaphysical scheme which I will employ in the remainder of this paper.

II. WHITEHEAD'S "PROCESS" METAPHYSICS

A. REALITY AS DIPOLAR

At the beginning of the modern era, Descartes posited two types of fundamental entities: matter (displaying extension) and mind (enjoying thought). Neither type required the other for the completion of its own makeup, nor therefore for its own explanation; though, since the two were observed usually to move in some kind of concert, both were deemed by Descartes to require God—a third type of fundamental entity—to supervise their external relations to one another. Subsequent philosophy, operating within this fundamental distinction, has taken the form, either of a dualism, or of one or another monism, materialist, idealist, or pantheist. Outright materialism, of course, is inimical to assertions of the intrinsic seriousness of value, purpose, spirit, and the like, and offers no viable frame-of-reference for the exposition of biblical thought. Idealist systems initially seem more promising, but have difficulty doing justice to the stubborn concern of the Old Testament for the concrete, material dimensions of existence. The radical blurring of distinctions between God and the world in pantheist monism goes against the grain of biblically oriented religious sensibility as well as theology. Whereas dualism, with its various "separate but equal" formulas, is a problem, as Hartshorne observes (PP, p. xxi), and not a solution. In any case, it provides a poor model within which to explicate the biblical anthropology, for which functional distinctions are valid, but not a fundamental body/mind or body/spirit dichotomy.

For Whitehead, the presumption that there is only one genus of actual entities constitutes an ideal of cosmological theory; and, accordingly, he posits that "the description of the generic character of an actual entity should include God, as well as the lowliest actual occasion" (PR, p. 130). For him, the notions of sheer physical energy (to which contemporary physics has reduced the older concepts of material substance) and of sheer cogitation are abstractions from the concrete character of an actual occasion. For, in those actual occasions with which we are most intimately acquainted—the occasions of human experience—"we think with our bodies" and, conversely, we feel with our minds ("mental activity is one of the modes of feeling belonging to all actual entities in some degree, but only amounting to conscious intellectuality in some actual entities" [PR, p. 71]). In this connection, "experience" is the basic notion. An actual entity is an occasion of experience, a "throb of experience," in which the universe as many is felt into a unity which becomes that particular entity. At one phase, and in one mode, of experience, the actual entity enjoys physical feelings, and at and in another, conceptual feelings; and though, in entities of the lowest grade of complexity, the conceptual feelings may be so trivial as to be safely disregarded for most purposes of analysis or use, yet metaphysically one should not posit a generic dichotomy.

The key notion from which a new cosmology should be constructed, is "that the energetic activity considered in physics is the emotional intensity entertained in life" (MoT, p. 168). In contrast, for example, to those who would maintain that "persons experience the world, whereas things behave in the world,"[6] Whitehead can insist that "apart from the experiences of subjects there is nothing, nothing, nothing, bare nothingness" (PR, p. 194). That is, while "behavior" is an appropriate term with which to characterize an entity as an element in *another's* experience, only the notion of "experience"—of the process of feeling (or "prehending") the world of multiplicity into the unity of the subject, with whatever grades of physical and mental feeling—is adequate to characterize any entity as it is *in and for itself*. It is this view of a single genus of dipolar entities which leads Whitehead to state, repeatedly, that his "organic" philosophy can be developed either from the fundamental notions of modern physics or "from our own psychological field, as it stands for our cognition, [taking] it for what it claims to be: the self-knowledge of our bodily event" (SMW, p. 73).

B. MUTUAL IMMANENCE

We come now to the heart of Whitehead's philosophy, in the notion of "mutual immanence." Again it will be helpful to introduce this notion by reference to that notion with which it sharply contrasts in the history of modern thought—the notion of "simple location." This notion, which is eminently obvious to unaided observation and persuasive to common sense, is, in Whitehead's view, "the very foundation of the seventeenth century scheme of nature" (SMW, p. 58), and a basic assumption underlying "the whole philosophy of nature during the modern period" (SMW, p. 48). In barest outline, the notion is this: that matter, envisioned as simple, self-sufficient, unchanging bits of primal stuff, is *either* here *or* there, in space and time. Space and time are held to be absolutes, together constituting a fixed, empty grid in four dimensions, and each capable of division into an indefinite number of instants, or an arbitrary series of variable quantities. Division of a volume leaves smaller but substantially unchanged units; similarly, throughout a given period a substance is equally in existence during any portion or at any point. Motion, or change, consists in the relocation of various bits of matter in this grid, whereby certain changes in the primary and secondary qualities, but not in the substances themselves, are effected.

The critique of this notion in view of recent developments in the sciences need not be reviewed here. We may simply remind ourselves that, for example, matter as formerly conceived has given way to energy viewed as vibratory and vectoral in character; that space and time no longer are multiples of instants in a fixed grid, but changeable functions of developing activity conceived in terms of durations, quanta, or "drops of energetic formation"; and that (as ecology is now rendering obvious to common observation and persuasive for common sense) "the environment enters into the nature of each thing" (MoT, p. 138). But though the Newtonian cosmology has now been dismantled, in the meantime, its presuppositions and implications had become firmly embedded in other disciplines of thought, where they may continue to operate[7] until correlated again with a more adequate cosmology or until rejected in a schizoid revolt from the world-view of science.

One problem inherent in the notion of simple location is what could be called the sense of the solidarity of history. How does history (not to speak of nature) cohere? How can the pragmatic presumption of cause and effect be justified? (Hume unanswerably abolished the notion of causation, for a metaphysics of simple location.) And what is to prevent the innumerable isolated bits of configural occurrence from resuming earlier positions in the space-time grid, once, twice, or however often, given enough time and the coincidences of sheer chance? There is, in this view, no rationale for our sense of the unrepeatability, the irreversibility, of time. Moreover, since fundamental substances undergo no change, time seems accidental to reality, and not inherent in it.

Closely related is the problem of memory and anticipation, posed by Whitehead in these terms:

> Either there is something about the immediate occasion which affords knowledge of the past and the future, or we are reduced to utter scepticism as to memory and induction. . . . [for] induction . . . is the divination of some characteristics of a particular future from the known characteristics of a particular past (SMW, p. 44).

For a metaphysics of simple location, there is no way from the present to either the past or the future; so that memory and anticipation (in spite of their great importance in biblical cult and thought) have no ontological significance, and work merely to alienate from the present.

In contrast to the notion of "simple location," Whitehead developed one of "mutual immanence." This doctrine he derived, in the first instance, from "the fundamental fact, according to the physics of the present day, . . . that the environment with its peculiarities seeps into the group-agitation which we term matter, and the group-agitations extend their character to the environment" (MoT, p. 138). Allowing for degrees of relevance, and for negligible relevance, "every actual entity is present in every other actual entity" (PR, p. 65; cf. MoT, p. 164). Indeed, "the philosophy of organism is mainly devoted to the task of making clear the notion of 'being present in another entity'" (PR, p. 65). The "seepage" by which this takes place, consists in the dynamic flow of what, at various levels, is termed vibratory energy, visceral feeling, emotion, sense perception, or thought. Whitehead uses the term "feeling" to cover the gamut of the various modes of transition (hence his description of *Process and Reality* as a Critique of Pure Feeling); he also coins the term "prehension" as a virtual synonym for feeling. "A feeling," he writes, ". . . is essentially a transition effecting a concrescence" (PR, p. 134), that is, a 'growing together' of the past many into the present one actual occasion. Again, "feelings are 'vectors'; for they feel what is *there* and transform it into what is *here*" (PR, p. 105). This vector character of feeling "transforms the cause into the effect" (PR, p. 278). And it is vector feeling, as "feeling *from* a beyond which is determinate and pointing *to* a beyond which is to be determined" (PR, p. 189; italics mine), which is the basis for memory and for induction or anticipation. Thus the immediate occasion itself, however short-lived, bears within itself as an essential part of its internal constitution, intimations of the reality which, though immanent in it, yet also transcends it.[8] In this way, the many actual occasions, which grow out of their ancestors and issue in their descendants, together constitute the actual world as a "prehensive manifold" (cf. SMW, p. 71), giving the world its solidarity and the historical process its irreversibility; and one can assert that "the historic character of the universe belongs to its essence" (MoT, p. 90). Which is simply to give the colloquialism that "time is of the essence" its metaphysical grounding.

Now, this "historic" universe is, in part, describable in terms of natural laws. In this respect the universe is the "realm of nature," and on this basis alone it would display a career rigidly determined by efficient cause. But, within a dipolar view of reality, mental and physical phenomena require one another for their respective complete descriptions. And the "psychological field" requires a description of things which takes seriously the sense of value, freedom, purpose, decision, and responsibility, and which takes seriously the importance attached to these in guiding the conduct of mankind (including that of the behavioristically minded members of the scientific community!). In this respect the universe is the "realm of history," and pursues a career which is shaped by self-determination, that is, by ends which are severally chosen for self-enjoyment by the manifold actual entities.

A sketch of Whitehead's doctrine of "concrescence" will serve to elaborate his notion of mutual immanence. The ultimate notion for Whitehead is Creativity, "by which the many, which are the universe disjunctively, become the one actual occasion, which is the universe conjunctively" (PR, p. 25). The "creative advance" is "the advance from disjunction to conjunction, *creating a novel entity* other than the entities given in disjunction" (PR, p. 26; italics mine). In other words, "the many become one, and are increased by one." Thus, "the 'production of novel togetherness' is the ultimate notion embodied in the term 'concrescence'" (PR, p. 26). The concrescent occasion, constituting the experience of an actual entity, may be described as follows.

The diverse entities of the past actual world present themselves as objectified vectoral feelings, physical in character, to be appropriated ("prehended") into a felt unity of experience. Though initially they constitute the objective data of experience, in the process of being ordered into compatibility for experience they are transformed into one objective datum. This ordering and transformation are effected by the aim of the emerging entity, and this "subjective aim" is aim at self-enjoyment, that is, enjoyment of feeling with maximum intensity and width.

In a secondary phase of concrescence, the simple physical feelings derivative from the past actual world are augmented by simple conceptual feelings, which envisage for the emerging entity certain abstract possibilities. These possibilities are presented in gradations of relevance to the past actual world, but in greater or lesser degree are novel in comparison with it. These simple conceptual feelings are then fused with the simple physical feelings, to give comparative feelings of varying degrees of complexity. Where the possibilities newly posed are virtually exact reproductions of the pattern of feelings in the past, the comparative feelings (in these instances termed "physical purposes") aim at a virtual reproduction of and conformation to the past; and the "self-enjoyment" of such an entity consists in a low-grade satisfaction over the mere fact of repetition. Here, efficient cause seems to reign virtually unchallenged; though the aeon-long process of change, however minute, even in rocks, should warn against assertions of absolute immutability.

But the possibilities newly posed for conceptual feeling may be significantly novel in comparison with the past actual world; in which case a requirement of selectivity is placed before the comparative feelings. In this case, the latter feelings may be termed "intellectual feelings," as feeling the contrast between what *might be* and what *is*. Now, not *all* presented possibilities can be appropriated for novel realization, by the requirements of compatibility (one may have one's cake, or eat it, but not both). Rather, some are appropriated ("positively prehended"), while others are barred from entry ("negatively prehended"). To the extent that, and in the precise manner that, the available possibilities are variously prehended, the result is the emergence of a unique, novel actual entity. And the manner of prehension involves selection and decision ("cutting off"—negative prehension) and therefore valuation, in accordance with subjective aim. But this means that value is inherent in the emergence of matter-of-fact.

Now, comparative feelings need not be conscious feelings; but if they achieve sufficient complexity, they result in consciousness, in a late phase of concrescence ("consciousness presupposes experience, and not experience consciousness" [PR, p. 67]). Yet, consciousness is not merely epiphenomenal. For in this phase subjective aim may be most decisively and intentionally pursued. Here freedom reaches its peak, extremely so in the almost unbounded reaches of the imagination; yet it is a freedom which operates within the limits of the determinations of the past as they enter into the emergent occasion. The past, which likewise was once a multiplicity of emergent entities, partly shaped by self-determination, now becomes the "stuff" out of which, by fusion with the prehended possibilities, the self-creation of the emergent entity takes place. When the latter reaches its maximum of self-enjoyment in what Whitehead calls its "satisfaction," it perishes as an actual occasion, and becomes an objective datum for ensuing entities, thereby exemplifying the principle of relativity, which is that "it belongs to the nature of a 'being' that it is a potential for every 'becoming'" (PR, p. 27).

In this view, the advancing universe is made up of centers of creativity, effecting emergent novelty in some determined relation to the past. In Hartshorne's words, "the causal conditions for each free act are previous acts of freedom; creativity feeds upon its own products and upon nothing else!" (PP, p. xviii).

The orders of existence, such as mineral, vegetable, animal, human, may be said to be differentiated according to the level of complexity achieved in the comparative feelings constituting the later phases of concrescence. At one extreme, *character* is the simple repetition of pattern through transmission of vibratory physical energy. At the other extreme, character is achieved, sustained, intensified, to the degree that successive decisions-amid-emergent-novelties are made in accordance with consistent subjective aim. Whereas character stagnates and becomes moribund when conformal feelings, by which the past is immanent, predominate over decisions for novel conceptual feelings; character dissipates by promiscuous enjoyment of random possibilities which have no significant relevance for the past actual world or the basic subjective aim. Character, then, emerges as a function of historical faithfulness. That is, it emerges when decisions are made in faithfulness to the past actual world accepted for what it is; in faithfulness to the future, envisaged in terms of what the self and the world realistically may become; and in faithfulness to the present, in seeking maximum intensity and width of immediate self-enjoyment.

Responsibility, in this view, is at least twofold. The actual entity is responsible for its own emerging character, resulting from its own decisions understood as self-creative. But, by the Principle of Relativity, in the very process of self-creation an entity is also unavoidably responsible for others. To recall Hartshorne's statement one's acts of freedom and self-creation become the causal conditions for the similar acts of others. The self one chooses to become enters into the determination of others by whom one is experienced and known. Responsibility has a transcendent reference. That is, to the extent that one recognizes the plurality of creative centers of self-enjoyment and of subjective aim, and relinquishes the temptation to make them merely subservient to his own, it is possible to envisage, and perhaps to achieve, a community of aims and enjoyments transcending, and in fact redefining, one's own aims and enjoyments. In this view, the claims of the individual and of the community are equally strong, and mutually enhancing. The ultimate moral principle here clearly is that one should love one's neighbor as himself. But if the universe is in any sense "orchestrated" in its creative advance; that is, if there is a divine subjective aim which constitutes a "lure" for every concrescent occasion in its self-enjoyment; then moral responsibility takes on a third dimension, and the moral principle of self-transcendence in love, in its first statement, becomes the requirement of love for God.

These two notions, of *character* as historical faithfulness, and *responsibility* as creative love, exemplify in a striking way, it seems to me, the way in which process metaphysics can serve biblical theology by providing it, in this instance, with ideas and terms of wide generality, for its analysis and explication of *ḥesed* and *'emet* in their application to both man and God.

C. CONCRETENESS AND LANGUAGE

The preceding section, developing Whitehead's doctrine of "mutual immanence," was introduced by way of contrast with what he terms "the fallacy of simple location." The aspect of his thought to which we shall now turn may be expounded in contrast to what he calls "the fallacy of misplaced concreteness."

Whitehead's definition of "concreteness" arises out of his understanding of concrescence: "an actual entity is concrete because it is . . . a particular concrescence of the universe" (PR, p. 65). That is, the concrete fact is the whole space-time universe as ingredient in, and viewed from the perspective of, a given actual entity. Whereas facts considered in isolation are abstractions from this whole. "A single fact in isolation is the primary myth required for finite thought, that is to say, for thought unable to embrace totality" (MoT, p. 9).

But the many actual entities of the universe are not ingredient in a particular concrescence in *all* of their respective aspects; each entity is represented in only some of its aspects (this is Whitehead's explanation of the phenomenon of "perspective"). Nor are the many entities appropriated in equal grades of relevance; rather, they are variously appropriated in accordance with the subjective aim of the concrescent occasion. As an actual entity grows through its phases of concrescence, and toward the deepening of its own individuality, the process of valuation, selection, and decision gives the occasion the character of an increasing abstraction. And consciousness, arising in the last phase of concrescence, involves a very high degree of abstraction from the fullness of concrete experience. Therefore, as immediate experience of the world moves to consciousness of the world, one should envisage a process of abstraction: from primary, or undifferentiated visceral, feelings; through vague emotions; to specific sense perceptions; on to conscious thoughts and negative perceptions; rising finally to "the peak of free imagination, in which the conceptual novelties search through a universe in which they are not datively exemplified" (PR, p. 187).

Now the fallacy of misplaced concreteness is the mistake of supposing that the clear and distinct impressions which arise in the latest, conscious, phase of concrescence directly report the most concrete and basic elements of experience. "It is tacitly assumed, except by Plato," Whitehead writes, "that the more fundamental factors will ever lend themselves for discrimination with peculiar clarity" (AI, p. 175). Whereas, in fact, "factors in our experience are clear and distinct in proportion to their variability[;] . . . the necessities are invariable, and for that reason remain in the background of thought, dimly and vaguely" (MoT, p. vii). Human experience may be described in terms of a luminous central point of consciousness, with its awareness of discrete sense perceptions and conceptions; a penumbral region of massive, vague associations, values, and emotions; and beyond this fringe, the vast hinterland of the universe of relations, vectorally present and experienced, but unillumined by consciousness. That is, we experience more than we know; and we know more than we can think; and we think more than we can say; and language therefore lags behind the intuitions of immediate experience.

All language thus is abstractive, and only an imperfect representation of concrete reality. Indeed, we may apply Whitehead's above-quoted statement to language, and say that "a single *word* in isolation is the primary myth required for finite *speech,* that is to say, for speech unable to embrace totality *in a word"* (cf. MoT, p. 9). Nevertheless, within this limitation, some modes of language are relatively more concrete while others are more abstract.

The languages of the special sciences, logic, mathematics, and rational philosophy, have as their ideal the development of terms that are univalent, conceptually focused, precisely defined. These languages—examples of what Philip Wheelwright[9] calls *steno-language*—are enormously useful for the formulation of rational explanations, and for exercising control over the world for specific purposes. But these "definitive"[10] languages constitute a high abstraction from, and therefore a quite limited representation of, the concrete totality of the world as experienced. Hence, as Whitehead says, "it is impossible to complete the description of an actual occasion by means of concepts" (SMW, pp. 169–170). The assumption, then, that steno-language is the most *adequate* language for the attempt to understand and report empirical reality, is in this view the linguistic version of the Fallacy of Misplaced Concreteness.

For "the deeper truths must be adumbrated by myths" (MoT, p. 10), the language of myth and poetry—what Wheelwright calls depth or *expressive* or *tensive language*. Employing multivalent words laden with innumerable associational and valuational and emotional ligatures, this mode of language conveys the essential connectedness and concrete particularity of things. With its disconcertingly capacious tolerance and even demand for referential congruity, contextual variation, plurisignation, soft focus, paralogical dimensionality, assertorial lightness, and paradox,[11] this mode of language is ill-designed to serve the limited functional purposes of, say, the special sciences. But these same features enable it to report the empirical world most richly and concretely for human understanding. And indeed, such language not only reports, but in some sense conveys, or re-enacts, what it reports. For "language is expression from one's past into one's present. It is the reproduction in the present of sensa which have intimate association with the realities of the past. . . . An articulated memory is the gift of language" (MoT, p. 33). From this point of view, the most concretely historical mode of language is the poetic, while the definitive languages of the sciences, including that of historical scholarship, are, for all their enormous utility, only in a secondary and abstract sense historical.

If one may describe steno-language as the language of rational discourse, and poetic language as that of empirical expression, it can readily be appreciated that, for Whitehead's rational empiricism (PR 6), neither mode has exclusive, or even preponderant, claims to credence. His own renowned work in mathematics sufficiently attests his commitment to rigorous expression. And the large number of neo-logisms and special usages with which he articulates his metaphysical scheme, indicates his concern for clarity and precision in definitive philosophical discourse. Yet, even in affirming the need for such definitive discourse, he acknowledges that "however such elements of language be established as technicalities, they remain metaphors mutely appealing for an imaginative leap" (PR 6). And in his comment that "philosophy is the endeavour to find a conventional phraseology for the vivid suggestiveness of the poet [; . . .] the endeavour to reduce Milton's 'Lycidas' to prose; and thereby to produce a verbal symbolism manageable for use in other connections of thought"—in this comment, and others like it, one detects a stubborn empiricism which insists on the eminent importance of poetic and mythical reportage on reality, and which refuses to give the last word to those whose sole normative use of language, and whose views on reality, consistently exhibit the fallacy of misplaced concreteness.

D. GOD

In this section, I will sketch the most salient features of Whitehead's conception of God. I may take as my starting point his preoccupation with "the puzzling fact that there is an actual course of events which is in itself a limited fact, in that metaphysically speaking it might have been quite otherwise" (SMW, p. 172). That is, why is there a cosmos at all—not necessarily a perfect cosmos, but one which displays enough order to be, at least up to now, viable? Why not sheer chaos devoid of value? It is, of course, possible that such order exists by the self-orchestration of the many self-created actual entities, "either by sheer luck or their own unimaginable wisdom and guidance" (Hartshorne, PP, p. xvii). But this explanation seems no more inherently likely than one that envisions the creative advance as guided by "some supreme form of self-creative power, a supreme form of process which, because of its superiority, exerts an attraction upon all the others" (ibid.). In the place of Aristotle's Prime Mover, Whitehead envisions God as "the principle of concretion," "the ground for concrete actuality" (SMW, pp. 174, 178). That is, He is the reason why reality as a whole exhibits order rather than sheer chaos, and why that order is, at any given stage, *this* order and not *another* order. This form of the cosmological argument for God constitutes the most significant application of Whitehead's ontological principle—that the reasons for things are to be sought in actual entities (PR, p. 23).

As the Principle of Concretion, God is primordially involved in each concrescent occasion, which may roughly be recapitulated as follows. The concrescent occasion emerges in a process of fusion of three factors: (1) the multiple actual entities of the past actual world, presented (in the form of vectoral physical feelings) for appropriation into the emergent occasion; (2) the various novel possibilities, presented (in the form of conceptual feelings) for appropriation to give uniqueness to the emergent occasion; (3) the subjective aim, which directs *how* the actualities and the potentialities are in fact appropriated into a novel concrescence by which "the many become one, and are increased by one." God's involvement in the concrescent occasion, His "activity," is such that: (a) He orders pure possibilities so that they are available in grades of relevance *vis-à-vis* the actual world; and thereby (b) He supplies the initial aim for each emergent actual entity. As Sherburne puts it, "every concrescence, which is *causa sui,* faces the question of what sort of entity it will make itself. The subjective aim, derived from God, is a rule . . . toward that way of becoming which is most in line with God's own aim of creating intensity of harmonious feeling in the world" (PRs, p. 28).

Now, in neither of these aspects is God's activity brusquely intrusive, in the manner of a *deus ex machina*. For, in Whitehead's conception, God is an actual entity, and as such exemplifies the principle of relativity, whereby "it belongs to the nature of a 'being' that it is a potential for every 'becoming.' "

Insofar, then, as each actual entity prehends, or feels, every other entity into its own real internal constitution, the prehension by each actual entity of God, the eminent actual entity, includes the prehension of His subjective aim for that occasion, and His envisagement of the novel possibilities relevant to the realization of that aim, and relevant to the current state of the actual world. But the finite entity is not coerced into response; it enjoys such freedom of self-creation as, in Buber's words, "at any definite moment really to take [its] choice, and by this [to share] in deciding about the fate of the moment after this."[12] "Such order as we find in nature," says Whitehead, ". . . presents itself as the one harmonious adjustment of complex detail. Evil is the brute motive force of fragmentary purpose, disregarding the eternal vision. Evil is overruling, retarding, hurting. The power of God is the worship He inspires" (SMW, p. 192). In these terms, the creative advance itself has religious character as the universe's worship of God, a "tropism to the beckoning light—to the sun passing toward the finality of things, and to the sun arising from their origin" (FR, p. 65).

The possibility of man's knowledge of God arises out of His role as the Principle of Concretion. Concerning knowledge in general, Whitehead posits that we can have knowledge about something, only because it is vectorally present in our own constitution:

> No statement, except one, can be made respecting any remote occasion which enters into no relationship with the immediate occasion *so as to form a constitutive element of the essence of that immediate occasion.* . . . The one excepted statement is—If anything out of relationship, then complete ignorance as to it. Here by 'ignorance,' I mean *ignorance* (SMW, p. 25; first italics mine; cf. PR, p. 6).

Our knowledge of God, then, arises from His unfailing presence in every actual occasion, as the principle of the concrescence of that occasion.

In the first place, then, no absolute distinction can be made between self-knowledge and knowledge of the external world, or between knowledge of persons and knowledge of "things." Likewise, no absolute distinction can be made between self-knowledge and the knowledge of God, or between the knowledge of God and knowledge of the world. But the supreme difficulty of coming to adequate self-knowledge, and knowledge of God, should now be clear. The difficulty rests in the fact that, as has already been quoted, "the necessities [in this case, the self, and God as the principle of concretion] are invariable, and for that reason remain in the background of thought, dimly and vaguely." On the one hand, Whitehead provides a metaphysical basis for understanding mystical experience. Yet on the whole, and for the vast generality of mankind, it would seem that the pursuit of self-knowledge and the knowledge of God may best be carried out, not by world-denying introspection or "theospection," but by a receptive interest in the concrete public world, viewed as potentially transparent, at every point, to its divine ground.

To this point, Whitehead's understanding of God may be taken as an unexceptionable, if interesting, exposition of God as Creator. But with the consideration of the divine knowledge of the world, his thought is seen to take a daring turn, which places it in direct confrontation with classical assertions of divine immutability and impassibility. As is by now clear, Whitehead's is a metaphysics of process or becoming, rather than one of being. In his view, immutability and impassibility are by no means preferable to change and experience, as characterizing the really real. Indeed, the art of persistent immutability in the midst of change could be termed the art of being stone dead—except that even stones are not totally immutable. For all its daring and controversial character, Whitehead's conception of a God for whom time and experience are real, is only a metaphysical articulation of the image of God as the living God. This conception arises out of the notion of internal relations, or mutual immanence.

As we have indicated, God is immanent in the world as the principle of concretion in its emergent occasions, and only on that basis is it possible to know Him. Analogously with human knowing, God can know the world only if it is immanent in Him "so as to form a constitutive element of the essence of that immediate occasion" of knowing. In fact, God's knowledge of the world is His prehension of it, whereby He becomes who He is in what Whitehead calls His Consequent Nature. (For example, after a certain point in ancient Near Eastern history, He becomes the God of Abraham and of Isaac and of Jacob, and that in two senses. He becomes such for them, in being known by them to be such; and He becomes such in and for Himself—as He was not hitherto—in knowing them and experiencing them as an enrichment in His consequent nature.) Inasmuch as His prehensive reception of the world is in accordance with His own subjective aim, He is eminent self-creativity. But inasmuch as what is prehended is the past actual world in its settledness, He is determined, or created, by the multiple finite centers of self-creative freedom. For all its boldness, this last conception seems to be required, not only by the other aspects of Whitehead's metaphysics, but by any world-view, such as the biblical, which depicts God in personal terms, and which uses the language of personal experiences to depict His relation to the world.

In His consequent nature, then, God is the recipient of the world, and as such is its transcendent Goal. He is *omnipresent,* as the primordial ground and the futuristic lure or aim of every concrescent occasion. He is *omnipotent,* not as overruling recalcitrant wills by preponderant power, but as possessing infinite patience and tender care (PR, p. 408) to lure the universe on toward His aim, by an inexhaustible resource of relevant possibilities (in this sense, He is the power of the future; and "the power of God is the worship He inspires" [SMW, p. 192]). He is *omniscient,* as knowing, in the appropriate mode, all that is there to be known: He knows, or *remembers,* the past actual world in its total facticity and value; He knows, or *enjoys,* the present concrescing universe of occasions in the richness of their several widths and intensities of self-employment; He knows, or *envisages,* the possibilities relevant to the universe in its passage into the future, a passage more or less consonant with His enduring subjective aim. He is the God of History; and He is a God with a History. And, in what constitutes perhaps His greatest power, His greatest capacity to inspire worship, He is a God who "rejoices with those who rejoice, and weeps with those who weep." For He is "the great companion—the fellow-sufferer who understands" (PR, p. 413).

In concluding this section, it should be noted that Whitehead does not suppose "any properly general metaphysics" could ever "lead . . . very far towards the production of a God available for religious purposes" (SMW, p. 173). Certainly, he argues that metaphysics requires the introduction of God for its own completion. But beyond this, he concludes,

> the general principle of empiricism depends upon the doctrine that there is a principle of concretion which is not discoverable by abstract reason. What further can be known about God must be sought in the region of particular experiences, and therefore rests on an empirical basis (SMW, p. 178).

It may be suggested, then, that the most promising resource for a theology will be found in those literatures whose content portrays particular experiences, reported and conveyed in the most concrete modes of language, that is, in myth and poetry and story. "The inspiration of religion lies in the history of religion. By this I mean that it is to be found in the primary expressions of the intuitions of the finest types of religious lives" (RM, p. 138). This, of course, in no way guarantees the credentials of the Bible as such a theological resource. But it does provide a frame of reference within which the Bible may most appreciatively be studied.

III. THE OLD TESTAMENT IN "PROCESS" PERSPECTIVE

In the preceding section I have presented a brief sketch of some fundamental notions of Whitehead's Process philosophy. Now it is time to bring these to bear upon the Old Testament. But a further word is necessary about what is being proposed.

I am not proposing that we attempt a simple and complete correlation between biblical and Process notions. Nor am I suggesting that biblical notions should be, or are capable of being, subsumed directly and completely under those of Process thought. What I do suggest is that, in general and unavoidably, our explicit or implicit metaphysical perspectives enter into our perceptions, assessments, and evaluations. Further, I suggest that certain fundamental notions and related basic imagery, developed in the sixteenth and seventeenth centuries and still prevalent in the modern world, may be rendering us incapable of taking seriously the biblical witness to reality; and that they may even tend to distort our perceptions of that witness, precisely when we are attempting to practice the utmost objectivity and philosophical and scientific integrity. The chief value of Process thought for biblical theology may be its provision of a new fundamental imagery, and fresh categories of thought and expressions, faithful to contemporary knowledge empirically derived and rationally organized, and yet in surprisingly close rapport at many points with the biblical witness. This new imagery, and these new categories, should make possible both a keener sensitivity to what the Bible actually attests, and a renewed readiness to take its attestations seriously. More than this we must not expect, or need desire. For, as Meland says, "what is thus seen and heard within this more sensitive stance will bring its own occasion of judgment and understanding" (RF, p. 136).

In the remainder of this paper, I want to point to some areas in which I believe such fresh possibilities are exemplified.

A. MAN

1. *Man the Individual.* A dipolar understanding of reality accords well with the biblical conception of man as a psychosomatic unity. The "organic" imagery in which Semitic psychology is couched is seen to be, not quaint or primitive, but empirically concrete, and meriting renewed study in its own terms. For example, the term *nepeš,* with its semantic range comprising "throat, appetite, desire, emotion, passion, life, self, soul," should be capable of exposition, not in substantial terms, but as the prehensive function (above, p. 488) of the experiencing organism. This is further suggested in the frequent use of the verb *śb‘* to connote experience generally, whether good (Ps. 63:6 "my soul is sated as with marrow and fat") or bad (Ps. 88:3 "My soul is sated with troubles"). In this connection, we may note the Old Testament's implicit affirmation of the goodness of earthly experience as such, whatever its particular character. (Salvation is anything but the cessation of desire.) This affirmation accords with Whitehead's description of concrescing individuality as "a certain absoluteness of self-enjoyment." Whatever transcendent considerations may enter in to complete the characterization of a specific occasion in terms of *ṭôb* and *ra‘,* its character is determined in part by how the individual experiences it, in and for himself. That is, "the occasion of experience is absolute in respect to its immediate self-enjoyment. How it deals with [or prehends] its data is to be understood without reference to any other concurrent occasions" (MoT, pp. 150, 151). To this extent, it may be said of Old Testament man that he exists for himself in his occasions of self-enjoyment (above, p. 490).

2. *Man in Community*. But further, the notion of mutual immanence, that is, of an actual entity as a concrescence of the universe, wherein "the many become one and are increased by one," affords new categories with which to explore the biblical understanding of man in community, especially as expressed in Covenant imagery. Individuals arise from community (they are $b^e nê-b^e rît$, sons of the covenant), and severally create community. Covenant responsibility is manifold: the community, as efficient cause, is responsible for the individual; the individual, as *causa sui,* is responsible for himself; and the individual, as a contributing cause, is responsible for the community. Thus, the Covenant with its laws is understood to be an internal bond of creative freedom and responsible concern. Man exists for others in their occasions of self-enjoyment; he ought to love them as himself. In this connection, the notion of "corporate personality," which has received wide diffusion within modern biblical scholarship, but which recently has been subjected to incisive critique as hitherto formulated,[13] should be susceptible of more adequate analysis and exposition in terms of the notion of mutual immanence.

3. *Man and God*. But perhaps the central, and most provocative, aspect of man in the Bible is his description as *imago dei,* with its corollary in the highly anthropomorphic terms with which God is depicted. It should be obvious that the former notion is functional only in a context where the latter is regarded as something more than a philosophical or theological embarrassment. Both notions take on fresh suggestiveness in the light of Whitehead's doctrine of internal relations, together with his doctrine that "there is only one genus of actual entities" and that "the description of the generic character of an actual entity should include God, as well as the lowliest actual entity" (PR, p. 130).

God, as part of man's actual world, is prehended in every actual occasion, most especially with regard to His subjective aim, or will, for that particular occasion. (The particularity of His will is only partially framed in moral laws, which function less as prescriptions for action than as exemplifications of the actions of a man who seeks to do justice and to love mercy and to walk humbly with his God.) Indeed, it is herein that each occasion derives its own subjective aim (above, p. 494; Ps. 40:7–8; Jer. 31:33), in terms of which man achieves self-creation. But self-creation is another way of speaking about freedom, the presupposition of man's three-dimensional responsibility. In these terms, sin is against self, against the community, and most deeply and "originally" against God (Ps. 51:4), insofar as it expresses "the brute force of fragmentary purpose, disregarding the eternal vision" (above, p. 495).

Now, in his self-creative freedom, and by the principle of relativity (above,

p. 494), man contributes to God's enjoyment, in his consequent nature, of his universe (Gen: 1:31; and usage of the verb *raṣah*). This may be said to provide the ultimate basis for biblical ethics (cf. also Hartshorne, DR, pp. 130–133). Man exists, then, for God in his occasions of self-enjoyment, as God, in His love for man, may be said to exist for him. Thus, the nature of biblical man is a three-dimensional covenant relation, whose Old Testament character is summarized by Jesus as the threefold law of love.

4. *Man and History.* The doctrine of creative advance through concrescent occasions likewise illuminates the biblical portrayal of the solidarity of historical Israel. For part of the character (above, p. 488) of an actual entity is the character given for it by the past, through its prehension of the past actual world. And this character is a *cumulative given,* which may be described as an ever deepening and widening "structure of experience," matrixally present within the individual and the community, as patterns of sensibility, perception, and understanding, and as "institutions, ceremonies, and public practices."[14] This structure of experience, deeper than conscious awareness, is expressed in cultic action and in epic narrative and articulated social custom. Thus, for example, the cultic confession of personal involvement in the events of the Exodus expresses one's participation in the common structure of experience; and memory (above, p. 487) has the character of efficacious re-presentation.

In the other direction, the forward dynamic of the Old Testament is an expression of Israel's sensitivity to the character of vector feeling as "feeling *from* a beyond which is determined and pointing *to* a beyond which is to be determined" (PR, p. 189; italics mine). The categories of Promise and Fulfillment, and the envisagement of the future in terms of New Exodus and Messianic hope, lend themselves to understanding in terms of the Whiteheadian denial of the future as sheer novelty, in favor of genuine novelty relevant to the actual occasion, such that there is at least the opportunity for the sustenance, and perhaps the intensification—in new forms, if need be—of enduring valuations and subjective aim.

(Parenthetically, it may be suggested that the above remarks point to a way of reconceiving the character and function of the Bible as canon. The canon may be thought of as that body of tradition which identifies and articulates for the community, in the deepest and most comprehensive way, and by the most concrete modes of expression, those structures of experience which give the community its present character and in terms of which it seeks its future. In this view, the Bible functions not so much as external norm, but as illuminator of the deep structures of experience, and of the vectoral character of the creative advance, yet so as in each instance to require of the community, in Meland's words, "its own occasion of judgment and understanding.")

5. *Man and Nature.* But the solidarity of the universe also embraces nature, which must be seen as more than the mere stage upon which the historical drama is played out. Though the higher animals and man may be favored with more complex roles, involving pronouncedly higher powers of decision and responsibility, yet the whole universe in some manner participates actively in the creative advance. Man and nature are energetically linked in a sympathetic bond or covenant (Hosea 2:20–25; cf. Gen. 2:15), within which one suffers on account of the other (Gen. 3:17–19; Hosea 4:1–3), and both share a hopeful destiny (Isa. 11:1–9, 55:12–13). Here again, Process thought would seem to yield categories capable of overcoming what has by now become an invidious bifurcation between nature and history.

B. GOD

Classical depictions of God, as externally related to the world, and as immutable and impassible, have always stood in some tension with the bold anthropomorphism of the Old Testament, so as to suggest the incompatibility of the God of the philosophers and the God of Abraham, of Isaac, and of Jacob. It is here that a metaphysics of process may be most helpful for biblical theology.

1. *Magnalia Dei.* The biblical emphasis on the mighty acts of God has become increasingly problematical, viewed as the intrusions of a *deus ex machina.* This problem seems now to be capable of more adequate treatment, if God and the world may be viewed metaphysically as mutually immanent (and also mutually transcendent), bonded together in a network of internal relations. In this connection, there can be no fundamental distinction between His acts in creation and His acts in history (cf. the use, in Second Isaiah, of the verb *bārā'*). Without exception, God is active in every occasion, as the principle of concretion: in the regularity of the rainfall (Job 37:6), and in the rain of quail (Ps. 78:27); in the Exodus, and in the migrations of the Philistines and the Syrians (Amos 9:7).

Now, granted the pervasiveness of the divine action, on what basis can the Bible depict certain specific events in the world process, certain "acts of God," as being uniquely redemptive and revelatory? If without exception God is active in *every* occasion, how may we properly claim to identify that activity in any special way, in any given occasion? Indeed, it may seem that we have merely traded the problem of a *deus ex machina* for that of a *deus absconditus intra machinam!* But, in my judgment, the latter problem is much the preferable traveling companion, demonstrably inherent in human experience. For differences in the efficacious and paradigmatic importance of public events are the universally assumed basis for history writing. Likewise, in the course of an individual life, the presence of the personal agent in all of his acts does not bleach out the differences between those acts which determine the main course of his life and disclose his character most deeply, and those other myriads of acts which are omitted in biography. That is to say, particularity *qua* particularity is no scandal. It is properly a scandal only when the wrong particulars are held up for emphasis. (And the difference between a good and a bad biographer is determined at least as much by sensitivity for the subject as it is by discrete information about it.) To repeat a quote from Whitehead, "the general principle of empiricism depends upon the doctrine that there is a principle of concretion (above, pp. 494f.) which is not discoverable by abstract reason. What further can be known about God must be sought in the region of particular experiences, and therefore rests on an empirical basis" (SMW, p. 178). The challenge to the biblical testimony concerning its particular emphases on the *magnalia Dei* is, then, empirical and not theoretical. The confessional character of the Bible is thus legitimized *vis-à-vis* philosophy, yet not hedged about with dogmas or notions of biblical positivism, which remove it from the arena of trial and testing.

2. *The Love of God.* The character of God, as depicted for example in Exod. 34:6–7, is experienced as the deepest character (above, pp. 495f.) of the successive particular occasions in the emergent process. And insofar as character is a function of historical faithfulness, the divine character as depicted in the Bible would seem to satisfy the requirements of religious concern for a locus or ground of dependability, which the notions of immutability and impassibility were designed to meet. But the biblical emphasis on the compassion and the love of God, as the ground of his righteous and redemptive acts, presents grave problems for interpretation in the categories of impassible divine being. For a love which can only give is monstrous (in Whitehead's words, "impulse without sensitiveness spells brutality"—SMW, p. 200). Only a love whose expressions are shaped by its own feelings for its effects on the beloved, and which can receive the reciprocal love of the beloved as an enrichment of its own experience and consequent nature, is worthy of the name of love. The Whiteheadian understanding of God as internally related to the world, and thereby affected by the world, gives the biblical language a metaphysical rationale which, in the proper function of a rationale (MoT, pp. 123–125), enables us to return to the concrete depictions of God in the Bible with enlarged capacity for appreciation and understanding.

3. *The Judgment of God.* In general, it is fair to say that Whitehead emphasizes patient persuasion—through presentation of the lure of relevant possibilities, and thereby of initial aim, to each actual occasion (above, p. 494)—as the mode of divine activity in the world. This would seem, on the face of it, to be incompatible with the prophetic announcements of dire judgment for sin. And indeed, on this as on some other counts White-

head's personal appreciation for the Old Testament was decidedly negative. Yet, I would argue, his metaphysical scheme requires no such conclusion of incompatibility. To be sure, according to Whitehead God's initial aim for even the most deplorably wicked state of affairs is "the best for that *impasse.*" But, he goes on to say, "if the best be bad, then the ruthlessness of God can be personified as *Atè,* the goddess of mischief. The chaff is burnt" (PR, p. 286). The language here is the appropriately moderate and dispassionate language of metaphysical discourse, free from the "body heat" of lived experience. But the upshot is no less realistic, in its recognition of occasions of judgment, than the prophetic warnings and verdicts, delivered with the dramatic urgency and vivid coloration that were appropriate to the subjective immediacy of those concrete occasions. Yet, as Whitehead implies in the above quotation, and as is clear from the total biblical emphasis, such occasions of judgment are properly understood only within the wider context of the continuing creative purpose of God. In passing, we may note that this is one of the points at which process thought carries forward the realistic emphases of neo-orthodoxy.

4. *God, Time, and History.* In the notion of God's consequent nature, we might say of his historical nature, time and history are given their adequate status in the really real, and hence their overwhelming importance. This point may be brought out by comparing it with some sentences of Hegel (or, for that matter, with theological doctrines of rigid predestination and foreknowledge):[15]

> The consummation of the infinite aim consists merely in removing the illusion which makes it seem yet unaccomplished. Good and absolute goodness is eternally accomplishing itself in the world: and the result is that it needs not wait upon *us,* but is already . . . accomplished.

Man's freedom and his moral acts, then, are illusory; for they are irrelevant to the outcome of things. For God's aim is already accomplished. He has already arrived, having never set out, and is already "satisfied," without ever having known aim. Time which is thus the moving image of eternity, must seem illusory—the rubber mask on the stony face of God. And the temporal preoccupations of both man and God in the Old Testament are an absorption with illusion, the future of which should properly be questioned. But the God of the Bible, and of Process metaphysics, waits upon man's decisions, and changes his own particular intentions (though not His fundamental subjective aim—on which see section c below) in response to them, as depicted for example in Jonah and in Jer. 18:1–11 (see also Buber, quoted above, p. 495). Moreover, if God must genuinely wait, then He does not already *know,* for if our decisions have any real status, He cannot know them (except as possibilities) until we have made them. In the notion of God as historical, and as the perfect recipient (*eis auton ta panta* as Paul says), the biblical concern for moral action, with its presupposition of human freedom, is given its metaphysical rationale.

5. *Worship and Sacrifice.* Finally, worship and sacrifice are placed within the very center of things. For man's worship is his participation in the cosmic worship (above, pp. 496f.) which is the response inspired by God as the power, or the lure, for creative advance. Whether in or out of the cult, therefore, man's deepest business is the worship of God. And sacrifice, in its most material forms, testifies to the requirement that man transcend the sole claims of his individual or corporate self-enjoyment. From this perspective, the scathing prophetic denunciations of hypocritical worship and unworthy sacrifice arise, not out of their irrelevance to what really matters, but out of their perversion as the explicit symbolic expression of the fundamental participation of man in the creative advance, his response to the tabernacling Glory.

C. PROMISE AND FULFILLMENT

In what remains, I would like to offer a brief sketch of some embryonic ideas, concerning God's subjective aim and His knowledge of the world, as exemplified in the Patriarchal and Exodus themes understood in terms of promise and fulfillment. Two texts will focus the discussion:

a) *Exodus 2:23b–25*

And the people of Israel groaned under their bondage, and cried out for help, and their cry under bondage came up to God. And God heard their groaning, and God remembered his covenant with Abraham, with Isaac, and with Jacob. And God saw the people of Israel, and God knew their condition.

b) *Psalm 81:6c–7a* (AB translation)

"I heard the speech of one unknown to me,
I removed the burden on his shoulder,
his hands were freed from the basket.
In distress you called, and I delivered you."

In the second passage I concur fully in Dahood's reading of 6c, as I hope to elaborate elsewhere. As thus read, the two texts are seen to be closely parallel—except for the apparent contradiction between *remembering,* in the one text, and *not knowing,* in the other. One way out is to say that text (a) is theologically profound, while text (b) is historically correct. This problem then receives the same solution as may be given that of the use of the divine names prior to Moses: E and P were historically correct, while J is theologically profound. But this forces us to "save" one text as a historical datum at the expense of its theological utility, and to "save" the other in just the reverse fashion. Moreover, it suggests that historical and theological interests do not really engage one another, but tip their hats politely in passing, one down the lane of historical knowledge, the other down the lane of faith statements. For a dipolar view of reality which eschews such bifurcations, other treatments than this must be attempted, perhaps so as to credit each of the texts with both a theological and a historical reference.

First, consider Ps. 81:6c. That with the Exodus and following events a novel phenomenon emerged in the history of ancient Near Eastern religions, seems a safe assertion. For a process metaphysics, there is likewise no problem in hearing that God entertains a novel experience. That thereafter He should know Israel (Amos 3:1–2) in a manner that He had not formerly (that is, that election is genuinely historical), simply attests, not only to the historical development of religion, but to the historical character of the experience of God.

But of course, such an exegesis, even if granted for the moment, seems to run against the plain statement of the other passage. For was not God's hearing a remembering, and thereby a recognizing? In addressing ourselves to this problem, it will be helpful to digress briefly to recapitulate the relation of novelty to the accumulative past.

Either there is novelty, or there is not. Either there is a new emergent, or there is the same old unchanged reality, rearranged like so many cold peas on a plate so as to slip by bored palates. Either novelty is the vivacious illusion which masks dead reality, or it is novel for God as well as for us.

On the other hand, novelty is not unrelated to the accumulative past. For were it so, such a thing as memory would be simply impossible (above, p. 487). And if novelty were not integrally, organically related to the past along defined routes, I would not remember the general past in terms of the distinction between my past and those pasts not immediately my own. Without an organic relation between novel emergence and the accumulative past, no past would be mine, and yet any and every past would be a candidate for arbitrary adoption as my own. Thus the metaphysical implications of memory and persistence of personal identity.

Now if, in the flow of things, the first movement is the emergence of novelty, the second movement would seem to be the integration of novelty with the accumulated past, through memory. The integration would occur through the vectoral character of feeling from the past, on the one hand, and through the character of the novelty as relevant to that past, on the other. The third movement, arising from the integration of the immediate novelty with the accumulated past, with its settled "structure of experience," would be a return to the novel present, now to *see* it for what it is, as a meaningful occurrence. To see it in its meaning would be to see it in relation to the valued and structured past, in its immediacy of self-enjoyment, and in its potential for the further achievement of subjective aim. But so to see the occasion would be truly to *know* it (on this paragraph, see above, pp. 488ff., 497).

I would venture to suggest that text (a) above may be understood in just these terms. God *heard*—which, as Psalm 81 asserts, constituted a novel emergent for Him. He *remembered*—the occasion was integrated with His experiences of the Patriarchs. He *saw*—and, in seeing, recognized an opportunity to carry forward the advance of His subjective aim as earlier expressed in terms of the general values of posterity and land. And He *knew* —the situation was open before Him in its full three-dimensional historicality.

The argument, then, is that the process of history is real for both Israel and God; and that each text is capable of both a historical and a theological reference. That is, Psalm 81 is not only historically correct, insofar as it attests to the Exodus as the beginning of the Yahweh-Israel relation; but it is also theologically significant insofar as it suggests the novel emergent in the experience and the knowledge of God. And conversely, Exod. 2:23–25 is not only theologically suggestive, in linking the Exodus action to the promises to the Patriarchs; it is also suggestive of antecedents in the historical experience of God. These antecedents may be said to be (a) the divine subjective aim, in the process of time conjoined with and determined by (b) the divine accumulative experience of the actual world. The argument at this point may be adumbrated with the help of Robert Frost's depiction of the experience of poetic creativity:[16]

> A poem is never a put-up job so to speak. It begins as a lump in the throat, a sense of wrong, a homesickness, a lovesickness. It is never a thought to begin with. It is at its best when it is a tantalizing vagueness. It finds its thought and succeeds, or doesn't find it and comes to nothing. . . . It finds the thought and the thought finds the words. Let's say again: A poem particularly must not begin in thought first.

> Every time a poem is written, every time a short story is written, it is written not by cunning, but by belief. The beauty, the something, the little charm of the thing to be, is more felt than known. . . . believing the thing into existence, saying as you go more than you even hoped you were going to be able to say, and coming with surprise to an end that you foreknew only with some sort of emotion.

> [A poem] has an outcome that though unforeseen was predestined from the first image of the original mood—and indeed from the very mood. It is but a trick poem and no poem at all if the best of it was thought of first and saved for the last.

Like the poem whose end is thought of first and written last, a historical process whose end is clearly thought out first and actualized after, is a trick history and no history we can find an interest in. Yet, though the thought does not come first, the final poem is the expression of a felt mood, the power and the aim of which sovereignly (if however gently in persuasion) has its way with the great poets. In regard to the creative advance, that felt mood, I suggest, is in the first instance the divine subjective aim. At the outset, it may be no more than the undetermined but intense mood which is the aim at "the attainment of value in the temporal world" (RM, p. 97), or, in William Temple's words, the aim at "the development of an ever wider fellowship of ever richer personalities." So that the goal of this aim, and therefore the goal of history, may be described abstractly as "the Commonwealth of Value."[17] But this initial mood, as Frost suggests, "assumes direction with the first line laid down." With the first concrete occasion, the final destiny of the divine subjective aim must incorporate the pattern of value achieved in that occasion, or the creative advance has no coherence, nor does the destiny of God.

To apply this now to our two texts: At one point God's subjective aim, in conjunction with the determinations of the past actual world, comes to expression in the as yet undefined and unfocused valuation of land and posterity, in the Patriarchal experience. But from this point, God becomes what He formerly was not (above, p. 496), the God of Abraham, and of Isaac, and of Jacob. And further concretions, as guided by His subjective aim, are woven in terms of these valuations. When, subsequently, the cry of oppressed slaves presents a novel opportunity for creative and redemptive action, it can be as no other than the God of the Fathers that He weaves this opportunity into a concrescence for the divine aim. In this way, what at the outset is abstractly felt as an aim for the Commonwealth of Value, becomes concretely determined in the particular Fellowship of historical individuals and societies, that is, in the Kingdom of God. Thus the God of the philosophers *becomes* the God of Abraham, and of Isaac, and of Jacob. And the career of history, its accumulative concrete character, is in the hands of God's creative faithfulness.

In proposing Process philosophy as a promising metaphysical perspective within which to do biblical theology, I do not mean to suggest that the two are at every point in harmony. Nor do I mean to imply that there are no problems internal to Process thought. But, apart from specific and detailed problems, at the heart of Process thought there is a basic conceptuality, and a central imagery, of such suggestive power, and so elucidatory of the world and human experience, that its application to biblical theology would contribute greatly to the deeper grasp of the biblical witness, in modes of thought which would at once be faithful to its historical meaning and expressive of its contemporary "cash value."

NOTES

1. B. S. Childs, *Biblical Theology in Crisis* (Philadelphia: Westminster, 1970), p. 9.
2. See p. 482.
3. *Encounter* 31 (1970), 311–324.
4. SMW, p. 8. Since frequent reference will be made to a number of works expounding

process thought, I will list them here, together with abbreviated titles by which they will be cited hereafter. In the case of Whitehead's books, the title and date of original publication will be followed by reference to the more recent printings which I use.

D. Browning, ed. "The Development of Process Philosophy," Introduction to *Philosophers of Process* (New York: Random House, 1965). *Cited as* PP.

C. Hartshorne, *The Divine Relativity* (Yale University Press, 1967). *Cited as* DR.

E. Meland, *Faith and Culture* (London: Allen & Unwin, 1955). *Cited as* FC.

———— *The Realities of Faith* (New York: Oxford University Press, 1962). *Cited as* RF.

D. W. Sherburne, ed. *A Key to Whitehead's Process and Reality* (Indiana University Press, 1969). *Cited as* PRs.

A. N. Whitehead, *Science and the Modern World*, 1925 (New York: Free Press, 1967). *Cited as* SMW.

———— *Religion in the Making*, 1926 (Cleveland and New York: World, 1960). *Cited as* RM.

———— *The Function of Reason*, 1929 (Boston: Beacon, 1958). *Cited as* FR.

———— *Process and Reality*, 1929 (New York: Free Press, 1969). *Cited as* PR.

———— *Adventures of Ideas*, 1933 (New York: Free Press, 1967). *Cited as* AI.

———— *Modes of Thought*, 1938 (New York: Free Press, 1968). *Cited as* MoT.

5. For an illuminating outline of the course of English poetry in relation to the development of modern science, see D. Bush, *Science and English Poetry: A Historical Sketch, 1590–1950* (London: Oxford University Press, 1967).

6. R. D. Laing, *The Politics of Experience* (New York: Ballantine, 1968), p. 2. On the tendency toward this sort of basic distinction in phenomenological thought, see R. J. Bernstein's Introduction to William James, *Essays in Radical Empiricism* (New York: Dutton, 1971), p. xii.

7. For example, in von Rad's discussion of "Israel's ideas about Time and History, and the Prophetic Eschatology," in *OTT*, II, Part I, ch. G. His characterization of western man's concept of time as absolute, linear, and independent of events is valid for those who work and think within the Newtonian abstractions. But as contemporary cosmological notions pervade the common mind, these abstractions will become increasingly limited in usefulness. A contrast, therefore, between Israelite and obsolescent ideas is of limited value in a new program for biblical theology.

8. From this point of view, radical contrasts and invidious comparisons between "epiphanic" and "epic" revelations or manifestations, made by Moltmann and others, are metaphysically misconceived. Of course the distinction is valid, and may be theologically significant; see e.g. A. Wilder, *The New Voice* (New York: Herder & Herder, 1969), esp. Part I. But the distinction is one of degree, not kind, and cannot provide the basis for a methodological means of distinguishing between "authentic" and "spurious" revelation.

In this connection, from within the perspective of the notion of simple location, the linking of tradition-units into larger complexes must seem externally imposed, and thereby disruptive of the earlier meanings. Whereas, from a Whiteheadian point of view, the units should be considered as already in some sense ligatured, or at least with latent extensions of reference ready to form ligatures, so that later joins are creative realizations of possibilities inherent in the units of material.

9. P. Wheelwright, *The Burning Fountain: A Study in the Language of Symbolism*, rev. ed. (Indiana University Press, 1968).

10. The term "definitive" as here used is Meland's. See his quotation above, p. 483, and his definition in *Higher Education and the Human Spirit* (University of Chicago Press, 1953), p. 62, where he writes: "Thinking definitively is always motivated by some functional purpose. The object in such instances is not to understand the person or the

object, but to deal with it. Under such circumstances, the penumbra of mystery and meaning which radiates from the clearly defined event is ignored, set aside as if it did not exist." The limits of definitive language are here clearly shown (compare the quotation from Willa Cather on p. 484). Against this he sets the metaphysical truth which, he asserts, "stares out from the analysis of experience by radical empiricism: namely, that reality is unfinished; that time makes a difference; that relations extend every event indefinitely, even making each event inexhaustible."

11. These seven are the main characteristics of expressive language, according to P. Wheelwright [N 9], ch. 5. In his subsequent book, *Metaphor and Reality* (Indiana University Press, 1968), where he explores the possibility of a metapoetics, "an ontology not so much of concepts as of poetic sensitivity," he arrives at a view of reality which is in close accord with the exposition of Whitehead in this section.

12. M. Buber, *The Prophetic Faith* (New York: Harper, 1960), p. 104.

13. J. W. Rogerson, "The Hebrew Conception of Corporate Personality: A Re-Examination," *JTS* 21 (1970), 1–18.

14. I am using the term "structure of experience" in the sense defined by Meland in RF [N 4], p. 210.

15. Quoted in William James, *A Pluralistic Universe* (New York: Dutton, 1971), p. 146.

16. The first quotation is from a letter to Louis Untermeyer, January 1, 1916. The last two are from *Selected Prose of Robert Frost,* eds. H. Cox and E. C. Latham (New York: Holt, 1966), pp. 44, 46, 18–19.

17. W. Temple, *Nature, Man and God* (London: Macmillan, 1951), p. 448.

26. *Historical and Canonical: Recent Discussion about the Old Testament and Christian Faith*

JAMES MAYS

UNION THEOLOGICAL SEMINARY, RICHMOND

"The primary question is not the importance of Israel's history for our history, but whether the God of Israel is the God and Father of Jesus Christ, and our God." That quotation from George Ernest Wright states the issue in the Christian use of the Old Testament. The Old Testament must be understood in its historical reality to be sure that it is indeed the Old Testament witness which is heard. But the issue is theological: whether the God who gives Himself to be known in the Old Testament proclamation is and must be the subject of faith in the Christian confession. The Old Testament must be taken up, not as a problem which the Christian scholar has to solve from an already established theological position, but with a question whether it has had its rightful say in making confession Christian.

The subject is as specific as the exposition of a single text and as broad as the question of Christian theology. But the scholar honored in this volume has kept it in focus so persistently and constructively throughout his career that it must be at least broached in this context. No more will be attempted here than to point to a selection of the work on the question and closely related areas during recent years to suggest one way to formulate the problem, and to sketch the way in which four contributions from American Old Testament studies have approached the question.

I

Work on the role of the Old Testament in Christian theology and preaching has always involved some conception of the whole which enters into its interpretation. The attempt to comprehend the Old Testament in terms of its theological character began a new chapter after the end of the first world war.[1] The new surge of activity in the discipline of "Old Testament Theology" was accompanied by a debate about the requirements of the term "theology." Is a comprehensive description of the Old Testament yet "theology" apart from a correlation with the New Testament or a coordination with the rubrics of dogmatics? Or can the subject matter of theology be clarified from within the Old Testament itself?

By 1960 the effort had produced a row of Old Testament Theologies which give different emphases to the demands of the term "theology." The works of W. Eichrodt, O. Procksch, L. Köhler, Th. C. Vriezen, E. Jacob, P. van Imschoot, G. A. F. Knight, P. Heinisch, and G. von Rad had appeared, to list only those works which bear the specific name.[2] The number and variety of approaches brought a pause during the decade of the sixties for discussion and assessment.[3]

Eichrodt's first volume (1933) and von Rad's concluding one (1960) stand like parentheses around this era of "Old Testament Theologies," and set forth two quite different approaches which have been the primary alternatives under discussion. Both decided to describe the Old Testament witness on its own so that in discussions of its relation to the New Testament and of its claims on Christian faith, it would really be the Old Testament's theological subject which comes into play. That decision has steadily gained dominance, and brought with it an intensification of questions about the relation to the New Testament and Christian theology. But Eichrodt selected a concept, the covenant broadly defined, as the appropriate instrument to display the distinctiveness of Old Testament religion in contrast to its environment and in connection with the New Testament. Von Rad instead focused on the forms and traditions in which specific testimony to Israel's God is given, leaving the characteristic distinctiveness of each witness to stand on its own, and bringing the history of tradition to the threshold of the New Testament. Both strategies have their strengths and correlated problems. In Eichrodt the Old Testament is heard in a unified testimony; he sought a way to expound the form of the whole, but in the process the kerygmatic actuality of the texts is dissolved. In von Rad the various witnesses are heard in the reality of their situations, but the theological claim of the Old Testament is left unsettled. Both strategies retain convincing influence and the discussion about Old Testament theology has unfolded in variations and preferences between these poles.

Recently the call has been heard to identify the central subject of the Old Testament, while holding to the focus of von Rad on the individuality of the kerygmatic entities. R. Smend, after a review of the search for a *Mitte* throughout the history of Old Testament studies, has proposed the double formula "YHWH, the God of Israel; Israel, the people of YHWH" as the unifying subject of the Old Testament witness.[4] W. Zimmerli sees the center in the proclamation "I . . . YHWH" heard through the history repeated in the tradition and the answering recognition "You . . . YHWH" of Israel's praise and prayer.[5] The task he undertakes is to describe the presence of this

Mitte which is decisively characteristic of the entire history of tradition and interpretation.

Renewed attention is being given to the fact that the Old Testament has already been the subject of an interpretation as scripture, which then has in turn been incorporated in the Bible.[6] The investigation and description of the use of the Old Testament by New Testament writers has been a constant, though not major, interest in New Testament exegesis.[7] The subject has probably been stimulated in recent years by the hermeneutical discussion among Old Testament scholars.[8] Because the subject is set about with hermeneutical concerns, a purely descriptive treatment is difficult to attain; questions which outrun historical method press into the discussion and evaluation.[9]

The tendency in the earlier decades of historical criticism to discount the importance of the use of the Old Testament in New Testament texts is gradually being overcome.[10] Studies of the purpose for which the Old Testament is cited uncover the essential theological interests at work.[11] The discovery of new sources for comparison, especially the Qumran texts, puts the New Testament procedures in sharper distinctive profile.[12] The approach of tradition-history shows how the New Testament writers continue directly a process of tradition and reinterpretation which begins at the origin of the Old Testament books.[13] The growing attention to Midrash as a way of interpreting scripture shows another continuity of understanding which runs from Deuteronomy through the New Testament.[14] The way in which New Testament writers understood Old Testament texts begins to appear less arbitrary and more closely coordinated with the context in which the texts stand and their theological subject.[15]

The reservation that a particular New Testament reading of an Old Testament text and the method employed are aspects of the writer's historical situation, and cannot determine its contemporary exegesis, is a guard against interpretation which would be artificial in an era of historical understanding.[16] On the other hand, should the conclusion that New Testament writers used the Old Testament simply as an accommodation to a particular audience, instead of as an assertion of an essential relationship,[17] be valid, the role of the Old Testament in Christian faith would be largely restricted to a phenomenon of its earliest history.

The question at issue, however, is not whether the contemporary interpretation of the Old Testament can resume the historical setting in which New Testament methods and interpretations were effective and relevant, but whether the Christian exegete can work within the theological setting created by the confession "Jesus is the Christ," heard from all the New Testament books. The historical description of the use of the Old Testament by the New points to a context in which both are to be understood. In this context it is not correct to say only that the interpretation of the Old Testament by the earliest Christians was based on the rule that what God had done in Christ is the key to understanding the scriptures. The historical description also shows that the Old Testament was the "key" to the recognition of the work of God in Jesus Christ. The situation was not that the primitive Christian community had an articulated faith and faced the Old Testament as a problem. The problem was the interpretation and exposition of Jesus, and they turned to the Old Testament for the construction of his theological significance, and even found in it the material to fill out the narration of God's work in him.[18] This historical relation points to a theological method in which one moves from within the Old Testament to show the way the God to whom it testifies is at work in Jesus Christ, as well as the move to hear the Old Testament from the side of the New Testament texts.

The vigorous activity in the disciplines of Old and New Testament theology stimulated an effort to reconceive the Christian interpretation of the Old Testament in the light of the positions being advocated.[19] In the context of discussion about hermeneutics it became even more apparent that the theological meaning of the Old Testament would not be settled within the horizons of Old Testament literature, and in the sixties work on this broader form of the question took up where the production of Old Testament Theologies had for the time left off.[20]

The question of how to formulate the relation between the Testaments in a way that would do justice to the distinctiveness of each occupied the first place on the agenda of discussion.[21]

The relation between the Testaments is both an inevitable and threatening preoccupation for approaches to the problem from the Old Testament side; from the Old Testament perspective the New can appear to be secure territory, but the issue of New Testament theology is at least as unsettled as that of the Old, if not more so; approaches from within the Old Testament meet uncertainty and resistance from decisions about the Old Testament in New Testament exegesis and theology.[22]

Proposals about the hermeneutical question naturally turn out to be correlates of decisions about the relation between the Testaments[23] and tend to fall in typical groups around either some thematic concepts of history or existentialist analysis of the texts.[24] Positions on the use of the Old Testament in preaching develop the implications of the basic hermeneutic choice which has been made.[25]

The pressure of this discussion about the relation between the Old Testament and the New, and about the consequences of formulations of that relation for dogmatics and preaching, keeps pulling the question of the Old Testament into a broader perspective than the one customary to Old Testament studies as a separate discipline. In the last few years, in spite of the disagreement about how Old and New Testament theology should be done, and in the face of the divergence in hermeneutical strategies and disarray in systematics, the call for a Biblical Theology has been heard.[26] The question is asked with increasing persistence whether the issues involved can be clarified apart from a broader attack than the now traditional fields on their own can mount. The time appears to be drawing near for a renewed discussion of the Bible as Canon.

II

The present situation in the discussion, as is often observed, has been created by the success of historical criticism at fixing the texts historically. For the sake of the integrity of the primary relation of literary units to historical situations, the integration of theological work was broken up. Biblical theology was separated from dogmatics; the two Testaments were assigned to different fields of study; the literary entities in each Testament were identified and their distinctiveness emphasized. The stages of the career of historical criticism have in turn become the profile of the program confronting theological work with the Bible. The way back from historical critical exegesis of individual texts to dogmatics and preaching, the settings in which the role of the Old Testament in Christian faith is actualized, is seen as a movement in the reverse direction through the stages of historical criticism's career.

The pathos of the current hermeneutical pilgrimage is the attempt to find the way back with the help of historical criticism. From the side of biblical studies historical criticism is cherished as the guardian of the reality of the Bible, the one dependable procedure for ensuring that it is the sense of the texts themselves which comes into play. And from the side of the history of dogmatics it has been recognized as the appropriate outcome of the Reformation's insistence on the authority of the Bible and the plain sense of the texts. Few are prepared to yield its rights or to develop a position which is not based on its results.

The similarity between the profile of the problem and the stages of tradition-history contributes to the appeal of tradition-history as a way of working at Biblical Theology. Tradition-history reconstructs the emergence of biblical literature in terms of a movement which runs from the earliest expressions of Israel's faith through new interpretations and reformulations in later situations and their articulation in literature, and can be extended to include the New Testament. The Bible appears as a continuity of tradition held together by a common process. The incompleteness of the approach lies in the fact that within the movement another concern was at work. A tendency sets in and reaches its completion in the transformation of tradition into a different genre. The process tended toward what the term "canon" means and produced a selected body of literature with the status and role implied in the term. The history of "canonization" is a movement in which the language of faith becomes tradition, tradition becomes scripture, and scripture becomes canon. The later official decisions of the church were only a recognition of what had happened in that history.

The selective recognition and collection of scriptures as "holy" draws a line through the history of tradition. History and tradition of course continue. But the scriptures are a fixed language, a constant which gives continuity to the change. The scriptures do not cancel, but make history. They assume a critical and a creative function. Their successive reinterpretation in new situations enters into the formulation of faith; their language stands as critical resource over against the what and how of the formulations. Their role is to maintain their subject as the decisive center of the continuing history of faith. Their canonization is a recognition that their subject transcends historical change; they become historical in the situations in which their subject is the subject of life and language.

This "intention" of the Bible to become historical in preaching and theology stands in tension with the intention of historical critical exegesis to fix the texts in a reconstructed historical setting and to fulfill their interpretation by describing the sense which the author of literary units meant to convey to those he addressed. The tension does not lie alone in the distance between the ancient and modern setting, the distance between "then" and "now." It is created primarily by the place of the texts in the history of the canon of scriptures, their preservation because they had a "sense" which was not in the end a function of a situation. It is no easy solution to say that biblical theology should be a descriptive discipline. The question is, descriptive of what and in which perspective. If the undertaking holds the focus of historical criticism in the original settings of the texts it will produce either a history of Israel or of Israel's religion or a history of tradition.

The assignment of the Old Testament scholar is the "Old Testament." To say so is not a tautology. The "Old Testament" is in view only when the question is asked which is appropriate to the dimension of history which brought it into existence as Holy Scripture. One way to think of the theological task of Old Testament study is to say that it seeks to identify and describe the characteristic of the texts which accounts for the existence of the Old Testament as such. What is the element in the historical nature of the texts which gives them a place in the history whose outcome is the Old Testament as Holy Scripture? What is the subject matter in the texts in all their variety of thought and function and setting which brings and holds the books together and so validates the historical existence of the Old Testament as more than an arbitrary and accidental collection? Where is the coincidence of historical and canonical? Around the answer to that question the other concerns which enter into the critical and creative role of the Old Testament for Christian faith—the relation to the New Testament, and the claim of the Old Testament on contemporary theology and preaching within that relation—come to expression.

III

Four contributions to the subject from American Old Testament studies in the last decade illustrate the centrality of the question and set forth quite distinctive options. All bring confessional assumptions about the literature into correlation with historical description; their distinctiveness lies in the point at which they see the coincidence of the two.

For G. Ernest Wright[27] the historical and the canonical coincide in the Old Testament in Israel's religion/faith as a distinctive way of viewing reality. That way of viewing reality was created in Israel's faith and recorded in the literature of the Old Testament; it constitutes its canonical claim on Christian theology. Wright coordinates confessional and historical approaches; the confessional view of the scripture supplies the basic assumptions that point to the material and goal of interpretation, while the historical uncovers the content which corroborates and implements the assumptions. His position is stated in the programmatic sentence: "The meaning and mode of this divine action (see below) is the central content of the canon of scripture through which God is revealed as *our* God and in the form by which he would be known as our God" (HR, p. 129).

The view of the Bible as a canon of scriptures has methodological weight in establishing a point of vantage. It is a theological recognition of the importance and extent of scripture, the identification of the creative and normative origin of the Christian faith (OT&T, pp. 167f.). The juxtaposition of Old and New Testaments is the church's confession that the canon as a whole is a prerequisite for a valid knowledge of Jesus Christ (HR, p. 187). The range of the canon comes to expression in the doctrine of the Trinity, "the Church's attempt to summarize the complexity of God's presentation of himself within the Canon's historical progression" (HR, p. 188). This means that the question appropriate for the Old Testament is nothing less than the question about God: "whether the God of Israel is the God and Father of Jesus Christ, and our God" (HR, p. 189). But the canon is not a dogmatic entity which settles questions, but must be viewed "dynamically" as the possibility of working out answers within its limits. The variety in the literature has led throughout the history of interpretation to decisions in favor of specific parts and themes of scripture as the central expression of its meaning and authority. Where and why the selection falls is a matter of the way scripture is understood in a particular era or theology. There is always a "canon within the canon" necessitated by the historical character of faith and theology. In effect, the problem of the limits of the material canon, the question of the "disputed books," is overrun by the function of a formal canon which always derives from the undisputed central core of literature (OT&T, pp. 169–183).

The question then facing the Old Testament scholar is to identify and describe what in the main body of Old Testament literature answers to and actualizes the canonical assumptions. The answer cannot be given from outside the Old Testament, either from the New Testament or from a theology, but must be sought objectively in a historical description of the way the Old Testament itself testifies to God (HR, pp. 184 f.). The criteria for identifying the Old Testament's own formal canon is the "characteristic" (what lends coherence to the central core of literature) and the "distinctive" (what features give it individuality in its own historical environment).

The historical phenomenon within the Old Testament which Wright describes is religion defined as "the structuring of a certain group of symbols which are understood to portray ultimate reality and the manner in which meaningful life is to be lived in relation to it" (HR, p. 183). This definition frees the term from its more limited reference to a cluster of institutions and beliefs of a specific time in the religious history of Israel and points to the theological character and capacity of an entire religious tradition.

The description of what is characteristic and distinctive of Israel's religion is a project which Wright along with colleagues has taken up repeatedly across his career. Its themes are history and covenant. The knowledge of God, revelation, came to Israel primarily through "event," the combination of happening and interpretation which had the effect of creating community and structuring life (HR, p. 186; OT&T, p. 44). These decisive events, the *magnalia Dei,* conveyed the type and direction of divine action in history. Around these events Israel was formed as a religious community of gratitude and loyalty. Their relation as community to God was given expression in two basic forms drawn from political life, both covenantal (Mosaic and Davidic); used analogically these forms furnished the structures of understanding by which Israel conceived the Real. Together, the *magnalia Dei* and the covenants were the sources of the symbols by which God was known and life lived meaningfully. In the process Israel developed a distinctive language which was indigenous to its symbolical structure (HR, pp. 191–195; and chs. 3–5 of OT&T, where the way the central images emerged and shaped appropriate language is developed in detail). This combination of a mode of divine action and a set of images clustered around the notion of the divine Suzerain institutes the actuality of the Old Testament. It is the unifying feature in the variety of the Old Testament; there is no place "where the conception is not central or does not stand as the background giving the foreground its meaning and setting," except in marginal books (OT&T, p. 165). It is the only appropriate rubric for a theology of the Old Testament (OT&T, ch. 2).

From the base of this description of the coincidence of historical and canonical in the Old Testament, Wright handles the question of its relation to the New Testament and Christian theology. The description uncovers the generic continuity of the New with the Old. The mode of divine action continues; all the New Testament literature is the expression of Jesus as "event," historical memory and interpretation structuring life (HR, pp. 187, 189). This "knowledge" of the New Testament's central figure is largely dependent on the Old Testament view of reality and its language by which alone the figure of Jesus Christ can be grasped (HR, p. 190). In the relation of the Testaments the Old has not only chronological but hermeneutical priority; a *Christo*centricity without a prior *theo*centricity is meaningless (OT&T, p. 29). The Old Testament furnishes the context for understanding the New and the criterion to prevent its misunderstanding.

The description also calls for a Christian theology based on the study of the creative symbols and the languages appropriate to them (HR, p. 196). The images of the divine suzerain and the cosmic government cannot be surrendered without the loss of the reality in which the symbols participate (HR, p. 189). Calvin's notion of God's accommodation to our knowledge and Tillich's reflection on the nature and role of symbol in human understanding would be basic (OT&T, ch. 6) in the hermeneutical task of reinterpreting the original images in relation to our world. God is not known directly, in biblical times or in our time, but the biblical Divine Monarch points to the manner in which the Bible's God would have us know him as God (OT&T, p. 165).

For J. Bright[28] the canonical and the historical in the Old Testament coincide in an overarching structure of theology which informs in one way or another all its texts. Participation in this theology is the objectively describable normative feature of the texts. It is what transcends the temporal and incidental features of their original historical setting. It is the locus of the relation of the Old Testament to the New. It is the function of the Old Testament that is authoritative for the Christian faith.

The fact of the Christian canon of scriptures does not settle the question of how the Old Testament works as canonical; instead it sets the problem which has been a constant concern of Christian thought throughout its history. That authority of the Bible with which biblical study can deal is its normative competence as the primary documents of the Christian faith (p. 30). "The Christian faith is a historical phenomenon: it is what it *was*. And our one primary authority regarding what is actually affirmed and taught remains the biblical record" (p. 109). The formation of the Bible sets the Old Testament in all its diversity and distinctiveness alongside the New Testament. With that definition of authority, obviously the New Testament has normative priority. It consists of documents of the Christian faith and is addressed to the church; the Old Testament is a document of the faith of Old Israel, a religion genetically related to, but different from, our own. The Old Testament requires a "hermeneutical transfer" to address the Christian faith in which the New Testament is "the final arbiter" (pp. 52, 182 ff.).

For the Old Testament's authority to come into play, its texts must be heard in their own right. The only method which preserves their individuality is grammatico-historical exegesis (p. 83). But exegesis has not completed its task until it goes beyond the verbal meaning of the text to lay bare the theological concern which animates all biblical texts (p. 170). It is in their expression, directly or indirectly, of a theology which transcends the temporal and incidental of the text's historical setting that the authority of Old Testament texts is manifested (p. 151). Old Testament theology working inductively from "the logical exegesis" moves through the entire Old Testament to develop a synthetic description of the Old Testament faith. It focuses on features of the faith which were "pervasive, constantly present, normative, that imparted to it its distinctive character, that made it both what it was and different from all other faiths" (p. 115).

The faith of Israel, "a phenomenon that is unique and is to be spoken of in the singular" (p. 123), is a "coherent, though never systematically articulated, structure of belief" whose overarching themes held the diversity of the Old Testament together (p. 136). Its genius is a theological interpretation of Israel's history. Among the essential features of the structure are: that complex of beliefs centered in the theme of God's election of Israel; an understanding of reality from the perspective of election expressed in the concept of covenant; an expectation of the future based on election and covenant. These features, and others, run through the whole of the Old Testament and inform all its parts (pp. 126–136). But it is precisely the reach for the future impelled by the character of the structure of belief which, for all its inclusiveness in comprehending the Old Testament, leaves it inconclusive within itself.

The New Testament's central theological concern is the announcement that this incompleteness has been fulfilled in the decisive act of the God of Israel's history in Jesus Christ. Like the Old Testament its center is a theological interpretation of events. In its affirmations it takes up the structure of theology of the Old Testament and reinterprets it in the light of Christ. "The *structure* of the New Testament's theology is the same as that of the Old, but with its *context* radically transformed in the light of what Christ has done" (p. 148). The place of the Old Testament in the Christian faith can be seen only from within the New Testament in its relation to and use of the Old. The two Testaments stand in a dual relation of continuity and discontinuity, continuous within the unity of God's purpose, discontinuous in the disparity of two aeons—B.C. and A.D. (p. 201).

The theological structure of the two Testaments and the relation established between them by the New Testament is the key that opens the whole of the Old Testament as a word to the church (p. 197). The key is not a single formula or pattern because the relation is complex, though its most important dimension is the *Heilsgeschichte* which moves through the Old Testament to completion in the New (p. 199). The Christian must read the Old Testament first in its plain historical meaning, and then second in the light of the

New Testament's affirmations about it. Each of the Old Testament texts has to be referred to the New "for verdict, whether it be ratification, modification, or judgment" (p. 200). And yet the Old Testament sense of the text must remain, seen in the New Testament perspective. Read so, it speaks an *objective* word about many essential features of the Christian faith simply assumed and not developed in the New Testament and guards the latter from misunderstanding; it speaks a subjective word regarding man and his condition without Christ, and so points to Christ (pp. 202–209). Thus the Old Testament interpreted within a biblical theology of the related belief-structures of both Testaments "is able to address all situations, since we as Christians stand under that theology, and since the human situations to which it was addressed are in a real sense 'typical' of our own human situation" (p. 173).

For J. Sanders, the canonical and the historical of the Old Testament coincide in the *Gestalt* which Israel's scriptures reached in becoming the Bible. The phenomenon in the Old Testament which can be described as its canonical character is the combination of function and form expressed in the final shape of the tradition as the guide to Israel's identity under God.[29]

To get at the canonical reality of the Old Testament books one must begin by moving behind questions about the disputed books and prior definitions of what constitute canonicity, bracket out the hermeneutical orientation of Judaism and Christianity, and learn what its authoritative character was from within the history of the material itself. All the historical disciplines, particularly tradition and redaction history, must be used to inquire about the function of tradition in the historical context in which it is cited and reformulated. From the vantage gained, "canonical criticism" then seeks to "take the measure of its activity," to uncover from the shaping of the tradition the way it was understood and to what purpose (pp. ix–xix, 120). The authoritative capacity of the tradition is evident in the way it was carried over from one situation to another, maintained itself in ever new reformulations, and gave continuity to Israel's understanding of its identity. The history of authoritative tradition moves toward invariability, the second and later characteristic of the canonical evident in the Old Testament. The goal of the investigation is ultimately a definition of the hermeneutics of that generation which gave the canon of scriptures its basic shape. The valid roles for reading the Old Testament as canon are embedded in the hermeneutics of that final shaping and its situation (pp. xvi, 88 f., 120).

Every arrangement of the Bible places the five books which came to be called "the Torah" at the beginning, a claim for their priority. The term *torah* can be correlated with each of the stages of the Pentateuch's formation. It points to the various confessional forms, simple and developed, which the story of Israel's origins took as Israel in successive eras found anew in the story the "mirror of its identity." In the tribal and monarchical period the laws and customs which guided Israel's life were incorporated in the story for authentication, and the story included the settlement in the Promised Land

and the founding of Israel's central religious institutions. But final shaping occurred in the exile after the land was lost and the institutions destroyed. In that crisis, and its loss of all that had come to represent its identity, Israel received once more from the Torah story, minus the narrative of its life in the land, its identity in final form. Through this henceforth invariable Torah "Israel passed from a nation in destitution to a religious community in dispersion which could never be destroyed" (p. 51). "The Torah was, therefore, essentially and forever a Diaspora Torah of hope" (p. 91). The severed portions of the old Torah story together with the record of the monarchy were grouped with the prophets whose work laid the foundations for understanding the destitution of old nationalist Israel (p. 96).

The classical prophets stand squarely within the Torah tradition. They were covenant mediators who spoke for the God known through Torah to raise the probing question whether the Israel to whom they spoke was the Israel of God's purpose. Their message was both judgment and transformation for Israel. The message of the "true" prophet was not heard in their time but passed over into the tragedy of the exile to gain authority when the devastated community heard in the word of judgment the continuity with their past and in the promise of transformation the clue to their identity in the future (pp. 71, 88).

The shape and character of the Bible as canon emerged in the catastrophe which ended Israel's national identity. By the late sixth century B.C. there was a fixed Torah and a dynamic collection of prophets in existence. The fundamental question of what it means to be "Israel" was settled, and the conclusion was expressed in the structure of priority and relationship in the yet forming canon, into which the rest of its literature was gathered. The Writings were added on the assumption that the identity question was settled and under the aegis of a different hermeneutic. In general they deal with the question of the life style which goes with the identity in the broadest ranges of ordinary life and in the situations in which a Diaspora had to live.

The result is a canon within the canon, with emphasis on both uses of the term. The whole is accounted for in tracing the emergence of the material. But a structure of priorities and functions sets the way interpretation is to follow. The Pentateuch declares that to be Israel means having an identity dependent on no institution other than the covenant of God. The prophets hold every institutionalization of faith under judgment and point to the existence which is wrought by the transformation of God. Moses is forever triumphant over David, Torah set over Temple, the true prophets overcome the false.

This structure of priority and function is not a settled unity of content. The "essential diversity" gathered into its order is a persistent call to the community which reads the Bible to receive its existence from the image mirrored in the scriptures. But the final *Gestalt* of the canon always in turn shapes the image in a specific way. The diversity reveals God's freedom and refusal to yield his sovereignty to any stance or conclusion of faith (pp. 85, 116). Every "old Israel" sees the reflection of a new which "participates in his [God's] absolute freedom to the extent of being free herself of any and every institution which she might have, and which God in his grace would give her" (p. 89). So here is a theological definition which is set by the invariable canon. Sanders does not pursue the consequences of "canonical criticism" into the New Testament. But his use of the rubric "crucifixion and resurrection" for the exilic experience suggests a continuity. Because the canon assumes this particular *Gestalt,* he concludes that it is "perhaps most relevant precisely to the sort of experience the heirs of Judaism now face, the church and synagogue today" (p. 119), for it is in such experiences that the actual authority of the canon, its "life giving quality in the midst of death" (p. 120) comes into force.

For B. S. Childs the historical and canonical cannot be said to coincide in a feature or dimension of the Old Testament.[30] Though he shows his particular interest by using Old Testament texts for illustrations of interpretation, he would regard the attempt to deal theologically with the Old Testament on its own as a misplaced question. The reality of the canon is the church's confessional recognition of Old Testament and New Testament together as normative theological source. Canon sets a context for interpretations, and the texts have canonical function when interpreted in that context. Historical investigation cannot find the canonical; the descriptive task already faces the identified canon and must be subordinated to the requirements set by the canon as context.

"Canon," a concern relegated usually to a few concluding paragraphs about the appearance and collection of the biblical books in introductions, must come to the fore as a "hermeneutical analogy for doing modern Biblical Theology" (BTC, p. 106). In this role of analogy the term means a great deal more than an external name given to the scriptures. It points to the status and function of the scriptures in the community of faith which alone explains their historical existence as this collection. Its methodological weight lies in its definition of the context in which the interpretation of the texts is to be carried out. Every textual unit can be investigated within the linguistic, literary, social, and cultural environment which is the setting for its origin. But the assembly of the units into books, and of the books into the arrangement and limits of a collection for exclusive use by a community as scripture creates a different environment for the texts which transcends reconstructed historical settings. That environment creates new possibilities and calls for different questions than those governed by the investigation of the text in its original historical setting. The canon is the context for theological interpretation of the texts (BTC, pp. 97 f.).

"Canon as context" means a specific area within which interpretation moves, a function which is expected of what is interpreted, a relation of the interpreter to the interpretation. The area is the Old Testament and New

Testament together without any preconception of their relationship. The function of the Testaments together is to be the medium of revelation, so that the expectation is theological. The relation of what is interpreted has the quality of normative authority for the interpreter (BTC, pp. 99–107). Only through an exegesis oriented to their structure of confessional assumptions is a viable biblical theology possible. Biblical theology cannot be restricted to a descriptive task; only when the description is framed so that it can be brought to bear on current questions of faith and life is it theological.

The urgency of this reorientation is seen against the background of the career of historical criticism and its consequences for theological work with the Bible, and of the "Crisis in the Biblical Theology Movement" in American biblical studies. Historical criticism dismantled the sense of the canon which had held the Bible in relation to the church's theological work with its focus on a reconstructed historical setting as the exclusive context for interpretation (surveyed in the first Sprunt Lecture). The "Biblical Theology Movement" attempted to exploit the results of historical criticism without an adequate notion of canon to give its work context (BTC, Part I).

Childs's call for a renewal of the sense of canon is not an attempt to turn back the clock. He wants "a method which is open to all the genuine advances of historical critical scholarship" (CC, II/3). The canon as form of the scriptures does not erase the individuality of the parts. This holds for particular texts and for the two Testaments. To be heard correctly each Old Testament text must be studied in the environment of its own period and within its Old Testament context (BTC, p. 112). Otherwise, "The witness of the whole canon is impaired" (BTC, p. 152); the integrity of the canon is already at stake in the accuracy with which an individual text is understood. In Old Testament exegesis it is imperative to give major attention to the final literary setting within which the texts are placed. The formation of books relocates the units in a new setting in which they have their function as scripture. The books represent the canonical shape of the tradition; "canonical criticism" must seek the hermeneutical clues given in the arrangement and redaction of the material to the way the witnesses were understood as they were preserved as witnesses to other historical situations beyond their original setting. The way the texts are interpreted by their relation to the book in which they stand turns out to be the reading with which they are used in the New Testament; disinterest in this stage of the text's history leaves a gap in the movement of thought between the Testaments (see case studies in the Sprunt Lectures).

The canon juxtaposes the two Testaments in their distinctness. The Old is not to be reduced to the New Testament's interpretation of it; "they speak of Christ in decidedly different ways" (BTC, p. 111). But they cannot be separated or one subordinated to the other. Their relationship cannot be adequately defined by patterns or formulas naming categories of history or theology. The Old Testament does not express a primitive level of faith that needs to be Christianized. The incorporation of both creates a new context which is more than the sum of its parts. Their individual validity rests in the claim of faith that both are testifying to the same God at work. The coherence to which this claim points is a "compatibility of the witnesses," evident in "characteristic approaches to divine reality, commensurate imperatives, and a sustained level of seriousness respecting the major questions of life and death" (BTC, p. 112). Childs describes this compatibility of the Testaments using New Testament quotations of the Old as the most appropriate category to reach a picture of the whole within which the interpreter can relate the texts of the two Testaments dialectically (BTC, pp. 114–118, 201–219).

The exegesis of Old Testament texts, then, holds a series of moments in their history in perspective, primarily the original situation, the final literary setting, and the context of the canon. Interpretation progressively subordinates the historical critical questions concerned with the sense of the text in its original situation to questions about its testimony to God's work in judgment and redemption raised by its setting in all of scripture. What comes into play is a concentrated interest in the theological capacity of the text expressed in language open to comparison and contrast with other appropriate witnesses within the range of the canon of scriptures. What is pursued in broadening the setting is not something typical or composite, an extraction from all the texts which represents the canonical, but an awareness of the text as a witness to divine reality in the function assigned it by the context of the canon. The Old Testament texts, and the New, become canonical in that function.

IV

Thus these four studies reach quite different conclusions in defining the canonical dimension of the Old Testament. Wright sees it in a unique view of reality expressed in images and language that convey the meaning and mode of divine action; he maintains the importance of this view of reality in relation to New Testament and Christian theology with a persistence that gives it an unqualified claim on both. Bright finds the canonical in a structure of theology which is shared by the New Testament and which allows Old Testament texts to be understood either in continuity or discontinuity with the normative content of the New. Sanders focuses on a correlation between the shaping of the canon's scriptures as Torah and the understanding of what it means to be Israel, an understanding always faced with the appropriation of "crucifixion and resurrection" as the way of God. For Childs the canonical is the meaning scripture has when interpreted in the context which the confessional recognition of them as canon sets.

Different as they are in their conclusions about method, all are expressions of the call for a biblical theology, and recognition of the need to give the canonical identity of Old Testament literature renewed emphasis alongside historical investigation. They show that the question of the "Old Testament" cannot really be reduced to anything less than the question about Christian faith. In developing their argument each is affected by the individual way he is working in Old Testament research, and each shows the influence of confessional and theological preferences as well as particular sensitivities to where the urgent questions of faith and life lie. As they must, and should.

The effort to speak of the significance of the Old Testament for Christian faith today has to overrun the unsettled questions about Old and New Testament theology, and work within the uncertainty created by the collapse of the theological fronts of the last generation into an almost individual pluralism of systematics. The word "problem" recurs with sobering frequency in all writing on the subject. G. E. Wright once observed that if a proper theology were given developed expression, then the importance of the Old Testament would no longer need to be argued and attention could concentrate on the more important task of a meaningful exposition of the Old Testament in the church (HR, p. 196). Yet every proposal about method is in a fundamental sense an expression of an interpretative understanding of the subject matter. The "how" of these, and of every proposal, is an articulation of the meaning of the Old Testament which convinces and illuminates. By holding the subject of the "Old Testament" in focus, they transcend the question of method and put the question of faith in the One who is God of Israel and Father of Jesus Christ.

NOTES

The literature cited in the following notes emphasizes work published since 1960 and indicates where bibliographies covering previous decades are available.

1. For a review of the discipline and analyses of significant contributions, see R. C. Dentan, *Preface to Old Testament Theology* (New Haven, 1962). For a discussion of the literature with full, though selective, bibliography, beginning with the discussions about method in the twenties, see E. Würthwein, "Zur Theologie des Alten Testaments," *Revue de l'Histoire des Religions* 36 (1971), 185–208.

2. Since all the books bear approximately the title "Theology of the Old Testament," and bibliographical data is given in the works listed in N 1, full citation is omitted. See the analysis of most of the mentioned works in *Contemporary Old Testament Theologians*, ed. R. B. Laurin (Valley Forge, 1970); and the review articles in *ET*, September 1961 through March 1962, July 1962, April 1963.

3. Representative discussions of the situation in Old Testament theology since 1960 are L. Alonso-Schokel, "Biblische Theologie des Alten Testaments," *Stimmen der Zeit* 172 (1962–63), 34–51; C. Barth, "Grundprobleme einer Theologie des Alten Testaments," *EvTh* 23 (1963), 342–362; R. E. Clements, "The Problem of Old Testament Theology," *London Quarterly and Holborn Review* 190 (1965), 11–17; E. Jacob, *Grundfragen alttestamentliche Theologie* (Stuttgart, 1970); J. P. M. van der Ploeg, "Une

'Théologie de l'Ancien Testament' est-elle possible?" *Ephemerides Theologicae Lovanienses* 38 (1962), 417–434; N. W. Porteous, "Second Thoughts II. The Present State of Old Testament Theology," *ET* 75 (1963), 70–74; G. von Rad, "Offene Fragen im Umkreis einer Theologie des Alten Testaments," *TLZ* 88 (1963), 401–416; H. Graf von Reventlow, "Grundfragen der alttestamentliche Theologie im Lichte der neueren deutschen Forschung," *Theologische Zeitschrift* 17 (1961), 81–98; M. Sekine, "Vom Verstehen des Heilsgeschichte. Das Grundproblem des alttestamentliche Theologie," *ZAW* 75 (1963), 145–154; H. J. Stoebe, "Überlegungen zur Theologie des Alten Testaments," in *Gottes Wort und Gottes Land* (Göttingen, 1965), pp. 200–220; R. de Vaux, "Peut on écrire une Théologie de l'Ancien Testament," in *Bible et Orient* (Paris, 1967), pp. 59–71 (Eng. tr., "Is It Possible to Write a 'Theology of the Old Testament'?" in *The Bible and the Ancient Near East*, tr. Damian McHugh [Garden City. N.Y., 1971], pp. 49–62); A. Weiser, "Die Theologische Aufgabe des alttestamentlichen Wissenschaft," *BZAW* 66 (1963), 207–224; G. E. Wright, "Reflections concerning Old Testament Theology," in *Studia Biblica et Semitica* (Wageningen, 1966), pp. 376–388.

4. R. Smend, *Die Mitte des Alten Testaments*. Theologische Studien 101 (Zurich, 1970). A crucial analysis of the situation and its demands on the subject.

5. Zimmerli's intention is outlined in "Alttestamentliche Traditionsgeschichte und Theologie," in *Probleme biblischer Theologie,* ed. H. W. Wolff (Munich, 1971), pp. 632–647. Cf. now *Grundriss der alttestamentliche Theologie* (Stuttgart, 1972).

6. See e.g. the recognition and differing conclusions in Part ɪ of S. Amsler, *L'Ancien Testament dans l'église* (Neuchâtel, 1960); and ch. 3 of F. Hesse, *Das Alte Testament als Buch der Kirche* (Gütersloh, 1966).

7. K. Stendahl, *The School of St. Matthew* (Lund, 1954), surveys the work on Old Testament quotations in the New Testament comprehensively.

8. A useful catalogue of recent research arranged in relation to the concerned texts is present in the footnotes to chs. ɪ–ɪɪɪ of H. von Campenhausen, *Die Entstehung des Christlichen Bibel* (Tübingen, 1968); Eng. tr., *The Formation of the Christian Bible* (Philadelphia, 1972).

9. E.g. A. Suhl, *Der Funktion der alttestamentlichen Zitaten und Anspielungen im Markus-Evangelium* (Gütersloh, 1965), and the review by M. Rese, "Die Rolle des Alten Testaments im Neuen Testament," in *Verkündigung und Forschung, Beiträge zur evangelischen Theologie* 2 (1967), 87–97.

10. See the assessment of C. K. Barrett, "The Interpretation of the Old Testament in the New," in *CHB,* I, 377–411.

11. On the apologetic function of the use of the Old Testament, see B. Lindars, *New Testament Apologetic. The Doctrinal Significance of the Old Testament Quotations* (Philadelphia, 1961). For the thesis that New Testament writers saw a "real presence" of Jesus in the Old Testament, see A. T. Hanson, *Jesus Christ in the Old Testament* (London, 1965).

12. For instance J. A. Fitzmyer, "The Use of Explicit Old Testament Quotations in Qumran Literature and in the New Testament," *New Testament Studies* 7 (1960–61), 296–333.

13. H. Gese writes, "Die neutestamentliche Traditionsbildung greift also in eine noch lebendige Traditionsbildung ein, d.h. wir haben es eben nur mit *einer,* der biblischen Traditionsbildung zu tun," in his article "Erwägungen zur Einheit der biblischen Theologie," *ZTK* 67 (1970), 420.

14. G. Vermes, "Bible and Midrash: Early Old Testament Exegesis," *CHB,* I, 199–231.

15. See the conclusions in E. Flesseman-van Leer, "Die Interpretation der Passionsgeschichte vom Alten Testament aus," and E. Lohse, "Die alttestamentliche Bezüge im neutestamentlichen Zeugnis vom Tode Jesu Christi," both in *Zur Bedeutung des Todes Jesu,* ed. F. Viering (Gütersloh, 1967), resp. pp. 79–96, 97–112.

16. J. Barr, *Old and New in Interpretation* (London, 1966), p. 133 and ch. 4 generally.

17. H. Braun, "Das Alte Testament im Neuen Testament," *ZTK* 59 (1962–63), 16 ff.

18. See the excellent formulation in J. A. Sanders, "The Vitality of the Old Testament," *USQR* 21 (1966), 164, and Barr [N 16], pp. 139 f.

19. Rather inclusive bibliographies for 1930 into the 1960s are given in Barr [N 16]; J. Bright, *The Authority of the Old Testament* (Nashville, 1967); Würthwein [N 1], 185–188. The collection of essays in *Probleme alttestamentlicher Hermeneutik*, ed. C. Westermann (Munich, 1960), Eng. tr., *Essays on Old Testament Hermeneutics* (Richmond, 1963), are representative of the discussion on the continent at the beginning of the 1960s.

20. Since 1960 books on the subject include: Amsler [N 6]; Barr [N 16]; Bright [N 19]; Childs, *Biblical Theology in Crisis* (Philadelphia. 1970); P. Grelot, *Sens chrétien de l'Ancien Testament* (Tournai, 1962); Hesse [N 6]; N. Lohfink, *The Christian Meaning of the Old Testament* (Milwaukee, 1968); K. H. Miskotte, *Wenn die Götter schweigen: Vom Sinn des Alten Testaments* (Munich, 1963), translated from the Dutch, *Als de goden zwijgen*, Eng tr., *When the Gods Are Silent* (New York, 1967); K. Schwarz-wäller, *Das Alte Testament in Christus*, Theologische Studien, 84 (Zurich, 1966); G. E. Wright, *The Old Testament and Theology* (New York, 1969).

Articles include: P. R. Ackroyd, "The Place of the Old Testament in the Church's Teaching and Worship," *ET* 74 (1963), 164–167; R. E. Brown, "The *Sensus Plenior* in the Last Ten Years," *CBQ* 25 (1963), 262–285; B. S. Childs, "Interpretation in Faith: The Theological Responsibility of an Old Testament Commentary," *Interpretation* 18 (1964), 432–449; H. Donner, "Das Problem des Alten Testaments in der Christlichen Theologie," in *Beiträge zur Theorie des neuzeitlichen Christentums,* ed. W. Trillhass (Berlin, 1968), pp. 37–51; D. Lys, "L'Appropriation de l'Ancien Testament," *Études théologiques et réligieuses* 41 (1966), 1–12; B. Vawter, "The Fuller Sense: Some Considerations," *CBQ* 26 (1964), 85–96; J. Wharton, "The Occasion of the Word of God," *Austin Seminary Bulletin* 84.1 (1968).

21. K. Schwarzwäller, "Das Verhältnis Altes Testament-Neues Testament im Lichte der gegenwärtigen Bestimmungen," *EvTh* 29 (1969), 281–307, reviews the relevant literature and develops the implications he sees in G. von Rad's *OTT.* Barr [N 16] offers a searching criticism of current approaches and expresses reservations about the procedures being used.

22. The best illustration is the literature provoked by R. Bultmann's definition of the Old Testament; see the essays in *The Old Testament and Christian Faith,* ed. B. W. Anderson (New York, 1963).

23. H.-J. Kraus, *Die Biblische Theologie* (Neukirchen, 1970), Parts II–III on the history of the relation between Old and New Testament theology.

24. Recent proposals in Hesse [N 20]; G. W. H. Lampe, "Hermeneutics and Typology," *London Quarterly and Holborn Review* 190 (1965), 17–25; F. Mildenberger, *Gottes Tat im Wort. Erwägungen zur alttestamentlichen Hermeneutik als Frage nach der Einheit des Testamente* (Gütersloh, 1964); R. Rendtorff, "Hermeneutik des Alten Testaments als Frage nach der Geschichte," *ZTK* 57 (1960), 27–40; H. W. Wolff, "Das Alte Testament und das Problem der existentialen Interpretation," *EvTh* 23 (1963), 1–17.

25. D. Rössler, "Die Predigt über alttestamentliche Texte," in *Studien zur Theologie der alttestamentliche Überlieferung,* eds. R. Rendtorff and K. Koch (Neukirchen, 1961), pp. 153–162; L. E. Toombs, *The Old Testament in Christian Preaching* (Philadelphia, 1961); A. H. J. Gunneweg; "Über die Prädikabilität alttestamentliche Texte," *ZTK* 65 (1968), 389–413; H. D. Preuss, "Das Alte Testament in der Verkündigung der Kirche," *Deutsches Pfarrerblatt* 63 (1968), 73–79.

26. G. Ebeling's remark—that Old and New Testament theology must take com-

prehensive account of the theological problems which arise when the question is put about the coherence in the variety of the biblical witness—is frequently cited ("The Meaning of 'Biblical Theology,'" in *Word and Faith* [Philadelphia, 1963], p. 79). See the opinions in Childs [N 20], pp. 91ff.; H. Gese, "Erwägungen zur Einheit der biblischen Theologie," *ZTK* 67 (1970), 417–436; F. Lang, "Christuszeugnis und biblische Theologie," *EvTh* 29 (1969), 523–534; Smend [N 4]; and most recently the attempt to state the need and problem comprehensively by H.-J. Kraus, *Die Biblische Theologie. Ihre Geschichte und Problematik* (Neukirchen, 1970).

27. The works by G. E. Wright referred to are: "History and Reality: The Importance of Israel's 'Historical' Symbols for the Christian Faith" (*cited as* HR) in *The Old Testament and Christian Faith,* ed. B. W. Anderson (New York, 1963), 176–199, and *The Old Testament and Theology* (cited as OT&T) (New York, 1969).

28. Page references in following paragraphs to Bright, *The Authority of the Old Testament* [N 19].

29. Page references in following paragraphs to J. A. Sanders, *Torah and Canon* (Philadelphia, 1972). Though Sanders does not deal with the New Testament or Christian faith directly, his method and conclusions bear significantly on the discussion.

30. The works by B. S. Childs referred to are: *Biblical Theology in Crisis* (cited as BTC) (Philadelphia, 1970), and the mimeographed form of the Sprunt Lectures of 1972, "Canon and Criticism: The Old Testament as Scripture of the Church" (*cited by* lecture number and page as on p. 523. CC, II/3).

V

Canon and Text

27. Adaptable for Life:
The Nature and Function of Canon

J. A. SANDERS

UNION THEOLOGICAL SEMINARY, NEW YORK CITY

I

THE STUDY of the canon of the Bible, and especially of the Old Testament, is today in a state of flux. One senses this especially if one rereads, at the present moment, the standard introductions and handbooks on the subject. For the most part they exhibit consensus on the meaning of canon without broaching the problems of canon as they should be put today. Discrepancy in judgment may appear on how early or how late one may speak of closure of the three sections of the Old Testament; but, save for a few hints otherwise, standard discussions of canon deal almost exclusively with last things in the canonical process rather than with the early factors which gave rise to the phenomenon of canon as Judaism inherited it.

The sense of flux comes in reading such discussions in the light of what has been happening in the last several years in biblical studies generally. Today, I am convinced, we cannot deal adequately with the question of the structure of canon, or what's in and what's out, until we have explored seriously and extensively the question of the function of canon. It is time to attempt to write a history of the early canonical process.[1] Out of what in ancient Israel's common life did the very idea of canon itself arise? The concept of canon is located in the tension between two poles: stability and adaptability; but discussions since Semler[2] in 1772 have dealt almost exclusively with the former and rarely with the latter. Hence, all the brave efforts to work on hermeneutics in the past fifteen years have failed, I think, for the lack of work on canonical criticism; for hermeneutics must be viewed as the midterm of the axis which lies between stability and adaptability.

Robert Pfeiffer's chapter in his introduction is one of the finest of the older Liberal discussions of canon.[3] And yet Pfeiffer started with the finding of the scroll in the temple in 621 B.C.: he started with the concept of stability and the necessary observations about Deut. 31:26. It seemed quite normal at the time, I am sure, and one can understand it today even though we are in a quite different *Zeitgeist,* to cast about for the earliest evidence of when a certain body of traditional literature became stabilized: and Deuteronomy seems to provide that evidence for the Pentateuch. The work of the exilic or priestly editors then is usually mentioned, followed by observations about the work of Ezra with evidence to substantiate it in the Chronicler. So much for the Law. In the case of the Prophets the discussions start with citations from Ben Sira 48 and 49, written about 190 B.C., to show that the books of the Three and the dodecapropheton must have become by that time the prophetic corpus as we know it now—with a door left ajar to allow for the embarrassing results of literary and historical criticism, that some isolated passages in the prophets may have dated from Ptolemaic, Seleucid, or even Maccabean times.

What is rather remarkable is the tendency to read back as far as possible the closure of some portions of the Writings. This has especially been the case for the Psalter. Before the discovery of the large Psalms Scroll from Qumran Cave 11 a general consensus had been reached placing the stabilization of the Masoretic collection of 150 psalms (give or take Psalm 151) in the late Persian period. Supported by what I suppose one might call a general neo-orthodox atmosphere, at least certainly a conservative one, conjoined with a growing nationalist hermeneutic in Jewish scholarship, assertions far outreached the evidence for such a judgment. A review of the evidence advanced by even the greatest names in scholarship for such an early dating of the closure of the MT-150 Psalter exposes rather dramatically the paucity of basis for it, as well as the range played by impertinent data. The only sound thesis that can be built on the now available evidence is that while the MT-150 collection may well have stabilized for some sects in Judaism already in the middle of the second century B.C. (considerably after the Persian period), for other segments of the Jewish community the Psalter was open-ended well into the first century A.D.[4] The prevailing view that the proto-MT text of the Law and the Prophets became the official text, and became largely stabilized, in the period of the some hundred years from Hillel to the fall of Jerusalem in A.D. 69, may possibly be a parallel and analogous historical picture for what happened to the Psalter in that same all-crucial period.[5] At any rate, the question of the dates of the individual psalms remains uninfluenced, and should remain uninfluenced, by the independent question of the stabilization of the contents and order of the MT Psalter, just as the text-critical question of the individual variants for the several psalms has to be dealt with on its own methodic grounds.[6] Social and political factors were at work in the period of Roman hegemony which just simply had not been there in such degree before and which caused an intensive, concentrated amount of scholarly effort on the part of Palestinian Jews resulting in the sorts of evidence of stabilization in that period available to us today.

Despite the apparent lack of clear reference to Jabneh,[7] there is abundant indirect evidence for the convening, at the end of the first century A.D., of a group of rabbis who felt constrained by the compelling events of the day, largely the threat of disintegration due to the loss of Jerusalem and her religious symbols, to make decisions regarding the contents of the Hagiographa.[8] The remarkable thing about the assumed council at Jamnia is not that it did not settle absolutely all questions. The remarkable thing, in the light of the way the question of canon should be broached today, is that so few questions remained after Jamnia about what was in (soiled the hands) and what was out. When one looks at the whole question of canon, from its inception in pre-exilic days, the authority of the supposed council of Jamnia is remarkable indeed. And the fact that some scattered debate continued into the second century about the canonicity of Esther, Song of Songs, Ecclesiastes and even Proverbs and Ezekiel, should, in that perspective, properly be viewed as minimal in the extreme. The effectiveness of the conciliar decisions at Jamnia (or what we extrapolate from the plethora of evidence for a Jamnia council) points as does very little else to the enormity of the fall of Jerusalem in A.D. 69 in the religious (not to speak of the social, economic, and political) history of Judaism. And it should caution us today against reading back into the earlier period what Judaism became in the first century.[9] Dramatic changes took place in Judaism in the first century of the common era which affected the bottom end of the canonical process.

Current discussions of the canon of the Old Testament have to begin, therefore, from a different perspective. This new approach to the question of canon I have called canonical criticism.[10] A new departure for the study of canon is necessary for a number of reasons: the need to move away from the peculiar views offered by the Jamnia mentality; the need to account for the fluidity (to a greater or less extent) both in text and content of the Prophets and Writings right up to the period of Pharisaic hegemony under Salome Alexandra;[11] the need to account for the great pluralism in Judaism in the Early Jewish period; and the need to account for a basic shift in hermeneutic techniques in proto-Pharisaic circles away from contextual to atomistic midrash.[12]

Largely because of the recovery of the Qumran literature, but also in part because of the intensive review that recovery has caused scholarship to engage in of the other Jewish literature datable to Early Judaism (including apocryphal, pseudepigraphic, and neotestamental),[13] we now know that the Jamnia mentality cannot dominate the way we must now think about the canonical process up to the first centuries B.C. and A.D. Not only is there no clear evidence of such punctiliar and conciliar decision-making in the period before Jamnia,[14] there is also no evidence prior to the first century A.D. of the kind of standardization of norms by which that century is now so well characterized. A new attitude is indicated in thinking about the canonical process and must be at the heart of canonical criticism.

II

Current thinking on Old Testament exhibits a kind of frustration about what is in and what is out of the canon. Behind the frustration is a tension between the Jamnia mentality and the modern question arising out of the ecumenical movement: what shall we say in answer to the question of what is canonical for church and synagogue today? Some of the deutero-canonical books, which Roman Catholics value to some degree as authoritative but which Jews and most Protestants do not consider at all canonical, were quite clearly authoritative for many Jews in the pre-Jamnia period. Are they in or out? Should they be graded separately and individually? Nor do these questions touch on the very sensitive problem for us of what is in the canon in the Eastern churches.[15] These modern, "relevant" questions serve but to stress the need for canonical criticism to turn, for the present, to the other pole of the canonical process. Let us begin at the beginning. Let us start at the top of the process. Exorcising the Jamnia mentality and turning our back on the frustrations it has engendered requires concentration on the basic concept of canon itself.

Because nearly all discussions of canon start with some etymological observation about the word canon (*Qaneh-kanōn*), the aspect of "normative rule" provides a mind-set from the beginning. Attention is drawn immediately to the question of the size of the rule. How long is it? Why is it that long? What were the criteria which determined its length? This is the pole of stability. But the other aspect of the idea of canon always in tension with it, is not its length or structure, but rather its nature and function. And it is on the nature and function of canon that canonical criticism puts the prior emphasis. What does it do? How did it get started in the first place? *A priori*, the first consideration of canonical criticism is the phenomenon of repetition. Repetition requires that the tradent be both stable and adaptable. Minimally speaking, it is the nature of canon to be "remembered" or contemporized. The fact that begs explanation is that of the earliest rise of a tradition.

Otto Eissfeldt is right to begin his chapter on canon with what he calls prehistory. "It was only in the second century A.D. . . . . that the formation of the Old Testament canon came to an end. But its prehistory begins centuries or even millennia earlier. Its starting point is the belief that particular utterances of men are in reality the word of God and as such can claim for themselves especial authority."[16] But because Eissfeldt limited himself in his prehistory to the concept of "word," he goes on only to speak of "six different kinds of words which rank as divine words." And in doing so he further limits his thinking to three of them, judgment, word, and directive (*mišpaṭ*, *dabar*, and *torah*) which narrows his cursive prehistory to collections of legal material and how they grew, "the replacement of older bodies of law by newer ones." And then, forthwith, he deals with the single aspect of inclusion-exclusion and leaves aside a discussion which could have been very fruitful indeed.

Aage Bentzen, in his introduction to the Old Testament, has a very pregnant sentence in his chapter on canon which he, too, fails to develop: "Another germ of a formation of Canon is probably also found in what has been called 'the historical *Credo* of Israel.' "[17] Bentzen is surely right, for concentration on how little legal codes became larger legal codes is not only a *Holzweg* for understanding the canonical process in general, it overlooks the essential nature of the Torah itself in which those codes are embedded. Two of the essential observations one must make about the Old Testament are (a) there are no laws, with the status of law, outside the Torah; and (b) the Torah itself is not primarily legal literature. It was in part to probe such observations that I wrote *Torah and Canon,* and I do not want to repeat all that here. But canonical criticism must deal with the observation that it is the Torah which gives authority to the laws within it, and not the other way around. Building on the observations of Gunnar Östborn, and on one's own unbiased reading, one must insist that a primary definition of Torah cannot be "law."[18] It is a story, first and foremost, with Yahweh, the God of Israel (in all his syncretistic makeup),[19] as the prime actor and speaker. Biblical scholarship has clearly shown that the laws in the Pentateuch actually date from widely varying times and were in large part the common property of the ancient Near East. Ancillary observations such as that of the lack of laws in Joshua (despite the formulary introduction in 24:25ff.), or in Samuel or Kings, despite the insistence therein that Israel's kings constantly made judicial decisions and ruled largely by royal decree, simply force the question of why Eissfeldt's "collections of judgments" are to be found *only* in the Pentateuch. (Ezekiel's so-called Temple Torah in chs. 40–48 did not make it in.)

III

The Torah is best defined as a story (*muthos*) with law (*ethos*) embedded in it.[20] The observation which has imposed itself most strongly in the past generation is that this Torah story is to be found in scattered places in the Bible, in shorter or longer compass—without the laws (or, to put it the way it is usually put, without Sinai). Gerhard von Rad has called these passages, especially those in Deut. 26:5–9 and Joshua 24, ancient Israel's ancient credo,[21] and George Ernest Wright has called them confessional recitals of God's mighty acts.[22] Touching directly on the question of the nature of canon, Wright calls the Bible the Book of the Acts of God.[23] Martin Noth in turn built on von Rad's thesis by a rather far-reaching tradition-critical study of the Pentateuch.[24]

The position generally shared by these three scholars and those that follow them is that the Pentateuch, or Torah, is the credo, or confessional recital, writ large. To it have been added, according to Noth, a number of other traditions, including Sinai. Wright's position differs largely in his insistence that the Torah including Sinai stems from actual historical occurrence indicated (though not proved) by archaeology.

Von Rad's work on the credo, and his and Noth's form-critical and tradition-critical work on the Hexateuch, have come under careful scrutiny in recent years.[25] The bulk of the criticism is to the effect that the so-called credo is not ancient at all, but rather Deuteronomic, and that in form Deut. 26: 5–9 is not a *Gattung* at all; rather all such passages are historical summaries embedded within larger forms such as the covenantal formulary, or simply parts of prayers of thanksgiving, petition, catecheses, or the like.[26]

These main points of criticism are in large part justified, especially the observation that the recitals are not ancient in the *form* that we inherit them. Surely Deut. 26:5–9 is in every crucial turn of phrase Deuteronomic.[27] The neo-orthodox *Zeitgeist* of the nineteen-thirties permitted the use of the term credo without criticism until 1948.[28]

Wright's term "recital" is a far more felicitous word for, as the critics of von Rad have pointed out, the summaries seem to be largely catechetical in form. But criticism of the main point of the summaries must itself not be permitted to get out of hand. The history of scholarship shows that often the pendulum-swing from one *Zeitgeist* to the following tends to annihilate what ought to remain of earlier work as well as what was tenuous about it. (One wonders if some of the fine work done in the last ten years on Wisdom in the Old Testament will be forced to languish for a while when the mood changes once more.) Critics of von Rad have seemed content to leave the impression, almost in the manner of assumptions made in the era of source criticism, that the Deuteronomists created the historical summary form, without probing the question of where it had itself come from.

Without faulting Wright's term "recital," I prefer the term *muthos,* or Torah story.[29] The idea of *muthos* admits of a wider range of questions concerning the function of the summaries. Form criticism is a useful tool in biblical criticism, or within criticism of any literature, but it can never stand alone. The form of a literary passage cannot possibly answer all the questions necessary concerning it. Indeed, its form may be deceptive, for the ancient speaker or writer may well have intended to pour new wine into an old wineskin, precisely in order to make a point which literary conformity might not have permitted him to make.[30] But more than that, as in the case of the larger question of canon, one must always ask what function a literary piece served, originally as well as in its subsequent contexts. What did these recitals or Torah stories do? The answers to that question will, I think, preclude any suggestion or assumption that the school of Deuteronomy invented them. There can be little question that Deuteronomy underscored their importance, just as there is little question that the intrusion of Deutronomy into the old J E story line (between Numbers and Joshua, and then eventual displacement of Joshua) had a profound effect on Judaism and its ability in the exile to arise out of the ashes of the old nationalist cult.[31]

IV

If one reflects on the basic idea of canon, what he must probe is the fact of repetition—*a priori,* the first time an idea was taken up again. It passed the immense barrier from a first telling to a second. One must dwell on that phenomenon above all others. My colleague, Theodor Gaster, insists that it may have been only for its entertainment or aesthetic value. And that is right, perhaps, in the case of songs and certain types of stories and proverbs. They afford distraction, release, or alter moods to some desired end. Aesthetics would clearly have been a determinant in the phenomenon of repetition. But there are many collections of such materials that do not make a canon.[32] One then must add the other criterion, function. Whatever else canon does it serves to engage the two questions: who am I, or we, and what are we to do? This is the classical understanding of the function of canon, and it has not been improved on. Canon functions, for the most part, to provide indications of the identity as well as the life-style of the on-going community which reads it. The history of the biblical concept of canon started with the earliest need to repeat a common or community story precisely because it functioned to inform them who they were and what they were to do even in their later situation.

But in the case of identity stories (and it is out of some sort of self-understanding that life-style is derived; a community's *ethos* issues from its *muthos*) it is most unlikely that there was ever a set form, either at the beginning or in the subsequent stages of repetition. Here Ernest Wright is surely correct: the basic elements in the recitals derive from history. And those basic elements were both the common property of the people and the constant factor in whatever form they might take, whether song, hymn, prayer, catechesis, covenant formulary, "creed," or what not. The more important such stories are to the life and existence of a people (that is, the more they are remembered or repeated) the less valuable they are apt to be to modern historians with *their* rather peculiar needs—since, of necessity, each repetition invites, so to speak, an increase of history, something from the period in which retold. Whenever a history belongs to the people and has existential value for them, it, of necessity, becomes *legendum* in some sense. Therefore, what we observe in the Old Testament is that Israel had a story of existential value for them communally, a historical *muthos* which took on a number of forms, and which functioned for the people in certain types of reflective situations. Since there might be several different forms, the aesthetic factor in repetition was clearly at best secondary. A quest for the reason for repetition has to be sought elsewhere.

The primary authority of Israel's central tradition, that of the escape from Egypt and entrance into Canaan, lay in its power to help the people answer the two questions of self-understanding and life-pattern. The fact that the story, in whatever form, passed the barrier from one generation to the following is, in this light, evidence enough of its validity. It spanned a generation gap at some point in Israel's early history. What scholars who try to meet their own needs (seeking answers to narrowly defined questions about history) must remember is that the needs of the people whom they study were for the most part quite different from theirs. And it is highly unlikely that a tradition arises and persists simply because there is a need to fill out a cultic order of service (the narrow sense of *Sitz im Leben*). As conservative as cults tend to be they were formed because of some gut-level existential need of the people they served, and from time to time, demonstrated the ability to meet the people at that level again.

A story that succeeded in passing from one generation to another did so, therefore, not because it had a set form or primarily because it distracted the people, but because (a) it spoke to a majority of the community; (b) it communicated to them a power they sought; and (c) this power met a common need of the community, probably the need to recapitulate their common self-understanding and to transcend a challenge borne to it. The challenge would have been some newness or strangeness which had to be dealt with—usually either by rejection or integration, by retaining a status quo, or by effecting some change. The challenge might range from the subtlest sort of threat to the existing societary structure; to a clear and present danger of its total disintegration.

In all such circumstances the imperative to any community is to review its understanding of who it is (a) to know if the moment of the review (and according to its *Zeitgeist*) the society should or can adapt to the measure indicated (*shalom*), or (b) in the event of rejection and violence at the other extreme (*milḥamah;* cf. Jer. 28:8–9), to relearn, in the situation presented by the threat, exactly who they are, so that when they emerge on the other side of the sword (Jer. 31:2) they will know (to put it very simply) if indeed they survived.

Survival is not a matter of living only, or breathing, or blood flowing through individual veins; for assimilation to another culture (which has another and different identifying *muthos*) is death as sure as slaughter is death. (What happened to the so-called northern ten tribes of Israel? They were assimilated into the dominant culture of the eighth-century neo-Assyrian empire. The majority lost their identity, even if most of the individuals involved survived and had children.)[33] So whether the whole of a society lives, or only a remnant, a dynamic source of identity-provision is absolutely necessary for that measure of continuity, within discontinuity, which can mean survival.

Other factors may seem of equal or greater importance at the moment, such as the foreign policy or statecraft of the threatening power: Assyria's sponsored disintegration of subject peoples; Babylonia's sponsored remnant or ghetto-type survival.[34] But statecraft in the sixth and fifth centuries was not, in fact, the more important factor; for many of her victims changed to such a point that many of the peoples existing in the Palestinian area from the Late Bronze Age through the Iron Age simply passed off the scene under Babylonian and Persian hegemony.

Why did Israel survive? That is the immense historical question that begs explanation. What happened to some of the other victim nations did not happen to Israel. Israel changed rather radically, to be sure, from being a nation with its own government and a highly nationalist cult to being a dispersed religious community (whether in Palestine or outside it) called Judaism. But the point is that Israel survived whereas others did not.

V

Why? What was Israel's dynamic identity source? It would have been (a) an indestructible element in society, (b) a commonly available element, (c) a highly adaptable element, and, if necessary, (d) a portable element. It would have been indestructible or the likelihood of its own survival in the midst of violence is precluded or greatly reduced. It would have been commonly available so that widely scattered segments of a remnant emerging from violence could consult it wherever they might be. It would have been adaptable so that it sponsored and did not preclude survival in new and strange situations. And it would have been portable so that territory loss or forced emigration could not sever the community from the survival power it needed.

Obviously a temple, or an elaborate cult, fails all four tests, though a portable shrine (Exodus 25–40) meets (d), and perhaps (c). An ark meets (c) and (d) beautifully, and in small communities that stay together may do for (b). Tradition affirms that the ark served identity purposes in the midst of violence very well indeed in Israel's early days.

But only a story meets all four criteria. It is, to the exclusion of all other religious "vessels," indestructible, commonly available to scattered communities, highly adaptable, and portable in the extreme.

The primary characteristic of canon, therefore, is its adaptability. Israel's canon was basically a story adaptable to a number of different literary forms, adaptable to the varying fortunes of the people who found their identity in it, adaptable to the needs of peace or the strains of war, adaptable to widely scattered communities themselves adjusting to new or strange idioms of existence but retaining a transnational identity, and adaptable to a sedentary or migratory life.

It is in this sense, therefore, that the study of canon cannot begin where the handbooks now start, with stability and the concept of inclusion-exclusion. There was no set creed, like Deut. 26:5-9, which was expandable. But there was a story existing in many forms from early days. In all likelihood, there were a number of such stories, but the Law and the Prophets as we inherit them highlight only two basic themes, those we call the Mosaic and the Davidic.[35] Only these survived, other traditions adhering to them; and only the Mosaic, less the Conquest, became the Torah. The nature of such an identifying story demanded that it be told in the words and phrases and senseterms of the generation and local community reciting it. Adaptability, therefore, is not just a characteristic; it is a compulsive part of the very nature of the canonical story. The story, in some part, is probably quite old, though no one *form* of it surviving in the Bible need of necessity be.[36] It is at least as old as Amos (Amos 2:9-11, 3:1-2, 4:10-11, 5:25, 9:7; cf. 6:5, 9:11). But it is Amos' use of the story, as we shall see, which precludes any thought of its being either invented by him or later inserted into the text of Amos.[37]

The second, and equally important character of a canonical story, is its ability to give life as well as survive in itself. One can characterize survival in any phenomenon as adaptability. And so canon. But that is only a part of the truth of canon. Another part is that canon is canon not only because it survives but because it can give its survival power to the community that recites it. It not only has survival qualities for itself; it shares those life-giving qualities with the community which finds identity in it.

Life, therefore, is the supreme character of canon. It has it and it gives it. It provides survival with identity to those who "remember" and repeat it, either in the essential demands of peace or the existential threat of upheaval. It can provide continuity within discontinuity because it offers to the community an essential identity which permits the people to adapt. Israel's story undoubtedly served this function many times from her origins until the Torah was shaped definitely in the exile, and the Torah, as we know it, emerged therefrom. But its power for life was so crucial to the remnant in Babylon in the sixth century B.C. that there was surely burnt into the community memory, indelibly, the knowledge that Torah both had life and gave life. To this Judaism in its later literature many times attests (cf. John 5:39; Pirqê Abōt 2:8, 6:7).[38] Professor Lewis Beck, of the University of Rochester, is an excellent example of the modern philosopher who has purposefully abandoned his Christian origins. Beck is one of the best of the anti-Christian polemicists today.[39] But Beck often points out that Judaism and Christianity simply cannot die. Even, he says, if earthlings should find life on a distant planet, the Bible religions would adapt to the new knowledge and probably flourish in it.

This is, in part, due to the high pluralism resident in the Bible.[40] But the qualities of survival and adaptability date from the earliest repetition of the story which became the essence or core of Israel's self-understanding. Ernest Wright's concept of there being in the Bible a canon within the canon is rather inescapable.[41] Brevard Childs has attacked the notion and argued for thinking of the Bible's authority in terms of the full canonical context.[42] I have argued that they are both right.[43] A canon-within-the-canon idea that does not perceive its high adaptability as essential, or, as put above, a compulsive part of its nature, but that too much relegates other parts of the final closed canon (such as the Jamnian) as of less power or authority, overlooks the dynamic nature of the canon's adaptability.[44] A crucial part of the canonical process, at all stages, was the historical accidents which caused the people to put certain questions to the traditions and not others. They did not rest back and, like scholars, make choices as to which questions they would ask of the story. Theirs was an existential dialogue, on-going, of greater or lesser moment, and no question, no part of that dialogue was, at the moment, of less importance or had less power than another. A full-canonical-context idea about the Bible, however, that does not appreciate the life-giving qualities of the central tradition, and its own nature of adaptability which ultimately afforded the vast pluralism in the Bible, can be misunderstood as a kind of unfortunate biblicism.[45]

VI

A new method of approach to the question of the relation between the Old and New Testaments is called comparative midrash.[46] If one studies the various ways in which Second Temple Judaism contemporized Old Testament traditions, one can actually trace the history of such midrashic tendency back into the Old Testament itself. In fact, since the older discipline of tradition criticism has begun to include in its purview the question of *why* a tradition would be repeated, or taken up again in another form, it has begun to sound more and more like the study of midrash.[47] This raises the question of what the difference between them (and redaction criticism in certain phases) actually is. Geza Vermès rightly says the difference is canonization.[48] But that difference needs clarifying.

As stressed above, certain traditions in ancient Israel bore repeating. Among these traditions, allowing for some aesthetic factor, the most important were those which told Israel's story about who she was and what her salient characteristics were.[49] Even stories that had little or nothing to do with Israel originally (such as common ancient Near Eastern myth, Canaanite legend, etc.) became attached to the growing number of such traditions. They were adapted by the fourfold process (where and when needed) of depolytheizing, monotheizing, Yahwizing, and Israelitizing. Sometimes one or more of these treatments did not take too well and the scholar today easily perceives beneath only a very slight veneer the original non-Israelite and polytheistic shape of the material. Some of this material shows up in the Old Testament more than once, and is hence available for tradition-critical work on it. The moment one asks why such material bore repeating, however, he is engaged in the question of authority. Such material, which met a need in one situation, was apparently able to meet another need in another situation. And that is precisely the kind of tradition that becomes canonical—material that bears repeating in a later moment both because of the need of the later moment and because of the value or power of the material repeated (the dialogue between them).

Early material repeated in this manner attains the status of tradition. Eventually it may attain the status of canon. Only the traditional can become canonical. One of the very real existential factors in the canonical process is that of the value or power of tradition, that is, material which had proved its worth in more than one situation, had already shown a measure of historical transcendence in its ability to address itself to two or more space-time parameters. One observation that impresses itself time and again in the study of history is that in crisis situations only the old, tried, and true has any real authority. Nothing thought up at the last minute, no matter how clever, can effect the necessary steps of recapitulation and transcendence needed by the threatened community, if it is to survive with identity. A new story will not do; only a story with old, recognizable elements has the power for life required, because it somehow can pierce beneath the immediate and apparent changes taking place to recover the irreducible core of identity left unthreatened, that which can survive the crisis. The early canonical process was precisely one of selectivity of such materials, and the major factor of selectivity was existential. In this sense may the criteria of antiquity, inspiration, and popularity be understood.[50] The older material, which had already shown its value in more than one situation, had in effect proved its status of being inspired. And certainly no private story or tradition would measure up in the breach: it had to have been widespread, or at least not esoteric.

The relationship, therefore, between the older (tradition-critical) materials within the Old Testament and the later midrashic use of those traditions, as well as of anything else available in the final canonical mass, is obviously very close indeed. To put it another way, one can extend tradition-critical study of the Old Testament well into post-biblical times simply by continuing on without an artificial or arbitrary halt. In the same manner, the student of midrash can push his work back into the earlier biblical period simply by continuing on without an artificial or arbitrary halt, even though he may be invading the tradition-critic's territory.

And what both disciplines find above all else, throughout the whole biblical and post-biblical period, is that the major characteristic of canonical material is its adaptability—not its rigidity. One of the major results of the new method of approach to Early Jewish literature, including Qumran and the New Testament, is the observation that adaptation of canonical material to a midrashic need (the old problem of "inaccurate quotation" that lies outside even the new observations about fluidity in text criticism), far from being impious, was a sign of the greater piety of the period—especially for eschatological groups.[51] In the long period before the marked tendency toward stabilization and standardization became the dominant trend among proto-Rabbinic Jews, convictions about God's activity in their own time brought them frequently to adapt the available text to the conviction. Again the salient character of canon was adaptability. And this was indeed its major trait from the earliest "moment" far back up the line in the canonical process until the other need, that of stabilization, became the more dominant in the later period.[52]

Morton Smith in a recent book on the canonical process stresses the political factor in selectivity almost to the exclusion of all others.[53] The existential factor may be thought of, academically, in political terms. That is, whenever a community or society has a need of any sort and tries, through one or more of its influential members or groups, to meet that need, there is without question a political situation *in sensu lato*. The difficulty with Smith's thesis is that it reads back a situation of fragmentary politics of a later period into the Late Iron Age problem of whether old Israel ought not to have passed off the scene of history the way some of her neighbors did.[54] That is an existential problem, a life and death situation which informs the political, if not transforms it. Smith's political theory also does not allow sufficient appreciation for the theological or mythic dimension in the exilic process of canonization; this is in contrast to the existential which underscores it. Smith's other major observation, however, is correct. We should assume that what we inherit in the Old Testament is only a fraction of what had been available, and that they were the needs of the community which shaped the surviving, earlier traditions into the Bible as we know it. I would see the process, however, dating well back into pre-exilic times and concentrating in the all encompassing life and death situation of the sixth century B.C., instead of, with Smith, as beginning in post-exilic times, for the most part, and concentrating in Hellenistic times.[55]

If adaptability was an abiding character of the canonical process well into Hellenistic times, and was completely overcome by the need for uniformity and stability of text only finally in the period of Roman occupation,[56] then von Rad's inability, in the light of all the recent criticism, either to establish a single form for his credo or to prove its high antiquity linguistically, should occasion no surprise. A basic story about a migration from Egypt to Canaan under Yahweh's tutelage pervades much of the literature of the Old Testament.[57] It would be utterly and completely foolhardy to gainsay that basic attainment of the work of the past generation. And it is with such traditions that the work of canonical criticism proceeds.

At the heart of canonical criticism will be not those introductory questions of source and unity which have so occupied the tradition critics, but rather the questions of the nature and function of the tradition cited. When a tradition is deposited in a particular situation, we must assume that it was found useful to that situation: it had a function to perform there and that is the reason it was called upon. At the heart of canonical criticism are the questions of the nature of authority and the hermeneutics by which that authority was marshalled in the situation where needed. What was the need of the community and how was it met?

VII

One of the remarkable observations one has to make about early biblical canonical materials is that the manner in which they were called upon to meet the people's needs was not necessarily popular. On the contrary, there is much evidence in the biblical process to indicate that authoritative traditions were used in particular situations to challenge the way the majority of the people and their political representatives, the establishment, or any political group, thought their needs ought to be met. (Did the phenomenon of the lectionary arise for this reason?)

Partly in response to Smith's otherwise very logical and cogent theory,[58] and partly in response to George Mendenhall's otherwise engaging theory about the place of the prophets in his five-part *schema* of Old Testament history,[59] the balance of this essay will center in the question of how the great judgmental prophets of ancient Israel marshalled the authority by which they declaimed their messages of pending change in Israel's basic self-understanding. Clearly Smith is right that "Yahweh-only" thinking won the day at the crucial junctures of Israel's history, and especially in the all-important exilic period, with respect to what finally became canon. But two decisive factors must not be overlooked in that process: (a) it won the day not because of some unknown political clout certain parties may have had, but because the theological view they espoused most met the existential needs arising out of historical circumstance; and (b) the Law and the Prophets as they emerged through that process (even though not stabilized for some time to come) do not present a single clear-cut political program. This second point is as important as the first. The Bible is highly pluralistic. A few years back many scholars were looking for the unity of the Bible, or of the Old Testament. They did not succeed. Today, the challenge for any student who thinks he has found a definite system, especially political program, in the Bible, is to return to the Bible and locate its contrapositive. Politicians can always proof text their position from the Bible. That is one of the reasons, the historian must avow, that the Bible has lasted so long. And whatever cannot be found there by one set of hermeneutic rules can almost certainly be located by another. This is the history of biblical interpretation, from the beginnings until today. And every party or denomination seeking authority in the Bible has been "right."

In Mendenhall's five-stage *schema* there is much that is still valid. He, resting his case largely on the work of William F. Albright, names the five stages thus: *praeparatio* (the Bronze Age or Genesis period), the Creative (or Mosaic) period, the Adaptive (or tribal federation-monarchic) period, the traditional (or prophetic) period, and the period of reformation (or exilic and early post-exilic era).

Much of what Mendenhall writes is in reaction to an earlier emphasis on the prophets having been the principal creative force in Israel's history as well as in the Old Testament as a whole. He scores the thinking of Wellhausen that the prophets introduced ethical monotheism into the religion of Israel. A historian might well say that Mendenhall was responding to the *Zeitgeist* of the neo-orthodox period by reacting to the *Zeitgeist* of the Liberal period.[60] Be that as it may, Mendenhall is right to attribute both the monotheizing process in Israel's history and the concern for ethics to the so-called Mosaic period. And he is right to insist that the prophets were dependent on authoritative traditions they inherited from the earlier period. What is questionable is his limiting their contribution to "the preservation and transmission of a tradition which was necessary to the preservation of the group." One needs to explore carefully his assertion that "in all the furor and violence of the whole period, there is no reason, no evidence, for the belief that anything important was added to the religious tradition." This is so in part because Mendenhall himself says, in the same section of his own work, "The prophets were proclaiming the necessity of change in the unchangeable," and again, ". . . the prophets added much of value to the tradition through their message to their own time."

The resolution between these apparent contradictions can perhaps be found in Mendenhall's claim that the message of the prophets "consisted largely of the fact that a group which was called into existence [chosen] to serve Yahweh ceased to have any excuse for being when it ceased to serve."[61] The difficulty with such an assertion can be found in recent work on the so-called false prophets, or establishment prophets. For it is not abundantly clear that the so-called false prophets relied on the same authoritative traditions as the so-called true prophets in propounding their message of no-change, or status quo, or continuity. They claimed that Israel was serving Yahweh. The utterly engaging aspect of current study of the false prophets is that their arguments, based in large measure on the same traditions from the Exodus-Wanderings-Entrance story, were very cogent and compelling.[62] And they apparently won the day!

The "false" prophets could and did cite Israel's story to support their view that the Yahweh who had brought Israel out of Egypt could surely maintain her in Palestine. On the basis of the same authority the "true" prophets argued the opposite—that the Yahweh who brought Israel out of Egypt could also take her out of Palestine.[63] Hananiah chided Jeremiah for not having enough faith in Yahweh's power to sustain his people (Jer. 28:2–11). The "false" prophets must not be viewed as having been somehow intrinsically wrong. They too believed in the "presence of God" and interpreted that presence to mean providence for continuity (Micah 2:6, 3:11; Jer. 5:12, 14:9; Isa. 36:15). The story itself was adaptable to whatever hermeneutics employed. Hermeneutics must be historically viewed as arising out of the need to keep a stabilized tradition adaptable. The difference between the hermeneutics of continuity and the hermeneutics of discontinuity, that is, between the hermeneutics of *shalom* and of *milḥamah* (Jer. 28:8–9 and 38:4) lay not so much between the Mosaic and Davidic views of the covenant with Yahweh, as between theological axioms.[64] Both the true and the false prophets offered hope, but the former held the higher view of God (Jer. 23:23; cf. Isa. 22:11) that he could offer continuity even in radically altered forms of the common life, that is, he could give by taking away. Amos rested his whole view of the taking away (Amos 1:3–2:8) on the authority of what God had done for Israel in the beginning (Amos 2:9–11; 3:1–2), as did Hosea (11:1–5; 13:4–8). Micah rested his three-point sermon on what Yahweh required of Israel out of the same Torah story (Micah 6:3–5) of what it was Yahweh had done for Israel, while Isaiah cited God's grace to David in giving him Jerusalem, precisely to give authority to his message of judgment and salvation (Isa. 1:21–27, 5:1–7, 22:2, 28:4, 21, 29:1–7, 32:13, *et passim*).[65] And Ezekiel, who had a developed view of what the old story meant (ch. 20) could adapt it with no difficulty to drive home his message of judgment (chs. 16 and 23). And it was the same Torah story which was called on to support the prophetic view of salvation in judgment (Hosea 2:16–17; Isa. 1:21–27, 32:1–18, 33:1–22; Jer. 16:14–15, 23:7–8, 31:31–34).[66]

VIII

The perspective that is needed here is that of canonical criticism. When would the criterion of "popularity," or widespread acceptance have come to play in the case of the judgmental prophets? Manifestly not in the pre-exilic period. There can be no doubt that these prophets had followers, or even small schools, to preserve their material. The family of Shaphan, as well as Baruch, would have been essential at the point of earliest preservation of the Jeremiah materials. And we must posit such small continuing groups, perhaps schools, for the others from Amos on. But, in contradistinction to Morton Smith's thesis, I cannot see these groups as forming a political movement or group. If so, they were not strong enough to prevent Jeremiah's being tried twice and imprisoned several times during the sieges of Jerusalem in the early sixth century.[67] A few continuing followers convinced enough to preserve (and adapt) the records of their masters' words and deeds is the most the evidence suggests.

When then did what the prophets had to say come to be perceived for its great value for Israel? Clearly the answer is the exile when what they had predicted occurred.[68] But even a prediction-fulfillment phenomenon is not sufficient to understand the canonical process so vigorously at work in the disintegrative experience of the national existence in the sixth and early fifth centuries. For some of what they predicted did not take place, and yet it too was preserved. The first step surely was the recognition in adversity that these men had been "right." But the next step in the process, gradually dawning on and pervading the consciousness of the remnant, was the really crucial one. And here is where the positive-thinking message of the old so-called false prophets when recalled would have turned to bitterness in their mouths. Both groups, so-called true and so-called false, had offered hope.[69] And they had both offered hope based on the old traditions about what God had done so effectively in the past. The great difference was that the judgmental prophets had offered an existential understanding of "Israel" which could survive the death of the body politic and which offered the means whereby a new corporate life could be accepted, though radically changed in form and venue.

The POWs in Babylon after 586 B.C., under either Babylonian or Persian hegemony, had two alternatives: life or death, not so much for themselves individually, but in terms of communal identity. They could pass off the scene the way others were doing—by assimilation to the dominant culture. There is a good bit in the Bible to suggest that this is what happened to many normal, rational Jews (Ps. 137:1–4; Ezek. 8:12–13, 18:25, 33:17, 20; Jer. 17:15; Isa. 40:27 *et passim;* Mal. 2:17). The evidence was in: Yahweh was bested in a fair fight. Israel's ancient Holy Warrior was defeated. One could not fly in the face of such proof as the utter defeat of Zedekiah's forces and the destruction of Jerusalem and the temple, especially the latter, afforded.

But a few, stunned and bewildered, asked a very crucial question: *'Ek niḥyeh?* "How shall we live?" (Ezek. 33:10). In what now does life obtain? All the symbols of the covenant relation were gone. What now? A fugitive ran with the message all the way from crumbling Jerusalem to the camp where Ezekiel was interned with the awful message, "The city has fallen" (Ezek. 24:26, 33:21). Some say the news arrived the morning after Mrs. Ezekiel had died (Ezek. 24:18). Be that as it may, Ezekiel used the occasion of the passing of the "delight of his eyes" to speak of the passing of the temple, which Ezekiel called the delight of the eyes of the people (24:21; cf. 7: 24; 16:24). They felt that as long as the temple was standing there was still hope. Therefore, when the impossible and unthinkable happened, that hope was dashed, and they turned to the resident, judgmental prophet with the

question, "How shall we live?" Ezekiel answered it in the way we should have
expected him to: Israel lives, moves, and has its being in the judgments of
God (Ezek. 33:10–16).[70] But following the thinking of Jeremiah (31:29–
34), and his own development of that thought (Ezekiel 18), Ezekiel stressed
the responsibility of the individual in the new dispersed situation. Between
the thinking of Jeremiah and Ezekiel in this regard, the exiles had a real
vehicle for understanding "Israel" corporately. Each stressed individual responsibility, but in two different ways: Jeremiah horizontally, as it were, and
Ezekiel vertically. Jeremiah's new covenant idea provided the means for
understanding how Israel could be scattered in far-flung places and still be
Israel: because each person would be responsible, wherever he was, for being
"Israel." Thinking of an individual as standing for the whole, wherever he
was, was already a part of royal tradition.[71] Ezekiel then stressed the vertical
aspect of individual responsibility, by generations, as it were. He spoke of
how the son would not suffer for the father's sin, and indeed, how within a
generation each man had to maintain rather strict obedience.

These two views of individual responsibility provided the means for Israel
to be Israel in diaspora.

It is clear that a great deal of reflection went on, in agonizing reappraisal,
of what Israel meant now that the temple and "holy city" were gone. A
number of the exiles reflected on the old story, the old adaptable canon.
Whether or not they recited the Deuteronomic *form* of the *"'Arami 'obed
'abi"* we do not know. But they surely came very close to it: "Abraham was
one man and came into possession of the land. We are many: therefore the
land is surely (all the more so) ours" (Ezek. 33:24; cf. Isa. 51:2). I have
inserted the expression in parenthesis to indicate that this is a typical midrashic *qal vaḥomer* or *argumentum a fortiori*. If the old story, or authoritative
tradition, started out talking about one man (wandering and perishing),
then the disintegrative experience of defeat and dispersion may not be the
end but yet another beginning.

I am quite convinced that it was precisely this kind of reflective dialogue,
as indicated in Ezekiel 33 and Isaiah 51, that formed the remnant in Babylon
(cf. Hab. 2:4). These would have been the ones whom Deutero-Isaiah addressed as "those who know righteousness, the people in whose heart is my
law" (Isa. 51:7)—as over against those whom he addresses as "stubborn of
heart, far away from righteousness" (Isa. 46:12).[72] Those who knew righteousness were those who could recognize a righteousness, that is, a mighty
act of God, when they saw one, and had been able to affirm the sovereignty
of Yahweh in Israel's terrible adversity and upheaval. They were also those
who, like the earlier prison-mates of Ezekiel, reflected on God's initial work
through Abraham (Isa. 41:8–9) and figured that if God had done such things
with Abraham he could surely do them with a remnant folk who remembered God's mighty acts well enough that they could recognize a new
one if they saw it (Isa. 52:8).

It is in the light of such agonizing reflection (Ezek. 4:17 *et passim*) that the canonical process with respect to the earlier judgmental prophets must be understood. When the positive-thinking message that God would never, no never, let them go, or let them down—precisely because he was powerful enough—had turned bitter to the decimated folk, and they had turned either to worship the gods of the Babylonians, *or* to engage in traumatic reappraisal of their faith and experience, then a few also asked, I think, to hear the messages of those earlier prophets whom they had called *mešugga'im* (Jer. 29:26), madmen, unpatriotic, blasphemous, seditious, and traitorous. I imagine that at some point after Ezekiel had given his famous answer to their existential question, one of the inquirers (Ezek. 36:37; contrast 14:7) asked to hear once more what they had so recently called unpalatable. Wasn't there a disciple of Amos around the camps the other day talking that nonsense again? And disciples of Hosea, Micah, Isaiah, and the others? Let us hear it once more, now.

And with the new ears to hear and the new eyes to see (every religious and national symbol now gone) they perceived in a way they had never been able to understand before. Was it that the prophets had predicted this? Yes, that was surely a primary factor. But within that was a far deeper element. For the messages of the madmen of God now offered a hope which no simple, magical prediction could possibly afford. For what they had said could not be fully appreciated until in the canonical process of agonizing reflection they were "heard" by many for what was existentially the first time: God was in charge of the adversity; God was challenging Israel's basic self-understanding; God was re-forming his Israel (Jer. 18:1–11) and reshaping his people into a new Israel (Ezek. 36–37). Those who embraced such an outrageous program before the discontinuity took place were viewed as traitorous, seditious, blasphemous, and mad. Does God want only masochists? But after the old national vessel had been broken to smithereens (Isa. 30:13–14), two options were open: either to join the First Church of Marduk (assimilate) or in agony to reflect on Israel's basic identity, that is, to ask, who are we and what are we to do?

It was then also that the anti-cultic and anti-royalist strictures of the judgmental prophets made "canonical" sense. What the prophets had kept saying, in effect, was that the cultic and royal institutions and practices did not derive from the Torah *muthos,* that is, they were unauthorized by the tradition the prophets adhered to (Amos 5:25; Hosea 8:4 *et passim;* Micah 6:6–7; Isa. 1:12–17; Jer. 7:22, etc.) as authoritative.[73] In the pre-exilic period that simply represented one of two points of view which one might hold: either cult (as practiced) and palace were authentic and properly authorized in Israelite society, or they were not. But in the period of intensive canonical process these strictures took on a much different meaning. When you are a POW pondering the awful experience of destitution, and are squarely facing the choice of whether your identity as "Israel" should live or die, then the prophetic strictures provide a means of survival as Israel, without temple or palace. If they did not derive from the Torah story (pre-Conquest) period, then they were not *essential* to identity. The community need not lose its identity because they were lacking. Because certain prophets had been saying this even when those institutions stood, their words bore all the more power for survival to those in destitution. *If need be,* Israel could be Israel even if reduced to one destitute man (Abraham, servant, Job, Christ). That this is canonical does not mean that Israel *should* be one destitute man, but it does mean that "Israel" can survive calamity with identity. The canon is adaptable to the worst and the best. It is for life.

IX

It is as though the old story, as well as the pre-exilic prophetic interpretations of it, were most vital in the death-and-resurrection experience of the exile.[74] That was the crucible for the old traditions, in which those which really spoke to the people's existential problems of identity and life-style became the core of the canon. If one thinks of all that we have called the Yahwist tradition or cycle of materials (including both the Mosaic and Davidic traditions) out of the monarchical period of pre-exilic Israel, then the Torah as it received its basic shaping (neither its creation nor its final form) is surprisingly apocopated: it is all pre-Conquest.[75] But it is precisely a Torah that would have offered life to a dispersed Israel, a transforming Israel, an emerging Judaism. The Joshua materials about the conquest are left to be the first book of the prophets, a hope integral to Judaism and all it meant, but not a part of the basic canon within the canon—not in the Torah. This is the greatest surprise of the canonical process, since none of von Rad's or Wright's ancient recitals lacks the conquest as part of the confession. But it is understandable that it could not be a part of the essential inner identifying tradition. Judaism could be the new Israel anywhere at all. This did not preclude a Return. Far from it. The Return has been an integral part of the hope of Judaism.

From this point the canonical process continued. Whatever Ezra brought back with him from Babylonia, it was surely the essential Torah (though not yet closed) as we know it (Neh. 8:1–12). It had been shaped by and edited in the agonizing reflection, and out of the existential questions, of the crucible of exile. The major judgmental prophets were gathered, read, and reread in the light of the new perspective of the shedding of false hopes which the crucible provided. The canon of the prophets was not closed until much, much later. It is becoming more and more difficult to suggest a probable date for its closure, but the basic *Gestalt* of the Law and the Prophets was being formed in the crucible.[76] Not only had some of the old traditions (some, but by no means all) survived, but they survived because they offered life in that crucial time. It was the old story reviewed in the shedding experience of exile which infused slain Israel with the spirit of life of which Ezekiel spoke (37:6). The whole of the passage on resurrection in Ezekiel 27 is told with the covenantal verbs of the old Exodus story (37:1, 2, 5–6, 11–14).[77] No one in antiquity who heard him would have missed the point Ezekiel was making: if Yahweh had created himself a people out of slaves in Egypt, he was now creating himself a renewed Israel. His use of those verbs was his authority for his idea of the resurrection.

It was surely in this same period that other old traditions took on new vibrant meaning: an old story about child sacrifice; whatever else Genesis 22 had said originally or in the pre-exilic period, it now said that the God who had given Isaac to the aged Abraham and the barren Sarah had every right to ask for him back; but instead, he gave the child a second time. Such a story, no matter what form criticism and source criticism may show it originally meant, to the exiles surely meant that the future of the believing community, of Israel, the question of the continuation of the people, the anxiety about whether there would be another generation, rested in the hands of the life-giver, of him who gives and gives again.[78] And no matter what form and source criticism may show the Garden of Eden story originally meant, to the exiles it was viewed in the light of their own expulsion from the garden of Canaan (Ezek. 36:35–36; cf. Isa. 5:1–7; Jer. 11:16–17, 12:10; Ezek. 28:12–19; Isa. 27:2–5). And no matter what must or must not be said about a Bronze Age Abraham, to the exiles when the canonical process was most decisively at work, he meant God's starting again: "Abraham was one man . . ." (Ezek. 33:23–29; Isa. 51:2).

Adaptability and stability. That is canon. Each generation reads its authoritative tradition in the light of its own place in life, its own questions, its own necessary hermeneutics. This is inevitable. Around this core were gathered many other materials, as time went on, adaptable to it.[79] There are many contradictions within the Bible; it is a highly pluralistic document. Hence, no tyranny can be established on its basis, for there is always something in it to challenge whatever is constructed on it. Its context is very broad and very wide and sponsors serious dialogue.[80] No single program, political, social, economic, or otherwise can escape the challenge of something in it. As the rabbis say, in another context, "It is the book with everything in it." There appears to be only one certainly unchallenged affirmation derivable from it: a monotheizing tradition which emerges through the canonical process. It gives the impression that Israel always doggedly pursued the integrity or sovereignty of God, his oneness.[81] The Bible is replete with polytheism often only thinly veiled. But it was finally the affirmation of the old Mosaic story, as well as the judgmental-prophetic insistence on it, that God is one, both judge and savior, saving as he judges, that afforded the true hope that disintegrated Israel in exile needed *lemiḥyah,* for life (Gen. 45:5; Ezra 9:8–9). It is abundantly clear that once the crisis had passed and Judaism was established, internal, normal, fractious politics came once more to the fore in the decision-making process. But by that time the existential experience of death and resurrection had burned itself forever into the cultic memory of Judaism. Torah was for life.[82] And that is, in the final analysis, the authority of canon.

NOTES

1. In a manner of speaking George Ernest Wright has been doing this, from his perspective of a canon within the canon, all along. If one reviews his published work in biblical theology from 1937 to the present (a most intriguing exercise) one witnesses a process at work: "Exegesis and Eisegesis in the Interpretation of Scripture," *ET* 48 (1937), 353–357; "The Terminology of Old Testament Religion and Its Significance," *JNES* 1 (1942), 404–414; "How Did Early Israel Differ from Her Neighbors?" *BA* 6 (1943), 1–10, 13–20; *The Challenge of Israel's Faith* (Chicago, 1944); "Neo-Orthodoxy and the Bible," *JBR* 14 (1946), 87–93; "Interpreting the Old Testament," *Theology Today* 3 (1947), 176–191; "The Christian Interpreter as Biblical Critic," *Interpretation* 1 (1947), 131–152; *The Old Testament Against Its Environment* (London, 1950); "The Unity of the Bible," *Interpretation* 5 (1951), 131–133, 304–317; *God Who Acts* (London, 1952); "Wherein Lies the Unity of the Bible?" *JBR* 20 (1952), 194–198; *The Biblical Doctrine of Man in Society* (London, 1954); "The Unity of the Bible," *Journal of Religious Thought* 13 (1955), 5–19; "The Unity of the Bible," *Scottish Journal of Theology* 8 (1955), 337–352; with R. H. Fuller, *The Book of the Acts of God* (Garden City, N.Y., 1957); *The Rule of God* (Garden City, N.Y., 1960); "History and Reality: The Importance of Israel's 'Historical' Symbols for the Christian Faith," in *The Old Testament and Christian Faith*, ed. B. W. Anderson (New York, 1963), pp. 176–199; *The Old Testament and Theology* (New York, 1969).

A beginning on a history of the canonical process is attempted in J. A. Sanders, *Torah and Canon* (Philadelphia, 1972)—hereinafter referred to as *T and C*. From a different perspective but congruous in certain presuppositions and basic theses is Morton Smith's *Palestinian Parties and Politics that Shaped the Old Testament* (New York, 1971)—hereinafter *PPP*. From the NT perspective see Albert C. Sundberg, Jr., *The Old Testament of the Early Church*, Harvard Theological Series, 20 (Cambridge, Mass., 1964), as well as articles in *CBQ* 30 (1968), 143–155, and in *Studia evangelica* (1968), 452–461. The trend of discussion on canon in NT can be seen in N. Appel, *Kanon und Kirche* (Paderborn, 1964); Ernst Käsemann, "The Canon of the New Testament and the Unity of the Church," in *Essays on New Testament Themes* (London, 1964), pp. 95–107; and especially now in *Das Neue Testament als Kanon*, ed. E. Käsemann (Göttingen, 1970). Käsemann's own contributions to the latter (pp. 336–410) are especially valuable; however, I would still insist that the problem of whether the Old Testament was Christian did not arise in the church until the second century A.D. The problem of the first century, and hence of the NT, was whether the NT was biblical, i.e. whether God really had done another righteousness, in Christ. Brevard Childs, while intensely and rightly interested in the nature and function of canon, is not primarily interested in a history of the early canonical process; see below NN 42–45.

2. Johann Salomo Semler, *Abhandlung von freier Untersuchung des Canon*[2] (Göttingen, 1776). (The first edition had apparently appeared in 1772.) Cf. Gottfried

Hornig, *Die Anfänge der historisch-kritischen Theologie; Johann Salomo Semlers Schriftverständnis und seine Stellung zu Luther* (Göttingen, 1961); and Wolfgang Schmittner, *Kritik und Apologetik in der Theologie J. S. Semlers* (Munich, 1963).

3. Robert H. Pfeiffer, *Introduction to the Old Testament*, 2d ed. (New York, 1948), pp. 50–70; cf. his article ad loc. in *IDB*, I.

4. See my article, "Cave 11 Surprises and the Question of Canon," first published in the *McCQ* 21 (1968), 284–298, reprinted in *NDBA*, pp. 101–116. The real value of the very flaccid references in the Ben Sira prologue, in Philo (*De vita contemplativa* 25) and Luke 24:44, must now be reviewed in the light of present evidence. See the excellent remarks of B. J. Roberts in *JTS* 18 (1967), 185, in this regard, contra his earlier thesis in *BJRL* 46 (1963–64), 164–178. Cf. P. R. Ackroyd, "The Open Canon," *Colloquium Australian and New Zealand Review* (1970), 279 ff.

5. I here reaffirm the judgment as stated in "Cave 11 Surprises" [N 4], pp. 106–109; to dismiss 11QPsᵃ as the earliest example of a Jewish prayer book is unwarranted: the Psalter itself, in whatever early form, is the earliest example of a Jewish prayer book! To the evidence adduced in fn. 10, p. 105, in my article, see now other evidence, especially from 4QIsaᶜ, adduced by Jonathan P. Siegel in *HUCA* 42 (1971), 159–172.

6. On the dating of individual psalms by linguistic criteria see the recent work of Avi Hurvitz of Hebrew University. In regard to the larger question of text transmission see: F. M. Cross, "The History of the Biblical Text in the Light of the Discoveries in the Judaean Desert," *HTR* 57 (1964), 281–299; "The Contribution of the Discoveries at Qumran to the Study of the Biblical Text," *IEJ* 16 (1966), 81–95; S. Talmon, "Aspects of the Textual Transmission of the Bible in the Light of the Qumran Manuscripts," *Textus* 4 (1964), 95–132. What is really needed now, as I tried to point out in my "Text Criticism and the NJV Torah," *Journal of the American Academy of Religion* 39 (1971), 193–197, is a critical review of method in text criticism—actually how in practice to make a judgment in "establishing the text." This is sharply indicated now by the work of the Hebrew University Bible Project and the International Old Testament Text Critical Committee of the United Bible Societies as over against the results now emerging in the fascicles of the Biblia Hebraica Stuttgartensia.

7. See Jack P. Lewis, "What do we mean by Jabneh?" *JBR* 32 (1964), 125–132.

8. See the recent work of Jacob Neusner, including *Development of a Legend* (Leiden, 1970) and *The Rabbinic Traditions about the Pharisees before 70* (Leiden, Parts I and II, 1971, and Part III, 1972).

9. Cf. J. A. Sanders, *The Dead Sea Psalms Scroll* (Ithaca, 1967), pp. 157–159.

10. *T and C* [N 1], pp. ix–xx.

11. See Dominique Barthélemy, in "Les tiqquné sopherim et la critique textuelle de l'A.T." in *VTS* 9 (1963), 283–304.

12. See the pivotal article on midrash by Renée Bloch in the *Dictionnaire de la Bible*, Supplément vol. V (1957), cols. 1263–1281. Parenthetically, it should be noted that because it is the nature of canonical or authoritative communal traditions that they are adaptable to the needs of the on-going communities, computer analyses of style are limited in value for determining authorship which do not use for control data literature (a) that is not canonical and (b) of absolutely known single authorship.

13. Pseudepigrapha studies have received a new impetus both in this country and abroad in the past ten years; cf. A. M. Denis, *Introduction aux pseudépigraphes grecs de l'A.T.* (Leiden, 1970), pp. ix–xx.

14. *Pace* L. Finkelstein, "The Maxim of the Anshe-Keneset ha-Gedolah," *JBL* 59 (1940) 455–469; cf. Sidney B. Hoenig, *The Great Sanhedrin* (New York, 1953). This is not to deny the need to explain what Finkelstein cites as his evidence, e.g. *ARNA*, fol. 65, n. 23, in Schechter's edition.

15. See the trenchant article, on the complex situation with the Enoch materials, by

J. T. Milik, "Problèmes de la littérature hénochique à la lumière des fragments araméens de Qumrân," *HTR* 64 (1971) 333–378.

16. O. Eissfeldt, *The Old Testament: An Introduction* (Eng. tr., New York, 1965), p. 560.

17. A. Bentzen, *Introduction to the Old Testament*[3] (Copenhagen, 1952), p. 24.

18. G. Östborn, *Tora in the Old Testament* (Lund, 1945) and *Cult and Canon* (Uppsala, 1950).

19. See Albrecht Alt, "The God of the Fathers," in *Essays on Old Testament History and Religion* (Oxford, 1966); O. Eissfeldt, "El and Yahweh," *JSS* 1 (1956), 35 ff.; F. M. Cross, "Yahweh and the God of the Patriarchs," *HTR* 55 (1962), 225–259; "The Divine Warrior in Israel's Early Cult," in *Biblical Motifs,* ed. Alexander Altmann (Cambridge, Mass., 1969); and Wright, *The Old Testament and Theology* [N 1], pp. 70–150. From a very different perspective, see Morton Smith, "The Common Theology of the Ancient Near East," *JBL* 71 (1952), 135–147.

20. *T and C* [N 1], pp. 31 ff.

21. G. von Rad, *Das formgeschichtliche Problem des Hexateuchs* (Stuttgart, 1938); Eng. tr. *The Problem of the Hexateuch and Other Essays* (New York, 1966), pp. 1–78.

22. Wright, *God Who Acts* [N 1]. Wright has clarified his confessional position *vis-à-vis* the systematic approach of Eichrodt, on the one hand, and the form-critical approach of von Rad, on the other, in *The Old Testament and Theology* (Eng. tr., New York, 1969); see my review of the latter in *Interpretation* 24 (1970), 359–368.

23. Wright and Fuller, *Book of the Acts of God* [N 1].

24. M. Noth, *Überlieferungsgeschichte des Pentateuch* (Stuttgart, 1948); Eng. tr.: *A History of Pentateuchal Traditions* (Englewood Cliffs, N.J., 1972). The translation is admirably done by B. W. Anderson who has greatly enhanced the volume by a critical introduction (pp. xiii–xxxii) and an analytical outline of the Pentateuch based on the source-critical and tradition-critical methods combined (pp. 261–276).

25. The most recent of these in English is J. P. Hyatt's "Were there an ancient historical credo in Israel and an independent Sinai tradition?" in *Translating and Understanding the Old Testament,* eds. H. T. Frank and W. L. Reed (New York, 1970), pp. 152–170. In addition to the criticism there of Artur Weiser, C. H. W. Brekelmans, Leonhard Rost, Georg Fohrer, Hyatt (pp. 156–165), and Calvin Carmichael (pp. 169–170), see now Lothar Perlitt, *Bundestheologie im AT* (Neukirchen-Vluth, 1969) and Norbert Lohfink, "Zum 'kleinen geschichtlichen Credo' Dtn 26, 5–9," *Theologie und Philosophie* 46 (1971), 19–39. Lohfink's is perhaps the most thoroughgoing critique of the lot (though I cannot read the Dutch of Breckelmans). Note also Lohfink's felicitous emphasis on the *Nachleben,* or continuing life, of a tradition. Hyatt's argument (p. 168) that Judaism "came to consider its confession of faith as embodied in the Shema' . . . and . . . the Shema' in the narrow sense says nothing about a saving act in history; only in Num. 15:14 . . ." is something of a *tour de force*. It is the same sort of observation as that of Sinai's not being mentioned in the recitals. The centrality to Judaism of the Torah *muthos* can be seen in Nehemiah 9; Daniel 9 . . . and throughout the Jewish prayer book. Is it possible to have a synagogue service without mention of it? Cf. Judah Goldin, *The Song at the Sea* (New Haven, 1971).

26. On OT catecheses see J. A. Soggin, "Kultätiologische Sagen und Katechese im AT," *VT* 10 (1960), 341–347; P. Laaf, *Die Pascha-Feier Israels* (Bonn, 1970); and J. Loza, "Les Catéchèses étiologiques dans l'AT," *RB* 78 (1971), 481–500.

27. But this means only that the story was adaptable to seventh–sixth-century idiom—not that Deuteronomy created the story.

28. Artur Weiser, *Einleitung in das AT* (Göttingen, 1948); see the Eng. tr.: *The Old Testament: Its Formation and Development* (New York, 1961), pp. 81–99.

29. The term *muthos* is chosen to avoid the problems of other words used to date. But I do not thereby wish to prejudice the question of historicity. So far as I am con-

cerned Israel's *muthos* was at base historical. See Brevard Childs's *Myth and Reality in the Old Testament* (London, 1960), pp. 101–102 and Wright, *The Old Testament and Theology* [N 1], pp. 39–69. I should really prefer the word "gospel," but since the form-critical study of "gospel" continues to be in a muddle one simply cannot use it. Dennis McCarthy's suggestion of "commonplace" (from Greek rhetoric, *topos*) in *Lexington Theological Quarterly* 4 (1969), 46–53, is a possibility, but not immediately appealing. I prefer the manner in which Jacob Neusner uses the term Torah-myth: see Neusner, *History and Torah* (New York, 1965); *The Way of Torah* (Belmont, Calif., 1970); and *There We Sat Down and Wept* (New York, 1972). See also the way Amos Wilder uses "story" as the means of God's speaking and the typically biblical medium of man's relating God's actions, in *The Language of the Gospel* (New York, 1964), 64 ff. Martin Buber used the word "myth" in the way I mean it in his *Legend of the Baal-Shem* (New York, 1955), xi: "The Jews are a people that has never ceased to produce myth. . . . The religion of Israel has at all times felt itself endangered by this stream, but it is from it, in fact, that Jewish religiousness has at all times received its inner life." The thesis being advanced by F. M. Cross and Paul Hanson, that ancient Near Eastern myth was, according to the period and the needs of the community, more or less historicized, is not, I think, contradicted by this use of the word *muthos:* cf. Hanson, "Jewish Apocalypic Against Its Near Eastern Environment," *RB* 77 (1970), 31–58; "Old Testament Apocalyptic Re-examined," *Interpretation* 25 (1971), 454–479; "Zechariah 9 and the Recapitulation of an Ancient Ritual Pattern," *JBL* 92 (1973), 37–59; see also the major study by Cross, *Canaanite Myth and Hebrew Epic* (Cambridge, Mass., 1973).

If Immanuel Kant and Max Weber described western man's maturity as transition from *muthos* to *logos,* and a process of rationalization of his thought processes and structures (cf. Thomas O'Dea, *The Sociology of Religion* [Englewood Cliffs, N.J., 1966], 41–47), then it must be admitted that there are many forces today contradicting the truth or validity of that transition as maturation. One thinks of the sociologists of knowledge (Mannheim, Berger, Luckman), on the one hand, and the structural anthropologists on the other, especially the work of Claude Lévi-Strauss, *Structural Anthropology* (New York, 1967), and of his student François Lacan; cf. Roland Barthes et al., *Analyse structurale et exégèse biblique* (Neuchâtel, 19). From another direction there is also the work of Joseph Campbell, as in his recent *Myths to Live By* (New York, 1972).

30. J. A. Sanders, "Dissenting Deities and Phil. 2:1–11," *JBL* (1969), 279–290, n. 12.

31. *T and C* [N 1], pp. 36–53.

32. Extreme caution should be used in treating ancient Near Eastern parallels to biblical material; the one has only in modern times been retrieved from some very ancient and remote moment in antiquity while the other is embodied in a canonical and cultic collection that has survived the "repetition" and handling of many generations, before becoming stabilized in the form we have it. The former might possibly be an autograph; the latter could never be. But more important still, precisely because the biblical material has been passed down through many generations of cultic usage it has had to pass all sorts of tests (precisely of its adaptability-stability quotient) in that canonical process which the other may never, or only rarely, have been submitted to.

33. The relation of some of these assimilating survivors, the "enemies of Judah" and the "people of the land" (Ezra 4), to the Samaritans of later date is still problematic.

34. Cf. John S. Holladay, "Assyrian Statecraft and the Prophets of Israel," *HTR* 63 (1970), 29–51.

35. Leonhard Rost, "Sinaibund und Davidsbund," *TLZ* 72 (1947), cols. 129 ff.; von Rad, *OTT,* I, 308 ff.; Murray Newman, *The People of the Covenant* (New York, 1962).

36. Even Rost in his critique of von Rad (*Das kleine Credo und andere Studien zum AT* [Heidelberg, 1965], 11–25) admits the antiquity of some parts of the summary.

37. Amos 2:9-11 is an integral part of Amos' address in 1:3-3:2 (though other parts of the pericope may conceivably be from later hands; Shalom Paul in *JBL* 90 [1971], 397–403). The argument of the "sermon" is clearly that though Yahweh had taken Israel's head out of the dust of the earth of Egypt and set her in a land of her own, Israel, when established in the land, instead of acting as indicated by Yahweh's acts in Egypt, treated the poor of the land as Pharaoh had treated her. The function of the *muthos* was to provide a basic identity and life-style pattern for Israel in terms of her own responsibility.

38. John 5:39 uses the expression *tas graphas.* A. C. Sundberg attempts to distinguish between "scriptures" and canon in his very cogent thesis that the canons of both the Old Testament and New Testament were fluid until dates considerably later than generally assigned; see N 1.

39. Cf. Lewis White Beck, *Philosophic Enquiry* (Englewood Cliffs, N.J., 1952) and *Six Secular Philosophers* (New York, 1960).

40. *T and C* [N 1], pp. x ff., and 116 ff.

41. This is Ernest Wright's major thesis about the canon. Eissfeldt uses the same expression in *The Old Testament: An Introduction* [N 16], 568.

42. B. Childs, *Biblical Theology in Crisis* (Philadelphia, 1970); see his Sprunt lectures delivered in February 1972 in Richmond. Two very instructive responses to Childs's book are by George M. Landes in *USQR* 26 (1971), 273–298, and B. W. Anderson in *Theology Today* 28 (1971), 321–327.

43. Sanders, *USQR* 26 (1971), 299 ff., and *Interpretation* 24 (1970), 359–368. Childs's position was anticipated in part in my "Habakkuk in Qumran, Paul and the OT," *Journal of Religion* 38 (1959), 232–244. Similar kinds of probing may be seen in James Barr's *Old and New in Interpretation* (New York, 1966), pp. 149–200; Norbert Lohfink, "Die historische und christliche Auslegung des AT," in *Bibelauslegung im Wandel* (Frankfurt, 1967), pp. 185–213; and Peter Stuhlmacher, "Neues Testament und Hermeneutik— Versuch einer Bestandsaufnahme," *ZTK* 68 (1971), 121–61.

44. Wright states its adaptability, obliquely, in relativistic terms in his *Old Testament and Theology* [N 1], pp. 183–185.

45. Wright's criticism of Childs in "Historical Knowledge and Revelation," in *Translating and Understanding the OT* [N 25], p. 298, is surely, in part, misunderstanding.

46. See the article on midrash by Renée Bloch [N 12]; Roger le Déaut, "Apropos a Definition of Midrash," *Interpretation* 25 (1971), 259–282; and Merrill P. Miller, "Targum, Midrash and the Use of the Old Testament in the New Testament," *Journal for the Study of Judaism* 2 (1971), 29–82. (The translation of the article by le Déaut was done by Mary Howard, graduate student in biblical studies at Union Seminary; Merrill Miller is in the same program.) See now G. Vermès, "Bible and Midrash: Early OT Exegesis," *CHB*, I, 199–231. James Barr in "Le Judaisme postbiblique et la théologie de l'AT," *Revue de Théologie et de Philosophie* (1968), 209–217, seems unaware of some of this new thrust.

47. See in this regard the probing study by E. W. Nicholson on the prose material in Jeremiah composed by disciples, in *Preaching to the Exiles* (Oxford, 1970); see also his *Deuteronomy and Tradition* (Philadelphia, 1967). Similarly see Gunther Wanke, *Untersuchungen zur sogenannten Baruchschrift* (Berlin, 1971).

48. *CHB*, I, 199; see also B. J. Roberts in *BJRL* 46 (1963–64), 164–178; but see above N 4.

49. This is, of course, the nature of the patriarchal blessings, Gen. 27:27–29 and 39–40; Genesis 49; and Deuteronomy 33. This appears to be the *function* of Melchizedeq's blessing of Abraham in Gen. 14:19–20. And it should be noted that the final or redactional form of the Book of Deuteronomy (hence, the Torah?) is that of a patriarchal blessing.

50. Josephus *Against Apion* I 38–42.

51. This is a major, axiomatic observation of work in Jewish exegesis clearly datable to the Early Jewish period. See the works cited in N 46, as well as B. J. Roberts, "Bible Exegesis and Fulfillment in Qumran," *Words and Meanings,* eds. P. R. Ackroyd and B. Lindars (Cambridge, 1968), pp. 195–207.

52. See the works of S. Talmon especially in *Textus* 4 (1964), 95–132, and CHB, I, 159–199; Dominique Barthélemy, *Les Devanciers d'Aquila* (Leiden, 1963); F. M. Cross, "The History of the Biblical Text in the Light of Discoveries in the Judaean Desert," *HTR* 57 (1964), 281–299; and Sanders, *The Dead Sea Psalms Scroll* [N 9], pp. 157–159.

53. Morton Smith, *PPP* [N 1].

54. Smith's thesis fits well into the situation as we know it (and none anywhere knows it better than he) in the Persian and Hellenistic periods (those parallel to the golden and Hellenistic periods in the Greek culture). See his contributions in the *Fischer Weltgeschichte* (1965), I and II. And there were surely religious parties (*PPP,* pp. 15–56) in the pre-exilic period. But Smith practically ignores the period all-important for the canonical process—the crucible of destitution and exile where the existential factor overshadowed all factious politics. (Smith's chapter on Hellenization, *PPP,* pp. 57–81, is brilliant and should be required reading of all Bible scholars, especially neotestamentlers.)

55. The most challenging section of Smith's book is the chapter on Nehemiah: *PPP,* pp. 126–147. I think it will cause a major review of our understanding of the work of Ezra and Nehemiah. Most scholars agree that the Torah Ezra brought with him from Babylonia to Jerusalem was essentially (though still unclosed, or adaptable) the Pentateuch. Smith thinks not. He argues that what is reported in Nehemiah 8 violates pentateuchal regulations on *Yom Kippur,* and assigns the stabilization of the Torah to the period 330–180 B.C. (*PPP,* pp. 187) to combat the "assimilationists." I would still hold that the Torah received its *shape* in the exilic period due to the existential question there faced and that what Ezra brought from Babylon to Jerusalem was the Torah (though not yet closed) very much as we know it: cf. Sanders, *T and C* [N 1]; D. N. Freedman, "The Law and the Prophets," in *VTS* 9 (1963), 250–265; and P. R. Ackroyd, *Exile and Restoration* (Philadelphia, 1968), esp. pp. 201–237.

56. Dynamically, adaptability and stability work hand in hand: it is only a question of which is needed the more in given historical circumstances. D Barthélemy's thesis that *tiqqune soferim* were halted in the period of Salome Alexandra, when hermeneutics could begin to shift to non-contextual techniques, is a parallel observation; cf. Barthélemy [N 11], 285–304.

57. There is no room or need to list all the passages: see e.g., von Rad, *The Problem of the Hexateuch* [N 21], pp. 3 ff.; Noth, *A History of Pentateuchal Traditions* [N 24], pp. 46 ff.; Wright, *God Who Acts* [N 1], pp. 70 ff.; Sanders, *The Old Testament in the Cross* (New York, 1961); D. R. Hillers, *Covenant* (Baltimore, 1969); Klaus Baltzer, *The Covenant Formulary.* Even criticisms of von Rad (largely from the Georg Fohrer school) confirm the point here made: cf. J. Vollmer, *Geschichtliche Rückblicke und Motive in der Prophetie des Amos, Hosea und Jesaja* (Berlin, 1971).

58. There is a lack of clarity in Smith between the *shaping* of traditions in the postexilic period and the creation of literary materials in the same period. Shades of Wellhausen's reconstruction of the literary history of the Old Testament lie scattered on Smith's otherwise valid thesis about shaping; cf. J. Wellhausen, *Prolegomena to the History of Ancient Israel* (1885, repr. New York, 1957).

59. G. E. Mendenhall, "Biblical History in Transition," in *BANE,* pp. 27–58.

60. Mendenhall himself rightly stresses the limitations of past scholarship in this regard, ibid., p. 28 *et passim.* I could not agree more if we, too, in our generation,

recognize our being sons of our own time and not pretend to be free of *Zeitgeist* ourselves: cf. Qoh 3:11. W. F. Albright in his great wisdom advised his students of archaeology to leave more of a tell intact than dug because the next generation will have a different perspective, and perhaps improved tools. The Reform principle of learning God's truth for any age and situation through Word *and* Spirit is a classical recognition of the canon's adaptability.

61. All these quotations are from Mendenhall, in *BANE*, pp. 46–48.

62. The most arresting of recent studies on the false prophets is that of Adam van der Woude, "Micah in Dispute with the Pseudo-prophets," *VT* 19 (1969), 244–260. Earlier valuable studies include G. Quell, *Wahre and falsche Propheten* (Gütersloh, 1952); E. Jacob, "Quelques remarques sur les faux prophètes," *Theologische Zeitschrift* 23 (1957), 47; Eva Osswald, *Falsche Prophetie im AT* (Tübingen, 1962); ibid., *Theologisches Wörterbuch zum Neuen Testament,* IX (1970), 805 ff. and *Religion in Geschichte und Gegenwart* 5, 621–622; Rolf Rendtorff, "Erwägungen zur Frügeschichte des Prophetentums in Israel," *ZTK* 59 (1962), 145–167; R. E. Clements, *Prophecy and Covenant* (London, 1965), pp. 11–44, 119–129; Barr, *Old and New in Interpretation* [N 43], pp. 149–170; D. N. Freedman, "The Biblical Idea of History," *Interpretation* 21 (1967), 32–49. A fair review of the problem in terms of cultic prophecy is Jörg Jeremias, *Kultprophetie und Gerichtsverkündigung in der späten Königszeit Israels* (Neukirchen-Vluyn, 1970); cf. esp. pp. 192–193 on the hermeneutic difference between true and false prophets. T. W. Overholt, *The Threat of Falsehood* (London, 1970), provides a good introduction to the whole problem by concentrating on *šeqer* in Jeremiah.

63. The "true" prophets had two bases or references of authority: (a) their own call, and (b) Israel's call (the Torah *muthos*): cf. *T and C* [N 1], 73 ff. We should assume that the "false" prophets did as well.

64. John Bright's view of this, especially in Isaiah, needs critique: cf. *A History of Israel* (Philadelphia, 1959), pp. 271 ff. I am convinced that Isaiah interpreted the Davidic covenant as conditional to the sovereign will of Yahweh without combining it with the Mosaic: Isa. 1:21–27 and chs. 28–31 offer ample evidence of this.

65. A brilliant example of Isaiah's basing his message of judgment squarely on the Davidic tradition is Isa. 28:21. The "providence" or status quo or "false" prophets would have cited the traditions we know from II Sam 5:17–25 and I Chron 14:10–17 to argue that Yahweh would act in their day as he had for David on Mount Perazim and in the vale of Gibeon—to prosper Israel. Isaiah agreed that Yahweh would act as he had on Perazim and in Gibeon but this time to judge his own people—a strange deed, and quite alien, as he says, to those who would employ the hermeneutic of false providence. Isaiah referred to the Davidic traditions only, precisely to counter the view that all one had to do was believe Yahweh was strong enough to save them, exactly what he himself had earlier thought (Isa. 7:9, etc.). Isaiah 36–39, if studied carefully to determine references of authority, shows itself to be largely alien to Isaiah. (This latter point is apart from the question of whether 36–39 reflects historical events.)

66. The Second Isaiah is omitted from the list partly because Isaiah 40–55 is obviously full of references to both the Mosaic and Davidic traditions; for there both the judgment and the salvation must be seen in the light of Israel's history: cf. e.g. Isa. 42:24–25 and 54:7–8; and see Sanders *Suffering as Divine Discipline* (Rochester, 1955), *The Old Testament in the Cross* [N 57], and *T and C* [N 1].

67. Smith, *PPP* [N 1], p. 46. If the great families who befriended Jeremiah early in his career were like the Whig party of England, Jeremiah must have disappointed them gravely to have been tried twice and imprisoned at least three times (cf. Jeremiah 34?). I suggest that the family of Shaphan were pro-Babylonian in political leanings and that they *thought* Jeremiah was also (Jer. 37:9–10). Nothing could be further from the

truth as Jeremiah's attitude and response to Nebuzaradan show when the defenses of the city were finally broken. The Babylonians naturally thought Jeremiah was politically anti-Egyptian and pro-Babylonian because of his identifying the foe from the north with themselves, and hence offered Jeremiah what he willed as soon as the city was taken (Jer. 39:11–14, 40:2–5). But Jeremiah's allegiances were neither to Egypt nor to Babylonia but to a vision of an Israel free to serve Yahweh by surrendering their enslavement to his gifts: he elected to stay in the destitute land and refused a pension and comfort in Babylon (40:6). Jeremiah's relations to Jehoiakim and Zedekiah were informed by an impolitic theological vision of Israel's identity (chs. 36–37), not by a politic quest for accommodation to a pro-Babylonian policy. The prose sections of Jeremiah are secondary in importance to the poetic oracles, in chs. 1–23, for judging the prophet's real alienation from *all* Judaic society (Jer. 5:4–5, 9:1, 15:17; 16, *et passim*). Smith himself at two points takes so much away from the word "party" that one is not altogether sure how he uses it in all instances; cf. pp. 13 and 29.

68. Cf. Jer. 28:9 and Deut. 18:22. Jeremiah's conviction was that God's message through prophecy was a challenge to, and judgmental of, existing structure and custom; only if prophecy sponsored a status quo, *shalom*, was it subject to historical proof.

By exile I mean not only the narrow period of 586 to 520 B.C., but the fuller experience of destitution plus the failure of Second Isaiah's vision, the failure of the Zerubbabel pretension, the destructive campaigns of Xerxes I throughout the area in the first quarter of the fifth century, up to the final successes of Ezra and Nehemiah within the apparently severe limitations imposed by Persian statecraft, and especially its rule of its provinces. Above all what must be accounted for is that not only was the final form of the Torah shaped by the Babylonian Diaspora but that it was upon that community that most of the hard decisions fell which shaped Judaism as it eventuated in Rabbinic Judaism after A.D. 70. Perhaps the historical way to put it is that what survived as the essence of "normative" (Pharisaic-Rabbinic) Judaism was the thinking about survival and identity and practice which went on among Babylonian Jewish communities of the "exilic" period, that is, from the time of Ezekiel until the time of Ezra and Nehemiah. See especially Jacob Neusner, *A History of the Jews in Babylonia,* vol. I (Leiden, 1966).

In this regard it would be well to ponder at great length the observation of Morton Smith at the close of his very challenging chapter on Nehemiah (*PPP,* p. 47): ". . . the connection between Judaism and the worship of the restored temple was, in the philosophical sense of the word, 'accidental.' It was demanded, indeed, by the traditions and aspirations of the religion, *but was not essential to its nature.* The national, political, territorial side of Judaism, by which it differed from the other Hellenistic forms of Oriental religions, was as a practical matter, the work of Nehemiah. He secured to the religion that double character—local as well as universal—which was to endure, in fact, for five hundred years and, in its terrible consequences, yet endures." (Italics mine— J.A.S.)

69. *T and C* [N 1], pp. 66–90. This hope is sometimes rendered more explicit by later hands, in the typically doxological and comforting closing verses of the prophetic books.

70. See the brilliant paper by Hartmut Gese of Tübingen, "The Idea of History in the ANE and the OT," *JTC* (1965), 49–64 [ANE=Ancient Near East].

71. See Otto Eissfeldt's seminal study of Isa. 55:1–5 on the democratization of the old royal theology in *Israel's Prophetic Heritage* (New York, 1962) ed. by B. W. Anderson and W. Harrelson, pp. 196–207.

72. These two phrases, in Isa. 46:12 and 51:7, are not only antithetic but chiastic in form, and were surely Isaianic epithets for the two groups, faithful and apostate.

73. The harmonistic efforts, in the recent neo-orthodox period, to see the prophets as

moralizing in favor of an ethical cult, are now seen as impertinent from the perspective of canonical criticism.

74. Richard L. Rubenstein, in *After Auschwitz* (Indianapolis, n.d.) observes on p. 138, "Death and rebirth are the great moments of religious experience." And with most Jews today, Rubenstein sees the modern state of Israel as the modern "rebirth" experience of Judaism.

75. *T and C*, pp. 45–53.

76. Freedman [N 55], pp. 259–263.

77. Ezek. 37:1 *wywṣ'ny*, 37:2 *wh'byrny*, 37:5 *mby'*, 37:6 *wh'lty*, and *wntty bkm rwḥ whyytm*, 37:12 *wh'lyty* and *whb'ty*, 37:14 *wntty* and *whnḥty*.

78. Cf. Geza Vermès, *Scripture and Tradition* (Leiden, 1961).

79. As Ernest Wright often points out; cf. e.g. *Old Testament and Theology*, p. 180. This was the early process of "dialogical revelation," of the necessary complementarity: "Word" and "Spirit."

80. This is what is right about B. Childs's thesis in *Biblical Theology in Crisis* [N 42]. And it is surely the meaning for today of the old principle of "salvation only through judgment."

81. As Yehezkiel Kaufmann apparently thought all ancient Israel did: cf. *The Religion of Israel* (1960) and the very open critique of Kaufmann's *magnum opus*, from which the work cited is extrapolated, by S. Talmon in *Conservative Judaism* 25 (1971), 20–28. The major thrusts of the canon within its pluralism indicate for the believing communities today, I think, (a) an ever expanding and syncretizing view of God [he is neither Jew *nor* Christian], and (b) a bias in favor of the powerless.

82. That the force of this historic memory should eventuate in the Pharisaic and Christian belief that God could give life again even after death, *teḥiyat ha-metim*, should occasion no surprise: it was a (theo)logical issue of Torah. According to Sir. 45:5, the Torah brings life; to Masseket Abot 2:8, acquiring the words of Torah acquires life in the world to come; to Abot 6:7, Torah gives life, now and in the world to come to those who practice it; cf. Rom. 7:10; Gal. 3:21; and John 5:39—all indirect witnesses to the same Jewish conviction of the period.

28. Jewish Palaeography and Its Bearing
on Text Critical Studies

RICHARD S. HANSON

LUTHER COLLEGE, DECORAH, IOWA

IT IS THE GENIUS of our learned friend, G. Ernest Wright, that he has been able to read history in the simplest artifacts left by our predecessors in the layers of debris that are now being dug by the spades of archaeologists. Be it fragments of pottery, the remains of buildings and walls or the soil itself, he has learned and taught others to regard it all as pages in a valuable record of the past. The genius of the palaeographer is akin to this. He is one who studies the ancient scripts as much for the sake of what the scripts themselves have to tell him as for the sake of reading whatever the ancient texts have to say, for palaeography has to do with the history and evolution of writing and writing technique. The palaeographer is often able to use script in the same way that a dirt-digging archaeologist uses a sherd of pottery: to determine dates and cultural data. Though it was not true as early as a half century ago, many of the ancient scripts—and notably the Jewish—have revealed the secrets of their development to such a degree that a great number of very old materials have been dated and classified on the basis of palaeographical data alone.

Our present concern is palaeography and its bearing on textual studies—which ought to embrace two areas beyond the study of scripts *per se:* (1) the unique contribution which palaeographers have made to the dating and reading of ancient texts, and (2) the restrictions and possibilities which methodical and careful palaeographical procedures have introduced into such matters as textual reconstruction. As a matter of plan, we shall begin with a review of the progress to date in the field of palaeography itself and, most specifically, in the narrower field of Jewish scripts.

One must necessarily be somewhat arbitrary in deciding where to begin a discussion of the subject of palaeography. If we should include any and all scholarly interest in Jewish scripts, it is necessary to go back very far in time, for rabbinical scholars and others have had a profound interest in the letters of their sacred records since Talmudic times at the latest. Inasmuch as none of this interest relates particularly to the scientific discipline of palaeography as practiced today, however, we shall pass it by and begin at the point where the collecting of valuable materials was begun and some attention paid to evolutionary development of scripts. That time was, of course, the late nineteenth century as signalled, perhaps, by the appearance of the *Corpus inscriptionum semiticarum*. Several of the great textual and archaeological scholars of that time became involved in the endeavor to the extent that they began to trace out evolutionary patterns in the script in an effort to determine sequence and dates.[1] Though their methods were crude and arbitrary by present standards, such men as Clermont-Ganneau and Lidzbarski did more than accumulate valuable collections of materials. They were among the first to attempt scientific description of the evolution of scripts.

It was William F. Albright who succeeded in moving palaeographical studies on to a new stage of sophistication. A publication which well displays the results of his work in this field was "A Biblical Fragment from the Maccabean Age: the Nash Papyrus."[2] In it he summarized all prior discussions concerning the date of the document, made a thoroughly fresh analysis, and developed a new outline of the typological development of late Aramaic and early Jewish scripts. Spotting the limitations of previous work done with ancient documents, he saw the importance of differentiating between types of script and criticized those who had grouped lapidary and cursive scripts together. He made it clear that one must have an overview of all available materials before making any judgments about the evolution of forms and he found himself able to distinguish script traditions and establish links between them, refining the knowledge of the evolutionary process considerably. He was able to observe that a script may evolve either slowly or rapidly, depending upon conditions of its use. He recognized the possibility of archaizing. He was able to distinguish calligraphic features from strictly evolutionary change. After the appearance of this article, palaeographical discussions had to be more careful, thorough, and methodical than they had ever been before.[3]

F. M. Cross, one of Albright's own students, made some of the next major steps in the field of palaeographical technique. Basing his work on thorough familiarity with the material and operating with extremely consistent procedures, Cross now occupies a front position among those who work with Northwest Semitic scripts and is very much the teacher of many other epigraphists.[4] His methods are so basic to the work that is now being done that we can do no better than to lay them out as the point at which we have arrived as far as procedure is concerned—and we do this by distilling our observations from his many valuable articles on the subject. The basic principles (many common to other palaeographical fields) are as follows.

(1) Awareness of an evolutionary development occurring in the script, but at varying rates of speed for the different letters of the alphabet. One letter may be evolving so slowly over a span of time as to be of little value in

establishing dates, while another may be changing at a rapid pace and be of great value.

(2) Beginning quite early, and until a relatively late period of time, viewing the Phoenician, Aramaic, and Hebrew scripts as hanging from a ceiling line rather than written upon a base.[5] Thus, when charts are made, tables of script should be constructed on the basis of horizontal lines rather than vertical columns, in order that letter position and length in relation to a ceiling (or, later, base) line may be easily noted.

(3) Exercising extreme precision in tracing letter forms for comparative charts, choosing samples only after a thorough study of all occurrences of a particular letter and choosing more than one sample form when more than one typical form of a letter actually occurs in the script. Wherever possible, tracing an actual form.

(4) Observing stance (or, more accurately, "swing," when working with a script that hangs from a ceiling line), relative length, width, and size as well as mere shape of a letter. (Early efforts tended to ignore all factors but general shape.)

(5) Being aware, at all times, of the model of a letter in the mind of the scribe and the fashion in which a letter is drawn. An actual form may at times be less "true" than a reconstruction and, when this is the case, a reconstructed form is preferable to an actual tracing.

(6) Noting such calligraphic techniques as thickness or thinness of lines (shading) but distinguishing them from other typological features in the forms of the letters.

(7) Being as watchful for historical "lag" or holdover of old forms in a script as for changes that are part of the evolutionary process. Though they are not so helpful in dating, such features do help determine the character of a given script.

(8) Being watchful for aberrations that do not fit within the evolutionary scheme (i.e. drop out of the scheme after an initial appearance or which identify loan forms from other script styles).

(9) Paying attention to such items as ligatures or other movements which begin as a matter of style but may result in radical changes in the form of the model when continued over a long period of time.

(10) Cataloguing manuscripts on the basis of at least two general rubrics: *formal* and *cursive*. (At an earlier stage, when flexible writing materials were first introduced, the categories would be *lapidary* versus *manuscript*.) Further vocabulary to describe the great variety of scripts which do occur can be subdivided quite conveniently under these rubrics. When a formal script under certain conditions begins to relax toward cursive, it can be called a *proto-cursive* script, while a style developed from the crossing of formal and cursive can be called *semi-cursive*. The term *semi-formal* (cf. uncial) is best reserved for a script style that develops similarly, but with only minor cursive features. Popular scripts that are the result of non-

professional hands are best termed *vulgar*. These terms apply, however, only to styles which crystalize and are used over a considerable period of time, at least several scribal generations. They do not apply to "tendencies" in a script.

(11) Locating phases within the evolutionary development by noting very general series of typological shifts (the emergence of a new style). In his treatment of the early Jewish scripts, Cross has distinguished three phases: (a) archaic: 250–150 B.C.E., (b) Hasmonaean: 150–30 B.C.E., and (c) Herodian: 30 B.C.E.–70 C.E.[6]

Though Albright and Cross may be credited with the major advances in methodology, there are others who have made many significant contributions. N. Avigad, who has worked constantly in the field of Hebrew, Aramaic, and related scripts, has published many important materials and made a most important contribution to the discussion of palaeographical features of the Jewish funerary scripts, Israelite seal scripts, and, of course, the Jewish hands of the Dead Sea Scrolls.[7] J. T. Milik has contributed much in the area of publishing and editing materials. He has an unusual flair for decipherment and is capable in the area of palaeography, having advanced the field in numerous ways, including his brilliant analysis of the late Jewish cursive.[8] E. L. Sukenik made some very valuable observations at the initial stages of research in the Scrolls.[9] John C. Trever has engaged in palaeographical discussion from time to time[10] and so, also, has W. H. Brownlee, though they rely heavily on Albright and more recently on Cross.[11]

Solomon A. Birnbaum, of recent memory, did some extraordinarily valuable pioneering in the field of palaeography and Jewish scripts. His contributions, though inconsistent in quality, have proven to be basically sound. He did some of the toughest spadework in the palaeographical discussions of the Dead Sea Scrolls and, in addition, published a collection of materials that must be rated as monumental in importance.[12]

Joseph Naveh has in recent years become a contributor of first rank in this field of endeavor. Though he has concentrated his efforts in Aramaic and Hebrew scripts to date, much of what he has done bears directly on the problems of the Jewish scripts. Receiving a good deal of his guidance from Avigad and Cross, Naveh has moved on to a position of independent insight and creative research. In *The Development of the Aramaic Script,* a revised version of a dissertation directed by Professor Avigad, he has clarified the origin and history of the script that is mother to the Jewish and other national scripts and provided a handbook for the study of palaeography that could well serve as an introduction for any student interested in the subject.[13]

Y. Yadin and Y. Aharoni have made valuable contributions in the area of publications, Yadin with the materials of Qumran, Masada, and Murabba'at,[14] Aharoni with the epigraphic material of Ramath-Raḥel and Arad.[15] Among the students of Cross who have made contributions in the field of palaeography we might mention the following: Paul Lapp for his study of Judaean stamps,[16] James Purvis for his discussion of the Samaritan script,[17]

Brian Peckham for his thorough survey and discussion of the late Phoenician scripts,[18] the author for his contribution to the dating of the palaeo-Hebrew fragments of the Dead Sea Scrolls and limited work with the Aramaic scripts of Asia Minor,[19] and Byron L. Haines for his study of the early Aramaic script.[20]

Regarding the Jewish scripts themselves, the present state of affairs can be summarized quite briefly. Methodology has been developed to such a point that, given materials to work on, we can trace the various lines of evolution within categories that are already known and date examples within a significant range of accuracy. The earliest phases of the Jewish script have been studied (with gaps in the Hasmonaean period where materials in cursive are scarce) to the end of the Herodian era—as has the Aramaic script tradition which precedes it. This point of arrival permits us to envision further studies in at least two directions: (1) the analysis of new materials as they are found and (2) a continuation of the systematic studies of available evidence, chiefly post-Herodian.[21]

When we speak of Jewish scripts, we are speaking primarily of scripts that derive from Aramaic rather than Hebrew prototypes. As is very well known, Jewish people all but completely stopped using the Hebrew forms of the letters in post-exilic times and adopted the current imperial chancellery hands instead.[22] The story behind these scripts is, then, the story of how the Aramaic developed into the Persian chancellery hands that are the mother of the Jewish scripts.[23] That evolution has been traced out most recently by Joseph Naveh[24] and is, in brief, as follows.

A distinctively Aramaic form of the Northwest Semitic alphabet begins to appear in the ninth century B.C.E.[25] Evidence reveals that cursive script became common in the eighth century, common enough to show its influence in lapidary inscriptions. It is at this time, apparently, that Aramaic is beginning to be used as a commercial *lingua franca*. A lack of materials makes it difficult to trace the development of the Aramaic script through the seventh and sixth centuries, but the lapidary script seems to have served as a powerful conservative influence while the cursive forms found on papyrus and sherds betray the currency of a vulgar as well as a semi-formal script. Inscriptions inscribed in soft clay typically contain a mixture of lapidary and cursive forms. A considerable wealth of materials from the fifth century B.C.E. permits us to see a variety of styles within an amazingly uniform and universal concept of the model. (Naveh subdivides the cursive types into the categories of *extreme, formal,* and *vulgar*. He chooses not to discuss the lapidary materials in detail but notes that formal cursive script was used for stone or metal engravings in a number of instances and that both extreme and vulgar cursive forms are common—evidence that the current cursive alphabet was actually replacing a lapidary tradition.[26] In sheer quantity, there is less material representing the fourth–third centuries than the fifth, but it is in the fourth-century examples that we see the forms from which the early Jewish script is derived. Naveh discusses the development of both *extreme* and *formal cursive* alphabets and then points out a truly stable Aramaic lapidary script: a script based on a well-developed cursive alphabet that does retain its own integrity alongside continuing cursive development.

It is in what he calls the fourth-century chancellery hand that Cross finds the origins of the earliest Jewish formal scripts.[27] The slightly later examples of cursive script are rooted in the cursive forms of Aramaic; they are not offshoots of the Jewish formal hand. Representing what he labels the archaic or proto-Jewish period (250–150 B.C.E.), Cross cites examples of (1) a formal script (4QSam[b] and 4QJer[a]), (2) a semi-formal script that could be considered a subtype of the first, made distinctive by influence of third-century cursive (early examples: 4QQoh[a] and 4QPrières lit.A), (3) a proto-cursive series that is influenced by the formal hand but is more directly connected with the Aramaic vulgar scripts of the third century B.C.E. (4QEx[f] is listed as an example of the true proto-cursive). For the Hasmonaean period (150–30 B.C.E.), he points to a formal tradition which grows out of the formal tradition of the archaic period but is strongly influenced by the semi-formal script (his examples: 4QDeut[a], 1QIsa[a], 4QDeut[c], 4QSam[a]) and several semi-cursive hands (examples: Nash Papyrus, a Murabba'ât ostracon, 4QXII[a], 4QDan[e]). Out of the relative abundance of palaeographical material available for the Herodian period, Cross sees a formal script distinctive to the period (examples: 4QSam[a] as its prototype; also 1QM, 4QDan[b], and 4QDeut[j]), but a rather elegant semi-formal script that does not descend directly from the earlier semi-formal (examples: 1QNum[b], 4QNum[b]) and a vulgar version—a crude and simplified form—of the Herodian formal hand. Concerning the Herodian cursive scripts, he simply has to say that they are not adequately represented by the materials at our disposal (which include the Bethphage lid, certain ossuary groups, and some fragments from Qumran, Murabba'ât, and Masada). Considerable quantities of Herodian cursive inscriptions require further study before definitive statements can be made about them and the same situation obtains for all the materials of the post-Herodian era. Even the dates of the latest materials are highly tentative.[28]

The Hebrew script is another story. Until now, the earliest known example of what can be called a truly Hebrew inscription is the famed Gezer Calendar, the date of which has been variously assigned around a central date of tenth or early ninth century B.C.E.[29] From that time until the fall of the Judaean Kingdom, there is a steady evolution of two different styles: the lapidary, which is found primarily on seals and stone monuments, and the cursive scripts that occur, for the most part, inscribed on sherds.[30] The latest materials of this era are the Gibeon stamps and various private stamps and seals of scattered or unknown provenance. The question of whether Hebrew script was used at all or with any frequency during the Persian-Hellenistic period is answered only with scattered evidence. The author and J. Naveh have both argued that it was in constant use,[31] but the more traditional viewpoint has been that the use of palaeo-Hebrew was virtually lost until Hasmonaean times.

The Hasmonaean rulers quite deliberately encouraged the use of Hebrew script—John Hyrcanus I, Judas Aristobulus, Alexander Janneus, and John Hyrcanus II all struck coins on which there appear legends in palaeo-Hebrew script[32]—and it is in conjunction with this that some scroll fragments in Hebrew script appeared among the finds of the Judaean wilderness. It is this group of materials which provides us with the script types that are antecedent to the Samaritan scripts that begin to appear from as early as the first century C.E.[33] The last examples of the Hebrew script in the hands of Jews are to be found on the coins of the First and Second Revolts.

As we have seen, there is still work to be done in the latest of the pre-Masoretic materials in which we find Jewish script. Many of these materials are currently being studied, however, and definitive articles will undoubtedly soon appear.[34]

Palaeographic studies have made several distinct and important contributions to the larger field of textual studies. In the first place, and most obviously perhaps, it has enabled us to read, date, and classify the precious textual materials that have come to light over the past three decades. The amount of material and the number of publications concerned with this is voluminous. Besides the critical editions of the materials themselves, there are a host of important articles in many journals that deal with such matters and a number of volumes and monographs too sizable to review. The most we can do here is to indicate some of the issues that have been resolved with the help of sound palaeographical techniques and the contributions that have resulted.

As soon as the Scrolls had been discovered, scholars of many traditions began an extremely hot debate concerning their date. Though internal evidence was immensely important in the discussion, we can safely say that those who applied themselves with discipline to the study of palaeographical development finally "saved the day" by offering the convincing evidence that tied down the dates and chronology which now seem to be agreed upon by those most concerned with the materials.[35] The variation of opinions was so extreme that it forced many scholars to master at least some of the techniques of palaeography in order to stay in the discussion. For some, the very reading of the materials required the learning of alphabet forms they had never before seen; for others it was an opportunity to show considerable skill in a new field of endeavor.[36]

One of the crucial by-products of this discussion was the discovery and recognition of letter forms which can be easily confused because of similarity and, therefore, a possible source of textual error or alteration. Many similarities of letter forms had of course been known for some time. Most notorious in the history of both Hebrew and Aramaic scripts has been the case of *daleth* and *resh*. The two are similar in size, shape, and stance over a considerable span of time. The difficulties that can result might be best illustrated by the epigraphical materials unearthed by J. B. Pritchard at Gibeon. The appearance of $g^d r^d r$ on a number of jar handles summoned a debate which could only be resolved with a most carefully detailed study of the palaeographical evidence—and then not resolved to the satisfaction of all.[37] For an illustration of lesser-known similarities, consult the literature on the Yabne-Yam letters, where the contest is an honest debate between two skilled palaeographers over a reading of *mem* versus *nun*.[38]

In the materials that have come from the caves of the Dead Sea, new pairs of similar letters have emerged. In *The Ancient Library of Qumran,* Cross has pointed out the possibility of confusing *waw* and *resh* in third-century book hand[39] and *waw* and *yodh* in the late first century B.C.E. In regard to the latter, even a cursory reading of the early Herodian manuscripts (4QSam[a], 4QM, 4QDan[b], 4QDeut[j], 4QNum[b], 1QNum[b]) is so convincing that it is easy to see how a host of later errors in transmission could result in such confusion of readings as the familiar confusion of *hw'* and *hy'* in the Masoretic text of the Pentateuch or a number of cases where there is confusion or possible confusion in the pronominal suffixes -*w* and -*y*.[40]

In addition to letters that are virtually identical in form, there are many cases of letters so similar in one or more crucial features that a slight amount of damage in a letter may result in a misreading. The author has tried to point out cases of this in the text of the Psalms. In MT, Psalm 19:5c reads *lšmš šm 'hl bhm,* a reading (supported by LXX) that strains the linguistic possibilities as it stands. If, however, we change *bhm* to *bym,* we come up with this lovely line that is thoroughly consistent with Israelite geography: "he set the sun's tent in the sea." The emendation is permitted by the similarity in stance and shape between *he* and *yodh* in palaeo-Hebrew script. If the bottom portion of a *yodh* was effaced, it could be misread as a *he*.[41] Or consider, by examination and comparison, how a combination of *š* and *w* could be emended to *ṣ* in order to change *bšwry* to *bṣry* in Ps: 92:12.[42] A somewhat damaged *'aleph* could be read as a *taw* in some palaeo-Hebrew scripts (due to similar swing and size), permitting an emendation of *bsk 'ddm* to *bskt [w]drm* in Ps. 42:5b.[43]

The conclusion we are leading up to is this: the textual scholar who knows the evolution and development of the Hebrew and Jewish scripts is aware of certain possibilities and restrictions which permit him to move with both freedom and control in the matter of textual restoration or emendation. In knowing what is really possible on palaeographical grounds, he adds one more important tool to his bag of tricks.[44] The discovery of Harry M. Orlinsky that the Greek translation of Job was based, not on a manuscript in the Jewish character, but on a manuscript in palaeo Hebrew could not be more important in this regard.[45]

Related to this, and just as important, is a knowledge of orthographic practice and its history. It was W. F. Albright and his students who first began to observe, in detail, the rules and regularity of Hebrew orthography and put them to use. The groundwork was laid in a series of textual studies[46] and in a manual of basic patterns and principles by F. M. Cross and D. N. Freedman entitled *Early Hebrew Orthography*.[47] This monograph is heavily quoted in textual literature, but further work of analysis has remained largely in the hands of the same persons.[48] There are, on the other hand, other matters of orthography which have been discussed by various scholars. A. R. Millard has made a most helpful contribution to one important matter in his article, "'Scriptio Continua' in Early Hebrew: Ancient Practice or Modern Surmise,"[49] showing how word division is an old practice in West Semitic orthography and the rule in the earliest manuscripts. In textual reconstruction, therefore, we cannot assume that scribal copiers were baffled by texts in which there is no indication of word division.

Among the pleasant orthographic surprises of the material from the Dead Sea is the discovery of scribal attention to strophic and stichometric divisions in poetry,[50] the use of palaeo-Hebrew script for the tetragrammaton in the midst of Jewish script,[51] the absence of any clear evidence for the use of abbreviations[52] and the appearance of various scribal marks to designate correction or other matters.[53] Indeed, one of the most helpful results of the reading and study of the texts from the Dead Sea is the actual knowledge of specific kinds of textual errors and corrections. M. Martin (see N 53) lists several types: corrections of erroneous letters and erroneous words, transference of letters to correct erroneous spacing, indication of alternative readings, insertion of either the tetragrammaton or *'dwny,* and the retracing of faulty letters. M. Burrows has pointed out two kinds of cases—a correction of errors by the original scribe and correction by a later hand—and notes instances where actual omissions of lines are filled in.[54]

Of greatest significance to textual studies, of course, are the many and valuable variant readings found in the old materials of recent discovery. Not merely because of occasional or frequent superior readings, but far more because of information they have provided for the comparative study of ancient texts and versions.

NOTES

1. Notably G. A. Cooke, F. C. Burkitt, A. H. Sayce, J. Euting, C. Clermont-Ganneau, J. Halévy, E. Sachau, and M. Lidzbarski in the earlier group, though the work that was begun by them was continued by such scholars as A. E. Cowley, F. Rosenthal, N. Aimé-Giron, C. C. Torrey, J. Cantineau, M. Dunand, R. Dussaud, and others. The most significant work done by this first group of researchers was the collection of materials. In addition to the *Corpus inscriptionum semiticarum,* we would call attention to Cooke, *A Textbook of North Semitic Inscriptions* (Oxford, 1903); Lidzbarski,

Handbuch der nordsemitischen Epigraphik (Weimar, 1898) and *Ephemeris für semit-
ische Epigraphik* (Leipzig, I Band, 1900–2; II Band, 1903–7; III Band, 1909–15);
D. Diringer, *Le iscrizioni antico-ebraiche palestinesi* (Florence, 1934); Cowley, *Aramaic Papyri of the Fifth Century B.C.* (Oxford, 1923); and *Corpus inscriptionum
iudicarum* by J. B. Frey (Rome, vol. I, 1936; vol. II, 1952). The work of collecting
materials has gone on. A. Reifenberg, *Ancient Hebrew Seals* (London, 1950) is a valuable collection to be replaced shortly by a corpus prepared by N. Avigad. So also is
S. Moscati, *L'epigrafia ebraica antica 1935–1950* (Rome, 1951). H. Donner and
W. Röllig, *Kanaanäische und Aramäische Inschriften* (Wiesbaden, 1966) is an invaluable catalogue of materials, as is the latest collection of Hebrew and Jewish materials,
S. Birnbaum, *The Hebrew Scripts* (London, 1954–57, and 1972). Needless to say, many
significant materials are to be found outside these collections and must be sought in
special publications devoted to particular corpora or in periodicals.

2. W. F. Albright, *JBL* 56 (1937), 145–176.

3. For the long bibliography of Albright's studies in Northwest Semitic epigraphy and
palaeography, see *BANE*, pp. 363–389 (1911–1958); and *EI* 9 (1969), 1–5 (1958–
1968).

4. Anyone interested in a serious study of palaeographical methods and development
will find the work of F. M. Cross crucial. To that end, we list a series of his articles
that deal with palaeography:

a) "Inscribed Javelin-heads from the Period of the Judges: A Recent Discovery in
Palestine" [with J. T. Milik], *BASOR* 134 (April 1954), 11–14

b) "The Evolution of the Proto-Canaanite Alphabet," *BASOR* 134 (April 1954),
15–24

c) "The Oldest Manuscripts from Qumrân," *JBL* 74 (1955), 147–172

d) "A Typological Study of the El Khadr Javelin- and Arrow-heads," *Annual of the
Department of Antiquities of Jordan* 3 (1956), 15–23 [with J. T. Milik; publication de-
layed]

e) "A Ugaritic Abecedary and the Origins of the Proto-Canaanite Alphabet" [with
T. O. Lambdin], *BASOR* 160 (Dec. 1960), 21–26

f) "The Development of the Jewish Scripts," in *BANE*, pp. 133–202

g) "Epigraphic Notes on Hebrew Documents of the Eighth-Sixth Centuries B.C.:
I. A New Reading of a Place Name in the Samaria Ostraca," *BASOR* 163 (Oct.
1961), 12–14 ". . . : II. The Murabba'ât Papyrus and the Letter Found Near Yabneh-
Yam," *BASOR* 165 (Feb. 1962), 34–46; ". . . : III. The Inscribed Jar Handles from
Gibeon," *BASOR* 168 (Dec. 1962), 18–23

h) "An Inscribed Seal from Balâṭah (Shechem)," *BASOR* 167 (Oct. 1962), 14–15

i) "An Archaic Inscribed Seal from the Valley of Aijalon," *BASOR* 168 (Dec.
1962), 12–18

j) "Excursus on the Paleographical Dating of the Copper Document," in *Les
'petites grottes' de Qumrân*, eds. M. Baillet, J. T. Milik et al., DJD, III (1962), 217–221
and fig. 12

k) "An Aramaic Inscription from Daskyleion," *BASOR* 184 (Dec. 1966), 7–10

l) "The Origin and Early Evolution of the Alphabet," in *EI* 8 [Sukenik Memorial
Volume] (1967), 8–24

m) "The Phoenician Inscription from Brazil: A Nineteenth Century Forgery,"
Orientalia, N.S. 37 (1968), 1–25

n) "Jar Inscriptions from Shikmona," *IEJ* 18 (1968), 226–233

o) "Judean Stamps," *EI* 9 [Albright Volume] (1969), 20–27

p) "Papyri of the Fourth Century B.C. from Dâliyeh," in *NDBA*, pp. 41–62, figs.
34–39

q) "Epigraphic Notes on the Ammân Citadel Inscription," *BASOR* 193 (1969),
13–19

r) "Two Notes on Palestinian Inscriptions of the Persian Age," *BASOR* 193 (1969), 19–24

s) "An Ostracon from Heshbon," *Andrews University Seminary Studies* 7 (1969), 223–229, pl. xxv

t) "The Cave Inscriptions from Khirbet Beit Lei," in *NEATC*, pp. 299–306

u) "Phoenician Incantations on a Plaque of the Seventh Century B.C. from Arslan Tash in Upper Syria" [with R. J. Saley], *BASOR* 197 (1970), 42–49

v) "An Inscribed Jar Handle from Raddana" [with D. N. Freedman], *BASOR* 201 (1971), 19–22

w) "The Old Phoenician Inscription from Spain Dedicated to Hurrian Astarte," in *HTR* 64:2–3 [Lapp Memorial Volume] (1971), 189–195

x) "The Stele Dedicated to Melcarth by Ben-Hadad of Damascus," *BASOR* 205 (1972), 36–42

5. The point at which this changes for the Jewish scripts is noted by Cross in *BANE*, p. 67, where we read, "By the end of the Hasmonean period, there is a feeling for a base line as well as a ceiling line, and in late Herodian manuscripts the scribe occasionally lines in a base line."

6. See the more detailed discussion of this on p. 566.

7. Avigad's studies of the Hebrew script include "The Epitaph of a Royal Steward from Siloam Village," *IEJ* 3 (1953), 137–152; "The Second Tomb-Inscription of the Royal Steward," *IEJ* 5 (1955), 163–166; "Some Notes on the Hebrew Inscription from Gibeon," *IEJ* 9 (1959), 130–133; "A Sculptured Hebrew Stone Weight," *IEJ* 18 (1968), 181–187; and the related study "Ammonite and Moabite Seals," in *NEATC*, pp. 284–295, a chapter in his forthcoming *Corpus of Northwest Semitic Seals*, which will include his many publications of seals over the last two decades. His studies of the Aramaic lapidary and Palaeo-Hebrew scripts include, "A New Class of *Yehud* Stamps," *IEJ* 7 (1957), 146–153; "New Light on the MṢH Seal Impressions," *IEJ* 8 (1958), 113–119; and "Yehûd or Haʿîr," *BASOR* 158 (April, 1960), 23–27. Of direct concern to Jewish scripts is his publication of the funerary inscriptions of Beth-Sheʿarim in "Excavations at Beth-Sheʿarim, 1955," *IEJ* 7 (1957), 73–92 and 239–255, and what he has published of the materials at Masada in *Masada, Survey and Excavations, 1955–1956*, by M. Avi-Yonah, N. Avigad et al. (Jerusalem, 1957), cf. pp. 59f. and pl. 16:C, D; "The Aramaic Inscriptions," *'Atiqot* 4 (1964), 32–38; and "Excavations in the Jewish Quarter of the Old City of Jerusalem, 1969/70," *IEJ* 20 (1970), 1–8, pls. 1–4; 129–140, pls. 29–34. For his discussion of the Dead Sea Scrolls, see "The Paleography of the Dead Sea Scrolls and Related Documents," *Scripta Hierosolymitana* 4 (1957), 56–87, a brilliant study in which he reviews much of the work done by others and applies his own keen insight to the materials at hand. His descriptions of scripts are general rather than detailed, but excellent nonetheless. Much of what he says in this article corroborates the work of Cross—and Avigad is almost too quick to pay tribute to the latter—but the judgments are independent and betray the eye of a master palaeographer. Included in it are many valuable comments concerning other materials of the Herodian period and what is available from the second–fourth centuries C.E.

8. See esp. *Gli scavi del "Dominus Flevit," Parte I*, eds. P. B. Bagatti and J. T. Milik (Jerusalem, 1958), but also the latter's "Trois tombeaux juifs," *Studii Biblici Franciscani Liber Annuus VII* (1956–57), 232–267; "Une lettre de Siméon bar Kokheba," *RB* 60 (1953), 276, n. 1; "Deux documents inédits du Désert de Juda," *Biblica* 38 (1957), 245–268, as well as his publications in *DJD*.

9. See esp. Sukenik's *'Ôṣār mĕgillôt gĕnuzôt* (Jerusalem, 1954).

10. Trever's article, "1Q Danᵃ, the Latest of the Qumran Manuscripts," *Revue de Qumrân* 26:7, fasc. 2 (April 1970), 277–286, is an example of his work in this area. His earlier study, "A Paleographic Study of the Jerusalem Scrolls," *BASOR* 113 (Feb. 1949), 6–23, reveals a combination of awareness and some inability to cope with the problems

(note: "strange irregularity of the base-line of the writing in contrast to the general regularity of the tops"; it did not occur to him, as it did to Cross and Birnbaum, that there was no base line in this script).

11. See e.g. Brownlee, "The Scroll of Ezekiel from the Eleventh Qumran Cave," *Revue de Qumrân* 13:4, fasc. 1 (Jan. 1963), 11–28.

12. We would call attention to a series of Birnbaum's articles: "The Date of the Hymns Scroll," *PEQ* 84 (1952), 94–103 (where he works with the concept of the ceiling line); "A Fragment in an Unknown Script," ibid., 118–120; "An Unknown Aramaic Cursive," *PEQ* 86 (1954), 23–32; "The Negeb Script," *VT* 6 (1956), 337–371 (his charts, which align the letter forms horizontally, are especially helpful here). Three of his articles, "The Beth Mashku Document," *PEQ* 87 (1955), 21 ff.; "The Kephar Beb-hayu Conveyance," *PEQ* 90 (1957), 108–132; and "Akiba and Bar Kokhba," *PEQ* 91 (1958), 137, seem to have been done with some carelessness. See esp. *The Qumran (Dead Sea) Scrolls and Paleography, BASOR,* SS 13–14 (New Haven, 1952) and, of course, *The Hebrew Scripts,* 2 vols. (London, 1954–57 and 1972).

13. J. Naveh, *The Development of the Aramaic Scripts,* The Israel Academy of Sciences and Humanities, V, no. 1 (Jerusalem, 1970). There are several noteworthy features about this work. It is a catalogue of all Aramaic inscriptions from the earliest through the third century B.C.E., a thorough discussion of the origin and development of the Aramaic scripts, a résumé of work done in the area of Aramaic palaeography, and a creative effort in methodology and interpretation of palaeographical findings. As an example of helpful analysis, we would call attention to Naveh's paragraph on p. 5: "The script as a whole develops as a result of modifications in its individual letters such as: (a) the dropping of elements; (b) the positional shift of strokes; (c) alterations in stance; (d) the joining of elements formerly written separately; and occasionally (e) the introduction of new elements." Summarizing a discussion of the work of individual scribes of Elephantine, he makes such significant statements as these: "On the basis of the above data, the handwriting of *Ntn br 'nny* can be traced for 15 or 21 years, his son's—for 18 years, and that of *Ḥgy br šm'yh*—for 35 years. It should be noted that the handwriting of these three scribes did not change over the years. A scribe's handwriting does not develop with his age; an elderly scribe could write in a script that he had evolved in his youth" . . . (p. 23). "The script of the Elephantine scribes, though formal, does not fit into the same category as that of the Arsham scribes. It would seem that while the scribes of Arsham preserved forms older by a hundred years, the Elephantine scribes were less conservative and preserved forms common only some fifty years prior to their time" (p. 24).

Other significant contributions by Naveh must include

a) "Canaanite and Hebrew Inscriptions (1960–1964)," *Leshonenu* 30 (1965), 65–80

b) "Phoenician and Punic Inscriptions (1960–1964)," ibid., 232–239

c) "Old Aramaic Inscriptions (1960–1965)," *Annali del Istituto orientale di Napoli,* N.S. 16 (1966), 19–36

d) "The Scripts from Two Ostraca from Elath," *BASOR* 183 (Oct. 1966), 27–30

e) "The Date of the Deir 'Alla Inscription in Aramaic Script," *IEJ* 17 (1967), 256–258

f) "A Palaeographical Note on the Distribution of the Hebrew Script," *HTR* 61 (1968), 68–74

g) "Aramaica Dubiosa," *JNES* 26 (1968), 317–325

h) "The Origin of the Mandaic Script," *BASOR* 198 (1970), 32–37

i) "The Ossuary Inscription from Giv'at Ha-mivtar," *IEJ* 20 (1970), 31–37

j) "The Aramaic Inscriptions of Asoka" (*hktwbwt h' rmywt šl 'swqh*)," *Leshonenu* 34 (1970), 125–136

k) "The Scripts in Palestine and Transjordan in the Iron Age," in *NEATC*, pp. 277–283

l) "Hebrew Texts in Aramaic Script in the Persian Period?" *BASOR* 203 (Oct. 1971), 27–32

His earlier publications, especially "A Hebrew Letter from the 7th Century B.C.," *IEJ* 10 (1960), 129–139, and "Old Hebrew Inscriptions in a Burial Cave," *IEJ* 13 (1963), 74–92, belong to an earlier stage of his career.

14. Cf. esp. Yadin, "The Expedition to the Judean Desert, 1960–1," *IEJ* 11 (1961) and 12 (1962); *The Finds from the Bar-Kokhba Period in the Cave of Letters,* Judean Studies I (Jerusalem, 1963); "The Excavation at Masada 1963–64," *IEJ* 15 (1965), 1–120; *Masada—Herod's Fortress and the Zealots Last Stand* (London, 1966); and *Bar-Kokhba* (London, 1971).

15. See the reports in Aharoni, *IEJ* 9 (1959), 55–56; 16 (1966), 1–7. See also *Excavations at Ramat Raḥel, Seasons 1959 and 1960* (Rome, 1962); and *BASOR* 197 (Feb. 1970), 16–42.

16. Lapp, "Late Royal Seals from Judah," *BASOR* 158 (April, 1960), 11–22; "Ptolemaic Stamped Handles from Judah," *BASOR* 172 (Dec., 1963), 22–35.

17. See Purvis's *The Samaritan Pentateuch and the Origin of the Samaritan Sect,* Harvard Semitic Monographs 2 (Cambridge, 1961) and especially chapter 2 for a discussion of the Samaritan script.

18. See Peckham's *The Development of the Late Phoenician Scripts,* Harvard Semitic Series 20 (Cambridge, 1966); "An Inscribed Jar from Bat-Yam," *IEJ* 16 (1966), 11–17; and "Notes on a Fifth-Century Phoenician Inscription from Kition, Cyprus (CIS 86)," *Orientalia* 37 (1968), 304–324, pls. XLIX–L.

19. Hanson, "Paleo-Hebrew Scripts in the Hasmonean Age," *BASOR* 175 (Oct. 1964), 26–42, and "Aramaic Funerary and Boundary Inscriptions from Asia Minor," *BASOR* 192 (Dec. 1968), 3–11.

20. Haines's treatise, *A Palaeographical Study of Aramaic Inscriptions Antedating 500 B.C.,* based on his Harvard dissertation of the same title (1966), is forthcoming.

21. For the post-Herodian period we can begin a relatively rich supply of (usually dated) documents in cursive script from Murabba'at, and some abundance of ossuary and funerary inscriptions. N. Avigad has a good appraisal of the materials in his important article, "The Paleography of the Dead Sea Scrolls and Related Documents" [N 7], esp. pp. 77–86. No systematic studies are available for the fourth to the twelfth centuries C.E., though Birnbaum has made a beginning.

22. The author has contended that there were small circles of scribes who kept the Hebrew script alive and that there is some sign of development between the last examples of the sixth century and the Hebrew script forms that appear in Hasmonaean times—with the meagre evidence of stamps and seals from the Persian period to back it up. See *BASOR* 175 [N 19], 30 and 42.

23. Cf. Cross, *BANE,* pp. 136 f.

24. See Naveh's monograph, *The Development of the Aramaic Script,* from which we derive the sketch that follows.

25. This is some seven hundred years after the first appearance of the alphabet. Cf. Cross and Lambdin in *BASOR* 160 [N 4e] for a review of materials to that date and a discussion of the palaeographical evidence. On ninth-century Aramaic scripts, see Cross, *BASOR* 193 [N 4q]. Naveh's date for the emergence of the Aramaic script in the early eighth century is too late.

26. The bulk of these materials are published by L. Delaporte in *Épigraphes araméens* (Paris, 1912). Naveh notes one other tablet as belonging to the corpus: the tablet published by G. R. Driver in *Iraq* 4 (1937), 16–18. That a lapidary tradition can actually

die out and be replaced by a well-developed cursive tradition is a reasonable expectation in the case of a script that belongs to a *lingua franca*. In the old period, Aramaic was used primarily for monumental inscriptions and such a tradition would be retained by those to whom the script is native. Once a language and its alphabet become the property of a commercial and political world, as Aramaic did, a whole new tradition is established by the professional scribes who ply their trade in all the major market cities. Lapidary inscriptions which (thus far) come from outside the area of the Aramaic homeland and its immediate environs have no choice but to use cursive scripts as a model.

27. Cf. his chapter in *BANE,* pp. 136–140, from which we draw the material that follows. For further discussion of when the Jews began to use Aramaic script, see Cross, *EI* 9 [N 4o], 26–27, and the critical essay by Naveh in *BASOR* 203 [N 131].

28. See N 21 above.

29. The earliest date assigned is late tenth century B.C.E., the date assigned by Cross in *BASOR* 168 [N 4i], p. 15. Naveh discusses this briefly in his chapter in *NEATC* [N 13k], pp. 277–283.

30. For a complete review of this period, see the series of three articles by Cross on epigraphic notes (N 4g).

31. Cf. Naveh, *BASOR* 203 [N 131], and the author, *BASOR* 175 [N 19].

32. For a discussion of this, see the author, *BASOR* 175, and J. Naveh, "Dated Coins of Alexander Janneus," *IEJ* 18 (1968), 20–25. Scroll materials discussed include Exodus fragments, the Genesis fragment from Cave IV, Leviticus fragments from Caves I and II, and the Leviticus fragments from Cave VI. Cross discusses a Herodian scroll of Numbers (4 QNum[b]) in *HTR* 57 (1964), 287, and classifies it as proto-Samaritan.

33. See esp. Purvis, *The Samaritan Pentateuch* [N 17].

34. To the knowledge of the writer, most of this material is being studied by Avigad, Naveh, and Cross. There is, of course, the matter of the great Jewish manuscripts from medieval to modern times, which we are omitting in this review.

35. The chief challenger to the early dating of the material was Solomon Zeitlin. For an expression of his point of view, see *The Dead Sea Scrolls and Modern Scholarship, JQR,* Monograph Series, No. 3 (Philadelphia, 1956). One of the stalwarts of the scholarly battle was the late Solomon A. Birnbaum, whose monograph, *The Qumran Scrolls and Paleography* [N 12], fairly blisters those who failed to recognize the importance of disciplined palaeographical study. A great deal of the total discussion was documented by Avigad in his important article, "The Paleography of the Dead Sea Scrolls and Related Documents" (N 7), and be Trever in "1Q Dan[a], the Latest of the Qumran Manuscripts" [N 10]. The most comprehensive summary of the total matter of dating is that of Cross in his chapter on the Jewish Scripts in *BANE* [N 4f].

36. Cross has paid special tribute to such scholars as Avigad and Milik in regard to the decipherment of the Scrolls; see e.g. *ALQ*[2], pp. 45–46.

37. See Pritchard's *Hebrew Inscriptions and Stamps from Gibeon,* Museum Monographs (Pennsylvania, 1959). See Cross in *BASOR* 168 [N 4g], 20, for a palaeographical analysis of the materials.

38. Cf. Cross in *BASOR* 165 [N 4g], 42–44, and J. Naveh, "Some Notes on the Reading of the Meṣad Ḥashavyahu Letter," *IEJ* 14 (1964), 158–159.

39. Cf. *ALQ*[2], pp. 188ff. The debated reading is *h'wyty/hr'wty/hr'ty* in II Sam. 24: 17a=MT I Chron. 21:17a. We quote as follows: "That *hr'ty* is the superior reading is evident. *Resh* and *waw* are virtually identical in the Jewish book hand of the third century B.C. The *matres lectionis waw* and *yodh,* probably introduced after the third century, were most easily confused in the late first century B.C." (p. 189).

40. In working with Psalms texts the author has made emendations of *'ḥr kbwd* to *'ḥrk byd* in Ps. 73:24b and actually follows 11QPs[a] in reading *'śyḥh* for MT *'śwḥh* in

Ps. 143:5c. A possible emendation of *zrym* to *zdym* suggests itself in Ps. 54:5a as an instance of confusion due to similarity of *resh* and *daleth*.

41. See, by the author, *The Psalms in Modern Speech,* vol. 1 (Philadelphia, 1968), 20, and accompanying n. 1. Compare the forms in the script of the Leviticus Fragment in DJD, III [א 4j], pl. xii. 5.

42. DJD III, 5 and n. 4.

43. *Les grottes de Murabba'at,* eds. P. Benoit, J. T. Milik et al., DJD, II (1961), 1 and n. 1. The resulting translation, "How I passed through Succoth and south," seems to be a considerable improvement over the conjectures one must make on the basis of MT.

44. The importance of using such an approach was stated as early as 1913 by S. R. Driver in his *Notes on the Hebrew Text and the Topography of the Books of Samuel* (Oxford, 1913). See the introduction, where he discusses the history of the Hebrew script as responsibly as it could be discussed at the time and brings up a number of matters in the realm of orthography as well.

45. "Studies in the Septuagint of the Book of Job," *HUCA* 36 (1965), secs. 1, 3–4, 17–20, and appendix. Here Orlinsky shows that in the *Vorlage* of the Greek *yod* and *waw,* the *bet* and *kaf,* frequently confused in the Jewish script, were in fact not readily confused. In a forthcoming study he will take up the matter anew.

46. By Albright, "The Oracles of Balaam," *JBL* 63 (1944), 207–234; "The Psalm of Habakkuk," *Studies in Old Testament Prophecy Presented to Theodore H. Robinson,* ed. H. H. Rowley (New York, 1950), pp. 1–18; and "A Catalogue of Early Hebrew Lyric Poems," *HUCA* 33 (1950–51), 1–39. By Cross and Freedman, "The Blessing of Moses," *JBL* 67 (1948), 191–210; "The Song of Miriam," *JNES* 14 (1955), 237–255; and "A Royal Song of Thanksgiving: II Sam. 22=Ps. 18," *JBL* 72 (1953), 15–34.

47. American Oriental Series, vol. 36 (New Haven, 1952).

48. We would call attention, especially, to two recent contributions by D. N. Freedman: "The Massoretic Text and the Qumran Scrolls: A Study of Orthography," *Textus* 2 (1962), 87–102, and "The Orthography of the Arad Ostraca," *IEJ* 19 (1969), 52–56. In the latter, he points out how the new materials confirm the conclusions reached in *Early Hebrew Orthography.* In the former, he reviews the orthographic practices of MT, then essays an appraisal of the Qumran Scrolls, showing that there is orthographic confusion in the Qumran materials and concluding that "Massoretic spelling was deliberately designed to combine the best features of the different orthographies current in the 3–4 c. B.C.," preserving continuity with conservative orthographies as that of the Samuel text but "incorporating the helpful features," of the fuller vowel spellings found in other materials from Qumran. D. W. Goodwin has attempted a harsh critique of the methods followed in the "Albright school" in his thesis, "Text Restoration Methods in Contemporary U.S.A. Biblical Scholarship" (Naples, 1969). At the surface level, it is accurate sometimes, but in attempting to assess the value of the textual methods followed by Albright and several of his students, Goodwin shows considerable lack of depth in his knowledge of linguistic principles and material. In the earlier part of his thesis he criticizes Albright for the alleged liberties he takes in relating Egyptian to West Semitic dialects but only exposes the fact that he, himself, knows very little Egyptian. It is in his third chapter (pp. 27–43) that he tackles the matter of orthography and, though he seems to be able to see what is going on in the work of Albright, Cross, and Freedman, he falls into the amateur's trap of confusing matters of linguistics with matters of orthography and fails to see how the data of linguistic evolution lend support to the patterns and principles that Cross and Freedman detect in the orthography. He seems most opposed to "rigid laws" in matters of either linguistics or orthography, as though that were an inherent evil in itself (a thorough exposure to the transformational theories of Noam Chomsky and his associates might lead him to be amazed at the

regularity that is normal to human speech), and is most critical when these men or Zellig Harris simply follow the principles that are made obvious by the data before them. When he attacks the notion of strictly consonantal spelling as a principle in Early Hebrew/Phoenician orthography by citing such words as *ra'š* as evidence against it, he fails to understand the phenomenon of historical spelling so common in the orthographies of almost all languages. In short, most of what he says to discredit the work done by Albright, Cross, and Freedman falls through because of his own lack of background and comprehension.

49. *JSS* 15 (Spring 1970). He cites data from as early as the Ras Shamra tablets or the Siloam inscription and notes the use of points and vertical marks as well as spaces to indicate division. The only exceptions in the age of our manuscripts are to be found on coins, tomb inscriptions, phylacteries, and the Copper Scroll. In the manuscripts, the principle of division excludes single-letter proclitic particles, at times the *nota accusativi* or such bound forms as construct plus regnant noun or infinitive absolute plus regnant verb.

50. Cf. J. A. Sanders, *The Psalms Scroll of Qumran Cave 11, DJD,* IV (1965), 14. Elsewhere, Sanders notes a case of haplography in the 11QSam Scroll which is detectable because of the stichometric divisions.

51. In the Habakkuk Commentary and in the Psalms Scroll.

52. Standing against many of the suggestions of G. R. Driver, most recently in "Abbreviations in the Massoretic Texts," *Textus* 1 (1960), 112–131. Though Driver claims to operate with caution, he seems to be opening the lid of a Pandora's box. There are simply too few controls to warrant much conjecture in this area. See also I. L. Seeligman, "Indications of Editorial Alterations and Adaptations in the MT and the LXX," *VT* 11 (1961), 207.

53. For a catalogue and discussion of the various kinds of scribal marks see, especially, M. Martin, *The Scribal Character of the Dead Sea Scrolls* (Louvain, 1958). His book lacks uniformity in its depth of understanding but it is a helpful catalogue of relevant data. For a most interesting comparison of what can be done in this area on the basis of MT and LXX alone, see Seeligman [N 52], 201–221.

54. As cited by Y. Yadin in *The Message of the Scrolls* (New York, 1957), pp. 85–87.

Appendix

THE BIBLIOGRAPHY
OF
G. ERNEST WRIGHT

1936

"The Chronology of Palestine in the Early Bronze Age," *BASOR* 63 (October), 12–21.

1937

"Exegesis and Eisegesis in the Interpretation of Scripture," *ET* 48 (May), 353–357.

"Palestine in the Chalcolithic Age," *BASOR* 66 (April), 21–25.

The Pottery of Palestine from the Earliest Times to the End of the Early Bronze Age (New Haven: American Schools of Oriental Research). ix+106 pages, 2 tables, 4 charts.

"The Troglodytes of Gezer," *PEQ* (January), 67–78.

1938

With Elihu Grant, *Ain Shems Excavations, Part IV* (Pottery), Biblical and Kindred Studies No. 7 (Haverford College). 70 plates.

"Herod's Nabataean Neighbor," *BA* 1.1 (February), 3–4.

"Iron in Israel," *BA* 1.2 (May), 5–8.

"A Gravestone of Uzziah, King of Judah," ibid., 8–9.

"Sun-image or 'Altar of Incense'?" ibid., 9–10.

"Some Personal Seals of Judean Royal Officials," ibid., 10–12.

Note on "Qosanal, Servant of the King," in *BA* 1.3 (September), 16.

"There Go the Ships," ibid., 19–20.

"Chronology of Palestinian Pottery in Middle Bronze I," *BASOR* 71 (October), 27–34.

"Lachish—Frontier Fortress of Judah," *BA* 1.4 (December), 21–30.

"Troglodytes and Giants in Palestine," *JBL* 57.3 (September), 305–309.

Review of "Tell Beit Mirsim II" (*AASOR* 17), in *Asia* (December).

1939

With Elihu Grant, *Ain Shems Excavations, Part V* (Text), Biblical and Kindred Studies No. 8 (Haverford College). vii+172 pages, 2 plates, 11 figures.

Note: "Cities Standing on their Tells," in *BA* 2.1 (February), 11–12.

"Palestine's First Great Artist," *BA* 2.2 (May), 16–20.

"Lamps, Politics, and the Jewish Religion," ibid., 22–24.

Review of Caiger, *Old Testament and Modern Discovery*, in *JBL* 58.2 (June), 191.

"Iron: The Date of Its Introduction into Common Use in Palestine," *AJA* 43.3 (July–September), 458–463.

"The Good Shepherd," *BA* 2.4 (December), 44–48.

1940

Review of Barrois, *Manuel d'archéologie biblique,* in *AJA* 44.3 (July–September), 400–401.

"Epic of Conquest," *BA* 3.3 (September), 25–40.

"The 1940 Conference," *Alumni Review* [of Presbyterian (McCormick) Theological Seminary] 16.2 (October), 116–118.

"The Syro-Palestinian Jar from Vounous, Cyprus," *PEQ* (October), 154–157.

Editorial: "To Our Readers," *BA* 3.4 (December), 42.

1941

"Archaeological Observations on the Period of the Judges and the Early Monarchy," *JBL* 60.1 (March), 27–42.

"Solomon's Temple Resurrected," *BA* 4.2 (May), 17–31.

Editorial: "Future Numbers" and "To All Subscribers," ibid., 18.

Review of Glueck, *The Other Side of the Jordan,* in *JBL* 60.2 (June), 189–194.

Review of Rowe, *The Four Canaanite Temples of Beth-shan, Part I* (1941), in *AJA* 45.3 (July–September), 483–485.

Review of Avi-Yonah, *Map of Roman Palestine,* in ibid., 485–486.

Review of Tufnell, Inge, Harding, *Lachish II, The Fosse Temple* (1940), in *AJA* 45.4 (October–December), 634–635.

Review of Ehrich, *Early Pottery of the Jebeleh Region,* in ibid., 635–636.

1942

Review of Loehr, *A History of Religion in the Old Testament,* in *WB* 1.2 (February), 13.

Review of Albright, *From the Stone Age to Christianity,* in ibid., 15–16.

Review of Rowe, *The Four Canaanite Temples of Beth-shan, Part I,* in *JQR* 32.2 (April), 445–448.

"Two Misunderstood Items in the Exodus-Conquest Cycle," *BASOR* 86 (April), 32–35.

Review of Ingholt, *Rapport Préliminaire sur Sept Campagnes de Fouilles à Hama en Syrie* (1932–1938), in *JBR* 10.3 (August), 173.

"The Terminology of Old Testament Religion and Its Significance," JNES 1.4 (October), 404–414.

Review of Gordon, *The Living Past,* in ibid., 496.

1943

"How Did Early Israel Differ from Her Neighbors?" *BA* 6.1 (February), 1–10, 13–20.

Notes: "Archaeological News and Views" (The New Museum of Hebrew University; Palestinian Agriculture—Ancient and Modern; Palestinian Population—Ancient and Modern; I Samuel 13:19–21), in *BA,* 6.2 (May), 32–36.

Review of McCown, *Ladder of Progress in Palestine,* in *WB* 3.1 (September–October), 29–30.

Notes: "Archaeological News and Views" (Glueck's work, McCown's *Ladder of Progress* . . . ; Tell Beit Mirsim III; Gordon's *The Loves and Wars of Baal and Anat* and Pritchard's *Palestinian Figurines* . . .), *BA* 6.4 (December), 68–70.

1944

The Challenge of Israel's Faith (University of Chicago Press). ix+108 pages.

Notes "Archaeological News and Views" (Cameron and Persepolis Elamite Tablets; Future Issues), in *BA* 7.2 (May), 30–32.

Note: Introduction to Symposium on "The Significance of the Temple in the Ancient Near East," in *BA* 7.3 (September), 41–44.

"The Significance of the Temple in the Ancient Near East. Part III, The Temple in Palestine-Syria," *BA* 7.4 (December), 65–77.

Review of Pritchard, *Palestinian Figurines in Relation to Certain Goddesses Known Through Literature,* American Oriental Series, Vol. 24, in *JBL* 63.4 (December), 426–430.

1945

With Floyd Vivian Filson, and an introductory article by W. F. Albright, *The Westminster Historical Atlas to the Bible* (Philadelphia: Westminster Press). 18 plates of maps, 77 figures, 114 pages.

"The Old Testament—Impediment or Bulwark of the Christian Faith" (Inaugural Address, September 5, 1945), *McCormick Seminary Addresses,* No. 4.

Review of Scott, *The Relevance of the Prophets,* in *WB* 4.3 (January–February), 3–6.

Review of M. S. and J. L. Miller, *Encyclopedia of Bible Life,* in *WB* 4.4 (March–April), 12–13.

Review of Benjamin Maisler et al., *The Graphic Historical Atlas of Palestine,* in *JBL* 64.4 (December), 558–560.

1946

The Challenge of Israel's Faith (London: SCM Press). November selection of British Religious Book-of-the-Month Club. 128 pages.

Review of Longacre, *The Old Testament: Its Form and Purpose,* in *WB* 4.3 (January–February), 15–16.

"The Literary and Historical Problem of Joshua 10 and Judges 1," *JNES* 5.2 (April), 105–114.

"Neo-Orthodoxy and the Bible," *JBR* 14.2 (May), 87–93.

"Interpreting the Old Testament," *Theology Today* 3.2 (July), 176–191.

Review of Finegan, *Light from the Ancient Past,* in *Theology Today* 3.3 (October), 421–422.

1947

Review of Glueck, *The River Jordan,* in *Journal of Religion* 27.1 (January), 75.

Review of Rowley, *The Re-Discovery of the Old Testament,* in *Presbyterian Tribune* 61 (January 11), 21.

Edited with Floyd Vivian Filson, *The Westminster Smaller Bible Atlas* (London: SCM Press). 16 plates.

"Biblical Archaeology Today," *BA* 10.1 (February), 7–24 (abbreviation of a paper prepared for *The Study of the Bible Today and Tomorrow,* 1947).

"The Present State of Biblical Archaeology," chapter 4 of *The Study of the Bible Today and Tomorrow,* ed. Harold R. Willoughby (University of Chicago Press), 74–97.

"The Christian Interpreter as Biblical Critic," *Interpretation* 1.2 (April), 131–152.

"Tell en-Nasbeh," *BA* 10.4 (December), 69–77.

Note: "Editor's Report," in ibid., 84–85.

Ceramic Notes in McCown, *[Excavations at] Tell en-Nasbeh* (Berkeley: Palestine Institute Pacific School of Religion; New Haven: American Schools of Oriental Research), pp. 223–227.

1948

One of the editors of *The Westminster Study Edition of the Holy Bible* (Philadelphia: Westminster Press).

"Dr. Waterman's View Concerning the Solomonic Temple," *JNES* 7.1 (January), 53.

"The God of Biblical Faith," *McCS* 1.3 (January), 7–10.

Notes: "Archaeological News and Views" (A New Journal, *Archaeology;* and Albright in Sinai), in *BA* 11.1 (February), 19–20.

"The Religion of the Good Man" (sermon outline), *McCS* 1.5 (March), 11.

"Palestinian Dilemma," *McCS* 1.7 (May), 12–13.

Note: "A Phenomenal Discovery," in *BA* 11.2 (May), 21–23.

Notes: "Archaeological News and Views" (New Law Codes Found; Some Recent Books), in ibid., 40–44.

Review of Baker, *The Witness of the Prophets,* in *WB* 7.5 (May–June), 20.

"The Bible in the Church," *The Christian News-Letter* (London), Supplement to 314, June 23.

Review of McCown et al., *Tell en Nasbeh,* Vols. I–II (Berkeley and New Haven, 1947), in *AJA* 52.3 (July–September), 470–472.

"The Old Testament Attitude toward Civilization," *Theology Today* 5.3 (October), 327–339.

"Amsterdam," *McCS* 2.2 (November), 12–13.

1949

"The World Council of Churches and Biblical Interpretation," *Interpretation* 3.1 (January), 50–61.

"The Biblical Teaching Concerning Divorce," *McCS* 2.6 (March), 3–6.

"Why the Old Testament?" *Growing* 1.3 (April–June), 6–7.

Notes: "Archaeological News and Views" (The Cave Excavated; Fragments of the Book of Daniel Found; The Extent of the Total Discovery; Photographs of the Jerusalem Scrolls), in *BA* 21.2 (May), 32–36.

Notes: "Archaeological News and Views" (Additional Comments on the Scroll Cave; A New Museum; The Excavation at Tell el-Far'ah; Some New Books), in *BA* 21.3 (September), 64–68.

"A Significant Document of the World Council of Churches," *McCS* 3.1 (October), 3–6, 14.

"The Problem of Archaizing Ourselves," *Interpretation* 3.4 (October), 450–456.

Notes: "Archaeological News and Views" (Commentary and slight expansion on articles by Diringer and Wylie; review of Reed's *The Asherah in the Old Testament*), in *BA* 21.4 (December), 91–92.

Review of Kelso, *The Ceramic Vocabulary of the Old Testament*, in *JBL* 68.4 (December), 380–381.

Review of Montgomery, *The Bible—The Book of God and of Man*, in ibid., 401.

1950

The Old Testament Against Its Environment. Studies in Biblical Theology, No. 2 (London: SCM Press; Chicago: Regnery).

"Archaeology and the Bible," *This Generation* 2.2 (January–March), 3, 18.

Notice of *A Remapping of the Bible World: Nelson's New Bible Maps*, eds. H. G. May and C. C. McCown, in *JBR* 18.2 (April), 149.

Review of Needler, *Palestine, Ancient and Modern: A Handbook and Guide to the Palestinian Collection of the Royal Ontario Museum*, in *AJA* 54.2 (April), 149.

"The Discoveries at Megiddo, 1935–39," *BA* 13.2 (May), 28–46.

Notes: "Archaeological News and Views" (Microfilming of Ancient Manuscripts; New Testament; Jericho), in ibid., 46–48.

Review of Welker, *The Painted Pottery of the Near East in the Second Millennium B.C. and Its Chronological Development*, in *JNES* 9.3 (July), 185–186.

"Freedom and Welfare," *The Presbyterian Tribune* 64 (July–August), 22–23.

"Recent European Study in the Pentateuch," *JBR* 18.4 (October), 216–224.

Review of Dentan, *Preface to Old Testament Theology*, in *JBL* 69.4 (December), 393–397.

Review of Baab, *The Theology of the Old Testament*, in ibid., 397–400.

Review of Loud (Field Director, The Megiddo Expedition), *Megiddo II, Seasons of 1935–39*, in *JAOS* 70.1, 56–60.

Bible note: "Election and Faith in Genesis," in *McCS* 3.6 (March), 11.

Bible note: "The Bible Versus Spiritualism, Astrology, and Magic," in *McCS* 4.2 (November), 11.

"B. A. Growth," *BA* 3.4 (December), 100.

1951

"From the Bible to the Modern World," in *Biblical Authority for Today*, eds. Alan Richardson and Wolfgang Schweitzer (London: SCM Press), 219–239.

"The Study of the Old Testament: The Changing Mood in the Household of Wellhausen," chapter 2 of *Protestant Thought in the Twentieth Century: Whence and Whither?* ed. Arnold S. Nash (New York: Macmillan), 17–44.

"The Israelite Law for the Common Life," *McCS* 4.4 (January), 7–10.

Review of *The Jews: Their History, Culture, and Religion,* ed. L. Finkelstein, in *JBR* 19.1 (January), 28.

Note: "Archaeological News and Views" (Some Radiocarbon Dates), in *BA* 14.1 (February), 31–32.

Editorial [on the Bible as Understandable to the Unlearned], in *McCS* 4.6 (March), 2.

"The Bible in the World Council of Churches," *Religion in Life,* 20.2 (Spring), 214–224.

"An Important Correlation Between the Palestinian and Syrian Chalcolithic," *BASOR* 122 (April), 52–55.

"The Unity of the Bible," *Interpretation* 5.2 (April), 131–133.

"The Unity of the Bible: A Summary," *Interpretation* 5.3 (July), 304–317.

"The Old Testament, a Bulwark Against Paganism," *International Review of Missions* 40.159 (July), 265–276.

With Emily DeNyse Wright, "He Speaketh Still," Lessons 1–6, *Crossroads* 1.3 (April–June), 46–60; with Scripture Exposition and Teaching Methods, *Westminster Teacher* 1.3 (April–June), 24–51.

"The Problem of Self-Will," *Growing* 3 (July–September), 3–4.

"Archaeological Discoveries at Megiddo: Megiddo in the Time of David and Solomon," *Bible League Quarterly* 207 (London, October–December), 5–7 (reprinted from *BA* 13.2 [May 1950]).

1952

God Who Acts: Biblical Theology as Recital. Studies in Biblical Theology, No. 8 (London: SCM Press; Chicago: Regnery). 132 pages.

With Floyd Vivian Filson, *Westminster Historical Maps of Bible Lands,* Westminister Aids to the Study of the Scriptures (Philadelphia: Westminster Press). 16 plates.

"The Faith of Israel," in *IB,* I, 349–389.

"From the Bible to the Modern World," in *Biblical Authority for Today,* eds. Alan Richardson and Wolfgang Schweitzer (London: SCM Press, 1951; Philadelphia: Westminster Press), 219–239.

Note: "Mystery and Knowledge" (Deut. 30:11–14), in *McCS* 5.7 (April), 11.

Notes: "Archaeological News and Views" (New Excavations at Jericho; More Cave Manuscripts, Dibon in Moab, Varia), in *BA* 15.2 (May), 43–46.

Review of Allis, "God Spake by Moses," in *The Presbyterian Tribune,* 66.9 (June), 8–9.

"Wherein Lies the Unity of the Bible," *JBR* 20.3 (July), 194–198.

"A Brief Rejoinder," ibid., 201.

"Weighing Zionism and the ACFJ" [American Council for Judaism], a review of E. Berger, *A Partisan History of Judaism,* in *The Presbyterian Tribune* 68.1 (October), 1–2.

"Many Volumes, One Book," *Crossroads,* 3.1 (October–December), 25–26, 50.

1953

Introduction and Exegesis of Deuteronomy, in IB, II, 311–537.

Notes: "Archaeological News and Views" (More News on the Manuscript Search; Qumran Excavations; Wadi Murabba^eat), in *BA* 16.1 (February), 17–20.

Notes: "Archaeological News and Views" (Tushingham and the Jericho Excavations; Future Numbers; The Qumran or Dead Sea Manuscripts), in *BA* 16.3 (September), 67–68.

"Holy War in Israel," *McCS* 6.4 (January), 3–6.

"The Rule of God," *McCS* 7.2 (November), 3–6.

"The Identity of God," *Anglican Outlook and News Digest* 9.1 (November), 12–16.

"Man in Society," *Anglican Outlook and News Digest* 9.2 (December), 14–15.

1954

With an ecumenical committee in Chicago, *The Biblical Doctrine of Man in Society,* Ecumenical Biblical Studies, No. 2 (published for the Study Department of the World Council of Churches; London: SCM Press). 176 pages. Chinese translation, 1959.

Review of Rowley, *From Joseph to Joshua,* in *Journal of Religion* 34 (January), 58.

"The Levites in Deuteronomy," *VT* 4.3, 325–330.

"Man in Society," *Anglican Outlook and News Digest,* 9.3 (January), 13–14.

"The Rule of God," *Anglican Outlook and News Digest,* 9.4 (February), 14–16.

Note: "Epitaph of a Judean Official," in *BA* 17.1 (February), 22–23.

"Ovid R. Sellers: Scholar Among His Books," *McCS* 7.7 (April), 6–10.

Notes: "Archaeological News and Views" (A New Atomic Clock; New Discoveries in Greece; Explorations in the Negeb; New Excavations), in *BA* 17.2 (May), 47–48.

Review of Rowley, *The Unity of the Bible,* in *JBR* 22.4 (October), 272–274.

Note: "Additional Note on Excavations," in *BA* 17.4 (December), 104.

"How Israelites Dressed," *McCS* 8.3 (December), 3–6.

"Tithes and Offerings," *Crossroads* 5.1 (October–December), 11–12, 14.

1955

With Floyd Vivian Filson, and an introductory article by W. F. Albright, *The Westminster Historical Atlas to the Bible,* revised edition (Philadelphia: Westminster Press, 1945).

"Biblical Archaeology," in *The Teachers' Commentary,* 7th ed., revised; eds. G. Henton Davis and Alan Richardson (London: SCM Press; Philadelphia: Westminster Press), pp. 36–45.

"Kingship in Israel," "Memorials and Sacred Stones," "Moses," "Palestine," "Red Sea," "Sinai," "Temples, Hebrew," in *Encyclopedia of Religious Knowledge,* eds. Loetscher et al. (Grand Rapids: Baker Book House).

"The Knowledge of God," *McCS* 8.5 (February), Alumni Supplement, 1–12.

"Judean Lachish," *BA* 18.1 (February), 9–17.

"The Stevens' Reconstruction of the Solomonic Temple," *BA* 18.2 (May), 41–44.

Note: "News and Books," in ibid., 44–46, 47–48.

"Israelite Daily Life," *BA* 18.3 (September), 50–79.

Note: "Archaeological News and Views: Hazor and the Conquest of Canaan," in
  BA 18.4 (December), 106–108.

"The Unity of the Bible," *Journal of Religious Thought*, 13.1 (Autumn–Winter
  1955–56), 5–19.

"The Unity of the Bible," *Scottish Journal of Theology* 8.4 (December), 337–
  352.

Review of Gross, *Weltherrschaft als religiöse Idee im Alten Testament*, in *JBL*
  74.2 (June), 130–131.

Review of Nielsen, *Oral Tradition*, in *JBL* 74.4 (December), 284–285.

Review of Barrois, *Manuel d'archeologie biblique*, Vol. II (Paris, 1953), in *JNES*
  14.2 (April), 133–135.

Review of Tufnell, *Lachish III: The Iron Age*, in *JNES* 14.3 (July), 188–189.

Review of Tufnell, *Lachish III: The Iron Age*, in *VT* 5.1, 97–105.

1956

Review of Alt, *Die Stadtstaat Samaria*, in *JNES* 15.2 (April), 124–125.

Review of Vincent, *Jérusalem de l'Ancien Testament. Tome I: Archéologie de la
  ville*, in ibid., 125–127.

Review of Napier, *From Faith to Faith*, in *The Pastor* 19 (January), 38–39.

"The Knowledge of God," *The Reformed Review* 9.2 (January), 1–11.

"Report on a Theological Conversation," *McCS* 9.5 (February), 3–6.

"Progressive Revelation," *The Christian Scholar* 39.1 (March), 61–65.

Review of Napier, *From Faith to Faith*, in *JBL* 75.2 (June), 149.

Review of Kaufman, *The Biblical Account of the Conquest of Palestine*, in ibid.,
  154–155.

With Frank M. Cross, "The Boundary and Province Lists of the Kingdom of
  Judah," *JBL* 75.3 (September), 202–226.

"Palestinian Excavation, 1956," *McCS* 10.2 (November), 3–6.

"The First Campaign at Tell Balatah (Shechem)," *BASOR* 144 (December),
  9–20.

1957

Biblical Archaeology (London: Gerald Duckworth; Philadelphia: Westminster
  Press). 288 pages.

With R. H. Fuller, *The Book of the Acts of God*, Christian Faith Series (New
  York: Doubleday). 372 pages.

With K. Galling, "Ausgrabungen. III. In Palastina," in *Die Religion in Geschichte und Gegenwart*, 3d ed., I (Tubingen: J. C. B. Mohr [Paul Siebeck]),
  cols. 759–762.

"Shechem, the 'Navel of the Land.' Part III. The Archaeology of the City," *BA*
  20.1 (February), 19–32.

Review of Burrows, *The Dead Sea Scrolls,* in *Archaeology* 10.1 (Spring), 77–78.

Review of Parrot, *Discovering Buried Worlds* (Philosophical Library, 1955), in *Archaeology* 10.2 (Summer), 146.

Review of Parrot, *The Flood and Noah's Ark* (Philosophical Library, 1955), in ibid., 146.

Review of Parrot, *The Tower of Babel* (Philosophical Library, 1955), in ibid., 146.

Review of Baly, *The Geography of the Bible: A Study in Historical Geography* (New York: Harper, 1957), in *BA* 20.3 (September), 79.

Review of Baly, *The Geography of the Bible,* in *JBR* 20.4 (October), 346–347.

"McCormick at Shechem, 1957," *McCS* 11.2 (November), 3–6.

"The Second Campaign at Tell Balatah (Shechem)," *BASOR* 148 (December), 11–28.

"Bringing Old Testament Times to Life," *National Geographic* 112.6 (December), 833–864.

1958

Biblische Archäologie. German translation by Christine von Mertens (Göttingen: Vandenhoeck & Ruprecht).

De Bijbel Ontdekt in Aarde en Steen (The Bible Discovered in Earth and Stone). Dutch translation by R. A. de Langhe and Th. C. Vriezen (Baarn, The Netherlands: Het Wereldvenster).

"Erwählung I. Im AT und im Judentum," in *Die Religion in Geschichte und Gegenwart,* 3d ed., II (Tübingen: J. C. B. Mohr [Paul Siebeck]), cols. 610–612.

"The Problem of the Transition between the Chalcolithic and Bronze Ages," *EI,* V (Mazar volume), 37–45.

"Report of the Representative on the Board of Trustees of the American Schools of Oriental Research," *JBL* 77.1 (March), xix–xxi.

"Archaeology and Old Testament Studies," ibid., 39–51.

Review of Parrot, *Nineveh and the Old Testament* (Philosophical Library, 1955), in *Archaeology* 11 (Spring), 70.

"Comment on Yadin's Dating of the Shechem Temple," *BASOR* 150 (April), 34–35.

With W. F. Albright, "Comments on Professor Garber's Article" (*in re* the Solomonic temple), *JBL* 77.2 (June), 129–132.

Note: "New Books Received," in *BA* 21.3 (September), 77–80.

Footnote: the dating of Hellenistic deposits at Shechem, in *BASOR* 151 (October), 37, fn. 46.

Note: "A Solomonic City Gate at Gezer," in *BA* 21.4 (December), 103–104.

"Chronique Archéologique, Sichem," *RB* 65, 253–260.

1959

With an ecumenical committee in Chicago, *The Biblical Doctrine of Man in Society* (published for the Study Department of the World Council of Churches; London: SCM Press, 1954). Translated into Chinese by Chan Kui

(Hong Kong: The Council on Christian Literature for Overseas Chinese, 1959). 168 pages.

Inclina tu Oido: Aspectos de la Fe de Israel (*The Rule of God: Essays in Biblical Theology*), Corrientes 728. (Buenos Aires [Catedra Carnahan]: Editorial La Aurora). 137 pages.

Review of Kenyon, *Digging Up Jericho* (1957), in *AJA* 63.1 (January), 91–92.

Review of Vincent, *Jérusalem de l'Ancien Testament,* Parts II–III (1956), in *JNES* 18.1 (January), 79–82.

"Report of the Representative on the Board of Trustees of the American Schools of Oriental Research," *JBL* 78.1 (March), xxi–xxiii.

Review of Reid, *The Authority of Scripture: A Study of Reformation and Post-Reformation Understanding of the Bible,* in ibid., 88–90.

Review of Koehler, *Old Testament Theology,* in *Religious Education,* 54.4 (July–August), 386–387.

"Philistine Coffins and Mercenaries," *BA* 22.3 (September), 54–66.

"Samaria," ibid., 67–78.

"The Biblical Story in the History of Civilization," *The Church School Worker* (E & R Church), 10.2 (October), 16–21.

"Israelite Samaria and Iron Age Chronology," *BASOR* 155 (October), 13–29.

"The Achievement of Nelson Glueck," and "Is Glueck's Aim to Prove that the Bible Is True," *BA* 22.4 (December), 98–108.

Review of Bright, *A History of Israel,* in *WB* 18.4 (December), 1–2.

Review of Schilling, *Isaiah Speaks,* in *The Christian Century* 76.49 (December 9), 1442.

1960

Biblical Archaeology (abridged) (Philadelphia: Westminster Press). xii+198 pages.

With R. H. Fuller, *The Book of the Acts of God* (Garden City, N.Y.: Doubleday Anchor). xvi+420 pages.

With R. H. Fuller, *The Book of the Acts of God,* revised edition (London: Gerald Duckworth).

Assisted by Roger Tomes, *Introduction to Biblical Archaeology* (London: Gerald Duckworth).

Edited with Floyd V. Filson, *Kleiner Historischer Bibelatlas.* Deutsche Bearbeitung von Théodor Schlatter (Stuttgart: Calwer Verlag). 30 pages.

The Rule of God: Essays in Biblical Theology (Garden City, N.Y.: Doubleday). ix+133 pages.

"Old Testament Scholarship in Prospect," *JBR* 28, 182–193.

Review of Jacob, *Theology and the Old Testament,* in *JBL* 79.1 (March), 78–81.

Review of Mowinckel, *The Old Testament as Word of God,* in *Religion in Life* 29.2 (Spring), 317–318.

"Modern Issues in Biblical Studies: History and the Patriarchs," *ET* 71 (July), 3–7.

Review of Simons, *The Geographical and Topographical Texts of the Old Testament,* in *JBL* 69.4 (December), 372–375.

"The Last Thousand Years Before Christ," *National Geographic* 115.6 (December), 812–853.

1961

Editor of *The Bible and the Ancient Near East: Essays in Honor of William Fox-well Albright* (Garden City, N.Y.: Doubleday). And author of chapter 4, "The Archaeology of Palestine," pp. 73–112.

Co-editor, with David Noel Freedman, *The Biblical Archaeologist Reader* (Garden City, N.Y.: Doubleday Anchor). And author of chapter 1 b & c; chapter 12, part III; chapter 20 c.

"Schöpfung II. Im AT," in *Die Religion in Geschichte und Gegenwart*, 3d ed., V (Tübingen: J. C. B. Mohr [Paul Siebeck]), cols. 1473–1477.

"The Old Testament Basis for the Christian Mission," in *The Theology of the Christian Mission*, ed. Gerald H. Anderson (New York: McGraw-Hill), 17–30.

With L. E. Toombs, "The Third Campaign at Balâṭah (Shechem)," *BASOR* 161 (February), 11–54.

Note: "More on King Solomon's Mines," in *BA* 24.2 (May), 59–62.

With Frank M. Cross, "The Study of the Old Testament at Harvard," *Harvard Divinity School Bulletin* 25.3–4 (April–July), 14–20.

Review of Tufnell, *Lachish IV. The Bronze Age*, in *JNES* 20.3 (July), 210–212.

"Praise and Thanksgiving," *McCQ* 15.1 (November), 18–22.

Review of Muilenburg, *The Way of Israel: Biblical Faith and Ethics*, in *USQR* 17.1 (November), 77–78.

1962

Biblical Archaeology, revised and expanded edition (London: Gerald Duckworth, 1962; Philadelphia: Westminster Press, 1963).

"The Lawsuit of God: A Form-Critical Study of Deut. 32," in *Israel's Prophetic Heritage*, Muilenburg *Festschrift*, eds. B. W. Anderson and Walter Harrelson (New York: Harper), pp. 26–67.

"Exodus, Book of," in *IDB*, II, 188–197; "Exodus, Route of," in *IDB*, II, 197–199; "Sinai, Mount," *IDB*, IV, 376–378; (with Joseph L. Mihelic) "Plagues in Exodus" in *IDB*, III, 822–824.

"Truth—Freedom or Slavery," *Harvard Divinity School Bulletin* 26.2 (January), 11–18.

"Cult and History: A Study of a Current Problem in Old Testament Interpretation," *Interpretation* 16.1 (January), 3–20.

Review of Barr, *The Semantics of Biblical Language*, in *USQR* 17 (May), 350–353.

Review of Kenyon, *Archaeology in the Holy Land*, in *AJA* 66.2 (April), 207.

"Archaeological Fills and Strata," *BA* 25.2 (May), 34–40.

Review of Steinmann et al., *Josué* in *JBL* 81.2 (June), 208–209.

Review of Steinmann et al., *Les Juges*, in ibid.

"History in Theological Education," *Harvard Divinity School Bulletin* 27.1 (October), 1–16.

"The Samaritans at Shechem," *HTR* 55 (October), 357–366.

"Selected Seals from the Excavations at Balâṭah (Shechem)," *BASOR* 167 (October), 5–13.

1963

God Who Acts: Biblical Theology as Recital, Studies in Biblical Theology, No. 8.
Translated into Japanese by Michiharu Shinya. (Tokyo: The Board of Publications, The United Church of Christ in Japan). 225 pages.

"The Unity of the Bible," in *American Christianity: An Interpretation with
Representative Documents,* II (New York: Scribner), Document 168, pp.
478–483 (reprint of "Wherein Lies the Unity of the Bible," *JBR* 20 (1952),
194–198).

With Lawrence E. Toombs, "The Fourth Campaign at Balâṭah (Shechem),"
BASOR 169 (February), 1–60.

With R. H. Fuller, *The Book of the Acts of God.* Translated into Japanese by
Tamotsu Hirano (Tokyo: The Board of Publications, the United Church of
Christ in Japan).

Review of Robert North, S.J., *Ghassul 1960, Excavation Report,* in *CBQ* 25.2
(April), 202–204.

Review of R. J. and L. J. Braidwood, *Excavations in the Plain of Antioch,* I:
The Earlier Assemblages, Phases A-J, in *JNES* 22.4 (October), 282–284.

Review of J. B. Pritchard, *The Water System of Gibeon,* in *JNES* 22 (July),
210–211.

"History and Reality: The Importance of Israel's 'Historical' Symbols for the
Christian Faith," in *The Old Testament and Christian Faith: A Theological
Discussion,* ed. by Bernhard W. Anderson (New York: Harper), 176–199.

"From the Hebrew Patriarchs to Alexander the Great and John Hyrcanus: 1600
Years of Shechem and its Pillars of the Covenant," Archaeological Section
No. 2144, *Illustrated London News,* Vol. 243, No. 6471 (August 10), 204–
208.

1964

Editor with Samuel H. Miller, *Ecumenical Dialogue at Harvard: The Roman
Catholic-Protestant Colloquium* (The Belknap Press of Harvard University
Press). And author of "Seminar I. Biblical Studies: Record and Interpreta-
tion," pp. 293–315.

The Book of Isaiah, The Layman's Bible Commentary, II (Richmond, Va.: John
Knox Press).

De boodschap van het Oude Testament (The Message of the Old Testament).
Dutch translation by J. Rinzema (Aalten, The Netherlands: de Graafschap).

"Antioch," "Astarte," "Baal," "Baalbek," "Byblos," "Canaanites," "Jericho,"
"Jerusalem: Early History," "Megiddo," "Palmyra," "Philistines," "Phoenicia," "Samaria," "Shechem," "Sinai, Mount," "Tyre," in *Encyclopedia International* (New York: Grolier).

"Philistine Coffins and Mercenaries" (revised from *BA* 22.3 [September 1959],
53–66); "The Discoveries at Megiddo, 1935–1939" (revised from *BA* 13.2
[May 1950], 28–46); "Samaria" (revised from *BA* 22.3 [September 1959],
67–78); "Judean Lachish" (revised from *BA* 18.1 [February 1955], 9–17),
in *The Biblical Archaeologist Reader,* 2, eds. David Noel Freedman and Ed-

ward F. Campbell, Jr. (Garden City, N.Y.: Doubleday Anchor), chapters 5, 12, 13, 15.

"The Semitic Museum," *Newsletter,* The Harvard Foundation for Advanced Study and Research (January 6), pp. 3–5.

"Archaeology, History and Theology," *Harvard Divinity Bulletin* 28.3 (April), 85–96.

Review of D. M. Beegle, *The Inspiration of Scripture* (Philadelphia: Westminster Press), in *Harvard Divinity Bulletin* 28.4 (July), 118–119.

"God of Gods, Lord of Lords," *Opening Doors* 17.1 (October–December), 1–3.

Introduction to Biblical Archaeology. Abridged by Roger Tomes. Translated into Japanese.

Review of J. Lindblom, "Prophecy in Ancient Israel," in *Interpretation* 18.3 (July), 360–363.

1965

Editor of *The Bible and the Ancient Near East: Essays in Honor of William Foxwell Albright* (Anchor edition). And author of chapter 4, "The Archaeology of Palestine," pp. 85–139.

Shechem: Biography of a Biblical City (New York: McGraw-Hill; London: Gerald Duckworth).

"Tyre," *Grolier Universal Encyclopedia,* Vol. 10, 200.

"God's Covenant—The Setting for the Common Life," *Opening Doors* 17.2 (January–March), 1–4.

Review of Emmanuel Anati, *Palestine before the Hebrews: A History, from the Earliest Arrival of Man to the Conquest of Canaan* (New York: Knopf, 1963), in *AJA* 69.1 (January), 68–70.

Review of H. J. Franken and C. A. Franken Battershill, *A Primer of Old Testament Archaeology* (Leiden: Brill, 1963), in *Archaeology* 18.1 (March), 74–75.

With Robert J. Bull, "Newly-Discovered Temples on Mount Gerizim in Jordan," *HTR* 58.2 (April), 234–237.

With R. J. Bull, J. A. Callaway, E. F. Campbell, Jr., J. F. Ross, "The Fifth Campaign at Balâṭah (Shechem)," *BASOR* 180 (December), 7–41.

With E. F. Campbell, Jr., "Sichem," *RB* 72, 415 ff.

"The Nations in Hebrew Prophecy," *Encounter* 26, Memorial Issue for Toyozo W. Nakari (Spring), 225–237.

1966

With Reginald Fuller, *The Book of the Acts of God* (New York: Penguin Books, 1966). First published in 1957 by Doubleday.

Review of Nelson Glueck, *Deities and Dolphins,* in the *Journal of the Central Conference of American Rabbis* 13.7 (October), 63–66.

"The Faith of Israel," translated into Japanese by Michiharu Shinya (Tokyo: Seibun-Sha, 1966, 1967) from *IB,* I (1952), 349–389.

"Fresh Evidence for the Philistine Story," *BA* 29.3 (September), 70–86.

"Reflections Concerning Old Testament Theology," *Studia Biblica et Semitica* (Wageningen), 376–388.

1967

"What is Theology?" *McCQ* 20.4 (May).

"The Provinces of Solomon," in *EI*, 8, the E. L. Sukenik volume, pp. 58–68.

"Ernst Sellin," in *ZDPV* 83, 84–85.

"Shechem," in *Archaeology and Old Testament Study*, ed. D. Winton Thomas, Jubilee Volume of the Society for Old Testament Study (Oxford), Part v, pp. 355–371.

1969

"Archaeological Method in Palestine—An American Interpretation," *EI* 9, (Albright Festschrift), 120–133.

The Old Testament and Theology (New York: Harper & Row).

With E. F. Campbell, Jr., "Tribal League Shrines in Amman and Shechem," *BA* 32.4 (December), 104–116.

"Biblical Archaeology Today," in *NDBA*, pp. 149–165.

1970

"The Phenomenon of American Archaeology in the Near East," in *NEATC*, pp. 3–40.

"Historical Knowledge and Revelation," in *Translating and Understanding the Old Testament: Essays in honor of Herbert G. May*, eds. Harry Thomas Frank and William L. Reed (New York and Nashville: Abingdon), pp. 279–303.

With E. F. Campbell, Jr., "Excavations in Shechem, 1956–1969," *Qadmoniot* 3.4, 126–133.

"The Significance of Ai in the Third Millennium B.C.," in *Archäologie und Altes Testament: Festschrift für Kurt Galling*, eds. Arnulf Kuschke and Ernst Kutsch (Tübingen), pp. 299–319.

With W. G. Dever and H. Darrell Lance, "Gezer I: Preliminary Report of the 1964–66 Seasons," *Annual of the Hebrew Union College Biblical and Archaeological School in Jerusalem*, Vol. 1.

1971

"Biblical Archaeology Today," in *NDBA* (Anchor edition), pp. 167–186.

"Thor Heyerdahl and His Papyrus Boat," *Buried History*, The Australian Institute of Archaeology (March), 16–17.

Review of "The Archaeology of Palestine from the Neolithic Through the Middle Bronze Age," in *JAOS* 91.2 (April–June), 276–293.

"The Theological Study of the Bible," in *The Interpreter's One-Volume Commentary on the Bible* (New York and Nashville: Abingdon), pp. 983–988.

"What Archaeology Can and Cannot Do," *BA* 34.3 (September), 70–75.

"A Problem of Ancient Topography: Lachish and Eglon," *BA* 34.3 (September), 76–86.

With Floyd V. Filson, Spanish translation of revised edition of *Westminster Historical Atlas to the Bible.*

"The Divine Name and The Divine Nature," *Perspective* 12, Essays in memory of Paul W. Lapp (Spring), 177–185.

1973

"The Theology of the Deuteronomic History of Israel in the Promised Land," *Encounter* (Christian Theological Seminary), forthcoming.

1974

"The Conquest Theme in the Bible," in *A Light Unto My Path: Old Testament Studies in Honor of Jacob M. Myers,* eds. H. N. Bream, R. D. Heim, C. A. Moore (Temple University Press), pp. 509–518.

Principal Advisor and Editorial Consultant for *Great People of the Bible and How They Lived.* The Reader's Digest Association, Inc., Pleasantville, N.Y.

With Lawrence E. Stager and Anita Walker, Co-editor of *American Expedition to Idalion, Cyprus. First Preliminary Report: Seasons of 1971 and 1972* (Supplement to the Bulletin of the American Schools of Oriental Research, No. 18), published by The American Schools of Oriental Research, Cambridge, Mass.

"The Tell: Basic Unit for Reconstructing Complex Societies in the Near East," in *Reconstructing Complex Societies, an Archaeological Colloquium,* edited by Charlotte B. Moore (Supplement to the Bulletin of the American Schools of Oriental Research, No. 20), published by The American Schools of Oriental Research, Cambridge, Mass.

Index of Authors

Abel, F.-M., 206
Abrahams, I, 387
Achtemeier, P. J., 186
Ackroyd, P., 382, 387, 527, 553, 557
Adams, J. L., 466, 477
Åstrom, P., 14, 34–35
Aharoni, Y., 5, 22, 149, 190, 197, 201, 205, 206,
   207, 208, 240, 241, 244, 247–48, 252, 258,
   259, 260, 266, 275, 277, 279, 281, 283, 287,
   288, 299, 300, 564, 573
Ahlström, G. W., 386
Aimé-Giron, N., 569
Akurgal, E., 221
Albeck, H., 445
Albrektson, B., 119
Albright, W. F., 4, 5, 6, 7, 10, 11, 12, 13, 20, 21,
   22, 23, 25, 26, 27–28, 30, 34, 36, 37, 48, 52,
   53, 55, 56, 57, 58, 60, 63, 82, 86, 87, 95,
   96–97, 98–99, 100, 101, 102, 105, 120, 150,
   157, 185, 189, 191, 192, 198, 199, 204, 206,
   208, 209, 218, 221, 239, 240, 242, 243, 244,
   245, 247, 248, 259, 277, 280, 290, 292, 294,
   295, 298, 299, 300, 303, 319, 323, 331, 337,
   338, 378, 386, 545, 558, 562, 564, 568, 570,
   575, 576, 580, 581, 585, 587, 589, 591, 592
Alleman, H. C., 476
Allis, O. T., 584
Alonso-Schökel, L., 378, 386, 525
Alt, A., 37, 39, 40, 52, 53, 118, 130, 157, 167,
   191, 198–99, 200, 204, 205, 206, 208, 367,
   375, 396, 554, 586
Altmann, A., 119, 241, 359, 386, 387, 412, 476,
   554
Amiram, Ruth, 5, 13, 14, 21, 22, 25, 31, 34, 35,
   36, 259, 275, 277, 279, 281, 282, 287, 288, 292
Amsler, S., 526, 527
Anati E., 591
Anderson, B. W., 53, 101, 358, 359, 477, 527,
   528, 552, 554, 556, 559, 589, 590
Anderson, G. H., 589
Anderson, G. W., 242
Appel, N., 552
Ap-Thomas, D. R., 185
Aptowitzer, V., 445
Arens, A., 381, 387
Arnold, M., 480, 483
Assaf, A., 25, 29
Astour, M. C., 52, 240, 246
Avigad, N., 246, 279, 299, 300, 564, 570, 571,
   573, 574
Avi-Yonah, M., 571, 580

Baab, O. J., 583

Bach, R., 53
Bacon, F., 482
Badawy, A., 250, 251
Badè, W. F., 291, 292
Bagatti, P. B., 571
Bahat, D., 25
Baillet, M., 570
Baker, G. P., 582
Baltzer, K., 359, 557
Baly, D., 52, 587
Barag, D., 248
Baramki, D. C., 277–78, 284
Barnes, W. E., 377
Barnett, R. D., 221, 222, 240, 244, 245, 251, 299
Barr, J., 387, 527, 556, 558, 589
Barrett, C. K., 526
Barrois, A., 580, 586
Barth, C., 385, 388, 525
Barth, Karl, 319, 320, 482
Barthélemy, D., 553, 557
Barthes, R., 555
Bass, G. F., 241
Battershill, C. A. Franken, 591
Bauer, Th., 185
Beaucour-Montet, C., 217
Beck, L., 540, 556
Becker, J., 387
Beckerath, J. von, 37
Beegle, D. M., 591
Beek, G. W. van, 244, 281, 282
Begrich, J., 203, 207, 358, 378, 386
Bendix, R., 166, 167, 168
Ben-Dor, I., 23, 26, 299
Bengston, H., 241
Benoit, P., 575
Bentzen, A., 361, 373, 399, 412, 535, 554
Benzinger, I., 303, 319
Berger, E., 584
Berger, P., 474–75, 476, 477, 478, 479
Berkeley, G., 483
Bernstein, R. J., 508
Bertholet, A., 386, 396, 411
Betz, H. D., 438, 439, 441, 443, 450, 451, 452
Beyerlin, W., 165, 386
Bietenhard, H., 447, 448
Biggs, R. D., 185
Bing, J. D., 245
Biran, A., 25, 37, 279
Birnbaum, S. A., 564, 570, 572, 573, 574
Bischoff, E., 445, 448
Bittel, K., 221
Blau, P. M., 166
Blázquez, J. M., 246, 247

Bleeker, C. J., 445
Blenkinsopp, J., 358–59
Bliss, F. J., 7, 23
Bloch, R., 553, 556
Boardman, J., 223
Bodenheimer, F. B., 125
Boecker, H. J., 321
Bölken, E., 411
Bogaert, P., 445, 446, 447
Boling, R. G., 100, 102, 378, 386
Bottéro, J., 20, 27, 28
Boulding, K., 148
Bousset, W., 396, 411, 412
Braidwood, L., 31, 32, 36, 590
Braidwood, R. S., 31, 32, 36, 590
Braun, H., 527
Bream, H. N., 476, 593
Breglia, L., 245
Brekelmans, C. H. W., 471, 478, 554
Bright, J., 53, 246, 360, 476, 479, 518–20, 524, 527, 528, 558, 588
Brinkman, J. A., 240, 247
Brock, J. K., 220
Brown, R. E., 374, 527
Browning, D., 508
Brownlee, W. H., 564, 572
Brueggemann, W., 359
Buber, M., 157, 167, 168, 495, 503, 509, 555
Buccellati, G., 27, 39, 40, 52, 205, 242
Buchholz, H. G., 220
Buhl, M. L., 53, 278
Bull, R. J., 591
Bultmann, R., 527
Burkitt, F. C., 569
Burney, C. F., 165, 320, 321, 322
Burridge, K. O. L., 184
Burrows, M., 569, 587
Busch, E., 319
Bush, D., 508
Buttenwieser, M., 377

Caiger, S., 579
Callaway, J. A., 591
Calvin, J., 481, 518
Caminos, R. A., 218
Campbell, E. F., Jr., 52, 53, 54, 100, 241, 590–91, 592
Campbell, J., 555
Campenhausen, H. von, 526
Cantineau, J., 569
Carlson, R. A., 319, 476
Carmichael, C., 554
Carroll, R. P., 359
Casson, S., 280
Cather, W., 484, 509
Catling, H. W., 35, 220, 222
Causse, A., 379, 476
Cazelles, H., 367, 374, 375, 387
Černý, J., 213, 214, 219, 220, 222
Charles, R. H., 391, 392, 401, 409, 410, 416, 424, 447, 449
Chehab, M., 29
Cheyne, T. K., 409
Childs, B. S., 51, 54, 99, 388, 480, 481, 507, 522–24, 527, 528, 541, 552, 555, 556, 560
Chomsky, N., 575

Christidès, V., 244
Cintas, P., 245, 247
Clapham, L., 338
Clemen, C., 337
Clements, R. E., 241, 525, 558
Clermont-Ganneau, C. S., 562, 569
Clines, D. J. A., 385, 386
Coats, G. W., 99
Cody, A., 207, 247
Cohen, R., 279
Cole, D. P., 37, 280
Conzelmann, H., 166
Cook, A. B., 220, 221
Cooke, G. A., 569
Coote, R. B., 247
Coppens, J., 385
Courbin, P., 220
Cowley, A. E., 569, 570
Cox, H., 509
Craigie, P. C., 99, 100
Crenshaw, J. L., 320, 324, 325
Crim, K. R., 463
Cross, F. M., 21, 66, 97, 99, 100, 101, 102, 109–10, 118, 119, 129, 168, 199, 200–01, 206, 207, 239, 246, 247, 248, 278, 299, 318, 319, 323, 336, 359, 371, 372, 375, 379, 386, 399, 412, 413, 441, 444, 446, 449, 451, 476, 553, 554, 555, 557, 562–64, 566, 568, 569, 570, 571, 572, 573, 574, 575, 576, 586, 589
Crowfoot, G. M., 277, 278, 280, 299
Crowfoot, J. W., 277, 278, 299
Culican, W., 247
Culley, R. C., 378, 386
Cumont, F., 336

Dahood, M., 66, 84, 100, 101, 102, 379, 386, 504
Dajani, R., 21
Dalglish, E. R., 386
Daniel, G., 240
Daube, D., 343, 344, 358, 359
Davis, G. H., 585
Debus, J., 303, 318–19, 322–23
Deissler, A., 387
Delaporte, L., 573
Delekat, L., 386, 388
Delougaz, P., 33
Denis, A. M., 451, 553
Dentan, R. C., 525, 583
Desborough, V. R. A., 220–21, 222
Descamps, A., 386
Descartes, R., 485
Deshayes, J., 220, 221
Dever, Wm. G., 21, 22, 25, 26, 27, 28, 30, 36, 277, 278, 279, 280, 282, 592
Díaz, R. M., 243
Dijk, H. J. van, 242, 244
Dikaios, P. 35
Dillmann, A., 392, 410
Diringer, D., 299, 300, 570, 583
Donner, H., 203, 207, 245, 246, 387, 527, 570
Dothan, M., 23, 26, 277, 278, 279
Dothan, T., 191, 215, 222, 260, 278, 279, 281
Doughty, Ch., 137
Drijvers, P., 385, 388
Driver, G. R., 573, 576

Driver, S. R., 575
Duhm, B., 390
Du Mesnil, R., 25, 29–30, 33
Dunand, M., 26, 32, 569
Dunayevsky, I., 260, 278, 279
Dupont-Sommer, A., 299
Dussaud, R., 29, 213, 220, 300, 569
Dyson, R. H., 34

Ebeling, E., 191
Ebeling, G., 450, 527
Edelstein, G., 278
Ehrich, R. W., 27, 28, 36, 580
Eichrodt, W., 157, 167, 378, 511, 554
Eisenstadt, S. N., 166, 185
Eissfeldt, O., 97, 101, 206, 246, 303, 319, 320,
    324, 325, 337, 359, 534, 535, 554, 556, 559
Eitan, A., 26, 279
Elgood, P. G., 213, 220
Eliade, M., 145, 151, 184, 484
Elizur, Y., 244–45
Ellermeier, F., 184
Elliger, K., 53, 204, 207
Engberg, R. M., 25, 26, 36, 277, 278
Engnell, I., 186, 378, 386, 397, 411
Epstein, C., 25
Erikson, E. H., 165
Ersch, J. S., 409
Euting, J., 569
Evans, A., 221
Evans, J. D., 240

Falkner, M., 251
Fangmeirer, J., 319
Faulkner, R. O., 240
Fensham, F. C., 206, 243
Filson, F. V., 581, 582, 584, 585, 588, 593
Finegan, J., 581
Finkelstein, L., 553, 584
Fishbane, M., 247
Fisher, C. S., 278
Fitzgerald, G. M., 23
Fitzmyer, J., 242, 336, 526
Flesseman-van Leer, E., 526
Flusser, D., 445
Fohrer, G., 167, 205, 241, 318, 554, 557
Forrer, E., 336, 337
Frank, H. T., 242, 554
Franken, H. J., 280, 591
Free, J. P., 53, 278
Freedman, D. N., 99, 100, 101, 102, 218, 277,
    278, 359, 360, 379, 386, 557, 558, 560, 569,
    571, 575, 576, 589, 590
Freedy, K. S., 248
Freund, J., 166
Frey, J. B., 570
Friedland, W. H., 166, 167
Friedmann, M., 430
Fritz, V., 52, 242
Frost, R., 506, 507, 509
Frost, S. B., 399–400, 411, 412, 413
Frye, R. N., 401, 413
Fugmann, E., 30
Fuller, R. H., 552, 554, 586, 588, 590, 591
Furumark, A., 191

Gall, A. von, 396, 411
Galling, K., 53, 205, 278, 281, 282, 288, 363,
    364, 365, 367, 370, 372, 374, 586, 592
Garber, P. L., 587
Garbini, G., 245, 247
Gardiner, A., 191, 218, 219
Gaster, T., 537
Gauthier, H., 219
Geiger, M., 319
Gelin, A., 387, 388
Genouillac, H., 336
Gershevitch, I., 150
Gerstenberger, E., 386
Gerth, H. H., 166
Gese, H., 526, 528, 559
Gibson, J. C. L., 246
Gilbert, G. H., 463
Giles, F. J., 52, 53
Gimbutas, M., 6
Ginsberg, H. L., 100, 119, 378, 386
Ginzberg, L., 208, 451
Giveon, R., 220
Glueck, J. J., 388
Glueck, N., 22, 36, 209, 244, 580, 581, 582, 588,
    591
Goedicke, H., 100, 149, 248
Goetze, A., 185, 240
Goldin, J., 463, 554
Goldman, H., 188, 191
Goldwasser, J., 213, 218, 220
Goldziher, I., 373
Goodenough, E. R., 446
Goodwin, D. W., 575
Gophna, R., 24, 25, 30, 31
Gordon, C., 102, 192, 192, 580, 581
Gordon, E. I., 191
Goshen-Gottstein, M., 382, 387
Gottwald, N. K., 463
Grant, E., 23, 35, 277, 278, 579
Gray, G. B., 100
Gray, J., 304, 318, 320, 321, 322
Grayson, A. K., 337
Greenberg, M., 165, 463
Greenfield, J., 47, 53, 243, 248
Grelot, P., 367, 375, 527
Gressmann, H., 221, 396–97, 398, 411
Grosjean, R., 240
Gross, H., 586
Gruber, J. G., 409
Grünwald, L., 443, 444, 451
Guariglia, G., 184
Güterbock, H. G., 337
Guiges, P. E., 29
Guilding, A., 387
Gunkel, H., 377, 378, 379, 380, 385, 393–96,
    397, 400, 402, 403, 405, 410, 411, 413
Gunneweg, A. H. J., 359, 475, 527
Gurney, O. R., 221, 336
Guy, P. L. O., 23, 26, 249

Hachmann, R., 29
Hahn, H. F., 464, 476
Haines, B. L., 565, 573
Halévy, J., 569
Hall, H. R., 215, 222
Hallevy, R., 323

Hallo, W. W., 246, 386
Hamilton, R. W., 278
Hanfmann, G. M. A., 217
Hankey, V., 280
Hanson, A. T., 526
Hanson, P. D., 119, 373, 410, 412, 413, 441–42, 443, 444, 449, 451, 555
Hanson, R. S., 573
Harding, G. L., 278, 580
Harnack, A. von, 463
Harrelson, W., 53, 101, 358, 477, 559, 589
Harris, Z., 576
Hartshorne, C., 485, 490, 491, 494, 500, 508
Harvey, J. W., 186
Haussig, H. W., 337
Hegel, G. W. F., 503
Heim, R. D. 593
Heinemann, I., 444
Heinisch, P., 511
Heintz, J. G., 184
Helck, W., 28, 46, 53, 219, 240, 241, 244, 337
Held, M., 207
Helfmeyer, F. J., 322
Henderson, A. M., 166
Hengel, M., 438–39, 445, 447, 448, 449, 450, 451
Hennessy, J. B., 280
Henry, M., 481
Henschel-Simon, E., 278
Henshaw, R. A., 320
Herder, J. G., 181
Herrmann, S., 242, 244
Herrmann, W., 242
Hertzberg, H. W., 382, 387
Hesse, F., 526, 527
Hilgenfeld, A., 390, 391, 409
Hillers, D., 100, 119, 557
Hirano, T., 590
Hirmer, M., 222
Hölscher, G., 175, 185, 368, 375, 392, 410
Hoenig, S. B., 553
Holladay, J. S., 277, 278, 280, 555
Holladay, W. L., 322
Holm-Nielsen, S., 53, 278, 380, 387
Honeyman, A. M., 542
Hooke, S. H, 386, 397, 411, 476
Hooser, J. B. van, 50–51, 54
Horn, S., 127, 210, 213, 217, 218, 219, 220, 221, 223, 278, 290
Hornig, G., 552–53
Hornung, E., 218, 219
Horovitz, H. S., 446
Houwink Ten Cate, Ph. H. J., 243
Howard, M., 556
Howells, W., 184
Hrouda, B., 34
Huffmon, H., 50, 53, 184–85
Hume, D., 487
Hurvitz, A., 553
Hutchinson, R. W., 220, 221
Huxley, G., 240
Hyatt, J. P., 554
Hyland, C. F., 99, 100

Iliffe, J. H., 23
Imschoot, P. van, 511

Inge, C. H., 580
Ingholt, H., 30, 580
Ishida, T., 165

Jacob, E., 511, 525, 558, 588
Jacobsen, Th., 116, 119, 336–37, 410, 411
James, F. W., 267, 277, 278, 282, 291
James, Wm., 508, 509
Jansen, H. L., 380, 381, 387
Japhet, S., 375
Jaussen, A., 149
Jenni, E., 53
Jepsen, A., 303, 318, 319, 320, 321, 324, 325
Jeremias, G., 450
Jeremias, J., 410, 558
Johnson, A. R., 180, 185, 385, 386

Käsemann, E., 409, 552
Kallai-(Kleinmann), Z., 165, 201, 207
Kant, I., 482, 555
Kantor, H. J., 28
Kapelrud, A. S., 385
Kaplan, J., 25, 34
Kappus, S., 53
Karageorghis, V., 35, 245
Katzenstein, H. J., 244, 246
Kaufman(n), Yehezkel, 128, 165, 204, 208, 445, 560, 586
Kellermann, U., 361, 362, 363, 364, 365, 366, 368, 370–71, 372, 373, 374, 375
Kelso, J. L., 25, 53, 277, 278, 583
Kenyon, K., 3, 4, 5, 6, 9, 10, 11, 12, 13, 18, 20, 21, 22, 23, 24, 26, 27, 28, 29, 31, 34, 37, 52, 247, 254, 256, 267, 273, 274, 277, 278, 279, 280, 282, 285, 291, 299, 361, 373, 588, 589
Kettering, Ch. F., 171
Kimbrough, S. T., 476
King, E. G., 387
Kitchen, K. A., 218
Kittel, R., 99
Klatt, W., 411
Klein, R. W., 376
Klein, S., 208
Klengel, H., 53
Klopfenstein, M. A., 303, 319, 324
Knight, G. A. F., 511
Knudtzon, J. A., 52
Koch, K., 389, 401, 409, 413, 440–41, 449, 450, 451, 527
Kochavi, M., 4, 5, 21, 25, 36
Köhler, L., 511, 588
Korošec, V., 47
Kortzfleisch, S. von, 463
Kraeling, E. G., 463
Kramer, S. N., 119, 336
Kraus, H. J., 109, 320, 359, 380, 386, 527, 528
Kuhl, C., 320
Kuhn, H. W., 450
Kuhn, K. G., 450
Kui, C., 587
Kuschke, A., 53, 278, 325, 592
Kutsch, E., 53, 278, 325, 592

Laaf, P., 554
Labadi, Y., 21
Lacan, Fr., 555

Laing, R. D., 508
Lambdin, T. O., 570, 573
Lambert, W. G., 191, 336, 337
Lamon, R. S., 277, 278, 299
Lampe, G. W. H., 527
Lance, H. D., 25, 26, 244, 267, 277, 278, 280, 281, 282, 592
Landes, G. M., 42, 556
Landsberger, B., 52, 337
Lane, W. R., 242
Lang, F., 528
Langdon, S., 185
Langhe, R. de, 385, 587
Lanternari, V., 184
Lapp, N , ?1, 279, 280
Lapp, P., 4, 5, 22, 24, 36, 44, 278, 279, 280, 281, 282, 288, 289, 293, 478, 564, 571, 573, 593
Laroche E., 150
Latham, E. C., 509
Laurin, R. B., 525
Layard, A. H., 251
LeClant, J., 240, 242
Le Déaut, R., 556
Lefèvre, A., 192
Lehmann, G. A., 240
Lemke, W. E., 375
Lévi-Strauss, C., 555
Lévy, I., 239
Lewis, I. L., 184
Lewis, J. P., 553
L'Heureux, C., 337
Licht, J., 165
Lichtheim, G., 477
Lidzbarski, M., 562, 569
Lindars, B., 526, 557
Lindblom, J., 591
Lipiński, E., 206, 246, 385, 386
Liverani, M., 30, 46, 53
Löhr, M., 208, 580
Loetscher, L. A., 585
Loewe, R., 463
Loewenstein, K., 166
Löwinger, D. S., 373
Lohfink, N., 319, 527, 554, 556
Lohse, E., 526
Longacre, L. B., 581
Lorimer, H. L., 217, 222, 223
Loud, G., 23, 26, 31, 35, 190, 191, 220, 277, 278, 583
Loza, J., 554
Luckmann, T., 476, 555
Lücke, F., 389–90, 409
Lugenbeal, E. N. 280
Luther, M., 481, 553
Lyon, D. G., 278
Lys, D., 527

Macalister, R. A. S., 23, 220
McCarthy, D. J., 53, 319, 347, 357–58, 359, 360, 555
McCown, C. C., 277, 278, 449, 581, 582, 583
McHugh, D., 526
McKane, W., 191
MacKenzie, D., 23, 34, 278
McKenzie, J., 358
Mair, L., 184

Malamat, A., 16, 27, 37, 164, 195, 196, 197, 206, 213, 217, 218, 220, 223, 240–41, 242, 243, 300
Mallowan, M. E. L., 14, 32, 33, 36
Mannheim, K., 413, 464, 466, 476, 477, 555
Marinatos, S., 222
Marquart, J., 207
Martin, M., 569, 576
Martin, M. F., 299
Martin, W. J., 244
Martindale, D., 166
Marvin, M. M., 217
Masson, O., 245
Matthiae, P., 30
Mauchline, J., 247
May, H. G., 583, 592
Mayer, L. A., 23
Mays, J. L., 479
Mazar (Maisler), Benjamin, 3, 10, 20, 27, 36, 37, 165, 190, 191, 204, 206, 207, 208, 239, 240, 243, 244, 260, 277, 278, 279, 283, 581, 587
Meland, B. E., 481–82, 483, 485, 498, 500, 508–09
Mellaart, J., 34, 36
Mellink, M. J., 34, 36, 221
Mendenhall, G., 48, 53, 54, 149, 151, 206, 357, 359, 476, 477, 544, 545, 557, 558
Mertens, C. von, 587
Mettinger, T. N. D., 244
Meyer, E., 364, 373, 396, 411
Middleton, J., 185
Mihelic, J. L., 589
Mildenberger, F., 527
Milik, J. T., 206, 278, 447, 554, 564, 570, 571, 574, 575
Millard, A. R., 337, 569
Miller, J. L., 581
Miller, J. M., 217, 246
Miller, M., 556
Miller, M. S., 581
Miller, P. D., 119, 359
Miller, S. H., 590
Millet, N. B., 217, 221, 223
Milton, J., 493
Minette de Tilesse, G., 319
Miskotte, K. H., 527
Mitzman, A., 166
Möhlenbrink, K., 192
Moffatt, J., 463
Moltmann, J., 508
Mommsen, W. J., 166
Montet, P., 27, 28, 209, 212–13, 214, 215, 219
Montgomery, J. A., 303, 319, 320, 321, 324, 583
Moore, C. A., 593
Moore, C. B., 593
Moore, G. F., 392–93, 410
Moortgat, A., 32
Moran, Wm. L., 47, 53, 184, 185, 337
Morgenstern, J., 304, 320, 324, 325
Moscati, S., 239, 245, 246, 247, 570
Moskowitz, S., 27
Moulds, L. G., 278, 290
Mowinckel, S., 365, 366, 368, 374, 375, 378, 379, 380, 382, 385, 386, 387, 388, 397–99, 411, 412, 476, 588

Mras, K., 337
Mühlmann, W. E., 167, 184
Muilenberg, J., 358, 360, 385, 589
Munch, P. A., 387
Murphy, R., 386
Murray, A. S., 222
Musil, A., 137
Myers, J. M., 99, 100, 373, 374, 375, 476, 593
Mylonas, G., 220, 221, 222, 223

Nakari, T. W., 591
Napier, B. D., 586
Nash, A. S., 584
Naveh, J., 239, 281, 564, 565, 566, 572, 573, 574
Needler, W., 583
Negbi, O., 21, 27, 35
Neiman, D., 241
Nelson, H. H., 219
Neusner, J., 446, 553, 555, 559
Newman, M., 555
Nicholson, E. W., 318, 319, 556
Nielsen, E., 586
Niemeyer, C. T., 387
Niemeyer, H. G., 245
Nilsson, M. P., 214, 220
Noack, L., 392, 410
North, C. R., 358
North, R., 365, 374, 590
Noth, M., 109, 121, 132, 133, 185, 200, 205,
    206, 241, 244, 246, 301, 302, 304, 318, 320,
    321, 322, 323, 324, 325, 359, 368, 370, 375,
    396, 535, 536, 554, 557
Nougayrol, J., 191, 337
Nyberg, H. S., 396, 411, 412

Oates, J., 282
O'Callaghan, R. T., 215, 223
O'Dea, T., 555
Östborn, G., 535, 554
Ohata, K., 25
Olmstead, A. T., 375
Oren, E., 4, 13, 21, 22, 23, 25, 26, 27, 29, 33, 35
Orlin, L. L., 245
Orlinsky, H. M., 133, 136, 144, 147, 148, 150,
    181–82, 183, 186, 205, 568, 575
Ory, J., 23, 25, 31, 34
Osswald, E., 558
Otto, R., 186, 396, 411
Overholt, T. W., 558

Page, S., 246, 247, 320
Parker, B., 185
Parker, S. B., 53, 337
Parr, P., 16, 30, 36, 37
Parrinder, G., 463
Parrot, A., 587
Parsons, T., 166, 185, 465, 467, 477
Paul, Sh., 556
Peckham, B., 242, 245, 565, 573
Pedersen, J., 386
Pendlebury, J. D. S., 250–51
Perlitt, L., 358, 554
Perrot, J., 279
Petrie, W. M. F., 7, 18, 22, 23, 26, 191, 215,
    221, 222, 278, 282
Pfeiffer, E., 448

Pfeiffer, R., 531, 553
Philibert, M., 477
Plein, I., 320
Ploeg, J. P. M. van der, 450, 525
Plöger, O., 326, 361, 373, 400, 407, 408, 413
Plumb, J. H., 135, 148–49, 150
Pohlmann, K. F., 363, 368–69, 371, 375
Pope, M. H., 119
Porada, E., 11, 27, 33, 34, 36, 191
Porten, B., 374
Porteous, N. W., 526
Posener, G., 16, 20, 27, 28
Poulssen, N., 359
Prag, K., 32
Prausnitz, M. W., 220
Preuss, H. D., 388, 412, 527
Prignaund, J. P., 279, 299
Pritchard, J. B., 24, 25, 26, 111, 249, 250, 251,
    278, 279, 568, 574, 581, 590
Procksch, O., 511
Przeworski, S., 221
Purvis, J. D., 375, 564, 573, 574
Pye, M., 244

Quell, G., 320, 558

Rabin, I. A., 446
Rabinowitz, L., 387
Rad, G. von, 109, 167, 318, 319, 323, 326, 350,
    351, 353, 358, 360, 365, 366, 374, 401, 410,
    413, 421, 422, 425, 426, 436, 437, 438, 446,
    447, 449, 450, 478, 508, 511, 526, 527, 535,
    536, 543, 550, 554, 555, 557
Rainey, A., 22, 28, 36, 52
Rast, W., 279
Ratman, K. J., 166
Redford, D. B., 248
Reed, H. T. F., 592
Reed, W. L., 242, 279, 554, 583, 592
Reid, J. K. S., 588
Reifenberg, A., 299, 570
Reimherr, O., 476
Reiner, E., 191
Reisner, G. A., 278
Reitzenstein, R., 396, 411, 412
Rendtorff, R., 185, 527, 558
Renger, J., 185
Rengstorf, K. H., 463
Rese, M., 526
Reuss, E., 390, 409
Reventlow, H. Graf von, 526
Reviv, H., 165, 167
Richardson, A., 477, 583, 584, 585
Richardson, H. N., 99, 100, 101, 102
Richter, W., 165, 167, 241, 318
Ringgren, H., 186
Rinzema, J., 590
Robert, A., 382, 387
Roberts, B. J., 553, 556, 557
Robertson, D. A., 96, 97, 99, 101, 102, 387
Robinson, T. H., 386, 575
Röllig, W., 245, 246, 570
Römer, W. H. Ph., 185
Rössler, D., 400, 407, 408, 413, 527
Rofé, A., 323–24
Rogers, M. G., 241

Rogerson, J. W., 509
Rosen, G., 185
Rosenthal, E. I. J., 463
Rosenthal, F., 185, 569
Ross, J. F., 185, 591
Rost, L., 344, 346, 357, 554, 555
Roth, G., 166
Rothenberg, B., 124
Rowe, A., 580
Rowley, H. H., 191, 361, 373, 375, 385, 386, 399, 412, 575, 582, 585
Rowton, M. B., 40, 52, 244
Rubenstein, R. L., 560
Rudolph, W., 364, 368, 375, 479
Russell, D. S., 399, 412, 441, 445, 451
Rustow, D. A., 165, 166, 167
Rylaarsdam, J. C., 358
Ryle, H. E., 383

Sabourin, L., 385, 386
Sachau, E., 569
Säve-Söderbergh, T., 37
Saggs, H. W. F., 185
Sakenfeld, K., 355, 359, 360
Saley, R., 370, 371, 372, 375, 376, 571
Saller, S. J., 278, 290
Sanda, A., 303, 319
Sanders, J. A., 381, 382, 387, 520–22, 524, 527, 528, 552, 553, 555, 556, 557, 558, 576
Sarna, N., 387
Sasson, J. M., 241
Sauer, J., 279, 280
Sawyer, J. F. A., 165, 384, 388
Sayce, A. H., 569
Schachermeyr, F., 240
Schader, E., 365, 374
Schaeffer, C. F. A., 14, 29, 30, 31, 32, 33, 34, 35, 221, 251, 252
Schaub, T., 22
Schechter, S., 553
Schildenberger, J., 385
Schilling, S. P., 588
Schlatter, Th., 588
Schmidt, H., 366, 374, 378, 386
Schmidt, J., 400, 409, 410
Schmidt, L., 167
Schmidt, W. H., 247
Scholem, G., 443, 451, 463
Schottroff, W., 365
Schreiner, J., 451
Schubart, H., 245
Schulman, A. R., 53
Schunk, K. D., 207, 243
Schwarzwäller, K., 527
Schweitzer, W., 583, 584
Scott, R. B. Y., 100, 191, 388, 581
Seeligmann, I. L., 167, 382, 387, 576
Seger, J. D., 52, 280
Séguy, J., 166
Sekine, M., 360, 526
Sellers, O. R., 277, 278, 585
Sellin, E., 292, 365, 592
Selms, A. van, 207
Semler, J. S., 531, 552, 553
Sergio, L., 184
Service, E. R., 148, 149, 150

Seters, J. van, 37, 478
Sethe, K., 336, 337
Seton-Williams, M. V., 31, 34
Several, M. W., 53
Seymour, St. J. D., 447
Shantur, B., 21
Sherburne, D. W., 494, 508
Shiloh, Y., 24, 251, 279
Shils, E., 165, 166, 167, 476
Shinya, M., 590, 591
Shipton, G. M., 25, 277, 278, 299
Shriver, D. W., 477
Siegel, J. P., 553
Simon, M., 463
Simons, J., 244, 588
Sinclair, L. A., 278–79
Sjöberg, E. K. T., 412
Sjöqvist, E., 14, 34
Skehan, P. W., 101
Smend, R., 241, 242, 318, 511, 526, 528
Smith, A. H., 222
Smith, G., 395
Smith, J. Z., 446
Smith, M., 543, 544, 546, 552, 554, 557, 558, 559
Smith, R. H., 4, 24, 25
Smith, S., 14
Smitten, W. T. in der, 373–74
Schmittner, W., 553
Snaith, N. H., 303, 319
Snodgrass, 217, 221, 222, 223
Soggin, J. A., 168, 208, 244, 554
Sohm, R., 157
Somogyi, J., 373
Speiser, E. A., 33, 119, 386
Stager, L. E., 593
Stamm, J. J., 385
Starcky, J., 243
Steck, O. H., 246, 324
Stegemann, H., 450
Steinmann, J., 589
Stendahl, K., 526
Stern, E., 248
Steve, A. M., 23
Stewart, J., 35
Stiebing, W. H., 222
Stiehl, I. R., 246
Stier, H. E., 246
Stinespring, W. F., 373
Stoebe, H. J., 526
Stolz, F., 167
Stone, M. E., 446, 448, 449, 451
Streck, M., 185
Stronach, D. B., 26
Strong, S. A., 185
Strugnell, J., 428, 434, 444, 446
Stubbings, F. H., 222
Stuhlmacher, P., 556
Suhl, A., 526
Sukenik, E. L., 299, 564, 570, 571, 592
Sundberg, A. C., 552, 556
Sussmann, V., 24, 30, 31
Swift, G. F., Jr., 31
Szörenyi, A., 386

Tadmor, H., 242, 246, 247

Tait, D., 185
Tal, U., 167
Talmon, S., 387, 553, 557, 560
Temple, Wm., 507, 509
Terrien, S., 244, 385, 388
Thackeray, H. St. J., 387
Theodor, J., 445
Thiele, E. R., 218
Thomas, C. G., 241
Thomas, D. W., 21, 53, 592
Thompson, T. L., 23
Thorndike, J. P., 447
Thureau-Dangin, G., 26, 32
Tillich, P., 413, 518
Tomes, R., 588, 591
Toombs, L. E., 527, 589, 590
Torrey, C. C., 373, 569
Toy, C. H., 409
Trask, W. R., 184
Trever, J. C., 564, 571, 574
Trillhass, W., 527
Troeltsch, E., 413
Trotsky, L., 171
Tucker, R. C., 166
Tufnell, O., 11, 23, 24, 27, 28, 36, 258, 266, 279, 282, 580, 586, 589
Tur-Sinai, N. H., 191, 388
Tushingham, A. D., 279, 585
Twain, M., 171

Ubach, B., 243
Uffenheimer, B., 445
Untermeyer, L., 509
Urbach, E. E., 444

Vaillant, A., 416, 426, 432, 434, 444, 448
Vanel, A., 248
Vatke, W., 120
de Vaux, R., 5, 22, 23, 53, 135, 203, 205, 206, 207, 208, 240, 241, 242, 245, 267, 277, 279, 299, 300, 526
Vawter, B., 527
Vermes, G., 526, 541, 556, 560
Vermeule, E. T., 217, 220, 221, 222
Viering, F., 526
Vincent, L. H., 23, 586, 588
Vink, J. G., 367, 374
Violet, B., 445, 446
Virolleaud, C., 337
Vischer, W., 358
Viteau, J., 383
Voegelin, E., 360
Vollmer, J., 557
Volterra, E., 374
Volz, P., 412
Vosté, J. M., 388
Vriezen, Th. Chr., 358, 511, 587

Wace, A. J. B., 222
Waddell, W. G., 218
Walcot, P., 337
Waldbaum, J. C., 217, 222
Walker, A., 280, 593
Wallace, A. F. C., 184
Walters, H. B., 222
Warmbacq, B. N., 102

Wampler, J. C., 259, 277, 279, 291
Wanke, G., 386, 556
Ward, W. A., 11, 27, 28, 36, 240
Waterman, L., 582
Watson, P. J., 34
Watzinger, C., 292
Weber, M., 157, 158–59, 166, 167–68, 185, 413, 479, 555
Webster, T. B. L., 217, 223
Weidner, E. F., 300
Weinberg, S., 191
Weippert, H., 165
Weippert, M. W., 478
Weiser, A., 100, 165, 380, 386, 526, 554
Weiss, M., 378, 386
Welker, 583
Wellhausen, J., 120, 303, 314, 319, 324, 389, 390, 391, 392, 393, 394, 409, 545, 557, 584
Wenig, S., 218
Wente, E. F., 53
Westermann, C., 343, 349, 356, 358, 359, 360, 381, 385, 386, 387, 463, 477, 479, 527
Wette, W. M. L. de, 390
Wevers, J. W., 386
Wharton, J., 527
Wheelwright, P., 484, 492, 493, 508, 509
White, W., 466, 467, 477
Whitehead, A. N., 482, 483, 485–97, 498, 499, 502–03, 508, 509
Widengren, G., 99, 476
Wiener, H. M., 129
Wijngaards, J., 51, 54
Wilder, A. N., 451, 508, 555
Willis, J. T., 186
Willner, A. R., 166, 167
Willner, D. 167
Willoughby, H. R., 582
Wilson, J. A., 185, 205
Wilson, J. V. K., 337
Winckelmann, J., 166
Winckler, H., 397
Winnett, F. V., 279
Wirth, L., 476
Wittich, C., 166
Wolf, E. R., 134, 137, 138, 139, 141, 148, 149, 150, 151
Wolff, H. W., 311, 318, 319, 322, 325, 411–12, 469, 477–78, 526, 527
Woolley, L., 31, 32
Worden, T., 388
Worsley, P., 184, 185
Woude, A. van der, 558
Wreszinski, W., 219, 222, 223
Wright, E. D., 584
Wright, G. E., 3, 5, 13, 20, 21, 22, 23, 24, 25, 26, 28, 30, 34, 35, 36, 37, 52, 53, 97, 101, 108, 135, 190, 193, 199, 200–01, 205, 206, 207, 209, 240, 241, 244, 246, 249, 253, 256, 265, 266, 277, 278, 279, 280, 299, 319, 339, 343, 358, 359, 360, 371, 375, 382, 387, 408, 455, 476, 477, 510, 516–18, 524, 525, 526, 527, 528, 535, 536, 537, 541, 550, 552, 554, 555, 556, 557, 560, 561
Wright, G. R. H., 36, 244
Würthwein, E., 525, 527
Wylie, C., 583

Yadin, Y., 5, 20, 22, 24, 26, 37, 131, 190, 207, 215, 219, 221, 222–23, 240, 245, 277, 279, 280, 283, 299, 445, 564, 573, 576, 587
Yeivin, S., 21, 144, 150, 192, 213, 220, 244

Zeitlin, S., 574
Ziegler, K., 191
Zimmerli, W., 167, 242, 244, 358, 511, 526
Zobel, H. J., 240

Index of Subjects

Aaron, 123
Abdi-Ashirta, 50
Abdi-Ḥepa, 47
Abel beth-Maacah, 206
Abibaal, 242
Abijah, 201
Abimelek ben Jerubbaal, 139, 140, 154, 162, 163–64, 167–68, 177, 294
Abimilki (of Tyre), 46
Abner ben-Ner, 243
Abraham, 67, 118, 294, 339, 342, 358, 12; 349, 446, 457, 467, 469, 477, 478, 496, 501, 504, 507, 556, 548 bis, 550, 551
    apocalypse of, 440–41, 442
Absalom, 294
Abydos, 243
Acco, 226, 227, 247
Achish, 196
Achzib, 220, 246, 247
Adad, 111, 331
Adadnirari III, 246, 237, 247, 320
Adoram, 207
Aesop, 189
Africanus, 211–12, 219
Ahab, 181, 182, 183–84, 236–37, 246, 253, 314, 324
Ahasuerus, 294
Ahaziah ben-Ahab, 181
Ahaziah ben-Jehoram, 237
Ahijah of Shiloh, 179, 180, 181, 182, 316
'Ain es-Sâmiyeh, 7
Akiba, 410
Akhenaten (see Amenophis IV)
Alalakh, 13, 14, 135, 122
Aleppo, 172
Alexander of Macedon, 372
Alexander Jannaeus, 567
Amalek, 57, 230, 324
Amanus (Mountain), 112, 337, 335
Amarna
    period, 39–54, 129, 146, 225, 228
    site, 32, 250
    texts, 121, 147, 240
Amawnet, 329
Amenemhet I, 10
Amenope, Onomasticon of, 191, 240, 421
Amenophis IV, 45, 129, 131
'amm, 61–2, 94–5, 471
Amman, 275
    citadel inscription, 130
Ammon, 130, 153, 194, 195, 230, 231, 233, 295, 472, 478
Amorite (MAR.TU), 10, 12, 13, 36

country, 50, 225, 228
people, 5–6, 22
religion, 118, 174
Amos, 238, 315–16, 324, 325, 470, 474, 540, 556, 546, 549
Amrit, 229
Amōn, 129, 175, 179, 329, 330, 332, 337
'Amûq, 13, 82, 90, 93, 105
'Anat, 111, 112, 117
Anatolia, 13, 136, 137, 214, 221, 231, 232 bis, 234, 235, 236, 237, 243
Anaximander, 334, 335, 337
Anaximenes, 335
Anshar, 112, 330
Anu, 112, 330–31
Anunnaki, 333
apocalyptic, 109, 116, 389–408; 409, 410, 411, 412, 413, 415–52 passim
apocalyptic eschatology, 398, 411, 441–42 bis, 443, 451–2
Apsu, 112, 113, 116, 330, 331, 332
Apuleius, 185
Aqhat, 11, 118
Arad, 126, 238, 281, 275, 283, 296, 546
Aramea, 224, 225, 231, 235, 237, 247, 324
    script, 562, 563, 564, 565–66, 572, 573, 574, 576
Aram-Naharaim, 153
Aram-Zobah, 195, 231
'Arâq eṭ-Ṭayiḥ, 42
Aristotle, 494
Ark of the Covenant, 145, 339, 345, 346, 383, 539
Artaxerxes I, 362, 363–4, 370
Artaxerxes II, 374, 370, 371, 372
Artaxerxes III, 364, 372
Arubboth, 199
Arumah, 43
Asa, 201
Asaph, 180, 181, 190, 383
Ashdod, 196, 275, 284
Asher, 156, 199, 226, 227, 228, 240, 241
Asherah, 117, 171, 175
Ashkelon, 192, 196, 227, 240
Ashtaroth (Tell Ashtarah), 127
Ashur (Aššur, see, too, Anshar), 111
Ashurbanipal, 175, 229, 238, 243
Ashurnasirpal II, 229, 251
Assyria, 34, 35, 47, 48, 175–76, 229, 235, 236, 237, 238, 246, 251, 272, 282, 274, 307, 398, 475, 538, 539
Astarte, 191, 232, 331, 335
Aten, 129

Athaliah, 236, 237, 246
Avaris, 125

Baal (Ba'l), 83, 111, 112, 114, 115, 116, 117, 140, 146, 171, 175, 184, 331, 333–4, 395
Baal Berit, 163
Baal-Ḥamon, 337
Baal-Shamen, 175, 232, 244
Baal Ṣapon, 337
Ba'lu-UR.SAG, 48
Baasha, 179, 180, 233–34, 236
Bâb edh-Dhrâ', 22
Babylon, 12, 49, 112, 172, 174, 185, 254, 298, 333, 343, 366, 367, 395, 396, 398, 403, 410, 475, 539, 540, 547, 548, 549, 550, 557, 558–59, 559
Baghouz, 13, 34
Bagoas, 364, 367, 370, 371–72, 374, 376
Balaam's Oracles (Num 23–4), 55 ff. passim, 66–8 passim, 127–8, 324, 444
Barak, 152, 153, 154, 156, 160, 178
Barqai, 7
Bashan, 127
Bathsheba, 179
Beersheba, 126, 143, 177, 209, 249, 282, 283, 275
Beirut, 230
Ben-Hadad, 314
Benjamin, 147, 154, 156, 162, 200, 201, 205, 227, 241
Bethel, 7, 44, 62, 67, 145, 147, 162, 183, 200, 267, 282, 284, 285, 286, 287, 288, 289, 290, 291, 292, 293, 302, 304, 305, 306, 307, 310, 313, 315–16, 321, 324, 325, 327, 346
Beth-Rehob, 195
Beth-Shan, 7, 147, 226, 267, 285, 286, 287, 288, 289, 290, 291, 292, 293
Beth-She'arim, 571
Beth-Shemesh
  site, 7, 31, 34, 196, 201, 253, 265–66, 275, 284, 285, 286, 287, 288, 289, 290, 291, 292, 293, 294, 298
Beth-Zur, 288
Biridiya (of Megiddo), 39
Biryawaza, 50
Boghazköy, 121, 221
Botrys, 229, 242
Byblos
  Amarna period, 47, 136, 175
  Phoenician period, 59, 225, 226, 228–30, 239, 240, 242
  site, 6, 10–11, 12–13, 29, 31, 37

Cain and Abel, 150
Caleb, 162
Canaan
  culture, 6, 124, 146, 148, 163, 172, 175, 188, 224–28
  land, 479, 538, 543, 551
  religion, 65, 71, 83, 109, 110, 111, 112, 113, 114, 117, 330–32, 336, 344, 346, 396, 398, 399, 400, 403, 404, 472, 541
Cappadocia
  ware, 14, 35–36
Carchemish, 13

Carmel (Mount), 171, 196, 241
Carthage, 234, 238, 243, 247
Cassius (Mount), 112, 335, 337
Chagar Bazar, 13, 32, 33
Chemosh, 111, 472
Cherethites and Pelethites, 196, 221
Cicero, 172, 182–83
Conquest, 109, 110, 115, 130, 147, 148, 149, 227–28, 242, 335–36, 350, 468, 470–73, 478, 479, 520, 540, 540, 556
Covenant
  "Davidic," 142, 342–43, 344–47, 348–49, 351, 353, 354, 357, 359, 473–74, 517, 546, 550, 559
  International, 45–52, 115, 122, 130, 148, 359, 360
  Israelite, 49, 50–52, 73–74, 114–15, 116, 118, 122, 130, 136, 138–39, 143–46, 148, 228, 336, 339–57, 357–58, 358, 360, 457, 465, 467, 470, 473, 474, 475, 499, 501, 511, 517, 519, 520, 536, 546, 548, 550, 551, 558
  lawsuit, 49, 115, 334, 337, 350
  renewal, 109, 341–42, 344, 350, 351, 353, 359, 500
Covenant Code, 121, 130, 136
Crete, 34, 213–14, 221, 226, 217
Cronos, 330
Cyprus, relations with Syria Palestine, 13, 14, 28, 31, 34, 209, 215, 220, 222, 226, 229, 234, 236, 242

Dagan (Dagon), 111, 112, 335
  of Tuttul, 173
Damascus
  city state, 50, 195, 197, 206, 225, 233, 234, 237, 239
  province of David, 203
Dan, 140, 150, 154, 162, 165, 196, 199, 200–1, 225, 226, 235, 240
Dan (Laish), 7, 16–20, 67, 140, 143, 145, 147, 150
Daniel
  Book, 391, 400, 404, 440, 442, 451
Darius I, 150, 375
Darius II, 370
Darius III, 371
David, 134, 139, 140, 145, 148, 149, 162, 177, 179–80, 187, 189, 190, 193–204, 207, 208, 209, 213, 228, 230–31, 232, 234, 238, 241, 243, 244, 294, 295, 296, 297, 302, 313, 323, 339, 343, 344, 345, 346–47, 348–49, 351, 353, 354, 356, 357, 360, 362, 363, 374, 383, 384, 473–74, 521, 540, 546, 550, 558, 66
David, Lament of
  55 ff. passim, 72, passim
David, Testament of
  55 ff. passim, 73–75 & passim, 345
Debir. See Tell Beit-Mirsim
Deborah, 140, 153, 154, 156, 160, 161, 162, 178
Deborah, Song of, 55 ff. passim, 61–63 & passim, 110, 154, 156, 241, 468
Deir 'Alla, 226
Delaiah of Samaria, 364
Deuteronomic Code, 365, 366, 368, 375, 472

Dibon, 147
Divine Council, 60, 112–15, 117, 333–34, 354, 356
Divine Warrior, 109, 110–17, 332–34, 335–36, 345–46, 547
Dor, 225, 227, 230, 239
Dothan, 44, 199

Ea, 112, 331, 332
Ebal, 42, 130
Eden, Garden of, 551
Edom, 124, 127, 194, 205–6, 195, 197, 203, 231, 232, 233, 236, 237, 247, 478
Egypt, 147, 188, 189, 191, 197, 202, 203–4, 209–17, 218, 225–26, 229, 230, 231, 232, 233–34, 238, 242, 255, 272, 280, 296, 297, 335, 342, 343, 359, 353, 356, 362, 363–64, 366, 371, 405, 404, 411, 417, 421, 459, 461, 538, 543, 545, 546, 556, 559, 575
   administration of provinces in Amarna period, 45–51
   in Mosaic era, 123–24, 126, 127, 129
   MB Synchronisms, 6, 10, 12, 27–28, 28, 35, 37
   texts, 122, 123
Ehud ben-Gera, 153, 154, 161, 162
Ein Gedi (Tell el-Jurn; Tell Goren), 254, 259, 260, 261, 264–65, 265–66, 272, 277, 281, 283, 284, 285, 286, 287, 288, 289, 290, 291, 292, 293
Ekron, 196, 206
'El
   epithets:
   'elyôn, 56, 63, 66, 67, 68, 70, 76, 78, 81, 82, 89, 90–91, 118, 332, 334, 335
   'ôlām, 56, 65–66, 68, 69, 70, 73–74, 89, 92, 118, 332, 335
   šadday, 56, 63–64, 66, 67, 68, 70, 71, 75–76, 82, 89, 90, 91–92, 118
   'elôhê, 58, 59, 61–62, 82
   'elôhîm, 58, 59, 62, 73, 80–81, 82–84, 86, 88–89, 94, 120
   in Canaan, 64, 111, 112, 113, 114, 117, 118, 331, 332, 334, 335
   in Israel, 60–61, 61–62, 64–65, 89–90
Elah ben-Baasha, 236
Elephantine
   garrison, 364, 367
   papyri, 364, 370, 371, 372, 572
Eli, 177
Elibaal, 242
Elijah, 171, 180, 181, 182, 294, 323, 324, 345
Elisha, 178, 189, 181, 182, 295, 296, 315, 323, 324
Elohist, 50, 504, 537
'Elpa'al, 243
Enki, 113, 116, 117, 330, 331–32
Enki and Ninki, 330, 332
Enkomi, 215
Enkur and Ninkur, 330
Enlil, 111, 330 bis, 331 bis
Enmešarra and Ninmešarra, 330 bis, 336
Enmul and Ninmul, 330
Ennun and Ninnun, 330

Enoch, 409, 416–17, 423–24, 426–27, 428–31, 433–34 & passim, 446
Enuma Eliš, 112, 113–14, 330, 331, 332–33, 395
Ephraim, 147, 150, 154, 156, 162, 199, 200, 227, 241, 326, 344
   district, 198, 199
Epic Sources, 120–21, 124–25, 345
Erebos, 112
Eros, 112
Esarhaddon, 48, 175 (bis), 229, 235, 238
Eshnunna
   code of, 121, 130
Eshtaol, 162
Ethan, 189, 190, 191, 192 21
Eusebius of Caesarea, 112, 114, 211–12
Exodus, 115, 120, 123–28, 138, 339, 340, 342, 343–46, 349, 350, 351, 352, 353, 354, 356, 357, 359, 500, 501, 504, 505, 506, 551
Exodus-Conquest, 109, 110, 335–36, 369, 538, 543, 545
Ezekiel, 229, 235, 310, 339, 343, 350, 352, 354, 360, 442, 444, 532, 535, 546, 547–48, 549, 551, 559
Ezion-Geber, 232, 233, 236
Ezra, 361–63, 364, 365, 366, 367, 368, 369, 370, 371–72, 375, 401, 414, 419, 420, 423, 532, 557, 559

Gad (tribe), 154, 198, 199, 296, 297
Gad the Seer, 179, 180
Gath, 196, 206
Gaza, 46, 127, 196, 206, 221, 222, 225, 227, 236
Gerizim, 42
Geshur, 195, 206, 231
Gezer, 7, 9, 13, 31, 34, 39, 45, 147, 187, 196, 197, 209, 210, 211, 213, 219, 220, 226, 227, 252, 280, 284
   calendar, 566
Gibeon, 7, 558
   stamps, 566, 568
Gideon, 140, 141, 144, 150, 151, 153, 154, 155, 156, 160, 161, 161–62, 163, 167, 168, 169, 177, 178, 294
Gilgal, 344, 346
Ginosar, 7
Goliath, 149, 214, 215, 223

Ḥabiru, 47, 48
Hadadezer, 195
Hadera, 7
Hades, 112, 114
Haggai, 339, 412
Hama, 13, 29, 30, 31, 33
Hamath, 175, 185, 195–96, 206, 230, 231, 237, 243
Hamman, 32
Hammurabi, 149
   code of, 121, 130
Hanani, 179
Hannah, Song of, 55 ff. passim, 71–72 & passim
Harran, 122
   site, 32
Hatti, 45–46, 50, 121, 214, 216, 225, 329, 334
   religion, 113, 117, 221, 330–31, 336
Hazael, 237
Hazor, 7, 16–20, 36, 51, 187, 227 bis, 249, 252,

254, 255, 257–58; 267 *bis,* 268, 272, 274, 281, 282, 285, 286, 287, 288, 289, 290, 291, 292, 293, 297
Hebron, 48, 147, 228, 230, 280
Hejar, 127
Heliopolis (On), 332
Heman, 188, 189, 190, 191, 192
Hermopolis, 329, 331, 334, 337
Herodian scripts, 564, 565, 566, 568, 571, 573, 574
Heshbon, 127, 147
Hesiod, 112, 113, 114, 330, 333
Hezekiah, 179, 201, 314, 369
Hillel, 532
Hiram I, 191, 231–32, 234, 243–44
Hiram II, 234, 238
Hiram III, 239
Hobab (see also Jethro), 124, 126
Hôdayôt, 383
Holy War, 109, 110, 115, 116, 228, 362, 470, 476, 478
Homer, 111, 113, 114, 137, 222
Honeyman Inscription, 234
Hosea, 316, 324, 343, 345, 350–51, 352, 360, 549
Ḥūḥ and Ḥawḥet, 329, 337
Ḥuḥ, 330
Humraiya, 31 n89
  Dhahrat el-Humraiya, 35
Hurrians, 37 n125; 113, 192, 330
Hyksos, 16, 125, 126

Igigi, 333
Isaac, 457, 468, 496, 501, 504, 507, 551
Isaiah, 71, 115, 345, 347, 360, 455, 462, 558, 579
  Second Isaiah, 70, 71, 339–57, 358, 359, 390, 398, 475–76, 501, 548, 558, 559
  Third Isaiah, 362, 370, 405
Ishbaal ben-Saul, 193
Ishtar, 117, 173, 180
Issachar, 154, 199, 226, 227, 228, 240
Ittobaal I, 236
Ittobaal II, 238
Ittobaal III, 239

Jabin, 227
Jacob, 62, 63, 65, 66, 95, 457, 461, 496, 501, 504, 507
Jacob, Testament of, 55 ff. *passim,* 63–66 & *passim,* 126
Jael, 227, 241
Jaffa, 7, 28, 196, 200, 225, 231, 239
Jahaziel, 180, 181
Jair, 154
Jamnia
  council of, 533, 534, 541
Jashar, Book of, 99
Jebusites, 145, 148
Jeduthun, 180, 190
Jehoahaz ben-Jehu, 237
Jehoash ben-Ahaziah (?), 183
Jehoiachin ben-Jehoiakim, 295, 298
Jehoiakim ben Josiah, 559
Jehoram ben-Jehosaphat, 236
Jehosaphat, 201, 205–6, 236, 246, 296

Jehu ben-Hanani, 179, 180
Jehu ben-Nimshi, 180, 237
Jephthah, 139, 140, 153, 154, 155, 160, 161, 162, 178, 472
Jeremiah, 49, 51, 115, 185, 296, 310, 322, 341, 350, 351–54; 360, 392, 393, 474, 546–47, 548, 556, 558, 559
Jericho, 7, 9, 254, 315
Jeroboam I, 179, 180, 207, 233, 302, 303, 304, 305, 306, 307, 308, 310, 312, 315–16, 319, 320, 324, 325, 345
Jeroboam II, 238, 315, 316
Jerome, 459–60
Jerusalem, 39, 40, 47, 65, 71, 145, 148, 181, 184, 193, 194, 210, 211, 232, 297, 298, 299, 318–19, 321, 323, 339, 342, 343, 345, 346, 352, 361, 364, 367, 368, 369, 370, 374, 383, 396, 398, 399, 407, 411, 415, 416, 445, 446, 455, 457, 462, 532, 533, 546, 547, 557
Jesus of Nazareth, 151, 390, 392, 456, 457, 500, 510, 512, 513, 516, 518, 519, 525, 526, 550, 552
Jethro, 124
Jezebel, 236
Jezreel, 39, 40, 187, 194, 226, 227
Job, 366, 393, 397, 421, 446, 451, 550, 568
John Hyrcanus I, 567
Jonah ben Amittai, 324, 503
Jonathan ben-Saul, 57, 230, 294
Joram ben-Ahab, 237
Joseph, 63, 448
  tribes, 138, 207, 345
Josephus, 191, 246, 364, 365, 368, 371, 437, 449
Joshua ben-Nun, 352, 360, 396, 535, 537, 550
Josiah
  reform, 151, 53; 307, 308, 312, 317, 321, 346, 369, 375
  reign, 200, 204, 238, 267, 275, 302, 304, 318, 322–23
Jotham's parable, 140
Judah, 154, 183, 193, 197, 199–200, 201, 205, 218, 226, 228, 230, 232, 233–34, 237, 238, 239, 242, 247, 253, 254, 260 *bis,* 261, 265, 266, 268, 272, 275, 280, 295, 298, 302, 303, 305, 309, 310, 312, 313, 314, 316, 322, 342, 344, 345, 362, 364, 366, 367, 374, 555, 559, 566
Judas Aristobulus I, 567
Judges
  office, 140, 152–64; 164, 165, 167, 177–78
  period of, 64, 67, 92, 135, 139, 152, 153–48; 152–64; 165, 167 177–78, 193, 227–28, 317

Kadesh (Qadesh), 214, 216, 240
Kadesh-Barnea, 126, 127
Kāmid el-Lōz, 13
Karatepe, 225–26, 236
Keilah, 40, 146
Kenites, 124, 128
Keret Cycle, 111, 118
Khabur ceramic, 30, 31, 32, 34, 35
Khirbet Beit Sêlûn, 44
Khirbet Bîr Shuweiḥa, 43
Khirbet edh-Dhûq, 44

Khirbet Kūfin, 7
Khirbet, Makhneh el-Fôqa, 43
Kingu, 114, 332, 395
Kishar, 112, 330
Kition, 234, 238, 245
Kothar (Koshar), 117
Kronos, 112, 113
Kūk and Kawket, 329
Kūk, 330
Kültepe, 14, 34, 36
Kumarbi, 330–31
Kûmeh, 42, 43
Kumidi, 46, 225

Lab'ayu, 39–40, 45, 47, 52
Lachish, 7, 20, 253, 258, 261, 265, 266–67, 275,
     279, 281, 283, 284, 285, 286, 287, 288,
     289, 290, 291, 292, 293, 299
Laish (see Dan)
Late Bronze Age
  Canaan, 39
  topography of central hills, 40–45
Levites, 139–40, 189, 189–190, 204–05, 208,
     228, 305, 318, 320–21, 362, 367, 369
Leviathan (see Lôtān)
Lôtān (Leviathan), 333, 334, 393
"love", 47, 351, 353
Lucian, 185
Luli, 238

Maacah, 195, 206
Maccabees, 151, 367, 450, 532, 562
Machir, 227
Malachi, 362, 368, 370
Manasseh, 147, 154, 156, 160, 199, 241
Manasseh ben-Hezekiah, 238, 398
Manetho, 211, 212
Marduk, 111, 112, 113, 114, 116, 117, 331, 332,
     333, 395, 549
Mari, 141, 149, 172–74, 175, 176, 189, 182,
     183, 185
  laws, 122
  site, 13
  texts, 16
Masada, 564, 566
Megiddo, 226
  Amarna period, 39, 45, 48, 156, 147
  site, 7, 9, 13, 31, 34, 35, 36, 37, 187, 189, 190,
     191, 192, 223, 249–51, 252, 253, 254, 255,
     267 bis, 268, 272, 273–74, 282, 284, 285,
     287, 290, 291, 292, 293, 297
Melchizedek, 67, 556
Melqart, 232, 236, 237
Mene'iye (Timna), 124
Merneptah, 225, 227
Mesad Hashavyahu, 275, 281, 283, 288
Mesha (Mēša'), 111, 246, 472
  stele, 111, 472
Mesopotamia, 10, 12, 13–15, 16, 20, 28, 122,
     142, 207, 233
  law, 121–22, 128
  religion, 109, 111, 113, 116, 173–74, 175–76,
     182, 183, 329–30, 332–33, 336, 396
Messianism, 345, 360, 361, 362, 363, 364, 368,
     393, 412, 500
Micah (of Judges 17–18), 115

Micah of Moreshet, 360, 546, 549
Michaiah, ben-Imla, 182, 183–84
Middle Bronze Age
  Middle Bronze Age I, 4–6, 21
  Middle Bronze Age II, 6–16
    burials, 7, 13, 16, 23, 35
    fortifications, 15–20, 41
    metallics, 8, 9, 13, 15, 23, 25–26
    pottery, 7–16, 41–42
    sites, 5–7
  Canaan, 3–20, 134
Midian, 120, 124, 126–27, 128, 141, 150, 153,
     164
Milk'asap, 229
Milkilu (of Gezer), 39
Miriam, 124
Miriam, Song of, 55 ff. passim, 57–60 & passim,
     110, 124–25, 344, 468
Mittin II, 238
Mizpah, 162
Moab, 124, 127, 153, 162, 194, 231, 237, 365,
     472, 478 n30
Moabite Stone (see Mesha')
Montet
  Jar, 10, 11
  Relief, 209, 212–17
Moses, 58, 64, 67, 69, 79, 87, 114, 120–131, 134,
     136, 138, 140, 141, 151, 179, 312, 313,
     317, 323, 339, 340, 341, 342, 343, 344,
     345, 346, 347, 348, 349, 350, 351, 352,
     353, 354, 355, 356, 359, 396, 414, 416,
     418, 421, 425, 432, 433, 444–45, 446, 504,
     517, 521, 540, 541, 546, 550, 551, 558
Moses, Blessing of, 55 ff. passim; 68–70 &
     passim, 95–96, 346, 468
Moses, Song of, 55 ff. passim, 77–80 & passim,
     477
Môt, 112, 114, 115, 117, 333
Moza, 7
Murabba'at, 564, 566, 573
Mursilis II, 174
Muṣri, 242
Mycenae, 147, 188, 214, 220, 221–22,

Nahariya, 7
Nahash of Ammon, 243
Nahor ben-Serug, 122
Naphtali, 154, 156, 199, 227, 241
Nash papyrus, 562, 566
Nāśî', 136, 146, 178, 362
Nathan, 179 bis, 180, 347, 359
Nazareth, 7
Nebuchadnezzar, 272, 298, 318
Nehemiah, 361–72, 373–74, 547, 557, 559
Nimrud, 251, 272, 275
Ninlil, 331
Ninurta, 111, 116
Nippur, 136
Noah, 342, 343, 348, 356, 359, 416
Nora stone, 130, 235, 236, 245
nqm, 48–49, 50
Nubia, 123
Nūn and Nawnet, 329
Nūn, 330, 335
Nuzi
  laws, 122

Og, 127
Ogdoad (of Hermopolis), 329, 330, 331, 332, 337
Okeanos, 112
Olympian gods, 111, 112
Omri, 236, 246
Ophir, 232, 236
Ophrah, 162
'Ormilk I, 229
Orpheus, 188
Osorkon I, 242
Osorkon II, 229, 242
Othniel ben-Kenaz, 152, 153, 154, 155, 161, 162
Ouranos, 330

Passover, 363, 367, 368, 369
Patriarchs, 63, 122, 126, 224, 504, 506, 507, 556
    religion, 56–57, 61–62, 64, 66, 67, 70, 71, 91, 98, 109, 118
Paul (Saul), 151, 166, 357, 503–04
Pella, 40, 147
Persia, 150, 239, 243, 254, 266, 281, 290, 336, 362, 363–64, 365, 367, 370, 372, 374, 375, 390, 396, 398, 399, 400–01, 411, 442, 532, 539, 547, 559, 566, 573
Pharisees, 409 n19; 533, 559, 560
Philistines, 153, 154, 165, 177, 187, 188, 189, 191, 194, 196–97, 212–13, 214, 215, 216, 217, 221, 222, 223, 226, 227, 230, 231, 233, 234, 235, 236, 238, 240, 241, 352, 501
Philo of Alexandria, 459, 553
Philo of Byblos, 335
Phoenicia, 127, 130, 220, 224–38, 239, 240, 255, 247, 297, 334, 335, 337, 563, 568, 576
Plato (Aristocles), 177, 492
Poetry, techniques of analysis, 55–57, 85–97, 377–84
Pontos, 112
Poseidon, 112, 114
pqd, 48, 49–51
Priestly source (see also Epic sources), 140, 342, 346, 366, 367, 368, 374, 504, 532
Prophecy, 109, 128, 140, 141, 145–46, 171–84, 303, 310–17, 320, 326, 345, 350–51, 353, 390, 391, 392, 393, 396–97, 398, 399, 404, 409, 412, 461, 463, 468, 473, 474, 479, 504, 521, 544–50, 558, 559, 560
Psusennes II, 211, 212, 213, 217, 219
Ptaḥ, 191
    of Ashkelon, 192
Ptolemies, 219, 532
Pumay, 235
Pyrgi, 229, 243

Qarqar, 229, 230, 237
Qaṭna, 6, 13, 29, 33, 35
Qena, 48
Que, 235, 238, 242
Qumran
    community, 407, 447 24; 449
    scrolls, 125, 131, 373, 379, 380, 381, 383, 440, 443, 447, 512, 530, 533, 542, 564 bis, 565, 566, 568, 569, 574, 575, 576
    11QPs, 381, 384, 450, 532, 553, 576

Rabbat (Ammon), 147
racism, 135, 143
Ramah, 162
Ramat Rachel, 254, 259, 260, 261, 264, 265, 272, 275, 279, 285, 286, 287, 288, 289, 290, 291, 292, 293, 294, 297, 298, 299, 564
Rameses (City), 13, 125
Rameses I, 214
Rameses II, 214, 227, 240
Rameses III, 214, 225, 240
Ramoth-Gilead, 237
Râs ed-Diyâr, 43
Ras el-'Ain, 7, 13, 29
Rehoboam, 134, 141, 207, 210, 211, 218, 233, 326
Reuel (see Hobab)
Rhea, 112
Rîb-Adda, 47, 240
Rome, 136, 532, 543
Royal ideology, 110, 302, 340, 344, 351–52, 378, 397–98, 399, 404, 411, 412, 441, 465, 469, 473, 548, 549–50, 559
Ruth, 64, 92

Safad (Ṣefat), 7
Salome Alexandra, 533, 557
Samaria, 200, 236, 242, 255, 256, 257, 267, 268, 272, 273, 282, 284, 285, 286, 287, 288, 289, 290, 291, 292, 293, 297, 307, 308, 320, 345, 361, 364, 366, 367, 370, 374, 398
    papyri, 365, 371, 372
Samaritans (see also Samaria), 361, 362, 363, 367, 375, 555
    script, 564, 567, 574
Samson, 153, 154, 155, 161, 162, 163, 189
Samuel, 140, 155, 171, 176–77, 177–78, 179, 180, 181, 182, 313, 314, 317, 361
Sanballaṭids, 362, 365, 370, 371, 374
Sanchuniaton, 330, 331, 333, 334, 335, 337
Sarah, 551
Sargon II, 236, 246
Saul ben-Kish, 57, 69, 70–71, 145, 147, 148, 152, 177, 189, 182, 187, 193, 205, 228, 230, 243, 295, 313–14, 324, 579
Sea-Peoples, 137, 212, 214–15, 225–27, 229, 230
Sede-Dov, 25
Sefire texts, 48, 49, 115, 334
Sennacherib, 229, 238, 247
Serabit el-Khadim, 127
"Servant", 47, 294–95, 340, 341, 349, 356, 357, 550
Sethos I, 124, 227
Shabaka, 289
Shalmaneser III, 237, 243
Shamgar ben-Anath, 153, 154, 227, 241
Shamshi-Adad I, 14, 16
Shechem (Tell Balaṭah)
    city-state, 39–45, 52, 147
    in Israel, 62, 66, 130, 162, 163, 167–68, 199, 255, 346, 350
    site, 7, 9, 36, 37, 256, 267, 268, 272, 280, 281, 282, 284, 285, 286, 287, 288, 289, 290, 291, 292, 293, 339
Sherden (šrdn), 214, 225, 226, 240

Shiloh, 44, 129, 162, 177, 314, 346, 352, 474, 479
Shiptibaal II, 229
Shishak I, 209, 210–11, 218, 229, 233, 242, 258
Shittim, 151
Shuppiluliumas, 45
Shuwardata, 48
Siamūn, 197, 209, 211, 212–13, 214, 215, 216, 217, 219, 19; 220, 221, 229, 232
Sidon, 13, 226, 227, 229, 230, 235, 238, 240, 241, 247, 248
Sihon, 127, 472, 478
Sile, 124
Siloam inscription, 576
Simeon (tribe), 228
Simyra (see Sumur)
Sin, 127
Sinai (see too, Sinai, Mount)
   desert, 120, 123, 124, 125–26, 129
   proto-sinaitic, 122–23
Sinai (Mount), 61, 110, 125, 126, 127, 145, 336, 341, 342, 343, 344, 345, 346, 354, 416, 421, 425, 444–45, 446, 457, 473, 474, 535, 536, 554
Sin el-Fil, 13
Sinuhe, 10, 28, 137, 149
Sippar, 172
Sirach, 379, 380, 381, 536
Sisera, 227
Socoh, 199
Sodom, 470
Solomon, 52, 99, 134, 140, 141, 146, 179, 187, 188–89, 190, 191, 194, 195, 196, 197, 198–201, 202, 203–04, 206, 207, 208, 209–11, 213, 218, 219, 231–32, 233, 234, 236, 238, 241, 243, 244, 249, 252, 253, 284, 297, 326, 345, 369, 383, 437, 449–50, 469
Sumur (Simyra), 46, 225, 230

Taanach (Taʻának)
   letters, 50
Tabernacle, 129, 418
Tabernacles, Feast of (Sūkkôt), 367, 369
Tabor, 227
Tanis, 123, 125, 212, 217
Tappuaḥ (Tell Sheikh Abû Zarâd), 40, 44, 199
Tarshish, 232, 235, 245
Tarsus, 151, 188, 235
Tartaros, 112, 330
Tēbēṣ, 44
Tell Abu Hawam, 239, 258
Tell al-Rimah, 247
Tell Balaṭah (see Shechem)
Tell Beit-Mirsim, 4, 6, 7, 9, 10, 21, 31, 45, 265, 275, 284, 285, 286, 287, 288, 289, 290, 291, 292, 294, 298
Tell Billa, 13
Tell Brak, 32, 36
Tell Chuera, 13
Tell ed-Damiyeh, 45
Tell el-ʻAjjul, 6, 7
ell el ʻAmr, 7
Tell el Farʻah (Tirzah), 7, 40, 44, 191, 215, 216, 222, 236, 255, 267, 268, 272, 282,

283, 284, 285, 286, 287, 288, 289, 290, 291, 292, 293
Tell el-Ḥesi, 7
Tell el-Yehudiyeh, 16
Tell en-Naṣbeh, 283, 291, 299
Tell esh-Shariʻah, 206
Tell es-Saʻidiyeh, 226, 249
Tell et-Tin, 13, 29
Tell Jemmeh, 272, 282
Tell Kisan, 7
Tell Mardikh, 13
Tell Miskeh, 94–95
Tell Poleg, 7, 37
Tell Qasila, 187, 188, 191, 275
Tell Rimah, 175
Tell Sôfar, 42–43
Tell Zeror, 7
Temple, First, 94, 189–90, 202, 229, 232, 323, 326, 345, 351, 352, 369, 531, 547–48, 550
   theology, 109, 339, 343, 415, 473, 474, 521, 547–48
Temple, Second, 303, 362, 369, 407, 541, 559
Temple Scroll (Qumran), 445
   heavenly Temple, 446
Tent of Meeting, 129
Tepe Gawra, 13
Terga, 173
Testaments of the twelve Patriarchs, 412, 440
Tešup, 331
Thales, 131, 334–45
Thoth, 191 n14; 331, 335, 337
Tiamat, 112, 113, 114, 330, 331, 332, 333, 335, 395
Tibni, 236
Tiglath-Pileser I, 229
Tiglath-Pileser III, 229, 238, 251
Til-Barsib (Tell Aḫmar), 13, 14
Timna (see Meneʻiye)
Tirhaqa, 238
Tirzah (see Tell el-Farʻah)
Titans, 329, 330
Tjeker, 225, 240
Tobiah, 362, 374
Tola ben-Puah, 153, 154
Tribal League, 62, 63, 66, 69–70, 94–5, 109, 110, 114, 126–27, 132–48, 149, 152–64, 193, 199–200, 205, 227–28, 345, 404, 441, 520, 545
Troy, 111
Tyre, 46, 112, 189, 191, 195, 226, 229, 230, 231, 232, 233, 234, 235–36, 237, 238, 239, 240, 241, 242, 255, 256, 247, 248

Ugarit
   city state, 46
   cult, 332, 337
   site, 6, 13, 34–35, 121, 251, 332–33
   texts, 175, 190, 576 n49
      texts, administrative, 44, 50, 185, n11
      texts, mythic, 60, 64, 65, 71, 113, 114, 117, 118, 124, 395, 399, 405
Ugaritic, 379
Upe (see, too, Damascus), 225
Ur
   Ur III, 12, 32

city, 122
    Lament over, 115
Uriah the Hittite, 179
Uruk, 174
Uzziah, 201, 238, 324, 325

Wadi ed-Dâliyeh, 21, 371
Wadi et-Tin, 7
Wen-Amun, 174–75, 229
Wisdom of Solomon, 423, 437–38

Xerxes I, 150, 559

Yabneh, 532
Yabneh-Yam, 7, 200, 247, 568
Yabrud, 13
Yahweh
    Divine Warrior, 109, 110, 114–15, 345
    epithets, 57–96, 128
    King, 110–111, 115–16, 342–43, 345, 346, 354
    name, 97–98, 118, 129
Yahwist (J) (see Epic sources) 50–51, 82, 242,
    395, 467, 468, 469–70, 477, 504, 537
Yamm, 112, 114, 333
Yehawmilke, 243
Yehimilk, 242
Yeno'am, 227

Zakarbaal, 229, 239
Zakir
    stele, 175, 180
Zarathustrianism, 150, 151, 390, 396, 400, 404,
    409, 413
Zebulun, 156, 199, 226, 227, 228, 240, 241
Zechariah ben-Berechyahu, 339, 412, 442
Zechariah ben-Jehoiada, 183
Zechariah ben-Josiah (King), 254, 298, 545,
    559
Zedekiah ben-Cenaanah, 175, 181, 183–84
Zerubbabel, 374, 559
Zeus, 111, 112, 114, 116, 117, 330
Ziklag, 193
Zimri, 236
Zinčirli, 223, 235
Zion theology, 342, 344, 345, 346, 356, 473,
    474, 479
zkr, 49, 51
Zoan, 123, 125
Zorah, 162

Psalm 29, 55 ff. *passim;* 66 ff. & *passim*
Psalm 68, 55 ff. *passim;* 82–85 & *passim,* 346
Psalm 72, 55 ff. *passim,* 82 & *passim*
Psalm 78, 55 ff. *passim,* 80–82 & *passim,* 345
II Samuel (= Psalm 18, Royal Psalm), 55 ff.
    passim, 75–77 & *passim*